A HISTORY OF
INDIAN LITERATURE

A HISTORY OF INDIAN LITERATURE:

VOL.1

INTRODUCTION, VEDA, EPICS, PURANAS AND TANTRAS

M. WINTERNITZ

TRANSLATOR

MRS.S.KETKAR

IN THREE VOLUMES

VOLUMS - I

GYAN

Published by

Gyan Publishing House
5, Ansari Road
Daryaganj, New Delhi-110002
Phone: 011-47034999, 9811692060
E-mail: books@gyanbooks.com

Distribution Network
gyanbooks.com
India, USA, Canada, UK, Australia

ISBN: 978-93-6920-702-2 (Set)
978-93-6920-382-6 (HB)
First Published, 1904

2nd Impression 2025

Printed at: Gyan Press, Delhi.

A HISTORY OF INDIAN LITERATURE (Vol. I)
Author: M. WINTERNITZ,
Translator: MRS.S.KETKAR

A HISTORY OF INDIAN LITERATURE

BY

M. WINTERNITZ, PH.D.

PROFESSOR OF INDOLOGY AND ETHNOLOGY AT THE GERMAN UNIVERSITY OF PRAGUE (CZECHOSLOVAKIA)

VOL. I

INTRODUCTION, VEDA, NATIONAL EPICS, PURĀṆAS, AND TANTRAS

TRANSLATED FROM THE ORIGINAL GERMAN BY
MRS. S. KETKAR

AND REVISED BY THE AUTHOR

Only Authorised Translation into English

PUBLISHED BY THE
UNIVERSITY OF CALCUTTA
1927

To

RABINDRANATH TAGORE

The Great Poet, Educator, and Lover of Man

This English Version of the "History of Indian Literature"

is dedicated

as a token of loving admiration and sincere gratitude

by the Author.

TABLE OF CONTENTS

PREFACE TO THE ENGLISH TRANSLATION.

Both in Santiniketan, where I held the visiting professorship at Viśvabhāratī University in 1922-23, and elsewhere in India, I often heard expressions of regret that my 'History of Indian Literature,' written in German, was not accessible to the majority of Indian students. I talked about this to some of my Indian friends, and one day Professor Taraporewala suggested that an English translation might be published by the University of Calcutta. He spoke about it to the late Sir Asutosh Mookerjee, the great champion and inspirer of Oriental Studies in Calcutta University, who at once showed great interest in the work, and at his suggestion the Syndicate of the University agreed to undertake the publication. It was not difficult to find a translator. When I came to Poona in November 1922, to visit the Bhandarkar Oriental Research Institute, I was introduced to Dr. S. V. Ketkar, the learned Editor of the Marathi Encyclopædia, and to my great surprise he showed me two big volumes, containing a typewritten English translation of the first two volumes of my "History of Indian Literature." The translation, I understood, was the work of Mrs. Ketkar, who had made it for the use of her husband, not for publication. Mrs. Ketkar, being German by her mother tongue, English by education, and Indian by marriage, seemed to me as if predestined for the work, and she agreed to revise and rewrite her translation for the purpose of publication.

But not only the translator had to revise her work, I myself had to revise mine. The first part of the German original, dealing with Vedic literature, had been published in 1905, the second part, treating the Epic and Puranic literature, in 1908. It was, therefore, necessary to revise the whole work for the English translation, in order to bring it up to date. Many chapters had to be rewritten entirely, smaller changes, corrections and additions, had to be made almost on every page, and the more important publications of the last twenty years had to be added to the references in the Notes. Thus this English translation is at the same time a second, revised and, I hope, improved edition of the original work.

It is not for me to say how far the translator has succeeded in her task. But I know that she has spared no pains to make her translation as accurate and as readable as possible. And for this it is my pleasant duty to thank her. I have also to thank my pupil Wilhelm Gampert for preparing the Index.

Prague, Sept. 5th, 1926. M. WINTERNITZ.

PREFACE TO THE GERMAN EDITION.

The publishers of this work have announced in a notice that the series in which the present volume, dedicated to the oldest period of Indian literature, appears, is intended, "not for learned circles, but for the educated people of the nation." With this idea in mind, the class of reader which I have kept constantly in view in the course of my work is the reader who as yet knows nothing of Indian literature, and possesses no special Indological knowledge of any kind:—and yet not that reader who merely desires a desultory acquaintance with Indian literature in a leisure hour, but him who wants to make himself as thoroughly acquainted with it as it is at all possible without a knowledge of the Indian languages. An English, German or French literary history need only be a bare presentation of the course of development of a literature which presumably is already familiar. A history of Indian literature, however, in all cases in which there are no German translations—and this is unfortunately so in the majority of cases—must also instruct the German reader as far as possible in the contents of the literary productions, by means of quotations and summaries of the contents. In other words: A history of the literature must be at the same time a description of the literature. Thus of the national epics and the Purāṇas, with which the second half of the present volume deals, only few portions have so far become known in German translations. Without extensive descriptive summaries and quotations it is impossible for the reader to gain any conception at all of the works treated.

In this way, indeed, the volume assumed larger proportions than it was originally anticipated. A second consideration also accounts for this increase in the size of the work. It is precisely the oldest Indian literature, treated in this volume, which, with reference to chronology, is to a certain extent "hovering in the air." Not a single one of the numerous and extensive works which belong to the Vedas, to the national Epics, or to the Purāṇas, can be ascribed with certainty even to this or that century. It is simply impossible, in one sentence or in a few lines, to give information on the age of the Vedas, of the Mahābhārata, of the Rāmāyaṇa and even of the Purāṇas. Even for the general reader it is not sufficient to tell him that we do not know anything definite about the date of these works. It is necessary to mark off the boundaries within which our ignorance moves, and to state the grounds on which an approximate, even though only conjectural, date of these works is supported. Therefore considerable sections had to be devoted to the enquiry concerning the age of the Vedas, the Epics and the Purāṇas. I emphasize expressly that these chapters, too, are not indeed written only for the specialist, but in the first place for the layman as characterised above, whom I had in view as my reader. If, notwithstanding, they contain something new for the specialist also,—and probably also some points which might challenge contradiction,—then it is because questions are here dealt with, which, just in recent years, have been the subject of new investigations, new discoveries, and manifold controversies.

The references given in the Notes are partly intended for the specialist, in whose eyes they are to justify the editor's standpoint in the most important debatable questions. For it is a matter of course, that a book which is addressed to the "educated people of the nation," must also stand before the judgment of the specialist, and submit entirely to the same. On the other hand, in the Notes intended for the non-specialist,

I have also made a point of referring to all German translations which are accessible by any means—and where these are wanting, to the English and French ones. I have utilised these translations only in a few cases, in which they appeared to me to reproduce the original in a particularly admirable manner. Where no translator is mentioned, the translations are my own.

After what has been said, it will not be surprising that the originally intended size of *one* volume proved to be too narrow for this Indian Literary History. I am sincerely thankful to the Publisher for raising no opposition to the reasons which were given for the widening of the originally planned size, and for giving his consent for a second volume. This widening also thoroughly corresponds with the extent and the significance of Indian literature,—for which I refer to the Introduction (p. 1 ff.). As the present volume deals in a certain sense with the "prehistoric" period of Indian literature,—at least in their beginnings, both the Vedas and the national epics reach back to far-off epochs which cannot be fixed by means of any dates—so the second volume shall begin with the Buddhist literature, and introduce the reader to the literature of the actually historical period of India.

Regarding the works upon which I have drawn and to which I am indebted, the Notes to the separate sections give information. What I owe to the "Akademische Vorlesungen über Indische Literaturgeschichte" by Albrecht Weber (2nd edition, Berlin 1876) which paved the way for Indian literary historiography, and to those stimulating and valuable lectures on "Indiens Literatur und Cultur in historischer Entwicklung" by Leopold v. Schroeder (Leipzig 1887) could naturally not be recorded in every single case. I also owe much, without always having specially mentioned it, to the valuable "Bulletins des Religions de l'Inde" by A. Barth in the Revue de l'Histoire des Religions, Tomes I, III, V, XI, XIV, XXVIIIf, XLIf, and XLV (1880-1902). The ingenious essays of H. Oldenberg, "Die Literatur des alten Indien" (Stuttgart and Berlin 1903) deal more with an aesthetic view and appreciation of Indian literature, which was somewhat outside the scope of my plans. The works of A. Baumgartner (Geschichte der Weltliteratur II. Die Literaturen Indiens und Ostasiens, 3. und 4. Aufl., Freiburg i. B. 1902), A. A. Macdonell (A History of Sanskrit Literature, London 1900) and V. Henry (Les Littératures de l'Inde, Paris 1904), though quite useful for their own purposes, hardly offered me anything new. The outlines of Indian literature by Richard Pischel in Part I, Section VII ("Die Orientalischen Literaturen"), of the series "Die Kultur der Gegenwart" (Berlin and Leipzig 1906), exceedingly short, but a masterpiece in their brevity, appeared only when my MS. was already finished and partly printed. I would not wish to leave unmentioned the services rendered to me by the "Orientalische Bibliographie" by Lucian Scherman, which is so indispensable to every Orientalist. Finally, I express my sincere gratitude to all those who have written friendly reviews or offered expert criticism on the first half volume which appeared two years ago.

Prag, Kgl. Weinberge, M. WINTERNITZ.
15th October, 1907.

LIST OF ABBREVIATIONS USED IN THE NOTES.

ABA=Abhandlungen der Berliner Akademie der Wissenschaften, Philol.-histor. Klasse.

ABayA=Abhandlungen der Bayerischen Akademie der Wissenschaften, Phil. Klasse.

AGGW=Abhandlungen der Königl. Gesellschaft der Wissenschaften zu Göttingen, Philol.-histor. Klasse.

AKM=Abhandlungen für die Kunde des Morgenlandes, herausg. von der Deutschen Morgenländischen Gesellschaft.

Album Kern=Album-Kern: Opstellen geschreven ter eere von Dr. H. Kern...op zijn zeventigsten verjaardag. Leiden 1903.

AMG=Annales du Musée Guimet (Paris).

Ann. Bh. Inst.=Annals of the Bhandarkar Institute, Poona.

ĀnSS=Ānandāśrama Sanskrit Series (Poona).

AR=Archiv für Religionsgeschichte.

ASGW=Abhandlungen der philol.-histor. Klasse der Königl. Sächs. Gesellschaft der Wissenschaften.

Aufrecht, Bodl. Cat.=Th. Aufrecht, Catalogus Codicum MSS. Sanscriticorum Bibliothecae Bodleianae, Oxonii 1859-64.

Aufrecht CC=Th. Aufrecht: Catalogus Catalogorum. Leipzig 1891; II, 1896; III, 1903.

Aufrecht, Leipzig=Katalog der Sanskrit-Handschriften der Universitätsbibliothek zu Leipzig, 1901.

BEFEO=Bulletin de l'école française d'Extrême Orient.

BenSS=Benares Sanskrit Series.

Bezz. Beitr.=Beiträge zur Kunde der indogermanischen Sprachen, herausg. von A. Bezzenberger.

Bhandarkar, Report 1882-83=R. G. Bhandarkar, Report on the Search for Sanskrit Manuscripts in the Bombay Presidency during the year 1882-83, Bombay 1884.

Bhandarkar, Report 1883-84=R. G. Bhandarkar, Report etc. during the year 1883-84, Bombay 1887.

Bhandarkar Comm. Vol.=Commemorative Essays presented to Sir Ramkrishna Gopal Bhandarkar, Poona 1917.

Bhandarkar, Vaiṣṇavism etc.=R. G. Bhandarkar, Vaiṣṇavism, Śaivism and Minor Religious Systems (Grundriss III, 6, 1913).

Bibl. Ind.=Bibliotheca Indica.

BSGW=Berichte über die Verhandlungen der Königl. Sächischen Gesellschaft der Wissenschaften zu Leipzig, Philol.-histor. Klasse.

BSOS=Bulletin of the School of Oriental Studies, London Institution.

BSS=Bombay Sanskrit Series.

Bühler, Report=G. Bühler, Detailed Report of a Tour in Search of Sanskrit MSS. made in Kaśmir, Rajputana, and Central India. (Extra Number of the JBRAS 1877).

Burnell, Tanjore=A. C. Burnell, A Classified Index to the Sanskrit MSS. in the Palace at Tanjore, London 1880.

Cambridge History=The Cambridge History of India, Vol. I. Ancient India. Ed. by E. J. Rapson, Cambridge 1922.

Deussen, AGPh=P. Deussen, Allgemeine Geschichte der Philosophie, I, 1—3, Leipzig 1894 (2nd ed. 1906)-1908.

DLZ=Deutsche Literaturzeitung.

Ep. Ind.=Epigraphia Indica.

ERE=Encyclopaedia of Religion and Ethics, edited by James Hastings.

Farquhar, Outline=J. N. Farquhar: An Outline of the Religious Literature of India, London 1920.

Festschrift Kuhn=Aufsätze zur Kultur-und Sprachgeschichte vornehmlich des Orients Ernst Kuhn...gewidmet... München 1916.

Festschrift Wackernagel=Antidoron, Festschrift Jacob Wackernagel zur Vollendung des 70. Lebensjahres, Göttingen 1924.

WZKM = Wiener Zeitschrift für die Kunde des Morgenlandes.

ZB = Zeitschrift für Buddhismus (Oskar Schloss, München).

ZDMG = Zeitschrift der Deutschen Morgenländischen Gesellschaft.

ZII = Zeitschrift für Indologie und Iranistik, herausg. von der Deutschen Morgenländischen Gesellschaft.

ZVV = Zeitschrift des Vereins für Volkskunde in Berlin.

OC=Transactions (Verhandlungen, Actes) of Congresses of Orientalists.

OTF=Oriental Translation Fund.

Pischel, KG=R. Pischel, Die indische Literatur, in Kultur der Gegenwart I, 7, 1906.

Proc. I (II, III) OC=Proceedings and Transactions of the First (Second, Third) Oriental Conference.

RHR=Revue de l'histoire des Religions, Paris.

RSO=Rivista degli studi orientali, Rome.

SBA=Sitzungsberichte der Berliner Akademie der Wissenschaften.

SBayA=Sitzungsberichte der Bayerischen Akademie der Wiss., Phil.-histor. Kl.

SBE=Sacred Books of the East (Oxford).

SBH=Sacred Books of the Hindus, published by the Panini Office, Allahabad.

Schroeder, ILC=L. von Schroeder, Indiens Literatur und Cultur, Leipzig 1887.

SIFI=Studi Italiani di Filologia Indo-Iranica.

Smith, Early History=Vincent A. Smith, The Early History of India. Fourth Edition, revised by S. M. Edwardes, Oxford 1924.

SWA=Sitzungsberichte der Wiener Akademie der Wissenschaften.

TSS=Trivandrum Sanskrit Series.

Weber, HSS. Verz.=A. Weber, Verzeichnis der Sanskrit und Prakrit-Handschriften der K. Bibliothek zu Berlin.

Weber, HIL=A. Weber, History of Indian Literature, Fourth Edition, 1904, Popular Re-issue, 1914.

Winternitz-Keith, Bodl. Cat.=Catalogue of Sanskrit Manuscripts in the Bodleian Library, vol. II begun by M. Winternitz, continued and completed by A. B. Keith, Oxford, 1905.

Festschrift Windisch = Festschrift Ernst Windisch zum 70. Geburtstag ..dargebracht...Leipzig 1914.

GGA = Göttinger Gelehrte Anzeigen.

GOS = Gaekwad's Oriental Series, Baroda.

Grundriss = Grundriss der indo-arischen Philologie und Altertumskunde.

GSAI = Giornale della societa Asiatica Italiana.

Gurupūjākaumudī = Gurupūjākaumudī, Festgabe zum fünfzigjährigen Doctorjubiläum Albrecht Weber dargebracht von seinen Freunden und Schülern, Leipzig 1896.

Haraprasād, Report I, II. = Haraprasād Śāstrī, Report on the Search of Sanskrit MSS. (1895-1900), Calcutta 1901 and (1901-02 to 1905-06), Calcutta 1905.

HOS = Harvard Oriental Series, ed. by Ch. R. Lanman.

Ind. Hist. Qu. = The Indian Historical Quarterly, edited by Narendra Nath Law.

Ind. Ant. = Indian Antiquary.

Ind. Off. Cat. = Catalogue of the Sanskrit Manuscripts in the Library of the India Office, London 1887 ff.

Ind. Stud. = Indische Studien, herausgegeben von A. Weber.

JA = Journal Asiatique.

JAOS = Journal of the American Oriental Society.

JASB = Journal of the Asiatic Society of Bengal.

JBRAS = Journal of the Bombay Branch of the Royal Asiatic Society.

JRAS = Journal of the Royal Asiatic Society of Great Britain and Ireland.

LZB = Literarisches Zentralblatt.

Mélanges Lévi = Mélanges d'Indianisme offerts par ses élèves à M. Sylvain Lévi...Paris 1911.

NGGW = Nachrichten von der Kgl. Gesellschaft der Wissenschaften Göttingen, Philolog.-histor. Klasse.

NSP = Nirṇaya Sāgara Press (Bombay).

Directions for Pronunciation of Indian (Sanskrit, Prākrit, Pāli) names and words, written in Roman characters.

Pronounce:

Vowels.

- *a* अ as a "neutral vowel" like English "short **u**" in b**u**t.
- *ṛ* ऋ as a vowel, like **er** in Scots English bak**er**.
- *e* ए, *o* ओ as long *ē* (in English th**ey**) and *ō* (in English st**o**ne), without diphthongal character.

Palatals.

- *c* च like **ch** in English **ch**ild.
- *j* ज like **j** in English **j**ust.

Cerebrals.

- *ṭ* ट, *ṭh* ठ, *ḍ* ड, *ḍh* ढ, *ṇ* ण like English "dentals", while the Sanskrit dentals (*t* त, *th* थ, *d* द, *dh* ध, *n* न) are pronounced like dentals in Italian and French.

Sibilants.

- *ś* (or *š*, *s̆*) श (palatal), *ṣ* ष (cerebral) like *sh* in English **sh**ip.

Nasals.

- *ṅ* ङ (guttural) like **ng** in English si**ng**
- *ñ* ञ (palatal) " **gn** in French monta**gn**e
- *ṃ* (Anusvāra) " **n** in French Jea**n**.

ḥ (Visarga) "a surd breathing, a final *h*-sound (in the European sense of *h*) uttered in the articulating position of the preceding vowel" (Whitney).

INTRODUCTION.

Extent and Significance of Indian Literature.

The history of Indian literature is the history of the mental activity of at least 3,000 years, as expressed in speech and writing. The home of this mental activity which has been almost uninterruptedly continuous through thousands of years, is a land which reaches from the Hindu-kush to Cape Comorin and covers an area of one and a half millions of square miles, equalling in extent the whole of Europe with the exception of Russia,—a land which stretches from 8° to 35° N. Lat., that is, from the hottest regions of the Equator to well within the temperate zone. But the influence which this literature, already in ancient times, exerted over the mental life of other nations, reaches far beyond the boundaries of India to Further India, to Tibet, as far as China, Japan and Korea, and in the South over Ceylon and the Malay Peninsula far away over the islands of the Indian and the Pacific Oceans, while to the West the tracks of Indian mental life may be traced far into Central Asia to Eastern Turkestan, where, buried in the sands of the desert, Indian manuscripts have been found.

As regards its contents, Indian literature embraces everything which the word "literature" comprises in its widest sense: religious and secular, epic, lyric, dramatic and didactic poetry, as well as narrative and scientific prose.

In the foreground stands the religious literature. Not only the Brahmans in their Vedas and the Buddhists in their Tipiṭaka, but also many others of the numerous religious sects, which have sprung up in India, can produce an enormous number of literary works—hymns, sacrificial songs, incantations, myths and legends, sermons, theological treatises, polemical writings, manuals of instruction on ritual and religious discipline. In this literature there is an accumulation of absolutely priceless material, which no investigator of religion can afford to pass by. Besides this activity in the sphere of religious literature, which reaches back through thousands of years, and is still being continued at the present day, there have been in India since the oldest times also heroic songs, which in the course of centuries have become condensed into two great national epics—the Mahābhārata and the Rāmāyaṇa. The poets of the Indian Middle Ages during centuries drew upon the legends of these two epics, and epic poems arose, which in contradistinction to these popular epics, are designated as—ornate epics. But, while these poems, on account of their exaggerated artificiality, which often exceeds all bounds, do not by any means always suit our Western taste, Indian poets have bequeathed to us lyrical and dramatic works, which bear comparison for delicacy and intensity of feeling, and partly also for dramatic creative power, with the most beautiful productions of modern European literature. In one department of literature, that of the aphorism (gnomic poetry), the Indians have attained a mastery which has never been gained by any other nation. India is also the land of the fairy-tale and fable. The Indian collections of fairy-tales, fables and prose narratives have played no insignificant part in the history of world-literature. Indeed, fairy-tale research—that most attractive study of fairy-tales and fairy-tale motives and of their wanderings from people to people—has only become an independent branch of knowledge through Benfey's fundamental work on the famous Indian book of fables, the Pañcatantra.

But one of the peculiarities of the Indian mind is that it has never drawn a distinct line between purely artistic production and scientific work, so that a division between "belles lettres" and didactic literature is not really possible in India. What appears to us a collection of fairy tales and fables is regarded by the Indians as a manual of political and moral instruction. On the other hand, history and biography have in India never been treated other than by poets and as a branch of epic poetry. Neither does a division between the forms of poetry and prose really exist in India. Every subject can be treated equally well in verses as in the prose form. We find novels which differ from the ornate epics in hardly anything except that the metrical form is wanting. Since the oldest times we find a special predilection for the mixture of prose and verse. For that which we call scientific literature, the prose form has been employed in India only for a small part, whereas verse has been used to a far greater extent. This is the case in works on philosophy and law, as also in those on medicine, astronomy, architecture, etc. Indeed, even grammars and dictionaries have been written by the Indians in metrical form. There is perhaps nothing more characteristic than that there exists a great classical epic in 22 Cantos, which pursues the definitely stated aim of illustrating and impressing the rules of grammar. Philosophy was very early a subject of literary activity in India, first in connection with the religious literature, but later also independently of the latter. Similarly, already in very early times, law and custom were,—also first in connection with religion,—made into subjects of a special law literature, written partly in verse and partly in prose. The importance of this law literature for the comparative study of law and social science is to-day appreciated to the full by prominent jurists and sociologists. Centuries before the birth of Christ, grammar was already studied in India, a science in which the Indians excel all the nations of antiquity. Lexicography, too, attains to a high age. The Indian court poets (Kavi) of later periods did not give utterance to that which a god revealed to them, but they studied the rules of grammar, and searched in dictionaries for rare and poetic expressions; they versified according to the teachings and rules which were laid down in scientific works on prosody and poetics. Since the earliest times the Indian mind had a particular predilection for detailed analysis and for the pedantic scientific treatment of all possible subjects. Therefore we find in India not only an abundant, and partly ancient, literature on politics and economics, medicine, astrology and astronomy, arithmetic and geometry; but also music, singing, dancing and dramatic art, magic and divination, and even erotics, are arranged in scientific systems and treated in special manuals of instruction.

But in each single one of the above enumerated branches of literature there has accumulated, during the course of the centuries, a mass of literary productions which it is almost impossible to survey, largely through the fact that in nearly all departments of religious literature, as well as of poetry and science, the commentators developed a very eager activity. Thus especially some of the most important and most extensive works on grammar, philosophy and law are only commentaries on older works. Very frequently other commentaries were again written on these commentaries. Indeed, it is not a rare thing for an author in India to have added a commentary to his own work. Thus, it is no matter for wonder, that the sum total of Indian literature is almost overwhelming. And in spite of the fact that the catalogues of Indian MSS. which can be found in Indian and European libraries contain many thousands of book-titles and names of authors, innumerable works of Indian literature have been lost, and many names of older writers are known only through quotations by later writers, or have even completely disappeared.

All these facts—the high age, the wide geographical distribution, the extent, and the wealth, the aesthetic value and still more the value from the point of view of the history of culture, of Indian literature—would fully suffice to justify our interest in this great, original, and ancient literature. Butt here is something else in addition to this, which gives, just to Indian literature, a quite particular interest. The Indo-Aryan languages, together with the Iranian, form the most easterly branch of that great family of languages, to which also our language and indeed most of the languages of Europe belong, and which is called Indo-European. It was indeed this very literature of India, the investigation of which led to the discovery of this affinity of languages, a discovery which was so truly epoch-making, because it threw such an astonishing new light upon the pre-historic relations between the peoples. For, from the affinity of languages, one was forced to conclude that there was a former unity of languages, and this again presupposed a closer tie between the peoples speaking these Indo-European languages. There certainly are widespread and considerable errors concerning this relationship of the Indo-European peoples prevailing even to-day. People speak of an Indo-European "race," which does not exist at all, and never has existed. One also hears at times that Indians, Persians, Greeks, Romans, Germanic peoples and Slavs are of the same blood, descendants of one and the same Indo-European "primitive stock." These were far too hasty conclusions. But though it is even more than doubtful whether the peoples which speak Indo-European languages are all descended from a common origin, still it must not be doubted that a common language, this most important instrument of all mental activity, implies a relationship of mind and a common culture. Though the Indians are not flesh of our flesh, or bone of our bone, we may yet discover mind of our mind in the world of Indian thought. In order, however, to attain to a knowledge of the "Indo-European mind," *i.e.* of that which may be called the Indo-European peculiarity in thought, reflection and poetry of these peoples, it is absolutely essential for the one-sided knowledge of the Indo-European character, which we have acquired by the study of European literatures, to be completed by an acquaintance with the Indo-European mind as evidenced in the distant East. It is for this reason that Indian literature, more especially, forms a necessary complement to the classical literature of Ancient Greece and Rome for all who would guard themselves against a one-sided view of the Indo-European character. Indian literature cannot, indeed, be compared with Greek literature in regard to artistic merit. The world of Indian thought has not, it is true, exercised by any means such an influence over modern European ideas as did Greek and Roman culture. But if we wish to learn to understand the beginnings of our own culture, if we wish to understand the oldest Indo-European culture, we must go to India, where the oldest literature of an Indo-European people is preserved. For whatever view we may adopt on the problem of the antiquity of Indian literature, we can safely say that the oldest monument of the literature of the Indians is at the same time the oldest monument of Indo-European literature which we possess.

Moreover, the immediate influence which the literature of India has exercised over our own literature, too, should not be under-estimated. We shall see that the narrative literature of Europe is dependent on the Indian fable literature in no small degree. It is more especially German literature and German philosophy which, since the beginning of the 19th century, have been greatly influenced by Indian ideas, and it is quite probable that this influence is still on the increase, and that it will be augmented still further in the course of the present century.

For that affinity of mind which is revealed to us in the unity of the Indo-European languages, is still clearly recognisable to-day, and nowhere so markedly as between Indians and Germans. The striking points of agreement between the

German and Indian mind have often been pointed out.[1] "The Indians," says Leopold von Schroeder, "are the nation of romanticists of antiquity: the Germans are the romanticists of modern times." G. Brandes has already referred to the tendency towards contemplation and abstract speculation as well as to the inclination towards pantheism in the case of both Germans and Indians. Moreover, the German and the Indian character meet in many other respects, in a striking manner. It is not only German poets who have sung of "Weltschmerz" (world-sorrow). "Weltschmerz" is also the basic idea upon which the doctrine of Buddha is built up; and more than one Indian poet has lamented the suffering and woe of the world, the transitoriness and the vanity of all earthly things in words which remind us forcibly of our great poet of "Weltschmerz," Nikolaus Lenau. And when Heine says:

> "Sweet is sleep, but death is better,
> Best of all is it never to be born,"

he expresses the same idea as those Indian philosophers, who aspire to nothing more ardently than to that death after which there is no further re-birth. Again, sentimentality and feeling for Nature are the common property of German and Indian poetry, whilst they are foreign, say, to Hebrew or Greek poetry. Germans and Indians love descriptions of Nature; and both Indian and German poets delight in connecting the joys and sorrows of man with the Nature which surrounds him. There is yet another, quite different province, in which we encounter the similarity between Germans and Indians. Mention has already been made of the tendency of the Indians to work out scientific systems; and we are justified in saying that the Indians were the

---

[1]) Thus especially by G. *Brandes*, "Hauptströmungen der Literatur des neunzehnten Jahrhunderts," Berlin 1872, I, p. 270, and by *Leopold von Schroeder*, "Indiens Literatur und Cultur," Leipzig 1887, p. 6 f.

nation of scholars of antiquity, just as the Germans are the nation of scholars of to-day. In the earliest ages the Indians already analysed their ancient sacred writings with a view to philology, classified the linguistic phenomena as a scientific system, and developed their grammar so highly that even to-day modern philology can use their attainments as a foundation ; likewise Germans of to-day are the undisputed leaders in all fields of philology and linguistic science.

In the field of Indian philology and in the research of Indian literature, too, the Germans have been the leaders and pioneers. Much as we are indebted to the English, who, as the rulers of India, took up the study of Indian language and literature as a result of practical needs, much as some prominent French, Italian, Dutch, Danish, American, Russian, and,—which should not be forgotten—native Indian scholars, have done for the investigation of Indian literature and culture,—the Germans have undoubtedly taken the lion's share in publishing critical editions of texts, explaining and investigating them, and in compiling dictionaries and grammars. A brief survey of the history of Indological studies will show us this.

THE BEGINNINGS OF THE STUDY OF INDIAN LITERATURE IN EUROPE.[1]

The enormous mass of Indian literary works, which to-day can hardly be surveyed by *one* investigator, has been made accessible for research only in the course of little more than a century.

Certainly already in the seventeenth, and still more in the eighteenth century, isolated travellers and missionaries acquired a certain knowledge of Indian languages, and made

[1]) For this chapter see *E. Windisch*, "Geschichte der Sanskrit-Philologie und indischen Altertumskunde," I, II (Grundriss I, 1, 1917 and 1920).

themselves acquainted with one or another of the works of Indian literature. But their efforts did not fall on fruitful soil. Thus in the year 1651 the Dutchman Abraham Roger who had lived as a preacher in Paliacatta (Puliat) to the north of Madras, reported in his work "Open Door to the Hidden Heathendom"[1] on the ancient Brahmanical literature of the Indians, and published some of the Proverbs of Bhartṛhari, which had been translated into Portuguese for him by a Brahman, and which were drawn upon by Herder in later years for his "Stimmen der Völker in Liedern." In the year 1699 the Jesuit Father Johann Ernst Hanxleden went to India and worked there for over thirty years in the Malabar Mission. He was himself conversant with Indian languages, and his "Grammatica Granthamia seu Samscrdumica" was the first Sanskrit Grammar written by a European. It was never printed, but was used by Fra Paolino de St. Bartholomeo. This Fra Paolino—an Austrian Carmelite, whose real name was J. Ph. Wessdin—is undeniably the most important of the missionaries who worked at the earliest opening-up of Indian literature. He was a missionary on the coast of Malabar from 1776 till 1789 and died in Rome in the year 1805. He wrote two Sanskrit Grammars and several learned treatises and books. His "Systema Brahmanicum" (Rome, 1792) and his "Reise nach Ostindien" (German by J. R. Forster, Berlin, 1798) show a great knowledge of India and the Brahmanical literature, as well as a deep study of Indian languages and especially of Indian religious thought. But yet his work too has left only faint traces behind.

At the same time, however, the English too had begun to concern themselves about the language and literature of the Indians. It was no less a person than Warren Hastings, the actual founder of British rule in India, from whom

[1]) The book appeared in Dutch in 1651 ("Open-Deure tot het verborgen Heydendom," in 1915 newly edited by W. *Caland*), and in a German translation in Nürnberg in 1663.

emanated the first fruitful stimulus for the study of Indian literature, which has never since been interrupted. He had recognised, what the English since then have never forgotten, that the sovereignty of England in India would be secure only if the rulers understood how to treat the social and religious prejudices of the natives with all possible consideration. At his instigation therefore a resolution was incorporated in the law which was to regulate the Government of India, to the effect that native scholars should attend the legal proceedings in order to make it possible for the English judges in India to consider the statutes of Indian law-books at the formulation of the verdicts. And when, in the year 1773, Warren Hastings was nominated as the Governor-General of Bengal and entrusted with the highest powers over the whole of the English possessions in India, he had a work compiled by a number of Brahmans, versed in the law, out of the ancient Indian law books, under the title of "Vivādārṇavasetu" ("Bridge over the Ocean of Disputes") containing everything important about the Indian law of inheritance, family law, and such like. When the work was finished, no one could be found who was capable of translating it directly from Sanskrit into English. It therefore had to be translated from Sanskrit into Persian, from which it was translated into English by Nathaniel Brassey Halhed. This translation was printed at the expense of the East India Company in the year 1776 under the title "A Code of Gentoo[1] Law."

The first Englishman who acquired a knowledge of Sanskrit was Charles Wilkins, who had been urged by Warren Hastings to take instruction from the Pandits in Benares, the chief seat of Indian learning. As the first-fruits of his Sanskrit studies he published in the year 1785 an English

---

[1]) A German translation appeared in Hamburg in 1778. "Gentoo" is the Anglo-Indian form of the Portuguese "gentio," "heathen," and is used to designate the Indian "heathens," *i.e.* the Hindus, in contradistinction to the Mohammedans.

translation of the philosophical poem "Bhagavadgītā," which was the first time a Sanskrit book had been translated directly into a European language. Two years later there followed a translation of the book of fables, "Hitopadeśa," and in 1795 a translation of the Śakuntalā episode from the Mahābhārata. For his Sanskrit Grammar, which appeared in 1808, Sanskrit type was used for the first time in Europe, a type which he himself had carved and cast. He was also the first who occupied himself with Indian inscriptions and translated some of them into English.

However, still more important for the opening-up of large departments of Indian literature was the work of the famous English orientalist William Jones [1] (born 1746, died 1794), who went to India in the year 1783 in order to take up the post of Chief Justice at Fort William. Jones had already in his youth occupied himself with oriental poetry, and translated Arabic and Persian poems into English. No wonder that, when he arrived in India, he transferred his enthusiasm to the study of Sanskrit and Indian literature. Already a year after his arrival in India he became the founder of the Asiatic Society of Bengal, which soon displayed an extraordinarily useful activity in the publication of periodicals, and especially in the printing of numerous editions of Indian texts. In the year 1789 he published his English translation of the celebrated drama "Śakuntalā" by Kālidāsa. This English translation was translated into German in the year 1791 by Georg Forster, and awakened in the highest degree the enthusiasm of men like Herder and Goethe. Another work of the same poet Kālidāsa, the lyric poem "Ṛtusaṃhāra," was published in the original text by Jones in Calcutta in the year 1792, and this was the first Sanskrit text which appeared

[1]) William *Jones* was not only a learned and enthusiastic Orientalist, but also the first Anglo-Indian poet. He composed suggestive hymns to Brahman, Nārāyaṇa, Lakṣmī, etc.; s. E. F. *Oaten*, "A Sketch of Anglo-Indian Literature," London 1908, p. 19 ff.

in print. Of still greater importance was the fact that Jones translated into English the most famous and most reputed work of Indian legal literature, the law book of Manu. This translation appeared in Calcutta in 1794 under the title "Institutes of Hindu Law, or the Ordinance of Manu." A German translation of this book appeared in 1797 in Weimar. Finally Jones was also the first who affirmed the certain genealogical connection of Sanskrit with Greek and Latin and its hypothetical connection with German, Celtic and Persian. He had already also pointed out the similarities between the ancient Indian and the Graeco-Roman mythology.

While the enthusiastic W. Jones, through the enthusiasm with which he brought to light Indian literary treasures, was primarily stimulating, the sober Henry Thomas Colebrooke, who continued the work of W. Jones, became the real founder of Indian philology and archaeology. Colebrooke had entered on his official career in Calcutta in 1782 as a youth of seventeen years, without troubling himself during the first eleven years of his sojourn in India about Sanskrit and Sanskrit literature. But when W. Jones died in 1794 Colebrooke had just learnt Sanskrit and had undertaken to translate from the Sanskrit into English, under Jones' guidance, a composition, prepared by native scholars, on the law of succession and contract, from the Indian law books. This translation appeared in 1797 and 1798 under the title "A Digest of Hindu Law on Contracts and Successions" in four folio volumes. From that time he devoted himself with untiring zeal to the investigation of Indian literature. His interest, contrary to that of Jones, lay not so much in the poetic as in the scientific literature. Therefore we are indebted to him not only for further works on Indian law, but also for pioneer essays on philosophy and religious life, on grammar, astronomy and the arithmetic of the Indians. Moreover it was he who, in the year 1805, in the now famous essay "On the Vedas," was the first to give definite and reliable information about the ancient sacred books of the Indians.[1] He was also the editor of the Amarakośa and other Indian dictionaries, of the famous grammar of Pāṇini, of the "Hitopadeśa," and of the epic poem "Kirātārjunīya." Further he is the author of a Sanskrit grammar, and edited and translated a number of inscriptions. Finally he amassed an exceedingly diversified collection of Indian manuscripts, which are supposed to have cost him about £10,000, and which, after his return to England, he presented to the East India Company. This collection of manuscripts is to-day one of the most valuable treasures of the library of the India Office in London.

Among the Englishmen who, like Jones and Colebrooke, learned Sanskrit at about the close of the eighteenth century, was Alexander Hamilton. The latter returned to Europe in 1802, travelling through France, and stayed for a short time in Paris. An event then happened, which, though unpleasant for himself, was extraordinarily favourable for Sanskrit learning. Just at that time the hostilities between France and England, which had been interrupted only for a short time by the Peace of Amiens, broke out anew and Napoleon issued a command that all English people who were in France when war broke out should be prevented from returning to their homes, and be detained in Paris. Alexander Hamilton was among these Englishmen. But, in the year 1802 the German poet Friedrich Schlegel[2] had also just come to Paris to

---

[1]) The alleged translation of the Yajurveda which appeared in the year 1778 in French under the title "Ezour-vedam" and in 1779 also in German, is a falsification, a pious fraud, which used to be ascribed to the missionary *Roberto de 'Nobili.'* But *W. Caland*, Th. *Zachariæ* (GGA 1921, p. 157), and others deny, that he was the author of the fraud. *Voltaire* received this alleged translation from the hands of an official returning from Pondicherry and presented it to the Royal Library in Paris, in 1761. *Voltaire* regarded the book as an old commentary on the Veda, which had been translated by a venerable centenarian Brahman into French, and he frequently refers to the "Ezour-Veda" as an authority for Indian antiquities. Already in the year 1782 *Sonnerat* declared the book to be a falsification. (A. W. *Schlegel*, Indische Bibliothek, II, p. 50 ff.)

[2]) *Cf.* A. F. J. *Remy*, "The Influence of India and Persia on the Poetry of Germany,'

stay there, except for a few intervals, till the year 1807, just during the time of A. Hamilton's involuntary sojourn. In Germany attention had for a long time already been drawn to the efforts of English scholars. Especially the above-mentioned translation of "Śakuntalā" by W. Jones had attracted much attention, and had been immediately (1791) translated into German. In the years 1795-97 W. Jones's treatises had already appeared in a German translation. Also Jones's translation of Manu's Law Book had been rendered into German already in the year 1797. The books of Fra Paolino de St. Bartholomeo too did certainly not remain unnoticed in Germany. Above all, however, it was the Romantic School, headed by the brothers Schlegel, for which Indian literature had a special attraction. It was indeed the time when people began to become enthusiastic about foreign literatures. Herder had already frequently directed the attention of the Germans to the Orient by means of his "Stimmen der Völker in Liedern" (1778) and his "Ideen zur Geschichte der Menschheit" (1784-91). It was the Romanticists, however, who threw themselves with the greatest enthusiasm into everything strange and distant, and who felt themselves most especially attracted by India. From India one expected, as Friedrich Schlegel said, nothing less than "the unfolding of the history of the primeval world which up till now is shrouded in darkness; and lovers of poetry hoped, especially since the appearance of the Sokuntola to glean thence many similar beautiful creations of the Asiatic spirit, animated, as in this case, by grace and love." No wonder, therefore, that, when he made the acquaintance of Alexander Hamilton in Paris, Friedrich Schlegel at once seized the opportunity of learning Sanskrit from him. In the years 1803 and 1804 he had the advantage of his instruction and the

---

New York, 1901, and P. Th. *Hoffmann*, "Der indische und der deutsche Geist von Herder bis zur Romantik" Diss., Tübingen, 1915.

remaining years of his stay in Paris he employed in study in the Paris Library, which already at that time contained about two hundred Indian manuscripts.[1] As the result of these studies there appeared in the year 1808 that book through which Friedrich Schlegel became the founder of Indian philology in Germany, namely, "Ueber die Sprache und Weisheit der Indier. Ein Beitrag zur Begründung der Altertumskunde." This book was written with enthusiasm and was suitable for awakening enthusiasm. It contained also translations of some passages from the Rāmāyaṇa, from Manu's Law Book, from the Bhagavadgītā, and from the Śakuntalā-episode of the Mahābhārata. These were the first direct translations from Sanskrit into German; for what had previously been known of Indian literature in Germany, had been translated from the English.

While Friedrich Schlegel's work was chiefly stimulating, it was his brother August Wilhelm von Schlegel who was the first in Germany to develop an extensive activity as a Sanskrit scholar by means of editions of texts, translations, and other philological works. He was also the first Professor of Sanskrit in Germany, in which capacity he was called to the newly-founded University of Bonn in the year 1818. Like his brother, he too had begun his Sanskrit studies in Paris, namely, in the year 1814. His teacher was a Frenchman, A. L. Chézy, the first French scholar to learn and teach Sanskrit; he was also the first Sanskrit Professor at the Collège de France, and has rendered valuable services as an editor and translator of Indian works. In the year 1823 appeared the first volume of the periodical "Indische Bibliothek," founded and almost entirely written by August Wilhelm von Schlegel, containing numerous essays on Indian philology. In the same year he published also a

[1]) A catalogue of these was published by *Alexander Hamilton* in Paris, 1807 (in conjunction with L. *Langlès*, who translated *Hamilton's* notes into French).

good edition of the Bhagavadgītā with a Latin translation, while in the year 1829 appeared the first part of Schlegel's most important work, his unfinished edition of the Rāmāyaṇa.

A contemporary of August Wilhelm von Schlegel was Franz Bopp, who was born in 1791, went to Paris in 1812, in order to devote himself to the study of Oriental languages, and there learned Sanskrit from Chézy, together with Schlegel. But while the brothers Schlegel, as romantic poets, were enthusiastic over India, and took up their work in Indian literature as a kind of adventure,[1] Bopp joined these studies as a thoroughly sober investigator, and it was he who became the founder of a new science, Comparative Philology, which was destined to so great a future,—and this by means of his book, published in 1816, "Ueber das Conjugations-system der Sanskritsprache in Vergleichung mit jenem der griechischen, lateinischen, persischen und germanischen Sprache." In the investigation of Indian literature, too, Bopp has rendered invaluable services. Already in his "Conjugations-system" he gave as an appendix some episodes from the Rāmāyaṇa and Mahābhārata in metrical translations from the original text, besides some extracts from the Vedas after Colebrooke's English translation. With rare skill he then singled out of the great epic Mahābhārata the wonderful story of King Nala and his faithful wife Damayantī, and made it universally accessible by means of a good critical edition with a Latin translation.[2] It is just this one, out of the countless episodes of the

---

[1]) Thus *Friedrich Schlegel* writes in a letter to *Goethe* that he has set himself the task "of bringing to light that which has been forgotten and unappreciated," and therefore had turned from Dante to Shakespeare, to Petrarch and Calderon, to the old German heroic songs, "In this manner I had to a certain extent exhausted the European literature, and turned to Asia in order to seek a new adventure." (A. *Hillebrandt*, "Alt-Indien" Breslau, 1899, p. 37.) *Aug. Wilh. von Schlegel* also writes (Indische Bibliothek, p. 8) that he desires, by means of his essays, to point the way to a certain extent for those of his compatriots "who wish to taste the adventure (for an adventure it remains after all)."

[2]) Nalus, Carmen Sanskritum e Mahabharato, edidit, latine vertit et adnotationibus illustravit *Franciscus Bopp*. London, 1819.

Mahābhārata, which most completely forms a separate whole, and not only is one of the most beautiful portions of the great epic, but also, as one of the most charming creations of Indian poetic art, is most peculiarly suitable for awakening enthusiasm for Indian literature, and love for the study of Sanskrit. It has, in fact, become almost traditional at all Western Universities where Sanskrit is taught, to select the Nala-episode as the first reading for the students, for which purpose it is especially suitable also on account of the simplicity of the language. A number of other episodes from the Mahābhārata, too, were published for the first time and translated into German by Bopp. His Sanskrit Grammars (1827, 1832 and 1834) and his "Glossarium Sanscritum" (Berlin 1830) have done very much to further the study of Sanskrit in Germany.

It was fortunate for the young science of comparative philology and for the study of Sanskrit, which was then still for a long time connected with it, that the ingenious, versatile and influential Wilhelm von Humboldt showed enthusiasm for these studies. In the year 1821 he began to learn Sanskrit because, as he once wrote in a letter to Aug. Wilh. von Schlegel,[1] he had perceived "that without as thorough as possible a study of Sanskrit, very little can be accomplished either in philology or in that kind of history which is connected with it." And when Schlegel, in the year 1828, took a retrospect of Indian studies, he emphasized as particularly fortunate for the new science the fact that it "had found a warm friend and patron in Herrn Wilhelm von Humboldt." Schlegel's edition of the Bhagavadgītā had directed Humboldt's attention to this theosophical poem. He devoted special treatises to it, and at the time he wrote to Fr. von Gentz (1827): "It is perhaps the deepest and loftiest thing the world has to show." Later, in 1828, when he sent to his friend his work on the Bhagavadgītā, which had in the meantime been

[1]) Indische Bibliothek, 1, p. 433.

criticized by Hegel, he wrote that, however indifferent he might be to Hegel's judgment, he greatly valued the Indian philosophical poem. "I read the Indian poem," he writes, "for the first time in the country in Silesia, and my constant feeling while doing so was gratitude to Fate for having permitted me to live long enough to become acquainted with this book." [1]

Yet another great hero of German literature remains to be mentioned, who fortunately for our science, had enthusiasm for Indian poetry. This is the German poet Friedrich Rückert, the incomparable master of the art of translation. Of the loveliest gems of Indian epics and lyrics there is indeed much which

> "Rustled thousands of years ago
> In the tops of Indian palms,"

and which, through him, has become the common property of the German people.[2]

Till the year 1830 it was almost entirely the so-called classical Sanskrit literature which occupied the attention of European students. The drama "Śakuntalā," the philosophic poem "Bhagavadgītā," the Law-Book of Manu, the proverbs of Bhartṛhari, the fable-book "Hitopadeśa," and selected portions of the great epics: these were practically the chief works with which research was occupied, and which were regarded as the original stock of Indian literature. The great and all-important province of Indian literature, the Veda, was almost entirely unknown, and of the whole of the great Buddhist literature nothing at all was known as yet. The little that was known of the Vedas up till the year 1830 was limited to meagre and incomplete information

[1]) Schriften von Friedrich *von Gentz*. Herausgegeben von Gustav Schlesier, Mannheim, 1840, Vol. V, pp. 291 and 300.

[2]) *Rückert's* translations from Indian classical poetry have been re-edited by H. *von Glasenapp*, Indische Liebeslyrik, München, 1921.

from the older writers on India. The first reliable information was given by Colebrooke in his abovementioned treatise on the Vedas in 1805.[1] Comparatively more was known about the Upaniṣads, the philosophic treatises belonging to the Vedas. These Upaniṣads had been translated in the 17th century into Persian by the brother of Aurangzeb, the unfortunate Prince Mohammed-Dara Shakoh,[2] the son of the Great Mogul Shah Jehan. From the Persian they were translated into Latin at the beginning of the 19th century by the French scholar Anquetil du Perron[3] under the title "Oupnek'hat." [4] Imperfect and full of misinterpretations as the Latin translation was, it has become of importance for the history of learning, through the fact that the German philosophers Schelling, and especially Schopenhauer, became enthusiastic for Indian philosophy by means of this book. It was not the Upaniṣads as we know and explain them now with all the material of Indian philology now accessible to us and our more definite knowledge of the whole philosophy of the Indians, but the "Oupnek'hat," that

---

1) Miscellaneous Essays, Madras, 1872, pp. 9 ff. A German translation was published in 1847. For the beginnings of Vedic research, see *W. Caland*, "De Ontdekkingsgeschiedenis van den Veda," Amsterdam 1918, and *Th. Zachariae*, GGA., 1921, 148 ff. (English in the Journal of Indian History, May, 1923.)

2) The fate of this prince forms the subject of a beautiful, unfortunately too little known tragedy by L. *von Schroeder*, "Dara oder Schah Dschehan und seine Söhne" (Mitau 1891).

3) *Anquetil du Perron*, too, was among those who were inspired by the Upaniṣads, and was himself a kind of Indian ascetic. See *E. Windisch*, "Die altindischen Religionsurkunden und die christliche Mission," Leipzig, 1897, p. 15, and "Geschichte der Sanskrit-Philologie," pp. 48 ff.

4) The complete title is: "Oupnek'hat *i.e.* secretum tegendum, opus ipsa in India rarissimum, continens antiquam et arcanam s. theologicam, et philosophicam doctrinam e quatuor sacris Indorum libris, Rak Beid, Djedir Beid, Sam Beid, Athrban Beid excerptam: ad verbum e persico idiomate, Sanscreticis vocabulis intermixto in latinum conversum... studio et opera *Anquetil du Perron*...Parisiis 1801-1802, 4, 2 Vol."

Partly translated into German, Nürnberg, 1808. "Oupnek'hat" is a corruption of "Upaniṣad" and "Rak Beid" etc. are corruptions of "Ṛg-veda," "Yajur-veda," "Sāma-veda" and "Atharva-veda."

absolutely imperfect Perso-Latin translation of Anquetil du Perron, which Schopenhauer declared to be "the production of the highest human wisdom." At the same time as Schopenhauer in Germany was putting more of his own philosophical ideas into the Upaniṣads of the Indians than he gleaned from them, there lived in India one of the wisest and noblest men that this land has produced, Rāmmohun Roy, the founder of the "Brahmo Samāj" (a new religious community which sought to unite the best of the European religions with the faith of the Hindus), an Indian who, out of the same Upaniṣads, gleaned the purest faith in God, and out of them tried to prove to his countrymen that, although the idolatry of the present Indian religions is objectionable, yet the Indians therefore need not embrace Christianity, but could find a pure religion in their own sacred writings, in the old Vedas, if they only understood them. With the object of revealing this new teaching, new though already contained in the ancient scriptures, and causing it to be propagated by means of the religious community founded by him, the Brahmo Samāj, or the "Church of God," and also with the purpose of proving to the Christian theologians and missionaries whom he esteemed highly, that the best of that which they taught was already contained in the Upaniṣads,—he translated in the years 1816-1819, a considerable number of Upaniṣads into English, and published a few of these in the original.[1]

The actual philological investigation of the Vedas, however, began only in the year 1838, with the edition, published in London, of the first eighth of the Ṛgveda, by Friedrich Rosen, who was only prevented by his premature death from completing his edition. But above all it was the great French orientalist Eugène Burnouf, who taught at the

---

[1]) Smaller fragments of the Upaniṣads appeared also in *Othmar Frank's* "Chrestomathia Sanscrita" (1820-1821) and in his "Vyāsa, über Philosophie, Mythologie, Literatur und Sprache der Hindu. (1826-1830).

Collège de France in the early forties of the nineteenth century, and who, by gathering around him a circle of pupils who afterwards became prominent Vedic scholars, laid the foundation of the study of the Vedas in Europe. One of these pupils was Rudolph Roth, who originated the study of the Vedas in Germany by his book "Zur Litteratur und Geschichte des Weda" (On the literature and history of the Veda) published in 1846. Roth himself and a goodly number of his pupils devoted themselves in the following years and decades with a burning zeal to the investigation of the various branches of this, India's oldest literature. Another celebrated pupil of Burnouf was F. Max Müller, who had been initiated into the study of the Vedas by Burnouf at the same time as Roth. Stimulated by Burnouf, Max Müller formed the project of publishing the hymns of the Ṛgveda with the great commentary of Sāyaṇa. This edition, essential for all further research, appeared in the years 1849-1875.[1] Before this was yet completed, Th. Aufrecht had rendered invaluable services to these investigations, by his handy edition of the complete text of the hymns of the Ṛgveda (1861-1863).[2]

The same Eugène Burnouf who had stood by the cradle of Veda study, had also, by the "Essai sur le Pali" published in 1826 in conjunction with Lassen, and by his "Introduction à l'histoire du Bouddhisme Indien" laid the foundation of the study of Pali, and the investigation of Buddhist literature.

With the conquest of this great department of Veda literature, and with the opening-up of the literature of Buddhism, the history of the infancy of Indology has reached its end. It has grown into a great department of learning, in which the number of collaborators increases year by year. Now rapidly, one after the other, appear critical editions of

---

[1]) A second improved edition was published in 1890-1892.

[2]) A second edition of *Aufrecht's* text of the hymns of the Ṛg-veda was published in Bonn, 1877.

the most important texts, and scholars of all countries strive in noble emulation to interpret them.[1] What has been done in the last decades in the different provinces of Indian literature, will have to be mentioned for the most part in the separate chapters of this history of literature. Here only the principal stages on the path of Indology, the most important events in its history can be briefly mentioned.

Above all, mention must be made of a pupil of A. Wilh. v. Schlegel, Christian Lassen, who tried to gather together the whole of the contemporary knowledge about India, in his "Indische Alterthumskunde" which, planned on a large scale, began to appear in the year 1843 and comprised four thick volumes, the last of which appeared in 1862. The fact that this book is obsolete already to-day is not the fault of the author, but a brilliant proof of the colossal progress which our science has made in the second half of the nineteenth century.

The most powerful lever, however, for this progress, and perhaps the chief event in the history of Sanskrit research was the appearance of the "Sanskrit-Wörterbuch" (Sanskrit Dictionary) compiled by Otto Böhtlingk and Rudolph Roth, published by the Academy of Arts and Sciences in St. Petersburg. The first part of this appeared in the year 1852, and in the year 1875 the work was complete in seven folio volumes —a brilliant monument to German industry.

In the same year 1852, in which the great St. Petersburg Dictionary began to appear, Albrecht Weber made an attempt for the first time to write a complete history of Indian literature. The work appeared under the title "Akademische Vorlesungen über indische Literaturgeschichte." A second

---

[1]) As early as 1823 A. W. *v. Schlegel* said very pertinently: "Will the English perhaps claim a monopoly of Indian literature? It would be too late. Cinnamon and cloves they may keep; but these mental treasures are the common property of the educated world." (Ind. Bibl. I, 15.)

edition appeared in 1876,[1] and it indicates not only a milestone in the history of Indology, but it has remained, in spite of its defects in style, which make it unpalatable for the general reader, for decades the most reliable and most complete handbook of Indian Literature.

However, if one desires to get an idea of the truly astonishing progress which the investigation of Indian literature has made in the comparatively short duration of its existence, then one should read A. Wilh. v. Schlegel's essay, written in the year 1819, "Ueber den gegenwärtigen Zustand der Indischen Philologie" (On the present condition of Indian philology), in which not many more than a dozen Sanskrit books are enumerated as having been made known through editions or translations. Next one should glance at Friedrich Adelung's book, which appeared in the year 1830 in St. Petersburg, "Versuch einer Literatur der Sanskrit-Sprache" (A Study on the literature of the Sanskrit language[2]) in which already the titles of over 350 Sanskrit books are mentioned. One should then compare with it Weber's "Indische Literaturgeschichte" which in the year 1852 (according to an approximate estimate), discusses close on 500 works of Indian literature. Then one should look at the "Catalogus Catalogorum" published by Theodor Aufrecht in the years 1891, 1896 and 1903, which contains an alphabetical list of all Sanskrit works and authors, based on the investigation of all the available catalogues of manuscripts. In this monumental work, at which Aufrecht worked for over forty years, all the catalogues of Sanskrit manuscripts of all the important libraries of India and Europe are incorporated,

---

[1]) An English translation of *Weber's* "History of Indian Literature" appeared in Trübner's Oriental Series.

[2]) This is rather a bibliography than a history of literature. About 230 edited texts are mentioned by J. *Gildemeister*, Bibliothecae Sanskritae sive recensus librorum Sanskritorum......Specimen Bonnae ad Rh. 1847.

and the number of available Sanskrit books in this "Catalogus Catalogorum" runs into many thousands. Yet this catalogue does not include the whole of the Buddhist literature, and all the literary works which were written in other Indian languages and not in Sanskrit. And how many new works have been discovered since 1903!

The investigation of Buddhist literature has been greatly furthered by the "Pali Text Society" founded in the year 1882 by T. W. Rhys Davids. Albrecht Weber, again, with his great treatise "Ueber die heiligen Schriften der Jaina"[1] (1883-1885) (on the sacred writings of the Jains) has opened up for science another great branch of literature, the writings of the Jains, a sect equal in antiquity to Buddhism.

So much indeed has the amount of Indian Literature, which has become known, gradually increased, that now-a-days it is hardly possible any more for *one* scholar to master all the provinces of the same, and that the necessity arose for giving in one work an encyclopaedic view of everything which has, up till now, been done in the separate branches of Indology. For this work which has been appearing since the year 1897[2] under the title "Grundriss der indo-arischen Philologie und Altertumskunde" (Encyclopaedia of Indo-aryan Philology and Archaeology) the plan was drawn up by Georg Bühler, the greatest and most versatile Sanskrit scholar of the last decades. Thirty scholars from Germany, Austria, England, Holland, India and America banded themselves together, in order to compile the separate parts of this work, first under the editorship of Bühler—afterwards under that of Franz Kielhorn and now under that of H. Lüders and J. Wackernagel. The publication of this, "Grundriss" is at one and the same time the latest and

1) "Indische Studien," Vols. 16 and 17.

2) Published by Karl J. Trübner in Strassburg, now Vereinigung wissenschaftlicher Verleger Walter de Gruyter & Co., Berlin and Leipzig.

most welcome, as well as most important, event in the history of the development of Indology. If we wish to compare the knowledge of India and its literature as laid down in the volumes of this "Grundriss" which have appeared up till now, with that which Lassen was able to record in his "Indische Altertumskunde" only a few decades before, then we can look with just pride at the progress which science has made in a comparatively short period of time.

The Chronology of Indian Literature.

Much as has been done with regard to the opening-up of Indian literature, yet its actual history is still to a great extent wrapped in darkness and unexplored. Above all, the chronology of the history of Indian literature is shrouded in truly terrifying darkness, and most of the riddles still remain to be solved by research. It would be so pleasant, so convenient, and, especially for a handbook, so desirable if one could divide Indian literature into three or four periods, separated by definite dates, and place the different literary productions in one or the other of these periods. But every attempt of such a kind is bound to fail in the present state of knowledge, and the use of hypothetical dates would only be a delusion, which would do more harm than good. It is much better to recognise clearly the fact that for the oldest period of Indian literary history we can give no certain dates, and for the later periods only a few. Years ago the celebrated American Sanskrit scholar W. D. Whitney [1] gave utterance to these words which since then have often been repeated: "All dates given in Indian literary history are pins set up to be bowled down again." For the most part this is still the case to-day. Even to-day the views of the most important investigators with

[1] In the Introduction to his "Sanskrit Grammar," Leipzig, 1879 (second edition, 1889).

regard to the age of the most important Indian literary works, differ, not indeed by years and decades, but by whole centuries, if not even by one or two thousands of years. What can be determined with some certainty, is at most only a kind of relative chronology. We can often say : this or that book, this or that class of literature is older than a certain other; however, with regard to its real age it is only possible to offer hypotheses. The surest mark of differentiation for this relative chronology still lies in the language. Less reliable are peculiarities of style; for it has often happened in India that later works have imitated the style of an older class of literature, in order to assume an appearance of antiquity. Often, indeed, also the relative chronology is spoiled, because many works of Indian literature, and just those which were the most popular, and therefore are the most important for us, have suffered manifold revisions, and have come to us in various modifications. If we find, for example, the Rāmāyaṇa or the Mahābhārata quoted in a book, the date of which can even only approximately be fixed, then the question always arises first, whether this quotation refers to the epics as we have them at present, or to the older versions of the same. Still greater does the uncertainty become through the fact that, of the majority of the works of the older literature, the authors' names are as good as unknown to us. They are handed down to us as the works of families, of schools, or monastic communities, or a mythical seer of primitive times is named as the author. When at last, we come to a time where we have to deal with the works of quite definite individual writers, then these are, as a rule, only mentioned by their family names with which the literary historian of India knows as little what to do, as probably a German literary historian with the names Meier, Schultze or Müller, when these are given without a first name. If, for example, a book under the name of Kālidāsa, or the name of Kālidāsa is mentioned anywhere, then it is by no means certain that the great poet of this name is meant, it can equally well be another Kālidāsa.[1]

In this ocean of uncertainty there are only a few fixed points, which, in order not to frighten the reader too much, I would like to mention here.

There is above all the evidence of language, which proves that the hymns and songs, prayers and magic formulas of the Veda, are indisputably the oldest which we possess of Indian literature. Further, it is certain that Buddhism arose in India about 500 years before Christ, and that it presupposes the whole Vedic literature, as represented by its chief works, as practically finished, so that one can assert: The Vedic literature apart from its latest excrescences is on the whole pre-Buddhist, *i.e.* it was concluded before 500 B.C. Also, the chronology of the Buddhist and Jain literature is fortunately not quite so uncertain as that of the Brahmanical literature. The traditions of the Buddhists and the Jains with regard to the formation, or rather the collection, of their canonical works, have proved themselves fairly trustworthy, and inscriptions on the preserved ruins of temples and topes of these religious sects give us appreciable indications of the history of their literature.

However, the safest dates of Indian history are those which we do not get from the Indians themselves. Thus, the invasion of Alexander the Great in India, in the year 326 B.C., is a certain date, which is of importance for Indian literary history, also, especially when it is the question whether, in any literary work or class of literature, Greek influence should be assumed. From the Greeks we also know that,

---

[1]) The history of Indian literature encounters an additional difficulty in the frequent occurrence of the same name in different forms, and in the circumstance that one and the same author often has two or several different names, as name synonyms and abbreviations of names are very general in India; s. R. O. *Franke*, "Indische Genuslehren," pp. 57 ff. and GGA, 1892, pp. 482 ff.

about 315 B.C. Candragupta, the Sandrakottos of the Greek writers, conducted successfully the revolt against the prefects of Alexander, took possession of the throne, and became the founder of the Maurya dynasty in Pāṭaliputra (the Palibothra of the Greeks, the present Patna). It was at about the same time, or a few years later, that the Greek Megasthenes was sent by Seleukos as ambassador to the court of Candragupta. The fragments which have been preserved of the description of India, written by him, give us a picture of the state of Indian culture at that time, and enable us to draw conclusions as to the dates of several Indian literary works. A grandson of Candragupta is the celebrated King Aśoka, who was crowned about 264 B.C.,[1] and from whom originate the oldest dateable Indian inscriptions which have been found up to the present. These inscriptions, partly on rocks, partly on pillars, are the oldest evidences of Indian script which we possess. They show us this powerful king as a patron and a protector of Buddhism, who made use of his sovereignty, which extended from the extreme north to the extreme south of India, for the purpose of spreading abroad everywhere the teaching of Buddha, and who, unlike other rulers, in his rock and pillar edicts, did not narrate his own conquests and glorious deeds, but exhorted the people to virtuous conduct, warned them against sin, and preached love and tolerance. These singular edicts of the King Aśoka are themselves precious literary monuments hewn in stone, but they are also of importance for the history of literature on account of their script and their language, as well as for evidences of religious history. In the year 178 B.C., 137 years after the coronation of Candragupta, the last scion of the Maurya dynasty was hurled from the throne by a king Puṣyamitra. The mention of this King Puṣyamitra, for instance, in a drama of Kālidāsa, is an important evidence for the determination

---

[1]) See *Fleet*, JRAS 1912, 239.

of the date of several works of Indian literature. The same is true of the Græco-Bactrian King Menander, who reigned about 144 B.C. He appears under the name Milinda in the famous Buddhist book "Milindapañha."

Next to the Greeks it is the Chinese to whom we are indebted for some of the most important date-determinations of Indian literary history. Since the first century after Christ we hear of Buddhist missionaries who go to China and translate Buddhist works into Chinese, of Indian embassies in China and of Chinese pilgrims, who make pilgrimages to India in order to visit the holy places of Buddhism. Works of Indian literature are translated into Chinese, and the Chinese give us exact dates at which these translations were made. There are especially three Chinese pilgrims Fa-hien, who went to India in the year 399, Hsüan-Tsang, who made great journeys in India from 630 to 645, and I-tsing, who sojourned in India from 671 to 695, whose descriptions of their travels are preserved. These accounts give us many a valuable datum on Indian antiquity and works of literature. The chronological data of the Chinese are, contrary to those of the Indians, wonderfully exact and reliable. It is only too true of the Indians, what the Arabian traveller Albērūni, who in the year 1030 wrote a book on India, which is very important for us, said of them: "Unfortunately the Hindus do not pay much attention to the historical order of things, they are very careless in relating the chronological succession of their kings, and when they are pressed for information and are at a loss, not knowing what to say, they invariably take to romancing." [1]

Nevertheless, one must not believe, as it has so often been asserted, that the historical sense is entirely lacking in the Indians. In India, too, there has been historical writing; and in any case we find in India numerous accurately dated inscriptions, which could hardly be the case if the Indians

---

[1]) See E. C. *Sachau*, Alberuni's India, English Ed., II, pp. 10

bad had no sense of history at all. It is only true that the Indians, in their writing of history, never knew how to keep fact and fiction strictly apart, that to them the facts themselves were always more important than their chronological order, and that they attached no importance at all, especially in literary matters, to the question of what was earlier or later. Whatever seems good, true and right, to the Indian, that he raises to the greatest possible age; and if he wants to impart a special sanctity to any doctrine, or if he wishes that his work shall be as widespread as possible, and gain respect, then he veils his name in a modest incognito, and mentions some ancient sage as the author of the book. This still happens at the present day, and in past centuries it was no different. It is for this reason that so many quite modern works pass under the time-honoured name of "Upaniṣads" or "Purāṇas," new, sour wine put into old bottles. The intention to deceive, however, is as a rule out of the question in these cases. It is only that extreme indifference reigns with regard to the right of literary ownership and the desire of asserting it. Only in the later centuries does it happen that authors give their own names with full details, together with the names of their parents, grandparents, teachers, patrons, and scanty biographical notes about themselves. The authors of astronomical books generally also give the exact date of the day on which they completed their work. Since the fifth century after Christ, inscriptions too begin to give us information about the dates of many writers. In the deciphering of inscriptions great progress has been made during the last decades. Witness thereof are the "Corpus Inscriptionum Indicarum," and the periodical "Epigraphia Indica." And it is the inscriptions to which we are not only indebted for the surest dates of Indian literary history, settled up to now, but from which we also hope to get the greater number of solutions of the chronological problems still unsolved at present.

The Art of Writing and the Transmission of Indian Literature.

The inscriptions are of such great significance for us because they also give us information on the question which is certainly not unimportant for Indian literary history, namely, the question regarding the age of the art of writing in India. As we shall soon see, the history of Indian literature does not by any means begin with the written literature, and it is not actual writings, but only orally transmitted texts which belong to the oldest periods of Indian literary history. Nevertheless it is clear that the question as to the time since when literary productions have been written down and thus transmitted, cannot by any means be an indifferent one for the history of the literature. Now the oldest dateable Indian inscriptions which have been found up till now, are the above-mentioned Edicts of King Aśoka of the third century before Christ. However, it would be quite wrong, if one were to form the conclusion—as Max Müller has done—that the use of writing in India does not date back to an earlier age. Palaeographic facts prove undeniably that writing cannot have been a new invention as late as the time of Aśoka, but must already have had a long history behind it. The oldest Indian script, from which the Nāgarī script, the best known in Europe, and all the numerous alphabets used in Indian manuscripts are derived, is called " Brāhma script," because it is supposed to have been invented, according to the Indian myth, by the Creator, the god Brahman himself. According to G. Bühler's comprehensive researches,[1] this script goes back to a Semitic origin, namely, to the oldest North Semitic characters, as they are found in Phœnician inscriptions, and on the stone

[1] "Indische Palaeographie" in the "Grundriss" I, 2, and "On the Origin of the Indian Brahma Alphabet," 2nd ed., Strassburg, 1898.

of Mesa about 890 B. C. Probably it was by merchants—perhaps already about 800 B. C.—that writing was introduced into India. For a long time, probably, it must have been used entirely for commercial purposes, records, correspondence, calculations, and so on. When afterwards writing began to be used also for the minutes of embassies, proclamations, records and so on in the Royal Chanceries, the kings must also have employed learned grammarians, Brahmans, who adapted the foreign alphabet more and more to the needs of Indian phonetics, and out of the 22 Semitic characters, elaborated a complete alphabet of 44 letters, as the oldest inscriptions already show it. However, since when writing has also been used in India for the recording of literary productions is a much debated question, which is hard to answer. Certain proofs of the existence of manuscripts, or even only authentic reports on the writing-down of texts do not exist from olden times. In the whole of Vedic literature it has not, up till now, been possible to find any proof of the knowledge of writing. In the Buddhist canon, which was probably completed about 240 B. C., there is no mention of manuscripts, although in it there are numerous proofs of an acquaintance with the art of writing, and its extensive use at that time. Writing is there spoken of as a distinguished branch of learning, it was expressly permitted to the Buddhist nuns to occupy themselves with the art of writing; we hear of monks, who through written praise of religious suicide, cause the death of others; it is said that "a registered thief" (*i.e.* a thief whose name is written down in the King's palace) may not be admitted into the order as a monk; a game of letters [1] is mentioned; and it is said that parents should have their children instructed in writing and arithmetic. Yet in the sacred books of Buddhism there is not to be found the least indication of the fact that the books themselves were copied

---

[1]) This consists of the guessing of letters drawn in the air or on a playmate's back.

or read. This is all the more striking because in the sacred texts of Buddhism we are informed of all possible, even most insignificant, details in the lives of the monks. "From morning till evening we can follow the monks in their daily life, on their wanderings, during their rest, in their solitude, and in their intercourse with other monks or laymen; we know the furniture of the rooms inhabited by them, their utensils, the contents of their store-rooms; but nowhere do we hear that they read or copied their sacred texts, nowhere that such things as writing materials or manuscripts were owned by anybody in the monasteries. The memory of the brethren "rich in hearing"—what we now call well-read was at that time called rich in hearing—took the place of monastic libraries; and if, in a community, the knowledge of an indispensable text, for instance, the confession formula which had to be recited in the assembly of brethren at every full-moon or new-moon threatened to disappear, then they followed the instructions prescribed in an old Buddhist rule for the community: "From amongst those monks one monk shall without delay be sent off to the neighbouring community. To him shall be said: Go brother, and when you have memorized the confession formula, the full one or the abridged one, then return to us." [1] Wherever the preservation of the teachings of the Master and of the sacred texts is spoken of, there is nowhere a mention of writing and reading, but always only of hearing and memorizing.

From such facts one would conclude that at the time, that is, in the fifth century B. C. the idea of the possibility of writing books had not as yet occurred at all. Such a conclusion, however, would be too hasty, for it is a strange phenomenon that in India, from the oldest times, up till the present day, the spoken word, and not writing, has been the basis of the whole of the literary and scientific activity.

---

[1]) H. *Oldenberg*, "Aus Indien und Iran," Berlin, 1889, pp. 22. f.

Even to-day, when the Indians have known the art of writing since centuries, when there are innumerable manuscripts, and when even a certain sanctity and reverence is accorded to these manuscripts, when the most important texts are accessible also in India in cheap printed editions, even to-day, the whole of the literary and scientific intercourse in India is based upon the spoken word. Not out of manuscripts or books does one learn the texts, but from the mouth of the teacher, to-day as thousands of years ago. The written text can at most be used as an aid to learning, as a support to the memory, but no authority is attributed to it. Authority is possessed, only by the spoken word of the teacher. If to-day all the manuscripts and prints were to be lost, that would by no means cause the disappearance of Indian literature from the face of the earth, for a great portion of it could be recalled out of the memory of the scholars and reciters. The works of the poets, too, were in India never intended for readers, but always for hearers. Even modern poets do not desire to be read, but their wish is that their poetry may become "an adornment for the throats of the experts." [1]

Therefore the fact, that in the older literary works there is no mention of manuscripts, is not absolutely a proof of the non-existence of the latter. Perhaps they are not mentioned only for the reason that the writing and reading of them was of no importance, all teaching and learning being done by word of mouth. Therefore it is yet possible that already in very ancient times also books were copied and used the same as now, as aids to instruction. That is the opinion of some scholars.[2] Yet it seems to me worthy of notice that in the later literature—in the later Purāṇas, in Buddhist Mahāyāna texts, and

1) G. *Bühler*, "Indische Palaeographie" (Grundriss I, 2), pp. 3 f.

2) On the age of the art of writing in India, s. also *Barth*, RHR 41, 1900, 184 ff. = Oeuvres II, 317 ff. The arguments brought forward by Shyamaji *Krishṇavarmâ*, OC VI, Leyden 1883, pp. 305 ff. for the knowledge and use of writing, even at the Vedic period, are well worthy of notice.

in modern additions to the old epic—the copying of books and the presentation of the same is praised as a religious act, while in the whole of the older literature no trace of it is to be found. It is also significant that the old works on phonetics and grammar, even the "Mahābhāṣya" of Patañjali in the second century B.C., take no notice whatsoever of writing, that they always treat of spoken sounds and never of written characters, and that the whole grammatical terminology always has only the spoken word, and never the written text in view. From all this it is after all probable, that in ancient times there were no written books in India.

For this strange phenomenon, namely that the art of writing had been known for centuries, without having been used for literary purposes, there are several possible reasons. First of all there was probably a want of suitable writing material; but this would have been found, if there had been a strong need of it. Such a need however, was not only not present, but it was to the interest of the priests, who were the bearers of the oldest literature, that the sacred texts which they taught in their schools, should *not* be committed to writing. By this means they kept a very lucrative monopoly firmly in their hands. He who wished to learn something, had to come to them and reward them richly; and they had it in their power to withhold their texts from those circles whom they wished to exclude from sacred knowledge. How important was the latter to them we are taught by the Brahmanical law-books, which repeatedly emphasize the law that the members of the lowest castes (the Śūdras and the Cāṇḍālas) may not learn the sacred texts; for impure as a corpse, as a burial place, is the Śūdra, therefore the Veda may not be recited in his vicinity. In the old law-book of Gautama[1] it is said: "If a Śūdra hears the Veda, his ears shall be stopped with molten tin or lac, if he repeats the sacred texts, his

---

[1]) XII, 4-6.

tongue shall be cut out, if he stores them in his memory his body shall be struck in two." Then how could they have written down their texts and thus exposed themselves to the danger that they might be read by the unauthorized? Moreover the transmission of the texts through the mouth of the teacher was an old-established method for their preservation,—why should they replace it by writing, this new-fashioned invention? And the chief reason[1] for the fact that writing was for so long not used for literary purposes, is probably to be found in the fact that the Indians only became acquainted with the art of writing at a period when they had already since a long time possessed a rich literature that was only orally transmitted.

Certain it is, that the whole of the most ancient literature of the Indians, Brahmanical as well as Buddhist, arose without the art of writing, and continued to be transmitted without it for centuries.[2] Whoever wished to become acquainted with a text had to go to a teacher in order to hear it from him. Therefore we repeatedly read in the older literature, that a warrior or a Brahman, who wished to acquire a certain knowledge, travels to a famous teacher, and undertakes unspeakable troubles and sacrifices in order to participate in the teaching, which cannot be attained in any other manner. Therefore to a teacher, as the bearer and preserver of the sacred knowledge, the highest veneration is due, according to ancient Indian law;—as the spiritual father he is venerated, now as an equal, now as a superior, of the physical father, he is looked upon as an image of the god Brahman, and to him who serves the teacher faithfully and humbly, Brahman's heaven is assured. Therefore also the introduction of the pupil to the teacher who is to teach him the sacred texts is

---

[1]) Compare especially *T. W. Rhys Davids*, "Buddhist India," London, 1903. pp. 112 f.

[2]) I-tsing (Trnsl. *Takakusu*, pp. 182 f.) mentions that in his time (7th century A.D.) the Vedas were still only handed down orally.

one of the most sacred ceremonies from which no Hindu could withdraw himself without risking to lose his caste. A book existed only when and only so long as there were teachers and pupils, who taught and learned it. What we call various branches of literature, different theological and philosophical systems, different editions or recensions of a work, were in ancient India in reality different schools, in which certain texts continued to be taught, heard and learned from generation to generation. Only if we keep this in view can we understand the whole development of the oldest Indian literature.

It also must be considered, that the method of handing-down was quite different in the case of the religious texts from that of the secular. The religious texts were held sacred, and accuracy in learning was in their case a strict requirement of religion. Word for word, with careful avoidance of every error in pronunciation, in accent, in the manner of recitation, the pupil had to repeat them after the teacher and impress them on his memory. There can be no doubt that this kind of oral transmission gives a greater guarantee for the preservation of the original text than the copying and re-copying of manuscripts. Indeed, we have—as we shall see later—direct proofs that, for example, the songs of the Ṛgveda, as we read them to-day in our printed editions, have remained almost unaltered, word for word, syllable for syllable, accent for accent, since the fifth century B.C. It was otherwise, no doubt, with secular works, especially with the epic poems. There the texts were certainly exposed to numerous disfigurements, there every teacher, every reciter, considered himself entitled to alter and to improve, to omit and to add, *ad libitum*—and criticism here faces a difficult, often impossible, task when it desires to restore such texts to their oldest and most original form. Nevertheless oral transmission, where it is still possible to resort to it—and this is so in the case of the oldest Veda text with the help of the old phonetic manuals of instruction (Prātiśākhyas) and in other cases often with the help of commentaries—is the most valuable aid to the reconstruction of our texts. For the manuscripts, from which we obtain most of our texts, reach but seldom to a great age. The oldest writing-materials on which the Indians wrote are palm-leaves and strips of birch bark; and it is significant of the conservative mind of the Indians that even to-day, in spite of their acquaintance with the much more convenient paper, and in spite of the general use of print, manuscripts are still written on palm leaves. Both materials are very fragile, and in the Indian climate quickly perishable. Thus it happens that the vast majority of manuscripts which we possess, and from which practically all our text editions are made, only date from the last few centuries. Manuscripts from the fourteenth century already are amongst the greatest rarities. Only a few manuscripts found in India proper date back to the eleventh and twelfth century.[1] However, the oldest Indian manuscripts were found in Nepal, Japan and Eastern Turkestan. The manuscripts found in Nepal date back as far as the tenth century, and in Japan manuscripts on palm leaves have been discovered which date from the first half of the sixth century. Since the year 1889 there have been finds of manuscripts in Kashgar and its environs which take us back to the fifth century, and M. A. Stein, in the year 1900, dug up out of the sand in the desert of Taklamakān near Khotan, five hundred small tablets of wood covered with writing, which reach back to the fourth century and are perhaps older still. Also by means of the Prussian Turfan Expedition and the more recent discoveries of M. A. Stein, fragments of manuscripts from the earliest centuries after Christ have been brought to light.[2]

1) *Kielhorn* discovered the oldest manuscripts of Western India, of the 11th century. (Report on the Search for Sanskrit MSS. in the Bombay Presidency during the year 1880-81, Bombay, 1881.)

2) See *Lüders*, "Ueber die literarischen Funde von Ostturkestan," SBA, 1914, pp. 90 ff.

Wood as a writing material is already mentioned in the Buddhist writings, and the use of it must be very old. The use of palm leaves also can be traced back to the first century after Christ. Rarely in India were cotton stuff, leather, metal and stones used as writing materials. The Buddhists mention here and there the writing, not only of documents, but also of verses and maxims, on gold plates. A gold plate with a votive inscription has also been preserved to us. Records and even small manuscripts, on silver plates, have often been found in India. Very frequently, however, copper plates were used for the writing of documents, especially deeds of gift, and such have been preserved in great numbers. The Chinese pilgrim Hsüan-Tsang reports that the King Kaniṣka had the sacred writings of the Buddhists engraved on copper tablets. Whether this is based on truth, we do not know, but it certainly is credible, for even literary works also have been found on copper tablets. It would hardly be credible that in India literary works were also hewn into stone, if, a few years ago, inscriptions on stone slabs had not been found in Ajmere, which contained entire dramatic writings, albeit, dramas of a king and his court poet.

The great majority, however, of the Indian manuscripts on which our texts rest, are written on paper. But paper was first introduced into India only by the Mohammedans, and the oldest paper manuscript is supposed to have been written in the year 1223-4 after Christ.

In spite of the above-mentioned predilection of the Indians for oral teaching and learning, yet already many centuries ago they began to collect manuscripts, and to preserve them in libraries. Such libraries—"treasure-houses of the Goddess of Speech" (sarasvatībhaṇḍāgāra) as the Indians call them—existed and even now exist in numbers in monasteries and temples, in the palaces of princes, and even in the private houses of the wealthy. It is reported of the poet

Bāṇa (about 620 after Christ) that he kept his own reader, so he must have possessed a considerable private library. In the eleventh century King Bhoja of Dhār had a famous library. In the course of centuries these libraries became exceedingly well stocked. Thus Bühler found in two Jain libraries in Khambay over 30,000 manuscripts, and in the Palace library of Tanjore in Southern India over 12,000 manuscripts. The systematic investigation of these Indian libraries, and the thorough search for manuscripts, extending over the whole of India, began in the year 1868, though Colebrooke and other Englishmen had, already before that, brought fairly large collections of manuscripts to Europe. However, in the year 1868 Whitley Stokes, well-known as a Keltic scholar and at that time Secretary of the Indian Council at Simla, started a complete cataloguing of all Sanskrit manuscripts, and since then the Indian Government has for years, in the Indian annual budget granted a large sum (24,000 Rupees) for the purpose of the "Search of Sanskrit manuscripts." Thus it is through the munificence of the Anglo-Indian Government and through the untiring industry of English, German and Indian scholars, that we now possess, to a considerable degree, a survey of the whole, enormous mass of Indian literature, so far as it is accessible in manuscripts.

Indian Languages in their Relation to Literature.[1]

The whole of this vast literature which has thus been handed down to us, is for the most part composed in Sanskrit. Yet the terms "Indian literature" and "Sanskrit literature" are by no means identical. The history of Indian literature in the most comprehensive sense of the word is the history of

---

[1]) See *R. G. Bhandarkar*, JBRAS 16, 245 ff.; 17, 1 ff., and *G. Grierson*, BSOS I, 3, 1920 pp. 51 ff.

a literature which not only stretches across great periods of time and an enormous area, but also one which is composed in many languages. Those languages of India which belong to the Indo-European family of languages, have passed through three great phases of development, partly consecutive in time, but partly also parallel.

These are:

I. Ancient Indian,
II. The Middle Indian languages and dialects,
III. The Modern Indian languages and dialects.

I. Ancient Indian.

The language of the oldest Indian literary monuments, of the songs, prayers and magic formulas of the Vedas, is sometimes called "Ancient Indian" in the narrower sense, sometimes also "Vedic" (inappropriately also "Vedic Sanskrit"). "Ancient High Indian"[1] is perhaps the best name for this language, which, while based on a spoken dialect, is yet no longer an actual popular language, but a literary language transmitted in the circle of priestly singers from generation to generation, and intentionally preserved in its archaic form. The dialect on which the Ancient High Indian is based, the dialect as it was spoken by the Aryan immigrants in the North-west of India, was closely related to the Ancient Persian and Avestic, and not very far removed from the primitive Indo-Iranian language.[2] Indeed, the difference between the language of the Vedas and this primitive Indo-Iranian language seems to be less, perhaps, than that between the Indian languages Sanskrit and Pāli. The Vedic language

---

[1] It is called thus by *Rhys Davids*, "Buddhist India," p. 153.

[2] This is the common original language to be inferred from a comparison of the language of the Veda with the Old Persian of the cuneiform inscriptions and the language of the Avesta.

hardly differs at all from Sanskrit in its phonetics, but only through a much greater antiquity, and especially through a greater wealth of grammatical forms. Thus for instance, Ancient High Indian has a subjunctive which is missing in Sanskrit; it has a dozen different infinitive-endings, of which but one single one remains in Sanskrit. The aorists, very largely represented in the Vedic language, disappear in the Sanskrit more and more. Also the case and personal endings are still much more perfect in the oldest language than in the later Sanskrit.

A later phase of Ancient High Indian appears already in the hymns of the tenth book of the Ṛgveda and in some parts of the Atharvaveda, and the collections of the Yajurveda. On the other hand, the language of the Vedic prose writings, of the Brāhmaṇas, Āraṇyakas and Upaniṣads, has preserved only a few relics of Ancient High Indian, on the whole the language of these works is already what is called "Sanskrit," while the language of the Sūtras belonging to the Vedāṅgas only in quite exceptional cases shows Vedic forms, but is essentially pure Sanskrit. Only the numerous Mantras, taken from the ancient Vedic hymns, *i.e.* verses, prayers, spells, and magic formulas, which we find quoted in the Vedic prose writings and the Sūtras, belong, as regards their language, to Ancient High Indian.

The Sanskrit of this most ancient prose-literature—of the Brāhmaṇas, Āraṇyakas, Upaniṣads and of the Sūtras—differs little from the Sanskrit which is taught in the celebrated grammar of Pāṇini (probably about fifth century B. C.). The best designation is perhaps "Ancient Sanskrit." It is the language which was spoken in Pāṇini's time, and probably earlier too, by the educated, principally by the priests and scholars. It is the Sanskrit of which Patañjali, a grammarian of the second century B. C., still says that in order to learn it correctly one must hear it from the "Śiṣṭas," that is, from the learned Brahmans who were well versed in literature. But that the sphere of people speaking Sanskrit extended much further—to all "educated people"—we learn from the same Patañjali, who tells us an anecdote, in which a grammarian converses in Sanskrit with a charioteer and the two have a discussion on etymologies. When in Indian dramas, the languages are so distributed that the king, the Brahmans, and nobles speak Sanskrit, while the women and all the common people use the vulgar tongues, only with the noteworthy exception that a few educated women (nuns and courtesans) occasionally speak Sanskrit, whereas uneducated Brahmans are introduced speaking popular dialects, then most probably the use of the languages in real life is reflected therein—and not only of the period after Christ, when these dramas were composed, but also of much earlier centuries. Sanskrit was certainly not a popular language, but the language spoken in wide circles of educated people, and understood in still wider circles. For, as in the drama dialogues occur between Sanskrit-speaking and Prākrit-speaking persons, so too in real life Sanskrit must have been understood by those who did not speak it themselves.[1] Also the bards, who recited the popular epics in the palaces of kings and in the houses of the rich and nobles, must have been understood. The language of the epics is

---

[1]) The linguistic conditions of ancient India, of which the dramas give us such a good idea, have altered very little up to the present day. It still happens that in a rich house with a large staff of servants who come from different districts, a dozen different languages and dialects are spoken and generally understood. *G. A. Grierson* describes a case known to himself, where in *one* house in Bengal, no less than thirteen languages and dialects are spoken. The master of the house speaks to Europeans in the refined Bengali language, while in ordinary life he uses the Bengali of every-day intercourse, which differs widely from the literary language. His wife comes from a place at a distance of one hundred miles, and speaks the peculiar women's dialect of that district. His secondary wife, whose ordinary colloquial language is the Urdu of Lucknow, lapses into a jargon when she is angry. The manager of his business speaks Dhākī, while among the servants some speak Uriyā, others Bhojpurī, Awadhī, Maithilī, Ahīrī, and Chaṭgaiyā. They all understand each other perfectly, although each one speaks his own dialect. It very rarely happens that one of them uses the dialect of the person whom he is addressing. (Ind. Ant., 30, 1901, p. 556.)

likewise Sanskrit. We call it "Epic Sanskrit," and it differs but little from the "Classical Sanskrit," partly in that it has preserved some archaisms, but more in that it keeps less strictly to the rules of grammar and approaches more nearly to the language of the people, so that one may call it a more popular form of Sanskrit. But there would never have been popular epics written in Sanskrit,[1] if Sanskrit had not once been a language that was widely understood—similarly as to-day in Germany Modern High German is universally understood, although it differs essentially from all spoken dialects.

That Sanskrit is a "high language" or "class language" or "literary language"—whatever we may call it in contrast to the actual language of the people—the Indians themselves express through the name "Sanskrit." For Sanskrit—Saṃskṛta, as much as "made ready, ordered, prepared, perfect, pure, sacred"—signifies the noble or sacred language, in contradistinction to "Prākrit"—prākṛta, as much as "original, natural, ordinary, common"—which signifies the "common language of the people."

Yet Sanskrit should never be spoken of as a "dead" language, rather as a "fettered" language, inasmuch as its natural development was checked, in that, through the rules of the grammarians, it was arrested at a certain stage. For through the Grammar of Pāṇini, in about the fifth century B. C., a fixed standard was created, which remained a criterion for the Sanskrit language for all future times. What we call "Classical Sanskrit" means Pāṇini's Sanskrit, that is, the Sanskrit which according to the rules of Pāṇini's Grammar, is alone correct.[2] In the "fetters" of this Grammar, however, the

---

[1]) It has been suggested that the popular epics were originally composed in dialect and were later translated into Sanskrit. This supposition, however, lacks all evidence from facts, as H. *Jacobi* (ZDMG., 48, 407 ff.) has shown.

[2]) Only this literary language as determined by the Indian grammarians is called Sanskrit by the Indians. If, as it is often done, people speak of "Vedic Sanskrit" the term "Sanskrit" is extended to Ancient Indian.

language still continued to live. The great mass of poetic and scientific literature, throughout a thousand years, was produced in this language, the "Classical Sanskrit." Moreover Sanskrit is not a "dead" language even to-day. There are still at the present day a number of Sanskrit periodicals in India, and topics of the day are discussed in Sanskrit pamphlets. Also the Mahābhārata is still to-day read aloud publicly, which pre-supposes at least a partial understanding. I have myself observed with pleasure and surprise, that scenes from such ornate Sanskrit dramas as Mudrārākṣasa and Uttararāmacarita, performed on a primitive stage at Santiniketan, were understood and greatly appreciated by a large audience of students, both men and women. To this very day poetry is still composed and works are still written in Sanskrit, and it is the language in which Indian scholars even now converse upon scientific questions. Sanskrit at the least plays the same part in India still as Latin in the Middle Ages in Europe, or as Hebrew with the Jews.[1]

---

[1]) There are epigraphical grounds for assuming that Sanskrit is a modification of a Northern Indian dialect, which was developed by schools of grammar, and which in historical times spread slowly throughout India among the educated classes; see *Bühler*, Ep. Ind., I, p. 5. Sanskrit is called a sacred language (brāhmī vāc) in the Mahābhārata I. 78, 13, and it probably always was the language of a certain class of society. *Cf. Windisch*, Ueber den sprachlichen Charakter des Pali (OC., XIV, Paris, 1906), pp. 14 ff.; *Thomas* JRAS., 1904, 747 f.; W. *Petersen*, JAOS., 32, 1912, 414 ff.; T. *Michelson*, JAOS 33 1913, 145 ff. About the wide use of Sanskrit in the India of to-day Paul *Deussen* ("Erinnerungen an Indien," Kiel, 1904, pp. 2 f.) says: "Not only the professional scholars, as especially the native Sanskrit Professors of the Indian Universities, speak Sanskrit with great elegance, not only their hearers are able to handle it as well as our students of classical philology can handle Latin, but the numerous private scholars, saints, ascetics, and even wider circles can speak and write Sanskrit with facility: I have repeatedly conversed in it for hours with the Maharaja of Benares: manufacturers, industrials, merchants, partly speak it or understand what is spoken: in every little village my first enquiry was for one who speaks Sanskrit, whereupon immediately one or another came forward, who usually became my guide, indeed often my friend." When he gave lectures in English, he was often invited to repeat in Sanskrit what he had said. "After this had been done, a discussion followed in which some spoke English, others Sanskrit, yet others Hindi, which therefore was also understood, to a

Summing up, I would, therefore, divide Ancient Indian in its relation to literature as follows:—

1. Ancient High Indian:

(*a*) Language of the oldest hymns and mantras, especially of those of the Ṛgveda.

(*b*) Language of the later hymns and mantras, especially those of the other Vedas, besides of the mantras occurring only in the Brāhmaṇas and Sūtras.

2. Sanskrit.

(*a*) Ancient Sanskrit, the language of the Vedic prose works (with the exception of the Mantras) and of Pāṇini.

(*b*) Epic Sanskrit, the language of the popular epics.

(*c*) Classical Sanskrit, the language of the Classical Sanskrit literature after Pāṇini.

II. The Middle Indian Languages and Dialects.

Simultaneously and parallel with the development of Sanskrit proceeded the more natural further development of the popular dialects spoken by the Aryan Indians. The languages and dialects which we distinguish as "Middle Indian" are not indeed derived directly from the Sanskrit, but rather from the Indo-Aryan popular languages which underlie the Ancient High Indian and the Sanskrit, or are related to the two latter. Considering the size of India, it is not to be wondered at that, with the gradual spreading of the Aryan

---

certain extent, because pure Hindi differs from Sanskrit in little more than by the loss of inflectional endings. Hence every Hindu understands as much of Sanskrit as an Italian of Latin, especially as, in the real Hindustan, the script has remained the same: and a smattering of Sanskrit can be traced down to the circles of servants and the lower classes wherefore a letter to Benares with only a Sanskrit address will without difficulty reach its destination, through every postal messenger." As to Sanskrit as a "living" language, see also S. *Krishṇavarmâ* in OC V, Berlin, 1881, II b, p. 222; R. G. *Bhandarkar*, JBRAS., 16, 1885, 268 ff., 327 ff.; *Windisch*, OC XIV, Paris, 1897, I. 257, 266; *Hertel*, Tantrākhyāyika, Transl. I., pp. 8 ff., and HOS., Vol. XII, pp. 80 ff.

immigrants from the West to the East and the South, a large number of varying dialects were formed. Of the diversity of these dialects we get an idea from the oldest Indian inscriptions, which are all written in Middle Indian and *not* in Sanskrit. Quite a number of such popular languages, moreover, have been raised to the rank of literary languages. Only these shall be briefly enumerated here:

1. The most important of the Middle Indian literary languages is *Pāli*, the ecclesiastical language of the Buddhists of Ceylon, Burma and Siam, the language in which the oldest preserved collection of sacred writings of Buddhism is written. The Buddhists themselves tell us that the Buddha did not, like the Brahmans, preach in the learned Sanskrit, but talked to the people in the language of the people. As Buddha first preached in the land of Magadha (Southern Bihar), and there displayed his best activity, therefore the Buddhists tell us that Pāli is the same as Māgadhī, the language of the province of Magadha. However, that cannot be right, as the dialect of Magadha which is otherwise known to us does not agree with Pāli. It is, however, probable that Pāli is a mixed language the foundation of which was Māgadhī.[1] The word Pāli really signifies "row," then "order, regulation, rule," hence also "sacred text" and finally the language of the sacred texts, in contradistinction to the Ancient Sinhalese, the language in which the commentaries to these texts were composed.

2. Besides the Pāli literature there exists also a Buddhist Sanskrit literature. Now in these Buddhist works there is frequently only the prose in Sanskrit, while the interspersed metrical pieces, the so-called "Gāthās" (*i.e.* "songs" or "verses") are composed in a Middle Indian dialect, which

---

[1]) This is the view of E. *Windisch*, "Ueber den sprachlichen Charakter des Pali" (OC., XIV., Paris, 1906) and of G. A. *Grierson*, Bhandarkar Com. Vol., 117 ff. The latter agrees with *Sten Konow* (ZDMG 64, 1910, 114 ff.), that Pāli is similar to Paiśācī-Prākrit The latter was probably the local dialect of Eastern Gāndhāra and the district of Taxila, a famous seat of learning at the time of Buddha

has therefore been called "Gāthā dialect." But this term is not quite appropriate, as the same dialect is found also in prose portions, and even whole prose works are written in it. It is an old Indian dialect, which through the insertion of Sanskrit terminations and other Sanskritisms in a rather crude manner, tries to approach the Sanskrit, wherefore Senart suggested for it the designation "mixed Sanskrit."[1]

3. Like the Buddhists, the Jains too did not use Sanskrit for their sacred writings, but Middle Indian dialects, indeed two different Prākrits:[2]

(*a*) The Jaina Prākrit (also called Ardhamāgadhī or Ārṣa), the language of the older works of the Jaina Canon.

(*b*) The Jaina-Māhārāṣṭrī, the language in which the commentaries to the Jaina Canon and the non-religious poetical works of the Jainas are written.[3] This dialect is closely related to that Prākrit, which has been used most frequently as a literary language for secular writing, namely—

4. The Māhārāṣṭrī, the language of Mahārāṣṭra, the land of the Marathas. This is universally considered the best Prākrit, and when the Indians speak simply of Prākrit then they mean Māhārāṣṭrī. It was used principally for lyric poetry, especially also for the lyric parts in the dramas. However, there are also epic poems in Māhārāṣṭrī. Other important Prākrit dialects which are used in the drama are:

5. The Śaurasenī, which in the prose of the dramas is chiefly spoken by high-born women. Its foundation is the dialect of Śūrasena, the capital of which is Mathurā.

---

1) See S. *Lefmann*. ZDMG, 212 ff.: and E. *Senart*, Ind. Ant., 21, 1892, 243 ff.

2) The Hindus do not designate popular languages generally by the term "Prākrit" but only those popular languages which are used in literature. For the whole of this chapter see R. *Pischel*, "Grammatik der Prākrit-Sprachen" (in Grundriss I, 8 Einleitung) and H. *Jacobi* in A Bay. AXXIX, 4, 1918, pp. 81 * ff.

3) See H. *Jacobi*, Ueber das Prākrit in der Erzählungs-litteratur der Jainas, in RSO, II, 1909, pp. 231 ff.

6. Persons of the lower classes speak Māgadhī in the dramas, the dialect of Magadha, and .

7. Paiśācī is spoken in the drama by the members of the lowest grades of society. The word probably originally designated the dialect of a branch of the Piśācas, although the Indians declared it to be the language of the demons called Piśācas. A famous book of narrative literature, Guṇādhya's Bṛhatkathā was also composed in this Paiśācī dialect.

8. Lastly the Apabhraṃśa which is used in popular poetry, in Jaina romances and occasionally in the drama, stands midway between the Prākrit and the modern Indian vernaculars : for "Apabhraṃśa" is a general term for literary idioms which, though based on the Prākrit, are more closely adapted to certain popular dialects.[1]

III. The Modern Indian Languages and Dialects.[2]

By about the year 1000 A.D. the modern Indo-Aryan vernaculars had developed out of the Middle Indian dialects, and from the 12th century onwards these languages can show literatures of their own, which are partly independent and partly dependent on the Sanskrit literature. The most important of these vernaculars is Hindī, the language of the ancient Madhyadeśa or midland, *i.e.* of the greater portion of the Gangetic Dōāb and of the adjacent plain to the Himalaya in the North, to the valley of the Nerbudda in the South, beyond Delhi in the West and nearly as far as Cawnpore in the East. Of the numerous Hindī dialects, Kanaujī and

---

[1]) On the Apabhraṃsas S. H. *Jacobi* in A Bay A XXIX, 4, 1918, pp. 53 * ff.; XXXI, 2, 1921, pp. xviii ff., 1 ff. and in Festschrift für Wackernagel, pp 124 ff. *Jacobi* is of opinion, that the Apabhraṃśa was first used by the poets of the Ābhīras and Gurjaras.

[2]) I follow the excellent survey of the Indo-Aryan Vernaculars given by Sir George *Grierson* in BSOS I., 1, 1918, pp. 47 ff. Compare also E. J. *Rapson*, Cambridge History I, 37 ff.

Bundēlī, and especially Braj Bhākhā (the language of the district of Mathurā), have produced literature worthy of the name. Hindōstānī or Urdu, a dialect with a strong admixture of Perso-Arabic elements,[1] is a form of the Hindī language. It originated in the twelfth century in the neighbourhood of Delhi, then the centre of the Mohammedan rule, in the camps (urdu) of the soldiers, hence also called "Urdu," *i.e.* "camp language." In the 16th century it also began to produce literature. Now-a-days it is the *lingua franca* of the whole of Northern India. High Hindī is a return to the vernacular of the Upper Dōāb, which is not as yet influenced by Persian. The following languages, belonging to the adjacent regions, are closely related to the language of the midland: Pānjābī in the North-West, Rājasthānī and Gujarātī in the West, Eastern Pahārī or Naipālī (the language of Nepal), Central Pahārī and Western Pahārī in the East. Rājasthānī and Gujarātī are closely related. Mārwārī, a dialect of Rājasthānī, can scarcely be distinguished from Gujarātī. Eastern Hindī, the language in which Tulsī Dās wrote, is more closely related to the "Outer" languages. Among the latter are: Lahndā (the language of Western Panjāb) and Sindhī in the North-West, Marāthī in the South, Bihārī, Oriyā, Bengālī and Assamese in the East. Maithilī is a dialect of Bihārī. Since the beginning of the 19th century literary Bengālī has diverged considerably from the vernacular by reason of the absorption of so many Sanskrit words. The High Hindī of Benares shows a similar tendency. Now-a-days, however, good authors, both in Bengālī and in Hindī, are aiming at keeping their language free from borrowed Sanskrit words.

The "Dardic" or modern Piśāca languages, among which Kāśmīrī (the language of Kashmir) possesses a considerable literature, form a separate group.

---

[1]) It is also written in Persian-Arabic characters.

Finally, Singhalese, the language of Ceylon, is an Indo-Germanic dialect descended from the Middle Indian. Through the introduction of Buddhism and the Buddhistic literature into Ceylon, an early literary activity began here, which was at first limited to the elucidation of the religious texts. In the later centuries we find, in addition, a secular literature influenced by Sanskrit poetry.[1]

All the Indian languages mentioned up to now belong to the Indo-Germanic group of languages. Besides these there are in India a number of non-Indo-Germanic languages, namely the Munda languages (scattered dialects in the Mahadeo Hills of the Central Provinces, in the Santal Parganās and Chotā Nāgpur), the Tibeto-Burmese languages (on the Northern and North-Eastern borders of India proper) and above all the Dravidian languages of Southern India. The latter must at one time have been common in the North as well,[2] for the Indo-Aryan languages show strong Dravidian influence.[3] The most important Dravidian languages are Malayalam (on the coast of Malabar), Kanarese, Telugu and Tamil. Although these languages are not Indo-Germanic, numerous Sanskritisms have penetrated into them: moreover, the not unimportant literature of these languages is greatly dependent on the Sanskrit literature.

In this book we shall have to limit ourselves mainly to the Sanskrit, Pāli and Prākrit literature. At most it will only be possible to touch on modern Indian literature in an Appendix.

---

[1]) See Wilhelm *Geiger*, Literatur und Sprache der Singhalesen, in "Grundriss" I, 10

[2]) Sporadic Dravidian dialects are found also in the Ganges valley and even in Baluchistan (Brahūī).

[3]) See *Grierson*, BSOS., I, 3, 1920, pp. 71 f.

SECTION I.

THE VEDA OR THE VEDIC LITERATURE.

WHAT IS THE VEDA ?

As the oldest Indian, and, at the same time, the oldest Indo-European literary monument, a prominent place in the history of world literature is due to the Veda. This is the case too when we remember that throughout at least 3,000 years millions of Hindus have looked on the word of the Veda as the word of God, and that the Veda has given them their standard of thought and feeling. As the Veda, because of its antiquity, stands at the head of Indian literature, no one who has not gained an insight into the Vedic literature can understand the spiritual life and the culture of the Indians. Also Buddhism, whose birth-place is India, will remain for ever incomprehensible to him who does not know the Veda. For the teaching of Buddha is in the same relation to the Veda, as the New Testament is to the Old Testament. No one can understand the new belief without having become acquainted with the old one taught by the Veda.

What then, is the Veda ?

The word "Veda" means "knowledge," then "the knowledge par excellence," *i.e.* "the sacred, the religious knowledge." It does not mean *one* single literary work, as for instance the word "Koran," nor a complete collection of a certain number of books, compiled at some particular time, as the word "Bible" (the "book par excellence"), or as the word "Tipiṭaka," the "Bible" of the Buddhists, but a whole great literature, which arose in the course of many centuries, and through centuries has been handed down from generation to generation by verbal transmission, till finally it was declared by a younger generation—but even then at some prehistoric period—to be "sacred knowledge," "divine revelation," as much on account of its great age, as on account of its contents. It is here not a matter of a "Canon" which might have been fixed at some council; the belief in the "sacredness" of this literature arose, as it were, spontaneously, and was seldom seriously disputed.

However, what is now called "Veda" or "Vedic literature" consists of three different classes of literary works; and to each of these three classes belongs a greater or a smaller number of separate works, of which some have been preserved, but also many lost.

I. Saṃhitās, *i.e.* "Collections," namely collections of hymns, prayers, incantations, benedictions, sacrificial formulas and litanies.

II. Brāhmaṇas, voluminous prose texts, which contain theological matter, especially observations on sacrifice and the practical or mystical significance of the separate sacrificial rites and ceremonies.

III. Āraṇyakas ("forest texts") and Upaniṣads ("secret doctrines") which are partly included in the Brāhmaṇas themselves, or attached to them, but partly are also reckoned as independent works. They contain the meditations of forest-hermits and ascetics on God, the world, and mankind, and there is contained in them a good deal of the oldest Indian philosophy.

There must once have existed a fairly large number of Saṃhitās, which originated in different schools of priests and singers, and which continued to be handed down in the same. However, many of these "collections" were nothing but slightly diverging recensions—Śākhās, "branches," as the Indians say—of one and the same Saṃhitā. Four Saṃhitās, however, are in existence, which differ clearly from each other, and which have been preserved in one or more recensions. These are :—

1. The Ṛgveda-Saṃhitā, the collection of the Ṛgveda. "Ṛgveda" is "the Veda or the knowledge of the songs of praise" (ṛc, plur. ṛcas).

2. The Atharvaveda-Saṃhitā, the collection of the Atharva-veda, *i.e.* "of the knowledge of the magic formulas" (atharvan).

3. The Sāmaveda-Saṃhitā, the collection of the Sāmaveda, *i.e.* "of the knowledge of the melodies" (sāman).

4. The Yajurveda-Saṃhitā, the collection of the Yajurveda, *i.e.* "of the knowledge of the sacrificial formulas" (yajus, plur. yajūṃṣi) of which there are two rather strongly diverging texts, namely :—

(*a*) The Saṃhitā of the Black Yajurveda, which has been preserved in several recensions, of which the most important are the Taittirīya-Saṃhitā and the Maitrāyaṇī-Saṃhitā; and

(*b*) the Saṃhitā of the White Yajur-veda, which has been preserved in the Vājasaneyi-Saṃhitā.

On account of these four different Saṃhitās the Indians distinguish between four different Vedas—and therefore one often speaks of the "Vedas" in the plural—namely, Ṛgveda, Atharvaveda, Sāmaveda, and (Black and White) Yajurveda. Every work that belongs to the class of the Brāhmaṇas, of the Āraṇyakas, or of the Upaniṣads, is joined to one of the enumerated Saṃhitās, and "belongs," as we say, to one of the four Vedas. There are, therefore, not only Saṃhitās, but also Brāhmaṇas, Āraṇyakas and Upaniṣads of the Ṛgveda, as well as of the Atharvaveda, of the Sāmaveda, and of the Yajurveda. Thus, for example, the Aitareya-Brāhmaṇa belongs to the Ṛgveda, the Śatapatha-Brāhmaṇa to the White Yajurveda, and the Chāndogya-Upaniṣad to the Sāmaveda, and so on.

Every work which belongs to one of the three above-mentioned classes, and to one of the four Vedas, must be designated as "Vedic," and the whole Vedic literature is thus presented to us as a long succession of works of religious content—collections of songs, prayer-books, theological and theosophical treatises—which belong to different successive periods of time, but which represent a unity, in so far as they all together form the foundation for the Brahmanical religious system, and have the same significance for Brahmanism as the Old Testament has for Judaism or the New Testament for Christianity. As Jews and Christians look on their "Holy Scripture," so the Brahmanic Indians look on their Veda, in its whole extent, as divine revelation. But it is significant that to the expression "Holy Scripture" there corresponds in the case of the Indians the expression "Šruti," "hearing," because the revealed texts were not written and read, but only spoken and *heard*. The whole history of Indian philosophy bears witness that not only the ancient hymns of the Ṛgveda were looked upon as "breathed out" by the God Brahman, and only "visioned" by the ancient seers, but that also every word in the Upaniṣads, the latest productions of the Vedic literature, was looked upon as indisputable wisdom emanating from the God Brahman himself. However much the different systems of Indian philosophy may vary, yet they are nearly all agreed in considering the Veda as revealed, and in appealing to the Veda, especially the Upaniṣads—although great freedom and arbitrariness prevail in regard to the explanation of these texts, and every philosopher gleans from them just what he wishes to. Most significant it is, that even the Buddhists, who deny the authority of the Veda, yet concede that it was originally given or "created" by God Brahman: only, they add, it has been falsified by the Brahmans, and therefore contains so many errors.

The expression "Veda" is justified only for this literature

which is regarded as revealed. However, there is another class of works, which has the closest connection with the Vedic literature, but yet cannot be said to belong to the Veda. These are the so-called Kalpasūtras (sometimes also called briefly "Sūtras") or manuals on ritual, which are composed in a peculiar, aphoristic prose style. These include:

1. The Śrautasūtras, which contain the rules for the performance of the great sacrifices, which often lasted many days, at which many sacred fires had to burn and a great number of priests had to be employed.

2. The Gṛhyasūtras, which contain directions for the simple ceremonies and sacrificial acts of daily life (at birth, marriage, death, and so on).

3. The Dharmasūtras, books of instruction on spiritual and secular law—the oldest law-books of the Indians.

Like Brāhmaṇas, Āraṇyakas and Upaniṣads, these works, too, are connected with one of the four Vedas; and there are Śrauta, Gṛhya, and Dharmasūtras which belong to the Ṛgveda, others which belong to the Sāmaveda, to the Yajurveda, or the Atharvaveda. As a matter of fact, they originated in certain Vedic schools which set themselves the task of the study of a certain Veda. Yet all these books of instruction are regarded as human work, and no longer as divine revelation; they do not belong to the Veda, but to the "Vedāṅgas," the "limbs," *i.e.* "the auxiliary sciences of the Veda."

These Vedāṅgas include, besides the works on ritual, also a number of works on phonetics, grammar, etymology, metrics and astronomy. We shall have to speak of these too at the end of the section.

After this general survey of the Vedic literature and the literature connected with it, we turn to the discussion of the most important works belonging to the Veda, above all, of the Sāṃhitas.

The Ṛgveda-Saṃhitā.

Indisputably the oldest and most important of all the works of Vedic literature, is the Ṛgveda-Saṃhitā, usually called simply the "Ṛgveda." Of the different recensions of this Saṃhitā, which once existed, only a single one has come down to us. In the text handed down to us, this [1] consisted of a collection of 1,028 hymns (Sūktas), which are divided into ten books (Maṇḍalas, "circles").[2]

That this collection of hymns is the oldest, or at least contains the oldest Indian literature which we possess, is proved indisputably by the *language* of the hymns.[3] But the language proves also that the collection is not a single work, but consists of older and later elements. As in the Hebrew Book of Psalms, so here also, songs which had been composed at widely separated periods of time, were united at some time in a collection, and ascribed to famous personages of prehistoric times, preferably to the earliest ancestors of those families in which the songs in question were handed down. The majority of the oldest hymns are to be found in Books II to VII, which are usually called the "Family Books," because each is ascribed by tradition to a particular family of singers. The names of the singers or *Ṛṣis* (*i.e.* "seers, prophets") who, as the Indians say, visioned these hymns, are mentioned, partly in the Brāhmaṇas, partly in separate lists of authors (Anukramaṇīs) connected with the Vedāṅga literature. They are: Gṛtsamada, Viśvāmitra, Vāmadeva, Atri, Bharadvāja

---

[1]) It is the recension of the Śākalaka-School. Regarding editions of the text, see above, pp. 20f.

[2]) Besides this there is also a purely external division, which takes into consideration only the size, namely into eight Aṣṭakas or "eighths," each of which is divided into eight Adhyāyas or "readings" which in their turn are again divided into smaller vargas or "sections," usually of five verses each.

[3]) See J. Wackernagel, "Altindische Grammatik" I, pp. xiii ff. on the language of the Ṛgveda.

and Vasiṣṭha. These and their descendants were regarded by the Indians as Ṛṣis or "seers"—we should say "authors"—of the hymns of Maṇḍalas II to VII. Book VIII contains hymns, which are ascribed to the singer race of the Kaṇvas and that of the Aṅgiras. But the Anukramaṇīs give us also the names of the Ṛṣis or "authors" of every single hymn of the remaining books (I, IX, X), and it is noteworthy that there are also women's names to be found amongst them. Unfortunately all these lists of names have practically no value at all, and in reality the authors of the Vedic hymns are quite unknown to us. For, as it has long since been proved,[1] the tradition which mentions Gṛtsamada, Viśvāmitra, and so on, *and* certain of their descendants, as the Ṛṣis of the hymns, disagrees with the statements of the hymns themselves. In the latter, *only* descendants of those ancient Ṛṣis are mentioned as authors of the hymns; the Ṛṣis, however, Gṛtsamada, Viśvāmitra, Vasiṣṭha, and whatever they may all be called—their names are well-known in the whole of Indian literature as the heroes of countless myths and legends—are already in the hymns of the Ṛgveda the seers of a long-past prehistoric time, and are only called the *fathers* of the singer families in which the songs were handed down. Book IX gains a character of unity through the fact that it contains exclusively hymns which glorify the drink of Soma, and are dedicated to the god Soma. Soma is the name of a plant, out of which an intoxicating juice was pressed, which already in the Indo-Iranian time was regarded as a drink pleasing to the gods, and therefore plays a prominent part at the sacrifices of the Indians as well as of the ancient Iranians, who called it Haôma. In ancient Indian mythology, however, the Soma drink is identified with the drink of immortality of the gods, and the seat of this divine drink is

---

1) *Oldenberg*, "Ueber die Liedverfasser des Ṛgveda" in ZDMG, Vol. 42, pp. 199 ff. Already previously A. *Ludwig*, "Der Ṛgveda," Vol. III, pp. xiii and 100 ff.

the moon, the golden-gleaming "drop"[1] in the sky. Therefore in Book IX of the Ṛgveda-Saṃhitā Soma is celebrated not only as the sacrificial drink dear to the gods, but also as the moon, the king of the sky. As the Soma-cult extends back into the Indo-Iranian period, we can also assume a fairly high age for the songs of Book IX, which are very closely connected with Soma sacrifice. The latest parts of our collection of hymns, however, are to be found in Books I to X, which are composed of very diversified elements.[2] Yet that does not mean that there are not some very old hymns which have been preserved in these books, while, on the other hand, some later hymns are also scattered in the "Family Books." Altogether, the question as to which hymns are "earlier" and which "later" is not easy to decide: for the language on which this decision chiefly rests, not only varies according to the age of the hymns, but also according to their origin and purpose, according to whether they arose more in connection with the priestly cult or with the popular religion.

An incantation, for example, can differ by its language from a song in praise of Soma or Indra, but it need not on that account be later.[3]

The so-called Khilas, which are found in a few manuscripts, represent, on the whole, a later stratum of Ṛgvedic hymn poetry. The word Khila means "supplement," and this name in itself indicates that they are texts which

---

[1]) Sanskrit "Indu" means "drop" and "moon." It is to the credit of A *Hillebrandt* to have shown in his "Vedische Mythologie" (Breslau 1891 ff.) that already in the Ṛgveda, Soma did not mean only the plant, but also the moon. In the whole of the later literature Soma is the moon.

[2]) See A. *Bergaigne*, J. A. 1886-7, on the arrangement of the hymns in Books II-VII, and A. *Barth*, RHR 19, 1889, 134 ff.=Oeuvres II, 8 ff. on those in Books I, VIII-X. See also *Bloomfield*, JAOS, 31, 1910, pp. 49 ff., for criteria for distinguishing between earlier and later hymns in the Ṛgveda.

[3]) See M. *Bloomfield*, "On the Relative Chronology of the Vedic Hymns" (JAOS, 21, 1900, pp 42-49).

were collected and added to the Saṃhitā only after the latter had already been concluded. This does not exclude the possibility that *some* of these Khilas are of no less antiquity than the hymns of the Ṛgveda-Saṃhitā, but for some reason unknown to us were not included in the collection. The eleven Vālakhilya hymns, which in all manuscripts are found at the end of Book VIII, without being included in it, are probably of this kind. Of comparatively high antiquity are probably also the eleven Suparṇa hymns, as well as the Praiṣasūktāni and the prose Nividas, small collections of sacrificial litanies.[1]

However, the question as to what we are to understand by "earlier" or by "later" hymns, can only be treated by us at the end of this section, where we shall have to discuss the question of the age of the Veda in general. It must here suffice that the general view of the great antiquity of the Ṛgveda, even of the "later" parts of it, is fully justified by the fact that, as Alfred Ludwig says: [2] "The Ṛgveda pre-supposes nothing of that which we know in Indian literature, while, on the other hand, the whole of Indian literature and the whole of Indian life pre-suppose the Veda."

Next to the language, however, the great age of the Vedic hymns is proved chiefly by the metres. For on the one hand, the Vedic metres are separated from those of classical Sanskrit poetry by a gulf, as in Vedic poetry there are numerous metres of which there is no trace to be found in the

---

[1]) The Khilas have been published by I. *Scheftelowitz*, "Die Apokryphen des Ṛgveda" (Indische Forschungen, I), Breslau 1906. See also Scheftelowitz, ZDMG 73, 1919, 30 ff.; 74, 1920, 192 ff.: 75, 1921, 37 ff.: ZTT, I, 1922, 50 ff.; 58 ff. *Oldenberg*, "Die Hymnen des Ṛgveda," I, Berlin, 1888, 504 ff., and GGA, 1907, 210 ff.; A. B. *Keith*, JRAS, 1907, 224 ff. The Khila Śivasaṃkalpa (edited, translated and explained by Scheftelowitz, ZDMG, 75, 1921, 201 ff.), is a regular Upaniṣad, the first part of which (1-13) is old, the rest late sectarian.

[2]) Der Rigveda, III, p. 183. Cf. also *ibid*, p. 3. "The claim to the highest age is proved not only internally by the contents as well as the linguistic form, but externally by the fact that the Veda formed the basis of literature, of the spiritual and religious life, and in the Veda again *the poetical pieces are the basis of the rest, but are not based on anything themselves.*"

later poetry, while on the other hand numerous metres in classical Sanskrit poetry have no prototype in the Veda. Again, some metres of the Vedic poetry do indeed re-appear in the later poetry, but with a much more strongly marked rhythm than in the Ṛgveda.

In the oldest Indian metre only the number of syllables is fixed, while the quantity of syllables is only partially determined. The Vedic verses are composed of lines of 8, 11 or 12, more rarely of 5 syllables. These lines, called Pādas,[1] are the units in ancient Indian metrics, and only the four (or five) last syllables are fixed with regard to the rhythm, the last syllable, however, being again a syllaba anceps. The regular form of the Pāda of eight syllables is thus :

o o o o ⏑ — ⏑ ⏓

Three such lines form the Gāyatrī and four such lines form the verse called the Anuṣṭubh. In the older poetry the Anuṣṭubh stands far behind the Gāyatrī in popularity. Later it is the reverse : the Anuṣṭubh becomes the usual verse, and out of it is developed the śloka, the proper metre of epic poetry. Metres of rarer occurrence are the Paṅkti, consisting of five lines of eight syllables, and the Mahāpaṅkti, consisting of six such Pādas.

The line of eleven syllables has a caesura after the fourth or fifth syllable, and its regular form is as follows :

o o o o ‖ o o o — ⏑ — ⏓
or o o o o o ‖ o o — ⏑ — ⏓

Four such Pādas form the verse called Triṣṭubh.

---

1) "Pāda" means "foot" but also "fourth part." The latter meaning is to be supposed here, because as a rule four Pādas make one line. The word "pāda" has nothing to do with the "foot" of Greek prosody. A breaking-up into such small units as the Grsek "feet" is impossible in the ancient Indian metre.

The line of twelve syllables differs from that of eleven only in so far as it has one more syllable, for the rest the two metres are formed exactly alike. The regular form of the Pāda of twelve syllables is thus:

o o o o ‖ o o o — ⏑ — ⏑ ⏓

or o o o o o ‖ o o — ⏑ — ⏑ ⏓

Four such Pādas of twelve syllables give a verse which is called Jagatī.

The regular form of the line of five syllables, four or eight of which together give the verse called Dvipadā-Virāj is thus:

⏓ — ⏒ — ⏓

By combinations of different kinds of Pādas into *one* verse, a number of more elaborate metres are formed, as the *Uṣṇih* and *Bṛhatī* verses. composed of lines of eight or twelve syllables.

How much, in old Indian metres, everything depends on the number of syllables,[1] is proved by the oft-recurring speculations, in the Brāhmaṇas and Upaniṣads, on the mystical significance of the metres, where the mysticism of numbers comes into play, when, for example, it is said, with strange logic: "The words bhūmi (earth), antarikṣa (atmosphere), and dyu (sky) form eight syllables. A Gāyatrī-Pāda consists of eight syllables. Therefore he who knows the Gāyatrī gains the three worlds."[2] But that the metres play such a highly important part in the mysticism of ritual, that considered as divine beings, they even receive sacrifices,[3] that mythology concern itself with them, especially with the

---

1) See *Weber*, Ind. Stud. 8, 178 f., and H. *Weller* ZTT, 1, 1922, 115 ff.

2) Bṛhadāraṇyaka-Upaniṣad V, 15. *Dyu* is to be pronounced as "diu."

3) Vāsiṣṭha-Dharmasūtra, XIII, 3 and elsewhere.

Gāyatrī, which in the form of a bird fetches the Soma from heaven, that they are *created* like other beings by Prajāpati,[1] —all this indicates the great age of these metres which were thought to have originated in times immemorial. Thus the age of the metres is also a proof of the age of the hymns themselves.[2]

The best idea, however, of the great age of these hymns is vouchsafed us by a glance at the geographical and cultural conditions of the time of which they tell us. There we see above all, that the Aryan Indians, at the time when the hymns of the Ṛgveda arose, had not nearly as yet spread over the whole of India. We find them still domiciled in the river-land of the Indus (Sindhu), the present Punjab.[3] From the West, over the passes of the Hindukush, Aryan tribes had penetrated into "the land of the five rivers," and in the songs of the Ṛgveda we still hear of the battles which the Aryans[4] had to fight with the Dasyu, or the "black skin", as the swarthy aboriginal inhabitants were called. Only slowly amidst continuous fighting against the hated "non-Aryans" (anārya)—the Dasyus or Dāsas, who know no gods, no laws, and no sacrifices—do they press forward towards the East up

---

[1]) See for instance, Śatapatha-Brāhmaṇa VIII, 1, 1-2. How great a rôle the metres play in the symbolism and mysticism of the ritual, may be seen from numerous passages in the liturgical Saṃhitās and in the Brāhmaṇas: See A. *Weber*, Ind. Stud. 8, pp. 8 ff., 28 ff.

[2]) See E. V. *Arnold*, "Vedic Metre," Cambridge 1905, and A. B. *Keith and Arnold*, JRAS, 1906, 484 ff., 716 ff., 997 ff., on the metre of the Ṛgveda as a criterion of its age.

[3]) According to E. W. *Hopkins* (the Punjab and the Ṛgveda, JAOS., 19, 1898, 19-28) the habitations of the Aryan Indians at the time when the majority of the hymns were composed, should be sought in the neighbourhood of Amballa, between the rivers Sarasouti and Ghuggar. The rivers of the Punjab are praised in the famous "Praise of the Rivers" (nadistuti), Rv. X, 75. Cf. A. *Stein*, JRAS. 1917, 91 ff. *Hertel* has not yet convinced me that the oldest parts of the Ṛgveda were composed in Iran and not in India (Indo-german. Forschungen, 41, 1923, p. 188).

[4]) Ssk. ārya = Avestic airya = Old Pers. ariya, "the faithful ones," "the people of the same race." Herodotus (VII, 62) says that the Medes called themselves *Αριοι*. Thus "Aryan" is the common designation of Indians and Iranians. On the close relationship between the language of the Veda with the old Iranian, see above, p. 41.

to the Ganges. It is significant that this river, without which we can hardly imagine the India of all later periods, and which up to the present day plays such a prominent part in the poetry as well as in the popular religion of the Indians, is hardly mentioned in the Ṛgveda. Heine's lyric :—

> " There are sweet smells and lights by the Ganges,
> And giant trees stand there,
> And beautiful silent figures
> Are kneeling by lotus flowers,"

so suggestive of people and scenes from the period of Kālidāsa, does not in the least fit into the times of the Ṛgveda. Even the lotus-flower, which in a manner belongs to the essentials of later Indian poetry, is not yet a subject for metaphors among the Vedic singers. Altogether the animal and plant worlds in the Ṛgveda are essentially different from those of later periods. The Indian fig-tree (Nyagrodha, Ficus indica) is missing in the Ṛgveda. The most dreaded beast of prey of the India of to-day, the tiger, is not yet mentioned in the hymns—his home is Bengal, into which the Aryan Indians at that time had not yet penetrated. Rice—later the chief product of agriculture and the staple food of the Indians—is still quite unknown to the Ṛgveda. Only barley is planted, and at the time of the hymns agriculture as yet played only a small part. The chief source of income was cattle-rearing, and the chief cattle was the bullock. The horse also was greatly valued and, harnessed before the chariot, bore the warrior to the field, and, at the popular chariot-races, gained praise and glory for the victor. Again and again in the songs and invocations to the gods, the prayer for cattle and horses occurs. Also the strife amongst the hostile aboriginal inhabitants turns on the possession of cattle. Therefore, too, the old word for "war" or "battle" is originally "desire for cattle" (gaviṣṭi). In the most extravagant expressions cows and bullocks[1] are praised as the most precious possessions. The lowing of cows hastening to the calves is looked on by the ancient Indian as the sweetest music. "The singers are shouting to the god Indra," says a poet, "as mother cows low to the calf." Gods are readily compared with bullocks, goddesses with cows. The milk of the cow was not only one of the chief articles of food, but milk and butter formed an essential part of the sacrifices to the gods. The milk was by preference consumed warm as it came from the cow, and Vedic poets marvel at the miracle that the "raw" cow gives cooked milk. As the German nursery rhyme has it:—

> "How can it be, O tell me now,
> The milk is white, but red the cow,"

so a Vedic singer praises the god Indra on account of the miracle that he has put the shining white milk into the red or black cows. However, the high esteem in which cattle were held proved no obstacle to the slaughtering of cows, and especially of bullocks, at the sacrifices, and to the eating of their flesh. An absolute prohibition of cow-killing did not exist in the oldest times, although the word "aghnyā," "she who is not to be killed" for "cow" indicates that cows were killed only under exceptional circumstances.[2] Also the skin of the oxen was used. The tanner worked it up into leather bottles, strings of bows and straps. There were also already different kinds of industries. There was above all the wood worker—at once carpenter, carriage-builder, and cabinet-maker—who made especially the chariot. There were metal-workers, smiths, who used a bird's wings as bellows. Shipping was still in its first beginnings. A canoe provided

---

1) It is quite similar among the Dinkas and Kaffirs in Africa, whose present form of economics must be fairly in agreement with that of the Vedic Aryans.

2) See A. A. *Macdonell* and A. B *Keith*, "Vedic Index of Names and Subjects," London 1912, II, 145 ff.

with oars, probably consisting only of a hollowed-out tree-trunk, served for the navigation of the rivers. Although the sea was known to the Vedic Indians, it is, to say the least, highly doubtful[1] whether there was yet an extensive maritime trade. However, it is certain that there were traders, and that an extensive trade was carried on, in which oxen and gold ornaments took the place of money. Besides oxen and horses, the Vedic singers implore the gods chiefly for gold, which they hope to receive as gifts from the rich sacrificers.

But while we hear in the Ṛgveda of cattle-rearing and agriculture, of trade and industry, as well as of deeds of war and of sacrifices, there is not yet to be found in the hymns that caste-division, which imparts a peculiar stamp to the whole of the social life of the Indians of later times, and which, up to the present day, has remained the curse of India. Only in one single hymn, evidently late, are the four castes—Brāhmaṇa, Kṣatriya, Vaiśya and Śūdra—mentioned. Certainly there were warriors and priests, but of an exclusive warrior-caste there is in the Ṛgveda as little mention as of one or several lower castes of farmers, cattle-traders, merchants, artisans, and labourers. As in later times, so indeed already in the Ṛgveda, it was the custom that, at the king's side there stood a house-priest (Purohita) who offered the sacrifices for him. But we still hear often enough—even in the later Vedic period—of sacrifices and ceremonies, which the pater-familias performs alone without priestly aid. The wife takes part in these sacrifices; indeed, it is reckoned as absolutely essential, that the husband and wife together perform the sacred ceremonies. This participation of the wife in the sacrifices proves at all events that the position of woman in

---

[1]) It is certainly not a mere accident, that in the songs of the Ṛgveda countless similes and metaphors are drawn from *cattle-rearing*, while only seldom a simile refers to *shipping*. Contrast with this Homer's wealth of figures of speech which refer to shipping.

the oldest period of the Ṛgveda was not yet so low as later, when the law-books absolutely *forbid* women to sacrifice, and to repeat sacred texts. In the Ṛgveda (VIII, 31) we read of the married couple (dampatī—"householder and housewife") who "with minds in harmony press the Soma, rinse and mix it with milk" and offer adoration to the gods. Manu, however, declares in his law-book, that it is displeasing to the gods when women sacrifice (IV, 206), and that women who offer the fire-sacrifice (Agnihotra) sink into hell (XI, 37). When we still hear in the Upaniṣads, that women also took an active share in the disputations of the philosophers, we must not wonder that in the hymns of the Ṛgveda women could without restriction—at feasts, dances, and such like—show themselves publicly. It is by no means necessary, as some scholars do, to think of courtesans, when it is said that beautiful women flock to the festival gathering. It is not to be denied, however, that already at the time of the Ṛgveda, many solitary, unprotected women—"brotherless maidens" as a poet calls them—gave themselves up to prostitution; but Pischel and Geldner,[1] in spite of all the trouble which they have taken to prove it, have not succeeded in proving that at that time already there existed a "grand system of courtesans" as in the time of Buddha in Vesali, or at the time of Perikles in Athens.

However, we must not form too exalted an idea of the moral conditions in ancient India, and not picture these to ourselves in such an idyllic manner, as certainly Max Müller has at times done. We hear in the hymns of the Ṛgveda of incest, seduction, conjugal unfaithfulness, the procuring of abortion, as also of deception, theft and robbery. All this, however, proves nothing against the antiquity of the Ṛgveda. Modern ethnology knows nothing of "unspoiled children of nature" any more than it regards all primitive peoples as

---

[1]) Vedische Studien, I, p. xxv.

rough savages or cannibal monsters. The ethnologist knows that a step-ladder of endless gradations of the most widely differing cultural conditions leads from the primitive peoples to the half-civilised peoples, and right up to the civilised nations. We need not, therefore, imagine the people of the Ṛgveda either as an innocent shepherd people, or as a horde of rough savages, nor, on the other hand as a people of ultra-refined culture. The picture of culture which is unfolded in these songs, and which Heinrich Zimmer in his still valuable book "Altindisches Leben"[1] has drawn for us in so masterly a manner, shows us the Aryan Indians as an active, joyful and warlike people, of simple, and still partly savage habits. The Vedic singers implore the gods for help against the enemy, for victory in battle, for glory and rich booty; they pray for wealth, heaps of gold and countless herds of cattle, for rain for their fields, for the blessing of children, and long life. As yet we do not find in the songs of the Ṛgveda that effeminate, ascetic and pessimistic trait of the Indian character with which we shall meet again and again in later Indian literature.

Now there have been scholars, who considered the hymns of the Ṛgveda to be so enormously old, that they thought to see in them not so much Indian as Aryan or Indo-European mental life; they held, that the epoch of these hymns was still so near to the Indo-European "pre-historic time," that in them we are still dealing rather with "Aryans" than with actual Indians. On the other hand, other scholars have shown that the Ṛgveda is above all a production of the *Indian* mind, and that for its explanation no other principles must be followed than for any other text of Indian literature. This is one of the many points on which the interpreters of the Ṛgveda diverge rather widely.[2]

---

1) Berlin 1879.

2) See *Barth*, Oeuvres II, 237 ff.; H. *Oldenberg*, Vedaforschung, Stuttgart, 1905; *Winternitz*, WZKM, 19, 1905, 419 ff.

We must here remember the important fact that the Ṛgveda is as yet by no means fully explained. There are, indeed, a large number of hymns, the explanation of which is as certain as that of any other Indian text. But on the other hand, there are many hymns and very many verses and isolated passages of the Ṛgveda whose right meaning is still in the highest degree doubtful. This is also of great importance for the just appreciation of these old writings. The outsider who takes a translation of the Ṛgveda in his hand often wonders that so much in these hymns is unpoetical, indeed unintelligible and senseless. But the reason is frequently only that the translators do not content themselves with translating that which is intelligible, but that they think they *must* translate *everything*, even that which has up till now not been rightly interpreted.

However it is not entirely our fault, that we as yet do not rightly understand the Ṛgveda, and that a *complete* translation of it *must* of necessity contain much that is incorrect. The reason lies in the great age of these hymns which *to the Indians themselves*, already in very early times, had become unintelligible. Within the Vedic literature we find already some verses of the Ṛgveda misunderstood and wrongly interpreted. Already in early times Indian scholars busied themselves with the interpretation of the Ṛgveda. So-called Nighaṇṭus or "Glossaries," collections of rare and obscure words which occur in the hymns, were prepared. The first commentator of the Ṛgveda, whose work is preserved to us, was Yāska, who on the basis of the Nighaṇṭus, explains a great number of Vedic verses in his work Nirukta (*i.e.* "Etymology"). This Yāska, who doubtless is older than Pāṇini,[1] already quotes no less than seventeen predecessors,

[1]) The great age of the Nirukta is proved by its language, which is more archaic than that of the remaining non-Vedic Sanskrit literature. s. *Bhandarkar*. JBRAS 16, 1885. 265 f. Lakshman *Sarup*, "The Nighaṇṭu and the Nirukta the oldest Indian Treatise on

whose opinions frequently contradict each other. Indeed, one of the scholars quoted by Yāska declares outright that the whole Veda-exegesis is worth nothing, as the hymns are obscure, senseless, and contradictory to each other—to which Yāska, however, observes that it is not the fault of the beam if the blind man does not see it. Yāska himself, in the explanation of difficult words, often relies on the etymology (which of course does not fulfil the scientific requirements of modern philology) and frequently gives two or more different interpretations of one and the same word. It follows from this, that already in Yāska's time the sense of many words and passages of the Ṛgveda was no longer established by an uninterrupted tradition. Of the work of the many successors whom Yāska has had, there is nothing preserved to us, any more than of that of his predecessors. Only from the 14th century after the birth of Christ do we possess a comprehensive commentary, which explains the Ṛgveda word by word. This is the famous commentary of Sāyaṇa. Some of the older European interpreters of the Ṛgveda—thus the English scholar H. H. Wilson, who has published a complete English translation of the Ṛgveda, which entirely follows the Indian commentary—depended entirely upon Sāyaṇa's commentary, taking it for granted that the latter rested on reliable tradition. On the other hand, other Veda investigators did not trouble themselves at all about the native interpretation. They denied

---

Etymology, Philosophy and Semantics," Introduction, Oxford 1920, p. 54, merely reflects the universal opinion (without offering any new proofs) that Yāska lived between 700 and 500 B.C. Yāska was acquainted with all the Vedic Saṃhitās and the most important Brāhmaṇas, including the latest Gopatha-Brāhmaṇa, the Prātiśākhyas and a few of the Upaniṣads; s. *Sarup, loc cit.*, pp. 54 f., and P.D. *Gune*, in Bhandarkar Com. Vol, pp. 43 ff. Yāska already considered the Veda as revealed; but even in his time there were men who doubted the sanctity of the Veda (s. Sarup, *loc. cit.*, pp. 71 ff.). Satyavrata *Sāmaśramin* in an appendix to his edition of the Nirukta has an interesting treatise in Sanskrit on the age of Yāska (about 1900 B.C. !) and the purpose of the Nirukta s. *Barth*, RHR. 27, 1893, 184 ff., = Oeuvres II, 94 ff. On Yāska, s. also *Liebich*, "Zur Einführung in die indischu einheim. Sprachwiss, II, 22 ff.

that a commentator, who lived more than two thousand years after the composition of the book explained by him, could know anything which we Europeans, with our philological criticism and with the modern resources of linguistic science, could not fathom and understand better. Among these investigators especially Rudolf Roth is conspicuous. One of his pupils and followers was H. Grassmann, who published in two volumes a complete metrical translation of the hymns of the Ṛgveda.[1] Most of the investigators to-day take up an intermediary position. While admitting that we must not blindly follow the native interpreters, they yet believe that the latter did *partly* at least, draw upon an uninterrupted tradition and therefore should not be disregarded, and that simply because they are Indians and moreover better acquainted with the Indian atmosphere, as it were, than we Westerners, they often hit the right meaning. Among these interpreters is Alfred Ludwig, who, in his complete German translation of the Ṛgveda, to which is added a comprehensive, most valuable commentary,[2] for the first time thoroughly utilized the explanations of Sāyaṇa, without rejecting other aids to interpretation. He is a forerunner of R. Pischel and K. F. Geldner, who, in their "Vedische Studien"[3] have

---

[1]) Leipzig, 1876 and 1877. The selection "Siebenzig Lieder des Ṛgveda übersetzt von Karl *Geldner* und Adolf *Kaegi.* Mit Beiträgen von R. *Roth.*" Tübingen 1875, which also proceeded from *Roth's* school, is much preferable to Grassmann's translation.

[2]) Prag 1876-1888, in six volumes. Though difficult to understand, *Ludwig's* translation is yet more reliable than the smooth verses in the translation of *Grassmann.* A good English translation is that of R.T.H. *Griffith*, Benares, 1889-1892. Selections from the Ṛgveda are translated into English by Max *Müller* and *Oldenberg* in SBE., Vols. 32 and 46; into German by K. F. *Geldner*, in A. Bertholet, "Religionsgeschichtliches Lesebuch" (Tübingen, 1908) p. 71 ff: A. *Hillebrandt*, "Lieder des Ṛgveda," Göttingen 1913: into English A. A. *Macdonell*, "Hymns from the Ṛgveda" (Heritage of India Series); and E. J. *Thomas* "Vedic Hymns" (Wisdom of the East Series), London 1923. The first part of a new and complete translation of the Ṛgveda by K.F. *Geldner* has been published in the series "Quellen der Religionsgeschichte," Göttingen, 1923.

[3]) Stuttgart, 1889-1901, 3 vols. Other important contributions to the interpretation of the Ṛgveda are: *Oldenberg*, "Ṛgveda, Textkritische und exegetische Noten", AGGW

rendered invaluable services to the clearing-up of many obscure passages of the Ṛgveda. They have also clung most firmly—certainly not without exaggeration—to the principle that the Ṛgveda must, above all, be interpreted as a production of the *Indian* mind, to the right understanding of which the Indian literature of later periods provides the best key.

Added to all this is yet another much-debated question, which is of no little importance for the interpretation of the Vedic hymns, namely the question whether these hymns arose independently of all sacrificial ritual as the naive expressions of a pious faith in the gods, as the outpouring of the hearts of divinely inspired singers, or whether they were, in a workmanlike manner, composed by priests, merely with the intention of using them for certain sacrifices and ceremonies.

But how differently these songs may be judged according to the line of interpretation taken by a scholar may be shown by contrasting the opinions of two eminent scholars. In his beautiful book, which is still worth reading, "Der Ṛgveda, die älteste Litteratur der Inder,"[1] Ad. Kaegi says of the hymns of the Ṛgveda: "The great majority of the songs are invocations and glorifications of the deities addressed at the time; their key-note is throughout a simple outpouring of the heart, a prayer to the Eternal Ones, an invitation to accept favourably the piously dedicated gift...... To that which a god placed in his soul and caused him to feel: to the impulse of his heart the singer wishes to give eloquent expression." He admits that also portions of inferior quality are to be found in the collection, "but there is in them all a fresh breath of vigorous primeval poetry. Whoever takes the trouble to transfer himself to the religious and moral thought

---

N.F., Vol. XI, No. 5, and Vol. XIII, No. 3, 1909 and 1912: *Geldner*, "Der Ṛgveda in Auswahl" I. Glossar, II Kommentar, Stuttgart 1907-1909, and ZDMG 71, 1917, 315 ff. M. *Bloomfield*, JAOS 27, 1906, 72 ff.: E. W. *Fay*, *ibid*, 403 ff.: A.B. *Keith*, JRAS 1910, 921 ff.

[1]) Second edition, Leipzig, 1881. An English translation (The Rig-Veda, the Oldest Literature of the Indians) with additions, by R. *Arrowsmith*, appeared 1886.

and action, the poetry and the working of a people and age, in which the first spiritual development of our own race is placed before our eyes at its best, will feel himself attracted in various ways by many of these songs, here through the childlike simplicity, there through the freshness or delicacy of feeling and in other parts by the boldness of metaphor, by the flight of the imagination." Now let us hear what H. Oldenberg, the ingenious and judicious expert on Indian literature, says about these songs in his "Religion des Veda." [1] He sees already in this "oldest document of Indian literature and religion" "the clear trace of an ever-increasing intellectual enervation." He speaks of the "sacrificial songs and litanies, with which the priests of the Vedic Aryans on a temple-less place of sacrifice, at the sacrificial fires strewn around with grass, invoked their gods—barbarian priests—the barbarian gods, who with horses and chariots came driving through the sky and air in order to feast on the sacrificial cake, butter, and meat, and to imbibe, with the intoxicating soma juice, courage and divine strength. The singers of the Ṛgveda, in a manner inherited of old, composing for the great and pompous ....Soma-sacrifice, do not want to tell of the god whom they are honouring, but they want to praise this god....So they heap upon him all the glorifying epithets which are at the disposal of the grossly flattering garrulousness of an imagination which loves the bright and the garish." "Such poetry," Oldenberg thinks, "could have arisen only in the exclusive circles of the priestly sacrificial experts."

To me both these opinions seem exaggerated, and the truth, in my opinion, here as in all the debateable questions regarding the interpretation of the Ṛgveda, lies midway. Let us remember that the hymn-collection of the Ṛgveda is composed of earlier and later portions. Just as there are hymns in the Saṃhitā, which belong to different periods of

[1]) Berlin 1894, p. 3.

time, so also in contents the hymns are of greatly varying value and of different origin. There is no doubt that a great number of these hymns arose independently of all sacrificial ritual, and that in them the breath of genuine primeval religious poetry is felt.[1] Even if many of these hymns were used later on for sacrificial purposes, that does not in the least prove that they were originally written for this purpose. On the other hand it is equally certain that very many portions of the Ṛgveda-Saṃhitā were from the first intended for nothing but sacrificial songs and litanies, and were glued together in a rather workmanlike fashion by priestly singers. It is also certainly exaggerated when W. D. Whitney[2] once said: "The Vedas appear rather like an Indo-European than an Indian record." But just as certainly is it an exaggeration when Pischel and Geldner (with H. H. Wilson) state that the Indians at the time of the Ṛgveda, had already attained a degree of culture, which was little different from that which Alexander the Great found in existence at the time of his invasion of India.[3]

Although the gulf which divides the hymns of the Ṛgveda from the rest of Indian literature may perhaps not be so wide as many older investigators have supposed, a gulf still exists.[4] This is proved by the language, by the cultural conditions indicated above, and most particularly by the stage of religious development, which we meet with in the hymns. So much is certain, that, whatever the

---

[1]) Enthusiasm should not, however, be allowed to obscure calm criticism, as is the case with H. *Brunnhofer*, who (in his essay "Ueber den Geist der indischen Lyrik," Leipzig 1882) makes the author of one of the later philosophical hymns of the Ṛgveda "A prince of poets towering up out of the mists of primitive times" (p. 15) and is carried away into saying that "the Veda is like the lark's morning trill, of humanity awakening to the consciousness of its greatness" (p. 41). That the Veda certainly is not !

[2]) Language and its Study, London 1876, p. 227.

[3]) Vedische Studien, I, pp. xxii, xxvi.

[4]) See also A. *Hillebrandt*, "Vedische Mythologie," II, 8.

poetical value of the songs of the Ṛgveda may be, there exists no more important source for the investigation of the earliest stages in the development of Indian religion, no more important literary source for the investigation of the mythology of the Indo-European peoples, indeed, of peoples in general, than these songs of the Ṛgveda.

To say it in a word: what renders these hymns so valuable for us is that we see before us in them a mythology in the making.[1]) We see gods, as it were, arising before our eyes. Many of the hymns are not addressed to a sun-god, nor to a moon-god, nor to a fire-god, nor to a god of the heavens, nor to storm-gods and water-deities, nor to a goddess of the dawn and an earth-goddess, but the shining sun itself, the gleaming moon in the nocturnal sky, the fire blazing on the hearth or on the altar or even the lightning shooting forth from the cloud, the bright sky of day, or the starry sky of night, the roaring storms, the flowing waters of clouds and of rivers, the glowing dawn and the spread-out fruitful earth—all these natural phenomena are, as such, glorified, worshipped, and invoked. Only gradually is accomplished in the songs of the Ṛgveda itself, the transformation of these natural phenomena into mythological figures, into gods and goddesses such as Sūrya (Sun), Soma (Moon), Agni (Fire), Dyaus (Sky), Maruts (Storms), Vāyu (Wind), Āpas (Waters), Uṣas (Dawn), and Pṛthivī (Earth), whose names still indubitably indicate what they originally were. So the songs of the Ṛgveda prove indisputably that the most prominent figures of mythology have proceeded from personifications of the most striking natural phenomena. Mythological investigation has succeeded, also in the cases of the deities

[1]) L. *de la Vallée Poussin*, ("Le Védisme," Paris 1909, pp. 61 ff., 68) contests this view that the Veda presents "a mythology in the making" and A. B. *Keith*, JRAS., 1909, p. 469, agrees with him. But I did not mean to say that all mythology first arose at the time of the Ṛgveda-Saṃhitā. The beginnings of the Vedic system of mythology and religion

whose names are no longer so transparent, in proving that they originally were nothing but just natural phenomena similar to sun, moon, and so on. Among such mythological figures, whose original nature is soon partly forgotten in the hymns, and who are honoured more as mighty, lofty beings, distinguished through all kinds of miraculous deeds, are Indra, Varuṇa, Mitra, Aditi, Viṣṇu, Pūṣan, the two Aśvins, Rudra and Parjanya. These gods' names, too, originally indicated natural phenomena, and natural beings. Epithets, which at first emphasized a particularly important side of a natural being, became gods' names and new gods. Thus Savitar, the "inspirer," "the life-giver," and Vivasvat, "the shining," were at first epithets, then names of the sun, and finally they became independent sun-gods beside Sūrya. Also the gods of different tribes and different periods are in many ways represented in the polytheism of the Vedic Indians.[1]) Hence it is that Mitra, Viṣṇu and Pūṣan also appear in the Ṛgveda as sun-gods. Pūṣan was probably the sun-god of a small shepherd-tribe, before he was received into the Vedic pantheon as the "Lord of the ways," the protector of travellers, the god who knows all the paths and also brings back to the right path the cattle which have strayed. Mitra, who is identical with the Mithra of the Avesta, is through this fact already distinguishable as an ancient Aryan sun-god, who still hails from the time when Indians and Iranians formed one people. It is not so easy with all gods to discover to which natural phenomenon they owe their origin. Still the opinions of investigators differ widely in the explanation of gods like Indra, Varuṇa, Rudra, Aditi, and the Aśvins—to mention

---

doubtless belong to a far earlier period than the compilation of the Saṃhitā. *Those hymns*, however, in which the natural phenomena and the deities embodied in them are as yet scarcely distinguished from one another, hark back to the time of the beginnings of Vedic mythology. This, of course, does not assume that the same thing is true of the whole Saṃhitā, or of the whole of Vedic religion.

[1]) See A. *Hillebrandt*, "Vedische Mythologie," II, 14 ff.

only the most important ones. Thus, to one, Indra is the god of the storm, to the other an old sun-god. Varuṇa is to some a god of the heavens, while others see in him a moon-god. Rudra, who is usually held to be a storm-god, because he is the father of the storm-gods (the Maruts), would be, according to Oldenberg, a mountain and forest god, according to Hillebrandt "a god of the horrors of the tropical climate."[1] Aditi is, according to one view, the expanse of the sky, according to another the endless, widespreading earth. The two Asvins, a pair of gods who are doubtless related to the Greek Dioskuri, and also reappear in Germanic and Lettic mythology, were already before Yāska a puzzle to the ancient Indian commentators. Some held them to be heaven and earth, others day and night, and still to-day some scholars see in them the two twilights, others sun and moon, yet others the morning and evening star, and again others the constellation of Gemini.[2] But what is the most important is that most mythologists to-day agree that by far the greatest majority of the Vedic gods has proceeded from natural phenomena or natural beings.[3] There were, indeed, some deities

---

[1]) See now the learned dissertation by E. *Arbman,* Rudra Untersuchungen zum altindischen Glauben und Kultus, Uppsala, 1922. He sees in Rudra a primitive popular deity, the prototype of Śiva.

[2]) This is not the place to express an opinion on all the controversial questions which concern Vedic Mythology. The best representation of the *facts* of Vedic Mythology is given by A. A. *Macdonell,* "Vedic Mythology" (in the "Grundriss" III, I, A.). Whoever desires information with reference to the *explanation* of the myths and religious belief of the ancient Indians, must at all events consult *both* H. *Oldenberg's* "Religion des Veda" (Berlin 1894) *and also* A. *Hillebrandt's* "Vedische Mythologie" (3 vols., Breslau 1891-1902). Different as are the results arrived at by the two investigators, both have greatly contributed to the extension and deepening of our knowledge of the Vedic religion. Even the outsider, however, must be quite clear that, in these questions, absolute truth can never be attained, in fact can always only be approached more or less closely. Great services have been rendered to the investigation of Vedic religion and still more to the explanation of the hymns of the Ṛgveda, by the French scholar Abel *Bergaigne,* ("La religion védique d'après les hymnes du Ṛg-veda," 3 vols., Paris, 1878-1883).

[3]) Sten *Konow,* The Aryan Gods of the Mitani People, Kristiania, 1921, p. 5, has not convinced me, "that the conception of Vedic religion as a worship of nature and natural phenomena is fundamentally wrong."

that have become divine beings out of abstractions, but they nearly all appear only in the latest hymns of the tenth book; thus Viśvakarman = "the world master-builder," Prajāpati = "the lord of creatures," or Śraddhā = "faith," Manyu = "anger," and some similar personifications. More important are certain gods of the so-called "lower" mythology, who also appear in the Ṛgveda: the Ṛbhus, who correspond with the elves, the Apsaras, who correspond with the nymphs, and the Gandharvas, who are a kind of forest and field spirits. Numerous demons and evil spirits too appear in the hymns as enemies of the gods, who are hated and fought against by the Devas or gods. The name Asura, however, by which in the later Vedic works these enemies of the gods are designated, appears in the Ṛgveda still with the old meaning "possessed of wonderful power" or "god,"[1] which the corresponding word "Ahura" has in the Avesta, and only in a few places also with the meaning of demons. In the Ṛgveda Dāsa or Dasyu—thus the non-Aryan aboriginal inhabitants also are called—is the usual name for the evil demons, besides also Rakṣas or Rākṣasas, by which, in the Ṛgveda, as well as in the whole of the later Indian literature, all kinds of mischievous, ghostly beings are designated. Also the Pitaras, the "fathers" or ancestral spirits, already in the Ṛgveda received divine worship. The king of these ancestral spirits, who rules in the kingdom of the deceased, high up in the highest heaven, is Yama, a god who belongs already to the Indo-Iranian prehistoric period; for he is identical with Yima who, in the Avesta, is the first human being, the primeval ancestor of the human race. As the first departed one—perhaps originally the daily setting sun or the monthly dying moon—he became the king in the realm of the dead. This kingdom of the dead is in the heavens, and the dying man is comforted by the belief that after death he will abide with King Yama in the highest heaven. Of the dismal belief

---

1) Cf. *Oldenberg*, Religion des Veda, pp. 162 ff.; V. K. *Rajwade*, Proc. IOC., II, pp. 1 ff.

in the transmigration of the soul and eternal rebirth—the belief which controls the whole philosophical thought of Indians in later centuries—there is, in the Ṛgveda, as yet no trace to be found. So we see here too, that in these hymns there breathes an entirely different spirit from that which pervades the whole of the later Indian literature.

Just these important differences between the religious views which appear in the songs of the Ṛgveda and those of the succeeding period prove also that these songs do as a matter of fact reflect the popular belief of the old Aryan Indians. Though it is true that the songs of the Ṛgveda cannot really be called "popular poetry," that—for the most part at least—they arose in certain singer-families, in narrow priestly circles, yet we must not think that these priests and singers created a mythology and a system of religion without any consideration of the popular belief. Certainly there may be some things that are told of the gods, which rest only on "momentary fancies of the individual poet," but on the whole we must take for granted that these priests and singers started from popular tradition, that they, as Hillebrandt aptly says, "stood above, but not outside, the people." [1)]

Thus, then, these songs are of incalculable value to us as evidence of the oldest religious faith of the Aryan Indians. As works of poetic art, too, they deserve a prominent place in the world literature. It is true, the authors of these hymns rise but extremely seldom to the exalted flights and the deep fervour of, say, the religious poetry of the Hebrews. The Vedic singer does not look up to the god whom he honours in song, with that shuddering awe and that faith, firm as a rock, with which the Psalmist looks up to Jehovah. The prayers of the priestly singers of ancient India do not, as with the former, rise from the inmost soul to the heavenly ones. These poets stand

---

[1)] See *Oldenberg*, "Aus Indien und Iran," p. 19; "Religion des Veda," p. 13; *Hillebrandt*, "Vedische Mythologie," II. 4.

on a more familiar footing with the gods whom they honour in song. When they sing a song of praise to a god, then they expect him to present them with wealth in cows and hero-sons, and they are not afraid to tell him this. "*Do, ut des,*" is the standpoint which they hold. Thus a Vedic poet says to the god Indra: (Ṛv. VIII, 14. 1, 2):

"If I, O Indra, were like thee,
Lord of all the goods that be,
My worshipper should never lack
For herds to call his own.

Gifts would I bestow on him,
On that wise singer blessings shower,
If I, as thou, O lord of power,
The Master of the cattle were."

And another poet addresses the god Agni with the following words (Ṛv. VIII, 19. 25, 26):

"If thou wert mortal, Agni, and I the immortal one,
Thou son of strength, like Mitra, to whom we sacrifice,
Thee would I not expose to curse, good God!
My worshipper should not suffer poverty, neglect, or harm."

Yet the character of the hymns—and I am now speaking of those which contain invocations or songs of praise to the gods, without being composed for definite sacrificial purposes—is very different, according to the deities to which they are dedicated. Amongst the loftiest and most inspired poems are indisputably the songs to Varuṇa. There are indeed not many of them. Varuṇa, however, is the only one amongst the Vedic gods, who stands nobly elevated above mortals, whom the poet ventures to approach only with trembling and fear, and in humble reverence. Varuṇa it is, too, who concerns himself more than any other god of the Vedic pantheon with the moral ways of men and punishes the sinners. Contritely, therefore, the poet approaches him and pleads for forgiveness of his sins. Thus the hymns addressed to Varuṇa are the only ones which lend themselves, to a certain extent, to comparison with the poetry of the Psalms. As a specimen I give the hymn Ṛv. V, 85 in the translation of R. T. H. Griffith :—

"Sing forth a hymn sublime and solemn, grateful to glorious Varuṇa, imperial Ruler,
Who hath struck out, like one who slays the victim, earth as a skin to spread in front of Sûrya.

In the tree-tops the air he hath extended, put milk in kine and vigorous speed in horses,
Set intellect in hearts, fire in the waters,[1] Sûrya in heaven and Soma on the mountain.

Varuṇa lets the big cask, opening downward, flow through the heaven and earth and air's mid-region.
Therewith the universe's Sovran waters earth as the shower of rain bedews the barley.

When Varuṇa is fain for milk he moistens the sky, the land, and earth to her foundation.
Then straight the mountains clothe them in the rain-cloud: the Heroes, putting forth their vigour, loose them.[2])

I will declare this mighty deed of magic, of glorious Varuṇa the Lord Immortal,
Who standing in the firmament hath meted the earth out with the Sun as with a measure.

None, verily, hath ever let or hindered this the most wise God's mighty deed of magic,
Whereby with all their flood, the lucid rivers fill not one sea wherein they pour their waters.

If we have sinned against the man who loves us, have ever wronged a brother, friend, comrade,
The neighbour ever with us, or a stranger, O Varuṇa, remove from us the trespass.

---

[1]) Namely, the lightning in the cloud.

[2]) The milk is the water of the clouds which are compared with cows. The "strong men" are the storm-god (Maruts) who, in the storm, cause the "milk" of the clouds to flow.

If we, as gamesters cheat at play, have cheated, done wrong unwittingly or sinned of purpose,
Cast all these sins away like loosened fetters, and, Varuṇa, let us be thine own beloved."

Varuṇa, too, already in the Ṛgveda, is, as he is in the later mythology, the god of the sea, a god of the waters, and therefore he punishes people who have sinned, particularly with dropsy. A simple prayer by one who is suffering from dropsy is Ṛv. VII, 89. I give it in the translation of R. T. H. Griffith:—

"Let me not yet, King Varuṇa, enter into the house of clay[1]):
Have mercy, spare me, Mighty Lord.

When, Thunderer! I move along tremulous like a wind-blown skin,
Have mercy, spare me, Mighty Lord.

O Bright and Powerful God, through want of strength I erred and went astray:
Have mercy, spare me, Mighty Lord.

Thirst found thy worshipper though he stood in the midst of water-floods:
Have mercy, spare me, Mighty Lord.

O Varuṇa, whatever the offence may be which we as men commit against the heavenly host,
When through our want of strength we violate thy laws, punish us not, O God, for that iniquity."

Quite a different note is struck in the songs to the god Indra. Indra can be designated as the actual national god of the Vedic Indians. As, however, the Indians at the time of the Ṛgveda, were still a fighting and struggling nation, so Indra is a thoroughly warlike god. His enormous strength and combativeness are described again and again, and fondly the Vedic singers dwell on the battles of Indra with the demons, whom he destroys with his thunderbolt. Especially

---

[1]) The grave, or the earthen urn in which the ashes of the cremated corpse are preserved, may be meant. On the methods of burial of the ancient Indians, see below pp. 95ff.

the battle of Indra with Vṛtra is celebrated by songs in numerous hymns. Again and again the splendid victory is spoken of, which the god achieved over the demon; countless times Indra is praised exultingly, because he slew Vṛtra with his thunderbolt. Vṛtra (probably "the Obstructor") is a demon in the form of a serpent or a dragon, who keeps the waters enclosed or imprisoned in a mountain. Indra wants to release the waters. With Soma he imbibes courage, hastens to the battle, and slays the monster—now the released waters flow in a rapid stream over the corpse of Vṛtra. This great deed of Indra is graphically described in the song Ṛv. I, 32, which begins with the verses [1]:—

> "I will proclaim the manly deeds of Indra,
> The first that he performed, the lightning-wielder.
> He slew the serpent, then discharged the waters,
> And cleft the caverns of the lofty mountains.
>
> He slew the serpent lying on the mountain:
> For him the whizzing bolt has Tvaṣṭar fashioned.
> Like lowing cows, with rapid current flowing,
> The waters to the ocean down have glided."

The songs leave no doubt that the myth of Indra's dragon-fight refers to some powerful natural phenomenon. Heaven and earth tremble when Indra slays Vṛtra. He does not destroy the dragon *once* only, but repeatedly, and he is invited also in the future always to kill Vṛtra, and to release the waters. Already the old Indian Veda-interpreters tell us that Indra is a god of the thunder-storm, and that by the mountains in which the waters are enclosed, we are to understand the clouds, in which Vṛtra—the demon of drought—keeps the waters imprisoned. Most of the European mythologists agreed with this opinion and saw in Indra, armed with a thunderbolt, a counterpart of the Teutonic Thunar, who swings the thunder-hammer Mjölnir, a thunder-god reaching

[1]) Translated by A. A. *Macdonell*, Hymns from the Rigveda, p. 47.

back into the Indo-European prehistoric period, and in the dragon-fight a mythological representation of the thunderstorm. Hillebrandt, however, has tried to prove that Vṛtra is not a cloud-demon and not a demon of drought, but a winter-giant whose power is broken by the sun-god Indra; the "rivers" which are imprisoned by Vṛtra and set free by Indra, are, according to him, not the torrents of rain, but the rivers of the North-West of India which dry up in winter and are re-filled only when the sun causes the masses of snow of the Himalaya mountains to melt.

However that may be, it is certain that the Vedic singers themselves had no clear consciousness of the original meaning of Indra and Vṛtra as nature-gods. For them Indra was a powerful champion, a giant of enormous strength, but Vṛtra the most dreaded of the demons, which were believed to be embodied in the black aborigines of the land. For Indra does not fight only with Vṛtra, but with numerous other demons. His demon-fights are only a copy of the battles which the Aryan immigrants had to fight. Therefore, too, Indra is above all a god of warriors. Of none of the gods of the Vedic pantheon are so many individual traits given us, none is portrayed so "true to life"—if one may use the expression with reference to a deity—as this warlike god in the 250 hymns which are dedicated to him. Big and strong are his arms. With beautiful lips he quaffs the Soma-drink, and when he has drunk, he moves his jawbones with pleasure, and shakes his fair beard. Fair as gold is his hair, and his whole appearance. He is a giant in stature,—heaven and earth would not be large enough to serve him as a girdle. In strength and vigour no heavenly nor earthly being approaches him. When he grasped the two endless worlds, they were for him only a handful. He is called by preference a bull. Boundless as his strength, is also his power of drinking, which is described, often not without humour, in the songs. Before he slew Vṛtra, he drank three ponds of soma; and once it is even said that he drank, in one gulp, thirty ponds of soma juice. Scarcely was he born—and his birth was no ordinary one, for still in his mother's womb he said: "I do not want to go out here, that is a bad way; across, through the side, I will go out" (Ṛv. IV, 18, 2)—when he already drank goblets of soma. Sometimes, too, he did too much of a good thing. In the song Ṛv. X, 119, a poet brings before us the intoxicated Indra, uttering a monologue and considering what he is to do—"Thus I will do it, no, thus," "I will place the earth here, no, I will place it there," and so on—where each verse ends with the significant refrain "Have I, then, drunk of the Soma?"

This warlike national god is much more suitable than any other to be the chief of gods. Although in the Ṛgveda almost every god is at some time or another praised as the first and highest of all gods—this is a sort of flattery, by means of which one wants to incline the god in one's favour, similarly to the way in which later court poets have celebrated many a petty prince as the ruler of the world—yet Indra is, in the earliest times, undoubtedly a king among the gods, like Zeus of the Greek Olympus.

As chief of gods he is celebrated in the song Ṛv. II, 12, which as a specimen of an Indra song, may here be given in the translation of A. A. Macdonell: [1]

"He who just born as chief god full of spirit
Went far beyond the other gods in wisdom:
Before whose majesty and mighty manhood
The two worlds trembled: he, O men, is Indra.

Who made the widespread earth when quaking steadfast
Who set at rest the agitated mountains,
Who measured out air's middle space more widely,
Who gave the sky support: he, men, is Indra.

[1]) Hymns from the Rigveda, pp. 48 ff

Who slew the serpent, freed the seven rivers,
Who drove the cattle out from Vala's cavern,[1]
Who fire between two rocks has generated,
A conqueror in fights: he, men, is Indra.

He who has made all earthly things unstable,
Who humbled and dispersed the Dasa colour,
Who, as the player's stake the winning gambler,
The foeman's fortune gains: he, men, is Indra.

Of whom, the terrible, they ask, "Where is he?"
Of him, indeed, they also say, "he is not."
The foeman's wealth, like player's stakes, he lessens.
Believe in him: for he, O men, is Indra.

He furthers worshippers, both rich and needy,
And priests that supplicate his aid and praise him.
Who, fair-lipped, helps the man that presses Soma,
That sets the stones at work: he, men, is Indra.

In whose control are horses and all chariots,
In whose control are villages and cattle;
He who has generated sun and morning,
Who leads the waters: he, O men, is Indra.

Whom two contending armies vie in calling,
On both sides foes, the farther and the nearer;
Two fighters mounted on the self-same chariot[2]
Invoke him variously: he, men, is Indra.

Without whose aid men conquer not in battle,
Whom fighting ever they invoke for succour,
Who shows himself a match for every foeman,
Who moves what is unmoved: he, men, is Indra.

---

[1] Next to the Vṛtra-killing this deliverance of the cows is the greatest heroic deed of Indra. It has been compared—I think, rightly—with the deed of Hercules, who kills the three-headed Geryoneus and leads away the herds of oxen stolen by him. In the same way Hercules and Cacus. *Cf. Oldenberg*, "Rel. des Veda," p. 143. f. *Hillebrandt*, "Ved. Myth," III, 260 ff.

[2] Namely, the warrior and the charioteer.

Who with his arrow slays the unexpecting
Unnumbered crew of gravely guilty sinners;
Who yields not to the boasting foe in boldness,
Who slays the demons: he, O men, is Indra.

He who detected in the fortieth autumn
Śambara [1] dwelling far among the mountains;
Who slew the serpent that put forth his vigour,
The demon as he lay: he, men, is Indra.

Who with his seven rays, the bull, the mighty, [2]
Let loose the seven streams to flow in torrents;
Who, bolt in arm, spurned Rauhiṇa, the demon,
On scaling heaven bent: he, men, is Indra.

Both Heaven and Earth, themselves, bow down before him;
Before his might the very mountains tremble,
Who, famed as Soma-drinker, armed with lightning,
Is wielder of the bolt: he, men, is Indra.

Who with his aid helps him that presses Soma,
That bakes and lauds and ever sacrifices; [3]
Whom swelling prayer, whom Soma pressings strengthen,
And now this offering: he, O men, is Indra.

Who, fierce, on him that bakes and him that presses
Bestowest booty: thou, indeed, art trusted,
May we, for ever dear to thee, O Indra,
Endowed with hero sons address the Synod."

---

[1]) Name of a demon.

[2]) Indra has a chariot provided with seven reins (Ṛv. II, 18, 1; VI, 44, 24), *i.e.*, many horses—"seven" in the Ṛgveda often means "many"—are harnessed to his chariot.

[3]) These are the four sacrificial priests of the older period.

While the hymns of Varuṇa and Indra show us that the Vedic poets are not lacking in pathos, vigour and raciness the songs to Agni, the fire or the fire-god, show us that these poets also often succeeded in touching the simple, warm, heart-felt tone. Agni, as the sacrificial fire and as the fire which blazes on the hearth, is esteemed as the friend of mortals; he is the mediator between them and the gods, and to him the poet speaks as to a dear friend. He prays to him, that he may bless him "as the father his son," and he takes for granted that the god is pleased with his song and will fulfil the wish of the singer. While Indra is the god of the warrior, Agni is the god of the householder, who protects his wife and children for him, and makes his homestead prosper. He himself is often called "master of the house" (gṛhapati). He is the "guest" of every house, "the first of all guests." As an immortal being he has taken up his abode amongst mortals; and in his hand lies the prosperity of the family. Since primitive times, the bride, when she came to her new home, was led around the sacred fire, and therefore Agni is also called "the lover of maidens, the husband of women" (Ṛv. I, 66, 8), and in a marriage benediction it is said that Agni is the husband of the maidens, and that the bridegroom receives the bride from Agni. Simple prayers are also addressed to him at the wedding, at the birth of children, and similar family events. During the marriage-sacrifice the prayer was offered on behalf of the bride: "May Agni, the lord of the house, protect her! May he lead her offspring on to a high age; may her womb be blessed, may she be the mother of living children. May she behold the joy of her sons!" As the sacrificial fire, Agni is "the messenger" between gods and mortals; and sometimes it is said that, as such, he bears the sacrificial food up to the gods, sometimes also that he brings the gods down to the sacrifice. Therefore he is also called the priest, the wise One, the Brahman, the Purohita (family priest) and by preference the title Hotar—the name of the chief priest at the great sacrifice—is given to him. Beginnings of mythology and poetic art can hardly be separated, especially in the songs to Agni. By means of abundant pourings of ghee the sacrificial fire was maintained in a state of radiant flame, and the poet says: Agni's countenance shines, or his back shines, his hair drips with ghee. When he is described as flame-haired, or red-haired, red-bearded, with sharp jawbones and golden gleaming teeth, when the flames of the fire are spoken of as Agni's tongues, when the poet, thinking of the bright fire radiating in all directions, calls Agni four-eyed or thousand-eyed, then all this may be called poetry just as well as mythology. Thus also the rattling and rustling of the fire is compared with the bellowing of a bull,[1]—and Agni is called a bull. The pointed, rising flames are imagined as horns, and a singer calls Agni "provided with a thousand horns," while another one says that he sharpens his horns and shakes them in anger. Just as frequently, however, Agni is also compared with a merrily neighing horse, a "fiery runner"; and in mythology as well as in religious worship, Agni stands in close connection with the horse. But, when Agni is also called the bird, the eagle of heaven, hastening along in rapid flight between heaven and earth, then we must think of the flame of the lightning which descends from the sky. Again, another appearance of fire is in the mind of the poet when he says (Ṛv. I, 143, 5): "Agni, with his sharp jaws, devours the forests; he masticates them, he lays them low as the warrior his foes." Similarly another poet (Ṛv. I, 65, 8): "When fanned by the wind, he has spread through the forests, Agni cuts off the hair of the earth." (*i.e.* grass and herbs).

Even the actual Agni-myths have only originated in the metaphorical and enigmatic language of the poets. Agni

---

[1]) In English, too, we speak of the "roaring fire."

has three births or three birthplaces: in the sky he glows as the fire of the sun, on the earth he is brought forth by mortals out of the two pieces of tinder wood, and as the lightning he is born in the water. As he is brought forth with the help of two pieces of tinder wood (Araṇis), it is said that he has two mothers,—and "scarcely is the child born, when he devours the two mothers." (Ṛv. X, 79, 4.) An older poet, however, says: "Ten indefatigable virgins have brought forth this child of Tvaṣṭar (*i.e.* Agni)" (Ṛv. I, 95, 2), by which are meant the ten fingers, which had to be employed in the twirling; and as it was only possible through great exertion of strength to bring the fire out of the pieces of wood by friction, Agni in the whole of the Ṛgveda is called "the son of strength."

With the extensive part which the fire-cult played among the ancient Indians, it is not to be wondered at, that the majority of the numerous songs in the Ṛgveda which are dedicated to Agni—there are about two hundred of them—have been used as songs of sacrifice, many of them having only been composed for sacrificial purposes. Yet we find among these songs many plain, simple prayers, which, perhaps are the work of priests, but certainly are the work of poets. As an example I give the first hymn of our Ṛgveda-Saṃhitā in the translation of A. A. Macdonell: [1]

"Agni I praise, the household priest,
God, minister of sacrifice,
Invoker, best bestowing wealth.

Agni is worthy to be praised,
By present a- by seers of old:
May he to us conduct the gods.

Through Agni may we riches gain,
And day by day prosperity
Replete with fame and manly sons.

---

[1]) Hymns from the Rigveda, pp. 72 f.

The worship and the sacrifice,
Guarded by thee on every side,
Go straight, O Agni, to the gods.

May Agni, the invoker, wise
And true, of most resplendent fame,
The god, come hither with the gods.

Whatever good thou wilt bestow,
O Agni, on the pious man,
That gift comes true, O Angiras.

To thee, O Agni, day by day,
O thou illuminer of gloom,
With thought we, bearing homage, come :

To thee the lord of sacrifice,
The radiant guardian of the Law,
That growest in thine own abode.

So, like a father to his son,
Be easy of approach to us ;
Agni, for weal abide with us."

Some pearls of lyric poetry, which appeal to us as much through their fine comprehension of the beauties of Nature, as through their flowery language, are to be found among the songs to Sūrya (the Sun), to Parjanya (the Rain-god), to the Maruts (the Storm-gods) and above all to Uṣas (the Dawn). In the hymns addressed to the latter the singers vie with each other in magnificent metaphors which are intended to depict the splendour of the rising dawn. Gleaming she approaches like a maiden decked by her mother, who is proud of her body. She puts on splendid garments, like a dancer, and reveals her bosom to the mortal. Clothed in light the maiden appears in the East and unveils her charms. She opens the gates of heaven and, radiant, steps forth out of them. Again and again her charms are compared with those of a woman inviting love. Thus we read (Ṛv. V, 80, 5.6)[1]:

"As conscious that her limbs are bright with bathing, she stands,
as 'twere, erect that we may see her.
Driving away malignity and darkness, Dawn, child of Heaven,
hath come to us with lustre.

The Daughter of the Sky, like some chaste woman, bends,
opposite to men, her forehead down.
The Maid, disclosing boons to him who worships, hath brought
again the daylight as aforetime."

The following hymn to Dawn (Ṛv. VI, 64) I also give in the translation of Griffith:

"The radiant Dawns have risen up for glory, in their white
splendour like the waves of waters.
She maketh paths all easy, fair to travel, and, rich, hath
shown herself benign and friendly.

We see that thou art good: far shines thy lustre; thy beams,
thy splendours have flown up to heaven.
Decking thyself, thou makest bare thy bosom, shining in majesty,
thou Goddess Morning.

Red are the kine and luminous that bear her the Blessed One
who spreadeth through the distance.
The foes she chaseth like a valiant archer, like a swift warrior
she repelleth darkness.

Thy ways are easy on the hills: thou passest Invincible!
Self-luminous! through waters.
So lofty Goddess with thine ample pathway, Daughter of Heaven,
bring wealth to give us comfort.

Dawn, bring me wealth: untroubled, with thine oxen thou bearest
riches at thy will and pleasure;
Thou who, a Goddess, Child of Heaven, hast shown thee lovely
through bounty when we called thee early.

---

[1]) Translated by *Griffith*.

As the birds fly forth from their resting-places, so men with store of food rise at thy dawning.
Yea, to the liberal mortal who remaineth at home, O Goddess Dawn, much good thou bringest."

To Vāta, the Wind, as the leader of the Maruts, the storm-gods, the following hymn (Ṛv. X, 168) is addressed, which I quote in the translation of Macdonell.[1]

"Of Vāta's car I now will praise the greatness:
Rending it speeds along; its noise is thunder.
Touching the sky it flies, creating lightnings;
Scattering dust it traverses earth's ridges.

The hosts of Vāta onward speed together:
They haste to him as women to a concourse.
The god with them upon the same car mounted,
The king of all this universe speeds onward.

In air, along his pathways speeding onward,
Never on any day he tarries resting.
The first-born, order-loving friend of waters:
Where was he born, and whence has he arisen?

Of gods the breath, and of the world the offspring,
This god according to his liking wanders,
His sound is heard, his form is never looked on:
That Vāta let us worship with oblation."

Beside these songs, which are worthy of being valued as works of poetic art, there is indeed a second class of hymns in the Ṛgveda, which are composed only as sacrificial songs and litanies, for quite definite ritual purposes. A strict line of demarcation is here, however, not possible. Whether we wish to accept a song as the spontaneous expression of pious faith, as the work of a divinely inspired poet, or as sacrificial prayer put together in a workmanlike fashion,

[1]) Hymns from the Rigveda, p. 62.

is often only a matter of taste. The extraordinary monotony of these prayers and sacrificial chants is certainly one of their characteristics. It is always with the same turns of expression that one god, like another, is praised as great and mighty: always the same formulas, with which the sacrificial priest beseeches the gods for wealth of cattle and riches. Many of these sacrificial songs are already distinguishable through the fact that in one and the same hymn several gods, sometimes even all the gods of the Vedic pantheon, are invoked one after another. For, at the great Soma sacrifice every god must receive his share, and every sacrificial offering must be accompanied by a verse. Compare, for instance, with the above-quoted songs to Varuṇa, Indra and Agni, a sacrificial litany like the following (Ṛv. VII, 35):

> "May Indra and Agni grant us happiness by their mercy, so also Indra and Varuṇa, to whom sacrifice is offered; may Indra and Soma grant us happiness, welfare and blessing! May Indra and Pūsan grant us happiness at the capture of booty.
>
> May Bhaga grant us happiness; our hymns of praise, Purandhi, our wealth, may they bring us happiness..................
>
> May Dhātar, Dhartar and the far-extending (Earth) freely grant us happiness; may the two great realms of space [1]), may the mountain, may the auspicious invocations to the gods grant us happiness.
>
> May Agni of shining countenance, may Mitra and Varuṇa, may the two Aśvins grant us happiness; may the good works of the pious grant us happiness! May the mighty Wind-god blow to us happiness"!

Thus it goes on through fifteen long verses.

To these sacrificial songs belong among others also the so-called Āprīsūktas, "propitiatory hymns" (*i.e.* hymns for the propitiation or reconciliation of certain deities, demons, and certain personified objects connected with the sacrifice). These hymns, of which there are ten in the Ṛgveda-Saṃhitā,

---

[1]) Heaven and Earth.

have a quite definite use at the animal sacrifice. They all consist of eleven or twelve verses, and Agni is invoked in them under various names, that he may bring the gods to the sacrifice. In the fourth or fifth verse the priests are invited to strew about the sacred grass, on which the gods are to sit down in order to receive the sacrificial gifts. Also certain goddesses are regularly invoked in the hymns, and the penultimate verse generally contains an invocation to the stake which serves in the binding of the sacrificial animal, *e.g.* "O divine tree, let the sacrificial meal go to the gods."

The hymns of Book IX which have already been referred to above, are throughout sacrificial songs, which are all addressed to Soma and are used in the great Soma-sacrifice. In sheer endless monotony the same procedure recurs, the pressing of the soma, the mixing and refining of the same, the pouring into the vats, and so on; again and again Indra is called to the drinking of the soma, Soma and Indra united are praised, and implored for riches, or for rain, of which the soma-juice trickling down through the sieve is a symbol. But rarely in these monotonous litanies do we come across a pretty metaphor, as for instance, when it is said of Soma (Ṛv. IX, 16, 6).

> " Clarified by the sieve of sheep's wool
> Soma rises to his fullest splendour,
> There he stands, as after battle
> Stands the hero by the stolen cows."

The fact that verses may be composed for ritual purposes and yet be of great poetic beauty, is proved by the funeral songs of which a few are preserved in Book X of the Ṛgveda. In Ancient India corpses were usually burnt, yet in the oldest times burial was probably the custom with the Indians, as with other Indo-European peoples. The following beautiful verses (Ṛv. X, 18, 10-13) refer to a burial : [1]

"Approach the bosom of the earth, the mother,
This earth, the far-extending, most propitious ;
Young, soft as wool to bounteous givers, may she
Preserve thee from the lap of dissolution.

Wide open, earth, O press not heavily on him ;
Be easy of approach to him, a refuge safe ;
As with a robe a mother hides
Her son, so shroud this man, O earth.

Now opening wide may here the earth stand steadfast,
May here a thousand columns rise to prop her ;
May here those mansions ever drip with butter,
And here be always shelter to protect him.

For thee I now prop up the earth around thee here ;
In lowering this clod may I receive no harm.
May the Fathers hold up for thee this column,
And Yama here provide for thee fit mansions."

It would indeed be possible also to fit in these verses, as Oldenberg [2] thinks, into the ritual of cremation. As we learn in the books of ritual, in ancient India the bones were collected after the cremation and placed in an urn, and this was buried. Accordingly these verses *could* have been uttered at the burial of this urn of bones. However I do not consider this probable. The words "wide open, Earth, O press not heavily on him" and so on, seem to me, only to be relevant at the erection of a mound over the actual corpse. The custom of burying the bones I consider to be a remnant of an older custom of the burial of the corpses, to which our verses refer.[3]

---

[1]) Translated by A. A. *Macdonell*, Hymns from the Rigveda, p. 88.

[2]) "Religion des Veda," p. 571.

[3]) At the time when cremation was already a general custom, children and ascetics were still buried. But in the above verse nothing indicates that it is a case of the burial of a child or of an ascetic. W. *Caland*, "Die altindischen Toten-und Bestattungsgebräuche," Amsterdam, 1896, pp. 163 ff., as against R. *Roth* (ZDMG 8, 1854, 467 ff.), has proved that the hymn Ṛgveda X, 18 is not one uniform production. Only the verses 10 to 13 form a separate poem. S. also W. D. *Whitney*, "Oriental and Linguistic Studies," New York, 1873, 51 ff., and L. v. *Schroeder*, WZKM 9, 1895, 112 f.

On the other hand, the hymn Ṛv. X, 16, 1-6, probably belonging to a later period, is intended for the ceremony of cremation. When the funeral pile is erected, the corpse is laid upon it, and the fire lighted. And when the flames unite above it, the priests pray :

"Burn him not up, nor quite consume him, Agni : let not his body or his skin be scattered.
O Jâtavedas,[1] when thou hast matured him, then send him on his way unto the Fathers.

When thou hast made him ready, Jâtavedas, then do thou give him over to the Fathers.
When he attains unto the life that waits him, he shall become the Deities' controller.

The Sun receive thine eye, the Wind thy spirit ; go, as thy merit is, to earth or heaven.
Go, if it be thy lot, unto the waters ; go, make thine home in plants with all thy members.

Thy portion is the goat : with heat consume him ; let thy fierce flame, thy glowing splendour, burn him.
With thine auspicious forms, O Jâtavedas, bear this man to the region of the pious.

Here we already find philosophical theories on life after death and on the destiny of the soul mixed up with the mythological ideas about Agni and the fathers. These are not the only allusions to philosophical ideas, but there are about a dozen hymns in the Ṛgveda which we can designate as philosophical hymns, in which, along with speculations on the universe and the creation, that great pantheistic idea of the Universal Soul which is one with the universe, appears for the first time—an idea, which since that time has dominated the whole of Indian philosophy.

Quite early there arose, among the Indians, doubts as to the power, even as to the existence of the gods. Already

---

[1]) A name of the god Agni.

in the hymn Ṛv. II, 12, translated above, which praises so confidently the might and the feats of strength of Indra, and the separate verses of which end in the refrain, which is flung out in such full faith: "He, O men, is Indra,"—even there we hear that there were people who did not believe in Indra: "Of whom they ask 'Where is he?' Of him indeed, they also say 'He is not'......Believe in him: for he, O men, is Indra." Similar doubts occur in the remarkable hymn Ṛv. VIII, 100, 3 f., where the priests are invited to offer a song of praise to Indra, "a true one, if in truth, he is; for many say: 'There is no Indra, who has ever seen him? To whom are we to direct the song of praise?'" Whereupon Indra personally appears, in order to give assurance of his existence and his greatness: "There I am, singer, look at me here, in greatness I tower above all beings" and so on.

But when people had once begun to doubt Indra himself, who was the highest and mightiest of all the gods, so much the more arose scruples concerning the plurality of the gods in general, and doubts began to arise whether indeed there was any merit in sacrificing to the gods. Thus in the hymn Ṛv. X, 121, in which Prajāpati is praised as the creator and preserver of the world and as the one god, and in which, in the refrain recurring in verse after verse: "Which god shall we honour by means of sacrifice?" there lies hidden the thought, that in reality there is nothing in all the plurality of the gods, and that alone the one and only god, the Creator Prajāpati, deserves honour. Finally, this scepticism finds its most powerful expression in the profound poem of the Creation (Ṛv. X, 129).[1] It begins with a description of the time before the creation:

> "Nor aught existed then, nor naught existed,
> There was no air, nor heaven beyond.
> What covered all? Wherein? In whose shelter was it?
> Was it the water, deep and fathomless?

---

1) Translation by R. T. H. *Griffith*.

No death was then, nor was there life immortal.
Of day and night there was then no distinction.
That *One* alone breathed windless by itself.
Than that, forsooth, no other thing existed."

Only very timidly does the poet venture on a reply to the question regarding the origin of the world. He imagines the state before the creation as "darkness shrouded in darkness," far and wide nothing but an impenetrable flood, until through the power of the Tapas,[1] "the One" arose. This "One" was already an intellectual being; and as the first product of his mind—" the mind's first fruit," as the poet says—came forth Kāma, *i.e.* "sexual desire, love,[2]" and in this Kāma "the wise searching in their hearts, have by meditation discovered the connection between the existing and the non-existing." But only gentle hints does the poet venture to give, soon doubts again begin to arise, and he concludes with the anxious questions:

" Who knoweth it forsooth, who can declare it here,
Whence this creation has arisen, whence it came?
The gods came hither by this world's creation only:[3]
Who knoweth then, whence this creation has arisen?

Whence this creation has arisen, whether
It has been made or not: He who surveys
This world in highest heaven, he may be knoweth,—
Or, it may be, he knoweth not." [4]

---

[1]) *Tapaç* may here have its original meaning of "heat" (some "creative heat" analogous to the heat by which the brood-hen produces life from the egg) or it may mean the 'fervour' of austerity; or, as *Deussen* thinks, both meanings may be implied in the word.

[2]) Not the "will" of Schopenhauer, as *Deussen* and others assume. As sexual desire leads to the procreation and birth of beings, so these ancient thinkers considered sexual desire as the primal source of all existence.

[3]) That is the gods themselves were created only with the rest of creation, therefore they cannot tell us whence the world originated.

[4]) Translated into English by the author. This famous hymn has been often translated and discussed, thus by H. T. *Colebrooke*, Miscellaneous Essays (2nd Ed., Madras,

In most of the philosophical hymns of the Ṛgveda the idea certainly comes to the foreground of a creator who is named now Prajāpati, now Brahmaṇaspati, or Bṛhaspati, or again Viśvakarman, but who is still always thought of as a personal god. But already in the above-quoted verse it appears doubtful to the poet whether the creation was "made" or whether it came into being by some other means, and the creative principle receives no name in this poem, but is called "the One." Thus already in the hymns the great idea of Universal Unity is foreshadowed, the idea that everything which we see in Nature and which the popular belief designates as "gods," in reality is only the emanation of the One and Only One, that all plurality is only imaginary—an idea which is really already expressed clearly and distinctly in the verse Ṛv. I, 164, 46:

> "They call him Indra, Mitra, Varuṇa,
> And Agni; he is the heavenly bird Garutmat:
> To what is one, the poets give many a name,
> They call it Agni, Yama, Mātariśvān."

While these philosophical hymns form, as it were, a bridge to the philosophical speculations of the Upaniṣads, there exist also a number of poems in the Ṛgveda-Saṃhitā—there might be about twenty of them—which form a connecting link with the epic and dramatic poetry. These are fragments of narratives in the form of dialogues (Saṃvādas), and may therefore be fitly called Samvāda or dialogue hymns. H. Oldenberg[1] called them "Ākhyāna hymns,"

1872), I, pp. 33 f.; Max *Müller* History of Ancient Sanskrit Literature, 2nd Ed., London 1860. p. 564; J. *Muir*, Original Sanskrit Texts, V, p. 356: H. W. *Wallis*, Cosmology of the Ṛigveda, London, 1887, pp. 89 ff.; W. D. *Whitney*, JAOS, XI, p. cix; P. *Deussen*, Allgemeine Geschichte der Philosophie I (where all the philosophical hymns of the Ṛgveda are discussed); L. *Scherman*, Philosophische Hymnen aus der Ṛig-und Atharvaveda-Sanhitâ, Strassburg, 1887, pp. 1 ff. It has also been translated by *Macdonell*, E. J. *Thomas*, etc.

1) "Das altindische Âkhyâna" in ZDMG 37 (1883) 54 ff. and Âkhyânahymnen im Ṛgveda" in ZDMG 39 (1885) 52 ff. *Âkhyâna* means "narrative."

and started a theory, in order to explain their fragmentary and enigmatic character. The oldest form of epic poetry in India, he said, was a mixture of prose and verse, the speeches of the persons only being in verses, while the events connected with the speeches were narrated in prose. Originally only the verses used to be committed to memory and handed down, while the prose story was left to be narrated by every reciter in his own words. Now in the dialogue hymns of the Ṛgveda only the verse portions, containing conversations, have been preserved, while the prose portions of the narrative are lost to us. Only some of these narratives can partly be restored with the help of the Brāhmaṇas or the epic literature, or even of commentaries. Where these aids fail, nothing remains for us but to try to guess the story from the conversations. This theory seemed to be supported by the fact that not only in Indian, but also in other literatures, the mixture of prose and verse is an early form of epic poetry. It is found, for instance, in Old Irish and in Scandinavian poetry.[1] In India we find it in some narrative portions of the Brāhmaṇas and Upaniṣads, in some of the old parts of the Mahābhārata, in Buddhist literature, in the literature of fables and tales, in the drama, and again in the campū. It is true that, in all these cases the prose has been handed down together with the verses, but as the Ṛgveda is professedly the Veda of the *verses*, it was not possible to include any prose in the Saṃhitā of the Ṛgveda. And if an Ākhyāna, consisting of prose and verse, was to find a place in the Ṛgveda-Saṃhitā, the prose portion would have to be omitted. This is the theory of Oldenberg, which for a long time was almost generally accepted by scholars.

---

[1] Already in the year 1878 in a lecture delivered at the 33rd meeting of German philologists and pedagogues at Gera, Ernst *Windisch* had pointed out the significance of quite similar phenomena in the *old Irish* legend-poetry, and on this occasion had also already drawn attention to the related phenomena in Indian literature.

Of late, however, the theory has also met with a great deal of opposition. Many years back Max Müller and Sylvain Lévi [1] had already suggested that the dialogue poems of the Ṛgveda might be a kind of dramas. This idea has been taken up by Joh. Hertel [2] and L. von Schroeder,[3] who tried to prove that these Saṃvāda hymns are really speeches belonging to some dramatic performances connected with the religious cult. We have only, they say, to supply dramatic action, and the difficulties which these hymns offer to interpretation will disappear. What kind of action has to be supplied can of course only be guessed from the dialogues themselves.

The fact is, that poems like the dialogue hymns of the Ṛgveda are of frequent occurrence in Indian literature. We shall find similar semi-epic and semi-dramatic poems, consisting chiefly or entirely of dialogues or conversations, in the Mahābhārata, in the Purāṇas, and especially in Buddhist literature. All these poems are nothing else but ancient ballads of the same kind as are found also in the literatures of many other peoples.[4] This ancient ballad poetry is the

---

1) Le Théâtre Indien, Paris, 1890, pp. 301 ff

2) WZKM 18, 1904, 59 ff, 137 ff.; 23, 1909, 273 ff.; Indische Märchen, Jena, 1921, pp. 344, 367 f.

3) Mysterium und Mimus im Rigveda, Leipzig, 1908.

4) A. *Barth* (RHR 19, 1889, 130 f.... Oeuvres, II, 5 f.) has already compared the Ākhyāna of Purūravas and Urvaśī in the Śatapatha-Brāhmaṇa with the ballad of King Rasālū in *Temple's* "Legends of the Panjâb." On the whole question see *Pischel*, GGA 1891, 355 ff.; *Oldenburg*, GGA 1909, 66 ff.; NGGW 1911, 459 ff.; *Bloomfield*, American Journal of Philology, 30, 1909, 78 ff.; A. B. *Keith*, JRAS, 1909, 200 ff.; 1911, 979 ff.; 1912, 429 ff.; ZDMG 64, 1910, 534 ff.; J. *Charpentier*, WZKM 23, 1909, 151 f.; 25, 1911, 307 ff.; Die Suparṇasage, Uppsala 1920, p. 13 ff. W. *Caland*, AR 14, 1911, 499 ff.; *Hillebrandt*, Lieder des Ṛgveda, passim; K. F. *Geldner*, Die indische Balladendichtung, Festschrift der Universität Marburg, 1913, pp. 93 ff.; E. *Windisch*, Geschichte der Sanskrit Philologie, pp. 404 ff.; M. *Winternitz*, WZKM 23, 1909, 102 ff.; Oesterreichische Monatsschrift für den Orient 41, 1915, 173 ff., and the Lecture on "Ancient Indian Ballad Poetry" in the Calcutta Review, December, 1923.

source both of the epic and of the drama, for these ballads consist of a narrative and of a dramatic element. The epic developed from the narrative, the drama arose from the dramatic elements of the ancient ballad. These ancient Ākhyānas or ballads were not always composed entirely in verse, but sometimes an introductory or a concluding story was told in prose, and occasionally the verses were linked together by short explanations in prose. Thus it may be that in some cases there might have been a connecting prose story (as Oldenberg assumed), which, if we knew it, would make the conversations of the hymns clear. But most of these hymns are simply ballads of the half-epic, half-dramatic type, though not real dramas, as some scholars have thought them to be.

The most famous of these Vedic ballads or Saṃvāda hymns is Ṛv. X. 95. This is a poem of 18 stanzas, consisting of a dialogue between Purūravas and Urvaśī. Purūravas is a mortal, Urvaśī a nymph (Apsaras). During four years the divine beauty lived on earth as the wife of Purūravas, until by him she became pregnant, when she vanished, "like the first of the dawns." He went out to seek her. At last he found her, playing with other water-nymphs, in a lake. That is about all we can glean from the obscure, often quite unintelligible verses, from the dialogues between the deserted one and the goddess who is romping about in the pond with her playmates. Fortunately this ancient myth of the love of a mortal king for a divine maiden is also preserved in other portions of Indian literature, and thus we can, to a certain extent, complete the poem of the Ṛgveda. The legend of Purūravas and Urvaśī is already told us in a Brāhmaṇa,[1] and the verses of the Ṛgveda are woven into the narrative. We are there told that the nymph, when she consented to become the wife of Purūravas, stipulated three conditions, one

[1] Śatapatha-Brāhmaṇa XI, 5, 1.

of which was that she might never see him naked. The Gandharvas—demi-gods of the same kingdom to which the Apsaras belong—wanted to get Urvaśī back. Therefore, in the night, they stole two little lambs which she loved like children, and which were tied to her bed. As Urvaśī complained bitterly that she was robbed as though no man were near, Purūravas jumped up—"naked as he was, for it seemed to him that the putting on of a garment would take too long" —to pursue the thieves. But at the same instant the Gandharvas caused a flash of lightning to appear, so that it became as light as day, and Urvaśī perceived the king naked. She then vanished; and when Purūravas returned, she was gone. Mad with grief, the king wandered about the country, until one day he came to a pond, in which nymphs in the form of swans, were swimming about. This gives rise to the dialogue which we find in the Ṛgveda. and which is reproduced with explanatory additions in the Brāhmaṇa.[1] Yet all the pleadings of Purūravas that she might return to him are in vain. Even when, in despair, he talked of self-destruction—he wanted to throw himself from the rocks as a prey to the fierce wolves—she only replied :

> "Nay, do not die, Purūravas, nor perish :
> let not the evil-omened wolves devour thee.
> With women there can be no lasting friendship,
> hearts of hyenas are the hearts of women." [2]

Whether and how Purūravas is reunited with his beloved is not quite clear either in the Ṛgveda or in the Śatapatha-Brāhmaṇa. It seems that he becomes transformed into a Gandharva and attains heaven, where at last the joy of reunion is his. The story of Purūravas and Urvaśī has often been retold in India : it is briefly hinted at in the Kāṭhaka

[1]) The Śatapatha-Brāhmaṇa has only fifteen of the eighteen verses of the Ṛgveda.

[2]) Translated by R.T.H. *Griffith*.

belonging to the black Yajurveda, it is retold in exegetic works attached to the Veda,[1] in the Harivaṃśa, an appendix to the Mahābhārata, in the Viṣṇu Purāṇa and in the book of tales Kathāsaritsāgara, and no less a poet than Kālidāsa has founded one of his immortal dramas on it. From the circumstance that, in spite of all efforts to bring the verses of the Ṛgveda into unison with the later narratives and to utilize the latter in the elucidation of the Ṛgvedic poem,[2] there is still so much that is obscure and unexplained in these verses, we see how very much earlier the Ṛgveda is than any other known work of Indian literature.

We have another valuable fragment of the art of narration in ancient times, in the dialogue of Yama and Yamī (Ṛv. X, 10). An old myth of the origin of the human race from a first pair of twins underlies the conversation.[3] Yamī tries to tempt her brother Yama to incest, in order that the human race may not die out. In passionate words, glowing with desire, the sister draws the brother on to love. In gentle, deliberate speech, pointing to the eternal laws of the gods, which forbid the union of blood-relations, Yama repulses her. These speeches, in which unfortunately there is still much obscurity, are full of dramatic strength. Yamī first says :

> "My friend I would draw near to me in friendship,
> Should he have gone e'en to the farthest ocean,
> That he beget a grandson to his sire
> On earth, remembering wisely future days." [1]

---

[1]) Baudhāyana-Śrautasūtra (s. *Caland*, in the Album Kern, pp 57 ff.) Bṛhaddevatā, Ṣaḍguruśiṣya's commentary on the Sarvānukramaṇī of the Ṛgveda.

[2]) See especially *Geldner* in the " Vedische Studien " I, 243-295. Also *Oldenberg*, ZDMG 39, 72 ff. and " Die Literatur des alten Indien," pp. 53 ff. The Purūravas-Urvaśī dialogue has also been translated by *Hertel*, Indogerm. Forschungen 31, 1912, 143 ff., and *Hillebrandt* , Lieder des Ṛgveda, pp 142 ff.

[3]) See A. *Weber*, SBA. 1895, 822 ff. Yama means "twin," and Yamī is a feminine form of Yama. A. *Winter* has attempted a mythological interpretation of the myth in the essay : "Mein Bruder freit um mich " (ZVV. VII, 1897, pp 172 ff.), where he compares

Thereupon Yama replies :

> "Thy friend loves not the friendship which considers her who is near in kindred as a stranger.
> Sons of the mighty Asura, the Heroes, supporters of the heavens, see far around them." [2]

Yamī, however, tries to persuade her brother that the gods themselves desire that he shall unite himself with her in order to propagate his race. As he will not listen, she becomes more and more persistent, more and more passionate :

> "I, Yamī, am possessed by love of Yama, that I may rest on the same couch beside him.
> I as a wife would yield me to my husband. Like car-wheels let us speed to meet each other." [7]

But Yama again refuses with the words :

> "They stand not still, they never close their eyelids, those sentinels of God who wander round us.
> Not me—go quickly, wanton, with another, and hasten like a chariot-wheel to meet him." [8]

More and more tempestuous, however, does the sister grow, ever more ardently does she desire the embrace of Yama, until—on his repeated refusal—she bursts forth into the words :

> "Alas! thou art indeed a weakling, Yama; we find in thee no trace of heart or spirit.
> As round the tree the woodbine clings, another will cling about thee girt as with a girdle." [13]

Rv. X, 10. with a Lettic popular song, in which a brother attempts to seduce his sister to incest. *Schroeder* (Mysterium und Mimus, pp. 275 ff.), explains the hymn as a drama connected with some rite of fertility. This is certainly wrong. See *Winternitz*, WZKM 23, 1909, 118 f. and *Charpentier*, Die Suparṇasage, p. 99.

Whereupon Yama concludes the dialogue with the words:

"Embrace another, Yamī; let another, even as the woodbine rings the tree, enfold thee.
Win thou his heart and let him win thy fancy, and he shall form with thee a blest alliance."[1] [14]

How the story of Yama and Yamī ended, we do not know; moreover no later source gives us any information upon it. Thus the poem of the Ṛgveda is unfortunately only a torso, but a torso which indicates a splendid work of art.

The Sūryāsūkta, Ṛv. X, 85,[2] may also be included in the Ṛgvedic ballad poetry. This particular hymn describes the marriage of Sūryā (the sun-daughter, as the dawn is here called) with Soma (the moon), at which the two Aśvins were the match-makers. This hymn consists of 47 verses, which are somewhat loosely connected. The verses nearly all refer to the marriage ritual, and most of them, as we know from the Gṛhyasūtras, the manuals of domestic ritual, were used also at the marriage of ordinary mortals. Yet I do not think that these verses were merely compiled from the ritual (as is the case with some of the funeral hymns) so that they would have to be regarded as a kind of compilation of all the benedictions used in the marriage-rites, like a chapter in a prayer-book. It is much more probable that it is an ancient ballad describing the marriage of Sūryā partly in narrative stanzas, partly in addresses to the Aśvins and Sūryā, and partly by the insertion of the mantras (benedictions, incantations) recited at the various stages of the marriage ceremony. But among the benedictions which we find in this Sūryāsūkta, there are many which, with their

---

1) Verses 2, 7, 8, 13, 14 translated by R. T. H. *Griffith*, the first verse by the author.

2) Translated into German by A. *Weber*, Ind. Stud. 5, 177 ff. See also J. *Ehni*, ZDMG, 23, 1879, 166 ff.; *Pischel*, Vedische Studien, I, 14 ff.; *Oldenberg*, GGA., 1889, p. 7.

simple, warm, hearty tone, remind us of the funeral hymns discussed above. Thus the bridal pair is addressed in the beautiful words:

> "Happy be thou and prosper with thy children here: be vigilant to rule thy household in this home.
> Closely unite thy body with this man, thy lord. So shall ye, full of years, address your company." [27]

The spectators past whom the marriage procession goes, are thus accosted:

> "Signs of good fortune mark the bride: Come all of you and look at her.
> Wish her prosperity, and then return unto your homes again." [33]

When the bridegroom, according to ancient Indo-European marriage-custom, clasps the hand of the bride, he recites this verse:

> "I take thy hand in mine for happy fortune that thou mayst reach old age with me thy husband.
> Gods, Aryaman, Bhaga, Savitar, Purandhi, have given thee to be my household's mistress." [36]

When at last the bridal pair enter the new home, they are received with the following words:

> "Be ye not parted; dwell ye here; reach the full time of human life.
> With sons and grandsons sport and play, rejoicing in your own abode." [42]

And upon the bride the blessing is invoked:

> "O Bounteous Indra, make this bride blest in her sons and fortunate.
> Vouchsafe to her ten sons, and make her husband the eleventh man!" [45][1]

---

[1]) The five verses translated by R. T. H. *Griffith*.

But some of the marriage benedictions have more of the character of magic formulas. Among them we find charms against the evil eye and other pernicious magic, by means of which the bride could injure her future husband, as well as exorcisms by means of which demons, which lie in wait for the bride, are to be scared away. These magic formulas by no means stand alone, for there are, besides, about thirty magic songs in the Ṛgveda. Some of these are benedictions and formulas for the healing of various diseases, for the protection of the embryo, for warding off the effects of bad dreams and unfavourable omens, while others are incantations for the scaring away of witches, for the destruction of enemies and malevolent wizards, or magic formulas against poison and vermin, verses for the supplanting of a rival; we also find a blessing on the field, a charm for the prosperity of cattle, a battle charm, a charm for inducing sleep, and so on. Of this kind is also the very remarkable "Frog song," Ṛv. VII, 103. Here the frogs are compared with Brahmans. In the dry season they lie there like Brahmans who have taken the vow of silence. Then when the rain comes, they greet each other with merry croaking "as a son his father." And the one repeats the croaking of the other, as the pupils repeat the words of the teacher when studying the Veda in a Brahman school. They modulate their voices in many ways. As priests at the Soma-sacrifice sit singing around the filled tub, so the frogs celebrate the commencement of the rainy season with their song. At the end follows a prayer for wealth:

> "Both Lowing Cow and Bleating Goat have given,
> Spotty and Tawny, too, have given us riches.
> The frogs give kine by hundreds; they for pressings
> Of Soma thousandfold, prolong existence." [1]

---

[1]) Translated by A. A. *Macdonell*, Hymns from the Ṛgveda, p. 96. A free poetical translation of the hymn is to be found in J. *Muir*, Metrical Translations from Sanskrit writers, pp 194 f.

All this sounds immensely funny, and almost generally the song was looked upon by scholars as a parody on the sacrificial songs and malicious satire against the Brahmans.[1] However, Bloomfield has proved conclusively[2] that this is a magic incantation, which was used as a rain-spell, and that the frogs, which, according to ancient Indian popular belief, can bring forth water, are praised and invoked as rain-bringers. The comparison with the Brahmans is not intended as a satire on the latter, but only as a flattery—a captatio benevolentiae—to the frogs. The frog-song was probably never a satire. It is only we who see something comic in it, and not the ancient Indians, who actually regarded frogs as great wizards. It appears, however, that incantations sometimes arose from secular poems. Thus, the song Ṛv. VI, 75, may originally have been a war song, which has been changed into a battle charm. While some verses of this song are distinguished by great poetic beauty and especially by bold images, other verses show only the dry, inartistic language of incantations. The first three verses sound more like a war-song than like an incantation :

"The warrior's look is like a thunderous rain-cloud's when, armed with mail, he seeks the lap of battle.

Be thou victorious with unwounded body : so let the thickness of thy mail protect thee.

With bow let us win kine, with bow the battle, with bow the victors in our hot encounters.

---

[1]) *Cf.* for instance, *Deussen*, Ag Ph 1, 1, pp. 100 ff.

[2]) JAOS 17, 1896, pp. 173 ff. Already before this M. *Haug* (Brahma und die Brahmanen, München, 1871, p. 12) had explained the song in the same way, and attached to it the following interesting information. "The song is used in connection with the foregoing, addressed to the rain-god (Parjanya), even to-day in time of great drought, when the ardently desired rain refuses to come. Twenty to thirty Brahmans go to a river and recite these two hymns, in order to cause the rain to descend."

See also L. v. *Schroeder* Mysterium und Mimus im Ṛgveda, pp. 396 ff., and J. W. *Hauer*, Die Anfänge der Yogapraxis, Berlin 1922, pp. 68 ff.

The bow brings grief and sorrow to the foeman : armed with the bow may we subdue all regions.

Close to his ear, as fain to speak, she presses, holding her well-loved friend in her embraces.

Strained on the bow, she whispers like a woman—this bow-string that preserves us in the combat." [1]

On the whole, however, the magic songs of the Ṛgveda differ in no wise from those of the Atharva-Veda, with which we shall deal later. But it is very significant that, besides the hymns to the great gods and the sacrificial songs, also incantations like these have been included in the Ṛgveda Saṃhitā—and that by no means only in the tenth book of the latter.

It is still more significant that also some apparently quite secular poems have got mixed amongst the sacred songs and sacrificial chants of the Ṛgveda. Thus, we find, for example, Ṛv. IX, 112, in the midst of the Soma songs a satirical poem, which derides the manifold desires of mankind. It is probably an old popular song of the "labour song" type. It could be sung as an accompaniment to any kind of work, and here the refrain "Flow, Indu,[2] flow, for Indra's sake"[3] indicates that it was adapted for the work of pressing Soma.[4]

---

[1]) Translated by R. T. H. *Griffith.*

[2]) Indu = Soma.

[3]) There is no justification for omitting this refrain, as some translators have done, for instance *Muir*, Metrical Translations from Sanskrit Writers, p. 190 ; *Macdonell*, Hymns from the Ṛgveda, p. 90. But see *Pischel*, Vedische Studien, I, 107.

[4]) Some of the Soma hymns (*e. g.* Ṛv. I, 28 ; IX, 2 ; 6 ; 8 etc.) are 'labour songs' in which the whole process of preparing the Soma juice is described. See K. *Bücher*, Arbeit und Rhythmus, 5. Aufl., Leipzig 1919, pp. 412 f. L. v. *Schroeder* (Mysterium und Mimus im Rigveda, pp. 408 ff.) has with bold imagination tried to show that the hymn was used at a popular procession during a Soma festival. But there are no facts on which this hypothesis could be founded. *Oldenberg* (GGA. 1909, 80 f.) thinks that the hymn was intended as a prayer at some Soma sacrifice offered for attaining special wishes. So also *Charpentier*, Die Suparṇasage, pp. 80 f.

I give the remarkable poem in the translation of R. T. H. Griffith:

"We all have various thoughts and plans, and diverse are the ways of men.

The Brahman seeks the worshipper, wright seeks the cracked, and leech the maimed. Flow, Indu, flow for Indra's sake.

The smith with ripe and seasoned plants, with feathers of the birds of air,

With stones, and with enkindled flames, seeks him who hath a store of gold. Flow, Indu, flow for Indra's sake.

A bard am I, my dad's a leech, mammy lays corn upon the stones. Striving for wealth, with varied plans, we follow our desires like kine. Flow, Indu, flow for Indra's sake.

The horse would draw an easy car, gay hosts attract the laugh and jest.

The male desires his mate's approach,[1] the frog is eager for the flood. Flow, Indu, flow for Indra's sake."

The most beautiful amongst the non-religious poems of the Ṛgveda collection is the song of the gambler, Ṛv. X, 34. It is the soliloquy of a penitent sinner, who by means of his irresistible attraction to dice-playing has destroyed the happiness of his life. In pathetic verses the gambler describes how the dice have caused him to lose his domestic happiness:

"She wrangles not with me, nor is she angry:
To me and comrades she was ever kindly.
For dice that only luckless throws effected
I've driven away from home a wife devoted. [2]
Her mother hates me, she herself rejects me:
For one in such distress there is no pity.
I find a gambling man is no more useful
Than is an aged horse that's in the market. [3]
Others embrace the wife of him whose chattels
The eager dice have striven hard to capture;
And father, mother, brothers say about him:
We know him not; lead him away a captive." [4]

---

[1]) Expressed much more coarsely in the original.

The uncanny power of the dice, too, is described in forceful terms:

" When to myself I think, I'll not go with them,
I'll stay behind my friends that go to gamble,
And those brown nuts, thrown down, have raised their voices,
I go, like wench, straight to the place of meeting." [5]

And of the dice it is said:

" The dice attract the gambler, but deceive and wound,
Both paining men at play and causing them to pain.
Like boys they offer first and then take back their gifts:
With honey sweet to gamblers by their magic charm. [7]

Downward they roll, then swiftly springing upward,
They overcome the man with hands, though handless.
Cast on the board like magic bits of charcoal,
Though cold themselves, they burn the heart to ashes." [9]

And however much he bewails his fate, yet he always falls again into the power of the dice.

" Grieved is the gambler's wife by him abandoned,
Grieved, too, his mother as he aimless wanders.
Indebted, fearing, he desiring money
At night approaches other people's houses. [10]

It pains the gambler when he sees a woman
Another's wife, and their well-ordered household.
He yokes those brown steeds early in the morning,[1]
And when the fire is low sinks down a beggar." [2] [11]

---

1) *i.e.* he begins to play with the brown dice.

2) Translated by A. A. *Macdonell*, Hymns from the Rigveda, pp. 88 ff. The hymn has also been translated by J. *Muir*, Metrical Translations from Sanskrit Writers, pp. 190 ff. L. v. *Schroeder* (Mysterium und Mimus im Rigveda, pp. 377 ff.) explains the poem as a drama in form of a monologue. *Charpentier* (Die Suparṇasage, pp. 83 ff.) thinks that it was composed for "didactic purposes." It seems to me more probable that this soliloquy of a gambler is part of a ballad, in which some epic story was told like that of Yudhiṣṭhira or Nala.

But finally he resolves to turn over a new leaf. He implores the dice to set him free, as, according to the command of Savitar, he desires to give up gambling, in order to look after his field and live for his family.

Lastly, a kind of intermediate position between religious and secular poetry is occupied by those hymns which are connected with so-called D ā n a s t u t i s, "Songs of praise to Generosity" (namely, that of the princes and patrons of the sacrifice, for whom the songs were composed.) There are about forty such hymns.[1] Some of them are songs of victory, in which the god Indra is praised, because he has helped some king to achieve a victory over his enemies. With the praise of the god is united the glorification of the victorious king. Finally, however, the singer praises his patron, who has presented him with oxen, horses, and beautiful slaves out of the booty of war, while incidentally with a few coarse, obscene jokes, the pleasure which the slaves give to the singer is recalled. Others are very long sacrificial songs,[2] also mostly addressed to Indra, which evidently were composed for quite definite occasions at the request of a prince or a wealthy man, and were recited at the sacrifice; and they also are followed by verses in which the patron of the sacrifice is praised, because he gave the singer a liberal priestly fee. These Dānastutis always mention the full name of the pious donor, and indubitably refer to historic events, or actual happenings. Hence they are not unimportant. As poems they are, of course, quite worthless; they are composed to order by artisan-like verse-writers, or accomplished with an eye to the expected payment. Even when they are not connected with any Dānastuti, some of the hymns of the

---

[1]) Only *one* hymn (Ṛv. I, 126) is entirely a Dānastuti. Otherwise it is usually only three to five verses at the conclusion of the hymns which contain the Dānastuti.

[2]) We get the impression that the honorarium was the greater, according to the length of the poem.

Ṛgveda certainly were "hammered together" for good payment in an equally artisan-like manner. Sometimes even the Vedic singers themselves compare their work with that of the carpenter.[1] Nevertheless it is remarkable that among those hymns which excel at all as works of poetic art, there is not a single one which ends in a Dānastuti. When, therefore, H. Oldenberg [2] says about Ṛgvedic poetry *in general*: "This poetry does not rank in the service of beauty, as this religion does not serve the aim of enlightening and uplifting the soul; but both rank in the service of class-interest, of personal interest, of fees,"—he evidently forgets that among the 1,028 hymns of the Ṛgveda there are only about 40 which end in Dānastutis. I think that among the composers of Vedic hymns there were certainly *artisans*, but equally certainly there were also *poets*.

There is one hymn in the Ṛgveda which is, in the higher sense, a Dānastuti, a "Praise of Generosity." It is the hymn Ṛv. X, 117, which is worthy of mention also because it strikes a moralizing note which is otherwise quite foreign to the Ṛgveda. The Ṛgveda is everything but a text-book of morals. And the hymn, which I give here in the translation of A. A. Macdonell,[3] is quite isolated in the Ṛgveda:—

> "The gods inflict not hunger as a means to kill:
> Death frequently befalls even satiated men.[4]
> The charitable giver's wealth melts not away;
> The niggard never finds a man to pity him.

[1]) Ṛv. I, 130, 6: "This speech has been built for thee by men desiring possessions, like a chariot by a clever master." Ṛv. I, 61, 4: "To him (to Indra) I send this song of praise, as a *coach builder* sends a chariot to him who has ordered it."

[2]) Die Literatur des alten Indien, p. 20.

[3]) Hymns from the Rigveda, pp. 92 f. Freely translated by J. *Muir*, Metrical Translations from Sanskrit Writers, pp. 193 f. See also *Deussen*, AGPh., I, I, pp. 93 f.

[4]) This is very well explained by A. *Ludwig* (Der Rigveda V, 561): "We do not interfere with the rule of the gods by giving nourishment to one who is nearly dying of starvation; this is said with bitter irony against the hypocrites who sought to justify

Who, of abundant food possessed, makes hard his heart
Towards a needy and decrepit suppliant
Whom once he courted, come to pray to him for bread:
A man like this as well finds none to pity him.

He is the liberal man who helps the beggar
That, craving food, emaciated wanders,
And coming to his aid, when asked to succour,
Immediately makes him a friend hereafter.

He is no friend who gives not of his substance
To his devoted, intimate companion:
This friend should turn from him—here is no haven—
And seek a stranger elsewhere as a helper.

The wealthier man should give unto the needy,
Considering the course of life hereafter;
For riches are like chariot wheels revolving!
Now to one man they come, now to another.

The foolish man from food has no advantage;
In truth I say: it is but his undoing;
No friend he ever fosters, no companion:
He eats alone, and he alone is guilty.

The plough that cleaves the soil produces nurture;
He that bestirs his feet completes his journey.
The speaking Brahmin earns more than the silent;
A friend who gives is better than the niggard.

The one-foot strides more swiftly than the biped;
The biped goes beyond him who has three feet.
The quadruped comes at the call of bipeds,
And watches near where groups of five are gathered.[1]

---

their hardness of heart by saying that the fate of the needy ones was determined by the gods. The irony or sarcasm becomes unquestionable through what follows; the poet concludes further that, if the poor were predestined by the gods to death by starvation, then the wealthy who had plenty of food, must live for ever."

[1]) The translation is hardly questionable, so much the more, then, the sense. It has been conjectured that by the "one-foot," the "one-footed ram," a storm-god, is meant, or, by others, the sun, and that the "three-footed" is the old man supported on a stick, and the "quadruped" the dog. This is by no means certain.

Two hands though equal make not what is equal;
No sister cows yield milk in equal measure;
Unequal is the strength even of twin children;
The gifts of even kinsmen are unequal." [1]

The last verse but one is an example of the **riddle-poetry**, very popular with ancient Indians as with other ancient nations. The hymn Ṛv. I, 164, contains a large number of such riddles, most of which, unfortunately, we cannot understand. For instance:

"Seven harness a one-wheeled cart; it is drawn by one horse with seven names; three naves has the immortal, never-stopping wheel, on which all these beings stand."

This *may* mean: The seven priests of the sacrifice harness (by means of the sacrifice) the sun-chariot, which is drawn by seven horses or *one* horse with seven forms: this immortal sun-wheel has three naves, namely, the three seasons (summer, rainy season and winter), in which the life of all mankind is passed. However, other solutions of the riddle are possible.

The meaning of the following riddles, too, is by no means clear:

"Bearing three mothers and three fathers the One stands erect, and they do not tire him; there on the back of the sky they consult with the all-knowing, but not all-embracing Vac (Goddess of Speech).

He who made him knows nothing of him; he who has seen him, from him he is hidden; he lies enwrapped in the womb of the mother; he has many children, and yet he has gone to Nirṛti. [2]

The sky is my father and my progenitor, there is the navel; my own mother is this great earth. Between the two spread-out Soma vessels is the womb; into it the Father placed the seed in the daughter."

---

[1] *Cf. Deussen*, AGPh I, 1, pp. 93 f.

[2] Nirṛti is the goddess of death and destruction. "To go to Nirṛti" means: to be completely ruined, to sink into nothingness.

On the other hand it is clear that the sun is meant when it is said :

"A shepherd I saw, who does not fall down, who wanders up and down on his paths: clothing himself in those which run together and those which disperse [1] he circles about in the worlds."

Equally clear is the meaning of the riddle :

"Twelve tyres, *one* wheel, three naves: who knows that? In it there are altogether about three hundred and sixty movable pegs."

The year is meant, with the twelve months, three seasons, and roughly three hundred and sixty days.[2]

Such riddle-questions and riddle-games were among the most popular diversions in ancient India; at some sacrifices they even formed a part of the ritual. We come across such riddles again in the Atharvaveda as well as in the Yajurveda.

If we now cast a glance over the varied contents of the Ṛgveda-Saṃhitā, of which I have here tried to give an idea, the conviction forces itself upon us that in this collection we have the fragments of the very oldest Indian poetry, that the songs, hymns and poems of the Ṛgveda which have come down to us are only a fragmentary portion of a much more extensive poetic literature, both religious and secular, of which probably the greater part is irretrievably lost. But as the great majority of these hymns are either sacrificial chants, or were used, or could have been used, as prayers and sacrificial songs, we may assume that these very hymns gave the actual stimulus for collecting and uniting them in one "book." Yet the collectors, who probably had a purely

---

1) The rays are meant.

2) The riddles of Ṛv. I, 164, have been treated in detail by Martin *Haug*, Vedische Rätselfragen and Rätselsprüche (SBay A 1875) and by *Deussen*, AGPh, I, 1, pp. 105-119. See also R. *Roth*, ZDMG 46, 1892, 759 f.; E. *Windisch*, ZDMG 48, 1894, 353 f.; H. *Stumme*, ZDMG 64, 1910, 485 f. and V. *Henry*, Revue critique, 1905, p. 403.

literary interest, as well as a religious interest in the collection, did not scruple to include in it also profane poems, which by language and metre, had proved themselves to be equally ancient and venerable as those sacrificial chants. Only through being included in a "book"—that is, a school-text intended for memorization—could they be saved from oblivion. Certainly there was much also which they considered too profane to be included in the Ṛgveda-Saṃhitā. Of this a certain amount has been saved through the fact that it was later included in another collection—the Atharvaveda-Saṃhitā.

The Atharvaveda-Saṃhitā.[1]

"Atharva-veda" means "the Veda of the Atharvan" or "the knowledge of Magic Formulas." Originally, however, the word *Atharvan* meant a fire-priest, and it is probably the oldest Indian name for "priest" in general, for the word dates back to the Indo-Iranian period. For the Athravans or "fire-people" of the Avesta correspond to the Indian Atharvans.[2] The fire-cult played no less a part in the daily life of the ancient Indians than in that of the ancient Persians, so often designated as "fire-worshippers;" the

---

[1]) There are two complete English translations of the Atharvaveda, one by R.T.H. *Griffith* (Benares 1895-6), and another by W.D. *Whitney*, revised and brought nearer to completion and edited by C.R. *Lanman* (HOS, vols. 7 and 8, Cambridge Mass. 1905), a selection of hymns in excellent English translation by M *Bloomfield* (SBE, vol. 42, 1897). A great number of hymns have been translated into German by A. *Ludwig* in the 3rd volume of his "Rigveda" (Prague 1878), pp. 428-551. A selection of hymns into German verse by J. *Grill* (Hundert Lieder des Atharva-Veda, 2. Aufl, Stuttgart 1888). German translations of books I-V and XIV by A. *Weber* (Ind. Stud., vols. 4, 5, 13, 17, 18), of book XVIII by the same (SBA 1895 and 1896), of book XV by Th. *Aufrecht* (Ind. Stud., vol. 1) and of VI, 1-50 by C.A. *Florenz* (Diss., Gottingen 1887). A French translation of books VII-XIII by V. *Henry* (Paris 1891-96). *Bloomfield* has treated of the Atharvaveda in detail in the "Grundriss" (II, I, B), and I am particularly indebted to this work for this chapter. For the contents and interpretation of the Atharvaveda, see also V. *Henry*, La magie dans l'Inde antique, Paris 1904; *Oldenberg*, AR 7, 1904, 217 ff.; F. *Edgerton*, American Journal of Philology, 35, 1914, 435 ff.

[2]) In Ancient Rome, too, the *Flamines*, who had to perform the burnt-sacrifice, belong to the oldest priests. (Th. *Mommsen*, Römische Geschichte, 4. Aufl. I p. 170 f.)

priests of this very ancient fire-cult, however, were still, like the Shamans of Northern Asia and the Medicine-men of the American Indians, "priests of magic," that is, priest and wizard combined in one person, as in the word "Magi"—as the Āthravans in Medea were called—the ideas of wizard and priest are merged together. Thus we can understand that the name Atharvan designated also the "incantations of the Atharvan or the wizard-priest," that is, the spells and magic formulas themselves. The oldest name, however, by which this Veda is known in Indian literature is Atharvāṅgirasaḥ, that is, "the Atharvans and the Aṅgiras." The Aṅgiras, similarly, are a class of prehistoric fire-priests, and the word also, like the word atharvan, attained the meaning of "magic formulas and spells." The two expressions *atharvan* and *aṅgiras*, however, designate two different species of magic formulas: atharvan is "holy magic, bringing happiness," while aṅgiras means "hostile magic, black magic." Among the Atharvans, for example, are the formulae for the healing of diseases, while among the Aṅgiras are the curses against enemies, rivals, evil magicians, and such like. The old name Atharvâṅgirasaḥ thus means these *two* kinds of magic formulae, which form the chief contents of the Atharvaveda. The later name Atharvaveda is merely an abbreviation of "Veda of the Atharvans *and Aṅgiras*."[1)]

Now the Atharvaveda-Saṃhitā, usually called simply "the Atharvaveda," is a collection of seven hundred and thirty-one hymns, which contain about six thousand verses, in the recension which is best preserved.[2)] It is divided into twenty

---

[1)] In later literature we meet also with the terms bhṛgvaṅgirasaḥ and bhṛguvistara (Culika-Upaniṣad 11) for the Atharvaveda. The Bhṛgus also were ancient firepriests.

[2)] It is the Śaunaka recension of the Saṃhitā text belonging to the Śaunaka school. The Paippalāda recension is known only in one single inaccurate manuscript. The text of the Saunaka recension is published by R. *Roth* and W.D. *Whitney*. Berlin 1856. The Atharvaveda-Saṃhitā, with the commentary of Sāyaṇa, has been published by Shankar P. *Pandit*, 4 vols., Bombay 1895-1898. The manuscript of the Paippalāda recension has

books.[1] The twentieth book was added quite late, and the nineteenth book, too, did not originally belong to the Saṃhitā. The twentieth book is almost entirely composed of hymns which have been taken literally from the Ṛgveda-Saṃhitā. Besides this, about one-seventh of the Atharvaveda-Saṃhitā is taken from the Ṛgveda ; moreover, more than half of the verses which the Atharvaveda has in common with the Ṛgveda, are to be found in the tenth book, most of the remaining verses in the first and the eighth book of the Ṛgveda. The arrangement of the hymns in the eighteen genuine books is according to a definite plan, and shows fairly careful editorial activity. The first seven books consist of numerous *short* hymns, the hymns in Book I having, as a rule, four verses, in Book II five, in Book III six, in Book IV seven. The hymns of Book V have a minimum of eight and a maximum of eighteen verses. Book VI consists of one hundred and forty-two hymns mostly of three verses each, and the seventh Book consists of one hundred and eighteen hymns, most of which contain only one or two verses. Books VIII-XIV, XVII and XVIII consist throughout of very *long* hymns, the shortest hymn (twenty-one verses) being at the beginning of this series (VIII, 1) and the longest (eighty-nine verses) at the end (XVIII, 4). Book XV and the greater part of Book XVI, which interrupt the series, are composed in prose, and are similar in style and language to the Brāhmaṇas. Although in this arrangement something quite external—the number of verses—has been considered first, yet some consideration is also given to the contents. Two, three,

---

been published in facsimile by M *Bloomfield* and R. *Garbe* (The Kashmirian Atharva-Veda, Stuttgart 1901). Books I, II, IV-X of the Kashmirian recension have been published with critical notes on the text by *Le Roy Carr Barret* and F *Edgerton* in JAOS, vols. 26, 30, 32, 34, 35, 37, 40-43, 1906-1923.

[1]) We can distinguish three main divisions of the Saṃhita, *cf. Lanman*, HOS, vol. 7, pp. CXXVII ff.) 1. Books I-VI. an appendix to which is contained in Book VII ; 2. Books VIII-XII and 3. Books XIII-XVIII, an appendix to which is contained in Book XIX.

four, and even more hymns, which deal with the same subject frequently stand side by side. Occasionally the first hymn of a book is placed at the beginning on account of its contents; thus Books II, IV, V and VII, begin with theosophical hymns, which, no doubt, is intentional. On the whole we can say thus : [1] the first section of the Saṃhitā (Books I to VII) contains the short hymns of miscellaneous contents, the second section (Books VIII to XII) the long hymns of miscellaneous contents, while Books XIII to XVIII are almost entirely uniform as to their contents. Thus Book XIV contains only marriage prayers and Book XVIII only funeral hymns.

The language and metre of the hymns of the Atharvaveda are in essentials the same as those of the Ṛgveda-Saṃhitā. Yet in the language of the Atharvaveda we find some decidedly later forms and some more popular forms : also the metre is not nearly so strictly handled as in the Ṛgveda. Apart from Book XV, which is wholly composed in prose, and Book XVI, the greater part of which is in prose, we occasionally find also other prose pieces among the verses ; and frequently it is not easy to distinguish whether a piece is composed in lofty prose or in badly-constructed verses. It also happens that an originally correct metre is spoiled through an interpolation or corruption of the text.[2] In certain cases, indeed, the facts of language and metre indicate that we are dealing with later pieces. In general, however, no conclusions can be drawn from the language and the metre with regard to the date of the composition of the hymns, still less with

---

[1]) On the divisions of the Atharvaveda-Saṃhitā see *Whitney* and *Lanman*, HOS, vol. 7, pp. cxxvii ff.

[2]) On the metre of the Atharvaveda see *Whitney*, HOS, vol. 7, pp. cxxvi f. Irregularities of metre are equally peculiar to the Atharvaveda as to all metrical Vedic texts other than the Ṛgveda. To correct the metre everywhere, would mean changing the text arbitrarily.

regard to the date of the compilation of our Saṃhitā. For it always remains an open question, whether the peculiarities of language and the freedom of metre, by which the magic incantations of the Atharvaveda are distinguished from the hymn-poetry of the Ṛgveda, are based upon a difference in the period of origin or on the difference between *popular* and *priestly* composition. (*Cf.* above, pp. 53 f.)

On the other hand there are other facts which prove indisputably that our text of the Atharvaveda-Saṃhitā is later than that of the Ṛgveda-Saṃhitā. Firstly, the geographical and cultural conditions show us a later period than that reflected in the Ṛgveda. The Vedic Aryans have now penetrated further to the South-east and are already settled in the Ganges country. The tiger, native to the marshy forests of Bengal, and therefore still unknown in the Ṛgveda, appears in the Atharvaveda already as the mightiest and most feared of all beasts of prey, and the king, at his consecration, steps upon a tiger-skin, the symbol of kingly power. The Atharvaveda knows not only the four castes—Brāhmaṇas, Kṣatriyas, Vaiśyas and Śūdras,—but in a number of hymns, the highest privileges are already claimed (as later happens more and more frequently) by the priestly caste, and the Brahmans are already often called the "gods"[1] of this earth. The songs of magic in the Atharvaveda, which, according to their main contents, are certainly popular and very ancient, have no longer even their original form in the Saṃhitā, but are *brahmanised.* These old charms and formulas, whose authors are equally unknown as the authors of the magic incantations and formulas of other peoples, and which originally were just as much "popular poetry" as the poetry of magic everywhere is, have already in the Atharvaveda-Saṃhitā partly lost

[1]) The expression "gods" for "priests" occurs *once* also in the Ṛgveda (Ṛv. I, 128, 8). Cf. *Zimmer*, Altindisches Leben, pp. 205 f.

their popular character. We see at every step, that the collection was made by priests, and that many of the hymns were also composed by priests. This priestly outlook of the compilers and partly also of the authors of the hymns of the Atharvaveda, reveals itself in occasional comparisons and epithets, as for instance, when, in a charm against field-vermin, it is said that the insects are to leave the corn untouched "as the Brahman does not touch unfinished sacrificial food." A whole class of hymns of the Atharvaveda, with which we shall deal below, is concerned only with the interests of the Brahmans, the feeding of priests, the fees for the sacrifice, and such like, and they are, of course, the work of priests.

And just as the brahmanizing of the ancient magic poetry indicates a later period of the collection, so the part which the Vedic gods play in the Atharvaveda points to a later origin for the Saṃhitā. We here meet the same gods as in the Ṛgveda: Agni, Indra and so on; but their character had quite faded, they hardly differ from each other, their original signification as natural beings is, for the greater part, forgotten, and as the magic songs deal mostly with the banishment and destruction of demons—the gods being invoked only for this purpose—they have all become demon-killers. Finally, also those hymns of the Atharvaveda which contain theosophical and cosmogonic speculations indicate a later period. We already find in these hymns a fairly developed philosophical terminology, and a development of pantheism standing on a level with the philosophy of the Upaniṣads. The fact that even these philosophical hymns themselves are used for magic purposes, that, for instance, a philosophical conception such as *Asat*, "the non-existent," is employed as a means of destroying enemies, demons, and magicians,[1] shews that here

---

[1]) Ath. IV, 19, 6.

already we have before us an artificial and very modern development of ancient witchcraft.

It is no sign of a later date that the sacredness of the Atharvaveda was not recognised by the Indians themselves for a long time, and even to-day is frequently disputed. The reason for this is to be found in the character of this Veda. The purpose of the Atharvaveda is, as the Indians say, "to appease, to bless and to curse." [1] Those numerous magic formulas, however, which contain curses and exorcisms, belong to the province of "unholy magic," which the priesthood and the priestly religion endeavoured more and more to renounce. On the whole there is no essential difference between cult and magic; by means of both man seeks to influence the transcendental world. Moreover, priests and magicians are originally one and the same. But in the history of all peoples there begins a time when the cult of the gods and witchcraft strive to separate (never quite succeeding), when the priest, who is friendly with the gods, renounces the magician, who is in league with the uncanny demon-world, and looks down on him. This contrast between magician and priest developed also in India. Not only the Buddhist and Jain monks are forbidden to devote themselves to the exorcisms of the Atharvaveda and to magic, but also the brahmanical law-books declare sorcery to be a sin, place the magician on a level with impostors and rogues, and invite the king to proceed against them with punishments.[2] Certainly in other places in the law-books of the Brahmans permission to make use of the exorcisms of the Atharvaveda against enemies is expressly given,[3] and the ritual texts, which describe the great sacrifices, contain numerous exorcism-formulas and descriptions of

---

[1]) *i.e.* to appease the demons, to bless friends and to curse enemies.

[2]) SBE X, II, p. 176. XLV, pp. 105, 133, 363. Manu IX, 258, 290; XI, 64. Viṣṇu-Smṛti 54, 25.

[3]) See Manu XI, 33.

magic rites by means of which the priest can annihilate—so runs the formula—"him who hates us, and him whom we hate." Yet a certain aversion to the Veda of the magic formulas arose in priestly circles; it was not considered sufficiently orthodox and was frequently excluded from the canon of sacred texts. From the beginning it held a peculiar position in the sacred literature. Wherever, in old works, there is talk of sacred knowledge, there the *trayī vidyā*, "the three-fold knowledge," that is, Ṛgveda, Yajurveda, and Sāmaveda, is always mentioned first; the Atharvaveda always follows *after* the trayī vidyā, and sometimes is even entirely passed over. It even happens that the Vedāṇgas and the epic narratives (itihāsapurāṇa) are represented as sacred texts, while the Atharvaveda remains unmentioned. Thus in a Gṛhyasūtra [1] a ceremony is described, by which the Vedas are to be "laid into" the new-born child. This takes place by means of a formula, which says: "I lay the Ṛgveda into thee, I lay the Yajurveda into thee, I lay the Sāmaveda into thee, I lay the discourses (vākovākya) into thee, the tales and legends (itihāsapurāṇa) I lay into thee, all the Vedas I lay into thee." Here, then, the Atharvaveda is intentionally passed over. Even in old Buddhist texts it is said of learned Brahmans that they are versed in the *three* Vedas.[2] The fact however that already in one Saṃhitā of the Black Yajurveda [3] and also occasionally in old Brāhmaṇas and Upaniṣads the Atharvaveda is mentioned by the side of the three other Vedas shows

[1]) Śāṅkhāyana-Gṛhyasūtra I, 24, 8.

[2]) Suttanipāta, Selasutta is especially remarkable, where it is said of the Brahman Sela that he is conversant with the *three* vedas, the Vedāṅgas and the Itihāsa as fifth (ed. Fausböll, p. 101). Also in Suttanipāta 1019 it is said of Bhāvarī that he has mastered th *three* Vedas. (SBE, vol. X, II, pp. 98 and 189).

[3]) Taittirīya-Saṃhitā, VII, 5, 11, 2, where the plural of Aṅgiras stands in the sense of "Atharvaveda." See above, pp 120 f.

that this non-mention of the Atharvaveda is no proof of the late origin of the Saṃhitā.

But even though it is certain that our *version* of the Atharvaveda-*Saṃhitā* is later than that of the Ṛgveda-*Saṃhitā*, yet it by no means follows from this that the *hymns* themselves are later than the Ṛgveda hymns. It only follows that the latest hymns of the Atharvaveda are later than the latest hymns of the Ṛgveda. However, certain as it is that among the hymns of the Atharvaveda there are many which are later than the great majority of Ṛgveda hymns, it is equally certain that the magic poetry of the Atharvaveda is in itself at least as old as, if not older than, the sacrificial poetry of the Ṛgveda, that numerous pieces of the Atharvaveda date back into the same dim prehistoric times as the oldest songs of the Ṛgveda. It will not do at all to speak of a "period of the Atharvaveda." Like the Ṛgveda-Saṃhitā, so too the collection of the Atharvaveda contains pieces which are separated from each other by centuries. Only of the later parts of the Atharvaveda-Saṃhitā it can be said that many of them were only composed after the pattern of the Ṛgveda-hymns. I consider as erroneous the opinion of Oldenberg,[1] that the oldest form of magic formulas in India was the prose form, and that the whole literature of magic verses and magic songs was only created after the "pattern of its elder sister, the poetry of the sacrificial hymns."

After all it is quite a different spirit that breathes from the magic songs of the Atharvaveda than from the hymns of the Ṛgveda. Here we move in quite a different world. On the one hand the great gods of the sky, who embody the mighty phenomena of Nature, whom the singer glorifies and praises, to whom he sacrifices, and to whom he prays, strong, helpful, some of them lofty beings, most of them friendly gods of life—on the other hand the dark, demoniacal powers,

[1]) Literatur des alten Indien, p. 41.

which bring disease and misfortune upon mankind, ghostly beings, against whom the wizard hurls his wild curses, or whom he tries to soothe and banish by flattering speeches. Indeed, many of these magic songs, like the magic rites pertaining to them, belong to a sphere of conceptions which, spread over the whole earth, ever recur with the most surprising similarity in the most varying peoples of all countries. Among the Indians of North America, among the Negro races of Africa, among the Malays and Mongols, among the ancient Greeks and Romans, and frequently still among the peasantry of present-day Europe, we find again exactly the same views, exactly the same strange leaps of thought in the magic songs and magic rites, as have come down to us in the Atharvaveda of the ancient Indians. There are, then, numerous verses in the Atharvaveda, which, according to their character and often also their contents, differ just as little from the magic formulas of the American-Indian medicine-men and Tartar shamans, as from the Merseburg magic maxims, which belong to the sparse remains of the oldest German poetry. Thus we read, for example, in one of the Merseburg magic incantations that "Wodan, who well understood it," charmed the sprained leg of Balder's foal with the formula:

> "Bone to bone,
> Blood to blood,
> Limb to limbs,
> As if they were glued."

And quite similarly it is said in Atharvaveda IV, 12, in a spell against the breaking of a leg:

> "With marrow be the marrow joined, thy limb united with the limb.
> Let what hath fallen of thy flesh, and the bone also grow again. [3]
> Let marrow close with marrow, let skin grow united with the skin,
> Let blood and bone grow strong in thee, flesh grow together with the flesh. [4]

Join thou together hair with hair,[1] join thou together skin with skin,
Let blood and bone grow strong in thee. Unite the broken part, O Plant." [2] [5]

The great importance of the Atharvaveda-Saṃhitā lies in the very fact that it is an invaluable source of knowledge of the real popular belief as yet uninfluenced by the priestly religion, of the faith in numberless spirits, imps, ghosts, and demons of every kind, and of the witchcraft, so eminently important for ethnology and for the history of religion. How very important the Atharvaveda is for the ethnologist, may be shown by the following glance at the various classes of hymns which the collection contains.

One of the chief constituent parts of the Atharvaveda-Saṃhitā consists of Songs and Spells for the Healing of Diseases, which belong to the magic rites of healing (bhaiṣajyāni). They are either addressed to the diseases themselves imagined as personal beings, as demons,[3] or to whole classes of demons who are considered to be the creators of diseases. And in India, as among other peoples, it is believed that these demons either oppress and torment the patient from outside, or that the patient is possessed by them. Some of these spells are also invocations and praises of the curative herb, which is to serve as the cure of the disease; others again, are prayers to the water to which special healing power is ascribed, or to the fire which is looked on by the Indians as the mightiest scarer of demons. These songs of magic, together with the magic rites attached to them, of which we learn in the Kauśikasūtra which will be mentioned later, form the oldest system of Indian medical science. The symptoms

---

1) The healing herb is addressed.

2) Translated by R. T. H. *Griffith.*

3) The name of the disease is at the same time the name of the demon. It is exactly the same, for instance, with the Malays: they have as many names of disease-spirits as of diseases known to them.

of the various diseases are often described with great clearness in the songs, and therefore they are not uninteresting for the history of medicine. This is true particularly of the spells against fever. In the later text-books of medicine the fever is still called "the king of diseases," on account of its frequency and violence. Numerous charms are addressed to Takman [1]—this is the name of the fever imagined as a demon in the Atharvaveda. Thus, for instance, hymn Ath. V. 22, from which a few verses may here be quoted:

"And thou thyself who makest all men yellow, consuming them with burning heat like Agni,
Thou, Fever! then be weak and ineffective. Pass hence into the realms below or vanish. [2]
Endowed with universal power! send Fever downward, far away,
The spotty, like red-coloured dust, sprung from a spotty ancestor. [3]
Go, Fever, to the Mūjavans, or, farther, to the Bahlikas,[2]
Seek a lascivious Śūdra girl and seem to shake her through and through. [7]
Since thou now cold, now burning hot, with cough besides, hast made us shake,
Terrible, Fever, are thy darts; forbear to injure us with these. [10]
Go, Fever, with Consumption, thy brother, and with thy sister, Cough,
And with thy nephew Herpes, go away unto that alien folk.[3] [12]

This pious wish, that the diseases may go to other people, may visit other lands, returns frequently in the songs of the Atharvaveda. In a similar manner the cough is sent away from the patient into the far distance with the spell Ath. VI, 105:

"As the soul with the soul's desires swiftly to a distance flies, thus do thou, O cough, fly forth along the soul's course of flight! (1)

As a well-sharpened arrow swiftly to a distance flee, thus do thou, O cough, fly forth along the expanse of the earth! (2)

---

1) On the hymn to Takman, see J. V. *Grohmann*, Ind. Stud. 9, 1865, 381 ff.

2) Names of tribes.

3) Translated by R. T. H. *Griffith*.

As the rays of the sun swiftly to a distance fly, thus do thou, O cough, fly forth along the flood of the sea"![1] (3)

On account of their picturesque, sublime language, some of these magic songs deserve to be valued as examples of lyrical poetry. Certainly we must not expect too much in this poetry; we must be content to be surprised here and there by a pretty simile, as when, in a spell against bleeding, the magician addresses the veins as red-robed maidens (Ath. I, 17):

"Those maidens there, the veins, who run their course in robes of ruddy hue,
Must now stand quiet, reft of power, like sisters who are brotherless. [1]
Stay still, thou upper vein, stay still, thou lower, stay, thou midmost one,
The smallest one of all stand still: let the great vessel e'en be still. [2]
Among a thousand vessels charged with blood, among a thousand veins,
Even these the middlemost stand still and their extremities have rest. [3]
A mighty rampart built of sand hath circled and encompassed you.
Be still, and quietly take rest."[2]

However, these sayings are not always so poetical. Very often they are most monotonous, and in many of them, in common with the poetical compositions of primitive peoples, it is chiefly that monotonous repetition of the same words and sentences of which their poetical form consists.[3] Often, too, as is the case with the magic incantations of all peoples, their meaning is intentionally problematic and obscure. Such a monotonous and, at the same time, obscure verse is, for instance, that against scrofulous swellings (Ath. VI, 25):

"The five and fifty (sores) that gather together upon the nape of the neck, from here they all shall pass away, as the pustules of the (disease called) apakit! (1)

---

[1]) Translated by M. *Bloomfield*, SBE, 42, p. 8.

[2]) Translated by R. T. H. *Griffith*.

[3]) On *repetition* as the crudest rudimentary form of poetry, *cf.* H. *Schurtz*, Urgeschichte der Kultur, Leipzig and Vienna, 1900, pp. 523 ff.

The seven and seventy (sores) that gather together upon the neck, from here they all shall pass away, as the pustules of the (disease called) apakit! (2)

The nine and ninety (sores) that gather together upon the shoulders from here they all shall pass away, as the pustules of the (disease called) apakit!"[1] (3)

There is here again a remarkable agreement between Indian and German magic incantations. Similarly as 55, 77, or 99 diseases are mentioned in the Atharvaveda, so in German incantations too, 77 or 99 diseases are often spoken of. For example in this German spell against fever:

> "This water and the blood of Christ is good for the
> seventy-seven kinds of fever."

A conception which the ancient Indians have in common not only with the Germans but also with many other peoples, is that many diseases are caused by worms. There are therefore a series of magic songs, which are intended to serve the purpose of exorcism and driving away all kinds of worms. Thus we read Ath. II, 31:

" The worm which is in the entrails, that which is in the head, and that which is in the ribs......these worms we crush with this spell. [4]

The worms which have settled down in the hills, in the woods, in the plants, in the cattle, in the waters, and those which have settled down in our bodies, this whole breed of worms I crush." [5]

These worms are regarded as demoniacal beings, their king and governor are mentioned, also male and female ones, worms of many colours and fantastical forms, and so on: for instance, in the spell against worms in children (Ath. V. 23):

Slay the worms in this boy. O Indra, lord of treasures! Slain are all the evil powers by my fierce imprecation! (2)

---

[1]) Translated by M. *Bloomfield*, SBE., 42, p. 19.

Him that moves about in the eyes, that moves about in the nose, that gets to the middle of the teeth, that worm do we crush. (3)

The two of like colour, the two of different colour ; the two black ones, and the two red ones ; the brown one ; and the brown-eared one ; the (one like a) vulture, and the (one like a) cuckoo, are slain. (4)

The worms with white shoulders, the black ones with white arms, and all those that are variegated, these worms do we crush. (5)

Slain is the king of the worms and their viceroy also is slain. Slain is the worm, with him his mother slain, his brother slain, his sister slain. (11)

Slain are they who are inmates with him, slain are his neighbours ; moreover all the quite tiny worms are slain. (12)

Of all the male worms, and of all the female worms do I split the heads with the stone, I burn their faces with fire." [1] (13)

Similarly, German spells are directed against "he-worm and she-worm" and worms of various colours are mentioned in the German spell against toothache :

"Pear-tree, I complain to thee,
Three worms are pricking me.
The one is grey,
The other is blue,
The third is red,
I wish they were all three dead." [2]

Very numerous, too, are the incantations which are directed against whole classes of demons, which are looked upon as the originators of diseases, especially against the *Piśācas* (goblins) and *Rākṣasas* (devils). The object of these spells is the scattering or exorcising of these demoniacal beings. An example is found in the song Ath. IV, 36 against

---

[1]) Translated by M *Bloomfield*, SBE., 42, p. 24.

[2]) The belief that toothache is caused by worms, is not only prevalent in India, Germany, England and France. In Madagascar, too, it is said of one who has toothache: "He is ill through the worm." And the Cherokees have a spell against toothache which says: "The intruder in the tooth has spoken, and it is only a worm" (James Mooney in the 7th Annual Report of the Bureau of Ethnology, 1885-86, Washington, 1891, pp. 357 f.).

the Piśācas, from which the following verses, here reproduced in prose, are taken, which indicated a boundless self-assertion on the part of the wizard.

"I am a pest to the Piśācas, as the tigor to the owners of oxen. Like dogs, when they have perceived the lion, they find no loophole. [6]

I cannot bear with the Piśācas, nor with thieves and prowlers in the forests. From the village which I enter, the Piśācas vanish. [7]

From the village which my violent strength encounters, the Piśācas vanish; they have no more evil intentions." [8]

Along with this belief in devilish beings which bring diseases upon mankind, we find in India also the world-wide belief in male and female demons (Incubi and Succubi), which visit mortal women and men by night. These are the *Apsaras* and *Gandharvas* of the ancient Indian popular belief, which correspond in every respect and in an amazing manner with the sprites and elves and fairies of the German popular belief. They are originally spirits of nature, river and forest deities. Rivers and trees are their dwelling places, which they leave only to entice mortals and to injure them by unnatural co-habitation. In order to drive away these spirits, the ancient Indian magicians made use of a pleasant-smelling plant, called Ajaśṛṅgī (*Odina pinnata*), and recited the song Ath. IV, 37, from which I quote the following verses:

"With thee do we scatter the Apsaras and Gandharvas. O ajaśringī (*Odina pinnata*), goad (aga) the Rakshas, drive them all away with thy smell! (2)

The Apsaras, Guggulû, Pílâ, Naladî, Aukshagandhi, and Pramandanî (by name), shall go to the river, to the ford of the waters, as if blown away! Thither do ye, O Apsaras, pass away, (since) ye have been recognised! [1] (3)

[1]) According to the magic lore of the Indians, as of other peoples, spirits and ghosts become powerless when recognized and called by name. Guggulū, and so on, are names of certain Apsaras.

Where grow the asvattha (*Ficus religiosa*) and the banyan-trees, the great trees with crowns, thither do ye, O Apsaras pass away, (since) ye have been recognised ! (4)

Of the crested Gandharva, the husband of the Apsaras, who comes dancing hither, I crush the two mushkas and cut off the sepas. (7)

One is like a dog, one like an ape. As a youth with luxuriant locks, pleasant to look upon, the Gandharva hangs about the woman. Him do we drive out from here with our powerful charm. (11)

The Apsaras you know, are your wives ; ye, the Gandharvas are their husbands. Speed away, ye immortals, do not go after mortals ! "[1] (12)

Just as in this song in the Atharvaveda, the elf in the German incantations is exhorted to leave the houses of mortals, and to depart to the rivers and trees. Just like the Apsaras and the Gandharvas, too, the Germanic water-fairies and elves love music and dancing, with which they lure mortal men and women. Just as in the ancient Indian magic song the Gandharva appears now as a dog, now as an ape, now as a youth with beautiful curls, the elf of the German legends makes his appearance in all kinds of transformations. Again, just as the Apsaras of the Indians have their swings in the branches of the banana and fig trees, the water-fairies of German popular belief swing in the branches and on the tree-tops. As here in the Atharvaveda a sweet-smelling plant serves to scare away the demons, so too sweet-smelling herbs (like thyme) were thought by the Germans to be an excellent means of driving away elves and other spirits. These points of agreement can scarcely be mere coincidences : and we may well agree with Adalbert Kuhn, who compared Indian and German incantations as long as sixty years ago,[2] in assuming that not only certain phenomena of magic lore, but also quite definitely developed forms of magic songs and magic

---

[1]) Translated by M. *Bloomfield*, SBE., Vol. 42, pp. 33 f.

[2]) In Vol. XIII of Zeitschrift für vergleichende Sprachwissenschaft (1864), pp. 49 ff, 113 ff.

formulas may be traced back to the Indo-European period, and that the German and Indian magic songs thus give us a clue to a kind of prehistoric poetry of the Indo-Europeans.

The prayers for health and long life, called by the Indians āyuṣyāṇi sūktāni, *i.e.* "hymns achieving long life," which form the second class of the hymns of the Atharvaveda, are but little different from the magic spells for healing. These are prayers, as they were used chiefly at family festivals, such as the first hair-cutting of the boy, the first shaving of the youth, and the initiation (upanayana). The prayer for a great age, for a life of "a hundred autumns" or "a hundred winters," for deliverance from the 100 or 101 kinds of death, and for protection against all sorts of diseases, here recurs again and again in a rather monotonous manner. Book XVII, consisting of a single hymn of thirty stanzas, belongs to this class of hymns. As in the spells of healing, the healing herb which the magic-doctor uses is often invoked, so some of these prayers for long life are addressed to amulets which are to ensure health and long life to the wearer.

In the closest connection with these prayers are the extremely numerous benedictions (pauṣṭikāni), by means of which the farmer, the shepherd, the merchant hope to gain happiness and success in their undertakings. Here we find a prayer which is used at the building of a house, benedictions for ploughing, for sowing, for the growth of the corn, and exorcisms against field-vermin, spells against the danger of fire, prayers for rain used in rain-magic, numerous benedictions for the prosperity of the herds of cattle, exorcisms of a herdsman against wild animals and robbers, prayers of a merchant for good business and good fortune on his journey, of a gamester for good luck with the dice, proscriptions and exorcisms against snakes, and so on. Only a few of these songs and spells are of any worth as poetry. It frequently happens, however, that in a very mediocre poem of considerable length, we find single verses of great beauty. The most beautiful is perhaps the rain-song Ath. IV, 15. Here we read: Driven by the wind may the clouds pass by, and "while the great, cloud-enwrapped bull roars,[1] may the rushing waters refresh the earth." Parjanya himself is invoked with the words:

> "Roar, thunder, set the sea in agitation, bedew the ground with thy sweet rain, Parjanya!
> Send plenteous showers on him who seeketh shelter, and let the owner of lean kine go homeward." [2]

The least amount of poetry is found in those benedictions which contain only quite general prayers for happiness and blessing or for protection against danger and evil. Among the latter are the so-called "mṛgārasūktāni" (Ath. IV, 23-29), a litany consisting of seven hymns of seven verses each. They are addressed respectively to Agni (1), Indra (2), Vāyu and Savitar (3), heaven and earth (4), the Maruts (5), Bhava and Śarva [3] (6), Mitra and Varuṇa (7), and every verse concludes with the refrain-like prayer for deliverance from affliction.

The word "aṃhas," however, which we here translate by "affliction," combines in itself the meanings "distress, affliction" on one side, and "guilt, sin" on the other. Therefore the above-mentioned litany can be reckoned among that class of Atharvaveda hymns which is connected with expiatory ceremonies (prāyaścittāni). These expiatory formulæ and spells for cleansing from guilt and sin are less different from the spells of healing than one might think. For, to Indian ideas, an expiation, a prāyaścitta, is necessary not only for "sins" in our sense, *i.e.* offences against the moral rule, or

---

[1]) The rain-god Parjanya.

[2]) Ath. IV. 15, 6, translated by R. T. H. *Griffith*. In time of drought the cows have become lean on account of scanty food. Now the herdsman must flee before the rain, and better times will come for the cattle (Weber, Ind. Stud., Vol. 18, p. 62).

[3]) Names or forms of *Rudra*, a god who plays a prominent part in witchcraft and in the magic songs of the Atharvaveda, while he occupies a more subordinate position in the hymns of the Ṛgveda.

transgressions against religion, but by the side of propitiatory formulae for imperfectly performed sacrifices and ceremonies, for crimes consciously and unconsciously committed, for sins of thought, for non-payment of debts, especially gambling debts, for the marriage prohibited by the law, of a younger brother before the elder, and beside general prayers for liberation from guilt and sin and their consequences, we find also propitiatory formulas, and, in connection with atonement ceremonies, songs and spells by which mental and physical infirmities, unpropitious omens (*e.g.* by the flight of birds or the birth of twins or the birth of a child under an unlucky star), bad dreams and sudden accidents are "expiated," *i.e.* warded off or weakened in their effects. The conception "guilt," "sin," "evil," "misfortune" are continually merged one into the other. The fact is that everything evil—disease and misfortune, just the same as guilt and sin—is looked on as caused by evil spirits. Like the invalid or the madman, so is the evil-doer, too, the sinner, possessed by a wicked demon. The same fiends which bring disease, also send the unfavourable omens and the accidents themselves. Thus, for example, Ath. X, 3, an amulet, which is tied on the person, is praised extravagantly in twenty-five verses and glorified as a mighty protection against dangers and evils of every kind, against evil magic, against bad dreams and unfavourable omens, against "the sin which my mother, which my father, which my brothers and which my sister and which we ourselves have committed," and at the same time as a universal remedy for all diseases.

Family discord, too, arises through the influence of evil demons or malicious wizards. Therefore we find in the Atharvaveda also a number of spells for the restoration of harmony, which stand midway between the expiatory formulas and the benedictions. For to this class belong not only the spells by which peace and harmony are to be restored in the family, but also formulas by which one can appease the wrath of a great master, or by which one desires to gain influence in an assembly, the art of persuasion in a court of law, and so on. One of the most pleasing of this kind of songs is Ath. III, 30, which begins with the words:

"Of one heart and of one mind,
Free from hatred do I make you,
Take delight in one another,
As the cow does in her baby calf.

Loyal to his sire the son be,
Of one mind, too, with his mother;
Sweet and kindly language ever
Let the wife speak to her husband.

Brother shall not hate the brother,
And the sister not the sister.
Of one mind and of one intent,
Speak ye words of kindness only." [1])

Of course some of these reconciliation-spells could also be employed in the restoration of unity between husband and wife. But the magic songs referring to marriage and love form a large separate class of hymns of the Atharvaveda; and in the Kauśikasūtra we become acquainted with the manifold kinds of love-magic and all the magic rites, which are called "strīkarmāṇi" or "women's rites," and for which these songs and spells were employed. There are, however, two sorts of spells belonging to this class. Those of the one kind have a sociable and peaceful character and refer to marriage and the begetting of children. They are pious spells connected with harmless magical rites by which a maiden tries to obtain a bridegroom, or a young man a bride, benedictions upon the bridal pair and the newly-married, magic songs and spells

[1]) This is an almost literal translation. The translation by J. *Muir*, Metrical Translations from Sanskrit Writers, p. 139, is rather free.

through which conception shall be accelerated and the birth of a male child effected, prayers for protection of the pregnant woman, also of the unborn and the new-born child, and so on. Of this kind is the whole of Book XIV, which contains a collection of marriage-verses and is, on the whole, a second, greatly enlarged edition of the marriage verses of the Ṛgveda.[1] More numerous is the second kind of these spells, consisting of wild exorcisms and curses, which refer to love-intrigues and disturbances of the married life. Still fairly harmless are the spells through which a wife wishes to pacify her husband's jealousy, or the verses which are to bring the unfaithful wife back to her husband, or the charm for inducing sleep (Ath. IV, 5), in which the following verse proves that the song is used by a lover who steals to his sweetheart: "May the mother sleep, may the father sleep, may the dog sleep, may the eldest in the house sleep, may *her* relations sleep, may all the people round about sleep."[2] Less harmless and partly of primeval savageness are the spells by which a person is to be forced to love against his or her will. The belief, existing all over the world, that by means of the *picture* of a person one can harm or obtain power over that person, is also found in ancient India. If a man wished to gain the love of a woman, he made a picture out of clay, took a bow with a string of hemp, an arrow the barb of which was a thorn, the feather of which came from an owl, the shaft of which was made of black wood, and began to pierce the heart of the picture through and through with the arrow—a symbolical piercing of the heart of the beloved with the arrow of the love-god Kama—while he recited the verses of the magic song, Ath. III, 25:

---

[1]) See above, pp. 107 f. The marriage prayers as also the love-charms of the Atharvaveda have been translated and explained by A. *Weber*, Ind. Stud., Vol. V.

[2]) *Bloomfield* (SBE., Vol 42, p. 105) calls the hymn a "charm at an assignation," *Whitney* (HOS., Vol. 7, p. 151) "an incantation to put to sleep." See also Th. *Aufrecht*, Ind. Stud. 4, 337 ff., on the two sleeping-spells, Ṛv. VII, 55 and Ath. IV, 5

"May (love) the disquieter, disquiet thee; do not hold out upon thy bed: with the terrible arrow of Kâma (love) do I pierce thee in the heart.

The arrow, winged with longing, barbed with love, whose shaft is undeviating desire, with that, well-aimed, Kâma shall pierce thee in the heart!

With that well-aimed arrow of Kâma which parches the spleen, whose plume flies forward, which burns up, do I pierce thee in the heart.

Consumed by burning ardour, with parched mouth, do thou (woman) come to me, pliant (thy) pride laid aside, mine alone, speaking sweetly and and to me devoted!

I drive thee with a goad from thy mother and thy father, so that thou shalt be in my power, shalt come up to my wish.

All her thought do ye, O Mitra and Varuṇa, drive out of her!

Then, having deprived her of her will, put her into my power alone!" [1])

A woman acts in a similar manner if she wants to compel the love of a man. She makes an effigy of the man, places it before herself, and hurls heated arrow-heads at it, while she recites the song, Ath. VI, 130 and 138 with the refrain: "Send forth Desire, ye Deities! Let him consume with love of me!" Thus she says:

"Madden him, Maruts, madden him. Madden him, madden him, O Air.
Madden him, Agni, madden him. Let him consume with love of me.
(130, 4.)

Down upon thee, from head to foot, I draw the pangs of longing love.
Send forth Desire, ye Deities! Let him consume with love of me.
(131, 1.)

If thou shouldst run three leagues away, five leagues, a horse's daily stage,
Thence thou shalt come to me again and be the father of our sons." [2])
(131, 3.)

---

1) Translated by M. *Bloomfield*, SBE., Vol. 42, p. 102.

2) Translated by R. T. H. *Griffith*. In the refrain (131, 1) I have corrected "send forth the charm" into "send forth Desire."—*The author.*

The wildest incantations, actually bristling with hatred, are those which women use in the attempt to oust their rivals. One example is Ath. I, 14:

"I have taken unto myself her fortune and her glory, as a wreath of a tree. Like a mountain with broad foundation may she sit a long time with her parents!

This woman shall be subjected to thee as thy wife, O King Yama [1]) (till then) let her be fixed to the house of her mother, or her brother, or her father!

This woman shall be the keeper of thy house, O king (Yama), and her do we make over to thee! May she long sit with her relatives, until (her hair) drops from her head!

With the incantation of Asita, of Kasyapa, and of Gaya[2]) do I cover up thy fortune, as women cover (something) within a chest." [3])

Language of unbridled wildness, of unmistakeable meaning is also found in the songs which are intended to make a woman barren (Ath. VII, 35) or to rob a man of his generative power (Ath. VI, 138; VII, 90).

These love-incantations really belong already to that class of hymns which are designated by the old name "Aṅgiras,"[4]) to the class of the curses and exorcisms against demons, wizards and enemies (ābhicārikāṇi). Some of the charms of healing, too, can just as well be included in this class inasmuch as they contain exorcisms against the demons of disease. Of this kind is among other things, also the second half of Book XVI, which contains an exorcism against nightmare in which this demon is told to visit the enemies. In these exorcisms no difference is made between demons and malicious

---

[1]) The god of death.

[2]) Probably names of famous wizards.

[3]) Translated by M. *Bloomfield*. (SBE., Vol. 42, p. 107) who was the first to give a correct interpretation of this difficult charm (*ib*. pp. 252 ff.) *Whitney* (HOS., Vol. 7, p. 15) describes it as an "imprecation of spinsterhood on a woman."

[4]) See above, pp. 120 f.

wizards and witches, and against them, Agni especially, the fire as a demon-destroyer, is called to the rescue. Numerous popular names of demons, otherwise quite unknown, are found in these hymns, in which indeed we continually meet with ideas more genuinely popular than usual. Thus we here come across the view, deeply-rooted in the popular belief—and that, of all peoples—that disease and misfortune can be caused not only by demons, but also by malicious people who are endowed with magic power. The magic by means of which these bad people work evil, is often personified in the songs, and a magic antidote—a healing herb, an amulet, a talisman—is confronted with it. The spells and songs connected with this hostile magic and its magic antidotes are often distinguished by a raciness and ferocity which are not without a certain beauty. In any case, in some of these curses and exorcisms of the Atharvaveda, there is more good popular poetry than in most of the sacrificial songs and prayers of the Ṛgveda. An example of this is the song for averting evil magic, Ath. V, 14, of which a few verses may here be quoted:

"An eagle found thee: with his snout a wild boar dug thee from the earth.
Harm thou, O Plant, the mischievous, and drive the sorcerer away. [1]
Beat thou the Yātudhānas back, drive thou away the sorcerer;
And chase afar, O Plant, the man who fain would do us injury. [2]
As 'twere a strip cut round from skin of a white-footed antelope,
Bind, like a golden chain, O God, his witchcraft on the sorcerer. [3]
Take thou his sorcery by the hand, and to the sorcerer lead it back.
Lay it before him, face to face, that it may kill the sorcerer. [4]
Back on the wizard fall his craft, upon the curser light his curse.
Let witchcraft, like a well-naved car, roll back upon the sorcerer. [5]
Whoso, for other's harm hath dealt—woman or man—in magic arts,
To him we lead the sorcery back, even as a courser with a rope. [6]

Go as a son goes to his sire : bite as a trampled viper bites,
As one who flies from bonds, go back, O Witchcraft to the sorcerer." [1] [10]

In a similar manner in the song Ath. VI, 37, the curse is personified and returned to the cursing one in the following vigorous verses :

" Hitherward, having yoked his steeds, came
Imprecation, thousand-eyed,
Seeking my curser, as a wolf the home of one who owneth sheep. [1]
Avoid us, Imprecation ! as consuming fire avoids the lake.
Smite thou the man who curses us, as the sky's lightning strikes the tree. [2]
Who curses us, himself uncursed, or, cursed, who curses us again,
Him cast I as a sop to Death, as to a dog one throws a bone." [2] [3]

Here we may mention the magnificent hymn to Varuṇa (Ath. IV, 16), the first half of which celebrates the almighty power and omniscience of God in language which is familiar to us from the Psalms, but which is extremely rarely heard in India, while the second half is nothing but a vigorous exorcism-formula against liars and libellers, such as are not infrequent in the Atharvaveda. I give the first five verses of this remarkable poem in the beautiful poetical translation of Muir,[3] and verses 6-9 in the prose translation of M. Bloomfield.[4]

" The mighty lord on high our deeds, as if at hand, espies ;
The gods know all men do, though men would fain their acts disguise, [1]
Whoever stands, whoever moves, or steals from place to place,
Or hides him in his secret cell,—the gods his movements trace.

[1]) Translated by R. T. H. *Griffith.*

[2]) Translated by R. T. H. *Griffith.*

[3]) Metrical Translations from Sanskrit Writers, p. 163.

[4]) SBE., Vol. 42, pp. 88 f.

Wherever two together plot, and deem they are alone,
King Varuṇa is there, a third, and all their schemes are known. [2]

This earth is his, to him belong those vast and boundless skies;
Both seas within him rest, and yet in that small pool he lies. [3]

Whoever far beyond the sky should think his way to wing.
He could not there elude the grasp of Varuṇa the king.
His spies, descending from the skies, glide all this world around;
Their thousand eyes all-scanning sweep to earth's remotest bound. [4]

Whate'er exists in heaven and earth, whatever beyond the skies,
Before the eyes of Varuṇa, the king, unfolded lies.
The ceaseless winkings all he counts of every mortal's eyes,
He wields this universal frame as gamester throws his dice. [5]

May all thy fateful toils which, seven by seven, threefold, lie spread out, ensnare him that speaks falsehood: him that speaks the truth they shall let go! [6]

With a hundred snares, O Varuṇa, surround him, let the liar not go free from thee, O thou that observest men! The rogue shall sit his belly hanging loose, like a cask without hoops, bursting all abont! [7]

With (the snare of) Varuṇa which is fastened lengthwise, and that which (is fastened) broadwise, with the indigenous and the foreign, with the divine and the human,— [8]

With all these snares do I fetter thee, O N. N., descended from N. N., the son of the woman N. N.: all these do I design for thee." [9]

Roth [1] says with regard to this hymn: "There is no other song in the whole of Vedic literature, which expresses the divine omniscience in such impressive words, and yet this beautiful work of art has been degraded into the exordium of an exorcism. Still, here as with many other portions of this Veda, we may surmise that available fragments of older hymns were used for the purpose of re-furbishing

[1]) Abhandlung über den Atharvaveda, Tübingen 1856, pp. 29 f. where the hymn is translated into German. For other translations of the hymn see *Whitney*, HOS., Vol. 7, p. 176.

magic formulæ. As a fragment of this kind the first five or even six verses of our hymn may be considered." I fully agree to these words. The supposition of Bloomfield,[1] that the whole poem, just as it is, was composed from the first for magic purposes, does not seem to me at all probable.

There exists a rather large class of magic songs, which are intended for the needs of the kings, partly exorcism formulas against enemies and partly benedictions. Every king was compelled, in India, from the earliest times, to have his Purohita or family priest, and this family priest had to be familiar with the magic rites which refer to the life of a king ('rājakarmāṇi,' 'kings' rites') and also with the songs and charms belonging to these rites. The Atharvaveda therefore is closely connected with the warrior caste. Thus we here find the songs which refer to the consecration of a king, when the king is sprinkled with the holy water and steps upon the tiger-skin; we find spells which are intended to ensure for the king mastery over other princes, and power and fame in general, prayers for the king when he girds on his armour, when he ascends his war-chariot, and so on. There is an interesting prayer (Ath. III, 4) at the election of a king, in which the heavenly King Varuṇa appears as the one who chooses the king, the name of the god being brought into etymological connection with the verb *var*, "to choose." A remarkable magic formula is that for the restoration of a banished king, in Ath. III, 3. Among the most beautiful hymns of this class are the battle-chants and magic songs of war, in particular the two songs to the drum, which is to call the fighters to the battle and to victory (Ath. V., 20 and 21). A few verses of V, 20, follow as an example :

---

[1]) SBE, Vol. 42, p. 389.

Formed out of wood, compact with straps of leather, loud is the
War-drum as he plays the hero.
Whetting thy voice and vanquishing opponents, roar at them like
a lion fain to conquer! [1]
Like a bull marked by strength among the cattle, roar seeking
kine and gathering up the booty.
Pierce through our adversaries' heart with sorrow, and let our
routed foes desert their hamlets. [3]
Hearing the Drum's far-reaching voice resounding, let the foe's
dame, waked by the roar, afflicted,
Grasping her son, run forward in her terror amid the conflict of
the deadly weapons.[1] [5]

The Brahmans, however, were from the beginning much too practical a people to have used the magic charms always only in the interest of kings or other people, and not also for themselves. Among the magic incantations belonging to the "kings' rites" we already find a few which are concerned more with the Purohita, the indispensable family priest of the king, than with the latter himself. And although attacks on witchcraft and exorcisms are not lacking[2] in brahmanical literature, yet the law-book of Manu (XI, 33) says clearly and distinctly: "Without hesitation the Brahman shall make use of the sacred texts of the Atharvaveda; the word, indeed, is the weapon of the Brahman; therewith may he kill his enemies." Thus also in the Atharvaveda we find a whole series of magic incantations and exorcisms in the interest of the Brahmans. In these hymns the inviolability of the Brahmans and their possessions is repeatedly emphasized in the strongest manner, and the heaviest curses are pronounced

---

[1]) Translated by R. T. H. *Griffith.* In Southern India, even in much later times, the Battle Drum was an object of worship, and "was regarded with the same veneration that regiments used to bestow upon the regimental flag in the armies of Europe." H. A. *Popley,* The Music of India, London, 1921, p. 11.

[2]) See above, pp. 125 f.

against those who assail the property and lives of the Brahmans. Besides this, the mystical meaning of the Dakṣiṇa, *i.e.* the sacrificial fee, is emphasized in the most extravagant expressions. The heaviest of all sins is to oppress Brahmans; the highest summit of piety is to give them liberal fees for sacrifice; these are the fundamental ideas running through all these songs, which are among the most unedifying of the whole Atharvaveda. Only a few of the better of these hymns contain prayers for enlightenment, wisdom, fame and theological knowledge. All songs belonging to this class might unhesitatingly be included amongst the latest parts of the Atharvaveda collection.

Among the later parts of the Saṃhitā are also the songs and charms composed for sacrificial purposes, which probably were included in the Atharvaveda only in order that the latter, like the other three Vedas, might be brought into connection with the sacrifice and be recognised as a real "Veda." Thus, for example, we find two Aprī[1] hymns and other songs corresponding to the sacrificial chants of the Ṛgveda. Prose formulæ, too, which correspond to those of the Yajurveda, are to be found, for example, in Book XVI, the entire first half of which consists of formulæ in which water is glorified, and which refer to some purification-ritual or other. Book XVIII, which contains the prayers pertaining to the death ritual and to ancestor-worship, should be included among this class of hymns. The funeral songs of Book X of the Ṛgveda,[2] recur here literally, though they are increased by many additions. Also Book XX, which was added quite late, and the hymns of which, with few exceptions, are all borrowed from the Ṛgveda, is related to the soma-sacrifice. The only new hymns in this book are the very curious

---

[1]) See above, pp. 94 f.

[2]) See above, pp. 95 ff.

"Kuntāpa hymns,"[1] Ath., XX, 127-136. They, too, form part of the sacrificial ritual as liturgies, while in content they coincide partly with the Dānastutis of the Ṛgveda,[2] by praising the liberality of certain princes; partly they are riddles and their solutions,[3] but partly also obscene songs and coarse jokes. At certain sacrifices, which lasted for many days, hymns of this kind constituted the prescribed conversation of the priests.[4]

The last class of hymns of the Atharvaveda which have still to be mentioned, are the hymns of theosophical and cosmogonic contents, which doubtlessly belong to the latest parts of the Atharvaveda. Nothing, indeed, seems further from magic than philosophy, and one might well wonder at the fact that the Atharvaveda-Saṃhitā contains, besides magic incantations, spells and benedictions, also hymns of philosophical content. However, if we look more closely at these hymns, we shall soon find that they, like the magic songs, mostly serve only practical purposes.[5] It is not the yearning and searching for truth, for the solution of dark riddles of the universe, which inspires the authors of these hymns, but they, too, are only conjurers who pose as philosophers, by misusing the well known philosophical expressions in an ingenious, or rather artificial, web of foolish and nonsensical plays of fancy, in order to create an impression of the mystical, the mysterious. What at the first glance

---

1) What the name "Kuntāpa" signifies is not known.

2) See above, pp. 114 f.

3) Like those of the Ṛgveda. See above, pp. 117 f.

4) A detailed account of the Kuntāpa hymns has been given by M. *Bloomfield*, The Atharvaveda (Grundriss, II, 1 B), pp. 96 ff. They were probably part of the jollification on the occasion of the bestowal of the dakṣiṇā, which "in many instances must have led to gormandizing and drunkenness,......followed......by shallow witticisms, by obscene talk, and worse" (l.c., p. 100).

5) *Cf. F. Edgerton*, The Philosophical Materials of the Atharva Veda (Studies in Honor of Maurice Bloomfield, New Haven, 1920, pp. 117 ff.).

appears to us as profundity, is often in reality nothing but empty mystery-mongering, behind which there is more nonsense than profound sense ; and indeed, mystery-mongering and the concealment of reality under a mystical veil, are part of the magician's trade. Yet these philosophical hymns presuppose a fairly high development of metaphysical thought. The chief ideas of the Upaniṣads, the conception of a highest god as creator and preserver of the world (Prajāpati), and even the ideas of an impersonal creative principle, besides a number of philosophical terms, such as brahman, tapas, asat, prāṇa, manas, must, at the time when these hymns originated, already have been the common property of large circles. Therefore, too, we must not look upon the theosophical and cosmogonic hymns of the Atharvaveda as representing a step in the development of Indian philosophy. The productive thoughts of the truly philosophical hymns of the Ṛgveda have attained their further development only in the Upaniṣads, and the philosophical hymns of the Atharvaveda can in no way be regarded as a transition-step from the oldest philosophy to that of the Upaniṣads. "They stand," as Deussen says, "not so much inside the great course of development, as, rather, by its side." [1]

Many a deep and truly philosophical idea occasionally flashes forth in these hymns out of the mystical haze, but in most cases, it may be said that the Atharvan poet is not the originator of these ideas, that he has only utilized for his own purposes the ingeniousness of others. Thus it is certainly an idea worthy of a philosopher, that *Kāla, Time,* is the first cause of all existence. Yet, it is the language of the mystic and not of the philosopher, when we read in Ath. XIX, 53 :[2]

---

[1]) *Deussen*, AGPh. I, 1, p. 209.

[2]) On this hymn see F. O. *Schrader* Uber den Stand der indischen Philosophie zur Zeit Mahāvīras und Buddhas, 1902, pp. 20 f.

"Time, the steed, runs with seven reins (rays), thousand-eyed, ageless, rich in seed. The seers, thinking holy thoughts, mount him, all the beings (worlds) are his wheels.

With seven wheels does this Time ride, seven naves has he, immortality is his axle. He carries hither all these beings (worlds). Time, the first god, now hastens onward.

A full jar has been placed upon Time; him, verily, we see existing in many forms. He carries away all these beings (worlds); they call him Time in the highest heaven." and so on.

Certainly, the idea that Kāla, Time, has brought forth everything, finds worthy expression in the two verses 5 and 6:

"Time begot yonder heaven, Time also (begot) these earths. That which was, and that which shall be, urged forth by Time, spreads out.

Time created the earth, in Time the sun burns. In Time are all beings, in Time the eye looks abroad."[1]

But immediately in the following verses and in the following hymn (Ath. XIX, 54) all kinds of things are enumerated in a quite mechanical manner as originating in Time, and especially the various names of the Divine, as they were known at that time, are enumerated as being created by Kāla, thus Prajāpati, thus Brahman, thus Tapas (asceticism), prāṇa (breath of life), and so on.

More mystery-mongering than true philosophy is to be found also in the long Rohita hymns, of which Book XIII of the Atharvaveda consists, in which, moreover, all kinds of disconnected matter appears to be thrown together in motley confusion. Thus, for instance, in the first hymn, Rohita, "the red one," *i.e.* the sun or a genius of the sun, is extolled as creative principle—"he created the heaven and the earth," "with strength he secured the earth and heaven"—; at the same time, however, an earthly king is

---

[1]) Translated by *Bloomfield*, SBE., Vol. 42, p. 224.

glorified, and the heavenly king Rohita brought into connection with the earthly king in an intentionally confused manner. In the middle of it, however, we find also imprecations against enemies and rivals and against those who strike a cow with their feet, or make water against the sun.[1] Again in hymn XIII, 3, in a few verses whose pathos recalls the above-quoted Varuṇa hymn, Rohita is extolled as the highest being, but a refrain is attached, in which the same Rohita is told to crush, in his anger, him who torments a Brahman. For example :

"He who engendered these, the earth and heaven,
who made the worlds the mantle that he weareth,
In whom abide the six wide-spreading regions
through which the bird's keen vision penetrateth,
This God is wroth offended by the sinner who wrongs
the Brahman who hath gained this knowledge.
Agitate him, O Rohita; destroy him : entangle in thy
snares the Brahman's tyrant. [1]
He from whom winds blow pure in ordered season,
from whom the seas flow forth in all directions,
This God, etc. [2]
He who takes life away, he who bestows it; from
whom comes breath to every living creature,
This God, etc. [3]
Who with the breath he draws sates earth and
heaven, with expiration fills the ocean's belly,
This God, etc." [2]

By the side of such sublime glorifications of Rohita, however, there are to be found instances of the mystical play of ideas, as when it is said that the two sacrificial melodies

---

[1]) Bloomfield compares this with Hesiod.

μηδ'αγιηελιου τετsαμμενος bσυος bμιγειν (Εργὰ × αι ημεραι 725).

Cf. Protagoras (Diog. Laert, VIII, 1, 19) :

προς ηλιου τετραμμενον μη ομιγειν.

[2]) Translated by R. T. H. *Griffith*.

Bṛhat and Rathantara have brought forth Rohita, or when the metre Gāyatrī is designated as "the lap of immortality." It would be vain to attempt to lighten the mystical semi-darkness which surrounds such and similar verses. I do not think, therefore, that we have to look for great philosophical truths in a hymn like Ath. IV, 11, where the Ox is extolled as the creator and preserver of the world:

> "The Ox bears the earth and the sky.
> The Ox bears the wide atmosphere.
> The Ox bears the six wide spheres of heaven,
> The Ox penetrates the whole universe."

Nor are we much impressed by the fact that this ox is identified with Indra and others of the highest gods, still less by the fact that he yields milk, "his milk is the sacrifice, the priestly fee is his milking," and we willingly believe that "he who knows the seven inexhaustible milkings of the ox, gains offspring and heaven." This ox is of no more importance than the bull that is extolled extravagantly in Ath. IX, 4—he bears all forms in his sides, he was in the beginning an image of the primeval water, and so on,—and that is finally discovered to be only an ordinary sacrificial bull which is to be slaughtered. The fact, however, that this pseudo-philosophy and mystery-mongering at bottom pursues a very practical purpose, is proved by such a hymn as Ath. X, 10. Here the great mystery of the cow is announced: heaven and earth and the waters are protected by the cow. A hundred pails, a hundred milkers, a hundred cow-herds are on her back. The gods who breathe in the cow, they know the cow. The cow is the mother of the warrior, sacrifice is the weapon of the cow, thought originated in her. In this manner it proceeds till this secret doctrine reaches its climax in the words: "The cow alone is called Immortality, the cow alone is worshipped as death; the cow became this universe, gods, people, asuras, manes and seers (they all are the cow)." But now follows the practical use: Only he who knows this great secret may accept a cow as a gift, and he who gives a cow to the Brahmans, gains all worlds, for in the cow is enclosed all the highest—Ṛta (the order of the universe), Brahman (the world-soul) and Tapas (asceticism)—and:

> "The gods live by the cow, and also man lives by the cow;
> The cow is this whole world, as far as the sun looks down."

Just as the Rohita, the Ox, and the Cow are praised as the Highest Being, so there is one hymn (XI, 5) in which the *Brahmacārin*, the Vedic student, is celebrated in a similar way. And again in the still more mysterious cycle of hymns forming Book XV of the Saṃhitā, the Highest Brahman is conceived and exalted as the *Vrātya*,—both as the heavenly Vrātya, identified with the Great God (mahādeva), the Lord (īśāna) Rudra, and as his prototype, the earthly Vrātya. The Vrātyas were certain, probably Eastern, tribes, whether Aryan or non-Aryan, but certainly living outside the pale of Brahmanism, roving about in bands—on rough waggons covered with boards in a rather war-like fashion, owners of cattle, having their own peculiar customs and religious cults, whose members however could be received into brahmanical society by means of certain sacrificial rites and ceremonies. Such a Vrātya who has already been converted to Brahmanism, seems to be glorified in the Vrātya-book of the Atharvaveda.[1)]

---

1) See A. *Weber* and Th. *Aufrecht* in Ind. Stud, I, 1850; A. *Hillebrandt*, Ritual-Litteratur (Grundriss III, 2), pp. 139 f.; M. *Bloomfield*, The Atharvaveda (Grundriss, II, 1 B) pp 96 ff.; Chas. *Lanman*, HOS., Vol. 8, pp. 769 ff. *Macdonell* and *Keith*, Vedic Index, II, pp. 341 ff. Rājārām Rāmkrishna *Bhāgavat*, JBRAS., 19, 1896, 357 ff. considers the Vrātyas to be non-Aryans. J. *Charpentier* (WZKM. 23, 151 ff.; 25, 355 ff.) considers the Vrātyas to be early worshippers of Rudra Siva, see *Keith*, JRAS. 1913, 155 ff. According to J. W. *Hauer*, Die Anfänge der Yogapraxis, Berlin 1922, pp. 11 ff. 172 ff they were ecstatics of the Kṣatriya class and fore-runners of the Yogins. (*f.* Winternitz in Festschrift für L. Scherman.

Deussen [1] has taken endless trouble to discover sense and meaning in the "philosophical" hymns of the Atharvaveda, and to establish certain coherent ideas in them. He finds, for instance, in Ath. X, 2, and XI, 8, the idea that deals with the "realisation of Brahman in man," and this in X, 2, "more from the physical teleological aspect," and XI, 8, "more from the psychical aspect." [2] I cannot discover so much philosophy in these hymns; I believe, rather, that here too we have only pseudo-philosophers, who did not announce a new doctrine of the world-soul in man, but who found this doctrine already existing in entirety and proclaimed it in mystically confused disconnectedness. While in a celebrated hymn of the Ṛgveda (X, 121) a deep thinker and a true poet refers in bold words to the splendour of the cosmos and sceptically asks about the creator, in Atharvaveda, X, 2, a verse-maker enumerates, one after the other, all the limbs of man, and asked who has created them:

> "By whom are the heels of man created? By whom the flesh, by whom the ankles, by whom the well-formed fingers? By whom the openings?...Why have they made the ankles of man below and the knee caps above? Why have the legs been placed apart from each other, and where are the joints of the knees? Who has thought that out?" etc.

Thus it proceeds throughout eight verses. Then follow nine verses, in which all kinds of things that belong to the human organism, and indeed to human life in general, are enquired about: "Whence come likes and dislikes, whence sleep, fear, fatigue, whence all joys and pleasures of mankind? Whence poverty and misery?" etc. In the same tone, all sorts of miscellaneous questions are asked, such as, who has

---

[1]) AGPh., I, 1, pp. 209 ff.

Cf. also Lucian *Scherman*, Philosophische Hymnen aus der Rig-und Atharva-Veda-Samhitā, verglichen mit den Philosophemen der älteren Upanishads, Strassburg, 1887.

[2]) Deussen, *loc. cit.*, pp. 264 ff.

placed water into the body, blood into the veins, whence man has obtained stature, height and name, who has endowed him with gait, intelligence, breath, truth and untruth, immortality and death, clothing, long life, strength and speed, and so on. Then further is asked whence man obtains his mastery over nature, and all these questions are answered with the reply that man as Brahman (world-soul) has become what he is, and attained all his power. So far the hymn is not exactly beautiful, but at least fairly clear. But now follows the usual mystical humbug in the closing verses 26-33, where, for instance, it is said :

> "Having sewn his heart and his head together, the Atharvan being above the brain as a purifier stimulated (him) from above the head. [26]
>
> To the Atharvan forsooth this head belongs, a firmly-locked box of the gods, and this head is protected by the breath, by food and by the mind." [27]

I think one would be honouring this kind of verses too much by seeking deep wisdom in them. Therefore, I cannot find such deep sense in the hymn Ath. XI, 8, as Deussen does, who tells us that it describes "the origin of man through the contact of psychic and physical factors which themselves are altogether dependent upon Brahman." Just as the liar must sometimes speak truth, in order that one may believe his lies, so the pseudo-philosopher, too, must introduce here and there into his fabrications a real, philosophical idea which he has "picked up" somewhere or other, in order that one may take his nonsense for the height of wisdom. Thus, the idea of Brahman as the first cause of all existence and of the oneness of man with the world-soul, is certainly at the basis of the hymn XI, 8. However, I do not think that the author had any idea in his mind while composing the words :

> "Whence was Indra, whence Soma, whence Agni born? Whence originated Tvaṣṭar ("the Fashioner")? Whence was Dhātar ("the Creator") born?

From Indra was Indra born, Soma from Soma, and Agni from Agni.
Tvaṣṭar came of Tvaṣṭar, and Dhātar is born of Dhātar."

Immeasurably higher than this verse-making, which is neither philosophy nor poetry, stands *one* hymn of the Atharvaveda, which, on account of a few verses which relate to the origin of the earth, is usually included among the cosmogonic hymns, but which is free from any and every kind of mysticism and really contains very little philosophy, but so much the more true poetry. It is the magnificent hymn to Earth, Ath. XII, 1. In sixty-three verses the Mother Earth is here extolled as the supporter and preserver of everything earthly, and entreated for happiness and blessing and protection from all evil. Just a few verses in R. T. H. Griffith's translation must suffice to give an idea of one of the most beautiful productions of the religious poetry of Ancient India:

"Truth, high and potent Law, the Consecrating Rite,
Fervour, Brahma, and Sacrifice uphold the Earth.
May she, the Queen of all that is and is to be, may
Pṛithivī make ample space and room for us. [1]

She who at first was water in the ocean, whom with their wondrous powers the sages followed,
May she whose heart is in the highest heaven, compassed about with truth, and everlasting,
May she, this Earth, bestow upon us lustre, and grant us power in loftiest dominion. [8]

She whom the Aśvins measured out, o'er whom the foot of Viṣṇu strode,
Whom Indra, Lord of Power and Might, freed from all foemen for himself,
May Earth pour out her milk for us, a mother unto me her son. [10]

O Pṛithivī, auspicious be thy woodlands, auspicious be thy hills and snow-clad mountains.
Unslain, unwounded, unsubdued, I have set foot upon the Earth,
On Earth, brown, black, ruddy and every-coloured, on the firm earth that Indra guards from danger. [11]

Produced from thee, on thee move mortal creatures : thou bearest them, both quadruped and biped.

Thine, Pṛithivī, are these Five human Races, for whom, though mortal, Sūrya as he rises spreads with his rays the light that is immortal. [15]

On earth they offer sacrifice and dressed oblation to the gods, men, mortals, live upon the earth by food in their accustomed way.

May that Earth grant us breath and vital power,
Pṛithivī give me life of long duration ! [22]

Let what I dig from thee, O Earth, rapidly spring and grow again,
O Purifier, let me not pierce through thy vitals or thy heart. [35]

May she, the Earth, whereon men sing and dance with varied shout and noise,
Whereon men meet in battle, and the war-cry and the drum resound,
May she drive off our foemen, may Pṛithivī rid me of my foes. [41]

Supporting both the foolish and the weighty she bears the death both of the good and evil.

In friendly concord with the boar, Earth opens herself for the wild swine that roams the forest. [48]

O Earth, my Mother, set thou me happily in a place secure,
Of one accord with Heaven, O Sage, set me in glory and in wealth." [63]

This hymn, which might just as well be found in the Ṛgveda-Saṃhitā, proves that in the Saṃhitā of the Atharvaveda, too, there are scattered manifold fragments of ancient poetry, although the latter Saṃhitā, more than the Ṛgveda, pursues one definite purpose. In this collection, too, as in that of the Ṛgveda, by the side of much that is of little value or absolutely worthless, there are rare gems of the oldest Indian poetic art. Only *both works together* give us a real idea of the oldest poetry of the Aryan Indians.

The Ancient Indian Sacrifice and the Vedic Samhitās.

The two Saṃhitās which have so far been discussed have in common the fact that they were not compiled for special liturgical purposes. Although most of the hymns of the

Ṛgveda could be, and actually were used for sacrificial purposes, and although the songs and spells of the Atharvaveda were almost throughout employed for ritualistic and magic purposes, yet the collection and arrangement of the hymns in these Saṃhitās have nothing to do with the various liturgical and ritualistic purposes. The hymns were collected for their own sake and arranged and placed, in both these collections, with regard to their supposed authors or the singer-schools to which they belonged, partly also according to their contents and still more their external form—number of verses and such like. They are as we may say, collections of songs which pursue a *literary* object.

It is quite different with the Saṃhitās of the two other Vedas, the Sāmaveda and the Yajurveda. In these collections we find the songs, verses, and benedictions arranged according to their practical purposes, in exactly the order in which they were used at the sacrifice. These are, in fact, nothing more than prayer-books and song-books for the practical use of certain sacrificial priests—not indeed written books, but texts, which existed only in the heads of teachers and priests and were preserved by means of oral teaching and learning in the priests' schools.[1] Now, in order to explain the origin of these Saṃhitās, it is necessary to insert here a few words about the cult of the Aryan Indians. This is the more advisable as a complete understanding of the Vedic literature in general is altogether impossible without a certain insight into the ancient Indian sacrificial cult.

So far back as we can trace the Vedic-Brahmanic religion there have always been two varieties of the cult. We have seen [2] that certain hymns of the Ṛgveda and a large number of songs and charms of the Atharvaveda were used as benedictions and prayers at birth and marriage and other

---

1) *Cf.* above, p. 36.

2) *Cf.* above, pp. 95 ff., 107 ff., 135 f.

occasions of daily life, at funerals and ancestor-worship, as well as at the various ceremonies which had to be performed by the herdsman for the prosperity of the cattle and by the farmer for the growth of the fruits of the field. The Indians call these ceremonies, mostly also connected with sacrifices, "*gṛhyakarmaṇī*," *i.e.* "domestic ceremonies." Concerning these the Gṛhyasūtras, which will be mentioned later, give us detailed information. At the sacrifices which this domestic cult required, the householder himself, who was assisted at most by *one single priest*, the "Brahman," occupied the position of the sacrificial priest.[1] So far as these sacrifices were burnt offerings, the *one fire* of the domestic hearth served as the altar for their presentation. Beside these sacrifices, which every pious Aryan, whether poor or rich, whether aristocratic or humble, performed according to ancient usage, there were also great sacrificial feasts—especially in connection with the Soma-cult relating to Indra, the god of the warriors,—which could only be celebrated by the aristocratic and wealthy, more especially by the kings. On an extensive sacrificial place set up according to firmly established rules, altars were erected for the *three sacred fires*, which were necessary at every sacrifice of this kind, and a multitude of priests, headed by *four chief priests*, were occupied with the performance of the innumerable, extremely intricate rites and ceremonies required for such a sacrifice. The Yajamāna or "sacrificer," the prince or great man, who offered the sacrifice, had very little to do; his chief duty lay in giving the priests a liberal payment for the sacrifice (dakṣiṇā). No wonder that the Brahmans selected these sacrifice-ceremonies, by which they gained the most, as the

[1]) Āśvalāyana—Gṛhyasūtra I, 3, 6: The appointment of a Brahman is optional at domestic sacrifices. Gobhila-Gṛhyasūtra I, 9, 8 f. The Brahman is the only priest at the Pākayajñas (*i.e.* the "simple sacrifices" of the domestic cult); the sacrificer himself is the Hotar (the priest who recites the verses).

subject of enthusiastic study, that they developed a regular science of sacrifice, which is set forth in those texts with which we shall become acquainted as Brāhmaṇas, and which form an essential part of the *Śruti*, the "Revelation," *i.e.* of that literature to which, in the course of time, divine origin has been ascribed. These sacrifices, therefore, were called *śrauta-karmāṇi*," "ceremonies based upon Śruti," in contrast to the domestic (gṛhya) ceremonies, which are based only upon *Smṛti*, "memory," *i.e.* tradition, and possess no divine authority.

Now the four chief priests who were occupied with the Śrauta sacrifices are: (1) The *Hotar* or "caller," who recites the verses (ṛcaḥ) of the hymns in order to praise the gods and invite them to the sacrifice; (2) the *Udgātar* or "singer," who accompanies the preparation and presentation of the sacrifices, especially of the Soma libations, with chants (sāman); (3) the *Adhvaryu* or "executor of the sacrifice," who performs all the sacrificial acts, at the same time muttering the prose prayers and sacrifice formulae (yajus), and (4) the *Brahman* or high priest, whose office it is to protect the sacrifice from harm. For every sacred act, therefore, every sacrifice too is, according to the Indian view, exposed to a certain amount of danger; if an act is not performed exactly in accordance with the ritualistic prescription, if a spell or a prayer formula is not spoken correctly, or if a melody is sung incorrectly, then the sacred act may bring destruction upon the originator of the sacrifice. Therefore the Brahman sits in the south of the place of sacrifice, in order to protect the sacrifice: the south being the haunt of the god of death, and the haunt from which the demons hostile to the sacrifice, threaten the people. He follows the course of the whole sacrifice mentally, and as soon as he notices the least mistake in a sacrificial act, in a recitation or in a chant, he must, by pronouncing sacred words, make good the harm. Therefore the Brahman is called in an old text "the best physician among the sacrificial priests." [1] But in order to be able to fulfil this office the Brahman must be "full of the veda"; he fulfils his office as sacrificial priest "with the threefold knowledge," *i.e.* by means of his knowledge of the three Vedas, which puts him in the position of being able instantly to detect every error.[2]

On the other hand, the three other priests need only know *one* Veda each. The verses with which the Hotar calls the gods to the sacrifice, the so-called "verses of invitation" (anuvākyās), and the verses with which he accompanies the gifts, the so-called "verses of sacrifice" (yājyās), the Hotar takes from the Ṛgveda. He must also know the Ṛgveda-Saṃhitā, *i.e.* he must have memorized it, in order to compile out of it the so-called Śastras or "songs of praise" which he had to recite at the Soma sacrifice. Thus the Ṛgveda Saṃhitā stands in a certain relationship to the hotar, although it is in no wise collected or arranged for the purposes of this priest.

However, to the Soma-sacrifice belong not only the songs of praise *recited* by the hotar, but also so-called stotras or "songs of praise," which are *sung* by the udgātar and his assistants.[3] Such stotras consist of song-stanzas, *i.e.* stanzas (ṛcah) which had been made the bearers of certain melodies (sāman). These melodies, as well as the song-verses with which they were connected, were learnt by the udgātar-priests

---

1) Śatapatha-Brāhmaṇa—XIV, 2, 2, 19. *Cf* Chāndogya-Upaniṣad IV, 17, 8 f.

2) Aitareya-Āraṇyaka, III, 2, 3, 6. Śatapatha-Brāhmaṇa XI, 5, 8, 7. Only at a later period was the Brahman brought into relationship with the *Atharvaveda*, so that the Atharvaveda was sometimes actually called "Brahmaveda" or "the Veda of the Brahman" and the adherents of the Atharvaveda declared that the Brahman must be a knower of the Atharvaveda-Samhitā. In reality the office of the Brahman at the Śrauta-sacrifice has nothing to do with the Atharvaveda. However, we can understand that the two were connected with each other. For, if the Brahman, as remarked above, officiated as the only priest at Gṛhya-sacrifices, he certainly had to be familiar with the benedictions which occur, for the most part, in the Atharvaveda.

3) In fact the chants (stotras) come *first*, and then the recitations (Śastras).

in the schools of the *Sāmaveda*, and the Sāmaveda-Saṃhitās are nothing but collections of texts which have been collected for the uses of the udgātars, not for their own sake, but because of the melodies the bearers of which they were.

Finally, the Adhvaryu-priest, at his innumerable sacrificial rites, has to utter, in low voice, partly short prose formulae, partly longer prayers in prose and verse—the prose formulae and prayers are called *yajus* (plur. yajūṃsi), the verses ṛc (plur. ṛcah).[1] In the Saṃhitās of the *Yajurveda* all these prose formulae and prayers, mostly accompanied by rules and discussions on the sacrificial acts at which they are to be uttered, are collected for the purposes of the Adhvaryu-priest, in the order in which they were used at the sacrifices.

We now turn to the discussion of the liturgical Saṃhitās, as, according to what has just been stated, we may call the Saṃhitās of the Sāmaveda and the Yajurveda, in contrast to those of the Ṛgveda and the Atharvaveda.

The Sāmveda-Saṃhitā.

Of the many Saṃhitās of the Sāmaveda which are said to have existed once—the Purāṇas even speak of a thousand Saṃhitās—,[2] only three have come down to us.[3] The best known of these, the Sāmaveda-Saṃhitā of the Kauthumas,[4]

[1]) The Hotar *recites* the hymns, *i.e.* he repeats them aloud in a kind of sing-song, the udgātar *sings* the songs of praise to certain melodies, the adhvaryu *mutters* the prayers. Only the " Nigadas," a variation of the Yajus-formulae, which serve the purpose of summoning the other priests to their various occupations, naturally had to be uttered loudly by the adhvaryu.

[2]) Later authors also speak of a thousand schools of the Sāmaveda. Cf. R *Simon*, Beiträge zur Kenntnis der vedischen Schulen (Kiel 1889), pp. 27, 30 f.

[3]) The Saṃhitā of the Rāṇayanīyas has been edited and translated by J. *Stevenson*, London, 1842; that of the Kauthumas by Th. *Benfey*, Leipzig, 1848, and by Satyavrata *Sāmaśramin*, Bibl. Ind., 1871 ff. The Jaiminīya-Saṃhitā has been edited by W *Caland* (Indische Forschungen, 2, Breslau 1907).

[4]) About this and the other two Saṃhitās see *Caland*, l.c., Introduction. See also *Oldenberg*, GGA, 1908, 711 ff.

consists of two parts, the Ārcika or the "verse-collection" and the Uttarārcika, the "second verse-collection." Both parts consist of verses, which nearly all recur in the Ṛgveda. Of the 1810—or, if we subtract the repetitions, 1549—verses, which are contained in the two parts together, all but 75 are also found in the Ṛgveda-Saṃhitā and, mostly in Books VIII and IX of the latter. Most of these verses are composed in Gāyatrī metre or in Pragātha stanzas which are made up of Gāyatrī and Jagatī lines, and doubtless the stanzas and songs composed in these metres were from the beginning intended for singing.[1] The seventy-five verses which do not occur in the Ṛgveda, are partly found in other Saṃhitās, partly in various works on ritual ; some may be taken from a recension unknown to us, but some are only pieced together out of sundry verses of the Ṛgveda without any proper meaning. Some of the verses of the Ṛgveda met with in the Sāmaveda offer divergent readings, and it has been believed that a more ancient text might be recognized in them. But Theodor Aufrecht,[2] has already shown that the divergent readings of the Sāmaveda are due only to arbitrary, intentional or accidental alterations—alterations such as also occur elsewhere where words are prepared for music. For in the Sāmaveda, in the Ārcika as well as in the Uttarārcika, the text is only a means to an end. The essential element is always the melody, and the purpose of *both* parts is that of teaching the melodies. The scholar, who wished to be trained as an udgātar-priest in the schools of the Sāmaveda, had first to learn the melodies : this was done with the aid of the Ārcika ; then only could he

---

[1]) This is proved by the very names "Gāyatrī" and "Pragātha," which are derived from the verb "gā" (resp. pragā) "to sing." See H. *Oldenberg*, ZDMG, 38, 1884, 439 ff., 464 ff.

[2]) In the preface to his edition of the hymns of the Ṛgveda (2nd ed., Bonn 1877) II, pp. xxxviii ff. See also J. *Brune*, Zur Textkritik der dem Samaveda mit dem achten Maṇḍala des Ṛgveda gemeinsamen Stellen, Diss, Kiel, 1909, who comes to the same conclusion as *Aufrecht*, l.c., and *Oldenberg*, Hymnen des Rigveda 1, pp. 289 f.

memorize the stotras as they were sung at the sacrifice, for which purpose the Uttarārcika served.

The first part of our Sāmaveda-Saṃhitā, the Ārcika, consists of five hundred and eighty-five single stanzas (ṛc) to which the various melodies (sāman) belong, which were used at the sacrifice. The word *sāman*, although frequently used for the designation of the text which had been either made or destined for singing, means originally only "tune" or "melody." As we say that a verse is sung "to a certain tune," thus the Indians say the reverse: This or that melody (sāman) is "sung upon a particular stanza." The Vedic theologians, however, conceive the relationship of melody and stanza in such a way that they say, the melody has *originated* out of the stanza. The stanza (ṛc) is therefore called the Yoni, *i.e.* "the womb," out of which the melody came forth. And although naturally a stanza can be sung to various melodies, and one melody can be used for different stanzas, yet there are certain stanzas, which as a rule, may be considered as the texts—the "yonis," as the Indian technical term goes—for certain melodies. The Arcika, then, is nothing but a collection of five hundred and eighty-five "yonis" or single stanzas, which are sung to about double the number of different tunes.[1] It may be compared to a song-book, in which only the text of the *first stanza* of each song is given as an aid to the recollection of the tune.

The Uttarārcika, the second part of the Sāmaveda-Samhitā, consists of four hundred chants, mostly of three stanzas each,[2] out of which the stotras which are sung at the chief sacrifices are formed. While in the Arcika the stanzas are arranged partly according to the metre, partly according to

---

[1]) See *Oldenberg*, GGA, 1908, 712 A.

[2]) 287 songs consist of 3 verses each, 66 of 2 each, 13 of one verse, 10 of 6 each, 9 of four each, 4 of 5 each, 3 of 9 each, the same number of 10 each, 2 of 7 each, and the same number of 12 each, and one song consists of 8 verses.

the gods to which they are addressed (in the sequence: Agni, Indra, Soma), the chants in the Uttarārcika are arranged according to the order of the principal sacrifices.[1] A stotra then, consists of several, usually three stanzas, which are all sung to the same tune, namely to one of the tunes which the Ārcika teaches. We may compare the Uttarārcika to a song-book in which the complete text of the songs is given, while it is presumed that the melodies are already known. It is usually assumed that the Uttarārcika is of later origin than the Ārcika.[2] In favour of this assumption is the fact that the Ārcika contains many "yonis," therefore also many melodies, which do not occur at all in the chants of the Uttarārcika, and that the Uttarārcika also contains some songs for which the Ārcika teaches no melody. On the other hand, however, the Uttarārcika is an essential completion of the Arcika: the latter is as it were, the first, the former the second course in the instruction of the udgātar.

Both parts of the Samhitā give us only the texts as they are *spoken*. The *melodies* themselves, in any case in the earliest times, were taught by oral, and probably also instrumental rendering. Of later origin are the so-called Gānas or "song-books" proper (from gā "to sing"), which designate the melodies by means of musical notes, and in which the texts are drawn up in the form which they take in singing, *i.e.* with all the extensions of syllables, repetitions and interpolations of syllables and even of whole words—the so-called "stobhas," as hoyi, hūva, hōi, and so on, which are partly not unlike our huzzas and other shouts of

---

1) On the stotras of the Sāmaveda and their use at the sacrifice, see A. *Hillebrandt*, Rituallitteratur, "Grundriss," III, 2, pp. 99 ff.

2) *Caland* (De wording van den Sāmaveda, Amsterdam (Akad.), 1907; Die Jaiminīya-Samhitā, pp. 4 f. and WZKM, 22, 1908, 436 ff.) endeavours to prove that the Uttarārcika is older. *Oldenberg*, GGA, 1908, 713, 722, disputes this on good grounds. For the question of the origin of the Sāmaveda, see *Caland*, Eene unbekende Recencie van den Sāmaveda, Amsterdam (Akad.), 1906.

joy. The oldest notation is probably that by means of syllables, as ta, co, ṇa, etc. More frequent, however, is the designation of the seven notes by means of the figures 1, 2, 3, 4, 5, 6 and 7, with which the F, E, D, C, B, A, G, of our scale correspond. When singing, the priests emphasize these various notes by means of movements of the hands and the fingers.[1] There are, attached to the Ārcika, a Grāmageyagāna ("book of songs to be sung in the village" and an Araṇyagāna ("book of forest songs"). In the latter those melodies were collected, which were considered as dangerous (taboo), and therefore had to be learnt in the forest, not in the village.[2] There are also two other books of songs, the Uhagāna and the Uhyagāna. These were composed for the purpose of giving the Sāmans in the order in which they were employed at the ritual, the Uhagāna being connected with the Grāmageyagāna, the Uhyagāna with the Āranyagāna.[3]

The number of known melodies must have been a very large one,[4] and already at a very early period every melody had a special name. Not only are they often mentioned by these names in the ritual-books, but various symbolical meanings are also ascribed to them, and they play no insignificant part in the symbolism and mysticism of the Brāhmaṇas, Âraṇyakas and Upaniṣads, especially a few of them, such as the two melodies "Bṛhat" and "Rathantara," which already appear in the Ṛgveda. The priests and theologians certainly did not invent all these melodies themselves. The oldest of them were presumably popular melodies, to which in very early times semi-religious songs were sung at solstice

---

[1]) More details about this the most ancient music of the Indians can be found in A. C. *Burnell*, The Ârsheya Brāhmaṇa ...... of the Sāma Veda (Mangalore 1876), Introd., pp. xxviii, xli-xlviii.

[2]) See W. *Caland*, Die Jaiminīya-Samhitā, p. 10; H. *Oldenberg*, GGA, 1908, pp. 722 f.

[3]) See *Caland*, Die Jaiminīya-Samhitā, pp. 2 ff

[4]) A later author gives the number of Sāmans as 8,000! (R. *Simon*, *loc. cit.*, p. 31.)

celebrations and other national festivals, and yet others may date back as far as that noisy music with which pre-brahmanical wizard-priests not unlike the magicians, shamans and medicine-men of the primitive peoples—accompanied their wild songs and rites.[1] Traces of this popular origin of the sāman-melodies are seen already in the above-mentioned stobhas or shouts of joy, and especially in the fact that the melodies of the Sāmaveda were looked upon as possessing magic power even as late as in brahmanical times.[2] There is a ritual-book belonging to the Sāmaveda, called Sāmavidhāna-Brāhmaṇa, the second part of which is a regular handbook of magic, in which the employment of various Sāmans for magic purposes is taught. We may also see a survival of the connection of the Sāman-melodies with the pre-brahmanical popular belief and magic, in the fact that the brahmanical law-books teach that the recitation of the Ṛgveda and the Yajurveda must be interrupted as soon as the sound of a sāman is heard. Especially distinct is the rule in Āpastamba's law book,[3] where the barking of dogs, the braying of donkeys, the howling of wolves and jackals, the hooting of the owl, the sound of musical instruments, weeping, *and the tone of sāmans* are enumerated as sounds at which the Veda-study must be interrupted.

Thus, then, the Sāmaveda-Saṃhitā is not without value

---

[1]) See A. *Hillebrandt*, Die Sonnwendfeste in Alt-Indien (Sep. aus der Festschrift für Konrad Hofmann), Erlangen 1889, pp. 22 ff. 34 ff., M. *Bloomfield*, The god Indra and the Sāma-veda, in WZKM, 17, 1903, pp. 156 ff.

[2]) The primary meaning of *Sāman* is probably "propitiatory song," "a means for appeasing gods and demons." The word sāman also occurs in the sense of "mildness, soothing words." In the older literature, when the Sāmaveda is quoted, it is usually with the words; "The Chandogas say." Chandoga means "Chandas-singer," and *chandas* combines in itself the meanings "magic song," "sacred text" and "metre." The fundamental meaning of the word must be something like "rhythmical speech"; it might be connected with the root chand "to please, to satisfy, or to cause to please," (*cf.* chanda, "pleasing, alluring, inviting").

[3]) 1, 3, 10, 19.

for the history of Indian sacrifice and magic, and the gānas attached to it are certainly very important for the history of Indian music,[1] even though as yet in no way exploited for this purpose. As a literary production, however, this Saṃhitā is practically worthless for us.

The Saṃhitās of the Yajurveda.

Just as the Sāmaveda-Saṃhitā is the song-book of the udgātar, so the Yajurveda-Saṃhitās are the *prayer-books* for the Adhvaryu priest. The grammarian Patañjali[2] speaks of "101 schools of the Veda of the Adhvaryus," and it is conceivable that many schools of just this Veda existed; for with reference to the separate sacrificial acts, such as the Adhvaryu had to execute and accompany with his prayers, differences of opinion and sectarian divisions could easily arise, which led to the formation of special manuals and prayer-books. The least deviation in the ceremonial or in the liturgy was sufficient cause for the formation of a new Vedic school. Up to the present we know the following five Saṃhitās and schools of the Yajurveda:

1. The **Kāṭhaka**, the Yajurveda-Saṃhitā in the recension of the Kaṭha-school.[3]

---

[1]) *Oldenberg* concludes his investigations of the Sāmaveda (GGA, 1908, 734) with the remark that these literary investigations "after all only touch upon the problems lying on the surface of the Sāmaveda"; for, in order to penetrate to greater depths, the philologist would have to be a student of the history of music as well. Since then we have gained an idea of the present-day mode of reciting the Sāmans in E. *Felber* (Die indische Musik der vedischen und der klassischen Zeit, mit Texten und Uebersetzungen von B. Geiger, SWA, 1912), based on the records of the Phonogramm-Archiv of the Vienna Academy. It is still doubtful, however, whether this necessarily teaches us how the ancient Udgātars sang 3,000 years ago. See also R. *Simon*, Die Notationen der vedischen Lieder-bücher (WZKM, 27, 1913, 305 ff.).

[2]) In the Introduction to his Mahābhāṣya.

[3]) Edited by L. v. *Schroeder*, Leipzig, 1900-1910, Index Verborum by R *Simon*, 1912. For the contents of the Kāṭhaka see A. *Weber*, Ind. Stud. 3,451 ff.; for the text and its interpretation s. *Keith*, JRAS, 1910, 517 ff.; 1912, 1095 ff.; *Caland*, ZDMG, 72, 1918, 12 ff.

2. The **Kapiṣṭhala-Kaṭha-Saṃhitā**, which is preserved only in a few fragments of manuscript.[1]

3. The **Maitrāyaṇī-Saṃhitā**, *i.e.* the Yajurveda-Saṃhitā in the recension of the Maitrāyaṇīya school.[2]

4. The Taittirīya-Saṃhitā, *i.e.* the Yajurveda-Saṃhitā in the recension of the Taittirīya school, also called "Āpastamba-Saṃhitā" after the Apastamba-school, one of the chief schools in which this text was taught.[3]

These four recensions are closely inter-related, and are designated as belonging to the "Black Yajurveda." Differing from them is

5. The Vājasaneyi-Saṃhitā or the Saṃhitā of the "White Yajurveda," which takes its name from Yājñavalkya Vājasaneya, the chief teacher of this Veda. Of this Vājasaneyi-Saṃhitā there are two recensions, that of the Kāṇva and that of the Mādhyandina-school, which however, differ very little from each other.[4]

The chief difference between the Saṃhitās of the "black" and the "white" Yajurveda lies in the fact that the Vājasaneyi-Saṃhitā contains only the Mantras, *i.e.* the prayers and sacrificial formulæ which the priest has to utter, while the Saṃhitās of the Black Yajurveda, besides the Mantras, contain a presentation of the sacrificial rites belonging to them, as well as discussions on the same. That is to say, in the Saṃhitās of the Black Yajurveda there is that which

---

1) See L. v. *Schroeder*, WZKM, 12, 362 f.

2) Edited by L. v. *Schroeder*, Leipzig, 1881-1886. Numerous passages from this Saṃhitā have been translated into German by L. *v. Schroeder*, Indiens Literatur und Kultur, Leipzig 1887, pp. 110-162. See also Schroeder, ZDMG, 33, 1879, 177 ff.; *Caland*, ZDMG, 72, 1918, 6 ff.

3) Edited by A. *Weber* in Ind. Stud. Vols. 11 and 12, 1871-72; with Sâyaṇa's commentary in Bibl. Ind, 1860-1899, and in Ān SS Nr. 42; translated into English by A. B. *Keith*, HOS, Vols. 18, 19, 1914.

4) Ed. by A. *Weber* (The White Yajurveda, Part I, The Vâjasaneyi-Saṃhitâ...... with the Commentary of Mahīdhara, Berlin-London 1852). Translated into English by R. T. H. *Griffith* (The Texts of the White Yajurveda), Benares, 1899.

is called "Brāhmaṇa" or "theological discussion," and which forms the contents of the Brāhmaṇas to be discussed in the next chapter, mixed with the Mantras. Now it is easily conceivable that in the prayer-books intended for the use of the Adhvaryus, the sacrificial rites themselves too were discussed, for these priests had above all to perform the separate sacrificial acts, and the muttering of prayers and formulas in the closest connection with these acts formed only a small part of their duties. It can therefore hardly be doubted that the Saṃhitās of the Black Yajurveda are *older* than the Vājasaneyi-Saṃhitā. Only later systematizers among the Yajurveda-theologians probably felt the necessity of having a Saṃhitā consisting only of Mantras analogous to the other Vedas, as well as a Brāhmaṇa separate from it.[1]

Significant, however, though the differences between the single Saṃhitās of the Yajurveda may have been for the priests and theologians of ancient India, yet for us they are quite inessential; and also as to time the various Saṃhitās of the Black and White Yajurveda are probably not very distant from each other. If, therefore, in the following lines I give a short description of the contents of the Vājasaneyi-Saṃhitā, then this is quite sufficient to give the reader an idea of the contents and character of the Saṃhitās of the Yajurveda in general.

---

[1]) It is usually assumed that the name "White" Yajurveda means "clear, well-arranged" Yajurveda, and that it indicates the clear distinction between sacrificial utterances and explanations of ritual in the same, while "black" Yajurveda means "unarranged" Yajurveda. This explanation, emanating from Indian commentators, seems very improbable to me. But already in Śatap. Br. XIV, 9, 4, 33 (*cf.* IV, 4, 5, 19) the "white sacrificial utterances" (Śuklāni yajūṃṣi) are called *ādityāni*, "revealed by the *sun*"; and the Purāṇas, too, relate that Yājñavalkya received new sacrificial utterances from the *sun* (Viṣṇu-Purāṇa, III, 5). I believe that the "*white* Yajurveda" owes its name to this connection with the sun. In contrast to this the older Yajurveda was then called the "black" one. It is most improbable "that the Saṃhitā of the white Yajurveda is most closely related to the original form of the Veda of the Adhvaryu," as Pischel thinks, KG, 172. *Cf. Keith*, HOS, Vol. 18, pp. lxxxv ff, on the mutual relationship of the Saṃhitās of the Yajurveda.

The Vājasaneyi-Saṃhitā consists of 40 sections, of which, however, the last 15 (perhaps even the last 22) are of later date. The first 25 sections contain the prayers for the most important great sacrifices. The first two sections give the prayers for the New and Full Moon sacrifices (Darśapūrṇamāsa) with the oblation to the Fathers (Piṇḍapitṛyajña) belonging to them. In the third section follow the prayers for the daily fire-cult, the laying of the fire, and the fire-sacrifices which have to be offered every morning and evening (Agnihotra), and the Sacrifices of the Seasons (Cāturmāsya) which take place every four months. The prayers for the Soma-sacrifice in general,[1] including the animal-sacrifice belonging to it, are to be found in sections IV to VIII. Among the Soma-sacrifices there are such as last *one* day, and such as last several days. To the one-day sacrifices belongs the Vājapeya or "Drink of Strength," a sacrifice offered originally probably only by warriors and kings, which was connected with a chariot-race, and at which, besides Soma, brandy (surā) also was offered, a drink otherwise proscribed according to brahmanical law.[2] Intended exclusively for kings is the "King's inauguration sacrifice" or Rājasūya, a sacrificial feast connected with many a popular usage: a symbolical military expedition, a play at dice, and all sorts of magic rites. The prayers for these two kinds of Soma-sacrifices are contained in sections IX and X. Then in sections XI to XVIII follow the numerous prayers and sacrificial formulæ for the Agnicayana or the "Building of

---

[1]) The sacrifices of the Ancient Indians fall into two great sub-divisions: *food sacrifices* (in which principally milk, butter, cake, pulp and grain were offered) and *Soma sacrifices* (whose chief component part is the soma-libations). The separate sacrifices may be classed under these two chief groups. The *animal sacrifice* is connected with sacrifices of the first division, as well as those of the second. In connection with every kind of sacrifice is the *fire-cult*, which is, to a certain extent, the preliminary of every kind of worship of the gods.

[2]) According to the law books, the drinking of brandy is as great a sin as the murder of a Brahman.

the Fire Altar," a ceremony which extends over a whole year, and to which a deep mystical-symbolical meaning is ascribed in the Brāhmaṇas. The fire-altar is named no other than "Agni" and is looked upon throughout as identical with the fire-god. It is built of 10,800 bricks, in the form of a large bird with outspread wings. In the lowest stratum of the altar the heads of five sacrificial animals are immured, and the bodies of the animals are thrown into the water out of which the clay for the manufacture of the bricks and the fire-pan is taken. The modelling and baking of the fire-pan and the separate bricks, many of which have special names and a symbolical significance of their own, is executed with much ceremoniousness accompanied by the continuous recitation of spells and prayer-formulæ. The following sections XIX to XXI give the prayers for the Sautrāmaṇī celebration, a remarkable sacrificial ceremony at which again, instead of the drink of soma, brandy is used and sacrificed to the Aśvins, to the goddess Sarasvatī and to Indra. The ceremony is recommended for one who has drunk too much Soma or with whom the Soma does not agree—and that may have been its original purpose—but also for a Brahman who desires success for himself, for a banished king who desires to regain his throne, for a warrior who desires victory, and for a Vaiśya who wishes to attain great riches. Many of the prayers belonging to this sacrifice refer to the legend of Indra, who was indisposed through intoxication from excessive enjoyment of Soma and had to be cured by the Aśvins and by Sarasvatī.[1] Finally, sections XXII to XXV, with which the old part of the Vājasaneyi-Saṃhitā ends, contain the prayers for the great Horse sacrifice (Aśvamedha), which only a powerful king, a mighty conqueror or "world-ruler," might offer. Old legends and epic poems tell of primeval kings, who performed this sacrifice, and it is looked upon as

---

[1]) *Cf.* above, p. 85.

the highest glory of a ruler, if it can be said of him: "He offered the Horse-sacrifice." The purpose of this great sacrifice is expressed very beautifully in the prayer Vāj.-Saṃh., XXII, 22:

> "O Brahman! May in this kingdom the Brahmin be born who shines through sacred knowledge! May the warrior who is a hero, a skilful shot, a good marksman, and a powerful chariot-fighter, be born here! Also the cow which yields good milk, the ox which draws well, the swift horse, the good housewife! May to this sacrificer a hero-son be born who is victorious, a mighty chariot-fighter and eloquent in the assembly! May Parjanya send us rain according to our desire! May our fruit-bearing plants ripen! May happiness and prosperity fall to our share!"

That the last fifteen sections are of later origin is not to be doubted. Sections XXVI to XXXV are designated even by Indian tradition itself as Khilas, *i.e.* "appendices," "supplements." Actually XXVI to XXIX contain only appendices to the prayers of the preceding sections. Section XXX is shown to be an addition even through the fact that it contains no prayers, but only an enumeration of the people who are to be sacrificed at the Puruṣamedha or "Human sacrifice" to the most diverse divine beings or to beings and powers for the moment elevated to divinity. No less than one hundred and eighty-four persons are to be slaughtered at this Puruṣamedha, there being offered, to give only a few examples, "to Priestly Dignity a Brahmin, to Royal Dignity a warrior, to the Maruts a Vaiśya, to Asceticism a Śūdra, to Darkness a thief, to Hell a murderer, to Evil a eunuch...........to Lust a harlot, to Noise a singer, to Dancing a bard, to Singing an actor.........to Death a hunter.........to the Dice a gambler ....to Sleep a blind man, to Injustice a deaf man.........to Lustre a fire-lighter.........to Sacrifice a washerwoman, to Desire a female dyer......to Yama a barren woman......to the Joy of Festival a lute-player, to Cry a flute-player... to

Earth a cripple..... to Heaven a bald-headed man," and so on. Surely it is hardly conceivable that all these classes of people should have been brought together and killed. We have to deal here probably only with a symbolical rite representing a kind of "human sacrifice" by which even the great horse-sacrifice was to be outdone, but which probably existed only as part of sacrificial mysticism and theory, and in reality hardly occurred.[1] With this agrees also the fact that section XXXI contains a version of the Puruṣasūkta, known to us from the Ṛgveda—*i.e.* of the hymn Ṛv. X, 90, in which the origin of the world through the sacrificing of the Puruṣa and the identification of the world with the Puruṣa are taught, Puruṣa, "Man," being conceived as the Highest Being,—and that this section, which the Brahman is to recite at the Puruṣamedha, is also called an Upaniṣad, *i.e.* a secret doctrine. Section XXXII, too, is in form and contents nothing but an Upaniṣad. The Creator Prajāpati is here identified with the Puruṣa and the Brahman. The first six verses of section XXXIV are similarly counted amongst the Upaniṣads, with the title Śivasaṃkalpa-Upaniṣad.[2] The prayers of sections XXXII to XXXIV are to be employed at the so-called Sarvamedha or "All-sacrifice." This is the highest sacrifice which exists at all, and which ends with the sacrificer's presenting the whole of his possessions to the priests as sacrificial fee and then retiring as a hermit into the forest there

---

[1]) So also *Oldenberg*, Religion des Veda, 2nd Ed., pp. 362 f. and *Keith*, HOS., Vol. 18, pp. cxxxviii, who says: "There can be no doubt that the ritual is a mere priestly invention to fill up the apparent gap in the sacrificial system which provided no place for man." *Hillebrandt* (Rituallitteratur, Grundriss III, 2, pp.153), however, considers the Puruṣamedha to be a real human sacrifice. There can be no doubt that human sacrifices occurred in ancient India, though not in the Brahmanical cult—only survivals of it can be traced in the rite of building the brick-altar for the fire, and in the Śunaḥśepa legend—, just as cruel human sacrifices occurred even in modern times among certain sects. But this does not prove that the Puruṣamedha was such a sacrifice.

[2]) Vāj. Saṃh. 34, 1-6, is found as an Upaniṣad in the Oupnekhat of Duperron, and translated by *Deussen*, Sechzig Upanishads des Veda, p. 837. See above pp. 19 f.

to spend the rest of his days. Section XXXV contains a few funeral verses, which are mostly taken from the Ṛgveda. Sections XXXVI to XXXIX contain the prayers for the ceremony called Pravargya, at which a cauldron is made red-hot on the sacrificial fire, to represent symbolically the sun; in this cauldron milk is then boiled and offered to the Aśvins. The whole celebration is regarded as a great mystery. At the end of it the sacrificial utensils are so arranged that they represent a man: the milk-pots are the head, on which a tuft of sacred grass represents the hair; two milking-pails represent the ears, two little gold leaves the eyes, two cups the heels, the flour sprinkled over the whole the marrow, a mixture of milk and honey the blood, and so on. The prayers and formulae naturally correspond with the mysterious ceremonies.[1] The XL and last section of the Vājasaneyi-Saṃhitā again contains an Upaniṣad, the very important Īśā-Upaniṣad, occurring in all Upaniṣad-collections, to which we shall have to refer in the chapter on the Upaniṣads.

If it is already clear from the contents of the last sections that they are of a later date, it is confirmed still more by the fact that the prayers contained in the Saṃhitās of the *Black Yajurveda* only correspond to those of the first half of the Vājasaneyi-Saṃhitā.[2]

Now as regards the prayers and sacrificial formulae themselves, which form the principal contents of the Yajurveda-Saṃhitās, they consist partly of verses (ṛc), partly of prose sentences. It is the latter which are called "Yajus," and from which the Yajurveda takes its name. The prose of these prayers is occasionally rhythmical and here and there

---

[1]) For details about all these sacrifices and festivals see *Hillebrandt*, "Rituallitteratur (Grundriss, III, 2), pp. 97-166; H. *Oldenberg*, Religion des Veda, 2nd Ed., pp. 437-474; E. *Hardy*, Die vedisch-brahmanische periode der Religion des alten Indiens, Münster i. W., 1893, pp. 154 ff. and *Keith*, HOS., Vol. 18, pp. ciii ff.

[2]) Only the first 18 Adhyāyas of the Vājasaneyi-Saṃhitā are completely given, word for word, and explained, in the Śatapatha-Brāhmaṇa of the White Yajurveda.

even rises to poetical flight.[1] The verses which occur are mostly found also in the Ṛgveda-Saṃhitā. The various readings, however, which the Yajurveda often presents, are not indeed more ancient than the text found in the Ṛgveda, but they are mostly intentional alterations which were made in the verses, in order to bring them more into line with the sacrificial acts. Only rarely were whole hymns of the Ṛgveda included in the Yajurveda-Saṃhitās; mostly they are only single verses, torn from their context, which just appeared suitable to some sacrificial ceremony or other, and were therefore included in the Veda of prayers. Therefore these verses are of less interest to us. The characteristic element of the Yajurveda is the prose formulae and prayers.[2]

The simplest prayer that we can imagine is the dedication of a sacrificial gift with the mere utterance of the name of the deity to which it is offered. Formulae of this kind are very numerous in the Yajurveda. "Thee for Agni," "thee for Indra," or "this for Agni," or also "for Agni Hail!" "for Indra Hail!" etc.—with such words the gift is laid down or thrown into the sacred fire. A shorter and simpler song of praise to a god can hardly be imagined than the words with which every morning and every evening the fire-sacrifice consisting of milk (Agnihotra) is offered: "Agni is Light, Light is Agni, Hail!" (in the evening), and "Sūrya is Light, Light is Sūrya, Hail!" (in the morning). In equally brief words the purpose of a sacred act is often indicated, when, for instance, the sacrificial priest cuts off the branch with which the calves are driven from the cows, and says at the same time: "Thee for juice, thee for

---

[1] See *Keith*, HOS., Vol. 18, pp. cxl ff., and H. *Oldenberg*, Zur Geschichte der altindischen Prosa (AGGW. N.F., Bd. 16, Berlin, 1917), pp. 2 ff. On the language of the Yajus.

[2] We also take no account here of the Brāhmaṇa-like theological explanations which the Saṃhitās of the *Black* Yajurveda contain besides the prayers and formulæ. What is said in the following chapter about the Brāhmaṇas is applicable to these too.

23

strength!" or the utensil which served for a sacred act is briefly named and a wish attached to it, when, for instance, the piece of wood with which the sacrificial fire is to be kindled, is dedicated with the words: "This, Agni, is thy igniter; through it mayst Thou grow and thrive. May we also grow and thrive!" If one apprehends evil or bad magic from an object used at the sacrifice, a short spell serves to avert it. The halter with which the sacrificial animal is bound to the stake, is addressed thus: "Become no snake, become no viper!" The razor with which the sacrificer, when he is consecrated for the sacrifice, has his beard shaved, is thus addressed by the priest: "O Knife, do not injure him!" At the consecration of a king, the king looks down upon the ground and prays: "Mother Earth, mayest Thou not injure me, nor I Thee!"[1]

The deities are not always invoked or praised in these sacrifice-formulæ, but in the most diverse ways sacrificial utensils and sacrificial acts are brought into relation to deities. Thus, for example, the priest binds with a rope the sacrificer's wife who takes part in the sacrifice, saying: "A girdle thou art for Aditi." At the consecration for the Soma-sacrifice the sacrificer binds himself with a girdle of hemp and reed-grass with the words: "Thou art the strength of the Aṅgiras,[2] soft as wool; lend me strength!" Then he makes a knot in his under-garment and says: "The knot of the Soma art thou." Hereupon he enwraps his head in his turban (or in his upper garment) muttering: "Thou art Viṣṇu's protection, the protection of the sacrificer." To the horn of a black antelope, which he wraps up in the hem of his garment he says: "Thou art Indra's womb." The priest takes the sacrificial food from the car with the words: "Thou art the body of Agni, thee for Viṣṇu. Thou art the body of

---

1) Vaj. IV, 1. VI, 12. II, 14. I, 1. III, 9. X, 23.

2) The ancient fire and magic-priests, conceived as semi-divine beings.

the Soma, thee for Viṣṇu." When the priest takes any sacrificial utensil into his hand, he does it with the oft-recurring formula: "At the god Savitar's instigation I take thee with the arms of the Aśvins, with the hands of Pūṣan." [1]

The sacred sacrificial fire must be twirled in the ancient manner with the fire-drill; [2] and the producing of the fire is already in the Ṛgveda compared with the process of procreation, the lower small board being regarded as the mother, and the upper friction-stick as the father of the child Agni (the fire).[3] Thus are explained the formulæ with which the fire-twirling is performed at the Soma-sacrifice, in which the two friction-sticks are addressed as the pair of lovers, Purūravas and Urvaśī,[4] already known to us, who bring forth Ayu. The priest takes the lower friction-stick with the words: "Thou art the birth-place of Agni," lays two blades of sacred grass upon it, and says: "You are the two testicles." Then he lays the small board down with the words: "Thou art Urvaśī," touches the frying pan with the twirling-stick, saying: "Thou art Āyu," and with the words: "Thou art Purūravas" places the twirling-stick into the lower friction-stick. Thereupon he twirls with the formula: "I twirl thee with the Gāyatrī metre, I twirl thee with the Triṣṭubh metre, I twirl thee with the Jagatī metre." [5]

---

[1]) Vāj. I, 30 IV, 10. V, 1. VI, 30.

[2]) This consists of the two "Araṇis" or friction-sticks, of which the one is a small board, the other a pointed stick which is turned round in the small board until a flame results. This is the fire-producing implement still used at the present day by many primitive peoples, *e.g.* the Eskimos,—doubtless one of the most primitive utensils of mankind.

[3]) The Malays of Indonesia still to-day call the small wooden board in which the fire drill is turned, "mother" or "woman," while the twirling-stick itself is called "man." The ancient Arabs, too, had two sticks for producing fire by friction, one of which was conceived as female, and the other as male.

[4]) See above, pp. 103 f.

[5]) Vāj, V. 2. Śatapatha-Br. III, 4, 1, 20 ff. *Cf.* Śatapatha Br., VIII, 5, 2, 1; *Weber*, Ind. Stud., 8, 1863, pp. 8 ff., 28 ff., and above, pp. 61 f.

Formula-like turns of this kind, which often convey little or no meaning, are extremely numerous in the Yajurveda. Comparatively rarely do we come across long prose prayers, in which the sacrificer expresses his desires to the deity in simple words, as in the above-quoted beautiful prayer, which was spoken at the horse-sacrifice. More frequent are the formula-like prayers, which, however, still convey a reasonable meaning, as the following :

"Thou, Agni, art the protector of bodies ; protect my body ! Thou, Agni, art the giver of life ; give me life ! Thou, Agni, art the giver of strength, give me strength ! Thou, Agni, make complete that which is incomplete in my body." (Vāj., III, 17.)

"May life prosper through the sacrifice ! May breath prosper through the sacrifice ! May the eye prosper through the sacrifice ! May the ear prosper through the sacrifice ! May the back prosper through the sacrifice ! May the sacrifice prosper through the sacrifice !" (Vāj. IX, 21.)

But still more frequently we find endless formulæ, the meaning of which is very doubtful, for example :

"Agni has gained breath with the mono-syllable ; may I gain it ! The Aśvins have gained the two-footed people with the two-syllabic, may I gain them ! Viṣṇu has gained the three worlds with the three-syllabic, may I gain them ! Soma has gained the four-footed cattle with the four-syllabic ; may I gain them ! Pūṣan has gained the five regions of the world with the five-syllabic ; may I gain them ! Savitar has gained the six seasons with the six-syllabic ; may I gain them ! The Maruts have gained the seven tamed animals with the seven-syllabic ; may I gain them ! Bṛhaspati has gained the Gāyatrī with the eight-syllabic ; may I gain it !... ..Aditi has gained the sixteen-fold Stoma with the sixteen-syllabic ; may I gain it ! Prajāpati has gained the seventeen-fold Stoma with the seventeen-syllabic ; may I gain it !" (Vāj., IX, 31-34.)

However, one of the chief causes of the fact that these prayers and sacrifice-formulæ often appear to us to be nothing but senseless conglomerations of words, is the identification and combination of things which have nothing at all to do with each other, so very popular in the Yajurveda. For instance, a cooking-pot is placed on the fire with the words:

"Thou art the sky, thou art the earth, thou art the cauldron of Mātariśvan."[1] (Vāj., I, 2.)

Or the cow with which the Soma is bought, is addressed by the priest in the words:

"Thou art thought, thou art mind, thou art intelligence, thou art the priestly fee, thou art suitable for mastery, thou art suitable for the sacrifice, thou art the double-headed Aditi." (Vāj., IV. 19.)

To the fire which is carried about in the pan at the building of the fire-altar the following prayer is addressed:

"Thou art the beautiful-winged bird, the song of praise Trivṛt is thy head, the Gāyatra melody thine eye, the two melodies Bṛhat and Rathantara are thy wings, the song of praise is thy soul, the metres are thy limbs, the Yajus-formulæ thy name, the Vāmadevya-Melody thy body, the Yajñāyajñiya-melody thy tail, the fire-hearths are thy hoofs; thou art the beautiful-winged bird, go to heaven, fly to the light!" (Vāj., XII, 4.)

Then the priest takes three steps with the fire-pan, and says:

"Thou art the rival-slaying stride of Viṣṇu, mount the Gāyatrī metre, stride along the earth! Thou art the foe-slaying stride of Viṣṇu; mount the Triṣṭubh metre, stride along the air! Thou art the hater-slaying stride of Viṣṇu; mount the Jagatī Metre, stride along the sky! Thou art the hostile-slaying stride of Viṣṇu; mount the Anuṣṭubh metre, stride along the regions of the world!" (Vāj., XII, 5.)

With reference to this kind of prayer Leopold von *Schroeder* says: "We may indeed often doubt whether these are the productions of intelligent people, and in this connection it is very interesting to observe that these bare and

---

[1]) Matariśvan is here the wind-god, hence "the cauldron of M." meaning "atmosphere."

monotonous variations of one and the same idea are particularly characteristic of the writings of persons in the stage of *imbecility*." He then gives a few examples of notes written down by insane persons which have been preserved by psychiaters, and these do indeed show a striking similarity with many of the prayers of the Yajurveda.[1] We must not forget that here we are not dealing with very ancient popular spells, as we find them in the Atharvaveda and in some cases even still in the Yajurveda, but with the fabrications of priests who had to furnish the countless sacrificial rites subtilised by themselves with equally countless spells and formulæ.

Some prayer-formulæ of the Yajurveda are indeed nothing but magic spells in prose. Even exorcisms and curses, quite similar to those with which we have become acquainted in the Atharvaveda, confront us also among the prayers of the Yajurveda. For there exist also sacrificial acts by which one can injure an enemy. Thus the priest says to the yoke of the car on which the sacrificial utensils are kept: "A yoke thou art, injure the injurer, injure him who injures us, injure him whom we injure." (Vāj., I, 8.)[2]

The following examples of such sacrificial prayers are given by L. von Schroeder,[3] from the Maitrāyaṇī-Saṃhitā:

"Him who is hostile to us, and him who hates us, him who reviles us and him who wishes to injure us, all those shalt thou grind to dust!"

"O Agni, with thy heat, glow out against him who hates us and whom we hate! O Agni, with thy flame, burn against him who hates us and whom we hate! O Agni, with thy ray, radiate against him who hates us and whom we hate. O Agni, with thy powerful strength, seize him who hates us and whom we hate!"

"Death, Destruction, shall seize the rivals!"

---

[1]) L. v. *Schroeder*, ILC., pp 113 f.

[2]) At the same time an example of the play of words, which is very popular in the Yajus-formulæ. The text reads: dhūr asi, dhūrva dhūrvantam, dhūrva taṃ yo'smān dhūrvati, taṃ dhūrva yaṃ dhūrvāmaḥ.

[3]) ILC., p. 122.

Just as these exorcism-formulæ have a primitive and popular air, so we find among the riddles, which have come down to us in the Yajurveda, besides genuinely theological riddles which well deserve the technical name "Brahmodya," as they presuppose an acquaintance with Brahman or sacred knowledge, also a few old popular riddles.[1] We have already become acquainted with this certainly very ancient literary type in the Ṛgveda and in the Atharvaveda. In the Yajurveda we also learn of the occasions at which the riddle-games were customary, indeed, even formed a part of the cult. Thus we find in the Vājasaneyi-Samhitā in section XXIII,[2] a number of riddles with which the priests amused themselves at the renowned ancient horse sacrifice. A few of these remind us of our juvenile riddles, while others refer to the sacrificial mysticism of the Brāhmaṇas and the philosophy of the Upaniṣads. As examples the riddles of Vāj. XXIII, 45-48, 51, may be quoted:

The Hotar: "Who wanders lonely on his way?
Who is constantly born anew?
What is the remedy for cold?
What is the great corn-vessel called?"

The Adhvaryu: "The sun wanders lonely on its way,
The moon is constantly born anew,
Fire is the remedy for cold,
The earth is the great corn-vessel."

The Adhvaryu: "What is the sun-like light?
What is the ocean-like flood?

---

[1]) On the Brahmodyas see *Ludwig*, Der Rigveda *Koegel*, III, 390 ff. Rud *Kœgel*, Geschichte der deutschen Litteratur, I 1, 1894, pp. 5, 61 ff includes the Brahmodyas, with which he compares the Old Germanic riddle poetry. in the poetic heritage of the Indo-European period.

[2]) Similarly also in Taittirīya-Saṃhitā, VII, 4, 18.

And what is greater than the earth ?
What is that of which no measure is known ? "

The Hotar : " Brahman[1] is the sun-like light,
The sky is the ocean-like flood,
And greater than the earth is God Indra,
But it is the cow, of which no measure is known."

The Udgātar : " Into what things has the Puruṣa penetrated ?
And what things are contained in the Puruṣa ?
This riddle, Brahman, I give thee to solve ;
What answer hast thou now to make ? "

The Brahman : " The five, it is, into which the Puruṣa has penetrated,
And these are they which are contained in the Puruṣa.[2]
That is the answer I have thought out for thee ;
In the magic strength of knowledge thou art not above me."

These riddle games form an equally important part of the worship of the gods as the prayers and sacrificial formulæ. However, the term "worship" of the gods expresses but inadequately the purpose of the prayers and formulæ, indeed, of the sacrifices themselves. The majority of the sacrificial ceremonies, as also the Yajus formulæ do not aim at "worshipping" the gods, but at influencing them, at compelling them to fulfil the wishes of the sacrificer. The gods too, love "panem et circenses," they, too, wish to be not only fed, but entertained as well : the Vedic texts very frequently assure us that the gods take a particular pleasure in the mysterious, the enigmatic, the barely hinted-at.[3]

---

[1]) This ambiguous word here probably means "the priest-hood," perhaps "the sacred knowledge."

[2]) Puruṣa means "human being," "person" and also "spirit," "universal spirit." "The five" are the five senses, which are contained in the Puruṣa, *i.e.* in the "human being" and are permeated by the Puruṣa, *i.e.* the "universal spirit."

[3]) "The gods love that which is hinted at, the mysterious," is a sentence often recurring in the Brāhmaṇas, *e.g.*, Śatapatha-Brāhmaṇa, VI, 1, 1, 2 ; 11 ; 2, 3 ; 7, 1, 23, VII, 4.

In the Yajurveda we find besides, already a mode of influencing the gods which prevailed very largely at later periods, and which consists of enumerating as many names and epithets as possible pertaining to a certain god and of worshipping him under all these names, in order to obtain something from him. Thus, in the later literature we find texts which enumerate a thousand names of Viṣṇu or a thousand names of Śiva, the recital of which is regarded as a particularly effective and meritorious work of devotion. The first beginnings of this kind of prayers we find in the Satarudriya, the enumeration of the hundred names of the god Rudra, in Section XVI of the Vājasaneyi-Saṃhitā and in the Taittirīya-Saṃhitā, IV, 5.

Finally, there is yet another kind of "prayers," as we cannot help calling them, with which we meet already in the Yajurveda, and with which also, at later periods, much mischief was done. They are single syllables or words, which convey no meaning at all, or whose meaning has been lost, which are pronounced in the most solemn manner at certain places in the act of sacrifice, and are regarded as immensely sacred. There is, first of all, the sacrificial cry *svāhā,* which we usually translate by "hail," with which every gift for the gods is thrown into the fire, while the cry *svadhā* is employed in the case of sacrificial gifts to the fathers. Other quite unintelligible ejaculations of the kind are *vaṣat, veṭ, vāt,* but above all the most sacred syllable *om.* This syllable, originally nothing but an expression of assent,[1] was regarded by the Indians for thousands of years, and still to the present

1, 10, etc. Bṛhadāraṇyaka-Upaniṣad, IV, 2. 2. "The gods love that which is hinted at darkly, and hate that which is uttered directly."

[1] According to Aitareya-Brāhmaṇa, VII, 18, *om* means, in the language used for the gods, that which is expressed among human beings by *tathā*, "so be it," "yes." In the same way Chāndogya-Upaniṣad I, 1, 8 : "This syllable *om* expresses assent, for when a person agrees to something, he says : 'om' ! It is probably purely a coincidence that the syllable *om* partly agrees with the Hebrew "amen" in meaning as well as in sound.

day is regarded, as inordinately sacred and full of mystical significance. In the Upaniṣads it is identified with Brahman, the world-soul, and recommended to the wise man as the highest subject of meditation. The Kaṭha-Upaniṣad (II, 16) says of it: "This syllable is indeed Brahman, this syllable is the Highest; for he who knows this syllable will have all his wishes, whatever they may be, fulfilled." To this syllable "*om*," are added the three "great words," namely *bhūr*, *bhuvaḥ*, *svar* (explained by the Indians as "earth, air, sky," which, however, is doubtful) of which it is said in an old text:[1] "This is indeed Brahman, this Truth, this Right; for without these there is no sacrifice."

Centuries later, in the Tantras, the religious books of more recent Indian sects, the use of such mystical syllables and words has become prevalent to such an extent that we frequently find nothing for pages, but inarticulated sounds such as uṃ, āṃ, hrīṃ, ūṃ, eṃ, kroṃ, phaṭ, aḥ, and so on. It is significant too, that the word *mantra*, which originally designated the verses and prayers (ṛc and yajus) of the Vedic Saṃhitās, later on had only the meaning of "magic formula." Already in the Yajurveda we can trace quite clearly the transition from prayer to magic formula—the two had, in fact, never been very strictly separated.

However bare and tedious, unedifying the Yajurveda-saṃhitās are if we want to *read* them as literary works, so supremely important, indeed, interesting are they for the student of religion, who *studies* them as sources not only for the Indian, but also for the general science of religion. Whoever wishes to investigate the origin, the development, and the significance of *prayer* in the history of religion—and this is one of the most interesting chapters of the history of religion—should in no case neglect to become acquainted with the prayers of the Yajurveda.

---

[1]) Maitrāyaṇī-Saṃhitā, I, 8, 5.

For the understanding of the whole of the later religious and philosophical literature of the Indians, too, these Saṃhitās are indispensable. Without the Yajurveda we cannot understand the Brāhmaṇas, and without these we cannot understand the Upaniṣads.

The Brāhmaṇas.[1]

Of the Brāhmaṇas, the second great class of works belonging to the Veda, Max Müller once said : "However interesting the Brāhmaṇas may be to students of Indian literature, they are of small interest to the general reader. The greater portion of them is simply twaddle, and what is worse, theological twaddle. No person who is not acquainted beforehand with the place which the Brāhmaṇas fill in the history of the Indian mind, could read more than ten pages without being disgusted."[2]

Indeed, it is even truer of these works than of the Yajurveda, that they are unpalatable as reading, but indispensable to the understanding of the whole of the later religious and philosophical literature of the Indians, and highly interesting for the general science of religion. The Brāhmaṇas are as invaluable authorities to the student of religion, for the history of sacrifice and of priesthood, as the Saṃhitas of the Yajurveda are for the history of prayer.

The word Brāhmaṇa[3] (neut.) means first a single

---

[1]) *Cf.* L. von *Schroeder*, I.L.C., pp. 127-167, 179-190. Sylvain *Lévi*, La doctrine du sacrifice dans les Brāhmaṇas (Bibliothèque de l'école des hautes études), Paris, 1898. H. *Oldenberg*, Vorwissenschaftliche Wissenschaft, die Weltanschauung der Bráhmaṇa-Texte, Göttingen, 1919, endeavours to do justice to the thoughts contained in the Brāhmaṇas. What *Oldenberg* calls "pre-scientific knowledge," should, however, be more correctly called "priestly pseudo-science." For the prose of the Brāhmaṇas, s. *Oldenberg*, Zur Geschichte der altindischen Prosa, pp. 13 ff., 20 ff.

[2]) Max Müller, Chips from a German Workshop, Vol. I.

[3]) The derivation of the word is doubtful. It can be derived either from brāhman

"explanation or utterance of a learned priest, of a doctor of the science of sacrifice, upon any point of the ritual." Used collectively, the word means, secondly, a collection of such utterances and discussions of the priests upon the science of sacrifice. For although the Brāhmaṇas fortunately contain much that has only a distant reference to the sacrificial cult, for instance, cosmogonic myths, ancient legends and narratives, yet the sacrifice is the one and only theme from which all the discussions start, on which everything hinges. For the Brāhmaṇas deal consecutively with the great sacrifices, with which we have become acquainted above in the contents of the Vājasaneyi-Saṃhitā,[1] and give instructions on the separate rites and ceremonies, attaching to them observations upon the relations of the separate sacrificial acts to each other and to the spells and prayers, partly quoted literally and partly quoted in abbreviated form.[2] To these are added symbolical interpretations and speculative reasons for the ceremonies and their connection with the prayer formulæ. Where, as is often the case, the views of the learned men differ on certain points of ritual, the one view is defended and the other rejected. Also there is sometimes talk of differences of the ceremonies in different districts, also of modifications of certain sacrificial rites in particular circumstances. The mention of what exactly constitutes the priests' payment, the dakṣiṇā, at every sacrificial act, is never omitted. In the same way it is explained to the sacrificer what advantages, whether in this life or in the life beyond, he can gain by means of the

---

(neut.) in the sense of "sacred speech, prayer, sacred knowledge," or from brahmān (masc.) "priest" in general or "Brahman priest," or also from brāhmaṇa (masc.) "the Brahman, the member of the priestly caste, the theologian."

[1]) Pp. 172-176

[2]) In several places in the Śatapatha-Brāhmaṇa, the word b a n d h u, "connection, relationship," *i.e.* "explanation of the deeper connection, the actual significance," occurs, whereas in later passages the word b r ā h m a ṇ a is used in the same sense. *Cf. Weber*, HIL., p. 11; Ind. Stud., 5, 60; 9, 351; *Oldenberg*, Vorwissenschaftl. Wissenschaft, p. 4.

various sacrificial rites. In short, if the use of the word "science" may be permitted with reference to theological knowledge then we can best designate the Brāhmaṇas as texts which deal with the "science of sacrifice."

Very many such texts must have existed. Of this we are assured by the Indians themselves, and it is also confirmed by the many quotations from lost Brāhmaṇas, which we find in our texts. However the number of even those Brāhmaṇas which are still preserved is by no means small, and moreover, all of them should be classed among the more extensive works of Indian literature. According to the four Vedic Saṃhitās with which we have become acquainted, the four Vedas, as we know, were distinguished, and to each of the latter several Brāhmaṇas usually belong, which issued from various schools (śākhās). We have seen that the Saṁhitās of the Black Yajurveda already contained, besides the mantras or prayers, also declarations of opinions and discussions on the purpose and meaning of the sacrifice. In these Brāhmaṇa-like parts of the Yajurveda-Saṃhitās we shall see the beginning of the Brāhmaṇa-literature. It was these very directions for the performance of the sacrificial ceremonies and the discussions on the meaning of the ritual, which in the Saṃhitās of the Black Yajurveda were directly connected with the Mantras themselves, it was just these which one Vedic school after another made the subject of individual works. Soon it was regarded as a rule that every Vedic school must possess a Brāhmaṇa. This explains on the one hand the large number of Brāhmaṇas, and on the other hand the circumstance that some works were designated as Brāhmaṇas, which deserve this name neither for their contents nor for their extent, and which belong to the latest productions of Vedic literature. Of this type are many so-called 'Brāhmaṇas' of the Sāmaveda, which are nothing but Vedāṅgas,[1] also the

[1]) See Chapter on the Vedāṅgas.

Gopatha-Brāhmaṇa of the Atharvaveda. The latter is one of the latest works of the whole of Vedic literature. There was obviously no Brāhmaṇa at all belonging to the Atharvaveda in early times. It was not until a later period, when a Veda without a Brāhmaṇa could not be imagined, that an attempt was made to fill this gap.[1]

The most important of the old Brāhmaṇas may here be enumerated.

To the Ṛgveda belongs the Aitareya-Brāhmaṇa. It consists of forty Adhyāyas or "lessons," which are divided into eight Pañcakas or "fifths." Tradition names Mahidāsa Aitareya as the author of the work. In reality he was probably only the compiler or editor of it. This Brāhmaṇa deals chiefly with the Soma-sacrifice, besides which with only the fire-sacrifice (Agnihotra) and the feast of the consecration of a king (Rājasūya). It is supposed that the last ten sections are of later origin.[2]

In the closest relationship with this Brāhmaṇa is the Kauṣītaki or Sāṅkhāyana-Brāhmaṇa, also belonging to the Ṛg-veda, and consisting of thirty Adhyāyas or "lessons." The first six Adhyāyas deal with the food-sacrifice (fire-laying, fire-sacrifice, new and full moon sacrifices and the sacrifices of the seasons), while Adhyāyas VII to XXX deal with the Soma-sacrifice fairly agreeing with the Aitareya-

1) For detailed treatment of the Gopatha-Brāhmaṇa see M. *Bloomfield*, The Atharva-veda ("Grundriss," II. I B.), pp. 101-124. The Gopatha-Brāhmaṇa has been edited by D. *Gaastra*, Leyden, 1919. Whilst *Bloomfield* considers the Gopatha-Brāhmaṇa later than the Vaitānasūtra (Der Atharvaveda, 101 ff, GGA. 1912, No. 1), *Caland* (WZKM 18, 1904, 191 ff) and Keith (JRAS, 1910, 934 ff.) consider it earlier.

2) Edited and translated into English by Martin *Haug*, Bombay, 1863. A much better edition with extracts from Sāyaṇa's commentary by Th. *Aufrecht*, Bonn, 1879. Edited with Sāyaṇa's commentary in ĀnSS No 32. Translated into English by A. B. *Keith*, HOS, Vol. 25, 1920. According to Keith (l. c., pp. 44 ff) the Aitareya-Brāhmaṇa is probably older than the Brāhmaṇa parts of the Taittirīya-Saṃhitā, and certainly older than the Jaiminīya-and Śatapatha-Brāhmaṇa On the language of the Ait-Br. see *Liebich*, Pāṇini, pp. 23 ff On Mahidāsa Aitareya s *Keith*, Aitareya Āraṇyaka, Introd., pp. 16 f.

Brāhmaṇa.[1] The Kauṣītaki-Brāhmaṇa is later than the Aitareya-Brāhmaṇa. However, while the latter is not the work of one hand and of one period, the Kauṣītaki-Brāhmaṇa is a uniform work.

To the Sāmaveda belongs the Tāṇḍya-Mahā-Brāhmaṇa,[2] also called Pañcaviṃśa, *i.e.* "Brāhmaṇa consisting of twenty-five books." This is one of the oldest Brāhmaṇas and contains some important old legends. Of special interest are the Vrātyastomas, and the description of sacrificial ceremonies by means of which the Vrātyas were received into the community of the Brahmans.[3] The Ṣaḍviṃśa-Brāhmaṇa, *i.e.* "the twenty-sixth Brāhmaṇa,"[4] is only a completion of the Tāṇḍya which consists of twenty-five books. The last part of the Ṣaḍviṃṣa is the so-called "Adbhuta-Brāhmaṇa," a Vedāṅga-text on miracles and omens.[5] The Jaiminīya-Brāhmaṇa of the Sāmaveda is even older than the Tāṇḍya-Mahā-Brāhmaṇa. This work is of special interest for the history both of religion and legend, but unfortunately the manuscript material is so fragmentary that it

---

1) The Kauṣītaki-Brāhmaṇa is edited by B. *Lindner*, Jena, 1887, also in ĀnSS No. 65, translated into English by A. B. *Keith*, HOS, vol. 25, 1920; chapter X translated into German by R. *Löbbecke*, Ueber das Verhältnis von Brāhmaṇas und Śrautasūtren, Leipzig, 1908. Āpastamba mentions the Kauṣītakins, but his quotations from a "Bahvṛca-Brāhmaṇa," that is "a Brāhmaṇa of the Ṛgvedins" do not occur either in the Aitareya or in the Kauṣītaki-Brāhmaṇa; they must therefore refer to another Ṛgveda-Brāhmaṇa which has not come down to us (Keith, l. c., p. 48). For critical and exegetical notes on Ait. Br. and Kauṣ Br. see W. *Caland*, ZDMG 72, 1918, 23 ff.

2) Edited in Bibl. Ind. 1870-1874. An analysis of it has been given by E. W. *Hopkins*, "Gods and Saints of the great Brāhmaṇa" (Transactions of the Connecticut Academy of Arts and Sciences, vol. 15, 1909, pp. 20-69). Critical notes on it by *Caland*, ZDMG 72, 1918, 19 ff.

3) See above p. 154, and Weber, HIL, pp. 67 f.

4) Edited by H. F. *Eelsingh*, Leyden, 1908, and the first Prapāṭhaka by Kurt *Klemm*, with extracts from Sāyaṇa's commentary, and a German translation (Gütersloh 1894). *Liebich* (Indogermanische Forschungen, Anzeiger, 1895, pp. 30 f.) has shown that the language of the Ṣaḍviṃśa is pre-pāṇinean.

5) Edited and translated into German by A. *Weber*, "Zwei vedische Texte über Omina und Portenta," ABA 1858.

cannot be edited. Hitherto only portions of it have been made known.[1]

The Taittirīya-Brāhmaṇa of the Black Yajurveda is nothing but a continuation of the Taittirīya-Saṃhitā,[2] for the Brāhmaṇas were already included in the Saṃhitās of the Black Yajurveda. The Taittirīya-Brāhmaṇa, therefore, contains only later additions to the Saṁhitā. We find here only a description of the Puruṣamedha, the symbolical "human sacrifice;"[3] and the fact that the sacrifice is missing in the Saṁhitā is one of the many proofs that it is only a rather late production of the science of sacrifice.

To the white Yajurveda belongs the Śatapatha-Brāhmaṇa, "the Brāhmaṇa of the Hundred Paths," so called because it consists of one hundred Adhyāyas or "lessons." This is the best known, the most extensive, and doubtless, also on account of its contents the most important of all the Brāhmaṇas.[4] As in the case of the Vājasaneyi-Saṁhitā, there are two recensions of this Brāhmaṇa, that of the Kāṇvas and that of the Mādhyandinas. In the latter the hundred Adhyāyas are distributed among 14 books (Kāṇḍas). The first nine books are simply a continuous commentary on the first eighteen sections of the Vājasaneyi-Saṁhitā. They

---

1) A selection from the Jaiminīya-Brāhmaṇa, texts with German translations, has been edited by W. *Caland* (Verhandeligen der kon. Akad. van Wetenschappen te Amsterdam, Afd. Lett. Deel I, N. R. D. XIX, No. 4) 1919. Legends from the Jaim. Br. have been made known before by A. C. *Burnell* and W. D. *Whitney*, Ind. Ant. 13, 1884, 16 ff., 21 ff., and by H. *Oertel* in JAOS, vols. 14, 15, 18, 19, 23, 26, 28, in OC XI, Paris 1897, I, 225 ff. and in Transactions of the Connecticut Academy of Arts and Sciences, vol. 15, 1909. See also *Caland*, WZKM 28, 1914, 61 ff. and "Over en uit het Jaiminīya-Brāhmaṇa" (Verslagen en Mededeelingen der kon. Akademie van Wetensch., Afd-Lett., 5, 1) Amsterdam, 1914. The Śaṭyāyana-Brāhmaṇa of the Sāmaveda is only known by quotations (especially in Sāyaṇa's Ṛgvedabhāṣya), see H. *Oertel*, JAOS 18, 1897, pp. 15 ff.

2) Editions in Bibl. Ind. 1855-1890, and ĀnSS No. 37. For the contents of the Taitt. Br., see *Keith*, HOS, vol. 18, pp. lxxvi ff.

3) See above, pp. 174 f.

4) The text was published by A. *Weber* (The White Yajurveda, Part II. The Çatapatha-Brāhmaṇa. Berlin and London, 1855). There is an excellent English translation

are decidedly older than the last five books. Probably also Books I to V are more closely connected. In them Yajñavalkya, who at the end of Book XIV is called the author of the whole Śatapatha-Brāhmaṇa, is often mentioned as the teacher whose authority is conclusive. On the other hand, in Books VI to IX, which deal with the fire-altar building (Agnicayana), Yajñavalkya is not mentioned at all. Instead of him another teacher, Śāṇḍilya, is quoted as an authority; and the same Śāṇḍilya is also regarded as the proclaimer of the Agnirahasya, *i.e.* of the "fire-altar mystery," which forms the contents of Book X. Books XI to XIV, besides appendices to the preceding books, also contain a few interesting sections on subjects which are otherwise not dealt with in the Brāhmaṇas, thus upon the Upanayana, the initiation of a pupil or the taking of the pupil to the teacher who is to instruct him in the sacred texts (XI, 5, 4), upon the daily Veda study (svadhyāya),[1] which is looked upon as a sacrifice to the god Brahman (XI, 5, 6-8), and upon the death-ceremonies and the raising of a burial mound (XIII, 8). The horse-sacrifice (Aśvamedha), the "human sacrifice (Puruṣamedha) and the "sacrifice of all" (Sarvamedha) are dealt with in Book XIII, and the Pravargya ceremony in Book XIV. At the close of this extensive work

with important introductions and notes, by Julius *Eggeling* in five volumes. (SBE, Vols. 12, 26, 41, 43 and 44). The Śatapatha-Brāhmaṇa is generally considered as one of the latest Brāhmaṇas; see *Keith*, HOS, Vol. 18, pp. cii f. According to P. *Oltramare* "L' histoire des idées théosophiques dans l'Inde," I, p. 96, many passages in the Śatapatha-Br. show the trace of the influence of the doctrines of the Upaniṣads. *Wackernagel*, Altind. Grammatik I, p. xxx declares that as to language, the Śatapatha-Br. and the Aitareya-Br. too is "comparatively modern," whilst he considers the Pañcaviṃśa-Br. and the Taittiriya-Br. as the most ancient Brāhmaṇas. (For the opposite view, see *Keith*, HOS, Vol. 25, pp. 46 f.). *Oldenberg*, "Zur Geschichte der altindischen Prosa," pp. 20 ff., gives the examples illustrating the "earlier" Brāhmaṇa period from the Taittirīya-Saṃhitā, and those for the "later" period from the Śatapatha-Brāhmaṇa.

[1]) The "learning" or reciting of the Veda by the Indians as a religious duty has an exact parallel in the Thora-reading or "learning" of the Jews.

is the old and important Bṛhadāraṇyaka-Upaniṣad with which we shall become acquainted in the next chapter.

The difference between the Brāhmaṇas which belong to the separate Vedas lies chiefly in the fact that the Brāhmaṇas of the Ṛgveda, in the presentation of the ritual, emphasize that which is of importance to the Hotar-priest, who has to recite the verses and hymns of the Ṛgveda, while the Brāhmaṇas of the Sāmaveda are chiefly concerned with the duties of the Udgātar, and those of the Yajurveda with the sacrificial acts to be performed by the Adhvaryu. In the essentials of their contents the Brāhmaṇas all agree fairly well with one another. In the main the same subjects are always dealt with; and all these works bear the same stamp. This is the more noticeable, as we are compelled to assume a period of several centuries for the origin and propagation of this literature. If we could believe the tradition which, in the so-called Vaṃśa[1] or "Genealogies," specifies genealogical trees of teachers with fifty to sixty names, then not even a thousand years would suffice to locate all the generations of teachers whose names are mentioned. These genealogies have indeed the object of tracing back the origin of the sacrifice theory to some deity or other—Brahman, Prajāpati or the Sun—but they also contain so many names which have certainly the appearance of being genuine family-names, that it is difficult

---

[1]) Connected with the Sāmaveda, there is a special so-called "Brāhmaṇa," the Vaṃśa.Brāhmaṇa (edited and explained by A. *Weber*, Ind. Stud. 4, 371 ff.) which contains only a list of 53 teachers, the last of whom, Kaśyapa, is said to have received the tradition from god Agni. There are four different Vaṃśas in the Śatapatha Brāhmaṇa. The one given at the conclusion of the work begins with the words: "We have this from the son of Bhāradvājī, the son of Bhāradvājī from the son of Vātsīmāṇḍavī," etc. Then follow 40 teachers, all only mentioned by their *maternal* names. Only as the 45th in the list does Yājñavalkya appear. Uddālaka, who is known to us from the Upaniṣads, being mentioned as his teacher. The last (55th) human teacher is Kaśyapa Naidhruvi, to whom the Brāhmaṇa is said to have been revealed by Vāc (the goddess of speech). She is said to have received it from Ambhṛṇī (the voice of thunder) and the latter from Āditya (the sun).

to look upon them as pure fiction. However, even quite apart from these lists of teachers, there still remain the numerous names of teachers who, in the Brāhmaṇas themselves, are quoted as authorities, and the fact remains that the collectors and compilers of the Brāhmaṇas shift the beginnings of the science of sacrifice as laid down in them, back to a far-distant past. This sacrifice-science itself, however, requires centuries for its development.

If we ask in which period we are to locate these centuries of the development of the Brāhmaṇa literature, there can be as little question of any definite dates as there is in determining the period of the Saṃhitās. The only certainty is, that the Saṃhitā of the Ṛgveda was already concluded and that the hymn-poetry already belonged to a far-distant past, when prayers and sacrifices were first made the subject of a special "science." It is probably certain, too, that the great majority of magic incantations, spells and formulae of the Atharvaveda and of the Yajurveda, as well as the melodies of the Sāmaveda, are much older than the speculations of the Brāhmaṇas. On the other hand it is likely that the final *compilation* of the Saṃhitās of the Atharvaveda and of the liturgical Saṃhitās was about contemporaneous with the beginnings of the Brāhmaṇa literature, so that the latest portions of these Saṃhitās might be of the same date as the earliest portions of the Brāhmaṇas. At least the geographical and cultural conditions indicate this, as they are represented to us on the one hand in the Saṃhitās of the Atharvaveda and Yajurveda, and on the other hand in the Brāhmaṇas, in comparison with those of the Ṛgveda. We have seen how, in the period of the Atharvaveda-Saṃhitā, the Aryan tribes of the Indus land, the home of the Ṛgveda, had already spread themselves further east into the region of the Ganges and the Jamnā. The region which is indicated by the Saṃhitās of the Yajurveda as well as by all the Brāhmaṇas, is the land of the *Kurus* and *Pañcālas*, those two tribes whose mighty battles form the nucleus of the great Indian epic, the Mahābhārata. *Kurukṣetra*, "the land of the Kurus," in particular, is regarded as a holy land, in which, as it is frequently put, the gods themselves celebrated their sacrificial feasts. This land Kurukṣetra lay between the two small rivers Sarasvatī and Dṛṣadvatī in the plain to the west of the Ganges and Jamnā; and the neighbouring region of the Pañcālas stretched from the north-west to the south-east between the Ganges and Jamnā. This part of India, the Doab between Ganges and Jamnā from the neighbourhood of Delhi to as far as Mathurā, is still in a later period, regarded as the actual "Brahman land" (Brahmāvarta), whose customs according to the brahmanical law-books should be adopted for the whole of India. This region is not only the land of the origin of the Saṃhitās of the Yajurveda and of the Brāhmaṇas, but also the home of the whole of brahmanical culture, which first spread from here over the whole of India

The religious and social conditions have changed very much since the time of the Ṛgveda. The old gods of the Ṛgveda still appear in the Yajurveda-Saṃhitās and in the Brāhmaṇas, just as in the Atharvaveda. But their significance has wholly faded, and they owe all the power they possess to the sacrifice alone. Furthermore, some gods who still play a subordinate part in the Ṛgveda, step into far greater prominence in the liturgical Saṃhitās and in the Brāhmaṇas, as *Viṣṇu*, and especially *Rudra* or *Śiva*. Paramount importance now also attaches to *Prajāpati*, "the lord of creatures," who is regarded as the father of the gods (devas) as well as of the demons (asuras). The word *Asura*,[1] which, corresponding to the Avestic Ahura, in the Ṛgveda still has the meaning of "endowed with miraculous powers" or "God," and appears especially often as an epithet of the god Varuṇa, henceforth has exclusively the meaning of "demon" which it always has

---

[1]) See above, p. 78.

in later Sanskrit, and again and again mention is made in the Brāhmaṇas of the battles between Devas and Asuras. Yet there is nothing titanic about these battles, as, for instance, the battle between Indra and Vṛtra in the Ṛgveda, but the gods and Asuras exert themselves to surpass each other by means of sacrifices. For in these Brāhmaṇas the gods actually have to make sacrifices if they wish to accomplish anything. Nothing is more significant for the Brāhmaṇas than the tremendous importance which is ascribed to the sacrifice. The sacrifice is here no longer the means to an end, but it is an aim in itself, indeed, the highest aim of existence. The sacrifice is also a power which overwhelms all, indeed, a creative force of Nature. Therefore the sacrifice is identical with Prajāpati, the creator. "Prajāpati is the sacrifice" is an oft-repeated sentence in the Brāhmaṇas. "The soul of all beings, of all gods is this, the sacrifice." "Truly, he who consecrates himself for the sacrifice, he consecrates himself for the All, for only after the sacrifice follows the All; in making the preparations for the sacrifice, for which he consecrates himself, he creates the All out of himself.[1] Equally endowed with magic power and equally significant is everything which is connected with the sacrifice, the sacrificial utensils no less than the prayers and formulae, the verses and their metres, the chants, and their melodies. Every single sacrificial act is treated with the greatest circumstantiality: enormous importance is attached to the most trivial circumstances, to the least details. Whether an action is to be performed to the left or to the right, whether a pot is to be put in this or in that spot on the place of sacrifice, whether a blade of grass is to be laid down with the point to the north or to the north-east, whether the priest steps in front of the fire or behind it, in which direction he must have his face turned, into how many parts the sacrificial cake is to be divided,

[1]) Śat., XIV, 3, 2, 1. III, 6, 3, 1

whether the ghee is to be poured into the northern or the southern half or into the centre of the fire, at which instant the repetition of a certain spell, the singing of a certain song has to take place,[1]—these are questions upon which generations of masters of the art of sacrifice have meditated, and which are treated in the most searching manner in the Brāhmaṇas. Upon the correct knowledge of all these details does the weal and woe of the sacrificer depend. "Such, indeed, are the wilds and ravines of sacrifice, and they (take) hundreds upon hundreds of days' carriage-drives; and if any venture into them without knowledge, then hunger or thirst, evil-doers and fiends harass them, even as fiends would harass foolish men wandering in a wild forest; but if those who know this do so, they pass from one deity to another, as from one stream into another, and from one safe place to another, and obtain well-being, the world of heaven."[2]

But "those who know," the guides through the wilderness of sacrificial art, are the priests, and it is no wonder that the claims of the *priestly caste*—for of such a caste we must now speak, as the caste system is already fully developed—in the Brāhmaṇas (as already in some parts of the Atharvaveda) exceed all bounds. Now the Brahmans are frequently declared to be gods. "Yes, they are the very gods, the Brahmans."[3] One Brāhmaṇa states plainly enough:

---

1) *Eggeling* (SBE., Vol. 12, p. X) recalls the fact that among the Ancient Romans, too, the *Pontifices* gained their power and influence through being the only people who understood all the details of the sacrificial ceremonial, which details, though small, had yet been declared tremendously important. It happened in Ancient Rome, that a sacrifice had to be repeated thirty times, because some little mistake had been made at one of the ceremonies; and in Ancient Rome, too, a ceremony was regarded as null and void, if a word was mispronounced or an act was not performed quite correctly, or if the music did not cease playing at the right moment. *Cf. Marquardt* and *Mommsen*, Handbuch der römischen Altertümer, VI, pp. 172, 174, 213.

2) Śat. XII, 2, 3, 12. Translated by J. *Eggeling*, SBE., Vol. 44, p. 160.

3) Taittirīya-Saṃhitā, I, 7, 3, 1.

"Two kinds of gods there are, indeed, namely the gods are the gods, and the learned and studying [1] Brahmans are the human gods. Between these two is the sacrifice divided: the sacrificial gifts are for the gods, the presents (Dakṣiṇās) for the human gods, the learned and studying Brahmans: by means of sacrificial gifts he pleases the gods, by presents he pleases the human gods, the learned studying Brahmans: these *two* kinds of gods transfer him, when they are satisfied, into the blessedness of heaven." [2]

Four duties has the Brahman: Brahmanic descent, corresponding conduct, fame (attained through erudition) and "ripening of the people" (*i.e.* offering of sacrifices, by means of which people are made ripe for the Beyond). But the "ripened" people also have four duties towards the Brahmans: They must show them honour, give them presents, may not oppress and not kill them. The property of a Brahman may under no circumstances be touched by the king; and if a king gives his whole country with all that is in it, to the priests as a sacrificial fee (dakṣiṇā), then it is always understood that the property of Brahmans is excepted. A king can certainly oppress a Brahman, but if he does so, evil will befall him. At the consecration of a king the priest says "this man, ye people, is your king; Soma is the king of us Brahmans," to which the Śatapatha-Brāhmaṇa observes: "By this formula he makes the whole nation as food for the king; [3] the Brahman alone he excepts; therefore the Brahman must not be utilised as food; for he has Soma as his king." [4] Only the murder of a Brahman is real murder. In a quarrel between a Brahman and a non-Brahman the judge must always decide in favour of the Brahman, for the Brahman may not be contradicted. [5]

---

1) Literally:—"who have heard and who repeat (recite what they have heard)."

2) Śat. II, 2, 2, 6; IV, 3, 4, 4.

3) *i.e.* the king lives by the people, who have to pay him taxes.

4) Śat. XI, 5, 7, 1; XIII, 5, 4, 24; XIII, 1, 5, 4; V, 4, 2, 3.

5) Śat. XIII, 3, 5, 3; Taittirīya-Saṃhitā, II, 5, 11, 9.

Everything which for some reason or another is taboo, which one may not touch, and cannot use otherwise, as, for example, the stone and earthenware vessels of a deceased person or a cow (intended for the Agnihotra milk) which becomes stubborn or ill, must be given to the Brahman, especially the remains of sacrifices and food which are taboo for others, for "nothing injures the stomach of a Brahman." [1]

Thus, at last, the conclusion is arrived at, that the Brahman is no longer a "human god" *by the side* of the heavenly gods, but that he raises himself *above* the gods. Already in the Śatapatha-Brāhmaṇa [2] it is said: "The Brahman descended from a Ṛṣi indeed *is* all deities," *i.e.* in him all deities are incorporated. This presumption on the part of the priests, the beginnings of which we meet with in the Brāhmaṇas, is not only of the greatest interest for the history of culture as an example of priestly arrogance, but it is also the precursor of a phenomenon which we can trace through the whole of Indian antiquity, and which, I think, is deeply rooted in the life of the Indo-European mind. While, for instance, the Hebrew poet says: "What is man, that Thou art mindful of him, and the son of man that Thou visitest him?" and adds "Man is like unto nothingness," a *Greek* poet uttered the great saying: "There is much that is powerful, but the most powerful is man." And a *German* poet—the same who created the super-man [3] Faust, who knocks violently

1) Taittirīya Saṃhitā II, 6, 8, 7. *Cf.* Goethe, Faust:

"The Church has a good digestion,
Has eaten up whole lands
And yet never over-eaten herself."

2) XII, 4, 4, 6. Later it is said in the law-book of Manu: "A Brahman, be he learned or unlearned, is a great deity," and immediately afterwards, "The Brahman is the highest deity." Manu, IX, 317, 319.

3) "What awful horror seizes thee, O Super-man!"

at the gates of the spirit-world—has sung the song of Prometheus, who calls to the gods:

> "I know nothing poorer
> Under the sun, than ye, O gods!"

And in India we see how, already in the Brāhmaṇas, the priest exalts himself over the gods through the *sacrifice*; in the epics we read countless stories of ascetics who, through *asceticism* attain to such ascendancy that the gods tremble upon their thrones. In Buddhism, however, the divine beings, with Indra the prince of gods, have fully dwindled into quite insignificant beings, who differ from ordinary mortals only in that they are somewhat better situated, and even that only so long as they remain devout Buddhists; and infinitely high above these gods stands not only the Buddha himself, but every man who, through *love for all beings* and through renunciation of the world, has become an Arhat or saint.[1]

Thus already in the Brāhmaṇas the way is prepared for that great movement to which Buddhism owes its origin: for it cannot be questioned that the old and genuine Brāhmaṇas belong to the Pre-Buddhist period. While in the Brāhmaṇas not the least trace is shown of any acquaintance with Buddhism,[2] the Buddhist texts pre-suppose the existence of a Brāhmaṇa literature. We can therefore say upon good grounds that the centuries in which the Liturgical Saṃhitās and the Brāhmaṇas originated, must fall into the period *after* the conclusion of the hymn-composition and the Ṛgveda-Saṃhitā and *before* the appearance of Buddhism.

As regards the actual contents of these works, a few examples will suffice to give the reader an idea. The

---

1) See A. *Weber*, SBA. 1897, 1, 594, ff.

2) It is significant that, in the list of human sacrifices in the Vājasaneyi-Saṃhitā, XXX (*cf.* above, pp. 147 f.) there is no mention of either monks or nuns, or of Buddhists at all. And yet this list is probably later than the oldest Brāhmaṇas.

Indians themselves usually arrange the contents of the Brāhmaṇas in two principal categories, which they call *Vidhi* and *Arthavāda*. Vidhi means "rule, precept," Arthavāda "explanation of meaning." For the Brāhmaṇas first give rules for the performance of the single ceremonies, and to these the interpretations and explanations of the purpose and meaning of the sacrificial acts and prayers are afterwards attached. Thus, for example, the Śatapatha-Brāhmaṇa begins with the precepts upon the vow of abstinence, which the sacrificer has to make on the day before the new-moon and full-moon sacrifice. There we read :

"He who is about to enter on the vow, touches water, whilst standing between the Āhavanīya and Gārhapatya fires, with his face turned towards east. The reason why he touches water is, that man is (sacrificially) impure on account of his speaking untruth ; and because by that act an internal purification (is effected),—for water is indeed (sacrificially) pure. 'After becoming sacrificially pure, I will enter on the vow,' thus (he thinks) ; for water is indeed purifying. 'Having become purified through the purifying one, I will enter on the vow,' thus (he thinks, and) this is the reason why he touches water." [1]

To such simple explanations there are often attached discussions of the views of various teachers upon some question of ritual. Thus here the controversy is raised whether, at the making of the vow in question, one should fast or not, and it is said :

"Now then of the eating (or) fasting. And on this point Āshāḍha Sāvayasa, on the one hand, was of opinion that the vow consisted in fasting. For assuredly (he argued), the gods see through the mind of man ; they know that, when he enters on this vow he means to sacrifice to them next morning. Therefore all the gods betake themselves to his house, and abide by (him or the fires, upa-vas) in his house : whence this (day) is called upa-vasatha. [7]

Now, as it would even be unbecoming for him to take food, before

1) Śat. I, 1, 1, 1. Translated by J. *Eggeling*, SBE. Vol 12, pp. 2 f.

men (who are staying with him as his guests) [1] have eaten; how much more would it be so, if he were to take food before the gods (who are staying with him) have eaten: let him therefore take no food at all. [8]

Yājñavalkya, on the other hand, said: "If he does not eat, he thereby becomes a sacrificer to the Fathers; [2] and if he does eat, he eats before the gods have eaten: let him therefore eat what, when eaten, counts as not eaten." For that of which no offering is made, even though it is eaten, is considered as not eaten When he therefore eats, he does not become a sacrificer to the Fathers; and by eating of that of which no offering is made, he does not eat before the gods have eaten. [9]

Let him therefore eat only what grows in the forest, be it forest plants or the fruit of trees."[3]

Etymologies, such as that of Upavasatha in the above-quoted place, are exceedingly frequent in the Brāhmaṇas. Moreover, it is regarded as a special advantage if an etymology is not quite accurate, for "the gods love that which is hidden." Thus, for instance, the name of the god *Indra* is derived from *indh*, "to kindle," and it is said: he is, therefore, actually named *Indha*, and he is called "Indra" only because the gods love what is concealed. Or the word "*ulūkhala*," which means "mortar," is derived from *uru karat*, "it shall make wide," and "ulūkhala" is declared to be a mystical designation for "urukara."[4] Like the etymologizing, *identifying* and *symbolizing* play an even greater part in the Brāhmaṇas than in the Yajurveda-Saṃhitās:[5] the most dissimilar things being put together and associated

---

[1]) The sentences in brackets have been completed from the context It is impossible to render the original accurately in English without such completions. The Brāhmaṇas are not *written for readers*, but *spoken* to hearers, hence much is omitted which the speaker can express by means of emphasizing certain words, manual gestures, and so on.

[2]) Because fasting is ordained for sacrifices to the fathers

[3]) Śat. I, 1, 1, 1, 7-10 Translated by J. *Eggeling*, SBE., Vol. 12, pp. 4 f.

[4]) Śat. VI, 1, 1, 2; VII, 5, 1, 22, *cf.* above, p. 184.

[5]) See above, p 181. On identifications in the Brāhmaṇas see *Oldenberg*, Vorwissenschaftliche Wissenschaft, pp. 110 ff.

with one another. On every page of the Brāhmaṇas we find explanations like the following:

"He now strews sacrificial grass all round (the fires), and fetches the utensils, taking two at a time, *viz.* the winnowing basket and the Agnihotra ladle, the wooden sword and the potsherds, the wedge and the black antelope skin, the mortar and the pestle, the large and the small mill-stones. These are ten in number; for of ten syllables consists the Virâj (metre), and radiant (virâj) also is the sacrifice; so that he thereby makes the sacrifice resemble the Virâj. The reason why he takes two at a time is, because a pair means strength; for when two undertake anything, there is strength in it. Moreover, a pair represents a productive copulation, so that a productive copulation (of those respective objects) is thereby effected." [1]

"Now the sacrifice is the man. The sacrifice is the man for the reason that the man spreads (performs) it; and that in being spread it is made of exactly the same extent as the man: [2] this is the reason why the sacrifice is the man. [1]

The juhū [3] (spoon) further belongs to that (man-shaped sacrifice and so does the upabhṛt [3]; and the dhruvā [3]; represents its trunk. Now it is from the trunk that all these limbs proceed, and for this reason the entire sacrifice proceeds from the dhruvā. [2]

The dipping-spoon [4] (sruva, masc.) is no other than the breath. This breath passes through (or, goes to) all the limbs, and for that reason the dipping-spoon goes to all the offering-spoons (sruc, fem.). [3]

That juhū further is to him [5] no other than yonder sky, and the upabhṛt this atmosphere, and the dhruvā this same (earth). Now it is from this (earth) that all the worlds originate: and from the dhruvā, therefore, the whole sacrifice proceeds. [4]

---

[1]) Śat. I, 1, 1, 22. Translated by J. *Eggeling*, SBE., Vol. 12, pp. 10 f.

[2]) Because, in measuring the sacrificial place, such measurements as "man's length," "arm's length," "span" and so on, are employed.

[3]) Names of different sacrificial spoons.

[4]) With this spoon (Sruva) the ghee is taken out of the ghee-pot and poured into the sacrificial spoons with which it is served.

[5]) "He" means Puruṣa, "man." But Puruṣa also means "spirit" and designates the "Great Spirit" too, which is one with Prajâpati, the creator of the universe. Hence the sacrifice is not only identified with man (the sacrificer) but also with the Universal Spirit and Prajâpati. *Cf.* above, p. 184, note 2.

The dipping-spoon then is no other than that blowing one (the wind); it is this that sweeps across all these worlds: and for that reason the sruva goes to all the offering-spoons." [1] [5]

In countless places in the Brāhmaṇas the *sacrifice* is identified with the god *Viṣṇu* and equally frequently with the creator *Prajāpati*. But the *year*, too, is identified with Prajāpati countless times, while on the other hand *Agni*, as the fire-altar, is also regarded as the year, because the building of the fire-altar takes a whole year. Thus we read: "Agni is the year, and the year is these worlds," and immediately afterwards: "Agni is Prajāpati, and Prajāpati is the year.' Or, "Prajāpati, indeed, is the sacrifice and the year, the new moon night is its gate, and the moon is the bolt of the gate." [2] A prominent part is here played by the symbolism of figures. Thus we read, for example:

"With *four* (verses) he takes (some of the ashes); he thereby supplies him (Agni) with *four*-footed animals; and animals being food, it is with food he thus supplies him. With *three* (verses) he takes (the ashes) down (to the water),—that makes *seven*, for of seven layers consists the fire-altar, seven seasons are a year, and the year is Agni: as great as Agni is, as great as his measure, so great does this become." [3]

Here and there these barren explanations gain a little interest through the fact that they throw some light upon the moral views and social conditions of the period to which the Brāhmaṇas belong. Thus, for example, at the soma-sacrifice one of the soma-libations is dedicated to Agni Patnīvat, *i.e.* "Agni accompanied by his wives." [4] This libation differs in certain details from other soma-gifts, and these deviations in the offering of the same are explained by

---

1) Śat. I, 3, 2, 1-5. Translated by J. *Eggeling*, SBE. Vol. 12, p. 78 f.
2) Śat. VIII, 2, 1, 17-18; XI, 1, 1, 1.
3) Śat. VI, 8, 2, 7. Translated by J. *Eggeling*, SBE., Vol. 41, p. 295.
4) *Cf.* above, p. 88.

reference to the weakness and helplessness of the female sex:

"With the remains of ghee left over in the sacrificial spoon he mixes (the soma). Other soma-libations he makes strong, by mixing them, but he weakens this one; for ghee is indeed a thunderbolt, and with the thunderbolt, the ghee, did the gods beat and weaken their wives; and thus beaten and weakened they had no right whatever either to their own bodies or to an heritage. And likewise he now beats and weakens the wives with the thunderbolt, the ghee, and thus beaten and weakened, the wives have no right whatever either to their own bodies or to an heritage." (Śat. IV, 4, 2, 13.)

This, then, would be a ritual argument for the bondage of woman.[1] In another place the relationship of the wife to the husband appears in a slightly pleasanter light. Namely, at the Vājapeya-sacrifice, the following ceremony occurs. A ladder is leaned against the sacrificial stake, and the sacrificer, with his wife, ascends it:

"When he is about to ascend, he addresses his wife in the following words: 'Wife, let us ascend to heaven,' and the wife answers: 'Yes, let us ascend.' The reason why he addresses his wife thus is this: She the wife, is indeed his own half; therefore as long as he has no wife, so long he does not propagate his species, so long he is no complete individual; but when he has a wife, then he propagates his species, then he is complete. 'As a complete individual will I go this way (to heaven),' he thinks; therefore he addresses his wife in this manner." (Śat. V. 2, 1, 10.)

The place of sacrifice or the altar (Vedi, fem.) is represented in the symbolism of the Brāhmaṇas as a woman. The following rule for the erection of the altar gives us information upon the ancient ideal of feminine beauty:

---

[1]) We also read in the Brāhmaṇas such sentences as: "Verily, the sacrifice is right and truth, woman is something wrong" (Maitrāyaṇīya-Saṃhitā, 1, 10, 11), "Nirṛti (*i.e.* Evil personified) is woman." (Maitr. 1, 10, 16), "Woman, the Śūdra, the dog, and the blackbird (the crow) are something wrong." (Śat, 14, 1, 1, 31), etc. See *Lévi*, La doctrine du sacrifice dans les Brāhmaṇas, pp. 156 ff.; *Oldenberg*, Vorwissenschaftliche Wissenschaft, pp. 44 f.; and *Winternitz*, Die Frau in den indischen Religionen, I, pp. 4 f., 10 ff, 43.

"It (the altar) should be broader on the west side, contracted in the middle, and broad again on the east side; for thus shaped they praise a woman: 'broad about the hips, somewhat narrower between the shoulders, and contracted in the middle (or, about the waist).' Thereby he makes it (the altar) pleasing to the gods."[1]

A glaring light is thrown upon the sexual morality of that period by a brutal sacrificial custom which occurs at one of the sacrifices of the seasons, and is described as follows:

"Thereupon the Pratiprasthātṛ[2] returns (to where the sacrificer's wife is seated). When he is about to lead the wife away,[3] he asks her, 'With whom holdest thou intercourse?' Now when a woman who belongs to one (man) carries on intercourse with another, she undoubtedly commits a (sin) against Varuṇa. He therefore thus asks her, lest she should sacrifice with a secret pang in her mind; for when confessed the sin becomes less, since it becomes truth; this is why he thus asks her. And whatever (connection) she confesses not, that indeed will turn out injurious to her relatives."[4]

This, by the way, is one of the few places in the Brāhmaṇas where morality is thought of. It is only very occasionally that we come across moral reflections, as for instance, when the Asuras defeated the gods by falsehood, but the gods gained the ascendancy in the end, we are told that in like manner when men speak the truth, they may suffer adversity at first, but will prosper ultimately, while though the liars may have success for a time, they will surely perish in the end.[5] Generally speaking, however, it is very characteristic of these texts that there is hardly any mention of morality in them at all. The Brāhmaṇas are a splendid proof of the fact that an enormous amount of religion can be connected with

---

1) Śat. I, 2, 5, 16 Translated by J *Eggeling*, SBE, Vol. 12, p. 68.

2) One of the priests, an assistant of the adhvaryu.

3) Namely to the altar, where she is to offer a gift to Varuṇa.

4) Śat. II, 5, 2, 20. Translated by J. *Eggeling*, SBE, Vol 12, pp. 396 f.

5) Śat. IX, 5, 1, 16 f. *Oldenberg* (Vorwissenschaftliche Wissenschaft, pp. 19 ff., 124 ff., 184 ff.) has taken great pains to collect all that can be found on ethical ideas in the Brāhmaṇas. It does not amount to much.

infinitely little morality. Religious acts, sacrifices and ceremonies, are the one and only subject of all these extensive works, but morality is a thing with which these works have nothing to do.[1] On the contrary, sacrificial acts are not only performed in order that the gods may fulfil the very materialistic wishes of the sacrificer, but also very frequently in order to injure an enemy. Indeed, the Brāhmaṇas give directions for the priests, how, by means of the sacrifice, they can injure the sacrificer himself by whom they are employed, if, for instance, he does not give them enough presents. They need only perform the prescribed ceremonies in reverse order, or employ spells at the wrong place, and the fate of the sacrificer is sealed.

But enough of this intricate science of sacrifice which forms the chief contents of the Brāhmaṇas. Fortunately, *one* of the component parts of the Arthavāda or the "explanation of meaning," consists of the so-called *Itihāsas*, *Ākhyānas* and *Purāṇas*, *i.e.* narratives, myths and legends, which are narrated in order to explain the reason for some ritual act or other. As in the Talmud, to which the Brāhmaṇas have some similarity, the blooming garden of the Hagada (so beautifully described in song by Heine) stands beside the theological jugglery of the Halacha, so also in the Brāhmaṇas the desert of desolate theological speculation is now and then pleasantly relieved by an oasis, in which the flower of poetry, a poetical narrative or a deeply thoughtful legend of the creation, blossoms.

---

[1] "Morals have found no place in this system: the sacrifice which regulates the relationship of man with the gods is a mechanical operation which acts by its innermost energy; hidden in the bosom of nature, it only emerges under the magic action of the priest." "It is indeed difficult to conceive of anything more brutal or more material than the theology of the Brāhmaṇas; the notions, which custom has slowly refined and clothed with a moral aspect, surprise us by their savage realism." Sylvain *Lévi*, La doctrine du sacrifice, p. 9; *cf.* 164 ff.

The very old myth, already known to the singers of the Ṛgveda, of **Purūravas** and **Urvaśī**, narrated in the Śatapatha-Brāhmaṇa,[1] is such an oasis in the desert. It is there related how the nymph (Apsaras) Urvaśī loved the king Purūravas, how she stated her conditions when she became his wife, and how the Gandharvas caused him to violate one of these conditions. Then she eluded him, and Purūravas, wailing and lamenting, wandered throughout the whole of Kurukṣetra until he came to a lotus-pond, where nymphs were swimming about in the form of swans. Among them was Urvaśī and there ensued the dialogue which is already known to us from the dialogue verses of the Ṛgveda.

"Then her heart took pity on him. She said, 'Come here the last night of the year from now : then shalt thou lie with me for one night, and then this son of thine,[2] will have been born.' He came there on the last night of the year, and lo, there stood a golden palace! They then said to him only this (word), 'Enter!' and then they bade her go to him.

She then said, 'To-morrow morning the Gandharvas will grant thee a boon, and thou must make thy choice.' He said, 'Choose thou for me!' She replied, 'Say, "Let me be one of yourselves!"' In the morning the Gandharvas granted him a boon ; and he said, 'Let me be one of yourselves!'"[3]

Thereupon, the Gandharvas taught him a particular form of fire-sacrifice, through which a mortal becomes changed into a Gandharva. To the description of this sacrifice we owe the insertion in the Brāhmaṇa of the old wonder-tale from which not even the doctors of the sacrificial art could strip all the magic of poetry.

In the Śatapatha-Brāhmaṇa we also find the Indian

---

[1]) XI, 5, 1. Translated by *Eggeling*, SBE, Vol. 44, pp. 68 ff., German translation by K. *Geldner*, Vedische Studien, I, 244 ff. See above, pp. 103 f.

[2]) Literally: "This thy son here." One of the many expressions which are only explicable in the *oral* presentation. Similarly, "this here" in the Brāhmaṇas often means "earth," "that yonder" means "sky," and so on.

[3]) Translated by J. *Eggeling*, SBE., Vol. 44, pp. 72 f.

27

legend of the flood, which in all probability is derived from a Semitic source, in its oldest form :

"In the morning they brought to Manu water for washing just as now also they (are wont to) bring (water) for washing the hands. When he was washing himself, a fish came into his hands. (1)

It spake to him the word, 'Rear me, I will save thee!' 'Wherefrom wilt thou save me?' 'A flood will carry away all these creatures: from that I will save thee!' 'How am I to rear thee?' (2)

It said, 'As long as we are small, there is great destruction for us: fish devours fish. Thou wilt first keep me in a jar. When I outgrow that, thou wilt dig a pit and keep me in it. When I outgrow that, thou wilt take me down to the sea, for then I shall be beyond destruction.' (3)

It soon became a jhasha (a large fish); for that grows largest (of all fish). Thereupon it said, 'In such and such a year that flood will come. Thou shalt then attend to me (*i.e.* to my advice) by preparing a ship; and when the flood has risen thou shalt enter into the ship, and I will save thee from it.' (4)

After he had reared it in this way, he took it down to the sea. And in the same year which the fish had indicated to him, he attended to (the advice of the fish) by preparing a ship; and when the flood had risen, he entered into the ship. The fish then swam up to him, and to its horn he tied the rope of the ship, and by that means he passed swiftly up to yonder northern mountain. (5)

It then said, 'I have saved thee. Fasten the ship to a tree; but let not the water cut thee off, whilst thou art on the mountain. As the water subsides, thou mayest gradually descend!' Accordingly he gradually descended, and hence that (slope) of the northern mountain is called 'Manu's descent.' The flood then swept away all these creatures, and Manu alone remained here.[1]

Thus far goes the old legend which must have related further how the human race was renewed through Manu. The Brāhmaṇa, however, related that Manu, in order to obtain descendants, offered a sacrifice; out of this sacrifice arose a woman, and through her the human race was propagated. This daughter of Manu is called Iḍā—and the

[1]) Śat. I, 8, 1. Translated by *Eggeling*, SBE., Vol. 1!, pp. 216 ff.

narrative is inserted only to explain the significance of a sacrificial gift designated by the name of Iḍā.

These narratives are also of importance to us as the oldest examples of Indian narrative prose which we possess. It has already been mentioned that this prose of the oldest epic compositions frequently alternates with verses. But while in the story of Purūravas and Urvaśī the verses appear not only in the Ṛgveda-collection, but in language and metre belong to the oldest Vedic compositions too, we find in the Aitareya-Brāhmaṇa an Ākhyāna in which the Gāthās or verses scattered among the prose approach the epic in language es well as in metre. This is the legend of Śunaḥśepa,[1] interesting in more ways than one. It begins as follows:

"Hariścandra, son of Vedhas, a king of the race of the Ikṣvākus, was childless. He had a hundred wives, but by none of them did he have a son. Once Parvata and Nārada[2] visited him, and he asked Nārada:

" As all men desire a son, wise men as well as fools,
Tell me, O Nārada, what a man gains by having
a son."

Asked thus in one verse, he replied with ten:

" The father, who looks upon the face of his son, born
living unto him,
Discharges his debt in him, attains to immortality
through him.[3]

---

[1]) Aitareya-Brāhmaṇa, VII, 13-18, English translation by *Max Müller*, "History of Ancient Sanskrit Literature," 2nd ed., London, 1860, pp. 408 ff., by M. *Haug*, and by A. B. *Keith* in their respective translations of the Aitareya-Brāhmaṇa. German translation by R. *Roth*, Ind. Stud., I. 457 ff. See also Roth, Ind. Stud., 2. 112 ff.; A. *Weber*, SBA., 1891, pp. 776 ff.; *Keith*, HOS., Vol. 25, pp. 61 ff.; *Charpentier*, Die Suparṇasage, pp. 58 f. The story is called an "Ākhyāna" in the text itself.

[2]) Two Ṛṣis or saints, who dwell now in heaven, now on earth, and often serve the gods as messengers.

[3]) The best explanation of this verse is given in two Brāhmaṇa passages. Taittirīya-Saṃhitā, VI, 3, 10, 5: "From the moment of his birth the Brāhman is burdened with three debts: to the Ṛṣis, he owes the vow of learning the Veda, to the gods he owes the

Of all the joys there are for creatures on this earth,
In fire, and in water, greatest is the father's in his son.

Always through the son have fathers conquered
darkness ;
He himself is again newly-born, the son is to him
a rescuing boat.

What avails the dirt, and what the goat-skin, what the
beard, and what asceticism ! [1]
Brahmans, desire a son for yourselves : in him ye have
the blameless world of heaven.

Food is life, clothing is protection and gold ornaments
are beauty ;
Marriage means cattle ; [2] a friend [3] is the wife, a sorrow
the daughter,[4]
Light in the highest regions of heaven is the son to his father.

The husband entereth his wife, becomes the embryo
in her womb,
And is by her brought forth again, in the tenth moon,
as a new man."

---

[5] After he had uttered the verses, he said to him ! 'Approach King Varuṇa and say : 'May a son be born to me ; I will sacrifice him to

---

sac ifice and *to the Fathers, offspring* ; he who begets a son, offers sacrifices and keeps the vow of learning the Veda, is freed from his debts ;" and Taittirīya-Brāhmaṇa I, 5, 5, 6 : "In descendants dost thou propagate thy race ; that, O mortal, is thy immortality." Already in the Ṛgveda V, 4, 10, it is said : "May I, O Agni, attain to immortality through descendants !"

[1]) The verse is directed against the forest-hermits and ascetics.

[2]) Because the purchase price for daughters was, among the ancient Indians as among the ancient Greeks, paid in cows. *Cf.* the "oxen-bringing maidens" in Homer.

[3]) At the marriage, in Ancient India, the bride and bridegroom took seven steps together, whereupon the bridegroom said : "At the seventh step become a *friend* (masc.)."

[4]) Female infanticide and child marriage have been the dismal consequences of the view that the birth of a daughter is a calamity. See *Winternitz*, Die Frau in den indischen Religionen, I, pp. 21 ff. The view that a daughter is "a misery" is, however, spread all over the world.

[5]) Here follow four verses more, in which the same ideas are varied.

thee.' 'So be it,' he said, and went up to King Varuṇa, praying: 'May a son be born to me; I will sacrifice him to thee.' 'So be it' (said Varuṇa). Then a son was born to him, Rohita by name. And Varuṇa said to him: 'Now a son has been born to thee; sacrifice him to me.' He, however, said: "Not until an animal is over ten days old is it suitable for sacrifice. Let him become over ten days old; then I will sacrifice him to thee.' 'So be it.' And he became over ten days old. The former said to him: 'Now he has become over ten days old; sacrifice him to me.' But the latter said: 'Not until an animal has got teeth is it suitable for sacrifice. Let him get teeth; then I will sacrifice him to thee.' 'So be it.'

In a similar manner Hariścandra puts the god Varuṇa off until Rohita has attained the age of manhood. Then at last he desires to sacrifice him, but Rohita escapes into the forest, where he wanders about for a year. Thereupon Hariścandra is attacked by dropsy, the disease sent by Varuṇa as a punishment. Rohita hears of it and desires to return, but Indra confronts him in the form of a Brahman, extols the fortune of the wanderer and advises him to continue wandering on. A second, a third, a fourth, a fifth year does the youth wander about in the forest, again and again he wishes to return, and again and again Indra confronts him and urges him to further wanderings. As he was wandering about in the forest the sixth year, he met the Ṛṣi Ajīgarta, who, tortured by hunger, was wandering about in the forest. The latter had three sons, Śuṇaḥpuccha, Śuṇaḥśepa, Śunolāṅgūla [1] by name, Rohita offers him a hundred cows for one of his sons, in order to ransom himself through him, and, as the father does not wish to part with the eldest and the mother does not wish to part with the youngest son, receives the middle one, Śuṇaḥśepa. With the latter Rohita goes to his

---

[1]) These strange names, which mean "dog's hinder part," "dog's pizzle," and "dog's tail," are probably chosen for the purpose of making the Ṛṣi Ajīgarta—the name means "who has nothing to eat"—appear in the worst possible light. Nevertheless these names also prove the more popular than priestly character of the narrative

father. And as Varuṇa agrees that Śunaḥśepa shall be sacrificed to him,—for "a Brahman is worth more than a warrior," said Varuṇa,—he is to be offered in the place of the sacrificial animal at the sacrifice of the consecration of the king (Rājasūya). Everything is prepared for the sacrifice, but no one is found who will undertake the binding of the sacrificial victim. Then said Ajīgarta, "Give me a second hundred, and I will bind him." And for a second hundred cows he binds his son Śunaḥśepa to the sacrificial stake; for a third hundred, however, he offers to slay him. The further hundred cows are given to him, and with a sharpened knife, he steps towards his son. Then thought the latter: "They want to slaughter me as though I were no human being; well, I will take refuge with the gods." And he praised in turn all the most prominent gods of the Vedic pantheon in a number of hymns which are found in our Ṛgveda-Saṃhitā. But when, finally, he glorified Uṣas, the Dawn, in three verses, one fetter after another fell from him, and the dropsical stomach of Hariścandra became smaller, and with the last verse he was free of his fetters and Hariścandra was well. Thereupon the priests received him into the sacrificial gathering, and Śunaḥśepa saw (by intuition) a particular kind of soma sacrifice. Viśvāmitra, however, the ṛṣi about whom there are so many legends, who occupied the position of hotar at the sacrifice of Hariścandra, adopted Śunaḥśepa as his son, and neglecting his own hundred sons, solemnly appointed him as his heir. Finally it is said:

"That is the tale (ākhyāna) of Śunaḥśepa which contains over a hundred Ṛgveda-verses and also stanzas.[1] This the hotar relates to the king, after he has been sprinkled with holy water at the Rājasūya. Seated on a golden cushion he tells the story. Seated on a golden cushion (the Adhvaryu) gives the responses. Gold, indeed, signifies glory. Thereby he causes his glory to increase. 'Om' is the response to a Ṛg-verse, 'yes'

[1] "Gāthās," epic verses, as those quoted above.

that to a Gāthā.[1] For "Om" is divine, and "yes" is human. In this way he releases him through the divine and the human word from misfortune and sin. Therefore a king who desires to be victorious, even though he be no sacrificer, may have the Śūnaḥśepa legend related to him; then not the least sin remains attached to him. A thousand cows shall he give to the narrator, a hundred to the priest who makes the responses, and to each of the two the golden cushions upon which he sat; moreover, also a silver chariot harnessed with mules is due to the hotar. Those, too, who desire a son, shall cause the story to be related to them; then they will assuredly obtain a son."

But if this Śunaḥśepa legend was already a time-honoured ancient myth for the editors or compilers of the Aitareya-Brāhmaṇa, and the narration of it at the consecration of the king[2] actually formed part of the ritual, how old must the legend itself be! It must be very old, also because in it is preserved the memory of human sacrifice, which must have been offered at the Rājasūya in pre-historic times, although nowhere else either in the Brāhmaṇas or in the ritual-manuals (Śrauta-sūtras) is there any mention of human sacrifices at the consecration of the king. Yet the Śunahśepa legend is late in comparison with the Ṛgveda. For the hymns,[3] which, according to the Aitareya-Brāhmaṇa, Śunaḥśepa is said to have "seen" are partly such as possibly a Ṛṣi Śunaḥśepa might have composed as well as any other ṛṣi, although there is not the least matter contained in them which might relate

---

[1]) *i.e.*, always when the Hotar recites a Ṛg-verse, the Adhvaryu cries at the conclusion of it: "Om;" when he has recited an epic verse, he cries "Yes." *Cf.* above, p. 185, note 1.

[2]) As an ākhyāna belonging to the Rājasūya it is also related in the Śāṅkhāyana-Śrautasūtra, 15, 17 ff. In the same Śrautasūtra, 16, 11, 1-3, it is mentioned as one of the ākhyānas to be told at the Puruṣamedha. It is also referred to in the Śrautasūtras of Kātyāyana, Āpastamba, and Baudhāyana. See *Keith*, HOS., Vol. 25, pp 29 f., 40 f., 61 f., 67.

[3]) Namely Ṛv. I, 24-30 and IX, 3. The Gāthās of the Śunaḥśepa-Ākhyāna are, of course, much later than the verses of the Ṛgveda. Yet from the metre, it seems that they are older than the metrical portions of the Upaniṣads; see *Keith*, HOS., Vol. 25, p. 50.

to our legend; partly, however, they are hymns which are not at all fitting for the lips of the Śunaḥśepa of the legend, as, for instance the song Ṛg-veda 1, 29, with the refrain; "Let us hope, O generously-giving Indra, for a thousand shining oxen and horses," or which like Ṛv. 1, 24, even contain verses which cannot possibly have been composed by the Śunaḥśepa of the Aitareya-Brāhmaṇa. For it says here: "He whom Sunaḥśepa invoked when he was seized, the king Varuṇa, may he deliver us!" and: "Śunaḥśepa, indeed, when he was seized and bound to three stakes, invoked the Aditya." These are verses which must refer to another much older Śunaḥśepa legend. If the Aitareya-Brāhmaṇa places these hymns in the mouth of Śunaḥśepa, then it can only be because the same tradition, in nowise reliable, which we have in our Anukramaṇis[1] at the time of the Aitareya-Brāhmaṇa already ascribed those hymns to a Ṛṣi Śunaḥśepa. We have here again a proof of how much earlier the Ṛgveda hymns are, chronologically, than everything else which belongs to the Veda.

Unfortunately few narratives have come down to us in such entirety in the Brāhmaṇas as that of Śunaḥśepa. Mostly, the stories are prepared for the purpose which they are to serve, namely the explanation or justification of a sacrificial ceremony, and it is sometimes not easy to extract from them the nucleus of an old legend or an old myth. Moreover, by no means all the narratives which we find in the Brāhmaṇas are derived from old myths and legends, but they are often only invented for the explanation of some sacrificial ceremony. Sometimes, however, even these invented tales are not without interest. To explain, for instance, why, in the case of sacrificial gifts which are dedicated to Prajāpati, the prayers are only to be uttered in a low voice, the following pretty allegory is related:

---

[1]) See above, pp. 57 f. and below in the section on Exegetic Vedāṅgas.

"Now a dispute once took place between Mind and Speech as to which was the better of the two. Both Mind and Speech said, 'I am excellent!' (8)

Mind said, 'Surely I am better than thou, for thou dost not speak anything that is not understood by me; and since thou art only an imitator of what is done by me and a follower in my wake, I am surely better than thou!' (9)

Speech said, 'Surely I am better than thou, for what thou knowest, I make known, I communicate.' (10)

They went to appeal to Prajâpati for his decision. He, Prajâpati, decided in favour of Mind, saying (to Speech), 'Mind is indeed better than thou, for thou art an imitator of its deeds and a follower in its wake; and inferior, surely, is he who imitates his better's deeds and follows in his wake.' (11)

Then Speech (vâc, fem.) being thus gainsaid, was dismayed and miscarried. She, Speech, then said to Prajâpati, 'May I never be thy oblation-bearer, I whom thou hast gainsaid!' Hence whatever at the sacrifice is performed for Prajâpati, that is performed in a low voice; for speech would not act as oblation-bearer for Prajâpati." [1] (12)

Vâc, speech, also forms the subject of many narratives, in which she is represented as the prototype of women. Thus we meet with her, for example, in the legend of the soma-theft, which frequently occurs in the Brāhmaṇas. The soma was in heaven, and Gāyatrī, in the form of a bird, fetched it down. But as she carried it away, it was stolen from her by a Gandharva. Now the gods took counsel together how they could get back the stolen soma.

"They said, 'The Gandharvas are fond of women: let us send Vâc (speech) to them, and she will return to us together with Soma.' They sent Vâc to them, and she returned to them together with Soma. (3)

The Gandharvas came after her and said, 'Soma (shall be) yours, and Vâc ours!' 'So be it!' said the gods; 'but if she would rather come hither, do not ye carry her off by force: let us woo her!' They accordingly wooed her. (4)

---

[1]) Śat. I, 4, 5, 8-12. Translated by J. *Eggeling*, SBE., Vol. 12, pp. 130 f.

The Gandharvas recited the Vedas to her, saying, 'See how we know it, see how we know it!' [1] (5)

The gods then created the lute and sat playing and singing, saying, 'Thus we will sing to thee, thus we will amuse thee!' She turned to the gods; but, in truth, she turned to them vainly, since she turned away from those engaged in praising and praying, to dance and song. Wherefore even to this day women are given to vain things; for it was on this wise that Vâc turned thereto, and other women do as she did. And hence it is to him who dances and sings that they most readily take a fancy." [2]

Just as this little story is invented to *explain* an attribute of women, there are numerous narratives in the Brāhmaṇas which deal with the *origin* of some matter or some institution. Such legends of origin, to which also the creation-legends belong, the Indians designate as Purāṇas,[3] in order to distinguish them from the Itihāsas (or Ākhyānas), as the stories of gods and men are called. Among these narratives, too, there are such as were merely invented by Brāhmaṇa theologians, while others date back to old, popular myths and legends, or at least are founded upon a tradition independent of the sacrificial science. Thus, the origin of the four castes is frequently related in the Brāhmaṇas. Already in one of the philosophical hymns of the Ṛgveda, the Puruṣasūkta,[4] it is reported how the Brahman arose out of the mouth, the warrior out of the arms, the Vaiśya out of the thighs and the Śūdra out of the feet of the Puruṣa sacrificed by the gods. In the Brāhmaṇas it is Prajāpati who produced out of his mouth the Brahman together with the God Agni, out of his breast and his two arms the warrior as well as Indra, out of the middle of his body the Vaiśya and the All-gods, but out of his feet

---

[1]) As the Veda is the knowledge *par excellence*. See above, p. 52.

[2]) Śat., III, 2, 4, 2-6. Translated by J. *Eggeling*, SBE., Vol. 26, p. 53. *cf.* Śat. III, 2, 1, 19 ff.

[3]) *Purāṇa* means "old," then "old legend," "old story," especially cosmogonic and cosmological myths. At a later period a peculiar class of works was designated as *Purāṇas*, with which we shall have to deal in a later section.

[4]) X, 90, 12, *cf.* above, p. 175. *Deussen*, AGPh, I, 1, pp. 150 ff.

the Śūdra. With the Śūdra no deity was created; therefore he is incapable for sacrifice. In consequence of this kind of origin the Brahman performs his work with his mouth, the warrior with his arms; the Vaiśya does not perish, however much he is "consumed," *i. e.* exploited, by priests and warriors, for he is created out of the middle of the body, where the reproductive power reposes; but of religious ceremonies, the Sūdra can perform only the foot-washing of members of the higher castes, for he arose out of the feet.[1] The following two suggestive tales of the creation of the night and of the winged mountains, found in the Maitrāyaṇī-Saṃhitā, are more pleasing.

"Yama had died. The gods tried to persuade Yamī [2] to forget him. Whenever they asked her, she said: "Only to-day he has died." Then the gods said: "Thus she will indeed never forget him; we will create night!" For at that time there was only day and no night. The gods created night; then arose a morrow; thereupon she forgot him. Therefore people say: "Day and night indeed let sorrow be forgotten!" (Maitr. I, 5, 12.)

"The oldest children of Prajāpati were the hills, and they were winged. They flew away and settled down just where they wished. But at that time the earth still swayed to and fro. Then Indra cut off the wings of the hills and made the earth fast with them. But the wings became storm-clouds; therefore these always hover in the direction of the mountains." (Maitr. I, 10, 13.)[3]

The creation-legends are very numerous in the Brāhmaṇas. An example will show how metaphysical thought here unites with desultory explanations of sacrificial directions. The daily fire-sacrifice (Agnihotra) [4] consisting in the offering of a gift of milk to the fire every morning and every

---

[1]) Taittirīya-Saṃhitā, VII. 1, 1, 4-6. Tāṇḍya-Brāhmaṇa, VI, 1. 6-11. *Cf. Weber*, Ind. Stud., X, 7-10.

[2]) Twin-sister of Yama. See above, pp. 105 ff.

[3]) The myth of the winged hills is already known to the singers of the Ṛgveda, and is still a favourite subject with later poets. *Cf. Pischel*, Vedische Studien, I, 174.

[4]) See above, p. 172.

evening, is one of the most important sacrifices. Upon the origin and significance of this sacrifice a Brāhmaṇa [1] has the following to say:

In the beginning only Prajāpati was here alone. He thought to himself: 'How can I obtain descendants?' He tortured himself and mortified himself.[2] Out of his mouth he produced Agni. And because he produced him out of his mouth, therefore Agni is a consumer of food. And truly, he who knows that Agni is a food-consumer, he himself becomes a consumer of food. Him, then, he produced first, *agre*, among the gods, and therefore he is called *Agni*, for the name Agni is really *Agri*.[3] Now thought Prajāpati to himself: 'This Agni I have produced as a food-consumer. But there is indeed no other food here than myself, would that he may not eat me up!' For at that time this earth was quite bare; there existed neither plants nor trees. About this Prajāpati was troubled. Hereupon Agni turned to him with open (mouth) and from (Prajāpati), because he was afraid, his own greatness fled. But his own greatness was his speech, and this his own greatness fled from him.' (It is then further related that Prajāpati desires a sacrifice for himself, and through rubbing his hands obtains an offering of butter or of milk, out of which the plants arise. As the result of a second offering of butter or of milk, there arise Sūrya, the sun, and Vāyu, the wind.) "And Prajapāti, in offering sacrifice, on the one hand propagated his species, and on the other hand also saved himself from Agni, from death, when the latter was about to consume him. And he who, knowing this, offers the fire-sacrifice, on the one hand propagates his species by means of descendants as

---

[1]) Sat. II, 2, 4.

[2]) Most of the creation-legends in the Brāhmaṇas begin in the same way. As the magician must prepare himself for his magic, and the priest must prepare himself for the sacrifice, by means of self-torture and mortification, so Prajapati, too, has to prepare himself in the same way for the great work of creation From the root *śram* "to exert oneself," is derived the word *Śramaṇa* "the ascetic" which later occurs frequently, particularly in the Buddhist literature. The word *Tapas* actually means "heat," then "ascetic fervour," then asceticism itself. "In fact, if by the designation Tapas the manifold forms of mortification are understood, then, especially in the earlier periods, the reference to heat as the vehicle of mortification stands in the foreground." (Oldenberg, Religion des Veda, 2. Aufl., pp. 401 ff.) According to Śat. X, 4, 4, 1 f., Prajapati once mortified himself for a thousand years until, as a result of the "heat" of the mortification, lights issued from his pores,—and these became the stars.

[3]) See above, p. 203.

Prajāpati did, and on the other hand saves himself from Agni, from death, when the latter is about to consume him. And when he dies, and he is laid upon the fire, he is born again out of the fire, the fire only consumes his body.[1] And as if he were born of his father and his mother, just so is he born of the fire. He, however, who does not offer the fire-sacrifice, never again arises to new life. Therefore one must of necessity offer the fire-sacrifice." (It is then further related very circumstantially how the gods Agni, Vāyu and Sūrya, brought forth by Prajāpati, themselves in their turn offer sacrifices, and how the cow was created.) "This cow, however, Agni, desired thinking: 'I would like to mate myself with her.' He united himself with her and poured forth his seed into her. This became milk. Therefore the latter is cooked, while the cow is raw, for the milk is Agni's seed; and therefore it is that milk, whether it is in a black cow or a red one, is always white and shining like fire, because it is Agni's seed. And therefore it is warm already at the milking, for it is the seed of Agni." [2]

Just as these creation-legends usually begin by relating that Prajāpati "torments and mortifies himself," so we often read also that, after the creation was accomplished, he was weak, exhausted and wearied, whereupon some sacrifice is described, through which his strength had to be restored. On one occasion it is the gods who offer this sacrifice, on another occasion Agni alone shows this favour to Prajāpati, and on yet another occasion he regains his strength, "after having sung hymns and tortured himself," by creating the sacrificial animals and sacrificing them.[3] It is indeed remarkable that this world-creator Prajāpati, who really is the highest god in the Brāhmaṇas, has nothing lofty about him and often plays a rather pitiful part. Once he is actually even offered as a sacrifice himself by the gods![4] In a legend which is referred to in several places, he is accused of incest, which he

---

[1]) One of the few places in the Brāhmaṇas where mention is made of life after death.

[2]) *Cf.* above p. 65.

[3]) Sat. IV, 6, 4, 1; VII, 4, 1, 16; and frequently. VI. 1, 2, 12 ff. III, 9, 1.

[4]) Sat. X, 2, 2.

has committed with his daughter Dyaus (heaven) or Uṣas (dawn). In order to punish him for this sin, the gods, out of their most frightful forms, formed the god Rudra. The latter pierced Prajāpati with his arrow, whereat Orion and other constellations arose.[1] Very noteworthy, too, is the fact that in the Brāhmaṇas (and in the Veda generally) there is no *one* Indian creation legend, which, as for instance the biblical legend in Europe, has found more or less general recognition in India, but that we find a great number of creation-legends, containing the most diversified ideas and speculations, which cannot be made to harmonize with one other at all. Thus we find, for example, in the Śatapatha-Brāhmaṇa, soon after the above quoted legend, an entirely different account of the creation. Prajāpati, here too,[2] tortured and mortified himself, in order to produce beings. He brought forth creatures, first the birds, then the small creeping things, then the snakes. But no sooner had they been created than they all vanished again, and Prajāpati was once more alone. He thought diligently about the reason for this, and at last the idea came to him that the creatures perished for lack of food. So he created new beings, from whose breasts he let milk flow forth, and these remained alive. Again, in another place in the same work,[3] Prajāpati creates the animals out of his vital organs, out of his mind he created man, out of his eye the horse, out of his breath the cow, out of his ear the sheep, out of his voice the goat. Because man is created out of Prajāpati's mind, and the mind is the first of the vital organs, therefore man is the first and strongest of all animals.[4]

In the majority of the legends, Prajāpati is indeed the

[1]) Aitareya-Brāhmaṇa III, 33. *Cf.* Śat. I, 7, 4, 1; II, 1, 2, 8; VI, 1, 3, 8.

[2]) Sat. II, 5, 1, 1-3.

[3]) Sat. VII, 5, 2, 6.

[4]) This refers to the sacrificial animals in particular.

only Creator, from whom the world and beings derive their origin. But, already in the Brāhmaṇas, there are places where Prajāpati himself is regarded as created, and the creation begins with the primeval water or with the non-existing or with the Brahman. Thus there is the following creation-legend :

"In the beginning there existed here nothing but water, a sea of water. These waters desired to propagate their kind. They tortured themselves, they mortified themselves. And when they had mortified themselves [1] a golden egg originated in them. The year did not yet exist at that time; but as long as the duration of a year, this golden egg swam about. After a year a man arose out of it; that was Prajāpati. Therefore a woman or a cow or a mare gives birth within a year, for Prajāpati was born after a year. He broke the golden egg open. But at that time there did not yet exist any standing-place. So this golden egg, which bore him, swam about as long as the duration of a year. After a year he tried to speak, and he said: "*bhūḥ*," and this (word) became this earth; (he said:) "*bhuvaḥ*" and this became yonder atmosphere, (he said) "*suvar*" [2] and this became the sky yonder. Therefore, a child tries to talk after a year, for after a year Prajāpati spoke. When Prajāpati first spoke, he uttered monosyllabic and bi-syllabic words, therefore a child, when it first speaks, utters mono-syllabic and bi-syllabic words. Those (three words) form five syllables. Out of these he made the five seasons of the year, therefore there are five seasons here.[3] This Prajāpati rose up above the worlds created in this manner after a year; therefore, after a year, a child tries to stand, for after a year Prajāpati rose up. He was born with the life of a thousand years. As one perceives the other bank of a river from a distance, so he perceived the other bank of his life.[4] And, singing praises and torturing himself

[1]) As the term *Tapas* not only means mortification, but also heat, it is possible, in the case of the words "when they had mortified themselves," which might also mean "when they had become heated," to think of "hatching-heat" and it is quite possible that there is an intentional ambiguity in the Sanskrit words. *Cf.* above p. 99. and 220, Note 2, and *Deussen*, AGPh., I, 1, p. 182; 2, pp. 60 ff.

[2]) *Cf.* above p. 186, on the three sacred words bhūḥ, bhuvaḥ, suvar (or svar).

[3]) Namely: Spring, summer, rainy season, autumn, and winter.

[4]) As Prajāpati was born, he must also be mortal.

he lived on, as he desired to propagate his species. He placed reproductive energy into himself, and with his mouth he created the gods .....After he had created them, he saw that there was, as it were, daylight (*divā*) for him, and that is the divinity of the gods (*deva*), that after he had created them, he saw that there was, as it were, daylight for him. Now he created with the breath of life which is below, the Asuras (demons) ..... And after they were created, he saw that there was, as it were, darkness. He knew: "Truly, I have created evil for myself, as there was darkness as soon as I had created them." And even at this early stage he smote them with evil, and their day was then already done. Therefore it is said: "It is not true what is reported of the battles between gods and Asuras, partly in narratives (anvākhyāna), partly in legends (itihāsa),[1] for at that time already Prajāpati smote them with evil, at that time already their day was done."......After he had created the gods, he made the day out of that which was light, and after he had created the Asuras, he made the night out of that which was dark. So there now existed day and night." (Śat. XI, 1, 6, 1-11.)

Another creation-legend is still more remarkable, though also much less clear (Sat. VI, 1, 1), beginning with the words: "In the beginning there was here only the non-existent (Asat)." But it is at once added that this non-existent was really the Ṛṣis, for these, by means of self-torture and self-mortification have brought forth everything. These Ṛṣis, however, were the Prāṇas or life-spirits, and these—how they did this is quite unintelligible—created first seven Puruṣas or "persons" and then united these to a single puruṣa, to Prajāpati.

"This puruṣa (person) Prajāpati desired to multiply himself, to propagate his species. He tortured himself, he mortified himself. After he had tortured and mortified himself, he created first the Brahman, namely, the three-fold knowledge (trayī vidyā). This was the foundation for him. Therefore it is said: 'The Brahman is the foundation of the All.' Therefore one stands firm, when one has learnt the Veda; for this, the Brahman (*i.e.* the Veda) is the foundation."

---

[1]) This is tantamount to declaring all the numerous legends of the Brāhmaṇas, which tell of the battles between gods and Asuras, to be lies!

It is then further related how Prajāpati, "standing firm upon this foundation," mortified himself, and then first created the water. With the aid of the Veda he brought forth an egg; out of the egg arose Agni, and the egg-shell became the earth, and so on. It is a very prolix and confused account. It is, however, important to see that the *Brahman*, originally signifying prayer or magic spell, then sacred knowledge or Veda, was here already made the foundation of all existence. From this only a step remained to the doctrine of the Brahman itself as a creative principle. This doctrine too is already found in the Śatapatha-Brāhmaṇa (XI, 2, 3, 1) where it says:

> "In the beginning there was here only the Brahman. This created the gods, and after it had created the gods, it gave them these worlds as dwellings,[1] (namely), this earth-world to Agni, the atmosphere to Vāyu and the heaven to Sūrya."

Thus we see how in the Brāhmaṇas—and therein lies their great significance for the history of Indian thought—all those ideas were already in the making, which attained their full development only in the Āraṇyakas and Upaniṣads. Even the fundamental doctrine of the Upaniṣads, as *Śaṇḍilya* enunciated it, is already found in the Śatapatha-Brāhmaṇa.[2]

Āraṇyakas and Upaniṣads.

When R. Garbe[3] calls the sacrificial science of the Brāhmaṇas "the only literary production of these barren centuries preceding the awakening of philosophical speculation," he gives expression to a universal, but in my opinion erroneous, view. It would be too terrible to think that, with such a gifted people as the Indians must have been,

[1]) Literally "it made them ascend these worlds."

[2]) X, 6, 3. *Cf.* below, pp. 249 f.

[3]) Beiträge zur indischen Kulturgeschichte (Berlin, 1903), p. 6.

even on the evidence of the Ṛgvedic hymns, the futile hair-splittings on the purpose and meaning of sacrificial ceremonies should have occupied the entire thought even of the priests, to say nothing of the warriors and the remaining classes of the people. As a matter of fact we do find in the Brāhmaṇas themselves, as Sāyaṇa has already emphasized, and as we have partly seen above, beside ritual-precepts (Kalpa) and the discussions on the same, also myths and legends (itihāsa), cosmogonic myths (purāṇa), epic song verses (gāthā) and songs in praise of heroes (nārāśaṃsī.[1]) In other words: the beginnings of epic poetry reach back into the period of the Brāhmaṇas. It is a matter of course that the great and costly sacrifices, with which the Brāhmaṇas deal, were only possible on the supposition of an active and industrious people; and it is unthinkable that the warriors and merchants, the farmers and herd owners, the craftsmen and labourers of that time should have sung no songs, related no stories. A little of what was sung and narrated in India at that early period, is preserved in the Vedic texts themselves (as, for example, the legend of Śunaḥśepa), but much is preserved in the later epics and Purāṇas. Moreover, the Brāhmaṇas presuppose the beginnings of grammar, phonetics, astronomy, *i.e.*, of those sciences which were later on pursued more independently as Vedāṅgas[2]; neither does the "awakening of philosophical speculation" come *after* the period of the Brāhmaṇas: It comes *before* this period. We have seen how in some hymns of the Ṛgveda doubts and scruples already arose concerning the popular belief in gods and the priestly cult.

---

[1]) *Max Müller*, "History of Ancient Sanskrit Literature," 2nd ed., London, 1860, p. 344. *Cf.* Śat. XI, 5, 6, 8; 7, 9. "Knowers of the narratives" (Ākhyānavidas) are mentioned, in the Aitareya-Brāhmaṇa, III, 25, as a special class of literary men.

[2]) On the beginnings of the Vedāṅgas in the Brāhmaṇas, *cf.* *Max Müller*, "History of Ancient Sanskrit Literature," pp. 110 ff.

These sceptics and thinkers, these first philosophers of ancient India certainly did not remain isolated. That they, too, founded schools of thought, that their teachings were diffused, is proved by the "philosophical" hymns of the Atharvaveda and isolated portions of the Yajurveda-Saṃhitās, in which, it is true, the teachings of the philosophers often appear only in caricature.[1] But even these caricatures prove that philosophical speculation was further pursued also during the centuries in which the sacrificial science flourished.

We are not, however, likely to find these oldest philosophers of ancient India among the priests, who were engaged in the science of sacrifice. For their teachings, which were directed against the plurality of gods, were in obvious contradiction to the interest of these priests. We can scarcely imagine that the Brahmans, who lived by the sacrifices, had many men amongst them who doubted the existence of Indra himself, and raised the question whether there were any sense in sacrificing to the gods.[2] It is much more probable that such sceptics and thinkers were to be found among those who were the most obnoxious to the priests, among the "misers," who did not *believe*, *i.e.*, who did not sacrifice and gave no gifts to the priests.

The fact that the warrior-caste was closely connected with the intellectual life and the literary activity of ancient times, is proved by numerous passages in the Upaniṣads, in fact already in the Brāhmaṇas. In the Kauṣītaki-Brāhmaṇa (XXVI, 5) a king Pratardana converses with the priests concerning the sacrificial science. In Book XI of the Śatapatha-Brāhmaṇa there is repeated mention of King Janaka of Videha, who confounded all priests by his knowledge. The passage in which Janaka questions the priests Śvetaketu,

---

[1]) *Cf.* above pp. 98 ff., 149 ff, 183 f.

[2]) *Cf.* above, p. 98.

Somaśuṣma and Yājñavalkya as to how they perform the fire-sacrifice (Agnihotra) is particularly instructive. None of them gives a satisfactory answer. But Yājñavalkya receives a gift of a hundred cows, because he has inquired the most deeply into the meaning of the sacrifice, although, as King Janaka remarks, even upon him the true meaning of the Agnihotra has not yet dawned. After the king has departed, the priests say to one another: "Truly, this warrior has confounded us by his speech. Well! We will challenge him to a theological debate (Brahmodya)." Yājñavalkya, however, dissuades them, saying: "We are Brahmans, but he is only a warrior. If we overcome him, whom shall we say that we have overcome? But if he should overcome us, the people would say of us: 'A warrior has overcome the Brahmans'; do not think of such a thing!" The two other priests agreed with him, but Yājñavalkya betakes himself to King Janaka and begs to be instructed by him.[1] Ayasthūṇa, too, the sacrificer, who instructs his priest Śaulvāyana,[2] can hardly be a Brahman, although Sāyaṇa declares him to be a Ṛṣi. According to tradition, even the Ṛṣis or composers of the hymns of the Ṛgveda were by no means always members of the priesthood. Thus it is said of a Ṛṣi Kavaṣa, that he was the son of a female slave, a non-Brahman. When he wanted to participate in a great sacrifice, the priests drove him away, to die of hunger and thirst in the desert. But the waters and the goddess Sarasvatī take pity on him, he 'sees' a hymn, whereupon the priests recognise him as a Ṛṣi and receive him back.[3]

In the Upaniṣads, however, we find not only kings, but also women and even people of dubious descent, taking an active part in the literary and philosophical aspirations and

---

1) Śat. XI, 6, 2; *cf.* XI, 3, 1. 2-4; XI, 6, 3.
2) Śat. XI, 4, 2, 17-20.
3) Aitareya-Brāhmaṇa, II, 19.

often possessors of the highest knowledge. Thus in the Bṛhadāraṇyaka-Upaniṣad, *Gārgī*, the daughter of Vacaknu, questions Yājñavalkya at great length upon the origin of all existence, until the latter says: "Ask not too much, Gārgī, that thy head may not burst. Truly, concerning divinity one must not ask too much. Thou dost ask too much, Gārgī; ask not too much!" And in another place the same Gārgī, in the midst of an assembly of disputative scholars, advances towards the famous teacher Yājñavalkya with the words: "I arise against thee, Yājñavalkya! As a hero's son from Benares or from Videha strings the slackened bow and arises with two foe-piercing arrows in his hand, so I arise against thee with two questions—answer me those!" In the same Upaniṣad Yājñavalkya instructs his wife Maitreyī in the highest knowledge of the Ātman.[1] How little this highest knowledge was the sole privilege of the priests, is again proved by the amusing story of Raikva with the bullock-team,[2] who is sitting under his cart and scratching the itch, but who, in the possession of the highest wisdom is proud as a king. Humbly the wealthy donor Janaśruti approaches him in order to be instructed by him. Raikva calls him a śūdra[3] and laughs at the presents which the rich man offers him. Only when the latter gives him his beautiful daughter in marriage, does he condescend to instruct him.[4] The following story is also delightfully ingenuous:

"1. Satyakāma, the son of Jabālā, addressed his mother and said: 'I wish to become a Brahmacārin (religious student), mother. Of what family am I?'

---

[1]) Bṛhadāraṇyaka-Upaniṣad, III, 6; III, 8; II, 4 and IV, 5.

[2]) The meaning of *sayugvan* translated by "with the bullock-team," is not certain. But other explanations (s. H. *Luders*, SBA., 1916, pp. 278 ff) are not satisfactory. Raikva is called a "Brāhmaṇa" in the sense of "one who knows the Brahman," not in the sense of "a member of the priestly class."

[3]) The word is here used as a term of abuse.

[4]) Chāndogya-Upaniṣad, IV, 1-3.

2. She said to him : 'I do not know, my child, of what family thou art. In my youth when I had to move about much as a servant (waiting on the guests in my father's house), I conceived thee. I do not know of what family thou art. I am Jabālā by name, thou art Satyakāma (Philalethes). Say that thou art Satyakāma Jābāla.'

3. He going to Gautama Hāridrumata said to him, 'I wish to become a Brahmacārin with you, Sir. May I come to you, Sir?'

4. He said to him: 'Of what family are you, my friend?' He replied: 'I do not know, Sir, of what family I am. I asked my mother, and she answered: "In my youth when I had to move about much as a servant, I conceived thee. I do not know of what family thou art. I am Jābāla by name, thou art Satyakāma," I am therefore Satyakāma Jābāla, Sir.'

5. He said to him: 'No one but a true Brāhmaṇa would thus speak out. Go and fetch fuel, friend, I shall initiate you. You have not swerved from the truth.' "[1]

The passage proves how lightly brahmanical descent was treated at that ancient period, while later—in the law-books—it is again and again emphasized that only the Brahman may teach the Veda, and only a member of the three highest castes may be instructed in the Veda. In the Upaniṣads, however, we are repeatedly told that kings or warriors are in possession of the highest knowledge, and that Brahmans go to them for instruction. Thus the Brahman Gautama, father of Śvetaketu, goes to King Pravāhaṇa in order to be instructed by him concerning the Beyond. And it is related that the desire of Gautama was very awkward for the king : for the doctrine which he had to proclaim, had never before penetrated to the Brahmans, "and therefore it is that in all the worlds the mastery has fallen to the share of the warrior-class." Finally, however, the king does

---

[1]) Chāndogya-Upaniṣad, IV, 4. Translated by *Max Müller*, SBE, Vol. I, p. 60. In the Vaṃśas or lists of teachers of the Śatapatha-Brāhmaṇa numerous teachers are only mentioned by their *maternal name*. *Cf.* above, p. 194 Note 1. Satyakāma means: "truth-loving." The passage has also been translated (into German) and explained by H. *Lüders*, SBA., 1922, pp. 227 ff.

impart the doctrine to him,—and it is the doctrine of *transmigration*, which here, where for the first time it appears clearly and distinctly, proves to be a doctrine which emanated from the warrior-class, and was originally foreign to brahmanical theology.[1] Another passage proves that the chief doctrine of the Upaniṣads, too, the doctrine of the *Ātman*, the All-One, originated in non-brahmanical circles. Here five highly learned Brahmans betake themselves to the wise Uddālaka Āruṇi, in order to learn from him the doctrine of the Ātman. He, however, thought to himself: "These great and learned scholars will question me, and I shall not be able to reply to everything. Well! I will direct them to some one else." And he directed them to *King* Aśvapati Kaikeya, to whom they actually went for instruction.[2]

While, then, the Brahmans were pursuing their barren sacrificial science, other circles were already engaged upon those highest questions which were at last treated so admirably in the Upaniṣads. From these circles, which originally were not connected with the priestly caste, proceeded the forest-hermits and wandering ascetics, who not only renounced the world and its pleasures, but also kept aloof from the sacrifices and ceremonies of the Brahmans. Different sects, more or less opposed to Brahmanism, were soon formed from these same circles, among which sects the Buddhists attained to such great fame. The extensive propagation of these sects, particularly of Buddhism, proves on what fruitful soil the doctrines of those ancient philosophers must have fallen, and how much response the doctrines which were opposed to the sacrifice found among the cultured classes.

---

[1]) Chāndogya-Upaniṣad, V, 3. Bṛhadāraṇyaka-Up., VI, 2. In the Kauṣitaki-Up., I, 1 the Kṣatriya Citra instructs the "first of the priests," Āruṇi, about the Beyond.

[2]) Chāndogya-Up., V, 11 ff. A version of this narrative is already to be found in Śat., X. 6. 1.

This is, however, by no means tantamount to saying that the Brahmans took no part in philosophical speculation; for warriors and members of the higher castes in general were educated in the Brahmans' schools, and there must have been a brisk exchange of philosophical ideas between the Brahmans and the other educated classes at all times.[1] Moreover, not every Brahman was a priest or an adept in the art of the sacrifice. There were Brahmans, both rich and poor, who pursued worldly professions,[2] and there must have been many of these who sympathised with the sceptics and the exponents of new doctrines. Lastly, as has so often been the case in the history of Indian thought, the Brahmans had the knack of bringing into line with their own priestly wisdom and orthodoxy even such ideas as were in opposition to them. They succeeded in doing this by means of the doctrine of the four Aśramas (stages of life),

---

[1]) *Cf. A. Hillebrandt,* Aus Brahmanas und Upanisaden, pp. 10 ff., with whom I quite agree when he says that the philosophy of the Upaniṣads should be called neither a "Brahmanical" nor a "Kṣatriya philosophy." But it should not be doubted that non-Brahmans, especially Kṣatriyas, had a considerable share in the spiritual and intellectual life of ancient India. See P. *Deussen,* System des Vedanta, Leipzig, 1883, pp. 18 f., AGPh. I, 1, 166; 1, 2, 17 ff.; R. *Garbe,* Beiträge Zur indischen Kulturgeschichte, Berlin, 1903, pp. 1 ff.; R. *Fick,* The Social Organisation in North-East India in Buddha's Time, transl. by S. *Maitra,* Calcutta, 1920, pp. 90 ff. The view that the Kṣatriyas had an essential share in the development of the Upaniṣad ideas, has been contested by H. *Oldenberg,* Die Lehre der Upanishaden und die Anfänge des Buddhismus, Göttingen, 1915, pp. 166 f.; P. *Oltramare,* L'histoire des idées théosophiques dans I, Inde, 1, 96 f.; A. B. *Keith,* Aitareya Āranyaka, p. 50 and JRAS., 1915, p. 550; also by S. *Dasgupta*, A History of Indian Philosophy, I Cambridge, 1922, pp. 33 ff., though he admits (p. 31) "that among the Kṣatriyas in general there existed earnest philosophic enquiries which must be regarded as having exerted an important influence in the formation of the Upaniṣad doctrines." The fact is that the ancient Upaniṣads as literary compositions were arranged in the Brahmanic schools and were "Brahmanical" in this sense. But it does not follow from this, that all or even the most essential *ideas* contained in these texts were first *conceived* in priestly circles. It is worth mentioning that even the Āpastambīya-Dharmasūtra (II, 2, 4, 25) permits a Brahman to learn under a Kṣatriya or a Vaiśya teacher "in time of need" (āpadi).

[2]) *Cf. Oldenberg,* Die Lehre der Upanishaden, etc., p. 5.

whereby the ascetic and hermit life was made an essential part of the brahmanical religious system. This doctrine consists of the principle that every "Aryan," *i.e.*, every man belonging to one of the three highest castes, who wishes to lead an ideal life, must pass through four stages of life. First, as a pupil (Brahmacārin), he must live with a teacher and learn the Veda; when his period of training is accomplished, he must found a household, and as a householder (Gṛhastha) beget children and offer the prescribed sacrifices to the gods, or have them offered. On approaching old age, however, he should quit his house, and, as a forest-hermit (Vānaprastha) henceforth perform only limited sacrificial service, but meditate the more upon the mystical and symbolical significance of the sacrifice. But only when he feels his end approaching, shall he give up this sacrifice and meditation also, renounce all good works, and as an ascetic fleeing from the world (Sannyāsin) henceforth ponder only over Brahman, the highest world-principle, and strive for union with it.[1)]

In the Brāhmaṇas or as appendices to them we find texts which were known as Āraṇyakas or "forest texts." These texts comprised everything which was of a secret, uncanny character, and spelt danger to the uninitiated, and which, for that reason, might only be taught and learnt in the forest, and not in the villages. The main contents of these Araṇyakas are no longer rules for the performance of the sacrifices and the explanation of ceremonies, but the mysticism and symbolism of sacrifice, and priestly philosophy. After the doctrine of the Āśramas had been set up as the

---

1) In the oldest Upaniṣads (Chāndogya-Up. II, 23; VIII, 1) three branches of an ideal life are spoken of, but there is no mention yet of three or four successive stages of life. Only in later Upaniṣads (Maitr. IV, 3; Āśrama-Up.), in the Mahabhārata and in the Dharmaśāstras the Āśrama theory is fully developed. See Deussen, Sechzig Upanishads, pp. 96 f; ERE., II, 128 ff.; and *Jacobi*, ERE., II, 802.

brahmanical ideal of life, these "forest texts" naturally came to be the prescribed portions of the Veda to be studied by forest-hermits.[1] Now, the oldest *Upaniṣads* are in part included in these "forest texts," and in part appended to them; and it is often difficult to draw the line between the Āraṇyakas and the Upaniṣads. These texts formed, in more senses than one, the *Vedānta, i.e.*, "the end of the Veda."[2] Firstly most of these texts are of later origin, and fall chronologically into the *end* of the Vedic period. Further, we must never forget that the whole of this Vedic literature did not consist of written books, but was only transmitted by word of mouth. What we find in the individual Brāhmaṇas, therefore, and usually call "works" or "books" is nothing but the subject of instructions of various priests' schools. The subject was taught to the pupils within a certain period embracing a number of years during which the pupil had to live with the teacher and serve him. The teaching of that which was the most difficult to understand, the mysteries, the mystical and philosophical doctrines, as they are contained in the Āraṇyakas and Upaniṣads, naturally fell into the *end* of this period of instruction. These texts form the *end*, too, of the Veda-recital, as a sacred act and religious duty. The later philosophers, lastly, saw in these doctrines of the Upaniṣads not the *end*, but the *final aim* of the Veda.[3]

---

[1]) *Cf. Oldenberg*, Die Hymnen des Rigveda, I, Berlin, 1888, p. 291 and NGGW., 1915, 382 ff. Rāmānuja (SBE., Vol. 48, p. 645) states that certain mantras and sacrificial rites are discussed at the beginning of Upaniṣads "owing to their having, like the latter, to be studied in the forest." In the Āruṇi-Upaniṣad, 2 (The Minor Upaniṣads, ed. F. O. *Schrader*, I, p. 7; *Deussen*, Sechzig Upanishads des Veda, p. 693) it is said that the hermit should study of all the Vedas only the Āraṇyaka and the Upaniṣad. Manu, VI, 29, says that the hermit should learn "the Upaniṣad texts" (aupaniṣadīḥ śrutīḥ). Strict rules of austerity are prescribed at the reading of the Upaniṣads, s. Baudhāyana-Dharmasūtra, II, 10, 18, 15 ff. *Cf.* also *Max Müller*, History of Ancient Sanskrit Literature, pp. 313 ff.

[2]) "Vedānta" means originally only the Upaniṣads. The word was only later used to mean the system of philosophy based on the Upaniṣads.

[3]) *Cf.* P. *Deussen*, System des Vedanta, pp. 3 f. AGPh., 1, 2, p. 5.

As Vedānta or "Veda-end," the Āraṇyakas, as well as the older Upaniṣads, belong to the various Vedic schools; they form, in fact, only component parts of the Brāhmaṇas. Thus an Aitareya-Araṇyaka, in which the Aitareya-Upaniṣad is included, is tacked on to the Aitareya-Brāhmaṇa of the Ṛg-veda. The Kauṣitaki-Brāhmaṇa, which also belongs to the Ṛg-veda, ends with the Kauṣitaki-Āraṇyaka, of which the Kauṣītaki-Upaṇiṣad (also called the Kauṣitaki-Brāhmaṇa-Upaniṣad) forms only a part.[1] In the Black Yajurveda the Taittirīya-Āraṇyaka[2] is only a continuation of the Taittirīya-Brāhmaṇa, and the conclusion of the Araṇyaka is formed by the Tattirīya-Upaniṣad and the Maha-Nārāyan-Upaniṣad. In the great Śatapatha-Brāhmaṇa of the White-Yajurveda, the first third of Book XIV is an Araṇyaka, while the end of the book is formed by the greatest and most important of all Upaniṣads, the Bṛhadāraṇyaka-Upaniṣad. The Chāndogya-Upaniṣad, the first section of which is nothing but an Āraṇyaka, belongs to a Brāhmaṇa of the Sāmaveda—probably the Tāṇḍya-Mahā-Brāhmaṇa. The so-called Jaiminīya-Upaniṣad-Brāhmaṇa[3] is an Araṇyaka of the Jaiminīya- or Talavakāra-school of the Sāmaveda, and the Kena-Upaniṣad, also called Talavakāra-Upaniṣad, forms a part of it.

With the exception of the Mahā-Nārāyaṇa-Upaniṣad, which was only added to the Taittirīya-Āraṇyaka at a later

---

1) The Aitareya-Āraṇyaka has been published and translated into English by A. B. *Keith* (Anecdota Oxoniensia, Aryan Series, Part IX, Oxford 1919) and as an appendix to it a portion of the Śāṅkhāyana-Āraṇyaka (VII-XV). Adhyāyas—I and II of this Āraṇyaka are published and translated by W. *Friedlander*, Der mahâvrata Abschnitt des Çāṅkhāyana-Āraṇyaka, Berlin 1900, Adhyāyas III to VI, by *Cowell*, Calcutta 1901. On the title, antiquity and contents of the Śāṅkhāyana- or Kauṣītaki-Āraṇyaka. S. *Keith*, JRAS., 1908, 363 ff. The Sāṅkhāyana Āraṇyaka, with an Appendix on the Mahāvrata, (translated) by A. B. *Keith*, OTF., London, 1908.

2) Ed. with Sâyana's Comm. in Bibl. Ind. and in An. SS. No 36.

3) The Jaiminīya or Talavakāra Upaniṣad Brāhmaṇa, Text, Translation and Notes by Hanns *Oertel*, in JAOS, Vol. XVI, 1896.

period, all the above-named Upaniṣads belong to the oldest works of this kind. In language and style they resemble the Brāhmaṇas, component parts of which they are, or to which they are immediately attached. It is the same simple, slightly clumsy *prose*, but—especially in the narrative portions—by no means lacking in beauty. Only half of the Kena-Upaniṣad is metrical, and it is the latest of the Upaniṣads enumerated. Although each one of the great Upaniṣads contains, as Deussen [1] says, "earlier and later texts side by side, hence the age of each individual piece must be determined separately," yet even the later portions of the above-mentioned Upaniṣads may claim great antiquity, if only on linguistic grounds.[2] We may take it that the greater Upaniṣads, like the Bṛhadāraṇyaka- and the Chāndogya-Upaniṣad, originated in the *fusion* of several longer or shorter texts which had originally been regarded as separate Upaniṣads. This would also explain the fact that the same texts are sometimes to be found in several Upaniṣads. The individual texts of which the greater Upaniṣads are composed, all belong to a period which cannot be very far removed from that of the Brāhmaṇas and the Āraṇyakas, and is before Buddha and before Pāṇini. For this reason the six above-mentioned Upaniṣads,—Aitareya, Bṛhadāraṇyaka, Chāndogya, Taittirīya, Kauṣītaki and Kena—undoubtedly represent the earliest stage of development in the literature of the Upaniṣads. They contain the so-called Vedānta doctrine in its pure, original form.

---

[1]) AGPh., 1, 2, p. 22.

[2]) On the language of the Upaniṣads see B *Liebich*, Panini, Leipzig, 1891, p. 62 ff.; Otto *Wecker*, Der Gebrauch der Kasus in der Upaniṣadliteratur, Göttingen 1905 (Bezz Beitr.); W. *Kirfel*, Beiträge zur Geschichte der Nominalkomposition in den Upaniṣads und im Epos, Diss, Bonn, 1908; A. *Fürst*, Der Sprachgebrauch der älteren Upaniṣads verglichen mit dem der früheren vedischen Perioden und des klassischen Sanskrit, Diss. (Tübingen), Göttingen, 1915; also *Oldenberg*, Zur Geschichte der altindischen Prosa, pp. 28 ff.

A few Upaniṣads which are written entirely or for the most part in *verse*, belong to a period which is somewhat later, though still early, and probably pre-Buddhistic. These, too, are assigned to certain Vedic schools, though they have not always come down to us as portions of an Araṇyaka. In this category we may include the Kaṭha- or Kāṭhaka-Upaniṣad,[1] the very name of which points to its connection with a school of the Black Yajurveda (see above p. 169). The Śvetāśvatara-Upaniṣad,[2] and the Mahā-Nārāyaṇa-Upaniṣad which has come down to us as an appendix to the Taittirīya-Āraṇyaka, are also counted among the texts of the Black Yajurveda. The short, but most valuable Īśā-Upaniṣad,[3] which forms the last section of the Vājasaneyi-Saṃhitā, belongs to the White Yajurveda. The Muṇḍaka-Upaniṣad,[4] and the Praśna-Upaniṣad,[5] half of which is in prose, half in verse, belong to the Atharvaveda. Though these six Upaniṣads, too, contain the Vedānta doctrine, we here find it interwoven to a great extent with Sāṃkhya and Yoga doctrines and with monotheistic views. We must, however, leave it to future scholars to decide to what degree the various philosophical doctrines mingled, and to what degree this mingling

---

[1]) Edited with Śaṅkara's commentary by Srīdhara-Śāstrī *Pāthaka*, Poona, 1919; translated by W. D. *Whitney*, Transactions of the American Philological Association, Vol 21. On text-criticism s. R. *Fritzsche*, ZDMG., 66, 1912, 727 f.; *Hillebrandt*, ZDMG., 68, 1914, 579 ff.; and *Hertel*, Die Weisheit der Upanischaden, pp. 42 ff.

[2]) On this Up. see *Weber*, Ind. Stud I, 420 ff. and R. G. *Bhandarkar*, Vaiṣṇavism, Śaivism and Minor Religious Systems (Grundriss III, 6, 1913), pp. 106 ff.

[3]) Translation (with text) and analysis by Aurobindo *Ghose*, Calcutta (Ideal and Progress Series, No. 5). Metrical translation by H. *Baynes*, Ind. Ant., 26, 1897, 213 ff. On text criticism s *Baynes*, l c., and *Hertel*, Die Weisheit der Upanischaden, pp. 25 ff.

[4]) J. *Hertel* (Muṇḍaka-Upaniṣad, kritische Ausgabe, Leipzig, 1924) has tried to restore the original text of this Upaniṣad. Its connection with the Atharvaveda (X, 7 and 8) has been pointed out by *Hertel*, l c., pp. 45 ff The title probably means "the Upaniṣad of the bald-headed," that is, of some sect of ascetics with shaven heads. *Hertel* (l c., pp. 64 ff) suggests some connection between the Muṇḍ.-Up, and the Jainas.

[5]) In this Upaniṣad the sage Pippalāda, the founder of the Paippalāda school of the Atharvaveda, appears as teacher. On text criticism s. *Hillebrandt*, ZDMG., 68, 1914, 581 f.

was consequent upon retouched versions of the text; for all these texts show distinct signs of having been touched up. There are for instance, as many as three separate recensions of the Mahā-Nārāyaṇa-Upaniṣad, and this shows how uncertain the text is.[1]

The Maitrāyaṇīya-Upaniṣad,[2] which, by reason of its title, is attributed to a school of the Black Yajurveda,[3] belongs to a considerably later period which must have been post-Buddhistic. It is again written in *prose*, like the earliest Upaniṣads. This prose, however, no longer shows any Vedic traces. On the grounds of language, style and contents, we may place the work in the period of classical Sanskrit literature. The Māṇḍūkya-Upaniṣad[4] of the Atharvaveda probably also belongs to this same later period. Śaṅkara, who quotes the twelve Upaniṣads previously enumerated as sacred and authoritative texts in his commentary on the

---

[1]) *Cf.* R. *Zimmermann*, Die Quellen der Mahā-nārāyaṇa-Upaniṣad und das Verhältnis der verschiedenen Rezensionen zu einander, Diss., Berlin, 1913, and Ind. Ant., 44, 1915, 130 ff., 177 ff.; *Barth.*, RHR. 19, 1889, 150 f = Oeuvres, II, 23. Edition by G. A. *Jacob*, BSS Nr. 35, 1888.

[2]) Other titles are: Maitrāyaṇa-Brāhmaṇa-Up., Maitrāyaṇa-Up., Maitrāyaṇī-Up., and Maitri-Up., s. *Max Müller*, SBE., Vol. 15, pp. xliii ff. There are several recensions of the text. The text (ed., with the commentary of Rāmatīrtha, by E. B. *Cowell*, 2nd ed. revised by Satischandra *Vidyabhusan*, Bibl. Ind, 1913 ff.) which has hitherto been translated consists of 7 Prapāṭhakas. But the two last Prapāṭhakas (declared to be supplementary by *Deussen*, Sechzig Upanishads, p. 330) are missing in the edition of Mahadeva *Sastri* (Sāmānya Vedānta Upanishads, pp. 388 ff.), where Prap., IV, 5 corresponds to the 5th Prapāṭhaka of the older editions. A different work is the metrical Maitreya-Upaniṣad (Minor Upaniṣads, ed. *Schrader*, I, pp. 105 ff.), which only in the prose introduction partly agrees with our Maitrāy.-Up.

[3]) In some MSS. it is given as part of the Maitrāyaṇīya-Saṃhitā.

[4]) On this Upaniṣad s. H. *Baynes*, Ind. Ant., 26, 1897, 169 ff. The Gauḍapādīya-Kārikās, one of the most important works of Indian philosophy, is based on the Māṇḍ.-Up. Pandit *Vidhusekhara Bhattacharya* (Sir Asutosh Mukherjee Silver Jubilee Volume, pp 103 ff.) has proved that Śaṅkara is not the author of the commentary ascribed to him on this Up. The same learned Pandit thinks, as he writes to me (in a letter dated 27th August, 1924) and as he intends to prove, that the Māṇḍūkya-Up. is later than Gauḍapāda's Kārikās, and was even unknown to Śaṅkara.

Brahmasūtras, mentions neither the Maitrāyaṇīya- nor the Māṇḍūkya-Upaniṣad.[1]

Though the two last-named texts must be among the latest offshoots of Vedic literature, they too may still be classed together with the twelve earlier texts as *Vedic Upaniṣads*; and these fourteen Upaniṣads only can be used as sources for the history of the earliest Indian philosophy.

Though the remaining Upaniṣads—and there are over 200 texts which have come down to us either independently as Upaniṣads or in larger collections—are also attributed by tradition to one or other of the Vedic schools, only a few of them have any real connection with the Veda. Most of them are religious rather than philosophical works, and contain the doctrines and views of schools of philosophers and religious sects of a much later period. Many of them are much more nearly related to the Purāṇas and Tantras chronologically as well as in content, than to the Veda. This latest Upaniṣad literature may be classified as follows, according to its purpose and contents: (1) those works which present Vedānta doctrines,[2]

---

[1]) *Cf. Deussen*, System des Vedanta, pp. 32 f., on the Upaniṣads quoted by Śaṅkara. As regards the chronological order of the fourteen Vedic Upaniṣads, absolute certainty cannot be obtained. *Keith* (The Aitareya Āraṇyaka, pp. 45 ff.) has tried to prove that the Aitareya-Upaniṣad is the oldest, dating back to about 700-600 B.C. Others consider the Bṛhadāraṇyaka-Up. to be the oldest. S. *Radhakrishnan*, Indian Philosophy, I, pp. 141 f., says that "the accepted dates for the early Upaniṣads are 1000 B.C. to 300 B.C." By whom are these dates "accepted"? *Cf. Deussen* in Transactions of the 3rd International Congress for the History of Religion, Oxford, 1908, II, pp. 19 ff.; *Oldenberg*, Die Lehre der Upanishaden, pp. 288 f., 341; *Hillebrandt*, Aus Brahmanas und Upanisaden, p. 170. *Benimadhab Barua*, A History of Pre-Buddhistic Indian Philosophy, Calcutta, 1921) has made a remarkable and creditable, though not always successful, attempt at establishing a chronology of the philosophical ideas contained in the Upaniṣads, apart from the chronology of the literary works. But his designation of the philosophy of the Upaniṣads as "post-Vedic" (pp. 39 ff.) is very confusing.

[2]) The Sāmānya Vedānta Upanishads with the commentary of Sri Upanishad-Brahma-Yogin, ed. by Pandit A. Mahadeva *Sastri*. Adyar Library (Theosophical Society), 1921.

(2) those which teach Yoga,[1] (3) those which extol the ascetic life (sannyāsa),[2] (4) those which glorify Viṣṇu,[3] and (5) those which glorify Śiva as the highest divinity, and (6) Upaniṣads of the Śāktas and of other more insignificant sects.[4] These Upaniṣads are written partly in prose, partly in a mixture of prose and verse, and partly in epic Ślokas. Whilst the latter are on the same chronological level as the latest Purāṇas and Tantras, there are some works among the former which may be of greater antiquity, and which might consequently still be associated with the Veda. The following are probably examples of such earlier Upaniṣads: the Jābāla-Upaniṣad[5] which is quoted by Śaṅkara as an authority, and which closes with a beautiful description of the ascetic named Paramahaṃsa; the Paramahaṃsa-Upaniṣad,[6] describing the path of the Paramahaṃsa still more vividly; the very extensive Subāla-Upaniṣad,[7] often quoted by Rāmānuja, and dealing with cosmogony, physiology, psychology and metaphysics;

---

[1]) The Yoga Upanishads with the Commentary of Sri Upanishad-Brahma-Yogin, ed. by A. Mahadeva *Sastri*. Adyar, 1920. The Cūlikā-Up., and Amṛtanāda-Up. have been edited and translated into German by A. *Weber*, Ind. Stud., 9, pp. 10ff., 23 ff.

[2]) The Minor Upaniṣads critically edited by F. Otto *Schrader*, Vol. I: Saṃnyāsa-Upaniṣads. The Adyar Library, Madras, S. 1912. The Mṛtyulāṅgala-Up. (ed. by A.C. *Burnell*, Ind. Ant., 2, 1873, pp. 266 f.) is a purely Tantric work.

[3]) The Vaishnava-Upanishads with the Commentary of Sri Upanishad-Brahma-Yogin, ed. by A. Mahadeva *Sastri*, Adyar 1923. The Rāma-Tāpaniya-Upaniṣad, text and German translation by A. *Weber*, ABA., 1864, pp. 271 ff.; the Nṛsiṃha-Tāpaniya-Up. by the same scholar, Ind. Stud., 9, 53-173. On Nirālamba-Up. and Garuḍa.Up. s. *Weber*, Ind. Stud., 3, 324 ff.; 17, 136 ff., 161 ff.

[4]) Edition of the Śaiva and Śākta Upaniṣads by Pandit Mahadeva *Sastri* of the Adyar Library are in preparation. This classification of the non-Vedic Upaniṣads was first proposed by *Deussen*, Sechzig Upanishads, pp. 542 f., and then adopted by F. O. *Schrader*, Minor Upaniṣads, pp. ii f. in an amplified form. It is useful for practical purposes, though not always strictly applicable. For some Upaniṣads teach brahmavidyā by means of Yoga, and might be classified as well with the Vedānta as with the Yoga Upaniṣads; and some Yoga Upaniṣads might as well be classified as Vaiṣṇava, etc.

[5]) Minor Upaniṣads, ed. F. O. *Schroder*, I, pp. 57 ff. *Deussen*, Sechzig Upanishads, pp. 706 ff.

[6]) Minor Upaniṣads, I, pp. 43 ff.; *Deussen*, l. c., pp. 703 ff.

[7]) Sāmānya Vedānta Upanishads, ed. Mahadeva *Sastri*, pp. 460 ff.

the Garbha-Upaniṣad,[1] part of which reads like a treatise on embryology, but which is obviously a meditation on the embryo with the aim of preventing rebirth in a new womb; and the Śivaite Atharvaśiras-Upaniṣad,[2] which is already mentioned in the Dharmasūtras[3] as a sacred text, and by virtue of which sins can be washed away. The Vajrasūcikā-Upaniṣad,[4] which teaches that only he who knows the Brahman as the One without a second, is a Brahmin, is not of very late origin. Another factor which makes it difficult to determine the date of these Upaniṣads is the fact that they are often to be found in various recensions of very uneven bulk.[5]

These *non-Vedic Upaniṣads*, as we may call them, have come down in large collections[6] which are not ancient as such. For the philosopher Śaṅkara (about 800 A.D.) still

---

[1]) Sāmānya Vedānta Upanishads, pp. 168 ff.; *Deussen*, Sechz ig Upanishads, pp. 605 ff.

[2]) *Deussen*, l. c., pp. 716 ff. See also *Bhandarkar*, Vaiṣṇavism, Śaivism, etc., pp. 111 f.

[3]) Gautama XIX, 12; Baudhāyana, III, 10, 10: Vāsiṣṭha, XXII, 9; XXVIII, 14 Viṣṇu, 56, 22.

[4]) Sāmānya Vedānta Upanishads, p. 416 ff. In some MSS. this Upaniṣad is ascribed to Śaṅkara. One version of it, expanded into an attack on the caste system, is ascribed to the Buddhist poet Aśvaghoṣa. Cf. A. *Weber*, ABA. 1859, 259 ff.

[5]) Thus *Deussen*, Sechzig Upanishads, pp. 743 ff., translates a Mahā-Upaniṣad which is so short, that it does not deserve its name "the Great Upaniṣad" at all, while in the South-Indian recension (Sāmānya Vedānta Upanishads, pp. 234 ff) it is indeed one of the longest Upaniṣads.

[6]) The collection translated into Persian in 1656, called Oupnek'hat (s. above, p. 19) contains 50 Upaniṣads. An analysis of these Upaniṣads from Duperron's Latin translation has been given by A. *Weber*, Ind. Stud., Vols. 1, 2 and 9. On a list of 52 Upaniṣads of the Atharvaveda s *Colebrooke*, Misc. Essays, I, pp. 93 ff., and *Bhandarkar*, Report, 1883-84, pp. 24 f. For another list s. *Weber*, HSS., Verz., p. 95. Editions: Eleven Ātharvaṇa-Upanishads, ed. by G. A. *Jacob*, BSS. Nr. 40, 1891. At the NSP., Bombay, a collection of 108 Upaniṣads has been published in 1913, one of 112 Upaniṣads in 1917, one of 28 Upaniṣads in 1918, the eleven (principal) Upaniṣads (Ekādaśopaniṣadaḥ), with commentaries, by Swami Achintya *Bhagawan*, ib. 1910. The most important Upaniṣads have been edited, with Śaṅkara's commentaries, in the Bibl. Ind. and in ĀnSS, Nos. 5-17, 29-31, 62-64. Bṛhadāraṇyaka-Up. and Chāndogya-Up. have been critically edited and translated into German by O. *Böhtlingk*, St. Petersburg and Leipzig, 1889, the Kaṭha-, Aitareya-, and Praśna-Up. by the same scholar in BSGW., 1890, and critical notes on these Upaniṣads by the same scholar in BSGW., 1891. Kena-Up. with comm. ed. by Śrīdhara-śāstrī Paṭhaka,

quotes the Upaniṣads as parts of the Veda texts to which they belong; and even Rāmānuja (about 1100 A.D.) speaks of the "Chandogas," the "Vājasaneyins" or the "Kauṣītakins" when quoting the Upaniṣads of the schools in question: the Subāla-Upaniṣad is the only one which he quotes by this title. In the Muktikā-Upaniṣad, which is certainly one of the latest, we read that salvation may be attained by the study of the 108 Upaniṣads, and a list of 108 Upaniṣads is set forth, classified according to the four Vedas: 10 Upaniṣads coming under the Ṛgveda, 19 under the White Yajurveda, 32 under the Black Yajurveda, 16 under the Sāmaveda and 31 under the Atharvaveda. This classification, however, can scarcely be based on an ancient tradition.[1] All these Upaniṣads which are, properly speaking, non-Vedic, are generally called "Upaniṣads of the Atharvaveda." They were associated with the Atharvaveda, because the authority of this Veda as sacred tradition was always dubious and it was therefore no difficult matter to associate all kinds of apocryphal texts with the literature belonging to the Atharva-

---

Poona, 1919. Translations: (Twelve principal) Upaniṣads translated by *Max Muller*, SBE, Vols. 1 and 15. The Thirteen Principal Upanishads translated by R. E *Hume*, Oxford, 1921. Sechzig Upanishads des Veda übersetzt von P. *Deussen*, Leipzig, 1897. Selections in German translation by A. *Hillebrandt*, Aus Brahmanas und Upaniṣaden, Jena, 1921, and J. *Hertel*, Die Weisheit der Upanischaden, München, 1921. Translations of Īśā-, Kena-, and Muṇḍaka-, and of Kaṭha- and Praśna-Up. with Śaṅkara's commentary by S. *Sitaram Sastri*, Madras, 1898; the Chāndogya-Up. with Śaṅkara's Comm. translated by *Ganganath Jhā*, Madras, 1899; Aitareya-Up. with Śaṅkara's Comm. transl. by H. M. *Bhadkamkar*, Bombay, 1899. Amritabindu and Kaivalya-Upanishads with Comm. transl. by A. *Mahadeva Sastri*; 2nd ed., Madras, 1921. The principal Upaniṣads with Madhva's commentary transl. by Rai Bahadur Śrīśa Chandra *Vidyārnava*, Īśā and Kena according to Śaṅkara by the same, and Śvetāśvatara transl. by Siddheśvarī *Prasad Varmā Sāstri* appeared in the Sacred Books of the Hindus, Pāṇini Office, Allahabad. A useful help for the study of the Upaniṣads is G. A. *Jacob's* Concordance, BSS., 1891. A selected and classified bibliography of the Upaniṣads is given by R. E. *Hume*, *l. c.*, pp. 459 ff.

[1]) Rāmānuja quotes the Garbha-Up. and the Mantrikā- (=Cūlikā-) Up. as Atharvaveda-Upaniṣads, although the list in the Muktikā-Up. counts the one as belonging to the Black, and the other to the White Yajurveda.

veda. Furthermore, the Atharvaveda, as we have seen, was above all the Veda of magic and the secretiveness connected with it.[1] The real meaning of "Upaniṣad"—and this meaning has never been forgotten—was "secret doctrine." What was more natural than that a large class of works which were regarded as Upaniṣads or secret doctrines, should be joined to the Atharvaveda, which itself was indeed nothing but a collection of secret doctrines!

The word "*Upaniṣad*" is, in fact, derived from the verb "upa-ni-sad," "to sit down near some one," and it originally meant the sitting down of the pupil near the teacher for the purpose of a confidential communication, therefore a "confidential" or "secret session." Out of thus idea of the "secret session," the meaning "*secret doctrine*" that which is communicated at such a confidential session—was developed.[2] The Indians generally give as a synonym of the word "*upaniṣad*" the word "*rahasyam*," which means "mystery, secret." In the Upaniṣad texts themselves the expressions "*iti rahasyam*" and "*iti upaniṣad*"

---

[1]) See above, p. 149 f.

[2]) See *Deussen*, AGPh. I, 2, pp 14 ff., with whom I fully agree in rejecting Oldenberg's explanation of *Upaniṣad* (ZDMG. 50, 1896, 458 ff.; 54, 1900, 70 ff.; Die Lehre der Upanishaden, etc., pp. 36 f., 155 ff., 348 f) as "a form of worship." *Upaniṣad* is used frequently enough as a synonym of *rahasyam*, but never synonymous with *upāsanā*. Besides, E. *Senart* (Florilegium Melchior de Vogüé, Paris, 1909, pp. 575 ff.) has shown that even the verb *upās* in the Upaniṣads does not mean "to worship," but "to have a profound knowledge, to know or to believe for certain." But even his translation of *upaniṣad* by "knowledge, belief" ("connaissance, croyance") does not hit the meaning of the word as well as "secret doctrine." M. *R. Bodas* (JBRAS., 22, pp. 69 f.) takes the original meaning of *upaniṣad* to be "sitting down near the sacrificial fire," as the conversations contained in the Upaniṣads are said to have taken place at the great sacrifices. This is not more probable than the explanation of J. W. *Hauer* (Anfänge der Yoga-praxis, p. 27), who gives "mysterious wisdom obtained by Tapas and meditation" as the original meaning of *upaniṣad*, connecting it with the quiet sitting as part of the Yoga practice. Nārāyaṇa in his commentary on Manu, VI, 29, defines upaniṣad as "that which is recited seated near," i e. "(a text) which is recited (while the pupils are) seated near (the teacher)"; s. *Bühler*. SBE., Vol. 25, pp. 203 n. *Cf.* also *Macdonell* and *Keith*, Vedic Index, I, pp. 91 f.

are frequently used side by side in the sense of "thus says the secret doctrine." Often enough we find in the Upaniṣads themselves the warning against communicating some doctrine to an unworthy one. "This doctrine of Brahman," it is said for example,[1] "may a father impart to his eldest son or to a trusted pupil, but not to another, whoever he may be, even if the latter should give him the whole earth, surrounded by the waters and filled with treasures." Very frequently it is also related in the Upaniṣads how a teacher is entreated to communicate some knowledge or other, but only after repeated entreaty and urging of the pupil, gives way and reveals his doctrine to him.[2]

According to this original meaning of the word "*Upaniṣad*," the oldest Upaniṣads already contain very heterogeneous matters. An Upaniṣad was above all else a "mystery," and every doctrine which was not intended for the masses, but was only communicated within a narrow circle of privileged persons—be it a profound philosophical doctrine or some futile symbolism or allegory, a symbolical sacrifice serving as magic, puzzled out by a Brahman, or some would-be wisdom serving as a magic formula—was called Upaniṣad. All this we actually find already in the *old* Upaniṣads side by side and jumbled up but particularly so in the so-called "Atharvaveda-Upaniṣads."[3]

---

1) Chāndogya-Upaniṣad, III, 11, 5 f. *Cf. Deussen, loc. cit.*, pp. 12 f.

2) The word *upaniṣad* occurs in the Upaniṣads themselves in three senses; it means:—(1) "mystic sense," *e g.*, the secret significance of the syllable Om; (2) "secret word," certain expressions and formulæ which are intelligible only to the initiated, as tajjalan, "in him growing, passing away, breathing," or satyasya satyam, "the truth of truth," as designation of the highest being; (3) "secret text," *i.e.*, "esoteric doctrine" and "secret knowledge," *cf. Deussen, loc. cit*, pp. 16 f.

3) According to Āśvalāyana-Gṛhyasūtra, I, 13, 1, certain rites connected with conception, procreation of male children, etc., are taught in an "Upaniṣad.' The charm in Ṛv. 1, 191 is called an "Upaniṣad" by Kātyāyana in his Sarvānukramaṇikā. In the manual of politics (Kauṭilīya-Arthaśāstra, XIV) all kinds of magic rites for the purpose of arson, assassination, blinding, etc., and in the manuals of erotics all sorts of secret prescriptions relating to sexual intercourse and to cosmetics are taught in an "Upaniṣadic chapter"

Thus the *Kauṣītaki-Upaniṣad* contains, besides psychological and metaphysical expositions and a detailed eschatology,[1] also descriptions of sacrificial rites, by which one can attain some good or other, or effect a love charm, ceremonies for the prevention of the death of children, and even an "Upaniṣad," *i.e.*, a secret doctrine, the knowledge of which serves as magic for the annihilation of enemies. Similarly the *Chāndogya-Upaniṣad* contains deep philosophical thoughts upon the creation, the universe and the soul, but among these also mystical speculations upon the syllable Om, secret rites for the healing of diseases and so on. In the Atharvaveda-Upaniṣads, indeed, we find for instance a whole Upaniṣad—"the *Garuḍa-Upaniṣad*,"[2]—which is nothing but a snake charm that might just as well be included in the Atharvaveda-Saṃhitā.

This should be borne in mind when a "philosophy of the Upaniṣads" or even a "system of the Upaniṣads" is spoken of. A philosophy of the Upaniṣads exists only in so far as, in these collections of all sorts of mysteries, the teachings of the philosophers were also included. A system of the Upaniṣad philosophy can only be said to exist in a very restricted sense.[3] For it is not the thoughts of one single philosopher or of one uniform *school* of philosophers, that might be traced back to one single teacher, which are before us in the Upaniṣads, but it is the teachings of various men,[4] even of various

---

(s. Kauṭilīya-Arthaśāstra, XIV; Vātsyāyana's Kāmasūtra, VII; and R. *Schmidt*, Beiträge zur indischen Erotik, Leipzig 1902, pp. 817 ff.). Rāmānuja (on Brahmasūtra II, 2, 43, s. SBE.; Vol. 48, p. 528) calls the Pāñcarātraśāstra "a great Upaniṣad."

1) On this chapter of the Kauṣītaki-Up. compared with another version of it in the Jaiminīya-Brāhmaṇa. s E. *Windisch*, BSGW., 1907, 111 ff.

2) *Deussen*, Sechzig Upanishads des Veda, pp 627 f.

3) "That the Upaniṣads teach not one but various systems, must follow from the fact that they are compilations just as the Ṛgveda-Saṃhitā is," R. G. *Bhandarkar*, Vaiṣṇavism, Śaivism, etc., p. 1. *Cf.* G. *Thibaut*, SBE, Vol. 34, pp. ci ff.

4) How far the persons mentioned by name in the Upaniṣads, such as Yājñavalkya, Śāṇḍilya, Bālāki, Śvetaketu and others, were really the teachers of the doctrines ascribed

periods, which are presented in the single sections of the Upaniṣads.

There are, it is true, a few *fundamental doctrines,* which lend an appearance of uniformity to the philosophical thoughts which stand out in the genuine Upaniṣads, and it is only of these that we wish to speak here: with respect to these fundamental doctrines alone is it possible to speak (as Deussen does)—though always with reserve—of a "system of the Upaniṣads." We must therefore not seek deep wisdom in every chapter of the Upaniṣads, or expect a Platonic dialogue in every Upaniṣad. It is indeed remarkable enough that in the very oldest and most beautiful portions of the Upaniṣads we find the same form of *dialogue* as in the works of the great Greek philosopher.[1] And just as Plato's dialogues reveal to us a wonderfully life-like picture of the life and doings of the Ancient Greeks, so the dialogues of the older Upaniṣads frequently afford us a surprising insight into life at the ancient Indian princely courts, where priests and famous wandering teachers, including learned women, flocked together, in order to hold their disputations before the king, who not infrequently entered into the theological and philosophical conversations and confounded the learned Brahmans by his knowledge; as well as insight into the school-life of those ancient times, when travelling scholars undertook long journeys in order to "hear" some famous teacher, to whom pupils came from all sides "as waters precipitate themselves

---

to them (as *Barua* in his "Pre-Buddhistic Indian Philosophy" takes them to be), is not quite certain. Yājñavalkya is said to be the author of the Bṛhadāraṇyaka-Up., as of the whole White Yajurveda (s. Bṛh.-Up., VI, 5, 3 and Yājñavalkya-Smṛti III, 110); but in the Bṛh.-Up. itself other teachers also are mentioned. Besides, so many different doctrines both of ritual and of metaphysics are ascribed to Yājñavalkya, that it seems difficult to credit him with all of them. On the other hand it is quite possible that Śaṇḍilya for instance was really the teacher of the famous doctrine ascribed to him.

[1]) On the dialogues of the Upaniṣads, *cf. Oldenberg,* Die Lehre der Upanishaden, pp. 160 ff.

into the abyss and mouths sink into the year."[1] But besides sections of deep philosophical content, and portions which very well bear comparison with Plato's dialogues, we also find in the Upaniṣads much that is inferior as philosophy or literature.

THE FUNDAMENTAL DOCTRINES OF THE UPANIṢADS.[2]

That which is of the greatest value in the Upaniṣads is those fundamental thoughts, on the basis of which we can speak of a "philosophy of the Upaniṣads," above all, the fundamental doctrine which pervades all the genuine Upaniṣads, and which can be summed up in the sentence: "*The universe is the Brahman, but the Brahman is the Ātman,*" which in our mode of philosophical expression would be equal to: "The world is God, and God is my soul."

The entire thought of the Upaniṣad philosophers revolves around the two conceptions of *Brahman* and *Ātman*; and it is necessary to get a clear idea of these conceptions, in order to be able to understand the philosophy of the Upaniṣads. The etymology of the word "*Brahman*" is doubtful.[3] If we

---

[1]) Taittirīya-Upaniṣad, I, 3.

[2]) See A. E. *Gough*, The Philosophy of the Upanishads, London, 1882; P. *Deussen*, The Philosophy of the Upanishads. Authorised English Translation by A. S. *Geden*, Edinburgh, 1919 (from AGPh., I, 2); G. *Thibaut*, SBE, Vol. 34, pp. cxv ff.; P. *Oltramare* L'histoire des idées théosophiques dans l'Inde, t. I, Paris, 1906, pp. 63 ff.; H. *Jacobi*, ERE., II, p. 801; H. *Oldenberg*, Die Lehre der Upanishaden und die Anfänge des Buddhismus, Göttingen 1915; B. *Barua*, A History of Pre-Buddhistic Indian Philosophy, Calcutta, 1921; R. E. *Hume*. The Thirteen Principal Upanishads, Introduction; S. *Dasgupta*, A History of Indian Philosophy, I, Cambridge, 1922, pp. 28 ff.; S. *Radhakrishnan*, Indian Philosophy, I, London, 1923, pp. 137 ff.

[3]) The most probable etymology is that suggested by H. *Osthoff* (Bezz. Beitr., 24, 1899, 113 ff.) who connects *brahman* with Old Irish *bricht*, "magic, magic formula." *Oldenburg* (Lehre der Upanishaden, pp. 44 ff., and "Zur Geschichte des Worts *brāhman*," NGGW., 1916, pp. 715 ff.) and *Hillebrandt* (ERE, II. pp. 796 ff.) have also accepted this etymology. An older etymology is that from the root *bṛh* "to grow" (M. *Haug*). *Hillebrandt* and *Dasgupta* (*l. c.*, p. 36) follow M. Haug in explaining *brahman* as "the

turn to the St. Petersburg Sanskrit Dictionary we find "Brahman" explained as "the devotion which appears as the craving and fulness of the soul," and strives after the gods, while according to Deussen,[1] the Brahman is supposed to be "the will of man, striving upwards to that which is sacred and divine." These explanations may correspond to Jewish-Christian ideas of divinity, but are diametrically opposed to the *Indian* conception of the relationship between gods and men, as we know it in the Saṃhitās and Brāhmaṇas.[2] What the word signifies etymologically is not certain. But in the Veda itself "Brahman" occurs countless times in the meaning of "prayer" or "magic formula"; there is nowhere any thought of devotion or exaltation to the divine, but it always means mere formulae and verses containing secret magic power, by which man desires to influence divine beings, or to obtain, or even to force something from them. When a later period united these magic formulae and prayers in "books" or school texts as the three Vedas these were called *trayī vidyā* or "threefold knowledge," also briefly "the Brahman." But as divine origin was ascribed to this Veda or Brahman—the two words being used with exactly the same meaning—and as the sacrifice, which, as we have seen, was itself conceived as a superhuman, nay superdivine power, was, according to the Indian view, derived from the Veda or contained in the Veda,[3] so at last this Brahman or sacred knowledge, came to be called the first created thing (brahma

---

magical force which is derived from the orderly co-operation of the hymns, the chants, and the sacrificial gifts." J. *Hertel* ("Das Brahman" in Indogerman. Forschungen, 41, 1923, pp. 185 ff.) connects *brahman* etymologically with Greek θλεχμα, Latin flagro, and tries to prove that the original meaning of *brahman* was "fire," *viz.*, both the internal fire in man and the cosmic fire. I, however, am not convinced by his arguments.

[1]) System des Vedanta, p. 128. AGPh., 1, 1, pp. 241 f.

[2]) *Cf.* above, pp. 79 f., 200 f., 221.

[3]) Śat. V, 5, 5, 10; "The whole sacrifice is as great as the three-fold Veda." According to Chāndogya-Up VII, 4, 1. "the sacrificial acts are contained in the mantras (*i.e.* in the Veda)."

prathamajam), and finally even to be made into the creative principle, the cause of all existence (brahma svayambhu). Thus the Brahman as divine principle is a conception of the priestly philosophy, and quite explicable in the light of the brahmanical views upon prayer and sacrifice.[1]

The history of the word "*Ātman*" is simpler. The etymology of this word, too, is uncertain. Some derive it from the root *an* "to breath" (German "atmen") and explain it as "exhalation, breath, soul, self." Others, like Deussen,[2] derive it from two pronominal roots, so that it would originally mean "This I." However that may be, Ātman is not only a philosophical conception, but a word which frequently occurs in Sanskrit, and whose meaning is perfectly clear. It signifies "self," is often used as a reflexive pronoun, and as a substantive denotes one's own person, one's own body in contrast to the outside world, sometimes the trunk in contrast to the limbs, but most frequently the *soul*, the true *self*, in contrast to the body.[3]

These two conceptions Brahman and Ātman have become united in the philosophy of Upaniṣads. Thus the famous *doctrine of Śāṇḍilya* begins with the words: "Truly, this All is Brahman," and ends, after a description of the

---

[1]) *Cf.* above, pp. 224 f. A. *Weber* already has compared Brahman with the logos-idea in Neo-Platonism and in Christianity. Thus also *Deussen*, System des Vedanta, p. 51 and Max F. *Hecker*, Schopenhauer und die indische Philosophie (Cologne, 1897), p. 3. Deussen desires to bring Brahman into accord with the "will" of Schopenhauer, but, as Hecker (p. 82) mildly expresses it, is forced "to offer some violence to the conception of Brahman." A comparison which is more justifiable is that with the "*mana*" of the Melanesians, which has been emphasised by N. *Söderblom*, in his "Das Werden des Götterglaubens," 1916, pp. 270 ff.

[2]) AGPh, I, 1, p. 285.

[3]) On the term Ātman s. *Deussen*, ERE. II, 195 ff.; *Jacobi*, ERE. II, 801; *Dāsgupta*, History of Indian Philosophy, I, 25 f. According to Deussen, Ātman is "the most abstract, and therefore the best name which philosophy has found for its sole and eternal theme." Schopenhauer named his white poodle "Ātman," whereby, following the Vedantic doctrine, he desired to acknowledge the inner being as equal in man and beast." (*Hecker, loc. cit.*, p. 8.)

Atman, with the statement that Brahman and Ātman are one:

"This my Ātman in my inmost heart is smaller than a grain of rice, or a barley-corn, or a mustard seed, or a millet grain. ....This my Ātman, in my inmost heart is greater than the earth, greater than the sky, greater than the heavens, greater than all spheres. In him are all actions, all wishes, all smells, all tastes; he holds this All enclosed within himself; he speaks not, he troubles about nothing;—*this my Ātman in my inmost heart is this Brahman.* With him, when I depart out of this life, shall I be united. For him to whom this knowledge has come, for him, indeed, there exists no doubt. Thus spake Sāṇḍilya yea Śāṇḍilya."[1]

Deussen expresses this fundamental idea of the Upaniṣads briefly and pertinently in the words: "The *Brahman*, the power which presents itself to us materialised in all existing things, which creates, sustains, preserves, and receives back into itself again all worlds, this eternal infinite divine power is identical with the *Ātman*, with that which, after stripping off everything external, we discover in ourselves as our real most essential being, our individual self, the soul."[2] This doctrine has found expression most pointedly and clearly in the Upaniṣad dictum which later became the confession of faith of millions of Indians, in the "*tat tvam asi*" (so often quoted by Schopenhauer), "that art thou," *i.e.*, the universe and the Brahman, that art thou thyself, or in other words: The world exists only in so far as thou thyself art conscious of it. Let us hear in what manner the poet-philosophers of the Upaniṣads endeavour to make clear this doctrine of the unity of the world with the Brahman and of the Brahman with the Ātman:[3]

"Śvetaketu was the son of Uddālaka Āruṇi. To him said his father: 'Śvetaketu, betake thyself as a Veda-student to a teacher. For, my dear

---

1) Chāndogya-Upaniṣad, III, 14. *Cf.* above, p. 225.

2) *Deussen*, "The Philosophy of the Upanishads," translated by A. S. *Geden*, Edinburgh, 1906, p 39.

3) Chāndogya-Upaniṣad, VI, 1 ff.

one, in our family it is not customary to be a Brahmin in name only, without having learnt the Veda.' So at the age of twelve years he was initiated as a pupil. And at twenty-four years of age, after he had learnt everything in all the Vedas he came home—proud, haughty, and regarding himself as a learned man. Then said his father to him: 'As thou art now, my dear Śvetaketu, so proud and haughty, and regardest thyself as a learned man, tell me, hast thou also inquired into that doctrine by which that which is unheard becomes heard, that which is unthought becomes thought, that which is unknown becomes known?' 'Venerable one, of what does this doctrine consist?' 'Just as, my dear one, through *one* lump of clay everything that is of clay is known and the difference lies only in the word, is merely a name—but in truth it is clay—; and just as, my dear one, through *one* copper trinket everything which is of copper is known and the difference lies only in the word, is merely a name—but in truth it is copper—; and just as, my dear one, through *one* pair of nail scissors everything which is of iron is known and the difference lies only in the word, is merely a name—but in truth it is iron—; so, my dear one, it is with this doctrine.' 'Surely my honourable teachers did not know this; for if they had known it, why should they not have told it to me? Then, venerable one, do thou expound it to me.' 'Very well, my dear one,' said his father.

'Only the *existent*, my dear one, was here in the beginning, and this only as One without a Second. To be sure, some people have said: Only the non-existent was here in the beginning, and this only as One without a Second, and out of this non-existent arose the existent. But how, my dear one, could this be so? How could the existent arise out of the non-existent? Only the existent, my dear one, was here in the beginning, and this only as One without a Second!' (He then demonstrates further, how this *existent* had created heat, which had created water, which, in its turn, had created food; and how the existent, penetrating those three elements, developed the material world out of itself. In the phenomena of sleep, of hunger and of thirst, he then explains how everything leads back to the three elements, heat, water, food—or, as we would say: fire, water, earth—while these three elements in their turn rest only upon the existent. But as this *existent* has, with the Ātman, its soul, penetrated into all beings, so it is also the soul in us. When, therefore, a man dies, he becomes again that which he originally was; he unites again with the existent, out of which he was produced. Now follow a number of similes which are all intended to illustrate the doctrine of the oneness of the world with the Alone-existing and the human soul.) 'As, my dear one, the bees, when they are preparing honey, collect the juices of the most diverse trees and then combine the juice in one unity;—as in this unity those juices do not retain any difference, so that they could say: I am the juice of this tree, I am the juice of that tree—so, my dear one, all these creatures here, when they have become absorbed in the *existent* have no consciousness of the fact that they have become absorbed in the existent. Whatever they may be here, whether tiger or lion, wolf or boar, worm or bird, fly or gnat,—*this* (namely, the *existent*) they become. And it is this very minute thing which constitutes the being of the All, that is the truth, that is the Ātman, *that art thou,* O Śvetaketu.' 'Venerable one, instruct me yet further.' 'Very well, my dear one...........'

'Fetch me a fruit from yonder fig-tree!' 'Here it is, venerable one.' 'Split it.' 'It is split, venerable one.' 'What dost thou see therein?' 'Very tiny grains, venerable one!' 'Split one of these!' 'It is split.' 'What seest thou therein?' 'Nothing, venerable one.' Then said the father to him: 'My dear one, it is as a result of that very quintessence which thou dost not perceive, that this big fig-tree stands here. Believe me, my dear one, it is this very minute thing which constitutes the being of the All, that is the truth, that is the Ātman, *that art thou,* O Śvetaketu!' 'Venerable one, instruct me yet further.' 'Very well, my dear one.'

'Place this piece of salt in water and come to me again to-morrow morning.' He did so. Then his father said to him: 'Bring me the salt which thou didst place in water last night.' He felt for it, but did not find it; it had vanished. 'Just taste the water from one side. How does it taste?' 'Salty.' 'Taste from the middle. How does it taste?' 'Salty.' 'Taste from the other side. How does it taste?' 'Salty.' 'Eat something with it and then return to me.' He did so, but the salty taste still remained. Then his father said to him: 'Truly, my dear son, here also (in the body) thou dost not perceive the *existent*, and yet it is there. And this very minute thing it is which constitutes the being of the All, that is the truth, that is the Ātman, *that art thou,* O Śvetaketu.'"

What inspires us with the highest respect for these ancient thinkers of India is the earnestness and the enthusiasm with which they endeavoured to fathom the divine principle, or what Kant would call the thing-in-itself whether they called it "the one" or "the existent," Brahman or Ātman. Thus we read in a dialogue, which recurs in two Upaniṣads in two different versions,[1] how Gārgya Bālāki, a proud and learned Brahman, comes to Ajātaśatru, the King of Benares, and pledges himself to explain the Brahman to him. One after another he explains the Puruṣa, *i.e.*, the personal spirit, in the sun, in the moon, in the lightning, in the ether, in the wind, in the fire, in the water, then the spirit which appears as a reflected image or shadow, in the echo, in sound, in dreams, in the human body, or in the eye, as the Brahman. Ajātaśatru, however, is not satisfied with any of these explanations, so that finally, the learned Brahman himself goes for instruction to the king, who then explains to him that the true Brahman is to be sought only in the *intelligent spirit* (Puruṣa) in man, *i.e.*, in the Ātman, in the self. "As a spider spins her web out of herself, as out of a fire the little sparks fly in all directions, so out of this Ātman emanate all vital breaths, all worlds, all gods and all beings."

Similarly, in a famous Upaniṣad passage, the difference between the true and the false Ātman is shown. There we read:

"'The Ātman, from which all evil has fled, which is free from old age, free from death and free from care, which is without hunger and without thirst, whose wishes are the true, whose intentions are the true, that Ātman should one investigate, that Ātman should one endeavour to know: he who has found and known this Ātman, attains to all worlds and the fulfilment of all wishes.' Thus spake Prajāpati. This was heard by the gods, as well as the demons, and they said: 'It is well, we will investigate this Ātman—the Ātman, through the investigation of which one obtains all worlds and the fulfilment of all desires.' From among the gods, Indra arose, and from among the demons Virocana arose, and both, without having communicated with each other, came

[1]) Kauṣītaki-Up. IV and Bṛhadāraṇyaka-Up. II, 1.

to Prajāpati with firewood in their hands.[1] They stayed with him as pupils for thirty-two years. Then said Prajāpati to them: 'What is your desire in living here as pupils?' and they said: 'The Ātman, from which all evil has fled, which is free from old age, free from death and free from care, which is without hunger and without thirst, whose wishes are the true, whose intentions are the true, that Ātman shall one endeavour to know: he who has found and known this Ātman, gains all worlds and the fulfilment of all desires. This thy speech, venerable one, we have heard. Our desire is for this Ātman; therefore we have lived with thee here as pupils. (Prajāpati now first explains to them that the Puruṣa in the eye or in the reflected image is the Ātman. Virocana is satisfied with this, returns to the demons and proclaims to them the doctrine that the body is the Ātman, and that one has only to please and care for the body in order to obtain all worlds. Indra, however, soon understands that the explanation given by Prajāpati cannot have been meant seriously. Dissatisfied he returns and again stays with Prajāpati as his pupil for thirty-two years.) Then the latter said to him: 'He (the spirit) who roams about blithely in dreams,[2] he is the Atman, that is the Immortal, the dangerless, that is the Brahman.' Then Indra departed thence with a quiet heart." (But even before he had reached the gods he comprehended that the vision in dream could not be the true Ātman, either. Once again he returns to Prajāpati and stays with him as a pupil for thirty-two years. Now Prajāpati declares the soul in dreamless, profound sleep to be the true Ātman. With that also Indra is not satisfied, he returns, and Prajāpati suffers him to live with him for another five years, when at last he reveals to him the doctrine of the true Ātman.) 'O Indra, mortal indeed is this body, of which death takes possession. It is the dwelling-place of that immortal, incorporeal Ātman. Possessed by pleasure and pain is the (Ātman) which

---

[1]) The pupil has to live with the teacher and serve him, and especially tend the sacred fire. "To come with wood in one's hand" therefore means "to go to someone as a pupil for instruction."

[2]) As in the Upaniṣads the development of the Ātman conception is traced to the true Ātman through the preliminary steps of the puruṣa in the eye, in the reflected image, in the shadow and in the dream-picture, to which the prāṇa or breath of life is often added, so we find in remarkable agreement also among the primitive races, the breath, the "little dweller in the eye," the reflected image, the shadow, and visions, as preliminary steps to the *belief in a soul*. (*Cf.* E. B. *Tylor*, "Primitive Culture," London, 1903. I, pp. 430 ff. Fritz *Schultze*, Psychologie der Naturvölker, Leipzig, 1900, pp. 254 ff.)

is united with the body, for so long as he is united with the body, there is no defence for him against pleasure and pain. But when he is incorporeal, then certainly pleasure and pain do not touch him............Now when the eye is directed to yonder ether, then *he* is the spirit (Puruṣa) in the eye, but the eye serves only for seeing. And it is the Ātman who *knows*: "this I will smell"; the organ of smell serves only for smelling. And it is the Ātman who *knows*: "this will I speak"; the voice serves only for speaking. And it is the Ātman who *knows*; "this will I hear"; the organ of hearing serves only for hearing. And it is the Ātman who *knows*: "this will I think"; the organ of thought is his divine eye. He it is who is pleased when, with the organ of thought, this divine eye, he sees the objects of his desires. *Him*, indeed, *this* Ātman, do the gods worship in the Brahman-world; therefore do they possess all worlds and all their desires are fulfilled. And he obtains all worlds and the fulfilment of all desires, who has found and recognises this Ātman.' Thus spake Prajāpati, so spake Prajāpati." [1]

Thus here again the true Ātman is explained as the knowing and intelligent spirit in man. But the doctrine that this Ātman is one with the universe and that everything exists only in so far as it is in the cognitive self, is taught by the beautiful conversation between Yājñavalkya and Maitreyī. Yājñavalkya is about to leave home in order to conclude his life as a hermit in the forest. So he wishes to make a settlement between his two wives, and tells this to the one, Maitreyī.

"Maitreyī said: 'My Lord, if this whole earth, full of wealth, belonged to me, tell me, should I be immortal by it?'

'No,' replied Yājñavalkya; 'like the life of rich people will be thy life. But there is no hope of immortality by wealth.'

And Maitreyī said: 'What should I do with that by which I do not become immortal? What my Lord knoweth (of immortality), tell that to me.'

Yājñavalkya replied: 'Thou who art truly dear to me, thou speakest dear words. Come, sit down, I will explain it to thee, and mark well what I say.'

---

[1]) Chāndogya-Upaniṣad, VIII, 7-12.

And he said: 'Verily, a husband is not dear, that you may love the husband; but that you may love the Self, therefore a husband is dear.

'Verily, a wife is not dear, that you may love the wife; but that you may love the Self, therefore a wife is dear.

'Verily, sons are not dear, that you may love the sons; but that you may love the Self, therefore sons are dear...........

'Verily, the Devas are not dear, that you may love the Devas; but that you may love the Self, therefore the Devas are dear.

'Verily, creatures are not dear, that you may love the creatures; but that you may love the Self, therefore are creatures dear.

'Verily, everything is not dear that you may love everything; but that you may love the Self, therefore everything is dear.

'Verily, the Self is to be seen, to be heard, to be perceived, to be marked, O Maitreyī! When we see, hear, perceive, and know the Self, then all this is known!"[1]

One of the most frequent appellations of the Ātman in the Upaniṣads is the word "prāṇa," *i.e.*, "breath of life, life, life-principle." And numerous portions of the Upaniṣads deal with this Prāṇa, which is one with the intelligent self; or with the relations of the same to the organs of the soul, the so-called Prāṇas (prāṇāḥ, plural of prāṇa). These organs—speech, breath, sight, hearing and the organ of thought—correspond to five forces of Nature in the universe: fire, wind, the sun, the quarters of heaven and the moon. And the Upaniṣads often talk of the reciprocal action between the organs and the forces of Nature. That is to a certain extent the psychology, which indeed cannot be separated from the metaphysics, of the Upaniṣads. The oft-related "psychological fable" of the dispute of the vital organs about rank, is very popular. It is there told how the Prāṇas, or vital organs, once fought for precedence. They went to the father Prajāpati, that he might settle their dispute.

"He said to them: 'That one of you after whose going off the body appears as if it were the very worst off—he is the most superior of you.'

[1]) Bṛhadāraṇyaka-Up., II, 4. Translated by *Max Müller*, SBE., Vol. 15, pp. 108-110.

8. Speech went off. Having remained away a year, it came around again, and said : 'How have you been able to live without me?'

'As the dumb, not speaking, but breathing with the breath, seeing with the eye, hearing with the ear, thinking with the mind. Thus.'

Speech entered in.

9. The Eye went off. Having remained away a year, it came around again, and said : 'How have you been able to live without me?'

'As the blind, not seeing, but breathing with the breath, speaking with speech, hearing with the ear, thinking with the mind. Thus.'

The Eye entered in.

10. The Ear went off. Having remained away a year, it came around again, and said : 'How have you been able to live without me?'

'As the deaf, not hearing, but breathing with the breath, speaking with speech, seeing with the eye, thinking with the mind. Thus.'

The Ear entered in.

11. The mind went off. Having remained away a year, it came around again, and said : 'How have you been able to live without me?'

'As simpletons, mindless, but breathing with the breath, speaking with speech, seeing with the eye, hearing with the ear, Thus.'

The Mind entered in.

12. Now when the Breath was about to go off—as a fine horse might tear out the pegs of his foot-tethers all together, thus did it tear out the other Breaths all together. They all came to it, and said : 'Sir! Remain. You are the most superior of us. Do not go off.'

15. Verily, they do not call them 'Speeches,' nor 'Eyes,' nor 'Ears,' nor 'Minds.' They call them 'Breaths' (prāṇa), for the vital breath is all these."[1)]

Just as the doctrine of the Prāṇa and the Prāṇas is connected with the fundamental doctrine of the Ātman, the same doctrine also affords the poet-philosophers of the Upaniṣads a motive for magnificent philosophical poems, as they can best be called, on the fortunes of the individual Ātman, *i.e.*, the human soul, in the conditions of waking and of dreaming, of sleep and of death, and in its wanderings in the Beyond up to its final "emancipation," *i.e.*, its complete absorption in the

[1)] Chāndogya-Up. V, I. Translated by R. E. *Hume*, "The Thirteen Principal Upanishads," pp. 227 f. *Cf.* Bṛhadāraṇyaka-Up. VI, 1, 7-14.

Brahman. Thus, above all, the Bṛhadāraṇyaka-Upaniṣad (IV, 3-4) sketches a picture of the fortunes of the soul, which, as Deussen [1] rightly remarks, "for richness and warmth of expression surely stands alone in Indian literature, and perhaps in the literature of all nations." Here we find also the doctrine of the *transmigration of souls*, and in the closest connection with it, developed clearly and distinctly for the first time, the *ethical* doctrine of *Karman*, *action*, which, with the unerringness of a law of Nature, must have its consequences. This great doctrine of *action*, which was later, especially in Buddhism, preached in every street and by-way, is still a great mystery in the Upaniṣads. Ārtabhāga asks Yājñavalkya:

"'Yājñavalkya,' said he, 'when after the death of this man here his voice enters into the fire, his breath into the wind, his sight into the sun, his organ of thought into the moon, his hearing into the quarters of heaven, his body into the earth, his soul (Ātman) into the ether, the hairs of his body into the herbs, the hairs of his head into the trees, and his blood and seed are laid down in the water,—where then is this man?' 'Take me by the hand, my dear one!' said Yājñavalkya. 'Ārtabhāga, let us two only know of this; let this discussion of ours not be in public.' And the two went out and discussed together; and it was *Action* of which they spoke; it was *Action* which they praised. Verily, he becomes good through good action, bad through bad action." [2]

This doctrine is then treated in a more detailed manner along with the magnificent description of the departure of the soul out of the body. It says there:

"The point of his heart begins to shine, and by this light the Ātman departs, be it out of the eye or out of the head, or out of other parts of the body. And while he is departing the breath of life (prāṇa) follows him; and behind the departing breath of life depart all the vital organs, the consciousness also follows them. But he, the cognitive one (the Ātman) is endowed with cognition. Knowledge and the *actions*, the experiences of the former life, remain attached to him. Just as a grass—leech,[3] when it has arrived at the end of a

[1]) Sechzig Upanishads, p. 463.

[2]) Bṛhadāraṇyaka-Up., III, 2, 13 f.

[3]) See *Barua*, Pre-Buddhistic Indian Philosophy, p. 175.

blade of grass, making another start (for another blade), draws itself together towards (this blade), so man, when he has stripped off the body and has rid himself of non-knowledge, making another start (for another body), draws himself together towards (that other body). Just as an embroideress undoes a small portion of a piece of embroidery, and out of it creates a different, quite new and more beautiful design, so man, when he has stripped off his body and has rid himself of non-knowledge, creates for himself a different, quite new and more beautiful form, that of the spirit of an ancestor or of a Gandharva, of a Brahman or of a Prajāpati, of a god or of a man, or that of some other being...........As he has acted, as he has lived, so he becomes ; he who has done good, is born again as a good one, he who has done evil, is born again as an evil one. He becomes good through good action, bad through bad action. Therefore it is said : 'Man here is formed entirely out of desire, and according to his desire is his resolve, and according to his resolve he performs the action, and according to the performance of the action is his destiny.'" [1]

In consequence of this doctrine of Karman the moral element plays a far greater part in the Upaniṣads than in the Brāhmaṇas. Moreover, we should not ignore the fact that the metaphysical doctrine of the Ātman, for whose sake we love our fellow-creatures[2] involves a deep ethical idea: as it is in reality the universal soul which we love in each individual, love for all creatures wells up from the recognition of the Ātman.[3] However, in the Upaniṣads, too, there is not much room left for actual moral teaching. Comparatively rarely do we meet with moral precepts, such as for example in the Taittirīya-Upaniṣad (I, 11) the teacher gives the scholar who is departing on his life's journey :

"Speak the truth, do thy duty, neglect not the study of the Veda. After thou hast brought thy teacher the agreeable gift (after completion of the period of training) see that the thread of thy race does not break

---

[1]) Bṛhadāraṇyaka-Up., IV, 4, 2-5.

[2]) See above, pp. 249 f.

[3]) On the ethics of the Upaniṣads, s. *Hume*, The Thirteen Principal Upanishads, pp. 58 ff. John *Mackenzie*, Hindu Ethics, London, 1922, pp. 67 ff. ; S. *Radhakrishnan*, Indian Philosophy, I, pp. 207 ff.

off............Neglect not the ceremonies for the gods and Fathers. A god be to thee thy mother, a god be to thee thy father, a god be to thee thy teacher, a god be to thee the guest," and so on.

There is another passage referring to ethics which we find in the Bṛhadāraṇyaka-Upaniṣad (V, 2) which is more interesting and much more Upanisad-like than these moral precepts:

"Three kinds of sons of Prajāpati, the gods, human beings, and the demons, sojourned with their father Prajāpati as pupils. After the gods had sojourned there as pupils, they said : 'Tell us something, O master!' And he uttered the syllable '*da*' and said: 'Did you understand that?' 'We understood it,' they said : 'thou didst say to us *dāmyata* (restrain yourselves).' 'Yes,' said he ; 'you understood it.' Then the human beings said to him : 'Tell us something, O master!' And he uttered the same syllable '*da*' and said : 'Did you understand that?' 'We understood it,' they said, 'thou didst say to us : *datta* (give).' 'Yes,' said he, 'you understood it.' Then the demons said to him : 'Tell us something, O master!' And he uttered to them the same syllable '*da*' and said : 'Did you understand that?' 'We understood it,' they said, 'thou didst say to us '*dayadhvam* (have pity).' 'Yes,' said he, 'you understood it.' And it is just this which yonder divine voice, the thunder, proclaims : da-da-da, that means dāmyata, datta, dayadhvam. Therefore shall he learn these three things : self-restraint, generosity and pity."

It is easy enough to see why we meet but seldom with such ethical doctrines in the Upaniṣads. According to the doctrine of the Upaniṣads the highest object to be aimed at is union with the Brahman, and this union can be attained only by giving up non-knowledge, by *cognition*. Only he who has *recognised* the oneness of the soul with the Divine will obtain deliverance, *i.e.*, complete union with the Brahman. But in order to attain this highest object it is necessary to give up all works, good as well as bad. For sacrifices and pious works only lead to new re-births, *knowledge* alone leads from this maze to the One and Eternally True. "As no water remains attached to the leaf of the lotus blossom, so no bad deed remains attached to him who knows this." [1]

[1] Chāndogya-Up. IV, 14, 3. *Cf.* Kauṣītaki-Up. I, 4 ; III, 8.

Already in the Brāhmaṇas and Āraṇyakas there is repeated mention of the advantages which accrue to him who knows some secret doctrine or other of sacrificial science,—" who knows this." Nothing is more characteristic of the Upaniṣads, however, than the ever-recurring promise of happiness and blessedness, of earthly possessions and heavenly joys as a reward for him " who knows this." The idea that knowledge is not only power, but the highest object to be aimed at, is traceable throughout all the Upaniṣads. Not only Indra serves Prajāpati for 101 years as a pupil, but it is also often reported that human beings serve a teacher for years as pupils in order to receive from him the transmission of some knowledge or other. Kings are prepared to present thousands of cows and piles of gold to the Brahman who can proclaim to them the doctrine of the true Ātman or Brahman. But Brahmans also humble themselves before kings, rich people before beggars, when these, as is not seldom the case, are in possession of higher wisdom.[1] This yearning for knowledge has found its most touching expression in the beautiful poem of *Naciketas*, which we find in the Kāṭhaka-Upaniṣad.

The youth Naciketas has descended into the lower world and the god of death has vouchsafed him three wishes. Naciketas wishes, firstly, that he may return alive to his father, secondly he wishes for heavenly bliss. When he is to express his third wish he says:

> " This doubt that there is in regard to a man deceased:
> ' He exists,' say some; ' He exists not,' say others—
> This would I know, instructed by thee!
> Of the boons this is boon the third."

Thereupon Yama replies that this question of what happens to man after death, is so difficult to investigate that even the gods were once in doubt about it, and he begs the youth to give up his wish.

---

[1]) *Cf.* above pp. 227 ff.

"Choose centenarian sons and grandsons,
Many cattle, elephants, gold and horses.
Choose a great abode of earth.
And thyself live as many autumns as thou desirest.
This, if thou thinkest an equal boon,
Choose—wealth and long life!
A great one on earth, O Naciketas, be thou.
The enjoyer of thy desires I make thee.
Whate'er desires are hard to get in mortal world—
For all desires at pleasure make request.
These lovely maidens with chariots, with lyres—
Such (maidens), indeed, are not obtainable by men—
By these, from me bestowed, be waited on!
O Naciketas, question me not regarding dying (maraṇa)!"

Naciketas, however, will not be deterred from his wish by these promises of earthly possessions:

"Ephemeral things! That which is a mortal's, O End-maker,
Even the vigor (tejas) of all the powers, they wear away.
Even a whole life is slight indeed.
Thine be the vehicles (vāha)! Thine be the dance and song!
Not with wealth is a man to be satisfied.
Shall we take wealth, if we have seen thee?
Shall we live so long as thou shalt rule?
—This, in truth, is the boon to be chosen by me......
This thing whereon they doubt, O Death:
What there is in the great passing-on—tell us that!
This boon, that has entered into the hidden—
No other than that does Naciketas choose."

Then Yama, the god of death, praises Naciketas for having chosen knowledge and not pleasures, and at last imparts to him the doctrine of the immortality of the Ātman.[1]

But how this high esteem of knowledge leads not only to the disregard of earthly pleasures, but to *contempt of the*

[1]) The above verses (Kāṭh.-Up., I, 20, 23-25, 26, 27, 29) are given in the translation of *Hume*, Thirteen Principal Upanishads, pp. 344 f. A fine poetical, but very free translation of the legend is given by J. *Muir*, Metrical Translations from Sanskrit Writers, pp. 54 ff.

world altogether,[1] is shown us by another Upaniṣad, in which for the first time that pessimistic trait of Indian thought appears, which we will meet with again and again in the later Indian literature. There we read: [2]

"A king named Bṛhadratha, after having installed his eldest son on the throne, thinking that his body is non-eternal, turned to renunciation and went forth into the forest. There he gave himself up to the severest mortification, standing with arms stretched upwards and gazing into the sun. After one thousand days had elapsed there approached him......... the Ātman-knowing, venerable Śākāyanya. 'Stand up, stand up and choose a wish!' thus spake he to the king. He made his obeisance to him and said: 'O venerable one! I am not cognizant of the Ātman. Thou knowest his nature, as we have heard; mayest thou explain this to us!' (The Brahman desires to dissuade him from this wish and invites him to wish for something else. Then the king bursts forth into the words:) 'O venerable one! In this evil-smelling, pithless body, composed of bones, skin, sinews, marrow, flesh, seed, blood, mucus, tears, gum of the eyes, faeces, urine, bile and phlegm,—how can one possibly enjoy pleasure! In this body burdened with passion, anger, desire, delusion, fear, cowardice, envy, separation from that which is beloved, attachment to that which is not beloved, hunger, thirst, age, death, disease, trouble and such like,—how can one possibly enjoy pleasure! We see also that this whole world is transitory, just like these flies, mosquitoes, and such like, these herbs and trees, which rise and again decay.' (There then follows an enumeration of ancient kings and heroes who had to perish, also gods and demigods, who all fall victims to annihilation.) 'But what of these! There are yet other things,—drying-up of great seas, falling down of the mountains, swaying of the Pole Star,.. ...sinking of the earth, the fall of the gods from their place,—in the course of a world in which such things happen, how indeed can one enjoy pleasure! When even he who is satiated with it, must return again and again! Therefore rescue me! For I feel in this world-cycle like the frog in a waterless well. Thou, O venerable one, art our refuge,"

It is noteworthy, however, that this passage, to which numerous parallels may be found in the Buddhist as well as

---

[1]) *Cf.* P. *Regnaud*, Le Pessimisme Brahmanique (Annales du Musée Guimet, t. I, pp. 101 ff)

[2]) Maitrāyana-Up, I, 2-4.

in the later Sanskrit literature, belongs to one of the *latest* Upaniṣads. For the Maitrāyana-Upaniṣad is, in language and style, nearer to the classical Sanskrit literature than to the Veda and is decidedly post-Buddhist.[1] The old *Vedic* Upaniṣads contain but the germs of pessimism in the doctrine of the non-reality of the world. Only the Brahman is real, and this is the Ātman, the soul, "which passes beyond hunger and thirst, sorrow and delusion, old age and death." "That which is different from it is full of suffering."—ato'nyad ārtam.[2] But "that which is different from it," does not exist at all in reality, and therefore also the suffering and misery of the world are not real. The knowing one, who has comprehended the doctrine of the Unity, knows no fear, no pain. "He who knows the joy of the Brahman, for him there is no fear." "Where is delusion, where sorrow, for him who knows the Unity?" Joy (ānanda) is a name of the Brahman. "Consisting of joy (ānandamaya) is the Ātman. And like a song of triumph of optimism sound the words of an Upaniṣad: Joy is the Brahman. For truly, out of joy arise all these beings, by joy they live after they have arisen, and when they pass away they are again absorbed into joy."[3]

Thus the doctrine of the Upaniṣads is at bottom not pessimistic. Certainly it is only a small step from the belief in the non-reality of the world to contempt of the world. The more extravagantly the joy of the Brahman was praised, the vainer, the more worthless did earthly existence appear.[4] Therefore, after all, the pessimism of later Indian philosophy has its roots in the Upaniṣads.

In fact the whole of the later philosophy of the Indians is rooted in the Upaniṣads. Their doctrines formed the

---

[1]) Maitr.-Up., VII, 8 f., contains distinct allusions to the Buddhists as heretics. On the style of the Maitrāyanīya-Upaniṣad, see *Oldenberg*, Zur Geschichte der altindischen Prosa, p. 33.

[2]) Bṛhadāraṇyaka-Up. III, 5.

[3]) Taittirīya-Up., II, 9. III,[6; Īśā-Up., 7.

[4]) *Cf.* M. F. *Hecker*, Schopenhauer und die indische Philosophie, pp. 116-120.

foundation for the *Vedānta-Sūtras* of *Bādarāyaṇa*, a work of which a later writer [1] says: "This text-book is the chief of all the text-books. All other text-books serve only as its complement. Therefore all who aim at deliverance, shall exalt it." The theological-philosophical systems of *Śaṅkara* and of *Rāmānuja*, whose adherents at the present day are still counted by millions, are built upon this text-book. Moreover, all other philosophical systems and religions which have arisen in the course of the centuries, the heretical Buddhism no less than the orthodox Brahmanical religion of the post-Buddhist period, have sprung forth from the soil of the Upaniṣad doctrines.

On the other hand it proved fatal for the development of Indian philosophy that the Upaniṣads should have been pronounced to be "revelations," and sacred texts; for in the Upaniṣads we still find vigorous, independent, creative philosophical thought, which grew rarer and rarer in the later development of Indian philosophy for the very reason that progress was not only hindered at every step by the fetters of the dogmatism of the schools—which is the case in other lands as well as in India—but still more by the orthodox belief that every word of an Upaniṣad must be regarded as divine truth.

However, it was not the belief in their divine revelation which gave these philosophical poems (there is hardly a better name for them) such enormous power over the minds of men: for even the silliest hymns and the most stupid Brāhmaṇa passages were regarded as uttered by the deity: but it was rather the circumstance that, arrayed in the language of *poetry*, they appealed just as much to the heart as to the intellect. And it is not because, as Schopenhauer asserts, they present the "fruit of the highest human knowledge and

---

[1]) Madhusūdana *Sarasvatī* in his Prasthānabheda.

wisdom," and contain "almost superhuman conceptions," "whose originators can hardly be regarded as mere men"[1) that across the space of thousands of years the Upaniṣads *still* have much to tell *us also*; not because, as Deussen thinks, these thinkers have obtained, "if not the most scientific, yet still the most intimate and immediate light upon the last secret of existence," and because (with which Deussen seeks to justify the belief of the Indians in revelation) in the Upaniṣads "there are philosophical conceptions unequalled in India or perhaps anywhere else in the world."[2) No, it is because these old thinkers *wrestle* so earnestly for the truth, because in their philosophical poems the eternally unsatisfied human yearning for knowledge has been expressed so fervently. The Upaniṣads do not contain "superhuman conceptions," but human, absolutely human attempts to come nearer to the truth—and it is this which makes them so valuable to us.

For the historian, however, who pursues the history of human thought, the Upaniṣads have a yet far greater significance. From the mystical doctrines of the Upaniṣads *one* current of thought may be traced to the mysticism of the Persian Sufism, to the mystic-theosophical logos-doctrine of the Neo-Platonics and the Alexandrian Christians down to the teachings of the Christian mystics Eckhart and Tauler, and finally to the philosophy of the great German mystic of the nineteenth century, Schopenhauer.[3) What Schopenhauer owed to the Indians he has himself told us often enough. He himself calls Plato, Kant and "the Vedas" (by which Schopenhauer always means the Upaniṣads) his teachers. In his manuscript written for University lectures he wrote: "The results of that which I intend to present to you, agree

---

1) *Hecker*, loc. cit., p. 7.

2) *Deussen*, System des Vedanta, pp. 50, 99 f. What exaggerations!

3) On Schopenhauer as a mystic, see *Hecker*, loc. cit., pp. 86 f.

with the oldest of all views of life, namely, the Vedas." He calls the opening up of Sanskrit literature "the greatest gift of our century," and prophesies that Indian pantheism might become the popular belief in the Occident also. The agreement of his own system with that of the Upaniṣads appears to him absolutely marvellous, and he tells us "that each of the separate and detached sayings which constitute the Upaniṣads might be taken as a conclusion from the idea communicated by himself, although on the other hand the same is by no means to be found there already." It is well known that the Oupnek'hat used to lie open on his table and that before retiring to rest he performed his "devotions" in it. And he says of this book: "It is the most satisfying and elevating reading (with the exception of the original text) which is possible in the world; it has been the solace of my life and will be the solace of my death."[1] The fundamental doctrine of the Upaniṣads, however, is the same which, according to Schopenhauer, "was at all times the ridicule of fools and the endless meditation of sages," namely, the *doctrine of Unity*, *i.e.* the doctrine "that all plurality is only apparent, that in all the individuals of this world, in whatever endless number they may present themselves after and beside one another, yet only one and the same, truly existing Being, present and identical in them all, manifests itself."[2] And if Ludwig Stein, who once said: "The philosophy of the present is Monism, that is the interpretation of all that happens in the universe," as one unity[3] is right, then this "philosophy of the present" was already the philosophy of the ancient Indians three thousand years ago.

---

[1]) Parerga und Paralipomena, published by J. *Frauenstädt*, II, p. 427. (§ 185) *Hecker*, loc. cit., pp. 6 ff.

[2]) *Schopenhauer*, Grundlage der Moral, § 22 (Works, publ. by J Frauenstädt, IV, pp. 268 ff.).

[3]) Supplement to the "Neue Freie Presse," July 10th, 1904.

The Vedāṅgas.

In one of the Upaniṣads we are told that there are two kinds of knowledge, a higher and a lower. The higher is that which teaches us to know the imperishable Brahman, but the lower consists of "Ṛgveda, Yajurveda, Sāmaveda, Atharvaveda, *phonetics*, *ritual*, *grammar*, *etymology*, *metrics* and *astronomy*.[1] This is the oldest enumeration of the so-called *six Vedāṅgas*, *i.e.* the six "limbs" or supplementary sciences of the Veda.[2] Originally this meant neither special books nor special schools, but only subjects of instruction, which had to be learned in the Vedic schools themselves, in order to understand the Vedic texts. The beginnings of the Vedāṅgas may therefore already be sought in the Brāhmaṇas and Āraṇyakas, where along with the explanations of the sacrificial ritual we also occasionally find discussions on matters of phonetics, grammar, etymology, metrics and astronomy. In the course of time, however, these subjects were treated more and more systematically, and separate special schools, though still within the Vedic schools, arose for each of the six supplementary sciences of the Veda. These then evolved special school texts, "manuals," the Sūtras, composed in a peculiar prose style intended for memorization.

The word *sūtra* originally means "thread," then a "short rule," a precept condensed into a few words. As a fabric is made out of several threads (thus the transition of meaning might be explained), so a system of instruction[3] is woven

---

1) Muṇḍaka-Up., I, 1, 5: ṛgvedo yajurvedaḥ sāmavedo 'tharvavedaḥ| śikṣā kalpo vyākaraṇaṃ niruktaṃ chando jyotiṣam.||

2) *Cf.* above p. 56, and Ludwig, Der Rigveda, III, pp. 74 ff.

3) Similarly, the word *tantra* originally signifies "web," then a system of instruction, a literary work, a book. In Chinese, too, the word "*king*" means "originally the warp of a texture, then standard, canon, and finally, in a metaphorical sense, any book which is considered as a rule or canon," s. W. *Grube*, Geschichte der chinesischen Litteratur, Leipzig, 1902, p. 31.

together out of these short precepts. A larger work consisting of a number of such sūtras strung together is then also called *Sūtra*.[1] These works serve a purely practical purpose. They are to present some science systematically in concise brevity, so that the pupil can easily commit it to memory. There is probably nothing like these sūtras of the Indians in the entire literature of the world. It is the task of the author of such a work to say as much as possible in as few words as possible, even at the expense of clearness and intelligibility. The saying of the grammarian Patañjali has often been quoted that the author of a sūtra rejoices as much over the saving of half a short vowel as over the birth of a son. An idea of the unique sūtra style, the aphoristic prose of these works, can only be given by means of examples. The words in *brackets* in the two following passages in our translation must be supplemented in order to make the sense of the detached words intelligible :

Āpastambīya-Dharmasūtra I, 1, 1, 4-8 :

Sūtra 4: (There are) four castes : Brahmans, Kṣatriyas, Vaiśyas and Śūdras.

Sūtra 5: Of these the preceding one (is) always better, according to birth (than every succeeding one).

Sūtra 6: For (them who are) not Śūdras and have not committed bad actions, (is prescribed :) initiation as a pupil, Veda-study, fire-laying ; and (these sacred) acts (are) productive (in this world and the next).

Sūtra 7: Obedience towards the other castes (is the duty) of the Śūdras.

Sūtra 8: With each preceding caste which he serves the bliss is greater (*i.e.* the higher the caste which a Śūdra serves, the greater is the bliss which shall fall to his share in the next world).

---

[1]) Compare the word *brāhmana*, which originally means "dictum of a theologian" and is then used collectively for the collections of such dicta, and the word *upaniṣad*, which signifies first *a* secret doctrine, then later means a larger work, a collection of secret doctrines. (See above pp. 187 f. and 243 f)

Gobhila-Gṛhyasūtra, I, 5, 1-5; 8-9.

Sūtra 1: Now at the new and full moon (*i.e.* on the day of the new moon and on the day of the full moon the following ceremonies are to be performed):

Sūtra 2: On the day of the full moon (when the moon rises) at (the time of the evening) twilight he shall fast.

Sūtra 3: Some (teachers say); on the following (day, *i.e.* when the moon rises shortly after sunset, he shall fast).

Sūtra 4: Furthermore (he shall fast) on the day on which the moon is not seen, (regarding) this day as the day of the new moon.

Sūtra 5: At the end of the half-months one shall fast, at the beginning of the half-months one shall sacrifice (*i.e.* a day of fasting shall always precede the sacrifices on the day of the new moon or on the day of the full moon).

Sūtra 8: But the day on which the moon is not seen, shall be made the day of the new moon (*i.e.* is to be celebrated as the day of the new moon).

Sūtra 9: Even if (the moon) is seen only (a little) once (in the day), (this day can be celebrated as the day of the new moon; for then one says) that (the moon has already) completed her course.

The Sanskrit-text, in the above, contains only the unbracketed words. The pupil memorised only these aphoristic sentences receiving the necessary explanations from the teacher. In later times these explanations by the teachers were also written down, and we have them in the extensive commentaries on all the sūtra-texts, without which the sūtras would mostly be unintelligible to us. This peculiar sūtra-style originated in the prose of the Brāhmaṇas. This prose of the Brāhmaṇas consists almost exclusively of short sentences; indirect speech is entirely absent; the sequence of principal sentences is but rarely interrupted by a relative or conditional clause, and its monotony is only relieved to some extent by participial constructions. Furthermore, in spite of a certain prolixity showing itself especially in awkward repetitions, much that is taken as a matter of course in oral presentation and instruction, remains unsaid, while we have to complete it in our translations.[1] Prose of this nature could easily, by more and more exaggerated simplification, be turned into such lapidary, detached sentences, connected only by the most essential particles, as we find in the sūtras. For the purpose of the greater saving of syllables and still shorter summarising only *one* new element was introduced: the formation of long compound words, with which we meet for the first time in the Sūtras, and which then became particularly characteristic of the classical Sanskrit literature and gained ever greater ascendancy at later periods. The frequent quotations from the Brāhmaṇas in the oldest Sūtra-texts, and even when there is no direct quotation, the many Brāhmaṇa-like passages in the midst of the Sūtras[2] make it apparent that the sūtra-style was developed from the piose of the Brāhmaṇas.

The Literature of Ritual.

The oldest Sūtra works are indeed those which even *in contents* are directly connected with the Brāhmaṇas and Araṇyakas. The Aitareya-Āraṇyaka actually contains passages which are nothing but Sūtras, and which tradition itself ascribes to the composers of Sūtras, Āśvalāyana and Śaunaka, and designates as non-revealed.[3] Sāmaveda literature, too, comprises a few works erroneously termed "Brāhmaṇas," which in reality are Sūtras, and on the grounds of their contents must be included in the Vedāṅga literature. Ritual (*Kalpa*), which constitutes the chief contents of the

---

[1]) See above, p 203, Note 1.

[2]) Thus certain sections of the Śaṅkhāyana-Śrautasūtra are similar in style and character to the Brāhmaṇas (*Weber*, HIL., p. 54. *Hillebrandt* in the preface to his edition of the Śāṅkhāyana-Srautasūtra). In the Baudhāyana-Kalpasūtra, too, there are numerous passages which read just like Brāhmaṇas. The Śrautasūtras were not however, written on the basis of the Brahmans, but on that of a long oral tradition; s. R. *Löbbecke* Über das Verhältnis der Brāhmaṇas und ŚrautasūtrenDiss., Leipzig, 1908.

[3]) *Cf.* Max *Müller*, History of Ancient Sanskrit Literature, pp. 314 f., 339.

Brāhmaṇas, is then the first Vedāṅga to receive systematic treatment in special manuals, the so-called K a l p a s ū t r a s. They arose out of the need for compiling the rules for the sacrificial ritual in a shorter, more manageable and connected form for the practical purposes of the priests. Kalpasūtras dealing with the Śrauta-sacrifices taught in the Brāhmaṇas are called Śrautasūtras, and those dealing with the domestic ceremonies and sacrifices of daily life, the Gṛhya-rites, are called Gṛhyasūtras.[1]

The Śrautasūtras thus contain directions for the laying of the three sacred sacrificial fires, for the fire-sacrifice (Agnihotra), the new and full moon sacrifices,[2] the sacrifices of the seasons, the animal sacrifice[3] and especially for the soma-sacrifice with its numerous variations.[4] They are our most important source for the understanding of the Indian sacrifice-cult, and their significance as sources for the history of religion cannot be estimated highly enough.[5]

The contents of the Gṛhyasūtras are still more manifold, and in some respects more interesting. They contain directions for all usages, ceremonies and sacrifices by virtue of which the life of the Indian receives a higher "sanctity," what the Indians call *saṃskāra*, from the moment when he is conceived in the womb, till the hour of his death and still further through the death-ceremonies and the cult of the soul. We thus find in these works a large number of genuinely popular customs and usages treated in detail, which refer

---

[1]) See above, pp. 56 and 160 f.

[2]) *Cf.* A. *Hillebrandt*, Das altindische Neu-und Vollmondsopfer, Jena, 1879.

[3]) *Cf.* Julius *Schwab*, Das altindische Tieropfer, Erlangen, 1886.

[4]) See above pp. 172 ff., and *Cf.* W. *Caland*, et V. *Henry*, L'Agniṣṭoma, description complète de la forme normale du sacrifice de Soma, I, Paris, 1906.

[5]) The entire ritual-literature, besides the chief features of the ritual itself, Śrauta as well as Gṛhya ceremonies, has been treated in detail by A. *Hillebrandt* in the "Grundriss," III, 2 (Ritualliteratur. Vedische Opfer und Zauber, Strassburg, 1897). The significance of the Śrautasūtras in the general science of religion was first fully appreciated by H. *Hubert* and M. *Mauss* in their "Essai sur la nature et la fonction du sacrifice," (Année Sociologique, Paris, 1897-1898, pp. 29-138.)

to conception, birth, the mother and the new-born child, the name-giving, the first outing and the first feeding of the child ; we find exact directions for the shaving of the boy's head, the introduction of the pupil to the teacher (Upanayana or " initiation of the pupil "), the mode of life of the Brahmacārin or Veda-student, the relationship between pupil and teacher, and the dismissal of the pupil from the service of the teacher. The customs at wooing, betrothal and marriage are presented in an especially detailed manner. Here in the Gṛhyasūtras, too, the " five great sacrifices " already mentioned in the Śatapatha-Brāhmaṇa (XI, 5, 6) are minutely described. "These are indeed great sacrificial feasts," it is said emphatically in the Brāhmaṇa, and they are called " great sacrifices " because their performance is among the most important religious duties of every head of a household, although in reality they consist only of small gifts and a few simple ceremonies. These are the daily sacrifices to the *gods*, *demons* and *fathers*, which need only consist of the pious laying of a log of wood upon the sacred fire of the hearth, a few scraps of food, a libation of water, further, hospitality to a guest (designated as "sacrifice to man ") and fifthly, the daily reading of a section of the Veda, considered as "sacrifice to the *Brahman* (or the Ṛṣis)." The simple evening and morning offerings, the new and full moon sacrifices, and the annual festivals connected with sacrifices (from which the Agnihotra, Darśapūrṇamāsa and Cāturmāsya sacrifices under the category of the Śrauta-sacrifices may have proceeded) are also presented in the Gṛhyasūtras. In addition, such customs and ceremonies are described as refer to house-building, cattle-breeding and farming, also those of the magic rites which are to serve for averting diseases and unpropitious omens, as also exorcisms and rites for love magic and such like. Finally the Gṛhyasūtras deal also with the funeral customs and the ancestral sacrifice (Śrāddhas), which, however, assumed such importance that they were soon treated with their minutest details,[1] in special texts (Śrāddha-kalpas).

Thus, then, these Gṛhyasūtras, insignificant though they may be as literary works, afford us a deep insight into the life of the ancient Indians. They are in truth a real treasure for the ethnologist. One need only remember how laboriously the student of classical antiquity has to collect the reports on the daily life of the ancient Greeks and Romans from the most diversified works. Here in India we have the most reliable reports, we may say reports of eye-witnesses, upon the daily life of the ancient Indians, in the form of rules and precepts in these apparently insignificant sūtra-texts. They are, as it were, the "Folklore Journals" of ancient India. It is true, they describe the life of the ancient Indian father of the family only from the religious side, but as religion permeated the whole existence of the ancient Indians to such an extent that actually nothing could take place without an attendant religious ceremony, they are for the ethnologist most invaluable sources for the popular customs and usages of that ancient period. The numerous parallels in the manners and customs of other Indo-European peoples, which have been discovered long ago, with the usages described in the Gṛhya-sūtras, make these documents all the more important. In particular, the comparison of the Greek, Roman, Teutonic and Slavonic marriage customs with the rules contained in the Gṛhyasūtras, has shown that the relationship of the Indo-European peoples is not limited to language, but that these peoples, related in language, have also preserved common features from prehistoric times in their manners and customs.[2]

---

[1]) In the investigation of funeral customs and ancestor-cult based on Indian ritual literature, W. *Caland* has rendered signal service by his works: Über Totenverehrung bei einigen der indogermanischen Völker. Amsterdam, 1888. Altindischer Ahnenkult. Leyden, 1893. Die altindischen Todten—und Bestattungsgebräuche, Amsterdam, 1896. *Cf. Winternitz*, Notes on Śrāddhas, WZKM., 4, 1890, pp. 199 ff.

[2]) *Cf.* E. *Haas* and A. *Weber*, Die Heiratsgebräuche der alten Inder, nach den Gṛihyasutra (in Vol. 5. of "Indische Studien"); L. v. *Schroeder*, Die Hochzeitsgebräuche der

No less important is a third class of text-books, directly connected with the Gṛhyasūtras, and probably originating only as a continuation of them, namely the Dharmasūtras, *i. e.* text-books which deal with the *Dharma. Dharma*, how ever, signifies "right, duty, law," as well as "religion, custom, usage." Therefore these works deal with secular as well as religious law, which indeed are inseparable in India. They give rules and regulations for the duties of the castes and the stages of life (āśramas). Through these works the Brahmans succeeded in transforming the law of ancient India to their own advantage, and in making their influence felt in all directions. We shall deal with these Dharmasūtras in detail in the section on legal literature. They are mentioned here only because, like the Śrauta and Gṛhyasūtras, they originated in the Vedic schools, and with these form a component part of the Kalpasūtras or text-books of ritual.

Lastly the Śulvasūtras, which are directly attached to the Śrautasūtras, should be mentioned in connection with these Kalpasūtras. They contain exact rules for the measurement (Śulva means "measuring-string") and the building of the place of sacrifice and the fire-altars, and as the oldest works on Indian geometry, are of no little importance for the history of science.

The Śrauta and Gṛhyasūtras are also of great importance for the interpretation of the Vedas. They contain not only

---

Esten und einiger anderer finnisch-ugrischer Völkerschaften in Vergleichung mit denen der indogermanischen Völker, Berlin, 1888. B. W. *Leist*, Altarisches Jus gentium. Jena, 1889; M. *Winternitz*, Das altindische Hochzeitsrituell nach dem Āpastambīya-Gṛhyasūtra und einigen anderen verwandten Werken. Mit Vergleichung der Hochzeitsgebräuche bei den übrigen indogermanischen Völkern. (Denkschriften der kais. Akademie der Wissenschaften in Wien, phil.—hist. Kl., Vol. XL. Vienna, 1892); M. *Winternitz*, On a Comparative Study of Indo-European Customs, with special reference to the Marriage Customs (The International Folk-Lore Congress, 1891, Papers and Transactions, London, 1892, pp. 267-291). O. *Schrader*. Reallexikon der indogermanischen Altertumskunde, Strassburg 1901, pp. 353 ff Th *Zachariæ*, Zum altindischen Hochzeitsritual, WZKM., Vol. XVII, pp. 135 ff., 211 ff.

the rules for the ritual, but also for the use (viniyoga) of the *Mantras, i.e.* of the prayers and formulas. They are mostly verses or Yajus-formulas, which occur in the Vedic Saṃhitās; and for their correct explanation their use in the sacrificial rites is by no means insignificant. Often enough, indeed, the mantras have nothing to do with the sacrificial acts for which they are prescribed, and it is extremely interesting, from the point of view of the history of religion, to see how often prayers are used for purposes to which they are not at all suited, and how often they have been entirely misunderstood, wrongly interpreted, or even arbitrarily altered.[1] Sometimes, however, their ceremonial use does give the key to the explanation of a difficult passage in the Veda. As a rule the mantras are enclosed in the sūtras, and are quoted there, now in their entirety, now only with the commencing words of the verses, which are assumed to be familiar.

It is the mantras too, which show most clearly the connexion of the Kalpasūtras with certain Vedic schools. Thus, for instance, the Śrauta and Gṛhyasūtras of the Black Yajurveda, give the prayers in the form which they assume in the Saṃhitās of the Black Yajurveda ; and they give only the first words of the verses or Yajus-formulas, which are taken literally from the Saṃhitā to which they belong, that is, taking for granted that they are known, while they give other mantras, for instance those out of the Ṛgveda or Atharvaveda, in entirety. There are, moreover, in all the sūtras also a number of mantras which do not occur in the Saṃhitās. There are two Gṛhyasūtras in which the mantras are altogether separate from the sūtra text and are combined in special prayer-books; these are the Mantrabrāhmaṇa,[2]

---

1) See *Winternitz* The Mantrapāṭha, pp. xxix f. and Edwin W. *Fay*, The Rig-Veda Mantras in the Gṛhya Sūtras, Diss. Roanoke. Va. 1899.

2) Edited, with commentary, by Satyavrata *Sāmaśrami* in the "Uṣā," Calcutta 1890; the first Prapāṭhaka with German translation by Heinrich *Stönner*. Halle a S. 1901 (Diss.); the second Prapāṭhaka, with Sāyaṇa's Comm. and German translation, by Hans *Jörgensen*, Darmstadt 1911 (Diss. Kiel).

which contains the prayers for the Gobhila-Gṛhyasūtra, and the Mantrapāṭha,[1] belonging to the Āpastambīya-Gṛhyasūtra.

Only in the Black Yajurveda schools of *Baudhāyana* and of *Āpastamba* do we find Kalpasūtras containing all the four kinds of sūtra texts, Śrauta, Gṛhya, Dharma and Śulvasūtras; and in these cases it can also be proved that these works are indeed so interconnected that, to a certain extent, they can be regarded as the four volumes of a uniform work. It is possible that Baudhāyana and Āpastamba were actually the authors of complete Kalpasūtras comprising all the four kinds of texts. But even if they were not the actual authors, at all events, the Śrauta, Gṛhya, Dharma and Śulvasūtras of the Baudhāyana and Āpastamba schools are works composed in each case on a uniform plan, of these two schools[2] of the Yajurveda.

Closely related to the sūtras of the Āpastamba school are those of the schools of *Bhāradvāja* and of *Satyāṣāḍha Hiraṇyakeśin.* The Śrautasūtra of the Bhāradvājas is only known in manuscripts, whereas the Gṛhyasūtra has been published.[3] Both the Śrauta and the Gṛhyasūtra[4] of the

---

[1]) The Mantrapāṭha, or the Prayer Book of the Āpastambins. Edited by M. *Winternitz.* Oxford (Anecdota Oxoniensia) 1897.

[2]) The Baudhāyana-Śrautasūtra has been edited by W. *Caland,* Bibl. Ind., 1904-1924; the Baudhāyana-Gṛhyasūtra by L. *Śrinivāsācharya,* Mysore 1904 (Bibliotheca Sanscrita, No. 32); selections from the Gṛhyasūtra translated by P. *Harting,* Amersfoort 1922; the Baudhāyana-Śulvasūtra has been edited and translated by G. *Thibaut* in the " Pandit, Vols. IX ff. On the Baudhāyana-Sūtras s. *Caland,* Das rituelle Sūtra des Baudhāyana, Leipzig 1903 (AKM., XII, 1),—The Āpastambīya-Śrautasūtra has been edited by R. *Garbe,* Bibl. Ind. 1882-1903, and Books 1-7 translated into German by W. *Caland,* Göttingen 1921; the Āpastambīya-Gṛhyasūtra ed. by M. *Winternitz,* Vienna 1887, and translated, with the Āpastamba-Paribhāṣāsūtras, by *Oldenberg,* SBE., Vol. 30; the Āpastambīya-Śulvasūtra ed. and translated into German by Albert *Bürk,* ZDMG., Vols. 55, 56, 1901-2 Critical and explanatory notes on the Āpast.-Śraut. by *Caland,* ZDMG. 72, 1918, pp. 27 ff. On the Śrautasūtras of the Black Yajurveda s. also A. B. *Keith,* HOS., Vol. 18, pp. xlii ff.

[3]) By Henriette J. W. *Salomons,* Leyden 1913.

[4]) Hiraṇyakeśī-Śrautasūtra ed. with Comm. in ĀnSS No. 53; Hiraṇyakeśi-Gṛhyasūtra ed. by J. *Kirste,* Vienna 1889, and translated by *Oldenberg* in SBE., Vol. 30.

Hiraṇyakeśins have been published, whilst the Hiraṇyakeśi-Dharmasūtra scarcely differs from the Āpastambīya-Dharmasūtra.

All these sūtras, to which we may add those of the hitherto less known schools of the *Vādhūlas*[1] and *Vaikhānasas*,[2] are closely associated with the Taittirīya-Saṃhitā. There can be no doubt that Baudhāyana is the earliest of these sūtra-writers,[3] his successors being Bhāradvāja, Āpastamba and Hiraṇyakeśin in chronological order. The Śrauta, Gṛhya and Śulvasūtras of the *Mānava* school,[4] and the Kāṭhaka-Gṛhyasūtra,[5] which is related to the Mānava-Gṛhyasūtra, come under the Maitrayaṇī-Saṃhitā.

Whether a Kalpasūtra embracing all four kinds of sūtras has always existed in every other Vedic school, as in the cases of the schools of Baudhāyana and Āpastamba, cannot be determined. Of those schools which do not belong to the Black Yajurveda we actually only possess here a Śrautasūtra, and there a Gṛhyasūtra, while the connection of a few Dharmasūtras with schools of the Ṛgveda or of the White Yajurveda is but a very loose one. To the White Yajurveda

---

1) On some fragments of the Vādhūla-Sūtras, which are related to those of Baudhāyana, s. *Caland*, Acta Orientalia I, pp. 3 ff.; II, pp. 142 ff.

2) On the Vaikhānasa-Sūtras s. Th. *Bloch*, Über das Gṛhya-und Dharmasūtra der Vaikhānasa, Leipzig 1896. The Vaikhānasadharmapraśna has been published by *Gaṇapati-Śāstrī* in TSS. No. 28, 1913.

3) This is also confirmed by Baudhāyana's style, which is sometimes intermediate between Brāhmaṇa and Sūtra style. Baudhāyana is sometimes called a *pravacanakāra*, and it seems that *pravacana* is the term for a literary type which forms a transitory stage between Brāhmaṇas and Sūtras; s. *Winternitz*, WZKM, 17, 1903, pp. 289 ff.

4) Mānava-Śrautasūtra, Books I-V, edited by F. *Knauer*, St. Petersburg 1900 ff.; the Cayana of the Mānava-Śrautasūtra by J. M. van *Gelder*, Leyden 1921 (Diss.); the Mānava-Gṛhyasūtra by F. *Knauer*, St. Petersburg 1897. The Mānava-Śrautasūtra is perhaps the oldest Śrautasūtra. *Garbe* (Āpastamba Śrauta Sūtra Ed., Vol. III, pp xxii f.) has shown that it is certainly older than Āpastamba who refers to it. On the Mānava-Gṛhyasūtra s. also P. v. *Bradke*, ZDMG, Vol. 36. The *Vārāhagṛhyasūtra* (ed. by R. *Sama-Sastry*, Gaekwad's Oriental Series, No. 18, Baroda 1921), belonging to a school of the Maitrāyaṇīya, is a late work.

5) An edition of the Kāṭhaka-Gṛhyasūtra by W. *Caland* is announced as being in the press by the D. A. V. College, Lahore.

belong: a Kātyāyana-Śrautasūtra,[1] a Pāraskara-Gṛhyasūtra[2] and a Kātyāyana-Śulvasūtra,[3] to the Ṛgveda an Aśvalāyana-Śrautasūtra,[4] and Aśvalāyana-Gṛhyasūtra[5] a Śrautasūtra and a Gṛhyasūtra of Śaṅkhāyana;[6] to the Sāmaveda the closely related Śrautasūtras of Lāṭyāyana[7] and Drāhyāyaṇa,[8] a Śrautasūtra and a Gṛhyasūtra of the Jaiminīya school,[9] and the Gṛhyasūtras of Gobhila[10] and Khādira.[11] Sāmaveda literature also includes the Arṣeyakalpa, also known as the Maśakakalpasūtra,[12] which teaches which melodies are to be sung to the various stanzas at the soma festivals.

---

1) Ed. by A. *Weber*, The White Yajurveda, Vol. III.

2) Ed. with a German translation by A. F. *Stenzler*, Indische Hausregeln, AKM. VI, 2 and 4, 1876-78; with Harihara's comm. by *Lādhāram Śarman*, Bombay 1890; translated by H. *Oldenberg*, SBE., Vol. 29.

3) A Pariśiṣṭa to this (Kātīyam Śulbapariśiṣṭam) ed. by G *Thibaut* in "Pandit," N.S., Vol. 4.

4) Edition in Bibl. Ind. *Cf. Keith*, HOS., Vol. 25, pp. 51 ff.; P. *Sabbathier*, L'Agnishṭoma d'après le Çrauta-sûtra d'Açvalāyana, JA. 15, 1890, 1 ff., 186 ff.

5) Ed. with commentary of Gārgya Nārāyaṇa in Bibl. Ind 1869; with commentary of Haradattācārya, by *Gaṇapati Sāstrī* in TSS. No. 78, 1923; with German translation by A. F. *Stenzler*, Indische Hausregeln, AKM, III, 4, 1864 and IV, 1, 1865; translated into English by H. *Oldenberg*, SBE., Vol. 29.

6) Śāṅkhāyana-Śrautasūtra ed. by A *Hillebrandt* in Bibl. Ind. 1888 ff. *Cf. Keith*, JRAS. 1907, pp. 410 ff. and HOS., Vol. 25, pp. 50 f. Śāṅkhāyana-Gṛhyasūtra, Sanskrit and German by H. *Oldenberg*, Ind. Stud , Vol 15; English translation by the same scholar, SBE., Vol. 29 Sāṃkhyāyanagrihyasaṃgraha by Pandita Vasudeva ed. by Somanāthopādhyāya, Nyāyopādhyāya and Kāvyatīrtha, and Kaushītakigrihyasūtras ed. by Ratna *Gopāla Bhaṭṭa*, BenSS. 1908.

7) Edition in Bibl. Ind. A few chapters translated into German by R. *Simon*, ZII., Vol. 2, 1923, pp. 1 ff.

8) Ed. by J. N. *Reuter*, Part I, London 1904.

9) D. *Gaastra*, Bijdrage tot de Kennis van het vedische ritueel, Jaiminīya-Śrautasūtra, Leyden 1906, being text and translation of the Agniṣṭoma chapter; text of the Śrautakārikā, ib. pp. 36-60. The Jaiminigṛhyasūtra ed. and translated by W. *Caland*, Lahore 1922 (Punjab Sanskrit Series, No. 2).

10) Ed. with Comm. by Chandrakanta *Tarkalankar*, 2nd Ed., in Bibl. Ind., 1906-1908. Critically edited, with German translation, by F. *Knauer*, Dorpat 1884, 1886. Translated into English by H. *Oldenberg*, SBE., Vol. 30.

11) Text and English translation by H. *Oldenberg* in SBE., Vol. 29.

12) Ed. by W. *Caland*; AKM. XII, 3, Leipzig 1908. Maśaka is the name of the author.

This sūtra is intimately connected with the Pañcaviṃśa-Brāhmaṇa and is earlier than the Lāṭyāyana-Śrautasūtra. Lastly, among Atharvaveda literature we have a Vaitāna-Śrautasūtra,[1] a work which originated very late, and which was added to the Atharvaveda in order to make it of equal value with the remaining three Vedas, and the much older and more important Kauśikasūtra.[2] This is only partly a Gṛhyasūtra, which, like the other Gṛhyasūtras, treats of domestic ritual; but it is much more extensive and also contains the most minute directions for the performance of those magic rites for which the songs and spells of the Atharvaveda were used. This Kauśikasūtra is thus a most valuable complement to the Atharvaveda-Saṃhita and an inestimable source for our knowledge of ancient Indian magic. The Sāmavidhāna-Brāhmana,[3] too, attached to the Sāmaveda, is an interesting book of magic, belonging, in spite of its title, to the Sūtra literature.

The Gṛhyasūtras are followed up by the Srāddhakalpas and Pitṛmedhasūtras, which contain rules for the Śrāddhas and the ancestral sacrifices. Some of these texts may be classed in the categories of the ritual texts of the Vedic schools after which they are named, whilst others are later productions.[4] The sūtra texts,

---

[1]) Edited and translated into German by R. *Garbe*, London and Strassburg 1878; the translation is superseded by that of W. *Caland*, Amsterdam (Akad.) 1910. On the position of the Vaitānasūtra in the Atharvaveda literature s. *Caland*, WZKM. 18, 1904, 185 ff.; *Keith*, JRAS. 1910, 934 ff.; *Bloomfield*, GGA. 1912, No. 1.

[2]) Edited by M. *Bloomfield*, New Haven 1890. Numerous extracts from this Sūtra have been given by the same scholar in the Notes to his English translation of selected hymns of the Atharvaveda (SBE., Vol. 42). The most important sections of the Kauśikasūtra referring to magic, have also been translated into German by W. *Caland* in his work: Altindisches Zauberritual, Amsterdam, 1900.

[3]) Edited by A. C. *Burnell*, London 1873. Translated into German by *Sten Konow*, Das Sāmavidhānabrāhmana, ein altindisches Handbuch der Zauberei, Halle a.S. 1893.

[4]) Mānavaśrāddhakalpa ed. by W. *Caland*, Altindischer Ahnencult, pp. 228 ff., Śrāddhakalpa of the Śaunakins, ib. pp. 240 ff., fragments of a Paippalādaśrāddhakalpa, ib. pp. 243 ff.. Kātyāyanaśrāddhakalpa, ib. pp. 245 ff. On the Gautamaśrāddhakalpa s. *Caland* in Bijdragen tot de taal, land en volkenkunde van Ned. Indië, 6e Volg. deel I,

however, do not exhaust the literature on ritual by any means. Just as the Upaniṣads of the Veda are followed up by the post-Vedic Upaniṣad literature, so the Vedic ritual literature is followed up by literary activity in the realm of ritual, which has continued down to the most recent times. Next after the Śrauta and Gṛhyasūtras follow the Pariśiṣṭas or "addenda," in which certain things are treated in greater detail, which have merely been briefly indicated in the Sūtras. The Pariśiṣṭas appended to the Gobhilagṛhyasūtra are of importance, namely the Gṛhyasaṃgrahapariśiṣṭa of Gobhilaputra,[1] and the Karmapradīpa.[2] The Pariśiṣṭas of the Atharvaveda,[3] which throw light more especially on all kinds of magical practices, omens and portents and the like, are of great value from the point of view of the history of religion. One of the oldest Pariśiṣṭas is the Prāyaścittasūtra,[4] which has come down as part of the Vaitānasūtra, and treats of the expiatory rites. Later ritual works are the Prayogas, "practical handbooks," the Paddhatis, "outlines," and the Kārikās, versified presentations of the ritual. All these works deal either with the complete ritual of some Vedic school or, which is more often the

---

1894. The Pitṛmedhasūtras of Baudhāyana, Hiraṇyakeśin, Gautama ed. W. *Caland* AKM. X, 3, 1896; the 2nd and 3rd Praśnas of Baudh.-Pitṛmedhasūtra by C. H. *Raabe*. Bijdrage tot de kennis van het hindoesche toodenritueel, Leyden 1911.

[1]) See M. *Bloomfield* in ZDMG., Vol. 35. Edited by Ch. *Tarkalankar*, Bibl. Ind. 1910. Other Gobhilya-Pariśiṣṭas (Sandhyāsūtra, Snānasūtra, Śrāddhakalpa, etc.), ed. by the same scholar, Bibl. Ind. 1909.

[2]) The first part of the Karmapradīpa ed. and translated into German by F. *Schrader* Halle a.S. 1889, the second part by A.v. *Staël-Holstein*, Halle a.S. 1900 (Diss.) Cf. *Hillebrandt*, Rituallitteratur, pp. 37 f., and *Caland*, Altindischer Ahnencult, pp. 112 ff.

[3]) Ed. by G. M. *Bolling* and J. *von Negelein*, Leipzig 1909-10. See also J.v. *Negelein*, Orientalististche Literaturzeitung 1908, 447 ff., *Winternitz*, WZKM. 23, 1909, 401 ff., and *Keith*, JRAS. 1912, 757 ff. The Śāntikalpa of the Atharvaveda (ed. by G. M Bolling, Transactions of the American Philological Association, Vol. 35. 1904, 77 ff.; JAOS. 33, 1913, 265 ff.) treats of rites for driving away the evil consequences of portents. The Ath.-Pariśiṣṭas sometimes give a clue to the explanation of the hymns of the Atharvaveda where the Kauśikasūtra fails; s. F. *Edgerton*, Studies in Honor of M. Bloomfield, p. 118.

[4]) The Atharvaprāyaścittāni have been edited by J v *Negelein*. New Haven 1915 (reprinted from JAOS. 1913-14). See also *Caland*, WZKM. 18, 1904, 197 ff.

case, with some special rites. The special works on marriage customs, burial of the dead and ancestral sacrifices (Śrāddhas), are of particular importance, though most of these works are known only through manuscripts and Indian prints.

The Exegetic Vedāṅgas.

Those Sūtra texts which deal with *Śikṣā* or "phonetics" are at least as old as the Kalpasūtras. While the Kalpasūtras are supplementary works to the Brāhmaṇa portion of the Veda, the sūtras of the Vedāṅga Śikṣā are very closely related to the Saṃhitās of the Vedas.

"*Śikṣā*" actually means "instruction," then in particular "instruction in reciting," *i.e.* in the correct pronunciation, accentuation, etc., of the Saṃhitā texts. The earliest mention of this Vedāṅga is to be found in the Taittirīya-Upaniṣad (I, 2), where the teaching of the letters, the accents, the quantity (of syllables) the stress, the melody and the combination of words in continuous recitation, are enumerated as the six chapters of the Śikṣā. Like the doctrine of the ritual, the Śikṣā also arose out of a religious need. For in order to perform a sacrificial act correctly it was not only necessary to know the ritual, but also to be able to pronounce the sacred texts accurately and recite them without errors, just as they were handed down in the Saṃhitās. This presupposes that, at the time when the text-books of the Śikṣā originated, the Vedic Saṃhitās were already established as sacred texts, that they had already obtained a definite form by the agency of editors trained in phonetics. It can actually be proved that, for instance, the Ṛgveda-Saṃhitā does not give the hymns in the form in which they were composed by the ancient singers. Though the editors did not alter the words themselves, yet in the matter of pronunciation, the initial and final sound of the words, the avoidance of the hiatus, and so on, they were led by their phonetic theories into deviating from the original manner of recitation. Thus, for instance, we read in our

Saṃhitā *tvaṃ hyagne*, but can prove (on the ground of metre), that the old singers said *tuaṃ hi agne*. The Vedic Saṃhitās themselves are then already the works of phoneticians. But beside the *Saṃhitā Pāṭhas, i.e.* the Saṃhitā-texts, as they had to be recited according to the teaching of the Śikṣā, there are also the so-called *Pada Pāṭhas* or "word-texts," in which the individual words appear separate from the phonetic connection in which they are presented in the Saṃhitā-text. One example will suffice to make the difference between Saṃhitā-Pāṭha and Pada-Pāṭha clear. A verse in our Ṛgveda-Saṃhitā runs :

agníḥ pū́rvebhirṛ́ṣibhirī́dyo nū́tanairutá | sá devā́m̐ ébá vakṣati

In the Pada-Pāṭha this verse runs :

agníḥ | pū́rvebhiḥ—ṛ́ṣi-bhiḥ | ī́dyaḥ | nū́tanaiḥ | utá | sá | devā́n ā́ | ihá | vakṣati. ||

These Pada-Pāṭhas are, of course, the work of theologians trained in phonetics, in fact of grammarians, for they present the text of the verses in a complete grammatical analysis. Yet they must be fairly old. The Pada-Pāṭha of the Ṛgveda is ascribed to Śākalya, a teacher who is already mentioned in the Aitareya-Āraṇyaka.[1]

Saṃhitā-Pāṭhas and Pada-Pāṭhas, then, are the oldest productions of the Śikṣā schools. The oldest text-books of this Vedāṅga which have come down to us are, however, the Prātiśākhyas, which contain the rules by the aid of which one can form the Saṃhitā-Pāṭha from the Pada-Pāṭha. Hence they contain instruction upon the pronunciation, the accentuation, the euphonic alterations of the sounds in the composition of words and in the initial and final sound of words in the sentence, upon the lengthening of vowels, in short upon the whole manner of the recitation of

[1]) On the Padapāṭha of Śākalya s. B. *Liebich*, Zur Einführung in die indische einheimische Sprachwissenschaft II, Heidelberg 1919, pp. 20 ff. On the Padapāṭha of the Taittirīya-Saṃhitā s. A. *Weber*, Ind. Stud. 13, 1-128, and A. B. *Keith*, HOS. Vol. 18, pp. xxx ff.

the Saṃhitā. Every Śākhā or recension of a Saṃhitā had a text-book of this nature, hence the name Prātiśākhyas, *i.e.* "text-books, each intended for a Śākhā." First of all we have a Ṛgveda-Prātiśākhya,[1] which is ascribed to *Śaunaka*, who is supposed to have been a teacher of *Aśvalāyana*. This work is in verse, and is probably a later revision of an earlier Sūtra-text: it is even called "Sūtra" in manuscripts and quotations. The Taittirīya-Prātiśākhya-sūtra,[2] belongs to the Taittirīya-Saṃhitā; a Vājasaneyi-Prātiśākhya-Sūtra,[3] ascribed to *Kātyāyana*, belongs to the *Vājasaneyi-Saṃhitā*, and the Atharvaveda-Saṃhitā has an Atharvaveda-Prātiśākhya-sūtra,[4] which is supposed to be of the school of the Śaunakas. There is also a Sāmaprātiśākhya,[5] and the Puṣpasūtra[6] is a kind of Prātiśākhya to the Uttaragāna of the Sāmaveda. A further work dealing with the manner of singing the Sāmans at the sacrifice, is the Pañcavidha-sūtra.[7]

These works are of twofold importance: firstly, for the history of grammatical study in India, which, as far as we know, commences with these Prātiśākhyas. Though they are

---

1) Edited, with a translation into German, by Max *Müller*, Leipzig 1856-69. On the metrics of the Ṛgveda-Prātiśākhya, s. H. *Oldenberg*. NGGW. 1919, pp. 170 ff.

2) Text, Translation and Notes by W. D. *Whitney*, New Haven 1871 (JAOS., Vol. 9). On the relation of the Taittirīya-Prātiśākhya to the Taitt.-Saṃhitā, s. *Keith*, HOS., Vol. 18, pp. xxxi ff. It is certainly older than Pāṇini.

3) Edited by P. Y. *Pathaka*. Benares 1883-88; text with German translation by A. *Weber*, Ind. Stud. 4, 65-160, 177-331. The *Pratijñāsūtra* (edited and explained by Weber in ABA. 1871, pp. 69 ff.) is an appendix to this Prātiśākhya.

4) Critically edited by *Vishva Bandhu Vidyārthī Śāstrī*, Part I, Punjab University 1923. This is different from the Śaunakīyā Caturādhyāyikā, which has been edited and translated as an "Atharvaveda-Prātiśākhya" by W. D. *Whitney*, New Haven 1862 (JAOS., Vol. 7).

5) Ed. by *Satyavrata Sāmaśrami* in "Uṣā," Calcutta 1890.

6) Ed. and translated into German by R. *Simon*, ABayA. 1909, pp. 481-780. On the mutual relation between Puṣpasūtra, Ārṣeyakalpa and Uttaragāna, s. *Simon*, l.c. 499 ff.; ZDMG. 63, 1909, 730 ff. and *Caland*, ZDMG. 64, 1910, 347 f.

7) Ed. and translated into German by R. *Simon*, Breslau 1913 (Indische Forschungen, Nr. 5).

not actually grammatical works themselves, they treat of subjects pertaining to grammar, and the quotations from so many grammarians prove that the study of grammar was already flourishing at their time. Secondly, they are still more important because they are pledges of the fact that the texts of the Saṃhitās as we have them to-day, have remained unaltered through all the centuries since the time of the Prātiśākhyas. Thus the rules of the Ṛgveda-Prātiśākhya take for granted that, at the period of the latter, the Ṛgveda-Saṃhita was not only firmly established in its division into ten Maṇḍalas, but that even the order of the hymns in each Maṇḍala was the same as it is now. Indeed, the minute rules of Śaunaka leave no doubt that, at the period of the latter, the text of the Ṛgveda-Saṃhitā read, word for word and syllable for syllable, almost exactly as we find it at the present day in our printed editions.

These Prātiśākhyas are the earliest representatives of the Vedāṅga Śikṣā. Beside them we find more modern works, short treatises on phonetics, which claim the title of Śikṣās and give famous names, such as Bhāradvāja, Vyāsa, Vāsiṣṭha, Yājñavalkya and so on, as their authors. They follow the Prātiśākhyas in much the same way as, at later periods, versified law-books followed up the ancient Vedic Dharmasūtras, also mentioning as their authors names famous in antiquity. Some of these Śikṣās are comparatively old and are more directly associated with some Prātiśākhya or other, *e.g.* the Vyāsa-Śikṣā [1] with the Taittirīya-Prātiśākhya, while others are of much later origin and of no importance either for grammar or for the history of the Vedic texts.[2]

---

[1]) *Cf.* H. *Lüders*, Die Vyâsa-Çikshâ besonders in ihrem Verhältnis zum Taittirīya-Pratiçâkhya, Kiel 1895.

[2]) On the Śikṣās s. F. *Kielhorn*, Ind. Ant. 5, 1876, 141 ff, 193 ff. On the Pāṇinīya-Śikṣā s. A. *Weber*, Ind. Stud. 4, 435 ff. and B. *Liebich*, Zur Einführung in die indische einheimische Sprachwissenschaft II, p. 20, who says that though late in form, it is old in contents. The Nāradīya-Śikṣā is edited in *Satyavrata Sāmaśrami's* "Uṣā," I, 4, Calcutta

Śaunaka and *Kātyāyana*, who are mentioned as authors of Prātiśākhyas, are also considered to be the authors of works very closely connected with the Vedāṅga literature because they deal also with the texts of the Vedic Saṃhitās, though they are not called Vedāṅgas. These works are the Anukramaṇīs, *i.e.* "catalogues," "lists," "indexes," which give the contents of the Vedic Saṃhitās with regard to different items.[1] Thus Śaunaka composed an Anukramaṇī or a catalogue of the Ṛṣis of the Ṛgveda hymns, also a catalogue of the metres, one of the deities and a further one of the hymns. Kātyāyana is the author of a Sarvānukramaṇī[2] *i.e.* a "catalogue of all things" for the Ṛgveda. This work gives, in the form of sūtras, the first words of every hymn, then the number of verses, the name and family of the ṛṣi to whom the hymn is ascribed, of the deities to whom the single verses are addressed, and the metre or metres in which the hymn is composed. The two metrical works Bṛhaddevatā and Ṛgvidhāna are again ascribed to Śaunaka. They are not, however, the work of Śaunaka himself, but that of his school. The Bṛhaddevatā[3] is an enlarged catalogue of the gods worshipped in the separate hymns of the Ṛgveda; for it contains also myths and legends referring to these deities, and is therefore at the same time an important work from the point of view of Indian narrative literature. The Bṛhaddevatā is obviously one of the earliest

---

1890; the Bhāradvāja-Śikṣā (cum versione latina, excerptis ex commentario etc.) by E. *Sieg*, Berlin 1892. A collection of Śikṣās (Śikṣāsaṃgraha) has been published in BenSS. 1893.

1) The Atharvavedīyapañcapaṭalikā (ed. by *Bhagwaddatta*, Lahore 1920) is an Anukramaṇī of the Atharvaveda-saṃhitā. The so-called Ārṣeya-brāhmaṇa of the Sāmaveda (ed. by A. C. *Burnell*, Mangalore 1876, and with commentary by *Satyavrata Sāmaśrami* in "Uṣā," II, 1, Calcutta 1892) is also an Anukramaṇī.

2) Edited by A. A. *Macdonell*, Oxford (Anecdota Oxoniensia) 1886. On a Kashmirian recension of the Sarvānukramaṇī s. *Scheftelowitz*, ZII. 1, 1922, 89 ff.

3) Ed. by Rajendralala *Mitra* in Bibl. Ind. 1892; critically edited and translated into English by A. A. *Macdonell*, HOS., Vols. 5 and 6, 1904.

Indian narrative works, for its metres, the triṣṭubh as well as the śloka, occupy a middle position in point of time between Vedic and epic metre; and furthermore, those legends which are common to the Bṛhaddevatā and the Mahābhārata, appear in a later form in the epic.[1] The Ṛgvidhāna,[2] also in the form of a catalogue following the division of our Ṛgveda-Saṃhitā, states the magic power which can be obtained by the recitation of each hymn or even of single verses. It is somewhat similar to the above-mentioned Sāmavidhāna-Brāhmaṇa.

Of importance are the Anukramaṇīs and the works related to them, on account of their affording additional proof that even in very early times the texts of the Vedic Samhitās were in almost exactly the same form, with the same divisions, the same number of verses, and so on, as we have them at present.

The same is true also of the Nirukta of *Yāska*,[3] which has already been mentioned on another occasion. This work, too, the only one of the Vedāṅga Nirukta which we possess, presupposes the Ṛgveda-Saṃhitā in essentially the same condition in which we know it to-day. Tradition erroneously ascribes also the Nighaṇṭus or "lists of words" to Yāska. In reality, however, the work of Yāska is only a commentary to these lists of words, of which Yāska himself says, that they were composed by the descendants of the ancient sages, for the easier understanding of the transmitted texts. The Nighaṇṭus are five lists of words, which are divided into three sections. The first section (Naighaṇṭukakāṇḍa) consists of

---

[1]) See A. *Kuhn*, Ind. Stud. I, 101 ff.; *Keith*, JRAS. 1906, pp. 1 ff.: 1912, pp. 769 ff. *Winternitz*, WZKM. 20, 1906, pp. 1 ff.; *Liebich*, Zur Einführung in die ind. einh. Sprachwiss. II. 30 ff.

[2]) Ṛgvidhânaṃ edidit cum praefatione Rudolf Meyer, Berolini 1878.

[3]) See above p. 69. The Nirukta was first edited by *R. Roth*, Göttingen 1852: with commentaries and useful indexes by *Satyavrata-Sāmaśrami* in Bibl. Ind., 1882-91; with commentary of Durgâcārya, Vol. 1, Adhy. 1-6, edited by *V. K. Rajavade*, ĀnSS. No. 88, 1921. On L. Sarup's edition s. above.

three lists, in which Vedic words are collected under certain main ideas. For instance, there are quoted 21 names for "earth," 15 for "gold," 16 for "air," 101 for "water," 122 verbs for "to go," 26 adjectives and adverbs for "quick," 12 for "much," and so on. The second section (Naigamakāṇḍa or Aikapadika) contains a list of ambiguous and particularly difficult words of the Veda, while the third section (Daivatakāṇḍa) gives a classification of the deities according to the three regions, earth, sky, and heaven.[1] Veda-exegesis probably began with the compilation of such glossaries; the composition of commentaries to these glossaries after the style of our Nirukta, with explanations of difficult Veda verses interwoven, was a further step in the development, and, at a still later period, detailed and continuous commentaries to the Vedic texts were written. Certain it is that Yāska had many predecessors, and that his work, though certainly very old and the oldest existing Veda-exegetic work, can nevertheless only be regarded as the last, perhaps also the most perfect, production of the literature of the Vedāṅga Nirukta.

Of the Vedāṅgas of metrics and astronomy, too, it is only the latest offshoots of an earlier scientific literature that remain. For the Sāmaveda there is the Nidānasūtra, containing not only metrical but other investigations into the various component parts of the Sāmaveda (Uktha, Stoma, Gāna). It is also important from the grammatical point of view, and some of the ancient teachers ascribe it to Patañjali.[2] The

---

[1]) On these Nighaṇṭus as the beginnings of Indian lexicography see Th. *Zachariae*, Die indischen Wörterbücher ("Grundriss," I, 3 B), Strassburg 1897, pp. 2 f. *S. K. Belvalkar* (Proc. SOC., pp. 11ff.) has shown that it is possible, with the help of the Nighaṇṭus, esp. the Aikapadika list, to distinguish literary strata in the Ṛgveda. Belvalkar dates Yāska's Nirukta from the 7th century B. C. This is likely enough, though not certain. But we have no idea how much earlier the Nighaṇṭus may be.

[2]) *Cf. Weber* HIL., pp. 81f., E. *Sieg*, Die Sagenstoffe des Ṛgveda, Stuttgart 1902, pp. 29, 35, 65; and *Caland*, Ārṣeyakalpa, pp. xvii ff. A Nidāna of the Sāmaveda is quoted

text-book of *Piṅgala* on metrics, though regarded by the Indians as a Vedāṅga of the Ṛgveda and Yajurveda, there being two recensions of it, is nevertheless the work of a later period; for it deals also with metres which only belong to later Sanskrit poetry. [1] The Jyotiṣa-Vedāṅga is a small text-book of astronomy in verse; in the Yajurveda recension it contains 43 verses, in that of the Ṛgveda 36. Its main contents are the positions of the moon and the sun at the solstices, as well as the new and full moon in the circle of the 27 Nakṣatras or stars of the zodiac, or rules are drawn up for their calculation. [2] The very circumstance that it is not written in verse, refers this little work which, moreover, has not yet been sufficiently explained, to a later period.

The old Vedāṅga texts on grammar are entirely lost. This science, too, certainly originated in connection with the Veda-exegesis, and proceeded from the Veda schools. For already in the Āraṇyakas we find isolated grammatical technical terms. But the oldest and most important text-book of grammar that has come down to us, that of *Pāṇini*, metes out to the Vedic language only casual treatment; it no longer stands in close relation to any Veda school, and altogether belongs to a period at which the science of grammar was already pursued in special schools, independent of theology. For in India also, as we shall see in the section on scientific literature, science has detached itself more and more from theology, within which it was originally included almost completely.

---

in the Bṛhaddevatā, V, 23. But the quotation is not found in the Nidānasūtra, printed in the "Uṣā," Calcutta, 1896.

[1]) The Sūtra of Piṅgala was edited and explained by A. *Weber* in Vol. 8 of Ind. Stud. Cf. also *A. Weber*, HIL., p. 60.

[2]) Cf. A. *Weber*, Uber den Vedakalender namens Jyotisham (ABA 1862) and G. *Thibaut*, Astronomie (in the "Grundriss," III, 9), pp. 17, 20 and 28. Ātharvaṇa Jyotiṣam edited by Bhagavad Datta, Lahore, 1924 (Punjab Sanskrit Series, No. 6).

The age of the Veda.

We have traced the whole of Vedic literature to its latest off-shoots and stragglers, and can now no longer evade the question of the age of the whole of this great literature. If it were possible to determine, even within a few centuries, the period into which the oldest hymns of the Ṛgveda and of the Atharvaveda reach back, then it were unnecessary to devote a special chapter to this question. It would suffice to give, in a few words, the approximate age of the Veda. Unfortunately, however, it is a fact, and a fact which it is truly painful to have to admit, that the opinions of the best scholars differ, not to the extent of centuries, but to the extent of thousands of years, with regard to the age of the Ṛgveda. Some lay down the year 1000 B.C. as the earliest limit for the Ṛgvedic hymns, while others consider them to have originated between 3000 and 2500 B.C. In view of the *very great* divergence in the opinions of the specialists, it is not enough, even in a book intended for the general reader, merely to give some approximate date, for even the general reader must have an idea of the circumstances supporting the various opinions on the greater or lesser antiquity of the Veda. This is the more necessary, as the question of the period of the oldest Indian literature coincides with the question of the beginning of the Indo-Aryan civilization, a question which is of the utmost importance to every historian, archæologist and philologist. If, indeed, it is at all possible to determine the periods of the development of Indo-Aryan culture, and, going still further back, those of Indo-European culture, it can only be done hand in hand with investigation as to the period of the earliest monuments of Aryan culture in India.

Under these circumstances, then, it seems to me absolutely necessary to render account of the whole question to the non-specialist also, and, as far as possible, to state the limits and the reasons both of our ignorance and of our knowledge.

On first becoming acquainted with Indian literature, people were inclined to ascribe tremendous antiquity to all Indian literary works. Did not Friedrich Schlegel expect from India nothing less than "enlightenment upon the history of the primitive world, so dark until now"?[1] As late as in 1852 A. Weber wrote in his "History of Indian Literature": "The literature of India passes generally for the most ancient literature of which we possess written records, and justly so," and it was only in 1876 in his second edition that he added: "In so far as this claim may not now be disputed by the Egyptian monumental records and papyrus rolls, or even by the Assyrian literature which has but recently been brought to light." The reasons for which, according to Weber, "we are fully justified in regarding the literature of India as the most ancient literature of which written records on an extensive scale have been handed down to us" are in part geographical, in part pertain to the history of religion. In the older parts of the Ṛgveda the Indian nation appears to us to be settled in the Punjab. The gradual spread eastwards across Hindustan towards the Ganges can be traced in the later portions of Vedic literature. The Great Epics then further show us the spread of Brahmanism towards the south. Centuries must have elapsed before such an enormous stretch of land, "inhabited by wild and vigorous tribes," could become brahmanized. Many centuries too, must have been required for the religious development from the simple nature worship of the Ṛgvedic hymns up to the theosophical-philosophical speculations of the Upaniṣads, and again to such phases of mythology and cult as Megasthenes, about 300 B.C., found prevalent in India. Weber did

[1]) *Cf.* above, p. 14

not attempt a more exact determination of the Vedic period; in fact, he expressly declares any such attempt to be entirely futile.[1]

The first, however, to make this attempt and to endeavour to construct a kind of chronology of the oldest Indian literature, was Max Müller in his "History of Ancient Sanskrit literature" which appeared in 1859. Starting from the few definite clues to Indian chronology which we possess, the invasion of Alexander and the appearance of Buddhism,[2] he argued further as follows. Buddhism is nothing but a reaction against Brahmanism, and it presupposes the existence of the whole Veda, *i.e.* the literature consisting of the hymns, the Brāhmaṇas, Āraṇyakas and Upaniṣads. The whole of this literature must therefore be *pre-Buddhist*, i.e. it must have originated before 500 B.C. The Vedāṅga or Sūtra literature might be approximately synchronous with the origin and the first spread of Buddhism. Now the origin of these Sūtra works, whose character is such that they necessarily pre-suppose the Brāhmaṇa literature, falls approximately into the period from 600 to 200 B.C. (It is at the fixing on these purely arbitrary dates that the untenable part of Max Müller's calculations begins.) The Brāhmaṇas, however, of which there are earlier and later ones, and which contain long lists of teachers, handed down by earlier Brāhmaṇas, cannot possibly be accommodated in less than 200 years. Therefore, argues Max Müller, we shall have to accept the period from 800 to 600 B. C. as the period of the origin of these prose works. The Brāhmaṇas, however, for their part, again pre-suppose the Vedic Saṃhitās. But the composition of all these collections of songs and prayers would take at least 200 years; hence the interval from roughly 1000 to 800 B. C. might be regarded as the

---

1) *Weber*, HIL., pp. 2 ff., 6 f.

2) Cf. above, pp. 27 f.

period in which these collections were arranged. However, before the compilation of these collections, which were already regarded as sacred sacrificial poetry and authorised prayer-books, there must have been a period at which the songs and chants contained in them arose as popular or religious poems. This period, Max Müller concluded, must have been before 1000 B. C. And as he had already assumed 200 years for the "Brāhmaṇa period" and 200 years for the period he called the "Mantra period," he now also assumed 200 years for the *arising* of this poetry (though without laying much stress on this figure), and thus arrived at 1200 to 1000 B. C. as the period of the beginning of Vedic poetry.

Now it is clear that the supposition of 200 years for each of the different literary epochs in the origin of the Veda is purely arbitrary. Even Max Müller himself did not really wish to say more than that such an interval *at least* must be assumed, and that in 1000 B. C. *at the latest*, our Ṛgveda-Saṃhitā must already have been completed. He always considered his date of 1200-1000 B. C. only as a *terminus ad quem*, and in his Gifford Lectures on "Physical Religion" in 1889,[1] he expressly states "that we cannot hope to fix a *terminus a quo*. Whether the Vedic hymns were composed 1000, or 1500, or 2000, or 3000 years B. C., no power on earth will ever determine." It is remarkable, however, how strong the power of suggestion is even in science. Max Müller's hypothetical and really purely arbitrary determination of the Vedic epochs in the course of years, received more and more the dignity and the character of a scientifically proved fact, without any new arguments or actual proofs having been added. It became a habit, a habit already censured by W. D. Whitney,[2] to say that Max Müller had proved 1200-1000 B. C. as the date of the Ṛgveda. It was only timidly that a

[1]) Published, London, 1901, p. 91.

[2]) Oriental and Linguistic Studies, First Series, New York, 1872, p. 78.

few scholars like L. von Schroeder [1] ventured to go as far back as 1500 or even 2000 B. C. And when, all at once, H. Jacobi attempted to date Vedic literature back to the third millenary B. C. on the grounds of astronomical calculations, scholars raised a great outcry at such heretical procedure, and even to-day most of the Western scholars shake their heads wondering how Jacobi could venture to assert so exaggerated an opinion on the age of the Veda. Strange to say, it has been quite forgotten on what a precarious footing stood the "opinion prevailing hitherto," which was so zealously defended.

The idea of drawing conclusions on the chronology of the earliest Indian literature with the assistance of *astronomical* data, is no new one. A. Ludwig already undertook an attempt of this nature on the basis of the eclipses of the sun. [2] The priests of ancient India, who had to determine the times of sacrifice, were, like the pontifices in ancient Rome, at the same time almanac-makers. They had to observe the firmament, in order to regulate and predetermine the times of sacrifice. Hence we find numerous astronomical and calendar data in the Brāhmaṇas and Sūtras. In these, the so-called Nakṣatras or "lunar mansions" play a particularly prominent part. The ancient Indians had observed that the moon requires about 27 days and nights for its siderial orbit and stays in a different constellation every night of the sidereal month. These stars or constellations, which all lie not far distant from the ecliptic, were combined into a kind of zodiac, a succession of 27 Nakṣatras embracing the spheres, and this lunar zodiac was employed for the purpose of estimating the position of the moon at a particular time. [3]

---

[1]) Indiens Literatur und Kultur, pp. 291 f.

[2]) Über die Erwähnung von Sonnenfinsternissen im Rigveda. (Sitzungsberichte der Königl. böhmischen Gesellschaft der Wissenschaften, Prag, 1885.

[3]) The lunar zodiac has been preserved in India down to the present day, side by side with the solar zodiac, which was probably not introduced into India until the

Thus there are many passages in Vedic literature in which it is said that a sacrificial act is to take place "under such and such a Nakṣatra," *i.e.* "when the moon stands in conjunction with this Nakṣatra." There are still more numerous passages in which the Nakṣatras are brought into definite relationship with the full moon and new moon. And already in the earlier literature there often appear only twelve of the 27 Nakṣatras connected with the full moon, from which may be traced the names of the months derived from the twelve Nakṣatras. These month-names were originally used only for lunar months, but were later extended also to the twelve divisions of the solar year. But as already in Vedic times attempts had been made to bring the solar and lunar year into accord by some means or another, the question arises whether, out of the combination of certain full-moon Nakṣatras with the seasons of the year and the commencement of the year, conclusions may not be drawn as to the period in which the respective calendar data originate. Such conclusions, which led to surprising results, were attempted in the year 1893, simultaneously and independently of each other, by H. Jacobi in Bonn and the Indian scholar Bál Gangádhar Tilak in Bombay.[1] Both scholars by different ways arrived at the opinion that at the period of the Brāhmaṇas the Pleiades

---

first century A.D. with the doctrines of the Greek astronomers. The problem of the origin of this lunar zodiac, and of the relationship between the Indian Nakṣatras and the Menāzil of the Arabs and the Sieou of the Chinese has not been solved even now. See especially A. *Weber*, Die vedischen Nachrichten von den Naxatra, 1, 2, ABA 1860, 1862; G. *Thibaut*, Astronomie (Grundriss III, 9), pp. 12 ff.; H. *Oldenberg*, Nakṣatra und sieou, NGGW 1909, 544 ff. *Macdonell* and *Keith*, Vedic Index, I, 427 ff., plead for Babylonian origin, which F. *Hommel* (ZDMG 45, 1891, 592 ff.) has tried to prove; but see B. V. Kameśvara *Aiyar*, Ind. Ant. 48. 1919, 95 ff.

1) A. *Ludwig*, Der Rigveda III, Prag 1878, pp. 183 ff. and R. G. *Bhandarkar*, Report, 1883-84, p. 39, have already pointed out the chronological significance of the Kṛttikas heading the list of the Nakṣatras in the Brāhmaṇas. But Bhandarkar places the Brāhmaṇas between 1200 and 900 B.C. Violent discussions were aroused by H. *Jacobi's* papers in "Festgruss an Rudolf von Roth," Stuttgart, 1893, pp. 68-73, in NGGW, 1894, pp. 105-116, and in OC X, Geneva 1894, I, pp. 103-108, and the book of B. G. *Tilak*. The

(Kṛttikās), which at that time formed the starting-point of the Nakṣatra series, coincided with the vernal equinox, but that in the Vedic texts there are also to be found traces of an older calendar, in which the vernal equinox fell in Orion (Mṛgaśiras). From the calculation of the value of the precession, however, it appears that about 2500 B. C. the vernal equinox lay in the Pleiades and about 4500 in Orion. But while Tilak goes so far as to date some Vedic texts back to the year 6000 B. C., Jacobi contents himself with placing "the beginnings of the period of civilization, as the mature, perhaps even late production of which the songs of the Ṛgveda have come down to us," at about 4500 B. C. This period of civilization stretches, according to him, roughly from 4500-2500 B. C., and he is inclined to ascribe "the collection of hymns which has come down to us, to the second half of this period." [1] Jacobi was confirmed in this opinion by a second astronomical observation. The Gṛhyasūtras tell us of a marriage-custom in ancient India, according to which the bride and bridegroom, after they had arrived at their new home, had to sit silently on the hide of a bull, till the stars became visible, whereupon the bridegroom showed his bride the *Pole star*, called *dhruva*, "the constant one," and at the same time uttered a prayer, as for example, "Be constant, prospering in my house," whereto she replied: "Constant art thou, may I be constant in the house of my husband." This marriage-custom, in which a "constant" star figures as the symbol of unchangeable constancy, must have originated at a time in which a brighter star stood so near the celestial

---

Orion or Researches into the Antiquity of the Vedas, Bombay 1893. Cf. G *Bühler*, Ind. Ant. 23, 1894, pp. 238 ff.; W. D. *Whitney* in JAOS Proceedings, March 1894 (reprinted Ind. Ant. 24, 1895, pp 361 ff.); G. *Thibaut*, Ind Ant. 24, pp. 85 ff.; and Astronomie (Grundriss III, 9) pp. 18 f.; A. *Barth*, JA 1894, pp. 156 ff.; Oeuvres II, 248 ff.; A. *Weber*, SBA 1894, pp. 775 ff.; H. *Oldenberg* in ZDMG 48, 1894, pp. 629 ff.; 49, pp. 470 ff.; 50, pp. 450 ff.; *Jacobi* in ZDMG 49, pp. 218 ff.: 50, pp. 69 ff.; E. W. *Hopkins*, The Religions of India, Boston 1895, pp. 4 ff.; A. A. *Macdonell*, History of Sanskrit Literature, London 1900, p. 12.

[1]) Festgruss an Roth, pp. 71 f.

pole that it seemed, to the observers of that time, to be standing still. Now it is again a result of the precession that, with the gradual alteration of the celestial equator, its North Pole also moves away, describing in about 26,000 years a circle of $23\frac{1}{2}$ degrees radius around the constant pole of the ecliptic. By this means, one star after another slowly moves towards the North Pole and becomes North Star or Pole Star; but only from time to time does a *brighter* star approach the Pole so closely, that it can, for all practical purposes, be regarded as "a constant one" (dhruva). At present Alpha, a star of the second magnitude, in the Little Bear, is the Pole Star of the Northern hemisphere. This star, of course, cannot be meant when the Pole Star is spoken of in Vedic times, because only 2000 years ago this star was still so far removed from the pole that it could not possibly have been designated as the "constant one." Not until 2780 B. C. do we meet with another Pole Star which merited this name. At that time Alpha Draconis stood so near to the Pole for over 500 years that it must have appeared immovable to those who observed with the naked eye. We must, then, place the origin of the name of Dhruva, as well as the custom of showing the "constant" star to the bride on her marriage evening as the symbol of constancy, into a period in which Alpha Draconis was Pole Star, that is, in the first half of the third millenary B. C. In the marriage-verses of the Ṛgveda, however, this custom is not yet thought of, wherefore Jacobi considers it probable "that the use of Dhruva in the marriage ceremony does not belong to the time of the Ṛgveda, but to the following period, and that, therefore, the Ṛgvedic period of civilization lies before the third millenary B. C." [1]

As has been said, the assertions of Jacobi and Tilak met with violent opposition. The most serious objection to the argument about the *Pleiades* was that the Indians of the

---

[1]) ZDMG., Vol. 50, p. 71.

most ancient times were concerned only with the position of the Nakṣatras in relation to the moon and not to the sun, and that there is not a single trace of any observation of the equinoxes to be found in the most ancient times. The passage [1] in which we read that the Pleiades "do not swerve from the East" should probably not be interpreted as meaning that they rose "due east" (which would have been the case in the third millenary B. C., and would point to a knowledge of the vernal equinox): the correct interpretation is more likely that they remain visible in the eastern region for a considerable time—during several hours—every night, which was the case about 1100 B. C.[2] Coming to the argument of the *New Year* in various millenaries, it is most difficult to decide these questions, primarily because in our texts the year sometimes begins with spring, sometimes with winter, and sometimes with the rainy season, and moreover the number of seasons varies between three, five and six.[3] The argument of the *Pole Star*, too, provoked serious

---

[1]) Śat.-Br. II, 1, 2, 3. See *Oldenberg* and *Jacobi*, ZDMG 48, p. 631 note; 50, pp. 72 and 452. Sankar B. *Dikshit* (Ind. Ant. 24, 1895, pp. 245 f.), B. V. Kameśvara *Aiyar* (The Age of the Brāhmaṇas, in the Quarterly Journal of the Mythic Society 1922, and previously in Proc. FOC I, pp. 1 ff. and Dhirendranath *Mukhopadhyaya*, The Hindu Nakshatras, pp. 41 f. (Reprint from Vol. VI of the Journal of the Department of Science, Calcutta University, 1923), have concluded from this passage, that the Śatapatha-Brāhmaṇa was written about 3000 B. C.

[2]) I am indebted for this explanation to Professor A. *Prey*, the astronomer of our University, who informs me that, in about 1100 B. C. the *Pleiades* rose approximately 13° to the north of the east point, approaching nearer and nearer the east line, and crossing it as late as 2 h 11m after their rise, at a height of 29°, when seen from a place situated at 25° North latitude. They thus remain almost due east long enough to serve as a convenient basis for orientation. This interpretation of the passage is proved to be the correct one, by Baudhāyana-Śrautasūtra 27, 5 (cf. W. *Caland*, Uber das rituelle Sūtra des Baudhāyana, Leipzig 1903, pp. 37 ff.), where it is prescribed that the supporting beams of a hut on the place of sacrifice shall face the east, and that this direction shall be fixed after the Pleiades appear, as the latter "do not depart from the eastern region." It is true that, about 2100 B. C. or about 3100 B. C., the Pleiades touched the east line earlier, but they proceeded southwards so rapidly that they were not suitable for orientation.

[3]) In the Śat.-Br. XII, 8,2,35, it is said: 'All seasons are the first, all are the intermediate, all are the last."

objections. We cannot deny the possibility of one of the lesser stars in the Little Bear having been visible (about 1250 B. C. and even later still) as the Pole Star in the clear Indian firmament.[1] At any rate it is not permissible to draw any conclusion from the non-mention of this custom in the Ṛgveda: for by no means all of the marriage-customs are mentioned in the marriage hymn in the Ṛgveda, and there is no reason why this particular custom should have been singled out for mention in preference to another.

Though the astronomical arguments of Tilak and Jacobi did not succeed in proving what was to be proved, they have stimulated the enquiry whether there are no other grounds for assuming a greater antiquity of Vedic culture. And indeed, from the point of view of Indian history, *nothing* speaks *against* the assumption that Vedic literature extends back into the third millenary, and ancient Indian culture to the fourth millenary, while the supposition of 1200 or even 1500 B. C., traceable to Max Müller, for the commencement of the Vedic period no longer agrees with the *present-day* state of our knowledge of the political history, as well as of the literary and religious history of ancient India. This has, I believe, been convincingly proved, especially by G. Bühler.[2]

Inscriptions prove that in the third century B. C. Southern India was conquered by the Aryan Indians and invaded by brahmanical culture. The fact, however, that some Vedic schools, such as those of Baudhāyana and Āpastamba, originated in the south of India, makes it probable that the conquest of the south by the Aryans must have taken place much earlier, perhaps as early as in the 7th or 8th

---

1) Professor Prey believes that Groombridge 2001 and 2029, stars of the fifth to the sixth magnitude in the Little Bear, the first of which approached the pole as far as 17, in about 1250 B. C., and the second of which approached the pole as far as 8' in 1500 B. C., are easily visible in view of the favourable atmospheric conditions of India.

2) Ind. Ant., 23, 1894, pp. 245 ff.

century B. C. For the whole country can hardly have been colonised and brahmanized immediately after the conquest to such an extent that Vedic schools could originate in the distant south. But, as Bühler says,[1] "with the conquest of Southern India about 700 or even about 600 B. C., the assumption that the Indo-Aryans inhabited about 1200 or even about 1500 B. C. the northern corner of India and Eastern Afghanistan becomes absolutely impossible. The dea that the Indo-Aryan nation of the Vedic times, with its many clan-divisions and its perpetual internal feuds, should have conquered the 123,000 square miles, which form the area of India (excluding the Punjab, Assam and Burma) and should have founded States, organised on the same model, all over this vast territory within the space of five, six or even eight hundred years, appears simply ludicrous; especially if it is borne in mind that this territory was inhabited not merely by forest tribes, but in part by peoples possessing a civilisation not much inferior to that of the invaders. More than double of the longest period named was required for such achievements.

Now it could be said, and it has been said by Oldenberg, that seven hundred years are a good span of time, in which much can happen. "One should consider," says Oldenberg,[2] "what 400 years have meant for the enormous plains of Northern and Southern America." This, however, is a poor comparison. The races and civilizations which came into contact with one another in America were, after all, very different from those with which we have to deal in ancient India. As far as the political conditions of ancient India are concerned, we learn from some of the songs of the Ṛgveda and from the epics that, just as is shown by the later history of India, continuous fighting took place between the separate

---

1) Ind. Ant. 23, 1894, p. 247.

2) ZDMG, Vol. 49, p. 479.

Aryan tribes in ancient and even the most ancient times. Under such circumstances the conquest of India could only proceed step by step, extremely slowly. Actually we see also, if we compare the two oldest strata of Indian literature with each other, that the advance of the Aryans towards the east and south proceeded only very slowly. In the hymns of the Ṛgveda we find the Indo-Aryan people still established exclusively in the extreme north-west of India, and in Eastern Afghanistan, and yet the period in which the hymns of the Ṛgveda originated, must have stretched over centuries. That is proved by the many different strata of earlier and later parts, which we find in these hymns; it is proved, too, by the circumstance that the Ṛṣis, who not only in the Anukramaṇīs, but already in the Brāhmaṇas, were *erroneously* called "seers" or composers of the hymns, are in the hymns themselves regarded as seers of a remote antiquity.[1] The composers of the hymns, too, very often speak of "*old* songs," of "songs composed after the *old* manner," as though this poetry had been practised since time immemorial.[2] M. Bloomfield[3] has shown that, of the approximately 40,000 lines of the Ṛgveda, nearly as many as 5,000 lines are repetitions. This proves that, at the time when the Ṛgveda was composed, the more modern poets would frequently borrow lines and expressions from older ones, and that there was actually in existence a large number of floating lines of verse, which any singer could incorporate in his song if he so fancied. But we have repeatedly seen how far, after all, the Ṛgveda lies behind all other literary works of the Veda. Even the language of the hymns is much more archaic than that of the Vedic prose works. The religious views and the conditions of civilization are quite different. The

---

1) See above pp. 57 f.

2) See *Ludwig*, Der Rigveda, III, pp. 180 f.

3) The Vedic Concordance, HOS, Vol. 10, 1906; Rig-Veda Repetitions, HOS, Vols. 20 and 24, 1916; JAOS 29, 1908, 287 f.; 31, 1910, 49 ff

Brāhmaṇas, Āraṇyakas and Upaniṣads pre-suppose not only the hymns of the Ṛgveda, but also the spells and prayers of the other Saṃhitās as sacred texts of hoary age. Indeed, these old hymns and spells were often no longer understood. The old legends had fallen into oblivion. I will recall only the distance separating the Śunaḥsepa legend of the Aitareya-Brāhmaṇa from the hymns of the Ṛgveda.[1]

Oral tradition, too, pre-supposes longer intervals of time than would be necessary, had these texts been written down. Generations of pupils and teachers must have passed away before all the existing and the many lost texts had taken definite shape in the Vedic schools.[2] On linguistic, literary and cultural grounds we must therefore assume that many centuries elapsed between the period of the earliest hymns and the final compilation of the hymns into a Saṃhitā or "collection," for the Ṛgveda-Saṃhitā after all denotes only the *close* of a period long past,[3] and again between the Ṛgveda-Saṃhitā and the other Saṃhitās and the Brāhmaṇas. The Brāhmaṇas themselves, with their numerous schools and branch schools, with their endless lists of teachers and the numerous references to teachers of antiquity, require a period of several centuries for their origin.[4] This literature itself, as well as the spread of brahmanical culture, theological knowledge, and not least, the priestly supremacy which went hand in hand with it, must have taken centuries. And when we come to the Upaniṣads, we see that they, too, belong to different periods of time, that they, too, pre-suppose generations

---

[1]) See above, p. 57, p. 60, pp. 62 ff., pp. 69 f., p. 75, pp. 79 f., p. 104, pp. 196 ff., pp. 215 f.

[2]) The circumstance that the texts were written down when they were no longer completely understood and after a gap had occurred in the tradition, also explains the fact that so frequently passages of diverse contents and different periods occur in all Vedic texts, so that, for instance, some Upaniṣads are to be found among the Saṃhitās and Brāhmaṇas. See above pp. 124, 149 ff., 226.

[3]) The Aitareya-Āraṇyaka already pre-supposed the Ṛgveda Saṃhitā in its division into ten books. (Max *Müller*, History of Ancient Sanskrit Literature, pp. 340 f.)

[4]) See above, pp. 194

of teachers and a long tradition.[1] Yet we see that, during the whole of this time, which lasted from the first beginnings till the last off-shoots of Vedic literature, the Indo-Aryan people conquered only the comparatively small stretch of land from the Indus as far as the Ganges, the actual Hindustan. If this advance from the extreme north-west over into the eastern Ganges-land already took so long, how many centuries must the conquest of the whole of Central and Southern India have taken! If we consider this, 700 years will no longer appear to us a great period of time.

There are other considerations besides this. It is indisputably to the credit of Max Müller to have shown that Buddhism at about 500 B.C. absolutely pre-supposes the existence of the whole of Vedic literature. In refutation of the view, held by some scholars,[2] that the earliest Upaniṣads should not be placed prior to the 6th century B.C., Oldenberg[3] has shown that centuries must have elapsed between the earliest Upaniṣads and the earliest Buddhist literature. Buddhist literature, however, pre-supposes not only the Veda, but the Vedāṅgas also,[4] and indeed brahmanical literature and science in a highly developed state. To-day, too, more light has been thrown on the religious conditions of ancient India than was the case in Max Müller's day, when it was thought possible to squeeze the whole development of the religious history of India up to the appearance of Buddhism within the limit of 700 years. Even *before* the appearance of Buddhism, there were sects in India, as Bühler has pointed out, which denied the sanctity of the Veda. The tradition of one of these sects, the Jainas, has in other respects proved so

---

[1]) See above, pp. 235 ff.

[2]) Cf. *Hopkins*, JAOS 22, 336 n.; *Rapson*, Ancient India, p. 181.

[3]) Die Lehre der Upanishaden und die Anfänge des Buddhismus, pp. 288, 357.

[4]) It is noteworthy that the Buddhists, too, call their didactic texts "Sūtras", although these are by no means composed in the "Sūtra" style indicated above, on pp. 268 f. They took "Sūtra" to mean "didactic text."

reliable as to chronology, that we may regard with some confidence a report which places the life of the first founder of this sect about 750 B.C. Bühler also thought he could prove that other sects antagonistic to the Veda and to Brahmanism went back to a much more hoary antiquity than had hitherto been supposed.[1] Unfortunately he did not live to demonstrate this proof.

The discoveries made by Hugo Winckler in Boghazköi in Asia Minor in the year 1907, gave an impetus to more recent discussions on the question of the age of the Ṛgveda and of Vedic culture.[2] The clay tablets from the archives of the capital of the ancient Hittite kingdom, which were found in Boghazköi, included records of treaties concluded by the king of the Hittites and the king of Mitani at the beginning of the 14th century B.C. The gods of both kingdoms are invoked as guardians of the treaties, and in the list of gods there appear, beside numerous Babylonian and Hittite deities, the names of Mitra, Varuṇa, Indra and Nāsatyau among the gods of Mitani.[3] How did the names

---

[1]) R. *Garbe*, too (Beiträge zur indischen Kulturgeschichte, pp. 27 ff), is inclined to date the origin of the sect of the Bhāgavatas or Pāñcaratras back to pre-Buddhist times.

[2]) Cf. Ed. *Meyer*, SBA 1908, pp. 14 ff. ; Zeitschrift für vergleichende Sprachwissenschaft, 42, 1909, pp. 1 ff. ; Geschichte des Altertums, 2. Aufl., I, 2 (1909), §§ 551, 574; H. *Jacobi*, JRAS 1909, 721 ff. ; 1910, 456 ff. ; Internat. Wochenschrift, 5, 1911, 387; A. B. *Keith*, JRAS 1909, 1100 ff, : 1910, 464 ff. ; Bhandarkar, Com. Vol., pp. 81 ff. and HOS., Vol. 18 Introd. (where the whole development of Vedic literature is crammed in between 1200 and 350 B.C., see esp. pp. clxv f.); A. A. *Macdonell* in Vedic Index I, pp. viii f and ERE 7, 1914, pp. 49 ff. ; H. *Oldenberg*, JRAS 1909, pp. 1095 ff. ; 1910, pp. 846 ff. ; L de la *Vallée Poussin*, Le Védisme, 3 ième ed. Paris, 1909, pp. 29 f. ; *Winternitz*, Oesterreichische Monatschrift für den Orient, 41, 1915 pp. 168 ff. ; Calcutta Review, Nov., 1923, pp. 119 ff. ; *Sten Konow*, The Aryan Gods of the Mitani People (Royal Frederik University Publications of the Indian Institute, Kristiania, 1921); F. E. *Pargiter*, Ancient Indian Historical Tradition, London, 1922, pp. 300 ff. ; P. *Giles*, Cambridge History of India, I, pp. 72 f.

[3]) At least, nearly all scholars agree with *Winckler* (Mitteilungen der Deutschen Orient-Gesellschaft No. 35, 1907, p. 51, s. Boghazköi-Studien VIII, Leipzig 1923, pp. 32 f., 54 f.) that these names of gods have to be recognised in the following cuneiform text : **ilāni Mi-it-ra aš-ši-il ilāni** U-ru-**wa**-na-**aš-ši-el** (in another text . **A**-ru-na—**aš-ši-il**) In-dar (other text : In-da-ra) **ilāni Na-ša-at-ti-ya-an-na**. Doubts against this identification have only been raised by J. *Halévy* in Revue Semitique, 16. 1908, pp. 247 ff.

of these deities reach the Mitanis in Asia Minor? Scholars diverge greatly in their reply to this question. The historian Ed. Meyer ascribes these gods to the Aryan period, *i.e.*, the period when the Indians and Iranians as yet formed an undivided nation in language and religion[1]; and he assumes that, at the same time as these "Aryans" appeared in western Mesopotamia and Syria, the separate development of the Aryans in north-western India had already begun: the Vedic hymns, the earliest of which arose "probably not later than about 1500 B.C." bearing witness to this development. A similar opinion has been expressed by P. Giles. Oldenberg[2] thinks it more likely "that these are the gods of some western Aryan tribe akin to the Indians, inherited from some common past, as the Indians on their part had inherited them from the same source." He leaves the question open whether these were Iranians before Zoroaster's time, or whether a third branch of the Aryans is meant, and takes the view that this discovery does not justify us in assuming greater antiquity for the Veda.

It is a fact, however, that this particular grouping of the gods Varuṇa and Mitra, Indra and Nāsatyau, with these forms of their names, can be traced *only in the Veda*. For this reason I agree with Jacobi, Konow and Hillebrandt in considering these gods to be *Indian, Vedic* deities and that there is no possible justification for any other view. We shall have to assume that, just as there were Aryan immigrations into India from the west, there must have been isolated migrations back to the west. We may think either of warlike adventurers or of connections by marriage. Nor should we forget that, at the time of the

---

[1]) H. *Winckler* (Orientalist. Literaturzeitung, 13, 1910, 289 ff.; Mitteilungen der Vorderasiatischen Gesellschaft 18, 1913, H. 4, pp. 75 ff.) even thinks that the *Harri* who in the inscriptions are mentioned as the ruling class in Mitani are identical with these very "Aryans." But this is quite uncertain. Cf. A. H. *Sayce*, JRAS 1909, pp. 1106 f.

[2]) NGGW, Geschäftliche Mitteilungen, 1918, p. 91.

Ṛgveda, the Aryan Indians were as yet much nearer the west from the geographical point of view.[1] As regards chronology, however, all that we can glean from the inscriptions at Boghazköi is that, about the middle of the second millenary B.C. Aryan tribes which worshipped Vedic gods must already have been established in north-western India for a very considerable time, as several of these tribes had migrated far back to the west as early as about 1400 B.C.[2] This small but important fact would be supported still further, if it should prove to be true that also traces of Indian numerals are to be found in the Boghazköi texts.[3]

The idea of so early a date as the third millenary B.C. for the Veda would certainly be out of the question, if it were proved that the individual Indo-European peoples had not yet separated from the primitive Indo-Europeans in the

---

1) See A. *Hillebrandt*, Aus Alt-und Neuindien, Breslau, 1922, pp. 1 ff. and ZII 3, 1924 pp. 1 ff. who points out traces of relations to Western countries especially in the eighth Book of the Ṛgveda. For other views about the Aryan Indians in Asia Minor see R. G. *Bhandarkar*, JBRAS 25, 1918, pp. 76 ff., and E. *Forrer*, Die acht Sprachen der Boghazköi-Inschriften, SBA 1919, pp. 1036 f.

2) *Konow* suggests that the Nāsatyas are mentioned in the Mitani treaty on account of their playing a role in the ancient marriage-rites, because the treaty, following upon a war between the Hittite king Subbiluliuma and the Mitani king Mattiuza, was confirmed by a marriage of the latter with the Hittite king's daughter. As this connection of the Aśvins with the marriage-ritual, however, occurs only in the late Sūryāsūkta, Konow concludes "that the extension of Indo-Aryan civilization into Mesopotamia took place after the bulk of the Ṛgveda had come into existence" so that the oldest portions of the collection would "have to be considered as considerably older than the Mitani treaty." I cannot see the force of this argument, as Indra and the Nāsatyau (Indranāsatyā) are invoked together in Rv. VIII, 26, 8, where they have nothing to do with marriage. K. *Chaṭṭopādhyāya* (Calcutta Review, May 1924, pp. 287 ff.) concludes from the mention of Vedic gods in the Boghazköi treaties that between 2000 and 1500 B.C. there were several arrivals of Aryan peoples in Asia Minor at the same time when other Aryan tribes entered India from Central Asia and became known as Vrātyas. This chronological combination of the Vrātyas with the Indians in Asia Minor has no foundation in fact whatsoever, hence Mr. Chaṭṭopādhyāya's chronological conclusions (Brāhmaṇa period from 2000 B.C. to 1400 B.C., Yajurveda and Atharvaveda about 2000 B.C. and Ṛgveda before 3,000 B.C.) are quite unfounded.

3) Cf. P. *Jensen*, Indische Zahlwörter in Keilschrifthittitischen Texten, SBA 1919, pp. 367 ff.

third millenary.[1] This view which, in my opinion, is very unlikely and has not been satisfactorily proved, is welcomed by those who wish to assign as low a date as possible to the Ṛgveda and to the beginnings of Indian culture. Thus J. Hertel[2] promises to demonstrate that the Ṛgveda originated, not in north-western India but in Iran, and at a time not far distant from that of Zoroaster, who, according to Hertel, lived about 550 B.C. G. Hüsing[3] goes still further, and turns and twists certain of the names of kings occurring in the cuneiform inscriptions so long that they are metamorphosed into those of Indian kings. On the basis of these "facts," he then concludes that from about 1000 B.C. the Indians wandered from Armenia to Afghanistan, which was the scene of the Ṛgvedic period, and that it was only later that they were driven further towards India. Following a suggestion of H. Brunnhofer, he even assumes that the king Kānīta Pṛthuśravas[4] who is mentioned in the Ṛgveda is identical with a Scythian king Kanitas who is mentioned in a Greek inscription and on a coin, and who lived in the 2nd century B.C. This would mean "that the collection of these songs was not yet completed in the 2nd century B.C." This must

[1]) Gunther *Ipsen* (Indogerman. Forschungen 41, 1923, pp. 174 ff.: Stand und Aufgaben der Sprachwissenschaft, Festsch ift für W. Streitberg, Heidelberg 1924, pp. 200 ff.) endeavours to prove that the Indo-European words for "copper," "cow" and "star" were borrowed from the Sumerian, and not earlier than between 3000 and 2100 B.C. However, when we consider that the domestic cow and copper are among the most ancient of prehistoric finds, we shall hesitate to accept Ipsen's theory.

[2]) Indogerman. Forschungen 41, 1923, p. 188; Die Zeit Zoroasters, Leipzig, 1924; Die Himmelstore im Veda und im Avesta, Leipzig, 1924, pp. 7 f. A book by Hertel on the age and home of the Ṛgveda is announced, but has not yet been published. Zoroaster's date is still uncertain, but there are good reasons for placing him about 1000 B.C. See C. *Clemen*, Die griechischen und lateinischen Nachrichten über die persische Religion, Giessen 1920, pp. 11 ff.; H. *Reichelt* in Festschrift für W. Streitberg, pp. 282 f.

[3]) Die Inder in Boghazköi, in Prace linguistyczne ofiarowane Janowi Baudouinowi de Courtenay...Krakow 1921, pp. 151 ff.

[4]) Ṛv. VIII, 46, 21; 24. The story of this King Pṛthuśravas is one of the old tales which, like the Ākhyāna of Śunaḥśepa, were recited at the Puruṣamedha, s. Śāṅkhāyana-Śrautasūtra XVI, 11, 23.

surely be the very latest date ever yet assumed as that of the Ṛgveda!

The strongest argument for a later dating of the Veda is undoubtedly the close relationship between the Veda and the Avesta with regard to language and religious views.[1] There are, however, very great differences to counteract the points of agreement in religion. Moreover the points of agreement can easily be explained, considering firstly that Indians and Iranians once formed *one* Aryan cultural unit at a pre-Vedic and pre-Avestic period, and secondly that they remained neighbours even after the separation. As regards the kinship of the languages, it is quite impossible to state definite chronological limits within which languages change. Some languages change very rapidly, others remain more or less unaltered for a long period.[2] It is true that hieratic languages, like those of the Vedic hymns and the Avesta, can remain unaltered much longer than spoken vernaculars.

Nevertheless, all that we know of the history of other languages and branches of languages compels us to say that languages do not remain unchanged for an indefinite number of millenaries, let alone tens of thousands of years. For this reason, the fantastic figures of 16000 or even 25000 B. C.[3] as the date of the Veda, built up on the basis of astronomical or geological speculations, are absolutely impossible. Figures like this imply, too, that scarcely any cultural progress worthy

---

1) Thus A. A. *Macdonell* (ERE. Vol. 7, 1914, pp. 49 ff.) says, that "it seems impossible to avoid the conclusion that the Indians cannot have separated from the Iranians much earlier than about 1300 B. C."

2) Cf. A. C. *Woolner* (Proc. FOC I, pp. xvii ff.; II, p. 20 ff.) who rightly says "that as far as any *philological* estimates go, 2000 B. C. remains quite as possible as 1200 B. C. for the earliest Mantra." See also B. V. Kameśvara *Aiyar*, Quarterly Journal of the Mythic Society XII, 1, p. 4.

3) I am thinking of Abinas Chandra *Das*, Ṛig-Vedic India, I, Calcutta 1921 (s. also Calcutta Review, March 1924, pp. 540 ff.) and D. N. *Mukhopadhyaya*, The Hindu Nakshatras (reprinted from Vol. VI of Journal of the Department of Science, Calcutta University, 1923).

of the name was made in the whole course of that overwhelmingly long aeon, which would be most surprising in the case of so talented a race as the Indians. These figures are impossible, too, because the continuity between the Vedic and the later brahmanical culture, which cannot be explained away especially as regards religion, would then become utterly inexplicable. Moreover, classical Sanskrit, as fixed by Pāṇini in his Grammar more especially on the basis of the language of the Brāhmaṇas which still formed part of the Veda proper, and again the language of the inscriptions of King Aśoka in the third century B. C., show too close a relationship with the language of the Veda for it to be feasible that a stretch of so very many thousands of years lay between.

In summing up, we may say:

1. Attempts to determine the period of the Veda by the aid of *astronomy* come to grief owing to the fact that there are certain passages in the Vedic texts which admit of various interpretations. However correct the astronomical calculations may be, they prove nothing unless the texts in question admit of an unambiguous interpretation.

2. The *historical* facts and hypotheses, such as the mention of Vedic gods in the cuneiform inscriptions, and the relationship of Vedic antiquity to the Aryan (Indo-Iranian) and Indo-European period, are so uncertain in themselves that the most divergent and contradictory conclusions have been drawn from them. Nevertheless, we have now such likely evidence of relations between ancient India and western Asia penetrating as far west as Asia Minor in the second millenary B. C., that Vedic culture can be traced back *at least* to the second millenary B. C.

3. The *linguistic* facts, the near relationship between the language of the Veda and that of the Avesta on the one hand, and between the Vedic language and classical Sanskrit on the other, do not yield any positive results;

4. they serve as a warning to us, however, to refrain from dating the Veda back to an inconceivably distant period on the strength of astronomical or *geological* speculations.

5. As all the external evidence fails, we are compelled to rely on *the evidence arising out of the history of Indian literature itself*, for the age of the Veda. The surest evidence in this respect is still the fact that Pārśva, Mahāvīra and Buddha pre-suppose the entire Veda as a literature to all intents and purposes completed, and this is a limit which we must not exceed. We cannot, however, explain the development of the whole of this great literature, if we assume as late a date as round about 1200 or 1500 B. C. as its starting-point. We shall probably have to date the beginning of this development about 2000 or 2500 B. C., and the end of it between 750 and 500 B. C. The more prudent course, however, is to steer clear of any fixed dates, and to guard against the extremes of a stupendously ancient period or a ludicrously modern epoch.

SECTION II.

THE POPULAR EPICS AND THE PURĀṆAS.

The Beginnings of Epic Poetry in India.

We have already seen the first traces of epic poetry in India in the Vedic literature—in the dialogue-hymns of the Ṛgveda as well as in the Ākhyānas, Itihāsas and Purāṇas of the Brāhmaṇas.[1] Moreover we know from the Brāhmaṇas and the ritual-literature, that the recital of such narrative poems formed a part of the religious ceremonies at the sacrificial and domestic festivals.

Thus the daily recitation of legends of gods and heroes belonged to the preliminary celebration, which lasted a whole year, of the great horse-sacrifice. In a regular succession which repeated itself every ten days, stories of certain gods and heroes were related ; and also two lute-players, a Brahman and a warrior, were present, who, in verses of their own composition (*gāthās*), glorified the generosity and the warlike deeds, respectively, of the prince who was celebrating the sacrifice. The lute-players, who sang to the accompaniment of the lute the praises of a real king or of Soma as the king of the Brahmans, had also to be present at the ceremony of parting the hair, which was performed on the expectant mother in the fourth month of pregnancy, with a sacrifice for the prosperity of the fruit of her womb. After a funeral, too, it was an old custom, to whose existence the poet Bāṇa still testifies in the 7th century A.D., for the mourners to sit

---

[1]) Cf. above pp. 101 ff., 208 ff., 226. The Indians are not consistent in their use of the expressions *ākhyāna*, *itihāsa* and *purāṇa*, for they sometimes use them as synonyms, but at other times to mean various kinds of narratives. The epic "Mahābhārata," in the Introduction, is called alternately *itihāsa*, *purāṇa* and *ākhyāna*. On these terms, *Cf.* also Emil *Sieg*, Die Sagenstoffe des Ṛgveda und die indische Itihāsatradition, I Stuttgart, 1902, Introduction.

down in a shady place outside the house and to be diverted and consoled by the recitation of old Itihāsas or Purāṇas. And when, after a death or some other heavy loss, the fire of the hearth had been carried out of the house in order to avert further misfortune, and a new fire kindled in the house by means of the two churning-sticks, then the members of the family, keeping the fire alive far into the silent night, sat listening to the tales of people who had reached a green old age, and Itihāsas and Purāṇas auspicious for the future.[1]

There were not only single ballads (Ākhyānas, Itihāsas) but also cycles of ballads. At least *one* cycle of this kind has come down to us in the *Suparṇākhyāna*, also called Suparṇādhyāya or Suparṇa.[2] This is an apocryphal work belonging to the later Vedic literature, the author trying his utmost to imitate the hymns of the Ṛgveda in language, accentuation and external form, so that his work should appear to belong to the Ṛgveda. The date of this work is quite uncertain, but on metrical grounds we may place it approximately in the period of the metrical Upaniṣads, such as the Kaṭha-Upaniṣad.[3] It is a cycle of ballads dealing with the legend

---

[1]) Śatapatha-Brāhmaṇa, XIII, 4, 3; Śāṅkhāyana-Gṛhyasūtra, I. 22, 11 f.; Āśvalāyana-Gṛhyasūtra, I, 14, 6 f., IV, 6, 6; Pāraskara-Gṛhyasūtra, I, 15, 7 f.; Āpastambīy Gṛhyasūtra, 14, 4 f. *Cf.* also A. *Weber*, Episches im vedischen Ritual (SBA 1891) and H. *Lüders*, in ZDMG, Vol. 58, pp. 707 ff. At the Puruṣamedha, too, the recitation of Ākhyānas forms part of the ritual, s. Śāṅkhāyana-Śrautasūtra 16, 11.

[2]) The text, which has come down in very bad condition, was first edited by E. *Grube*, Berlin, 1875 (reprinted in Ind. Stud., Vol. 14); newly edited, translated into German and annotated by J. *Charpentier*, Die Suparṇasage, Uppsala 1920, pp. 190 ff.; *Cf.* J. v. *Negelein* in GGA, 1924, pp. 65 ff., 87 ff. J. *Hertel* considers this work to be a dramatic poem after the style of the Swāng described by R. Temple (WZKM 23, 1909, 273 ff.; 24, 1910, 117 ff.; Indische Märchen, pp. 344, 367 f.); and he has translated it into German as a drama (Indische Märchen, Jena 1919, pp. 344 ff.). *Cf. Winternitz*, Oesterreichische Monatsschrift für den Orient 41, 1915, pp. 176 f., *Oldenberg*, Zur Geschichte der altindischen Prosa, pp. 61 ff. and NGGW 1919, pp. 79 ff. This Suparṇādhyāya has no connection with the Suparṇa songs belonging to the Khilas of the Ṛgveda, which are also called "Suparṇādhyāya" (s. above p. 60, and *Scheftelowitz*, ZDMG 74, 1920, p. 203).

[3]) *Charpentier*, l. c. pp. 196 f., J. v. *Negelein* (l. c. pp. 196, f.) doubts the justification of Charpentier's conclusions.

of Kadrū, the snake-mother, and Vinatā, the bird-mother, and the enmity between Garuḍa and the snakes, a legend which dates far back into Vedic times,[1] and which appears in epic form in the Āstīkaparvan of the Mahābhārata.

In the later Vedic texts *Itihāsa* and *Purāṇa* are very frequently enumerated beside the Vedas and other branches of learning; the study of them counts as a work pleasing to the gods: in fact the *Itihāsapurāṇa* is actually called "the fifth Veda."[2] They are generally mentioned immediately after the Atharvaveda, to which they are said to be closely related.[3] This has led to the conclusion that, similar to the Vedic Saṃhitās, there existed one or several collections of Itihāsas and Purāṇas, made up of myths and legends, legends of gods and tales of demons, snake deities, old sages (Ṛṣis) and kings of ancient times. There is no proof, however, that such collections actually existed in the form of "books" in Vedic times.[4] All that we know is that there were professional story-tellers (Aitihāsikas, Paurāṇikas) in very ancient times.

---

[1]) *Charpentier*, l. c., pp. 288 ff.; Śatapatha-Br. III, 6, 2.

[2]) As Chāndogya-Up VII, 1 f. and 7. In the Buddhist Suttanipāta III, 7 (Selasutta), Itihāsa is called "the fifth" after the three Vedas and the Vedāṅgas *Cf.* A. *Weber*, l. c., and J. *Dahlmann*, Das Mahābhārata als Epos und Rechtsbuch, Berlin 1895, pp. 281 ff.

[3]) According to Chāndogya-Up III, 3, 4, the magic songs of the Atharvaveda stand in the same relationship to the Itihāsapurāṇa as the hymns (ṛc) to the Ṛgveda, the prayer formulae (yajus) to the Yajurveda, and the melodies (sāman) to the Sāmaveda. According to the Kauṭilīya-Arthaśāstra, p. 7, the Atharvaveda and the "Itihāsaveda" together with the trayī, "the threefold knowledge," form the Vedas. *Cf.* above, p. 126, and M. *Bloomfield*, SBE., Vol. 42, pp. xxxvi f.

[4]) The theory that there was a *book* called "Itihāsaveda" or "Itihāsapurāṇa" is advanced by K F. *Geldner*, Vedische Studien I, pp. 290 f.; E. *Sieg*, Die Sagenstoffe des Ṛgveda und die indische Itihāsatradition I, p. 33 and ERE VII, 1914, 461 ff.; J. *Hertel*, WZKM 23, 1909, p. 295; 24, p. 420, R. *Pischel* KG 168; H. *Oertel*, WZKM 24, p. 121; H. *Jacobi*, SBA 1911, p. 969. But the very passage in Kauṭilīya I, 5, p. 10, which is quoted by these scholars, proves that "Itihasa" should be interpreted, not as a single work, but as a class of literary productions: for "Veda" only means a certain kind of learning, not a book: Āyurveda is "medical science," Gandharvaveda is "music," Ṛgveda, Sāmaveda, etc., are classes of texts, and not single books. Thus "Itihāsaveda" is not any particular book, but that branch of learning which consists of legends, stories, etc.

It is certain, moreover, that as early as the time of Buddha there was in existence an inexhaustible store of prose and verse narratives—Ākhyānas, Itihāsas, Purāṇas and Gāṭhās—, forming as it were *literary public property* which was drawn upon by the Buddhists and the Jains, as well as by the epic poets.

The "songs in praise of men" (*gāthā nārāśaṃsī*)[1] are often mentioned beside the Itihāsas and Purāṇas, among the texts which are pleasing to the gods. These songs are connected on the one hand with the Dānastutis of the Ṛgveda and the Kuntāpa hymns of the Atharvaveda, but on the other hand they are the direct precursors of the actual Heroic Epic itself, for their contents are the glorious deeds of the warriors and princes. These "songs in praise of men" probably soon developed into epic poems of considerable length, *i.e. heroic songs*, and into entire *cycles* of epic songs, centring around *one* hero or *one* great event; for the only two national epics which have come down to us, the *Mahābhārata* and the *Rāmāyaṇa*, represent but the last remnants of a long past period of epic poetry. Long before these two epics existed as such, songs must have been sung of the great combat of nations around which the Mahābhārata centres, and of the deeds of Rāma, the hero of the Rāmāyaṇa. Neither is it conceivable that the battles of the Kauravas and Pāṇḍavas and the adventures of Rāma should have been the only subjects of poetry. Many other heroes and great events in other royal houses also must have been sung. These old heroic songs, whose existence we must take for granted, have not all vanished without trace; in remnants and fragments some of them have been preserved in our two epics.[2]

---

1) Śatapatha-Br. XI, 5, 6, 8; Āśvalāyana-Gṛhyas. III, 3. The fact that, in these songs, panegyrics were more important than historical truth, is evident from the Vedic texts themselves, for they declare these Gāthās to be "lies" (Maitrāyaṇī-Saṃhitā 1, 11, 5: Kāṭhaka 14, 5).

2) *Cf.* H. *Jacobi*, Uber ein verlorenes Heldengedicht der Sindhu-Sauvīra, in Mélanges Kern, Leide 1903, pp. 53 ff.

The authors, reciters and preservers of this heroic poetry were the bards, usually called *Sūtas*, who lived at the courts of kings and recited or sang their songs at great feasts in order to proclaim the glory of the princes. They also went forth into battle, in order to be able to sing of the heroic deeds of the warriors from their own observations. Thus, in the Mahābhārata itself, it is the Sūta Sañjaya who describes to King Dhṛtarāṣṭra the events on the battlefield. These court-singers formed a special caste,[1] in which the epic songs were transmitted from generation to generation. Epic poetry probably originated in the circle of such bards, who certainly were very closely related to the *warrior class*. Besides there were also travelling singers, called *Kuśīlavas*, who memorised the songs and publicly sang them to the accompaniment of the lute,[2] and to them the circulation of the heroic songs among the *people* was due. Thus it is related in the Rāmāyaṇa, though in a late, interpolated song,[3] how the two sons of Rāma, Kuśa and Lava, travelled about as wandering singers and recited in public assemblies the poem learned from the poet Vālmīki.

But what we know as the popular epics of the Indians, the Mahābhārata and the Rāmāyaṇa, are not the old heroic songs as those court-singers and travelling minstrels of

---

[1]) According to the law-book of Manu (X, 11 and 17), the Sūtas are a mixed caste descended from the intermarriage of warriors with Brahman women, while the Māgadhas, who, as well as the Sūtas, are usually called singers, are said to be descended from the intermarriage of Vaiśyas with Kṣatriya women. In war, the Sūtas are also the charioteers of the princes. Originally the Māgadhas were undoubtedly bards from the land of Magadha, and the Sūtas, too, were probably inhabitants of a country situated to the east of Magadha. *Cf.* F. E. *Pargiter,* Ancient Indian Historical Tradition, London 1922, p. 16. J. J. *Meyer*, Das Weib im altindischen Epos, Leipzig, 1915, p. 62 note, compares the modern Bhāts of the Rājputs to the Sūtas. On the Bhāts and other kinds of singers in the India of to-day, *cf.* R. C. *Temple*, the Legends of the Panjâb, Vol. I (1884), p. viii; and A. *Baines*, Ethnography (Grundriss II, 5, 1912), pp. 85 ff.

[2]) *Cf.* A. *Holtzmann*, Das Mahābhārata I, p. 54 f., 65 f.

H. *Jacobi*, Das Râmâyaṇa, pp. 67.

[3]) I, 4.

ancient India sang them, compiled into unified poems by great poets or at least by clever collectors with some talent for poetry, but accumulations of very diverse poems of unequal value, which have arisen in the course of centuries owing to continual interpolations and alterations. Though ancient heroic songs do indeed form the nucleus of both these works, the more devotional Itihāsa literature was included in them to so great an extent, and such long poems of a religious-didactic nature were inserted, that the Mahābhārata, in particular, has almost completely lost the character of an epic.

WHAT IS THE MAHĀBHĀRATA ?[1)]

It is only in a very restricted sense that we may speak of the Mahābhārata as an "epic" and a "poem." Indeed, in a certain sense, the Mahābhārata is not *one* poetic production at all, but rather a *whole literature.*

---

1) For information on the contents of the epic, the best help is H. *Jacobi*, Mahābhārata, Inhalts-Angabe, Index und Konkordanz der Kalkuttaer und Bombayer Ausgaben. Bonn 1903. For the problems of the Mahābhārata see especially E. W. *Hopkins*, The Great Epic of India, Its Character and Origin, New York 1901. A rich, though unfortunately not handy, collection of materials, is contained in A. *Holtzmann*, Das Mahābhārata und seine Teile. In 4 vols. Kiel 1892-95. The value of this great work is considerably prejudiced by the untenable theories of the author upon the remodellings of the Mahābhārata. Untenable, too, are the opposite theories upon the origin of the epic as one work, which *Joseph Dahlmann* has upheld in his books "Das Mahābhārata als Epos und Rechtsbuch," Berlin, 1895, "Genesis des Mahābhārata," Berlin 1899, and "Die Sâṃkhya-Philosophie als Naturlehre und Erlösungslehre, nach dem Mahābhārata," Berlin 1902. The first of these books, however, has the great merit of having given new life to studies of the epic; it has given rise to a veritable "Dahlmann-literature." *Cf.* H. *Jacobi* in GGA 1896. No. 1 and 1899, No. 11; A. *Ludwig* in Sitzungsber. der kgl. böhmischen Ges. der Wiss. cl. f. Phil Prague 1896; C. H. *Tawney*, Asiatic Quarterly Review 1896, pp. 347 ff.; J. *Jolly*, Ind. Ant. 25, 1896, 343 f. A. *Barth* in the Journal des savants, April, June and July, 1897, and RHR, t. 45, 1902, pp. 191 ff. (Oeuvres II, 393 ff.); M. *Winternitz* in JRAS, 1897, pp. 713 ff. and WZKM XIV, 1900, pp. 53 ff., E. W. *Hopkins* in the American Journal of Philology, 1898, XIX, No. 1, W. *Cartellieri* in WZKM, 13, 1899, pp. 57 ff.; J. *Kirste* in Ind. Ant., 31, 1902, pp. 5 ff. Among the older literature on the Mahābhārata (it is summarized by *Holtzmann*, loc. cit., IV, pp. 165 ff.) the following deserve special notice: Monier *Williams*, Indian Wisdom, 4th

Mahābhārata [1] means "the great narrative of the battle of the Bhāratas." The *Bharatas* are already mentioned in the Ṛgveda as a warlike tribe, and in the Brāhmaṇas we encounter Bharata, the son of Duḥṣanta and Sakuntalā, who is regarded as the ancestor of the royal race of the Bhāratas. The home of these Bharatas or Bhāratas was in the country of the Upper Ganges and the Jumnā. Among the descendants of Bharata, a ruler named *Kuru* was specially prominent, and his descendants, the *Kauravas* (Kuruides), were so long the ruling race of the Bhāratas, that the name Kuru or Kaurava in the course of time assumed the character of a name for the tribe of the Bharatas, and their land is that *Kurukṣetra* or "Kuru-land" with which we are already acquainted from the Yajurveda and the Brāhmaṇas.[2] A family feud in the royal house of the Kauravas leads to a bloody battle, a truly internecine struggle in which the ancient race of the Kurus, and with it the family of the Bhāratas, is almost entirely ruined. The history of this bloody battle, which we shall probably have to regard as an historical event, though we hear of it only in the Mahābhārata, was told in songs, and some great poet whose name has been lost, combined these songs into an heroic poem of the great battle in the field of the Kurus. Thus, as in the Iliad and in the Nibelungen-song, the tragedy of a terrible war of annihilation forms the actual subject of the heroic poem. This old heroic poem forms the *nucleus* of the Mahābhārata.

---

edit. London 1893; Sören *Sörensen*, Om Mahābhārata's stilling i den Indiske literatur (with a "Summarium" in the Latin language), Copenhagen 1893; A. *Ludwig*, Uber das Râmâyaṇa und die Beziehungen desselben zum Mahābhārata (II. Jahresbericht des Wiss. Vereins f. Volkskunde und Linguistik in Prague 1894). See also *Hopkins*, ERE VIII, 1915, 325 ff. and H. *Oldenberg*, Das Mahabharata, seine Entstehung, sein Inhalt, seine Form, Göttingen, 1922.

[1]) Bhārata means "battle of the Bharatas" (bhārataḥ saṃgrāmaḥ, Pāṇini IV, 2, 56). In the Mahābhārata itself we find mahābhārata-yuddha (XIV, 81, 8) "the great Bharata battle," and Mahābhāratākhyānam (I, 62, 39)," "the great story of the Bharata battle" the title "Mahābhārata" being an abbreviation of the latter.

[2]) See above p. 196.

In the course of centuries, however, an enormous mass of the most diverse poetry has collected *around this nucleus.* First numerous legends whose connection with the old heroic poem is more or less casual, legends referring to the early history of the heroes, or giving reports of all kinds of adventures of these men, without having any reference whatever to the great battle, were added to the poem. Then, too, fragments of other heroic legends and cycles of legends, which refer to various famous kings and heroes of primeval times, found their way into the poem, even though they had nothing at all to do with the song of the great Kuru battle. How much of this old bard poetry already belonged to the original poem as secondary tales (*episodes*) and how much was only added later, will probably never be determined. We have reason to believe that in ancient times many of these episodes were recited by the minstrels as independent poems.[1] In any case, our Mahābhārata is not only the heroic poem of the battle of the Bhāratas, but at the same time also a *repertory of the whole of the old bard poetry.*

However, it is very much more than this. We know that the literary activity of ancient India was for the most part in the hands of the priests, the Brahmans; and we have seen how they brahmanised the old popular magic songs of the Atharvaveda, and how they intermingled with their priestly wisdom, the philosophy of the Upaniṣads which was really foreign, even antagonistic, to the priesthood.[2] The more the heroic songs grew in favour and the more popular they became, the greater the anxiety of the Brahmans to take possession of this epic poetry also; and they had the art of compounding this poetry which was essentially and

[1]) It seems that individual bards made a speciality of the recitation of certain poems; for Patañjali (Pāṇini IV, 2, 60) teaches the formation of words like Yāvakrītika, "one who knows the story of Yavakrīta" Yāyātika, "one who knows the story of Yayāti etc. *Cf.* F. *Lacôte*, Essai sur Guṇāḍhya et la Bṛhatkathā, Paris, 1908, pp. 138 f.

[2]) See above pp. 123, and 231 ff.

purely *secular* in origin, with their own *religious* poems and the whole stock-in-trade of their theological and priestly knowledge. Thus it happens that legends of gods, *mythological narratives of brahmanical origin*, and to a great extent even *didactic sections referring to brahmanical philosophy and ethics and brahmanical law*, were received into the Mahābhārata. This priestly caste welcomed the popular epic as the very medium for the propagation of their own doctrines, and thereby for the strengthening and consolidation of their influence. It was they who inserted into the epic all the numerous myths and legends (Itihāsas) [1] in which wonderful feats are related of the famous seers of ancient times, the Ṛṣis, the ancestors of the Brahmans, how by dint of sacrifices and asceticism, they obtain tremendous power not only over men, but even over the gods, and how, when they are offended, their curse causes the fall of princes and great men, and even of the kings of the gods.

The Mahābhārata was, however, too much of a popular book, too much the property of extensive circles of the people, in particular of the warrior caste, for it ever to have become an actual brahmanical work or the property of any one Vedic school. And it was not so much the Veda-knowing and learned Brahmans who took part in the development of the Mahābhārata; hence the noticeably scanty knowledge of actual brahmanical theology and sacrificial science, which we find even in those parts of the epic in which brahmanical influence is unmistakable. It was the *Purohitas*, the court-priests, who like the Sūtas (bards) were in the service of the kings, and on that account came more into contact with epic poetry. It was this less learned class of priests, too, which later on furnished temple-priests at famous holy places and places

[1]) Some of these legends can still be traced. In Brahmanic texts, for instance, the story of Bhaṅgāsvana who was changed into a woman, in Mahābh. XIII, 12, is found in the Baudhāyana-Śrautasūtra; s. *Winternitz* and *Caland* in WZKM 17. 1903. 292 f.; 351 ff.

of pilgrimage, mostly dedicated to the gods Viṣṇu or Śiva, and devoted itself to the literary cultivation of local myths attached to such sacred spots, and the legends woven around the gods Viṣṇu and Śiva. This, as we shall see, was done chiefly in the Purāṇas, but also in the Mahābhārata, into which crept numerous *local myths in true Purāṇa style, Viṣṇu and Śiva myths, and Purāṇa-like cosmologies, geographical lists and genealogies.*

But an epic poetry seems to have been cultivated more in those regions of India where the worship of Viṣṇu as the highest deity prevailed. This accounts for the fact that, in the religious-didactic portions of the Mahābhārata, this god stands so prominently in the foreground, that the work at times gives the impression of a *religious book dedicated to the worship of Viṣṇu.* It is true, *Śiva-legends* and passages referring to the Śiva cult are not wanting, but they are in every case easily recognisable as later additions. They were inserted as the epic was propagated also over regions in which Śiva worship had its home.[1]

But there existed yet other religious circles in India which, already in early times, showed literary activity, and tried partly even more than the Brahmans, to win over the great masses of the people. These were the ascetics, forest-hermits and mendicants, the founders of sects and monastic orders, which at the time of Buddha were already very numerous in India. These, too, had their own poetry; *legends of saints, aphorisms,* in which they preached their doctrines of renunciation and contempt of the world, of self-sacrifice and love for all beings, and also *fables, parables, fairy-tales, and moral stories,* which were intended to illustrate the philosophy and ethics of the ascetics by means of examples. This *ascetic poetry,* too, was incorporated into the Mahābhārata to a considerable extent.

---

1) *Cf.* H *acobi* in GGA 1892, pp. 629 f.

To such an extent had the Mahābhārata become a compendium of narratives of all descriptions rather than an epic, that even *prose pieces*, brahmanical legends and moral tales, some entirely in prose form and others partly in verse and partly in prose, were incorporated into the epic.[1]

We find, then, in this the most remarkable of all literary productions, side by side and intermingled, warlike heroic songs with highly coloured descriptions of bloody battle-scenes; pious priestly poetry, with dissertations, which are often tedious enough, upon philosophy, religion and law; and mild ascetic poetry full of edifying wisdom and full of over-flowing love towards man and beast.

Therefore the Indians themselves regard the Mahābhārata, though always as an epic, as a work of poetic art (kāvya), but also at the same time as a manual (Śāstra) of morality, law and philosophy, supported by the oldest tradition (smṛti) and hence furnished with incontestible authority; and since more than 1,500 years it has served the Indians as much for entertainment as for instruction and edification.

At least 1,500 years ago,[2] this Mahābhārata was already just as we possess it to-day in our manuscripts and editions—or at least very similar—*one work* which was of about the same extent as our epic of to-day. Like the latter, it already contained a long introduction with a framework, a story of the legendary origin of the poem and a glorification of it as a text-book of religion and morals; it was divided into eighteen books called *Parvans*, to which a nineteenth book *Harivaṃśa* had already been added as a "supplement" (Khila);

---

[1]) In the Pauṣyaparvan (Mahābh. I, 3), in the Mārkaṇḍeya section of the Vanaparvan, and in the sectarian Nārāyaṇīya. All these are pieces which are really outside the scope of the epic proper. I therefore cannot agree at all with *Oldenberg* (Zur Geschichte der altindischen Prosa, pp. 65 ff.; Das Mahabharata, pp. 21 ff.) in seeing an earlier stage of the epic in these very pieces. *Cf. Hopkins*, The Great Epic of India, pp. 266 ff.; *Winternitz*, DLZ 1919, No. 44.

[2]) See, further on, the chapter on the age and history of the Mahābhārata.

and it attained the extent of about 100,000 verses (Ślokas). And up to the present day this gigantic work, in spite of all the diverse elements of which it consists, is regarded by the Indians as a unified work, complete in itself,[1] whose author is the most venerable Ṛṣi *Kṛṣṇa Dvaipāyana*, also called *Vyāsa*. This same Ṛṣi is also said to be the compiler of the four Vedas[2] and the author of the Purāṇas. According to the legend, he was not only a contemporary, but also a close relative of the heroes of the Mahābhārata, and occasionally also appears in the action of the poem. His history is told us in great detail in the Mahābhārata.

He is the son of a famous ascetic, the Ṛṣi Parāśara. This great saint one day catches sight of Satyavatī, who came into the world in a fish and was brought up by fisherfolk, and is so charmed with her beauty that he desires her love. But she will yield to him only on the condition that, after she has borne him a son, she may regain her maidenhood. The great saint grants her this wish, and also the wish that she may lose her fish-odour and may diffuse a wonderful perfume. Immediately after he has co-habited with her, she gives birth to a son, on an island in the Jumnā, who is named Dvaipāyana, "the island-born." The boy grows up and soon gives himself up to asceticism. When taking leave of his mother, he tells her that he will appear immediately at any time she, needing him, thinks of him. Satyavatī, however, once more a virgin, later on became the wife of the Kuru king, Śāntanu, and bore the latter two sons, Citrāṅgada and Vicitravīrya. After the death of Śāntanu and Citrāṅgada, Vicitravīrya was appointed heir. He died young and childless, but left two wives. In order that the race may not die out, Satyavatī

---

1) Therefore, too, it is called a *saṃhitā*, *i.e.* "a (complete) compilation," "a connected text," thus Mahābh. I, 1, 21.

2) Hence his name *Vyāsa* or *Vedavyāsa*, *i. e.* "classifier" "classifier of the Veda. This is the explanation of the name given in the Mahābhārata itself (1, 63, 88 : Vivyāsa vedān yasmāt sa tasmād Vyāsa iti smṛtah, cf. I, 60. 5 ; 105, 13).

decides to call her illegitimate son Dvaipāyana, so that, according to the legal custom of the Levirate, he may beget descendants by his sisters-in-law. Now although this Dvaipāyana is a great ascetic and saint, yet he is an extremely ugly man with bristly hair and beard and darkly rolling eyes, dark in complexion (hence probably his name Kṛṣṇa, "the black one") and an evil smell emanates from him. Therefore, when he approaches the one princess she cannot bear the sight of him, and closes her eyes: the consequence of this is that her son is born blind. He later became king *Dhṛtarāṣṭra.* The saint then approaches the second lady, and she grows pale at sight of him. As the result of this she gives birth to a son who is pale, and is therefore called *Pāṇḍu,* "the pale one." He is the father of the five principal heroes of the epic. Once again Dvaipāyana is to approach the first woman; but grown wiser, she sends her maid to the saint, who notices nothing of the substitution, and with the maid he begets *Vidura,* to whom in the epic is allotted the part of a wise and well-wishing friend of Dhṛtarāṣṭra as well as of the sons of Pāṇḍu.[1]

This saint, Kṛṣṇa Dvaipāyana *Vyāsa,* whom legend has made into a kind of grandfather [2] of the heroes of the epic, is regarded by the Indians, up to the present day, as the author of the whole Mahābhārata. Only after his three "sons" had died, so says the introduction to the Mahābhārata,[3] did Vyāsa publish among the people the poem composed by him. He imparted it to his pupil *Vaiśampāyana,* and the latter recited the whole poem in the intervals of the great snake-sacrifice of King Janamejaya. On this occasion it was heard by the Sūta Ugraśravas, the son of Lomaharṣana; and our Mahābhārata

---

1) Mahābh. I, 63; 100 ff.

2) According to the law of the Levirate, Vyāsa is only the progenitor, not the father, of Dhṛtarāṣṭra and Pāṇḍu. The deceased husband of the two widows is regarded as their father.

3) I, 1, 95 ff.

commences with the Ṛṣis, who are assembled at the twelve-yearly sacrifice of Śaunaka in the Naimiṣa forest, entreating the Sūta Ugraśravas to tell them the story of the Mahābhārata as he has heard it from Vaiśampāyana. The Sūta declares himself willing, and tells the story of the snake-sacrifice of Janamejaya, before proceeding to the repetition of the narrative of Vaiśampāyana.

The fact that the Mahābhārata consists almost entirely of *speeches* is certainly a trait of antiquity.[1] Ugraśravas is the reciter of the outline story, and in the poem itself Vaiśampāyana is the speaker. Within the narrative of Vaiśampāyana innumerable inserted tales are put in the mouth of various persons, this insertion of stories within stories being a very popular device in Indian literature. In most cases the narratives, as well as the speeches of the persons appearing, have no introduction but the prose formulae: "Vaiśampāyana spake," "Yudhiṣṭhira spaken, "Draupadī spake," and so on.

Fantastic as is all the information imparted to us in the introduction to the Mahābhārata about its supposed author, yet we find a few noteworthy statements in it. Thus we are told that the Ṛṣi Vyāsa narrated his work in a short summary as well as in detailed presentation; further, that different reciters begin the poem at three different places, and that its length was not always the same. Ugraśravas says that he knows the poem as consisting of 8,800 verses, while Vyāsa declares that he composed the Saṃhitā of the Bhārata poem in 24,000 verses, "and without the secondary stories

---

[1]) "We may observe in the Iliad, too, that the old epics all contain very much dialogue; only in the later epics does this dramatic element recede further into the background... But the epic poem only reaches completion when, in addition to the speeches, the outline of the narrative, too, is composed in metrical form. The final stage is the withdrawal of the speeches, and the narration of events only in the form of verse." Ernst *Windisch*, Māra und Buddha (Abhandl. der philolog.—histor. Klasse der K. sächsischen Ges. der Wiss. Leipzig 1895), pp. 222 ff. The Mahābhārata is still a long way from that "final stage."

the Bhārata is recited in this length by the experts." Immediately afterwards it is said, rather fantastically, that Vyāsa also composed an epic of 60 hundred thousand verses, *viz.* 30 hundred thousand for the gods, 15 for the fathers, 14 for the Gandharvas and *one* hundred thousand for man.[1] Of course this only hints at the present extent of the Mahābhārata, which has also acquired for it the designation *śatasāhasrī saṃhitā*, "collection of one hundred thousand verses." One sees from these statements that the Indians themselves, in spite of their firm belief in the unity of the work, have at least retained a recollection of the fact that the Mahābharata only gradually grew, from an originally smaller poem, to its present extent.

What the Mahābhārata means *to the Indians*, the introduction to the work tells us in the most extravagant fashion. It is there said, for example :

"As butter excels among curds, as the Brahman excels among Aryans, as the Āraṇyakas among the Vedas, the drink of immortality among medicines, the ocean among all waters, and the cow among four-footed beasts, even so the Mahābhārata is the best of all narrative works (Itihāsas)."

"Whosoever has once heard this story, can no longer take pleasure in any other story though it be well worth hearing; just as he who has heard the song of the kokila[2] can take no pleasure in the harsh voice of the crow."

"The thoughts of the poets arise from this most excellent of all narrative works, as the three realms of the universe from the five elements."

"Whosoever presents a veda-knowing and deeply learned Brahman with a hundred cows with gilded horns, and he who hears daily the sacred stories of the Bhārata poem—these two acquire equal (religious) merit."

"Verily this narrative work is a song of victory: a king who desires victory, should hear it, and he will conquer the earth and triumph over his enemies."

---

[1]) Mahābh. I, 1, 51 ff.; 81; 101 ff.

[2]) The Kokila, the Indian cuckoo, is to Indian poets what the nightingale is to our poets.

"This is a sacred manual of morals (dharma); it is the best manual of practical life (artha), and Vyāsa, of boundless wisdom, recited it also as a manual of salvation (mokṣa).[1]

"All sins, whether of thought, word or deed, depart immediately from the man who hears this poem."

"The sage Kṛṣṇa Dvaipāyana, rising daily (to perform his devotional and ascetic exercises) composed this marvellous story, the Mahābhārata, in three years. What we find in this book relating to morals, relating to practical life, relating to sensual pleasure and relating to salvation,[2] can be found elsewhere; but what is not written therein, can be found nowhere else in the world." [2]

For us, however, who do not look upon the Mahābhārata with the eyes of believing Hindus, but as critical historians of literature it is everything but a work of art; and in any case we cannot regard it as the work of *one* author, or even of a clever collector and compiler. The Mahābhārata as a whole is a literary monster. Never has the hand of an artist attempted the well-nigh impossible task of combining the conflicting elements into one unified poem. It is only unpoetical theologians and commentators and clumsy copyists who have succeeded in conglomerating into a heterogeneous mass parts which are actually incompatible, and which date from different centuries. But in this jungle of poetry, which scholarship has only just begun to clear, there shoots forth much true and genuine poetry, hidden by the wild undergrowth. Out of the unshapely mass shine out the most precious blossoms of immortal poetic art and profound wisdom. The very fact that the Mahābhārata represents

[1]) *Dharma,* "law and custom" or "morality," *artha* "utility," "advantages" "practical life" and *kāma,* "sensual gratification" are the three aims of life, to a certain extent the be-all and end-all of human existence, according to Indian ethics. The final aim of all striving, however, is *mokṣa,* "deliverance," to which the various sects and philosophical systems indicate different paths.

[2]) I, 1, 261 f.: 2, 382 f., 393; 62, 20 f., 23, 25, 52 f. To the last verse compare the Bengali saying: "Whatever is not in the Mahābhārata is not to be found in Bharatavarṣa" (*i.e.* in India).

a whole literature rather than one single and unified work, and contains so many and so multifarious things, makes it more suited than any other book, to afford us an insight into the deepest depths of the soul of the Indian people.

This may be shown by the following survey of the contents of the Mahābhārata and its various component parts.[1]

The Principal Narrative of the Mahābhārata.

Years ago Adolf Holtzmann (Senior) undertook the bold endeavour "to open up for the first time for German poetry lovers, the essence of the Mahābhārata, the old Indian national epic itself."[2] He started from the undoubtedly correct point of view that the Mahābhārata is not "*the* Indian epic," but that rather only "the remains, the ruins of the ancient Indian heroic songs ...., after much retouching, extension, and disfigurement, are contained in the Mahābhārata." But with enviable self-confidence he believed

[1] The whole of the Mahābhārata has been translated into English prose by Kisori Mohan *Ganguli* and published by Protap Chandra *Roy* (Calcutta 1884-1896), and by Manmatha Nath *Dutt* (Calcutta 1895-1905). A fine poetical rendering, partly in metrical translations, partly in prose extracts, has been given by Romesh *Dutt* in his "Maha-Bharata, the Epic of Ancient India condensed into English Verse," London 1899. Extracts from the Mahābhārata will also be found in John *Muir's* "Original Sanskrit Texts" (1858-1872), and "Metrical Translations from Sanskrit Writers" (London 1879), and in Monier *Williams*, "Indian Wisdom," 4th ed., London 1893. A Summary of the 18 Parvans has been given by Monier Williams, Indian Epic Poetry, London 1863; an outline of the story and extracts by J. C. *Oman*, The Great Indian Epics, London 1899, pp. 93 ff. Books I-X have been translated into French by H *Fauche*, Paris, 1863-1870, a collection of larger extracts by Ph. E. *Foucaux*, Le Mahābhārata, onze épisodes tirés de ce poème épique, Paris, 1862. Several episodes have been translated into Italian by P. E. *Pavolini*, 1902, and into German by F. *Bopp* (Berlin, 1824), by the poet Friedrich *Rückert* (s. R. *Boxberger*, "Rückert-Studien," 1878, pp. 84-122 and "Rückert-Nachlese" I, 270; II, 315 ff.), by A. *Holtzmann*, Indische Sagen, 1845-1847 (new edition by M. Winternitz, Jena, 1912, and 1921), by J. *Hertel*, Indische Märchen, Jena, 1919, No. 10-14, and by W. *Porzig* in the series "Indische Erzähler" (Vols. 12 and 15, Leipzig 1923, 192 ff). The philosophical texts of the Mahābhārata have been translated into German by O. *Strauss* and P. *Deussen*, Vier philosophische Texte des Mahâbhâratam: Sanatsujâtaparvan, Bhagavadgîtâ, Mokshadharma, Anugitâ, Leipzig 1906.

[2] Indische Sagen. Part 2: Die Kuruinge. Karlsruhe 1846.

himself to be endowed with the ability to reconstruct the *ancient original* heroic poem from these retouched and disfigured "ruins." He thought that by means of omissions, abridgments, and *alterations*, he had created in German verse an Indian heroic poem, which gave a better idea of the actual Mahābhārata as sung by the ancient Indian bards, than a literal translation of the existing original text would probably give. Now Holtzmann, with ingenious insight and deep poetic feeling, certainly often hit upon the right thing, but then he departed so arbitrarily from the Sanskrit text, that his work can only be regarded as a very free recast of the ancient Mahābhārata, but in no case as a faithful representation of it. In fact Holtzmann attempted an impossible task. Every endeavour *to reconstruct* "the ancient Indian national epic itself" in its original shape will always be attended by so great an element of arbitrariness, that it can only have a purely subjective value.

On the other hand, it is comparatively easy to extract *a kernel* from the enormous mass of songs of the Mahābhārata, namely, *the narrative of the battle of the Kauravas and the Pāṇḍavas*, which in any case formed the subject of the actual epic. This shall be done in the following, necessarily short outline. We trace the story of the great fight, taking into consideration also, as far as possible, the important secondary stories referring to the principal heroes. In this we shall not digress into doubtful hypotheses upon the "original" epic, but faithfully follow *the Mahābhārata text now available to us*, *leaving aside*, for the present, everything which has no reference to the principal narrative.

The Descent of the Kauravas and the Pāṇḍavas.

In the land of the Bharatas there once ruled a king of the house of the Kurus, Śāntanu by name. By the goddess Gaṅgā [1] who had

[1] Goddess of the River Ganges.

become a mortal woman, this king had a son called *Bhīṣma,* whom he had appointed as his successor to the throne. One day, when the latter had already grown up into a superb hero endowed with all warlike virtues, Sāntanu met the beautiful fisher girl Satyavatī, fell in love with her and desired her as a wife. Her father, the king of the fisherfolk, would, however, only give her to him on condition that the son born by his daughter should inherit the throne. But Śāntanu would not consent to this, though he found it difficult to give up his beloved. Now Bhīṣma soon noticed how depressed his father was, and when he had learned the cause of this depression, he himself went to the king of the fishermen to woo Satyavatī on his father's behalf. He not only announces his intention to renounce his right to the throne, but takes a vow of chastity, so as to make it impossible for any son of his to claim the throne, whereupon the fisherman gladly gives him his daughter. So Śāntanu marries Satyavatī and has two sons by her, *Citrāṅgada* and *Vicitravīrya.* Soon after this, Śāntanu died and young Citrāṅgada was killed in battle by a Gandharva: then Bhīṣma, as the senior of the family, annointed Vicitravīrya as king. The latter, however, died young and without issue, though he had two wives. In order that the race may not die out, Satyavatī begs Bhīṣma to beget descendants by the surviving widows of Vicitravīrya, in accordance with the ancient usage of the Levirate. But Bhīṣma, mindful of his vow of chastity, declares that though the sun may give up its brilliancy, the fire its heat, the moon may give up the coolness of its rays, the god Indra his bravery, and the god Dharma [1] his justice, he could never break his promise. Then Satyavatī remembers her illegitimate son *Vyāsa,* and with Bhīṣma's consent invites him to see to the propagation of the race. And as we have already seen,[2] the saint Vyāsa begets *Dhṛtarāṣṭra, Pāṇḍu* and *Vidura.* As Dhṛtarāṣṭra was born blind, the younger brother Pāṇḍu became king. Dhṛtarāṣṭra married *Gāndhārī,* daughter of the king of Gāndhāra, and she bore him a hundred sons, the eldest of whom was named *Duryodhana.* Pāṇḍu had two wives, *Pṛthā* or *Kuntī,* daughter of a king of the Yādavas, and *Mādrī,* sister of *Śalya,* king of the Madras. Kuntī bore him three sons: *Yudhiṣṭhira,* the eldest, *Arjuna* and *Bhīma,* who was born on the same day as Duryodhana, whilst Mādrī gave birth to the twins *Nakula* and *Sahadeva.*

Here the epic relates the following very fantastic story (which could scarcely have belonged to the old poem), according to which these five

---

[1]) The god of death, and at the same time the god of justice. [2]) See above, pp. 322f.

principal heroes of the epic are supposed to have been begotten not *by*, but *on behalf of* Pāṇḍu. Pāṇḍu killed a pair of antelopes at the time of copulation. In reality, however, it was a ṛṣi who had assumed the form of an antelope in order to enjoy love. This ṛṣi now pronounces a curse that Pāṇḍu shall die during the enjoyment of love. Pāṇḍu therefore determines to lead the life of an ascetic, and to renounce sexual pleasures. In order to provide descendants, however, Kuntī invokes the gods to beget children with her. Dharma, the god of justice, begets Yudhiṣṭhira with her, Vāyu, the god of the wind, begets strong Bhīma and Indra, the king of the gods, begets Arjuna. At Kuntī's request, the two Aśvins cohabit with Mādrī, and beget the twins Nakula and Sahadeva with her.

The Pāṇḍavas and Kauravas at the Court of Dhṛtarāṣṭra.

When Pāṇḍu died soon afterwards, blind Dhṛtarāṣṭra assumed the reins of government. The five sons of Pāṇ u accompanied their mother Kuntī—Pāṇḍu's second wife Mādrī had thrown herself on to his funeral pyre—to the court of king Dhṛtarāṣṭra at Hastināpura, where they were educated with the princes, their cousins.

Even in their juvenile games, the sons of Pāṇḍu excelled over those of Dhṛtarāṣṭra, arousing the jealousy of the latter. Bhīma, in particular, evinced great exuberance of spirits and gave many an exhibition of unruly strength which were most displeasing to Dhṛtarāṣṭra's children. For instance, if the children climbed a tree, he would shake it so that his cousins tumbled down together with their fruits. For this reason Duryodhana hated Bhīma intensely, and made several attempts on his life without however being able to harm him. The boys grew up, and two famous Brahmans, skilled in the use of weapons, *Kṛpa* and *Droṇa*, were engaged as their tutors. There were among their pupils besides the sons of Dhṛtarāṣṭra and of Pāṇḍu, also *Aśvatthāman*, one of Droṇa's sons, and *Karṇa*, son of a Sūta or charioteer. Duryodhana and Bhīma soon became Droṇa's best pupils with the clubs, Aśvatthāman in magic arts, Nakula and Sahadeva in sword exercises, and Yudhiṣṭhira in chariot fighting. But Arjuna was not only the best archer, but excelled all the others in every respect. For this reason the sons of Dhṛtarāṣṭra were extremely jealous of him.

When the princes had completed their studies, Droṇa organised a tournament at which his pupils were to show their skill. It is a brilliant and festive assembly, the king, the queens and numerous heroes are present. Bhīma and Duryodhana give a performance of club-fighting which threatens to become so deadly earnest that the combatants have to be separated. Arjuna is universally praised for his skill in archery. But Karṇa also enters the ring, and executes the same feats as Arjuna, which greatly angers the latter, whilst Duryodhana joyfully embraces Karṇa and swears eternal friendship. Karṇa challenges Arjuna to a duel, but as the descendant of a charioteer he is laughed to scorn by the Pāṇḍavas.

Yudhiṣṭhira becomes heir to the throne. Conspiracy against him and his brothers. (*The lac house.*)

After a year had elapsed, Dhṛtarāṣṭra appointed as heir to the throne, Yudhiṣṭhira, the first-born of the Kuru family, who had distinguished himself by his bravery as well as by all other virtues. The other Pāṇḍavas perfected themselves still further in arms, and even went forth on victorious campaigns of conquest off their own bat. When Dhṛtarāṣṭra learned of these exploits of the Pāṇḍavas who were growing mightier and mightier, he felt some anxiety as to the future of his own line. Therefore when Duryodhana, his younger brother *Duśśāsana*, his friend Karṇa and his maternal uncle *Śakuni* concerted a plot against the Pāṇḍavas, they found a willing supporter in the aged king. They persuaded Dhṛtarāṣṭra to remove the Pāṇḍavas to Vāraṇāvata on some pretext or other. At Vāraṇāvata Duryodhana engaged a skilful builder to construct a house of lac and of other highly inflammable materials, in which the Pāṇḍavas were to live. At night when they would all be asleep, the house was to be set on fire, so that the Pāṇḍavas would meet their doom. But Vidura tells Yudhiṣṭhira privately of the treacherous plan, and for this communication he makes use of a Mleccha language, *i.e.* the language of a non-Indian tribe, which was not understood by the others. Now to avoid arousing suspicion, as they feared that Duryodhana would otherwise have them killed in some other fashion by assassins, they pretend to fall in with the plan, journey to Vāraṇāvata and occupy the lac house. However, they flee into the forest by a subterranean passage which they had previously had dug, after setting fire to the house, in which, in addition to the builder, there is only a drunken low-caste woman lying asleep with her five sons. While everyone believes that the Pāṇḍavas have been burned with their mother Kuntī, and the funeral ceremonies are being performed at Dhṛtarāṣṭra's court, the five brothers are wandering about with their mother in the forest on the other side of the Ganges. At dead of night they are in the midst of dense jungle, weary, hungry and thirsty. Kuntī complains of thirst, and Bhīma conducts his mother and four brothers to a banyan tree where they are to rest while he is seeking water. Following the water-birds, he comes to a lake, where he bathes and drinks and dips his upper garments into the water, so as to take water to the others. He hastens back, to find all his people asleep under the tree. At the sight of his mother and brothers lying asleep thus, he bemoans their sad fate in bitter words.

Hiḍimba, the giant, and his sister.

Near this banyan tree there lurks a horrible, man-eating giant, the *Rākṣasa Hiḍimba.* He smells human flesh, and from a high tree sees the sleeping forms. His mouth waters for the delicacy which has so long been denied to him, and he asks his sister, the giantess Hiḍimbā, to go and see what manner of people they be; they would then enjoy a feast of fresh human flesh and blood together, and dance and sing merrily afterwards. The giantess approaches them, but no sooner does she set eyes on Bhīma than she is seized by violent love for the strong young hero. She therefore transforms herself into a beautiful human woman and steps smilingly towards Bhīma, tells him that this forest is haunted by a man-eating Rākṣasa, her brother, who has sent her here, but that she loves Bhīma and desires no other man but him as her lord, that he may take delight in her, and that she will rescue him. Bhīma replies that it would not enter his head to yield to passion, and to leave his mother and brothers in the lurch. Hiḍimbā answers that he may awaken his relatives by all means, and she will save them all. Bhīma retorts, however, that he would not dream of awakening his mother and brothers from their sweet slumber: Rākṣasas, Yakṣas (elves), Gandharvas and such-like riff-raff do not alarm him in the least, and he will find a way of dealing with the man-eater himself. At this juncture the giant Hiḍimba, thinking that his sister is too long away, appears in person, and would slay the love-sick Hiḍimbā in his anger. But Bhīma confronts him and challenges him to fight. After a terrible conflict, during which the brothers awake, Bhīma slays the giant. When he is about to despatch Hiḍimbā likewise, Yudhiṣṭhira exhorts him not to slay a woman. At her earnest entreaties, he at last agrees to be united to her until a son is born to her. Yudhiṣṭhira arranges that Bhīma may stay with the giantess all day, but that he must always return before sunset. So Hiḍimbā flies through the air with Bhīma to the pleasant hill-tops, where they give themselves up to the pleasures of love, until she conceives, and bears a son, who grows into a mighty Rākṣasa. They call him *Ghaṭotkaca,* and later on, in the great fight, he does good service to the Pāṇḍavas.

The giant Baka and the Brahman family.

Disguised as ascetics, the Pāṇḍavas now wander from forest to forest, experiencing many an adventure, and come at last to a city Ekacakrā where, without being recognised, they stay at a Brahman's house. During the day they beg for their food and in the evening they bring it home, where Kuntī divides all the food into two halves, the one for Bhīma, and the other for all the rest. One day Kuntī is alone at home with Bhīma. Loud groans and lamentations are heard proceeding from the apartments of the Brahman whose hospitality they are enjoying. First of all they hear the Brahman give vent to bitter lamentations over the lot of humanity in general, and declare that it would be best for him to perish together with his family, for he would never have the heart to sacrifice his faithful wife, his beloved daughter or his dear little son, and yet on the other hand, were he to die alone, he would be leaving his dear ones to sure distress. Then the Brahman's wife begins to speak, and says that he must live on, so as to provide for his children and to preserve the race: she herself, having borne him a son and a daughter, has fulfilled the purpose of her life, and can die in peace. Were he to die, she could never nourish and protect her two children single-handed; she would be able neither to protect her daughter from unworthy men nor to give her son an education worthy of a Brahman. Whereas he could take a second wife, she herself, as a widow, would lead but a pitiable existence. "As birds swoop greedily down upon a piece of flesh that is cast away, thus do men abuse a woman who is bereaved of her husband." Therefore she will sacrifice her life. The daughter, who has listened to what her parents have said, now has her say, and seeks to prove that for her alone is it fitting to die for the family. "Is it not said: A son is as one's own self, a wife is a friend, but a daughter is misery. Rid thyself of this misery, therefore, and let me fulfil my duty." While these three converse in this fashion, and finally burst into tears, the little son, his eyes wide open, approaches each one individually, and says, smiling, in his sweet, childish voice: "Do not weep, father! Do not weep, mother! Do not weep, sister!" And the little fellow gaily takes a blade of grass from the ground, saying: "I am going to kill the man-eating Rākṣasa with this!" And in the midst of their sore distress, their hearts were filled with joy when they heard the boy's sweet voice. It is this moment which Kuntī, the mother of the Pāṇḍavas, chooses to enter and to enquire what it is that has gone wrong. She is then told that a man-eating Rākṣasa, the giant Baka, lurks in the vicinity of the city, and that at certain intervals the inhabitants of the city are obliged to supply him with a cartload of rice, two buffaloes and a human being by way of tribute. The families are chosen in rotation, and it is now the turn of the family in question. Then Kuntī consoles the Brahman and suggests that one of her five sons shall pay the tribute to the Rākṣasa. But the Brahman will not hear of a Brahman, and a guest at that, sacrificing his life for him. Then Kuntī explains to him that her son is a great hero, which fact is not to be disclosed, and that he will surely slay the Rākṣasa. Bhīma is prepared to carry out his mother's proposal immediately, and the next morning he drives into the forest haunted by the monster, with the cart containing the food intended for the Rākṣasa. As soon as he reaches the forest, he begins to eat the food himself (this is most humorously described), and is in no wise perturbed by the stormy approach of the giant. Even when the infuriated Rākṣasa showers blows on him with both hands, he calmly continues eating. It is not until he has eaten everything up that he prepares for the combat. They uproot the mightiest trees in the forest and hurl them at each other. A stupendous struggle then ensues, the result of which is that Bhīma breaks the giant in two across his knee. Bhīma extracts a promise from the remaining Rākṣasas, the relatives and subjects of Baka, that they will never again kill a human being, and he then returns to his brothers. There is great joy in the city, but the Pāṇḍavas preserve their incognito.

The self-choice and marriage of Draupadī

After a time the Pāṇḍavas decide to leave Ekacakrā and to migrate to Pāñcāla. On the road thither they hear that *Drupada*, king of the Pāñcālas, is about to hold a "self-choice" [1] for his daughter. The brothers decide

[1] *Svayamvara*, *i.e.* "bride's self-choice," is a form of engagement or betrothal in which the king's daughter herself chooses her husband from amongst the assembled princes and heroes (after her father has issued a solemn invitation), placing a garland around the neck of the chosen one, whereupon the marriage takes place. While the Svayamvara is very frequently described in *epic poetry*, this custom is not mentioned at all in the brahmanical *law-books*, which otherwise treat the various kinds of betrothal in great detail. *Cf.* J. J. *Meyer*, Das Weib im altindischen Epos, pp. 60 ff.

to take part in the festival, and, disguised as Brahmans, they go to the residential town of Drupada, where they live unrecognised at the house of a potter, and beg for their food as Brahmans. Now Drupada had had a very stiff bow made, and had had a target set high up in the air by means of a mechanical contrivance, and he proclaimed that only the hero who could draw the bow and hit the mark, would be qualified to win his daughter Kṛṣṇā at the Svayamvara. Princes of all lands, among them the Kauravas, Duryodhana and his brothers and Karṇa, accept King Drupada's invitation and assemble in the festively decorated hall in which the self-choice of a husband is to take place. Innumerable Brahmans, too, flock in as spectators, and among them are the five Pāṇḍavas. There are brilliant festivities for several days, and the foreign kings and the Brahmans enjoy splendid hospitality as guests. At last, on the sixteenth day, attended by the usual ceremonies, the radiant *Kṛṣṇā*, beautifully dressed and adorned, steps into the hall, holding the garland of flowers in her hand. Her brother *Dhṛṣṭadyumna* proclaims in a loud voice :

> "Mark this bow, assembled monarchs, and the target hung on high,
> Through yon whirling piercéd discus let five glitt'ring arrows fly!
> Whoso born of noble lineage, hits the far suspended aim,
> Let him stand and as his guerdon Drupad's beauteous maiden claim!" [1]

After this he tells his sister the names of all the kings present, beginning with Duryodhana. All of them are at once enamoured of the charming *Kṛṣṇā*, each is jealous of the other, and every single individual hopes to win her. One after the other now attempts to bend the bow, but none succeed. Then Karṇa steps forward; he has already bent the bow, and is prepared to hit the mark, when Kṛṣṇā calls out in a loud voice: "My choice shall not be a charioteer." With a bitter laugh and a glance towards the sun, Karṇa throws the bow down again. In vain do the mighty kings Śiśupāla, Jarāsandha and Śalya strive to bend the bow. Then Arjuna arises from the midst of the Brahmans. Amid loud murmurs of applause from those who admire the stately youth, and amid the sounds of disapproval of those who are angry at the presumption of a Brahman in entering the lists with warriors, he strides to the bow, bends it in the twinkling of an eye, and shoots the target down. When Kṛṣṇā sees the

[1]) Translated by Romesh *Dutt*, Maha-Bharata, p. 19.

godlike youth, she hands him the garland joyfully, and followed by the princess, Arjuna leaves the hall.

However, when the assembled kings perceive that Drupada really intends to give his daughter to the Brahman, they take it as an insult; for in their opinion, the self-choice of a husband is for warriors, but not for Brahmans. They attempt to kill Drupada, but Bhīma and Arjuna hasten to his aid. Bhīma uproots a mighty tree, and stands there, terrible as the god of death. Arjuna stands beside him, with the bent bow. Karṇa fights with Arjuna, and Śalya with Bhīma. After a hard fight, Karṇa and Śalya confess themselves beaten. The kings give up the fight, and return to their homes. But the Pāṇḍavas go on their way with Kṛṣṇā, and wend their way to the potter's house, where Kuntī anxiously awaits them. Arjuna now declares in the presence of his mother and his brothers that he will not wed Kṛṣṇā, daughter of Drupada, whom he has won, for himself alone, but that, in accordance with the ancient custom of their family, she must become the common wife of all five brothers.

Among those present at the self-choice was *Kṛṣṇa*, the chieftain of a clan of the Yādavas and the cousin of the Pāṇḍavas (for Vasudeva, Kṛṣṇa's father, was Kuntī's brother). He was the only one who had recognised the Pāṇḍavas, in spite of their disguise. He therefore followed the Pāṇḍavas, accompanied by his brother *Baladeva*, visited them at the potter's house, and disclosed to them that he was their relative. This greatly rejoiced the Pāṇḍavas, but in order that they might not be recognised, Kṛṣṇa and Baladeva soon took their departure.

Prince Dhṛṣṭadyumna had also secretly followed the Pāṇḍavas in order to find out who the hero who had won his sister for his consort, really was. He conceals himself in the potter's house, and observes how the brothers return home and respectfully greet their mother, how Kuntī instructs Draupadī [1] regarding the preparation and distribution of the food, how after the evening meal they betake themselves to rest, the youngest brother spreading a mattress of kuśa grass whereon the five brothers stretch themselves in turn, each one on his antelope-skin, whilst their mother and Draupadī put up their beds at their head and foot respectively: and he hears how the brothers still regale one another with all kinds of conversation upon arms and warlike deeds before falling asleep. Then Dhṛṣṭadyumna hastens back to his father, to tell him that,

---

[1]) Kṛṣṇā, "the black one" is usually called Draupadī, *i.e.* "daughter of Drupada."

judging from their conversation, the supposed Brahmans must be warriors, at which the king rejoices exceedingly. The next morning, Drupada invites the Pāṇḍavas to the palace, in order to celebrate his daughter's wedding with due festivity. It is only now that Yudhiṣṭhira informs him that they are the sons of Pāṇḍu, whom people had thought dead; Drupada is much rejoiced at this, for it had always been his wish to have the brave Arjuna as a son-in-law. Just when he is about to perform the ceremonial marriage of his daughter with Arjuna, he is, however, somewhat astonished and disillusioned to learn from Yudhiṣṭhira that Kṛṣṇā must become the common wife of all five brothers. The scruples which he puts forward are, however, appeased when he learns of the ancient family custom of the Pāṇḍavas, and Draupadī is wedded before the sacred fire first to Yudhiṣṭhira as the eldest brother, and then to the other four brothers in order of age.[1] Kuntī blesses her daughter-in-law, and Kṛṣṇa sends rich and most costly wedding presents to the newly-wedded people.

---

[1]) In this marriage to five husbands, the epic has indubitably faithfully preserved an old feature of the legend; for polyandry, or rather group-marriage, of which the marriage of the Pāṇḍavas affords an example, though still occurring in certain regions of India at the present day, was by no means attested as a legitimate form of marriage in ancient India, and is directly opposed to the brahmanical views. When Drupada says (I, 197, 27): "The law teaches that *one* man has many wives; but one has never heard that *one* woman has many men as her husbands," he only gives expression to the general Indian opinion. When, in spite of this, the five principal heroes of the epic have only *one* wife between them, it is a proof that this feature was so closely interwoven with the whole legend and the ancient epic, that, even at a later time, when the Mahābhārata acquired a more and more brahmanical character and became a religious text book, the elimination of this feature could not be dreamed of. All that was done was to try to *justify* the marriage to five husbands, by means of several clumsily inserted stories. On one occasion Vyāsa relates the silly story of a maiden who could not obtain a husband, and implored the god Śiva to procure a husband for her. Now because she had cried *five times* "Give me a husband," Śiva promises her five husbands—in a future birth. This maiden is reborn as Kṛṣṇā, Drupada's daughter, and therefore receives the five Pāṇḍavas as husbands. A second story is not much more ingenious. The Pāṇḍavas, who live in the potter's house as begging Brahmans, come home with Draupadī, and announce to their mother that they have brought "the alms" which they have collected while out begging. Without looking up, Kuntī says, according to her custom, "Enjoy it all together." Only then does she notice that "the alms" is a woman, and is very much perturbed; but the word of a mother may not be made untrue, and therefore the five brothers must enjoy Draupadī in common. A third story, which Vyāsa related to Drupada, is the śivaitic "Five Indra story" (pañcendropākhyānam), a most fantastic and confused account, according to which Indra, as a punishment for having offended Śiva, is reborn on earth in five parts

43

The Pāṇḍavas get their kingdom back.

The report that the Pāṇḍavas are still alive and that it was Arjuna who had won Draupadī at the self-choice, is soon noised abroad. Duryodhana and his friends return sadly to Hastināpura, and they are much cast down by the Pāṇḍavas' having gained two mighty allies by their marriage, namely, Drupada and the Pañcālas, and Kṛṣṇa and the Yādavas. Duryodhana is of opinion that they should be on their guard against the Pāṇḍavas, and suggests that they should get rid of them by treachery. Karṇa, on the other hand, is for open combat. But Bhīṣma, supported by Vidura and Droṇa, advises Dhṛtarāṣṭra to cede one-half of the kingdom to the Pāṇḍavas and to live peaceably with them. Dhṛtarāṣṭra agrees to this proposal and cedes one-half of his kingdom to the Pāṇḍavas, and it is arranged that they shall settle in the desert of Khāṇḍavaprastha. Yudhiṣṭhira gladly accepts the offer, and, accompanied by Kṛṣṇa, the Pāṇḍavas journey to Khāṇḍavaprastha, where they found as their residence the great city and fort of *Indraprastha* (near modern Delhi).

Arjuna's banishment and adventures.

The Pāṇḍavas live happy and contented in Indraprastha with their common wife. In order to avoid any jealousy among them, they had mutually agreed (on the advice of the divine sage Nārada) that if any one of the brothers should intrude on a private interview of any other of the brothers with Draupadī, the former should go into banishment and lead a life of chastity for twelve years. Owing to this understanding they lived at peace with one another.

One day some robbers steal some cattle from a Brahman, who comes running into the palace violently reproaching the king for not protecting his

---

and an incarnation of Lakṣmī or Śrī (goddess of good fortune and beauty) is destined to be his wife. The five Pāṇḍavas are incarnations of the *one* Indra, Draupadī is an incarnation of Lakṣmī, so that Draupadī has actually only *one* husband! There is not even an attempt made to bring these three justification stories into accord with one another or with the principal narrative. On the other hand, it is repeatedly distinctly emphasized that it was an *ancient family custom*, *not* indeed a general Indian custom, but a special *family usage* of the *Pāṇḍavas*. In Buddhist and Jain stories, Draupadī's self-choice of a husband is so described that she chooses, not Arjuna, but all the five Pāṇḍavas simultaneously. Strangely enough, even a few European scholars have tried to *interpret* and *justify* the marriage to five husbands mythologically, allegorically and symbolically, instead of accepting it as an ethnological fact. (*Cf.* my "Notes on the Mahābhārata," JRAS, 1897, pp. 733 ff.).

subjects sufficiently. Arjuna wishes to hasten to his aid immediately. Chance will have it that the weapons are hanging in a room in which Yudhiṣṭhira happens to be together with Draupadī. Arjuna is in a dilemma. Is he to fail in his duty of a warrior towards the Brahman, and to break the rule with regard to their common wife, or is he to violate the former so as to be able to conform to the latter? He decides to enter the room and fetch the weapons; he pursues the robbers and restores the cattle to the Brahman. Then he returns home and announces to Yudhiṣṭhira that, in accordance with the agreement, he will go into banishment for twelve years. Though Yudhiṣṭhira tries to restrain him, as he had taken no offence whatsoever, Arjuna nevertheless retires to the forest, on the principle that what is right is right, whatever the circumstances.

Here he has many adventures. On one occasion he is bathing in the Ganges, and is about to come out of the water, after sacrificing to the fathers, when *Ulūpī*, the daughter of a Nāga king, draws him down into the kingdom of the Nāgas (snake demons). She explains to him that she has fallen in love with him, and begs him to take delight in her. Arjuna replies that he cannot do this, as he has taken the vow of chastity. But the snake virgin objects, saying that this vow can only refer to Draupadī, and that, as a matter of fact, it is his duty as a warrior to aid the unfortunate; and that if he would not grant her request, she would end her life—he must therefore save her life. Arjuna is powerless against these arguments, and "keeping his eye on his duty," he grants beautiful Ulūpī's request and spends a night with her.

On another occasion his wanderings bring him to Citravāhana, king of Maṇipūra, and he falls in love with the king's beautiful daughter *Citrāṅgadā*. But she is a "son-daughter," [1] and the king only gives her to him on condition that a son born of her be accounted as his (Citravāhana's) son. Arjuna agrees to this, and lives with her in Maṇipūra[2] for three years. After she has borne a son, he takes leave of her and continues his wanderings.

After having visited various holy places and had many more adventures, he meets Kṛṣṇa and visits him in his city of Dvārakā, where he is received with great festivity. A few days later there was a great feast

---

[1]) A *putrikā* or "son daughter" is a daughter whose son does not belong to the husband, but to the *father* of the girl. For if a man has no son, he can appoint his daughter as *putrikā*, whereby a son born of her becomes the continuator of *her father's* race, *i.e.* he is bound in duty to the ancestral sacrifice and entitled to the inheritance.

[2]) We hear no more of the vow of chastity.

of the Vṛṣṇis and Andhakas—clans of the Yādavas—on the hill Raivataka. Noblemen and citizens go forth with music, singing and dancing, and there is great merriment. Baladeva, Kṛṣṇa's brother, gets drunk with his wife Revatī; Ugrasena, king of the Vṛṣṇis, comes with his thousand wives, and many other princes with their wives. On this occasion Arjuna sees *Subhadrā*, Kṛṣṇa's beautiful sister, and becomes enamoured of her. He asks Kṛṣṇa how he can obtain her, and the latter advises him to carry her off by force after the fashion of warriors, as a self-choice is always an uncertain affair [1]). Then Arjuna sends a messenger to Yudhiṣṭhira to ask his permission for the abduction of Subhadrā. Yudhiṣṭhira gives his consent, and Arjuna goes forth in his chariot in full battle array, as though he were going to the chase. Subhadrā is taking a stroll on Raivataka, and just as she is about to return to Dvārakā, Arjuna seizes her, places her on his chariot and drives off with her in the direction of Indraprastha. Great excitement prevails in Dvārakā; the drunken Baladeva is furious at Arjuna's having violated the laws of hospitality. But Kṛṣṇa pacifies his relatives by telling them that Arjuna has not offended them at all. On the contrary, he had not considered the Yādavas so avaricious that they would sell a maiden like a head of cattle, and he had not wanted to take the chance of an uncertain self-choice, so his only course had been to carry Subhadrā off. There was no objection to the marriage itself, but they should recall Arjuna, and effect a reconciliation. This actually takes place, and Arjuna and Subhadrā are married. He stays in Dvārakā for another year, enjoying the society of Subhadrā. He spends the remainder of the twelve years at the sacred place of Puṣkara, after which he returns to Indraprastha. Draupadī reproaches him for his marriage with Subhadrā, but is appeased when Subhadrā offers herself to Draupadī as a maidservant. Thenceforth Draupadī, Subhadrā and Kuntī live happily together. Subhadrā bore Arjuna a son, *Abhimanyu*, who became a favourite with his father and his uncles, but Draupadī bore *one* son to each of the five Pāṇḍavas.

Yudhisthira becomes the Ruler of the World

King Yudhiṣṭhira reigned justly and piously in his kingdom, and his subjects, who loved him devotedly, lived in peace and happiness. The king's brothers, too, led a happy life. But Arjuna enjoyed a still more

[1]) Obviously the Yādavas were a rough shepherd-tribe, with whom *marriage by theft* was still legitimate.

intimate friendship with Kṛṣṇa. Once when the two friends were conversing in the groves by the Jumnā (where they had veritable orgies with many beautiful women, and in which even Draupadī and Subhadrā participated) the god Agni approached them in the form of a Brahman, and besought them to assist him in burning the Khāṇḍava forest. The fact was that the god had indigestion after eating the numerous offerings at some great sacrifice, and Brahman had told him that he must burn the Khāṇḍava forest if he wished to recover from it: but every time he had attempted to set the forest afire, the forest animals extinguish it again. Arjuna and Kṛṣṇa are to prevent this, and Agni procures heavenly weapons for them for the purpose: for Arjuna the mighty bow Gāṇḍīva with two inexhaustible quivers and a splendid chariot with silvery-white horses and recognisable from afar by a monkey banner; and for Kṛṣṇa a sure discus and an irresistible club. With these weapons they support Agni and kill all creatures which attempt to escape from the burning forest. They spare only the demon Maya, who is a great artist among the heavenly host.[1]

In thankfulness at the sparing of his life, the demon Maya builds for Yudhiṣṭhira a marvellous palace with all kinds of most ingenious devices. After some time Yudhiṣṭhira, in agreement with Kṛṣṇa, decided to offer the great sacrifice for the consecration of a king (rājasūya). Now only a ruler of the world, a great conqueror, is entitled to offer this sacrifice. But as Jarāsandha, king of Magadha, is the mightiest ruler for the time being, he must be removed. He is killed in a duel with Bhīma. After this, Arjuna, Bhīma, Sahadeva and Nakula go forth on victorious campaigns of conquest in the north, east, south and west respectively, on the strength of which Yudhiṣṭhira becomes possessed of a world-kingdom. The kings' consecration sacrifice may now be offered, and it is celebrated with great pomp. Numerous kings, including the Kauravas, are invited to it. At the close of the sacrifice, gifts of honour are distributed. At Bhīṣma's suggestion, Kṛṣṇa is to receive the first gift of honour. Śiśupāla, king of Cedi, objects to this. A quarrel ensues, ending in the death of Śiśupāla at the hands of Kṛṣṇa.

When the sacrifice is accomplished, the foreign kings take their departure. Kṛṣṇa, too, returns to his home. Only Duryodhana and his uncle Śakuni stay on in the palace of the Pāṇḍavas for some time. When viewing the superb building Duryodhana meets with all kinds of mishaps.

---

[1]) Here ends the *Ādiparvan*, or First book of the Mahābhārata.

He mistakes a crystal surface for a lake, and undresses in order to bathe; on the other hand, he mistakes an artificial pond for dry land, and has an involuntary dip, at which Bhīma and Arjuna burst out laughing loudly.[1] This scorn wounded Duryodhana very deeply, for he was already consumed with envy. It is with feelings of the deepest envy and hate that he takes leave of his cousins and returns to Hastināpura.

The game of dice.

Duryodhana tells his tale of woe to his uncle Śakuni in bitter words. He tells him that he cannot bear the disgrace of seeing his enemies celebrating such triumphs; and that, as he cannot see any way of getting at the Pāṇḍavas, he will put an end to his life by fire, poison or water. Then Śakuni proposes that a game of dice should be arranged, and that Yudhiṣṭhira be invited to it; and Śakuni, who is a skilled player, is to win Yudhiṣṭhira's whole kingdom from him with ease. They repair forthwith to the aged king Dhṛtarāṣṭra, in order to obtain his consent to the plan. At first the king will have nothing to do with it, wishing at all events to consult his wise brother Vidura; but when Duryodhana points out to him that Vidura always takes the part of the Pāṇḍavas, the feeble old king allows them to talk him over, and orders the game of dice to be held. He sends Vidura in person to Yudhiṣṭhira to invite him to the game. Vidura warns the king and does not conceal from him his fear that great mischief may arise from this game of dice. Dhṛtarāṣṭra himself entertains this fear too, but believes that he must let Fate have its course. So Vidura goes to the court of King Yudhiṣṭhira to deliver the invitation to the game of dice. The latter, too, refers to the irresistible power of Fate, and accepts the invitation, though reluctantly. Accompanied by his brothers and Draupadī and the other women of the household, he sets out for Hastināpura. In Dhṛtarāṣṭra's palace the guests are greeted affably by their relatives and are received with great honours.

The next morning Yudhiṣṭhira and his brothers repair to the gaming-hall, where the Kauravas are already assembled. Śakuni challenges

---

[1]) Duryodhana's adventures in the marvellous palace of Yudhiṣṭhira remind us of the story of the Queen of Sheba, who mistakes a glass floor in Solomon's palace for a sheet of water, and bares her legs. *Cf.* Qurān, 27, 38; W. Hertz Gesammelte Abhandlungen, (1905), p. 427; *Grierson*, JRAS 1913, 684 f. There is also a similar story in the legend of the wonders of the new Babylon, built by Nebuchadnezzar; s. A. *Wesselofsky* in Archiv für lavische Philologie II, 310 ff., 321.

Yudhiṣṭhira to play, the last-named stakes something—and loses. One after the other, he stakes all his treasures, all his wealth of gold and precious stones, his state chariot, his male and female slaves, elephants, chariots and steeds—and he loses every time. Then Vidura turns to Dhṛtarāṣṭra and advises him to sever from his son Duryodhana who bids fair to bring on the ruin of the entire family, and to forbid the continuation of the game. Duryodhana now begins to inveigh most bitterly against Vidura, calling him a traitor, a viper which the Kauravas have nourished in their bosom, for he never speaks but in the interests of their enemies. Vidura turns in vain to Dhṛtarāṣṭra. Śakuni scornfully asks Yudhiṣṭhira whether he has anything more to stake. Yudhiṣṭhira is now possessed by the uncontrollable passion for gambling, and stakes all his possessions, his oxen and all his cattle, his city, his land and the whole of his kingdom—and all is lost. He stakes even the princes, and then the brothers Nakula and Sahadeva, and loses them. Incited by Śakuni, he is even led away to stake Arjuna and Bhīma, and he loses even these. Finally he stakes *himself*, and Śakuni again wins. Śakuni remarks with scorn that Yudhiṣṭhira has not done wisely in staking himself, since he still possesses a treasure which can be gambled away, namely Draupadī, the daughter of the Pañcāla king. And to the horror of all the aged people present,[1] of Bhīṣma, Droṇa, Kṛpa and Vidura, Yudhiṣṭhira announces that he will stake beautiful Draupadī. The dice are cast amid universal excitement, and Śakuni gains yet another victory.

Laughing, Duryodhana asks Vidura to bring Draupadī along, so that she may sweep the rooms and take her place among the maidservants. Vidura admonishes him, and warns him that his behaviour will only serve to bring about the downfall of the Kauravas; he says that, as a matter of fact, Draupadī has not become a slave at all, for Yudhiṣṭhira only staked her when he was no longer master of himself. Then Duryodhana sends a sūta as a messenger to Draupadī, to fetch her. The latter sends the messenger back to ask whether Yudhiṣṭhira gambled *himself* or *her* away first. Duryodhana sends the reply that she was to come to the gaming-hall and ask this question herself. As she refuses, and sends the messenger back each time without fulfilling his task, Duryodhana calls on his brother Duśśāsana to go and fetch her by force.

---

[1]) It is very noteworthy that these impartial and well-disposed men accept so calmly the fact that Yudhiṣṭhira has gambled away *his brothers and himself*, while it appears to them monstrous that he should stake their common *wife*.

Duśśāsana repairs to the women's apartments, and soon drags the struggling Draupadī into the assembly by the hair; she is unwell and therefore clad only in scanty garments. She laments bitterly that no one takes her part, not even Bhīṣma and Droṇa, and she casts a despairing glance at the Pāṇḍavas. Now the loss of their possessions and of their kingdom does not pain them so deeply as this glance of Draupadī's, filled with shame and anger. Then Bhīma can restrain himself no longer, he reproaches Yudhiṣṭhira violently for having staked Draupadī, and is about to lay hands on him.[1]) But Arjuna admonishes him: Yudhiṣṭhira must always be recognised and respected as the eldest. Now Vikarṇa, one of Duryodhana's youngest brothers, calls on those assembled to reply to Draupadī's question whether she has been gambled away by right. As they are all silent, he himself answers the question *in the negative.* Karṇa, however, retorts that the Kauravas have won *everything*, and that therefore the wife of the Pāṇḍavas also belongs to them. He adds that the Pāṇḍavas, and Draupadī too, should be stripped of their very clothes, as the Kauravas have won their clothes from them. The Pāṇḍavas take off their upper garments, while Duśśāsana, at a sign from Karṇa, proceeds to tear Draupadī's garment from her. She, however, prays to Kṛṣṇa, the incarnation of the god Viṣṇu, and by his help she remains clothed, however many times Duśśāsana seizes her draperies.[2]) But Bhīma now pronounces the terrible oath:

"Give heed to my oath, ye warriors of the whole world, an oath such as has never before been uttered by men, and such as will never again be uttered by a man. May I never attain to the resting-place of my ancestors if I do not fulfil the words which I have spoken—if I do not tear open the breast of this evil, foolish outcast of the Bhāratas in the fight, and drink his blood!"

---

[1]) Bhīma says he will burn both of Yudhiṣṭhira's arms, and asks Sahadeva to bring fire for this purpose (II, 68, 6; 10). J. J. *Meyer* ("Das Weib im altindischen Epos," p. 226) translates differently, interpreting the passage as meaning that Bhīma wishes to burn his own hands, and Meyer calls this "a typically Indian method of revenge and branding," similar to the "prāyopaveśa" (threat of suicide by hunger, in order to force a right). Nilakaṇṭha's commentary (te tava pura iti śeṣaḥ) would confirm this interpretation. Even if the usual translation be accepted, Bhīma's threat sounds very strange.

[2]) Not only the Southern Indian manuscripts, but also the play "Dūtavākya" ascribed to Bhāsa, make it seem probable that this miracle of the garments is a very late interpolation; s. *Winternitz* in Festschrift Kuhn, pp. 299 ff. *Oldenberg* ("Das Mahabharata," pp. 45 ff.) makes an attempt to distinguish generally between the earlier and later parts in the present narrative of the gambling scene.

Horror seizes all the warriors and heroes at these fearful words. In vain does Vidura remind those present of their *duty* to decide the legal question whether Draupadī has been won by the Kauravas or not. In vain does Draupadī weep and lament, and implore her relatives to answer her question. Even the pious Bhīṣma, learned in the law, can say no more than that justice is a ticklish matter, and that might is right in this world. As Yudhiṣṭhira is a model of justice, he himself should decide. Duryodhana, too, scornfully asks Yudiṣṭhira to give his opinion whether he considers Draupadī has been won or not. And as Yudhiṣṭhira sits there absent-minded, and makes no reply, Duryodhana goes so far as to offer the most unheard-of insult to the Pāṇḍavas: he bares his left thigh before Draupadī's very eyes. Then Bhīma utters the terrible words: "May Bhīma never be united to his fathers, if I do not crush this thigh of yours in the fight!"

Whilst still further speeches are being exchanged, the loud cry of a jackal and other sounds of ill omen are heard in Dhṛtarāṣṭra's house. Terrified by these, the old king Dhṛtarāṣṭra at last feels himself called upon to intervene. He blames Duryodhana in violent words. Then he pacifies Draupadī, and tells her to wish for something. She wishes for the freedom of her husband Yudhiṣṭhira. He grants her a second wish, and she chooses the liberation of the four remaining Pāṇḍavas. However, when he asks her to wish a third time, she says that she has now nothing more to wish for, as the Pāṇḍavas themselves will win all things needful, as soon as they are set free. Karṇa now begins to mock, saying that Draupadī is the boat in which the Pāṇḍavas have saved themselves from danger. Bhīma is consumed by rage, and is in doubt whether he should not slay the Kauravas on the spot. But Arjuna calms him, and Yudhiṣṭhiar forbids any fighting. King Dhṛtarāṣṭra, however, returns Yudhiṣṭhira his kingdom and exhorts him to let bygones be bygones. Thus they return to Indraprastha in a calmer frame of mind.

The second game of dice and the banishment of the Pāṇḍavas.

No sooner have the Pāṇḍavas departed, however, than Duryodhana, Duśśāsana and Śakuni again besiege the old king, pointing out to him the danger which threatens from the Pāṇḍavas who have now been so grievously insulted, and persuade him to give his consent to a second game of dice This time the loser is to go into banishment into the forest for twelve years, sojourn somewhere among people in the thirteenth year incognito, and is only to be allowed to return in the fourteenth year. Should he be recognised in the thirteenth year, however, he would have to go into banishment for another twelve years. In vain does Gāndhārī, the king's consort, strive to persuade him to sever himself from his wicked son Duryodhana, in order that he may not be guilty of causing the downfall of all the Kauravas. But he is deluded, and gives his consent; and a messenger is sent out, who catches up with the Pāṇḍavas, who are still on their homeward journey. Bewildered by fate, Yudhiṣṭhira accepts the invitation to the second game of dice. They all return, the game begins afresh, and he again loses. Now they must all go into banishment for thirteen years.

Clad in antelope-skins, the Pāṇḍavas prepare to go into the forest. Duryodhana and Duśśāsana rejoice in their triumph, and joke about them, but Bhīma hurls terrible threats at them. As Duryodhana pierces their hearts with sharp words, he says, even so will he pierce Duryodhana's heart in the fight. And once again he swears to drink the blood of Duśśāsana. Arjuna promises to slay Karṇa, Sahadeva, Śakuni and Nakula, the remaining sons of Dhṛtarāṣṭra. But Yudhiṣṭhira takes leave of Dhṛtarāṣṭra, Bhīṣma and the other Kauravas, and most affectionately of all, of wise, good Vidura. Kuntī, the mother of the Pāṇḍavas, stays behind in Vidura's house, but Draupadī follows her husbands into banishment, and her farewell from her mother-in-law is touching indeed. With tearful lamentations Kuntī sees her children go forth into banishment, but, with the exception of the gentle Yudhiṣṭhira, all of them swear to have their bloody revenge on the Kauravas in the fourteenth year. Omens of evil portent, and the prophetic words of the heavenly messenger Nārada announce to King Dhṛtarāṣṭra the downfall of his race, and he feels bitter remorse for having given his consent to the game of dice and the banishment.[1]

The twelve years' forest life of the Pāṇḍavas.[2]

Numerous citizens of Hastināpura accompany the Pāṇḍavas into the forest, and it cost Yudhiṣṭhira some trouble to persuade them to return home. Several Brahmins stayed with him for some considerable time. In order to be able to feed them, he practised asceticism, and prayed to the sun-god, whereupon he received from the latter a copper cooking-pot which filled itself at will. He fed the Brahmins with this,

---

[1]) Here ends the *Sabhāparvan*, the second book.

[2]) This forms the contents of the extensive third book, called *Vanaparvan* or "forest section."

and then journeyed northward to the Kāmyaka forest. Bhīma soon slew the man-eating rākṣasa Kirmīra, a brother of Baka and a friend of Hiḍimba, who haunted this forest.

In the meantime Dhṛtarāṣṭra had a consultation with Vidura. The latter advises the king to recall the Pāṇḍavas from banishment and to effect a reconciliation with them. Dhṛtarāṣṭra is angry that Vidura always takes the part of the Pāṇḍavas, and ungraciously dismisses him with words intimating that he may go where he likes. Vidura goes to the Pāṇḍavas in the Kāmyaka forest, and tells them what has happened. The aged king, however, soon repents of his violence, and sends the charioteer Sañjaya to have his brother Vidura recalled. Vidura soon returns accordingly, and there is a complete reconciliation between the two brothers.

When the friends and relatives of the Pāṇḍavas heard of their banishment, they went to them in the forest, to visit them. One of the first was, of course, Kṛṣṇa. At the time of the game of dice, he had been entangled in a war, and thus had been unable to stand by his friends. Had he been with them, he would certainly have prevented the game. When, however, Kṛṣṇa suggests making war on Duryodhana and reinstating Yudhiṣṭhira in power, Yudhiṣṭhira will not fall in with it, though Draupadī complains in bitter terms of the disgrace which the Kauravas have brought upon her. Later on, too, Draupadī and Bhīma repeatedly urge Yudhiṣṭhira to pull himself together and regain his throne by force. Yudhiṣṭhira declares each time that he must remain true to his promise and spend twelve years in the forest. Bhīma reproaches him with unmanliness, telling him that the first duty of a warrior is to fight, that thirteen months have now elapsed, which Yudhiṣṭhira may count as thirteen years, or that he can make up for the breaking of the promise by performing an expiatory sacrifice. Thereupon Yudhiṣṭhira also objects that Duryodhana has mighty and unconquerable allies in Bhīṣma, Droṇa, Kṛpa and Karṇa. At this moment the old ṛṣi Vyāsa appears once again and gives Yudhiṣṭhira a charm by the help of which Arjuna is to obtain heavenly weapons from the gods, which will assist them in gaining a victory over the Kauravas. Soon afterwards, therefore, Yudhiṣṭhira sends Arjuna to Indra to obtain the heavenly weapons. Arjuna wanders to the Himālayas, where he meets Indra in the form of an ascetic. The latter sends him to Śiva, who must first give his consent for the weapons to be delivered to Arjuna. Then Arjuna practises severe asceticism, whereupon Śiva appears to him in the form of a Kirāta, a wild hill-man. Arjuna gets involved in a fierce fight with the supposed Kirāta, until the latter reveals himself as the god Śiva and presents him with irresistible weapons. The world-protectors Yama, Varuṇa and Kubera soon also appear, and lend him their weapons, but Mātali, Indra's charioteer, conducts him to Indra's celestial city, where he receives still more weapons. He lives very happily in Indra's heaven for five years, and at Indra's command, a gandharva gives him lessons in singing and dancing.

Meanwhile the other Pāṇḍavas live in the forest by the chase, obtaining scanty nourishment from wild animals, roots and fruits. As Arjuna is so long absent, they are most anxious about him. Though the ṛṣi Lomaśa, who has just been on a visit to Indra's heaven, comes to them and consoles them by telling them that Arjuna is dwelling safely with Indra, they are unsatisfied, and prepare to go and seek Arjuna. They wander forth into the Gandhamādana hills, where they are very much terrified by a fearful storm and awful thunder and lightning. Draupadī faints from fear and fatigue. Then Bhīma thinks of his son Ghaṭotkaca, whom he had begotten with the giantess Hiḍimbā; and this rākṣasa appears immediately and takes Draupadī on his back; he also fetches other rākṣasas, who carry the Pāṇḍavas on their backs, and thus all of them are carried to a hermitage on the Ganges near the divine mountain Kailāsa, where they rest under a mighty Badarī tree.

As Draupadī expresses a longing for the heavenly lotus flowers, Bhīma scours the mountain wilderness, to the terror of the wild beasts, for he slays one wild elephant with another one, and one lion with another lion, or simply kills them with a blow of his fist. Here he also encounters *Hanumat*, the ape king, who obstructs his path and warns him not to proceed further, where only immortals may tread. Bhīma, however, tells him who he is, and orders him out of his path. The ape does not move, pretends to be ill, and says that Bhīma need only push his tail aside, in order to be able to pass by. In vain does Bhīma now endeavour to raise the ape's tail. The latter now smilingly discloses that he is Hanumat, "so very well known from the Rāmāyaṇa."[1] Bhīma now rejoices exceedingly at seeing his brother, for both of them are sons of the wind god, and he engages in a conversation with him. Finally Hanumat shows Bhīma the way to Kubera's garden, but warns him not to pluck flowers there, whereupon they take affectionate leave of each other. Bhīma soon reaches the lotus lake and garden of Kubera, where

---

[1]) Thus Bhīma speaks of him, Mahābh., III. 147, 11 Hanumat here gives a short extract from the Rāmāyaṇa.

the divine lotuses grow. He is confronted with rākṣasas who forbid him to pluck flowers, and inform him that, at any rate, he must first obtain Kubera's permission. Bhīma retorts that a warrior does not ask permission, but takes what he wants. He fights with the rākṣasas, puts them to flight, and plucks the flowers

After various adventures and fights with rākṣasas, the fifth year approaches, when Arjuna is to return from heaven. The brothers repair to the "white mountain" (the heavenly mountain of Kailāsa) to meet him. Bhīma again engages in a fight with yakṣas and rākṣasas, the guardians of Kubera's garden, and slays many of their number, among others Maṇimat, who had once spat on the head of the holy ṛṣi Agastya, wherefore Kubera had been cursed by the ṛṣi. Bhīma's deed now released Kubera from the curse, and for this reason he is by no means enraged at the bloodshed caused among the demons; on the contrary, he bids Bhīma and his brothers a very cordial welcome.

On the glorious mountain they at last meet Arjuna again, who comes careering along in Indra's chariot driven by Mātali. After the most cordial of greetings, Arjuna tells them of all his experiences and adventures, and especially how he has fought victoriously with the Nivātakavaca demons who dwell by the sea, and with the inhabitants of Hiraṇyapura, the city which flies through the air.

The Pāṇḍavas now live happily in the pleasure groves of Kubera, and four years pass, as if they had been a single night. However, in order not to be diverted from their earthly cares and fights, they resolve to quit the heavenly regions. Having descended Kailāsa, they repair to the hills and forests on the bank of the Jumnā.

Here Bhīma had an unpleasant adventure, and his life was saved by Yudhiṣṭhira. Roaming in the woods, Bhīma espies an immense snake which hurls itself at him furiously, and clings around him so tightly that he cannot extricate himself. His brother Yudhiṣṭhira finds him in this predicament. Now the snake is none other than the famous old king *Nahuṣa*, who had been cast out from heaven as the result of a curse of Agastya, and transformed into a serpent. He is not to be released from this curse until he can find somebody who can answer all the questions which he puts. Yudhiṣṭhira gives satisfactory answers to all his philosophical questions, whereupon he sets Bhīma free, and himself released from the condition of a snake, Nahuṣa returns to heaven.

Soon after this, they return to the Kāmyaka forest. Here they are again visited by Kṛṣṇa. He brings Draupadī the desired news of her children, and exhorts Yudhiṣṭhira to make sure of allies for the fight against the Kauravas, and to make other preparations for the war. As usual, however, Yudhiṣṭhira assures him that he must remain faithful to his promise, and that he does not wish to think of war until the thirteenth year shall have elapsed.

Pious Brahmins, too, often visit the Pāṇḍavas in the forest. One of these Brahmins goes straight from the Pāṇḍavas to the court of King Dhṛtarāṣṭra, where he relates how much the Pāṇḍavas, and especially Draupadī, have to suffer in their struggle with the elements in the wilderness. Whilst the old king laments at this, and is overcome with remorse, his son Duryodhana is much rejoiced, and, incited by Śakuni and Karṇa, he decided to visit the Pāṇḍavas in the forest, so as to gloat over their distress. As a pretext they represent to Dhṛtarāṣṭra that they must visit the cattle-pens situated in the vicinity of the forest, to inspect the herds, count the heads of cattle and mark the young calves. They ride forth in a great cavalcade, inspect the cattle, and give themselves up to the pleasures of the chase. However, when they wish to proceed in the neighbourhood of the spot where the Pāṇḍavas are staying, they are held up by gandharvas. A fight ensues, and Duryodhana is ignominiously taken prisoner by the king of the gandharvas. The Kauravas hasten to the Pāṇḍavas for aid, which the noble Yudhiṣṭhira does not refuse. After a hard fight, Duryodhana is liberated by the Pāṇḍavas from the captivity of the gandharva king. Filled with shame and pain at this humiliation, Duryodhana is about to end his life, and it is only with some difficulty that his friends succeed in diverting him from his suicidal frame of mind.

Karṇa has now a new plan to annoy the Pāṇḍavas. He sallies forth on a great campaign of conquest in all the four regions of the earth, to win the rule over the whole earth for Duryodhana, so that he too may be able to offer a great king's sacrifice. After the campaign of conquest has been brought to a successful conclusion, a great sacrifice is indeed performed; but as the Rājasūya sacrifice can only be performed once in one and the same family, and as Yudhiṣṭhira has already offered a sacrifice of this kind, it has to be a different sacrifice, called the *Vaiṣṇava*, which is supposed to have been offered only by the god Viṣṇu himself. In order to vex the Pāṇḍavas, Duryodhana invites them to this great sacrificial feast. Yudhiṣṭhira declines politely, while Bhīma sends a message that the Pāṇḍavas will pour out the sacrificial ghee of their anger over the Kauravas after the thirteenth year, in the sacrifice of battle.

During the last year of their sojourn in the forest, the Pāṇḍavas were threatened by a great loss. One day when all the brothers were out hunting, their wife Draupadī, who had stayed behind alone, was stolen away by *Jayadratha*, king of the Sindhus, who passed by. The Pāṇḍavas immediately pursue him, and he is overcome, and chastised and humiliated by Arjuna and Bhīma. Bhīma would fain have killed him, but as he is Dhṛtarāṣṭra's son-in-law, Yudhiṣṭhira grants him his life.

The Pāṇḍavas are very sorrowful about the rape of Draupadī. Though Jayadratha has been punished, they nevertheless feel humiliated. Yudhiṣṭhira, especially, is often in a sad mood, reproaches himself for the misfortune of which he is the cause, and laments above all the sad fate of Draupadī. Now Yudhiṣṭhira fears none of the Kauravas so greatly as Karṇa, who had come into the world with a natural coat-of-mail and ear-rings which make him invulnerable. In order to release Yudhiṣṭhira from his fear of Karṇa, Indra appears before Karṇa in the form of a Brahmin, and begs him for the coat-of-mail and the ear-rings. Karṇa, who can refuse nothing to a Brahmin, gives him the coat-of-mail and the ear-rings, which he cuts from his body without blinking an eye-lash. By way of a return gift, Indra presents him with a never-failing spear, which, however, he is only to use against one enemy and in the case of extreme emergency.

Distressed by the rape of Draupadī, the Pāṇḍavas left the Kāmyaka forest and went to Dvaitavana. There they met with their last forest adventure An antelope which is roaming through the forest happens to catch a Brahmin's fire-sticks with her antlers, and hurries away. The Brahmin, who requires the sticks for the sacrifice, requests the Pāṇḍavas to get them for him, and they pursue the animal in full chase, but cannot come up with it, and finally the animal vanishes from sight. They lament their bad luck. Wearied by the bootless chase and tortured by thirst, they look around for water. Nakula climbs a tree, and sees a lake in the distance. At the request of Yudhiṣṭhira, he goes thither, to fetch water in the quivers. He comes to a pretty lake, with beautiful, clear water, surrounded by cranes. However, just as he is about to drink, an invisible spirit (yakṣa) speaks from the air: "Do no violence, O friend, this is my property; first answer my questions, then drink and take water!" But Nakula gives no heed to these words, drinks and sinks lifeless to the ground. As he is so long away, Sahadeva goes to seek him, but he meets with the same fate. Yudhiṣṭhira now sends Arjuna, who fares no better, and finally Bhīma, who vainly endeavours to fight with the invisible yakṣa. He, too, drinks from the lake, and falls lifeless to the ground. Boding no good, Yudhiṣṭhira at last goes himself, to see what has become of his brothers. Horror-stricken, he sees them all lying dead, and begins to lament and complain. Now when he approaches the lake, he too hears the voice of the yakṣa warning him not to drink before he has answered his questions. Yudhiṣṭhira declares himself willing to answer the questions, and there ensues a most interesting play of questions and answers, in which, with the exception of a few riddles in the style of the ancient Vedic brahmodyas,[1] almost the whole of Indian ethics is recited. Only a few examples will be quoted here:

The yakṣa: "What is weightier than the earth? What is higher than the sky? What is swifter than the wind? What is more numerous than grass?"

Yudhiṣṭhira: "A mother is weightier than the earth. The father is higher than the sky. The spirit is swifter than the wind. Thoughts are more numerous than grass."

The yakṣa: "Who is the friend of the traveller? Who is the friend of him who remains at home? Who is the friend of the sick? Who is the friend of the dying?"

Yudhiṣṭhira: "A caravan is the friend of the traveller. The wife is the friend of him who remains at home. The doctor is the friend of the sick. Charity is the friend of the dying."

The yakṣa: "Who is the foe who is difficult to conquer and which is the never-ending disease? Which man is considered good, and which bad?"

Yudhiṣṭhira: "Anger is the foe that is difficult to conquer. Greed is the never-ending disease. He who is friendly towards all creatures is considered good; he who knows no mercy, is considered bad."

The yakṣa: "What, O king, is called delusion, and what is pride? What do we mean by idleness, and what is sorrow?"

Yudhiṣṭhira: "To be deluded with regard to Dharma,[2] is delusion; to be proud of oneself is pride. Inactivity with regard to Dharma is idleness, and ignorance is true sorrow."

The yakṣa: "What do the ṛṣis call constancy, and what is known as bravery? What is the best bath? What is charity?"

Yudhiṣṭhira: "Steadfastness in the fulfilment of one's duty is constancy; bravery is the control of the senses. The best bath is getting rid

---

[1]) *Cf.* above pp. 183 f. The riddle there quoted from the Vājasaneyi-Saṃhitā XXIII, 45 f. here recurs (Mahābh. III, 313, 65 f.).

[2]) There is no word in any European language which is quite synonymous with the Sanskrit word *dharma*. *Dharma* signifies "the norm of action," and includes the conceptions "law *and* custom, morality *and* religion, duty *and* virtue." It is therefore impossible to translate the word in the same way in each case. *Cf.* above p. 326.

of uncleanliness of thought; but charity consists of affording protection to all creatures."

The yakṣa: "Tell me, O king, of what does Brahman-hood really consist, of descent, of the way of life, of the reading of the Veda, or of erudition?"

Yudhiṣṭhira: "Listen, dear Yakṣa! Brahman-hood is based neither on descent, on the reading of the Veda, nor on erudition, but solely on a good life; of this there can be no doubt. The Brahmin must pay more attention to the ordering of his life than to all else; so long as his good life is unimpaired, he himself is unimpaired; if his good life is ruined, he himself is ruined. Those who learn and teach and meditate on the sciences, are fools if they humour the passions. The wise man is he who does his duty. A scoundrel, though he know all the four Vedas, is worse than a Śūdra. He who but offers the fire-sacrifice, but curbs his senses, may count as a Brahmin."[1]

The yakṣa is so pleased with Yudhiṣṭhira's answers that he is willing to call one of his brothers back to life. Yudhiṣṭhira is to choose which of his four brothers shall be brought back to life. He chooses Nakula, on the grounds that his father had two wives, and that it is only right and fair that a son of the second wife, Mādrī, be alive too. This answer pleases the yakṣa so immensely that he calls all the brothers to life again. Now in reality the yakṣa is none other than the god Dharma himself, the "father"[2] of Yudhiṣṭhira, the god of right and morality. Before he vanishes, he grants the Pāṇḍavas the additional favour that they may remain unrecognised in the *thirteenth* year; for the twelve years of their life in the forest are now over, and, in accordance with the arrangement, they must still spend the thirteenth year unrecognised among people.

The Pāṇḍavas at the court of King Virāṭa.[3]

The Pāṇḍavas decide to go to the court of Virāṭa, king of the Matsyas, and to stay there under false names in appropriate disguise.

---

[1]) III, 313. Similar definitions of the "brahman" are frequent in Buddhistic texts, *cf.* for instance, Vinayapiṭaka, Mahāvagga I, 2, 2 f. Suttanipāta, Vāsetthasutta and Milindapañha IV, 5, 26. A version of this story of Yudhiṣṭhira and the Yakṣa is found in the Jaina Hemavijaya's "Kathāratnākara," No. 21 (German translation by J. *Hertel*, Vol. I, pp. 58 ff.).

[2]) See above p. 330.

[3]) The events at the court of Virāṭa form the contents of the *fourth* book, called *Virāṭaparvan*.

They conceal their weapons near the cemetery outside the city on a tree, upon which they hang a corpse so that no one shall venture near; they tell the herdsmen who watch them do this, that it is their mother who is one hundred and eighty years old, and whom they are "burying" in this way according to the custom of their ancestors. First of all Yudhiṣṭhira goes to Virāṭa, gives himself out as an excellent dice-player, and is appointed as the king's companion and counsellor. The others then come in their turn. Bhīma takes service as a cook. Arjuna, taking the feminine name Bṛhannalā, gives himself out as an eunuch, and is appointed as dancing-master to the king's daughter Uttarā. Nakula is engaged as a horse-tamer, Sahadeva as an overseer of cattle, whilst Draupadī is engaged by the queen as her chambermaid.

The Pāṇḍavas soon gain great popularity at Virāṭa's court, especially as Bhīma has distinguished himself by killing the world-famous athlete Jīmūta at a wrestling match organised in honour of the god Brahman.

Draupadī, on the other hand, had an unpleasant adventure. Kīcaka, a brother-in-law of the king and commander of his army falls in love with the beautiful chambermaid, and accosts her. Now Draupadī, at the time of her appointment by the queen, had given out that she was the wife of five gandharvas who would protect her in case of need. By promising him a rendezvous, Draupadī entices her pursuer at dead of night into the dancing hall, where Bhīma is on the watch for him and strangles him after a mighty struggle. Thereupon Draupadī summons the watchmen and says that one of her gandharvas has killed Kīcaka, because he had persecuted her with love-making. Kīcaka's mighty relatives wish to burn the chambermaid on the funeral pyre with the corpse; but Bhīma again comes to the rescue, and in his guise of a gandharva, kills 105 sūtas (for Kīcaka is a sūta) and releases Draupadī. Then the citizens of the town demand the dismissal of the chambermaid who is so dangerous by reason of her gandharvas, and the king gives a command accordingly. However, Draupadī begs the queen to let her remain for another thirteen days, after which time the gandharvas would fetch her away. (For all but thirteen days of the thirteenth year has expired.)

In vain does Duryodhana send out spies to find out the whereabouts of the Pāṇḍavas. The spies only bring back the news that Kīcaka has been killed by gandharvas, which is quite agreeable to Duryodhana, as the Matsyas are a hostile nation. Moreover Kīcaka had often oppressed Suśarman, the king of the Trigartas. Now the Trigartas arrange with the Kauravas to organise a joint raid on the land of the Matsyas. Just as the thirteenth year of banishment expires, there is news that the Trigartas have invaded the country and have stolen King Virāṭa's cattle. Virāṭa prepares for the fight, provides Yudhiṣṭhira, Bhīma, Nakula and Sahadeva with weapons too, and sallies forth into the battle-field against the Trigartas. A mighty battle ensues. Virāṭa is taken prisoner, but is liberated immediately by Bhīma, and finally the Trigartas are defeated, thanks to the assistance of the Pāṇḍavas, who, nevertheless, remain unrecognised.

While Virāṭa is fighting against the Trigartas, the Kauravas invade the land of the Matsyas at another point, and steal much cattle. The cowherds approach the young prince *Uttara*, who has stayed behind in the city, and request him to go forth to battle against the Kauravas. Now he has no charioteer. Then Draupadī, through the agency of the princess, persuades him to take Arjuna as his charioteer. He receives a suit of armour, and they go forth to battle. When Uttara sees the mighty hosts of the Kauravas, he is seized with fear, leaps from the chariot and is about to flee; but Arjuna catches him up, drags him back on to the chariot by the hair, and exhorts him to courage. Then they drive to the tree on which the weapons are concealed, and Arjuna fetches his weapons. When he reveals himself to Uttara as the mighty hero Arjuna, the former takes courage again. Uttara now becomes Arjuna's charioteer. A mighty battle is now fought, in which Arjuna fights with Duryodhana, Karṇa, Bhīṣma and the other heroes of the Kauravas, and of course gains a glorious victory. Though the Kauravas harboured a suspicion that it was Arjuna who was fighting against them, they did not recognise him.

After he has won the victory, Arjuna takes the weapons back to the tree, and returns to the city as the dancing-master Bṛhannalā and Uttara's charioteer, having impressed upon Uttara that he must not betray him. In the meantime Virāṭa and the Pāṇḍavas have returned after defeating the Trigartas. The king is very anxious when he hears that his son has gone forth against the Kauravas, but the news of the victory soon reaches him. Uttara is received in triumph. He relates that it is not he who has defeated the Kauravas, but that a god in the form of a beautiful youth has aided him. Three days later the thirteenth year comes to an end. To the astonishment of the king, the five Pāṇḍavas appear in their true form in the hall, and disclose their identity. Virāṭa rejoices greatly, and immediately offers Arjuna his daughter as a wife. Arjuna accepts her, not for himself, but for his son *Abhimanyu*, for by making her his daughter-in-law, he would be testifying to the fact that, though he had lived in such close association with her for a whole year, she had remained pure. The wedding of Abhimanyu and Uttarā is soon celebrated with great pomp, and numerous kings amongst whom are, of course, Drupada and Kṛṣṇa, arrive with costly presents.

Peace negotiations and preparations for war.[1]

At this wedding feast the Pāṇḍavas and their friends consult together as to what attitude should be taken up with regard to the Kauravas. Kṛṣṇa proposes that an ambassador be sent to Duryodhana to request him to give back to the Pāṇḍavas their half kingdom. After a long consultation it is then accordingly decided to send the old family priest of King Drupada as an ambassador to the Kauravas.

But even before the beginning of the negotiations, the Pāṇḍavas as well as the Kauravas are seeking to enlist as many allies as possible on their respective sides; and both parties are simultaneously endeavouring to win over several mighty kings. Thus Duryodhana seeks to win Kṛṣṇa himself over to his side, whom we have hitherto known only as the intimate friend of the Pāṇḍavas. As chance will have it, Duryodhana comes to Kṛṣṇa while the latter is asleep, and Arjuna arrives immediately after him. When Kṛṣṇa awakens, his eyes first light on Arjuna. Now as Duryodhana had come first, but as Arjuna has first been beheld by Kṛṣṇa, Kṛṣṇa thinks that he ought not to give either of them an answer containing a refusal; he therefore says that he will assist the one with his advice, whilst he will place an army of herdsmen at the disposal of the other. Duryodhana chooses the latter, Arjuna the former. For this reason Kṛṣṇa promises that he will not actually participate in the fight, but will only stand by the Pāṇḍavas as a counsellor, as Arjuna's charioteer. Śalya, too, king of the Madras, who, accompanied by a host of warriors, is already on his way to Yudhiṣṭhira in order to join his side, is invited by Duryodhana to fight on the side of the Kauravas. Śalya agrees to do so, but goes to Yudhiṣṭhira nevertheless. The last named, who is otherwise always represented as a model of virtue, agrees upon disgraceful treachery with Śalya. Śalya is to fight on the side of the Kauravas, but as Karṇa's charioteer, he is to drive the chariot badly and thus cause Karṇa's fall, should there be single combat between him and Arjuna.

While both sides are thus already thinking of war, Drupada's venerable priest comes to King Dhṛtarāṣṭra as an ambassador, and puts the

---

[1]) These form the contents of the *fifth* book (*Udyogaparvan*).

peace terms of the Pāṇḍavas before him. The king receives him in a very worthy manner, but gives him no definite answer, saying that he himself will send his charioteer Sañjaya as an ambassador to Yudhiṣṭhira. He does this after a few days; but Sañjaya's message is merely that Dhṛtarāṣṭra desires peace, and no offer is made to the Pāṇḍavas. Thereupon Yudhiṣṭhira sends back the reply that he must either receive Indraprastha and half of the kingdom back, or the fight shall commence. In order to avoid bloodshed among relatives, he even declares his willingness to accept the peace on condition that Duryodhana will place five villages at his disposal. The Kauravas now confer upon this reply which Sañjaya brings back. Bhīṣma, Droṇa and Vidura vainly strive to persuade Duryodhana to yield and make peace. As Dhṛtarāṣṭra shows himself entirely feeble and powerless, even this conference breaks up without the achievement of any result.

The Pāṇḍavas, too, again debate on the peace, and Kṛṣṇa offers to make another attempt, and to go in person to the Kauravas as a messenger of peace The Pāṇḍavas gratefully accept this offer. Even the defiant Bhīma speaks in favour of the peace in words whose mildness is so astonishing, " as if mountains had grown light and fire cold," that Kṛṣṇa himself is surprised. On the other hand some of the heroes, and more especially Draupadī, the wife of heroes, are impatient of any negotiations for peace, and would much prefer to declare war at once; but Yudhiṣṭhira insists upon the message of peace. In tender words he remembers their mother Kuntī, and he begs Kṛṣṇa to visit her, as she is living with Vidura at the court of the Kauravas, and to ask after her welfare.

Kṛṣṇa repairs to the Kauravas, taking benedictions on his way. He is received splendidly by Dhṛtarāṣṭra, but only accepts Vidura's hospitality. He immediately visits Kuntī and gives her Yudhiṣṭhira's greetings. The mother of heroes laments the separation from her sons in bitter words, but she is still more pained at the insult offered to Draupadī, and reproaches Yudhiṣṭhira with weakness. She asks Kṛṣṇa to tell her sons that they should not forget their duty as warriors, and should not hesitate to stake their lives. She says that the moment has now come "for the sake of which a warrior's wife brings children into the world." The next morning Kṛṣṇa goes to the assembly of the Kaurava princes in festive array, and makes a speech as to peace. Dhṛtarāṣṭra announces that he, for his part, desires nothing better than peace, but that he is powerless to do anything against his son Duryodhana. Then Kṛṣṇa turns his peace exhortations to Duryodhana, and Bhīṣma, Droṇa and Vidura also do their utmost to persuade Duryodhana to accept the peace terms. The latter, however, announces that he will not cede to the Pāṇḍavas even as much land as will cover the point of a needle. After he has left the assembly in anger, Kṛṣṇa proposes that the well-disposed among the Kauravas should deliver Duryodhana and his associates as prisoners to the Pāṇḍavas. Dhṛtaraṣṭra does not agree to this, but he sends for his wife Gāndhārī, in order that she may endeavour to persuade the obstinate son to make peace. Gāndhārī comes in, and reproaches the aged king violently for having abdicated in favour of his son; but her exhortations to Duryodhana are just as fruitless as those of the others. On the contrary, Duryodhana and his associates hatch a plan to take Kṛṣṇa prisoner, so as to dispose of a powerful foe in this way. The plan, however, does not remain a secret, and Duryodhana is severely admonished by Dhṛtarāṣṭra and Vidura for having planned this violation of the law of embassy. After Bhīṣma and Droṇa, too, have vainly spoken in favour of peace, even this peace embassy of Kṛṣṇa's must be regarded as having failed.

Before Kṛṣṇa departs, he still has a secret interview with Karṇa. This brave hero is generally regarded as the son of a charioteer (sūta). The story goes, however, that in reality he was begotten by Sūrya, the sun-god, and Kuntī, when the latter was as yet a virgin, in a marvellous fashion, so that Kuntī's virginity was not violated. But after she had given birth to Karṇa, she was ashamed, and put the boy out on the river in a little water-tight basket. There he was found by a charioteer, who brought him up. Karṇa is therefore really an elder brother to the Pāṇḍavas. Kṛṣṇa refers to this, and tries to persuade him to seize the throne and to appoint his younger brother Yudhiṣṭhira as his successor, as the Pāṇḍavas would agree to this. Karṇa, however, refuses to listen to such treachery to his friend Duryodhana; and when Kuntī, supported by Sūrya himself, tries in similar fashion to persuade him to go over to the side of the Pāṇḍavas, Karṇa only answers her in hard words: he says that she has never been a good mother to him, and that he does not now want to be her son.

Kṛṣṇa therefore returns to the Pāṇḍavas with his mission unaccomplished, and reports on his vain attempts to establish peace. A wild battle-cry is raised when Kṛṣṇa relates that there was even an attempt to take him prisoner. Both sides now actively prepare for war. The Pāṇḍavas choose Dhṛṣṭadyumna, son of King Drupada, as their field-marshal, and the Kauravas choose Bhīṣma. The ranks for the battle are drawn up and arranged. Bhīṣma enumerates the heroes to Duryodhana as chariot fighters according to their rank; he places Karṇa lower than all the other heroes, therefore offering him deadly insult. Karṇa swears that he will not participate in the fight until Bhīṣma has fallen. Then Bhīṣma enumerates the principal heroes of the Pāṇḍavas, and declares that he is willing to fight with all of them, except with *Śikhaṇḍin.* The latter had come into the world as a maiden, the daughter of Drupada, and had only been transformed into a man later, when a yakṣa exchanged sexes with her.[1] Bhīṣma still regards this warrior as a woman, and he will not fight with a woman.

When the preparations for war have been completed, *Ulūka*, the son of a gambler, is sent to the camp of the Pāṇḍavas by the Kauravas with a declaration of war in the form of insulting speeches. He is sent back by the Pāṇḍavas with no less insulting and defiant words. Thereupon the two hosts march to Kurukṣetra.

The great eighteen day's fight.[2]

The two hosts range themselves with their auxiliaries on either side of the great Kuru field. Watchwords and signs are determined, by which friend can be distinguished from foe. Then certain covenants are agreed on among the combatants: only opponents of equal birth and bearing the same kind of arms are to fight each other; chariot-fighters are to fight only chariot-fighters, warriors on elephants only warriors on elephants, riders with riders, and foot-soldiers with foot-soldiers; no one is to fight without first having challenged his opponent to fight; those who have surrendered, or who are hors de combat, also the fugitives, are not to be killed; drivers, beasts of burden, armour-bearers and musicians are also to be spared.

Before the beginning of the battle, the saint Vyāsa appears and bestows on *Sañjaya*, King Dhṛtarāṣṭra's charioteer, the gift of being able to see everything that takes place on the field of battle. He also makes him invulnerable, so that he may be able to report daily to the old, blind king. The descriptions of the battle, which now follow, are put in the mouth of Sañjaya as an eye-witness, and this lends them a most realistic vividness.[3]

---

1) On this and similar changes of sex in fairy-tale literature *cf.* Th. *Benfey,* "Das Pantschatantra," I, pp. 41 ff.

2) The *sixth* book (*Bhīṣmaparvan*) begins here and ends with the fall of the leader Bhīṣma.

3) Similarly the Langobardian poets frequently resort to the artifice "of observing the progress of the battle through the eyes of a scout who is set on an eminence, and then

The venerable *Bhīṣma*, the great-uncle of the Kauravas as well as of the Pāṇḍavas, commands the Kaurava armies during the first ten days of the battle. In fiery speech he exhorts the warriors to fight bravely: "The great gate of heaven stands wide open to-day, O warriors! Enter in by this gate to the world of Indra and of Brahman!...It is not right for a warrior to die at home of a disease; the eternal duty of the warrior is to seek death in the fight."[1] Thus they go forth courageously to battle, and brilliantly adorned with the shining armour and weapons, the two hosts face each other.

Thundering war-cries and loud battle music give the signal for the commencement of the fight. Kauravas and Pāṇḍavas now meet in terrible conflict, without regard for relationship, for the father knows not the son, nor the brother his brother, the uncle knows not his sister's son, nor the friend his friend. The elephants cause dreadful devastation, and there is bloody slaughter. Now it is this, now that hero who is seen engaged in single combat; victory is now with the Pāṇḍavas, now with the Kauravas. But when night falls, the combatants retire, and it is not until the next morning that the armies are drawn up again in fresh battle array, and the fight begins anew. Bhīṣma and Arjuna encounter each other repeatedly, and both of them fight so bravely that gods and demons watch the conflict in astonishment. But every time that things go badly for the Kauravas, Duryodhana reproaches Bhīṣma for showing too much regard whilst fighting against the Pāṇḍavas; and when the Pāṇḍavas suffer losses, Kṛṣṇa reproaches Arjuna for not shooting direct at Bhīṣma. Many of Duryodhana's brothers have already fallen in the fight. Now Duryodhana again blames Bhīṣma for showing too much mercy to the Pāṇḍavas. He is to defeat the foe, or else let Karṇa take command. Overwhelmed by pain and anger, Bhīṣma promises to fight mercilessly next day against all, with the sole exception of Śikhaṇḍin, who had once been a woman. "Sleep in peace, O son of Gāndhārī," says he (VI, 99, 23), "I shall gain a great victory to-morrow, which shall be spoken of, as long as the world endures." The Pāṇḍavas do, indeed, suffer heavy losses on the ninth day of the battle. Bhīṣma rages in the host of the foe like the god of death, whilst

---

reports what he has seen; by this means the artist avoids a tedious description, and has the twofold advantage of being in a position to limit himself to the main incidents, and of thrilling his hearers to a greater degree." (R. *Koegel*, Geschichte der deutschen Litteratur, I, 1, Strassburg 1894, p. 120.)

[1]) VI, 17, 8 ff.

Arjuna, who still reveres Bhīṣma as his "grandfather,"[1] shows too much consideration in fighting. When Kṛṣṇa observes this, he rushes himself upon Bhīṣma to kill him, but Arjuna holds him back forcibly, reminding him of his oath not to fight. Put to wild flight by Bhīṣma, the Pāṇḍava warriors return to their camp at nightfall.

The Pāṇḍavas use the night for a council of war. As they know that Bhīṣma will not fight against Śikhaṇḍin, they decide[2] to place the latter in the van the next day; but Arjuna is to be concealed behind Sikhaṇḍin, and direct his arrows against Bhīṣma. It is only unwillingly that Arjuna agrees to this treachery, and he remembers with pain and shame that, as a boy, he had played on Bhīṣma's lap and called him "daddy." Kṛṣṇa, however, succeeds in persuading him that only he can conquer Bhīṣma, and it is only by killing the mighty opponent that he will fulfil his warrior's duty.

Thus dawn breaks on the tenth day of the battle, and Śikhaṇḍin is placed in the van by the Pāṇḍavas, while the Kauravas advance with Bhīṣma at their head. All day long the conflict rages between the Pāṇḍavas and the Kauravas around Bhīṣma. Thousands and thousands sink to the ground on both sides. At last Śikhaṇḍin, behind whom Arjuna is concealed, succeeds in coming up with Bhīṣma. The latter smilingly awaits Śikhaṇḍin's arrows, without defending himself against him. But however violently the latter aims at Bhīṣma, the arrows do not hurt him. But soon Arjuna, hidden behind Śikhaṇḍin, begins to shower arrow upon arrow on the venerable hero. And Bhīṣma, turning to Duśśāsana who is fighting beside him, says: "*These* arrows, which are completely destroying my life-spirits like messengers of Yama, are not Śikhaṇḍin's arrows; these arrows, which penetrate into my limbs like raging, writhing serpents distended with venom, are not Śikhaṇḍin's arrows, they are shot by *Arjuna*."[3] Once more he pulls himself together, and hurls an arrow at Arjuna,

---

[1]) The *great-uncle* Bhīṣma is usually called thus by the sons of Pāṇḍu.

[2]) In the old poem it was probably *Kṛṣṇa* who gave this advice. The version given in our present "Mahābhārata" is simply absurd. The sons of Pāṇḍu, we are told, betake themselves at night time to Bhīṣma in the hostile camp, and ask him quite naively how they can best kill him. Bhīṣma *himself* then advises them to place Śikhaṇḍin opposite him, and to let Arjuna fight behind him. So it is narrated at the beginning of Canto VI, 107; in the middle of the same Canto we have the beautiful speeches in which Arjuna, full of tenderness, lets his thoughts dwell on his "grandfather" Bhīṣma, who had rocked him on his knees as a child; and at the end of the same Canto it is the same Arjuna who comes forward with the plan of killing Bhīṣma in so unfair a manner. *Cf.* Ad. *Holtzmann*, "Das Mahābhārata," II, 172 f.

[3]) VI, 119, 63 f.

which the latter catches and shivers into three pieces. Then he takes his sword and shield to defend himself, but Arjuna smashes his shield into a hundred pieces. Then Yudhiṣṭhira orders his people to attack Bhīṣma, and the Pāṇḍavas rush from all sides on the warrior who is standing alone, until, just before sunset, bleeding from innumerable wounds, he falls headlong from his chariot.[1] And there are so many arrows sticking in his body on all sides that he does not touch the ground in his fall, but rests on a bed of arrows.

Loud is the jubilation among the Pāṇḍavas, but boundless the lamentation in the camp of the Kauravas. It is agreed to call a truce in honour of the fallen hero, who had been so closely related to both the belligerent parties. And Pāṇḍavas as well as Kauravas stand around the dying hero, filled with admiration and sorrow. He greets the warriors, and tries to speak to them. The head of the dying man hangs feebly down. He begs for a cushion. They hasten to bring fine cushions, but he waves them aside smilingly. Then Arjuna takes three arrows from his quiver and supports Bhīṣma's head on them.

Bhīṣma declares contentedly that this is what he wanted, and that this is a fitting bed for a hero. The dying hero exhorts Duryodhana in impressive words to conclude peace: "Let this battle end with my death, O my son," he says. "Make peace with the Pāṇḍavas." But like a man sick unto death who refuses medicine, Duryodhana refuses the wise counsel of Bhīṣma.

The defiant, but noble Karṇa also approaches to pay his respect to the dying hero. With dim eyes, the aged chief embraces him with *one* hand and exhorts him also to make peace with the Pāṇḍavas, the more so as, being the son of Kuntī, he is their brother. But Karṇa declares that he must remain faithful to Duryodhana and do his duty as a warrior in the fight against the Pāṇḍavas. He says that he cannot do otherwise. Reconciled, Bhīṣma gives the brave warrior permission to fight, though it is

---

[1]) The foolish tale (VI, 116) in which Bhīṣma explains to Yudhiṣṭhira in the midst of the battle that he is weary of life, whereupon the latter, with cheap courage, exhorts his men to fight against the hero, is just as much in contradiction with this description (VI, 120, 58 ff.) as the childish story (VI, 120, 32 ff.) which tells how Vasus (divine beings) and Ṛṣis appear in the sky and approve of Bhīṣma's determination to die. These are later interpolations, which pursue the two-fold aim of whitewashing the Pāṇḍavas and making Bhīṣma himself into a demi-god. In the old poem Bhīṣma was surely only a mighty hero, whom the Pāṇḍavas brought low in an unchivalrous manner. But the story of VI. 116, is known in the "Dūtaghaṭotkaca" (v. 19), ascribed to Bhāsa.

truly painful to him that all his efforts towards peace have been in vain.[1]

Now that Bhīṣma has fallen, Karṇa again participates in the battle, and at his suggestion the old teacher Droṇa is consecrated as commander-in-chief.[2] The fight is carried on under his command from the eleventh till the fifteenth day.

On the thirteenth day of the battle there is a sad event for the Pāṇḍavas. The youthful, but valiant son of Arjuna, Abhimanyu, ventures too far into the ranks of the enemy, is separated from his protectors by the Sindhu king Jayadratha, and is killed by Duśśāsana's son. Arjuna swears to take a terrible revenge on the murderer of his son, meaning Jayadratha. So the principal event of the fourteenth day of the battle is the combat between Arjuna and Jayadratha, which drags on all day, and ends in the death of the latter. As Arjuna swore, he is killed before sundown. At the same time Bhīma has been raging in the Kaurava army, killing many of Dhṛtarāṣṭra's sons.

But on this day the fight is not interrupted as usual when the sun goes down. The combatants on both sides are so embittered that they can brook no interval, in spite of the approaching darkness. They fight on, by the light of torches and lamps. Individual heroes perform astounding feats. But Karṇa bears down especially hard on the Pāṇḍavas, and on Kṛṣṇa's advice the rākṣasa Ghaṭotkaca is sent out against Karṇa. The hero wrestles manfully with the giant monster, and the rākṣasa does fearful damage in the Kaurava host, until he is at last killed by Karṇa. But even in his very fall the giant Ghaṭotkaca tears an entire army of the Kauravas to the ground and crushes it. The Pāṇḍavas are very sorrowful

[1]) In the old poem Bhīṣma surely did not live longer after his downfall than was necessary to address a few words to Duryodhana and Karṇa. Our Mahābhārata relates the curious story that Bhīṣma fell in the sun's southerly course, *i.e.* in the half-year before the winter solstice, but postponed his death until the time of the sun's northerly course (*uttarāyaṇa*) *i.e.* the half-year before the summer solstice. The Upaniṣads teach that the soul, which traverses along the path of the gods to the world of Brahman, must pass the *uttarāyaṇa* (Chānd. Up. V, 10, 1; Bṛh. Up. VI, 2, 15). Out of this the theologians have derived the rule that a saint or yogin, who desires to be united with the Brahman, must die in the *uttarāyaṇa*. (Thus Bhagavad-gītā, VIII, 24.) The philosopher Śaṅkara (on Vedānta-sūtra IV, 2, 20 f.) already speaks of the fact that Bhīṣma had chosen the uttarāyaṇa for his death. At that time therefore, (8th century A.D.) the story of Bhīṣma's death must already have been related as in our present Mahābhārata.

[2]) The battle under the leadership of Droṇa forms the contents of the *seventh* book (*Droṇaparvan*).

at the death of Bhīma's son Ghaṭotkaca, only Kṛṣṇa rejoices; for the fact is that Karṇa had used the spear given him by Indra, which he had saved up for Arjuna,[1] against the rākṣasa. This was the very thing that Kṛṣṇa had intended.

The fight rages on, until the warriors of both sides are overpowered by sleep. It is only with difficulty that the most conscientious of the warriors keep up. Many of them, weary and drowsy, drop on their elephants, chariots and horses, whilst others, blinded by sleep, reel about and even slay their own friends. Then Arjuna the warrior takes pity, and in a resounding voice gives the combatants permission to devote some time to sleep. The foes, too, joyfully welcome this proposal, and both gods and men bless Arjuna for these words. And in the midst of the field of battle, steeds, elephants and warriors lie down to slumber.

(The following literal prose translation of a few verses can only give a feeble impression of the poetic beauty of the nocturnal scene here described; the style recalls in some places the lyrics of a Kālidāsa.[2])

"Then, overpowered by sleep, all the great chariot-fighters grew silent. And they lay down, some on their steeds' backs, others in the body of their chariots, yet others on the necks of their elephants, and many others stretched themselves on the ground. With their weapons, with clubs, swords, battle-axes and lances, fully armed, they lay down to sleep, some here, others there......The elephants, lying on the ground breathing heavily, looked like mounds, over which giant snakes hissed by......And this slumbering host, lying there unconscious, in its deep repose, resembled a wondrous picture painted on the canvas by a skilful artist...Then the sublime moon appeared suddenly in the East with its ruddy beams of light...In the twinkling of an eye the earth was flooded with light, and the deep, unfathomable darkness sped swiftly away... But in the radiant moonlight this host of warriors awoke, as a grove of hundred-leaved day lotus blossoms awakens at the touch of the sun's rays. And as the tide of the ocean arises when the moon shines forth, so this sea of troops awoke at the rising of the constellation of night. But then, O King, the fight for the annihilation of the world began afresh among these people, who longed for the highest region of heaven."[3]

And the bloody strife lasts uninterrupted till the grey dawn. The fifteenth day of the battle is at hand. The sun rises in the East, and the

---

1) He might only use it once, see above p. 351.

2) Even apart from a few verses inserted by a later writer of ornate poetry.

3) VII, 185, 37 ff.

warriors of both armies dismount from their horses, elephants and chariots; gazing upwards towards the sun-god, they perform their morning devotions with folded hands. This interlude only lasts a moment, however, and the battle rages on. Two of the most excellent heroes, Kings Drupada and Virāṭa, fall by Droṇa's hand. The Pāṇḍava heroes try in vain to cut down this knight. An astonishing hand-to-hand fight between Droṇa and Arjuna, teacher and pupil, which even the celestial ones watch with admiration, leads to no result, as the pupil is not inferior to his teacher in any of his feats of arms. It is now again Kṛṣṇa who conceives a devilish trick. At his instigation, Bhīma kills an elephant which happens to answer to the name of Aśvatthāman, and then calls out loudly, approaching Droṇa, that Aśvatthāman, which is also the name of Droṇa's son, has been killed. Droṇa is frightened, but does not yet believe the report. It is only when Yudhiṣṭhira, who is famous for his love of truth, repeats the lie, at the persuasion of Kṛṣṇa, that Droṇa is compelled to believe it. Overcome with sorrow, he casts his weapons aside and stands, lost in deep meditation. This is the moment utilised by Drupada's son Dhṛṣṭadyumna to cut off the head of the eighty-five years old Droṇa. Vainly does Arjuna shout that the venerable teacher must not be slain. Dhṛṣṭadyumna has accomplished the deed, and thrown the commander-in-chief's head in the midst of the Kauravas, who, horror-sticken, take to flight. It is only now that Aśvatthāman hears the news of the death of his father, and he swears bloody vengeance on the Pañcālas and the Pāṇḍavas.

After the fall of Droṇa, *Karṇa* is chosen as commander-in-chief of the Kauravas, but he is in command for only two days.[1] On the sixteenth day of the battle, Bhīma and Aśvatthāman, Arjuna and Karṇa perform marvels of bravery, but there is no decisive result. On the morning of the seventeenth day of the battle, Karṇa demands that Śalya, king of the Madras, be given to him as his charioteer, for only then could he be a match for Arjuna, who had so excellent a charioteer in Kṛṣṇa. At first Śalya is unwilling to render service to a man of lower rank, but he finally consents on condition that he may be allowed to say what he pleases in Karṇa's presence. He then makes full use of this concession. While he is driving Karṇa's chariot, he heaps insult and scorn on the latter. It is true that Karṇa is not outdone by him: he abuses the Madras, Salya's people, in cutting words, and describes them as being false, hypocritical, addicted to drunkenness, immorality and incest. On the other hand Salya

---

[1] This fight forms the contents of the *eighth* book (*Karṇaparvan*).

tells Karṇa that the Aṅgas, over whom he rules, sell their wives and children.[1] At length Duryodhana restores the peace between the two, and they go forth to the battle.

While Arjuna seeks to get at Karṇa, Bhīma causes dreadful slaughter among the sons of Dhṛtarāṣṭra, again killing many of them. With his weighty club he hurls Duśśāsana down from his chariot, springs at him, tears open his breast and drinks his warm life-blood, as he had once sworn.[2] The foes retreat shuddering at this sight. Meanwhile Arjuna and Karṇa have come to close quarters, and a terrible duel is fought, in which even the gods take part: Indra for Arjuna, and Sūrya for Karṇa. Like two wild elephants goring each other with their tusks, the two heroes shower each other with arrows. In vain does Arjuna endeavour to bring Karṇa to earth. Then one wheel of Karṇa's chariot begins to sink into the ground.[3] Karṇa now tries to pull the chariot out, and asks Arjuna to make a break in the combat, in accordance with the rules of warfare. Kṛṣṇa, however, persuades Arjuna to have no regard to this; and Arjuna, generally a model of chivalry, kills Karṇa *treacherously*, while the latter is still busy with his chariot. A light radiates from the body of the fallen hero, and he retains his beauty even in death.

There is great joy in the camp of the Pāṇḍavas, but the Kauravas flee in fear.

It is only with much trouble that Duryodhana succeeds in assembling and inspiriting his troops for further fighting. *Śalya* is the commander-in-chief on the eighteenth day of the battle.[4] Yudhiṣṭhira is selected to undertake single combat with Śalya. After a long and fierce contest, Yudhiṣṭhira slays Śalya at about midday. The Kauravas flee. Only Duryodhana and Śakuni with a small band still offer desperate resistance. Sahadeva kills Śakuni. Arjuna and Bhīma cause fearful carnage. The host of the Kauravas is now entirely annihilated.

---

[1]) The whole of the very remarkable section (VIII, 33-45) is extremely interesting from the point of view of ethnology and the history of civilization.

[2]) See above, p. 344.

[3]) Although we already know (see above p. 356) that this happens in consequence of the treachery of Śalya, the matter is here presented as though this mishap had befallen Karṇa as the result of the curse of a Brahman whom he had offended (VIII, 42, 41 and 90, 81). The entire narrative of the fight between Arjuna and Karṇa (VIII, 86-94) has been touched up to a great extent. *Cf. Oldenberg*, Das Mahabharata, pp. 50 ff., where he says that in this instance nothing is left of the old poem, but that "a new poem was created on the old theme."

[4]) This day of battle forms the contents of the *ninth* book (*Śalyaparvan*).

Duryodhana flees alone to a pond, where he hides himself. Besides him, there are only three surviving heroes, Kṛtavarman, Kṛpa and Aśvatthāman. The sun has already set. The camp of the Kauravas lies there, empty and forsaken. The Pāṇḍavas seek the fugitive Duryodhana and at length find him. Yudhiṣṭhira challenges him to single combat. Duryodhana says that he is not prepared to fight until the following morning, and that he has fled to the pond from fatigue and not from fear. But Yudhiṣṭhira insists upon the duel being fought on the spot, and he promises him that he shall remain king, even if he kill only one of them. The duel is to be fought between Duryodhana and Bhīma. The fight with clubs is introduced by the usual duel of words. Baladeva, Kṛṣṇa's brother, who had not taken part in the battle, comes from a long distance, in order to be a spectator of the club fight. The gods, too, watch the spectacle in astonishment and admiration. As two bulls butt each other with their horns, so the two heroes rain blows on each other with their clubs. Covered with blood all over they both continue fighting. They lacerate each other with their clubs like two cats which are quarrelling over a piece of meat. They both accomplish marvels of valour, and the issue remains indecisive. Then Kṛṣṇa tells Arjuna that Bhīma will never be able to defeat Duryodhana in fair fight, for though Bhīma is the stronger fighter, Duryodhana is more skilful. But he reminds him of the words of Bhīma, when on the occasion of the insult to Draupadī,[1] the former had sworn to smash Duryodhana's thigh. Then Arjuna slaps his own left thigh, before Bhīma's eyes. Bhīma understands this hint, and whilst his opponent is taking a leap preparatory to striking, Bhīma smashes his thigh, so that he breaks down like a tree uprooted by the storm. But Baladeva, who has been watching the fight, hurls angry words at Bhīma, accusing him of fighting *dishonestly*, for in an honest club fight it is forbidden to strike one's opponent below the navel. His brother Kṛṣṇa has some difficulty in restraining him from chastising Bhīma; but in vain does Kṛṣṇa seek to persuade his brother by his sophistry that Bhīma has acted rightly. Honest Baladeva mounts his chariot in anger and drives away, promising that Bhīma shall always be known in the world as a dishonest fighter, but Duryodhana as an honest one.

Thereupon Yudhiṣṭhira sends Kṛṣṇa to Hastināpura to console and pacify Dhṛtarāṣṭra and Gāndhārī, and Kṛṣṇa performs his errand to the

---

[1] See above, p. 345.

best of his ability. The Pāṇḍavas decide to spend the night outside the camp, on the bank of a river.

No sooner do Aśvatthāman and his two companions hear the news of the fall of Duryodhana, than they hasten to the scene of the fight, and lament the hero, who lies there with his thighs smashed. But Aśvatthāman swears that he will annihilate all the Pāṇḍavas, whereupon the dying Duryodhana solemnly appoints him commander-in-chief, though it is not quite obvious os what, as there is no army left.

The nocturnal slaughter in the camp of the Pāṇḍavas.[1]

The three surviving Kaurava heroes, having taken leave of Duryodhana, have repaired to the shade of a tree at some distance from the field of battle, in order to spend the night there. Kṛpa and Kṛtavarman have fallen asleep, but Aśvatthāman is kept awake by rage and thirst for revenge. Then he sees a flock of crows nestling in the branches of the tree beneath which they are resting, and how suddenly, in the middle of the night, a dreadful-looking owl comes along and kills all the sleeping birds.[2] This sight suggests to him the idea of falling upon his foes in their sleep and murdering them. He awakens the two other heroes, and tells them of his plan. Kṛpa seeks to dissuade him, as it is wrong to fall upon the sleeping and the defenceless. Aśvatthāman, however, retorts that the Pāṇḍavas have long ago "broken the bridge of right in a hundred fragments," that they need now only obey the dictates of revenge, and that no man living shall prevent him from carrying out his intention. "I shall kill the Pañcālas, the murderers of my father, in the sleep-time of night, even though I be reborn as a worm or as a winged insect for the deed!"[3] With this resolve, he mounts his chariot and drives to the hostile camp. Like a thief he creeps in, whilst the two other heroes keep guard at the gate of the camp, so as to kill any who might attempt flight. He breaks into the tent of Dhṛṣṭadyumna (who had killed his father) awakens him with a kick, and strangles him like a head of cattle. Then he passes like the god of death from tent to tent, from bed to bed, and murders without mercy all the sleeping and drowsy heroes, one after another, including the five sons of Draupadī, and Śikhaṇḍin. Before

[1]) This forms the contents of the *tenth* book (*Sauptikaparvan*).

[2]) *Cf.* with this scene Th. *Benfey*, Das Pantschatantra 1, pp 336 ff

[3]) X, 5, 18-27.

midnight all the warriors of the hostile army are dead. Thousands are wallowing in their gore. Rākṣasas and Piśācas, the flesh-eating demons who swarm in the night, come prowling into the camp in their multitudes, to feast on the flesh and blood of the murdered. When morning light appears, deathly stillness again reigns supreme far and wide over the camp.

But the three heroes hasten to the spot where the dying Duryodhana still lies, so as to tell him the news of the slaughter of the hostile warriors. When Duryodhana has heard what to him are glad tidings, he gives up the spirit gratefully and joyfully.

In the meantime Dhṛṣṭadyumna's charioteer, the only survivor, has secretly informed the Pāṇḍavas of the terrible news that their and Drupada's sons have been murdered and the entire host annihilated. Yudhiṣṭhira loses consciousness, and is only supported at some pains by his brothers. Then he sends for Draupadī and the other women of the family. He goes to the camp, and almost breaks down at the sight which meets his eyes. Then Draupadī approaches, and in her overwhelming sorrow for her murdered sons and brothers, she congratulates her husband Yudhiṣṭhira on his splendid victory in words of bitterest irony. But as boundless as her mourning is her hatred for the murderer Aśvatthāman, and she refuses to take nourishment until this fearful deed be avenged.

Whether and how, in the original epic, the deed of Aśvatthāman was avenged, is no longer evident from our Mahābhārata, owing to insertions and recastings. The following is related in a rather unintelligible and confused manner:

Bhīma pursues Aśvatthāman and fights with him, but really gets the worst of it. At all events he does not kill him, but Aśvatthāman voluntarily gives him a jewel desired by Draupadī, which has grown on his head. (There was never any previous mention of this remarkable head-ornament.) He is, moreover, in possession of a wonderful weapon, with which he destroy- the last scion of the Kuru race, who is still lying in the womb of Uttarā, Arjuna's daughter-in-law, as an embryo; for this reason Uttarā later on gives birth to a dead child, which is, however, revived by Kṛṣṇa. This is *Parikṣit,* the father of that *Janamejaya,* at whose snake-sacrifice the Mahābhārata is supposed to have been first recited. But Kṛṣṇa pronounces a curse on Aśvatthāman, condemning him to wander about the world for three thousand years—a kind of

Ahasuerus—alone, avoided by all human creatures, spreading the odour of blood and festering discharge, and laden with all diseases.

It is difficult to say whether any of all this belongs to the old poem. Certainly the lament for the dead still belonged to it.

The women's lament for the dead.[1]

In vain do Sañjaya and Vidura endeavour to console the old, blind King Dhṛtarāṣṭra in his unspeakable grief. He breaks down again and again, and at length Vyāsa also comes to give him consolation. The funeral ceremonies for the dead must now, however, be performed. The king therefore sends for his consort Gāndhārī and the other ladies of the court, and, lamenting loudly, they wend their way out of the city towards the field of battle. On the way they meet the three surviving Kaurava heroes, who tell them of the terrible carnage which they have made in the night in the hostile camp. They do not stay, however, but make good their escape, as they fear the vengeance of the Pāṇḍavas. Soon afterwards, indeed, the five sons of Pāṇḍu come along with Kṛṣṇa, and fall in with the procession of the mourners. After some difficulty, Kṛṣṇa succeeds in effecting some kind of reconciliation between the Pāṇḍavas and the aged king and queen, though it is very difficult for Gāndhārī to forgive Bhīma who has not left alive a single one of her hundred sons. But Draupadī, too, has lost all her sons, and community of grief contributes towards the reconciliation.

Here follows the *Lament of Gāndhārī*, which is one of the most beautiful parts of the whole epic, as a masterpiece of elegiac poetry, as well as for the clear descriptions of the battlefield, recalling the pictures of a Wereschagin. The whole scene becomes so much the more impressive, owing to the fact that the poet does not himself tell the story, but lets the aged mother of heroes recount what she sees with her own eyes.[2]

---

[1]) It forms the contents of the *eleventh* book (*Strīparvan*).

[2]) Although it is expressly stated (XI, 16,10 f.) that Dhṛtarāṣṭra and the women have arrived at Kurukṣetra and see the bloody battle-field before them, yet it is related

The procession of the mourners reaches the battlefield. Awful is the sight of the mangled corpses, around which birds of prey, jackals and flesh-eating demons swarm, whilst the mothers and wives of the fallen heroes wander about, lamenting, among the corpses. All this is seen by Gāndhārī who begins her lament addressed to Kṛṣṇa. She also espies Duryodhana, and painfully remembers how he had said farewell to her on the eve of the battle. "He, whom once lovely women cooled with their fans, is now fanned only by the birds of prey with their wings." But still more than at the sight of her valiant son, at the sight of all her hundred sons lying there in the dust but nevertheless assured of a place in heaven, she is moved with compassion toward her daughters-in-law who are running hither and thither among the corpses of their husbands and sons, in wild despair, and with their hair flying. She sees her intelligent son Vikarṇa lying, with dismembered limbs, in the midst of slain elephants—"as when the moon is surrounded by dark clouds in the autumnal sky." Then she sees the youthful Abhimanyu, Arjuna's son, whose beauty even death has not been able entirely to destroy. His unfortunate young wife draws near to him, strokes him, removes his heavy armour, binds his bloody curls together, lays his head on her lap, and speaks to the dead hero in the tenderest words: she begs him to remember her sometimes, when he is taking delight in beautiful heavenly women in the divine regions. Then her gaze rests on Karṇa, the hero who had once been so much feared by all, and who now lies there like a tree brought low by the storm. Then she sees her son-in-law, the Sindhu king Jayadratha, whose wives vainly strive to chase the greedy birds of prey from the corpse, whilst her own daughter Duśśalā is seeking her husband's head amid lamentations. There, again, she sees Śalya, the Madra king, whose tongue is just being eaten by vultures, while his lamenting wives sit around him, "like passionate female elephants around an elephant that has sunk into the mire." She sees Bhīṣma, too, reposing on his bed of arrows—"this sun among men goes to his rest, as the sun sets in the sky." And after she has lamented also for Droṇa and Drupada and all the great heroes who have fallen, she turns with angry words to Kṛṣṇa and reproaches him with not having prevented

at the beginning of the canto that Gāndhārī, by her pious austerities, has received divine vision by the mercy of Vyāsa, enabling her to survey the battle-field from a great distance. This is certainly a feature which is foreign to the old poem, the clumsy idea of a later pedant.

the annihilation of the Pāṇḍavas and the Kauravas. And she pronounces a curse upon him, that after thirty-six years he shall cause the destruction of his own race, and that he himself shall perish miserably in the wilderness.

Then Yudhiṣṭhira gives orders for the performance of the funeral ceremonies for all the fallen. Pyres are erected and butter and oil are poured over them. Sweet-scented woods and costly silk garments, broken chariots and weapons are burned with the corpses. After the rites and lamentations for the dead have been completed, at which the strangers and the friendless are not forgotten, they all repair to the bank of the Ganges, in order to offer the usual libations for the dead.

This is probably the point at which the old poem ended. Our Mahābhārata continues the story of the heroes.

The horse-sacrifice.[1]

It is only on the occasion of the offering of the gifts to the departed, that Kuntī first tells her son Yudhiṣṭhira that Karṇa, too, was one of her sons, and asks him to offer the libation for Karṇa as his eldest brother. Yudhiṣṭhira is now sad, not only at having caused the downfall of so many relatives and friends, but at having been guilty even of fratricide to Karṇa. Inconsolable, he announces his intention of going into the forest and becoming an ascetic. In vain do his brothers and Kṛṣṇa endeavour to persuade him to take over the reins of government—he insists upon his resolve, until at length Vyāsa comes and advises him to offer a horse-sacrifice, thereby purging himself of all his sins. Yudhiṣṭhira acts on this advice. Arrangements are made for the great sacrifice. As required by the ritual, the sacrificial horse is let loose, to wander about at will for one year. Arjuna is selected to accompany and protect the horse. He follows the horse from land to land throughout the world. In these wanderings he has to fight many a battle, for everywhere he encounters tribes whose warriors have been defeated in the Kuru battle, and which take up a hostile attitude towards him. He performs feats of great heroism, but avoids unnecessary bloodshed as far as possible, and invites all the defeated kings to the horse-sacrifice. At the end of a year he returns with the

[1]) This forms the contents of the *fourteenth* book (*Aśvamedhikaparvan*). Regarding Books XII and XIII see below.

sacrificial horse to Hastināpura, where he is received amid great rejoicings. Now the sacrificial feast begins, and all the invited kings flock in. The horse is killed with exact observance of all the sacrificial requirements and is sacrificed in the fire. The Pāṇḍavas breathe the smoke of the burnt marrow, whereby all their sins are made as nought. After the completion of the sacrifice, Yudhiṣṭhira presents Vyāsa with "the whole earth." The latter generously returns the gift to him, and exhorts him to give the priests much gold. After Yudhiṣṭhira has accordingly given away vast quantities of gold to the priests, he is free of his sins, and thenceforward rules his kingdom as a good and pious king.

Dhṛtarāṣṭra's end.

The old king Dhṛtarāṣṭra,[1] as head of the family, is still consulted on all matters, and he and his consort Gāndhārī are always held in high esteem. Thus the old king still lives for fifteen years at the court of Yudhiṣṭhira in the best understanding with the Pāṇḍavas, which is only spoilt to some extent by the king's relation to Bhīma. The king could never find it in his heart entirely to forgive this man who had robbed him of all his sons, and the defiant Bhīma hurt his aged uncle's feelings only too often by his unseemly speech. Thus after fifteen years the aged king resolved to retire into the forest as a hermit. Yudhiṣṭhira consented only unwillingly. But Kṛṣṇa says that it has always been the custom for pious kings to end their days either as a warrior on the field of battle or else as a hermit in the forest. Thus Dhṛtarāṣṭra and Gāndhārī go forth into the forest, and Kuntī, Sañjaya and Vidura join them. After a time the Pāṇḍavas visit their relatives in the forest hermitage, just as the sage Vidura is dying. Two years later the Pāṇḍavas receive the news that Dhṛtarāṣṭra, Gāndhārī and Kuntī have lost their lives in a forest fire, whilst Sañjaya has gone to the Himālayas.

The destruction of Kṛṣṇa and his race.[2]

Thirty-six years after the great battle in the Kuru field the Pāṇḍavas receive the sad news that Gāndhārī's curse[3] has come true, and that Kṛṣṇa has perished with all his race. At a drinking bout the chiefs of

---

[1]) Here begins the *fifteenth* book (*Āśramavāsikaparvan*).

[2]) Related in the *sixteenth* book (*Mausalaparvan*).

[3]) See above, p. 372.

two clans fall to quarrelling, in which they are soon joined by others. A general club fight ensues, Kṛṣṇa transforming sedges into clubs, and the men of the Yādava clans kill each other. Kṛṣṇa looks around for his brother Baladeva, but is just in time to witness his dying hour. A white snake runs out of Baladeva's mouth, and hastens to the ocean,[1] where it is received by the most famous snake demons. Then Kṛṣṇa lies down in the desolate forest, and becomes absorbed in deep meditation. Here he is mistaken by a hunter named Jarā (*i.e.* "Old Age") for an antelope, and is shot and killed by an arrow in the sole of his foot, the only spot at which he is vulnerable.

The last journey of the Pāṇḍavas.

The Pāṇḍavas are inconsolable for the death of their faithful friend, and soon afterwards they resolve to go forth upon their last journey.[2] Yudhiṣṭhira appoints Parikṣit as king, and says farewell to his subjects. Then the five brothers and their wife Draupadī, all clothed in garments of bast, and accompanied only by a dog, wander forth to the Himālayas which they ascend, and reach the divine mountain Meru. On the way to heaven Draupadī first falls dead, then Sahadeva, next Nakula, soon afterwards Arjuna, and lastly Bhīma. Then Indra comes driving in his celestial chariot, to fetch Yudhiṣṭhira to heaven.[3] The latter, however, does not wish to accompany him, as he does not desire to dwell in heaven without his brothers. Then Indra promises him that he shall see his brothers as well as Draupadī again in heaven. But Yudhiṣṭhira also insists upon his dog entering heaven as well, and this Indra will not allow under any circumstances. At length the dog reveals himself as the god Dharma, and evinces his great satisfaction at Yudhiṣṭhira's faithfulness. Thus they reach heaven, but Yudhiṣṭhira by no means wants to stay there,

---

[1]) A beautiful example of the idea of the soul assuming the form of a snake, prevalent among so many peoples. In the German legend, too, of King Guntram, the soul, in the form of a snake, issues *out of the mouth* of the sleeping king into a hill.

[2]) With this begins the *seventeenth* book (*Mahāprasthānikaparvan*).

[3]) In an essay "Points de contact entre Mahâbhârata et le Shâh-nâmah" JA. s. 8 t. X, 1887, pp. 38 ff., *cf.* JBRAS 17, Proceed, pp. ii ff.) J. *Darmesteter* has compared Yudhiṣṭhira's ascent to heaven with the disappearance of *Kai Khosru* in the Persian heroic epic. Kai Khosru, too, climbs a high mountain and reaches heaven in the flesh. Like Yudhiṣṭhira's brothers, the Pehlevans (heroes) accompanying Kai Khosru, also perish on the way. Nevertheless the two episodes are fundamentally so different that I cannot believe in any connection (*Cf.* also *Barth* in RHR t. 19, 1889, pp. 162 ff.)

as he does not see either his brothers or Draupadī. Now when he even[1] sees Duryodhana seated upon a heavenly throne, and honoured by all, he has had enough of heaven, and demands to be conducted to the worlds where his brothers and heroes like Karṇa are. Then the gods give him a messenger to accompany him to hell, where he sees the terrible tortures of the damned. He is already turning away from this awful sight, when he hears voices imploring him to stay, as a beneficent breath of air emanates from him. Full of pity he asks the tortured souls who they are, and he is informed that they are his brothers and friends. Then he is seized by pain and anger at the injustice of Fate, and he sends the messenger back to the gods to tell them that he will not go to heaven, but will remain in hell. But soon the gods come down to him, and Indra explains to him that those who have sinned most are sent first to heaven and then to hell, whereas those who have only committed a few sins, atone for these rapidly in hell, and then enjoy eternal blessedness in heaven. He himself had to visit hell first, owing to his having deceived Droṇa, and in the same way his brothers and friends had to be purged of their sins in hell. Soon, however, all the horror of hell vanishes ; they all find themselves in heaven, and assume the form of gods.[2]

This principal story, which has here been briefly sketched, constitutes not quite one-half of the eighteen books of the Mahābhārata.[3] The other half consists of those parts of the work, partly narrative and partly didactic, which have no bearing, or only a very slight one, on the conflict of the Kauravas and the Pāṇḍavas. An account of this will be given in the following chapters.

Ancient Heroic Poetry in the Mahābhārata.

Among the tasks of the ancient Indian bards was also that of tracing the genealogical trees of the kings, or, if

---

[1] Here begins the *eighteenth* (last) book (*Svargārohaṇaparvan*).

[2] *Cf.* with this episode the legend of Vipaścit in the Mārkaṇḍeya Purāṇa (below) and see also L *Scherman*, Materialien zur Geschichte der indischen Visionslitteratur, Leipzig, 1892, pp. 48 ff.

[3] The eighteen parvans or books of the Mahābhārata contain together 2,109 Adhyāyas or cantos (in the Bombay edition) : of these about 1,000 deal with the principal narrative.

necessary, of inventing them. Genealogical verses (anuvaṃśa-śloka) therefore, form an essential part of the old heroic poetry. And the first book of the Mahābhārata contains a whole section, entitled Sambhavaparvan or "section of the origins," in which the genealogy of the heroes is traced back to their first ancestors who were descended from the gods, and many interesting legends about these old kings of ancient times are related. Of course, among these ancestors of the Kauravas and Pāṇḍavas belonging to the Bhārata race, that *Bharata* is not missing, from whom the Mahābhārata itself has derived its name. Bharata is the son of King *Duṣyanta* and of *Śakuntalā*, so famous from the drama of Kālidāsa, and whose story is also told in the Sambhavaparvan.

Unfortunately, however, this very *Śakuntalā episode* of the Mahābhārata [1] has been handed down to us in a much deteriorated and probably also mutilated, form which seems to have retained only a few features of the old heroic poem and could hardly have formed the prototype of Kālidāsa's poem. The descriptions of the forest, the chase and the hermitages, are spun out not to "epic" but to pedantic length partly after the pattern of the later ornate poetry. The story itself is unattractive and has no artistic basis. The fact that Śakuntalā is not acknowledged by the king is not accounted for, as in Kālidāsa's play, by a curse and the story of the lost ring, but by the king's desire to remove every doubt, on the part of his courtiers, as to the genuineness of the royal birth of his son. Therefore he provokes as it were, a divine judgment. He pretends not to know Śakuntalā, and refuses to

---

[1] I, 68-75. An English translation of the Śakuntalā episode by Charles *Wilkins* appeared as early as 1794 in A. Dalrymple's Oriental Repertory and separately, (London, 1795); a French translation by A. *Chézy* as an appendix to his edition of Kālidāsa's Śakuntalā drama (Paris, 1830); German translations by B. *Hirzel* (1833), A. F. Graf *von Schack* (1877, Stimmen vom Ganges, pp. 32 ff.), J. J. *Meyer*, Das Weib im altindischen Epos, pp. 68 ff., and W. *Porzig* (Indische Erzähler, Vol. 12, Leipzig 1923, pp. 50 ff.). The Kumbhakonam edition has enlarged and spoiled the traditional text still more, S. M. *Winternitz*, Ind. Ant. 1898, p. 136; J. J. *Meyer*, l.c., p. 76 note, and *Porzig*, l.c., pp. 123 ff.

acknowledge his son, until a heavenly voice announces, before the whole court, that Sakuntalā has spoken the truth and that her child is really the son of King Duṣyanta. Here we meet the two verses which we know for certain belong to the oldest part of the Śakuntalā poem and are taken from the old bard poetry.[1]

"The mother is but the leathern bag (for the preservation of the seed), it is to the father that the child belongs; the son, whom he has begotten, is himself.[2] Cherish[3] thy son, Duṣyanta, do not scorn Śakuntalā!

A son, O King, who begets offspring again, leads (the fathers) up (to heaven) out of Yama's abode. And thou art the creator of this seed, Śakuntalā has spoken the truth."

There are very probably also many old and genuine verses preserved in the dialogue between Śakuntalā, who stands up for her rights and those of her son, and the king who does not wish to acknowledge her. In any case a dialogue of this kind must have formed one of the principal parts of the old narrative, and moralising maxims, like the following beautiful verse, may have occurred in Śakuntalā's speech:

"None sees me": so when bent on sin,
The fool imagines, madly bold;
For gods his evil deeds behold;
The soul, too, sees the man within."[4]

Śakuntalā also probably spoke of the happiness and blessing which a son brings to his father, as in the verses:

"He himself has begotten himself again as a son,[5] thus say the wise ones. Therefore shall a man look upon his wife, the mother of his sons, as upon his own mother."

---

[1]) This is proved by their repeated occurrence, for we find the same verses (I, 74,109 f.) quoted again as "genealogical verses" (anuvaṃśaślokau) in the Mahābhārata (I, 95, 29 f), and they recur in the Harivaṃśa (32, 10 ff.), Viṣṇu-Purāṇa (IV, 19), Vāyu-Purāṇa (99, 135 f. AnSS ed.), Matsya-Purāṇa (49, 12 f. ĀnSS ed.) and Bhāgavata-Purāṇa (IX, 20, 21 f.).

[2]) *Cf.* the verses translated above, on pp. 211 f.

[3]) Because of this word "cherish" (*bhara*), the boy received the name *Bharata.*

[4]) I, 74, 17. Translated by J. *Muir*, Metrical Translations from Sanskrit Writers, p. 8.

[5]) Similarly Aitareya-Brāhmaṇa VII, 13; *cf.* above, pp. 211 f.

48

"Is there any higher blessedness than to see the little son return from play, covered with dust, and run to embrace his father's knees?"

"He has sprung from thy loins, from one soul another soul has sprung forth. Behold thy son, like a second self in a lake clear as a mirror!"[1]

Yet it is not probable that *all* the beautiful sayings which are placed in the mouth of Śakuntalā really belonged to the old heroic poem, sayings which deal with the happiness of marriage, and the duties of husband and wife, with paternal duties, and with truthfulness. Some of the verses, which refer to matrimonial laws and right of succession and which have been taken directly from the legal literature, rather indicate that Brahmanical *scholars* utilised the speeches of Śakuntalā for the purpose of bringing in as many sentences as possible on morality and law. This does not prevent our finding in these very speeches some of the most magnificent examples of Indian gnomic poetry, like the following:

"A wife is half the man, transcends
In value far all other friends.
She every earthly blessing brings,
And even redemption from her springs."

"In lonely hours, companions bright,
These charming women give delight;
Like fathers wise, in duty tried,
To virtuous acts they prompt and guide.
Whene'er we suffer pain and grief,
Like mothers kind they bring relief."

"The weary man whom toils oppress,
When travelling through life's wilderness,
Finds in his spouse a place of rest,
And there abides, refreshed and blest."[2]

Among the ancestors of the heroes of the Mahābhārata a king *Yayāti* is mentioned, whose history is also related in

---

[1]) I, 74, 47; 52; 64.

[2]) I, 74, 40, 42; 49 translated by J. *Muir*, l. c., pp. 134 f.

the "Sambhavaparvan," the section of the genealogical bard-poetry.[1] But just as the old Śakuntalā poem was utilised for the purpose of pointing Brahmanical teachings on law and morality, so also the old Yayāti legend, which seems originally to have been a kind of Titan legend, was transformed into a moral narrative, whereby it became a popular subject for ascetic poetry. However, the traces of the old heroic poetry are by no means entirely effaced; they are discernible particularly in a certain racy humour, with which the story of the two wives of the king is related. Out of the contents of the Yayāti episode only the following extract can be given:

Devayānī, daughter of the Asura priest Śukra, has been insulted by Śarmiṣṭhā, daughter of the Asura king. For this reason the priest wishes to leave the king. Now the latter, in order to appease the priest, gives his daughter to Devayānī as her handmaiden. Soon afterwards Devayānī becomes the wife of King Yayāti, who has to promise to have no intercourse with her "servant," Princess Śarmiṣṭhā. But the king breaks his promise, marries Sarmiṣṭha secretly, and begets three sons with her. Jealous Devayānī finds it out, and complains to her father Śukra. The latter pronounces a curse upon Yayāti that he shall immediately lose his youth and become old and decrepit; however, at the request of Yayāti, he tones the curse down in as much as Yayāti may transfer his old age to someone else.

Now Yayāti, after having become suddenly old and wrinkled and grey, asks his sons, one after the other, to relieve him of his old age and to give him their youth, as he has not yet enjoyed life sufficiently. None of the elder sons will agree to this exchange, whereupon they are cursed by their father. Only the youngest, Pūru, declares his willingness. He

---

[1]) The story is first told briefly in I, 75, then repeated with many details in I, 76-93. The last part of the legend, with a few additions, is then told once again in V, 120-123. The episode has been translated into German by A. *Holtzmann* (Indische Sagen), J. J. *Meyer* (Das Weib im altindischen Epos, pp. 8 ff.) and W. *Porzig* (Indische Erzähler, Vol. 12, pp. 12 ff.). On the different versions of the story in Sanskrit literature, s. Porzig, l.c., pp. 105 ff. On a mythological interpretation of the legend s. A. *Ludwig* in Sitzungsberichte der K. böhmischen Gesellschaft der Wissenschaften, Prague 1898.

relieves his father of the burden of old age and gives him his own youth in exchange. Then Yayāti rejoiced in another thousand years of the most blooming youth, and enjoyed the pleasures of life to the very full. Not only did he take delight in his two wives, but also in a heavenly nymph, the beautiful Apsaras Viśvācī ("gracious to all"). But however much he enjoyed, he was never fully satisfied. And when the thousand years had elapsed, he came to the conclusion as expressed in the following verses:

> "Truly, desire is not satisfied by the gratification of desires;
> Nay, it grows and waxes stronger, as the fire fed by sacrificial ghee.
> The earth filled with treasures, gold, cattle and women too,
> Is not enough for one man:—think on this, and seek thy soul's contentment.
> Only he who has never wrought evil to any creature,
> In thought, word or deed, only he may dwell with the Brahman.
> He who is unafraid, and who is feared by no creature,
> Who has no desires and knows no hate, only he may dwell with the Brahman." [1]

Then he returned his son Pūru his youth, took up the burden of his own old age, and after having instated Pūru on the throne, repaired to the forest, where he lived as a hermit, practising the severest austerities for a thousand years. On the strength of this he attained to heaven, where he lived for a long time, honoured by all the gods and saints. One day, however, he boasted during a conversation with Indra, and was cast out from heaven for this offence. Later on, however, he returns to heaven with his four pious grandchildren.

---

[1] I, 75, 49-52. Only the first verse recurs literally in all the other places where the Yayāti legend is related. (It also occurs in Manu II, 94.) The remaining verses are found again with variations in I, 85, 12-16, Harivaṃśa 30, 1639-1645, Viṣṇu-Purāṇa IV, 10, Bhāgavata-Purāṇa IX, 19, 13-15. But only in I, 75, 51-52 and Harivaṃśa 30, 1642 is there any talk of union with the Brahman in the sense of the Vedānta philosophy. In all other places the corresponding verses only talk of the curbing of desires as the worthy aim of the morality of asceticism, and this morality is the same for Buddhists and Jainas as for the Brahmanical and Viṣṇuite ascetics. Hence we find quite similar sayings amongst all Indian sects which practise asceticism.

The legend of Nahuṣa, the father of Yayāti, which is related in the Mahābhārata several times,[1] is also a kind of Titan legend, which ends with a fall from heaven:

Nahuṣa, a grandson of the Purūravas of Vedic fame,[2] was a mighty king, who annihilated the robber bands (dasyusaṃghātān). But he levied taxes on the ṛsis, too, and commanded them to carry him on their backs, like beasts of burden. He even overpowered the gods, and ruled the heavens for a long time in Indra's stead. He desired Indra's wife Śacī as his wife, and grew so overbearing that he yoked the divine ṛṣis to his chariot, treading on Agastya's head. Now this was a bit too much for this great saint, and he cursed Nahuṣa, with the consequence that he fell out of heaven and was obliged to live on the earth as a snake for ten thousand years.[3]

Some of the poems which have found admission into the Mahābhārata are of such proportions, and form a complete whole to such an extent, that we can speak of them as epics within the epic. Of this kind is above all the rightly famous poem of Nala and Damayantī.[4] While the Pāṇḍavas are in banishment in the forest they receive a visit from the Ṛṣi Bṛhadaśva. Yudhiṣṭhira complains to him of his own misfortune and that of his people, and asks him the question whether there has ever been a more unfortunate king than himself. Thereupon Bṛhadaśva relates the story of the unfortunate king Nala, who loses all his possessions and his kingdom in a game of dice with his brother Puṣkara, and then goes forth into the forest as an exile with his beautiful and faithful wife Damayantī; pursued and blinded still further by the wicked demon of gambling, he deserts his

[1]) First in I, 75 as an introduction to the Yayāti episode, then in greater detail in V, 11-17; in a short extract also XII, 342 and XIII, 100. A free poetical adaptation by Ad. *Holtzmann*, Indische Sagen I, pp. 9-30.

[2]) Purūravas too (*cf.* above, pp 103 f., 209 f.) was like Nahuṣa, according to the Mahābhārata (I, 75, 20 ff.) an enemy of the priests, oppressing the ṛṣis and being annihilated by their curse.

[3]) He was then redeemed by Yudhiṣṭhira (III, 179 f.), see above, p. 349.

[4]) III, 52-79: Nalopākhyāna.

faithful wife in the midst of the forest, while she lies deep in slumber, fatigued from her wanderings. The adventures of King Nala, and of Damayantī, deserted by her husband, how they wander about in the forest separated from each other, how Damayantī, after much sorrow and hardship, obtains a friendly reception from the queen-mother of Cedi, how Nala, after the snake-king Karkoṭaka has made him irrecognisable, serves King Ṛtuparṇa as charioteer and cook, until finally the husband and wife, after a long and painful separation, are reunited in love, all this is related in the touchingly simple, genuinely popular, tone of the fairy tale, which also is not lacking in humour.

Since the year 1819 when Franz Bopp first published this poem of King Nala, together with a Latin translation, it is recognised as one of the gems of Indian literature, nay more, as one of the gems of universal literature. Bopp's edition and translation of the poem was welcomed by A. W. v. Schlegel[1] with the words: "I will only say that, in my estimation, this poem can hardly be surpassed in pathos and ethos, in the enthralling force and tenderness of the sentiments. It is made expressly to attract old and young, the high-born and the lowly, the connoisseurs and those who are merely guided by instinct. Also, the fairy-tale is tremendously popular in India,......there the courageous constancy and devotion of Damayantī is equally famous as that of Penelope amongst us; and in Europe, the gathering-place of the productions of all continents and all ages, it deserves to become equally so." And indeed it has become so The German poet Friedrich Rückert, that past master in the art of translation, rendered the poem into German verse in the year 1828[2] with his incomparable talent, making it as

---

[1]) Indische Bibliothek, I, 98 f.

[2]) New editions appeared in 1838, 1845, 1862 and 1873. A very free poetical rendering was given by Ad. *Holtzmann* in his "Indische Sagen."

popular in Germany as it has become famous in England by means of Dean H. H. Milman's version.[1]

Nala Naiṣadha, the hero of the narrative, is surely no other than the Naḍa Naiṣidha, mentioned in the Satapatha-Brāhmaṇa, of whom it is there said, that "day after day he bears Yama (the god of death) to the South." He must therefore have lived at that time, and undertaken warlike expeditions towards the South. The name of the hero thus indicates high antiquity. The poem itself probably belongs among the old parts of the Mahābhārata, though not among the oldest. In any case it is free from all purāṇa-like accessories, and only the old Vedic gods, like Varuṇa and Indra, are mentioned, but not Viṣṇu or Śiva. The state of civilisation, too, described in the poem is, on the whole, quite simple and has the appearance of antiquity. On the other hand we find hardly anywhere in the oldest poetry such delicacy and so much romance in the representation of courtship and of love itself, as especially in the first cantos of the Nala poem. Only the very ancient poem of the love of Purūravas and Urvaśī allows us to suspect that love-romance was no stranger to India even in the most ancient times. But how very congenial romance is to the Indian mind in general, is proved by the enormous popularity of this poem, which has again and again been imitated by later poets, in Sanskrit as well as in modern Indian languages and dialects.[2] Few Indian poems also suit European taste so extremely well as the Nala poem. It has been translated into practically all the languages of Europe,[3] and a dramatic adaptation by A. de Gubernatis

---

[1]) Nala and Damayantī and other Poems translated from the Sanskrit into English verse, Oxford, 1835.

[2]) *Cf.* the enumeration in A. *Holtzmann*, Das Mahabharata, II, 69 ff.

[3]) A. *Holtzmann*, loc. cit., II, 73 ff. mentions translations into German, English, French, Italian, Swedish, Czech, Polish, Russian, Modern Greek and Hungarian. I will only mention the translations into English by Monier *Williams* (1860), Charles *Bruce* (1864), Edwin *Arnold* (Indian Idylls, 1883, Poetical Works, 1885); into German by E.

was even produced on the stage in Florence in 1869. And since a long time it has been the custom, at almost all Western universities, to begin the study of Sanskrit with the reading of this poem, for which purpose it is excellently adapted in language as well as contents.[1]

The Rāma[2] episode, too, is a kind of epic within an epic. But while the Nala poem (in spite of some disfiguring additions and insertions, from which indeed *no* part of the Mahābhārata is quite free) is a work of art and a valuable survival of the ancient bard-poetry, the narrative of Rāma has only a purely literary significance for the history of the second great epic of the Indians, the Rāmāyaṇa. For the Rāma episode can scarcely be regarded as anything but a rather inartistically abridged rendering of either the Rāmāyaṇa itself,[3] or of those heroic songs from which Vālmīki composed his great poem. In no case is it these oldest heroic songs of Rāma themselves, which we find in the Mahābhārata. The Rāma episode is related by the ṛṣi Mārkaṇḍeya to console Yudhiṣṭhira, who is much depressed on account of the rape of Draupadī[4]; for Rāma's wife, too, Sītā, was abducted, and was held in captivity for a long time by the demon Rāvaṇa. References to the Rāma legend are not rare in other parts

---

Lobedanz (1863), H. C. *Kellner* (in Reclams Universalbibliothek), L. *Fritze* (1914); into French by S. *Lévi* (Paris, 1920 in "Les classiques de l'orient," Paris 1920).

1) The text of the Nala story has often been published, with glossary and notes, for beginners in Sanskrit, *e g.*, by G. *Bühler* (Third Book of Sanskrit, Bombay, 2nd Ed. 1877), Monier *Williams* (London, 1879), J. *Eggeling* (London, 1913), H. C. *Kellner* (Leipzig 1885), W. *Caland* (Utrecht, 1917).

2) III, 273-290 : Rāmopākhyāna.

3) H. *Jacobi* (Das Râmâyaṇa, (Bonn, 1893), pp. 71 ff.) has given such good reasons for this assumption that it seems to me the most probable one, in spite of the objections of A. *Ludwig*, Über das Râmâyaṇa und die Beziehungen desselben zum Mahâbharata, pp. 30 ff., and *Hopkins*, The Great Epic of India, pp. 63 f. *Cf.* also A. *Weber*, Über das Rāmāyaṇa, pp. 34 ff.

4) See above, pp. 350 f. Probably this story of the rape of Draupadī is itself only a clumsy imitation of the stealing of Sītā in the Rāmāyaṇa.

of the Mahābhārata either. I point out only the meeting of Bhīma with the monkey Hanumat.[1]

A much more valuable remnant of ancient Indian bard-poetry, unfortunately preserved only as a fragment, is found in the fifth book of the Mahābhārata. It is the episode of the *hero-mother Vidulā.*[2] Kuntī sends a message by Kṛṣṇa to her sons, the Pāṇḍavas, telling them not to forget their duty as warriors,[3] and on this occasion relates how the warrior's wife Vidulā once urged her son Sañjaya on to fight. The latter was quite discouraged after a shameful defeat which he had suffered at the hands of the king of the Sindhus, and lived with his wife and his mother Vidulā in misery. Then, in extremely forceful language Vidulā reproaches him with his cowardice and inactivity, and with fiery words spurs him on to new deeds of heroism. In order to give an idea of the racy vigour of the language of this fragment of ancient heroic poetry, I give a few verses from this speech in literal prose translation: [4]

"Up, coward! Lie not there so idle, when thou hast suffered defeat, to the joy of thy foes, to the sorrow of thy friends!"

"A shallow brooklet is soon filled, the fist of a mouse is easy to fill. The coward is soon satisfied, he is contented even with little."

"Die not like a cur before thou hast at least robbed the serpent of its fangs! Be brave, though it cost thee thy life!"

"Why liest thou there like a dead man, like one who has been struck by lightning? Up, coward! Sleep not, when thou hast been defeated by the foe!"

---

[1]) Above, p. 348.

[2]) V, 133-136: Vidulāputrānuśāsana. *Cf.* H. *Jacobi*, Über ein verlorenes Heldengedicht der Sindhu-Sauvīra (in Mélanges Kern, Leyden, 1903, pp. 53 ff.). A free poetical rendering of the poem is given by J. *Muir*, Metrical Translations from Sanskrit Writers, pp. 120-133. He justly refers to the women of Rājputānā who "maintain in more recent times the character of heroism ascribed to Vidulā in this passage of the Mahābhārata. (l.c., p. 132).

[3]) See above, p. 357.

[4]) The translation by *Muir*, l.c., pp. 121 f. gives no sufficient idea of the raciness of the original.

"Flare up like a torch of tinduka wood,[1] though it be but for a moment, but smother not like a fire of chaff, just to prolong life!"

"Better flare up for a moment than smother for hours! O that a mild ass should have been born in a royal house!

"That man whose deeds do not form the subject of tales of wonder, serves but to increase the great heap, he is neither woman nor man."[2]

To all the admonitions and reproaches of his mother, the son, who is sharply characterised by his short speeches, has only the reply that he lacks the means for a victorious battle, and that, in any case, his death would not benefit her:

"Thou hast a hard, an iron heart,
And play'st no loving mother's part,—
True daughter of a warrior line;
A fierce unbending soul is thine.
To all thy Kshatriya instincts true,
Thou dost not yield to love its due;
Nor seek to guard me as thy one
Supreme delight, thine only son!
But spurr'st me on, devoid of ruth,—
As if I were an alien youth,—
To join again in hopeless strife,
And all in vain to peril life.
What worth would earth, its wealth, its joys,
Its power, its state, its glittering toys,—
What worth would life—possess for thee,
My mother, if thou hadst not me?"[3]

But his mother always answers him again with fresh exhortations, that a warrior may not know fear, and must in any case fulfil his duty as a warrior. And at last she succeeds in rousing her son, "even though he had little intelligence."

---

[1]) Tinduka, the *Diespyros embryopteris* tree.

[2]) V, 132, 8-10, 12, 15, 22.

[3]) V, 134, 1-3. Translated by J. *Muir*, l.c., pp. 127 f.

"Like a noble steed when it is chastised, the son, goaded by the shafts of his mother's words, did all she asked of him." [1]

This torso of a heroic poem is one of the few portions of the Mahābhārata which have remained almost entirely untouched by brahmanical influence. Only too often has the old bard-poetry, which was inspired by the warrior-spirit, been quite watered down in form and contents under the influence of the Brahmin scholars. Thus we find—this is one of the many instances—an "old itihāsa" quoted in the twelfth book of the Mahābhārata, which Nārada relates to Sṛñjaya, in order to console him after the death of his son. Many kings of primitive times are named, who all had to die, though they were famous heroes. But of what do the "heroic deeds" of these kings consist? They offered countless sacrifices, and what was still more important, gave enormous presents to the priests. One king, for example, gives the priests as sacrificial gift "a thousand times a thousand" maidens adorned with gold, each of whom sits on a four-horse chariot; each chariot is accompanied by a hundred elephants garlanded with gold; behind each elephant follow a thousand horses, and behind each horse a thousand cows, behind each cow a thousand goats and sheep.[2] It is often difficult to say whether they are remnants of ancient heroic poetry, spoilt through the priests' attempts at recasting, or independent brahmanical compositions.

BRAHMANICAL MYTHS AND LEGENDS IN THE MAHĀBHĀRATA.

The fact that the old Indian bard-poetry has not been preserved in its pure originality is due to the circumstance that the Brahmans took possession of the Mahābhārata. To the same circumstance, however, we are indebted for the

[1] V, 135, 12; 16.

[2] XII, 29. A similar list of ancient kings who were noted for their generosity is to be found in VII, 56-71.

preservation in the Mahābhārata not only of numerous myths of gods, and legends, important for the history of mythology and tradition, but also of some remarkable creations of Brahmanical poetic art and valuable specimens of Brahmanical wisdom.

Interesting from the point of view of mythology and tradition is the frame-story of the Snake sacrifice of Janamejaya,[1] into which there is again interwoven a tangle of stories, snake-legends, myths of the bird Garuḍa and others. But what is here called "*Snake-sacrifice*" is in reality a snake-charm, *i.e.* an exorcism for the annihilation of snakes. Janamejaya's father, Parikṣit, had been bitten to death by the snake-king Takṣaka. In order to avenge the death of his father, King Janamejaya arranges a great sacrifice,[2] at which all the snakes of the earth are compelled, by the exorcisms of the priests, to come from near and far and cast themselves into the fire. This is described in our epic with great vividness :

"The sacrificial ceremonial now began in accordance with the prescribed rules for the snake-sacrifice. Hither and thither hurried the priests, each one eagerly fulfilling his appointed task. Wrapped in black garments, their eyes inflamed by the smoke, they poured the sacrificial ghee into the blazing fire, whilst saying the incantations. They caused the hearts of

---

1) I, 3, 13-58; XV, 35. Freely rendered in German verses by A. *Holtzmann*, "Indische Sagen"; literally translated into German prose by W. *Porzig* (Indische Erzähler, Vol. 15, Leipzig, 1924). Similar legends also exist in Europe, especially in the Tyrol; *cf.* my treatise "Das Schlangenopfer des Mahābhārata (in Kulturgeschichtliches aus der Tierwelt, Festschrift des Vereins für Volkskunde und Linguistik," Prague, 1904).

2) The Mahābhārata is supposed to have been recited in the intervals of this sacrifice. See above, p. 324. *Porzig* (l.c.) suggests that the Āstīkaparvan was originally much more closely connected with the Mahābhārata as a frame-story, and that it was not Vaiśampāyana, but Āstīka himself who related the whole of the Mahābhārata, and thereby saved the snake-king Takṣaka. There are but very weak grounds for this hypothesis. It is more probable that the whole of the Āstīkaparvan was originally an independent poem, which was only later connected with the recitation of the Mahābhārata. *Cf.* V. *Venkatachellam Iyer*, Notes of a Study of the Preliminary Chapters of the Mahābhārata, Madras, 1922, pp. 352 ff.

all snakes to quake, and called them all forth into the jaws of the fire. Then the snakes fell into the flaming furnace, distorting their bodies and calling piteously on one another. Palpitating and hissing, embracing one another with their heads and their tails, they hurled themselves in their masses into the brightly glowing fire......great snakes and small snakes, many, of many colours, terrible biters of mighty strength as that of a club, snakes full of venom; driven by the curse of the mother, the snakes fell into the fire."[1]

With this legend of the snake-sacrifice, the ancient myth of Kadrū and Vinatā, occurring already in Vedic texts,[2] is here combined. Kadrū, "the red-brown one," is the earth and the mother of the snakes, Vinatā, "the curved one," is the vault of heaven and the mother of the mythical bird Garuḍa. And there is also interwoven the myth of the *twirling of the ocean*,[3] which occurs also in the Rāmāyaṇa and in the Purāṇas, and is again and again related, or used for purposes of illustration and comparison by poets of later times. How gods and demons, united in ardent labour, twirl the ocean in order to obtain the draught of immortality, the mountain Mandara serving as a twirling-stick and the snake-prince Vāsuki as a rope, how the moon then arises out of the foaming mass, then Lakṣmi, the goddess of good fortune and of beauty, the intoxicating drink Surā and other precious things, until at last the beautiful god Dhanvantari, holding the draught of immortality in a shining white goblet, appears from out of the ocean,—all this is described, if one may say so, with "life-like" graphicness.

One more of the snake-legends interwoven into the frame-story deserves mentioning, namely the story of Ruru partly only a duplicate of the legend of the snake-sacrifice

---

1) I, 52.

2) Taittirīya Saṃhitā, VI, 1, 6, 1; Kāṭhaka, 23, 10; Śatapatha-Br. III, 6, 2. The myth of Kadrū and Vinatā from the Āstika-parvan translated by J. *Charpentier*, Die Suparṇasage, pp. 167 ff. On the same myth in the Suparṇādhyāya S. above, pp. 312 f.

3) I, 17-19.

itself, for, like Janamejaya, Ruru vows to annihilate all snakes. This happens as follows:

Ruru, son of a Brahman, once saw the lovely virgin Pramadvarā, daughter of an Apsaras, and was seized with love for her. She becomes his bride, but a few days before the wedding, she is bitten by a poisonous snake while she is at play. She lies there lifeless, as though asleep, more lovely than ever. All the pious hermits approach, and, moved by pity, burst into tears, but Ruru goes forth into the depth of the forest in his sorrow. Lamenting loudly, he invokes the gods to have regard to his penance and his pious life, and to give his beloved back to him. Then a messenger from the gods appears, and announces that Pramadvarā can only be recalled to life if Ruru will yield half of his own life for her. Ruru agrees at once, and the King of Law, *i.e.* the god of death, gives his consent for Pramadvarā to be recalled to life. Soon afterwards, on a happy day, the two are wedded. Now Ruru vowed to destroy all the snakes in the world, and thenceforth, whenever he saw a snake, he killed it. But one day he happened on a non-poisonous snake, which asked him to spare it. It was in reality a ṛṣi who was compelled to live as a snake in consequence of a curse, and who was now released from the curse by his meeting with Ruru. In his human form he admonishes him to desist from destroying living creatures.[1]

Ruru, the hero of this legend, is a descendant of that *Cyavana*, of whom it is already related in the Ṛgveda,[2] that the Aśvins made him young again. The story of this rejuvenation is told in detail in the Brāhmaṇas,[3] and a version of the legend is to be found in the Mahābhārata too.[4] It is instructive to compare the Vedic form of the legend with that in the epic. I therefore give below the contents

[1]) Extract from I, 8-12.

[2]) Rv. 1, 116, 10, where he is called Cyavāna.

[3]) Śatapatha-Brāhmaṇa IV, 1, 5. Translated into German by A. *Weber* Indische Streifen I (Berlin, 1868), pp. 13 ff. Jaiminīya-Brāhmaṇa, III, 120 f. *Cf.* the interesting study of E. W. *Hopkins*, "The Fountain of Youth" (JAOS., Vol. XXVI, 1905, pp. 1-67, and 411 ff.), in which the legend of the *fountain of youth* is traced not only in India, but also among other peoples.

[4]) III, 122-125. References to the last part of the narrative also XII, 342; XIII, 156 and XIV, 9.

according to the Mahābhārata, and draw attention in the notes to the most important deviations of the Brāhmaṇa narratives.

Cyavana, a son of Bhṛgu, practised severe austerity on the shore of a lake. He stood motionless as a post for so long that a mound of earth formed over him, on which the ants crawled about, and he himself looked like an ant-hill.[1] Into the neighbourhood of this lake King *Śaryāti* once came with many followers. His young daughter *Sukanyā*, rom,ing about in the forest with her playmates, came upon the ant-hill, in which only the two eyes of the ascetic were visible like glow-worms. Out of wantonness and curiosity the young girl poked about in the two shining things with a thorn and—poked out the eyes of the ascetic.[2] Filled with anger, the saint caused retention of urine and constipation in the army of Śaryāti.[3] The king for a long time sought the cause of the misfortune, and when it transpired that the great ascetic had been offended, he went to him to obtain his forgiveness. The latter will only be reconciled if the king gives him his daughter as his wife. So the young girl becomes the wife of the frail old man. One day the two Aśvins see the young wife just as she is stepping out of her bath, and try to persuade her to choose one of them as her husband instead of the ugly old man. She, however, declares that she wishes to remain faithful to her husband. Then the two physicians of the gods propose to her that they should make her husband young, and she should then choose between them both and the rejuvenated Cyavana. As Cyavana agrees to this, she consents also. Thereupon the Aśvins let the old ascetic step into the lake and they themselves also dive into the water, whereupon they all three come out quite alike and in the dazzling beauty of youth. Now Sukanyā is to choose, and after mature consideration, she decides for her own husband Cyavana.[4] The latter, in return for having been rejuvenated, promises

---

[1]) The Brāhmaṇas know nothing of these ascetic practices. Cyavāna is there only an "old, ghostly-looking" saint.

[2]) In the Brāhmaṇas it is the young lads in the retinue of the king who insult the old ṛṣi, pelting him with lumps of earth.

[3]) According to the Brāhmaṇas the punishment consisted in the arising of discord in the retinue of the king. "The father fought with his son, the brother with his brother." (Śat-Br.) "The mother did not know her son, nor the son his mother" (Jaim-Br.)

[4]) The Śat-Br. knows nothing of the fact that the Aśvins also step into the lake. But the Jaim.-Br. records that Cyavāna had already previously given Sukanyā a sign by which she would recognise him.

to make the Aśvins into Soma-drinkers. At a great sacrifice which he performs for Śaryāti, he presents the Aśvins with the Soma. The king of the gods, Indra, however, will not concede that the Aśvins, who wander about as physicians among mortals, can be worthy of the Soma. But Cyavana takes no notice of the objections of Indra, and continues to sacrifice to the Aśvins. The enraged Indra is about to hurl the thunderbolt upon him. At that moment, however, the saint paralyses the arm of the god; and in order to humble him thoroughly,[1] he creates, by virtue of his asceticism, a terrible monster, *Mada, Intoxication*. With his huge mouth (the one jaw touches the earth, while the other reaches up to the sky) he approaches Indra and threatens to swallow him. Trembling with fear, the prince of gods implores the saint to have mercy, and the latter, satisfied, lets *Intoxication* vanish again, dividing him among the intoxicating drink Surā, women, dice and the chase.[2]

We see here clearly, as in many other cases, that the brahmanical poetry which is contained in the epic, represents a much later phase of development than that of Vedic literature. The characteristic of this later brahmanical poetry, however, is exaggeration, lack of moderation in general, and especially immoderate exaltation of the saints—Brahmans and ascetics—over the gods. Even in the actual *Indra-myths* connected with the Vedic legends of the gods, Indra is no longer the mighty champion and conqueror of demons, as we knew him in the hymns of the Ṛgveda.[3] It is true that the old legend of the battle between Indra and Vṛtra survives, it is even related twice in considerable detail in the Mahābhārata,[4]

---

[1]) In the Śat. Br. there is no question of any humiliation of the god; Cyavāna only provides the Aśvins with the means by which they are voluntarily made participators in the Soma-drink by Indra and the other gods. In the Jaim. Br. there is, it is true, a trial of strength between ṛṣis and gods, and the ṛṣis create *Mada* to *support* them. But as Indra and the gods flee from the monster, the sacrifice threatens to become an Indra-less and god-less one, and the ṛṣi begs Indra most politely, with prayers and invocations, to return. It is only in the version of the Mahābhārata that the god is completely humiliated by the saint.

[2]) In the Jaim.-Br. the demon Intoxication is transferred *only* to the Surā (brandy).

[3]) *Cf.* above, pp. 82 ff.

[4]) III, 100 f.; V, 9-18. The references to this fight are numerous. The legend of the fight of Indra with *Namuci*, IX, 43, is a duplicate of that of the Vṛtra-battle.

but the main stress is laid upon the circumstance that Indra, by killing Vṛtra, burdened himself with the guilt of Brāhman-murder. It is related in great detail how he first had to free himself from this terrible guilt, suffering many humiliations. We have seen, that for a time he was even robbed of his heavenly throne, and Nahuṣa occupied his place.[1] The belief that the supremacy of Indra may be shaken by the austerities of pious Brahmans is exemplified by numerous legends. It is even said[2] that asceticism can compel Indra himself to enter the home of Yama (the god of death). And often indeed does Indra have recourse to the proved expedient of allowing a beautiful Apsaras to seduce a saint who, through his severe austerities, threatens to become dangerous to the gods.[3]

Agni, too, the friend of Indra, has, in the myths of the Mahābhārata, lost much of his old glory as a god. Yet the myths related of him are still connected with the Vedic ideas of fire and of the god of fire. Already in the Ṛgveda he is called "the lover of maidens, the husband of women."[4] But the Mahābhārata tells of Agni's definite love affairs. Thus he once became enamoured of the beautiful daughter of King *Nīla*, and the sacred fire in the king's palace would burn only if fanned by the beautiful lips and the sweet breath of the king's daughter. There was nothing for it but the king must give his daughter in marriage to Agni. In gratitude for this, the god grants him the favour that he may become invincible and that the women of his town may enjoy complete freedom with regard to sexual intercourse.[5] The gluttony, too, of Agni, is already spoken of in the Veda. The legends of the Mahābhārata relate, however, that in consequence

---

[1]) See above, p. 381.

[2]) III, 126, 21.

[3]) *Cf.* A. *Holtzmann*, in ZDMG. 32, 1878, pp. 290 ff., about Indra in the Mahābhārata.

[4]) See above, p. 88.

[5]) II, 31. A similar love-story of Agni, XIII, 2.

of the Ṛṣi *Bhṛgu's* curse he became an "eater of all things." That Agni has several brothers and that he conceals himself in the water or in the friction-sticks, are also Vedic ideas, which already in the Brāhmaṇas led to the formation of myths[1]; but it is only in the Mahābhārata that detailed stories are told about the reason why Agni hid himself, and how the gods found him again.[2]

To the legends which are known already in the Veda and which recur in the Mahābhārata belongs also the flood-legend of Manu and the fish, which has been related above[3] according to the Śatapatha-Brāhmaṇa. The narrative of the Mahābhārata, the "fish episode,"[4] as it is called, differs from the legend as it is related in the Brāhmaṇa, in its greater detail and the poetical presentation, which is not lacking in poetic flights—as when it is described how the ship, "like a drunken wench," staggers to and fro on the agitated ocean. As regards the details of the story it is of importance that in the Mahābhārata, exactly as in the Semitic flood-legends, the taking of *seeds* in the ship is mentioned.[5] I see in this one of the strongest proofs that the Indian flood legend was borrowed from the Semitic one.[6] The conclusion of the legend in the Mahābhārata differs from that in the Brāhmaṇa. In the epic the fish declares that he is the god Brahman, and

---

1) *E. g.*, Śatapatha-Br. I, 2, 3, 1; Taittirīya-Saṃhitā, II, 6, 6.

2) *Cf.* A. *Holtzmann*, Agni nach den Vorstellungen des Mahâbhârata, Strassburg, 1878.

3) Pp. 209 f.

4) Matsyopākhyāna, III, 187. German translations by F. *Bopp* (1829), F. *Rückert*, and H. *Jacobi* (in H. *Usener*, Die Sintflutsagen, Bonn 1899, pp. 28 ff.).

5) Similarly in the Matsya-Purāṇa and in the Bhāgavata-Purāṇa, where the legend recurs.

6) *Cf.* my treatise "Die Flutsagen des Altertums und der Naturvölker in Vol. XXXI of the Mitteilungen der Anthropologischen Gesellschaft in Wien (Vienna), 1901, especially pp. 321 f. and 327 ff. I do not know how those who, like R. *Pischel*, Der Ursprung des christlichen Fischsymbols (SBA., XXV, 1905) deny the connection between Indian and Semitic flood-legends, account for this remarkable agreement.

invites Manu to create the world anew, which the latter does by means of undergoing severe austerities.[1]

Less familiar is the profound and beautiful myth of the Goddess Death, which is related twice in the Mahābhārata.[2] "Whose child is Death? Whence comes Death? Why does Death sweep away the creatures of this world?" Thus asks Yudhiṣṭhira, sorrowing at the departure of so many heroes who had fallen in the battle. Then Bhīṣma (resp. Vyāsa)[2] tells him the story which Nārada once related to King Anukampaka, when the latter was inconsolable at the death of his son. The contents of the narrative are briefly as follows:

When Grandfather Brahman had created the beings, they multiplied unceasingly and did not die. The worlds became over-filled, and the Earth complained to Brahman that she could no longer bear her burden. Then the Grandfather considered how he could reduce the number of beings, but he could think of no remedy. This enraged him, and the fire of his wrath issued from all the pores of his body, flames engulfed the world and threatened to annihilate everything. But god Śiva felt pity for the beings, and at his intercession Brahman withdrew into himself the fire which had arisen from his wrath, and ordered the origin and passing away of the beings; while so doing, however, there came forth out of the pores of his body, a dark-eyed, beautifully adorned woman, draped in a dark red garment. She wished to go on her way towards the South, but Brahman called to her and said: "Death, kill the beings of this world! For thou art born of my thought about world-annihilation and out of my wrath,

---

[1]) At the new creation of the world there is no longer any mention of the "seeds" which he took with him!

[2]) VII, 52-54, where Vyāsa comforts Yudhiṣṭhira, who is in deep distress at the death of Abhimanyu (see above, p. 363), with the story; and XII, 256-258, where Bhīṣma again tells the same story of consolation to Yudhiṣṭhira, who is lamenting at the departing of so many heroes who have fallen in the great battle. Probably the story was originally *only* in Book XII, for verses XII, 256, 1-6, in which there is mention of the many fallen ones *in the plural number*, are found again literally in VII, 52, 12-18, although here it is really only the lament for Abhimanyu which provides occasion for the narration. The poem has been translated into German by Friedrich *Rückert* (in Rob. Boxberger's "Rückert-Studien," Gotha 1878, pp. 114 ff.), and by *Deussen*, Vier philosoph ische Texte des Mahābhāratam," pp. 404-413.

therefore annihilate the creatures, the fools and the sages, all together!" Then the lotus-crowned *Goddess Death* wept aloud, but the lord of creatures caught up her tears in his hands. She implored him to release her from this gruesome task:

"I bow to thee, O lord of beings, be merciful to me, that I may not sweep away innocent creatures—children, old men and people in the prime of life: beloved children, trusted friends, brothers, mothers and fathers! I shall be reproached if they die away thus. Of this I am afraid. And I fear the tears of the unhappy ones, whose moisture will burn me in eternity."

But a decision of Brahman is irrevocable. She must submit to it, but the Grandfather grants her the favour that greed, anger, jealousy, envy, hatred, infatuation and shamelessness may ruin men and that the tears which were shed by the goddess and which he holds in his hand, may become diseases to kill the creatures. Thus no blame for the death of the beings rests upon her. On the contrary, the sinners perish through their own sin. But she, the Goddess Death, free from love and free from hate, is justice itself and mistress of justice,[1] sweeping away the living creatures.

A proof of the fairly high antiquity which must be ascribed to this myth, as well as to that of Manu and the flood, is the exalted position which is allotted to the god *Brahman* in them. In the myth of the Goddess Death, the god Śiva is subordinate to Brahman, who addresses him as "little son." Myths in which the god Śiva occupies a position far above all gods, indicate a much later stratum of brahmanical poetry in the Mahābhārata. The same is true also of the myths in which the god *Viṣṇu* plays the principal part. Frequently older brahmanical myths and legends were revised in accordance with Viṣṇu- or Śiva-worship, which is mostly not difficult to recognise. Such Viṣṇuite and especially Śivaite additions often appear like blots on a painting. They are easy to distinguish, and their removal only enhances the value of the poetry. As poetical productions, the narratives

[1]) VII, 54, 41.

which are dedicated to the glorification of the gods Viṣṇu and Śiva, are quite inferior.[1]

A *Goddess Death* plays no part elsewhere in Indian mythology.[2] But, just as, in the above-related myth, the goddess of death becomes the goddess of justice, so in the whole of the Mahābhārata the idea prevails that *Yama*, the god of death, is one with *Dharma*, the personification of Law.[3] But nowhere is the identification of the king of the realm of death with the lord of law and justice expressed so beautifully as in the most magnificent of all brahmanical poems which the epic has preserved, the wonderful poem of faithful Sāvitri.[4] The partly religious character of the poem, the intermingling of mythology, indeed of the ancient brahmanical mythology, in which Grandfather Brahman determines the destinies of mankind, and neither Śiva nor Viṣṇu plays a part—and the scenery of the forest hermitage in which the greater part of the action takes place, induce me to classify the Sāvitrī-episode among the *brahmanical* legend-poetry. Yet I am not quite certain whether it may not be a pious legend belonging to the old bard-poetry. For the independent action of the princess Sāvitrī, who goes forth in search of a husband, and remains steadfast to her choice, although the saint and her father raise warning protestations, the independence with which she practises asceticism,

---

[1]) Devoted exclusively to the sectarian cult are portions such as the *Viṣṇusahasranāmakathana* (XIII, 149), the enumeration of the thousand names of Viṣṇu, the *Śatarudriya* (VII, 202), "the hundred names of Śiva," and the *Śivasahasranāmastotra* (XII, 284, 16ff.) "Praise of Siva in a thousand names." *Cf.* above, pp. 185 f.

[2]) To my knowledge it only recurs once again in the Brahmavaivartta-Purāṇa by the side of Yama (Th. *Aufrecht*, Catalogus codicum MSS. Sanscriticorum in Bibl. Bodleiana, p. 22*a*).

[3]) Concerning the god Dharma also see above pp. 330 and 374.

[4]) III, 293-299: *Sāvitryupākhyāna* "episode of Sāvitrī" or *Pativratāmāhātmya* "the song in praise of the faithful wife." The story is told by the seer *Mārkaṇḍeya*, who, though many thousand years old, is eternally young, to Yudiṣṭhira in order to comfort him with regard to the fate of Draupadī.

offers sacrifices, and takes vows upon herself,[1] and above all, her courageous intercession for the life of her husband, as well as her knowledge of wise sayings, by means of which she even impresses the god of death—all this recalls more the women of heroic poetry, such as Draupadī, Kuntī and Vidulā, than the brahmanical ideal of woman.[2] But whoever it was who sang the song of Sāvitrī, whether a Sūta or a Brahman, he was certainly one of the greatest poets of all times. Only a great poet was capable of placing this noble female character before us so that we seem to see her before our eyes. Only a true poet could have described in such a touching and elevating manner the victory of love and constancy, of virtue and wisdom, over destiny and death, without even for an instant falling into the tone of the dry preacher of morality.[3] And only an inspired artist could have produced as if by magic such wonderful pictures before us. We see the deeply distressed woman walking by the side of her husband who is doomed to death; the husband, mortally ill, wearily laying his head on his wife's lap, the dreadful form of the god of death, who binds the man's soul with fetters and leads it away; the wife, wrestling with the god of death for the life of her husband; and finally, the happily re-united pair, wandering homewards in the moonlight with their arms around each other. And we see all these pictures in the splendid setting of a primeval Indian forest, whose

---

[1]) According to brahmanical precept a woman as such (separate from her husband) is not entitled to perform sacrifices nor to undertake fasts and other vows. (Manu, V. 155.)

[2]) This ideal is, in short, the "Griselda ideal"—the unconditionally obedient, submissive wife, of whom Manu teaches, V, 154: "Even if a husband is lacking in all virtues, only indulges in sensual pleasure and possesses no good qualities of any kind, he must ever be honoured as a god by a virtuous wife."

[3]) The conversation between Sāvitrī and Yama, the god of death, who is at the same time Dharma, forms the nucleus of the poem. Some of the verses may have been badly transmitted Yet the fundamental thought of all the verses by means of which Sāvitrī so greatly pleases the god and vanquishes him, is sufficiently clear; it is the doctrine of wisdom that is one with love and goodness.

deep stillness we seem to feel, and whose delicious fragrance we seem to breathe, when we surrender ourselves to the magic of this incomparable poem.

How well the Hindus themselves appreciate the treasure which they possess in this immortal poem, is shown in the closing words which have been added to the poem in our Mahābhārata:

> "He who has heard with devotion the glorious story of Sāvitrī, that man is fortunate, his affairs will prosper, and never will sorrow visit him."

Still at the present day, Hindu women annually celebrate a festival (Sāvitrīvrata) in remembrance of faithful Sāvitrī, to secure married happiness for themselves, in which festival the recitation of this poem from the Mahābhārata, forms an essential part of the celebration.[1]

The poem has frequently been translated into European languages including German.[2] But all translations, adaptations and imitations can only give a feeble idea of the incomparable charm of the Indian poem.

Not all brahmanical legends are so pious and moral as that of Sāvitrī. Indeed, a whole volume could easily be filled with disgusting and obscene stories from the Mahābhārata which pleased the Brahmans. One of these legends has, however, rightly attained fame as a poem, and is, moreover, very important for the criticism of the Mahābhārata. This is the legend of *Ṛṣyaśṛṅga*,[3] the ṛṣi who had never seen a

---

[1] *Cf. Shib Chunder Bose*, The Hindoos as they are, 2nd ed., Calcutta, 1883, pp. 293 ff.

[2] English translations by R. T. H. *Griffith* (1852, and Idylls from the Sanskrit, Allahabad 1912, pp. 113 ff.) and J. *Muir* (Edinburgh, 1880). German renderings by F. *Bopp* (1829), F. *Rückert* (in "Brahmanische Legenden," 1836), H. C. *Kellner* (Reclams Universal bibliothek, 1895). For other translations s. *Holtzmann*, Das Mahābhārata II, pp. 92 f. The Sāvitrī poem has also been adapted for the stage by Ferdinand Graf *Sporck*, with music by Hermann *Zumpe*, and produced in German theatres.

[3] III, 110-113. Freely rendered into German by A. *Holtzmann* in "Indische Sagen," and by J. V. *Widmann* (Buddha, Bern 1869, pp. 101 ff.). Very freely dramatised by A. Christina *Albers* in Calcutta Review, Nov. 1923, pp. 231 ff. ("The Great Drought"). J. *Hertel* (WZKM. 18, 1904, pp. 158 f.) and L. v. *Schroeder*, Mysterium und Mimus im

woman. The contents of this ancient Indian tale are briefly as follows:

Ṛṣyaśṛṅga,[1] born miraculously of an antelope, is the son of a saint, who grows up in a hermitage in a forest, without ever having seen any person besides his father. Above all, he has never seen a woman. Now there was once a great drought in the kingdom of King Lomapāda, and the sages declared: the gods are angry, and the rain will fall only if the king succeeds in bringing Ṛṣyaśṛṅga into his country. The king's daughter Śāntā [2] undertakes the task of enticing the young saint into the land. A floating hermitage is constructed of artificial trees and shrubs, and in this Śāntā sails to the dwelling place of Ṛṣyaśṛṅga. Arriving in the vicinity of the forest hermitage, the king's daughter steps ashore and takes advantage of the absence of the father of Ṛṣyaśṛṅga, in order to approach the youthful ascetic. She gives him magnificent fruits and delicious wine, plays coquettishly with a ball, and clings in a tender embrace to the youth, who thinks he sees before him a hermit lad like himself. Thereupon the maiden returns to the ship, as the father of Ṛṣyaśṛṅga approaches the hermitage. The old man notices the excitement of his son, and asks him what has happened. The latter then describes his adventure with the beautiful "youth" and his rapture at meeting him, in glowing terms, and says that he would fain practise the same "ascetic discipline" as yonder youth, for the yearns to see him again. But the father warns him that these are evil demons (rakṣas) who go about in that shape to disturb the asceticism of pious men.

But no sooner has the father departed again, than Ṛṣyaśṛṅga goes in search of his young "friend." Soon he has found beautiful Śāntā, is

---

Rigveda, pp. 292 ff., have tried to explain the Ṛṣyaśṛṅga poem as an ancient drama, a kind of "mystery play." It is really a *ballad* of the type of the Vedic Ākhyānas. H. *Lüders* (NGGW., 1897, pp. 1 ff.; 1901, pp. 1 ff.) has traced the older forms of this ballad, by comparing its different versions in Indian literature.

[1]) The name means "the antelope-horned." As he has *one* horn on his head, he is also in Buddhistic versions called *Ekaśṛṅga*, *i.e.* "Unicorn."

[2]) In our Mahābhārata it is not Śāntā, but a courtesan, who seduces the saint. *Lüders* (l. c.) has proved convincingly, however, that not only in the original form of the legend, as it has come down to us in the *Jātaka*-book of the Buddhist Tipiṭaka but also in an earlier form of the Mahābhārata itself, the princess Śāntā was the seducer. Only some later rhapsodist or copyist took exception to a king's daughter being said to have seduced Ṛṣyaśṛṅga, and put a courtesan in her place, so that we do not know why the king finally gives his daughter in marriage to the saint. It may be mentioned that *Holtzmann*, in his free rendering (l. c.) has already made the princess Śāntā the seducer of Ṛṣyaśṛṅga.

enticed by her into the floating hermitage, and is carried away into Lomapāda's kingdom. The moment the young saint enters the land, the rain begins to fall in torrents. The king makes him his son-in-law, after he has conciliated the old father by means of rich gifts.

Various versions of this legend may be found in other Indian works of literature, especially in the Rāmāyaṇa, in the Padma-Purāṇa and in the Buddhist Jātaka book. It is easy to recognize that though the ballad is based on an old legend with a religious background, it was related in its original form with a racy humour whose indecencies the various revisors endeavoured to mitigate. The scene in which the ascetic's son, who has never seen a woman, catches sight of the beautiful maiden, whom he takes for an ascetic, though her charms do not leave him unmoved, was certainly the central point of the story in the original version, and was described with a coarse humour, of whose rudeness some examples are still preserved in the Buddhistic Jātaka.[1] But how popular this humorous tale was, is shown by its being familiar in different versions in Tibet, China and Japan, and in its having left traces behind even in the unicorn-legend of the West.[2]

The Ṛṣyaśṛṅga-legend is in the so-called *Tīrthayātrā*-section.[3] The Ṛṣi Lomaśa, who has come in order to console the brothers of Arjuna,[4] makes a pilgrimage with them. At every sacred place (Tīrtha) which they visit, the ṛṣi relates

---

[1]) In the Gāthās of the Jātakas Nos. 523 and 526. These Gāthās are, according to *Lüders* (l. c., 1897, p. 38), "the oldest remnants of a literary setting of the Ṛṣyaśṛṅga-legend," "and these verses were, at any rate, partly known to the author of the Mahābhārata version, and, translated into Sanskrit and more or less transformed, were included in his work."

[2]) *Cf.* F. W. K. *Müller*, Ikkaku seunin, eine mittelalterliche japanische Oper, transkribiert und übersetzt, Nebst einem Exkurs zur Einhornsage (in the Festschrift für Adolf Bastian zu seinem 70. Geburtstag, Berlin 1896, pp. 513-538).

[3]) *i.e.*, "section of pilgrimages," III, 80-156. Sacred places to which pilgrimages (yātrā) are undertaken, are called *Tīrthas*.

[4]) See above, p. 348.

a story referring to that place. Thus there are collected in this section (certainly not belonging to the oldest parts of the Mahābhārata) numerous brahmanical legends. Here we find, for example, the above-related legend of Cyavana,[1] similarly the legends of the famous Ṛṣi *Agastya*. This great saint is asked by the gods, among other things, to dry up the ocean, so that they may fight against certain demons who dwell on the bottom of the ocean. The saint does this quite simply by drinking up the whole ocean. He is also the hero of numerous other brahmanical legends.[2]

While these Agastya-legends are intended to show the tremendous ascendancy of the brahmanical saint over gods and men, we find in the Mahābhārata also a whole cycle of legends, the heroes of which are the famous Ṛṣis *Vasiṣṭha and Viśvāmitra*,[3] and in which, though in the end they also serve for the glorification of the Brahmans, there can still be perceived distinct traces of the struggle for supremacy between priests and warriors. The roots of these legends reach back far into the Vedic period, and they recur in various versions also in the Rāmāyaṇa epic and in the Purāṇas. The contents of the legend according to the Mahābhārata are briefly as follows:

Viśvāmitra was a warrior, the son of King Gādhin of Kanyākubja (Kanauj). One day, in the course of his hunting, he came to the hermitage of Ṛṣi Vasiṣṭha. The latter had a marvellous cow which fulfilled all his wishes. When he desired anything, whether food or drink, jewels or garments, or whatever it might be, he had only to say: "Give," and the cow Nandinī granted it to him. When Viśvāmitra saw the excellent cow, he desired to have it, and offered Vasiṣṭha ten thousand ordinary cows for it. But the latter would not give it up, as it gave him everything he

1) Pp. 391 f.

2) III, 96-109.

3) I, 177-182; V, 106-119; IX, 39 f.; 42 f.; XII, 141; XIII, 3 f. *Cf.* J. *Muir*, Original Sanskrit Texts. Vol. I, 3rd ed. (London 1890), pp. 388 ff., 411 ff., and F. E. *Pargiter* in JRAS. 1913, pp. 885 ff.

ever wanted for sacrificial purposes. Viśvāmitra now wanted to steal the cow, according to "warriors' custom." Vasiṣṭha, as a gentle Brahman, did not hinder him in this, but the marvellous cow itself brought forth out of its body, mighty hosts of warriors, by whom the troops of Viśvāmitra were defeated and put to flight. Then the proud king sees that the power of Brahmans is after all greater than that of warriors; he gives up his kingdom and performs severe austerities in order to become a Brahman, in which he succeeds after unutterable efforts.

I may quote one other remarkable legend in this cycle of myths, because it recalls certain features of the Ahasuerus-legend:

Even after Viśvāmitra has become a Brahman, his enmity with Vasiṣṭha continues. Instigated by Viśvāmitra, Kalmāṣapāda, who is possessed by a Rākṣasa, kills the sons of Vasiṣṭha. But the latter is so full of mildness that he will rather die than give vent to his anger. He is about to end his life, and throws himself down from Mount Meru, but falls on a pile of wool. He enters the fire, but it does not burn him. With a stone around his neck he throws himself into the sea, but is thrust out again living. So he returns with a sorrowful heart to his hermitage. But when he sees his home empty of children, grief brings him back anew to thoughts of suicide. He hurls himself into a swollen mountain stream, after having tied his limbs fast with ropes, but the current tears his fetters and throws him on to a bank. Wandering further, he comes to a river which is full of crocodiles and horrible monsters; he throws himself in, but the wild animals timidly shrink away from him. As he sees that he cannot die by his own hand, he returns again to his hermitage, after having wandered over hills and countries. On the way he meets his daughter-in-law Adṛśyantī, and he hears a voice like that of his son singing Veda hymns. It is the voice of his as yet unborn grandchild, who already in his mother's womb—Adṛśyantī has been pregnant with him since twelve years—has learned all the Vedas. As soon as he knows that he is to have descendants, he gives up his thoughts of suicide.

While the literary value of this kind of brahmanical legends cannot be gainsaid, there are also numerous stories in the Mahābhārata which are invented purely for the purpose of the glorification of the Brahmans or for the inculcation of some brahmanical doctrine or other. We have, for instance, tales of pupils who go to the utmost extremes in obedience towards their teacher, like that Uddālaka Āruṇi, who is commissioned by his teacher to block a leaking dam, and does this, as no other way presents itself to him, with his own body. Or the story is told of a king who, as a punishment for having given a Brahman's cow to someone else, was changed into a lizard.[1] Other stories are intended to prove that there is no greater merit than giving cows to Brahmans. In a famous Upaniṣad the youth Naciketas, thirsting for knowledge, utilises his sojourn in the underworld to question the god of death about the Beyond. In the Mahābhārata, the youth, who is here called Nāciketa, asks to see the paradise of the cow-givers, and Yama delights him with a long lecture upon the merit which one acquires by presenting cows.[2] In order to prove that it is meritorious to give sunshades and shoes, it is related that Ṛṣi Jamadagni was once angry with the sun, and was just about to shoot it down from the sky, when the sun-god pacified him in the nick of time, by giving him a sunshade and a pair of shoes.[3] Such stories are frequent especially in the didactic sections and books (XII and XIII). In these didactic portions of the Mahābhārata we find finally also numerous frame-stories called " Itihāsas " which serve only to introduce and give a certain form to the talks upon law, morality or philosophy. It is noteworthy that, in these Itihāsas, we occasionally meet with the same personages as speakers whom we met in the Upaniṣads, *e.g.*, Yājñavalkya and Janaka.[4] And as in the Upaniṣads and the Buddhistic dialogues, so in the didactic Itihāsas of the

---

[1]) I, 3; XIII, 70 f.

[2]) XIII, 71. *Cf.* above, pp. 261 f.

[3]) XIII, 95 f.

[4]) XII, 18; 290; 310-320.

Mahābhārata too, we meet learned women[1] as well as kings and sages.[2]

Fables, Parables and Moral Narratives in the Mahābhārata.[3]

These Itihāsa-Saṃvādas, as we may call those discourses clothed in the form of narratives (saṃvāda), for the greater part no longer belong to the brahmanical legend-poetry, but to what, for lack of a better expression, we have called Ascetic poetry.[4] The latter is clearly distinguishable from the brahmanical poetry connected with the ancient legends of the gods, which are already forgotten to a considerable extent among the people; it is far more closely related to the *popular* literature of fables and fairy-tales, partly because it draws upon the latter, and partly because it approaches it as closely as possible. And while the brahmanical legends, like the brahmanical Itihāsa-Saṃvādas, serve the special interests of the priests and teach a narrow priestly morality, reaching its climax in the sacrificial service and in the worship of the Brahmans (more than of the gods), the ascetic poetry rises to a general morality of mankind, which teaches, above all, love towards all beings and renunciation of the world. Traces of this literature are first to be found in the Upaniṣads, but later just as much in the Mahābhārata and in some Purāṇas, as in the sacred texts of the Buddhists and the

---

1) King Janaka disputes with the nun Sulabhā, XII, 320. King Senajit is comforted by the verses of the courtesan Piṅgalā, XII, 174.

2) Occasionally also gods, e.g., Indra and Bṛhaspati, XII, 11; 21; 68; 84; 103; XIII, 111-113.

3) A selection of moral narratives, especially out of Book XII, from the Mahābhārata, is given in French translation by A. *Roussel*, Légendes Morales de l'Inde empruntées au Bhagavata Purāṇa et au Mahabharata traduites du Sanskrit. (Les littératures populaires t. 38 et 39). Paris 1900. On fables and parables s. *Oldenberg*, Das Mahābhārata, pp. 66 ff.

4) See M. *Winternitz* in Calcutta Review, Oct. 1923, pp. 1 ff.

Jainas. Therefore it is not to be wondered at, that in these different literatures we often meet with the same legends of saints and the same maxims of wisdom and ethics, often literally the same.

The oldest Indian fables are to be found, indeed, already in the actual epic, and they serve for the inculcation of rules of *Nīti*, *i.e.* worldly wisdom, as well as of *Dharma* or morality. Thus a minister advises Dhṛtarāṣṭra to deal with the Pāṇḍavas in a similar manner as a certain jackal, who utilised his four friends, a tiger, a mouse, a wolf and an ichneumon, for the purpose of obtaining his prey, but then cunningly got rid of them, so that the prey remained for him alone.[1] In another place Śiśupāla compares Bhīṣma with that old hypocritical flamingo, which always talked only of morality and enjoyed the confidence of all its fellow-birds, so that they all entrusted it with the keeping of their eggs, until they discover too late, that the flamingo eats the eggs. Delightful also is the fable of the treacherous cat, which Ulūka, in the name of Duryodhana, relates to Yudhiṣṭhira, at whom it is aimed. With uplifted arms the cat performs severe austerities on the bank of the Ganges; and he is ostensibly so pious and good that not only the birds worship him, but even the mice entrust themselves to his protection. He declares himself willing to protect them, but says that in consequence of his asceticism he is so weak that he cannot move. Therefore the mice must carry him to the river—where he devours them and grows fat.[2] The wise Vidura, into whose mouth many wise sayings are placed, also knows many fables. Thus he advises Dhṛtarāṣṭra not to pursue the Paṇḍavas out of self-interest, that it may not befall him as it befell the king who, out of

---

[1]) I, 140. On similar fables, *cf.* Th. *Benfey*, Pantschatantra I, pp. 472 f.

[2]) II, 41; V, 160. Such fables, in which animals appear as hypocritical ascetics, are not at all rare in Indian fable literature, *cf.* Th. *Benfey*, l. c., I, pp. 177 f., 352; and M. *Bloomfield*, JAOS. 44, 1924, pp. 202 ff.

greed, killed the birds which disgorged gold, so that he then had neither birds nor gold.[1] In order to bring about peace, he also relates the fable of the birds which flew up with the net which had been thrown out by the fowler, but finally fell into the hands of the fowler, because they began to quarrel with one another.[2]

Most of the fables, as well as all the parables and moral narratives, are to be found in the didactic sections and in Books XII and XIII. Many of these recur in the Buddhistic and later collections of fables and fairy-tales, and some have been transmitted into European narrative literature. Thus Benfey has traced through the literature of the world a series of fables which all deal with the subject of the impossibility of friendship between cat and mouse.[3]

Many a pretty parable, too, is to be found in the didactic portions of the Mahābhārata. Thus "the old Itihāsa, the conversation between the river and the ocean,"[4] is related in order to inculcate the wise theory that it is good to stoop :

" The ocean asks the rivers how it is that they uproot strong mighty trees and bring them to him, while they never bring the thin weak reed. Gangā answers him : 'The trees stand, each in its place, firmly rooted to one spot. Because they oppose the current, they must move from their place. Not so the reed. The reed bends as soon as it sees the current

---

1) II, 62. Related to this is the fairy-tale of Suvarṇaṣṭhīvin (*i.e.*, " he who drops gold out of his mouth"), the son of King Sṛñjaya. The latter had desired a son whose entire evacuations should be gold. The wish is fulfilled, and the gold accumulates in his palace. But finally the son is kidnapped by robbers (dasyus) and murdered, and all the gold vanishes. VII, 55. *Cf. Benfey*, l. c., I, 379.

2) V, 64. *Cf.* also the fable of the crow which desires to enter on a flying-race with the flamingo, VIII, 41, translated by *Benfey*, l. c., I, pp. 312 ff., where also other related fables are indicated.

3) XII, 111 ; 138 ; 139 (also Harivaṃśa, 20, 1117 ff.) translated and traced in other literatures by *Benfey*, l. c., I, 575 ff., 545 ff., 560 ff. Other fables of the Mahābhārata which are part of universal literature, are that of the three fishes XII, 137 (*Benfey*, l. c., I, 243 f.) and that of the saint's dog which is changed into a leopard, a tiger, an elephant, a lion, a Śarabha and finally again into a dog, XII, 116 f. (*Benfey*, l. c., I, 374 f.).

4) XII, 113.

approaching—not so the trees—and when the force of the current has passed by, it stands erect again."

Great fame and almost universal propagation has been attained by the parable of the "Man in the well" which the wise Vidura relates to King Dhṛtarāṣṭra.[1] For its own sake as well as on account of its significance in universal literature, it deserves to be quoted in an extract and partly in translation :

A Brahman loses his way in a dense forest full of beasts of prey. In great terror he runs here and there, looking in vain for a way out. "Then he sees that the terrible forest is surrounded on all sides by traps and is embraced by both arms of a dreadful-looking woman. Great and terrible five-headed dragons, which reach up like rocks to the sky, surround this great forest." And in the middle of this forest, covered by underwood and creeping plants, there is a well. The Brahman falls into it and is caught on the intertwined branches of a creeper. "As the great fruit of a bread-fruit tree, held by its stalk, hangs down, so he hung there, feet upwards, head downwards. And yet another even greater danger threatens him there. In the middle of the well he perceived a great, mighty dragon, and at the edge of the lid of the well he saw a black, six-mouthed and twelve-footed giant elephant slowly approaching." In the branches of the tree which covered the well, swarmed all kinds of dreadful-looking bees, preparing honey. The honey drips down and is greedily drunk by the man hanging in the well. For he was not weary of existence, and did not give up hope of life, though white and black mice gnawed the tree on which he hung. The forest, so Vidura explains the metaphor to the king who was filled with pity, is the saṃsāra, existence in the world : the beasts of prey are the diseases, the hideous giantess is old age, the well is the body of beings, the dragon at the bottom of the well is time, the creepers in which the man was caught, the hope of life, the six-mouthed and twelve-footed elephant, the year with six seasons and twelve months: the mice are the days and nights, and the drops of honey are sensual enjoyments.

There can be no doubt that this parable is a genuine Indian production of ascetic poetry. It has been called

---

[1]) XI, 5.

"originally Buddhistic," [1] but it does not correspond more with the Buddhists' view of life than with that of the Jainas and of other Indian ascetic sects. However, it probably was the Buddhistic versions of the parable which paved the way for it to the West; for it penetrated into the literature of the West principally with that stream of literature which flowed to the West through the popular books "Barlaam and Joasaph" and "Kalîlah and Dimnah," which originated in *India*, but later became absolutely international. But in Germany it is most familiar through Rückert's beautiful poem "Es war ein Mann in Syrerland," whose immediate source is a Persian poem by Jelâled-dîn Rûmî.[2] Ernst Kuhn has traced throughout all the literatures of the world the "circulation of this truly non-sectarian parable which has served equally for the edification of Brahmans, Jainas, Buddhists, Mohammedans, Christians and Jews." [3]

As with this parable, so with many *moral narratives* of the Mahābhārata, one might be inclined to trace them back to Buddhistic sources. On closer scrutiny, however, they could equally well have been drawn from that source of popular narratives which was alike at the disposal of Brahmans, Buddhists and other sects. Thus, for example, the stories of King Śibi not only look very Buddhistic, but, in a text belonging to the Tipiṭaka [4] the legend is actually already related, how this self-sacrificing king tears out both his eyes in order to give them to a beggar. In the Mahābhārata the

---

[1]) Thus *Benfey*, l. c., I, pp. 80 ff., and M. *Haberlandt*, Der altindische Geist (Leipzig 1887), pp. 209 ff.

[2]) Friedrich *Rückerts* Werke, publ. by C. Beyer, Vol. I, pp. 104 f. The Persian poem from the second Diwan of Jelâl-ed-dîn Rûmî, translated by Joseph v. *Hammer*, Geschichte der schönen Redekünste Persiens, Vienna 1818, pp. 183. *Cf.* also R. *Boxberger*, Rückert Studien, pp. 85 f., 94 ff.

[3]) In the "Festgruss an O. v. Böhtlingk," Stuttgart 1888, pp. 68-76.

[4]) Cariyāpiṭaka, I, 8. *Cf.* also the Sivi-Jātaka (Jātakas ed. V. *Fausböll*, IV, 401 ff., No. 499) and *Benfey*, l. c., I, 388 ff.

story is told in three different versions,[1] how the king cuts the flesh from his own body piecemeal and gives up his life, in order to save the life of a dove which is pursued by a hawk. This same king Śibi, however, already plays a part in the old heroic legends of Yayāti. He is one of the four pious grandsons of this king, who offer him their places in heaven and finally ascend to heaven with him.[2] The description, too, of the immeasurable riches and the tremendous generosity of Śibi in another place, where he is glorified as a pious sacrificer, who gives the Brahmans as many oxen as raindrops fall upon the earth, as there are stars in the sky and grains of sand in the bed of the Ganges, is distinctly brahmanical in colouring.[3]

To the stories of self-sacrifice so popular in ascetic poetry, belongs also the touching narrative of the huntsman and the doves,[4] which has also been included in *one* recension of the Pañcatantra.[5] Love of one's enemy, and self-denial can hardly go further than in this "sacred, sin-destroying Itihāsa," which relates how the male dove burns himself in the fire for the wicked hunter, who has caught his beloved wife because he has no other food to offer the "guest;" how the dove follows her husband into death, and how the wicked hunter, deeply touched by the great love and self-sacrifice of the pair of doves, gives up his wild

---

[1]) III, 130f; 197, XIII, 32. See *Griffith*, Idylls from the Sanskrit, pp. 123 ff. (The Suppliant Dove).

[2]) I, 86 and 93. *Cf.* above, p. 380.

[3]) VII, 58. The legend of Śibi, too, which is related in III, 198, is quite brahmanical. Here, at the wish of a Brahman, he unhesitatingly kills his own son and—even eats him himself, because the Brahman commands it. On the other hand the narrative of King Suhotra and Śibi (III, 194) looks more Buddhistic, and, in fact, though no longer referring to Śibi, actually recurs in Buddhist literature (Jātaka No. 151). *Cf.* T. W. *Rhys Davids*, Buddhist Birth Stories, London 1880, pp. xxii-xxviii, R. O. *Francke*, WZKM, 20, 1906, pp. 320 ff.

[4]) XII, 143-149.

[5]) See *Benfey*, l. c., I, pp. 365 f., II, 247 ff.

life, becomes an ascetic and finally also seeks death in the fire.[1]

Another side of ascetic morality is illustrated by the story of the pious ascetic Mudgala, who does not want to go to heaven :

As Mudgala is so wise and pious, a messenger of the gods appears, in order to lead him up to heaven. But Mudgala is careful enough to enquire first what the heavenly life is like. The messenger of the gods then describes to him all the glories of heaven and all the bliss which there awaits the pious. Certainly, he cannot conceal the fact that this bliss is not of eternal duration. Everyone must reap the fruits of his actions. When once the *Karman* is exhausted, then one must descend again from heaven and begin a new existence. Then Mudgala will have none of such a heaven; he devotes himself afresh to ascetic practices and finally through deep meditation (dhyānayoga) and complete indifference towards the sense-world attains to that highest place of Viṣṇu, in which alone the eternal bliss of Nirvāṇa is to be found.[2]

The doctrine of *Karman*, Action, which is the fate of man, the first appearance of which we observed in the Upaniṣads,[3] forms the subject of many profound narratives in the Mahābhārata. One of the most beautiful is that of the Snake, Death, Fate and Action. The contents are briefly as follows :

Gautamī, an old and pious Brahman woman, one day finds her son dead. A snake has bitten him. The grim hunter Arjunaka drags the snake along by a rope and asks Gautamī how he shall kill the wicked murderer of her son. Gautamī replies that through the killing of the snake her child will not be restored to life; nor would any good arise from it; for by the killing of a living being one only burdens oneself with guilt. The hunter objects, saying that it is good to kill enemies, even as Indra

---

[1]) The story can hardly be Buddhistic, as Buddhism does not advise religious suicide. Other sects, *e.g.*, the Jainas, recommend it.

[2]) III, 260 f. E. *Windisch* (Festschrift Kuhn, pp. 4 f.) sees in this Mudgala the prototype of the Buddhist Maudgalyāyana who visits the heavens and hells.

[3]) See above, pp. 258 f.

killed Vṛtra. But Gautamī can see no good in torturing and killing enemies. Then the snake also joins in the conversation. It says that it is not to blame for the death of the boy. It was *Mṛtyu*, Death, who only employed it as his instrument. Now, while the snake and the hunter are in violent dispute as to whether the snake was to blame for the death of the child or not, the god of death, Mṛtyu, appears himself and declares that neither the snake nor he himself were to blame for the boy's death, but *Fate* (*Kāla*, "time"): for everything that happens, happens through Kāla; everything that exists, exists through Kāla. "As the clouds are driven hither and thither by the wind," so also death is under the sway of fate. While the hunter insists on the point of view that both the snake and Mṛtyu are guilty of the child's death, *Kāla* himself appears, and declares: "Neither I nor death (Mṛtyu) nor this snake here are to blame for the death of any being, O hunter, we are not the cause. *Action* (*Karman*) it is, which has driven us to it; there is no other cause of his destruction, only through his own action was he killed............As the potter shapes out of a lump of clay everything he desires, so man attains only that fate which he has prepared for himself by his action. As light and shade are always most closely connected with each other, so also the deed and the doer are closely connected through everything which he himself has done." Then Gautamī consoles herself with the thought that the death of her son was the necessary effect of his and her own Karman.[1]

How human beings are to behave towards *death*, is a question which Indian thinkers and poets have again and again treated in innumerable maxims, and also in many a consolatory story.[2] One of the most beautiful of these stories is that of the Vulture and Jackal and the Dead Child, the contents of which shall again only be briefly indicated:

The only little son of a Brahman had died. Lamenting and weeping, the relatives carried the corpse of the little child out to the place of burial. In their grief they could not bear to part from their dead darling. Attracted by the sounds of lamentation, a vulture comes flying to the place, and

---

[1]) XIII, 1.

[2]) See above, p 313, and *Lüders* in ZDMG. 58, 1904, pp 707 ff.

explains to them how futile are all lamentations for the dead. No mortal returns to life when he has once succumbed to Kāla;[1] therefore they should return home without delay. Consoled to some extent, the mourners begin the homeward journey. Then a jackal comes towards them and reproaches them with want of love, because they leave their own child so quickly. Sadly they turn back again. Here the vulture awaits them and reproves them for their weakness. One should not mourn for the dead, but for one's own self. This one should above all cleanse from sin, not weep for the dead; for all the weal and woe of man depends only on the Karman. "The wise man and the fool, the rich man and the poor man, they all come into the power of Kāla, with their good and bad deeds. What do you want with your mourning? Why do you complain of death?" and so on. Again the mourners turn homewards and again the jackal exhorts them not to give up their love towards their offspring; one should make efforts against fate, for it may perhaps after all still be possible to restore the child to life. Whereupon the vulture remarks: "A thousand years old am I, but I have never seen a dead person come to life again.......Those who do not care for their mother and father, their relatives and friends *so long as they are alive*, commit a crime against morality. But of what benefit is your weeping to one who does not see with his eyes, who does not move and is absolutely dead?" Again and again does the vulture urge the mourners to return home, whilst the jackal tells them to return to the burial place. This is repeated several times. Vulture and jackal thereby pursue their own ends, for they are both hungry, and greedy for the corpse. At last god Śiva, urged by his wife Umā, has pity on the poor relatives and lets the child become alive again.[2]

But it is not only the morality of asceticism which finds expression in the moral narratives of the Mahābhārata. Many of them appeal to us particularly for the reason that they teach more the every-day morality which is rooted in the love between husband and wife, parents and children. One of the prettiest of these narratives is that of Cirakārin or the Youth Ponder-well,[1] who is instructed by his father to

---

[1]) *Kāla* is not only "time" and "fate", but also "destiny of death."

[2]) XII, 153.

kill his mother who has sinned grievously. As he is by nature slow and considers everything at length, he delays the execution of the command, and considers from this and that point of view, whether he should carry out his father's command and burden himself with matricide, or neglect his duty to his father. While he is pondering so long, his father returns, and, as his anger has in the meantime vanished, he rejoices deeply that his son Ponder-well has, true to his name, pondered the matter so long. In the centre of this narrative, which is presented in simple popular tone with a certain humour, stands the soliloquy of the youth. In beautiful words he speaks of paternal love and filial duties, and in still more beautiful words, of maternal love :

> "So long as one has a mother one is well cared for; when she is lost, one is without protection. He who enters his house with the cry 'O mother!' is oppressed by no sorrow, is undisturbed by age though he were robbed of all his wealth. Though one has sons and grandsons, even though one is full a hundred years old, when he comes to his mother he behaves like a two-year old child......When he has lost his mother, then a man becomes old, then he becomes unhappy, then the world is empty for him. There is no cool shade like a mother, there is no refuge like a mother, there is no beloved like a mother......"

The main point of all these narratives lies in the speeches of the characters. But I have already mentioned that many so-called *Itihāsas* are actually only short introductions and frames of didactic *dialogues*, so that we can call them *Itihāsa-saṃvādas*. Some of these dialogues rank equally with the best similar productions of the Upaniṣad-literature and of the Buddhistic literature. The saying of King *Janaka* of Videha, after he has obtained peace of mind sounds as though it had been taken from an Upaniṣad: "O, immeasurable is my

---

¹) XII, 265, translated by *Deussen*, "Vier philosophische Texte des Mahâbhâratam," pp, 437-444.

wealth; for I possess nothing. Though the whole of Mithilā burn, nothing of mine burns." [1] And the verses of the courtesan *Piṅgalā*, who is bereft of her lover at the trysting-place, and after overcoming her grief, attains to that deep calmness of soul which has always been the highest aim of all Indian ascetic wisdom, verses which end in the words: "Calmly sleeps Piṅgalā, after she has put non-desire in the place of wishes and hopes," [2] recall the Buddhist nun-songs (Therīgāthā). As occasionally in the Upaniṣads, [3] so also in the dialogues in the Mahābhārata, it is often people of despised caste and low rank, who are in the possession of the highest wisdom. Thus the Brahman Kauśika is instructed by *Dharmavyādha*, the pious hunter and dealer in meat, upon philosophy and morality, and especially about the theory that not birth, but virtuous life, makes one a Brahman. [4] Thus also the pedlar *Tulâdhāra* appears as the teacher of the brahmanical ascetic Jājali. [5] This Itihāsa-dialogue is so important in the history of Indian ethics, that it merits being given here in extract:

The Brahman Jājali lived as a hermit in the forest, and gave himself up to the most frightful austerities. Clothed in rags and skins, stiff with dirt, he wandered through the forest in rain and storm undertook severe fasts, and defied every inclemency of the weather. Once he stood in the forest, deep in yoga, like a wooden post, without moving. There a pair of

---

[1]) XII, 178. J. *Muir* (Metrical Translations, p. 50) translates:

"How vast my wealth, what joy I taste,
Who nothing own and nought desire!
Were this fair city wrapped in fire,
The flame no goods of mine would waste."

Mithilā is the residence of Janaka. *Cf.* Jātaka (ed. Fausböll), Vol. V, p. 252 (Verse 16 of the Sonakajātaka No. 529), and Vol. VI, p. 54 (No. 539). R. O. *Franke*, WZKM., 20, 1906, pp. 352 f.

[2]) XII, 174; 178, 7 f. *Cf.* O. *Böhtlingk*, Indische Sprüche, Nos. 1050 f. Buddhistic parallels are quoted by R. O. *Franke*, WZKM., 20, 1906, pp. 346 f.

[3]) See above, pp. 228 f.

[4]) III, 207-216.

[5]) XII, 261-264; translated by *Deussen*, "Vier philosophische Texte des Mahâbhâratam," pp. 418-435.

birds came flying towards him, and in the hair of his head, which was dishevelled by the storm and matted with the dirt and rain, they built a nest. When the yogin noticed this, he did not stir, but remained standing immovable as a pillar, till the female bird had laid eggs in the nest on his head, till the eggs were hatched and the young birds were fledged and had flown away After this mighty feat of asceticism, Jājali, filled with pride, shouts exultingly into the forest: "I have reached the essence of all devotion." Then a heavenly voice answered him out of the regions of the air: "In devotion thou art not even equal to Tulādhāra, O Jājali, and not even this very wise Tulādhāra, who dwells in Benares, may speak of himself as thou speakest." Then Jājali becomes very disheartened, and went to Tulādhāra at Benares, to see in what manner the latter had advanced so far in devotion. Tulādhāra, however, is a pedlar in Benares, where he keeps an open shop and sells all kinds of spices, healing herbs, and so on. To the enquiry of the Brahman Jājali as to whereof his renowned devotion consists, he replies in a long speech upon morality, beginning with the words:

"I know, O Jājali, the eternal law with all its secrets: it is known to men as the old doctrine, beneficial to all, the doctrine of *love.*[1] A manner of life which is combined with complete harmlessness, or only with slight harm, to all beings, that is the highest devotion; in accordance with this I live, O Jājali. With wood and grass which others have cut, I have built myself this hut. Red lac, lotus-root, lotus-fibres, all kinds of sweet perfumes, many kinds of juices and drinks, with the exception of intoxicating drinks, I buy and sell without deception. He, O Jājali, who is a friend of all beings and always rejoices in the well-being of all in thought, word and deed, he knows the moral law. I know neither favour nor disfavour, neither love nor hatred. I am the same towards all beings: see, Jājali, that is my vow. I have equal balances[2] for all beings, O Jājali......If one fears no being, and no being fears one, if one has preference for nobody and hates nobody, then he becomes united with Brahman......"

Then follows a long explanation of *Ahiṃsā*, the commandment of non-violence. There is no higher law than forbearance towards all living

---

[1]) *Maitra* (in the Pāli of the Buddhists, *mettā*) means "friendship" and is the technical expression for *love towards all beings*, which differs from the Christian brotherly love n extending beyond human beings to the animals also.

[2] The name of the pedlar, *Tulādhāra*, signifies: "He who holds the scales."

beings. Therefore the breeding of cattle is cruel, because it involves the torturing and killing of animals. Cruel, too, is the keeping of slaves, and traffic in living creatures. Even agriculture is full of sin, for the plough wounds the earth and kills many innocent animals. Jājali objects that without agriculture and cattle-breeding people could not exist and could not find food, and that sacrifices, too, would be impossible if animals might not be killed and plants not be destroyed. Thereupon Tulādhāra replies with a long discourse upon the true sacrifice, which should be offered without the desire for reward, without priestly deception, and without the killing of living beings. Finally Tulādhāra calls on the birds which had nested in the hair of Jājali's head as witnesses for his doctrine, and they, too, confirm that the true religion consists in forbearance towards all human beings.

The sharp contrast between the brahmanical morality and that of Indian asceticism can nowhere be so well observed as in the Dialogue between Father and Son,[1] in which the father represents the standpoint of the Brahman, and the son that of the ascetic who has severed himself from the priestly religion. The view of life represented by the son is that of the Buddhists and the Jainas,[2] without, however, being limited to these. It would be premature to declare the dialogue, of which a partial translation here follows, or even only single verses of it, to be "Buddhistic" or "borrowed from the Buddhists":

A Brahman, who took delight in learning the Veda, had an intelligent son, *Intelligent* (Medhāvin) by name. This son, who was learned in all things pertaining to salvation, morality and practical life, and saw clearly into the true nature of the world, spoke in this wise to his father, who took delight in learning the Veda:

Son.

"Since soon the days of mortals end,
How ought the wise their lives to spend?

---

[1]) XII, 175, repeated in but slightly different wording in XII, 277; translated into English by J. *Muir*, Metrical Translations from Sanskrit Writers, pp. 28-32; into German by *Deussen*, "Vier philosophische Texte des Mahâbhâratam," pp. 118-122.

[2]) Almost every verse which is uttered by the son here in the Mahābhārata could just as well occur in a Buddhistic or Jainistic text. As a matter of fact XII, 174, 7-9,

What course should I, to duty true,
My sire, from youth to age pursue?

Father.

"Begin thy course with study; store
The mind with holy Vedic lore.
That stage completed,—seek a wife,
And gain the fruit of wedded life,
A race of sons by rites to seal,
When thou art gone, thy spirit's weal.
Then light the sacred fires, and bring
The gods a fitting offering.
When age draws nigh, the world forsake,
Thy chosen home the forest make;
And there, a calm, ascetic sage,
A war against thy passions wage,
That, cleansed from every earthly stain,
Thou may'st supreme perfection gain.[1]

Son.

"And art thou then, my father, wise,
When thou dost such a life advise?
What wise or thoughtful man delights
In formal studies, empty rites?
Should such pursuits and thoughts engage
A mortal more than half his age?
The world is ever vexed, distressed;
The noiseless robbers never rest.

Father.

"Tell how the world is vexed, distressed;
What noiseless robbers never rest?
What means thy dark, alarming speech?
In plainer words thy meaning teach.

---

does recur in the Uttarādhyāyana-Sūtra (14, 21-23) of the Jainas, and XII, 174, 13 corresponds almost literally with the verses of the Buddhist Dhammapada, 47 f. A similar dialogue occurs also in the Jātaka No. 509, *cf.* J. *Charpentier*, ZDMG. 62, 1908, 725 ff.

[1]) That is the brahmanical doctrine of the Āśramas, see above, pp. 232 f.

Son.

" The world is vexed by death ; decay
The frames of mortals wears away.
Dost thou not note the circling flight
Of those still robbers, day and night,
With stealthy tread which hurrying past,
Steal all our lives away at last ?
When well I know how death infests
This world of woe, and never rests,
How can I still, in thoughtless mood,
Confide in future earthly good ?
Since life with every night that goes,
Still shorter, and yet shorter grows,
Must not the wise perceive how vain
Are all their days that yet remain ?
We, whom life's narrow bounds confine,
Like fish in shallow water, pine.

While men on other thoughts are bent,—
Like those on gathering flowers intent,—
As lambs by wolves are snatched away,—
They fall to death a sudden prey,
Before they yet the good have gained
For which they every nerve had strained.

No moment lose; in serious mood
Begin at once to practise good ;
To-morrow's task to-day conclude ;

The evening's work complete at noon :—
No duty can be done too soon.
Who knows whom death may seize to-night ?
And who shall see the morning light ?
And death will never stop to ask,
If thou hast done, or not, thy task.
While yet a youth, from folly cease;
Through virtue seek for calm and peace.
So shalt thou here attain renown,
And future bliss thy lot shall crown.

Death interrupts the futile dreams
Of men who, plunged in various schemes,
Are thinking: "This or that is done;
This still to do; that just begun."
As torrents undermine the ranks
Of stately trees that crown their banks,
And sweep them downwards to the main,
Death tears from earth those dreamers vain.

While some are all on traffic bent,
And some on household cares intent,
Are fighting hard with pressing need,
And struggling wives and babes to feed,
Or with some other ills of life
Are waging an incessant strife;
Death these hard toiling men uproots,
Before they yet have reaped the fruits
Of all their labour, all their thought,
Of all the battles they have fought.

Death spares no class, no rank, no age;
He carries off the fool, the sage,
The knave, the saint, the young, the old,
The weak, the strong, the faint, the bold.

As soon as men are born, decay
And death begin to haunt their way.
How can'st thou, thoughtless, careless, rest,
When endless woes thy life infest;
When pains and pangs thy strength consume,—
Thy frame to dissolution doom?

Forsake the busy haunts of men,
For there has death his favourite den.
In lonely forests seek thy home,
For there the gods delight to roam.

Fast bound by old attachment's spell,
Men love amid their kin to dwell,
This bond the sage asunder tears;
The fool to rend it never dares.

Thou dost advise that I should please
With sacrifice the deities.
Such rites I disregard as vain;
Through these can none perfection gain.
Why sate the gods, at cruel feasts,
With flesh and blood of slaughtered beasts?
Far other sacrifices I
Will offer unremittingly;
The sacrifice of calm, of truth,
The sacrifice of peace, of ruth,
Of life serenely, purely, spent,
Of thought profound on Brahma bent.
Who offers these, may death defy,
And hope for immortality.

And then thou say'st that I should wed,
And sons should gain to tend me, dead,
By offering pious gifts, to seal,
When I am gone, my spirit's weal.
But I shall ask no pious zeal
Of sons to guard my future weal.
No child of mine shall ever boast
His rites have saved his father's ghost." [1]

There is no greater treasure for the Brahman than solitude, equanimity, truth, virtue, steadfastness, mildness, uprightness, and the renunciation of all dealings. How shall treasures, relatives, or a wife, profit thee, O Brahman, as thou must die? Seek the self (the ātman) which is hidden within thee! Whither have thy ancestors, whither has thy father departed?"

Thus this dialogue, apparently moving entirely in Buddhistic ranges of thought, leads into the ātman-theory of the

[1]) Translated by J. *Muir*, l.c.

Vedānta, with which we became acquainted in the Upaniṣads. And this is by no means remarkable. The ancient Indian sects of ascetics hardly differed more distinctly from one another than, for instance, the various Protestant sects in Great Britain to-day. It is therefore no wonder that, in the edifying stories, dialogues and maxims of the ascetic poetry which has been embodied in the Mahābhārata, there are to be found so many thoughts which are in accord with the Upaniṣads, as well as with the sacred texts of the Buddhists and the Jainas.

The Didactic Sections of the Mahābhārata.[1]

Most of the Itihāsas and Itihāsa-saṃvādas discussed in the preceding chapter are to be found in the numerous and extensive didactic sections of the Mahābhārata. Such sections, now shorter, now longer, are scattered in almost all the books of the Mahābhārata, and they deal with the three things which the Indians term *Nīti*, *i.e.* worldly wisdom, especially for kings, therefore also "politics," *Dharma*, *i.e.* systematic law as well as general morality, and *Mokṣa*, *i.e.* "liberation," as the final aim of all philosophy. These things are, however, not always presented in the form of pleasing narratives and beautiful sayings; we also find long sections containing dry-as-dust discussions, especially upon philosophy in Book XII and upon law in Book XIII.

It may already be seen from our outline of the contents that Books XII and XIII have nothing at all to do with the actual epic, but that the events related in Book XIV are connected directly with the end of Book XI. The interpolation of these two extensive books is made possible by the singular legend which we have already considered above. Bhīṣma, pierced by countless arrows, lies on the battle-field,

---

[1]) On the style and contents of these didactic sections *cf.* O. *Strauss*, ZDMG. 62 1908, pp. 661 ff., and Ethische Probleme aus dem Mahābhārata, Firenze 1912 (from GSAI. 24, 1911).

but, as he can determine the hour of his death for himself, decides to die half a year later.[1] The intervening period is used by the mortally wounded hero, who is at the same time a lawyer, a theologian, and a yogin, to lecture Yudhiṣṭhira upon philosophy, morality and law. Book XII begins with Yudhiṣṭhira being in despair because so many brave warriors and near relatives have been massacred. He bursts out into self-accusations, and resolves, in his despair, to withdraw from the world and end his life as a forest hermit. The brothers try to dissuade him from it, and this gives rise to long detailed discussions whether renunciation and retirement from the world, or whether the fulfilment of the duties of a householder and king are right. The wise Vyāsa also is present, and declares that a king should first fulfil all his duties, and retire into the forest only in the evening of his life. However, he refers Yudhiṣṭhira to Bhīṣma, who will instruct him fully in all the duties of a king. So Yudhiṣṭhira, after he has been consecrated as king, actually goes with a great retinue to Bhīṣma, who is still lying on the battle-field, in order to question him first upon the duties of a king, and further upon other matters. The speeches of Bhīṣma upon law, morality and philosophy fill Books XII and XIII.

The first half of Book XII (*Śānti Parvan*), consisting of the two sections "Instruction in a king's duties" and "Instruction in the law in cases of distress and danger,"[2] deals above all with the dignity and duties of a king, teachings of politics (nīti) being occasionally inserted, and further also with the duties of the four castes and the four stages of life (āśramas) generally, with duties towards parents and teachers, the right conduct in distress and danger, self-restraint, asceticism and

---

[1]) *Cf.* above, p. 363 Note 1. V. V. *Iyer*, Notes of a Study of the Preliminary Chapters of the Mahâbharata, pp. 271 ff. ; and *Oldenberg*, Das Mahābhārata, pp. 76 ff. *Hopkins*, Great Epic of India, pp. 381 ff., applies to these books (XII, XIII) the term "pseudo-epic."

[2]) Rājadharmānuśāsanaparvan (1-130) and Āpaddharmānuśāsanaparvan (131-173).

love of truth, the relationship between the three aims of life,[1] and so on. The second half of the book, containing the section of the "Instruction in the duties which lead to liberation,"[2] is principally of philosophical content. Yet we find here besides long, dry and often confused discussions upon cosmogony, psychology, the principles of ethics or the doctrine of liberation, many of the most beautiful legends, parables, dialogues and moral aphorisms, some of which have already been discussed in the preceding chapter. And though this Book XII as a whole only presents an inartistically jumbled compilation, it yet contains many a priceless gem of poetry and wisdom. This book is of inestimable value, too, as a source for Indian philosophy.

While Book XII can be termed, in a certain sense, a "manual of philosophy," Book XIII (*Anuśāsana-Parvan*) is essentially nothing but a manual of law. Indeed, there are large portions in this book which contain nothing but quotations from, or exact parallels to, well known law-books, *e.g.* that of *Manu*. We shall see in a later section that Indian legal literature, too, consists mainly of metrical text-books and can be classed as didactic poetry. The only distinction between Book XIII of the Mahābhārata and the law-books (Dharmaśāstras) is that in the former the dry presentation is frequently interrupted by the narration of legends, which indeed are mostly extremely silly and insipid.[3] While Book XII, even though it did not belong to the original epic, yet was probably inserted at a comparatively early date, there can be no doubt with regard to Book XIII, that it was made a component part of the Mahābhārata at a still later time. It bears all the marks of a later fabrication. Nowhere in the

---

[1]) Dharma, artha and kāma, *cf.* above, p. 326 Note.

[2]) Mokṣadharmānuśāsana (174 ff.), completely translated in *Deussen's* "Vier philosophische Texte des Mahâbhâratam."

[3]) Of the kind quoted above, pp. 402ff.

Mahābhārata, to mention only one thing, are the claims of the Brahmans to supremacy over all other strata of society vindicated in such an arrogant and exaggerated manner as in Book XIII. A large part of the book deals with the Dānadharma, *i.e.* the laws and precepts upon generosity; generosity, however, is always to be understood only in the sense of the giving of presents to the Brahmans.

Besides in these two books, and apart from smaller passages not exceeding one or two cantos, we also find large didactic sections in Books III, V, VI, XI and XIV. We find in Book III (28-33) a long conversation between Draupadī, Yudhiṣṭhira and Bhīma upon ethical questions, in which Draupadī quotes a dialogue between Bali and Prahlāda and a "Nīti of Bṛhaspati."[1] In the same book we find (205-216) the dissertations of *Mārkaṇḍeya* upon the virtues of women (205 f.), upon forbearance towards living beings (Ahiṃsā, 206-208), upon the power of destiny, renunciation of the world and liberation, upon doctrines of the Sāṅkhya philosophy (210) and of the Vedānta (211), upon the duties towards parents (214 ff.) and others. Book V contains long lectures of *Vidura* upon morality and worldly wisdom (33-40) and the philosophical doctrines of the eternally young *Sanatsujāta* (41-46). In Book VI (25-42) we meet with the famous Bhagavadgītā, to which the *Anugītā* in Book XIV (16-51) forms a kind of continuation or supplement.[2] The consolatory speeches of Vidura in Book XI (2-7) again move in the province of ethics.

Of all these didactic portions of the Mahābhārata, none has attained to such popularity and fame as the Bhagavadgītā[3]

---

[1]) III, 32, 61.

[2]) The three philosophical poems Bhagavadgītā, Sanatsujātīya and Anugītā have been translated into English by Kâshinâth Trimbak *Telang* in SBE., Vol. 8, and into German by *Deussen*. "Vier philosophische Texte des Mahâbhâratam."

[3]) The full title is *Bhagavadgītā upaniṣadaḥ*, "the esoteric doctrines delivered by the Exalted One." *Bhagavat* "the Exalted One, the Adorable," is the epithet of the god

or the "Lord's Song." In India itself there is scarcely any book which is read so much and esteemed so highly as the Bhagavadgītā. It is the sacred book of the Bhāgavatas, a Viṣṇuite sect, but it is a book of devotion and edification for every Hindu, to whatever sect he may belong. The historian Kalhaṇa[1] relates of a king of Kashmir, Avantivarman, who died in 883 A. D., that in the hour of his death he had the Bhagavadgītā read to him from beginning to end, whereupon, thinking of Viṣṇu's heavenly abode, he gladly yielded up his spirit. And he was not the only Hindu to find consolation in this book in the hour of his death. There are many educated Hindus to-day who know the whole poem from memory. Countless are the manuscripts of it which have been preserved. And since it was printed for the first time in the year 1809 in Calcutta, hardly a year elapses without a new reprint of the work appearing in India. Countless also are the translations into modern Indian languages.

Outside India, too, the Bhagavadgītā has gained many admirers. The Arabian traveller Albērūnī knew the poem perfectly and appreciated it very highly.[2] In Europe the poem was first made known by means of the English translation by Chas. Wilkins (London, 1785). The critical text-edition by August Wilhelm von Schlegel, which appeared in 1823, with a Latin translation appended, was of great importance. It was through this work that Wilhelm von Humboldt became acquainted with the poem, and his great enthusiasm about it has already been mentioned.[3] He placed the Bhagavadgītā far above Lucretius and even above Parmenides and Empedokles, and declared "that this episode

---

Viṣṇu incarnated as Kṛṣṇa, who recites to Arjuna the doctrines contained in the poem. Besides "Bhagavadgītā the short title "Gītā" (*i.e.* "the song" *par excellence*) is current in India.

[1]) Rājataraṅgiṇī, V, 125.

[2]) See E. C. *Sachau*, Alberuni's India, I, p. xxxviii; II, Index s.v. Gītā.

[3]) See above, pp. 17 f. *Cf.* Ges. Werke of W. v. Humboldt, I, pp. 96 and 111.

of the Mahābhārata is the most beautiful, nay perhaps even the only truly philosophical poem which we can find in all the literatures known to us." Wilhelm von Humboldt dealt in detail with the poem in a long dissertation of the Berlin Academy (1825-26), "Über die unter dem Namen Bhagavadgītā bekannte Episode des Mahābhārata,"[1] and in a lengthy review of Schlegel's edition and translation.[2] It was translated repeatedly into European languages.[3]

The poem is to be found in a place where one would least of all expect it, at the beginning of Book VI, where the descriptions of the great fight commence. All preparations for the battle have been made. The two armies confront each other ready for the fray. Then Arjuna lets his war-chariot halt between the two armies and surveys the hosts of the Kauravas and Pāṇḍavas armed for the fight. And as he sees on both sides "fathers and grandfathers, teachers, uncles and brothers, sons and grandsons, friends, fathers-in-law and companions," he is overcome by a feeling of deepest pity; horror seizes him at the thought that he is to fight against relatives and friends; it appears to him sin and madness to intend to murder those for whose very sake one otherwise goes to war. When Kṛṣṇa reproaches him with weakness and soft-heartedness Arjuna declares that he is quite at a loss, that he does not know whether it is better to be victorious or to be defeated, and finally he implores Kṛṣṇa

---

[1]) Also Ges. Werke, I, 26-109.

[2]) In Schlegel's "Indische Bibliothek," Vol. II, 1824, pp. 218 ff., 328 ff. Also Ges. Werke, I, 110-184.

[3]) English translations by J. C. *Thomson*, Hertford, 1855; K. T. *Telang* (in verse, Bombay, 1875; prose in SBE., Vol. 8); John *Davies* (1882); Edwin *Arnold* (1885); C. C. *Caleb* (1911); L. D. *Barnett* (in Temple Classics). Sanskrit text with English Translation by Annie *Besant* and Bhagavan *Das*, Benares, 1905. German translations by C. R. S. *Peiper* (1869); F. *Lorinser* (1869); R. *Boxberger* (1870); P. *Deussen* (in "Vier philosophische Texte des Mahâbhâratam"); R. *Garbe* (1905, 2nd ed. 1921); and L. v. *Schroeder* (Jena, 1912). For other translations both in Indian vernaculars and in European languages s. *Holtzmann*, Das Mahābhārata, II, 129 ff.

to instruct him as to what he should really do in this conflict of duties. Thereupon Kṛṣṇa answers him with a detailed philosophical discourse,[1] whose immediate purpose is to convince Arjuna that it is his duty as a warrior to fight, whatever the consequences may be. Thus he says:

"Thou hast grieved over them for whom grief is unmeet, though thou speakest words of understanding. The learned grieve not for them whose lives are fled nor for them whose lives are not fled.

"Never have I not been, never hast thou and never have these princes of men not been; and never shall time yet come when we shall not all be.

As the Body's Tenant goes through childhood and manhood and old age in this body, so does it pass to other bodies; the wise man is not confounded therein.........

It is these bodies of the everlasting, unperishing, incomprehensible Body-Dweller that have an end, as it is said. Therefore, fight, O thou of Bharata's race.

He who deems This to be a slayer, and he who thinks This to be slain, are alike without discernment; This slays not, neither is it slain.

This never is born, and never dies, nor may it after being come again to be not; this unborn, everlasting, abiding Ancient is not slain when the body is slain.........

As a man lays aside outworn garments and takes others that are new, so the Body-Dweller puts away outworn bodies and goes to others that are new.

Weapons cleave not This, fire burns not This, waters wet not This, wind dries it not.........

Unshown is This called, unthinkable This, unalterable This; therefore, knowing it in this wise, thou dost not well to grieve........."[2]

So Kṛṣṇa says: There is no cause for mourning over the imminent murder, for *man* himself, *i.e.* the *spirit*, is eternal

---

[1]) On the teaching of the Bhagavadgītā see R. G. *Bhandarkar*, Vaiṣṇavism, Śaivism, etc. (Grundriss III, 6), pp. 14 ff.: and J. E. *Carpenter*, Theism in Mediaeval India, London, 1921, pp. 250 ff. Some less known monographs on the Gītā are discussed by P. E. *Pavolini*, GSAI., 24, 1911, pp. 395 ff.

[2]) II, 11-13. 18-20. 22. 23. 25, translated by L. D. *Barnett*.

and indestructible, it is only the bodies which are destroyed.[1] And from this he leads on to exhort Arjuna to go forth into the righteous war in the spirit of his duty as a warrior. Happy the warrior to whose lot such a fight falls, which opens the gates of Heaven for him! If he does not fight he burdens himself with shame worse than death. If he falls in the battle, he is assured of heaven; if he is victorious he will rule the earth. Therefore he must in any case fight. However, all the subsequent explanations of the *sage* Kṛṣṇa and later of the *god*, for in the course of the poem it is more and more the *god* Kṛṣṇa who speaks to Arjuna, are in irreconcilable contradiction to this speech of the *hero* Kṛṣṇa. For all the other expositions of the Bhagavadgītā upon the ethics of action culminate in the doctrine that man should, indeed, act according to his duty, but without any consideration for success or failure, without troubling about the possible reward. For it is only such *desire-less* action which is to a certain extent compatible with the real ethical ideal which consists in the giving-up of all works, in non-action, in complete renunciation of the world. In fact, in spite of this, there still runs through the whole poem an unsolved contradiction between the quietistic *morality of asceticism* which points to meditation pursued quite apart from the world and the striving for the highest knowledge as the way to salvation, and the *morality of action* which, at least among the philosophers, has never been properly acknowledged in India. It is true that Kṛṣṇa teaches that there exist two paths to salvation, the path of knowledge and the path of action. But so long as the spirit is bound to the body, it would only be hypocrisy to say that man can live without performing

---

[1]) There is no murder or act of violence which could not be justified by this miserable sophistry. It is surprising that the pious readers of the Gītā do not see this. On the unsolved and insoluble contradiction between the principles of the Gītā and the morality of war forming the starting-point of Kṛṣṇa's speeches, see W. L. *Hare*, Mysticism of East and West, London, 1923, pp. 159 ff.

actions. For matter is always connected with Guṇas[1] (constituents)—sattva (lightness, goodness), rajas (energy, passion), tamas (darkness, heaviness, ignorance)—through which of necessity actions arise. All that man can do, therefore, is to fulfil his duty without wishes, without desires. For "as the fire is concealed by smoke, as the mirror is covered by dirt, as an embryo is protected by the amnion, so knowledge is surrounded by desire, that eternal enemy of the knower."[2] Therefore, he who acts without desire approaches the most closely to the real ideal, which lies on the path of knowledge. How high the Bhagavadgītā places *knowledge* as a way to salvation is shown by these verses (IV, 36 f.) :

> "Even if you are the most sinful of all sinful men, you will cross over all trespasses by means of the boat of knowledge alone. As a fire well kindled, O Arjuna ! reduces fuel to ashes, so the fire of knowledge reduces all actions to ashes."[3]

And according to the Bhagavadgītā, too, he who, turned away entirely from all earthly things, strives for knowledge in meditation only, is a *yogin*, the ideal of the saint and the sage. The yogin maintains his calmness of soul "in cold and heat, in joy and sorrow, in honour and dishonour." A block of earth, a stone and a lump of gold are alike in value to him. He is one and the same to friends and foes, to strangers and relatives, to good people and bad. Sitting in a lonely place deep in contemplation, "he gazes without moving, at the tip of his nose." 'As a light does not flicker in a place where there is no wind': that is the simile, known from of old, for the yogin, who curbs his thoughts and yields himself entirely to absorption (yoga)."[4] But while

---

1) On the Sāṃkhya doctrine of the three Guṇas see R. *Garbe*, Die Sâṃkhya-Philosophie, 2nd ed., Leipzig, 1917, pp. 272 ff. ; and S. *Dasgupta*, History of Indian Philosophy, I, pp. 243 ff.

2) III, 38 f.

3) Translated by K. T. *Telang*, SBE., Vol. 8, p. 62.

4) VI, 7-19. In a letter to Gentz, Wilh. v. *Humboldt* writes that the former will

in the Upaniṣads meditation and thought are regarded as the only path to knowledge and salvation, the Bhagavadgītā knows yet another path, that of *Bhakti*, *i.e.* love and devotion towards God.[1] In answer to the question of Arjuna whether he who is unable to lend his spirit absolutely and entirely to abstraction is lost, Kṛṣṇa replies: "No one who

---

understand how deeply the Indian poem must have impressed him. "For I am not so unlike the *absorbed ones* (*i.e.* yogins) who are described in it." (Schriften von Friedrich von Gentz, published by G. Schlesier. Mannheim, 1840, V, p. 300.)

[1]) It is this idea of *Bhakti* which, more than anything else in the Bhagavadgītā, reminds us of *Christian* ranges of thought. Elsewhere too, the accord with Christian ideas is so marked that the attempt of F. *Lorinser*, in the appendix to his translation (Breslau 1869), to prove Christian influence in the Bhagavadgītā, must not be repudiated from the outset. But Lorinser's thorough investigation in itself proves that this is parallelism of development, highly interesting for the history of religion, and not a case of borrowing. Lorinser is convinced "that the author of the Bhagavadgītā not only knew and frequently utilised the scriptures of the New Testament, but also wove into his system Christian ideas and views in general," and he wishes to prove "that this much-admired monument of the ancient Indian mind, this most beautiful and most exalted didactic poem, which can be regarded as one of the most precious blossoms of heathen philosophy, owes its purest and most highly praised doctrines for the most part" to Christian sources. Guided by such tendencies, Lorinser has compared *everything* which in any way admits of comparison. But of the more than a hundred passages from the Gospels which Lorinser quotes as parallel with passages in the Bhagavadgītā, I have found twenty-five at the most that are of such a kind that a case of borrowing could be at all *thought of.* Not in one single instance, however, is the resemblance such that the supposition of borrowing were more probable than that of an accidental agreement. Mystical love towards God, too, is not limited to Christianity. I need refer only to Sufism, in which it plays no less a part than with the Christian mystics. The expositions of Lorinser have indeed convinced few Indologists up to the present. Even A. *Weber*, who himself ("Griechen in Indien," SBA., 1890, p. 930) traces Bhakti back to Christian influences, is of opinion that Lorinser goes too far. E. W. *Hopkins*, India, Old and New, New York, 1902, 146 ff.) is the only scholar who has expressed a decided opinion in favour of the theory that the Bhagavadgītā was influenced by Christianity. G. *Howells* (The Soul of India, London, 1913, 425 ff) compares the doctrines of the Gītā with those of the New Testament, and seeks to trace points of agreement, without asserting that the Gītā was dependent on Christianity. Most scholars agree that the doctrine of Bhakti can be explained by earlier Indian teachings, and that the hypothesis of Christian influence on the Bhagavadgītā is unlikely, on historical grounds. *Cf.* J. *Muir*, Ind. Ant., 4, 1875, pp. 77 ff.; A. *Barth*, RHR., 11, 1885, pp. 57 f. (Oeuvres I, 370 f.) and The Religions of India, transl., London, 1889, 220 f.; J. *van den Gheyn*, Le Muséon 17, 1898, pp. 57 ff.; L. J. *Sedgwick*, JBRAS., 23, 1910, 111 ff.; A. B. *Keith*, JRAS. 1907, 490 ff.; *Grierson*, ERE. II (1909), pp. 547 ff.; and esp. R. *Garbe*, Die Bhagavadgītā (2nd Ed.), pp. 66 ff., and Indien und das Christentum, 1914, pp. 227 ff.

has done good is quite lost." He who has done his duty in this world, is after death born again according to his merits, in a good, pious family, and after several rebirths gradually obtains the capability of becoming a yogin. "And even among all devotees," says Kṛṣṇa,[1] "he who, being full of faith, worships me, with his inmost self intent on me, is esteemed by me to be the most devoted." Out of the *love of God* arises the knowledge of God, and true liberation. Kṛṣṇa teaches this again and again:

"Even if a very ill-conducted man worships me, not worshipping any one else, he must certainly be deemed to be good, for he has well resolved. He soon becomes devout of heart, and obtains lasting tranquillity. (You may) affirm, O son of Kuntī! that my devotee is never ruined. For, O son of Pṛthā! even those who are of sinful birth, women, Vaiśyas, and Śūdras likewise, resorting to me, attain the supreme goal. What then (need be said of) holy Brahmans and royal saints who are (my) devotees?............"[2]

The moral action and all the virtues of the yogin, too, gain their chief value through the love of God:

"Hateless toward all born beings, friendly, and pitiful, void of the thought of a Mine and an I, bearing indifferently pain and pleasure, patient,

ever content, the Man of the Rule subdued of spirit and steadfast of purpose, who has set mind and understanding on Me and worships Me, is dear to Me.

He before whom the world is not dismayed and who is not dismayed before the world, who is void of joy, impatience, fear and dismay,

desireless, pure, skilful, impartial, free from terrors, who renounces all undertakings and worships Me, is dear to Me."[3]

The kernel of all the ethical teachings of the Bhagavadgītā, however, is contained in the verse which the commentators rightly call the "quintessence verse":

---

[1]) VI, 47. Transl. by K. T. *Telang*, SBE., Vol. 8, p. 73.

[2]) IX, 30-33. Transl. by K. T. *Telang*, SBE., Vol. 8, p. 85.

[3]) XII, 13-16. Transl. by L. D. *Barnett*,

"He who does My work, who is given over to Me, who is devoted to Me, void of attachment, without hatred to any born being, O son of Pāṇḍu, comes to Me." [1]

Here is also expressed what, according to the Bhagavadgītā, constitutes liberation or the highest good: coming to, or union with, God. This is to be understood "as elevation of the soul to a god-like state, as individual perpetuation in the presence of God." [2]

There are, then, *three* paths which lead to this goal: the path of dutiful, desireless action, the path of knowledge, and the path of the love of God. And it is at least attempted, though not always successfully, to bring the three paths into harmony with one another. The first path can, indeed, be combined with the third, and the love of God leads to the knowledge of God, thus meeting the second path. Thus the contradictions in the ethical teachings of the Bhagavadgītā can to a certain extent be overcome.[3]

There are, however, other contradictions in the poem staring us in the face at every turn. Kṛṣṇa invariably speaks of himself as a *personal god*, as the creator, who is eternal and imperishable, but is nevertheless born into the world or creates himself at such times when a decrease in religion is imminent; this is especially the case in the passages dealing with bhakti (IV, 5 ff.). In other places, again, he teaches that *he* is in all beings, and all beings in *him* (VI, 30 f.). "This All is strung on me, like pearls on a string. I am the taste in the water, O son of Kuntī, I am the light in the sun and moon, the syllable Om in all the Vedas, the sound in the atmosphere and the bravery in men," etc. (VII, 7 ff.). This doctrine, according to which God is separate from the

---

1) XI, 55. Transl. by L. D. *Barnett*.

2) *Garbe*, Die Bhagavadgîtâ (2nd Ed.), p. 65.

3) Otto *Strauss*, Ethische Probleme aus dem "Mahābhārata," Firenze 1912 (GSAI. 24, 1911), pp. 309 ff., gives a good summary of the ethics of the Gītā, which he presents as a compromise between the contradictory doctrines.

world, though at the same time immanent in it, is taught as a great secret (IX, 1 ff.). There is, however, a third category of passages where Kṛṣṇa is not mentioned at all, but which speak quite abruptly of the brahman (neuter) as the sole and highest world principle in the sense of the monism of the Upaniṣads. Moreover, side by side with verses mentioning the Veda in an almost scornful tone (II, 42 ff.), we find other passages recommending the sacrifices prescribed in the Veda, and even describing the sacrifice as "a magic cow which fulfils all wishes" (III, 10), which is difficult to reconcile with that "desireless action" that is so often praised.

This doctrine of desireless action is sometimes described by the term *Yoga*. The same term is, however, used to denote various things. The usual meaning is what is generally understood by Yoga in Indian literature, *i.e.*, the doctrine of absorption, and of the methods by which man can withdraw from the sense-world and become entirely absorbed in the deity. It is in this sense that the Bhagavadgītā is sometimes called a *Yogaśāstra*, or manual of Yoga. This "practical philosophy" of the yoga has its psychological and metaphysical foundation in the *Sāṃkhya*.[1] The Sāṃkhya, however, teaches differentiation between spirit (puruṣa) and matter (prakṛti), plurality of souls, and independence and eternity of matter, and explains the creation as an unfolding of the world from original matter. Now all these are doctrines diametrically opposed to the doctrine of unity taught by the Upaniṣads and the Vedānta. In spite of this, the passages dealing with the brahman, teach the doctrine of universal unity as well.

How can all these contradictions be explained? Scholars are by no means unanimous on this point. Some are content

[1]) In V, 4 f., it is explained with great emphasis that Sāṃkhya and Yoga are one. In XVIII, 13, sāṃkhye kṛtānte cannot mean anything but "in the Sāṃkhya system." In XVIII, 19, guṇasaṃkhyāna is explained by Śaṅkara as Kāpila Śāstra. Kapila, the founder of the Sāṃkhya system, is called the first of the perfect sages, in X, 26.

to say that all these contradictions simply result from the fact that the Bhagavadgītā is not a systematic philosophical work, but a mystical poem, and that, in the words of Franklin Edgerton, the most decided and consistent exponent of this opinion, it is "poetic, mystical, and devotional, rather than logical and philosophical." W. von Humboldt had already said: "It is a sage, speaking out of the fulness and inspiration of his knowledge and of his feeling, not a philosopher trained in a school, classifying his material in accordance with a definite method, and arriving at the last principles of his doctrine by a skilful chain-work of ideas."[1] On the other hand, other scholars maintain that there are limits even for mystical poetry, and that the contradictions in the Gītā can better be explained by the assumption that the poem has not come down to us in its original form, but like most parts of the Mahābhārata has only received its present form as a result of interpolations and revisions. Some scholars had assumed that the Bhagavadgītā had originally been a pantheistic poem, which was remodelled later by the devotees of Viṣṇu into a theistic poem. This is very improbable, for in spite of all the contradictions the whole character of the work is predominantly theistic. God appears as an essentially personal god, who, as a teacher, and in human incarnation, requires devotion (bhakti) of his worshippers.

---

[1]) "Ueber die unter dem Namen Bhagavadgītā bekannte Episode des Mahābhārata," 1825 (Gesammelte Schriften V, p. 325). The following take up more or less the same point of view: K. T. *Telang*, SBE., Vol. 8, pp. 11 ff.; E. W. *Hopkins*, JRAS. 1905, pp. 384 ff., and Cambridge History I, 273; L. v. *Schroeder* in the Introduction to his German translation; B. *Faddegon*, Çaṃkara's Gītābhāṣya, toegelicht en beoordeeld, Diss., Amsterdam 1906, pp. 12 ff.; D. van Hinloopen *Labberton*, ZDMG. 66, 1912, 603 f.; R. G. *Bhandarkar*, Vaiṣṇavism, Śaivism, etc., pp. 157 ff.; O. *Strauss*, Ethische Probleme aus dem Mahābhārata. (GSAI. 24, 1911), p. 310; ZDMG. 67, 1913, 714 ff.; A. B. *Keith*, JRAS. 1913, p. 197; 1915, p. 548. H. *Oldenberg*, NGGW. 1919, 321 ff., and Das Mahabharata, pp. 39, 43, 70 ff.; J. N. *Farquhar*, Outline of the Religious Literature of India, London 1920, pp. 90 f.; H. *Jacobi*, DLZ. 1921, 715 ff.; 1922, 266 ff.; F. *Edgerton*, The Bhagavad Gita interpreted, Chicago 1925.

Taking this for granted, R. Garbe[1] made a direct attempt to reconstruct the original poem, by printing in small type in his translation all verses which he considers unauthentic i.e. interpolated from the view-point of the Vedanta philosophy and the orthodox brahmanical religion. I was formerly in entire agreement with Garbe.[2] However, after repeated readings of the Gītā and the most thorough investigation of the passages cut out by Garbe, I have come to the conclusion that even the original poem did not teach pure theism, but theism tinged with pantheism. I do not now believe that we are justified in pronouncing as interpolated all those passages where Kṛṣṇa speaks of himself as immanent in the world, as for instance the beautiful verses VII, 7 ff. On the other hand, I still agree with Garbe that those passages where mention is suddenly made of the *brahman* (neut.) without any reference to Kṛṣṇa whatsoever, are interpolated (*e.g.* II, 72; V, 6, 7, 10; VII, 29—VIII, 4 etc.), as well as the passages where ritual and sacrifices are recommended or glorified (*e.g.* III, 9-18; IX, 16-19 etc.). I think, too that the original Bhagavadgītā was much shorter, and that the work in its present form contains many more interpolations and additions than are assumed by Garbe. The very fact that the Bhagavadgītā contains exactly 18 Adhyāyas, just as the Mahābhārata is divided into 18 Parvans and as there are 18 Purāṇas, is suspicious.[3] Canto XI, where Kṛṣṇa reveals himself to Arjuna in his godlike form, is of the nature of a Purāṇa rather than like the work of the poet of the first sections.

---

[1]) In his translation of the Bhagavadgītā, see also ERE. II, 535 ff. and DLZ. 1922, 98 ff.; 605 f.

[2]) Also F. O. *Schrader*, ZDMG. 64, 340, and A. *Hillebrandt*, GGA. 1915, p. 628, agree with Garbe. *Grierson*, too (ERE. II, 540 f.; Ind. Ant. 37, 1908, 257) agrees with Garbe in counting the passages where "Brahmaism" is taught, among the "later" portions of the Gītā. The scholars mentioned in Note 2 are the opponents of the view adopted by Garbe.

[3]) *Cf. Hopkins*, Great Epic, p. 371.

It is this very conviction of mine that the author of the original Gītā was a great poet, that makes me hesitate to attribute to him such verses as XI, 26 ff., where the heroes of the epic are visioned as hanging between the teeth of the god,—a vision by which a further excuse for the killing of the enemy is added to those already given in Canto II: namely Arjuna need not hesitate to kill the enemies, because in reality they have "already been killed (by God)."[1)]

There can hardly be any doubt that the Bhagavadgītā did not belong to the original heroic poem. It is scarcely imaginable that an epic poet would make his heroes hold a philosophical conversation of 650 verses in the midst of the description of a battle. In all probability the original epic included only a very short dialogue between Arjuna and the hero and charioteer (not the god) Kṛṣna. This dialogue was, as it were, the germ from which the present didactic poem grew.[2)] This didactic poem was originally, by its very nature, a text of the Bhāgavatas, wherein the doctrine of bhakti in conjunction with the yoga doctrine of desireless action was taught on the foundation of the Sāṃkhya. There is evidence from inscriptions that, as early as the beginning of the 2nd century B. C. the religion of the Bhāgavatas had found adherents even among the Greeks in Gandhāra.[3)]

---

¹) Those scholars, too, who reject Garbe's views, do not all believe in the unity of the Gītā. *Hopkins* (Great Epic, pp. 215, 234 f.) speaks of the Gītā as "clearly......... rewritten by a modernising hand." *Oldenberg*, too, thinks it likely that the earliest Gītā concluded with II, 38, and that Adhyāyas XIII-XVIII are an appendix or appendices (NGGW. 1919, 333 f., 336 f.). See also *Strauss*, Ethische Probleme, pp. 312 f.

²) H. *Jacobi* (ZDMG. 72, 1918, 323 ff.) has endeavoured to trace in the poem those verses (of Adhyāyas I and II) which belonged to the old epic. But it is not impossible that there was no dialogue whatsoever between Kṛṣṇa and Arjuna in the old heroic poem, and that the whole poem was originally a text independent of the epic, an Upaniṣad, which was inserted bodily into the epic.

³) See J. H. *Marshall*, JRAS. 1909, pp. 1053 ff.; J. F. *Fleet*, ib., 1087 ff.; D. R. *Bhandarkar*, JBRAS. 23, 1910, 104 ff.; R. G. *Bhandarkar*, Ind. Ant. 41, 1912, pp. 13 ff.; Vaiṣṇavism, Śaivism, etc., pp. 3 f.; H. *Raychaudhuri*, Early History of the Vaishnava Sect, Calcutta 1920, pp. 13, 52 f., 58 ff.

It is perhaps not too bold to assume that the old Bhagavadgītā was written at about this time as an Upaniṣad of the Bhāgavatas.[1] Its language, style and metre, too, prove the work to be one of the earlier parts of the Mahābhārata. There are references to the Gītā in later sections of the epic,[2] and the *Anugītā* (XIV, 16-51) is surely nothing but a late imitation and continuation of the Bhagavadgītā, than which it contains a still greater variety of doctrines.

The Bhagavadgītā was already known to the poet Bāṇa (in the 7th century A.D.) as a portion of the Mahābhārata,[3] and side by side with the Upaniṣads and Vedānta-sūtras it formed one of the foundations of the philosophy of Śaṅkara. Most likely it was already in the early centuries A.D. that it received its present form at the hands of orthodox Brahmans; in this form it became and has remained until to-day the most popular religious book for all Hindus. The work owes this great popularity to the very circumstance that the most conflicting philosophical doctrines and religious views are united in it, so that adherents of all schools and sects could make use of it, and even to-day the strictest Brahman is just as much edified by it as the adherent of the Brahmo-Samaj and the believing theosophist under the leadership of Annie Besant.

It is scarcely possible, however, that the Bhagavadgītā can have arisen from the start on the basis of syncretism, as the latter only made its appearance more and more in later times. It is certain that the old and authentic Gītā was the work of a true and great poet. It is on the strength

---

[1]) According to K. T. *Telang* (SBE., Vol. 8, p. 34) the Gītā is "earlier than the third century B.C.," according to R. G. *Bhandarkar* (Vaiṣṇavism, Śaivism, etc., p. 13) it is "not later than the beginning of the fourth century B. C." I agree with *Edgerton* when he says (l. c., p. 3): "All that we can say is that it was probably composed before the beginning of our era, but not more than a few centuries before it."

[2]) XII, 346, 11 with "Harigītāḥ" and XII, 348, 8.

[3]) K. T. *Telang*, SBE., Vol. 8, p. 28.

of its poetic value, the forcefulness of its language, the splendour of the images and metaphors, the breath of inspiration which pervades the poem, that it has made such a deep impression on impressionable minds of all ages; and I am convinced that the poetical beauties as well as the moral value of the poem would find still greater appreciation, had the poem not been mutilated by additions and interpolations.[1)]

Another text-book of the Bhāgavatas is the Nārāyaṇīya (XII, 334-351); this is certainly a later work than the Bhagavadgītā, but even this has been augmented by additions.[2)] It is a work in true purāṇa style, which teaches that perfection can only be attained by bhakti and the grace of God, who appears here under the name of Nārāyaṇa. Here, too, we find the Bhāgavata religion and the philosophy of Saṃkhya and Yoga mingled with Vedānta ideas. The paradise of the pious devotees of Nārāyaṇa, Śvetadvīpa or "the white island," is described in very fantastical fashion:

The sage Nārada desires to look upon the only god Nārāyaṇa, whose faithful worshipper he is, in his original nature. He therefore raises himself aloft by the strength of yoga, and reaches the divine mountain Meru. Gazing thence to the north-west, he espies north of the ocean of milk the famous "white island" lying 32,000 yojanas from Meru. On this island he sees "white men without sense organs, who take no nourishment, whose eyes do not blink, from whom a most pleasant scent emanates, who are free from all sin, at the sight of whom evil men are dazzled, whose bodies are of bone hard as diamond, who are indifferent both to honour and scorn, like unto the children of heaven in form, endowed with shining

1) Attention has often been called to the fact that, notwithstanding the many beauties and lofty thoughts, the poem has many weak points. *Cf.* O. *Böhtlingk*, Bemerkungen zur Bhagavadgītā (BSGW. 1897); E. W. *Hopkins*, Religions of India, pp. 390, 399f, quoted in assent by R. *Garbe*, Die Bhagavadgîtâ, p. 16; and V. K. *Rajwade*, Bhandarkar Com. Vol., pp. 325 ff.

2) See R. G. *Bhandarkar*. Vaiṣṇavism, Śaivism, *etc.* pp. 4 ff., *Grierson*, Ind. Ant. 37, 1908, 251ff., 373ff. Translated into German by *Deussen*, Philosophische Texte des Mahâbhâratam, pp. 748 ff., into Dutch by C. *Lecoutere* in Mélanges Charles de Harlez, Leyden 1896, pp. 162 ff.

strength, with heads in the shape of sunshades. Their voice resembles the rushing of torrents of rain, they have four equal testicles, feet like lotus-leaves, sixty white teeth and eight fangs; they lick their sun-like faces with their tongues, and are full of love for God." [1]

It seems evident that the "white island" as well as the divine mountain Meru and the ocean of milk, belongs to the province of mythology, and not to that of historical geography. A few scholars have, however, tried to identify the ocean of milk with Lake Issyk-Kul or Lake Balkhash, and the "white island" with a land of "white men" in the north, inhabited by Nestorian Christians,[2] so that we should have to assume that there was Christian influence in the Nārāyaṇīya. In my opinion, the description of Śvetadvīpa does not remind us of the Christian Eucharist, but of heavenly regions such as Vaikuṇṭha, Goloka, Kailāsa and the Sukhāvatī paradise of the Buddha Amitābha.

Though Sāṃkhya and Yoga stand in the foreground of most of the philosophical sections of the Mahābhārata, we nevertheless find everywhere interpolated passages where the Vedānta is taught, and a few longer passages like the *Sanat-sujātīya* (V, 41-46) have been inserted with an entirely Vedāntist teaching.[3] However, as regards poetical value, there is none of the philosophical sections of the

---

[1]) XII, 335, 6-12. A tongue of this kind also belongs to the 32 characteristics of a Buddha, who, however, has only forty white teeth, *e.g.*, Suttanipāta, Selasutta (SBE., Vol. 10, II, p. 101).

[2]) *Cf.* J. *Kennedy*, JRAS. 1907, 481f., R. *Garbe*, AR. 16, 1913, 516ff, and Indien und das Christentum, Tübingen 1914, pp. 192 ff., *Grierson*, ERE. II, p. 549. On the other hand, s. *Winternitz*, Oesterreich. Monatsschrift fur den Orient, 41, 1915, pp. 185 f., and H. *Raychaudhuri*, Early History of the Vaishnava Sect, pp. 79 ff.

[3]) For the philosophical doctrines contained in the Mahābhārata s. E. W. *Hopkins*, The Great Epic of India, pp. 85-190, J. *Dahlmann*, Die Saṃkhya-Philosophie als Naturlehre und Erlösungslehre nach dem Mahābhārata, Berlin 1902, P. *Deussen*, AGPh I, 3, pp. 8-144. Contrary to Deussen and Dahlmann, I consider it wrong to speak of an "epic philosophy" as a "transition philosophy" between the philosophy of the Upaniṣads and that of the later systems. The epic proper has no connection with philosophy at all, and the "pseudo-epics" contains a mixture of philosophical doctrines belonging to widely different times.

Mahābhārata which could bear the least comparison with the Bhagavadgītā.

On the other hand, many a precious gem of Indian poetry is to be found in those didactic pieces which deal with *ethical* questions, *e. g.*, the oft-discussed question regarding the relationship of destiny and human action (karman), or contain general ethical doctrines—without regard to any particular philosophical or religious views. The following translations may serve at least as a small sample of the abundance of beauty and wisdom which lies hidden in these verses of the Mahābhārata:

"The wound a foeman's trenchant steel
Inflicts, in time again will heal;
The tree a woodman's axe o'erthrows
Soon sprouts again, and freshly grows;
But never more those wounds are closed,
Which harsh and cutting words have caused."

"The gods no club, like herdsmen, wield
To guard the man they deign to shield:
On those to whom they grace will show
They understanding sound bestow;
But rob of sense and insight all
Of whom their wrath decrees the fall.
These wretched men,—their minds deranged,—
See all they see distorted, changed;
For good to them as evil looms,
And folly wisdom's form assumes."

"With meekness conquer wrath, and ill with ruth,
By giving niggards vanquish, lies with truth."

"Reviling meet with patience; ne'er
To men malignant malice bear.
Harsh tones and wrathful language greet
With gentle speech and accents sweet.
When struck return not thou the blow.

Even gods their admiration shew
Of men who thus entreat a foe."

"That foe repel not with a frown
Who claims thy hospitable aid;
A tree refuses not its shade
To him who comes to hew it down."

"Thou mark'st the faults of other men,
Although as mustard seeds minute;
Thine own escape thy partial ken,
Though each in size a Bilva fruit." [1]

"A man should do with all his might
The good his heart has once designed.
Ne'er let him wrong with wrong requite,
But be to others ever kind."

"The good kind actions recollect,
But base injurious deeds forget;
On doing good to others set,
They never recompense expect."

"'Tis not for gain, for fame, from fear,
That righteous men injustice shun,
And virtuous men hold virtue dear;
An inward voice they seem to hear
Which tells that duty must be done."

"Whene'er thy acts the source must be
Of good or ill to other men,
Deal thou with them in all things then
As thou would'st have them deal with thee." [2]

---

[1]) Matthew vii, 3f.

[2]) V, 33, 77, 80 f., 34, 41, III, 194, 7, V, 35, 11, XII, 146, 5, I, 74, 82, III, 206, 44, II, 72, 7, XII, 158, 58, V, 38, 72 (Roy's edition), translated by J. *Muir*, Metrical Translations from Sanskrit Writers, pp. 93, 9, 88, 110, 85, 81 and 84.

The Harivaṃśa, an Appendix to the Mahābhārata.[1]

What has been said in the preceding chapters must suffice to give an idea of the *eighteen books* (parvans) of the Mahābhārata. The Indians, however, regard also the Harivaṃśa, a work which is in reality a Purāṇa and is also occasionally called "Harivaṃśa-Purāṇa" as part of the Mahābhārata. Yet the book is not even by the Indians termed a nineteenth "Parvan," but a *Khila, i.e.* a supplement or appendix to the Mahābhārata. This "appendix," it is true, is a work of 16,374 verses (Ślokas), that is, longer than the Iliad and the Odyssey put together. But its literary value is by no means in direct proportion to its size. It is above all not a "poem," in no sense the work of any *one poet*, but a jumbled or quite loosely connected mass of texts—legends, myths and hymns—serving for the glorification of the god Viṣṇu. The Harivaṃśa is not even the work of *one compiler*. The last third of it is surely only a later appendix to the appendix, and also in the remaining parts of the work many portions were probably inserted at quite different times.

The connection of the Harivaṃśa with the Mahābhārata itself is purely external and is limited essentially to the fact that the same Vaiśampāyana who is said to have recited the whole Mahābhārata to Janamejaya,[2] is also regarded as the reciter of the Harivaṃśa. In connection with the frame story of the Mahābhārata, Śaunaka, at the beginning of the appendix, requests Ugraśravas, after he has told him all the beautiful stories of the Bhāratas, to relate something about the Vṛṣṇis and Andhakas—the families to which Kṛṣna belongs.

---

[1]) *Cf.* A. *Holtzmann*, Das Mahābhārata, II, pp. 272-298, and E. W. *Hopkins*, Gleanings from the Harivaṃśa in Festschrift Windisch, pp. 68 ff. The Harivaṃśa has been translated into French by S. A. *Langlois*, Paris, 1834-35.

[2]) See above, pp. 323 f.

Thereupon Ugraśravas remarks that exactly the same request had been made by Janamejaya to Vaiśampāyana after the recitation of the Mahābhārata, and the latter had then related all that which he himself was now going to repeat. Thus all that follows is placed in the mouth of Vaiśampāyana. Besides this, in a few verses at the beginning and a complete lengthy song at the end of the appendix,[1] the praise of the Mahābhārata including the Harivaṃśa is sung in extravagant verses, and the religious merit acquired by the reciting and hearing of the whole poem is emphasized. This exhausts practically everything whereby the Harivaṃśa itself shows its connection with the Mahābhārata. As far as the contents are concerned, the Harivaṃśa has no more in common with the Mahābhārata than the Purāṇas ; for many legends, in particular brahmanical legends and myths, which occur in the Mahābhārata, reappear in different versions in the Harivaṃśa as well as in the Purānas.

The Harivaṃśa consists of three great sections, the first of which is entitled Harivaṃśaparvan. The title "Harivaṃśa," *i.e.* "genealogy of Hari,"[2] which was given to the whole appendix is in reality only applicable to this first book. It begins in the manner of the Purāṇas with a rather confused account of the Creation and all sorts of mythological narratives, thus of Dhruva, who became the Pole Star (62 ff.), of Dakṣa and his daughters, the female ancestors of the gods and demons (101 ff.), and others. The story of Vena, the Titan who was opposed to the Veda and to sacrifice, and his son Pṛthu, the first king of men, is narrated in detail.[3] Numerous legends, for instance those of Viśvāmitra and Vasiṣṭha (706 ff.) are worked into the genealogy of the solar dynasty (545 ff.), *i.e.* of King Ikṣvāku and his descendants,

---

1) Adhyāya 323, see below.

2) *Hari* is one of the most usual of the innumerable names of the god Viṣṇu.

3) *Pṛthūpākhyānā*, Adhy. 4-6, vss. 257-405

who trace their origin back to the sun-god. Regardless of any connection with this genealogy there is then inserted a ritual portion about the fathers and the sacrificial service due to them.[1] Then follows (1312 ff.) the genealogy of the lunar dynasty, which sprang from Atri, the son of the moon-god (Soma). One of Soma's grandsons was the renowned *Purūravas*, whose love adventures with *Urvaśī* are related in a very archaic form which rather closely approaches the Śatapatha-Brāhmaṇa.[2] Among the descendants of Purūravas are Nahuṣa and Yayāti. Yadu, the son of the latter, is the ancestor of the Yādavas, to whom Vasudeva belongs, as whose son Kṛṣṇa the god Viṣṇu is born on earth. After the genealogy of the human Kṛṣṇa has thus been given, there follow a series of songs (2131 ff.) dealing entirely with the *god Viṣṇu* and thus, to a certain extent, containing the divine previous history of Kṛṣṇa.

The second great section of the Harivaṃśa, entitled Viṣṇuparvan,[3] deals almost exclusively with Kṛṣṇa, the god Viṣṇu become mortal. All the stories of the birth and childhood, the heroic deeds and love adventures of the human, often all-too-human, cowherd-god, are related here at great length; they are also related in greater or less detail in some of the Purāṇas, and have made the name *Kṛṣṇa* one of the most familiar to every Hindu. While the best and wisest among the Viṣṇu-worshippers honour Kṛṣṇa above all as the herald of the pious doctrines of the Bhagavadgītā, it is the Kṛṣṇa of the *legends*, as they are related in the Harivaṃśa and in the Purāṇas, who is now honoured and

---

[1]) *Pitṛkalpa*, "ancestral ritual," Adhy. 16-24, vss. 835-1311. The story of Brahmadatta, who understands the languages of the animals, is inserted in Adhy. 21, vss. 1185 ff.; this is translated and discussed by Th. *Benfey* in "Orient und Occident," Vol. II, 1862, pp. 133-171, and by *Leumann*, WZKM., 6, 1892, pp. 1 ff.

[2]) Adhy. 26, vss. 1363-1414, translated by K. *Geldner* in "Vedische Studien" I, p. 249 ff. Cf. above p. 209.

[3]) Adhy. 57 ff. = vss. 3180 ff.

worshipped as a lofty god, and now exalted as an ideal of the most perfect manhood, by the millions of Hindus of all classes throughout India till the present day. It is this god of the legends, and not the Kṛṣṇa of the Mahābhārata, the cunning friend of the Pāṇḍavas, of whom the Greek Megasthenes already talked as the "Indian Hercules." In order to give at least an idea of these Kṛṣṇa legends which are important alike in the history of literature and the history of religion, the contents of the second section of the Harivaṃśa shall here be briefly sketched.

In the town of Mathurā there reigned a bad king *Kaṃsa*. To him Nārada announced that he would meet his death at the hands of the eighth son of *Devakī*, the sister of his father and the wife of *Vasudeva*. Then Kaṃsa determines to kill all Devakī's children. He has Devakī closely guarded by his servants, and six of her children are killed immediately after birth. The seventh child, that brother of Kṛṣṇa who is later known as "*Rāma* with the ploughshare," "Balarāma," or "Baladeva," is rescued by Nidrā,[1] the goddess of sleep, by her transferring the boy, before he is born, from the womb of Devakī to that of *Rohiṇī*, another wife of Vasudeva. The eighth son, however, and this was Kṛṣṇa, was exchanged by Vasudeva himself, immediately after birth, in order to rescue him from Kaṃsa, with the daughter of the cowherd *Nanda* and his wife *Yaśodā*, who was born at the same time. So the little daughter of the latter is dashed against a rock by Kaṃsa, while Kṛṣṇa is regarded as the son of a cowherd and grows up among the cowherds. Rāma, too, is entrusted to the protection of the cowherd family by Vasudeva, and the two boys grow up together in the cowherds' station. Even as a suckling Kṛṣṇa performs wondrous miracles. One day, when his foster-mother Yaśodā, after having laid the sleeping child under a waggon, lets him wait too long for food, he begins to struggle impatiently with hands and feet, and finally overthrows the heavy waggon with one foot. In mad merriment the boys Kṛṣṇa and Rāma later rush through forest and field, and make much trouble for the simple cowherd's wife. On one occasion

[1] Perhaps the circumstance that Nidrā is also the name of *Durgā*, gave rise to the interpolation of a hymn to this goddess, the *Āryāstava* (Adhy. 59 = vss. 3268-3303). But the interpolation of such hymns (stotras) is characteristic of all Purāṇas.

she hardly knows what to do, so she ties a rope round little Kṛṣṇa's body and fastens him tightly to a heavy mortar, saying angrily: "Now run, if thou canst." But the boy not only drags away the mortar with him, but as the mortar gets caught between two gigantic trees, he tears out the mighty trees by their roots. Horrified, the cowherds and the foster-mother see the boy sitting laughing between the branches of the trees, but he himself is uninjured.

After seven years had elapsed, the boys grew tired of the cowherds' station. So Kṛṣṇa caused innumerable wolves to issue from his body, which frightened the cowherds so much that they decided to wander further. They wandered with their flocks to the Vṛndā-forest. Here the boys now run happily through the forest. But one day Kṛṣṇa strolls alone—now playing now singing, now whistling on a leaf, now blowing on the cowhard's flute—along the banks of the river Jumnā, and reaches the deep lake in which the snake-king *Kāliya* dwells, who, with his retinue, poisons the water of the Jumnā and makes the whole neighbourhood unsafe. With swift determination, Kṛṣṇa plunges into the lake, in order to overcome the frightful dragon. Soon the five-headed, fire-breathing monster appears, and a host of snakes rush furiously upon the youthful hero, surrounding and biting him. But he soon frees himself, presses the heads of the monster on the ground, and jumps with force on to the middle head, so that the dragon confesses himself conquered and retreats into the deep with the whole brood of snakes.

Soon afterwards he also slays the demon *Dhenuka*, who, in the form of an ass, guards the mountain Govardhana. Another demon, the giant *Pralamba*, does not venture to tackle Kṛṣṇa, but is slain by Rāma, the brother of the latter.

In the autumn the cowherds, according to their custom, wish to arrange a great feast in honour of the rain god *Indra*. Kṛṣṇa will have none of this worship of Indra. "We are cowherds who wander through the forests, who always live by the wealth of cows, the cows are our deity, the hills and forests." (3808) In such words he invites the cowherds to arrange a mountain-sacrifice instead of the Indra celebration, which the cowherds do. At this Indra is so enraged that he sends down a frightful storm. But Kṛṣṇa lifts up the mountain Govardhana and holds it like an umbrella over the cowherds and their flocks, so that they are entirely sheltered. After seven days the storm ceases, Kṛṣṇa restores the mountain to its place, and Indra humbly recognises in Kṛṣṇa the exalted god Viṣṇu.

Then the cowherds praise and worship him as a god, but he smilingly declares that he only desires to be their relative ; the time will come later when they will recognise his true nature. And, as a cowherd among cowherds, he lives in youthful happiness. He organises bull-fights and tournaments with the strongest among the cowherds. On the lovely autumn nights, however, his heart rejoiced in the round dances,[1] which the beautiful cowherdesses, who are all enamoured of the hero-youth, perform in the moonlight, singing of his deeds and jestingly imitating his play, his merry glance, his gait, his dancing and his singing.

Once, when Kṛṣṇa was enjoying himself with the cowherdesses, *Ariṣṭa*, a demon in the form of a bullock, appeared. Kṛṣṇa tears out one of his horns and slays him with it.

The fame of all the heroic deeds of Kṛṣṇa reaches the ears of Kaṃsa and causes him anxiety. In order to get him out of the way, he sends for the two youthful heroes to come to Mathurā, where, at a festival, they are to fight with his best wrestlers. But no sooner has he arrived in the town than Kṛṣṇa performs wonderful miracles and feats of strength. Thus he bends the king's great bow, which even the gods cannot bend, with such strength that, with a tremendous crash, it breaks in twain. Kṛṣṇa pulls out the tusk of an elephant which Kaṃsa lets loose upon the youths, and kills the elephant with it. The two powerful champion wrestlers with whom Kaṃsa confronts the youths are also killed by them. Filled with rage, the king now commands that the cowherd-youths and all cowherds shall be driven out of his kingdom. Then Kṛṣṇa springs like a lion upon Kaṃsa, drags him by his hair into the centre of the arena and kills him.

After some time the two brothers go to Ujjein, in order to learn the art of archery from a famous teacher there. A son of this teacher has perished in the sea, and as his fee, he demands that Kṛṣṇa shall bring him back this son. Then Kṛṣṇa descends into the underworld, overcomes the god of death, Yama, and brings the boy back to his father.

In order to avenge the death of Kaṃsa, his father-in-law *Jarāsandha* goes forth with many allied princes to fight against the Yādavas, besieges Mathurā, is repeatedly repulsed by Kṛṣṇa, but always renews his attacks, until at last he is compelled to retreat. These battles with Jarāsandha are described in a long series of narratives.

---

[1]) These are the dances called *Rāsa* or *Hallīśa*, accompanied by pantomimic representations, and which still to-day take place in some parts of India, and, for instance, in Kathiawad are still known by a name corresponding to the Sanskrit "Hallīśa." (*Cf.* the Indian monthly magazine "East and West," Vol. I, 748 f., May, 1902.)

In the same way the following narrative of the rape of *Rukmiṇī* is spun out.[1] King Bhīṣmaka of Vidarbha has promised his daughter Rukmiṇī in marriage to King Śisupāla, and the wedding was about to be celebrated. Then Kṛṣṇa comes with his brother Rāma to the marriage-feast and *kidnaps* the bride. The deeply-offended princes pursue him, but are repulsed by Rāma. Rukmin, the brother of the kidnapped girl, swears he will never return to his native town, unless he has killed Kṛṣṇa and brought his sister back. A fierce fight takes place, in which Rukmin is defeated; but in response to the entreaties of Rukmiṇī Kṛṣṇa grants him his life. In order not to break his oath, Rukmin founds a new town for himself. In Dvārakā the marriage of Kṛṣṇa with Rukmiṇī takes place. With her he begets ten sons, but later marries s·ven queens and sixteen thousand other wives, with whom he begets thousands of sons. *Pradyumna*, a son of Kṛṣṇa and Rukmiṇī,[2] later marries a daughter of Rukmin, and their son Aniruddha marries a grand-daughter of Rukmin. At the marriage of Aniruddha, Rāma and Rukmin quarrel over a game of dice, and the latter is slain by Rāma. In connection with this there is a glorification of the deeds of Rāma.[3]

Then follows the story of the slaying of *Naraka*.[4] This Naraka is a demon, who has stolen the ear-rings of Aditi, and also otherwise gives the gods much trouble. At the request of Indra Kṛṣṇa fights against him and kills him.

The next narrative [5] shows us Kṛṣṇa in a battle against Indra. The seer Nārada once brought Kṛṣṇa a blossom from the heavenly tree *Pārijāta*, which Kṛṣṇa gave to his beloved Rukmiṇī. Then Satyabhāmā, one of his other wives, grows terribly jealous, and sulks until Kṛṣṇa promises to bring her the whole Pārijāta-tree from heaven. But as Indra will not willingly surrender the tree, Kṛṣṇa challenges him to fight. This leads to a long and violent battle between the two gods, which, however, is finally settled peaceably by Aditi, the mother of gods.

There follows a rather extensive didactic portion,[6] only very

---

[1]) Into the old legend, in which Kṛṣṇa appears as *hero* later portions are here interpolated, in which he appears as god Viṣṇu in his full divinity.

[2]) He is an incarnation of the god of love.

[3]) *Baladevamāhātmyakathana*, Adhy. 120, 6766-6786.

[4]) *Narakavadha*, Adhyāyas 121-123=6787-6988.

[5]) *Pārijātaharaṇo*, Adhy. 124-140=6989-7956. A hymn to Śiva is inserted (*Mahādevastavana*), Adhy. 131=7415-7455.

[6]) *Puṇyakavidhi*, Adhy. 136-140=vss. 7722-7956.

slightly connected with this long section, and really belonging to scientific eroticism, the *Kāmaśāstra*. This is an instruction (in the form of a conversation between the wives of Kṛṣṇa and the wise Nārada, who, however, refers to *Umā*, the wife of Śiva, as his authority) upon *Puṇyakas* and *Vratakas*, *i.e.* ceremonies, festivals and vows, by means of which a wife can make her body pleasing to her husband and assure herself of his favour. But as these ceremonies are efficacious only for virtuous wives, a few instructions upon the duties of wives (7754 ff.) are given at the beginning.

The next section [1] again relates Kṛṣṇa's battles with the demons. The Asuras of the "six towns" (*Ṣaṭpura*) steal the daughters of the pious Brahmadatta. Kṛṣṇa comes to his rescue and kills Nikumbha, the king of the Asuras, and restores the Brahman his daughters.

Then follows an entirely Śivaite passage,[2] which has nothing to do with Kṛṣṇa, and relates how the thousand-headed demon *Andhaka* is killed by Śiva.

The following section[3] reverts to Kṛṣṇa and relates another story of the killing of the Asura Nikumbha. The Yādavas, with Kṛṣṇa and Rāma at their head, undertake a pilgrimage to the sea to a sacred bathing-place in order to celebrate a great joyous festival there. Kṛṣṇa with his sixteen thousand wives, Rāma with his only wife Revatī, and youths of the Yādavas with thousands of courtesans give themselves up to playing and singing, feasting and drinking, and all kinds of enjoyments in the water and on the sea-shore.[4] During these festivities the demon Nikumbha kidnaps *Bhānumatī*, a daughter of the Yādava Bhānu. Kṛṣṇa's son Pradyumna pursues the Asura and brings the stolen one back, while Kṛṣṇa himself kills Nikumbha.

The following cantos [5] deal almost exclusively with *Pradyumna*, the son of Kṛṣṇa. First the story of the marriage of Pradyumna with *Prabhāvatī*, the daughter of the Asura *Vajranābha*, is related, in which the heavenly flamingoes intervene in bringing about the bond of love just as in the Nala-song flamingoes are the messengers of love between Nala and

---

[1] *Ṣaṭpuravadha*, Adhy. 141-144 = vss. 7957-8198.

[2] *Andhakavadha*, Adhy 145 f. = vss. 8199-8300.

[3] *Bhānumatīharaṇa*, Adhy. 147-149 = vss. 8301-8549.

[4] The brilliant description of these voluptuous scenes fills two cantos (147 f. = 8301-8470).

[5] Adhy. 150 ff. = vss. 8550 ff. Freely rendered into German in the beautiful poem "Pradyumna" by *Schack*, "Stimmen vom Ganges," pp. 67 ff.

Damayantī. In order to win Prabhāvatī, Pradyumna, disguised as an actor, comes with a whole troupe of actors to the court of Vajranābha. Then all sorts of plays are performed,[1] with which the Asuras are greatly charmed. But Pradyumna uses the lovely nights for secretly enjoying the pleasures of love with Prabhāvatī. Finally Vajranābha hears of the love-intrigue, and, full of anger, he is about to have Pradyumna thrown into fetters. But the latter kills the warriors who rush towards him, and the Asura king himself. Thereupon he enters Dvārakā with his beloved one.

The second narrative [2] treats of the youthful love of *Pradyumna*: how he is kidnapped by Asuras seven days after his birth and grows up in the house of the demon *Śambara*; how Māyāvatī, the wife of the latter, burns with love for the beautiful youth and enlightens him on the fact that he is not her son, but the son of Kṛṣna and Rukmiṇī; how Pradyumna then kills Śambara after a desperate fight [3] and finally, united with Māyāvatī, returns to his native town, where he is joyfully received by his parents.

For no reason at all, the daily prayer of Rāma,[4] a litany consisting of an enumeration of divine beings, is inserted here.

After a few shorter pieces, legends and speeches in praise of Kṛṣṇa, the book concludes with the story of the "battle of Bāṇa" [5] and the love affair of *Aniruddha*, the son of Pradyumna, with *Ūṣā*, the daughter of the Asura-king Bāṇa. The latter is a favourite of the god Śiva. Kṛṣṇa comes to the aid of Aniruddha, who is hard pressed by Bāṇa; and the fighting with Bāṇa leads to a violent battle between Śiva and Viṣṇu, by which the whole world is seriously menaced. But Brahman comes to the aid of the earth and creates peace between the two gods, by declaring that

---

[1]) This (8672 ff.) is *perhaps* one of the oldest, certainly one of the most interesting mentions of dramas and dramatic performances in Indian literature. Not only scenes from the life of Kṛṣṇa are here produced, but dramatizations of the great epic Rāmāyaṇa and of the story of Ṛṣyaśṛṅga (*cf.* above pp. 399 ff.) are also expressly mentioned. Unfortunately the age of this piece called "Pradyumnottara," is quite uncertain. *Cf.* Sylvain *Lévi*, "Le théâtre indien," Paris, 1890, pp. 327 ff., and A. B. *Keith.* The Sanskrit Drama, Oxford 1924, pp. 28, 47 f.

[2]) *Śambaravadha*, Adhy. 163-167 = vss. 9208-9487.

[3]) In this he is helped by Durgā, whom he invokes in a hymn (*Pradyumna-kṛta Durgāstava*, Adhy. 166 = 9423-9430).

[4]) *Baladevāhnika*, Adhy. 168 = vss. 9488-9591.

[5]) *Bāṇayuddha*, Adhy. 175-190 = 9806-11062.

Śiva and Viṣṇu are one. Here follows a hymn (stotra) glorifying these two as identical deities.[1] With the marriage of Aniruddha and Ūṣā, which is celebrated with great magnificence in Dvāravatī, the book ends.

The intermingling of stotras (hymns) as that of Viṣṇu-Śiva here, shows particularly to how great an extent the Harivaṃśa is a collection of texts for *religious* purposes, and not an epic poem.[2]

But while in Book II there are still some remains of a *Kṛṣṇa epic* which must certainly once have existed, Book III, called Bhaviṣyaparvan (11063 ff.), is only a loose collection of Purāṇa texts. The title Bhaviṣyaparvan, *i.e.* "section of the future" refers only to the first cantos of this book, which contain prophecies regarding the coming ages of the world. Here is related the story of a horse-sacrifice which Janamejaya wished to offer; but Vyāsa foretells him that this sacrifice would not be successful, for the godless age of Kali will dawn, which will be followed only a long time later by the Kṛta-age of virtue and piety. This section [3] forms a complete whole and is even termed an independent poem. Then follow, without any connection, two different accounts of the Creation.[4] A third section deals in great detail with the incarnations of Viṣṇu as a boar, a man-lion and dwarf.[5]

---

1) *Hariharātmakastava*, Adhy. 184 = vss. 10660-10697. This is one of the *few* places in Indian literature where there is a mention of *Trimūrti*. For *Hari* (Viṣṇu) and *Hara* (Śiva) are not only identical with each other, but also with *Brahman*.

2) How largely the Harivaṃśa is regarded as a religious book, is proved by the circumstance that it is the custom in the courts of justice in Nepal to place a copy of the Harivaṃśa on the head of the witness, if he is a Hindu, in the same way as the Koran is placed upon the head of a Mohammedan. (A. *Barth*, Religions of India, p. 156 note).

3) Adhy. 191-196 = vss. 11063-11278. The passage is commended, in 11270 ff., as a great ornate poem (mahākāvyam). But verses 11082 ff. already say clearly that the Harivaṃśa is *concluded*, and that the story of Janamejaya's horse-sacrifice only forms *an appendix to the Harivaṃśa*. The subsequent sections are most probably only later additions.

4) *Pauṣkaraprādurbhāva*, Adhy. 197-222 = vss. 11279-12277.

5) Adhy. 223-263 = vss. 12278-14390. Brahman begins a hymn to Viṣṇu (Viṣṇu-stotra) 12880 ff. (Adhy. 238). Kaśyapa utters a hymn in prose to the "Great Spirit" (Mahāpuruṣastava) 14114 ff. (Adhy. 259).

Next follows a section which, like the last one in Book II, pursues the tendency to harmonise Viṣṇu- and Śiva-worship. Alternately Viṣṇu sings a hymn to Śiva and Siva to Viṣṇu.[1] The next passage again deals with a heroic deed of Kṛṣna, namely the slaying of King *Pauṇḍra*, who rises up against Kṛṣṇa.[2] The last longer section of the Harivaṃśa is the legend (upākhyāna) of the two Śiva-worshippers *Haṃsa* and *Ḍimbhaka*, who are humiliated by Kṛṣṇa-Viṣṇu.[3]

There is appended yet another long canto which, in most extravagant fashion, tells of the merit of reading the Mahābhārata and the reward of heaven which awaits the reader, and further prescribes the presents which one should give to the readers (vācaka) after the close of every parvan, and finally ends with a song in praise of the Mahābhārata as the most sacred and most exalted of all "text-books" (śāstra).[4] Above all, however, it is boasted that the work serves for the glorification of Viṣṇu, for: "In the Veda, in the Rāmāyaṇa and in the sacred Bhārata, O bravest of Bharata's descendants, everywhere, at the beginning, at the end, and in the middle *Hari* is glorified."[5]

Strange to say, after all the glorifications of Viṣṇu, and after the actual conclusion of the book, there still follows a canto[6] in which the god Śiva comes into his own, and it is related how he destroyed the three castles (Tripura) of the demons. Yet even here a final verse in praise of the "great yogin" Viṣṇu is added.

---

[1]) *Kailāsayātrā*, Adhy. 264-281 = vss. 14391-15031. Adhy. 278; Īśvarastuti, Adhy. 279 and 281. Viṣṇustotra.

[2]) *Pauṇḍrakavadha*, Adhy. 282-293 = vss. 15032-15375.

[3]) *Haṃsaḍimbhakopākhyāna*, Adhy. 294-322 = vss. 15376-16139.

[4]) Adhy. 323 = vss. 16140-16238: *Sarvaparvānukīrttana*. The enumeration of the parvans partly contains other names than our editions. The contents of this adhyāya coincide with similar songs of praise in Book I of the Mahābhārata. *Cf.* above, pp. 325 f.

[5]) Verse 16232.

[6]) *Tripuravadha*, Adhy. 324 = vss. 16239-16324.

The book finally concludes with a short summing-up of the contents of the Harivaṃśa and an enumeration of the religious gains one acquires by hearing this "Purāṇa."

The fact that the Harivaṃśa is absolutely and entirely a *Purāṇa* is also shown by the numerous, often literally identical, coincidences with passages in several of the most important Purāṇas.[1] Nevertheless, it was necessary to speak of the Harivaṃśa here, and not only later in the chapter on the Purāṇas, not only because this work is regarded by the *Indians* as belonging to the Mahābhārata, but also because this supplement and the way in which it is added to the epic is peculiarly adapted for throwing light on the history of the Mahābhārata itself. We will now turn to this history.

THE AGE AND HISTORY OF THE MAHĀBHĀRATA.

We have now given a survey of all that has come down to us as "Mahābhārata" in manuscripts and editions, and are now faced with the question: How and when did this gigantic work originate?

Already in the short account of the contents of the actual heroic poem (pp. 328-375) the reader must have noticed a contradiction, which is still more noticeable in the reading of the Mahābhārata itself. While the poem in its present form absolutely takes the part of the *Pāṇḍavas,* and describes the Pāṇḍavas as not only brave beyond measure, but also as noble and good, and on the other hand represents the *Kauravas* as treacherous and mischievous,—the poem, in remarkable self-contradiction, relates that all the heroes of the Kauravas fall through treachery or in unfair fight.[2]

---

[1] Brahma-, Padma-, Viṣṇu-, Bhāgavata-, and especially Vāyu-Purāṇa. The Garuḍa-Purāṇa communicates the contents of the Mahābhārata *and of the Harivaṃśa* in extract. See A. *Holtzmann,* Das Mahābhārata, IV, pp. 32, 35, 37 ff., 40, 42 ff., 47 ff., 56.

[2] See above, pp. 361 f.

It is still more striking that all the treachery emanates from *Kṛṣṇa*, that *he* is always the instigator of all the deceit and defends the conduct of the Pāṇḍavas. And this is the same Kṛṣṇa who in many parts of the Mahābhārata and more especially in the Harivaṃśa, is praised and glorified as an incarnation of Viṣṇu, the highest god, and as the ideal and prototype of every virtue.

How can these remarkable contradictions be explained? Upon this there can only be conjectures. First, there is probably justification for the supposition, although we have only the authority of the Mahābhārata itself for it, that a change of dynasty did actually once take place in the North-west of India as the result of a great war, and that these quasi-historical events form the foundation of the epic itself.[1] Starting out from this, we can well imagine that the original heroic songs dealing with the fight between the hostile cousins, were sung among the bards who were still near Duryodhana himself or the house of the Kauravas, but that, in the course of time, as the rule of the victorious Pāṇḍavas was more and more firmly established, these songs were transmitted to bards who were in the employ of the new ruling race. In the mouths of these bards those alterations were then undertaken which made the Pāṇḍavas appear in a favourable light and the Kauravas in an unfavourable one, without its being possible to eradicate completely the original tendency of the songs. In our Mahābhārata the nucleus of the epic, the

---

[1]) Even those who find a *mythological* nucleus in the legend underlying the epic, admit that there are also historical elements in it. Thus A. *Ludwig* "Über das Verhältnis des mythischen Elementes zu der historischen Grundlage des Mahâbhârata." (Abhandlungen der k. böhmischen Ges d. Wissensch. VI, 12.) Prague, 1884. *Pargiter* and *Grierson* (JRAS., 1908, pp. 309 ff., 602 ff.) have expressed the opinion that, underlying the war between the Kauravas and the Pāṇḍavas there may be the historical fact of a battle of nations (a fight between the nations of Madhyadeśa and the other nations of India) and at the same time a fight between a warrior party on the one side and a priestly party on the other. I do not consider that there is any justification of this historical construction. *Cf. Hopkins*, Cambridge History, I, p. 275.

description of the great battle, is placed in the mouth of Sañjaya, the charioteer of Dhṛtarāṣṭra, that is, in the mouth of the bard of the *Kauravas*. It is precisely in these battle-scenes that the Kauravas appear in the most favourable light. The whole Mahābhārata, on the other hand, is recited, according to the frame-story contained in Book I, by Vyāsa's pupil, Vaiśampāyana at the snake-sacrifice of Janamejaya. This Janamejaya, however, is regarded as a descendant of the *Pāṇḍava* Arjuna, which agrees well with the fact that, in the Mahābhārata as a whole, the Pāṇḍavas are preferred to the Kauravas.[1)]

As regards Kṛṣṇa, the race of the Yādavas to which he belongs, is described in several places in the Mahābhārata as a cowherd-tribe of rough manners, and he himself is repeatedly scorned by hostile heroes as "cowherd" and "slave." In the ancient heroic poem, he was certainly nothing more than a prominent leader of that cowherd-tribe and had nothing divine about him. Even behind the Kṛṣṇa-legends of the Harivaṃśa there seems to be a foundation of older legends, in which Kṛṣṇa was not yet a god, but the hero of a rough tribe of cowherds. It is difficult to believe that *Kṛṣṇa*, the friend and counsellor of the Pāṇḍavas, *Kṛṣṇa*, the herald

---

1) I do not think that there was a systematic remodelling (as is the view of *Holtzmann*), but that gradual changes were made. J. v. *Negelein* (OLZ. 1908, 336 f.) refutes this theory by observing that the ancient epic took no stock whatsoever of the moral point of view, that it portrayed both parties in almost equal light and shade, and that it merely rejoiced in the actual display of strength. A similar view is taken by *Oldenberg* (Das Mahābhārata, pp. 35 ff.) who, like *Hopkins* (Cambridge History, I, 265) believes that the moral reflections cast on the conduct of the Pāṇḍavas belong to a more modern age, "when a finer morality had begun to temper the crude royal and military spirit." *Hertel* (WZKM. 24, 1910, 421) seeks to explain the contradiction of the treacherous behaviour of the Pāṇḍavas and the poet's siding with them, by saying that the Mahābhārata has the character of a nītiśāstra and that, according to the rules of politics, the king is justified in or even in duty bound to the utilisation of cunning. These scholars, however, forget that the speeches in which the Pāṇḍavas' manner of fighting is condemned as dishonourable, do not belong to the didactic additions to the epic, but are interwoven with the description of the fight itself, and do not in the least bear the stamp of later additions.

of the doctrines of the Bhagavadgītā, *Kṛṣṇa*, the youthful hero and demon-slayer, *Kṛṣṇa*, the favourite and lover of the cowherdesses, and finally *Kṛṣṇa*, the incarnation of the exalted god Viṣṇu, can be one and the same person. It is far more likely that there were two or several traditional Kṛṣṇas, who were merged into *one* deity at a later time. Kṛṣṇa, the son of Devakī, is mentioned in the Chāndogya-Upaniṣad (III, 17) as a pupil of Ghora Āṅgirasa, who expounds doctrines which at least in a few points coincide with those of the Bhagavadgītā. For this reason we can scarcely separate this old sage of the time of the Upaniṣads from the Kṛṣṇa of the Bhagavadgītā.[1] It is possible that this Kṛṣṇa was the founder of the Bhāgavata religion, and that like so many other founders of religions in India, he was made into an incarnation of the god worshipped by his adherents.[2] It is possible, moreover, that Kṛṣṇa did not figure at all in the original epic, and was introduced only later, perhaps with the express intention of justifying the actions of the Pāṇḍavas, which were shady from the moral point of view, by representing them as inspired by the "god" Kṛṣṇa.[3] Much as has been written on the problem of Kṛṣṇa, we must admit, nevertheless, that no satisfactory solution has been found.[4] In any case, it is a far cry from Kṛṣṇa the friend of the Pāṇḍavas, to the Kṛṣṇa of the Harivaṃśa and the exalted god Viṣṇu.

---

[1]) *Cf.* H. *Raychaudhuri*, Early History of the Vaishnava Sect, pp. 23, 30 f., 48 ff.

[2]) This view is advocated especially by *Garbe*, Die Bhagavadgītā, 2nd Ed., pp. 27 ff.

[3]) Thus *Oldenberg*, Das Mahābhārata, pp. 37, 43. *Cf.* also *Jacobi*, ERE. VII, 195 f. and Sir Charles *Eliot*, Hinduism and Buddhism (London, 1921), II, 154, who emphasizes the point that Kṛṣṇa is not so essentially important in the story of the Mahābhārata as is Rāma in that of the Rāmāyaṇa. It seems to me, however, that the *warrior* Kṛṣṇa, *not the god* Kṛṣṇa, is too closely bound up with the main narrative for the epic to be imaginable entirely without him.

[4]) *Cf. Holtzmann*, Das Mahābhārata I, 132 ff.; A. *Weber*, Zur indischen Religionsgeschichte (Sonderabdruck aus "Deutsche Revue" 1899), pp. 28 f.; L. J. *Sedgwick*, JBRAS,

The political and religious development which is reflected in those songs of the Mahābhārata which refer to the great fight—the passing of the supremacy from the Kauravas to the Pāṇḍavas, and the deification of Kṛṣṇa—thus already presupposes a long period of time, and it is unthinkable that even these songs only, which form the nucleus of the work, should originate with one single poet. Such an assumption becomes still more impossible if we consider the countless *contradictions* which occur in the *details* of the principal narrative. I will recall only the narratives of the marriage of the Pāṇḍavas (see above, pp. 336 f.) and the adventures of Arjuna (p. 339). In Book IV we find a duplicate of the whole battle in the Kuru-field: Bhīṣma and all the other heroes of the Kauravas are put to flight by Arjuna almost in no time; which does not fit in well with the fact that later on it is only possible to overcome the Kauravas in eighteen days, and then only by the employment of guile on the part of the Pāṇḍavas. There can scarcely be any doubt that the whole of Book IV (Virāṭa-parvan) is a later production [1] than the magnificent battle-descriptions in the following books. But even in those books which unquestionably contain the oldest parts of the epic, there are constantly to be found contradictions which cannot possibly be explained by the "ingenious carelessness" of any *one* poet.[2] Beside the most splendid descriptions full of raciness and vigour, there are also to be found long songs, in which the description of the

---

23, 1910, pp. 115 ff.; *Grierson*, ERE. II, 539 ff: *Jacobi*, ERE. VII, 193 ff. and Streitberg-Festgabe, p. 168; A. B. *Keith*, JRAS. 1915, 548 ff; R. G. *Bhandarkar*, Vaiṣṇavism, etc., pp. 3 f., 8 ff., 33 ff.; *Raychaudhuri*, l. c., pp. 18 ff. and passim; *Garbe*, l. c.; *Eliot*, Hinduism and Buddhism II, 152 ff.; *Hopkins* in Cambridge History I, 258; *Oldenberg*, Das Mahābhārata, pp. 37 ff.

1) Thus already *Holtzmann*, Mahābhārata II, p. 98, and *Hopkins*, The Great Epic of India, pp. 382 f. *Cf.* N. B. *Utgikar*, The Virāṭaparvan of the Mahābhārata (Poona, 1923), pp. xx f. and my remarks in Ann. Bh. Inst. V, 1, p. 23.

2) *Cf.* above, notes on pp. 361, 362 f.; 366, 370 f.

eighteen-day battle is spun out as long as possible with dull monotony and continual repetitions.

Thus even what we can term the "actual epic," as it has come down to us, is certainly not the work of *one* poet. Even this "nucleus" of the Mahābhārata *is* no longer the old heroic poem; but the latter is *contained* in it, in a much diluted condition.

We have now seen that around this nucleus an enormous mass of the most miscellaneous poems has accumulated; heroic songs from various cycles of legends, brahmanical myths and legend poetry, ascetic poetry and didactic poems of all kinds from the simplest moral maxims to extensive philosophical poems, formal law-books and complete Purāṇas. Though J. Dahlmann has applied an enormous amount of erudition in an attempt to prove that the Mahābhārata is one unified work which was composed by *one* poet in pre-Buddhist times both as an epic and a law-book,[1] only few scholars agree with him. Sylvain Lévi,[2] too, has recently attempted to explain the Mahābhārata as "a deliberate composition organically and artistically spread around a central fact and inspired by a dominant sentiment which penetrates and permeates it." He compares the Mahābhārata with the Vinaya, the code of discipline of the Mūla-Sarvāstivādin Buddhists,

---

[1]) In his book "Das Mahābhārata als Epos und Rechtsbuch" (Berlin, 1895) (see above, p. 316, note 1), *Dahlmann*, it is true, only speaks of a "unified diaskeuasis" but yet he ascribes to the "diaskeuast" an activity which could certainly stamp him as a poet; and in conclusion (p. 302) he speaks of the Mahābhārata as the work of "*one single* poetical creative genius." In his book "Genesis des Mahābhārata" (Berlin, 1899) he says directly: "The poet was a diaskeuast, the diaskeuast a poet." It is noteworthy that even such a rather orthodox Indian as C. V. *Vaidya* (The Mahābhārata: A Criticism, Bombay, 1905), who speaks with reverence of Vyāsa, the contemporary of Kṛṣṇa, as the "poet" of the Mahābhārata (whom he places high above Homer, Milton and Shakespeare) and in all earnestness computes that Vyāsa and Kṛṣṇa might have lived at the time of the Mahābhārata war about 3101 B. C., yet frankly admits that the Mahābhārata in its present form is the extension of an originally much smaller work and contains numerous additions and interpolations.

[2]) Bhandarkar Com. Vol., pp. 99 ff. (English in Ann. Bh. Inst. I, 1, 13ff.)

and is of opinion that the whole great epic "with all its exaggerations and episodes, with all its varied and luxuriant mass of detail" is based on nothing but "a code of Kṣatriya discipline as practised by the Bhāgavatas." Of course, if we take it that the nucleus of the epic is to be found in the Bhagavadgītā, Nārāyaṇīya and Harivaṃśa, such a point of view is justifiable. If, however, as I myself believe, the real nucleus of the Mahābhārata is a heroic poem of the conflict between the Kauravas and the Pāṇḍavas, Lévi's interpretation is just as impossible as that of Dahlmann. Those scholars who see in the Mahābhārata a "scripture of the warrior caste,"[1] forget that the Mahābhārata as we have it in our present-day text contains much which would be quite out of place in a work intended for warriors. The ascetic morality of ahiṃsā which is preached in so many passages in the didactic sections, of the love towards all creatures and complete resignation, is just as incompatible with the very sensual pleasures promised to the warrior in Indra's heaven, as with the eating of meat and the drinking of strong drinks in which the heroes and even their wives indulge, in many a vivid description of the warriors' life in the actual epic.[2] Anyone who has really read the whole of the Mahābhārata and not only the most magnificent portions of it, is bound to admit that our present-day text of the epic contains not only much that is diverse in content, but also much that is diverse in value. In truth, he who would believe with the orthodox Hindus and the above-mentioned Western scholars, that our Mahābhārata, in its present form, is the work of one single man, would be forced to the conclusion that this man was, *at one and the same time*, a great poet and a wretched scribbler, a sage and an idiot, a talented artist and a ridiculous

---

1) *Eliot*, Hinduism and Buddhism I, pp. xc f. *Cf.* also *Hopkins* in Cambridge History I, p. 256.

2) See *Hopkins*, Great Epic, pp. 373, 376 ff.

pedant—apart from the fact that this marvellous person must have known and confessed the most antagonistic religious views, and the most contradictory philosophical doctrines.[1]

With regard to *language*, *style* and *metre*, too, the various parts of the Mahābhārata show absolutely no uniformity. It is in only quite a general sense that one can speak of "epic Sanskrit" as the language of the popular epics.[2] In reality the language of the epic is in some parts *more archaic*, *i. e.* more closely related to the Ancient Indian of the Vedic prose works, than in other parts. And beside linguistic phenomena which recall the Pāli, and which can be called *popular*, there are others which one is compelled to call *solecisms*, such as are often committed by uneducated and inferior authors like the Purāṇa composers. The style, too, can only in a general sense be said to be far removed from the so-called "Kāvya style" *i. e.* the style of the later ornate poetry, which is characterised by the *excessive* use of embellishments (Alaṃkāras). However, there is no lack of passages in the Mahābhārata which remind us of this Kāvya style.[3] Beside these, we also find portions which retain the naïve style of the old Itihāsas, as they are related in the Brāhmaṇas and Upaniṣads, while again in numerous other portions the most negligent Purāṇa style prevails. As regards the metre,[4] the *Śloka* which originated in the old Anuṣṭubh is certainly the metre *par excellence.* But there are earlier and later forms of this

---

[1] *Oldenberg* (Das Mahābhārata, p. 32) calls it a "scientific monstrosity" to suppose that the Mahābhārata was a unified composition.

[2] The epic language is treated by H. *Jacobi*, Das Râmâyaṇa, pp. 112 ff. *Cf.* also above, p. 44, and *Hopkins*, The Great Epic, p. 262. A. *Ludwig*, Mahâbhârata als Epos und Rechtsbuch, pp. 5 ff.; J. *Wackernagel*, Altindische Grammatik I, pp. xliv ff.; W. *Kirfel*, Beiträge zur Geschichte der Nominalkomposition in den Upaniṣads und im Epos, Bonn 1908; *Keith*, JRAS, 1906, pp. 2f; *Oldenberg*, l. c., pp. 129 ff., 145 ff.

[3] *Cf.* above, p. 364. But these passages are not numerous, at all events not nearly as numerous as in the Rāmāyaṇa.

[4] See *Hopkins*, Great Epic, pp. 191 ff.; J. *Zubatý*, ZDMG, 43, 1889, pp. 619 ff.; *Ludwig* l. c., p. 37; *Jacobi* in Gurupūjākaumadī, pp. 50 ff.; *Oldenberg*, l. c., pp. 137 ff.

Śloka, which are all represented in the Mahābhārata. Moreover our epic also contains old prose passages, in which the prose is occasionally rhythmical, and sometimes alternates with verses.[1] Also of the Triṣṭubh metre which is often used in the Mahābhārata, though the Śloka is about twenty times as frequent as the Triṣṭubh, we find the ancient form, still similar to the Vedic form, as well as later forms; and even the elaborate metres of classical Sanskrit poetry are already to be found in certain parts of the Mahābhārata.

Lastly, we must not forget that the opening sections of the Mahābhārata themselves give clear indications that the epic had not always its present form and extent. Even the tables of contents which we find in the first two adhyāyas, are not always in agreement with our text.[2]

Thus everything indicates that the Mahābhārata is not the work of one single author or of one time, but consists of earlier and later portions which belong to different centuries. Contents and form alike confirm the fact that some parts of the Mahābhārata reach back to the times of the Veda, while others must be synchronous with the late productions of the Purāṇa literature.

Now it has been assumed, especially by A. Holtzmann, that an ancient heroic poem of the Kauravas existed, which was the "original Mahābhārata," that this later underwent a "revision with a tendency" in favour of the Pāṇḍavas; and that it was then on *several* consecutive occasions—first by

---

[1]) *Cf. Hopkins*, Great Epic, pp. 266 ff. The view taken by *Oldenberg* (Das Mahābhārata, pp. 21 ff. and elsewhere) that these prose-poetry passages are the oldest portions of the Mahābhārata, is quite wrong in my opinion.

[2]) See above, p. 271; V. V. *Iyer*, Notes of a Study of the Preliminary Chapters of the Mahābhārata, pp. 17 ff. and passim; *Oldenberg*, l. c., pp. 33 ff., 43 ff. Though the division into 18 parvans is traditional, it is not certain that the division was originally the same as we find it in our text at the present day. Albērūnī mentions other titles of the 18 parvans, s. E. *Sachau*, Alberuni's India, I, pp. 132 f. The Southern Indian MSS. and the Javanese translation also have other titles. *Cf.* also *Brockhaus*, ZDMG. 6, 1862, pp. 528 ff.

Buddhists, then by Brahmans—"revised with a tendency." The "second Purāṇa-like revision" must have taken place, according to Holtzmann, about 900-1100 A. D., "after which followed, a few centuries later, the definite establishment and completion of the text."[1]

It is important to state at once that this last supposition, according to which the Mahābhārata received its present form only in the 15th or 16th century, is absolutely false. For it is *proved* by literary and inscriptional evidence,[2] that already about 500 A. D. the Mahābhārata was no longer an actual epic, but a sacred text-book and religious discourse, and was, on the whole, not essentially different, in extent and contents, from the work as we have it at present. The philosopher *Kumārila* (about 700 A. D.) quotes numerous passages from almost all the books of the Mahābhārata, which to him was a great smṛti expounded by Vyāsa.[3] The poets *Subandhu* and *Bāṇa* (about 600-650 A. D.) knew the Mahābhārata chiefly as a poem, indeed Bāṇa considered it as the culmination of all poetry.[4] In his romance "Kādambarī," however, the latter also relates that the Queen Vilāsavatī was present at a recitation of the Mahābhārata on the occasion of a festival in a temple at Ujjein. Such public readings of the Mahābhārata still at the present day take place in India in temples on festive occasions—and naturally not only for entertainment, but also for edification and religious instruction.[5] As early

[1]) *Holtzmann*, Das Mahābhārata, I, 194.

[2]) See R. G. *Bhandarkar*, JBRAS. 10, 1871-2, pp. 81 ff.; K. T. *Telang*, SBE., Vol. 8, pp. 28 ff.; and especially G. *Bühler* and J. *Kirste*, Indian Studies II, SWA. 1892.

[3]) See *Bühler*, l. c., pp. 5 ff.

[4]) Harṣacarita, introductory verses 4-10. But from this passage it does not follow, as *Peterson* (Kādambarī, Introd., p. 68) thinks, that in Bāṇa's time the Mahābhārata "was as yet comparatively a fresh wonder in the world," but rather that its fame had already "penetrated the three worlds," as Bāṇa himself says. On the Mahābhārata in the works of Subandhu and Bāṇa s. W. *Cartellieri*, WZKM. 13, 1899, 57 ff.

[5]) In another place in the "Kādambarī" (ed. Peterson, p. 209) we read that Kādambarī listens to a recitation of the Mahābhārata, Nārada's daughter reciting it "in a

as about 600 A.D. an inscription from Cambodia testifies to similar public readings of the Mahābhārata, and this by utilising *manuscripts*, presented expressly for this purpose in this distant Indian colony in Further India. Finally, we also possess deeds of land grants from the 5th and 6th centuries, in which the sections of Book XIII (see above, p. 425), dealing with the morality of giving (dānadharma) are quoted as sacred texts; and in *one* inscription of this kind the Mahābhārata is already called the "collection of a hundred thousand verses." The number of a hundred thousand verses, however, is not even approached, unless Books XII and XIII and even part of the Harivaṃśa are included.[1] But if the Mahābhārata already in the 5th century received its unquestionably latest sections such as Book XIII and the Harivaṃśa,[2] if it was at

---

gentle singing voice," whilst a pair of Kinnaras seated behind her accompany the recitation on the flute.

[1]) In the Mahābhārata itself there is already mention made of its "hundred thousand" verses (I, 1, 107; XII, 343, 11; *cf.* above, p. 325 and *Hopkins*, l. c., p. 9). The 18 books of the Mahābhārata have, in the Calcutta edition, 90,092 verses, of which 13,935 fall to the share of Book XII and 7,759 to Book XIII. With the whole Harivaṃśa the number of verses is 106,466. If the Bhaviṣyaparvan (see above, p. 452) is omitted, there remain 101,154 verses, which number best agrees with the round number of "a hundred thousand." But the different *recensions* of the Mahābhārata, which often differ from each other in that the one recension omits a number of verses which are included in another, but, on the other hand, in another place inserts just as many verses which are missing in the latter, prove that the *contents* of the Mahābhārata could vary without the *extent* being changed.

[2]) We cannot form any definite conclusion as to the date of the Harivaṃśa ("about the third century of the Christian era," R. G. *Bhandarkar*, Vaiṣṇavism, etc., p. 36) on the basis of the occurrence of the word "dīnāra" = denarius. We may assume, however, that this appendix to the Mahābhārata did not come into existence very long before the 4th century A. D.; for though *Roman* gold coins were known in India as early as in the 1st century A. D. (s. E. J. *Rapson*, Indian Coins, Grundriss II, 3 B., pp. 4, 17 ff., 25, 35; R. *Sewell*, JRAS. 1904, 591 ff.), the *Indian* word dīnāra is only traceable from 400 A. D. onwards in Gupta inscriptions (*Sewell*, l. c., p. 616). *Cf.* B. C. *Mazumdar*, JRAS. 1907, pp. 408 f.; A. B. *Keith*, JRAS. 1907, pp. 681 ff.; 1915, pp. 504 f. If the Buddhist poet Aśvaghoṣa should really be the author of the Vajrasūcī which is ascribed to him, the Harivaṃśa would already have been a part of the Mahābhārata in the 2nd century A. D., for two verses from the Harivaṃśa (1292 f.) are quoted in the Vajrasūcī 3 (s. *Weber*, Indische Streifen I, p. 189) with the words "for it is written in the Bhārata."

that time already a religious text-book and discourse, and if, a hundred years later, manuscripts of the Mahābhārata had already reached Further India and were read in temples there, then we are justified in concluding that at least one or two centuries earlier, that is, in the 3rd or 4th century A.D., it must already have received that form which it still has to-day. On the other hand,[1] however, it can only have received this form after the origin and spread of Buddhism, to which it contains many references, indeed, only after Alexander's invasion of India, as the Yavanas, *i.e.* the Greeks (Ionians), are frequently mentioned. *According to this the Mahābhārata cannot have received its present form earlier than the 4th century B.C. and not later than the 4th century A.D.*[2]

Therefore, a great *re-modelling* of the Mahābhārata, or even the addition only of one of the great Books, cannot have taken place after the 4th century A.D. In fact, I cannot consider the hypothesis of one or indeed several remodellings to be either at all necessary or probable.[3] As in later periods the copyists deal rather arbitrarily with their text, so,

---

[1]) See *Hopkins*, Great Epic, pp. 391 ff. If *Dio Chrysostomos'* statement that even the Indians sang Homer's poems and that they were well acquainted with the sufferings of Priam, etc., alluded to the Mahābhārata (as is the view of A. *Weber*, Ind. Stud. II, 161 ff.; *Holtzmann*, Das Mahābhārata IV, 163; *Pischel*, KG, 195; H. G. *Rawlinson*, Intercourse between India and the Western World, Cambridge, 1916, pp. 140 f., 171), then this statement would constitute our earliest external evidence of the existence of the Mahābhārata in the 1st century A.D. It is possible, however (in fact, according to *Jacobi* in Festschrift Wackernagel, pp. 129 f., probable), that Dio's statement, which was repeated by Aelian, refers to an actual Indian translation of Homer. On various Greek words in the Mahābhārata s. *Hopkins*, l. c., p. 372; *Rawlinson*, l. c., p 172 note.

[2]) *Hopkins*, Epic Mythology (Grundriss III, 1 B 1915, p. 1) considered 300-100 B. C. to be the probable date of the Mahābhārata, but in Cambridge History I, p. 258, he also gives the limits 4th century B. C. to 4th century A. D. S. *Lévi* (JA. s. 11, t. V, 1915, p. 122) concludes from the agreement between the geography of the Buddhist Mahāmāyūrī with that of the Mahābhārata, that the latter received its final redaction in the first three or four centuries A. D.

[3]) But that does not say that separate parts, as for example, the Virāṭa-parvan, have not been remodelled. *Cf. Hopkins* in the JAOS. 24, 1903, p. 54.

in more ancient times, the rhapsodists, among whom the heroic songs must have been transmitted orally during centuries, probably took every possible liberty in the presentation of their songs: they lengthened scenes which pleased their audiences, and abridged others which made less impression. But the greatest alterations, by means of which the ancient heroic poem *gradually* became a compilation, which offered "much" and therefore offered "everyone something," can probably be explained by the fact that the transmission and preservation of the ancient heroic songs passed from the original singers to other classes, that the songs themselves were transplanted to other regions, and adapted to other times and a changing public. Already in very early times, as we have seen, the songs must have passed from the bards who were connected with the race of the Kurus to such as had relations with the race of the Pāṇḍavas. They spread from such districts where the Viṣṇu-cult prevailed to those where Śiva was worshipped as the highest god. The phases, too, through which the Kṛṣṇa-cult passed, left their traces in the epic poetry. As with other peoples, so with the Indians a time must have come when the creative poetic genius no longer manifested itself in works of heroic poetry, which latter ceased to be living poetry, and when only the *ancient* songs were still sung by the bards.[1] The old heroic time, too, came to an end, the time when the bards went forth into battle with the warriors as charioteers, so that after the victory was achieved, perhaps at a great sacrificial feast, they could sing of the glorious deeds of the heroes. The epigones of these bards were an inferior class of literary men—the same who also devoted themselves to the handing down of the Purāṇas. These people were probably neither proper warriors nor proper Brahmans; it is not for nothing

---

[1]) *Cf.* H. *Jacobi* in GGA. 1892, p. 632.

that the law-books describe the Sūtas as bastards, who were said to be descended from the intermarriage of warriors with Brahman women or of Brahmans with Kṣatriya women. This very thing constitutes the peculiarity of the Mahābhārata in its present form: it is neither proper warrior-poetry nor proper religious poetry; it is no longer an epic, but not yet a real Purāṇa.

The Mahābhārata may not have received a final form of some kind until after centuries of oral tradition it was first *written down.* Probably only Brahmans, Paṇḍits, participated in this editing and writing-down. If, however, we have come to the conclusion that the Mahābhārata, even in the 4th century A.D. or still earlier, was *not essentially* different, *on the whole*, in extent and contents, from the work as we have it now, then the words "on the whole" and "not essentially" must be very strongly emphasized. For additions and alterations, and, in fact, additions not only of single verses, but also of whole songs (such as hymns to Durgā and so on) have been made even during later centuries,[1] and a *critically established text of the Mahābhārata does not exist at all.*

When we speak of the "Mahābhārata," we usually mean the text as we have it in the two standard editions which were published in India and were arranged by Indian paṇḍits, *viz.* the "Calcutta Edition" of 1834-1839[2] and the "Bombay Edition" with Nīlakaṇṭha's commentary.[3] These

[1]) R. G. *Bhandarkar* (JBRAS. 20, 1900, p. 402) points out that interpolations were made in the Anuśāsanaparvan as late as at the Gupta period.

[2]) This edition was begun by the Committee of Public Education and completed under the auspices of the Asiatic Society of Bengal, and contains also the text of the Harivaṃśa.

[3]) It has appeared in several editions since 1862. See *Holtzmann*, Das Mahābhārata, III, pp. 2 ff., 9 ff., on this and other Indian editions. The edition by Pratapa Chandra *Roy* (Calcutta, 1882 ff.) is very handy, but is unfortunately spoiled by misprints. This edition is a work of true Indian piety and charity: it was printed by the aid of collections organised by the editor, for the purpose of free distribution, and 10,000 copies were given away gratis.

two editions differ but slightly, and may be regarded as good representatives of the text as commented by Nīlakaṇṭha.[1] The Bengali and especially the Southern Indian manuscripts, however, often deviate from the latter text.[2] A *critical edition of the Mahābhārata* made on the basis of all the various classes of manuscripts from all parts of India is one of the greatest desiderata of Indology, and we hope that this need may be supplied in the near future.[3] Not until the publication of a critical edition of this nature will it be possible to sift out many a passage at present included in our texts of the Mahābhārata as being certainly or at least very probably interpolations.[4] Moreover, apart from the

---

1) Nīlakaṇṭha, one of the latest commentators, worked on a text which already contained a strong admixture of interpolations (s. *Utgikar*, Virāṭaparvan, pp. xii f.). Arjunamiśra is earlier than Nīlakaṇṭha, and the commentary Viṣamapadavivaraṇa is still earlier. Editions of the Virāṭaparvan and Udyogaparvan with several commentaries have been published in Bombay, at the Gujarati Printing Press, 1915 and 1920.

2) Bengali MSS., though not only Bengali ones, were used for the "Burdwan Edition." On the Southern Indian MSS., *cf.* M. *Winternitz*, Ind. Ant. 27, 1898, 67 ff., 92 ff., 122 ff. and H. *Lüders*, "Uber die Grantharecension des Mahābhārata," AGGW. 1901. Southern Indian MSS. were utilised for the "Kumbhakonam Edition"; this is by no means a critical edition of the Southern recension, but a mixed recension, containing the interpolations of the Northern as well as the Southern MSS. In the Sabhāparvan of the Southern recension there is a long inserted passage about Kṛṣṇa, a kind of Kṛṣṇa-epic, in which *Hopkins* (Festschrift Windisch, pp. 72 ff. *cf.* Cambridge History I, p. 255) has traced many literal points of agreement with the Harivaṃśa.

3) The preparation of a critical edition of the Mahābhārata was agreed upon in 1905 by the *International Association of Academies* (*cf.* Almanach der Wiener Akademie 54, 1904, 248f., 267ff., 55, 1905, 238ff.), but the preliminary work which had already been begun, was interrupted by the world war. A critical edition of the Mahābhārata is now in course of preparation by the *Bhandarkar Oriental Research Institute, Poona*; s. A prospectus of a New and Critical Edition of the Mahābhārata undertaken by the Institute under the Auspices of Shrimant Balasaheb Pant Pratinidhi, B.A., Chief of Aundh, 1919; R. *Zimmermann* and C. V. *Vaidya* in JBRAS. 25, 1920, pp. 358 ff., N. B. *Utgikar* in Ann. Bh. Inst. II, 2, 1921, pp. 155 ff.; and the Virāṭaparvan of the Mahābhārata edited from original MSS. as a tentative work.........Poona, 1923; M. *Winternitz*, Ann. Bh. Inst. IV, 2, 1923, pp. 145 ff.; V. 1, 1924, pp. 19 ff.

4) Even now we can say with certainty, on the basis of the MSS., that, for instance, the story of Gaṇeśa, who writes down the Mahābhārata, in the Ādiparvan 1 (s. M. *Winternitz*, JRAS. 1898, pp. 380 ff. and *cf.* V. V. *Iyer*, Preliminary Chapters of the Mahābhārata, pp. 32 ff., 97 ff., 340 f.) and the Durgāstotra in the Virāṭaparvan 6 (s. *Utgikar*, The Virāṭaparvan Ed., p. xxii) are interpolations.

manuscripts, it will be possible to distinguish with some degree of certainty between what is authentic and what is spurious.[1] For this purpose the older translations in the vernaculars, as well as the Javanese and Persian translations of the Mahābhārata will have to be taken into account.[2]

As long as there is no such critical edition of the text of the Mahābhārata available, the date of each section, nay sometimes of each single verse of the Mahābhārata must be determined separately, and there is very little meaning in, and no sort of justification for, saying, as it is so frequently said, that a certain name or subject "*already*" occurs in the Mahābhārata. So much the less justification is there for connecting definite dates with the Mahābhārata as a whole, as not only were later insertions made in decidedly "early" parts, but also, just as frequently, very ancient passages are found in the "later" portions. Thus the whole of Book I of the Mahābhārata is certainly not "ancient"; but that does not prevent many of the myths, legends and genealogical verses occurring in it from being very old.[3] Even in the Harivaṃśa, which was certainly only added late, we find very old verses and legends. But the expressions "early" and

---

[1]) See above, notes to pp. 282, 305, 306, 310, 314, 319, 342 f.; and A. *Ludwig* on interpolations in the Rājasūya and Jarāsandha Parvans (Mahābh. II, 12 ff.) in OC xii, Paris, I, pp. 187 ff.

[2]) For vernacular versions of the Mahābhārata see *Holtzmann*, Das Mahābhārata, III, pp. 100 ff. On the Tamil translation said to belong to the 11th century A. D., s. V. V. *Iyer*, l. c., p. 97 ff. and passim. The old Javanic translation is dated 996 A. D., s. K. *Wulff*, Den old javanske Wirātaparva, Kopenhagen, 1917; D. van Hinloopen *Labberton*, JRAS. 1913, pp. 1 ff.; and H. *Kern*, Verspreide Geschriften, 1920, Vol. ix, pp. 39 ff., 215 ff. On the Mahābhārata on the island of Bali, s. R. *Friederich*, JRAS. 1876, pp. 176 f., 179 ff. On the Persian translation s. *Holtzmann*, l. c., III, p. 110, and A. *Ludwig*, Das Mahâbhârata als Epos und Rechtsbuch, pp. 66 ff., 93 ff.

[3]) The Yayāti legend, for instance, is surely at least as early as Patañjali, who teaches the formation of the word Yāyatika "he who knows the Yayāti legend" in the Mahābhāṣya (4, 2, 60). F. *Lacôte* (Essai sur Guṇāḍhya, p 138 f.) is most probably right in assuming that in olden times the episodes of the great epics were recited as independent poems, and I should like to add that this was most likely the case long before they were inserted into the epic.

"late" with reference to whole books and large portions of the Mahābhārata, must always be used with caution and reserve.

This leads us to the most difficult question: What do we mean when we speak of "old" and "oldest" parts of the Mahābhārata? In other words: To what time do the beginnings of the Mahābhārata reach back?

Let us keep to facts. In the whole of *Vedic* literature there is no mention of a Mahābhārata, though in Brāhmaṇas and Upaniṣads there is frequent talk of Ākhyāna, Itihāsa, Purāṇa and Gāthā Nārāśaṃsī (see above, p. 314). Even of the great, and probably historical, event which constitutes the central point of the epic, the bloody battle in the Kuru field, the Veda says not a word, though in the Brāhmaṇas this very Kuru field is so often mentioned as a place where gods and mortals celebrated great sacrificial feasts, that this event, if it had already taken place, would most certainly have been mentioned.[1] It is true that Janamejaya, the son of Parikṣit, and Bharata, the son of Duḥṣanta and of Sakuntalā, already appear in the Brāhmaṇas; and already in a Kuntāpa-song of the Atharvaveda Parikṣit is praised as a peace-loving king under whose rule the land of the Kurus prospered. In the works belonging to the Yajurveda there is frequent mention of Kurus and Pañcālas or Kurupañcālas; and in connection with a sacrificial feast of the Kurupañcālas an anecdote is told in the Kāṭhaka (X, 6) of Dhṛtarāṣṭra, the son of Vicitravīrya. On the other hand, nowhere in the whole Veda is the name of Pāṇḍu or of his sons, the Pāṇḍavas, to be found, nowhere do such names as Duryodhana, Duḥśāsana, Karṇa, etc., appear. The name Arjuna does, it is true, occur in a Brāhmaṇa, but as a secret name of the god Indra. The Sāṅkhāyana-Srautasūtra (XV, 16) is the first place where we find mention of a war in

[1]) See A. *Ludwig*, Über das Verhältnis des mythischen Elementes zu der historischen Grundlage des Mahâbhârata, p. 6.

Kurukṣetra which was disastrous for the Kauravas.[1] In the Āśvalāyana-Gṛhyasūtra,[2] "Bhārata and Mahābhārata" are mentioned in a list of teachers and sacred books which are honoured by libations at the end of the study of the Veda. Pāṇini[3] teaches the formation of the names "Yudhiṣṭhira," "Bhīma" and "Vidura," and the accent of the compound word "Mahābhārata." Patañjali, however, is the first to make definite allusions to the story of the battle between the Kauravas and the Pāṇḍavas.

What of *Buddhist* literature? In the Tripiṭaka, the Pāli-canon of the Buddhists, the Mahābhārata is not mentioned. On the other hand, we find, in the oldest texts of the Tripiṭaka, poems after the style of the Ākhyānas with which we became acquainted in the Brāhmaṇas as a preliminary step to the epic.[4] The Jātakas, whose metrical portions (the Gāthās) belong to the Tripiṭaka, betray an acquaintance

---

[1]) *Cf. E. Leumann*, ZDMG. 48, 1894, 80 ff.; *Ludwig*, Das Mahābhārata als Epos und Rechtsbuch, pp. 77 ff.; *Hopkins* in Cambridge History I, 252 f. B. C. *Mazumdar* (JRAS. 1906, 225 f.) suggests that the author of the Mahābhārata grafted the Kuru-Pāṇḍava story upon an older story of a war between Kurus and Pañcālas.

[2]) III, 4, 4. This passage has been much discussed. *Cf. Hopkins*, Great Epic, pp. 389 f.; *Dahlmann*, Das Mahābhārata als Epos und Rechtsbuch, pp. 152 ff.; *Winternitz*, WZKM. 14, 1900, pp. 55 f.; *Utgikar* in Proc. I OC, Vol. II, pp. 46 ff.; *Oldenberg*, Das Mahābhārata, pp. 18, 33. Utgikar is right in explaining the mention of the Mahābhārata in the Āśvalayana-Gṛhyasūtra (and not in other Gṛhyasūtras) by the fact that Āśvalāyana counts as the pupil of Śaunaka, and, according to the frame-story of the Mahābh., Ugraśravas relates the Mahābhārata to Śaunaka. The date of the Āśv.-Gṛhyas is, however, entirely unknown, and lists of this nature could easily have been enlarged at any time in Āśvalāyana's *school*. For this reason we are not justified in drawing a chronological conclusion from this passage.

[3]) VIII, 3, 95, III, 2, 162; 4, 74; VI, 2, 38 But these scanty references do not admit of our drawing any conclusion as to the contents and extents of the epic known to Pāṇini.

[4]) See above, p. 311. E. *Windisch*, Māra und Buddha (ASGW., Vol. XV, Leipzig, 1895), pp. 222 ff., and T. W. *Rhys Davids*, Buddhist India, London, 1903, pp. 180 ff. Recitations of Ākhyānas are mentioned in the Brahmajālasutta, as well as conversations and exhibitions which the monk is to avoid (Dialogues of the Buddha, translated from the Pāli by T. W. *Rhys Davids*, London, 1899, p. 8). If, as the commentator says, recitations of the Mahābhārata and of the Rāmāyaṇa were to be understood by this, the author would surely have mentioned them by name.

with the Kṛṣṇa-*legend*, but not with the Harivaṃśa and the Mausalaparvan of the Mahābhārata.[1] The names occurring in the Jātaka-book, Pāṇḍava, Dhanañjaya (in the Mahābhārata an ordinary epithet of Arjuna), Yudhiṭṭhila (Pali form of Yudhiṣṭhira), Dhataraṭṭha (Pāli form of Dhṛtarāṣṭra), Vidhura or Vidhūra (the Vidura of the Mahābhārata), and even the narrative, appearing in this work, of the self-choice of a husband and the five-husband marriage of Draupadī, bear testimony only to slight acquaintance with the Mahābhārata. For Pāṇḍava occurs in the Jātaka as the name of a horse,[2] Dhṛtarāṣṭra as the name of various kings,[3] Dhanañjaya and Yudhiṣṭhira are only mentioned as Kuru kings who dwelt in Indraprastha, and Vidura is a wise man, who appears now as domestic priest, and now as a minister of the court of Dhanañjaya or of Yudhiṣṭhira.[4] Draupadī, however, one of the most magnificent female characters of the epic, appears in the Jātaka as an example of feminine depravity, as she is not content with her five husbands, but also commits adultery with a hunchbacked servant.[5]

---

1) The legend of Kṛṣṇa (Kaṇha) is told in the Ghatajātaka (No. 454), allusions to it are found also in Jātakas No. 512 and No. 530 (gāthā 20). See *Lüders* in ZDMG., 58, 1904, pp. 687 ff., also E. *Hardy* in ZDMG., 53, 1899, pp. 25 ff. The Jainas have already in the third or second century B. C. made the Kṛṣṇa cult part of their religion, s. *Jacobi* in OC VII, Vienna 1886, pp. 75 ff. and ZDMG, 42, 1888, pp. 493 ff.

2) Jātaka No. 185.

3) Dhataraṭṭha is a king of the gods in Jāt. No. 382, a king of the Nāgas in Jāt. No. 543, a king of the flamingoes in Jāt. Nos. 502, 533, 534. In Jāt. No. 544 he heads a list of righteous kings. In the Mahāvastu Dhṛtarāṣṭra is the name of a Buddha, and once the name of a palace, s. E. *Windisch*, Buddhas Geburt (ASGW., 1908), pp. 101, 168.

4) In Jātaka No. 413 Dhanañjaya is a Kuru king residing in the city of Indapatta (Indraprastha) of the family of Yudhiṭṭhila (Yudhiṭṭhilagotta), and Vidhūra is his purohita. In Jāt. No. 515 Dhanañjaya Korabya is a pious Kuru king, called Yudhiṭṭhila in the Gāthās, while the sage Vidhura is living at Benares. In the Vidhurapaṇḍita-Jātaka (No. 545, already mentioned in the second century B. C. with the title "Vitura-Punakiya jātakam" in a Bharhut inscription, s. E. *Hultzsch*, Ind. Ant, 1892, p. 234) Vidhura s a minister of the Kuru king Dhanañjaya who (like Yudhiṣṭhira in the Mahābhārata) is fond of playing at dice. But there is no allusion at all to the story of the Mahābhārata. In Jāt. No. 329 Dhanañjaya is a king of Benares. Vidhura also occurs as the name of a wise monk in the Therīgāthā 1188 and in the Majjhimanikāya 50.

5) Jātaka No. 536 (gāthā 288). *Cf. Winternitz*, JRAS., 1897, pp. 752 ff.

From these facts we must conclude that, before the conclusion of the Veda, there could *not* have existed an epic Mahābhārata, *i. e.* an epic poem which dealt with the war with the Kauravas and Pāṇḍavas and the battle on the Kuru field, and bore the title "Bhārata" or "Mahābhārata"; but that, on the other hand, such a poem must have existed already in the 4th century B. C., as the Sūtra works of Śāṅkhāyana, Aśvalāyana and Pāṇini can scarcely be later. Now as the Pāli-canon of the Buddhists, which originated in the 4th and 3rd centuries B. C., betrays only quite a superficial knowledge of the Mahābhārata, it was probably at that time still little known in the *east* of India, where Buddhist literature originated.

We have seen, however, that some elements of our present Mahābhārata reach back into the Vedic period, and that much, especially in the didactic sections, is drawn from a *literary common property*, from which also Buddhists and Jainas (probably already in the 5th century B. C.) have drawn.[1)]

Finally, it must still be mentioned, that not only the events described in the epic, but also the innumerable names of kings and royal races, however historical some of the events and many names may appear, do not belong to Indian *history* in the true sense of the word. It is true that the Indians set the reign of Yudhiṣṭhira and the great war of the Mahābhārata at the beginning of the Kaliyuga, or Iron

---

[1)] Verses Mahābh. XI, 7, 23 ff., which H. *Raychaudhuri* (JASB., N. S., 18, 1922, pp. 269 ff.) believes to be quoted in the Besnagar inscription, also belong to this literary common property. See above, pp. 314, 409 f., 415, 417. On the Ṛṣyaśṛṅga-legend in the Jātaka *cf.* above, pp. 399 ff. and H. *Lüders* in the treatise there cited. Another legend which the Mahābhārata (I, 107 f.) has in common with the Jātaka (No. 444) is that of Māṇḍavya, who, as a punishment for having in his childhood impaled a fly on a thorn, was taken for a robber and impaled. (*Cf.* L. *Scherman*, Materialien zur Geschichte der indischen Visionslitteratur, Leipzig, 1892, pp. 53 f., and N. B *Utgikar* in Proc. II OC 1922, pp. 221 ff. In the Jātaka this Māṇḍavya is a friend of Kaṇhadīpāyana, *i.e.* of Kṛṣṇa Dvaipāyana Vyāsa).

Age, *i. e.* 3102 B. C.; but this date for the beginning of the Kaliyuga is based upon the artificial calculation of Indian astronomers, and the association of this date with the conflict of the Kauravas and Pāṇḍavas is, of course, quite arbitrary.[1] The political history of India commences with the Śiśunāga kings Bimbisāra and Ajātasattu of Magadha, who are known to us as contemporaries of the Buddha, and we may also ascribe historical character to the kings of the Śiśunāga and Nanda dynasties mentioned in the Purāṇas.[2] With the great King Candragupta (321 B. C.), the founder of the Maurya dynasty, we step on to firm historical ground in India. Of all these historical personalities there is no trace to be found in the Mahābhārata.[3] This "prehistoric" character of the narrative and of the heroes certainly indicates the great antiquity of the epic.

Summing up, we can say the following about the age of the Mahābhārata:

1. Single myths, legends and poems which are included in the Mahābhārata, reach back to the time of the Veda.

2. An epic "Bhārata" or "Mahābhārata" did not exist in the Vedic period.

3. Many moral narratives and sayings which our Mahābhārata contains, belong to the ascetic-poetry, which was drawn upon, from the 6th century B. C. onwards, also by Buddhists and Jainas.

4. *If* an epic Mahābhārata already existed between the 6th and 4th centuries B. C., then it was but little known in the native land of Buddhism.

---

[1]) See R. Ramkrishna *Bhagwat*, JBRAS., 20, 1899, pp. 150 ff. and J. F. *Fleet*, JRAS. 1911, pp. 479 ff., 675 ff. In a similar way the Arabian astronomers have connected the same era with the Deluge.

[2]) These kings reigned between 642 (or 600) B. C. and 322 B. C. *Cf. Smith*, Early History, pp. 44, 46 ff., and E. J. *Rapson*, Cambridge History, I, pp. 312 ff., 697.

[3]) E. W. *Hopkins* (in Album Kern, pp. 249 ff.), it is true, believes to have found references to the Mauryas, Aśoka and Candragupta in the Mahābhārata. But why should these be so hidden?

5. There is no certain testimony for an epic Mahābhārata before the 4th century B. C.

6. Between the 4th century B. C. and the 4th century A. D. the transformation of the *epic* Mahābhārata into our present compilation took place, probably gradually.

7. In the 4th century A. D. the work already had, on the whole, its present extent, contents and character.

8. Small alterations and additions still continued to be made, however, even in later centuries.

9. *One* date of the Mahābhārata does not exist at all, but the date of every part must be determined on its own account.

THE RĀMĀYAṆA, BOTH A POPULAR EPIC AND AN ORNATE POEM.

The Rāmāyaṇa differs essentially from the Mahābhārata in more respects than one. Above all it is much shorter and of much greater uniformity. While the Mahābhārata in its present form can scarcely be called an actual epic, the Rāmāyaṇa, even in the form in which we have it to-day, is still a fairly unified heroic poem. Moreover, while indigenous tradition names Vyāsa, an entirely mythical seer of ancient times, who was supposed to be at the same time the compiler of the Vedas and of the Purāṇas, as the author or editor of the Mahābhārata, it attributes the authorship of the Rāmāyaṇa to a poet named Vālmīki, and we have no reason to doubt that a poet of this name really lived and first shaped the ballads, which were scattered in the mouths of the bards, into the form of a unified poem. The Indians call this Vālmīki " the first Kavi or author of ornate poetry " (*ādikavi*) and like to call the Rāmāyaṇa " the first ornate poem " (ādikāvya). The beginnings of ornate epic poetry do indeed lead back to the Rāmāyaṇa, and Vālmīki has always remained the pattern to which all later Indian poets admiringly aspired. The essential factor of Indian ornate poetry, of the so-called "*kāvya*," is that greater importance is attached to the form than to the matter and contents of the poem, and that so-called *alaṃkāras*, *i.e.* "embellishments," such as similes, poetic figures, puns, and so on, are used largely, even to excess. Similes are heaped on similes, and descriptions, especially of nature, are spun out interminably with ever new metaphors and comparisons. We find the first beginnings of these and other peculiarities of the classical ornate poetry in the Rāmāyaṇa. While we found in the Mahābhārata a mixture of popular epic and theological didactic poetry (purāṇa), the Rāmāyaṇa appears to us as a work that is popular epic and ornate poetry at the same time.

It is a true popular epic, just like the Mahābhārata, because, like the latter, it has become the property of the whole Indian people and, as scarcely any other poem in the entire literature of the world, has influenced the thought and poetry of the nation for centuries. In the introduction to the epic (a later addition) it is related that god Brahman himself invited the poet Vālmīki to glorify the deeds of Rāma in verse; and the god is said to have promised him:

> "As long as in this firm-set land
> The streams shall flow, the mountains stand,
> So long throughout the world, be sure,
> The great Rāmāyan shall endure."[1]

This dictum has proved itself truly prophetic to the present day. Since more than two thousand years the poem of Rāma has kept alive in India, and it continues to live in all grades and classes of the people. High and low, prince and peasant, nobleman, merchant and artisan, princesses and shepherdesses, all are quite familiar with the characters and

---

[1]) I, 2, 36 f. Translated by R. T. H. *Griffith*.

stories of the great epic. The men are elevated by the glorious deeds of Rāma and are edified by his wise speeches, the women love and praise Sītā as the ideal of conjugal fidelity, the highest virtue of woman. Old and young enjoy the wonderful feats of the true-hearted monkey Hanumat, and they enjoy no less the gruesome tales of the man-eating giants and the demons endowed with magic power. Popular sayings and proverbs bear witness to the familiarity of the people with the stories of the Rāmāyaṇa. But also the teachers and masters of the various religious sects refer to the Rāmāyaṇa and draw upon it, when they wish to propagate religious and moral doctrines among the people; and the poets of all later times, from Kālidāsa down to Bhavabhūti and their epigones, have ever again drawn their materials from the Rāmāyaṇa and worked them up anew.[1] When we come to the modern Indian literature of the vernaculars, we find a Tamil translation of the Sanskrit epic as early as in the 11th century, and soon there follow imitations and translations in the vernaculars from the North to the South of India. The religious-philosophical Hindi poem Rām-caritmānas, based on the ancient epic, and composed about 1574 A.D. by the celebrated *Tulsī Dās*, has become almost a gospel for millions of Indians. Generations of Hindus in all parts of India have made the acquaintance of the old legend of Rāma in such modern translations. In the houses of the wealthy, recitations of the poem are arranged even in our own day. Dramatic versions, too, of the story of Rāma, as mentioned already in the Harivaṃśa (see above p. 451 Note), may still be seen performed at religious festivals in villages and towns in India at the present day. Thus, in Northern India, *e.g.* in Lahore, the Dassara feast is celebrated annually by the "Rāma-play" (Rām Līla), at which the most

---

[1]) A. *Baumgartner*, Das Râmâyana und die Râmaliteratur der Inder, Freiburg i. B. 1894, has given a survey of the whole Râma literature.

popular scenes from the Rāmāyaṇa are performed before an enormous audience.[1] Whether the worship of the monkey-king Hanumat as a local deity— wide-spread over India—and monkey-worship in general can be traced back to the popularity of the Rāmāyaṇa, or whether, on the contrary, the prominent part played by monkeys in the Rāma legend must be explained by an older monkey-cult, remains an open question. It is certain, at all events, that none of the larger villages of India is without its image of the monkey-king Hanumat, and that monkeys are swarming in many temples, and are treated with great forbearance and love. This is particularly the case in Oudh, the ancient town of residence of Rāma.[2]

Rāma himself, the hero of the Rāmāyaṇa, was probably only later made into an incarnation of the god Viṣṇu and then worshipped as a god. The fact that the epic dealing with this divine Rāma then assumed the character of a sacred book cannot surprise us. Thus it is said at the end of the first canto (certainly not composed by Vālmīki):

> " Whoe'er this noble poem reads
> That tells the tale of Rāma's deeds,
> Good as the scriptures, he shall be
> From every sin and blemish free.
> Whoever reads the saving strain,
> With all his kin the heavens shall gain.
> Brahmans who read shall gather hence
> The higher praise for eloquence.

---

1) A vivid description of this festival from personal observation is given by J. C. *Oman*, The Great Indian Epics, The Stories of the Ramayana and the Mahabharata, London, 1899, pp. 75 ff. *Cf.* M. M. *Underhill.* The Hindu Religious Year, Heritage of India series, 1921, pp. 79 f.

2) *Cf.* W. *Crooke*, Popular Religion and Folklore of Northern India, 2nd Ed., 1896, I, pp. 85 ff., W. J. *Wilkins*, Hindu Mythology, 2nd Ed., Calcutta, 1882, p 405, *Underhill*, l. c., pp. 119 f.

The warrior o'er the land shall reign
The merchant luck in trade obtain ;
And Śūdras listening ne'er shall fail
To reap advantage from the tale.[1] "

Significant also is the legend of Dāmodara II, a king of Kashmir, who was changed into a snake through a curse, and could not be released from the curse until he had had the whole Rāmāyaṇa read to him in one single day.[2]

But it is the very popularity of the Rāmāyaṇa, as in the case of the Mahābhārata, which became a reason for the fact that the poem has not come down to us in its original form, but much increased and disfigured by additions and alterations. The work, as we have it before us, consists of seven books and contains about 24,000 couplets (ślokas): but which of these are early or late, genuine or spurious, we shall only be able to determine when we have given a short summary of the contents of the poem.

Contents of the Rāmāyaṇa.[3]

Book I, called *Bālakāṇḍa* (section of childhood), begins with an introduction upon the origin of the poem, and relates the story of the youth of Rāma. But in this book, too, exactly as in the Mahābhārata, the course of the narrative

---

[1]) Translated by R. T. H. *Griffith.*

[2]) Kalhaṇa's Rājataraṅgiṇī, I, 166.

[3]) Translated into English verse by R. T. H. *Griffith* (in 5 vols. 1870-1874, in one vol., Benares, 1895, new ed. with a memoir by M. N. *Venkataswami*, Benares, 1915) ; into English prose by *Manmathanath Dutt*, Calcutta, 1892-94 ; condensed into English verse by *Romesh Dutt*, London, 1900; translated into Italian by G. *Gorresio*, Parigi, 1847-58, into French by H. *Fauche*, Paris, 1854-58, and by A. *Roussel*, Paris, 1903-1909 ; only Book I into German by J. *Menrad*, München, 1897, and a few extracts by Fr. *Rückert*, s. Rückert Nachlese, I, 271 ff. An outline of the story is given by J. C. *Oman*, The Great Indian Epics, pp. 19 ff. ; a full account of the contents by H. *Jacobi*, Das Râmâyaṇa, Bonn, 1893. Scenes from the Ramayan, by R. T. H. *Griffith*, reprinted and published by the Panini Office, Allahabad, 1912.

is interrupted by the insertion of numerous brahmanical myths and legends; and some of these are the same which also appear in various versions in the Mahābhārata. Thus a mention of *Ṛṣyaśṛṅga* serves as a pretext for relating the legend with which we are already familiar.[1] The appearance of *Vasiṣṭha* and *Viśvāmitra* gives rise to the narration of numerous legends referring to these ṛṣis, famous from ancient days. Thus especially, the story of Viśvāmitra's austerities, which he performed in order to become a Brahman, and of the temptations of this ṛṣi by the Apsarases Menakā and Rambhā is told in detail.[2] The cycle of Viśvāmitra-legends also includes the ancient legend of Śunaḥśepa.[3] Of the other myths and legends we may mention those of the *dwarf-incarnation of the god Viṣṇu* (I, 29), the birth of the war-god *Kumāra* or *Kārttikeya* (I, 35-37), the 60,000 sons of Sagara (the ocean) and the *descent of Gaṅgā* from heaven,[4] and the *twirling of the ocean* by the gods and demons.[5]

From the introduction we shall call attention only to the pretty story of the *invention of the śloka*[6]:

Vālmīki was wandering through the forest along the bank of a river, when he noticed a pair of curlews which were hopping about on the grass singing sweetly. Suddenly a wicked fowler comes along and kills the male bird with his arrow. Now, when the bird is weltering in his blood and his mate mourning for him in pitiful tones, Vālmīki is seized with the deepest pity, and he utters a curse on the fowler. But the words of the curse of their own accord take the form of a śloka. Then god Brahman appears and bids the poet to sing of the deeds of Rāma in this very metre.

---

[1]) I, 9-11. See above, pp. (399 ff.) and *Lüders*, NGGW., 1897, 1, pp. 18 ff.

[2]) I, 51-65.

[3]) I, 62, *cf.* above, pp. 211 ff.

[4]) I, 38-44. An outline of this story is given by J. C. *Oman*, The Great Indian Epics, pp. 87 ff. It has been translated into German by A. W. von *Schlegel* in his "Indische Bibliothek," I (1823), pp. 50 ff.

[5]) I, 45. *Cf.* above, p. 389.

[6]) I, 2. Translated by F. von *Schlegel*, Uber die Sprache und Weisheit der Indier, p. 266. H. *Jacobi* (Das Râmâyaṇa, pp. 80 f.) suggests that the basis of this legend may be the fact that the epic śloka in its final form is to be traced back to Vālmīki.

Book I gives the following history of Rāma's youth :

In the land of the Kosala (north of the Ganges), in the city of Ayodhyā (the present Oudh), there ruled a mighty and wise king, named *Daśaratha.* He was long childless. Then he resolved to offer a horse-sacrifice. The seer *Ṛṣyaśṛṅga* is engaged as the conductor of this great sacrifice, and he presents a specially powerful sacrificial offering efficacious in causing the begetting of sons. Just at that time the gods in heaven were much troubled by the demon Rāvaṇa. They therefore turn to *Viṣṇu* begging him to become a mortal, and as such kill Rāvaṇa. Viṣṇu agrees and resolves to be born on earth as the son of Daśaratha. So, after the horse-sacrifice was concluded, the three wives of King Daśaratha bore him four sons: *Kausalyā* bore *Rāma* (in whom Viṣṇu had incarnated himself), *Kaikeyī* bore *Bharata*, *Sumitrā* bore *Lakṣmaṇa* and *Śatrughna.* Of these four princes Rāma, the eldest, was the declared favourite of his father. But from his youth Lakṣmaṇa was deeply devoted to his elder brother. He was as his second self, and fulfilled all his wishes even before they were uttered.

When the sons had grown to manhood, the great ṛṣi *Viśvāmitra* came to the court of Daśaratha. Rāma and Lakṣmaṇa went forth with him to slay demons, for which they were rewarded by the ṛṣi with magic weapons. Viśvāmitra also accompanies the princes to the court of King Janaka of Videha. The latter had a daughter named *Sītā.* She was no common mortal, for once when the king was ploughing the field, she had come forth out of the earth—hence her name "Sītā," "the field-furrow"—and Janaka had brought her up as a daughter. But the king possessed a wonderful bow and had announced that he would give his daughter Sītā in marriage only to the man who could bend the bow. Many princes had already tried in vain. Then Rāma came and bent the bow, so that with a thundering crash, it broke in two. Highly delighted the king gives him his daughter in marriage. Daśaratha is informed and fetched, and then, amid great rejoicings the marriage of Rāma and Sītā is celebrated. And for many years they both lived in happiness and joy.

The real story begins with *Book* II, which describes the events at the royal court of Ayodhyā, and is therefore entitled *Ayodhyā-Kāṇḍa.*[1]

---

[1]) A free poetical rendering of this Book in German by A. *Holtzmann*, "Indische Sagen."

61

When Daśaratha felt old age approaching, he resolved to appoint his favourite son Rāma as heir to the throne, and caused all the necessary preparations for the consecration to be made by his domestic priest Vasiṣṭha. This is noticed by the hunchbacked maid of Queen Kaikeyī, and she urges her mistress to procure from the king the nomination of her own son Bharata as heir to the throne. The king had once promised to grant her two wishes, which she has up till now kept pending. Now she requests of the king that he will banish Rāma for fourteen years and appoint her son Bharata as heir to the throne. The king is much cast down, but Rāma himself, as soon as he hears of the matter, does not hesitate for a moment to go into banishment, so that his father may not be guilty of breaking his word. In vain his mother Kausalyā and his brother Lakṣmaṇa try to keep him back. He insists that it is his highest duty to help his father to keep his word. He immediately also tells his wife Sītā that he is determined to go into banishment into the forest. He asks her to be friendly to Bharata, to live piously and continently at the court of Daśaratha and to serve his father and his mothers [1] obediently. But Sītā answers him in a magnificent speech on the duties of a wife, that nothing shall prevent her from following him into the forest:

"My lord, the mother, sire and son
Receive their lots by merit won;
The brother and the daughter find
The portions to their deeds assigned.
The wife alone, whate'er await,
Must share on earth her husband's fate.
So now the king's command which sends
Thee to the wild, to me extends.
The wife can find no refuge, none,
In father, mother, self, or son:
Both here, and when they vanish hence,
Her husband is her sole defence.
If, Raghu's son, [2] thy steps are led
Where Daṇḍak's pathless wilds are spread,

---

[1]) It is interesting to note that Rāma always speaks of all the wives of his father as his "mothers."

[2]) Rāghava, "descendant of Raghu," i.e. Rāma.

My feet before thine own shall pass
Through tangled thorn and matted grass...
And as with thee I wander there
I will not bring thee grief or care.
I long, when thou, wise lord, art nigh,
All fearless, with delighted eye,
To gaze upon the rocky hill,
The lake, the fountain, and the rill;
To sport with thee, my limbs to cool,
In some pure lily-covered pool,
While the white swan's and mallard's wings
Are playing in the water-springs.
So would a thousand seasons flee
Like one sweet day, if spent with thee.
Without my lord I would not prize
A home with gods above the skies;
Without my lord, my life to bless,
Where could be heaven or happiness?" [1])

Rāma describes to her all the terrors and dangers of the forest, in order to dissuade her from her resolve. But she remains firm and will hear nothing of a separation; as Sāvitrī once followed Satyavat, so, she says, will she not leave him.

Then Rāma at last consents that Sītā shall go forth with him into the forest. Nor will faithful Lakṣmaṇa, of course, be hindered from following his brother into banishment. Clothed only in garments of bark, the banished ones go forth into the forest amidst the sympathy of the whole population.

But King Daśaratha cannot overcome his grief at the loss of his son. A few days after Rāma had gone into banishment, the king awakes from uneasy sleep about midnight. Then he remembers a crime he had committed in his youth; he tells Kausalyā how he had once killed a young hermit by accident, when hunting, and how the blind father of the latter had cursed him, that he should die of grief at the loss of his son. Now this curse is being fulfilled:

"'I see thee not: these eyes grow blind,
And memory quits my troubled mind.

[1]) II, 27. Translated by *Griffith*.

Angels of Death are round me : they
Summon my soul with speed away.
What woe more grievous can there be,
That, when from light and life I flee,
I may not, ere I part, behold
My virtuous Rāma, true and bold?
Grief for my son, the brave and true,
Whose joy it was my will to do,
Dries up my breath, as summer dries
The last drop in the pool that lies...
Ah Raghu's son, ah mighty-armed,
By whom my cares were soothed and charmed,
My son in whom I took delight,
Now vanished from thy father's sight!
Kausalyā, ah, I cannot see;
Sumitrā, gentle devotee!
Alas, Kaikeyī, cruel dame,
My bitter foe, thy father's shame!'
Kausalyā and Sumitrā kept
Their watch beside him as he wept.
And Daśaratha moaned and sighed,
And grieving for his darling died." [1]

After the death of the king, Bharata, who is staying in Rājagṛha, is sent for, and invited by his mother Kaikeyī, as well as by the counsellors, to ascend the throne. But Bharata will hear nothing of it, and declares with determination that the sovereignty belongs to Rāma, and that he will bring him back. With a great retinue he sets out to fetch his brother. Meanwhile, Rāma is sojourning in the Citrakūṭa hills, and is just describing the beauties of the landscape to Sītā,[2] when clouds of dust are seen to rise and the noise of an approaching army is heard. Lakṣmaṇa climbs up a tree and sees the army of Bharata drawing near. He believes that it is a hostile attack, and is greatly enraged. But he soon observes that Bharata leaves his army behind and draws near alone. He approaches Rāma, throws himself at his feet, and the brothers embrace one another.

---

1) II, 64. Translated by *Griffith*.

2) II, 94. A magnificent description of nature, such as are not rare in the Rāmāyaṇa.

Now Bharata, with many 'ears and reproaches against himself and his mother Kaikeyī, reports to Rāma the death of his father, and asks him to return and commence his reign. Rāma says he could not reproach either him or his mother; but that which his father had commanded, must even now be dear to him, and he will never depart from his decision to spend fourteen years in the forest. In vain are all the entreaties of Bharata, who reminds him of the departure of their father. Rāma, with many lamentations, offers the funeral libation for the departed one, but remains firm in his resolve. Rāma comforts his mourning brother in a magnificent speech on the natural, necessary transitoriness of existence, and the inevitableness of death, which makes every lament seem unreasonable.

"In scatterings end collections all;
High towering piles at length must fall;
In parting every meeting ends;
To death all life of creatures tends.
The early fall to earth is sure,
Of fruits on trees that hang mature.
Of mortals here behold a type;
They, too, succumb, for death when ripe.
As houses fall when long decay
Has worn the posts which formed their stay,
So sink men's frames, when age's course
Has undermined their vital force.........
As logs that on the ocean float,
By chance are into contact brought,
But, tossed about by wind and tide,
Together cannot along abide;—
So wives, sons, kinsmen, riches, all
Whate'er our own we fondly call,—
Obtained, possessed, enjoyed, to-day,
To-morrow all are snatched away.
As, standing on the road a man
Who sees a passing caravan,
Which slowly winds across the plain,
Cries, "I will follow in your train,"
So men the beaten path must tread
On which their sires of yore have led.

Since none can nature's course elude,
Why o'er thy doom in sorrow brood?" [1]

The counsellors, too, come in order to invite Rāma to begin his reign. One of these, *Jābāli*, a great heretic and representative of nihilistic views, tries to drive away his moral scruples. Everyone lives only for himself, he says, one need not trouble about father and mother, death is the end of all things, the talk of a Beyond is only spread abroad by crafty priests, in order to procure presents,—therefore he should only consult his common-sense and ascend the throne. Rāma energetically rejects these teachings of the nihilist.[2] Even the representations of the pious priest Vasiṣṭha cannot make him change his mind. And finally Bharata is compelled to consent to conduct affairs for Rāma. Rāma gives him his sandals as a symbol of sovereignty,[3] and Bharata returns to Ayodhyā, where Rāma's sandals are solemnly placed on the throne as the representatives of the king, while he himself transfers his residence to Nandigrāma, in order from there to manage the affairs of the country for Rāma, as his representative.

Beginning with *Book III*, which describes the forest-life of the exiles, and hence is called *Araṇya-kāṇḍa*, "Forest section," we leave, as it were, the world of reality, and enter a miraculous fairy-tale world, from which we do not emerge before the end of the poem. While Book II shows us the life at an Indian prince's court, and begins from a court

---

[1]) II, 105, 16 ff. Translated by J. *Muir*, Metrical Translations from Sanskrit Writers, pp. 41 f. Sayings of this kind belong to the *common property* of Indian poets, which has already been mentioned several times. We meet them again almost literally in the Mahābhārata, in Purāṇas, in the legal literature (*e g.* Viṣṇusmṛti XX, 32), in the Buddhist proverbial wisdom, in the sayings of Bhartṛhari, and so on. Rāma's speech of consolation also forms the nucleus of the *Dasaratha-Jātaka, cf.* below p.

[2]) The expression corresponds exactly to the Sanskrit *nāstika*, "one who teaches that nothing exists (nāsti)." Here these words are placed in the mouth of Rāma: "Like a thief is *the Buddha*, and know thou that the Tathāgata is a nāstika." This verse, which does not even appear in all the recensions, has long ago been proved spurious. *Jacobi* (l. c., pp. 88 f.) considers the entire Jābāli episode to be an interpolation. A. *Hillebrandt*, however, observes (Festschrift Kuhn, p. 23): "The situation is described very well, and such an effective contrast has been made between the materialist and the pious Rāma that I cannot consider this passage as spurious."

[3]) On the shoe as a symbol of law in old Norse and old German law, *cf.* Jacob *Grimm*, Deutsche Rechtsaltertümer, 4th Ed., 1899, I, 213 ff. A. *Holtzmann* has already compared the strikingly similar Hebrew custom, Ruth 4, 7.

intrigue, such as in reality occurred in India more than once, the only fabulous element in it being perhaps the exaggerated generosity of the two brothers Rāma and Bharata, Book III begins the battles and adventures of Rāma with fabulous and demoniacal beings.

When the exiles had lived in the Daṇḍaka forest for a long time, the forest-hermits living there besought Rāma for protection against the Rākṣasas. Rāma promises this protection, and from that time is incessantly engaged in battles against these devilish monsters. The man-eating giant Virādha is the first to be killed.[1] Fateful for the exiles is the meeting with *Sūrpaṇakhā* ("having claws as big as winnows"), the sister of Rāvaṇa. This she-devil falls in love with Rāma and makes amorous proposals to him. But he refers her to his brother Lakṣmaṇa who is not yet married.[2] Lakṣmaṇa scornfully declines her advances. Full of rage she is about to swallow Sītā, when Lakṣmaṇa cuts off her ears and nose. Howling she flees to her brother *Khara*. The latter sets out against Rāma, first with 14, then with 14,000 Rākṣasas, but Rāma slays them all. After Khara too has fallen, Śūrpaṇakhā hastens to *Laṅkā*, a fabulous land beyond the ocean,[3] and incites her brother *Rāvaṇa*, a ten-headed monster and ruler of Laṅkā, to revenge against Rāma. At the same time she describes to him the wondrous beauty of Sītā in the most alluring colours, and incites him to gain possession of her and to make her his wife. Then Rāvaṇa arises, drives in his golden chariot through the air across the ocean and there meets his friend, the demon *Mārīca*, who is living there as an ascetic. With Mārīca's aid he succeeds in parting Sītā from her protectors and stealing her away. He bears her away on his chariot through the air. Sītā cries loudly for help. The vulture Jaṭāyus, an old friend of Daśaratha's, comes flying along; he succeeds in smashing Rāvaṇa's chariot, but finally he himself is overcome by Rāvaṇa. The demon again seizes Sītā with his claws and flies away with her. As she

---

[1]) Here again follow (in Cantos 8-14) all sorts of legends, *e.g.* of the Ṛṣi *Agastya* and others, just as in Book I, and in the Mahābhārata.

[2]) This passage is one of the many proofs of the spuriousness of the first Book, in which it is related that the brothers of Rāma were married at the same time as Rāma.

[3]) *Not*, as is usually assumed, Ceylon. It was not till a much later time that Laṅkā was identified with Ceylon. See *Jacobi*, Râmâyana, pp. 90 ff. M. V. *Kibe*, Rawana's Lanka Discovered, 2nd Ed, 1920, attempts to determine the geographical position of Laṅkā.

is borne flying through the air, the flowers fall from her hair, and the jewelled bands slip from her feet to the ground. The trees, in whose branches the wind rustles, seem to call to her: "Be not afraid!" the lotuses droop their heads, as though they were mourning for their beloved friend; lions, tigers and other wild beasts run behind the shadow of Sītā, as if in rage; with tear-washed faces, *i.e.* the waterfalls, and up-stretched hands, i.e. the towering peaks, the hills seem to make moan for Sītā. Even the great sun, whose rays are darkened and whose orb pales at sight of the stolen Sītā, seems to lament: "There is no more justice, no truth, no righteousness, no innocence, if Rāvaṇa steals Sītā, the wife of Rāma." (III, 52, 34-39). But Rāvaṇa flies with the stolen lady across the ocean to Laṅkā, where he accommodates her in his harem. He conducts her round his palace, shows her all its splendours, and describes to her the immeasurable riches and marvels over which he rules. With coaxing words he tries to persuade her to become his wife. But Sītā answers him full of anger, that she will never break her faith with Rāma, and will never allow herself to be touched by him. Then Rāvaṇa threatens that, if she does not yield herself to him within twelve months, he will have her cut in pieces by the cooks and will eat her for his breakfast. Thereupon he has her taken to a grotto, and delivers her to the strict guardianship of the Rākṣasa women.

Meanwhile Rāma and Lakṣmaṇa have returned, and, to their horror, find the hut empty. In vain they seek Sītā in the forest. Rāma raises a bitter lament, he questions the trees, the rivers, the hills and the animals—but none can give him news of Sītā. At last they find the flowers and ornaments which fell from Sītā in her flight, soon they find the ruins of Rāvaṇa's chariot, scattered weapons and other traces of a fight. Rāma cannot but believe that Sītā has been killed by Rākṣasas, and in mad passion, he declares his intention of destroying the whole world. He will fill the air with his arrows, stay the course of the wind, annihilate the rays of the sun and envelop the earth in darkness, hurl down the summits of the hills, dry up the lakes, destroy the ocean, uproot the trees, nay more, even annihilate the gods themselves if they do not give him back his Sītā. Only with much trouble does Lakṣmaṇa succeed in soothing the raving one and in persuading him to renew the search. Then they find the vulture Jaṭāyus weltering in his blood. Dying, he still relates to them what has occurred, but dies in the middle of his story. Wandering towards the south the brothers encounter a roaring, headless monster, *Kabandha*, whom they deliver from a heavy curse. In gratitude for this, he advises Rāma to ally himself with the monkey-king *Sugrīva*, who will be helpful to him in the recovery of Sītā.

Book IV, the *Kiṣkindhā-kāṇḍa*, tells of the alliance which Rāma forms with the monkey, in order to win back Sītā.

The brothers reach the lake Pampā, the sight of which causes Rāma to fall into a melancholy mood; for it is spring, and the sight of the awakening of nature arouses in him great longing for the distant loved one.[1] Here they soon meet with the monkey-king Sugrīva. He tells them that he has been robbed of his wife and his dominion by his brother *Vālin*, and driven from his kingdom. Rāma and Sugrīva now form a close bond of friendship. Rāma promises to help Sugrīva against Vālin, while Sugrīva promises to aid Rāma in the recovery of Sītā. Before *Kiṣkindhā*,[2] the residence of Vālin, a battle takes place between the hostile monkey brothers. Rāma comes to Sugrīva's aid and kills Vālin. The monkey Sugrīva is consecrated as king, and *Aṅgada*, the son of Vālin, as heir to the throne.

Among the counsellors of Sugrīva, *Hanumat*,[3] the son of the wind-god, is the wisest. Sugrīva has the greatest confidence in him, and commissions him to find Sītā. Accompanied by a host of monkeys under the leadership of Aṅgada, the clever Hanumat starts on his way to the south. After many adventures they meet with *Sampāti*, a brother of the vulture Jaṭāyus. The latter tells them how once, when he wanted to fly to the sun in a race with his brother,[4] his wings were scorched, so that he had now to stay helpless on the Vindhya hills. But he had seen how Rāvaṇa had stolen Sītā away and taken her to Laṅkā. He describes to them the position of Laṅkā, and the monkeys descend to the ocean. But when they saw the immeasurable billowing sea before them, they simply despaired of getting across it. Aṅgada, however, tells them not to be despondent, "for despondency kills a man, as the angry snake kills a boy" (IV, 64,9). Then they take counsel together, as to who can jump the furthest, and it appears that none can jump so far as Hanumat. The

[1]) The whole first canto is an elegy, which might be entitled "Longing for the beloved in spring," quite in the style of the later ornate poetry.

[2]) Hence the title of Book IV.

[3]) Also *Hanūmat*. The name signifies: "He with the jaws." According to IV, 66, 24, he is so called because Indra crushed his jaws with the thunderbolt.

[4]) Like Icarus. This myth is at first briefly touched upon (IV, 58), then (IV, 59-63) related in purāṇa-like diffusiveness.

latter then ascends the hill Mahendra and prepares to leap across the ocean.

Book V describes the wonderful island of Laṅkā, the town of residence, the magnificent palace and harem of Rāvaṇa, and relates how Hanumat gives Sītā news of her beloved Rāma, and at the same time finds out the strength of the enemy. The book may have received the title *Sundara-kāṇḍa*, "the beautiful section," on account of the many poetical descriptions,[1] or because it contains even more fabulous stories than all the other books. If the whole second half of the Rāmāyaṇa is already a "romantic" epic, then this fifth book is very specially "romantic," and for Indian taste the romantic is always the most beautiful.

With a mighty leap, which causes the hill Mahendra to tremble in its depths and terrifies all the living beings on the hill, the monkey Hanumat rises into the air and flies across the ocean. After a flight of *four days*, on which he encounters various adventures and performs miracles, he finally reaches Laṅkā. From a hill he looks at the town, which seems to him almost impregnable. He makes himself as small as a cat,[2] and after sunset, penetrates into the town. He views the whole demon-city, the palace of Rāvaṇa and the wonderful chariot called Puṣpaka, on which the Rākṣasa is wont to drive through the air. He also penetrates into Rāvaṇa's harem, where he sees the powerful demon prince reposing in the midst of his beautiful women.[3] After long fruitless searching, he at last finds Sītā, consumed by grief, in the Aśoka-grove. He makes himself known as

---

[1]) Thus according to *Jacobi*, Râmâyana, p. 124.

[2]) According to another explanation: "as a horse-fly." Hanumat can change his form at pleasure.

[3]) The nightly seraglio-scene (V, 9-11) is described vividly in the style of ornate poetry, and forcibly recalls the description in the Buddha legend, where Prince Siddhārtha, surrounded by his wives, awakens at the hour of midnight, and is seized with disgust at sensual pleasure. The similarity of the situation and of the description is sufficiently striking to justify the supposition that it is an imitation of the description in *Aśvaghoṣa's Buddhacarita* (V, 47 ff.). For as E. B. *Cowell* rightly remarks (in the preface to his edition of the Buddhacarita), this scene forms an essential part of the Buddha legend, while in the Rāmāyaṇa, it is only an entirely unnecessary embellishment. Of course we must not ascribe the piece to Vālmīki himself, but the imitation must be ascribed to a later interpolator.

a friend and messenger of Rāma. She tells him that Rāvaṇa has threatened to devour her, and that she must die after two months, if Rāma does not deliver her before then. Hanumat assures her of the certainty of Rāma's coming to deliver her.[1]

Thereupon Hanumat returns to the hill, flies across the ocean and relates his adventures in Laṅkā to the monkeys awaiting him there. Then he goes to Rāma, reports to him how he found Sītā, and delivers him her message.

Book VI, which describes the great battle between Rāma and Rāvaṇa, hence called "*Yuddha-kāṇḍa*," "battle section," is the most extensive of all.

Rāma praises Hanumat for the successful execution of his errand, and heartily embraces him. But he despairs at the thought of the difficulty of getting across the ocean. Sugrīva advises the construction of a bridge to Laṅkā. Hanumat gives an exact description of the city of Rāvaṇa and its fortification, and declares that the principal heroes of the monkey-host would be able to overcome it. So Rāma commands that the army shall be prepared for the march, and soon the tremendous monkey-army sets out southwards towards the sea-shore.

When the news of the approaching army of monkeys had reached Laṅkā, Rāvaṇa summoned his counsellors, all great and powerful Rākṣasas, to a council. Now while all the other relatives and counsellors urge Rāvaṇa in boasting speeches to fight, *Vibhīṣaṇa*, Rāvaṇa's brother, points to unfavourable omens and advises him to return Sītā. Rāvaṇa is much enraged at this, and accuses him of envy and ill will ; relatives, he says, are always the worst enemies of a king and hero. Feeling deeply offended by his brother, Vibhīṣaṇa renounces him, flies across the ocean with four

---

[1]) With this, Hanumat's mission is fulfilled, and the following narrative (41-55) is doubtless a later interpolation : in order to test the strength of the enemy, Hanumat instigates a quarrel by destroying the Aśoka-grove. In tremendous battles with thousands of Rākṣasas he alone remains the victor. But finally he is put into fetters and taken before the demon-king. Hanumat introduces himself as the messenger of Rāma and demands the return of Sītā. Rāvaṇa decides to kill him, but is persuaded to spare him as an ambassador. However, in order to punish him, he causes cotton rags soaked in oil to be wrapped round the monkey's tail and to be set alight. Sītā hears of it, and prays to Agni, the fire-god, that he may not burn Hanumat. The monkey now leaps with his burning tail from house to house, and sets the whole town on fire, while he himself escapes uninjured. The spuriousness of this passage has been indisputably proved by *Jacobi*, l. c., pp. 31 ff.

other Rākṣasas and allies himself with Rāma. On the advice of Vibhīṣaṇa Rāma appeals to the Ocean-god himself to aid him in crossing the sea. The latter calls the monkey Nala, the son of the divine masterbuilder Viśvakarman, and instructs him to bridge the ocean. At Rāma's command, the monkeys bring rocks and trees, in a few days a bridge is built over the ocean, and the whole of the great army passes over to Laṅkā.

Now Rāvaṇa's residence town is surrounded by the army of monkeys. Rāvaṇa gives the command for a general sortie. A battle takes place, also many cases of single combat between the chief heroes of the two fighting armies. Lakṣmaṇa, Hanumat, Aṅgada and the bear-king Jāmbavat are the most prominent fellow-combatants of Rāma, while on Rāvaṇa's side, his son Indrajit is the most conspicuous. The latter is versed in all magic arts and knows how to make himself invisible at any moment.

Thus, on one occasion, he inflicts dangerous wounds on Rāma and Lakṣmaṇa. But in the night, on the advice of the bear-king Jāmbavat, the monkey Hanumat flies to Mount Kailāsa, in order to fetch thence four particularly powerful healing herbs. As these herbs are concealed, the monkey simply takes the whole mountain-peak with him and carries it to the battle-field, where, through the fragrance of the healing herbs, Rāma, Lakṣmaṇa and all the wounded are immediately healed. Hereupon Hanumat puts the mountain back into its place.

On another occasion, Indrajit, versed in magic, comes out of the city carrying on his war-chariot a magically produced image of Sītā, which he ill-treats and beheads before the eyes of Hanumat, Lakṣmaṇa and the monkeys. Horrified, Hanumat reports to Rāma that Sītā is killed; Rāma falls into a swoon. Lakṣmaṇa breaks into lamentations and utters a blasphemous speech with bitter complaints against Fate that has no regard to virtue (VI, 83, 4 ff.) but he is soon enlightened by Vibhīṣaṇa that the whole affair is only a delusion produced by Indrajit. Finally, Indrajit is killed by Lakṣmaṇa after a violent duel.

Furious at the death of his son, Rāvaṇa himself now appears on the field of battle. A dreadful duel between Rāma and Rāvaṇa takes place, continuing day and night. The gods themselves come to Rāma's aid, especially Indra with his chariot and his projectiles. But as many times as Rāma strikes off Rāvaṇa's heads, so often a new head grows again. At last he succeeds in piercing Ravaṇa's heart with a weapon created by god Brahman himself. There is great rejoicing in the army of the monkeys, and wild flight of the Rākṣasas.

Now Rāvaṇa is solemnly buried and Vibhīṣaṇa is installed as king in Laṅkā by Rāma.

Only now does Rāma send for Sītā, and proclaim to her the joyous news of the victory—but then, in the presence of all the monkeys and Rākṣasas, he rejects her. He has (so he declares) had his revenge for the ignominy he has had to suffer, but with her he will have no more to do ; for a woman who has sat on the lap of another man, and who has been looked at with lustful eyes by another, could no longer be received as a wife by a Rāma. Then Sītā raises a bitter complaint against the unjust suspicion of Rāma, and asks Lakṣmaṇa to erect a pyre : for now nothing remained for her but to enter the fire. Rāma gives his consent, the pyre is erected and lighted, and Sītā, invoking the fire as witness of her innocence, rushes into the flames. Then the god Agni arises out of the burning pyre with the uninjured Sītā and delivers her to Rāma, assuring him, in a solemn speech, that she has always kept her faith with him, and even in the palace of the Rākṣasa remained pure and innocent. Thereupon Rāma declares that he himself never had any doubts concerning Sītā's innocence, but that it was necessary to prove her innocence before the eyes of the people.

Now Rāma and his people, accompanied by Hanumat and the monkeys, return to Ayodhyā, where they are received with open arms by Bharata, Śatrughna, and the mothers. They enter amidst the rejoicings of the populace. Rāma is consecrated as king and rules happily and for the welfare of his subjects.

This really concludes the story of Rāma, and there can be no doubt at all that the original poem ended with Book VI, and that the following *Book VII*, is a later addition. This seventh book—it is called *Uttara-kāṇḍa*, " last section," again contains numerous myths and legends similar to those which also occur in the Mahābhārata and the Purāṇas, which have nothing at all to do with the Rāma-legend. The first cantos deal with the origin of the Rākṣasas and the battles of Indra with *Rāvaṇa*,[1] after which the story of the youth of *Hanumat* is related (VII, 35 f.). Only about a third of

---

[1]) VII, 1-34. *Jacobi* calls the piece " Rāvaneïs."

the book deals with Rāma and Sītā, and the following is related :

One day Rāma is informed that the people are expressing their disapproval at his having received Sītā back after she (during her abduction) had sat on the lap of Rāvaṇa; it was feared that this might have a bad effect on the morals of the women in the land. The model king Rāma is very sad about this; he cannot bear the reproach that he is setting the people a bad example, and requests his brother Lakṣmaṇa to take Sītā away and desert her in the forest. With a heavy heart Lakṣmaṇa takes her on his chariot, leads her to the Ganges and brings her to the further bank of the river, where he discloses to her that Rāma has rejected her on account of the suspicions of the people. In deep grief, but yet full of submission to her fate, Sītā only sends Rāma friendly greetings. Soon after, some hermit-boys find the weeping Sītā in the forest and lead her to the hermitage of the ascetic *Vālmīki*. The latter delivers her into the protection of hermit-women. After some time she gives birth, in the hermitage, to the twins *Kuśa* and *Lava*.

Several years pass. The children have grown up and become pupils of the ascetic and singer Vālmīki. At this time Rāma organises a great horse-sacrifice. This is also attended by Vālmīki and his pupils. He instructs two of them to recite, in the sacrificial assembly, the Rāmāyaṇa composed by him. All listen with rapture to the wonderful recitation. But Rāma soon discovers that the two youthful singers Kuśa and Lava,[1] who recite the poem to the accompaniment of the lute, are sons of Sītā. Then he sends messengers to Vālmīki and asks him to arrange that Sītā may purify herself by an oath before the sacrificial assembly. The next morning Vālmīki brings Sītā, and, in a solemn speech, the great ascetic declares that she is pure and innocent, and that her children, the twin-brothers Kuśa and Lava, are the true sons of Rāma. Thereupon Rāma declares that, though he is satisfied with the words of Vālmīki, he still desires that Sītā shall purify herself by means of an oath. Then all the gods descended from heaven. But Sītā, with downcast glance and folded hands, said: "As truly as I have never, even with one thought, thought of another than Rāma—may Goddess Earth open her arms to me! As truly as I have always, in thought, word and deed, honoured only Rāma

---

[1]) Professional "travelling singers," who sang epic songs to the accompaniment of the lute, were called *kuśīlava*; the names Kuśa and Lava were invented as a kind of etymological interpretation of the word kuśīlava. *Cf. Jacobi*, l. c., pp. 62 f., 67 f.

—may Goddess Earth open her arms to me! As I have here spoken the truth and never known another than Rāma—may Goddess Earth open her arms to me!" Scarcely was the oath finished, than there arose out of the earth a heavenly throne, borne on the heads of snake-demons, and Mother Earth, seated on the throne, embraced Sītā and vanished with her into the depths. In vain Rāma now adjures the Goddess Earth to give him back his Sītā. Only god Brahman appears and comforts him with the hope of reunion in heaven. Soon afterwards Rāma gives up the government to his two sons Kuśa and Lava, and himself enters heaven, where he again becomes Viṣṇu.

The thread of this narrative in Book VII is constantly interrupted by the interpolation of numerous myths and legends. There we find again the familiar legends of *Yayāti* and *Nahuṣa* (VII, 58f.), of the *slaying of Vṛtra by Indra*, who by this becomes guilty of Brahman-murder (VII, 84-87), of *Urvaśī*, the beloved of the gods Mitra and Varuṇa, who in a marvellous manner beget the Ṛṣis *Vasiṣṭha* and *Agastya* VII, 56f.), of King *Ila*, who as the woman *Ilā* bears *Purūravas* (VII, 87-90), and so on. Many truly brahmanical legends with an exaggerated tendency compare well with similar stories of Book XIII of the Mahābhārata. Thus the story of the ascetic *Śambūka*, belonging to the Śūdra caste, whose head Rāma strikes off, for which he is commended by the gods, because a Śūdra should not take it upon himself to practise asceticism; or of the god who is compelled to eat his own flesh because, in a former incarnation, he practised asceticism, but omitted to make presents to the Brahmans (VII, 73-81), and similar "edifying" legends. The whole of the book bears the character of the latest parts of the Mahābhārata.

The Genuine and the Spurious in the Rāmāyaṇa.[1]

There can be no doubt that the whole of *Book VII* of the Rāmāyaṇa was added later to the work; but it has also

[1] The problems of the Rāmāyaṇa have been fully dealt with first by A. *Weber*, "Uber das Râmâyana," (ABA., 1870). The fundamental work on these problems is that

long been recognised that the whole of *Book I* cannot have belonged to the original work of Vālmīki. Not only are there numerous internal contradictions in the book, but the language and style, too, stand out as inferior to those of Books II to VI. Moreover, in the genuine parts of the poem there is never any reference to the events in Book I, in fact there are details in this book which directly contradict the statements of later books.[1]

Only in Books I and VII is Rāma throughout conceived as a divine being, an incarnation of the god *Viṣṇu.* In Books II to VI, apart from a few passages which are doubtless interpolated,[2] he is always only a mortal hero, and in all indisputably genuine parts of the epic there is no indication whatever of his being conceived as an incarnation of Viṣṇu. Where mythology enters into the genuine parts of the poem, it is not Viṣṇu, but the god *Indra* who, as in the Veda, is regarded as the highest god.

It is characteristic, too, of the two Books I and VII that, as we have seen, the thread of the narrative is frequently interrupted, and, in the manner of the Mahābhārata and of the Purāṇas, numerous brahmanical myths and legends are inserted. There are only very few passages in Books II to VI (*e. g.* at the beginning of Book III) where this kind of thing occurs also. The additions and extensions in *these* books—and they are numerous enough—are generally of quite a different kind. They consist chiefly of the *spinning out* of the most beautiful and most popular passages by the singers by means of their own additions. We must imagine the Rāmāyaṇa as having been *orally* transmitted for a long time

---

of H. *Jacobi*, Das Râmâyana, Geschichte und Inhalt, Bonn, 1893. See also C. V. *Vaidya*, The Riddle of the Ramayana, Bombay and London, 1906; and *Dineshchandra Sen*, The Bengali Ramayanas, Calcutta, 1920.

1) *E. g.* the marriage of Lakṣmaṇa, see above p. 487 Note 2.

2) Thus, for instance, at the end of Book VI, where, at the moment when Sītā ascends the pyre, all the gods come on the scene and praise Rāma as god Viṣṇu.

—perhaps through centuries—in the circles of travelling singers like the brothers Kuśa and Lava in the Uttara-kāṇḍa. These singers or minstrels regarded the epic songs as their property, with which they took every kind of liberty. If they noticed that the audience was deeply moved by the touching plaints of Sītā, Daśaratha or Kausalyā, they would fabricate a number of additional verses, so that they could linger over it for a longer time; if the battle-scenes met with greater appreciation from a more warlike public, then it was easy for the singer to gather together more and more new heroes for duels, to have a few more thousands or tens of thousands of monkeys or Rākṣasas slaughtered or to relate again with a little variation a heroic deed which had already been related; if the audience enjoyed comical scenes, especially those in which the monkeys appear, then it was tempting for the singer not only to spin out such scenes, but also to add new similar ones; if he had a learned audience of Brahmans before him, he sought to win their favour by spinning out the didactic portions, adding new moral maxims or inserting aphorisms taken from elsewhere; especially ambitious rhapsodists would extend the descriptions of nature, probably already popular in the ancient and genuine poem, by means of additions in the style of the ornate court poetry.[1] Probably the Rāmāyaṇa, like the Mahābhārata, only received a more or less definite form when it was *written down.*[2] But this must have happened at a time when the poem was already so famous and so popular, that it was already regarded as of religious merit to read and to hear it, and that heaven was

---

[1]) It was favourable for the amplifications, though unfavourable for the preservation of the genuine, that the śloka is a metre easy to handle. To produce any amount of ślokas almost in no time, is an easy matter for any tolerably educated Indian who knows Sanskrit.

[2]) The activity of the *commentators*, by which the text was made still more secure, began much later still.

promised to him who copied it.[1] The more one copied of so magnificent and so salutary a poem, "that imparts long life, health, renown, good brothers and intelligence,"[2] the more certain one was of entering heaven. Therefore the first compilers and editors to handle the written poem, did not regard it as their task to view the transmitted material critically, to distinguish the genuine from the spurious, but, on the contrary, welcomed everything which presented itself under the title of "Rāmāyaṇa."

We can, however, only speak of a "*more or less*" definite form of the Rāmāyaṇa, for the manuscripts in which the epic has come down to us, differ greatly from one another, and there are at least *three different recensions* of the text, representing the transmission in different regions of India. These recensions differ from one another not only in reference to various readings of certain passages, but also in the fact that in each of them verses, long passages and even whole cantos occur, which are missing in others; also the order of the verses is very frequently different in the different recensions. The recension most widely spread (in the North as well as in the South of India), is the one which Jacobi designates as "C," which has several times been printed in Bombay.[3] The only complete edition which has appeared in Europe, by G. Gorresio.[4] contains the *Bengal* recension. The text of the *North-Western Indian* (Western Indian, Kashmiri) recension

1) VI, 128, 120: "Those men who, full of love towards Rāma, write down this collection (saṃhitā) compiled by the Ṛṣi, attain to a dwelling in Indra's heaven."

2) VI, 128, 122. Also see above, pp. 478 f.

3) I quote from this recension in the edition of the NSP. by K. P. *Parab*, 2nd Ed., Bombay, 1902. It was a mistake to call this recension "Northern Indian," for the Southern Indian MSS. give the same text; see *Winternitz*, Catalogue of South Indian Sanskrit Manuscripts, London, 1902, p. 67; M. *Winternitz* and A. B. *Keith*, Catalogue of Sanskrit MSS. in the Bodleian Library, II, pp. 145 f.

4) Turin, 1843-1867. See on this edition E. *Windisch*, Geschichte der Sanskrit-Philologie (Grundriss I, 1 B), pp. 145 f. Only the two first Books have been edited (with a Latin translation) by A. W. von *Schlegel*, Bonnae, 1829, 1838, on eclectic principles.

is now being printed at Lahore.[1] The only explanation for the great differences between the recensions is the fact that the text of the epic was for a long period only handed down by oral transmission. It is conceivable that the order of the verses became dislocated in the memory of the rhapsodists, that the wording must often have suffered considerable changes, and that the singers of different regions made different additions and extensions respectively.

All these recensions agree, however, in that they contain all the seven books, and that in all of them, spurious passages are side by side with genuine ones. For this reason none of the recensions represent an "original text" of the Rāmāyaṇa. But the omission of a passage in one of the recensions is always justifiable ground for suspecting its genuineness; and on the whole it is certainly easier to detect what is spurious and later in the Rāmāyaṇa, than it is in the Mahābhārata. "As on many of our old, venerable cathedrals," says Jacobi,[2] "every coming generation has added something new and repaired something old, without the original construction being effaced, in spite of all the added little chapels and turrets; so also many generations of singers have been at work at the Rāmāyaṇa; but the old nucleus, around which so much has grown, is to the searching eye of the student, not difficult to recognise, if not in every detail, yet in its principal features." Jacobi himself, in his work "Das Rāmāyaṇa"

An edition from a Bengali MS. with comparative foot-notes was published by Pandit Rasiklal *Bhattāchārya* in the "Pandit," N. S., Vols. 28-34. A comparative study of the recensions C and B (Bengali) has been made by M. *Vallauri*, GSAI. 25, 1912, pp. 45 ff.

[1]) Critically edited by Pandit *Ram Labhaya*, published by the Research Department, D. A. V. College, Lahore, 1923 ff. *Cf.* Hans *Wirtz*, Die westliche Recension des Rāmāyaṇa. Diss. Bonn, 1894; S. *Lévi*, JA. 1918, s 11, t. xi, pp. 5 ff. Only when we shall have critical editions of all the three recensions, will it be possible to decide which of them contains the more authentic text.

[2]) Das Râmâyaṇa, p. 60.

* * *

has indisputably proved a large number of additions and extensions to be such. The fact that, in an attempt at a critical reconstruction of the text, perhaps only a quarter of the transmitted 24,000 verses of the Rāmāyaṇa would prove to be "genuine," does not speak against the justification of the criticism.[1] It is only on account of the *great mass* of the "spurious" in the Indian epics, that the reading of them, which often carries us away to the greatest admiration, still oftener disappoints us. And if a comparison between the Indian and the Greek epics with reference to artistic value must necessarily result unfavourably for the former, the blame rests far more with those versifiers who increased and disfigured the ancient songs with their own additions and alterations, than with the ancient Indian poets. The "formless fermenting verbiage," with which Friedrich Rückert reproaches the Rāmāyaṇa, is surely more often to be placed to the account of the imitators of Vālmīki than to that of Vālmīki himself. But on the whole the German poet is probably right when he seeks the beauty of the Indian epic *elsewhere* than that of the Greek, saying:

> "Such fantastic grimaces, such formless fermenting verbiage
> As Rāmāyaṇa offers thee, that has Homer
> Certainly taught thee to despise; but yet such lofty thoughts
> And such deep feeling the Iliad does not show thee." [2]

The Age of the Rāmāyaṇa.[3]

Closely connected with the question of the genuine and the spurious in the Rāmāyaṇa is the question of the age of the poem. For in order to answer this question it is certainly of importance whether we can form some idea, at least, of

---

[1]) In Vol. 51 of ZDMG. (1897), pp. 605 ff., *Jacobi* made an attempt to deal critically with a considerable connected portion of the Rāmāyaṇa, in which, out of 600 verses, not quite a quarter remained.

[2]) F. *Rückert*, Poetisches Tagebuch, Frankfurt a. M., 1888, p. 99.

[3]) *Cf. Jacobi*, l.c., p. 100 ff.; A. B. *Keith*, JRAS 1915, p. 318 ff.

the interval of time which may have elapsed between the original poem, whose genuine parts are to be found in Books II-VI, and the two added Books I and VII.

We have now seen that in the genuine books Rāma is merely a human hero, and that it is only in Books I and VII (and in a few interpolated passages of the other books) that he appears as the incarnation of the god Viṣṇu. It is the epic itself which has made Prince Rāma a national hero. This transformation of Rāma from a man into a semi-divine national hero and finally into the Universal God Viṣṇu must necessarily have taken a very long time. Moreover, the poet Vālmīki appears as a pious forest hermit and Ṛṣi and a contemporary of the hero Rāma in the first and last books of the Rāmāyaṇa. Thus Vālmīki had already become a legendary personage in the minds of the poets of these later books. All this makes it seem likely that centuries elapsed between the genuine and the spurious portions of the poem.[1]

We should immediately add here, though, that also in our Mahābhārata, which knows not only the Rāma legend, but the Rāmāyaṇa of Vālmīki, Rāma is regarded as an incarnation of Viṣṇu, and Vālmīki is mentioned as an ancient Ṛṣi. It has already been mentioned above (p. 384) that the *Rāmopākhyāna* of the Mahābhārata is in all probability only a free abridged rendering of the Rāmāyaṇa, and we may add, of the Rāmāyaṇa in a very late form, fairly nearly approaching the present one. For, to the author of the Rāmopākhyāna Rāma is already Viṣṇu become man,[2] he knows that Hanumat "burned" Laṅkā—a passage proved to be spurious—,[3] and he is already acquainted with that

[1]) *Jacobi*, l. c. p. 65.

[2]) Mahābh. III, 147, 31; 275, 5 ff.

[3]) Mahābh. III, 148, 9. *Cf.* above p. 491 Note 1.

part of Book VII which refers to Rāvaṇa.[1] The story of Rāma is related in the Mahābhārata in order to console Yudhiṣṭhira for the stealing of Draupadī. But this whole episode of the stealing of Draupadī is surely only an imitation of the stealing of Sītā in the Rāmāyaṇa. In the latter, indeed, this abduction is the nucleus of the legend and of the poem, while in the Mahābhārata the abduction of Draupadī has practically no significance for the course of the narrative. Other striking coincidences in single features in the two epics have been pointed out, especially the resemblance between the heroes Arjuna and Rāma. The banishment into the forest for twelve to fourteen years, the bending of the bow, and endowment of the heroes with divine weapons which they fetch from the gods[2]—these are points in which the influence of the one epic upon the other is *possible*, but can hardly be proved. Nevertheless it is more likely that the Mahābhārata borrowed motives from the Rāmāyaṇa than the reverse. For while the Rāmāyaṇa shows no kind of acquaintance with the Pāṇḍava legend or the heroes of the Mahābhārata,[3] the Mahābhārata, as we have seen, knows not only the Rāma legend, but the Rāmāyaṇa itself. In the Harivaṃśa there is even already a mention of a dramatic representation of the Rāmāyaṇa (see above, p. 451 Note). It is still more important, however, that the Mahābhārata (VII, 143, 66) quotes a "śloka once sung by Vālmīki," which is actually to be found in our Rāmāyaṇa, (VI, 81, 28). Vālmīki is mentioned in several places in

---

1) *Jacobi*, l. c., pp. 73 f. Also in Mahābh., VII, 59, and XII, 29, 51 ff., the Rāma legend is briefly touched on, and a few verses partly agreeing with Rām. VI, 128, 95 ff., refer to the paradisiacal condition of the subjects of Rāma "who ruled for ten thousand and ten hundred years."

2) *Cf.* *A. Holtzmann*, Das Mahābhārata, IV, 68 f. *E. Windisch*, LZB., 1879, No. 52, col. 1709.

3) It is true that the poet of the Rāmāyaṇa knew the poem of Sāvitrī and the song of Nala (Rām. II, 30, 6; V, 24, 12), but it is not certain that he knew them as parts of the Mahābhārata (as is assumed by *Hopkins*, Great Epic, p. 78 note).

the Mahābhārata as a "great ascetic" and venerable Ṛṣi, by the side of Vasiṣṭha and other Ṛṣis of ancient times.[1] On one occasion he tells Yudhiṣṭhira that, in the course of a disputation with holy Munis he was once reproached with being a "Brahman-murderer," and that through this reproach the guilt of Brahman-murder had come upon him, from which he could only cleanse himself by the worship of Siva.[2] All these facts justify our agreeing with Jacobi (l. c., p. 71) when he says that the Rāmāyaṇa must already "have been generally familiar as an *ancient* work, before the Mahābhārata had reached its final form." It is quite in accord with this that the "process of degeneration," if one may say so, *i.e.* the superseding of the genuine by the spurious, and the penetrating of later elements into the old parts has gone so far in the Mahābhārata as to pervade the whole work, while in the Rāmāyaṇa it was checked in the beginning and extends only to Books I and VII and a few parts of the remaining books.

But if the Mahābhārata already had, on the whole, its present form in the fourth century A. D. (see above, p. 465), then the Rāmāyaṇa must have received its "final" form (the word "final" is to be taken *cum grano salis*) at least one or two centuries earlier.

However, this does not by any means answer the question as to which is the older of the two epics. After all that we have said about the history of the Mahābhārata as well as of the Rāmāyaṇa, it is clear enough that this question

---

[1]) Mahābh. I, 2, 18; II, 7, 16; V, 83, 27; XII, 207, 4; Hariv. 268, 14539.

[2]) Mahābh. XIII, 18, 8. According to the Adhyātma-Rāmāyaṇa, Vālmīki lived among robbers when he was a young man, though he was a Brahman by birth. The same tradition is to be found in the Bengali Rāmāyana. *Cf. Jacobi,* l. c., p. 66 note; D. *Ibbetson* and A. K. *Mojumdar* in Ind. Ant., 24, 1895, p. 220; 31, 1902, p. 351; D. Ch. *Sen*, Bengali Ramayanas, p. 125 (a similar Mohammedan legend, pp. 127f.). Bālmīk, *i.e.* Vālmīki, is worshipped as a kind of saint by the caste of the scavengers in Eastern Punjab, s. R. C. *Temple.* The legends of the Punjāb, 1 (1884), pp. 529 f.

in itself has no sense at all, but naturally resolves itself into three different questions, namely: I. Which of the two works, *in the form in which they are now before us*, is the older? II. What relation does the period of time in which an original *Mahābhārata epic* gradually became the great *compilation* combining heroic songs and didactic poetry, bear to that period of time in which *the ancient poem of Vālmīki* became enlarged into the *present Rāmāyaṇa* by means of greater or smaller additions in the older books, and finally by the addition of Books I and VII? III. Was there, generally speaking, a Mahābhārata epic or a Rāmāyaṇa epic first in existence?

Only to the first of these three questions a definite answer could be given, namely that our present Rāmāyaṇa is older than the Mahābhārata in its present form. As regards the second question, we may assume that the Rāmāyaṇa, being so much shorter, required a shorter time for its gradual growth than the Mahābhārata. It has already been pointed out that the character of the two spurious books of the Rāmāyaṇa is strikingly similar to that of the Mahābhārata, and that the same brahmanical myths and legends often recur in both. The stories which are common to both works are, however, told with such variations that we are compelled to assume that they are derived from the same source, the Itihāsa literature orally transmitted in brahmanical circles, rather than that borrowing took place. Furthermore, all the books of the Rāmāyaṇa and of the Mahābhārata have numerous phrases, hemistiches, proverbial idioms and whole verses in common,[1] and in language, style and metre there is a far-reaching conformity in the two works.[2] From

---

[1]) This has been proved especially by E. W. *Hopkins* in the American Journal of Philology, Vols. XIX, pp. 138 ff. and XX, pp. 22 ff., and in his book, The Great Epic of India, pp. 58 ff., 403 ff.

[2]) On the Śloka in the two epics see *Jacobi*, l. c., pp. 24 ff., and Gurupūjākaumudī, pp. 50 ff.

these facts we conclude that the period of the growth of the Rāmāyaṇa *falls within* the longer period of the development of the Mahābhārata.

The third and most important question, which of the two *original* epics is the earlier, can only be answered by way of hypothesis. The Hindus declare the Rāmāyaṇa to be earlier than the Mahābhārata, because, according to the traditional list of Viṣṇu's incarnations, the incarnation as Rāma preceded that as Kṛṣṇa.[1] This argument has no force, because in the old, genuine Rāmāyaṇa, as we have seen, Rāma does not as yet appear as an incarnation at all. It is a fact, however, that allusions to Vāsudeva (Kṛṣṇa), Arjuna and Yudhiṣṭhira already occur in Pāṇini's grammar, whereas Rāma is not mentioned either by Pāṇini or Patañjali, nor in inscriptions of the pre-Christian era.[2] It is likely, too, that the theory of incarnation arose out of the Kṛṣṇa cult, and that the transformation of the hero Rāma into an incarnation of Viṣṇu resulted only later, by analogy to the Kṛṣṇa incarnation.[3] A few scholars[4] have declared the Rāmāyaṇa to be the earlier of the two epics, because the *burning of widows* does not occur in it, whilst it is mentioned in the Mahābhārata. The fact of the matter, however, is that in the old, genuine Mahābhārata the burning of widows is just as much absent as in the genuine Rāmāyaṇa, whilst there *are* allusions to it in the later portions of the Rāmāyaṇa, though less frequent than in the Mahābhārata.[5]

---

[1]) According to the Purāṇas, Rāma appears in the Kṛtayuga, but Kṛṣṇa not until the Dvāparayuga. *Cf.* A. *Govindācārya Svāmin* in JBRAS., 23, 1911-12, pp. 244 ff.

[2]) *Cf.* R. G. *Bhandarkar*, Early History of the Deccan, 2nd Ed., Bombay, 1895, p. 10: Vaiṣṇavism, etc., pp. 46 f.

[3]) *Jacobi* in ERE., VII, 194 f. R. *Chanda*, The Indo-Aryan Races, 1, 1916, pp. 88 f., 111 ff.

[4]) *Jacobi*, l. c., pp. 107 f., and before him A. W. v. *Schlegel* and Monier *Williams*, also J. *Jolly*, Recht und Sitte, p. 68.

[5]) *Cf. Winternitz*, Die Frau in den indischen Religionen, I, 1920, pp. 58 f.; J. J. *Meyer*, Das Weib im altindischen Epos, pp. 307 f.

Jacobi (l. c., pp. 78, 81 ff.) is so sure about the Rāmāyaṇa being the older poem, that he even takes for granted that the Mahābhārata only became an epic under the influence of the poetic art of Vālmīki. This seems to me to go far beyond what is warranted by facts, indeed it seems to be in contradiction with some facts. In more than one respect the Rāmāyaṇa, as compared with the Mahābhārata, indicates progress in the art of epic poetry. In the Mahābhārata we still have a distinct remnant of the ancient ballad form in the *prose formulae* such as "Yudhiṣṭhira spake," "Kuntī spake," "Duryodhana spake," and so on, introducing the speeches of the various characters, while in the Rāmāyaṇa the speakers throughout are introduced in verses.[1] It has also already been pointed out to how great an extent the Rāmāyaṇa already shows the peculiarities of the style of ornate court poetry, the kāvya.[2] Of course it is hard to say which of it is old, and which parts have been added later. Nevertheless, this peculiarity of the Rāmāyaṇa which separates it considerably from the Mahābhārata and brings it nearer to the epics of Kālidāsa, must make us chary of assuming a greater antiquity for the Rāmāyaṇa.[3]

There is a second point, too, in which the Mahābhārata makes a much more archaic impression than the Rāmāyaṇa. Throughout the Mahābhārata—at least in the nucleus of the poem, which treats of the Pāṇḍava story and the Kuru battle—we encounter rougher manners and a more warlike spirit than in the Rāmāyaṇa. The battle scenes of the Mahābhārata read quite differently from those described in the Rāmāyaṇa.

---

1) See above, p. 324. The Purāṇas have always retained these prose formulas in order to preserve the appearance of antiquity.

2) See above, pp. 475 f., 489 note 1, 490 and *cf.* p. 461.

3) E. W. *Hopkins* (Cambridge History, I, p. 251) says of the Rāmāyaṇa "Whatever may have been the date of its germ as a story, as an art-product it is later than the Mahābhārata." *Cf.* also *Oldenberg*, Das Mahabharata, pp. 53 ff., and H. *Raychaudhury* in Calcutta Review, Mar. 1922, pp. 1 ff.

Those in the Mahābhārata give the impression that the poet belonged to a rough race of warriors, and had himself seen bloody battle-fields, while those in the Rāmāyaṇa sound rather as though a story-teller is relating battles of which his only source of information is the reports he has heard. There is not that embittered hatred, that fierce resentment between Rāma and Rāvaṇa, Lakṣmaṇa and Indrajit, as in the Mahābhārata when we read of the battles between Arjuna and Karṇa or Bhīma and Duryodhana. The Sītā of the Rāmāyaṇa, when she is stolen, abducted and persecuted by Rāvaṇa, or when she is rejected by Rāma, always maintains a certain calmness and meekness in her accusations and lamentations, and in her speeches there is not a trace of the wild passion which we so often find in Draupadī in the Mahābhārata. Kuntī and Gāndharī, too, are true hero-mothers of a warlike race, while Kausalyā and Kaikeyī in the Rāmāyaṇa can rather be compared with the stereotyped queens of the classical dramas. This seems to indicate that the Mahābhārata belongs to a ruder, more warlike age, while the Rāmāyaṇa shows traces of a more refined civilization; unless, in order to explain this sharply marked difference between the two epics, we assume that the Mahābhārata reflects a rougher civilization of *Western* India, while the Rāmāyaṇa reflects a more refined civilization of *Eastern* India, and that the two epics do not represent the poetry of different *periods*, but of different *regions* of India. Even from this point of view, however, it is difficult to conceive that the Mahābhārata should only have become an epic under the influence of Vālmīki's poetic art.

There can be no doubt that the Mahābhārata belongs to the West of India, and the Rāmāyaṇa to the East. Western peoples play the principal part in the Mahābhārata, while the chief events of the Rāmāyaṇa take place in the the land of the Kosala, where, according to tradition, Vālmīki is said to have lived, and where, in all probability, he did really live.[1] But in *Eastern* India *Buddhism* originated, and in Magadha, as in the neighbouring Kosala land, it was first propagated. So much the more important is the question: What is the relationship of the Rāmāyaṇa to Buddhism?

It has already been pointed out above (p. 471) that, in the oldest Buddhist literature, we still find examples of the Ākhyāna or ballad poetry, in which we have recognised a forerunner of the epic. T. W. *Rhys Davids*[2] has concluded from this that the Rāmāyaṇa could not have yet existed as an epic at the time of the origin of these Buddha-ballads. Now it could be objected that perhaps the ancient Ākhyāna or ballad poetry might have lived on beside the new literary form of the epic which had developed out of it, in the same way as we find ballad and epic poetry side by side in modern literatures. It is remarkable, notwithstanding, that we find nothing but Buddha-ballads throughout early Buddhist literature, whilst a Buddha epic was not written until centuries later. It is still more important that in the Tipiṭaka we find the *Dasaratha-Jātaka*,[3] which relates how Bharata brings the news of the death of Dasaratha, whereupon Rāma tells Lakṣmaṇa and Sītā to step into the water to offer the libations for the departed. This gives rise to a conversation, in which Bharata asks Rāma how it is that he shows no sign of sorrow,[4]

---

1) *Jacobi*, l. c., pp. 66 ff., 69.

2) Buddhist India, London, 1903, p. 183.

3) The Pāli text of this Jātaka (No. 461) was first published with an English translation by V. *Fausböll*, Copenhagen, 1871. It has been treated in detail by *Weber*, l. c., 1 ff.; *Jacobi*, l. c., 84 ff. E. *Senart*, Essai sur la légende du Buddha, 2nd Ed., Paris, 1882, pp. 317 f.; *Lüders*, NGGW., 1897, 1, pp. 40 ff: D. Ch. *Sen*, The Bengali Ramayanas, pp. 9 ff.; G. A. *Grierson*, JRAS., 1922, 135 ff.; N. B. *Utgikar* in Centenary Supplement to JRAS., 1924, pp. 203 ff. Only the gāthās of the Jātaka belong to the Tipiṭaka. The prose narrative is the fabrication of the compilers of the commentary (about the fifth century A. D.), and all conclusions drawn from this story, such as those of D. Ch. Sen and others, are faulty.

4) Here we see that even the Jātaka-gāthās were remodelled with a Buddhist tendency. In the Rāmāyaṇa Rāma himself laments exceedingly at the news of his father's death, before making the speech of consolation, s. Rām. II, 102-105, and the same thing probably holds good for the ancient ballad too.

and Rāma replies with a lengthy speech of consolation, explaining how futile it is to lament over the dead, as death comes to all mortals. The fact that only *one* of the twelve ancient gāthās of the Jātaka appears in our Rāmāyaṇa,[1] proves that our epic cannot be the source of these verses, but that the Jātaka is based upon an ancient Rāma ballad. In the same Jātaka book there is also the Sāma-Jātaka,[2] which we may probably consider as an older form of the tale about the hermit-boy killed in the chase, which is told by Daśaratha in Rāmāyaṇa II, 63 f. There are a few other Jātakas, too, in which we find passages reminding us of the Rāmāyaṇa, but only very seldom literal agreement.[3] It is striking, too, that in the whole of the Jātaka, which tells so many tales of demons and fabulous animals, we hear not a word of the Rākṣasa Rāvaṇa or of Hanumat and the monkeys. All this makes it seem likely that, at the time when the Tipiṭaka came into being (in the fourth and third centuries B.C.) there were ballads dealing with Rāma, perhaps a cycle of such ballads, but no Rāma epic as yet[4]

Another question is whether traces of Buddhism can be proved in the Rāmāyaṇa. It can probably be answered with

---

1) Parallels to other verses in Rāma's speech of consolation (Rām. II, 105, 21: 22) have been traced by *Lüders* (ZDMG., 58, 1904, 713f.) in Jātaka 328, gā. 2-4. In the commentary on the Dasaratha-Jātaka there is also a verse about the ten thousand years' reign of Rāma, which corresponds to Rām. VI, 128 ; 104. An allusion to the Rāma legend also occurs in Jātaka 513, gā. 17.

2) Jātaka 540, also in Mahāvastu II, 209 ff. *Cf. Charpentier*, WZKM., 24, 1910, 397; 27, 1913, 94. *Oldenberg*, NGGW., 1918, 456ff.; D. Ch. *Sen*, l. c., pp. 15 ff.

3) There are a few scenes and situations in the Vessantara-Jātaka which remind us of the Rāmāyaṇa, but there is not a single case of literal agreement between the Rāmāyaṇa and the Jātaka-gāthās. In Jātaka 519, however, there is a stanza in which a demon tries to persuade faithful Sambulā to desert her sick husband and to follow him, uttering the same threat as is used by Rāvaṇa to Sītā in Rām. V, 22, 9, namely, that if she is not willing, he will devour her for his breakfast. *Cf.* D. Ch. *Sen*, l. c., pp. 18 ff. The Jātaka-gāthās, too, contain earlier and later portions, and some parts may be later than the Rāmāyaṇa.

4) *Cf.* T. W. *Rhys Davids*, Buddhist India, p. 183.

an absolute negative; for the only place in which the Buddha is mentioned (see above, p. 486, Note 2) is decidedly spurious. However, there may be one, though very distant, relation to Buddhism. Weber had still believed that the Rāmāyaṇa was based on an "ancient Buddhist legend of the pious prince Rāma, in whom the legend glorified the ideal of Buddhist equanimity."[1] That is surely not the case. Nevertheless, the idea of explaining the exceeding mildness, gentleness and tranquillity which are ascribed to Rāma, by Buddhistic undercurrents, should perhaps not be rejected. At the least, it is conceivable that, in a land strongly influenced by Buddhism, an epic was composed by a non-Buddhist, the hero of which, in spite of all his splendid demon-battles, is more a sage after the heart of the Buddha, than a hero of war. It appears, then, that the authors of the ancient Buddhist texts in the fourth and third centuries B.C. had as yet no knowledge of the Rāmāyaṇa, but that they knew ballads utilised by Vālmīki for his Rāma epic, and that on the other hand the Rāmāyaṇa was influenced at least indirectly by Buddhism. From this we may probably argue that the Rāmāyaṇa came into being at a time when Buddhism had already spread in Eastern India and the Buddhist Canon was in course of formation.

This is in harmony with the circumstance that the *metre* (the śloka) of the Rāmāyaṇa appears to represent a later stage of development than that of the Buddhist Pāli poetry, and that it approximates more nearly to the metre of the later portions of the Mahābhārata.[2]

H. Jacobi thought it possible to assume a pre-Buddhist time of origin of the epic on *linguistic* grounds. This epic language is a popular *Sanskrit*. About 260 B.C., for his

---

1) "Über das Rāmāyaṇa," pp. 6 f.

2) *Cf.* H *Oldenberg* in Gurupūjākaumudī, pp. 9 ff., and E. W. *Hopkins*, Great Epic, pp. 286 ff. *Jacobi*, l. c., p. 98, and *Keith*, JRAS., 1915, pp. 321, 324 ff., contest the soundness of this argument.

inscriptions addressed to his people, King Aśoka used, not Sanskrit, but dialects similar to Pāli. Buddha, too, as early as the sixth and fifth centuries B.C. preached, not in Sanskrit, but in the popular language. But popular epics, so he said,[1] cannot be composed in an already "extinct" language, but must be composed in the living language of the people. Now, as in Aśoka's time and even already in Buddha's time, Sanskrit was no longer the language of the people, the popular epics (in their original form) must belong to an older pre-Buddhist period when Sanskrit was still a living language. Against this, it may be urged that Sanskrit has always "lived" in India as a *literary language*, side by side with the popular languages, and has also been understood in extensive circles in which it was not spoken. There is nothing strange in the fact that, at the same time as Buddhist and Jain monks composed and preached in popular dialects, Sanskrit epics also were composed and listened to. Down to the present day in India it is not at all unusual for two or more languages to be current side by side in the same district. And in a great part of Northern India there is current, even to-day, (besides Sanskrit) a *modern Indian* literary language, which differs strongly from the colloquial language.[2] Therefore, if we here and there encounter the same verses which we find in the Rāmāyaṇa or in the Mahābhārata, in Pāli or in Prākrit, in Buddhist or in Jainistic texts, it does not always follow that the Sanskrit verses must have been translated from the popular languages. Still less justification is there for the view of some prominent scholars that the epics as a whole were originally composed in popular dialects and only translated into Sanskrit later. It is highly improbable that such a translation could have occurred without any record of it

---

1) *Jacobi*, l. c, pp. 116 ff.

2) *Cf.* above p. 43 note, and *Grierson* in JRAS., 1906, pp. 441 f.

having been kept anywhere. Jacobi[1] has convincingly shown how unacceptable this hypothesis is on other grounds also. But when he here, in opposition to the view that "a popular epic must be recited in the language of the people," recalls the fact "that the songs of the Iliad and the Odyssey also were presented in the Homeric language, although the language of the audience differed considerably from it," and when he emphasizes the fact hat the conception "nation" could never, in India, have the meaning which we connect with the word, he refutes his own view that the Rāmāyaṇa must have been composed when Sanskrit was still the "popular language," and that it must therefore be pre-Buddhist.[2]

During the first centuries of the Christian era, Sanskrit was used by the Buddhists also. The Buddhacarita of the great Buddhist poet *Aśvaghoṣa* is an ornate epic (kāvya) in

---

[1]) ZDMG., 48, 1894, pp. 407 ff. The view that the epics were originally composed in Prākrit was first expressed by A. *Barth* (Revue Critique, 5 avril 1886) and later defended by him in detail (RHR., t. 27, 1893, pp. 288 ff.; t. 45, 1902, pp. 195 f.: Oeuvres II, 152 ff., 397 f.). *Cf.* also *Grierson*, Ind. Ant., 23, 1894, p. 55.

[2]) The question as to whether Sanskrit was a living language at the time when the epics were composed, has been much discussed. It is a fact that all our ancient inscriptions (beginning approximately about 300 B. C.) are written in popular dialects, and that it is only inscriptions of the Christian era which are also written in Sanskrit. (*Cf.* R. O. *Franke*, Pali und Sanskrit, Strassburg, 1902, and T. W. *Rhys Davids*, Buddhist India, pp. 148 ff.) However, the inscriptions only prove that, in those pre-Christian centuries, Sanskrit was not as yet used as the *language of the royal offices*: they prove nothing against its use as a *literary* language. R. G. *Bhandarkar* (JBRAS., 16, 1885, 268 ff., 327 ff) has already shown that, at the time of the grammarians Pāṇini, Kātyāyana and Patañjali, Sanskrit was by no means a "dead" language. See also E J. *Rapson* and F. W. *Thomas*, JRAS., 1904, pp. 435 ff. 460 ff., 747 ff. The objections of *Rhys Davids*, *Grierson*, and *Fleet* (*ib.* pp. 457 ff., 471 ff., 481 ff.) prove nothing against the assumption that, at the time when the epics came into being, Sanskrit was a literary language understood in wide circles and spoken to some extent. *Cf.* also *Keith* and *Grierson*, JRAS., 1906, pp. 1 ff., 441 f.; 1915, 318 f.; and *Windisch* in OC., XIV, Paris, 1, 257, 266. The fact that in the drama the sūtas speak only Sanskrit, also tends to show that the sūta poetry, *i. e.* the epic, was composed in Sanskrit. On archaisms in the language of the Rāmāyaṇa s. T. *Michelson*, JAOS., 25, 1904, 89 ff. and Transactions and Proceed. American Philol. Assoc. 34, pp. xl f.; M. A. *Roussel*, JA., 1910, s. 10, t xv, pp. 1 ff.; *Keith*, JRAS., 1910, pp. 1321 ff.

Sanskrit, for which the poetry of Vālmīki certainly served as a model.[1] On the other hand we find, in a spurious portion of the Rāmāyaṇa, a scene [2] which is most probably an imitation of a scene of the Buddhacarita. Now, as Aśvaghoṣa is a contemporary of *Kaniṣka*, we may conclude that at the beginning of the second century A.D.,[3] the Rāmāyaṇa was already regarded as a model epic, but that it had not yet received its final form to such an extent as to exclude further interpolations. Towards the end of the second century, however, it must have already had its final form, as follows from what has been said above concerning the relationship of the Rāmāyaṇa to the Mahābhārata.

A public recitation of the Rāmāyaṇa is already mentioned in Kumāralāta's Kalpanāmaṇḍitikā,[4] which was probably written towards the close of the second century A.D. In Chinese translations of Buddhist tales, which are said to date back to the third century A.D., the Rāma legend is related in a form prepared to suit Buddhist purposes.[5] We glean from Chinese sources, too, that, at the time of the Buddhist philosopher Vasubandhu (fourth century A.D.,) the Rāmāyaṇa was a well known and popular poem also among the Buddhists in India.[6] As early as in the second half of the first century A.D. the Jain monk Vimala Sūri recast the Rāma legend in his Prākrit poem Paümacariya (Padmacarita), bringing it

---

1) *Cf.* A. *Gawronski*, Studies about the Sanskrit Buddhist Literature, w. Krakowie, 1919 (Prace Komiji Orj. Pol. Akad. Um. No. 2), pp. 27 ff.

2) The seraglio scene, above p. 490, note 3.

3) Much as has been written about the period of Kaniṣka, it is not yet definitely settled. However, there is ever increasing evidence for the theory that he reigned during the first half of the second century A. D. *Cf. Smith*, Early History, pp. 271 ff., 276n.

4) Translated from the Chinese as "Aśvaghoṣa's Sūtrālaṃkāra" by Ed. *Huber*, Paris, 1908 p. 126.

5) *Cf.* S. *Lévi* in Album Kern, pp. 279 ff.; Ed. *Chavannes*, Cinq cents contes, III, p. f.; Ed. *Huber* in BEFEO., 4, 1904, 698 ff.

6) See K. *Watanabe*, JRAS., 1907, pp. 99 ff.

into line with the religion and philosophy of the Jains.[1] It was obviously his intention to offer his co-religionists a substitute for the poem of Vālmīki which was already famous at that time. In about 600 A.D. the Rāmāyaṇa was already famous in far-off Cambodia as a sacred book of Hinduism, for an inscription reports that a certain Somaśarman presented "the Rāmāyaṇa, the Purāṇa, and the complete Bhārata" to a temple.[2]

The circumstance that the *ancient* poem already served as a model for Aśvaghoṣa, and hence must have been composed long before the time of the latter, agrees well with the entire absence, in the old and genuine Rāmāyaṇa, of any traces of *Greek* influence or of an acquaintance with the Greeks. For two allusions to the *Yavanas* (Ionians, Greeks) have been proved to be spurious. And it is quite out of the question that, as was once suggested by Weber, the Homeric poems should have had any sort of influence on Vālmīki's composition. There is not even a remote similarity between the stealing of Sītā and the rape of Helen, between the advance on Laṅkā

---

1) According to the concluding verses belonging to the poem itself, it was written in the year 530 after Mahāvīra (*i.e.* about 62 A.D.). E. *Leumann* (to whom I am indebted for valuable information about the Paümacariya) considers this date as unassailable. H. *Jacobi* (ERE., VII, p. 467) assumes that it was written in the third century A. D. The later Jain recensions of the Rāma legend (in the 68th Parvan of Guṇāḍhya's Uttarapurāṇa and in the 7th Parvan of Hemachandra's Saṣṭiśalākāpuruṣacaritra) are based on the Paümacariya. On Hemachandra's "Jain Rāmāyaṇa" s. D. Ch. *Sen*, Bengali Ramayanas, pp. 26 ff. (The Jain Rāmāyaṇa influenced the Bengali versions of the Rāmāyaṇa, as is shown by D. Ch. Sen, l. c., pp. 204 ff.). However, the appearance of Rāvaṇa as a great sage and ascetic, and of Sītā as Rāvaṇa's daughter in Buddhist and Jain versions of the poem of Rāma, should not be looked upon as traits pointing to ancient traditions, as is done by D. Ch. Sen. In the *Adbhutottarakhaṇḍa*, too, Sītā appears as the daughter of Mandodarī, Rāvaṇa's queen. This, however, is a late appendix to the Rāmāyaṇa, written in praise of Sītā as Śakti, and is popular among the Śāktas in Kashmir. *Cf. Weber*, HSS., Verz. I, pp. 123 f., *Eggeling*, Ind. Off. Cat. VI, p. 1183; D. Ch. *Sen*, l. c., pp. 35, 59, 227 f.; *Grierson*, JRAS, 1921, pp. 422 ff.

2) See A. *Barth*, Inscriptions Sanscrites du Cambodge (Notices et extraits des MSS. de la bibliothèque nationale, t. xxvii, 1, Paris, 1885), pp. 29 ff. On the Old Javanic Rāmāyaṇa see R. *Friederich*, JRAS 1876., pp. 172 ff. and H. *Kern*, Verspreide Geschriften, Vol. 9, pp. 251 ff., 297.

and that on Troy, and only a very remote similarity of motive between the bending of the bow by Rāma and that by Ulysses.[1]

As an epic the Rāmāyaṇa is very far removed from the *Veda*, and even the Rāma *legend* is only bound to Vedic literature by very slender threads. Whether that King *Janaka* of Videha who is frequently mentioned in the Upaniṣads[2] is the same as the father of Sītā, must remain an open question. Weber[3] has pointed out a few slight connections between the Rāmāyaṇa and the Yajurveda. *Sītā*, the heroine of the epic, probably belongs to the oldest elements of the Rāma legend. Her name signifies "field furrow," she came forth out of the earth, and Mother Earth receives her again. Although the latter feature of the legend only occurs in the late Book VII, yet it may be very old. The idea of a goddess of agriculture, *Sītā*, who is already invoked in a blessing on the land, in the Ṛgveda (IV, 57, 6) is extremely ancient, and certainly reaches back far into the Vedic period. The Gṛhyasūtras have preserved for us prayer-formulas, in which she is personified in an extremely life-like manner—" lotus-crowned, radiant in every limb ... black-eyed," and so on.[4] Yet Weber[5] is probably right when he remarks that this Vedic idea of Sītā as the goddess Field-furrow is "separated *by a wide gulf* from the representation of her in the Rāma legend." Neither is there anything to indicate that

---

1) See *Jacobi*, l. c., pp. 94 ff.

2) Rāma does not appear in the old Upaniṣads. The Rāmapūrvatāpanīya-Upaniṣad and the Ramottaratāpanīya-Upaniṣad (The Vaiṣṇava-Upanishads ..., ed. by Mahadeva Sastri, Adyar, 1923, pp. 305 ff., 326 ff.; Deussen, Sechzig Upanishads, pp. 802 ff., 818 ff.) are very late fabrications, which are " Upaniṣads " only in name; and in them Rāma is honoured as an incarnation of the god Viṣṇu.

3) Uber das Rāmāyaṇa, pp. 8 f.

4) Kauśikasūtra 106. See A. *Weber* " Omina und Portenta " (ABA. 1858, pp. 368 ff.)

5) " Episches im vedischen Ritual " (SBA., 1891., p. 818).

songs of Rāma and Sītā already existed in Vedic times.[1] Even if, with Jacobi, we were inclined to find in the legend of the battle of Rāma with Rāvaṇa, another form of the ancient myth of the battle of Indra with Vṛtra,[2] the "wide gulf," which separates the Veda from the epic, would still remain.

If we briefly summarise the results of our investigations into the age of the Rāmāyaṇa, we can say the following :—

1. The later parts of the Rāmāyaṇa, especially Books I and VII, are separated from the genuine Rāmāyaṇa of Books II to VI by a long interval of time.

2. The whole Rāmāyaṇa, including the later portions, was already an old and famous work when the Mahābhārata had not yet attained its present form.

3. *It is probable* that the Rāmāyaṇa had *its present extent and contents* as early as *towards the close of the second century A.D.*

4. The older nucleus of the Mahābhārata, however, is probably older than the ancient Rāmāyaṇa.

5. In the Veda we find no trace of the Rāma epic and only very faint traces of the Rāma legend.

6. The ancient Buddhist texts of the Tipiṭaka betray no knowledge of the Rāmāyaṇa, but contain traces of ballads in which the Rāma legend was sung.

7. There are no obvious traces of Buddhism to be seen in the Rāmāyaṇa, but the characterisation of Rāma may possibly be traceable to remote Buddhist influence.

8. There can be no question of Greek influence in the Rāmāyaṇa, and the genuine Rāmāyaṇa betrays no acquaintance with the Greeks.

---

1) I am unable to follow the fantastic expositions of Julius v. *Negelein*, who thinks he is able to discover in the Veda the "outline of the Rāma-Sītā legend" (WZKM., 16, 1902, pp. 226 ff.)

2) *Jacobi*, l. c., p. 131.

9. *It is probable* that *the original Rāmāyaṇa* was composed *in the third century B.C.* by Vālmīki on the basis of ancient ballads.

The Purāṇas and their Position in Indian Literature.[1]

It is difficult to determine the exact position of the Purāṇas in the history of Indian literature, both according to contents and chronologically. Actually they belong to the *religious* literature, and are, for the later Indian religion, which is generally called "*Hinduism*," [2] and which culminates in the worship of Viṣṇu and Śiva, approximately what the Veda is for the oldest religion or Brahmanism. On the other hand, how closely the Purāṇas are connected with the *epic* compositions can already be deduced sufficiently from the fact that in the preceding chapters we repeatedly had to speak of them. Indeed, the Mahābhārata for the greater part and the Harivaṃśa almost entirely, are nothing other

---

[1]) The first to make a thorough study of the Purāṇas was H. H. *Wilson*, in his "Essays on Sanskrit Literature" which first appeared in 1832 ff. and in the Introduction and Notes to his translation of the Viṣṇu-Purāṇa (see Works by the late H. H. Wilson, ed. by R. Rost and Fitzedward Hall, Vol. III, pp. 1-155, and Vol. VI, Preface). He had a predecessor in *Vans Kennedy*, Researches into the Nature and Affinity of Ancient and Hindu Mythology, London, 1831. Valuable services have also been rendered to the investigation of the Purāṇa literature by Eugène *Burnouf* (Preface to his edition and translation of the Bhāgavata-Purāṇa) and by the compilers of the great catalogues of manuscripts, especially Th. *Aufrecht* (Bodl. Cat, pp. 7 ff.) and Julius *Eggeling* (Ind. Off Cat., Part VI, London, 1899). For *Wilson's* services in the investigation of the Purāṇas, *cf. Windisch*, Geschichte der Sanskrit-Philologie, pp. 41 ff. For more recent researches on the Purāṇas see R. G. *Bhandarkar*, A Peep into the Early History of India, JBRAS., 20, 1900, 403 f., new ed. 1920, pp. 66 ff.; W. *Jahn* Festschrift Kuhn, pp. 305 ff.; F. E. *Pargiter*, ERE., X, 1918, 448 ff.; Ancient Indian Historical Tradition, London. 1922, pp. 15 ff. and *passim*; J. N. *Farquhar*, An Outline of the Religious Literature of India, London, 1920, pp. 136 ff.; E. J. *Rapson*, Cambridge History, I, pp. 296 ff.

[2]) On this religion *cf.* A. *Barth*, Religions of India, 2nd ed., London, 1889, pp. 153 ff.; M. Monier *Williams*, Brahmanism and Hinduism, London, 1891; E. W. *Hopkins*, Religions of India, Boston, 1895, pp. 434 ff.; Sir Charles *Eliot*, Hinduism and Buddhism, London, 1921, Vol. II; H. v. *Glasenapp*, Der Hinduismus, Munich, 1922.

than Purāṇas, and even the later books and sections of the Rāmāyaṇa partake of the character of Purāṇas. Furthermore, the Purāṇas undoubtedly reach back to great antiquity and are rooted in Vedic literature; many a legend, already familiar from Ṛgvedic hymns and from the Brāhmaṇas, reappears in the Purāṇas;[1] but, just as undoubtedly, those works which have come down to us under the title of "Purāṇa" are of a later date, and up to the present day books are fabricated which assume the proud title "Purāṇa," or claim to be parts of ancient Purāṇas. What has been said in the Introduction (see above, p. 30) about "new wine in old bottles," applies especially to these works. Even the latest productions of this literature have the external form and the archaic frame of the oldest Purāṇas.

The word "purāṇa" means originally nothing but *purāṇam ākhyānam, i.e.* "old narrative."[2] In the older literature, in Brāhmaṇas, Upaniṣads and old Buddhist texts, we generally find the word in connection with *itihāsa.* But it has already been remarked (see above, p. 314) that the "Itihāsas and Purāṇas" or "Itihāsapurāṇa" so often mentioned in olden times, do not mean actual books, still less, then, the epics or Purāṇas which have come down to us. On the other hand, definite works may have been thought of, when, in the *Atharvaveda,*[3] beside the four Vedas, "the Purāṇa" also is enumerated. Only in the Sūtra literature is the existence of *real Purāṇas* definitely proved, *i.e.*

[1]) Instances are the myths of Purūravas and Urvaśī, of Saraṇyū (s. A. *Blau*, ZDMG., 62, 1908, pp. 337 ff.), of Mudgala (s. *Pargiter*, JRAS., 1910, pp. 1328 ff.), of Vṛṣakapi (s. *Pargiter*, JRAS., 1911, 803 ff.).

[2]) The Kauṭilīya-Arthaśāstra I, 5 (p. 10) in its definition of *itihāsa*, enumerates *purāṇa* and *itivṛtta* as belonging to the content of *itihāsa.* As *itivṛtta* can only mean a "historical event," *purāna* probably means "mythological and legendary lore."

[3]) XI, 7, 24. In the verse Ath. V. 19, 9 the Ṛṣi Nārada is addressed in such a manner as to make one believe that the verse is taken out of a Purāṇa dialogue. *Cf.* M. *Bloomfield*, SBE., Vol. 42, p. 435.

of works whose contents approximately agreed with our present Purāṇa texts. In the *Gautama-Dharmasūtra*,[1] which is regarded as the oldest of the preserved law-books, it is taught that the king is to take as his authorities on the administration of justice, the Veda, the law-books, the Vedāṅgas, and "the Purāṇa." The expression "the Purāṇa" can here, like "the Veda" only denote a species of literature. It is still more important that another law-book, the *Āpastambīya-Dharmasūtra*, contains not only two quotations from "the Purāṇa," but also a third quotation from a "Bhaviṣyat-Purāṇa." The latter quotation, it is true, is not to be found in the Purāṇa which has come down to us under that title, neither can the other two quotations be found literally in our Purāṇas. However, there certainly are similar passages in our texts.[2] As there are good grounds for assigning the abovementioned Dharmasūtras to the fifth or fourth century B.C., there must have been even at that early period works resembling our Purāṇas.[3] It is indeed likely enough that our Purāṇas are only recasts of older works *of the same species*, namely, of works of religious

---

[1]) XI, 19. Thus also in the law-books of *Bṛhaspati*, which are many centuries later (SBE., Vol. 33, p. 280) and *Yājñavalkya*, I, 3. In still later law-books the Purāṇas are not only enumerated generally among the sources of law, but also quoted as such in innumerable instances. *Cf. Jolly*, Recht und Sitte (Grundriss, II, 8) pp. 30 f. The lawyer *Kullūka* (Manu I, 1) quotes "from the Mahābhārata" the verse: "The Purāṇa Manu's law-book, the Veda with the Vedāṅgas and the science of therapeutics are four things that are established by authority, they cannot be refuted with reasons." I have not found the verse in our Mahābhārata editions.

[2]) *Cf.* G. *Bühler*, Ind. Ant., 25, 1896, pp. 323 ff. and SBE., Vol. 2, 2nd ed., 1897, pp. xxix ff., and *Pargiter*, Anc. Ind. Hist. Trad., pp. 43 ff.

[3]) It does not, however, follow from these quotations that the Purāṇas contained separate sections on *dharma* at that time, as is the case with our present Purāṇas; we need only assume that, in connection with the "ancient lore" they also handed down all kinds of ancient legal principles and maxims. *Cf. Pargiter*, Anc. Ind. Hist. Trad., pp. 48 f. The Kauṭilīya-Arthaśāstra recommends that misguided princes be instructed by means of Purāṇas (V, 6, p. 257), and counts Paurāṇikas, i.e. "Purāṇa specialists," among the court officials (V, 3, p. 247). However, I cannot agree with *Pargiter* (l. c., pp. 54 f.) in regarding this as a proof of the existence of definite Purāṇas in the fourth century B. C., as I consider the Kauṭilīya as a work of the 3rd or 4th century A. D.

didactic contents, in which were collected ancient traditions of the Creation, the deeds of the gods, heroes, saints and ancient ancestors of the human race, the beginnings of the famous royal families, and so on.

Also the relationship of the *Mahābhārata* to the Purāṇas[1] indicates that the latter reach back to great antiquity, and that Purāṇas certainly existed already long before the final redaction of the Mahābhārata. Our Mahābhārata not only calls itself a Purāṇa, but also begins exactly as the Purāṇa texts usually begin, Ugraśravas, the son of the Sūta Lomaharṣaṇa, appearing as narrator. This Ugraśravas is called "versed in the Purāṇas," and Śaunaka, when inviting him to narrate, says to him: "Thy father once learned the whole Purāṇa;... in the Purāṇa are told the stories of gods and the genealogies of the sages, and we heard them once long ago from thy father." Very frequently legends in the Mahābhārata are introduced with the words "it is heard in the Purāṇa"; gāthās and ślokas, especially genealogical verses, "sung by those versed in the Purāṇas," are quoted; an account of the Creation, composed in prose (Mahābh. XII, 342) is called "a Purāṇa," the snake-sacrifice of Janamejaya is taught "in the Purāṇa," and those versed in the Purāṇas recommend it; "in remembrance of the Purāṇa proclaimed by Vāyu,"[2] the past and future ages of the world are described, and the Harivaṃśa not only quotes a Vāyu-Purāṇa, but in many places agrees literally with the Vāyu-Purāṇa transmitted to us. Numerous myths, legends, and didactic passages are common to the Purāṇas and the epics. Lüders[3] has proved that the Ṛṣyaśṛṅga legend has an older

[1]) *Cf.* A. *Holtzmann*, Das Mahābhārata, IV, pp. 29 ff. and E. W. *Hopkins*, The Great Epic of India, pp. 47 ff.

[2]) Mahābh. III, 191, 16. As *Hopkins*, l. c., pp. 48 f., has shown, the description in our Vāyu-Purāṇa is more ancient than the one given in the Mahābhārata.

[3]) NGGW., 1897, pI, p. 8 ff.

form in the Padma-Purāṇa than in our Mahābhārata: In a verse of the Mahābhārata, which, it is true, was added very late,[1] the "eighteen Purāṇas" are already mentioned. From all this it appears that Purāṇas, as a species of literature, existed long before the final redaction of the Mahābhārata, and that even in the Purāṇas which have come down to us there is much that is older than our present Mahābhārata.

It is, however, only an apparent paradox, when we say that the Mahābhārata is older than the Purāṇas, and that the Purāṇas are older than the Mahābhārata. For the Purāṇas are just as little unified works as the epic, and in them too, early and late portions are found side by side. In the numerous cases in which the Purāṇas agree with each other, and with the Mahābhārata, more or less literally, it is more probable that they all are derived from the same old source, than that one work is dependent on the other.[2] This old source was, on the one hand, oral tradition, comprising Brahman traditions reaching back to Vedic times, as well as the bard poetry handed down in the circles of the Kṣatriyas,[3] and on the other hand, it was certain definite texts, probably far less in bulk than our present Purāṇas. The number of these was probably not exactly eighteen from the outset. Perhaps there were only four, as indicated by the legendary report in the Viṣṇu-Purāṇa.[4] It is, however, most unlikely indeed that, as is assumed by some scholars,[5]

---

[1]) XVIII, 6, 95. Another verse, XVIII, 5, 46, is not to be found in all editions.

[2]) Of course we do not wish to deny that, in isolated cases, one Purāṇa may have copied from another.

[3]) I doubt, however, whether we are justified in drawing the line between the Kṣatriya tradition and the brahmanical tradition as definitely as is assumed by *Pargiter*.

[4]) III, 6. According to this, the Sūta Romaharṣaṇa and three of his pupils wrote the four fundamental Purāṇasaṃhitās (mūlasaṃhitā). Similarly Bhāgavata-Pur. XII, 7. *Cf.* *Burnouf*, Bhāgavata-Purāṇa, I, Préface, pp. xxxvii.ff. However, we should not place much reliance on these legends.

[5]) A. M. T. *Jackson*, JBRAS., 21, 1905, Extra Number, pp. 67 ff.; A. *Blau*, ZDMG., 62, 1908, 337; *Pargiter*, Anc. Ind. Hist. Trad, 35 ff., 49 ff.

all the Purāṇas originated in a *single* original Purāṇa. There was never *one* original Purāṇa, any more than there was *one* original Brāhmaṇa whence all the Brāhmaṇas sprang, or *one* original Upaniṣad whence all the Upaniṣads sprang. When, as we have seen above, ancient works here and there mention "the Purāṇa," they only mean "the old tradition" or "Purāṇa literature," in the same way as the expressions "Veda" or "Śruti" or "Smṛti" are used in the singular. That our present Purāṇas are not the ancient works themselves which bore this title, can already be deduced from the fact that, in content, none of them agrees with the definition of the term Purāṇa as given in themselves. According to this certainly very old definition,[1] every Purāṇa is to have "five characteristics" (pañcalakṣaṇa) *i. e.* it is to treat five subjects: (1) Sarga, "creation," (2) Pratisarga, "re-creation," *i. e.* the periodical annihilation and renewal of the worlds, (3) Vaṃśa, "genealogy," *i. e.* the genealogy of the gods and Ṛṣis, (4) Manvantarāṇi, "the Manu-periods of time," *i. e.* the great periods, each of which has a Manu or primal ancestor of the human race, and (5) Vaṃsānucarita, "the history of the dynasties, *viz.* "the early and later dynasties whose origin is traced back to the sun (solar dynasty) and the moon (lunar dynasty). These five things only partly form the contents of the Purāṇas handed down to us; some contain much more than what is included in the "five characteristics," while others scarcely touch upon these subjects, but deal with quite different things. What is especially significant of almost all our Purāṇas, their *sectarian* character, *i. e.* their being dedicated to the cult of some god or other, of Viṣṇu or Śiva, is completely ignored by the old definition.[2] In most

---

[1]) It is found in the more important Purāṇas, also in the ancient Indian lexicon, the Amarakośa, as well as in other lexicons.

[2]) In the Brahmavaivarta-Purāṇa it is certainly said that the "five characteristics" are only for the *upapurāṇas*, while the *mahāpurāṇas* ("the great Purāṇas") have *ten*

of these works there are also considerable sections on the rights and duties of the castes and of the Āśramas, on the general brahmanical rites, especially the funeral sacrifices (śrāddhas),[1] as well as on particular ceremonies and feasts (vratas) in honour of Viṣṇu or Śiva, and frequently also sections on Sāṅkhya and Yoga philosophy.

In such Purāṇas as have preserved an old nucleus, we find sections on cosmogony and history of primeval times, corresponding to the "five characteristics." We find, too, genealogical lists of the ancient royal houses, continued from the first kings, whose origin is traced back to the sun and moon, down to the heroes of the great war of the Mahābhārata. As our Purāṇas are ascribed to Vyāsa, who is said to have lived at the beginning of the Kaliyuga contemporaneously with the heroes of the Bhārata battle, the history of "the past" ends with the death of the Pāṇḍavas or shortly afterwards.[2] In several of these Purāṇas,[3] however, the royal dynasties of the "past" are followed by lists of the

---

"characteristics," including "praise of Viṣṇu and the gods individually." The Bhāgavata-Purāṇa likewise mentions "ten characteristics" of the "Purāṇa" in two places (II, 10, 1 and XII, 7, 8 ff.). (See E. *Burnouf*, Le Bhâgavata Purâṇa, t. I. Préf., pp. xlvi ff.) But these definitions, too, only partly correspond to the contents of the actually existing Purāṇas.

[1]) Here the Purāṇas often agree literally with later law-books. *Cf.* W. *Caland*, Altindischer Ahnenkult, pp. 68, 79, 112.

[2]) When the Kaliyuga era had become current the Indians felt the need of associating the starting-point of the era with some important "historical" event, and they used the Bhārata battle for this purpose. There was, however, a school of astronomers, thus Varāhamihira (died A. D. 587) with whom the historian Kalhaṇa agrees, which does not date the beginning of the Kaliyuga from the battle of the Mahābhārata, but reckons this battle as having been fought in the 653rd year of the Kaliyuga (2449 B. C.). In the Aihoḷe inscription (634 A. D.) the date "after the Bhārata battle" is already mentioned. *Cf.* J. F. *Fleet*, JRAS., 1911, 675 ff. Indian kings were just as fond of tracing their ancestry back to those who fought in the Bhārata battle as European princes were anxious to prove their descent from the heroes of the Trojan war. *Cf. Rapson*, Cambridge History, I, p. 307. I consider it as entirely contrary to historical criticism to draw chronological conclusions as is done by *Pargiter* (Anc. Ind. Hist. Trad., pp. 175 ff.) from this fiction of the coincidence of the Bhārata battle with the beginning of the Kaliyuga.

[3]) Matsya-, Vāyu-, Brahmāṇḍa-, Bhaviṣya-, Viṣṇu-, Bhāgavata,- and Garuḍa-Purāṇas.

kings of the "future" in the form of *prophecies*.[1] In these lists of kings of the Kali era, we meet, among others, the dynasties of the Śiśunāgas, Nandas, Mauryas, Śuṅgas, Andhras and Guptas which are well known in history. Among the Śiśunāgas are Bimbisāra and Ajātaśatru, who are mentioned in Jain and Buddhist writings as contemporaries of Mahāvīra and Gautama Buddha (6th to 5th century B. C.); and with the Maurya Candragupta, who came to the throne in 322 B. C., we emerge into the clear daylight of history. Though these lists of kings of the Kaliyuga can only be utilised as historical sources, with caution and discrimination,[2] V. A. *Smith*[3] has shown that the Viṣṇu-Purāṇa is very reliable as regards the Maurya dynasty (326-185 B. C.) and that the Matsya-Purāṇa is also very reliable as regards the Andhra dynasty (which came to an end about 225 A. D.) whilst the Vāyu-Purāṇa describes the rule of the Guptas as it was under Candragupta I (about 320-330 A. D.). At the end of the lists of kings, these Purāṇas enumerate a series of dynasties of low and barbarian descent (Śūdras and Mlecchas), such as Abhīras, Gardabhas, Śakas, Yavanas, Tuṣāras, Hūṇas and so on, which were contemporary with the former, and then follows a dreary description of the Kali age. This prophecy reminds us of the account given by the Chinese pilgrim Sung-yun[4] of the barbarian invasions in the northern Punjab in about 465 A. D.

---

[1]) In Rāmāyaṇa IV, 62, 3 *purāṇa* means "a prophecy made in olden times."

[2]) F. E. *Pargiter* has rendered valuable services to the criticism of these lists of kings, by his book: The Purāṇa Text of the Dynasties of the Kali Age, London, 1913. It is probable that the sources of these prophecies are ancient annals and chronicles; for this reason we find occasional expressions such as "abhavat," "smṛta" in our texts, in spite of the prophetical future tense (*cf.* Pargiter, l. c., p. ix). Pargiter gives good reasons for the hypothesis that these sources were written in Prākrit; but we should not therefore jump to the conclusion that the Purāṇas as a whole were translated from the Prākrit. Pargiter's views have been contested by A. B. *Keith*, JRAS., 1914, 1021 ff.; 1915, 328 ff. *Cf.* the discussion *ib.* 141 ff., 516 ff., 799 ff.

[3]) Early History, pp. 11 ff.; ZDMG., 56, 1902, 654, 672 f.; 57, 1903, 607 f. *Cf.* D. R. *Bhandarkar*, JBRAS., 22, 155 f.

[4]) *Cf.* S. *Beal*, Buddhist Records of the Western World, I, p. c; *Smith*, Early History, p. 328.

and of Kalhaṇa's[1] vivid description of the rule of the Hun chieftains Toramāṇa (about 500 A. D.) and Mihirakula (about 515 A. D.) who ruled " like the god of death in the kingdom swamped by the barbarian hordes," and, surrounded day and night by thousands of murderers, took no pity even on women and children. Moreover, foreign dynasties ruled in India over and over again as early as in the first centuries of the Christian era. It is possible that we may have to interpret the prophecies about the evil Kaliyuga as an echo of these various barbarian invasions and foreign rules. The data are, however, too confused to serve as a basis for safe conclusions as to the date of origin of the Purāṇas. All that we can safely conclude is that the earlier Purāṇas must have come into being *before the 7th century*, for neither later dynasties nor later famous rulers such as for instance Harṣa, occur in the lists of kings.

Another point which would seem to bear out the theory that the *earlier* Purāṇas had come into being, with, to all intents and purposes, their present form, as early as in the first centuries of the Christian era, is the striking resemblance between the Buddhist Mahāyāna texts of the first centuries of the Christian era, and the Purāṇas. The Lalitavistara not only calls itself a "Purāṇa," but really has much in common with the Purāṇas. Texts like Saddharmapuṇḍarīka, Kāraṇḍavyūha and even some passages of the Mahāvastu, remind us of the sectarian Purāṇas not only by reason of the boundless exaggerations but also on account of the extravagance in the praise of *Bhakti*. The Digambara Jains, too, composed Purāṇas from the 7th century onwards.[2]

It used to be the general opinion of Western scholars that our Purāṇas belong to the latest productions of Sanskrit

---

[1] Rājataraṅgiṇī I, 289 ff. *Cf. Smith*, Early History, 328 ff., 333 ff.

[2] Raviṣeṇa wrote the Padmapurāṇa in 660 A. D. See also *Pargiter*, Mārkaṇḍeya Purāṇa Transl., p. xiv.

literature and only originated in the last thousand years.[1] This view is certainly no longer tenable. For the poet *Bāṇa* already (about 625 A.D.) knows the Purāṇas well, and relates in his historical romance Harṣacarita, how he attended a reading of the Vāyu-Purāṇa in his native village. The philosopher *Kumārila* (about 750 A.D.) relies on the Purāṇas as sources of law, while *Śaṅkara* (9th century) and *Rāmānuja* (12th century) refer to them as ancient and sacred texts in support of their philosophical doctrines. It is also important that the Arabian traveller *Albērūnī* (about 1030 A.D.) is very familiar with the Purāṇas, gives a list of the "eighteen Purāṇas," and not only quotes Āditya, Vāyu, Matsya, and Viṣṇu-Purāṇa, but has also studied one of the later Purāṇa texts, the Viṣṇudharmottara, very minutely.[2] The erroneous opinion that the Purāṇas must be "quite modern" is also connected with the formerly prevalent notion that the Purāṇa religion, the Viṣṇu and Śiva worship, was of a late date. More recent investigations have proved, however, that the sects of the Viṣṇu and Śiva worshippers at all events

---

[1]) This view was first expressed by H. H. *Wilson* and often repeated after him. He saw references to the Mahomedan conquest in the description of the Kaliyuga. *Vans Kennedy* (see Wilson, Works X, 257 ff.) already advocated emphatically a greater antiquity of the Purāṇas.

[2]) *Cf.* G. *Bühler*, Ind. Ant., 19, 1890, 382 ff.; 25, 1896, 328 ff.; P. *Deussen*, System des Vedānta, Leipzig, 1883, p. 36; *Smith*, Early History, pp. 22 ff. A manuscript of the Skanda-Purāṇa in Gupta script is assigned by *Haraprasād Śāstrī* (JASB., 1893, p. 250) to the middle of the 7th century. In records of land-grants of the 5th century B. C. verses are quoted, which, according to *Pargiter* (JRAS., 1912, 248 ff., Anc. Ind. Hist. Trad., p. 49), occur only in the Padma-, Bhaviṣya-, and Brahma-Purāṇa, and hence he concludes that these particular Purāṇas are earlier. It is more probable, however, that these verses both in the inscriptions and in the Purāṇas were taken from earlier Dharmaśāstras. *Cf. Keith*, JRAS., 1912, 248 ff., 756, and *Fleet*, *ib.*, 1046 ff. *Fleet* himself believes that chronological deductions could be made from the fact that in some of the Purāṇas the planets, beginning with the sun, are enumerated in the same order in which they appear in the days of the week, which points to the period after 600 A. D. However, any arguments of this nature are conclusive merely for isolated chapters, and not for complete Purāṇa texts.

reach back to pre-Christian and perhaps pre-Buddhist times.[1]

The orthodox Hindus themselves regard the Purāṇas as extremely ancient. They believe that the same Vyāsa who compiled the Vedas and composed the Mahābhārata was also, in the beginning of the Kaliyuga,[2] the present age of the world, the author of the eighteen Purāṇas. But this Vyāsa is a form of the exalted god Viṣṇu himself, "for" (says the Viṣṇu-Purāṇa) "who else could have composed the Mahābhārata?" His pupil was the Sūta Lomaharṣaṇa, and to him he imparted the Purāṇas.[3] Thus the Purāṇas have a divine origin. And the Vedānta philosopher *Śaṅkara*, for a proof of the personal existence of the gods, turns to Itihāsas and Purāṇas, because these, as he says, rest not only upon the Veda, but also upon sense-perception, namely on the perception of people like Vyāsa, who personally spoke with the gods.[4] The authority of the Purāṇas certainly cannot be compared with that of the Vedas. Itihāsa and Purāṇa are, to a certain extent, merely a supplement to the Veda, principally intended for the instruction of women and Śūdras, who are not entitled to the study of the Veda. Thus already an ancient verse says: "By Itihāsas and Purāṇas the Veda is to be strengthened: for the Veda fears an unlearned man, thinking that the latter might injure it." [5] Only the Veda, says

---

[1]) *Cf.* G. *Bühler*, Ep. Ind. II, 1894, p. 95. Kadphises II (about 78 A. D.) was so ardent a Śiva-worshipper that he had a picture of Śiva stamped on his coins (V. A. *Smith*, l. c., p. 318).

[2]) Thus according te Mahābh. XII, 349 and Śaṅkara in his commentary on the Vedānta-Sūtras III, 3, 32.

[3]) Viṣṇu-Purāṇa III, 4 and 6. The name Lomaharṣaṇa (or Romaharṣaṇa) is explained etymologically in the Vāyu-Purāṇa I, 16, as "one who, by his beautiful narrations, causes the *hairs* (loman) on the bodies of the hearers to *stand on end* (harṣaṇa) with joy."

[4]) Ved.-Sū. I, 3, 33. SBE., Vol. 34, p. 222. Śaṅkara adds: From the fact that men no longer to-day speak with the gods, it in no wise follows that this was not the case in ancient times.

[5]) The verse is quoted by Rāmānuja (SBE., Vol. 48, p. 91) as a Purāṇa text. It is to be found in Vāyu-Pur. 1, 201; Mahābhār. I, 1, 267, and Vāsiṣṭha-Dharmas. 27, 6.

Rāmānuja,[1] serves for the attainment of the highest knowledge, the knowledge of Brahman, while Itihāsa and Purāṇa lead only to the cleansing from sins. The Purāṇas, then, are sacred books of the second grade.[2] This is easily explained, for originally the Purāṇas were not priestly literature at all. The *Sūtas* or bards were undoubtedly the creators and bearers of the oldest Purāna poetry as well as of the epic.[3] This is also borne out by the circumstance that in almost all the Purāṇas the *Sūta* Lomaharṣaṇa or his son Ugraśravas, "the Sauti," *i.e.* "the son of the Sūta," appears as narrator. This is so much the case that *Sūta* and *Sauti* are used almost as proper names in the Purāṇas. But the Sūta was certainly no Brahman, and he had nothing to do with the Veda.[4] But when this old bard poetry ceased, we do not know when, this literature did not pass into the hands of the *learned* Brahmans, the Veda-knowers, but the lower priesthood, which congregated in temples and places of pilgrimage, took possession of it; and these rather uneducated temple-priests used it for the glorification of the deities whom they served, and in later times more and more for the recommendation of the temples and places of pilgrimage in which

---

1) SBE., Vol. 48, pp. 338 f.

2) This is expressed most clearly by *Rāmānuja* (on Ved.-Sū. II, 1, 3, SBE., Vol. 48, p. 413) when he says that the Purāṇas have indeed been proclaimed by the Creator Hiraṇyagarbha, but that they, just as Hiraṇyagarbha himself, are not free from the qualities of passion (rajas) and of darkness (tamas) and are therefore subject to error.

3) According to the Vāyu- and the Padma-Purāṇa, the preservation of the genealogies of the gods Ṛṣis and famous kings, is the duty of the Sūtas. *Cf. Pargiter*, Anc. Ind. Hist. Trad., pp. 15 ff. Thus even at the present day the Bhātas preserve the genealogies of the Kṣatriyas; see C. V. *Vaidya*, History of Mediaeval Hindu India, II, Poona, 1924, pp. 260 ff.

4) "The Sūta has no claim at all to the study of the Vedas," says the Vāyu-Purāṇa, I, 33, and also according to Bhāg. Pur. I, 4, 13, the Sūta is conversant "with the whole realm of literature *with the exception of the Veda.*" *Cf.* E. *Burnouf*, Le Bhâgavata-Purâṇa I, pp. xxix and liii ff.

they maintained and often enriched themselves.[1] But how very strongly, nevertheless, even to the present day, the Hindus believe in the sanctity of the Purāṇas, is best shown by a lecture delivered by Manilal N. *Dvivedi* at the Congress of Orientalists in Stockholm (1889).[2] As a man of Western education he spoke of anthropology and geology, of Darwin and Haeckel, Spencer and Quatrefages, but only in order to prove that the view of life of the Purāṇas and their teachings upon the Creation are scientific truths, and he finds in them altogether only the highest truth and deepest wisdom—if one only understands it all correctly, *i.e.* symbolically.

The Purāṇas are valuable to the historian and to the antiquarian as sources of political history by reason of their genealogies, even though they can only be used with great caution and careful discrimination.[3] At all events they are of inestimable value from the point of view of the history of religion, and on this head alone deserve far more careful study than has hitherto been devoted to them. They afford us far greater insight into all aspects and phases of Hinduism—its mythology, its idol-worship, its theism and pantheism, its love of God, its philosophy and its superstitions, its festivals and ceremonies and its ethics, than any other works.[4] As literary productions, on the other hand, they are by no means a pleasing phenomenon. They are in every respect regardless

---

[1]) According to Manu III, 152, temple-priests (devalaka) cannot be invited to sacrifices any more than physicians and vendors of meat. The historian *Kalhaṇa* speaks of these priests with undisguised contempt. *Cf.* M. A. *Stein*, Kalhaṇa's Rājataraṅgiṇī...... translated...Westminster, 1900), Vol. I, Introduction, p. 19 f. The epics, as well as the Purāṇas, are now-a-days recited by special reciters" (Pāṭhakas) or "narrators" (Kathakas) belonging to the Brahman caste.

[2]) OC, VIII Stockholm, II, pp. 199 ff.

[3]) As historical sources they surely do not deserve such confidence as is placed in them by F. E. *Pargiter* (JRAS 1914, 267 ff.; Bhandarkar Com. Vol., p. 107 ff., and Anc. Ind. Hist. Trad, 77 ff., 119 ff. and *passim*).

[4]) *Cf. Pargiter*, ERE X, pp. 451 ff. and J. N. *Farquhar*, Outline of the Religious Literature of India, p. 136 ff. and *passim*.

of form and proportions. The careless language and poor versification, in which the grammar often suffers for the sake of the metre, are just as characteristic of these works as are the confused medley of contents and the boundless exaggerations. Just a few examples of the latter. While in the Ṛgveda Urvaśī sojourns with Purūravas for *four* years, the two lovers in the Viṣṇu-Purāṇa spend 61,000 years in pleasure and delight. While even the older Purāṇas know only *seven* hells, the Bhāgavata-Purāṇa speaks of "hundreds and thousands" of hells, and the Garuḍa-Purāṇa counts no less than 8,400,000.[1] The later the Purāṇa—this may be regarded as a general rule—the more boundless are the exaggerations. This, too, indicates that it was an inferior class of literary men, belonging to the lower, uneducated priesthood, which was engaged in the transmission of the Purāṇas. Yet, many of the old legends of kings and some very old genealogical verses (anuvaṁśaśloka) and song-verses (gāthās) have been saved from the original *bard poetry* and incorporated into the later texts which have come down to us. Fortunately, too, the compilers of the Purāṇas, who collected their materials from anywhere and everywhere without choice, did not despise the good either, and received into their texts many a dialogue, in form and contents recalling the Upaniṣads, as well as some profound legends, taken from the old ascetic poetry. Thus the following short survey of the most important Purāṇas and their contents will show that even in the desert of Purāṇa literature oases are not wanting.

Survey of the Purāṇa-Literature.

In the Purāṇas themselves which have come down to us, the number of existing Purāṇas "composed by Vyāsa" is

---

[1]) *Scherman*, Visionslitteratur, p. 32 f.

unanimously given as *eighteen*; and also with reference to their titles there is almost complete agreement. Most of the Purāṇas also agree in the order in which they enumerate the eighteen Purāṇas, *viz.*:

1.	Brāhma	10.	Brahmavaivarta
2.	Pādma	11.	Laiṅga
3.	Vaiṣṇava	12.	Vārāha
4.	Śaiva or Vāyavīya	13.	Skānda
5.	Bhāgavata	14.	Vāmana
6.	Nāradīya	15.	Kaurma
7.	Mārkaṇḍeya	16.	Mātsya
8.	Āgneya	17.	Gāruḍa
9.	Bhaviṣya or Bhaviṣyat	18.	Brahmāṇḍa [1]

It is peculiar that this list of "eighteen Purāṇas" is given in each one of them, as though none were the first and none the last, but all had already existed when each separate one was composed. All these Purāṇas point out in extravagant terms the advantages to be attained both in this world and in the world beyond, by reading and hearing these

---

[1]) The list is given thus in Viṣṇu-P. III, 6; Bhāgavata-P. XII, 13 (varying only slightly XII, 7, 23 f); Padma-P. I, 62; Varāha-P. 112; Matsya-P. 53; Agni-P. 272 and at the end of the Mārkaṇḍeya-P. Padma-P. IV, III; VI, 219; and Kūrma-P. I, 1 only diverge by putting 6 after 9. Padma-P. IV, iii has also the order 16, 13, 12, 15, 14 instead of 12-16, and Padma-P. VI, 263 has the order 17, 13, 14, 15, 16 instead of 13-17. Saura-P. IX, 6 f. has the order 5, 8, 7, 9, 6 instead of 5-9. The Liṅga-P. (see Aufrecht, Bodl. Cat., p. 44) has the order: 1-5, 9, 6, 7, 8, 10, 11, 12, 14-17, 13, 18. A list in which the order is quite different, is that of the Vāyu-P. 104, 1 ff. Matsya, Bhaviṣya, Mārkaṇḍeya, Brahmavaivarta, Brahmāṇḍa, Bhāgavata, Brahma, Vāmana, Ādika, Anila (*i.e.* Vāyu), Nāradīya, Vainateya (*i.e.* Garuḍa), Pādma, Kūrma. Śaukara (Sankara ? Varāha ?), Skānda. (These are only 16, though "18 Purāṇas") are spoken about; a verse has probably been omitted. For a similar list in the Purāṇasaṃhitāsiddhāntasāra, see F. R *Gambier-Parry*, Catalogue of Sanskrit MSS. purchased for the Max Müller Memorial Fund, Oxford, 1922, p. 43.) The list in the Devībhāgavata-P. (quoted by *Burnouf*, Bhāgavata-Pur., Préface, I, p. lxxxvi) also begins with the Matsya, but otherwise diverges. Albērūnī (Sachau, I, p. 130) gives a list of the 18 Purāṇas, which was read to him from the Viṣṇu-Purāṇa, and which agrees with our list, and also a second, widely diverging list, which was dictated to him. A list which is very different from the usual one is given in the Bṛhaddharma-Purāṇa 25, 18 ff.

works. In some places [1] the length (number of ślokas) of the various Purāṇas is mentioned, but the texts which have come down to us are mostly shorter. In one passage of the Padma-Purāṇa (I, 62) all of the eighteen Purāṇas are enumerated as parts of Viṣṇu's body (the Brahma-Purāṇa is his head, the Padma-Purāṇa is his heart, etc.), and are thus all stamped as sacred books. In another text of the same work,[2] on the other hand, we find the Purāṇas classified according to the three Guṇas [3] from the standpoint of Viṣṇuism. According to this classification, only the Viṣṇuite Purāṇas (Viṣṇu, Nārada, Bhāgavata. Garuḍa, Padma, Varāha) are of the quality of "goodness" (sāttvika) and lead to salvation ; the Purāṇas dedicated to Brahman (Brahmāṇḍa, Brahmavaivarta, Mārkaṇḍeya, Bhaviṣya, Vāmana, Brahma) are of the quality of "passion" (rājasa) and only serve to attain heaven ; whilst the Purāṇas in praise of Śiva (Matsya, Kūrma, Liṅga, Śiva, Skanda, Agni) are described as charged with "darkness" and as leading to hell. The texts which have come down to us, only partially agree with this artificial classification.[4] All this is additional confirmation of the fact that none of the Purāṇas has come down to us in its original form.

Besides the eighteen Purāṇas, which are often called the "great Purāṇas" (mahāpurāṇa), some of the Purāṇas themselves make mention of so-called Upapurāṇas or "secondary

---

[1]) Matsya-P. 53, 13 ff. ; Bhāgavata-P. XII, 13 ; Vāyu-P. 104, 1-10 : Agni-P. 272.

[2]) In the Uttarādhyāya of the Padma-P. 263, 81 ff.

[3]) See above, p. 430.

[4]) For instance, the Matsya-P., which is condemned as a tāmasa, has both Viṣṇuite and Śivaite chapters in our text ; the Brahmavaivarta-P. is dedicated rather to Kṛṣṇa than to Brahman, the Brahma-P. teaches sun-worship as well as Viṣṇu and Śiva worship, the Mārkaṇḍeya-P. and the Bhaviṣya-P. are not sectarian at all, and so on. The above classification of the Purāṇas also shows that we can hardly talk of a "canon of eighteen Purāṇas" (s. *Farquhar*, Outline, p. 225) ; for the Purāṇas are not the books of *one* religion, neither do they form a unified whole in any respect. For the religious views of the Purāṇas, *cf. Pargiter*, ERE X, 451 ff.

Purāṇas," whose number also is occasionally given as eighteen.[1] While, however, in the enumerations of the Purāṇas there is almost complete agreement with regard to the titles, this is by no means the case with the titles of the Upapurāṇas. Obviously there was a definite tradition about the existence of eighteen Purāṇas, while any modern religious text could assume the title of an "Upapurāṇa," if the author did not prefer to declare his work as a part of one of the "eighteen Purāṇas." The latter is the case especially with the exceedingly numerous *Māhātmyas*, *i.e.* "glorifications" of sacred places (places of pilgrimage, tīrthas).[2] But also many *Stotras*, *i.e.* "songs of praise" (usually to Viṣṇu or Śiva, but also to other deities), *Kalpas*, *i.e.* "rituals" and *Ākhyānas* or *Upākhyānas*, *i.e.* "legends," give themselves out as belonging to one or the other of the ancient Purāṇas.

We now give a short summary of the contents of the eighteen Purāṇas, in which we can only dwell a little longer on the most important ones.

1. The *Brāhma* or *Brahma-Purāṇa*.[3] This is given as the first in all the lists, and hence is sometimes called *Ādi-Purāṇa*, *i.e.* "the first Purāṇa."[4] In the introduction it is related that the Ṛṣis in the Naimiṣa-forest are visited by Lomaharṣaṇa, the Sūta, and they invite him to tell them of the origin and the end of the world. Thereupon the Sūta declares himself prepared to impart to them the Purāṇa which the creator *Brahman* once revealed to Dakṣa, one of the

---

[1]) But the Matsya-Purāṇa mentions only four Upapurāṇas. The Brahmavaivarta-P., without enumerating them, says that eighteen Upap. exist. The Kūrma-P. enumerates them.

[2]) The "Māhātmyas" of sacred texts or of rites and festivals are not so numerous.

[3]) *i.e.* "The Brahmaic Purāṇa" or "The Purāṇa of Brahman"; all the other double titles, *e.g.* Vaiṣṇava-("the Viṣṇuite") or Viṣṇu-Purāṇa ("the Purāṇa of Viṣṇu") are similarly explained. The Brahma-Purāṇa has been published in ĀnSS No. 28.

[4]) But there are other Purāṇas also which occasionally call themselves "Ādipurāṇa." *Eggeling*, Ind. Off. Cat., VI, p. 1184 f., describes, for instance, an Upapurāṇa which calls itself Ādipurāṇa and is devoted to the praise of Kṛṣṇa and Rādhā.

primal ancestors of the human race. Then follow the legends, more or less common to all the Purāṇas, of the creation of the world, the birth of the primal man Manu and his descendants, the origin of the gods, demigods and other beings, about the kings of the solar and lunar dynasties, as well as a description of the earth with its various divisions, of the hells and heavens. By far the major portion of this Purāṇa is devoted to glorifications (māhātmyas) of sacred places (tīrthas). Oṇḍradeśa or Utkala (the present-day Orissa) with its sacred places and temples is described in very great detail. As Utkala owes its sanctity to sun-worship, we find here also myths of the origin of the Ādityas (the gods of light) and of the sun-god Sūrya. The description of a forest sacred to Śiva in Utkala gives rise to stories of the birth of Umā, the daughter of the Himālaya, and her marriage with Śiva, as well as other Śiva myths. A hymn to Śiva (Chapt. 37) is also inserted here. Nevertheless the Purāṇa is by no means Śivaite, for the Mārkaṇḍeyākhyāna (Chapt. 52 ff.) contains numerous Viṣṇu legends, and rituals and stotras of the Viṣṇu cult. Here, too, (Chapt. 178) the charming legend of the ascetic *Kaṇḍu* [1] is related, who spends many hundred years in sweet love dalliance with a beautiful Apsaras, and finally awaking from the intoxication of love, thinks that only a few hours of a single day have passed. A large section (Chapt. 180-212) is devoted to Kṛṣṇa. The well-known legends of Kṛṣṇa's childhood, adventures and heroic deeds are told in exact, often literal agreement with the Viṣṇu-Purāṇa. The introduction to this passage mentions the incarnations of Viṣṇu, which are then described in detail in Chapt. 213. The last chapters contain rules for the

---

[1]) Printed in Ch. *Lassen's* "Anthologia Sanscritica," translated into German by A. W. v. *Schlegel*, Indische Bibliothek, I, 1822, p. 257 ff., and into French by A. L. *Chézy* in JAI., 1822, p. 1 ff. The legend is also related in the Viṣṇu-P. I, 15.

Śrāddhas, for a moral life, the duties of the castes and āśramas, the rewards of heaven and the punishments of hell, and the merit of Viṣṇu worship. Then come a few chapters on the periods of the world (yugas) and the periodical destruction of the world, and in conclusion explanations on Sāṃkhya and Yoga and the path leading to salvation.

The Gautamīmāhātmya, the glorification of the sacred places on the Ganges (Chapt. 70-175), frequently appears in manuscripts as an independent text. The Uttara-Khaṇḍa (*i.e.* "last section") of the Brahma-Purāṇa, which occurs in some manuscripts, is nothing but a māhātmya of a sacred river Balajā (Banās in Marwar ?).

Surely only a small portion of what has come down to us as the Brahma-Purāṇa can lay claim to be an ancient and genuine Purāṇa. About the middle of the 7th century A.D. Hsüan-Tsang still found over a hundred Buddhist monasteries with a myriad monks, but he also already found 50 Deva temples in Orissa. Śivaism was introduced in Orissa in the 6th century, and Viṣṇuism still later.[1] As the sun temple of Konārka, which is mentioned in our Purāṇa, was not built until 1241, at least the large section on the sacred places of Orissa cannot be earlier than the 13th century.[2] It is probable, however, that the Māhātmyas do not belong to the original Purāṇa.

The *Saura-Purāṇa*,[3] which claims to be a supplement (khila) of the Brahma-Purāṇa, but which is quoted as an authority by Hemādri as early as in the 13th century, proves

---

[1]) See Th. *Watters*, On Yuan Chwang's Travels in India (London, 1905), II, p. 193; W. *Crooke*, ERE, Vol. 9, p. 566.

[2]) See *Wilson*, Works III, p. 18.

[3]) Text published in ĀnSS No. 18, 1889. An analysis with extracts and partial translation of the work has been given by W. *Jahn*, Das Saurapurāṇam, Strassburg, 1908. The Saura-P. is sometimes also called Āditya-P. However, there is another Āditya-Purāṇa, which is different from, though related to the Saura-P. See Jahn, l. c, pp. ix, xiv and Festschrift Kuhn, p. 308 The Brahma-P., too, is sometimes called "Saura-P." *Cf. Eggeling*, Ind. Off. Cat. VI, p. 1185 ff

that there must have been an earlier Brahma-Purāṇa. The Saura-Purāṇa (the "Purāṇa of the sun-god") which is mentioned in the lists of the Upapurāṇas, is of great value as regards our knowledge of Śivaism, especially of the Liṅga cult. Its main purpose is to glorify god Śiva. In many places, however, Śiva is identified with the sun-god who reveals the Purāṇa, or else the sun-god recommends Śiva worship. The advantages of Śiva worship are praised in the most extravagant terms, instructions are given for the worship of the god and the liṅga, and many Śiva legends are told. A few chapters also deal with the genealogies; in Chapter 31 on the descent of Yadu there is a version of the Urvaśī legend.[1] In the philosophical sections the work takes up an intermediate position between the orthodox systems. On the one hand Śiva is explained as the Ātman, in accordance with the Vedānta, and on the other hand the creation from the primal matter (prakṛti) is explained, as in the Sāṃkhya. Three chapters (38-40) are devoted to polemics against the system of Madhva (1197-1276), which is important from the point of view of chronology.[2]

II. The *Pādma* or *Padma-Purāṇa*. There are two different recensions of this voluminous work.[3] The printed edition,[4] consisting of the six books Ādi, Bhūmi, Brahma,

---

[1]) See P. E. *Pavolini*, GSAI 21, 1908, p. 291 ff, and *Jahn*, Das Saurapurāṇam, p. 81.

[2]) See A. *Barth* in Mélanges Charles de Harlez, Leyden, 1896, p. 12 ff. As Madhva lived from 1197-1276 and Hemādri wrote between 1260 and 1309, the Saura-Purāṇa would have been compiled approximately between 1230 and 1250. However, as Chapters 38-40 do not occur in all the MSS. (s. Edition, p. 125 note, and *Eggeling*, Ind. Off Cat. VI, p. 1188), it is more probable that they have been interpolated, and that the work is earlier. *Cf. Jahn*, l. c., p. xiv.

[3]) In the Purāṇa itself (V, 1, 54; VI, 219, 28) and in the lists, the number of Ślokas is said to be 55,000. However, according to *Wilson*, the Bengali recension only contains nearly 45,000 ślokas, whilst the edition contains 48,452.

[4]) Edited by V.N. *Mandlick* in ĀnSS No. 28, 1894, 4 vols. At the end of the Bhūmi-Khaṇḍa in this edition there is a verse which enumerates the Khaṇḍas with the same titles and in the same order as in the Bengali MSS. The printed recension thus itself proves that the Bengali recension is the earlier one. *Cf. Lüders*, NGGW 1897, 1, p. 8.

Pātāla, Sṛṣṭi and Uttara-Khaṇḍa, is a later recension. The earlier one, which has come down to us only in Bengali manuscripts, consists of the following five books or Khaṇḍas.[1]

Book I, *Sṛṣṭikhaṇḍa, i.e.* "section of the Creation," commences with the usual introduction:[2] Lomaharṣaṇa sends his son, the Sūta Ugraśravas, to the Naimiṣa forest to recite the Purāṇas to the Ṛṣis assembled there. At the request of Śaunaka he tells them the Padma-Purāṇa, so-called after the lotus (padma) in which the god Brahman appears at the creation. The Sūta then reproduces the account of the creation as he has heard it from Brahman's son Pulastya. The cosmological and cosmogonic myths are here too related similarly as in the other Purāṇas. But in this book, it is not Viṣṇu who is assumed as the first cause, but the highest Brahman in the form of the personal god Brahman. Nevertheless, even this book is Viṣṇuite in character, and contains myths and legends for the glorification of the god Viṣṇu. After the account of the Cr. ation come the usual genealogies of the solar dynasty, into which a section about the Pitṛs, the "fathers" of the human race and their cult by means of Śrāddhas has been interwoven,[3] and of the lunar dynasty down to the time of Kṛṣṇa. Myths are then told of the conflicts between gods and demons, followed by a chapter which is

---

In the Sṛṣṭi-Khaṇḍa 1, 53-60, the Padma-Purāṇa is described as consisting of five Parvans: (1) Pauṣkaram, treating of the creation, (2) Tīrthaparvan, about mountains, islands and oceans, (3) a chapter on the kings who offered rich sacrificial gifts, (4) a chapter on the genealogies of the kings, and (5) a chapter on salvation. This, too, corresponds to the arrangement in the Bengali recension in all essentials.

[1]) My account of the Bengali recension is based on the Oxford manuscripts, which I inspected in 1898, and on the descriptions by *Aufrecht*, Bodl. Cat. I, p. 11 ff. and *Wilson*, Works III, p. 21 ff.; VI, p. xxix ff.

[2]) In the ĀnSS edition, too, the Sṛṣṭi-Khaṇḍa begins as though it were the beginning of the Purāṇa, but it has 82 Adhyāyas here, whilst in the Bengali recension it only consists of 46 (Wilson) or 45 (Aufrecht).

[3]) Chapt. 9-11 in ĀnSS edition.

of interest from the point of view of the history of religion,[1] and from which we here give a short extract.

At first the gods were defeated by the demons. However, Bṛhaspati, the teacher of the gods, finally caused the gods to triumph in the following manner. In the guise of Śukra, the teacher of the Asuras, he goes to the Asuras, and by means of heretical speeches, lures them from their pious faith in the Vedas. He tells them that the Veda and the tenets of the Vaiṣṇavas and the Śaivas are full of violence (hiṃsā), and that they are preached by married teachers. How then can there be any good in them? How can Śiva, the god in the form of a semi-female (ardhanārīśvaraḥ), surrounded by hosts of evil spirits and even adorned with bones,[2] tread the path of salvation? How can Viṣṇu, who uses violence, attain to salvation? If the path to heaven consists of felling a tree to make a sacrificial stake out of it, of killing a sacrificial animal and causing slaughter, what is the path to hell? How is it possible to attain heaven by sexual intercourse, or purity by earth and ashes? Soma seduced Tārā, the wife of Bṛhaspati; Budha, the son whom she bore, violated her; Indra committed adultery with Ahalyā, the wife of the Ṛṣi Gautama. Then the demons beg him to tell them to which god they can fly for safety. Bṛhaspati considers in what way he can demoralise them. Viṣṇu now comes to his aid, by causing the phantom figures of a nude Jain monk (digambara) and a Buddhist monk (raktāmbara, "red-mantle") to appear, to initiate the demons into Jain and Buddhist doctrines. After thus giving up their old (brahmanical) way of life, they yield dominion to god Indra.

One of the principal parts of the book consists of the description of the lake Puṣkara (Pokher in Ajmir),[3] sacred to Brahman, which is recommended and glorified as a place of pilgrimage. Numerous myths and legends, many of which occur in different connections in other Purāṇas, are told in praise of Puṣkara. Moreover various feasts and vows (vrata) in honour of the goddess Durgā are mentioned here.

---

1) V, 13, 316 ff. in ĀnSS edition. Cf. Viṣṇu-Purāṇa III, 17, 41-18, 33.

2) One of Śiva's forms is that of the half-female. His adornment is a wreath of human skulls, and his retinue is formed by the Bhūtas or ghosts.

3) The Sṛṣṭi-Khaṇḍa is therefore also called Pauṣkara-Khaṇḍa.

Thereupon the theme of the Creation is resumed. The book concludes with myths of Viṣṇu as the destroyer of demons, and the birth and marriage of Skanda.[1]

Book II, *Bhūmikhaṇḍa*,[2] *i.e.* "section of the earth," begins with legends of Somaśarman, who in a later rebirth became the famous Viṣṇu worshipper Prahlāda.[3] The aim of the legends is to explain why on the one hand he was born among the demons, and yet, on the other hand, was able to become so great a devotee of Viṣṇu. Besides a description of the earth, this book contains numerous legends which are intended to prove the sanctity of various tīrthas or holy places. Not only sacred places are regarded as tīrthas, but also persons, such as the teacher, the father, or the wife. As a proof of the fact that a wife can be a "tīrtha" there is told,[4] for instance, the story of Sukalā, whose husband goes on a pilgrimage and leaves her behind in want and misery; the love-god Kāma and the king of gods, Indra, try in vain to seduce her: she remains faithful to her husband, and when he returns from the pilgrimage, *he* (!) receives a divine reward on account of the virtues of his wife. Here, too, in order to prove that a son can be "a tīrtha," the story of Yayāti and his son Pūru, already known to us from the Mahābhārata, is told.

Book III, *Svargakhaṇḍa*,[5] *i.e.* "section of the heavens," gives a description of the various worlds of the gods, of the

---

[1]) The contents of the Sṛṣṭi-Khaṇḍa are still more variegated in the ĀnSS edition, where among other things, Chapt. 61-63 are devoted to the cult of Gaṇeśa and the final chapters to the cult of Durgā. The Ādi-Khaṇḍa, with which the edition begins, consists almost entirely of Māhātmyas of various Tīrthas. Only the last chapters (50-60) deal with Viṣṇu-bhakti and the duties of the castes and āśramas.

[2]) On the whole it corresponds to the Bhūmikhaṇḍa in the ĀnSS edition.

[3]) It is here taken for granted that the actual legend of Prahlāda, as told in the Viṣṇu-Purāṇa (see below) is known.

[4]) Sukalācarita in ĀnSS edition Adhy. 41-60.

[5]) There is an English translation of the Svargakhaṇḍa by Panchánan Tarkaratna, Calcutta, 1906, which I have not seen.

highest heaven of Viṣṇu, Vaikuṇṭha, the worlds of the Bhūtas, Piśācas, Gandharvas, Vidyādharas and Apsaras, the worlds of Sūrya, Indra, Agni, Yama, and so on, into which are woven numerous myths and legends. A mention of King Bharata gives rise to the narration of the story of Śakuntalā, which is here not told as in the Mahābhārata, but more in agreement with the drama of Kālidāsa. A comparison of Kālidāsa's drama with the versions of the Mahābhārata and of the Padma-Purāṇa shows that in all probability Kālidāsa used the last-mentioned as a source.[1] A description of the world of the Apsaras is the occasion for narrating the legend of Purūravas and Urvaśī. Also numerous other legends, which are known from the epics, recur in this book. It further contains instructions upon the duties of the castes and of the āśramas, upon the modes of Viṣṇu-worship and much upon ritual and morality.

Book IV, *Pātālakhaṇḍa*, *i.e.* "section of the nether world," first describes the subterranean regions, in particular the dwellings of the Nāgas or snake-deities. A mention of Rāvaṇa is the cause of the narration of the whole Rāma-legend, which is here given partly in conformity with the Rāmāyaṇa, but also often in literal agreement with Kālidāsa's epic Raghuvaṃśa.[2] Here we also find the Ṛṣyaśṛṅga-legend in a version which is older than that in our Mahābhārata.[3] The actual Rāma-legend is preceded by a story of the forefathers of Rāma, beginning with Manu, the

---

[1]) This has been shown by *Śarmā*, Padmapurāṇa and Kālidāsa, Calcutta, 1925 (Calcutta Oriental Series, No. 17 E. 10). Professor Śarmā here also gives the text of the Śakuntalā episode according to the Bengali MSS. *Wilson* (Works III, p. 40) had maintained that the Purāṇa utilised Kālidāsa's drama.

[2]) H. *Śarmā*, l. c., has made it appear probable that, in this case also, the Padma-Purāṇa was Kālidāsa's source, and not, as *Wilson* (Works III, p. 47) assumed, that the compiler of the Purāṇa drew from the Raghuvaṃśa. H. *Śarmā*, l. c., has published a critical edition of the text of this chapter (which is missing in the ĀnSS edition).

[3]) This has been proved by *Lüders*, NGGW 1897, 1, p. 8 ff. This circumstance is further proof of the greater antiquity of the Bengali recension of the Padma-P.

son of the sun-god, and his rescue from the flood. The slaying of Rāvaṇa, who was a Brahman, has laid the guilt of the murder of a Brahman on Rāma. By way of expiation he arranges a horse-sacrifice. In accordance with the prescribed rules, the horse destined for the sacrifice is let loose to roam at will for the space of one year, accompanied by a host of warriors with Śatrughna at their head. The adventures of the steed and his followers on their wanderings over the whole of India take up a considerable portion of the book; many sacred places are described, and legends attached to them are told. At length the horse reaches Vālmīki's hermitage, which is an occasion for narrating that part of the Rāma-legend which concerns Sītā.[1] Detailed instruction on the eighteen Purāṇas then follows. Here it is said that Vyāsa first proclaimed the Padma-Purāṇa, then sixteen others, and finally the Bhāgavata-Purāṇa, which is glorified as the most sacred book of the Viṣṇu-worshippers. The book ends with a few chapters, probably added at a very late date, on Kṛṣṇa and the cowherdesses, with mention of Rādhā, on the duties of Viṣṇu-worshippers, the sanctity of the Śālagrāma stone and other details of the Viṣṇu cult.[2]

Book V, *Uttarakhaṇḍa, i.e.* "last section," is a very long book expounding the Viṣṇu cult and the feasts and ceremonies connected with it, in the most impressive manner. A large portion is devoted to the glorification of the month Māgha, which is especially sacred to Viṣṇu. The silliest of legends are related as evidence of the great merit of bathing during this

---

[1]) *Wilson* (Works, III, p. 51) says: "This part of the work agrees in some respects with the Uttara-Ráma Charitra, but has several gossiping and legendary additions."

[2]) The Pātālakhaṇḍa in the ĀnSS edition only partly agrees with that of the Bengali recension. The sequence of the chapters is different, and it also contains a few chapters devoted to the Śiva cult (105-111). In the edition the Pātālakhaṇḍa is preceded by the short Brahmakhaṇḍa, which consists mainly of descriptions of Viṣṇuite feast days. Chapt. 7, treating of the birthday feast of Rādhā (rādhājanmāṣṭamī), indicates late origin. The cult of Rādhā is mentioned neither in the Mahābhārata and the Harivaṃśa, nor in the Rāmāyaṇa or the earlier Purāṇas. See below (Brahmavaivarta-Purāṇa)

month. Another section glorifies the month Kārttikeya, in which the giving away of lamps is especially meritorious. In order to give especial prominence to the Viṣṇuite standpoint, the author causes Śiva himself, in a conversation with his wife Pārvatī, to declare the glory of Viṣṇu and to recite a long account of Viṣṇu's avatāras, which involves a repetition of the entire Rāma-legend in summary and the Kṛṣṇa-legend with a fair amount of detail. In answer to Pārvatī's question who the heretics are, it is Śiva himself who declares that the Śivaite teachers and the adherents of the Śivaite Pāśupata sect are among the heretics. In another passage we find, curiously enough, the cruel goddess Durgā holding forth upon Ahiṃsā. Śiva also explains what Viṣṇu-Bhakti is, and the various forms of the Viṣṇu cult. This book also contains a glorification of the Bhagavadgītā,[1] in fact there are legends to illustrate the merit of reading each single canto. One chapter contains the enumeration of the thousand names of Viṣṇu, in another Rādhā is identified with the great goddess Lakṣmī, and the celebration of her birthday is described The sectarian bias of this book cannot be better illustrated, however, than by the following legend :

A quarrel once arose among the Ṛṣis as to which of the three great gods, Brahman, Viṣṇu or Śiva, was deserving of greatest worship. In order to dissolve their doubts, they request the great ascetic Bhṛgu to go to the gods and convince himself personally which of them is the best. Accordingly Bhṛgu at first repairs to the mountain Kailāsa to visit Śiva, and is announced by Śiva's janitor Nandin. But Śiva is just enjoying the love of his wife, and does not admit the Ṛṣi at all. Thus insulted, the Ṛṣi pronounces a curse on Śiva, condemning him to take on the shape of the generative organs,[2] and to be worshipped not by Brahmans, but

---

[1]) Gītāmāhātmya, Adhy. 171-188 in ĀnSS edition, where a glorification of the Bhāgavatapurāṇa (Adhy. 189-194) follows after it. This Bhāgavatamāhātmya also appears as an independent work in MSS. as well as in printed editions. The Māghamāhātmya and other parts of the Uttara-khaṇḍa also occur as independent works.

[2]) This refers to the worship of the Yoni and the Liṅga as symbols of the god Śiva.

only by heretics. Thereupon Bhṛgu goes to the world of Brahman. The god is seated upon his lotus-throne, surrounded by the gods. The Ṛṣi bows before him in reverential silence, but filled with pride, Brahman does not even rise to greet him and to honour him as a guest. Spurred to anger, Bhṛgu pronounces a curse whereby Brahman is to enjoy no worship at all from the human race.[1] The saint now goes to the mountain Mandara in Viṣṇu's world. There he sees the god reposing upon the world-snake, while Lakṣmī caresses his feet. He awakens the god roughly by a kick on his chest. Viṣṇu awakens, gently strokes the sage's foot, and declares that he feels highly gratified and honoured by the touch of his foot. He and his wife hasten to rise, and do honour to the Ṛṣi with divine garlands, sandalwood oil, etc. Then the great ascetic bursts into tears of joy, bows before the "treasury of mercy," and praises Viṣṇu as the highest god, when he exclaims: "Thou alone shalt be worshipped by the Brahmans, none other of the gods is worthy of worship. They shall not be worshipped, Brahman, Śiva and the other gods, for they are charged with passion (rajas) and darkness (tamas): thou alone, endowed with the quality of goodness (sattva), shalt be worshipped by the first-born (*i.e.* the Brahmans). Let him who honours other gods, be counted among the heretics." Then Bhṛgu returns to the assembly of the Ṛṣis and tells them the result of his visit to the gods.[2]

A kind of appendix to the Uttarakhaṇḍa is formed by the *Kriyāyogasāra*,[3] *i.e.* "the essence of Yoga by works," which teaches that Viṣṇu should be worshipped not by meditation (dhyānayoga), but by pious acts, above all by pilgrimages to the Ganges and the celebration of the festivals dedicated to Viṣṇu. In evidence of the fact that the fulfilment of all possible desires can be attained by worshipping

---

[1]) This is an allusion to the fact that there is scarcely any cult of Brahman in India.

[2]) In the Bengali recension this legend is found in the middle, in the ĀnSS edition at the end of the Uttara-khaṇḍa, which contains only 174 Adhyāyas in the Bengali recension, but 282 in the edition.

[3]) Many extracts from this book which is mentioned in the list of Upapurāṇas, Bṛhaddharma-P. 25, 24, have been translated into German by A. E. *Wollheim da Fonseca*, Mythologie des alten Indien, Berlin, s. a. The same scholar has given an analysis of the book in the "Jahresbericht der deutschen morgenländischen Gesellschaft," 1846, p. 153 ff.

Viṣṇu on the bank of the Ganges, many silly legends are told, but also the beautiful love story of Mādhava and Sulocanā.[1]

It is quite impossible to say anything definite as to the date of the Padma-Purāṇa. It is obviously a rather loose compilation, the parts of which belong to totally different periods, and are probably many centuries apart. The common characteristic of the five or six books is merely their rigidly sectarian character, for all of them inculcate the cult of Viṣṇu.[2] Moreover, all these books contain references to fairly modern aspects of the Viṣṇu cult, such as the adoration of Rādhā as a goddess, the sanctity of the Śālagrāma stone, of the Tulsī plant, and the like. The latest portions are certainly later than the Bhāgavata-Purāṇa, which belongs to the latest works of Purāṇa literature. Nevertheless there is sure to be an ancient nucleus at least in the Sṛṣṭi, Bhūmi, Svarga and Pātāla Khaṇḍas. It remains the task of future research to extract this ancient nucleus.[3]

III. The *Vaiṣṇava* or *Viṣṇu-Purāṇa*.[4] This is the main work of the Vaiṣṇavas or Viṣṇu-worshippers, and is frequently quoted as an authority by the philosopher Rāmānuja, the founder of the Viṣṇuite sect of the Rāmānujas, in his commentary on the Vedānta-sūtras. In this work Viṣṇu is praised and glorified as the highest being, as the one and only god, with whom Brahman and Śiva are one, and as the creator and preserver of the world. Yet it is precisely this Purāṇa which lacks all references to special feasts,

---

1) Freely rendered into German verse by A. F. Graf von *Schack*, Stimmen vom Ganges, p. 156 ff.

2) The Sṛṣṭi-khaṇḍa, where Brahman is in the foreground, is an exception.

3) An essential preliminary for this would be a critical edition of the Padma-Purāṇa on the basis of the Bengali manuscripts.

4) Edited, with Ratnagarbha's commentary, Bombay śake 1824. An older commentary is that of Śrīdhara, from which Ratnagarbha has copied, s. *Eggeling*, Ind. Off. Cat. VI, p. 1310. Translated by H. H. *Wilson*, London 1840 (and Works, Vols. VI-X) and by Manmatha Nath *Dutt*, Calcutta, 1894.

sacrifices and ceremonies dedicated to Viṣṇu; not even Viṣṇu-temples are mentioned, nor places sacred to Viṣṇu. This already leads to an assumption of the great antiquity of the work. The Viṣṇu-Purāṇa, too, approaches the most closely to the old definition of Purāṇa (see above p. 522), containing but little that is not included in those "five characteristics." Its character is more that of a unified composition than of a mere compilation, which is the case with most of the other Purāṇas. The fact that the title "Viṣṇu-Purāṇa" was hardly adopted at all for later works, Māhātmyas and such like,[1] likewise indicates that we are here dealing with a work of the earlier Purāṇa literature, which, on the whole, at least, has been preserved in its original form.[2]

A more detailed summary of the contents of this Purāṇa will best serve to give the reader an idea of the contents and significance of the Purāṇas altogether.

The work, which consists of six sections, begins with a dialogue between Parāśara, the grandson of Vasiṣṭha, and his pupil Maitreya. The latter asks his teacher about the origin and nature of the universe. To this Parāśara replies that this question reminds him of that which he had once heard from his grandfather Vasiṣṭha; and he prepares to

---

[1]) *Aufrecht* CC. I, 591; II, 140; III, 124, mentions only a few stotras and minor texts which claim to be parts of the Viṣṇu-Purāṇa. Nevertheless it is noteworthy that Matsya- and Bhāgavata-Purāṇa give the number of ślokas of the Viṣṇu-Purāṇa as 23,000, while in reality it has not quite 7,000 verses, and that also a "Great Viṣṇu-Purāṇa" (Bṛhadviṣṇu-purāṇa, *Aufrecht*, CC. I, 591) is quoted.

[2]) It is no more possible to assign any definite date to the Viṣṇu-Purāṇa than it is for any other Purāṇa. *Pargiter* (Anc. Ind. Hist. Trad., p 80) may be right in thinki g that it cannot be earlier than the 5th century. A. D. However, I do not think that it is much later. Cf. *Farquhar*, Outline, p. 143. C. V. *Vaidya* (History of Mediaeval Hindu India, I, Poona 1921, p. 350 ff.; JBRAS 1925, 1, p. 155 f.) endeavours to prove that the Viṣṇu-P. is not earlier than the 9th century, for he assumes that the Kailakila or Kaiṅkila Yavanas mentioned in IV, 24 reigned in Andhra between 575 and 900 A.D, and were at the height of their power about 782 A.D. This assumption is, however, purely hypothetical and not proven.

repeat that which he had heard. Contrary to the tradition (occurring, moreover, in the Viṣṇu-Purāṇa itself), which ascribes all the Purāṇas to Vyāsa, Parāśara is here directly called the *author* of the work. After he has first glorified Viṣṇu in a hymn, he gives an account of the *creation of the world*, as it recurs, fairly uniformly, in most of the Purāṇas.[1] Philosophical views, essentially belonging to the Sāṅkhya-philosophy, are here in a remarkable manner mingled with popular mythical ideas, for which we can find many parallels among primitive peoples.

Attached to the account of the creation of the gods and demons, of the heroes and the primal ancestors of the human race, are numerous mythological narratives, allegories and legends of ancient kings and sages of primeval times. We have already become acquainted with many of these narratives in the Mahābhārata; thus that of the *twirling of the ocean*.[2] There is here a particularly poetical description of the goddess of Fortune and Beauty, *Śrī*, arising in radiant beauty out of the twirled milk-ocean, and throwing herself on Viṣṇu's breast. In a splendid hymn she is glorified and invoked by Indra as the mother of all beings, as the source of all that is good and beautiful, and as the giver of all happiness. Just as this piece serves, above all, for the glorification of *Viṣṇu*, whose wife *Śrī* is, so it is in all the other narratives always Viṣṇu, whose praise is sung in an extravagant manner. In the description of the power which can be gained by the worship of Viṣṇu, Indian fancy knows no bounds. One example is the myth of the prince *Dhruva*, who, vexed by the preference shown to his brother, entirely gives himself up, still as a boy, to austerities and Viṣṇu-worship,

---

[1]) A summary of the accounts of the creation in the Purāṇas is given by Wilhelm *Jahn*, Uber die kosmogonischen Grundanschauungen im Mānava-Dharma-Śāstram. Diss., Leipzig, 1904

[2]) See above, p. 389. A collection of all the passages that are common to the Viṣṇu-Purāṇa and the Mahābhārata is given by A. *Holtzmann*, Mahābhārata, IV, 36 ff.

so that Viṣṇu finds himself compelled to grant him his wish of becoming something higher than his brother, and even than his father; he makes him the Pole-star, which is higher and of greater constancy than all the other stars of the heavens.[1] The power of faith in Viṣṇu, however, finds its most magnificent expression in the legend of the boy *Prahlāda* (I, 17-20), whom his father, the proud demon-king Hiraṇyakaśipu, in vain tries to dissuade from his Viṣṇu-worship. No weapon can kill him, neither snakes nor wild elephants, neither fire nor poison nor magic spells can harm him. Hurled down from the balcony of the palace, he falls gently on the bosom of the earth. He is thrown fettered into the ocean, and mountains are piled upon him—but on the floor of the ocean he sings a hymn to Viṣṇu, his fetters drop off, and he hurls the mighty hills from him. Questioned by his father whence his marvellous powers are derived, Prahlāda replies:

"Whatever power I possess, father, is neither the result of magic rites, nor is it inseparable from my nature; it is no more than that which is possessed by all in whose hearts Acyuta[2] abides. He who meditates not of wrong to others, but considers them as himself, is free from the effects of sin, inasmuch as the cause does not exist; but he who inflicts pain upon others, in act, thought, or speech, sows the seed of future birth, and the fruit that awaits him after birth is pain. I wish no evil to any, and do and speak no offence; for I behold Keśava[2] in all beings, as in my own soul. Whence should corporeal or mental suffering or pain, inflicted by elements or the gods, affect me, whose heart is thoroughly purified by him? Love, then, for all creatures will be assiduously cherished by all those who are wise in the knowledge that Hari[3] is in all things."[4]

---

[1]) I, 11 f. A more detailed version of the myth is to be found in the Bhāgavata-Purāṇa (IV, 8 f.); on this is based the poem by *Schack*, Stimmen vom Ganges, p. 189 ff.

[2]) Names of Viṣṇu.

[3]) Also a name of Viṣṇu.

[4]) I, 19, 1—9. Translated by H. H. *Wilson*. A version of the same legend is found in the Bhāgavata-P. VII, 4-6, on which the poetical rendering by *Schack*, Stimmen vom Ganges, p. 1 ff. is based.

Book II of the Viṣṇu-Purāṇa first gives (Chapt. 1-12) a fantastic description of the world. The seven continents and the seven oceans are described, in the midst of which is situated Jambudvīpa with the golden mountain Meru, the dwelling of the gods. In Jambudvīpa is Bharatavarṣa, *i.e.* "India," whose lands, mountains and rivers are enumerated. After this description of the earth follows a description of Pātāla, the nether world, in which the snake-gods dwell; next follow an enumeration and description of the still deeper-situated Narakas or hells. As a contrast there now follows a description of the heavenly spheres, the sun, the chariot of the sun and the sun-horses, with astronomical expositions on the sun's course, the planetary system, and the sun as giver of rain and preserver of beings. Next follows a description of the moon, of its car, its horses, its course, and its relation to the sun and planets. The section concludes with the statement that the whole world is but Viṣṇu, and that he alone is the only reality.

In connection with the name Bharatavarṣa there is then related (Chapt. 13-16) a legend of king *Bharata* of old,[1] which, however, only serves as an introduction to a philosophical dialogue in which the ancient *doctrine of the Unity of All*, familiar from the Upaniṣads, is presented from the Viṣṇuite standpoint. The style of the whole section recalls that of the Upaniṣads in many respects. The substance of the legend is as follows:

King Bharata was a devout worshipper of Viṣṇu. One day he went to bathe in the river. While he was bathing, a pregnant antelope came out of the forest to drink. At the same moment there was heard in close proximity, the loud roar of a lion. The antelope is startled, and, with a mighty leap, darts away. In consequence of her leap, her young

[1] Cf. E. *Leumann*, Die Bharata-Sage, ZDMG, 48 1894, p. 65 ff., and August *Blau*, Das Bharatopākhyāna des Viṣṇu-Purāṇa (Beiträge zur Bücherkunde und Philologie August Wilmanns zum 25 März 1903 gewidmet, Leipzig, 1903, p. 205 ff.)

one is born and she herself dies. Bharata took the young one with him and reared it in his hermitage. From that time onwards nothing but the antelope concerned him. She was his one thought, his one care. And when at last, still thinking only of the antelope, he died, he was soon afterwards born again as an antelope, but with the remembrance of his former existence. In this antelope-existence also, he worshipped Viṣṇu and practised austerities, so that, in his next birth, he came into the world as the son of a pious Brahman. Although, as such, he had acquired the highest knowledge, the doctrine of the unity of all, yet he troubled about no Veda-study, performed no brahmanical rites, spoke disconnectedly and ungrammatically, went about dirty and in torn garments—in short he behaved absolutely like an idiot.[1] He was universally despised, and employed in the low work of a slave. Thus it happened that he was once employed by a servant of king Sauvīra as the king's palanquin-bearer. On this occasion a conversation takes place between the apparent idiot and the king, in which Bharata soon reveals himself as a great sage, and to the great joy of the king, reveals to him the doctrine of the unity of all. In elucidation of this he tells him the story of *Ṛbhu and Nidāgha*:

The wise and holy Ṛbhu, son of the creator Brahman, had been the teacher of Nidāgha. After a thousand years he once visited his pupil, was hospitably entertained by him, and was asked where he dwelt, whence he came, and where he was going. Ṛbhu answered him that these were quite unreasonable questions, for man (namely, the ātman) is everywhere, for him there is no going and no coming, and he makes the doctrine of the unity so clear to him that Nidāgha, enraptured, falls at his feet and asks who he is. Only now does he learn that it is his old teacher Ṛbhu who had come in order to teach him the true wisdom once again. After another thousand years Ṛbhu again comes to the town where Nidāgha lives. There he observes a crowd of people and a king, who is

---

[1]) The corresponding story in the Bhāgavata-P. V, 9; 10 has the title Jaḍabharata-carita, "Life of Bharata the Idiot," in the colophons. Jaḍabharata is mentioned, along with Durvāsas, Ṛbhu Nidāgha and other Paramahaṃsa ascetics, who "though not mad, behave like madmen," in the Jābāla-Upaniṣad 6. In Viṣṇu-P. I, 9 a legend is related of the ascetic Durvāsas (*i.e.* "Badly Clad") "who observed the vow of a madman." Cf. also A. *Barth*, Religions of India, p. 83. Similarly there were in the Middle Ages certain Christian saints, like St. Symeon Salos and St. Andreas, who wandered about like fools or idiots, exposing themselves to mockery and insults as a kind of asceticism. Cf. H. *Reich*, Der Mimus, Berlin, 1903, I, 2, p. 822 f., and J. *Horovitz*, Spuren griechischer Mimen im Orient, Berlin, 1905, p. 34 ff.

entering the city with a great retinue. Far away from the crowd stands his former pupil Nidāgha. Ṛbhu approaches him and asks him why he thus stands apart. Thereupon Nidāgha replies: "A king is entering this city, there is a great crush, therefore I stand aside." Ṛbhu asks: "Which, then, is the king?" Nidāgha: "The king is he who sits on the great stately elephant." "It is well," says Ṛbhu, "but who is the elephant and who is the king?" Nidāgha: "The elephant is below and the king is above." Ṛbhu: "Now, what is the meaning of below, and what is the meaning of above?" Then Nidāgha jumps on the back of Ṛbhu and says, "I am above like the king, thou art below like the elephant." "Very well," says Ṛbhu, "but now tell me, my dear one, *which of us two art thou and which am I?*" Only now does Nidāgha recognise his old teacher Ṛbhu, for nobody is so filled with the doctrine of unity as *he*. Then the doctrine of the unity of the universe was so deeply impressed on Nidāgha that from now on he looked on all beings as one with himself, and attained complete liberation.

Book III of the Viṣṇu-Purāṇa begins with an account of the Manus (primal ancestors of the human race) and the ages (manvantaras)[1] over which they ruled. Then follows a discussion on the four Vedas, on their division by Vyāsa and his pupils, and on the origin of the various Vedic schools. Then comes an enumeration of the eighteen Purāṇas and a list of all sciences.

Then the question is raised and discussed, how one may attain to liberation as a devout Viṣṇu-worshipper. In a beautiful dialogue (Chapt. 7) between Yama, the god of death, and one of his servants, it is explained that he who is pure in heart and leads a virtuous life and has directed his mind to Viṣṇu, is a true Viṣṇu-worshipper and therefore is free from the bonds of the god of death. This is followed by an exposition on the duties of the castes and āśramas, on birth and marriage ceremonies, ritual ablutions, the daily sacrifices, the duties of hospitality, conduct at meals, and so on. A long treatise (Chapt. 13-17) on the funeral oblations and ceremonies

---

[1]) On the Ages of the World according to the Purāṇas s. *Jacobi*, ERE I, 200 ff.

for the worshipping of spirits of ancestors (śrāddhas) concludes this section, in which the Vedic-brahmanical religious customs are represented as the right kind of Viṣṇu-worship. The last two chapters of the book describe the origin of the heretical sects hostile to the Veda, whose adherents, especially the Jains, called Digambara, and the Buddhists known as "Red-mantles" (raktāmbaras),[1] are represented as the worst evil-doers. In order to show how sinful it is to have any sort of intercourse with such heretics, the story of the ancient king *Śatadhanu* (Chapt. 18) is told, who otherwise was a devout worshipper of Viṣṇu, but once, out of mere politeness, exchanged a few words with a heretic, and in consequence was re-born consecutively as a dog, jackal, wolf, vulture, crow and peacock, till at last—thanks to the constant faithfulness and piety of his wife *Śaibyā*—he again came into the world as a king.

Book IV of the Viṣṇu-Purāṇa contains chiefly genealogical lists of the ancient royal races, of the solar dynasty, which traces its origin back to the sun-god, and the lunar dynasty, which traces its origin to the moon-god. Long lists of ancient kings—many of them purely mythical, some probably historical—are only occasionally interrupted in order to relate some legend about one or other of them. The marvellous plays a great part in all these legends. There is Dakṣa, who is born out of Brahman's right thumb; Manu's daughter Ilā, who becomes transformed into a man; Ikṣvāku, who owes his existence to the sneezing of Manu; King Raivata, who, with his daughter Revatī, goes to heaven, in order to have a husband for his daughter recommended to him by god Brahman;[2] or indeed King Yuvanaśva, who

---

[1]) The rise of the heretical sects is here (III, 17 f.) explained by the legend according to which Viṣṇu sent a phantom figure to the demons in order to alienate them from the Veda religion, whereupon they can be defeated by the gods. Cf. Padma-Purāṇa, above p. 536 ff.

[2]) IV, 1. A poetical rendering by *Schack*, Stimmen vom Ganges, pp. 120 ff.

becomes pregnant and brings a son into the world, whom Indra suckles with the drink of immortality, the child putting his finger into the mouth of the god and then sucking it. Because Indra said: "He will be suckled by me" (mān dhāsyati), the child received the name *Māndhāṭṛ*. The latter became a powerful king and the father of three sons and fifty daughters. How he acquires a son-in-law, is related, with that peculiar humour which occasionally makes a pleasant break in the deep earnestness which usually prevails in the Indian legends of saints, in the legend of the pious ascetic *Saubhari*, who practises asceticism in the water for twelve years, until the sight of a fish-king enjoying himself with his young ones, awakens in him the desire for paternal joys.[1]

In this book we meet with many legends already familiar from the epics, for example, those of Purūravas and Urvaśī,[2] of Yayāti, and others. There is also here a short summary of the Rāma-legend. There is an account of the birth of the Pāṇḍavas, and of Kṛṣṇa, and the story of the Mahābhārata is briefly touched upon. The conclusion of this extensive genealogical book is formed by prophecies concerning the "future" kings of Magadha, the Śaiśunāgas, Nandas, Mauryas, Śuṅgas, Kāṇvāyanas and Andhrabhṛtyas (see above, p. 523 f.), concerning the foreign barbarian rulers who will succeed them, and the terrible age brought about by them, an age without religion and without morality, which will only be ended by Viṣṇu in his incarnation as Kalki.

Book V is a complete whole in itself. It contains a detailed biography of the divine cowherd Kṛṣṇa, in which practically the same adventures are told in the same order as in the Harivaṃśa.[3]

---

[1]) IV, 2. A poetical rendering by *Schack*, l. c., p. 87 ff.

[2]) Translated by *Geldner*, Vedische Studien, I, p. 253 ff.

[3]) See above p. 446 ff. This chapter has been translated into German by A. *Paul*, Krischnas Weltengang, Munich, 1905.

Book VI is quite short. Once again the four consecutive ages of the world (yugas)—Kṛta, Tretā, Dvāpara and Kali—are recalled, and the evil Kaliyuga is described in the form of a prophecy, to which is attached a presentation of the various kinds of dissolution (pralaya) of the universe. Next are described in a pessimistic manner (Chapt. 5) the evils of existence, the pain of being born, of childhood, of manhood, old age and death, the torments of hell and the imperfection of the bliss of heaven, and from this the conclusion is drawn that only liberation from existence, freedom from re-birth, is the highest happiness. But for this it is necessary to know the nature of God; for only *that* wisdom is perfect by which God is seen, all else is ignorance. The medium for obtaining this wisdom is *Yoga*, meditation upon Viṣṇu. The two penultimate chapters of the work give information on this medium. The last chapter recapitulates briefly the contents of the whole Purāṇa and ends with a praise of Viṣṇu and a final prayer.

IV. The *Vāyava* or *Vāyu-Purāṇa.*[1] This appears in some lists under the name of *Śaiva* or *Śiva-Purāṇa,*[2] a title which is given to the work because it is dedicated to the worship of the god Siva. A "Purāṇa proclaimed by the Wind-god," *i.e.* a Vāyu-Purāṇa, is quoted in the Mahābhārata as well as in the Harivaṃśa, and the Harivaṃśa in many cases agrees literally with our Vāyu-Purāṇa.[3] It has already been mentioned (see above p. 526) that the poet Bāṇa (about 625 A.D.) had a Vāyu-Purāṇa read to him, and that in this Purāṇa the rule of the Guptas is described as

---

[1]) Editions in Bibl. Ind. 1880-1889 and in ĀnSS No. 49. 1905.

[2]) Thus in the Viṣṇu and Bhagavata-P. But there is also a *Śiva-Purāṇa*, which is quite a different work and belongs to the Upapurāṇas. It consists of 12 Saṃhitās, including a Vāyavīya and a Dharma-Saṃhitā. Cf. *Eggeling*, Ind. Off. Cat. VI, p. 1311 ff. The Brahmāṇḍa-P. also is called Vaiyavīya, "proclaimed by Vāyu," and *Pargiter* (ERE X, 448) believes that Vāyu and Brahmāṇḍa were originally *one* Purāṇa and only differentiated later.

[3]) Cf. *Hopkins*, Great Epic, p. 49. *Holtzmann*, Das Mahābhārata IV, p. 40 f. and above, p. 520 f.

it was in the 4th century A.D. There certainly existed an ancient Purāṇa under this name, and undoubtedly there is still preserved in our texts much of the ancient work, which is probably not later than the 5th century A.D.[1] This work also deals with the same subjects, characteristic of the ancient Purāṇas—creation of the world, genealogies, etc., as the Viṣṇu-Purāṇa. Only here the legends which are related serve for the glorification of Śiva, not of Viṣṇu. Like the Viṣṇu-Purāṇa, so also the Vāyu-Purāṇa in its last part gives a description of the end of the world, and deals with the efficacy of Yoga, but ends with a description of the splendour of Śivapura, "the city of Śiva," where the Yogin arrives who has entirely lost himself in meditation upon Śiva. Even in this Śivaite work two chapters are devoted to Viṣṇu.[2] The Purāṇa deals in detail with the fathers (pitṛs) and their cult by means of Śrāddhas.[3] One chapter is devoted to the art of song.[4] The Gayāmāhātmya printed at the end of the editions is certainly a later addition.[5] There are also other Māhātmyas, Stotras and ritual-texts, which claim to belong to the Vāyu-Purāṇa.

V. The *Bhāgavata-Purāṇa.* This is indisputably that work of Purāṇa literature which is most famous in India. Still to-day it exerts a powerful influence on the life and thought of the innumerable adherents of the sect of the Bhāgavatas (worshippers of Viṣṇu under the name of "Bhagavat"). The extremely numerous manuscripts and prints of the text itself, as well as of many commentaries on the whole work

---

1) Cf. *Bhandarkar*, Vaiṣṇavism etc., p. 47, *Farquhar*, Outline, p. 145. C. V. *Vaidya's* argument (JBRAS 1925, 1, p. 155 f.) for ascribing the Vāyu-P. to the 8th century is not convincing.

2) Adhyāyas 96, 97.

3) Śrāddhaprakriyārambha and Śrāddhakalpa, Adhy. 71-86.

4) Adhy. 87: gītālaṃkāranirdeśaḥ.

5) Adhy. 104-112. It is missing in some MSS. and appears as an independent text in MSS. as well as in Indian prints.

and of separate explanatory writings on parts of it,[1] in addition to the many translations into Indian vernaculars,[2] bear witness to the enormous popularity and the extraordinary reputation of the work in India. It is in accordance with this its significance, that it is the first Purāṇa that has been edited and translated in Europe.[3] Nevertheless it belongs to the later productions of Purāṇa literature. In contents it is closely connected with the Viṣṇu-Purāṇa, with which it often agrees literally, and it is undoubtedly dependent upon the latter. Even in India doubts as to the "genuineness" of the Bhāgavata as one of the ancient eighteen Purāṇas "composed by Vyāsa" have already been expressed, and there are polemic treatises[4] discussing the question whether the Bhāgavata—or the *Devībhāgavata-Purāṇa*,[5] a Śivaite work, belong to the "eighteen Purāṇas." In this connection the question is raised and discussed whether the grammarian *Vopadeva* is the author of the Bhāgavata-Purāṇa.[6] Rather

---

[1]) See *Eggeling*, Ind. Off. Cat. VI, p. 1259 ff., and *Aufrecht*. CC. I, p. 401 ff.

[2]) In Bengali alone there are 40 translations, especially of the Kṛṣṇa-book. See. D. Ch. *Sen*, History of Bengali Language and Literature, Calcutta, 1911, p. 220 ff.

[3]) Le Bhâgavata Purâna ou histoire poétique de Krichṇa, traduit et publié par M. Eugène *Burnouf*, t, 1-III, Paris 1840-47. T. IV et V publiés par M. *Hauvette-Besnault* et P. *Roussel*. Paris 1884 et 1898. A few legends from the Bhāg.-P. have been translated into French by A. *Roussel*, Légendes Morales de l'Inde. Paris 1900, I, 1 ff. and II, 215 ff. English translation by Manmatha Nath *Dutt*, Calcutta, 1895. A French translation of the Tamil version of the Bhāgavata was published as early as 1788 at Paris, and this was rendered into German, Zürich 1791 (s. *Windisch*, Geschichte der Sanskrit-philologie, p. 47 f.).

[4]) Thus the "box on the ear for villains" (durjanamukhacapeṭikā), the "big box on the ear for villains" (durjanamukhamahācapeṭikā) and the "slipper in the face of villains" (durjanamukhapadmapādukā). They are translated by *Burnouf*, l. c., I, Préface p. lix ff. These are quite modern writings.

[5]) This is also called simply Śrībhāgavatamahāpurāṇa in the MSS. Editions have been published in Bombay, and an English translation in the SBH. Cf. *Aufrecht*, Bodl. Cat., p. 79 ff.; *Eggeling*, Ind. Off. Cat. VI, p. 1207 f. There is also a Mahā-Bhāgavata-Purāṇa differing from it, which is described by *Eggeling* (l. c., p. 1280 ff.) as "an apocryphal Purāṇa recounting the story and exploits of Devī and urging her claims to being worshipped as the supreme deity."

[6]) This supposition seems to rest only on the fact that Vopadeva is the author of the *Muktāphala*, a work dependent on the Bhāgavata, and of the *Harilīlā*, an Anukramaṇī (index) to the Bhāgavata.

hastily Colebrooke, Burnouf and Wilson have concluded from this, that Vopadeva really was the author of the Purāṇa, and therefore that it only originated in the 13th century.[1] In any case the work cannot possibly be as late as that, as it already passed as a sacred book in the 13th century.[2] There are good grounds for assigning it to the 10th century A.D.[3] Rāmānuja (12th century) did not yet recognise the Bhāgavata as an authority, for he does not mention it, and only alludes to the Viṣṇu-Purāṇa. But though it may have originated at a comparatively late date, it certainly utilised very ancient materials. Moreover it is the one Purāṇa which, more than any of the others, bears the stamp of a unified composition, and deserves to be appreciated as a literary production on account of its language, style and metre.[4]

The work is divided into twelve books (skandhas) and consists of about 18,000 ślokas. The cosmogonic myths agree on the whole with those of the Viṣṇu-Purāṇa, but in some interesting details also differ from it.[5] The incarnations of Viṣṇu are described in detail, especially that as a wild boar. It is remarkable that *Kapila*, the founder of the Sāṅkhya philosophy, is also mentioned as an incarnation of Viṣṇu and (at the end of Book III) himself recites a long exposition on

---

1) Vopadeva was a contemporary of *Hemādri*, who lived between 1260 and 1309.

2) Ānandatīrtha Madhva (1199-1278), who himself wrote a commentary on the Bhāg.-Pur., places it on a level with the Mahābhārata.

3) C. V. *Vaidya* (JBRAS 1925, 1, 144 ff.) makes it seem probable that it is later than Śaṅkara (beginning of the 9th century) and earlier than Jayadeva's Gītagovinda (12th century). *Bhandarkar* (Vaiṣṇavism etc., p. 49) says that it "must have been composed at least two centuries before Ānandatīrtha." *Pargiter* (Anc. Ind. Hist Trad, p. 80) places it "about the ninth century A.D.," *Farquhar* (Outline, p. 229 ff.) about 900 A.D., C. *Eliot* (Hinduism and Buddhism, II, p. 188 note) remarks that "it does not belong to the latest class of Purāṇas, for it seems to contemplate the performance of Smārta rites, not temple ceremonial." *Vaidya* (l. c., p. 157 f.) adduces arguments for the hypothesis that the author of the Bhāg.-P. lived in the land of the Dravidas. Cf. *Grierson*, JRAS 1911, p. 800 f.

4) Side by side with the śloka, metres of ornate poetry also appear. Cf. *Burnouf*, I, Préface, p. cv f.

5) See A. *Roussel*, Cosmologie Hindoue d'après le Bhâgavata-Purâṇa, Paris, 1898.

Yoga. Buddha, too, already appears among the incarnations of Viṣṇu.[1] The legends which are told for the glorification of Viṣṇu are numerous. Most of them, like those of Dhruva, Prahlāda, and so on, are the same as are already familiar to us from the Viṣṇu-Purāṇa. With the Mahābhārata, too, the work has much in common; a few verses from the Bhagavadgītā are quoted literally.[2] The Śakuntalā episode is related in IX, 20, in quite a short extract, but probably after a very ancient source.[3] *Book X* is the most popular and the most frequently read of all. It contains the biography of *Kṛṣṇa* which is here given in much greater detail than in the Viṣṇu-Purāṇa and in the Harivaṃśa. In particular the love scenes with the cowherdesses (gopīs) occupy a much larger space.[4] This book is translated into almost all the Indian vernaculars and is a favourite book with all classes of the Indian people. The annihilation of the Yādavas and the death of Kṛṣṇa are related in *Book XI*, while the last book contains the usual prophecies concerning the Kaliyuga and the destruction of the world.

VI. The *Bṛhannāradīya-Pūrāṇa*, *i.e.* "the great Purāṇa of Nārada." It is generally so called to distinguish it from the Nārada—or Nāradīya—Upapurāṇa. It is doubtful, however, whether even the Bṛhannāradīya-Purāṇa[5] deserves to be

---

1) Though he appears, "to delude the foes of the gods" (I, 3, 24), he is among the avatāras, and as such (in the Nārāyaṇavarman, VI, 8, 17) he is invoked, whilst in the Viṣṇu-P. (III, 17 f.), Viṣṇu in order to delude the Daityas, causes a phantom form to issue forth from himself, which comes into the world as Buddha.

2) See *Holtzmann*, Das Mahābhārata, IV, 41-49, and J. E. *Abbott*, Ind. Ant. 21, 1892, p. 94.

3) In IX, 20, 16, *om* is used in the sense of "yes," which is very archaic. Cf. Ait.-Br. VII, 18; Chānd.-Up. I, 1, 8 and above p. 185, note. In Kurma-P. I, 23 (p. 248) and I, 27 (p. 294) *om* is also used in the sense of "yes" in the style of the old legends, though the Kūrma itself is a late work.

4) Rādhā, however, does not appear, from which *Vaidya*, l. c., rightly concludes that the Bhāg.-P. is earlier than the Gītagovinda.

5) Edited by Pandit *Hrishīkeśa Śāstrī*, Bibl. Ind. 1891, who calls the work an "Upapurāṇa." Cf. *Wilson*, Works, VI, p. li ff.; *Eggeling*, Ind. Off. Cat. VI, p. 1208 ff.

counted among the ancient Purāṇas; for it is a purely sectarian text, wherein the Sūta repeats a conversation between Nārada and Sanatkumāra, and the sage Nārada appears in the character of a teacher of Viṣṇu-bhakti, the pious adoration of Viṣṇu. The real themes of the Purāṇas, the creation of the world, etc., are not touched upon; the main themes are descriptions of the feasts and ceremonies of the Viṣṇu-cult, illustrated by all manner of legends. Inserted in the legends we also find didactic sections upholding a rather intolerant brahmanical standpoint. Chapter XIV, a lengthy chapter containing a catalogue of the principal sins and the corresponding punishments of hell, is characteristic.

By way of example, the following are included among the sinners for whom there is no atonement, and who must irrevocably be condemned to hell: He who venerates a Liṅga or an image of Viṣṇu which is worshipped by a Śūdra or a woman; he who bows down before a Liṅga worshipped by a heretic, or who himself becomes a heretic. Śūdras, uninitiated persons, women, outcasts, who touch an image of Viṣṇu or Śiva, go to hell. He who hates a Brahman, can in no wise hope for atonement. There is no expiation for the Brahman who enters a Buddhist temple, even though he did so in a great emergency; even hundreds of expiation ceremonies are of no avail. The Buddhists are despisers of the Vedas, and therefore a Brahman shall not look at them, if he is truly devoted to the Vedas.[1] These sinners for whom there is no expiation, are not only condemned to roast in hell for hundreds and thousands of years—the author actually revels in the enumeration of the tortures of hell—but they are subsequently reborn again and again as worms and other animals, as Cāṇḍālas, Śūdras and Mlecchas. Dreadful torments of hell await him who recites the Veda in the presence of women or Śūdras. Nevertheless, in contradiction to all these damnations, the same chapter teaches that Viṣṇu-bhakti annihilates all sins, and that Ganges water, too, washes away the blackest sins.

In the Bṛhaddharma-P. I, 25, 23 both the Bṛhannāradīya and the Nāradīya are enumerated among the Upapurāṇas.

1) Pandit *Hrishīkeśa* concludes from this passage that the work was compiled when Buddhism "was rooted out and was universally despised." I think, on the contrary, that such violent outbreaks against the Buddhists could only have a meaning at a time when Buddhism was still a living power in India.

Several chapters (22-28) deal in detail with the duties of the castes and āśramas, and with Śrāddhas and the ceremonies of expiation (prāyaścitta). The last chapters deal with the misery of transmigration (saṃsāra) and with salvation (mokṣa) by means of Yoga and Bhakti. Devotion to Viṣṇu is again and again declared to be the only means of salvation. Thus we read (28, 116): "Of what avail are the Vedas, the Śāstras, ablutions in sacred bathing-places, or austerities and sacrifices, to those who are without the worship of Viṣṇu (Viṣṇubhakti)?"

The *Nāradīya-Upapurāṇa* includes the Rukmāṅgadacarita, which also occurs as an independent book. The "edifying" legend of King Rukmāṅgada is here told in 40 chapters. King Rukmāṅgada has promised his daughter Mohinī that he will grant her a wish, whatsoever it may be. She demands that he shall either break his fast on the Ekādaśī (the eleventh day of the half-month sacred to Viṣṇu) or slay his son; the king decides upon the latter, this being the lesser of the two sins.

VII. The *Mārkaṇḍeya-Purāṇa.*[1)] This is one of the most important, most interesting, and probably one of the oldest works of the whole Purāṇa literature. Yet even this Purāṇa is no unified work, but consists of parts which vary in value and probably belong to different periods.

The work takes its name from the ancient sage Mārkaṇḍeya, who enjoyed eternal youth, and who also appears in a large section of the Mahābhārata (see above p. 397 Note 4 and p. 425) as a narrator. We may probably regard those sections as the oldest,[2)] in which Mārkaṇḍeya is actually the speaker and instructs his pupil Krauṣṭuki upon the creation of

---

[1)] Edited by K. M. *Banerjea*, Bibl. Ind. 1862 and translated into English by F. Eden *Pargiter*, Bibl. Ind. 1888-1905.

[2)] These are chapters 45-81 and 93-136 (conclusion). Cf. *Pargiter*, Introd., p. iv. Verse 45, 64 is quoted twice by Śaṅkara (Vedānta-Sūtras I, 2, 23 and III, 3, 16, see P. *Deussen*, Die Sûtras des Vedânta aus dem Sanskrit übersetzt, Leipzig 1887, p. 119 and 570); but it is by no means certain that Śaṅkara knew the verse from the Mārkaṇḍeya-Purāṇa, for he does not mention it, but only says "It is said in the Smṛti."

the world, the ages of the world, the genealogies and the other subjects peculiar to the Purāṇas. Special evidence for the great antiquity of these sections which contain the *old* Purāṇa is found in the circumstance that in them neither Viṣṇu nor Śiva occupies a prominent position, that, on the other hand, Indra and Brahman are much in the foreground, and that the ancient deities of the Veda, Agni (Fire) and Sūrya (Sun) are glorified by hymns in a few of the cantos, and that a large number of sun-myths are related.[1] This oldest part of the Purāṇa, as Pargiter considers, may belong to the third century A.D., but may perhaps be earlier. A large part of this section also consists of moral and edifying narratives.

This is still more the case in the first sections of the work, which are closely connected with the Mahābhārata and have very much in common with the character of Book XII of the epic. The Purāṇa actually commences with Jaimini, a pupil of Vyāsa, approaching Mārkaṇḍeya, and, after a few eulogies of the Mahābhārata,[2] asking him for the answers to four questions, which the great epic leaves unanswered. The first question is, how it was that Draupadī was able to become the common wife of the five Pāṇḍavas, and the last, why the children of Draupadī were killed at a youthful age. Mārkaṇḍeya does not answer these questions himself, but refers him to four wise birds, in reality Brahmans who were born as birds in consequence of a curse.[3] These tell

---

1) Chapters 99-110. An impression of great antiquity is also created by the narrative of Dama who, in order to avenge the death of his father, cruelly kills Vapuṣmat and offers his flesh and blood to the spirit of his father, with the funeral cakes (136). The very fact that in the Bengali manuscripts the narrative ceases without any mention of the human sacrifice, is a proof of the great antiquity of traditions which could no longer be reconciled with the views of a later time. (Cf. *Pargiter*, p. vii.)

2) These partly agree literally with the praises at the beginning and end of the Mahābhārata itself (cf. above p. 325 f. and 453).

3) This is again a duplicate of a legend also occurring in the Mahābhārata (I, 229 ff.), where, however, one of the birds is called Droṇa, while in the Mārk.-P. the four birds are Droṇa's sons.

Jaimini a series of legends in reply to the propounded questions. In reply to the last question it is related, how five angels (viśve devās) once took the liberty of finding fault with the great saint Viśvāmitra, when he treated King Hariścandra cruelly, for which they were cursed by the saint to be born again as human beings, which curse he mitigated so that they should die young and unmarried. The five sons of Draupadī were those angels. In connection with this is related the touching, but genuinely Brahmanical legend of King *Hariścandra*, who, through fear of the wrath and curse of Viśvāmitra, suffers endless sorrow and humiliation, until at last he is taken into heaven by Indra himself.[1]

After the answering of the four questions, there begins a new section (Chapts. 10-44) in which a conversation between a father and his son is communicated; this is a very lengthy amplification of the dialogue between father and son which we met with in the Mahābhārata (see above, p. 417 ff.). It is significant that the son, in the Mahābhārata, is called "Intelligent" (Medhāvin), while in the Purāṇa he bears the nickname *Jaḍa*, "the Idiot."[2] As in the Mahābhārata, here too, the son despises the life of the pious Brahman, which his father places before him as an ideal, he recalls all his previous births and sees salvation only in an escape from the Saṃsāra. In connection with this the "Idiot" gives a

[1]) Chapters 7 and 8. This famous legend has been translated into English by J. *Muir*, Original Sanskrit Texts, I, 3rd ed., p. 379 ff. and by B. H. *Wortham*, JRAS 1881, p. 355 ff., into German by F. *Rückert* (ZDMG 13, 1859, 103 ff.; Rückert-Nachlese II, 489 ff.). The legend was a favourite theme for later dramatists, thus it forms the subject of the Caṇḍakauśika by the poet Kṣemīśvara (10th or 11th century A.D.). It is also told in a ballad that is still popular in the Punjab, s. R. C. *Temple*: The Legends of the Panjâb No. 42 (Vol. III, p. 53 ff.). The Śunaḥśepa legend, the Buddhist Vessantara-Jātaka, and the Hebrew Book of Job have been compared with the Hariścandra legend. Cf. *Weber* SBA 1891, p. 779 f. Ind. Stud. 15, p. 413 ff. On the legends of Viśvāmitra, Vasiṣṭha, Hariścandra, and Śuṇaḥśepa in the Brāhmaṇas, Purāṇas and Epics, see F. E. *Pargiter*, JRAS 1917, p. 37 ff.

[2]) This "wise fool" also, like Jaḍabharata (see above, p. 549) is a proclaimer of the Yoga.

description of the Saṃsāra and of the consequences of sins in various rebirths, and especially of the hells and the punishments of hell, which await the sinner. In the midst of this description of hell, magnificent of its kind, though not very enjoyable,[1] stands one of the gems of Indian legend poetry, the story of the noble king *Vipaścit* ("the Wise"),[2] which well deserves to be briefly reproduced here.

The extremely pious and virtuous king *Vipaścit* is, after his death, taken to hell by a servant of Yama. In answer to the king's amazed question as to why he should have to go to hell, Yama's servant explains to him that he once neglected to cohabit with his wife at the time suitable for conception, and he must atone for this light offence against the religious precepts, at least by a very short stay in hell. Thereupon he gives the king instruction upon good and bad deeds (karman), which must inevitably have their effects, and the punishments of hell which are laid down for every single sin. After these explanations the servant of the god of death is about to take him out of hell again. The king turns to go, when dreadful screams of agony smite on his ear, and the inhabitants of hell assail him with entreaties to stay only a minute longer, as an inexpressibly pleasant breath emanates from him, which alleviates the torments of hell which they are enduring. At his amazed question, Yama's servant gives him the explanation that, from the good works of a pious man, a refreshing breath is wafted towards the inhabitants of hell and alleviates their torments. Then says the king :

"Not in heaven, nor in Brahman's world, methinks,
Does man find such bliss as when
He can give refreshment to beings in torment.

If through my presence, racking torture
Of these poor ones is alleviated,
Then will I stay here, my friend,
Like a post, I will not move from this spot."

---

[1]) This is the most detailed description of hell in the Purāṇa literature, but similar descriptions also occur in other Purāṇas. They are discussed by L. *Scherman*, Visionslitteratur, p. 23 ff., 45 ff.

[2]) Chapt. 15, Verses 47-79 translated into German by F. *Rückert* (ZDMG 12, 1858, p. 336 ff; Rückert-Nachlese II, 485 ff.).

Yama's servant spake:

"Come, O King, let us go, do *thou* enjoy
The fruits of thy good deeds and leave the torments
To those who, through bad deeds, deserve them."

The king spake:

"No, I will not go hence, while these
Poor dwellers in hell are happy through my presence.
A disgrace and a shame is the life of a man
Who feels no pity for the tortured, poor ones,
Who implore him for protection—even for bitter foes.
Sacrifices, gifts, austerities serve neither here nor beyond
For his salvation, who has no heart for protecting tortured ones,
Whose heart is hardened to children, old men and the weak,
Not as a man do I regard him—he is a devil.
Even though, through the presence of these dwellers in hell
I suffer the torment of purgatory, the stink of hell,
And the pain of hunger and of thirst rob me of my senses—
Yet I deem it sweeter than the joy of heaven,
To give them, the tortured ones, protection and help.
If through *my* suffering many unhappy ones become glad,
What more do I want?—Do not tarry, depart and leave me."

Yama's servant spake:

"Behold! *Dharma* [1] comes, and *Śakra*, to fetch thee hence.
Thou must go indeed, King: up, and away from here!"

Dharma spake:

"Let me lead thee to the heaven which thou hast well deserved;
Enter this chariot of the gods without delay—away from here!"

The King spake:

"Here in this hell, Dharma, men are tortured a thousandfold;
'Protect us!' full of agony they cry to me; I will not move from
here."

[1]) On *Dharma* as the name of the god of death see above p. 397. *Śakra* is a name of *Indra*, the king of the gods. In genuine old Ākhyāna-style, it is *not related* that the two gods came there, but their coming is communicated in *conversation*, and they then immediately appear speaking.

Śakra spake :

" The reward of their *deeds*, these evil ones receive in hell ;
Thou, prince, must for thy *good* deed ascend to heaven."

But for the king the dwellers in hell are not sinners, only *sufferers*. And as, in answer to his question how great his good works are, Dharma himself replies that they are as numerous "as the drops of water in the sea, the stars in the heavens,... the grains of sand in the Ganges," he has only the *one* desire, that, through these good works of his, the dwellers in hell may be delivered from their torments. The king of gods grants him this wish, and as he ascends to heaven, all the inmates of hell are released from their pain.[1]

In language and style this splendid dialogue reminds one very much of the Sāvitrī poem of the Mahābhārata. But just as in the great epic the most absurd productions of priestly literature stand by the side of the most beautiful poems, so also in our Purāṇa. Immediately after the above-told legend follows that of *Anasūyā*, which appears like a caricature of the Sāvitrī legend :

Anasūyā[2] is the extremely faithful wife of a loathsome, leprous, rough and vulgar Brahman. In accordance with the brahmanical principle: " The husband is the deity of the wife," his wife tends him with the greatest love and care, and bears his coarseness with patience. One day the good man, who is also a libertine, expresses the urgent desire of visiting a courtesan who has excited his admiration. As he himself is too

[1]) The story of Yudhiṣṭhira's visit to hell and ascent to heaven in Book 18 of the Mahābhārata (see above, p. 374 f.) seems to me but a poor imitation of the Vipaścit legend. The very fact that Yudhiṣṭhira only has a vision (māyā) of hell, shows a considerable falling-off. In the Pātāla-Khaṇḍa of the Padma-Purāṇa (s. *Wilson*, Works, III, p. 49 f., not in the ĀnSS edition) King Janaka goes to hell as a matter of form, because he has struck a cow, and he releases the damned souls in a similar fashion. A Jewish fairy-tale tells of a selfless man who spent his whole life in succouring the distressed, and after his death refused to go to Paradise because there was nobody there in need of aid; he prefers to go to hell, where there are creatures with whom he can feel sympathy and whom he can help. (I. L. *Perez*, Volkstümliche Erzählungen, p. 24 ff.). The original source of all these legends is probably to be found in a Buddhist Mahāyāna legend of the Bodhisattva Avalokiteśvara.

[2]) The name signifies the " not jealous one."

ill to go, his faithful wife takes him on her back, in order to carry him there. He then accidentally touches a saint with his foot, and the latter curses him that he shall die ere the sun rises. Then Anasūyā says: "The sun shall not rise." In consequence of her devotion the sun actually does not rise, which causes the gods great embarrassment, as they receive no sacrifices. There remains nothing but for them to arrange that the charming husband of Anasūyā remains alive.

Just as in the Mahābhārata, so here too, there are besides legends purely didactic dialogues upon the duties of the householder, upon Śrāddhas, upon conduct in the daily life, upon the regular sacrifices, feasts and ceremonies,[1] and also (Chapts. 36-43) a treatise upon Yoga.

A work complete in itself, which doubtless was only later inserted into the Mārkaṇḍeya-Purāṇa, though not later than the 6th century A. D., is the *Devīmāhātmya*,[2] a glorification of the goddess Durgā, who, till the most recent times, has been worshipped with human sacrifices. In the temples of this terrible goddess the Devīmāhātmya is read daily, and at the great feast of Durgā (Durgāpūja)[3] in Bengal it is recited with the greatest of solemnity.

---

[1] Chapters 29-35. The chapter on Śrāddhas partly agrees literally with the *Gautamasmṛti*, according to W. *Caland*, Altindischer Ahnenkult, Leyden 1893, p. 112.

[2] Chapts. 81-93. Edited and translated into Latin by L. *Poley*, Berolini 1831. Translated into English by *Pargiter*, Mārkaṇḍeya-P. Transl., pp. 465-523; Extracts rendered in French by *Burnouf* (JA 4, 1824, p. 24 ff.). As an independent work, also with the titles Caṇḍī, Caṇḍīmāhātmya, Durgāmāhātmya and Saptaśatī, it occurs in innumerable MSS., and has often been printed in India, sometimes with a Bengali translation. On the numerous translations in Bengali, s. D. Ch. *Sen*, Bengali Language and Literature, p. 225 ff. There are also many commentaries on the text, s. *Aufrecht*, CC. I, p. 261. One MS. of the Devīmāhātmya is dated 998 A.D., and the work probably originated even earlier than the 7th century, for a verse from the Devīmāhātmya seems to have been quoted in an inscription of the year 608 A.D. (D. R. *Bhandarkar*, JBRAS 23, 1909, p. 73 f.); and Bāṇa's poem "Caṇḍīśataka" is perhaps based on the Devīmāhātmya; Cf. G. P. *Quackenbos*, The Sanskrit Poems of Mayūra...together with the Text and Translation of Bāṇa's Caṇḍīśataka, New York 1917, pp. 249 ff., 297; *Farquhar*, Outline, p. 150; *Pargiter*, Mārkaṇḍeya-P., Transl., pp. xii, xx.

[3] On this most popular of all religious festivals in Bengal cf. Shib Chunder *Bose*, The Hindoos as they are, p. 92 ff.

VIII. The *Āgneya-* or *Agni-Purāṇa,*[1] so called because it is supposed to have been communicated to Vasiṣṭha by Agni. It describes the incarnations (Avatāras) of Viṣṇu, among them also those as Rāma and Kṛṣṇa, where it confessedly follows the Rāmāyaṇa, Mahābhārata and Harivaṃśa. Although it commences with Viṣṇu, gives directions for the ritual of the Viṣṇu-cult and contains a Dvādaśasahasrī-Stotra to Viṣṇu (Chapt. 48), it is yet essentially a Śivaite work and deals in detail with the mystic cult of the Liṅga and of Durgā. It also mentions Tantric rites, gives instructions for the production of images of gods and their consecration, and refers to the cult of Gaṇeśa (Chapt. 71) and the sun-cult (Chapt. 73). A few chapters (368-370) treat of death and transmigration and Yoga (371-379), Chapt. 380 contains a summary of the doctrines of the Bhagavadgītā, and Chapt. 381 a Yamagītā. But the cosmological, genealogical and geographical sections peculiar to the Purāṇas are not missing. The especially distinctive feature of this Purāṇa is, however, its encyclopædic character. It actually deals with anything and everything. We find sections on geography, astronomy and astrology, on marriage and death customs, on omina and portenta, house building and other usages of daily life, and also on politics (nīti) and the art of war, on law (in which it is closely connected with the law-book of Yājñavalkya), on medicine, metrics, poetry, and even on grammar and lexicography.

To which age this remarkable encyclopædia or its separate parts belong, it is impossible to say. In spite of the fact that the work itself contains so much that is heterogeneous, there are still many Māhātmyas and similar texts which claim to belong to the Agni-Purāṇa, but do not occur in the manuscripts of the work itself.

---

1) Editions in Bibl. Ind. 1873-1879, and ĀnSS No. 41, translation by M. N. *Dutt*, Calcutta, 1901. It is also called Vahni-Purāṇa. There is, however, also an Upapurāṇa with the same title, s. *Eggeling*, Ind. Off. Cat. VI, p. 1294 ff.

IX. The *Bhaviṣya* or *Bhaviṣyat-Purāṇa.* The title signifies a work which contains prophecies regarding the future (bhaviṣya). However, the text which has come down to us in manuscript under this title is certainly not the ancient work which is quoted in the Āpastambīya-Dharma-sūtra.[1] The account of the Creation which it contains, is borrowed from the law-book of *Manu,* which is also otherwise frequently used.[2] The greater part of the work deals with the brahmanical ceremonies and feasts, the duties of the castes, and so on. Only a few legends are related. A description of the Nāgapañcamī-feast, dedicated to the worship of snakes, gives an opening for an enumeration of the snake-demons and for the narration of some snake-myths. A considerable section deals with the sun-worship in "Śākadvīpa" (land of the Scythians ?) in which sun-priests named *Bhojaka* and *Maga* are mentioned, and which undoubtedly is related to the Zoroastrian sun and fire cult.[3]

The *Bhaviṣyottara-Purāṇa,* which, though it contains a few ancient myths and legends, is more a handbook of religious rites, is a sort of continuation of this Purāṇa.

Very numerous are the Māhātmyas and other modern texts which claim to be parts of the Bhaviṣya and especially of the Bhaviṣyottara-Purāṇa.

X. The *Brahmavaivarta-* or *Brahmakaivarta-Purāṇa.*[4]

---

[1]) See above, p. 519 f. There is still less claim to authenticity for the edition of the Bhaviṣya-Purāṇa which appeared in Bombay in 1897 in the Srīveṅkata Press, and which Th. *Aufrecht* (ZDMG 57, 1903, p. 276 ff.) has unmasked as a "literary fraud."

[2]) Cf. *Wilson,* Works, VI, p. lxiii; G. *Bühler,* SBE Vol. 25, p. cx f.; 78 n; W. *Jahn,* Ueber die kosmogonischen Grundanschauungen in Mānava-Dharma-Śāstram, p. 38 ff.

[3]) Cf. *Aufrecht,* Bodl. Cat., p. 31 ff.; *Wilson,* Works, X, p. 381 ff. We learn from an inscription written in 861 A.D., by one Maga Mātṛrava, that the Magas lived in Rājputāna as early as in the 9th century. "Maga" is a name for the Śākadvīpa Brahmins, who at the present day are still living in the district of Jôdhpur, and trace their history back to the Sūrya-Purāṇa and the Bhaviṣya-Purāṇa. See D. R. *Bhandarkar,* Ep. Ind. IX, p. 279.

[4]) Editions published at Calcutta 1887 and 1888. English translation in SBH,

The latter is the name current in Southern India. This extensive work is divided into four books. The first book, the Brahma-Khaṇḍa, deals with the creation by Brahman, the First Being, who is, however, none other than the god Kṛṣṇa.[1] Many legends, especially about the sage Nārada, are included. One chapter (16) contains a treatise on medicine. The second book, the Prakṛti-Khaṇḍa, deals with Prakṛti, the original matter, which, however, here seems to be conceived quite mythologically, resolving itself, at the command of Kṛṣṇa, into five goddesses (Durgā, Lakṣmī, Sarasvatī, Sāvitrī and Rādhā). The third book, the Gaṇeśa-Khaṇḍa, relates legends of the elephant-headed god Gaṇeśa, who is unknown to the oldest Indian pantheon, but is one of the most popular of the more modern Indian deities.[2] In a very curious way Gaṇeśa is here represented as a kind of incarnation of Kṛṣṇa. The last and most extensive book, the Kṛṣṇajanma-Khaṇḍa, "section of the birth of Kṛṣṇa," deals not only with the birth, but with the whole life of Kṛṣṇa, especially his battles and his love adventures with the cowherdesses (gopīs). It is the chief part of the whole Purāṇa, which throughout pursues no other object than to glorify the god *Kṛṣṇa* and his favourite wife Rādhā, in myths, legends and hymns. Rādhā is here Kṛṣṇa's Śakti.[3] According to this Purāṇa, Kṛṣṇa is so much the god above all gods, that

---

Brahmavaivarta-purani specimen ed. by A. F. *Stenzler*, Berolini, 1829. A detailed analysis of the work by *Wilson*, Works, III, p. 91 ff.

[1]) The title Brahmavaivarta-P, which can be translated "Purāṇa of the transformations of Brahman," probably refers to this. The Southern Indian title is not intelligible to me.

[2]) B. C. *Masumdar* says that he has proved in the Bengali journal Vangadarśana, "that the worship of Gaṇeśa 'as an affiliated son of Pārvatī was wholly unknown to the Hindus previous to the 6th century A. D." (JBRAS 23, 1909, p. 82.)

[3]) Nimbārka, probably in the 12th century, regards Rādhā as the eternal consort of Kṛṣṇa, who, in his view, is not merely an incarnation of Viṣṇu, but the eternal Brahman (Cf. *Farquhar*, Outline, p. 237 ff.) It was not until the 16th century that the sect of the Rādhāvallabhis, who attach great importance to the worship of Rādhā as Śakti, arose. s. *Grierson*, ERE X, p. 559 f.; *Farquhar*, l. c. p. 318.

legends are related in which not only Brahman and Śiva, but even Viṣṇu himself, are humiliated by Kṛṣṇa.

A large number of Māhātmyas claim to belong to this Purāṇa, which is altogether a rather inferior production.

XI. The *Laiṅga-* or *Liṅga-Purāṇa.*[1] The principal theme of the work is the worship of Śiva in his various forms, but especially in the Liṅga symbol.[2] There is a somewhat confused account of the legend of the origin of the Liṅga-cult: on the occasion of Śiva's visit to the Devadāru forest, the hermits' wives fall in love with the god, who is cursed by the Munis.[3] In the account of the creation Śiva occupies the position which is otherwise ascribed to Viṣṇu. Corresponding to the Avatāras of Viṣṇu, legends of twenty-eight incarnations of Śiva are told in the Liṅga-Purāṇa. Some passages show the influence of the Tantras; [4] this fact, and the character of the work as a manual for the use of Śiva-worshippers would seem to indicate that it can scarcely be a very ancient work.

XII. The *Vārāha-* or *Varāha-Purāṇa.*[5] The work owes its title to the fact that it is related to the goddess

---

[1]) Editions have been published in Calcutta, Bombay, Poona and Madras, also with a commentary.

[2]) The Liṅga (the phallus), generally in the form of a small stone column, is for the worshippers of Śiva only a symbol of the productive and creative principle of Nature as embodied in Śiva; and it is worshipped by simple offerings of leaves and flowers and the pouring of water. The Liṅga cult certainly bears no trace of any phallic cult of an obscene nature. Cf. H. H. *Wilson*, Works, Vol. VI, p. lxix; *Monier-Williams*, Brāhmanism and Hinduism, 4th Ed., London 1891, pp. 83, 90 f.; *Eliot*, Hinduism and Buddhism, II, 142 ff. The Liṅga cult can be traced in Cambodia and Champa as early as about 550 A. D.; s. *Eliot*, l. c. p. 143 note 3.

[3]) I, 28-33, translated into German by W. *Jahn*, ZDMG 69, 1915, pp. 539 ff. The same legend also occurs in other Purāṇas, s. Jahn, l. c. pp. 529 ff.; 70, 1916, p. 301 ff. and 71, 1917, 167 ff.

[4]) Cf. *Farquhar*, Outline, p. 195 f.

[5]) Ed. by *Hrishīkeśa Śāstrī*, Bibl. Ind. 1893. According to 218, 1 the Purāṇa was "written" by Mādhava Bhaṭṭa and Vīreśvara in Benares in the year 1621 of the Vikrama era (1564 A. D.). However, this cannot be the date of the work itself, but only of a copy of it.

Earth (Pṛthivī) by Viṣṇu in his incarnation as a wild boar (varāha). Though it contains brief allusions to the creation, the genealogies, etc., it is not a Purāṇa in the ancient sense of the word, but rather a manual of prayers and rules for the Viṣṇu-worshippers. In spite of the Viṣṇuite character of the work, it yet contains a few legends relating to Śiva and Durgā. Several chapters are devoted to the Mothers and the female deities (Chapts. 90-95). We find the story of the birth of Gaṇeśa, followed by a Gaṇeśa-stotra. Furthermore, it deals with Śrāddhas (Chapt. 13 ff.), Prāyaścittas (Chapt. 119 ff.), the erection of images of the gods (Chapt. 181 ff.), etc. A considerable section (Chapts. 152-168) is nothing but a Mathurā-Māhātmya, a glorification of the sacred city which is Kṛṣṇa's birthplace. Another considerable section (Chapts. 193-212) tells the legend of Naciketas, but the narrator is more concerned with the description of heaven and hell than with the philosophical ideas contained in the ancient poem in the Kaṭha-Upaniṣad.[1]

XIII. The *Skānda-* or *Skanda-Purāṇa.* This Purāṇa is named after Skanda, son of Śiva and commander of the celestial armies, who is said to have related it and proclaimed Śivaite doctrines in it.[2] The ancient Purāṇa of this name, however, is probably entirely lost ; for though there is a considerable number of more or less extensive works claiming to be Saṃhitās and Khaṇḍas of the Skanda-Purāṇa, and an almost overwhelming mass of Māhātmyas which give themselves out as portions of this Purāṇa, [3] only one, very ancient, manuscript contains a text which calls itself simply " Skanda-

---

[1]) See above, p. 261 f. Cf. L. *Scherman*, Visionslitteratur, p. 11 f. The name is Nāciketa here, as in the Mahābhārata XIII, 71.

[2]) Matsya-P. 53, 42 f. The length of the Skanda-P. is here, as elsewhere, stated as 81,100 ślokas. In Padma-P., VI, 263, 81 f., too, the Skanda-P. is counted as among the " tāmasa," *i.e.* the Śivaite Purāṇas.

[3]) Cf. *Eggeling*, Ind. Off. Cat. VI, pp. 1319-1389.

Purāṇa." [1] Even this text, however, is scarcely identical with the ancient Purāṇa : for, though it contains all manner of legends of Śiva, especially of his battles with Andhaka and other demons, a few chapters on the hells and Saṃsāra, and a section on Yoga, there is hardly anything in it that corresponds to the "five characteristics" of a Purāṇa.[2] Texts which are considered as belonging to the Skanda-Purāṇa inform us [3] that there are six Saṃhitās, namely Sanatkumarīyā, Sūta, Brāhmī, Vaiṣṇavī, Śāṅkarī and Saurī Saṃhitā, and fifty Khaṇḍas of the Skanda-Purāṇa. The Sūta-Saṃhitā is a work of some bulk.[4] It consists of four Khaṇḍas, the first of which is devoted wholly to the worship of Śiva. The second section (jñānayogakhaṇḍa) deals not only with Yoga, but also with the duties of the castes and Āśramas. The third section teaches ways and means of attaining salvation; and the fourth section begins with rules about Vedic-brahmanical ceremonies, and then deals with "the sacrifice of meditation" and "the sacrifice of knowledge," as well as with devotion to Śiva (Śiva-bhakti). A second part contains a Śivaite Brahmagītā and a Vedāntist Sūtagītā. The Sanatkumāra-Saṃhitā, too, contains Śivaite legends, more especially relating to the sacred places of Benares.[5] The Saura-Saṃhitā, which is supposed to have been revealed to Yājñavalkya

---

[1]) This is the old manuscript in Gupta script, which was discovered in Nepal by *Haraprasād Śāstrī*, and has been assigned to the 7th century A. D. by him and C. *Bendall* on palaeographical grounds. See Haraprasād Śāstrī, Catalogue of Palm Leaf and Selected Paper MSS. belonging to the Durbar Library, Nepal, Calcutta 1905, pp. lii, 141 ff.

[2]) According to the short table of contents given by *Haraprasād*, l. c. As no khaṇḍa is named in the colophons of the MS., Haraprasād considers the text to be the original Skanda-P. The supposition that it might be the Ambikā-Khaṇḍa (Haraprasād, Report I, p. 4), turned out to be erroneous. The Ambikā-khaṇḍa (*Eggeling*, l. c. p. 1321 ff.) contains a collection of legends about Śiva and Durgā, told by Sanatkumāra to Vyāsa.

[3]) *Eggeling*, l. c., pp. 1321, 1362.

[4]) Ed. with the commentary of Mādhavācārya in ĀnSS No. 25, 1893 in 3 vols.

[5]) The Sahyādri-khaṇḍa (publ. by J. G. da *Cunha*, Bombay 1877) belongs to the Sanatkumāra-saṃhitā. Cf. *Eggeling*, l. c., p. 1369 ff. The Veṅkaṭeśa-Māhātmya of the

by the sun-god, contains chiefly cosmogonic theories. The Śaṅkara-Saṃhitā is also called Agastya-Saṃhitā, because Skanda is supposed to have communicated it to Agastya. It is doubtful, however, whether this is the Agastya-Saṃhitā which teaches the cult of Viṣṇu especially in his incarnation as Rāma.[1] There is a Kāśī-Khaṇḍa,[2] dealing with the Śiva-temples in the neighbourhood of Benares and with the sanctity of this city itself. A Gaṅgāsahasranāman, a litany of the "thousand names of the Ganges" belongs to the same section. The above-mentioned are only a few of the many texts which are said to belong to this Purāṇa.

XIV. The *Vāmana-Purāṇa.*[3] This Purāṇa, too, has not come down to us in its original form, for the five themes of the Purāṇas, *i.e.* Creation, etc., are scarcely mentioned, and the information given in the Matsya-Purāṇa[4] as to the contents and length of the work does not tally with our text. The text begins with an account of the incarnation of Viṣṇu as a dwarf (vāmana), whence it takes its name. Several chapters deal with the Avatāras of Viṣṇu in general.[5] On the other hand, a considerable section

---

Sahyādri-khaṇḍa, a glorification of the temple of Mañjgunī, is translated by G. K. *Betham*, Ind. Ant. 24, 1895, pp. 231 ff. The same khaṇḍa probably also includes the Ṛṣyaśṛṅga-legend, which was transformed into a local legend, and which has been translated by V. N. *Narasimmiyengar* (Ind. Ant. 2, 1873, pp. 140 ff.).

[1]) Cf. *Eggeling*, l. c., p. 1319 ff.; 1321. In the Śivarahasya-khaṇḍa of the Śaṅkara-saṃhitā (Eggeling l. c., p. 1363 f.) the 18 Purāṇas are enumerated, of which ten (Śaiva, Bhaviṣya, Mārkaṇḍeya, Laiṅga, Vārāha, Skānda, Mātsya, Kaurma, Vāmana, Brahmāṇḍa) are declared to be Śivaite, four (Vaiṣṇava, Bhāgavata, Nāradīya, Gāruḍa) Viṣṇuite, whilst Brāhma and Pādma are said to be dedicated to Brahman, Āgneya to Agni, Brahmavaivarta to Savitṛ. It is added, however, that the Viṣṇuite Purāṇas teach the identity of Śiva and Viṣṇu, and the Brahma-P., the identity of Brahman, Viṣṇu and Śiva.

[2]) Published (with commentaries) in Benares, 1868, Calcutta 1873-80 and Bombay 1881.

[3]) Published, with Bengali translation, Calcutta, 1885.

[4]) 53, 45 f. Cf. *Wilson*, Works, Vol. VI, p. lxxiv f.

[5]) According to *Aufrecht* (Bodl. Cat. p. 46) these chapters (24-32) are mainly taken from the Matsya-P.

deals with Liṅga-worship, and in connection with the glorification of sacred places, the Śivaite legends of the marriage of Śiva and Umā, the origin of Gaṇeśa and the birth of Kārttikeya are related.

XV. The *Kaurma-* or *Kūrma-Purāṇa.* In the work itself we read that it consists of four Saṃhitās, namely Brāhmī, Bhāgavatī, Saurī and Vaiṣṇavī; but the Brāhmī-Saṃhitā is the only one which has come down under the title "Kūrma-Purāṇa."[1] This work begins with a hymn to the incarnation of Viṣṇu as a tortoise (kūrma) on which the mountain Mandara rested when the ocean was twirled. At that time Lakṣmī arose from the ocean and became Viṣṇu's consort. When the Ṛṣis ask him who this goddess is, Viṣṇu replies that she is his highest Śakti. The Introduction then relates further how Indradyumna, who in a former birth had been a king, but was born again as a Brahman by reason of his devotion to Viṣṇu, desired to gain knowledge of the glory of Śiva. Lakṣmī refers him to Viṣṇu. Then he worships Viṣṇu as the Universal God, the Creator and Preserver of the universe, but also as "Mahādeva," "Śiva" and as "father and mother of all beings." At length Viṣṇu, in his incarnation as the tortoise, imparts the Purāṇa to him. As in this Introduction, Śiva is the Highest Being throughout the work, but it is emphasized over and over again that in reality Brahman, Viṣṇu and Śiva are one.[2] The worship of *Sakti, i.e.* "Energy" or "Creative force" conceived as a female deity, is also emphasized. Devī, the "Highest Goddess" (Parameśvarī), the consort and Śakti of Śiva, is praised under 8,000 names.[3] In like manner as Viṣṇu is none other than

---

[1]) Published by Nīlmaṇi *Mukhopādhyāya* in Bibl. Ind. 1890. It contains 6,000 ślokas. According to the statements made in the Bhāgavata- ., Vāyu-P. and Matsya-P., the Kūrma-P. contains 17,000 or 18,000 ślokas.

[2]) In I, 6 (p. 56) Brahman is worshipped as Trimūrti. I, 9 especially inculcates the unity of the three gods. Cf. also I, 26.

[3]) I, 11 and 12. Śiva divides himself into two parts, a male and a female, the

Śiva, Lakṣmī, Viṣṇu's śakti, is in reality not apart from the Devī.[1] When the sons of Kārttavīrya, some of whom worshipped Viṣṇu and the others Śiva, could not agree as to which god was the more worthy of worship, the seven Ṛṣis decided the dispute by declaring that the deity worshipped by any man is that man's deity, and that all the gods deserve the worship of at least some beings.[2] Notwithstanding, Śiva is the god above all gods to such a degree that, though Kṛṣṇa is praised as Viṣṇu Nārāyaṇa, he obtains a son for his wife Jāmbavatī only after strenuous asceticism and by the mercy of Śiva.[3] Moreover, in spite of the tolerance as regards the recognition of all the gods, there are allusions in several places to the false doctrines which have been sent into the world to deceive mankind, and to false manuals which will come into existence during the Kaliyuga.[4]

The five themes of the Purāṇas, namely the Creation, the genealogies, etc., are also treated in the Kūrma-Purāṇa, and in this connection a few of Viṣṇu's Avatāras are touched upon. However, an entire chapter (I. 53) is devoted to the incarnations of Śiva. A considerable section of the first part consists of a description and glorification of the holy places of Benares (Kāśīmāhātmya) and Allahabad (Prayāgamāhātmya). The second part begins with an *Īśvaragītā* (a counterpart to the Bhagavadgītā), teaching the knowledge of God,

---

former gives rise to the Rudras, and the latter to the Śaktis. Cf. *Farquhar*, Outline, p. 195 f.

1) I, 17 (p. 206 f.) Prahlāda praises Viṣṇu and Lakṣmī as Viṣṇu's Śakti.

2) I, 22 (p. 239 ff.).

3) I, 25-27. Here (p. 269) there is also a reference to a Yogaśāstra written by the great Yogin Yājñavalkya, which is perhaps an allusion to the Yājñavalkyagītā, where Yoga is taught. Cf. F. E. *Hall*, A Contribution towards an Index to the Bibliography of the Indian Philosophical Systems, Calcutta 1859, p. 14. In I, 26 Kṛṣṇa recommends the Liṅga cult and explains its origin.

4) This appellation is given to the Śivaite sects and Śāstras of the Kāpālas, Bhairavas, Yāmalas, Vāmas, Ārhatas, Nākulas (*i.e.* Lākulīśa-Pāśupata, cf. *Bhandarkar*, Vaiṣṇavism etc., p. 116 f.), Pāśupatas and the Viṣṇuite Pāñcarātra : I, 12; 16; 30 (pp. 137, 184, 305). The Vāmas or "left-hand ones," are those Śakti worshippers whose cult is connected with orgiastic rites. See below in the chapter on the Tantras.

i.e. Śiva, through meditation. This piece is followed by a Vyāsagītā, a larger section in which Vyāsa teaches the attainment of the highest knowledge through pious works and ceremonies, and therefore delivers a lecture on the duties of the householder, the forest-hermit and the ascetic. A few chapters deal with expiatory ceremonies for all sorts of crimes, where there is also mention of chastity. This gives rise to the narration of a story of Sītā (not occurring in the Rāmāyaṇa), how she is rescued from the hands of Rāvaṇa by the fire-god.

XVI. The *Mātsya* or *Matsya-Purāṇa.*[1] This, again, is one of the older works of the Purāṇa literature, or at least one of those which have preserved most of the ancient text, and do fair justice to the definition of a "Purāṇa." It commences with the story of the great *flood* out of which Viṣṇu, in the form of a fish (matsya) saves only Manu alone. While the ship in which Manu is sailing along is being drawn through the flood by the fish, there takes place between him and Viṣṇu, incarnated as a fish, the conversation which forms the substance of the Purāṇa. Creation is treated in detail, then follow the genealogies, into which is inserted a section about the Fathers and their cult (Chapts. 14-22). Neither are the usual geographical, astronomical and chronological sections, absent, and, according to V. A. *Smith* (see above, p. 524) the lists of kings in this Purāṇa are particularly reliable for the Andhra dynasty. It has very much in common with the Mahābhārata and the Harivaṃśa; thus the legends of Yayāti (Chapts. 24-43), Sāvitrī (Chapts. 208-214), the incarnations of Viṣṇu (Chapts. 161-179, 244-248); and there is often literal agreement. There are, however, very numerous later additions and interpolations. For instance we find a considerable

---

[1]) Published in ĀnSS No. 54. (The quotations are given according to this edition.) Translated into English in SBH. Vol. 17. The edition has 291 adhyāyas, but the MS. described by *Aufrecht*, Bodl. Cat., p. 38 ff., has only 278.

section about all manner of festivals and rites (Vratas, Chapts. 54-102), a glorification of the sacred places of Allahabad (Prayāgamāhātmya, Chapts. 103-112), Benares (Vārāṇasi= and Avimuktamāhātmya, Chapts. 180-185), and of the river Narmadā (Chapts. 186-194); then sections on the duties of a king (Chapts. 215-227), on omina and portenta (Chapts. 228-238), ceremonies at the building of a house (Chapts. 252-257), the erection and dedication of statues of deities, temples and palaces (Chapts. 258-270), the sixteen kinds of pious donations (Chapts. 274-289), etc. As far as the religious content is concerned, the Matsya-Purāṇa might be called Śivaite with just as much reason as it is classed as Viṣṇuite. Religious festivals of the Vaiṣṇavas are described side by side with those of the Śaivas, and both Viṣṇu and Śiva-legends are related. In Chapter 13 Devī ("the Goddess," Śiva's wife Gaurī) enumerates to Dakṣa the one hundred and eight names by which she wishes to be glorified. It is obvious that both sects used the work as a sacred book.

XVII. The *Gāruḍa-* or *Garuḍa-Purāṇa.*[1] This is a Viṣṇuite Purāṇa. It takes its name from the mythical bird Garuḍa, to whom it was revealed by Viṣṇu himself, and who then imparted it to Kaśyapa. It treats some of the five themes, *viz.* Creation, the ages of the world, the genealogies of the solar and lunar dynasties; but far more attention is given to the worship of Viṣṇu, to descriptions of Viṣṇuite rites and festivals (Vratas), to expiatory ceremonies (Prāyaścittas) and glorifications of sacred places. It is also cognisant of Śakti-worship, and gives rules for the worship of the "five gods" (Viṣṇu, Śiva, Durgā, Sūrya and Gaṇeśa).[2] Moreover, like the Agni-Purāṇa, it is a kind of encyclopaedia, in which the most diversified subjects are dealt with: thus,

---

[1]) Published by Jibānanda *Vidyāsāgara*, Calcutta 1890. English translation by Manmatha Nāth *Dutt*, Calcutta 1908 (Wealth of India, Vol. VIII).

[2]) Cf. *Farquhar*, Outline, p. 178 f.

the contents of the Rāmāyaṇa, the Mahābhārata and the Harivaṃśa are retold, and there are sections on cosmography, astronomy and astrology, omina and portenta, chiromancy, medicine, metrics, grammar, knowledge of precious stones (ratnaparīkṣā) and politics (nīti). A considerable portion of the Yājñavalkya-Dharmaśāstra has been included in the Garuḍa-Purāṇa.

What is counted as the Uttarakhaṇḍa or "second part" of the Garuḍa-Purāṇa is the *Pretakalpa*, a voluminous though entirely unsystematic work, which treats of everything connected with death, the dead and the beyond. In motley confusion and with many repetitions, we find doctrines on the fate of the soul after death, Karman, rebirth and release from rebirth, on desire as the cause of Saṃsāra, on omens of death, the path to Yama, the fate of the Pretas (*i.e.*, the departed who still hover about the earth as spirits, and have not as yet found the way to the world beyond), the torments of the hells, and the Pretas as causing evil omens and dreams. Interspersed we find rules of all kinds about rites to be performed at the approach of death, the treatment of the dying and of the corpse, funeral rites and ancestor-worship, the especial funeral sacrifices for a Satī, *i.e.*, a woman who enters the funeral pyre with her husband. Here and there we also find legends recalling the Buddhist Petavatthu, telling of encounters with Pretas who relate the cause of their wretched existence (sins which they committed during their lifetime).[1] An "extract" (*Sāroddhāra*) of this work was made by *Naunidhirāma*.[2] In spite of its title, this work

[1]) A detailed analysis of the contents of the Pretakalpa is given by E. *Abegg*, Der Pretakalpa des Garuḍa-Purāṇa (Naunidhirāma's Sāroddhāra). Eine Darstellung des hinduistischen Totenkultes und Jenseitsglaubens ...... übersetzt... Berlin und Leipzig 1921, p. 8 ff.; chapters X-XII translated p. 229 ff.

[2]) This Sāroddhāra was published under the title "Garuḍa-Purāṇa" in Bombay NSP in 1903 and with an English translation by E. *Wood* and S. V. *Subrahmaṇyam* in SBH, Vol. IX, 1911. There is a good German translation by *Abegg*, Pretakalpa etc. (s. the preceding Note).

is not a mere extract from the Pretakalpa, for the author also utilised material from other Purāṇas, and treated the subject more systematically. Among other works he drew on the Bhāgavata-Purāṇa, whence it follows that he was later than this Purāṇa.

Among the Māhātmyas which claim to be parts of the Garuḍa-Purāṇa, especial mention should be made of a Gayā-māhātmya in praise of Gayā, the place of pilgrimage, where it is particularly meritorious to perform Srāddhas.

XVIII. The *Brahmāṇḍa-Purāṇa.*[1] In the list in the Kūrma-Purāṇa the eighteenth Purāṇa is called "Vāyavīya Brahmāṇḍa," the "Purāṇa of the Brahman-egg proclaimed by Vāyu," and it is possible that the original Brahmāṇḍa was but an earlier version of the Vāyu-Purāṇa.[2] According to the Matsya-Purāṇa (53, 55f.) it is said to have been proclaimed by Brahman, and to contain a glorification of the Brahman-egg[3] as well as a detailed account of the future kalpas in 12,200 ślokas. It appears, however, that the original work of this name is lost, for our manuscripts for the most part contain only Māhātmyas, Stotras and Upākhyānas which claim to be parts of the Brahmāṇḍa.

The *Adhyātma-Rāmāyaṇa,*[4] *i.e.,* "the Rāmāyaṇa in

[1]) Published in Bombay, Śrī-Veṅkateśvara Press, 1906.

[2]) Cf. *Pargiter,* Anc. Ind. Hist. Trad., p. 77 f. H. H. *Wilson* (Works, Vol. VI, p. lxxxv f.) mentions a MS. of the Brahmāṇḍa-P. the first part of which agrees almost entirely with the Vāyu-P., whilst the second part is dedicated to Lalitā Devī, a form of Durgā, and teaches her worship by Tantric rites. On the island of Bali a Brahmāṇḍa-P. is the only sacred book of the local Śiva-worshippers. Cf. R. *Friederich,* JRAS 1876, p. 170 f.; *Weber,* Ind. Stud. II, p. 131 f.

[3]) Even the Brāhmaṇas and Upaniṣads already tell of the golden egg out of which the universe was created. Cf. Satapatha-Br. XI, 1, 6 (above p. 223) and Chāndogya-Upaniṣad III, 9, 1. According to the cosmogony of the Purāṇas Brahman (or Viṣṇu in the form of Brahman) dwells in the egg in which the whole of the universe is locked up, and out of which it unfolds itself by the will of the Creator. Cf. Viṣṇu-P. I, 2: Vāyu-P. 4, 76 ff.; Manu I, 9 ff.

[4]) There are numerous Indian editions (the Bombay NSP 1891 edition is recommended) and several commentaries, among them one by Śaṅkara. English translation by Lāla Baij *Nath* in SBH 1913.

which Rāma is the Supreme Ātman," in which Advaita (the monism of the Vedānta) and Rāma-bhakti are taught as paths to salvation, is a very well known book, which is considered as a part of the Brahmāṇḍa-Purāṇa. As in the case of Vālmīki's poem, the work is divided into seven books, bearing the same titles as in the ancient epic; but it is only an epic in its external form—in reality it is a manual of devotion, Tantric in character. Like the Tantras it is in the form of a dialogue between Śiva and his wife Umā. Throughout the work Rāma is essentially the god Viṣṇu, and the Sītā who is abducted by Rāvaṇa is only an illusion, whilst the real Sītā, who is identical with Lakṣmī and Prakṛti, does not appear until after the fire ordeal at the end of the book. The Rāmahṛdaya (I, 1) and the Rāmagītā (VII, 5) are texts which are memorised by the devotees of Rāma. The fact that the Marathi poet-saint Eknātha, who lived in the 16th century, calls it a modern work, proves that the work cannot be very ancient.[1)]

The *Nāsiketopākhyāna*, which also claims to be a part of the Brahmāṇḍa-Purāṇa, is nothing but a most insipid, amplified and corrupted version of the beautiful old legend of Naciketas.[2)]

As regards the *Upapurāṇas*, they do not in general differ essentially from the Purāṇas, except inasmuch as they are even more exclusively adapted to suit the purposes of local cult and the religious needs of separate sects. Those of the Upapurāṇas which claim to be supplements to one or other of the "great Purāṇas" have already received mention. We shall now only refer to a few of the more important among the other Upapurāṇas.

---

1) Cf. *Bhandarkar*, Vaiṣṇavism etc., p. 48; *Farquhar*, Outline, p. 250 f.

2) Cf. F. *Belloni-Filippi* in GSAI 16, 1903 and 17, 1904: *Eggeling*, Ind. Off. Cat. VI, p. 1252 ff.

The *Viṣṇudharmottara* is occasionally given out as a part of a Purāṇa, namely the Garuḍa-Purāṇa, but generally it is counted as an independent Upapurāṇa. It is repeatedly quoted by Albērūnī as the "Viṣṇudharma."[1] It is a Kashmiri Vaiṣṇava book of encyclopædic character in three sections. Section I deals with the usual themes of the Purāṇas: the Creation of the world, cosmology, geography, astronomy, division of time, genealogies, Stotras, rules about Vratas and Śrāddhas.[2] Among the genealogical legends, that of Purūravas and Urvaśī is also related—more or less in agreement with Kālidāsa's drama. Section II deals with law and politics, but also with medicine, the science of war, astronomy and astrology. There is here a prose section with the special title "Paitāmaha-Siddhānta." If, as is probable, this is an extract from the Brahma-Sphuṭa-Siddhānta written by Brahmagupta in 628 A.D., the Viṣṇudharmottara must have been compiled between 628 and 1000 A.D.[3] Section III, too, is of a very miscellaneous character, treating of grammar, lexicography, metrics and poetics, dancing, singing and music, sculpture and painting (the making of images of gods)[4] and architecture (construction of temples).

The *Bṛhad-Dharma-Purāṇa*,[5] "the Great Purāṇa of

---

1) Edition of the text in Bombay, Śrī-Veṅkateśvara Press 1912. Analysis of the contents according to Kashmiri MSS. and a comparison with the quotations of Albērūnī by G. *Bühler*, Ind. Ant. 19, 1890, p. 382 ff. According to Bühler, Albērūnī used two separate works with the same title, and mixed the two together. *Eggeling*, Ind. Off. Cat. VI, p. 1308 f., describes a MS. which contains six chapters more than the edition. In the MS. the title of the work is "Viṣṇudharmāḥ."

2) As regards the Śrāddhas, W. *Caland*, Altindischer Ahnenkult, Leyden 1893, pp. 68, 112, has traced connections with the Viṣṇu-Smṛti. Cf. *Abegg*, Der Pretakalpa, p. 5 f.

3) Cf. G. *Thibaut*, Astronomie etc. (Grundriss III, 9), p. 58. The commentators of Brahmagupta's work maintain that this author drew upon the Viṣṇudharmottara. MSS. of the "Viṣṇudharma" are dated 1047 and 1090; see *Haraprasad*, Report I, p. 5.

4) On this extremely interesting section s. Dr. Stella *Kramrisch*, Calcutta Review, Feb. 1924, p. 331 ff. and Journal of Letters, Calcutta University, Vol. XI, 1924.

5) Edited by *Haraprasād Śāstrī* in Bibl. Ind. 1897. The work consists of a "first," "middle" and "last" khaṇḍa.

the Duties," which appears as the eighteenth in a list of the Upapurāṇas,[1] only devotes the beginning of its first section, and its last section to Dharma, with the glorification of which it begins. The greater portion of the first section is in the form of a conversation between the Devī and her two friends Jayā and Vijayā, which gives it a Tantric stamp. In the second section, too, the Devī appears as the Great Goddess, to whom Brahman, Viṣṇu and Śiva come singing her praises, and II, 60 teaches that the universe and all the gods have their existence in Śiva and Śakti. The fact that it is not a Tantra is, however, shown by the contents of the work, which, by reason of its relations with the epic and the legal literature, is deserving of some interest, though the work cannot be a very ancient one.

In the opening chapters the duties towards one's parents, especially the mother, and the Gurus in general, are inculcated in great detail. By way of illustrating the importance of these duties, a legend of a "hunter Tulādhāra" is told, which, though having some reference to the Mahābhārata stories [2] of Dharmavyādha and Tulādhāra, has little in common with them except the name. Then come sections on the Tīrthas, the incarnation of Viṣṇu as Rāma, the story of Sītā and the origin of the Rāmāyaṇa. The latter work is called the root of all Kāvyas, Itihāsas, Purāṇas and Saṃhitās. It was only after Vālmīki had completed this poem at the command of the god Brahman, and had declined to write the Mahābhārata also, that Vyāsa set to work to compile both the Mahābhārata and the Purāṇas.[3] Vālmīki in his hermitage converses with Vyāsa on the composition of the Mahābhārata, which is then praised extravagantly. A prayer, which also contains the titles of the most important Parvans of the Mahābhārata, is recommended as an amulet (I, 30, 41 ff.). The second section consists mainly of legends of the origin of Gaṅgā, but all manner of other myths and legends are interwoven with

---

[1]) In the Bṛhad-Dharma-P. itself (I, 25, 26).

[2]) See above p. 415 ff.

[3]) There is here a list of the 18 Purāṇas and the 18 Upapurāṇas (I, 25, 18 ff.) and also an enumeration of the Dharmaśāstras (I, 29, 24 f.).

them. Among the Avatāras of Viṣṇu, mention is made of those as Kapila, Vālmīki, Vyāsa and Buddha. Śiva sings a song in praise of Viṣṇu.[1] A section of considerable length (II, 54-58) contains rules for the cult of the Ganges (gaṅgādharmāḥ). The legend of the miraculous origin of Gaṇeśa is told in the last chapter (II, 60). The last section deals with the duties of the castes and Āśramas, the duties of women, the adoration of various gods, the festivals of the year, the worship of the sun, the moon and planets, with the Yugas, the origin of evil and wickedness in the world (III, 12) and with the intermixture of castes (III, 13-14).

The *Śiva-Purāṇa*, which is said to consist of no less than twelve Saṃhitās, is one of the most voluminous Upapurāṇas.[2] The *Gaṇeśa-Purāṇa*[3] and the *Caṇḍī-* or *Caṇḍikā-Purāṇa*[4] are also Śivaite Upapurāṇas. The *Sāmba-Purāṇa*[5] is dedicated to the cult of the sun. The deeds of Viṣṇu in the future age at the close of the Kali-Yuga are described in the *Kalki-Purāṇa*.[6] The *Kālikā-Purāṇa*[7] treats of the deeds of the goddess Kālī in her numerous forms, and of the worship dedicated to her. One chapter[8] deals in detail with the animal and human sacrifices which should be offered to her. Curiously enough it also contains a chapter on politics.

The majority of the Māhātmyas which are connected with or included in the Purāṇas and the Upapurāṇas, is, on

---

[1] Śivagānam (II, 44). Previously Nārada delivers a lecture to Viṣṇu on the significance of the Rāgas and Rāgiṇīs in the art of singing.

[2] *Eggeling*, Ind. Off. Cat. VI, p. 1311 ff. Editions of a Śiva-Purāṇa appeared in Bombay (1878, 1880, 1884).

[3] *Aufrecht*, Bodl. Cat., p. 78 f.; *Eggeling* l. c., p. 1199. An edition appeared in Poona in 1876. In the *Maudgala*-P., too (Eggeling, l. c., 1289 ff.), Gaṇeśa is worshipped as the highest deity.

[4] *Eggeling* l. c., p. 1202 ff.

[5] *Eggeling* l. c., p. 1316 ff. A Sāmba-Purāṇa was published in Bombay in 1885.

[6] *Eggeling* l. c., p. 1188 f. Editions have appeared in Calcutta.

[7] *Eggeling* l. c., p. 1189 ff. Edition Bombay, 1891.

[8] The "chapter of blood" (rudhirādhyāya) translated into English by W. C. *Blaquiere* in Asiatick Researches, Vol. 5 (4th ed., London 1807), p. 371 ff.

the whole, inferior literature. They arose as hand-books for the Purohitas of the Tirthas praised in them, and tell legends which in part belong to tradition, and in part are inventions, with the purpose of proving the holiness of these places of pilgrimage. They describe, too, the ceremonies which the pilgrims are to perform and the route they are to follow. For this reason they are not unimportant from the point of view of the topography of India. Thus in particular, the *Nīlamata,*[1] the Kāśmīra-māhātmya, is an important work from the point of view of the history, legendary lore and topography of Kashmir.[2] The Nāga king Nīla is a kind of cultural hero of Kashmir, and the work contains " the doctrines of Nīla " which he imparted to the Brahman Candradeva.[3] It tells the legends of the primeval history of Kashmir (verses 1-481), whereupon there is a description of the ceremonies and festivals prescribed by Nīla. Many of these are the usual Brahmanical and Puranic rites, but we find some which are peculiar to Kashmir. Thus joyous festivals are celebrated with singing, music and drinking bouts at the New Year, on the first of the month Kārtika, on which Kashmir is said to have arisen (v. 561 ff.), and then again on the occasion of the first fall of snow (v. 579 ff.). On the fifteenth day of the bright half of the month Vaiśākha, the birthday of Buddha as an incarnation of Viṣṇu is solemnly celebrated by the Brahmans; a statue of Buddha is erected, Buddhist speeches are made and Buddhist monks are honoured (v. 809 ff.). The historian Kalhaṇa (about 1148 A.D.) drew on the Nīlamata in his Rājataranginī for the ancient history of Kashmir; and he regarded it as a venerable

---

[1]) Nīlamatapurāṇam (Sanskrit Text) edited with Introduction etc. by Ram Lal *Kanjilal* and Pandit Jagad-dhar *Zadoo*, Lahore 1924 (Punjab Sanskrit Series).

[2]) Cf. *Bühler*, Report, p. 37 ff., LV ff.; M. A. *Stein*, Kalhaṇa's Rājataranginī, Translated, I, p. 76 f.; II, p. 376 ff.; Pandit Ānand *Koul*, JASB 6, 1910, p. 195 ff.

[3]) Cf. Nīlamata, vss. 424 ff.; Rājataranginī I, 182-184.

"Purāṇa."[1] It must, therefore, be several centuries earlier than Kalhaṇa's work.

Among the offshoots of the Purāṇa literature mention should also be made of the Nepalese Vaṃśāvalis ("Genealogies"), which are partly Brahmanical and partly Buddhist, the Nepāla-Māhātmya and the Vāgvatī-Māhātmya, which claims to be part of a Paśupati-Purāṇa.[2]

Finally we here mention another work, which, though an epic and not a Purāṇa, nevertheless has the sectarian character of the Purāṇas: this is the Āśvamedhikaparvan of the Jaimini-Bhārata,[3] *i.e.*, of the Mahābhārata-Saṃhitā ascribed to Jaimini.[4] This poem, written in the ornate style, describes the combats and adventures of the heroes Arjuna, Kṛṣṇa etc., who accompanied the sacrificial steed destined for Yudhiṣṭhira's horse-sacrifice, but it diverges greatly from the Mahābhārata story. Besides, the narrative of the horse-sacrifice merely provides a welcome opportunity to insert numerous legends and tales of which there is not the slightest trace in the Mahābhārata. A considerable section (Kuśalavopākhyāna, "the episode of Kuśa and Lava") contains a brief reproduction of the entire Rāmāyaṇa. Among other lands the heroes go the realm of the Amazons

---

1) Kalhaṇa calls the work "Nīlamata" (Rājataraṅgiṇī I, 14; 16) or "Nīlapurāṇa" (l. c. I, 178). *Bhandarkar*, Report 1883-84, p. 44, mentions a MS. in which the work is described as a Kāśmīramāhātmya with the title Nīlamata. The pandits of Kashmir usually call it "Nīlamata-purāṇa."

2) See S. *Lévi*, Le Népal, AMG, Paris 1905, I, 193 ff., 201 ff., 205 ff.

3) Editions published in Bombay, Poona and Calcutta. There are numerous MSS. Cf. *Holtzmann*, Das Mahābhārata, III, p. 37 ff.; *Weber*, HSS. Verz. I, p. 111 ff.; *Aufrecht*, Bodl. Cat., I, p. 4; *Eggeling*, Ind. Off. Cat. VI, p. 1159.

4) In the Mahābhārata (I, 63, 89 f.) it is related that Vyāsa taught the Mahābhārata to his five pupils Sumantu, Jaimini, Paila, Śuka and Vaiśampāyana, and that each one of these published a Saṃhitā of it. It is open to doubt, however, whether there was actually a complete Mahābhārata-Saṃhitā by Jaimini and whether this Āśvamedhikaparvan is the sole remnant of it. Talboys *Wheeler*, The History of India, London 1867, I, 377, has unwittingly reproduced the contents of the Jaimini-Āśvamedhikaparvan in the chapter on "The Horse Sacrifice of Raja Yudhishthira."

(strīrājya) and we hear of the adventures which happened to them there. The story of Candrahāsa and Viṣayā (Candrahāsopākhyāna)[1] is of importance in the literature of the world. It is a version of the story recurring so frequently in Indian (Buddhist and Jain) and in Western narrative literature, of a youth who has been born under a lucky star and always escapes the infamous machinations of the wicked adversary who seeks his destruction. Finally the persecuted young man is made to deliver a letter ordering his own death; when a maiden alters or exchanges the fatal letter, and becomes the bride of the youth, who attains to wealth or power, whilst the fate which had been destined for him befalls the adversary or the adversary's son. Now the youth Candrahāsa, in the Jaimini-Bhārata was immune from all dangers solely because, from his childhood onwards, he was a devout worshipper of Viṣṇu and always carried a Śālagrāma stone (the sacred symbol of Viṣṇu) about with him.[2] The

[1]) Told by T. *Wheeler* l. c., p. 522 ff. Text and German translation by A. *Weber* (Monatsberichte der preuss. Akademie der Wissenschaften 1869, pp. 10 ff., 377 ff.), who was the first to call attention to the Western parallels, and more recently by J. *Schick*, Corpus Hamleticum I, 1, Das Glückskind mit dem Todesbrief, Orientalische Fassungen, Berlin 1912, p. 167 ff. In this book *Schick* deals in detail with the Buddhist and Jain versions of this story (which will be dealt with in Vol. II), the popular modern Indian versions and the Western Asiatic adaptations through the medium of which the story reached Europe. In Europe we find the story, among other places, in Chapter XX of the Latin "Gesta Romanorum" (cf. M. *Gaster*, JRAS 1910, p. 449 ff.), in *Dasent's* Norse Tales (cf. C. H. *Tawney* in Ind. Ant. 10, 1881, p. 190 f.), in the French romance of the Emperor Constantine after whom Constantinople is named (cf. Joseph *Jacobs* in his Introduction to Old French Romances done into English by William Morris, London 1896, p. viii ff.) and in the story of Amleth by Saxo Grammaticus. Only the motif of the altered fatal letter has been adopted in Shakespeare's "Hamlet." In German the narrative is best known through *Schiller's* poem "Der Gang nach dem Eisenhammer." Cf. Th. *Benfey*, Pantschatantra, I, 321, 340; E. *Kuhn*, in Byzantinische Zeitschrift IV, 242 ff.; E. *Cosquin*, La légende du page de sainte Elisabeth de Portugal, Paris 1912 (Extrait de la Revue des questions historiques). The earliest of all versions hitherto known is that in the Chinese Tripiṭaka (Ed. *Chavannes*, cinq cents contes et apologues extraits du Tripiṭaka Chinois I, No 45), which was translated into Chinese by Seng-houei who died in 280 A. D.

[2]) Among the Bhāgavatas Candrahāsa became a Vaiṣṇava saint, and in Nābhādāsa's Bhakt-Māla his story is narrated, as in the Jaimini-Bhārata, as that of the thirty-first

conclusion of the legend takes the form of a glorification of the sacred stone and the tulasī plant, which is also sacred to Viṣṇu, in the extravagant style of the later Purāṇas. In the whole poem Kṛṣṇa is not only a hero, but is honoured as the god Viṣṇu. He appears, as a helper, to all who appeal to him with love (bhakti). He works all manner of miracles, he restores a dead child to life, he feeds multitudes of munis with a single leaf of a vegetable, and so on, and whosoever beholds Kṛṣṇa's countenance, is freed from all his sins. Nothing definite can be said regarding the date of the Jaimini-Bhārata, resp. its Āśvamedhikaparvan. Judging by the nature of the Viṣṇu-worship appearing in the work, it is probably not earlier than the later works and sections of the Purāṇa literature. At any rate it is later than the Bhāgavata-Purāṇa quoted at the end of the Candrahāsa legend.[1]

THE TANTRA-LITERATURE.

Saṃhitās, Āgamas, Tantras.

"Tantric" influences have already been noticed in several of the later Purāṇas, namely isolated allusions to the cult of the Śaktis, the female deities, considerable sections in the form of dialogues between Śiva and Pārvatī and the occasional use of mystic syllables and formulas (mantras) and

---

of the "forty-two beloved ones of the Lord"; s. *Grierson*, JRAS 1910, p. 292 ff. Cf. N. B. *Godabole*, Ind. Ant. 11, 1882, p. 84 ff. The story also occurs in Kāśīrām's Bengali version of the Mahābhārata (see Calcutta Review, December 1924, p. 480 ff.). The motif of the changed "letter of death" alone occurs in folk-tales from Bengal, the Punjab, and Kashmir. Cf. Hatim's Tales Kashmiri Stories and Songs by Sir Aurel *Stein* and Sir G. A. *Grierson*, London 1923, p. 97, with Notes by W. *Crooke*, ib. p. xliv ff.

1) The astrologer Varāhamihira (6th century A. D.) is mentioned in 55, 8. The scene of the story of Candrahāsa is laid in the South in the land of the Keralas. A Canarese version of the Jaimini-Aśvamedhikaparvan by the Brahmin Lakṣmīśa is the most popular work in Canarese literature. Lakṣmīśa lived after 1585 and before 1724. Cf. E. P. *Rice*, Kanarese Literature (Heritage of India Series), 1921, p. 85 ff. and H. F. *Mögling*, ZDMG 24, 1870, 309 ff.; 25, 22 ff.; 27, 1873, 364 ff.

diagrams (yantras). Whereas, however, the Purāṇas always maintain a certain connection with epic poetry, and are, as it were, a repertory of Indian legend poetry, the Tantras, and the Saṃhitās and Āgamas, which differ from them but slightly, rather bear the stamp of purely theological works teaching the technicalities of the cult of certain sects together with their metaphysical and mystical principles. Strictly speaking, the "Saṃhitās" are the sacred books of the Vaiṣṇavas, the "Āgamas" those of the Śaivas and the "Tantras" those of the Śāktas. However, there is no clear line of demarcation between the terms, and the expression "Tantra" is frequently used as a general term for this class of works.[1)]

As a matter of fact all these works really have characteristic features in common. Though they are not positively hostile to the Veda, they propound that the precepts of the Veda are too difficult for our age, and that, for this reason, an easier cult and an easier doctrine have been revealed in them. Moreover these sacred books are accessible not only to the higher castes, but to Śūdras and women too. On the other hand, it is true that they contain Secret Doctrines which can only be obtained from a teacher (guru) after a ceremonial initiation (dīkṣā), and which must not be communicated to any uninitiated person.[2)] A complete Tantra (Saṃhitā, Āgama) should consist of four parts according to the four main themes treated, *viz.*, (1) Jñāna, "knowledge,"

---

1) Thus the Viṣṇuite Pādma-Saṃhitā is also called Pādma-Tantra. The "sāttvataṃ tantram" mentioned in the Bhāgavata-P. 1, 3, 8 is probably the Sāttvata-Saṃhitā. Lakṣmī-Tantra is a Viṣṇuite work, and Pāñcarātra-Āgama is spoken of as well as Pāñcarātra-Saṃhitās. Cf. *Eliot*, Hinduism and Buddhism, II, p. 188 f. *Tantra* means "a system of doctrines," "a book," *i.e.* "Bible;" *Āgama* means "tradition" and *Saṃhitā* a "collection of sacred texts."

2) "The Vedas, Śāstras and Purāṇas are like harlots accessible to all, but the Śivaite science is well concealed like a woman of good family." (*Avalon*, Principles of Tantra, I, p. ix.) In the Kulacūḍāmaṇi-Tantra, Chapt. I, we read that the doctrine is not to be communicated to any uninitiated person, not even to Viṣṇu or to Brahman. The Kulārṇava-Tantra III, 4 says: Vedas, Purāṇas and Śāstras may be propagated, but the Śaiva and Śākta Āgamas are declared to be secret doctrines.

comprising actual philosophical doctrines, sometimes with a monotheistic bias, and sometimes leaning towards monism, but also a confused occultism including the "knowing" of the secret powers of the letters, syllables, formulas and figures (mantraśāstra, yantraśāstra); (2) Yoga, *i.e.*, "meditation, concentration," also more especially with a view to acquiring magic powers, hence also "magic" (māyāyoga); (3) Kriyā, "action," *i.e.*, instructions for the making of idols and the construction and consecration of temples; (4) Caryā, "conduct," *i.e.*, rules regarding rites and festivals, and social duties. Though in reality all these four branches are not treated in every single one of these works, they all contain a medley of philosophy and occultism, mysticism and magic, and ritual and ethics.

Hitherto little is known about the Śaiva-Āgamas.[1] There are 28 Āgamas, which are said to have been proclaimed by Śiva himself after the creation of the world, and each Āgama has a number of Upāgamas. As we know scarcely anything of the contents of these works, we are not in a position to determine their date.[2]

We have a little more information about the Saṃhitās of the Viṣṇuite Pāñcarātra sect.[3] Though the traditional

---

1) Cf. H. W. *Schomerus*, Der Çaiva-Siddhānta, Leipzig, 1912, p. 7 ff., a list of the 28 Āgamas ib. p. 14. Only fragments of 20 Āgamas have been preserved. Portions of two Upāgamas, Mṛgendra and Pauṣkara, are printed. Cf. *Eliot*, Hinduism and Buddhism, II, p. 204 f.

2) According to *Schomerus* (l. c., p. 11 f.) the Āgamas were used by Tirumūlār and other Tamil poets as far back as the first or second century A.D., and would therefore originate in pre-Christian times. However, it is more likely that these poets should be assigned to the 9th century and the Āgamas to the 7th or 8th century A.D. Cf. *Farquhar*, Outline, p. 193 ff.

3) Especially by the researches of F. O. *Schrader*, Introduction to the Pāñcarātra and the Ahirbudhnya Saṃhitā, Adyar, Madras, S. 1916. Cf. A. *Govindacarya Svamin*, JRAS 1911, p. 935 ff.; *Bhandarkar*, Vaiṣṇavism, etc., p. 39 ff.; *Eliot*, Hinduism and Buddhism, II, p. 194 ff.; *Farquhar*, Outline, p. 182 ff. There are various explanations of the name "Pañcarātra," it is probably connected with the Pañcarātra-Sattra, a sacrifice lasting five days, which is taught in the Śatapatha-Brāhmaṇa. Cf. *Schrader*, l.c., p. 23 ff.; *Govindacarya* l. c., p. 940 f.

list enumerates 108 Pāñcarātra-Saṃhitās, there is actually mention of more than 215, of which, however, only twelve have been published.[1] One of the earlier Saṃhitās is the Ahirbudhnya-Saṃhitā,[2] a Kashmiri work which probably originated not long after the fourth century A. D.[3]

The work takes the form of a conversation between Ahirbudhnya, *i.e.*, Śiva and Nārada. The smaller portion of the work is philosophical in content, and the greater portion occult.[4] Several chapters deal with the Creation.[5] When Nārada asks how it is that men hold such varied opinions regarding the Creation, Ahirbudhnya replies (Chap. 8) that it is due to various causes, (1) it is impossible to express the truth about the Absolute in the language of human beings, (2) human beings often take various names to be various objects, (3) human beings vary in intelligence, and (4) the deity has an endless number of forms, of which the philosophers usually comprehend only one or another. In connection with the Creation Chapts. 12 and 13 give a very interesting survey of the "sciences," *i.e.*, the various systems of religion and philosophy. Then come the rules for the castes and Āśramas. The paterfamilias and the forest hermit attain to the heaven of Brahman, but the ascetic (sannyāsin) "is extinguished like a lamp" (15, 26 ff.). Chapt.

---

1) See the lists in *Schrader* l.c., pp. 4-13. A list of 25 Pāñcarātra "Tantras" is enumerated in the Agni-Purāṇa, Chapt. 39. Most of the published texts are difficult of access. A few extracts from the Sāttvata-Saṃhitā are given by *Schrader* l.c., p. 149 ff. in translation. On the Pādma-Saṃhitā cf. *Eggeling*, Ind. Off. Cat. IV, p. 847 ff.; on the Lakṣmī-Tantra, in which Lakṣmī is worshipped as the Śakti of Viṣṇu-Nārāyaṇa and the final cause of the world, cf. *Eggeling* ib., p. 850 f.

2) Edited for the Adyar Library by M.D. *Rāmānujācārya*, under the supervision of F. Otto *Schrader*, Adyar, Madras, S., 1916. This is the only critical edition of a Saṃhitā.

3) As it is acquainted with the three great schools of Buddhism, and as the astrological term *horā* occurs (XI, 28), it cannot possibly have originated before the 4th century A.D. From its presentation of the Sāṃkhya system as a Ṣaṣṭitantra (XII, 18 ff.) *Schrader* (ZDMG 68, 1914, 102 ff.; Introduction, p. 98 f.) concludes that it is earlier than Īśvarakṛṣṇa's Sāṃkhyakārikā. As Īśvarakṛṣṇa himself describes the Sāṃkhya as a Ṣaṣṭitantra, we might be justified in assuming that the Ahirbudhnya-Saṃhitā and the Sāṃkhyakārikā belong to about the same period.

4) Cf. the table of contents in *Schrader*, Introduction, p. 94 ff.

5) On the philosophy of the Pāñcarātras as connected with the theory of the Creation, s. *Schrader*, l.c., p. 26 ff.

16-19 deal with the mysterious significance of the letters of the alphabet. Chapt. 20 on Dīkṣā begins with a fine description of the ideal Vaiṣṇava teacher: He is not only to know the truth of the Veda and the Vedānta and be ever mindful of the ceremonies due to the gods and the fathers, but also he should be "a non-speaker of evil speech, a non-doer of evil deeds, free from envy of the good fortune of others, full of sympathy for the misfortune of others, pitying all creatures, rejoicing at the joy of his neighbour, full of admiration of the good man, forbearing towards the wicked, rich in asceticism, contentment and uprightness, devoted to Yoga and study," and he is not only to possess a detailed knowledge of the Pāñcarātra, the Tantras, Mantras and Yantras, but also the knowledge of the Highest Soul, and must be calm, passionless, having control over his senses, and born of a good family. Chapts. 21-27 then describe diagrams which are also to be used as amulets. Further chapters deal with the cult, the theory and practice of Yoga, "the hundred and two magic weapons," *i.e.*, secret powers by which might can be attained. A few chapters deal with ceremonies to be performed by a king when in danger during time of war, in order to ensure victory. Sorcery forms the subject-matter of several chapters. An Appendix (Pariśiṣṭa) contains a hymn of the thousand names of the divine Sudarśana.

Though the Pāñcarātra-Saṃhitās probably originated in the North, the earliest of them perhaps dating from the 5th-9th century A.D.,[1] it is mainly in the South that they circulated. One of the earlier of these Southern Saṃhitās is the Īśvara-saṃhitā, quoted by Rāmānuja's teacher Yāmuna, who died in about 1040 A.D. Rāmānuja himself quotes the Pauṣkara[2] Parama and Sāttvata-saṃhitās. On the other hand, the Bṛhadbrahma-saṃhitā,[3] which is supposed to belong to the Nārada-Pāñcarātra, already contains prophecies regarding Rāmānuja, and cannot, therefore,

---

1) The Viṣṇuite Upaniṣads of those sects which worship Viṣṇu as Nṛsiṃha or Rāma in Mantras and Yantras, such as the Nṛsiṃhatāpanīya-Upaniṣad (already commentated by Gauḍapāda) and the Rāmatāpanīya-Upaniṣad, possibly belong to the same period. Cf. *Farquhar*, Outline, p. 188 ff.

2) On the Pauṣkara-Saṃhitā cf. *Eggeling*, Ind. Off. Cat. IV, p. 864 f.

3) Published in ĀnSS No. 68.

be earlier than the 12th century. The Jñānāmṛtasāra-saṃhitā, which is published with the title "Nārada-Pāñcarātra,"[1] and is entirely devoted to the glorification of Kṛṣṇa and Rādhā, is quite a modern and apocryphal work. As the cult taught in this book agrees most with that of the Vallabhācārya sect, it appears to have been written a little before Vallabha at the beginning of the 16th century.[2]

However, when we speak of "Tantras," we think primarily of the sacred books of the Śāktas, *i.e.*, the worshippers of the Śaktis or "energies" conceived as female deities, or of the "Great Śakti," the "Great Mother," the "Goddess" (Devī), who, in spite of her countless names (Durgā, Kālī, Caṇḍā etc.), is only *one*, the one "Highest Queen" (Parameśvarī). To an even greater degree than is the case with other forms of Hinduism, Śāktism, the religion of the Śāktas, presents a curious medley of the highest and lowest, the sublimest and the basest conceptions ever thought out by the mind of man. In Śāktism and its sacred books, the Tantras, we find the loftiest ideas on the Deity and profound philosophical speculations side by side with the wildest superstition and the most confused occultism; and side by side with a faultless social code of morality and rigid asceticism, we see a cult disfigured by wild orgies inculcating extremely reprehensible morals. In former years people laid stress only on the worst aspects of this religion or else deemed it best to enshroud this episode in the development of Indian religion in the charitable veil of oblivion.[3] It is Sir John Woodroffe (under the

---

[1]) Ed. by K. M. *Banerjea*, Bibl. Ind. 1865. Translated in SBH, Vol. 23, 1921. Cf. A. *Roussel*, Étude du Pāñcarātra in Mélanges Charles de Harlez, Leyde, 1896, p. 251 ff.

[2]) See *Bhandarkar*, Vaiṣṇavism etc., p. 40 f.

[3]) Cf. H. H. *Wilson*, Works, Vol. I, pp. 240-265; M. *Monier-Williams*, Brāhmanism and Hinduism, 4th Ed., London 1891, p. 180 ff.; A. *Barth*, The Religions of India, 2nd Ed., London 1889, p. 199 ff.; *Bhandarkar*, Vaiṣṇavism etc., p. 142 ff.

pseudonym of Arthur Avalon) who, by a series of essays and the publication of the most important Tantra texts, has enabled us to form a just judgment and an objective historical idea of this religion and its literature.[1]

A few of the Tantras themselves say that there are 64 Tantras, or 64 Tantras *each*, in three different parts of the world.[2] However, the number of Tantras existing in manuscripts is far larger.[3] Their original home seems to have been Bengal, whence they spread throughout Assam and Nepal, and even beyond India to Tibet and China through the agency of Buddhism. In reality they are known throughout the length and breadth of India, even in Kashmir and the South. As a rule the Tantras take the form of dialogues between Śiva and Pārvatī; when the goddess asks the questions like a pupil and Śiva replies like a teacher, they are called "Āgamas": when the goddess is the teacher and answers Śiva's questions, they are called "Nigamas."

The class of Āgamas includes the very popular and widely known Mahānirvāṇa-tantra,[4] in which we see

---

[1]) A. *Avalon*, Principles of Tantra, Part I, London 1914, Part II, 1916; Sir John *Woodroffe*, Shakti and Shâkta, 2nd Ed., Madras and London 1920, and the Introductions to the translation of the Mahānirvāṇa-Tantra and to the "Tantrik Texts" edited by him. Cf. also N. *Macnicol*, Indian Theism, 1915, p. 180 ff.; *Eliot*, Hinduism and Buddhism, II, p. 274 ff., and *Farquhar*, Outline, pp. 199 ff., 265 ff.

[2]) *Avalon*, Tantrik Texts, Vol. I, Introduction.

[3]) Numerous Tantras have been catalogued and described by *Haraprasād Śāstrī*, Notices of Sanskrit MSS., Second Series I, Calcutta 1900, pp. xxiv-xxxvii; Catalogue of Palm-Leaf and Selected Paper MSS. belonging to the Durbar Library, Nepal, Calcutta, 1905, pp. lvii-lxxxi; Report II, 7 ff., 11 f.; M. *Rangacharya*, Descriptive Catalogue of the Sanskrit MSS. in the Government Oriental MSS. Library, Madras, Vols. XII and XIII. On the Tantras in Malabar s. K. *Ramavarma Raja*, JRAS 1910, p. 636. Cf. also *Wilson*, Works, II, 77 ff.; *Aufrecht*, Bodl-Cat. I, p. 88 ff.; *Eggeling*, Ind. Off. Cat. IV, p. 844 ff.; *Bhandarkar*, Report 1883-84, p. 87 ff.

[4]) "The great work which enjoys a popularity next perhaps to the Bhagavadgītā," says *Haraprasād*, Notices I, p. xxxiv. Several editions have appeared in Calcutta, the first being in 1876 by the Ādi Brāhma Samāj. A Prose English Translation by M. N. *Dutt*, Calcutta 1900. Tantra of the Great Liberation (Mahānirvāṇa Tantra), a Translation from the Sanskrit, with Introduction and Commentary by A. *Avalon*, London 1913. The work seems to have been written in Bengal, because in VI, 7, 3, it recommends three species of

the best aspect of Śāktism. Though it is not an ancient work, it is an example of the superior Tantras, and as such we may accord somewhat more detailed treatment to it, because the same thoughts also occur in the earlier works of this nature, and much has been taken literally from earlier Tantras.

This Tantra speaks of the Brahman, the highest divine principle, in the same expressions as the Upaniṣads. Now according to the doctrines of the Śākta philosophers the Brahman is nothing but the eternal and primeval force (Śakti), out of which all things have been created. Śakti, "Energy," is not only feminine as far as grammar is concerned, for all human experience teaches that all life is born from the womb of woman, from the mother. Hence these Indian thinkers believed that the conception of the Highest Deity, the loftiest creative principle, must be made comprehensible to the human mind, not by the word "Father" but by the word "Mother." Just as every human being calls upon his mother in his sorest distress, the great mother of the universe is the sole being who can remove the great misery of existence.[1] All the philosophical conceptions to which language has assigned the feminine gender—first and foremost prakṛti, primeval matter, which is identical with Śakti—as well as all the mythological figures which popular belief imagined as being female—Pārvatī, Śiva's consort, also called Umā, Durgā, Kālī, etc., and Lakṣmī, Viṣṇu's consort, or Rādhā, the beloved of Kṛṣṇa—become divine mothers. In reality all these are but different names for the *one* great universal mother, Jaganmātā, "the mother of all living creatures." The Indian mind had long been accustomed to recognise the unity of what appears in manifold forms. Just as *one* moon is reflected in innumerable waters, thus Devī, "the Goddess," by whatever other name she may be described, is the embodiment of all the gods and all the "energies" (śaktis) of the gods. In her are Brahman, the Creator, and his Śakti, in her are Viṣṇu, the Preserver, and his Śakti, in her too, is Śiva as Mahākāla, "the great Father Time," the great Destroyer; as she herself

---

fish for the sacrifice, which are found especially in Bengal (s. *Eliot*, Hinduism and Buddhism, II, 278 note 4). *Farquhar* (Outline, p. 354 f.) regards it as quite a modern work, not earlier than the eighteenth century (?). The Nirvāṇa-Tantra, in which Rādhā is glorified as the wife of Viṣṇu, is an entirely different work, s. *Haraprasād* l.c.

[1]) *Avalon*, Principles of Tantra I, p. 8.

devours the latter, she is also Ādyā Kālikā, "the primeval Kālī," and as a "great sorceress," Mahāyoginī, she is at the same time the female Creator, Preserver and Destroyer of the world. She is also the mother of Mahākāla, who, drunk with wine pressed from the Madhūka blossoms, dances before her.[1] Since the Highest Deity is a woman, every woman is regarded as an incarnation of this Deity. Devī, "the Goddess," is in every female creature. This conception it was which led to a cult of women, which, though in some circles it assumed the form of wild orgies, could, and no doubt did appear also in a purer and ennobled form.

The cult of Devī, the Goddess, who is the joyous creative principle of nature, includes the "Five Essentials" (Pañcatattva) by which man enjoys his existence, preserves his life and obtains issue: Intoxicating drink (*madya*) which is "the great medicine for humanity, helping it to forget deep sorrows, and is the cause of joy"; meat (*māṃsa*) of the beasts bred in villages, in the air, or forest, which is nourishing, and increases intelligence, energy and strength; fish (*matsya*) which is "pleasing and of good taste, and increases the generative power of man"; delicacies of parched food (*mudrā*) which is "easily obtainable, grown in the earth, and is the root of the life of the three worlds"; and fifthly sexual union (*maithuna*)[2] which is "the cause of intense pleasure to all living things, is the origin of all creatures, and the root of the world which is without either beginning or end."[3] However, these "five essentials" may only be used in the circle (*cakra*) of the initiated, and even then only after they have been "purified" by sacred formulas and ceremonies. In these "circles" of initiated men and women, in which each man has his "Śakti" on his left hand,[4] there are no distinctions of caste, but evil and unbelieving persons cannot be admitted into the "circle." Neither is there to be any abuse of the "five essentials." He who drinks immoderately, is no true devotee of the Devī. In the sinful Kali age a man is to enjoy only his own wife as a "Śakti." If a householder is unable to control his senses, sweet things (milk, sugar, honey) shall be used instead of intoxicating drink, and the worship of the

---

1) Mahānirvāṇa-T. IV, 29-31; V. 141.

2) As all the "five essentials" begin with an "m," they are also called "the five m's."

3) Mahānirvāṇa-T. VII, 103 ff. (Avalon's Transl., p. 156). Detailed description of the "five essentials," VI, 1 ff.

4) Even in the Śatapatha-Brāhmaṇa (VIII, 4, 4, 11) we already read that "the woman's place is on the *left*" of the man. Hence most probably comes the term *vāmācāra*," left-hand ritual," for this kind of "cult in the circle" (cakrapūjā).

lotus feet of the goddess shall take the place of sexual union.[1] It is true that the "hero" (*vīra*), *i.e.*, he who has secret powers and is suited to be a Sādhaka or "sorcerer" is entitled to unite himself in the "circle" to a "Śakti" who is not his wife. He has only to make her his "wife" by a ceremony prescribed especially for this purpose. It is only in the highest "heavenly state" (*divyabhāva*), *i.e.*, in the case of the saint who has completely overcome earthly things, that purely symbolical acts take the place of the "five essentials."[2]

The cult of the Devī attaches especial importance to Mantras, *i.e.*, prayers and formulas, and Bījas, *i.e.*, syllables of mysterious significance, such as "aiṃ," "klīṃ," "brīṃ," etc.; as well as Yantras, *i.e.*, diagrams of mysterious significance, drawn on metal, paper or other material, Mudrās, *i.e.* especial positions of the fingers and movements of the hands, and Nyāsas. The last-named consist of placing the finger-tips and the palm of the right hand on the various parts of the body, whilst reciting certain mantras, in order thus to imbue one's body with the life of the Devī.[3] By using all these means, the worshipper causes the deity to show goodwill towards him, he compels the deity into his service, and becomes a *Sādhaka*, a sorcerer: for *Sādhana*, "sorcery," is one of the principal aims, though not the final goal of the worship of the Devī.

This final goal is that of all Indian sects and systems of religion, namely Mokṣa or salvation, the becoming one with the deity in Mahānirvāṇa, the "great extinction." The perfect saint, the Kaula, who sees everything in the Brahman and the Brahman in everything, whether he fulfil the rites laid down in the Tantras or not, attains this state even in this life, and is "released though living." (*Jīvanmukta*).[4] However, the path of salvation can only be found through the *Tantras*; for the Veda, the Smṛti, the Purāṇas and the Itihāsas,

---

[1]) Mahānirvāṇa-T. VI, 14 ff.; 186 ff. VIII, 171 ff., 190 ff.

[2]) The distinction of the three classes of mankind: *paśu*, "the animal," "the brutish man," *vīra*, "the hero" and *divya*, "the heavenly one," occurs very frequently in all the Tantras. It is not quite clear what *paśu* means; for a *paśu* is not necessarily a stupid or bad man. The term appears to be applicable to a person who is not suited to comprehend occult matters. Cf. *Avalon*, Tantra of the Great Liberation, Introduction, p. lxv ff.

[3]) *Eliot*, Hinduism and Buddhism II, p. 275, compares the Nyāsa with the Christian sign of the Cross, and points out further analogies between the Tantric and the Christian ritual.

[4]) Mahānirvāṇa-T. X, 209 ff. *Kaula* or *Kaulika* is "one who belongs to the family (*kula*) of the goddess Kālī." Cf. *Haraprasāda Śāstrī*, Notices of Sanskrit MSS. I, pp.

all these were the sacred books of bygone periods of the world's existence, whereas the Tantras were revealed by Siva for the welfare of humanity, for our present evil age, the Kali period (I, 20 ff.). In this way the Tantras describe themselves as comparatively modern works. In this age Vedic and other rites and prayers are of no avail, but only the mantras and ceremonies taught in the Tantras are of value (II, 1 ff.). Just as the cult of the Devī leads to the grossest material issues by means of sorcery, as well as to the loftiest ideal of Nirvāṇa, even so the sensual and spiritual elements are well mixed in the cult itself.

There is a meditation on the Devī, which is characteristic of the above. It is taught in the following manner: The devotee first offers Devī spiritual adoration by bestowing the lotus of his heart as her throne, the nectar which trickles from the petals of this lotus-flower as water wherein to wash her feet, his mind as a gift of honour, the restlessness of his senses and his thoughts as a dance, selflessness, passionlessness, etc., as flowers, but afterwards—sacrifices to the Devī an ocean of intoxicating drink, a mountain of meat and fried fishes, a heap of parched dainties in milk with sugar and butter, the nectar of the "woman flower" (*strīpuṣpa*) and the water which has been used for washing the Śakti.[1] Besides the "five essentials" and other elements of a most sensual cult and one based upon the intoxication of the senses, from which even bells, incense, flowers, candles and rosaries are not missing, there is also calm meditation on the deity (*dhyāna*). In like manner, beside mantras which are devoid of all meaning and insipid, we find such beautiful lines as for instance V, 156: "O Ādyā Kālī, thou who dwellest in the inmost soul of all, who art the inmost light, O Mother! Accept this the prayer of my heart. I bow down before thee."

Along with the Tantric ritual, the Mahānirvāṇa-Tantra also teaches a philosophy which is little different from the orthodox systems of the Vedānta and Sāṃkhya,[2] and

---

xxvi, xxxiii. For a different interpretation s. *Avalon*, Tantrik Texts, Vol. IV, Introduction, where *Kaula* is derived from *Kula* in the sense of "community" or "combination of soul, knowledge and universe." The Tantras speak of the Kaula sometimes as the loftiest sage and sometimes as a person to whom all is permitted as regards the "five essentials." The last verse of Chapt. X of the Jñānatantra teaches that only Brahmins of the fourth Āśrama may fulfil "the left-hand cult," whilst householders may perform only the "right-hand cult." (Haraprasāda Śāstrī l. c., pp. xxxi, 126).

1) Mahānirvāṇa-T. V, 139-151.

2) On the philosophy of the Tantras see S. *Das Gupta* in Sir Asutosh Mookerjee Silver Jubilee Vol. III, 1, 1922, p. 253 ff.

which is at times recognisable even in that chaos of nonsensical incantations. As regards the ethics, the doctrine of the duties in Chapter VIII of the Mahānirvāṇa-Tantra reminds us at every turn of Manu's Law-book, the Bhagavadgītā and the Buddhist sermons. Though there are no caste distinctions in the actual Śākta ritual, all castes and sexes being accounted equal, the castes are nevertheless recognised in agreement with Brahmanism, except that in addition to the usual four castes a fifth one is added, namely that of the Sāmānyas, which arose through the mingling of the four older castes. Whilst Manu has four Āśramas or stages of life, our Tantra teaches that in the Kali epoch there are only two Āśramas, the state of the householder and that of the ascetic. For the rest, all which is taught here about duties to one's parents, to wife and child, to relatives and to one's fellow men in general, might be found exactly the same in any other religious book or even in a secular manual of morality. We quote only a few verses from this Chapter VIII by way of example:

A householder should be devoted to the contemplation of Brahman and possessed of the knowledge of Brahman, and should consign whatever he does to Brahman. (23)

He should not tell an untruth, or practise deceit, and should ever be engaged in the worship of the Devatās and guests. (24)

Regarding his father and mother as two visible incarnate deities, he should ever and by every means in his power serve them. (25)

Even if the vital breath were to reach his throat,[1] the householder should not eat without first feeding his mother, father, son, wife, guest and brother. (33)

The householder should never punish his wife, but should cherish her like a mother. If she is virtuous and devoted to her husband, he should never forsake her even in times of greatest misfortune. (39)

A father should fondle and nurture his sons until their fourth year, and then until their sixteenth they should be taught learning and their

[1] *i.e.*, even if he were about to die of hunger.

duties. (45) Up to their twentieth year they should be kept engaged in household duties, and thenceforward, considering them as equals, he should ever show affection towards them. (46) In the same manner a daughter should be cherished and educated with great care, and then given away with money and jewels to a wise husband. (47)

The man who has dedicated tanks, planted trees, built rest-houses on the roadside, or bridges, has conquered the three worlds. (63) That man who is the happiness of his mother and father, to whom his friends are devoted, and whose fame is sung by men, he is the conqueror of the three worlds. (64) He whose aim is truth, whose charity is ever for the poor, who has mastered lust and anger, by him are the three worlds conquered. (65)[1]

The duties of the separate castes as well as the duties of the king, as prescribed here, do not greatly differ from those laid down by Manu. The value of family life is put very high. Thus there is a strict injunction that no man who has children, wives or other near relatives to support, shall devote himself to the ascetic life.[2] In complete agreement with the regulations in the brahmanical texts, Chapter IX describes the "sacraments" (*saṃskāras*) from conception till marriage, and Chapter X similarly gives instructions for the burial of the dead and the cult of the departed (*śrāddhas*). A peculiarity of the Śāktas as regards marriage is that, in addition to the *Brāhma*-marriage, for which the brahmanical rules provide, there is also a *Śaiva*-marriage, *i.e.*, a kind of marriage for a certain time, which is only permitted to members of the circle (*cakra*) of the initiated.[3] However, the children of such marriages are not legitimate and cannot inherit. This shows to how great an extent brahmanical law is valid for the Śāktas too. Thus also the section on civil and criminal law in Chapters XI and XII agrees in essentials with Manu.

Nevertheless the Kauladharma which is recited in the Tantra, is declared in extravagant terms to be the best of all religions, and the adoration of the Kula saint is praised as supremely meritorious. In words similar to those of a famous Buddhist text we read in our Tantra: "As

---

1) Translated by *Avalon*, pp. 161 f., 163, 165 f.

2) In the Kauṭilīya-Arthaśāstra II, 1, 19 (p. 48) a fine is prescribed for him who becomes an ascetic without first having provided for his wife and children.

3) See above p. 595.

the footmarks of all animals disappear in the footmark of the elephant, so do all other Dharmas disappear in the Kula-Dharma." [1]

One of the principal works of the Kaulas, *i.e.*, the most advanced of the Śāktas, is the Kulārṇava-Tantra,[2] which teaches that there are six forms of life (ācāra),[3] which are but an introduction to the Kulācāra, and that release from suffering, and the highest salvation can only be attained through the Kulācāra or Kula-Dharma.

When the Devī asks: "Whereby is release from suffering to be attained?" Śiva replies: Only through the knowledge of the Unity; for the creatures, surrounded by Māyā, are but as sparks emanating from the fire of Brahman. There are people who boast of their knowledge of Brahman, smear their bodies with ashes, and practise asceticism, but are yet only devoted to the pleasures of their senses. "Asses and other animals, go about naked without shame, whether they dwell in the house or in the forest: does this make them Yogins?" (I, 79). In order to become a Kaula a man should avoid all external things and strive only for true knowledge. Ritual and asceticism are of value only as long as a man has not yet recognised the truth. The Kula-Dharma is *Yoga* (meditation) as well as *Bhoga* (enjoyment), but only for the man who has purified his mind and has control over his senses. We can well understand the statement, so often repeated in the Tantras, that it is easier to ride on a drawn sword than to be a true Kaula, when in one and the same book we find, not only doctrines on the true knowledge of the Brahman and Yoga, but also the minutest details concerning the preparation of twelve kinds of intoxicating drinks and everything connected with the "five essentials," which bestow *bhukti* (enjoyment) and *mukti* (salvation) at the same time.[4] "The Brahmin," we read, "should drink at all times, the warrior at the beginning of the battle, the Vaiśya when purchasing cows, the Śūdra when

---

[1]) Mahānirv-T. XIV, 180, transl. *Avalon*, p. 356. Cf. Majjhimanikāya 26 (at the beginning).

[2]) Ed. by Tārānāth *Vidyāratna* in Tantrik Texts, Vol. V, 1917.

[3]) These are Vedācāra, Vaiṣṇavācāra, Śaivācāra, Dakṣiṇācāra, Vāmācāra, Siddhāntācāra (or Yogācāra). Cf. *Avalon*, Tantra of the Great Liberation, Introduction, p. lxxviii ff.

[4]) Though the *surā* drink is extolled in the most extravagant fashion (V, 38 f.), the others are also recommended (V, 30). The eating of meat at the *Kulapūjā* is a permissible exception to the rule of non-killing (*ahiṃsā*).

performing the funeral sacrifices" (V, 84). On the other hand, when these and similar rules have been formulated, we again read that true drinking is the union of Kuṇḍalinī Śakti with Ciccandra ("moon of thought"), others being merely imbibers of intoxicants, that the true "flesh-eater" is he who merges his thought in the highest Being, and a true "fish-eater" is he who curbs his senses and unites them with the Ātman—"others merely kill animals"; and that true *maithuna* is the union of the highest Śakti or Kuṇḍalinī with the Ātman—"others are merely slaves to women." This comes at the close of Chapter V. In Chapter VII, however, the necessity of drink in the cult of Śakti is again emphasized. It is true that one should only drink in moderation, but this moderation is reckoned very liberally: "As long as the eye, the understanding, speech and the body do not become unsteady, a man may continue drinking, but drink taken in excess of this is the drinking of a brute beast" (VII, 97). Though it is true that only the initiated are allowed to drink, it is to them that the oft-quoted maxim is addressed: "He is to drink, drink and drink again, till he falls to the ground, and when he has arisen, he is to drink yet again—then there will be no rebirth" (VII, 100).[1]

Another oft-quoted work of the Kaula School of the Śāktas is the "Head jewel of the Kula," Kulacūḍāmaṇi,[2] an example of a Nigama in which Devī proclaims the doctrine and Śiva listens in the character of a pupil. In reality Śiva and Devī are one, and the latter says at the end of the book:

"Thou appearest now as the father, now in the form of the teacher, then thou becomest the son, then again a pupil..........Everything whatever exists in the world, consists of Śiva and Śakti. Thou, O God of gods, art all, and I, too, am all to all eternity. Thou art the teacher when I

---

[1]) The saying occurs frequently in the Tantras. According to *Avalon* these and similar verses do not refer to actual drinking, but to the symbolical "drinking" of the Yoga. This, however, is difficult to believe

[2]) Ed. by Girīsha Chandra *Vedāntatīrtha*, with an Introduction by A. K. *Maitra* in Tantrik Texts, Vol. IV, 1915. The ritual of the Kaulas is also treated in the *Nityāṣoḍaśī-Tantra*, which is a part of the *Vāmakeśvara-Tantra* (publ. in ĀnSS Vol. 56, 1908) and the *Adīśvaracaritra*, an analysis of which is given by L. *Suali* (SIFI Vol. 7).

am the pupil, but then there shall be no distinction. Therefore be thou the teacher, O Lord, and I shall be thy Pupil, O Highest Lord!"

The work begins with an enumeration of the Kulasundarīs or Devīs, and then describes the worship of the Śaktis with Yantras as well as meditations on the unity of the Great Mother. Instructions are given for the worship not only of one's own wife but also for that of an outside "Śakti." He who would be admitted to the Cakra rites, must first have walked in the path of the love of God (bhaktimārga) according to Vaiṣṇavism, and he must be good and patient to others. The last three chapters deal solely with magic.

One of the more important texts of the Tantras is the Prapañcasāra-Tantra,[1] which is ascribed to the philosopher Śaṅkara or the god Śiva in his incarnation as Śaṅkara. Though the name Śaṅkara appears not infrequently in the Tantra literature, it is by no means certain that the texts attributed to him were really his work. *Prapañca* means "the expansion," "the expanded universe," hence *Prapañcasāra*, "the Essence of the Universe."

The work begins with an account of the Creation.[2] This is followed by treatises on chronology, embryology, anatomy, physiology and psychology, which are no more "scientific" than the succeeding chapters on the occult doctrines of Kuṇḍalinī and the secret significance of the Sanskrit alphabet and the Bījas. According to the general teaching of the Tantras the human organism is a microcosm, a miniature copy of the universe, and contains countless canals (*nāḍī*) through which some secret power flows through the body. Connected with these canals there are six great centres (cakra) lying one above the other, which are also furnished with occult powers. The lowest and most important of these centres contains the Brahman in the form of a Liṅga, and coiled round this Liṅga like a serpent, lies the Śakti called Kuṇḍalinī.[3] This

---

[1]) Ed. by Tārānātha *Vidyāratna* in Tantrik Texts, Vol. III, 1914. The author Śaṅkara is supposed to be identical with the commentator of the Nṛsiṃhapūrvatāpanīya-Upaniṣad. Cf. Vidhushekhara *Bhattacharya*, Ind. Hist. Qu. I, 1925, p. 120.

[2]) On the Creation theories of the Tantras s. J. G. *Woodroffe*, Creation as explained in the Tantra (read at the Silver Jubilee of the Chaitanya Library, Calcutta, 1915)

[3]) Kuṇḍalinī, "the coiled one." The theory of the Nāḍīs and Cakras is also to be found in the Varāha-Upaniṣad V, 22 ff. and in the Śāṇḍilya-Upaniṣad (Yoga Upanishads ed. Mahadeva Sastri, pp. 505 f, 518 ff.).

Kuṇḍalinī is forced up into the highest centre by Sādhana and Yoga, and then salvation is attained. The Bījas and Mantras,[1] that is, the letters and syllables and the formulas composed from them, in all of which, according to an ancient doctrine already foreshadowed in the Brāhmaṇas and Upaniṣads,[2] a potent influence on the human organism and the universe lies concealed, are means to the attainment of the highest perfections (*siddhi*).

The chapters on the ritual for the consecration (dīkṣā), the worship of the mothers and the meditations on the Devī are of considerable significance from the point of view of the history of religion. The very prominent part played in the whole of this cult by the erotic element is exemplified in IX, 23 ff., where it is described how the wives of the gods, demons and demigods, compelled by Mantras, come to the sorcerer "scattering their ornaments in the intoxication of love, letting their silken draperies slip down, enveloping their forms in the net of their flying tresses, their every limb quivering with intolerable torments of love, the drops of sweat falling like pearls over their thighs, bosom and armpits,.........torn by the arrows of the love god, their bodies immersed in the ocean of the passion of love, their lips tossed by the tempest of their deep-drawn breath" etc. Chapter XVIII teaches the Mantras and Dhyānas (meditations) for the worship of the love god and his Śaktis, and the union of man and woman is presented as a mystical union of the ego (*ahaṃkara*) with knowledge (*Buddhi*) and as a holy act of sacrifice. If the man honours his beloved wife in this manner, then, wounded by the arrows of the love god, she will follow him as a shadow even into the other world (XVIII, 33). Chapter XXVIII is dedicated to Ardhanārīśvara, the god who is half female—the right half of his body is in the form of Śiva who is represented as a wild-looking man, and the left half is his Śakti, represented as a voluptuous woman. Chapter XXXIII, with which the work originally seems to have closed, devotes its first part to a description of ceremonies to prevent childlessness,

---

[1]) The monosyllabic meaningless sounds such as "hrīṃ," "Śrīṃ," "krīṃ," "phaṭ," *etc.*, are Bīja, "seeds," because they are the seed from which the fruit of magic powers (siddhi) is produced, and because they are the "seed" of the Mantras. Cf. *Avalon*, The Tantra of the Great Liberation, Introd. p. lxxxiii ff.

[2]) There is considerable truth in the contention of B. L. *Mukherji* (in *Woodroffe*, Shakti and Shâktas, p. 441 f.) that the occultism of the Tantras is already foreshadowed n the Brāhmaṇas, and that allusions to sexual intercourse play a prominent part in the symbolism of the Brāhmaṇas as well as in the Tantras.

which is the result of carelessness in the worship of the gods and of scorning the wife. The second part deals with the relationship between teacher and pupil, which is of paramount importance in the Śakti religion.

The ritual and the Mantras described in this Tantra are not limited to the worship of the various forms of Devī and Śiva, but frequently also Viṣṇu and his avatāras are referred to. Chapter XXXVI contains a reflection on Viṣṇu Trailokyamohana ("the confounder of the triple world"). This description is replete with sensual fire: Viṣṇu shines like millions of suns and is of supreme beauty. Full of kindness his glance rests upon Śrī his consort, who embraces him lovingly. She, too, is incomparably beautiful. All the gods and demons and their wives do honour to the lofty, divine couple; but the divine women press around Viṣṇu full of the fiery longing of love, and exclaim: "Be our consort, our refuge, O highest Lord!" [1]

The first part [2] of the Tantrarāja-Tantra bearing the proud title "king of Tantras" treats of the Śrīyantra, the "famous diagram," which consists of nine triangles and nine circles cleverly drawn one within the other and each one of which has a special mystical significance. By meditation with the aid of this Śrīyantra one attains knowledge of the Unity, *i.e.*, the knowledge that everything in the world is one with the Devī. The Kālīvilāsa-Tantra,[3] which belongs to the "prohibited" Tantras, *i.e.*, those which are valid not for our age but only for a bygone period, is a later text. The attitude adopted towards the Pañcatattva ritual is very ambiguous indeed. All that we can glean clearly from the text is that there were two different schools of Śāktas, one of which condemned this ritual, while the other considered it as compulsory. A few chapters deal with Kṛṣṇa as the lover of Rādhā, who is identical with the

---

1) XXXVI, 35-47, translated by *Avalon* in the Introduction, p. 61 ff.

2) This one alone (Part I, Chapters I-XVIII) has been published by M. *Lakṣmaṇa Shâstrî* in Tantrik Texts, Vol. VIII, 1918.

3) Ed. by Pârvatī Charaṇa *Tarkatīrtha* in Tantrik Texts, Vol. VI, 1917. One chapter contains a Mantra in a dialect which is a mixture of Assamese and East Bengali, another contains Mantras with the words written backwards.

goddess Kālī. The Jñānārṇava-Tantra[1] deals with the various kinds of Tantra ritual and the meditations on the various forms of Devī. The Kumārīpūjana, the worship of young maidens, is described as the highest sacrifice. The Śāradātilaka-Tantra,[2] written by Lakṣmaṇa Deśika in the 11th century, begins with a theory of the Creation and the origin of human speech, but treats chiefly of Mantras, Yantras, and magic.

In addition to the actual "revealed" Tantras there are innumerable manuals on separate branches of Tantric ritual[3] and great collections compiled from the various Tantras.[4]

The earliest Nepalese manuscripts of Tantras date from the seventh to the ninth century,[5] and it is not very likely that this literature originated further back than the fifth or sixth century. Even in the latest portions of the Mahābhārata, with their frequent allusions to Itihāsas and Purāṇas, there is never mention of Tantras, and the Amarakośa, among the meanings of the word "*tantra*" does not give that of a

---

[1]) Published in AnSS No. 69, 1912.

[2]) An analysis of its contents by A. H. *Ewing*, JAOS, 23, 1902, p. 65 ff. Cf. *Farquhar*, Outline, p. 267.

[3]) Thus there are glossaries and dictionaries to explain the mysterious significance of the letters, Bījas and Mantras, as well as the Mudrās or positions of the fingers to be observed with the Yoga. A few of these texts (Mantrābhidhāna from the Rudrayāmala, Ekākṣarakoṣa by Puruṣottamadeva, Bījanighaṇṭu by Bhairava, Mātṛkānighaṇṭus by Mahīdhara and by Mādhava, Mudrānighaṇṭu from the Vāmakeśvara-Tantra) are published by A. *Avalon*, Tantrik Texts, Vol. I, 1913. Cf. also Th. *Zachariæ*, Die indischen Wörterbücher (Grundriss I, 3 B, 1897) para. 27, and *Leumann*, OC VI, Leyden, Vol. III, p. 589 ff. The six centres (cakra) and the Kuṇḍalinī are treated in the Ṣaṭcakranirūpaṇa from the Śrītattvacintāmaṇi by Pūrṇānanda Svāmī and the Pādukāpañcaka, both published by Tārānātha *Vidyāratna* in Tantrik Texts, Vol. II, 1913 and translated into English by A. *Avalon*, The Serpent Power, 2nd. ed, Madras 1924.

[4]) Thus the Tantrasamuccaya, very popular in Malabar, written by Nārāyaṇa of the Jayanta-mangala family of N. Travancore about 1426 A.D., published by T. *Gaṇapati Śāstri* in TSS Nos. 67 and 71.

[5]) A Kubjikāmata-Tantra is said to date from the 7th century, and a Niśvāsatattva-Saṃhitā from the 8th century. A Parameśvaramata-Tantra was written in 858 A.D. Cf. *Haraprasād*, Report I, p. 4.

religious book.[1] Neither do the Chinese pilgrims as yet mention the Tantras. In the seventh and eighth centuries they began to penetrate into Buddhism, and in the second half of the eighth century Buddhist Tantras were translated into Chinese [2] and in the ninth century into Tibetan also. The fact that the worship of Durgā, which plays so great a part in the Tantras, harks back to the later Vedic period,[3] does not prove that Tantrism and the Tantras are of an equally venerable age. There is no doubt that this goddess and her cult do unite traits of very different deities, Aryan as well as non-Aryan. It is probable, too, that the system of the Tantras adopted many characteristics from non-Aryan and non-brahmanical cults.[4] On the other hand, some essential traits of the Tantras can be found as far back as in the Atharvaveda, as well as in the Brāhmaṇas and Upaniṣads. Śāktism was prevalent from the twelfth to the sixteenth century in Bengal especially among the aristocracy, and even at the present day its adherents are to be found not in

---

[1]) Amarakoṣa III, 182 gives for *tantra* the meaning *siddhānta*, which is really "a system of doctrines" in general, and not a particular class of texts. Cf. *Wilson*, Works, I, 250. The other Kośas, too, give all kinds of meanings for *tantra*, but not that of the sacred book of a sect. When *mantra* and *tantra* are mentioned side by side (Ahirbudhnya-Saṃhitā XX, 5; Pañcatantra, text. simpl., ed. F. Kielhorn I, v. 70; Daśakumāracarita II, NSP edition, p. 81; mudrātantramantra-dhyānādibhiḥ), *tantra* means "magic rite," and *mantra* "incantation." The passage in the Daśakum. probably presupposes a knowledge of Tantras. Daṇḍin, however, did not live earlier than the 7th century A.D. The Bhāgavata-Purāṇa (IV, 24, 62; XI, 3, 47 f., 5, 28; 31) is the first work to mention the Tantras as a class of works apart from the Veda.

[2]) According to L. *Wieger*, Histoire des croyances religieuses et des opinions philosophiques en Chine, Paris 1917 (quoted by *Woodroffe*, Shakti and Shâkta, p. 119 ff.), as early as in the 7th century. It is not likely that the *nigamas* mentioned side by side with the *nirghaṇṭu* in Lalitavistara XII (ed. Lefmann, p. 156) are identical with the Tantras known as "nigama," as is the view of *Avalon* (Principles of Tantra I, p. xli). As in Manu IV, 14; IX, 14, texts of Veda-exegesis are no doubt meant.

[3]) *Jacobi* in ERE V, 117 ff.

[4]) In the Jayadrathayāmala it is said that Parameśvarī is to be worshipped in the house of a potter or oil-presser (who belong to the lowest castes). Cf. *Haraprasād*, Report I, p. 16; Catalogue of the Durbar Library, Nepal, p. lxi.

the lower castes, but among the educated.[1] On the whole the Tantras and the curious excrescences and degenerations of religion described in them, are not drawn from popular belief or from popular traditions either of the aboriginal inhabitants or of the Aryan immigrants, but they are the pseudo-scientific productions of theologians, in which the practice and theory of Yoga and doctrines of the monist (advaita) philosophy are seen mingled with the most extravagant symbolism and occultism.

Neither the Purāṇas nor the Tantras make enjoyable reading, and this is much more applicable to the latter. They are the work of inferior writers, and are often written in barbarous and ungrammatical Sanskrit. On the other hand neither the literary historian nor the student of religion can afford to pass them by in silence; for during centuries and even at the present time these writings are the spiritual food of millions of Indians. "The Purāṇas," says a learned Hindu,[2] "form an important portion of the religious literature of the Hindus, and, together with the Dharmaśāstras and Tantras, govern their conduct and regulate their religious observances at the present day. The Vedas are studied by the antiquarian, the Upaniṣads by the philosopher; but every orthodox Hindu must have some knowledge of the Purāṇas, directly or vicariously, to shape his conduct and to perform the duties essential to his worldly and spiritual welfare." Whatever also may be our opinion of the literary, religious and moral value of the Tantras, the historian of Indian religion and culture cannot afford to neglect them, and from the point of view of comparative religion, too, they contain valuable material.

---

[1]) The present-day Śāktas are probably for the most part such as will have none of the Pañcatattva ritual. At any rate I was assured in Kashmir that the Śāktas there all abhor rites of this nature.

[2]) N. *Mukhopādhyāya* in the Introduction to his edition of the Kūrma-Purāṇa (Bibl. Ind.), p. xv.

CORRECTIONS AND ADDITIONS.

P. 5 l. 1 read *more the.*
l. 4 " *But there.*
" 38 " 19 " *seventh* for *tenth.*
" 48 note 1 add: *Haraprasād Śāstrī* (Ind. Hist. Qu. I, 1925, p. 204 f.) thinks that it is not a Sanskritised vernacular, but "the spoken language of N. India."
" 49 note 1, l. 1 read *Apabhraṃśas see H.*
Pp. 53, 55 etc., to 71 the head line should be "*Vedic Literature*" instead of "*Introduction.*"
P. 59 l. 9 read I and X for I to X.
" 60 note 1, l. 3 read ZII for ZIT.
" 62 " 1 " ZII " ZTT.
" 63 " 3 l. 5 " *nadīstuti.*
" 71 l. 14 read *therefore* for *moreover.*
" 76 " 4 " *already* " *soon.*
" 81 note 2, l. 2 read *storm-gods.*
" 98 " 1 should be note 2 on p. 97, l. 21.
" 99 l. 20 read 3) for 2)
note 1, l. 1 read *Tapas* for *Tapaç.*
" 100 notes, l. 2, after V, p. 356, add: Metrical Translations from Sanskrit Writers, p. 188 f.
" 102 " 4, l. 4 read *Oldenberg* for *Oldenburg.*
" 117 line 7 from below, read *Vāc* for *Vac.*
" 120 " 1, l. 2 read *Cūlikā-Upaniṣad.*
" 2 l. 3 after 1856 add: second edition by Max *Lindenau*, Berlin, 1924.
" 131 l. 5 from below read *spell* for *verse.*
" 1 " " " *apacit* " *apakit.*
" 132 ll. 3, 6 read *apacit* for *apakit.*
" 134 l. 2 read *indicate* " *indicated.*

	Page	Place	Correction
P.	138	l. 13	read *conceptions of* for *conception.*
"	152	note 1	the Greek quotation is hopelessly wrong.
"	154	" 1	add at the end of the note: ZB VI, 1924-25, p. 48 ff.
"	160	l. 6	read *gṛhyakarmāṇi.*
"	163	" 18	" *Sāmaveda-Saṃhitā.*
"	167	ll. 13, 15, 16	read *Ūhagāna, Ūhyagāna.*
"	179	l. 14	" *Āyu* for *Ayu.*
		note 5, l. 1,	read *Śatapatha* for *Śatapaṭha.*
"	187	note 3,	" *bráhman* for *brāhman.*
"	188	notes, line 1,	" *brahmán* for *brahmān.*
"	190	l. 19	" *Śāṅkhāyana.*
"	194	note, l. 6	" *Bhāradvājī* for *Bhāradvājō.*
"	201	" 2	" *174 f.* for *147 f.*
"	215	l. 4	" *Śunaḥśepa* for *Śūnaḥśepa.*
"	222	l. 12	" *another* for *other.*
"	225	l. 21	" *Śāṇḍilya* for *Śaṇḍilya.*
"	232	l. 16	" *Āśramas* for *Aśram as*
		note 1, l. 7	" *Fick* for *Pick.*
		l. 12	" *l'Inde* for *l, Inde.*
"	235	ll. 12 and 13	" *Taittirīya-Upaniṣad and Mahā-Nārāyaṇa-Upaniṣad.*
		note 1, l. 4	" *Friedlaender* for *Friedlander.*
"	243	l. 13	" *this* for *thus.*
"	247	note 3, l. 3	" *Oldenberg* for *Oldenburg, and brahman* for *brāhman.*
"	248	note, l. 3	" *phlegma* for the Greek word.
"	259	note 3	Add.: E. W. *Hopkins*, Ethics of India, New Haven 1924, p. 63ff.
"	271	note 2, l. 5	read *Brāhmaṇas* for *Brahmans.*
"	288	" 1, l. 3	" *Proc. IIOC* for *Proc. SOC.*
"	298	" 1, l. 4	" *Proc IOC* for *Proc. FOC.*
"	299	" 1.	" *17′* and *8′*.
"	300	" l. 20	put the inverted commas (") after *achievements.*

P. 302 l. 5 read *Śunaḥśepa.*
" 302 note 4 read *194 f.*
" 308 note 2, l. 1 read *Proc. IOC.* for *Proc. FOC.*
" 312, note 1, l. 2 read *Āpastambīya.*
l. 5 " *Śrautasūtra.*
" 313, " 4, l. 6 " *Itihāsa.*
" 316, " 1, l. 5 from below, read *Winternitz.*
" 317, " l. 5 read *seine* for *scine.*
" 319, " 1, line 1, " *traced in* for *traced. In*
" 320, " l. " *H. Jacobi.*
" 322, ll. 5 and 3 from below, read *Śāntanu* for *Sāntanu.*
" 322, note 2, l. 2 read *vivyāsa.*
l. 3 " *smṛtaḥ, cf.*
" 324, l. 17 " *spake* for *spaken.*
" 324, note 1, l. 2 from below, read *saechsischen* for *sáchsischen.*
" 325, l. 5 read *men* for *man.*
" 327, l. 6 " *parts* 1).
" 327, note 1, line 1 " *Kisari* for *Kisori.*
l. 4 from below, read *1924* for *192ff.*
" 329, l. 4 read *Śāntanu* for *Sāntanu.*
" 334, l. 2 from below, " *Pañcālas* for *Pāñcālas.*
" 345, l. 12 from below, " *Yudhiṣṭhira.*
" 349, l. 9 from below, " *Nahuṣa* for *Nahusa.*
" 359, l. 13 " *days'* for *day's.*
" 368, l. 8 " *of* for *os.*
" 376, note 1, l. 6 " *Porzig* for *Perzig.*
" 379, l. 19 " *Śarmiṣṭhā* for *Sarmiṣṭha.*
" 385, note 2, l. 5. put inverted commas (") after *Mahābhārata.*
" 386, note 1 read *diospyros* for *diespyros.*
" 389, " 2, l. 3 " *s.* for *S.*
" 393, l. 3 " *Brahman-* for *Brāhman-*
" 397, l. 12 " *Sāvitrī* for *Sāvitri.*
note 4, l. 3 " *Yudhiṣṭhira.*

P. 410, note 3, l. 6 read *Franke* for *Francke*.
" 413, last line, the reference is to note 1 on page 414.
" 417, note 2, l. 2 read *Jinistic* for *Jainistic*.
" 418, " , line 1 " *Uttarādhyayana*.
" 426, " , l. 2 " *excellence* for *excetlence*.
" 431, " 1, l. 2 from below, read *Garbe* for *Carbe*.
" 439, l. 7 read *disfigured* for *mutilated*.
l. 16 " *Sāṃkhya* for *Saṃkhya*.
note 1, line 1 " *late* for *ten*.
" 440, " 3, last line " *epic* for *epics*.
" 443, " 1, add : *and into English by Manmatha Nath Dutt, Calcutta 1897*.
" 444, note 3 read *Pṛthūpākhyāna*.
" 447, l. 14 " *cowherd* for *cowhard*.
" 449, l. 3 " *Śiśupāla*.
" 450, l. 6 from below " *Naraka* for *Nikumbha*.
" 453, note 1 " *Adhy. 278 : Īśvarastuti. Adhy. 279 and 281 : Viṣṇustotra.*
" 3 " *Haṃsa*° for *Hamṣa*°.
" 470, l. 2 from below " *Śāṅkhāyana-Śrautasūtra*.
" 471, lines 10, 13, 16 " *Tipiṭaka* for *Tripiṭaka*.
" 471, note 3, l. 2 " *extent* for *extents*.
" 472, l. 4 " *Yudhiṭṭhila*.
l. 5 " *Dhataraṭṭha*.
note 4, l. 6 " *is*.
" 473, l. 4 " *of* for *with*.
l. 8 " *Āśvalāyana* for *Aśvalāyana*.
" 479, note 3, line 1 " *Griffith* for *Crifith*.
" 486, " 1, l. 6 " *below, p. 508f*.
" 487, line 11 " *Śūrpaṇakhā*.
" 489, l. 4 " *monkeys* for *monkey*.
" 492, l. 30 " *14ff.* for *4ff.*
" 507, l. 15 " *Gāndhārī*.
" 511, l. 7 from below " *Jinistic* for *Jainistic*.

P. 512, l. 8 read *that* for *hat*.
" 512, note 2, l. 9 " *Pāṇini* and *Patañjali*.
" 513, " 5 " *p. 1 f.*
" 518, " 1 After *Urvaśī* read (*cf. T. Michelson, JAOS* 29, 284 *f.*)
" 522, l. 20 read *Vaṃśānucarita*.
l. 21 " *dynasties,*" *viz.* "*the*
" 527, note 2 " *to* for *te*.
" 528, " 2 " *the most clearly* for *most clearly*.
" 540, " 1, line 1 " *Haradatta Śarmā*.
" 553, " 2, l. 4 " *Vāyavīya* for *Vaiyavīya*.
" 557, l. 20 " *-Purāṇa* for *-Pūrāṇa*.
" 562, l. 28 " *the racking torture* for *racking torture*.
" 566, l. 7 from below, read *poetics* for *poetry*.
" 576, note 1 " *Jibananda Vidyasagara* for *Jibānanda Vidyāsāgara*.
" *Nath* for *Nāth*.
" 580, l. 1 " *Viṣṇudharmottara*.
" 587, note 2, last line " *Śaiva* for *Saiva*.
" 589, l. 7 read *Śiva, and Nārada* (comma after Śiva).
" 589, note 1, l. 5 read *the* for *t e*.
" 589, " 3, l. 6 read *Ṣaṣṭitantra*.
" 590, l. 4 from below, put *comma* after *Pauṣkara*.
" 593, l. 20 read *Prakṛti* for *prakṛti*.

Note.—In order not to swell the list of corrections, smaller errors such as *s* for *ś* or *a* for *ā*, and the like, have not been mentioned in the above list.

INDEX.

COMPILED BY W. GAMPERT.

A HISTORY OF
INDIAN LITERATURE

A HISTORY OF INDIAN LITERATURE:

VOL.II

BUDDHSIT AND JAINA LITERATURE

M. WINTERNITZ

TRANSLATOR

MRS.S.KETKAR

IN THREE VOLUMES

VOLUMS - II

GYAN

Published by

Gyan Publishing House
5, Ansari Road
Daryaganj, New Delhi-110002
Phone: 011-47034999, 9811692060
E-mail: books@gyanbooks.com

Distribution Network
gyanbooks.com
India, USA, Canada, UK, Australia

ISBN: 978-93-6920-702-2 (Set)
978-93-6920-204-1 (HB)
First Published, 1904

2nd Impression 2025

Printed at: Gyan Press, Delhi.

A HISTORY OF INDIAN LITERATURE (Vol. II)
Author: M. WINTERNITZ,
Translator: MRS.S.KETKAR

A HISTORY OF INDIAN LITERATURE

A HISTORY OF INDIAN LITERATURE

BY

MAURICE WINTERNITZ, Ph.D.

PROFESSOR OF INDOLOGY AND ETHNOLOGY AT THE GERMAN UNIVERSITY OF PRAGUE (CZECHOSLOVAKIA)

VOL. II

BUDDHIST LITERATURE AND JAINA LITERATURE

TRANSLATED FROM THE ORIGINAL GERMAN BY

MRS. S. KETKAR AND MISS H. KOHN, B.A.

AND

REVISED BY THE AUTHOR

Only Authorised Translation into English

PUBLISHED BY THE

UNIVERSITY OF CALCUTTA

1933

To

RABINDRANATH TAGORE

The Great Poet, Educator and Lover of Man

This English Version of the "History of Indian Literature"

is dedicated

as a token of loving admiration and sincere gratitude

by the Author

TABLE OF CONTENTS

PREFACE TO THE GERMAN EDITION, THE FIRST HALF OF VOLUME II

Just five years ago, when I wrote the preface to Volume I of this "History of Indian Literature," I had hoped that it would be possible to publish Volume II complete two years later; but the task of dealing, for the first time, with Buddhist literature presented far greater difficulties than I had foreseen. For this reason, even now only the first half of Volume II is appearing. I hope, however, that the second half—the conclusion of the work—will follow in the course of next year.

I am only too conscious of the fact that a presentation of Buddhist literature, which forms the subject-matter of this half-volume, is, at the present stage of our knowledge, a hazardous enterprise. A great part of this literature has only just been opened up, while a still greater part, especially of the Buddhist Sanskrit literature, but also some important Pāli texts, is still waiting for translators and researchers, and even for editors. In addition to this, with the small number of workers in the province of Sinology, the light which the Chinese translations throw upon the history of Buddhist literature has scarcely begun to shine. Here we may surely hope for help and improvement in the near future from French and Japanese scholars. We may also expect very shortly considerable enrichment of our knowledge of Buddhist literature and its history from the investigation of the Central Asian finds—the wealth of manuscripts which M. A. *Stein* has brought back from Khotan, and A. *Grünwedel* and A. von *Le Coq* from Turfan. Nevertheless it will take decades before all the results of these investigations will be available. An American colleague of mine hit the mark when he recently wrote to me: 'I can easily understand that your History of Buddhist Literature is the devil's own job to write.' And yet, the attempt to present Buddhist literature had to be ventured now; for it simply will no longer do, now-a-days, to write a history of Indian literature without doing justice to the Buddhist literature. Buddhism, after all, is and remains that production of the Indian mind, which is the most important in the history of the world. And how can we understand Buddhism without knowing its literature? Just as in a history of Indian religion the religion of Buddha would have to occupy a large space, just as a history of Indian art could not exist without Buddhist art, so too the history of Indian literature would show a gaping chasm if Buddhist literature were not presented therein. Even though this literature is to-day more at home in Ceylon and Burma, in Nepal and Tibet, than in India proper, yet it grew up on Indian soil, it bears all the characteristics of a genuine product of the Indian mind, it has, through far more than a thousand years, influenced Indian spiritual life, and naturally is most intimately connected with all the rest of Indian literature. However defective a presentation of Buddhist literature must necessarily still be to-day, it is nevertheless of some use for the progress of knowledge. We must have the courage to err. Our errors will serve as stepping-stones over which the knowledge of future generations of scholars will stride to new truths.

The literary references in the notes give sufficient information concerning the works from which I have drawn and the scholars to whom I am indebted. I should not, however, like to omit in this place the expression of my sincere thanks to my honoured colleague, Professor Louis de *La Vallée Poussin* in Brussels, and my dear friend and former pupil, Professor Jyun *Takakusu*, for several valuable printed papers and written communications.

M. WINTERNITZ

Prague—Smichow,
17th October, 1912.

FROM THE PREFACE TO THE GERMAN EDITION, VOLUME II, SECOND HALF

The second half of Volume II (p. 289 ff.) is devoted to the literature of the Jainas, which, as in the case of Buddhist literature is presented here for the first time as a connected whole.

Since the publication of the first half of this volume, seven years have elapsed. During this period much work has been done in the field of Buddhist literature. I have utilised everything of importance, in as far as I was informed of it,[1] in the "Corrections and Additions," as also the valuable reviews which individual scholars—J. *Charpentier* (WZKM 27, 1913, pp. 85-96), H. *Haas* (Zeitschrift für Missionskunde und Religionswissenschaft 28, 1913, pp. 111-123), P. E. *Pavolini* (GSAI 25, 1912, pp. 323-325), T. W. *Rhys Davids* (JRAS, 1913, 479-483) and H. *Kern* (Ostasiatische Zeitschrift II, 1913-14, pp. 471-481)—devoted to my book. I had to deal somewhat more exhaustively (p. 357 ff.) with the latest studies of R. O. *Franke* and with the criticism which the same scholar has devoted to my book, as these concern the most essential part of my work. The fact that, in his views regarding the person of the Buddha and the historical significance of the Buddhist writings, *Franke* occupies a rather isolated position among the competent scholars, would certainly not be a reason against his being right after all. However, I

---

1 Unfortunately much may have escaped my notice. The terrible world-war which lies between the appearance of the first and second half of this volume, has also hit our science badly, and made it very difficult, often impossible, for us to avail ourselves of the studies of our English, American, Indian, French and Italian colleagues.

hope I have shown that neither the extreme scepticism of *Franke* nor his attitude towards the Nikāyas, which diverges so very widely from the current conception, are so convincing as to induce me to make any essential alteration in what I have said about the Pāli canon...

I am indebted to my pupil Dr. Otto *Stein* for his assistance in the correction of the proofs of the second half of this volume and in the revision of the Index.

* * * *

During the time which has elapsed since the publication of the first half of this volume, death has made deep gaps in the ranks of the scholars whose studies afforded some of the most valuable basic material of this work. Heinrich *Kern*, the patriarch among Buddha researchers, Ernst *Windisch*, to whom we are indebted for some of the most valuable researches into Buddhist literature, Paul *Deussen*, the enthusiastic pioneer of ancient Indian philosophy, and Hermann *Oldenberg*, who had so profound a knowledge of both Buddhist and Vedic literature and religion, coupled with so great a talent in presenting them, who scarcely left a single field of the culture of India uncultivated, have passed away in rapid succession. My dear friend Leopold von *Schroeder*, too, who more than thirty years ago, undertook to write a history of Indian literature and culture, and to whom I was permitted to dedicate this work as a token of grateful admiration, and who ever followed its progress with affectionate interest, is no longer among the living. The memory of these men will not fade in the history of our science,—*na hi karma kṣīyate*— for "deeds are not lost."

Prague, *29th July, 1920.*

M. WINTERNITZ

PREFACE TO THE ENGLISH TRANSLATION

Owing to various unfortunate circumstances both the revision and the printing of this volume have taken much longer time than I ever anticipated. As the German original of Part I on Buddhist Literature was published in 1913 and that of Part II on Jaina Literature in 1920 it is only natural that this volume, no less than Volume 1, is not a mere translation, but a new edition as well, in which much had to be altered, added and, I hope, improved. I had to revise my presentation of Buddhist literature in the light of the numerous excellent publications we owe to the Pāli Text Society during the last twenty years, and I had to avail myself of the valuable work done during the same period by European, Indian and Japanese scholars in the field of Sanskrit Buddhist literature.

To Mrs. *Rhys Davids* I am greatly indebted for sending me, along with some valuable notes of her own, the critical notes which her husband, the late Professor *T. W. Rhys Davids*, had entered in his copy of my German book, and which I did not fail to make use of in the course of revising the chapters on Pāli literature.

Thanks to the zeal and efforts of the Jaina community a great number of Jaina texts, both in new editions and in translations, has become accessible since the publication of my German account of Jaina literature. But not only that. Not a few Jaina texts that were already published before 1920, were not available to me at the time when I first wrote on the subject. I owe a great debt of gratitude to my Jaina friends—above all to my revered friend the Itihāsa-Tattva-Mahodadhi

Vijaya Indra Suri, the worthy successor of the late venerable Jainācārya *Vijaya Dharma Suri*, but also to Mr. *Chotelall Jain* of Calcutta, to the Dharm-Sewak *Ummed Singh Musaddi Lal Jain* of Amritsar, and many others—for having provided me with a great number of rare and valuable publications, both old and new, which enabled me to make the section on Jaina literature in the English version far more complete than it was in the German original.

As the first batch of manuscript was sent to press already in 1927, and the last sheets were printed only in the summer of 1932, many "Additions and Corrections" became necessary, in order to bring the work up to date (that is, up to June, 1932). But I am glad to say, the number of printer's errors that had to be corrected, is comparatively small. For this I have to thank Dr. *Niranjan Prasad Chakravarti*, M. A., Ph. D. (Cantab.), Lecturer in Sanskrit at the University of Calcutta, to whom the difficult task of reading the proofs had been entrusted and who has done his work most carefully.

My thanks are due to the translators of the volume, Mrs. *Ketkar* and her sister Miss *Helen Kohn*, who have spared no pains to make as accurate and readable a translation as possible.

Finally I have to thank again my pupil Dr. *Wilhelm Gampert* for the great care he has bestowed on the compilation of the Index.

Prague, *February, 1933.* M. WINTERNITZ

LIST OF ABBREVIATIONS USED IN THE NOTES

ABA = Abhandlungen der Berliner Akademie der Wissenschaften, Philol.-hist. Klasse.

ABayA = Abhandlungen der Bayerischen Akademie der Wissenschaften, Phil. Klasse.

AGGW = Abhandlungen der Königl. Gesellschaft der Wissenschaften zu Göttingen, Philol.-histor. Klasse.

AKM = Abhandlungen für die Kunde des Morgenlandes, herausg. von der Deutschen Morgenländischen Gesellschaft.

Album Kern = Album-Kern: Opstellen geschreven ter eere von Dr. H. Kern...op zijn zeventigsten verjaardag, Leiden 1903.

AMG = Annales du Musée Guimet (Paris).

Ann. Bh. Inst. = Annals of the Bhandarkar Institute, Poona.

AR = Archiv für Religionsgeschichte.

ASB = Asiatic Society of Bengal.

ASGW = Abhandlungen der Philol.-histor. Klasse der Königl. Sächs. Gesellschaft der Wissenschaften.

ĀUS = Āgamodaya Samiti.

Bagchi = Prabodhachandra Bagchi, Le Canon Bouddhique en Chine, tome I, Paris 1927.

BB = Bibliographie Bouddhique (Paris).

BEFEO = Bulletin de l'école française d'Extrême Orient.

Bezz. Beitr. = Beiträge zur Kunde der indogermanischen Sprachen, herausg. von A. Bezzenberger.

Bhandarkar, Report 1882-83 = R. G. Bhandarkar, Report on the Search for Sanskrit Manuscripts in the Bombay Presidency during the year 1882-83, Bombay 1884.

Bhandarkar, Report 1883-84 = R. G Bhandarkar, Report, etc., during the year 1883-84, Bombay 1887.

Bibl. Buddh. = Bibliotheca Buddhica (Leningrad).

Bibl. Ind. = Bibliotheca Indica (Calcutta).

BSGW = Berichte über die Verhandlungen der Königl. Sächsischen Gesellschaft der Wissenschaften zu Leipzig, Philol.-histor. Klasse.

BSOS = Bulletin of the School of Oriental Studies, London Institution.

BSS = Bombay Sanskrit Series.

Cambridge History = The Cambridge History of India, Vol. I, Ancient India. Ed. by E. J. Rapson, Cambridge 1922.

Comm. Wogihara = Journal of the Taisho University, Vols. VI-VII, in commemoration of the Sixtieth Birthday of Professor Unrai Wogihara, Sugamo, Tokyo, the Taisho University, 1930, Part II.

CUIS = Columbia University Indo-Iranian Series, New York.

DJGK = Digambara Jaina Granthabhāṇḍāra, Kāśī Kā, ed. by Pannālāl Chaudhari, Benares 1924-25.

DLZ = Deutsche Literaturzeitung.

Duff = C. Mabel Duff, The Chronology of India, Westminster 1899.

EB = The Eastern Buddhist (Kyoto, Japan).

Eliot = Sir Charles Eliot, Hinduism and Buddhism, London 1921.

Ep. Ind. = Epigraphia Indica.

ERE = Encyclopædia of Religion and Ethics, edited by James Hastings.

Festgabe Jacobi = Beiträge zur Literaturwissenschaft und Geistesgeschichte Indiens. Festgabe Hermann Jacobi zum, 75. Geburtstag...Bonn 1926.

GGA = Göttinger Gelehrte Anzeigen.

GOS = Gaekwad's Oriental Series, Baroda.

GSAI = Giornale della societa Asiatica Italiana.

Hiralal, Catalogue = Rai Bahadur Hiralal, Catalogue of Sanskrit and Prākrit MSS., published under the Orders of the Government of the Central Provinces and Berar, Nagpur 1926.

HOS = Harvard Oriental Series, ed. by Ch. R. Lanman.

Ind. Ant. = Indian Antiquary.

Ind. Hist. Qu. = The Indian Historical Quarterly, edited by Narendranath Law, Calcutta.

Ind. Stud. = Indische Studien, herausgegeben von A. Weber.

JA = Journal Asiatique.

JAOS = Journal of the Americen Oriental Society.

JASB = Journal of the Asiatic Society of Bengal.

JBORS = Journal of the Bihar and Orissa Research Society.

JBRAS = Journal of the Bombay Branch of the Royal Asiatic Society.

JBTS = Journal of the Buddhist Text Society.

JDL = University of Calcutta, Journal of the Department of Letters.

JPTS = Journal of the Pāli Text Society.

JPU = Sheth Devchand Lalbhai Jaina Pustakoddhara.

JRAS = Journal of the Royal Asiatic Society of Great Britain and Ireland.

Km = Kāvyamālā.

Lanman Studies = Indian Studies in honour of Charles Rockwell Lanman, Harvard University Press, Cambridge Mass. 1929.

LZB = Literarisches Zentralblatt.

MDJG = Māṇikacandra Digambara Jaina Granthamālā.

Nanjio = Bunyiu Nanjio, Catalogue of the Chinese Translation of the Buddhist Tripiṭaka, Oxford 1883.

NGGW = Nachrichten von der Kgl. Gesellschaft der Wissenschaften Göttingen, Philol.-histor. Klasse.

NSP = Nirṇaya-Sāgara Press (Bombay).

OC = Transactions (Verhandlungen, Actes) of International Congresses of Orientalists.

Oldenberg, Buddha = Hermann Oldenberg, Buddha. Sein Leben, seine Lehre, seine Gemeinde. 7. Aufl. Berlin 1920.

OTF = Oriental Translation Fund.

OLZ = Orientalistische Literaturzeitung.

OZ = Ostasiatische Zeitschrift.

Peterson, Report 1882-83 = P. Peterson, Report on the Search for Sanskrit Manuscripts in the Bombay Circle, 1882-83 (JBRAS, Vol. 16, Extra Number).

Peterson, Report II = P. Peterson, A Second Report of Operations in Search of Sanskrit MSS., etc., 1883-84 (JBRAS, Vol. 17, Extra Number).

Peterson, 3 Reports = P. Peterson, Three Reports on a Search for Sanskrit MSS. with an Index of Books (JBRAS, Vol. 18, Extra Number). 1887.

Peterson, Report IV = P. Peterson, A Fourth Report, etc., 1886-92 (JBRAS, Vol. 18, Extra Number).

Peterson, Report V = P. Peterson, A Fifth Report, etc., April, 1892—March, 1895, Bombay 1896.

Peterson, Report VI = P. Peterson, A Sixth Report, etc., April, 1895—March, 1898, Bombay 1899.

Proc. I etc., OC = Proceedings and Transactions of the First, etc., Oriental Conferences.

PSS = Punjab Sanskrit Series (Lahore).

PTS = Pāli Text Society.

PTS Dic. = The Pāli Text Society's Pāli-English Dictionary, edited by T. W. Rhys Davids and William Stede.

RGG = Die Religion in Geschichte und Gegenwart (Tübingen).

RHR = Revue de l' histoire des Religions, Paris.

RSO = Rivista degli studi orientali, Rome.

SBA = Sitzungsberichte der Preussischen Akademie der Wissenschaften in Berlin.

SBB = Sacred Books of the Buddhists (London, Oxford University Press).

SBE = Sacred Books of the East (Oxford).

SBJ = Sacred Books of the Jainas (Arrah).

SIFI = Studi Italiani di Filologia Indo-Iranica.

SJG = Sanātana-Jaina-Granthamālā.

Smith, Early History = Vincent A. Smith, the Early History of India. Fourth Edition, revised by S. M. Edwardes, Oxford 1924.

TSS = Trivandrum Sanskrit Series.

Weber HSS. Verz. = A. Weber, Verzeichniss der Sanskrit und Prakrit-Handschriften der K. Bibliothek zu Berlin.

WZKM = Wiener Zeitschrift für die Kunde des Morgenlandes.

YJG = Yasovijaya Jaina Granthamālā.

ZB = Zeitschrift für Buddhismus (München).

ZDMG = Zeitschrift der Deutschen Morgenländischen Gesellschaft.

ZII = Zeitschrift für Indologie und Iranistik, herausg. von der Deutschen Morgenländischen Gesellschaft.

ZVV = Zeitschrift des Vereins für Volkskunde in Berlin.

DIRECTIONS FOR PRONUNCIATION OF INDIAN (SANSKRIT, PRAKRIT, PALI) NAMES AND WORDS WRITTEN IN ROMAN CHARACTERS.

Pronounce

Vowels
- a अ as a 'neutral vowel,' like English short *u* in b*u*t
- ṛ ऋ as a vowel, like *er* in Scots English bak*er*.
- e ए, o ओ as long ē in English th*e*y and ō in English st*o*ne, without diphthongal character.

Palatals
- c च like *ch* in English *ch*ild.
- j ज like *j* in English *j*ust.

Cerebrals
- ṭ ट, ṭh ठ, ḍ ड, ḍh ढ, ṇ ण like English 'dentals,' while the Sanskrit dentals t त, th थ, d द, dh ध, n न are pronounced like dentals in Italian and French.

Sibilants
- ś श (palatal), ṣ ष (cerebral) like *sh* in English *sh*ip.

Nasals
- ṅ ङ (guttural) like *ng* in English si*ng*.
- ñ ञ (palatal) like *gn* in French monta*gn*e
- ṃ (Anusvāra) like *n* in French Jea*n*.
- ḥ (Visarga) "a surd breathing, a final *h*-sound (in the European sense of *h*) uttered in the articulating position of the preceding vowel."—*Whitney*.

SECTION III.

BUDDHIST LITERATURE.

THE PĀLI CANON OR THE TIPIṬAKA.[1]

Vedic literature led us well-nigh into "prehistoric" times; and for the beginnings of epic poetry, too, we had to dispense with all certain dates. It is only with the Buddhist literature that we gradually emerge into the broad daylight of history, and we have seen that the darkness of the history of the Vedic and the epic literature is somewhat illuminated by this light. The approximate period of Buddha can be determined with some degree of probability, and that gives a starting-point, from which we can calculate the origin of a Buddhist literature. Gotama Buddha died probably a few years before or after 485 B. C.,[2] and according to a tradition

---

[1]) See H. *Oldenberg*, Vinayapiṭaka, Vol. I, London, 1879, Introduction; ZDMG 52, 1898, 613ff.; NGGW 1912, 197ff.; Reden des Buddha (1922), Einleitung; H. *Jacobi* and *Oldenberg*, ZDMG 34, 1880, 184ff.; 751ff.; *Oldenberg* and T. W. *Rhys Davids*, SBE, Vol. 13, Introduction; *Rhys Davids*, Buddhist India, London, 1903, 167ff.; Cambridge History I, 192ff.; W. *Geiger*, Pāli Literatur und Sprache (Grundriss I, 7, 1916), p. 6ff.; R. S. *Copleston*, Buddhism, 2nd Ed., London, 1908, 45f., 167ff.; H. *Kern*, Manual of Indian Buddhism (Grundriss III, 8, 1896), 1ff., 101ff.; *Eliot* I, 275ff. The following are more or less sceptical about the authenticity of the Pāli Canon: I. P. *Minayeff*, Recherches sur le Bouddhisme (AMG, Bibliothéque d'études, t. 4, Paris, 1894); A. *Barth* in RHR, t. 5, 1882, 237ff.; t. 28, 1893, 241ff.; 277ff.; t. 42, 1900, 74ff. (= Oeuvres I, 340ff.: II, 156ff., 187ff., 356ff.; V. A. *Smith*, *Ind. Ant.* 32, 1903, 364ff.; L. de *La Vallée Poussin*, Bouddhisme, Études et Matériaux (Mémoires......publié par l'Académie roy. des sciences de Belgique, t. LV), Bruxelles, 1897, 1ff., 27ff., 44ff., 53ff.; Le Muséon, 1905, 213ff.; *Ind. Ant.* 37, 1908, 1ff., 81ff.; Bouddhisme, Paris, 1909, pp. 29ff., 155, 166ff., 248; ERE. Vol. IV, p. 179ff. (*Cf.* E. J. *Rapson*, JRAS, 1898, 909ff.); R. Otto *Franke*, JPTS, 1908, pp. 1-80; Dīghanikāya (1913), p. xliiff.; A. B. *Keith*, Buddhist Philosophy in India and Ceylon, Oxford, 1923, pp. 3, 16ff.

[2]) See Appendix I.

whose authenticity we are scarcely justified in questioning, he attained the age of 80 years. As a young man of 29 years he is said to have taken up the life of a wandering ascetic, and thus begun to seek the way of salvation. After severe internal struggles he began, as a mature man, to proclaim the doctrine he had discovered. The activity of the Buddha might, then, fall into the period of about 535-485 B. C.: the foundation and propagation of that Indian religion which was destined to become one of the three great religions of the world. The Ganges district in North-East India was the scene of his activity. Here—in the kingdoms of Magadha (Bihar) and Kosala (Oudh)—he wandered from place to place, preaching his doctrine and gathering ever more adherents about him.

Does this work of many decades include any literary activity? Certainly not. It is true that in the Tipiṭaka, the Pāli canon of the Buddhists, most of the speeches and sayings are placed in the mouth of Buddha himself; it is even related exactly and circumstantially where and on what occasion the master delivered a speech or made an utterance. How much, out of all this, should really be attributed to Buddha, will probably never be decided; for Gotama Buddha has not left behind him any written matter, even as little as Yājñavalkya, Śāṇḍilya, or Śaunaka. However, as much of the contents of the speeches and utterances of these sages has probably been handed down in the Upaniṣads, so, doubtless, many speeches and utterances of Buddha were faithfully preserved in the memory of his disciples and handed down to posterity. We may, without laying ourselves open to the charge of credulousness, regard as originating with Buddha himself, speeches such as the famous sermon of Benares on the "four noble truths" and the "noble eightfold path," which recurs always in the same wording, not only in many parts of the Pāli canon, but also in Buddhist Sanskrit texts, some of the farewell speeches handed down in the Mahāparinibbānasutta, which the master is supposed to have addressed to his disciples before his passing, and some of the verses and short utterances handed down as "words of the Buddha" in the Dhammapada, in the Udāna, in the Itivuttaka and in more or less the same form also in Sanskrit texts of Nepal, as well as in Tibetan and Chinese translations. Gotama Buddha, however, did not only preach his new doctrine of suffering and the end of suffering, but also founded a monastic order; he gathered around himself a community of disciples who, according to strict precepts, led a holy life in the way of the master, in order to reach the end of suffering—the much praised Nirvāṇa. And some of the rules and laws for this monastic community probably originated with Buddha himself, above all "the ten commandments for mendicant monks" (dasasikkhāpadāni), perhaps also the list of transgressions (pātimokkha), though in an earlier and shorter form than that in which we have it now.[1]

Now, though none of the works which belong to Buddhist literature can date back to the period of Buddha himself, isolated texts preserved in these works may probably be correctly regarded as words of Buddha. Also, among the first disciples of Buddha there must have been a few prominent leaders and some of the speeches, sayings and poems [2] contained in our collections might have been composed by some of these disciples of Buddha.

Almost the whole of the oldest literature of the Buddhists consists of collections—collections of speeches or conversations, of sayings, songs, narratives and rules of the order.

[1]) *Cf. Eliot*, I, 294f.; *Oldenberg*, Reden des Buddha, p. xxiiiff.

[2]) The metre, too, indicates that the verse aphorisms (gāthā) in particular are very old. According to *Oldenberg* (Gurupūjākaumudī, pp. 9ff.) the metres of the Pāli gāthās are more archaic than those of the Rāmāyaṇa. See also R. *Simon* in ZDMG, 44, 1890, 83-97 on the Śloka in Pāli, and *Oldenberg* "Zur Geschichte des Śloka" (NGGW, 1909, p. 244).

The Tipiṭaka is nothing but a great collection of such collections. It is clear that such collections can only form the conclusion of a considerable preceding literary activity, and that their component parts must belong to different times.

According to Buddhist tradition one such conclusion had already been made very early. It is recorded that, a few weeks after the death of Buddha, an assembly of the monks—the so-called first Buddhist Council—organised by the immediate disciples of Buddha, was held in the city of Rājagaha (the present Rajgir) in order to establish a canon of the religion (dhamma) and of the discipline of the order (vinaya).[1] The very fact that this report expects us to believe too much speaks against its trustworthiness in its oldest form, as it has come down to us in the Tipiṭaka itself;[2] for, it is absolutely impossible that the two great sections of the Tipiṭaka which deal with the doctrine and the discipline of the order—Suttapiṭaka and Vinayapiṭaka—should soon after the death of Buddha have been essentially such as we find them in our Pāli canon.[3] We need not, on this account, assume that the tradition is entirely unfounded. There is probably preserved in it a recollection of the not improbable fact that the elders of the community assembled immediately after the death of the master, in order to agree upon the principal points of the doctrine and of the discipline of the order.[4] But surely too

[1]) The Pāli *Dhamma* (*i.e.*, Sanskrit dharma) is the technical expression for the religion of Buddha, and *Vinaya* for the "discipline of the order," *i.e.*, rules and regulations for the order of mendicants.

[2]) Vinayapiṭaka, Cullavagga XI.

[3]) Other arguments against the authenticity of the tradition of the first Council have been raised by *Oldenberg* (Vinayapiṭaka, Introd., p. xxvff., ZDMG, Vol. 52, 625f.).

[4]) *Cf.* H. *Kern*, Manual of Indian Buddhism, p. 103; R. *Pischel*, Leben und Lehre des Buddha, 4 aufl., 1926, p. 11, 99f.; E. *Windisch* in OC XIV, I, 284f.; L. de *La Vallée Poussin*, *Ind. Ant.* 37, 1908, 2ff.; S. *Lévi* (JA, 1915, s. 11, t. V, 401ff.) has compared the reports as to the first Council in the Pāli Vinayapiṭaka, the Udāna, the Divyāvadāna, as well as the Vinaya of the Mūlasarvāstivādins and the Sarvāstivādins, and has shown that they hark back to an early age.

short a time had elapsed immediately after the death of Buddha for the compilation of a canon of sacred texts such as our Tipiṭaka. The tradition of a second council, which is supposed to have been held at Vesāli, a hundred years after the death of Buddha, is more credible. According to the older report,[1] however, the sole object of this gathering was to do away with ten heresies regarding the discipline of the order. Only the later reports [2] add that at the same time during a session of eight months a revision of the doctrine took place. If we keep to the earlier report, we may accept it as an historical fact that, about a hundred years after the passing of the Buddha, a schism occurred, which stirred up so much controversy that a great assembly of monks had to be summoned, to decide what should be regarded as right with reference to the debatable points. Now this pre-supposes that there was in existence at that time some criterion or other for the decision of such questions, and that could only have been some canon of precepts for the life of the monks such as we find in the Vinayapiṭaka. Hence, though the first century after Buddha may not have witnessed the formation of a canon, at least a fundamental stock of texts for such a canon must have been formed.

According to the report of the chronicles of Ceylon, a real canon of sacred texts was compiled on the occasion of the third Council, at the time of the famous King Aśoka. It is certain that, at that time, the Buddhist community was already divided into a number of schools or sects.[3] For this reason it is not at all unlikely that the need for compiling a canon of texts for orthodox believers, *i.e.*, those who wished to be regarded as the adherents of the original doctrine of

---

[1]) Vinayap., Cullavagga XII, s. SBE, Vol. XX, p. 409ff.

[2]) Thus Dīpavaṃsa V, 27ff., Mahāvaṃsa IV.

[3]) 18 different schools are mentioned. We are familiar with the fact that the number 18 is a favourite number in India; hence the existing schools, whether they numbered more or less than 18, were fitted into a scheme of 18.

Buddha, was felt. Moreover, it is likely enough that a compilation of this kind should have been made precisely during the reign of King Aśoka, the great patron and adherent of the Buddhist community, for, in one of his edicts, the king himself decrees that heretical monks and nuns shall be excommunicated.[1] Consequently, it would have been only natural for him to take an active interest in establishing what tenets constituted the true religion of Buddha. On the other hand, we find no mention in any of his numerous edicts of a council to determine the canon. It is true that he would have had no reason for so doing, because, even according to the tradition, it was not the king himself, but the learned monk Tissa Moggaliputta who, 236 years after the death of Buddha, convened an assembly of a thousand monks in the city of Pāṭaliputra (Patna), with the object of compiling a canon of texts of the true religion or the Theravāda, *i.e.*, the "doctrine of the elders," the immediate disciples of Buddha. The school of the Vibhajjavādins,[2] to which Tissa, the President of the council, belonged, adhered to this Theravāda, and it is the canon of this school which was compiled during the nine months' session of the Council of Pāṭaliputra. Tradition has it, too, that Tissa also compiled the "Kathāvatthu," a book refuting all the heretical doctrines of those times, and incorporated it with the canon.

---

1) See E. *Hultzsch*, Inscriptions of Aśoka, Corpus Inscriptionum Indicarum, X, Oxford, 1925, pp. xliii f., 160 n. 5.

2) There is no distinction in the chronicles between Theravāda and Vibhajjavāda ; but *Theravāda* is probably a general term meaning merely "authentic doctrine." The word is used in this sense also with reference to the schools of Buddha's predecessors (Majjh. 26, I. 164f.). The *Vibhajjavādins* declared that they taught the Theravāda. However, the same thing was also maintained by other sects, such as the Mahīśāsakas and the Sarvāstivādins (s. *Kern*, Manual of Buddhism, p. 110f.). In Majjh. II, 197 (99) Buddha says, referring to himself, that he is a vibhajjavāda, *i.e.*, "one who explains everything with careful distinctions," and not an ekaṃsavāda, "who answers questions from one point of view only." *Cf.* Majjh. III, 208 (136) ; Aṅgutt. III, 67 (I, p. 197); Milindap., 144f. ; Mrs. *Rhys Davids*, Points of Controversy, p. xl sq.; M. *Walleser*, Die Sekten des alten Buddhismus, Heidelberg, 1927, p. 13f.

It has been much disputed whether or not there is any historical foundation for the tradition about the councils.[1] In the nature of things it is likely that, in the course of time, the orthodox Buddhists would feel the need of compiling a canon of doctrines, monastic rules and authentic texts as a defence against the schismatics; and this could only be done by one or several meetings of monks. This would be an argument in favour of there being at least a nucleus of historical truth in these reports, even though they are not attested in all their details. It has been rightly remarked [2] that the tradition about the councils would not have arisen, had not at least one council been a historical fact. As a matter of fact, it is probable that even more than three councils were held. Singhalese and North Indian records of a "great council" (mahāsaṅgīti) which is said to have led to the schism of the Mahāsaṅgītikas or Mahāsaṅghikas, would seem to indicate that the council of the orthodox Buddhists at Pāṭaliputra was preceded by a great assembly of the schismatics. It is true, nevertheless, that these reports contradict one another very considerably. It is possible that the canon was not compiled all at once, but at several meetings of the monks, the most important of which was the Pāṭaliputra session.

The chroniclers of Ceylon then go on to relate that it was Tissa, the President of the council, who first sent out missionaries to the North and the South and prepared the way for the propagation of Buddhism in foreign lands. A pupil of Tissa was Mahinda, the younger brother (according to another tradition, the son) of Aśoka, who is supposed to have brought

---

[1]) *Cf. Kern*, Manual of Buddhism, p. 101ff., *La Vallée Poussin* ERE IV, 1911 170ff.; *Geiger*, Mahāvaṃsa, Transl., p. li ff.; *Eliot* I, 254ff.; Nalinaksha *Dutt*, Early History of the Spread of Buddhism and the Buddhist Schools, London, 1925 (Calcutta Oriental Series), pp. 225ff., 249ff. See also p. 1 note 1 above.

[2]) By *Copleston*, Buddhism, p. 174f.

Buddhism and the Buddhist texts to Ceylon. It is conceivable that legends took up this apostle of Ceylon; and even though we shall not believe the chronicler when he says that Mahinda and the monks who were accompanying him flew, like flamingoes, through the air to Ceylon, yet we need not reject the whole tradition,[1] but may suppose that underlying the many legends, there is the one historical fact that Mahinda actually introduced Buddhism into Ceylon and brought with him the texts of the canon. These texts are said to have been first transmitted orally, until, under the Singhalese king Vaṭṭagāmani, in the first century B.C., they were committed to writing. This again sounds quite trustworthy.[2]

Now, in the opinion of the Buddhists of Ceylon, that canon which was compiled at the third council, was brought to Ceylon by Mahinda, and was recorded in writing under Vaṭṭagāmani, is the same as our Pāli canon or Tipiṭaka, as we still possess it to-day. This Tipiṭaka—the word means "three baskets"—consists of three so-called piṭakas or "baskets,"[3] namely:

1. Vinayapiṭaka, "basket of the discipline of the order." This section contains all that refers to the monastic community (saṅgha), the rules of the discipline of the order, precepts for the daily life of the monks and nuns, and so on.

---

[1]) As is done by *Oldenberg*, Vinayapiṭaka, Introd. p. li ff., for the opposite view, *cf.* *Kern*, Manual, p. 116f. When the chroniclers report that Mahinda was sent to Ceylon and Majjhima to the Himavat (Dīpavaṃsa VIII, 10) and when we find a reliquary in the stūpa at Sānchi with the inscription: "(relics) of Majjhima, teacher of Himavat," it speaks strongly in favour of the authenticity of the Ceylon chronicles. (*Copleston*, Buddhism, p. 173f.).

[2]) See Vol. I, p. 32f. The Chinese pilgrim *Fa-hien* (s. A Record of Buddhistic Kingdoms...transl. by J. *Legge*, Oxford, 1886, Chap. XXXVI), when he travelled through North India during the years 399-414 A.D., did not as yet find any manuscripts of the Vinayapiṭaka, but only oral tradition. It was not until he came to Pāṭaliputra that he found a copy of the Vinaya in a Mahāyāna monastery.

[3]) In the opinion of V. *Trenckner* (JPTS 1908, p. 119f.), which is accepted by T. W. *Rhys Davids* (SBE, Vol. 35, p. 28 note) the word *piṭaka* does not mean "receptacle" but

2. Suttapiṭaka, "basket of the Suttas." The Pāli word sutta corresponds to the Sanskrit sūtra, but with the Buddhists it has lost the old meaning of "short rule," [1] and here means "discourse," "sermon." Every long or short explanation, frequently in the form of a dialogue, on one or more points of religion (dhamma) is called a sutta and often also suttanta (Sanskrit sūtrānta). The Suttapiṭaka consists of five nikāyas, *i. e*, great collections of these suttas or suttantas.

3. Abhidhammapiṭaka, "basket of the higher subtleties of the doctrine." [2] The texts contained in this section, like those of the Suttapiṭaka, deal with the religion (dhamma); but they do so after a more learned and catechistical fashion, in the form of dry enumerations and formal divisions, which refer chiefly to the psychological foundations of Buddhist ethics.

In the Tipiṭaka itself there is in various places [3] mention of a division of the Canon into 9 Aṅgas or "limbs," *viz.*, 1. Sutta,

rather "tradition." In ancient times, when excavations were in progress, baskets were used which were passed along the line from one labourer to the next, in order to remove the dug-out earth from the site of the excavation : thus the treasure of the doctrine was transmitted in the "piṭakas" down a long line of teachers and pupils from olden times down to the present day. The Majjhima Nikāya 95 (II, p. 169) speaks of a "basket-like tradition" (piṭakasampradāya) of the ancient Vedic mantras. But is it not simpler to interpret it as receptacles in which gems, family treasures, were preserved from generation to generation? According to G. *Bühler* (on the Origin of the Indian Brāhma Alphabet, Indian Studies III, 2nd Ed., Strassburg 1898, p. 86ff.) *piṭaka* is a basket, in which manuscripts were preserved, so that the division of the Buddhist sacred texts into piṭakas would be evidence of their having been *written*, though it is true that, according to Singhalese tradition, this would not have happened until towards the close of the first century B. C. Cf. *Keith*, Buddhist Philosophy, p. 24 n. 2.

[1]) See Vol. I, 268ff. The Buddhist "sūtras" are generally very prolix. *Trenckner* also tried to explain Sutta as "thread of tradition" (JPTS 1908, p. 121), but this is improbable.

[2]) According to Buddhaghosa (Sumaṅgalavilāsinī, p. 18 : Atthasālinī, p. 2) *abhi* in *abhidhamma* means "higher," "especially," "specifically." Side by side with *abhidhamma*, *abhivinaya* also occurs ("the higher subtleties of the Dhamma and of the Vinaya"), thus Vinayap., Mahāvagga I, 36, 12f. ; 37, 11 ; Dīghanikāya III, p. 267 ; Majjhimanikāya I, p. 472 ; Milindapañha, p. 344 (SBE, Vol. 36, p. 237 n.).

[3]) Majjh. 22 (I, p. 133) and in several passages in the Aṅguttaranikāya. Cf. Milindapañha, p. 345 ; Sumaṅgalavilāsinī I, p. 23ff.; Atthasālinī, p. 26 ; Gandhavaṃsa in JPTS 1886, p. 57 ; H. *Kern*, Manual, p. 7. E. *Senart*, JA 1901, s. 9, t. XVII, p. 407f. The texts

prose sermons, 2. Geyya, sermons in a mixture of prose and verse, 3. Veyyākaraṇa (Vyākaraṇa), explanations, commentaries,[1] 4. Gāthā, stanzas, 5. Udāna, pithy sayings, 6. Itivuttaka, short speeches beginning with the words: "Thus spake the Buddha," 7. Jātaka, stories of former births of Buddha, 8. Abbhutadhamma, reports of miracles, 9. Vedalla, teachings in the form of questions and answers. This division[2] does not allude to a canon complete in itself, or to definite books, but is only meant to classify the various types of Buddhist texts according to their form and contents.

The list of the Aṅgas is evidence of the fact that, at the time when the Canon was compiled in its present form, all these diverse forms of Buddhist literature were already in existence. Moreover, there are other passages of the Canon which show us that there was at that time a great mass of short texts, rules of the order, speeches, dialogues, aphorisms in verse, and even minor collections of texts,[3] which passed as "the word of Buddha" (Buddhavacanam), and were memorised and recited by the monks. They were recited as a kind of recitative, as all sorts of sacred texts are still recited to this day in India and Ceylon.[4] Among the monks there were

dealing with Vinaya also belong to the "Sutta," whilst the Abhidhamma texts—at least according to Buddhaghosa—belong to the Veyyākaraṇa. However, they might also be included in the "Vedalla." Lord *Chalmers* (SBE V, pp. 93, 207ff.) renders *vedalla* by "miscellany." But it is doubtful whether there is any thought of Abhidhamma texts in the list of the Aṅgas.

1) In Buddhist Sanskrit, *vyākaraṇa* frequently means prophecy, especially the prediction of a future Buddha; thus also in Pāli in the Nidānakathā (Jātaka ed., Fausböll, pp. 34, 44).

2) A similar division into 9 Aṅgas, sometimes into 12 Dharmapravacanas, is also found in Sanskrit Buddhist texts. Cf. *Kern*, l.c.; Saddharmapuṇḍarīka II, 48 (SBE, Vol. 21, p. 45); Mahākaruṇāpuṇḍarīka in SBE, Vol. 10 (i), p. xxxiii.

3) Such as the Aṭṭhakavagga, which we now find in the Suttanipāta, and which is already mentioned in the Vinayapiṭaka (Mahāv. V, 13, 9) and in the Udāna V, 6, (p. 59). Cf. Dhammapada 19, 20, 102, 185, 352; Suttanipāta 87.

4) Cf. *Rhys Davids*, SBE, Vol. 20, p. 72 n. 3. The reciters (or leaders of a common recitation) were known as sarabhāṇakā "intoners." Later on, the entire Canon was divided into "lessons" (bhāṇavāra) for the purposes of recitation. Cf. SBE, Vol. 20, p. 415ff. In Cullavagga V, 3, it is expressly forbidden to *sing* the texts of the Dhamma to melodies, as if they were songs.

Suttantikas, reciters of the Suttantas, Dhammakathikas, preachers of the doctrine, and Vinayadharas, experts in the discipline.[1] In order to ensure the continuance of the knowledge of the doctrine and the rules of the order, the texts had to be memorised, recited and expounded again and again. When, during the rainy season, many learned monks assembled at a place, there was an opportunity to obtain enlightenment on knotty points. It happened that some learned monk or perhaps a whole community of monks in some monastery would declare as Dhamma or Vinaya something which had first to be investigated before it could be sanctioned as being really in accord with the "teaching of the Master" (satthusāsanam).[2] This means that there must have been authoritative texts which could be consulted. It is often said of prominent monks that they are "very learned, masters of the tradition, and well versed in the Dhamma, Vinaya and the Mātikās."[3] The Mātikās are the "lists" or "tabulated summaries" of those ideas which are of importance in the doctrine and the monastic order. These Mātikās were subsequently worked into the texts of the Abhidhammapiṭaka.[4] From this it would appear that the texts of the Abhidhamma were merely in their beginnings before the Canon was compiled.

In our Pāli Canon we find the Kathāvatthu, traditionally ascribed to Tissa, as one of the books of the Abhidhammapiṭaka.

[1]) Cullavagga IV, 4, 4 and in many other passages. Cf. N. *Dutt*, Early History of the Spread of Buddhism, p. 207f. Upāli is mentioned as one of the first Vinayadharas, Cullavagga VI, 13; IX, 5; XI, I, 7 ff. Cf. SBE, Vol. XIII, p. xiii.

[2]) Aṅgutt. VI, 51; IV, 180; Dīghanikāya XVI. 4, 7-11. The fact that there is always mention here of the Sutta and Vinaya but not of the Abhidhamma, proves that, at the time when this Sutta was completed, only *two* Piṭakas were recognised as authorities.

[3]) Vinayapiṭaka, Mahāv. II, 21, 2; X, 1, 2; Cullav. I, 11, 1; XII, 1, 9f.; 2, 1; Dīgha. II, p. 125; Aṅgutt. I, p. 117. The phrase is: bahussutā āgatāgamā dhammadharā vinayadharā mātikādharā.

[4]) In the Sanskrit Buddhist texts the corresponding word *mātṛkā* is used for "Abhidharmapiṭaka." Cf. *Kern*, Manual, pp. 3, 104; *Oldenberg* and *Rhys Davids*, SBE, Vol. 13, p. 273; Mrs. *Rhys Davids*, Buddhist Manual of Psychological Ethics, 2nd Ed., pp. ix, cv-xiii.

It presupposes oot only the texts of the Vinayapiṭaka and of all the Nikāyas of the Suttapiṭaka, but other books of the Abhidhammapiṭaka too.[1] It is therefore certainly one of the latest works of the Tipiṭaka, and, in the nature of things, it would be quite feasible to assume that this book was not written until the time of the compilation of the Canon by Tissa himself, and that the members of the Council appended it to the whole work by way of a crowning piece.

We must, however, consider the question as to whether we can agree with the Buddhist believers of Ceylon that the Canon compiled at the Third Council is really the same canon which has come down to us in the Pāli Tipiṭaka.

First of all, the language of our Tipiṭaka can scarcely be the same as that of the Canon of the third century B. C. Buddha himself spoke the dialect of his native province Kosala (Oudh), and it was most likely in this same dialect that he first began to proclaim his doctrine. Later on, however, when he wandered and taught in Magadha (Bihar) he probably preached in the dialect of this province. We must, however, take into account the fact that, in the early days of Buddhism, little importance was attached to the linguistic form of texts. An utterance of Buddha has come down to us, in which he affirms that he cares not for mere wording, but only for the meaning itself.[2] When, in course of time, the doctrine spread over a large area, the monks of various districts preached each in his own dialect. It is probable that monks coming from Brahman circles also attempted to translate the speeches of Buddha into Sanskrit verses. In the Vinayapiṭaka, however, this procedure is expressly declared as a transgression against the monastic discipline, because it "contributes neither to the conversion of the unconverted nor to the augmentation of the converts," and it is declared to be right that each one

---

[1]) Cf. Mrs. *Rhys Davids*, Points of Controversy, pp. xxixf., 401ff.

[2]) Majjhimanikāya, 103 (II, p. 240).

should learn the doctrine in a version adapted to his own language.[1] The monks who compiled the Canon in Pāṭaliputra, most probably used an ancient Māgadhī dialect. *Pāli*,[2] however, the literary language of the Buddhists of Ceylon, Burma and Siam, though called "Māgadhī" by these people themselves, deviates essentially from the dialect, otherwise known to us through inscriptions, literary works and grammarians. On the other hand, it agrees just as little with any other dialect. The fact is that Pāli is a literary language, which was used exclusively as such only by the Buddhists, and like all literary languages, it developed more or less out of a mixture of dialects. Of course a literary language of this kind, even if it represents a kind of compromise between two different dialects, could at all events only have proceeded out of *one* certain dialect. This was very likely an old Māgadhī, so that the tradition which makes Pāli and Māgadhi the same, though it is not to be taken literally, has some historical background.

The time and place of the origin of this literary language cannot be determined with any degree of certainty.[3] It is probable that, during the period immediately after Aśoka, when Buddhism had already spread throughout the whole of Central India and in the North-west too, it developed as a compromise between the various dialects spoken in this vast territory, among the monks engaged in handing down the Theravāda Canon. It is for this reason that Pāli bears traces of so many different Indo-Aryan dialects.[4] When the Canon of the Vibhajjavādins was written down in the first century B.C., there was already an older and a more modern

---

[1]) Cullavagga V, 33; SBE, Vol. 20. p. 150f. W. *Geiger*, Pāli Literatur und Sprache, p. 5, offers a different explanation for this passage, s. Appendix II.

[2]) See Appendix II.

[3]) See Appendix II.

[4]) Cf. S. K. *Chatterji*, Origin and Development of the Bengali Language, Calcutta, 1926, I, 55 ff.

form of Pāli,[1] so that, even at that early period, Pāli must have been a language with a considerable development behind it. The monks of Ceylon were, however, bent on preserving and passing on the texts written in the language once established for them in India.[2] In all probability these monks were just as conscientious regarding the contents as regarding the language, and preserved and handed down to us the texts of the Tipiṭaka which was written down in the Pāli language, with rare fidelity during the last two thousand years. However, *before* they were fixed in Pāli and had reached Ceylon, they probably also passed through changes in contents.

Thus, as regards language and contents, our Pāli Tipiṭaka, though closely approaching the canon compiled under Aśoka, is yet not identical with it. For we must admit that, in the period from the third to the first century before Christ, when the writing-down took place, and occasionally even still later, the texts suffered many a change, that especially much was added, and that in many cases commentaries penetrated into the texts and became mixed with them. Thus the collections as well as the separate texts contained in them, must have increased in extent. The centuries have surely not passed them by without leaving traces. This accounts, too, for the

---

[1]) Cf. *Geiger*, l. c., p. 1 f.

[2]) The fact that a Pāli Canon was known in North India as late as in the 2nd and 3rd centuries A.D., is proved by a quotation (from the Saccasaṃyutta of the Saṃyuttanikāya ?) about the "four noble truths" in an inscription dating from this period in Sarnath, s. *Konow*, Ep. Ind. IX, 1908, 291 ff. and Dharmananda *Kosambi*, Ind. Ant. 1910, 217. In inscriptions from Swat in the extreme North-west of India, written at the close of the first century B.C. or in the first half of the first century A.D., we find Sanskrit verses which seem to be literal translations from the Pāli of verses of the Mahāparinibbānasutta and the Dhammapada (G. *Bühler*, Ep. Ind. IV, 133ff.) A fragment of the Cullavagga discovered by C. *Bendall* (OC XIII Hamburg 1902, p. 58ff.) would seem to prove that the Pāli Canon was in existence in Nepal in the 8th and 9th centuries. But it is possible that the MS. was taken from Ceylon to Tibet. So also, when we find that Chinese and Tibetan translations betray familiarity with Pāli texts, it is possible that the translators had been in Ceylon.

numerous contradictions within the Canon,[1] the many instances of juxtaposition of early and late traditions, and the frequent occurrence of the same texts in different collections.[2]

With these reservations and limitations, we can nevertheless say that our Pāli Tipiṭaka, at least the Vinaya and the Suttapiṭaka,[3] does, on the whole, correspond to the Māgadhī Canon of the third century B.C. Our main witnesses to this are the inscriptions of King Aśoka. Not only do these edicts breathe the same spirit as the moral maxims which have come down in our Pāli Canon,[4] but they show verbal similarities to

---

[1]) Such contradictions have been pointed out, for instance, by R. Otto *Franke* (WZKM 24, 1910, 1ff.). Cf. also *Minayeff*, Recherches, etc., p. 62ff., and Mrs. *Rhys Davids*, Buddhist Psychology, 2nd Ed., London, 1924, pp. 280 f., 291 f.

[2]) In particular, the same Gāthās occur in various collections, s. the concordance of the Gāthās, by R. O. *Franke* in ZDMG 63, 1909, 1ff.; WZKM 24, 1910, 1 ff.; 225 ff.; 26, 1912, 171 ff. However, these repetitions and the contradictions occurring in them are not sufficient reason for our immediately jumping to the conclusion, as has been done by *Franke* (ZDMG 63, 1909, 8 ff.) that the entire Canon is "not authentic and not original." For, if a verse is ascribed in the one text to Buddha, and in the other to Sāriputta, or if an utterance was, according to the one text, made at Rājagaha, and according to the other at Benares, it merely proves that these legendary adornments are not authentic, but does not in any way confute our assumption that the verses and utterances are "authentic" in themselves, *i.e.*, that they faithfully reproduce the old doctrine of Buddha. The arguments of *Franke* and other critics destroy the belief of the orthodox Buddhist that every single word of the Canon is genuine and was spoken by Buddha himself, but they prove nothing against the hypothesis of those scholars who acknowledge the Canon to have a certain, though limited, genuineness and reliability.

[3]) Doubts against the Abhidhammapiṭaka are justifiable, because, with the exception of the Vibhajjavādins, only the Sarvāstivādins have a corresponding Abhidharmapiṭaka, and the latter contains totally different texts from the Pāli Abhidhammapiṭaka. Cf. *La Vallée Poussin*, Bouddhisme, p. 44; *Farquhar*, Outline, p. 68 f.; *Keith*, Buddhist Philosophy, p. 22. When, in the Dīpavaṃsa V, 35-37, we are told that, at the "great Council" of Vesāli, the Mahāsaṅgītika Bhikkhus rejected certain passages of the Suttas and the Vinaya, especially the Parivāra, Abhidhamma, Paṭisambhidā, Niddesa texts and portions of the Jātakas, and wrote down other texts in their place, it is noteworthy that it is precisely these texts which we, too, are inclined to suspect of being later additions to the Canon.

[4]) Parallel passages from the Dhammapada, which are in accord with the Dhamma of Aśoka, are quoted by *Hultzsch*, Inscriptions of Asoka, p. xlvii ff. We can only compare such texts as have reference to the morals of the laity, as Aśoka had only these in view, and not the philosophy and dogmas of Buddhism.

the texts of our Canon, and quotations which can also be traced in our texts with but slight deviations.[1] But this is not all. In the edict of Bairāt (or Bhābrū) of the year 249 B.C., the king says to the monks of Magadha: "All that the Lord Buddha has said, is well said," and he names the titles of seven texts, the study of which he most particularly recommends to them. These texts have been traced in our Suttapiṭaka, though not all in an entirely satisfactory manner.[2]

The majority of the inscriptions on the famous stūpas of Bharhut and Sānchī are written in the same characters as the inscriptions of Aśoka, and the stūpas were formerly regarded as monuments of the time of Aśoka. Now-a-days, however, authoritative archæologists are inclined to ascribe the bulk of the sculptures rather to the 2nd and 1st centuries B.C.[3] The

[1]) Cf. G. *Bühler*, ZDMG 48, p. 57 ff.; F. W. *Thomas*, JRAS 1903, p. 831 ff.; K. E. *Neumann*, WZKM 11, 1897, p. 156 ff. However, when the last named scholar (Reden Gotamo Buddhos, III, p. 41 note) speaks of Aśoka as "brought up on our texts," he is saying more than he can prove. E. *Hardy* (JRAS 1901, 314) compares Aṅgutt. III, pp. 247, 340: yena...saddhammo ciraṭṭhitiko hotī ti, with Aśoka's Bhābrū Edict: hevaṃ sa dhammo cilaṭhitiko hāsatī ti.

[2]) See Appendix III.

[3]) The stūpa at Bharhut (Bharahut, Bharaut, Barāhat) was discovered by General A. *Cunningham* in the year 1874, and described by him in the work "The Stūpa of Bharhut," London, 1879. The inscriptions have been published and translated by E. *Hultzsch*, ZDMG 40, 1886, p. 58 ff. and Ind. Ant. 21, 1892, 225 ff., and B. M. *Barua*, Barhut Inscriptions, Calcutta, 1926. According to Cunningham, the inscriptions date from the period between 250 and 150 B.C. L. A. *Waddell* (JRAS 1914, p. 138 ff.) believes that most of the sculptures date from the 3rd century B.C., and that only the Eastern Gateway should be attributed to the 2nd or 1st century. The sculptures of the Sānchī stūpas have been described by F. C. *Maisey*, Sanchi and its Remains, London, 1892, and Sir J. H. *Marshall*, A Guide to Sanchi, Calcutta, 1918. G. *Bühler*, On the Origin of the Indian Brāhma Alphabet, p. 17, dates the stūpas of Bharhut and Sānchī in the 3rd century B.C. on palaeographic grounds (with repairs and additional buildings in the 2nd century). V. A. *Smith*, A History of Fine Art in India and Ceylon, Oxford, 1911, p. 73 ff. ascribes the Sānchī stūpas to the period between 150 and 100 B.C., but in his Early History (1924), p. 173, he speaks of them as "buildings of the Asokan period." See also A. *Grünwedel*, Buddhistische Kunst in Indien, Berlin, 1900, 22 ff.; A. *Foucher*, The Beginnings of Buddhist Art, London, 1917, pp. 29 ff., 61 ff.; J. H. *Marshall* in Cambridge History, I, 618 ff., 627 ff. Only the earliest portions of the monuments, of which little has been preserved, go back to Aśoka's time. Cf. *Grünwedel*, l. c., p. 24; *Foucher*, l. c., p. 34 and *Marshall*, l.c., p. 627; *Rapson* in Cambridge History, I, p. 523.

remnants of the stūpa of Bharhut are at present among the most precious treasures in the Indian Museum at Calcutta, while we are as yet able to admire the magnificent remains of the stūpas of Sānchī in their original place. (The railings and gateways of the stūpas of Bharhut and Sānchī are covered with reliefs and inscriptions of inestimable value. The sculptures represent scenes from the life of the Buddha, testifying to an abundantly developed Buddha legend, such as we find in a few of the Pāli Suttas, but more especially in such works as the Nidānakathā, Lalitavistara and the Mahāvastu.[1] Many of the reliefs are, however, illustrations to fables and tales, the titles of which are generally mentioned in the inscriptions, in the case of the stūpa of Bharhut. These inscriptions prove beyond the shadow of a doubt, that the reliefs depict Jātakas, *i.e.*, "stories from former births of the Buddha," and most of these have also been traced in the Jātaka book of the Tipiṭaka. Moreover, we also find on the monuments of Bharhut and Sānchī votive inscriptions, in which monks are given the epithets bhāṇaka, "reciter," sutaṃtika, "Sutta reciter,"[2] pacanekāyika, "knower of the five Nikāyas," peṭakin, "knower of the Piṭakas," and dhammakathika, "preacher of the doctrine."[3]

From all this, it follows that, some time before the second century B.C. there was already a collection of Buddhist texts, which was called "Piṭakas" and was divided into five "Nikāyas," that there were "Suttas" in which the "Dhamma," the religion of Buddha, was preached, that some of these Suttas agreed with those contained in our Tipiṭaka, and that "Jātakas" of exactly the same kind as those

[1]) Cf. B. M. *Barua* in Ind. Hist. Qu. I, 1925, 50 ff., 245 ff.

[2]) In one of the Sānchī inscriptions, a nun, sutātikinī, "female reciter of the Sutta," is also mentioned.

[3]) Such experts for preaching and recitation are also mentioned in the Canon, s. above p. 11. In the days of Buddhaghosa there were also reciters of special texts, such as Dīghabhāṇakas, Majjhimabhāṇakas, etc.

contained in the Tipiṭaka, already belonged to the stock of Buddhist literature—in short, that, at some period prior to the 2nd century B.C., probably as early as at the time of Aśoka or a little later, there was a Buddhist Canon which, if not entirely identical with our Pāli Canon, resembled it very closely.

It is true that the earliest literary evidence of the existence of the "three baskets" as a triad of piṭakas (piṭakattayaṃ) and of Nikāyas is only to be found in the Milindapañha,[1] a work whose authentic portion probably belongs to the beginning of the first century A.D. But the whole of the remaining Buddhist literature other than the Pāli Canon, proves that the texts contained in the latter hark back to an early period, not so very far removed from the time of Buddha himself, and in any case may be regarded as the most trustworthy evidences of the original doctrine of Buddha and the Buddhism of the first two centuries after Buddha's death.

This is proved firstly by the non-canonical Pāli literature, including the dialogues of the Milindapañha, the chronicles of Ceylon Dīpavaṃsa and Mahāvaṃsa, and a rich commentary literature in connection with the Tipiṭaka. All these works indicate that the Tipiṭaka was in existence at least as early as the early centuries of the Christian era.[2]

[1]) Ed. *Trenckner*, p. 22, about monks who are tepiṭakā, *i.e.*, "knowers of the three piṭakas," and those who are pañcanekāyikā and catunekāyikā, "knowers of the five Nikāyas" and "knowers of the four Nikāyas." I see no reason for regarding this passage as interpolated, as does F. O. *Schrader*. Sanskrit *trepiṭaka* occurs in an inscription of King Kaniṣka (2nd century A.D.), s. J. Ph. *Vogel*, Ep. Ind. VIII. 176.

[2]) The entire Pāli literature, canonical as well as non-canonical, is frequently termed "Southern Buddhist," because, at the present day it is preserved and spread among the Buddhists of Ceylon, Burma and Siam. This term is, however, to be deprecated owing to the fact that the texts of the Pāli Canon and the Milindapañha are in no wise related to the South, and do not even give indications of a knowlege of South India and Ceylon, but in all probability originated in North India. The occasional occurrence of the expression tāmraparṇīyanikāya in some manuscript or other, is not sufficient ground to justify our talking about "the Singhalese Canon" as does *La Vallée Poussin* (JA s. 9. t.XX, 1902 p. 287). Cf. *Rhys Davids* in JRAS 1896, 378 f.

Moreover, the Buddhist Sanskrit literature [1] testifies to the antiquity and the fidelity of the Pāli transmission. This literature, composed partly in good Sanskrit, partly in "mixed Sanskrit," [2] comprises works of the most varied kinds and of the most widely differing sects. One of these sects, namely that of the Mūlasarvāstivādins, had a canon of its own in Sanskrit, and it is only in recent times that fragments of it have been discovered in Central Asia. We find that this canon, though not translated from the Pāli, yet affords splendid evidence of the fidelity of the Pāli transmission: for, in spite of numerous deviations in the wording and the arrangement, there are yet so many literal agreements between the Sanskrit Canon and the Pāli Canon, that we must take it for granted that there is a uniform tradition behind both collections. In the Sanskrit texts of the Buddhists of Nepal, as well as in the works of the various Buddhist sects, known only through Tibetan and Chinese translations, we can establish a fundamental stock not only of doctrines, but also of texts, agreeing in all essentials with the transmission of the Pāli Canon. The more this Buddhist Sanskrit literature is opened up, and the more minutely it is compared with the Pāli Canon,[3] the more it is proved that Oldenberg is right when he says: "The Pāli copy, though naturally not of infallible accuracy, must still be judged as

---

[1]) The term "Northern Buddhist" as applied to the Sanskrit Buddhist literature as well as to the Buddhist literatures of Tibet, China and Japan which are based upon it, is even more unsuitable than the term "Southern Buddhist" for the Pāli literature: for by this term the texts of entirely different sects, such as Hinayāna and Mahāyāna, are all lumped together.

[2]) See Vol. I, English edition, p. 48.

[3]) For comparisons of this kind we are especially indebted to E. *Windisch*, Māra und Buddha (ASGW XV, 4), Leipzig, 1895, and Buddhas Geburt (ASGW XXVI, 2), Leipzig, 1908, and M. *Anesaki* in OC XIII Hamburg 1902, p. 61, and Le Muséon, N. S. VI, 1905 23ff., VII, 1906, 33ff., who shows that even Pāli quotations occur in the Mahāyāna texts. E. *Waldschmidt*, Bruchstücke des Bhikṣuṇī-Prātimokṣa der Sarvāstivādins, Leipzig 1926, has come to the conclusion, after a careful and unbiassed comparison of the Bhikṣuṇī-Prātimokṣa in the

eminently good."[1] There is indeed neither a canon nor any Buddhist text which has come down from such early times as the Pāli Canon which was written down in the first century B.C., in which there is as yet not even a single word of mention of the great Buddhist King Aśoka.[2] In language, style and contents the Pāli texts are most closely connected with the Upaniṣads, while the Buddhist Sanskrit literature reminds us far more of the Purāṇas. Finally, the fact that in these texts, written down and transmitted in Ceylon, there are no references of any kind to Ceylon, again confirms the view that they are not a "canon of the Buddhists of Ceylon," but a canon of that Buddhist sect of India which, as a matter of fact, has preserved the most of ancient Buddhism and might, with some justification, call its doctrine "Theravāda," the doctrine of the first disciples of Buddha.

If we had only the Pāli texts and nothing besides, we should certainly form merely a one-sided idea of Buddhism. On the other hand, if only the Sanskrit and semi-Sanskrit Buddhist texts and none of the Pāli Canon had come down to us, we should have an entirely distorted picture of Buddhism and only a scanty notion of the original teaching and personality of Buddha. We may say this without any bias in favour of the Pāli transmission, and without denying that our knowledge of Buddhism and especially of its history is very

---

recensions of six different schools, that "the *Pāli version* of the school of the Theravādins proves itself to be *the most faithful preserver* of an earlier tradition" (p. 187). S. also *Oldenberg*, AR 13, 1910, 596 ff.; NGGW 1912, 171 ff. *Barth*, RHR, t. 41, 1900, 166 ff. (= Oeuvres II, 300 ff.); *La Vallée Poussin* and T. W. *Rhys Davids*, JRAS 1903, 359 ff. A canon similar to the Tipiṭaka is also recognised by the Mahāyāna Buddhists, s. *Kern*, Manual, p. 3 n. 4, and *La Vallée Poussin*, Bouddhisme, p. 29 f.

1) ZDMG 52, p. 673. Even A. *Barth* RHR 1900, t. 42, p. 57 (= Oeuvres II, 340), cf. Journal des savants 1899, p. 631, and RHR 1900, t. 41, p. 170 (= Oeuvres II, 303 f.), admits that there are very much surer guarantees to support the Pāli tradition than the disconnected mass of writings of the North.

2) The Indians have never been such deliberate forgers that, if Aśoka had been mentioned, they would have eliminated the references, in order to create the appearance of antiquity. Cf. *Rhys Davids*, Buddhist India, p. 174.

materially completed and extended by the Sanskrit Buddhist literature of Nepal, as well as by the Chinese and Tibetan translations from the Sanskrit.

The Pāli texts, moreover, surpass all other productions of Buddhist literature, not only as a source for our knowledge of Buddhism, but also—which here concerns us first and foremost—from a purely literary standpoint. This will be shown by the following survey of this literature.[1]

The Vinayapiṭaka of the Pāli Canon

The Buddhists themselves place the Vinayapiṭaka[2] at the head of the canon, and we may follow their example, without committing ourselves to the opinion that this is earlier than the Suttapiṭaka.[3] The Vinayapiṭaka comprises the following texts :

I. The Suttavibhaṅga, consisting of 1. Mahāvibhaṅga, and 2. Bhikkunīvibhaṅga.

II. The Khandhakās, consisting of 1. Mahāvagga and 2. Cullavagga.

III. The Parivāra or Parivārapāṭha.

---

[1]) A complete edition of the sacred writings of the Tipiṭaka in 30 volumes (in Siamese type) was printed by the order of King *Cuḷālaṅkaraṇa* of Siam on the occasion of the twenty-five years' jubilee of his reign, in 1894 in Bangkok, and, with admirable generosity, he had it distributed to European and American libraries. Cf. R. *Chalmers*, JRAS 1898, p. 1. ff. and Ch. *Lanman*, JAOS, Vol. XVI, 1895, Proceedings CCXLIV ff. Most of the texts have also been published by the *Pali Text Society*. Extracts from the Tipiṭaka have been translated by K. E. *Neumann*, Buddhistische Anthologie, Leiden, 1892 ; Henry Clarke *Warren*, Buddhism in Translations, Cambridge, Mass. 1896 (HOS, Vol. 3); Julius *Dutoit*, Das Leben des Buddha, Leipzig, 1906 ; M. *Winternitz*, Buddhismus, in A. *Bertholet*, Religionsgeschichtliches Lesebuch, Tübingen, 1908, Einzelausgabe 1911 (new edition in preparation ; Karl *Seidenstücker*, Pāli-Buddhismus in übersetzungen, Breslau, 1911, 2nd Ed., 1923; H. *Oldenberg*, Reden des Buddha, München, 1922; E. J. *Thomas*, Buddhist Scriptures, London, 1913 (Wisdom of the East Series); F. L *Woodward*, Some Sayings of the Buddha according to the Pāli Canon, Oxford, 1925.

[2]) Edited by H. *Oldenberg*, London, 1879-1883.

[3]) *Kern*, Manual, p. 2, and *La Vallée Poussin*, Buddhisme, E'tudes et Matériaux, p. 27, regard the Vinayapiṭaka as earlier. In the opinion of R. Otto *Franke* (JPTS 1908,

The nucleus of the Vinayapiṭaka is the Pāṭimokkha,[1] a list of transgressions against the rules of discipline of the order, together with the corresponding atonements. The life of the monk was regulated by this code of rules, which formed the bond[2] holding the community together. Its immense significance as regards the stability of the Buddhist order becomes evident from a speech attributed to Ānanda,[3] in which he declares that though Buddha had not appointed any one of his disciples as his successor nor invested him with the supreme authority, the community of monks would continue, because the Sublime One had proclaimed the Sikkhāpada (the ten commandments for the conduct of the monks) and the Pāṭimokkha to the monks. In an oft recurring phrase, it is said of a good monk that his life is "restrained by the restraints of the Pāṭimokkha."[4] This code of

---

pp. 8 ff., 68 ff.,74) the Mahāvagga and Cullavagga of the Vinayapiṭaka would be later than the Dīghanikāya. K. E. *Neumann* (Prefaces to Vols. I and III of the "Reden Gotamo Buddhos") believes that "the Vinayapiṭaka and later the Abhidhammapiṭaka gradually partly became eliminated, and partly were further developed, out of the Suttapiṭaka." In support of this view, we could adduce the fact that some of the Suttas deal with Vinaya, and some resemble the texts of the Abhidhamma very closely both in form and contents. However, as the Vinayapiṭaka and the Suttapiṭaka have some texts in common, I think it likely that the final compilation of these two took place at about the same time.

[1]) Cf. *Oldenberg*, Vinayapiṭaka, Introd., p. xv ff.; T. W. *Rhys Davids* in ERE IX, 1917, 675 ff.: Sukumar *Dutt*, Early Buddhist Monachism, London, 1924, pp. 75 ff., 99 ff.

[2]) S. *Dutt*, l. c., p. 90 f. thinks that, even etymologically pāṭimokkha means "bond" in this sense. The PTS Dic. s. v. (also R. C. *Childers*, Dict. of the Pāli Language, s. v.) explains it by pratimokṣya "that which should be made binding," "obligatory," "obligation," with reference to Jātaka V, p. 25, where it explains saṃgaraṃ paṭimokhaṃ by "a binding promise." In my opinion, the correct explanation of this phrase is "a promise to be redeemed," and, accordingly, I am inclined to explain pāṭimokkha as "that which is to be redeemed." For other etymologies s *Rhys Davids* and *Oldenberg*, SBE., Vol. XIII, p. xxvii f. ("Disburdening, Getting free"), *Oldenberg*, Buddha, p. 419 n. 1, *Kern*, Manual, p. 74 n. 5 ("a spiritual cuirass"), and R. O. *Franke*, Dīghanikāya, p. 66 n. 7. The earliest etymology is the one in the old commentary Mahāvagga II, 3, 4, which was also accepted by Buddhaghosa, pāṭimokkha being taken as a derivative of mukhaṃ, which is quite impossible.

[3]) Majjhimanikāya 108 (Vol. III, p. 9 f.).

[4]) Pātimokkhasaṃvarasaṃvuto, see Dīghanikāya II, 42; XIII, 42; XXVI, 28; cf. Dhammapada 185.

rules was recited in the form of a confession formulary in solemn conclave of the monks, twice every month, on the new moon and the full moon days.[1] After the recital of each chapter—there are eight different kinds of greater and lesser sins, the treatment of which takes up eight chapters—the conductor of the ceremony would ask whether any one had committed the sin in question: and if this was the case, he had to confess his guilt.[2] This Uposatha ceremony, as it is called, was probably already instituted by Buddha himself, being modelled on ceremonies of a similar character among earlier sects of ascetics,[3] and the very earliest Buddhist literature must have included a Pāṭimokkha.[4] Originally it probably contained only 152 rules,[5] but they were extended to

---

[1]) According to Dīghanikāya XIV, 3, 22-28, at an earlier period—the legend is here dealing with the period of the former Buddha Vipassi—the Buddhist monks' appear to have assembled every six years at some large centre, for the recital of the Pāṭimokkha, which then was merely a kind of confession of faith, though the expression pāṭimokkhopadesāya is the same as in Majjh. 77 (Vol. II, p. 8), where there is mention of the fortnightly celebration.

[2]) At least this was the original idea, according to the wording of the formulas of the Pāṭimokkha. However, even in the Vinayapiṭaka itself the procedure was simplified and toned down, inasmuch as a monk who felt himself guilty of some transgression, had to confess it to one of the brethren *before* the Uposatha ceremony, so that he might be pure when he took his place in the assembly. Cf. *Oldenberg*, Buddha, pp. 381 f., 418 ff.

[3]) There may possibly be some historical foundation for the story told in Mahāvagga II, 1, that the heretical Paribbājakas convened assemblies for the recital of their Dhamma on the 14th, 15th and 8th days of each half-month, and that King Bimbisāra proposed to Buddha that similar assemblies should be organised. The Pāli word *Uposatha* is the Sanskrit Upavasatha, which means "fasting." From time immemorial the Brahmanical Indians observed the new moon and full moon days by sacrifices, prayers and fasting. The Uposatha ceremony, as performed in Ceylon at the present day, is described by J. F. *Dickson*, JRAS 1875 (reprinted in *Warren*, Buddhism in Translations, p. 405 ff.).

[4]) This is proved by the fact that we have a Prātimokṣa (Sanskrit for Pāṭimokkha) also in a Sanskrit version, and in one Tibetan and four Chinese versions. Cf. L. *Finot* and Ed. *Huber* in JA 1913, s. 11, t. II, p. 462 ff.; Mahāvyutpatti paragraphs 256-264; *Oldenberg*, ZDMG, 52, 645 f.; *Kern*, Manual, 74 f., 85 ff.

[5]) Aṅguttaranik. I, pp. 236, 230 (III, 83, 1; 87, 1) and Milindapañha, pp. 243, 272 speak of 150 Sikkhāpadas, which probably mean the rules of the Pāṭimokkha. Most likely the figure 150 is only a round number for the 152 rules remaining out of the total of 227 rules, after deducting the 75 sekhiyā dhammā which are merely rules of

227 at the time of the origin of the Vinayapiṭaka of the Theravādins. Though the text of these 227 rules of the Pāṭimokkha has come down independently in manuscripts, it does not, as such, form a part of the Canon, but is included in the Suttavibhaṅga, for this last-named work is nothing but an ancient commentary on the Pāṭimokkha consisting of 227 rules—a commentary which attained to the honour of being included in the canon. Suttavibhaṅga means "explanation of the Suttas," and in this case we should take "Sutta"[1] to mean the separate clauses or articles of the Pāṭimokkha. Each Sutta, *i.e.*, each single article, is explained word for word, and in an introduction it is related where and on what occasion the Buddha issued the decree in question. The Mahāvibhaṅga consists of eight chapters, corresponding to the eight classes of transgressions against the discipline. By analogy with the Pāṭimokkha for the monks, a similar code was compiled later for the nuns. The Bhikkhunīvibhaṅga, a much shorter work, is a commentary on it.

The Khandhakās, *i.e.*, "sections,"[2] which give the pre cepts for the various arrangements of the order (Saṅgha) and regulate the entire conduct of the monks and nuns in their daily life, form a kind of continuation and supplement of the Suttavibhaṅga. The ten sections of the Mahāvagga, *i. e.*, the "great section," contain the special precepts for

---

etiquette. The Prātimokṣa of the Sarvāstivādins gives the number of Pātayantikā dharmāḥ as 90 (in the Pāli 92 Pācittiyā dhammā), and it also gives us a total of 150, excluding the Śaikṣā dharmāḥ. The Sarvāstivādins have 113, the Mūla-Sarvāstivādins 106, the Dharmaguptas 100 Śaikṣā dharmāḥ (corresponding to the 75 sekhiyā dhammā in the Pāli), and the Mahāvyutpatti, para. 256 reads only : sambahulāḥ śaikṣadharmāḥ. Cf. *Finot*, JA 1913, s. 11, t. II, p. 469 f. ; S. *Dutt*, Early Buddhist Monachism, p. 92 f.

[1]) In the sense of the ancient meaning of the word *Sūtra*, see Vol, I, p. 268 f. The text of the Pāṭimokkha is published separately and translated by J. F. *Dickson*. JRAS 1876, p. 62 ff. and translated once again by *Rhys Davids* and *Oldenberg* in SBE vol. 13, p. 1 ff.

[2]) Translated into English by *Rhys Davids* and *Oldenberg* in SBE vols. XIII, XVII and XX.

admission into the order, for the Uposatha celebration, for life during the rainy season and for the Pavāraṇā celebration taking place at the end of the rainy season, and further, the rules for the wearing of shoes, facilities for seats and vehicles, medicine and clothing of the monks, and finally for the regulation of the legal conditions and the legal procedure within the order, especially in the case of schisms. The first nine sections of the Cullavagga, *i.e.*, the "lesser section," deal with the disciplinary methods in lesser matters, with various atonements and penances, the adjustment of disputes, the daily life of the monks, dwellings and furnishing of dwellings, the duties of monks towards one another and the exclusion from the Pāṭimokkha ceremony. Section X of the Cullavagga deals with the duties of the nuns. In the same way as the Pāṭimokkha underlies the Suttavibhaṅga, there are also, underlying the acts and ceremonies prescribed in the Khandhakās, old formulae, the so-called Kammavācā, *i. e.*, "words for the acts." These do not form a part of the Tipiṭaka any more than the Pāṭimokkha does,[1] but are merely included in the Khandhakās, in a similar manner as the mantras or prayers are included in the Vedic Brāhmaṇas and Sūtras. Sections XI and XII, in which the story of the first two councils of Rājagaha and Vesālī[2] is told, are no doubt later additions, and form a kind of appendix to the Cullavagga.

---

[1]) Upasampadā-Kammavācā, formularies for admission into the Order. These were first published by F. *Spiegel* (Kammavakya, liber de officiis sacerdotum Buddhicorum, Bonnae ad. Rh. 1841), with Latin translation, then by J. F. *Dickson* (JRAS 1875, p. 1 ff.) with English translation The last-named also describes the ceremony of admission, as it is still performed to-day in Ceylon. Other Kammavācā have been published and translated by O. *Frankfurter*, Handbook of Pāli, London, 1883, Herbert *Baynes* (JRAS 1892, p. 53 ff.; cf. also p. 380), Sarat Candra *Das* in JASB 63, Part I, 1894, p. 20 ff. and G. L. M. *Clauson* (JPTS 1906-1907, pp. 1-7).

[2]) See above, p. 4 ff. The fact that the last two books were added later, also appears from the title Cullavagga, "lesser section," which would only be justified if this work, like the Mahāvagga, were composed of ten parts only. Cf. *Rhys Davids* and *Oldenberg* in SBE, Vol. 13, p. xxi, n. 3.

As this appendix, too, only deals with the history of the order, we can say that the one and only subject of the books of the Vinayapiṭaka is the monastic community, or the Order (Saṅgha).

The Pāṭimokkha already indicates a fairly complicated organisation of the community.[1] The Khandhakās presuppose a still more advanced organisation. We are struck by the far-reaching liberality, if not laxity, in the rules for monastic life. According to the strict regulation the monk is to live only on what he obtains by begging, but he is also allowed to accept invitations to meals. He is to clothe himself in cast-off rags, but he may also wear garments of linen, cotton and even silk. He is to live at the foot of a tree, but he may also seek a more comfortable lodging in houses, huts or caves. Urine is to be his sole medicament, but he may also take butter, oil and honey. He may even eat fish, as long as the fish have not been killed for him.[2] All this indicates that there must have been a fairly long development of the discipline of the community prior to the final compilation of the Vinayapiṭaka, and that the bulk of the rules originated, not all at once, but gradually. On the other hand it has been shown that many of the regulations of the order of the community are identical with those which were in vogue among other sects of ascetics before Buddha.[3] Nevertheless, all the rules and regulations of the Vinaya are attributed to Buddha himself; for just as in the Suttavibhaṅga, the rules and regulations in the Khandhakās too, are introduced by narratives recording when and on what occasion they were declared by Buddha. As regards style, too, the stories in the Khandhakās agree with those in the Suttavibhaṅga to so great an extent that we are bound to assume

---

1) Cf. E. *Waldschmidt* Bruchstücke des Bhikṣuṇī-Prātimokṣa der Sārvāstivādins, p. 3 f.

2) Mahāvagga, I, 30; Cullavagga VII, 3, 14 f.

3) S. *Dutt*, Early Buddhist Monachism, pp. 16, 28, 37.

that they belong approximately to the same time.[1] In a few cases these stories may possibly have reference to actual events. In the majority of cases, however, they were probably invented *ad hoc*. On the whole, they are stereotyped, and of little value as literature.

Fortunately this is not true of all the narratives. The very commencing chapters of the Mahāvagga[2] contain one of the oldest fragments of a Buddha legend. In beautiful, archaic language, it is here related how Gotama Buddha obtained enlightenment (bodhi), how he decided to proclaim his doctrine, and how he gained his first disciples. Here is related, for instance, the legend of the noble youth Yasa, who grows up in a life of luxury, spends the nights among a band of female singers and dancers, but once waking up in the middle of the night and seeing the beautiful women in various ugly positions, is seized by disgust and satiety with the pleasures of this world; he flees from the life of voluptuousness, hastens to Buddha and becomes a monk. The later Buddha legend relates this story of Prince Siddhārtha, the subsequent Buddha, himself. A strange picture of manners is revealed by the story of the conversion of a band of young men, who are going out with their wives to enjoy themselves; one of them, who has no wife, takes a harlot with him; the latter steals the belongings of the men, and runs away. While the young men are pursuing her, they meet with Buddha, and ask him whether he has not seen a woman. The Buddha asks whether they would not do better to seek *themselves*, rather than a woman, and avails himself of the opportunity to preach the doctrine to them, whereupon they all become monks. There is no lack of marvellous stories, in which snake kings

---

[1]) If the rule dealt with in the Khandhakās is the same as the one dealt with in the Suttavibhaṅga, then the introductory story is also the same. Cf. *Oldenberg*, Vinayapiṭaka, Introd., p. xxii f.

[2]) I, 1—24. SBE, Vol. 13, p. 73 ff.

and gods play a part. The most beautiful of all these conversion-stories is that of the conversion of the two friends Sāriputta and Moggallāna, who were afterwards among the favourite disciples of the Buddha.[1] The first sermons of Buddha, for instance, the "sermon of Benares" and the "fire sermon," are also included in this old report.

In a later section of the Mahāvagga,[2] the story is told how the Buddha visits his native town and admits his son Rāhula into the order. In the Cullavagga we then find the narratives of the rich merchant Anāthapiṇḍaka, who presents his park to the order; of Devadatta, the enemy and rival of Buddha, who causes the first schism in the community; of the founding of the order of nuns, to which Buddha unwillingly gives his consent at the prayers and entreaties of his foster-mother Mahāpajāpati, who finds a noble advocate in the disciple Ānanda, and so on.[3]

Even among those of the introductory stories which, presumably, were only invented *ad hoc* and have no value otherwise, either historical or legendary, there is many a beautiful and valuable passage to be found. A narrative of this kind, touching in its simplicity, is the following:

"Now at that time a certain Bhikkhu had a disturbance in his bowels, and he lay fallen in his own evacuations. And the Blessed One on going round the sleeping-places accompanied by the venerable Ānanda came to that Bhikkhu's abode, and found him so. And he went up to him, and asked him, 'what is the matter with you, O Bhikkhu?'

'I have a disturbance, Lord, in my bowels.'

'Then have you, O Bhikkhu, any one to wait upon you?'

'No, Lord.'

---

1) Mahāvagga, I, 7 f.; 14; 15 ff.; 23 f. SBE, Vol. 13, pp. 102 ff., 116 ff., 118 ff., 144 ff. All these stories end with the admission of the converts into the Order. For this reason they form quite a natural introduction to the section about admission into the Order.

2) I, 54. SBE, Vol. 13, p. 207 ff.

3) Cullavagga VI. 4, 9; VII. 2—4, X. 1 f.; SBE, Vol. 20, pp. 187 ff., 233 ff., 320 ff.

'Why do not the Bhikkhus wait upon you?'

'Because I am of no service, Lord, to the Bhikkhus.'

Then the Blessed One said to the venerable Ānanda: 'Go, Ānanda, and fetch some water. Let us bathe this Bhikkhu.'

'Even so, Lord,' said the venerable Ānanda, in assent to the Blessed One, and fetched the water. And the Blessed One poured the water over that Bhikkhu; and the venerable Ānanda wiped him down. And the Blessed One taking hold of him at the head, and the venerable Ānanda at the feet, they lifted him up, and laid him down upon his bed.

Then the Blessed One, on that occasion and in that connection, convened a meeting of the Bhikkhu-saṃgha, and asked the Bhikkhus, 'Is there, O Bhikkhus, in such and such an apartment, a Bhikkhu who is sick?'

'There is, Lord.'

'Then what, O Bhikkhus, is the matter with that Bhikkhu?'

'He has a disturbance, Lord, in his bowels.'

'And is there any one, O Bhikkhus, to wait upon him?'

'No, Lord.'

'Why, then, do not the Bhikkhus wait upon him?'

'That Bhikkhu, Lord, is of no service to the Bhikkhus; therefore do they not wait upon him.'

'Ye, O Bhikkhus, have no mothers and no fathers who might wait upon you! If ye, O Bhikkhus, wait not one upon the other, who is there indeed who will wait upon you? Whosoever, O Bhikkhus, would wait upon me, he should wait upon the sick.' [1]

Others of these stories are valuable to us because they afford us some insight into the everyday life of the ancient Indians.[2] Thus, for instance, when it is related how the parents of the boy Upāli take counsel together, with regard to what they shall let the boy become, how they consider that

---

[1]) Mahāvagga, VIII, 26, translated by *Rhys Davids* and *Oldenberg* in SBE, Vol. 17, p. 240 f. However forcibly this passage may remind us of St. Matth. 25, 40 ("Inasmuch as ye have done it unto one of the least of these my brethren, ye have done it unto me"), the situation is, after all, quite different in this case, and the resemblance cannot be more than pure chance.

[2]) In this respect the Vinayapiṭaka is a valuable complement to the Brahmanical Gṛhyasūtras. See Vol. I, p 272 ff. Moreover, some of the sections, *e.g.*, the detailed

he might get sore fingers from writing, or pains in his chest from arithmetic, or spoil his eyes with painting, and therefore determine to let him become a monk, because this is the most comfortable way of earning a livelihood.[1] Not only extremely interesting from the point of view of the history of civilisation, but full of delightful humour too, are the stories of the doctor Jīvaka,[2] from which at least a very short extract shall here be given:

The town of Rājagaha vies with the great city of Vesālī in renown and splendour. The magnificence of the latter is not a little enhanced by the famous courtesan Ambapālī, who demands fifty florins for one night. In order to make Rājagaha, too, as flourishing as Vesālī, the beautiful and well-educated Sālavatī is installed there as courtesan at the command of the king and she demands a hundred florins for one night. She becomes pregnant, but on account of her profession keeps her pregnancy secret and after she has given birth to a child, she has it turned adrift in a little basket. The child is found by Prince Abhaya, who has it brought up and gives it the name of Jīvaka.

When Jīvaka is grown up, he goes as apprentice to a famous doctor in Takkasilā (Taxila). After a seven years' course of instruction he passes his "examination." This consists of his teacher's giving him a spade and commissioning him to bring him all the plants from the environs of Takkasilā which cannot be used as herbs of healing. Jīvaka comes back, and declares that far and wide he did not find one such plant. With this the teacher is satisfied, gives him some money for his journey, and lets him depart.

The money is soon spent and in order to earn something, he announces himself as a doctor in a town where he hears that the wife of a rich merchant is very ill. Jīvaka puts a little melted butter into her nose,

---

enumerations of thefts, sexual offences (cf. P. E. *Pavolini*, GSAI, Vol. 17, p. 325 ff.) and crimes of all descriptions, are of interest, because they add to our store of knowledge of the laws and customs of ancient India.

1) Mahāvagga, I, 49.

2) Mahāvagga, VIII, 1. The stories end with Jīvaka's making Buddha a present of clothes, and therefore they form the introduction to the section on the clothing of the monks. The stories of Āmrapālī (Ambapālī) and Jīvaka also occur in the Chinese Tripiṭaka, s. Éd. *Chavannes*, Cinq cents contes, III, p. 325 ff.

this comes into her mouth and she spits it out, whereupon she instructs the maid to preserve the melted butter. Jīvaka is at once anxious about his fee, as he regards the woman as mean. She reassures him, however, that she is merely a good house-wife, for the melted butter could still be used by the servants as grease or for the lamp. She recovers, and rewards the doctor with 4,000 florins; in addition, her son, her daughter-in-law and her husband, each gives him 4,000 florins, and the latter also gives him a male slave, a female slave and a carriage with a team.

Thus he returns to Rājagaha, where he hands over the money he has earned to Prince Abhaya, as a recompense for having brought him up. The latter does not accept it, but desires that Jīvaka shall take up his residence in Rājagaha. After he has cured the old King Bimbisāra of an unpleasant disease, he becomes the court physician and effects many remarkable cures. Once a great merchant in Rājagaha becomes very ill. All the doctors have already given him up. Then the king gives permission for his court physician to treat the merchant. Jīvaka first stipulates for an honorarium of a hundred thousand florins for himself and the same for the king, then he asks him whether he will be able to lie quietly first on one side, then on the other, and finally on his back, for seven months in each position. The invalid answers in the affirmative, whereupon the doctor ties him to the bed, cuts open his scalp, pulls out two worms, for it was they which had threatened the life of the merchant, and sews the wound up again. But the invalid is not able to lie for seven months on each side, but can always only endure it for seven days. After three times seven days, however, he is well. Jīvaka now explains that he only spoke of seven months, because otherwise the patient would not even have managed to lie still for seven days.

Many other stories are told of the cunning and the skill of the doctor Jīvaka.[1] He also treated Buddha professionally and was a great friend of the order.

This is not the only example which shows that the authors or compilers of the Vinayapiṭaka sometimes got tired of the dry tone, and interspersed the enumeration of prohibitions

---

[1]) He passed as an authority on the diseases of children, and was called the "children's doctor." Cf. *Jolly*, Medicin (in Grundriss III, 10), p. 68. In later times, too, the Buddhists took an active interest in medical science. (*Jolly*, l.c, pp. 8 and 15 f.)

and regulations with narratives in lighter vein. Thus, for instance, as an introduction to the rules regarding the precedence of age among the monks, Buddha relates the following fable: [1]

"Long ago, O Bhikkhus, there was a great banyan tree on the lower slopes of the Himālaya range; and near it there dwelt three friends—a partridge, a monkey, and an elephant. And they dwelt together without mutual reverence, confidence, and courtesy. Then, O Bhikkhus, it occurred to those friends, "Come now, let us find out which of us is the oldest by birth; and let us agree to honour and reverence and esteem and support him, and by his counsels let us abide." So, Bhikkhus, the partridge and the monkey asked the elephant,

"How far back can you, friend, remember?"

"Friends! when I was little I used to walk over this banyan tree, keeping it between my thighs, and its topmost twig brushed my stomach. So far back, friends, can I remember."

Then, O Bhikkhus, the partridge and the elephant asked the monkey (the same question).

"Friends, when I was little, sitting once on the ground, I gnawed at the then topmost twig of this banyan. So far back can I remember."

Then, O Bhikkhus, the monkey and the elephant asked the partridge (the same question).

"Friends! there was formerly a lofty banyan tree in yonder open space. One day after eating one of its fruits, I voided the seed here; and from that this banyan tree grew up. So I must be older than either of you."

Thereupon, O Bhikkus, the elephant and the monkey said to the partridge, "You, friend, are the oldest of us all. Henceforth we will honour and reverence and esteem and support you, and by your counsels will we abide."

Serious narratives, too, embodying the purest and most genuine Buddhist morality, are occasionally inserted; thus, the

[1]) Cullavagga, VI, 6, 3. Translated by *Rhys Davids* and *Oldenberg* in SBE, Vol. 20, p. 193 f.

touching story of Prince Dīghāvu ("Longlived"), who makes every effort to avenge the murder of his parents, but who, at the very moment when the murderer, King Brahmadatta, is entirely in his power, sheathes his already drawn sword and foregoes his revenge.[1] Finally, similes too, which play such a large part in the sermons and sayings, are not wanting in the Vinayapiṭaka. Thus, for example, in the Cullavagga (IX, 1, 3f.) in a carefully worked out simile, eight qualities of the ocean are compared with eight peculiarities of the Buddhist doctrine and discipline of the order. Here we meet with the oft-quoted sentence:

> "Just as, O Bhikkhus, the great ocean has but *one* taste, the taste of salt, so, O Bhikkhus, this religion and discipline has but *one* taste, the taste of liberation."

The Vinayapiṭaka texts bear a certain resemblance to the Vedic Brāhmaṇas. In both cases we find "rule" (vidhi) and "explanation of meaning" (arthavāda) side by side, and to the latter belong, in both cases, narrative poems, which appear like oases in the desert of religious technicalities.[2]

The Parivāra, the last book of the Vinayapiṭaka, is an insignificant and much later production, probably only the work of a Singhalese monk.[3] This comprises nineteen shorter texts, catechisms, indices, appendices, lists, and so on, very similar to the Anukramaṇīs and Pariśiṣṭas of the Veda and Vedāṅga texts. They are in the form of questions and answers, just like the texts of the Abhidhammapiṭaka, which probably date from the same time.

[1]) Mahāvagga, X, 2, 3-20; SBE, Vol. 17, p. 293 ff. I do not think it very likely that the legend is influenced by the Biblical story of David and Saul (I Sam. 24) as is suggested by *Copleston*, Buddhism, p. 103 note.

[2]) See Vol. I, pp. 202 and 208.

[3]) SBE, Vol. 13, p. xxiv.

The Suttapiṭaka of the Pāli Canon.

1. *The Speeches and Dialogues.*

Just as the Vinayapiṭaka is our best source for the Saṅgha, *i.e.*, the regulations of the ancient Buddhist order and the life of the monks, so the Suttapiṭaka is our most reliable source for the Dhamma, *i.e.*, the religion of Buddha and his earliest disciples. In the Suttapiṭaka, in the prose of the dialogues and narratives, as well as in sayings and songs, we also find—and this is our primary concern here—the greatest literary works which Buddhism has produced.

The Suttapiṭaka consists of five Nikāyas or "collections," [1] namely : (*i*) Dīghanikāya, (*ii*) Majjhimanikāya, (*iii*) Saṃyuttanikāya, (*iv*) Aṅguttaranikāya, and (*v*) Khuddakanikāya. The last-named comprises the following texts : 1. Khuddakapāṭha, 2. Dhammapada, 3. Udāna, 4. Itivuttaka, 5. Suttanipāta, 6. Vimānavatthu, 7. Petavatthu, 8. Theragāthā, 9. Therīgāthā, 10. Jātaka, 11. Niddesa, 12. Paṭisambhidāmagga, 13. Apadāna, 14. Buddhavaṃsa and 15. Cariyāpiṭaka.

The contents of the first four Nikāyas or " collections " consist of Suttas [2] or " discourses." These are eitherspeeches of the Buddha (sometimes also of one of his disciples), preceded only by a short introduction, in which is related where and on what occasion Buddha made the speech ;[3] or they are dialogues with outline narratives (Itihāsa-saṃvāda, Itihāsa dialogues) of the kind with which we have already become acquainted in the Upaniṣads and the Mahābhārata. The Suttas are,

1) According to Buddhaghosa (Sumaṅgalavilāsinī, p. 22 f.), however, it is the *whole Tipiṭaka* (not the Suttapiṭaka) which is divided into 5 Nikāyas, and he counts the Vinayapiṭaka and the Abhidhammapiṭaka with the Khuddakanikāya. Likewise Gandhavaṃsa (JPTS 1886, p. 57).

2) The expression *Suttanta* is also often used for *Sutta.*

3) Hence the typical beginning of each Sutta with the words : " Thus I heard (evaṃ me sutam) ; once the Lord sojourned, etc. (*e.g.*, in Sāvatthī in the garden of Anāthapiṇḍaka)."

however, as a rule, in prose form. Only here and there, in some of the Suttas, the prose is interrupted by verses (gāthās) which are partly quotations and partly interposed verses, such as were at all times popular in Indian literature for elevating the prose at particularly striking passages.[1]

1. The Dīghanikāya, "the collection of the long sermons,"[2] consists of 34 Suttas of considerable length, each of which deals minutely with one or more points of the doctrine, and could equally well be regarded as an independent work. The whole work is divided into three books, which differ in contents and character, but all of which contain earlier and later strata of tradition.[3] The earliest stratum is represented principally in the first book, and the later one mainly in the third book, whilst the second book is composed of the longest Suttas, some of which have grown to their present bulk owing to interpolations.[4] In form, too, the Suttas are by no means homogeneous. Whilst all the Suttas in Book I and a number of Suttas in Books II and III are written entirely in prose,

---

[1]) For instance, when stanzas are introduced by the words : "Here the following is said" (tatth' etaṃ vuccati) they are self-evidently quotations (*e.g.*, in Dīghanikāya 30). On the other hand, when significant words in verse form are put in the mouth of Buddha, and these verses begin with such sentences as "Thus spake the Master" or "The Lord addressed him in the following verses" (*e.g.*, Dīghanikāya 31 ; Majjhimanikāya 7, Vol. I, p. 39 ; 34, Vol. I, p. 34), we may take it that they are verses composed by the author of the Sutta himself : at least this would generally be the case, for in ancient India no clearly defined distinction was ever made between one's own literary work and that others.

[2]) Edited by T. W. *Rhys Davids* and J. E. *Carpenter*, London PTS, Vols. I, 1890, II 1903, III, 1911 ; translated by *Rhys Davids*, Dialogues of the Buddha, I–III=SBB, Vols. II—IV, 1899, 1910, 1921 ; into German by K. E. *Neumann*, München 1907-1918. Selections are translated by *Rhys Davids* in SBE, Vol. 11, 1 ff., 158 ff., 235 ff. ; into German by R. O. *Franke*, Göttingen 1913, and P. *Dahlke*, Suttapiṭaka II, Berlin, 1920.

[3]) Cf. P. V. *Bapat* in Ann. Bh. Inst. VIII, 1926, p. 1 ff.

[4]) Book I is called Sīlakkhandhavagga after its contents (it treats of sīla, "virtue"). Book II is called Mahāvagga after its bulk (it contains mostly Suttas, the titles of which begin with mahā,—"great"), Book III is called Pāṭikavagga, *i.e.*, "the section beginning with the Pāṭika-Sutta."

there are many Suttas in Books II and III written in a mixture of prose and verse, a form so popular in India. The verses are either ballad verses (as in Nos. 16, 18, 19, 21) or momentous utterances (as in Nos. 16, 17). Elsewhere we find (as in Nos. 30, 31) a constant interchange between prose and gāthās, such as we shall frequently come across in the Sanskrit and half-Sanskrit Buddhist texts. Suttas Nos. 20 and 32 are almost entirely in verse.

The majority of Suttas in Book I deal with ethical questions, more especially with virtue (sīla), concentration (samādhi) and insight (paññā) which lead to the state of an arhat, the ideal of the devout life. The ethical doctrines of Buddha are frequently set up controversially as against the teachings of the Brahmans and of other masters. The very first Sutta the Brahmajāla-Sutta, the "discourse on the Brahman-net," is of first-rate importance from the point of view of the history of religion, not only for Buddhism, but for the entire religious life and thought of ancient India.[1] In connection with the rules for the moral conduct of his disciples, Buddha here enumerates in long lists all kinds of occupations, conversations, modes of life and thought of the Brahmans and ascetics, from which the Buddhist monk is to keep aloof. There are Brahmans and ascetics who accumulate riches, who delight in dances, musical entertainments, dramatic performances and games of all kinds (the ethnologist finds here an interesting enumeration of popular amusements); others, who indulge in every possible luxury; others again, who earn their livelihood by sacrifices, divination and magic (we find here a catalogue which is most instructive from the point of view of Indian folk-lore); and finally, many who yield themselves up

---

1) For this see *Rhys Davids*, Buddhism, American Lectures, 2nd Ed., 1904, p. 30 ff., and F. O. *Schrader*, Über den Stand der indischen Philosophie zur Zeit Mahāvīras und Buddhas, Strassburg 1902, p. 8 ff. At the conclusion the Sutta calls itself a Veyyākaraṇa ("commentary," "exposition")

to every imaginable speculation upon being and non-being, on the beginning and the end of the world, on the soul, its nature and its history—no less then 62 different philosophical views are here enumerated. From all these things the disciple of Buddha is to keep aloof. As a skilful fisherman catches all the fish, great and small, when he casts a fine-meshed net into a pond, so Buddha knows how to "catch" in the "Brahman-net" all sophists and philosophers, and to prove their doctrines and speculations to be worthless and obstacles to true salvation.

The second Sutta, too, the Sāmañña-phala-Sutta, "the discourse on the reward of asceticism," is a valuable piece of evidence for ancient Indian life and thought at the time of Buddha ; for it acquaints us with the views of a whole series of prominent non-Buddhist teachers and founders of sects. A most vivid description of the visit of King Ajātasattu to Buddha forms the introduction to this dialogue.[1] For the history of the Indian caste system and the attitude of Buddha towards the problem of caste, the Ambaṭṭha-Sutta (No. 3) is of the utmost importance. Owing to its references to the history of the Sakya race and to the Ṛṣi Kṛṣṇa (Kaṇha), a mythological, and perhaps even historical interest, is attached to this Sutta. Suttas No. 5, the Kūṭadanta-Sutta, "the discourse on (the Brahman) Sharp-tooth," [2] and No. 13, the Tevijja-Sutta, "the discourse on the knowers of the three Vedas," in which with refined, but absolutely inoffensive irony, Buddha ridicules the Brahmanical cult with its bloody sacrifices and the striving of the Veda-knower for union with the Brahman, and contrasts with them Buddhist "sacrifices" and ideals of

---

[1]) According to *Oldenberg*, Zur Geschichte der altindischen Prosa, AGGW XVI, 6, 1917, p. 40 note, this introduction is an imitation of the Yājñavalkya dialogue in the Bṛhadāraṇyaka-Upaniṣad IV, 1. However, inspite of the similarity, this seems doubtful to me.

[2]) In this Sutta as in No. 17 (Mahā-Sudassana-Sutta), we find the Jātaka type.

life, are eminently instructive regarding the relation between the old and the new faith, Brahmanism and Buddhism. The fundamental doctrine of Buddhist philosophy of the interconnection of causes, is treated in No. 15, the Mahānidāna-Sutta, "the great discourse on causes." One of the most important duties of the Buddhist monk is "mindfulness." The four kinds of mindfulness are treated in No. 22, the Mahā-Satipaṭṭhāna-Sutta, "the great discourse on the kinds of mindfulness." It also deals with the fundamental doctrines of Buddhism, and closes with a detailed presentation of the "four noble truths."[1] For Buddhist ethics from a popular point of view, one of the most important texts in the Pāli Canon is No. 29, the Sigālovāda-Sutta, "the sermon: the exhortation of Sigāla," in which the entire domestic and social duties of the Buddhist layman are presented in detail.[2]

That Sutta of the Dīghanikāya which is the most important in every respect is No. 16, the Mahā-Parinibbāna-Sutta, "the great discourse on the perfect Nirvāṇa of (Buddha),"[3] which differs essentially in form and contents from all the other Suttas. It is neither a dialogue nor a speech on one or more chief points of doctrine, but a continuous record of the latter part of Buddha's life, his last speeches and sayings, and his death. The oldest parts of this extensive record surely belong to the oldest part of the Tipiṭaka and to the earliest beginnings of a poetic treatment of the life of Buddha. It is remarkable that in the Pāli Canon there is no biography of the Buddha; but the beginnings of one are to be found partly

1) This conclusion is absent in the Satipaṭṭhāna-Sutta of the Majjhimanikāya (No. 10). F. *Heiler*, Die buddhistische Versenkung, 2nd Ed., München. 1923, p. 13, calls this Sutta "the exercise manual of the Buddhist monk."

2) Cf. R. C. *Childers*, Ind. Ant. 12, 1883, p. 23 ff.; T. W. *Rhys Davids*, Buddhism (SPCK), p. 143 ff., and Mrs. *Rhys Davids*, SBB, Vol. IV, p. 168 ff.

3) Translated by *Rhys Davids*, SBE, Vol. 11 and SBB, Vol. II, 78 ff., into German by J. *Dutoit*, Leben des Buddha, p. 221 ff., K. E. *Neumann*, München, 1911, R. O. *Franke*,

in the Vinayapiṭaka,[1] and partly in the Suttapiṭaka. It is quite comprehensible that the memory of the latter part of the Master's life and of his last speeches was most firmly impressed on the minds of the disciples of Buddha, and that these have been preserved and handed down with loving fidelity. I do not hesitate to see the beginnings of a Buddha biography in the oldest parts of this Sutta, though there are only few passages in the Mahā-Parinibbāna-Sutta which can be regarded as really ancient and original. For, the Sutta is by no means a unified work, but is composed of parts which belong to different ages. At a very early period—probably soon after the death of Buddha—there must already have been a short "Sutta of the perfect Nirvāna (of the Buddha)," which, by means of interpolations and additions, grew longer and longer in course of time, till it became the "*great* Sutta of the perfect Nirvāṇa" which we now have in our Pāli Canon. Such passages as those in the second section, where the story is related of the first illness of Buddha, which befell him at Beḷuva, and which he overcame by the strength of his will, where he assures Ānanda that he is not one of those teachers "with the closed fist," who keep something for themselves, but that he has proclaimed the whole truth, and where he disclaims the idea that he should ever have wished to pose as a leader of the community, are surely ancient and original. The order, he says, had never been dependent upon him and would therefore not be "without a leader" even after his departure, if it would only be guided by the religion he had proclaimed. "Therefore, Ānanda, be your own lights! Be your own refuge! Hold steadfastly to the religion as your light, hold steadfastly to the religion as your refuge!" Equal

Dīghanikāya, 179 ff., H. *Beckh*, Stuttgart, 1925. Extracts from it have been translated in all books on Buddhism. *Cf.* also E. *Müller*, JRAS, 1913, 1087 ff. ; H. *Kern*. OZ II, 1913-14, 229 f. ; P. *Oltramare* in RHR 66, 1912, 118 ff., *Eliot* I, 161 ff.

[1]) See above, p. 27f.

antiquity and originality can most probably be claimed for the passage in the fifth section, in which we read how Ānanda, no longer able to control his grief at the approaching departure of the Master, goes out and stands weeping, leaning against the doorpost, whereupon the Buddha has him called back, and tells him the most kindly words of consolation and of recognition of his loving attachment. The verses, too, which are scattered in the Sutta, bear the stamp of the greatest antiquity. Some of them contain significant sayings of the Buddha and his disciples, and others effectively emphasize the most striking events of the narrative.[1] While, in all these passages, Buddha speaks entirely as man to man, we see him, in other parts of the same text, performing miracles like a demigod or a magician; indeed, he boasts of his magic power, by means of which he could, if he only desired it, prolong his life till the end of an age of the world, and reproaches Ānanda because the latter had not understood the hint at the given time and implored him, Buddha, to live on (III, 34-47). Buddha's resolve to die causes an earthquake, and he avails himself of the opportunity to enumerate the eight causes of an earthquake, and to follow it up by the enumeration of other things, likewise eight in number (III, 11-33). These are additions and insertions of epigones, who no longer felt even a breath of the spirit which had inspired the authors of the ancient record. In most cases, moreover, it is not difficult to point out the sources whence the additions came; for large portions of the Sutta, all together amounting to almost the whole Sutta, recur in other texts of the Tipiṭaka and are obviously borrowed from them.[2] Nevertheless all the

[1]) *Copleston* (Buddhism, pp. 46, 53) is of the opinion that this Sutta is based on an earlier epic poem, from which these stanzas were taken. I rather think that these verses are the *first beginnings* of a poetical version of the life of Buddha (in the form of *sacred ballads*).

[2]) However, in some cases, passages were originally in the Mahā-Parinibbāna-Sutta, and thence found their way into other texts. The parallel texts have been collected by

interpolations and extensions have not succeeded in destroying the character of this text, which recalls our gospels more than any other text of the Tipiṭaka.

It is evident that it was a favourite practice to utilise this famous and popular Sutta for inserting especially important texts into it, with a view to enhance their prestige by this means; thus, for instance, also the Dhammādāsa, or "mirror of religion," the solemn confession of faith in the Buddha, the doctrine and the community, was inserted.[1] The final redaction of the Mahā-Parinibbāna-Sutta can nevertheless only be of comparatively late date; for one passage speaks of the transmission and authority of the Suttas and of the Vinaya texts;[2] and in the concluding section of the Sutta, mention is even made of Buddha relics[3] and the erection of Stūpas, *i.e.*, the same Buddha who, in the beautiful dialogue with Ānanda, still stood before us as a simple man and teacher, already appears here as the object of a cult, which is not attested by monuments until the time of Aśoka.

Whilst the Mahā-Parinibbāna-Sutta is a mosaic composed of earlier and later pieces, other Suttas belong entirely to a

---

Rhys Davids, Dialogues of the Buddha, II, p. 72. It is only by comparing the Pāli text minutely with the Sanskrit texts, in which fragments of a Parinirvāṇa-Sūtra have come down to us, and with the Tibetan and Chinese translations, that we can discern which parts of the Sutta are ancient and genuine. Cf. *Windisch*, Māra und Buddha, p. 33 ff., *Oldenberg*, ZDMG 52, 1898, p. 628, J. S. *Speyer*, ZDMG 53, 1899, p. 121 ff., J. *Edkins*, JRAS 1881, p. 66 ff. For the Chinese translation of the Mahā-Parinirvāṇa-Sūtras. Carlo *Puini*, in GSAI 21, 1908, 59 ff. ; 22, 1909, p. 1 ff. For a comparative study of the different Parinirvāṇa texts see M. *Przyluski* in JA 1918-1920, s. II, t. XI, 485 ff. ; XII, 401 ff. ; XV, 5 ff.

[1]) II, 8-10. Cf. Saṃyuttanikāya 55, 8 (Vol. V, p. 357) and Theragāthā 395. H. *Baynes* has published an enlarged form of the Dhammādāsa, as it is still recited at the present day at the Pāṭimokkha (WZKM 10, 1896, 242 ff.).

[2]) IV, 7-11, Dīgha, Vol. II, p. 123 ff.; cf. Aṅguttara-Nikāya, IV, 180 (Vol. II, 167 ff.) and *Copleston*, Buddhism, p. 45. In IV, 10 f. (Vol. II, p. 125) the knowers of the Mātikās are also mentioned (s. above p. 11, note 3).

[3]) Cf. J. F. *Fleet*, JRAS 1906, 657 ff., who (l. c. 667 ff.) tries to prove that the Sutta could not have been composed before 375 B. C. I believe that the final redaction must be placed a good deal later.

later stratum of tradition. The Suttas (especially in Book I) in which Buddha appears as a human teacher only, cannot possibly have been written at the same time as the Mahā-Apadāna-Sutta (No. 14), "the great discourse on the miracles (of Buddha)" in which the dogma of the six Buddhas,[1] who are said to have been the precursors of Gotama Buddha, is already taught, and in which the entire Buddha legend, adorned by numerous miracles, especially all the miracles of the conception and birth of Buddha, is recited.[2] The Lakkhaṇa-Sutta (No. 30) also belongs to the same stratum of tradition. This Sutta enumerates the 32 signs of a "great man"; the man who has these physical marks, must become either a ruler of the world, or a saviour of the world, a Buddha. There is no doubt that Buddha, like the majority of his contemporaries, believed that by continued meditation one could attain to all sorts of supernatural powers (iddhis) and become a kind of superman. However, he expressly declared it unworthy of a monk and dangerous for the doctrine, to attempt to exert influence over a layman by means of magic of this nature, rather than by means of teaching and persuasion, and the "miracle of instruction."[3] For this reason it is certain that the main portion of the Pāṭika-Sutta (No. 24) in which Buddha not only takes part in a miracle-working competition with other ascetics, but also boasts grandiloquently of his marvellous powers, represents a

---

[1]) It is perhaps more than mere coincidence that, in this Sutta, Buddha Vipassi's favourite pupil is named Aśoka.

[2]) There is absolutely no foundation for the supposition of L. A. *Waddell* (JRAS 1914, 661 ff.) that the title of the Sutta was originally Mahā-Padhāna-Sutta, "Sutta of the highest being." However, he may be right in saying that this Sutta and the Lalitavistara can be traced back to a common source, and that the Sutta corresponds to the tradition of about the 3rd to the 1st century B. C.

[3]) Kevadha-Sutta (No. 11), Vol. I, p. 214. Similarly in No. 28 (Vol. III, p. 112 f.). In the Vinayapiṭaka (Culla. V, 8, 2) it is declared as a Dukkaṭa offence for a monk to perform miracles before laymen for the sake of worldly gain. A monk who does this, is compared to a woman who displays her charms for money.

later stage of the tradition. As a matter of fact, this Sutta is a very miserable compilation, in which only the beginning is ancient, and all the rest is an inferior admixture.[1]

The semi-poetical and mythological Suttas, Nos. 17-21, probably also belong to the later stage of the tradition. Just as in the Purāṇas and in some sectarian sections of the epic, Indra is presented as paying homage to the god Śiva or Viṣṇu, so, in these Suttas, which *Rhys Davids*[2] so aptly calls "Tendenzschriften," *i.e.*, 'pamphlets with a purpose,' we find Indra and the other gods and demi-gods as devout worshippers of Buddha. The most interesting is the Sakkapañha-Sutta (No. 21), "the Sutta of the questions of Sakka." Sakka, *i.e.*, Indra, king of the gods, scarcely dares to approach the sublime Buddha. He first sends one of his Gandharvas, or heavenly musicians, in advance, in order to put the sublime sage into a favourable frame of mind, and strangely enough the Gandharva does this by singing a love-song.[3] Needless to say, Buddha receives the god with his habitual friendliness, expounds the truths of religion to him, and replies to all his questions, whereupon Sakka bursts forth into an enthusiastic hymn of praise to the Sublime One. The Cakkavatti-Sīhanāda-Sutta (No. 26), which mentions Buddha Metteyya, the Buddhist Messiah, and must, if only for that reason, be a later work, is a kind of mythological story of the origin of moral ideas, and is a remarkable medley of vision, prophecy and sermon. The first beginnings (aggañña) are treated in still greater detail in the Aggañña-Sutta (No. 27). These fancies regarding the origin of the universe and the beings, and regarding the beginnings of culture and social order are also reminiscent of the Purāṇas. Nevertheless, the purpose

---

[1] Cf. Friedrich *Weller* in Asia Major I, p. 620 ff.

[2] SBB, Vol. III, p. 298.

[3] It appears that a fragment of an ancient non-Buddhist poem has been worked into the Sutta here.

of this Sutta is the same as that of the Ambaṭṭha-Sutta, namely, to demonstrate that the life of the saints (arhat) and the attainment of Nirvāṇa are independent of caste.

One of the best dialogues in the Dīghanikāya is No. 23, the Pāyāsi-Sutta, the dialogue between the unbelieving chieftain Pāyāsi, who denies the soul and the Beyond, and the monk Kumāra Kassapa. While elsewhere in the "dialogues" of the Suttapiṭaka the person who takes the secondary part in the conversation mostly interrupts the principal speaker, who is usually the Buddha himself, only with words of assent, the Pāyāsi-Sutta is a real, lively dialogue, which sometimes recalls the Platonic dialogues. However, even this Sutta is not original, but is an Itihāsa dialogue enlarged to its disadvantage, which has been borrowed from another sect.[1] The last three Suttas also serve to indicate that the final redaction of the Dīghanikāya must have been completed at a late date: these are the Āṭānāṭiya-Sutta, which is merely an incantation to ward off snakes and demons, and the Saṅgīti and the Dasuttara-Sutta, which are written after the style of the Aṅguttaranikāya, and which, like the texts of the Abhidhamma, which they resemble in contents, are in the form of a catechism.[2]

To anyone who has followed this survey of the contents of the Dīghanikāya, it will scarcely be credible that a prominent Pāli scholar[3] attempts to prove that this text should be regarded as "a literary work which was drawn up as a

---

[1]) Kumāra Kassapa wants to prove to Pāyāsi that there is a soul, and yet we know that Buddha himself denies the existence of a soul substance. We also find a version of this dialogue among the Jains. Probably both sects borrowed it from an earlier source. Dhammapāla says (in his commentary on the Vimānavatthu) that this dialogue was written subsequently to the death of Buddha and the erection of a stūpa over his ashes, s. *Rhys Davids*, SBB, Vol. III, p. 347.

[2]) A text corresponding to the Saṅgīti-Sutta, entitled Saṅgītiparyāya, appears among the Sarvāstivādins as a book of the Abhidharmapiṭaka. Cf. J. *Takakusu*, JPTS 1904-5, p. 99 ff.

[3]) R. O. *Franke*, ZDMG 67, 1913, 409 ff.; WZKM 27, 1913, 198 ff., 276 ff.; Dīghanikāya, p. x ff.

uniform whole."[1] It is a matter of course that the compiler or the committee of compilers were desirous of arranging the Suttas according to some principle, classing together such Suttas as seemed to belong together by reason of association of ideas or wording;[2] but this does not prove that the whole work is the work of *one* author. When the same scholar seeks to trace a uniform idea underlying the whole of the Dīghanikāya, namely, that Gotama Buddha was a Tathāgata, *i.e.*, that he had trodden the path of salvation in order to encourage his disciples to tread the same path, and that the doctrine of the path leading to liberation or Nirvāṇa is the nucleus of the work, it is merely saying in other words that the alleged author wished to present the tenets of the Buddha on the ideal life. Now this comprises practically all Buddha's teaching, and therefore, in this way, one could puzzle out a "uniform underlying idea" in all the texts of the Tipiṭaka dealing with the Dhamma, and claim that they are the work of *one* author.[3]

If, as we have shown, the Dīghanikāya is composed of earlier and later portions, it cannot be the earliest work of the Canon, as *Franke* endeavours to prove,[4] and there is no justification for the attempt to construct "the doctrine of Buddha in its earliest accessible form" from the Dīghanikāya. It is only by comparing *all* the ancient Buddhist texts, which are scattered in the *various* collections, that we can attempt

---

[1]) Dīghanikāya, p. xlii.

[2]) However, in the Chinese translation of the Dīrghāgama, the Sūtras are arranged in an entirely different order from that in which they appear in the Dīghanikāya; cf. M. *Anesaki* in Transactions of the Asiatic Society of Japan, Vol. XXXV, part 3, 1908, p. 35 ff. The fact is that the compiler of the Sanskrit version arranged the material in a different way.

[3]) *Franke's* view is also repudiated by *Oldenberg* (AR 17, 1914, 626 f.), C. A. F. *Rhys Davids* (JRAS 1914, 459 ff.), *Geiger* (Pāli Literatur und Sprache, p. 11 f.) and *Eliot* I, 278 n. 1.

[4]) ZDMG 69, 1915, 455 ff.; 71, 1917, 50 ff.

to reconstruct the doctrine of Buddha in its earliest accessible form.

II. The Majjhimanikāya, "the collection of the medium-sized Suttas,"[1] consists of 152 speeches and dialogues, which differ from those of the Dīghanikāya only in being, on the whole, shorter. But in this collection, too, each Sutta forms a complete whole, and they are as different in kind as they are in value. The great number of the Suttas is one reason for their contents being much more varied than that of the Dīghanikāya. We find in them discourses on almost all the points of the religion of Buddha, on the four noble truths, on the Karman, the vanity of desires, the objectionableness of the belief in a soul, Nirvāṇa, the various kinds of meditation, and so on. Though these discussions are often only tedious sermons, they frequently have the popular and agreeable form of dialogues with a long or short introduction, or a frame story (Itihāsa dialogues). Instruction by means of similes is a favourite device, whether *one* simile is spun out through an entire speech, or whether a whole series of similes runs through a speech in order to impress one and the same doctrine again and again. Myths and legends, too, are related for the sake of introducing some doctrine or other, as in No. 37, where the visit of Moggallāna, the renowned disciple of Buddha, to Indra's heaven is described. The monk Moggallāna, with his great toe, causes the whole heavenly palace to shake[2]—a trait strongly reminiscent of the Brahmanical legends of the Mahābhārata and the Purāṇas. Some of the frame narratives give the impression of actual events as, for instance, the story of Pukkusāti, who desires admission into

---

[1]) Ed. by V. *Trenckner* and R. *Chalmers*, London PTS 1888-1902. Translated by Lord *Chalmers*, Further Dialogues of the Buddha in SBB, Vols. V and VI, 1926-27; into German by K. E. *Neumann*. Selections translated by T. W. *Rhys Davids* in SBE, Vol. II, and (into German) by P. *Dahlke*, Suttapiṭaka, Vol. III, Berlin, 1923.

[2]) A trick which is again alluded to, in No. 50.

the order, and, while he goes to fetch a cloak and a begging bowl, is killed by a cow (No. 140), in which connection Buddha inculcates the lesson that this man attained Nirvāṇa, in spite of not having been a monk. There is, again the story of the monk Channa (No. 144), who was overtaken by a serious illness, and who took his own life by opening a vein, which Buddha approves. Suicide, he says, is blameworthy if by that means one merely desires to gain another body (in a new re-birth), but not if one enters Nirvāṇa. The beautiful Assalāyana-Sutta (No. 93) strikes us, as though taken from the actual life of the time of Buddha. Gotama's doctrine of the "purity of all the four castes" must have been very awkward for the proud Brahmans. Such dialogues about the problem of caste, as that between the young Brahman Assalāyana and Gotama Buddha, must frequently have occurred in real life. The reasoning against the caste claims of the Brahmans is excellent. Assalāyana says to Buddha:

"The Brahmans, Lord Gotama, say thus: The Brahmans alone are the best caste, every other caste is low; the Brahmans alone are the white caste, every other caste is black, only the Brahmans become pure, not the non-Brahmans: only the Brahmans are the actual sons of the god Brahman, produced out of his mouth, begotten by Brahman, formed by Brahman, heirs of Brahman. What does the Lord Gotama say to that?"

Thereupon Buddha asks Assalāyana a series of questions which the latter is compelled to answer in the affirmative, thereby admitting that the statements of the Brahmans are unfounded. He says, for example:

"What dost thou think, Assalāyana? Suppose that an anointed king of the warrior race causes a hundred men of different castes to be assembled together; men shall come from the families of warriors, of Brahmans, of the nobility, and they shall take an upper friction-stick from a Sāl tree or Salaḷa tree or sandal tree or Padmaka tree,[1] produce a fire by turning

[1]) Various kinds of fine wood.

it (in the lower friction-stick) and bring forth a flame. And there shall come men from the families of Caṇḍālas, hunters, basket-makers, chariot-builders, Pukkusas,[1] and they shall take an upper friction-stick from a dog's trough, or a hog's trough, or a washing trough, or a stick of ricinus wood, produce a fire through turning, and bring forth a flame."[2] Now, will the fire that the warriors, Brahmans, *etc.*, have produced with the fine wood have flame, brightness and light, and will this fire be useful for all fire purposes? And will the fire which the Caṇḍālas, hunters, *etc.*, have produced with wood from the dog's trough, *etc.*, have no flame, no brightness and no light, and will this fire not be useful for all fire purposes? Assalāyana naturally has to reply that there is no difference between the two kinds of fire, and Gotama concludes that it is the same with the castes."[3]

Some of the Suttas, however, are neither dialogues nor sermons, but simply narratives. Thus No. 86 is a regular old Ākhyāna, telling, in prose and verse, the tale of the terrible robber Aṅgulimāla, who became a monk and rose to be an Arhat (a saint who has attained to Nirvāṇa even in this life)—a valuable piece of ancient Buddhist poetry. Another Sutta (No. 83) tells the legend (recurring in the Jātakas) of King Makhādeva who, at the appearance of the first grey hair, gives up the reigns of government, and becomes a monk. One of the most splendid passages of this kind is the Raṭṭhapāla-Sutta (No. 82). In beautiful old ballad-style, the following—I give only a short extract—is related :

The young prince Raṭṭhapāla desires to become a monk. His parents absolutely refuse to consent, but, by refusing to take any food, he compels them to give their permission. Years later, he returns as a monk to his native town, and begs at the door of his parents' home. His father does not recognise him, and drives him from the threshold with abuse. "By these shaven monks," he cries, "our only dearly beloved son was induced to renounce the world." Meanwhile the nurse comes out to throw

1) Sanskrit Pukkaśas, a very low caste.

2) Abridged from here.

3) Majjhimanikāya, Vol. II, p. 151 ff. A discussion on the caste problem is also to be found in Sutta No. 84. Cf. R. *Chalmers*, JRAS 1894, p. 341 ff.

away some scraps of food. The mendicant monk begs for these scraps for his meal. Then the servant recognises him as the son of the house, and announces this to her master. The latter comes out and invites his son to enter the house. The latter politely declines, saying "Not so, I have already dined to-day." However, he accepts an invitation for the next day. His father prepares for him not only a meal, but heaps up gold and ornaments in the dining-room, and instructs the former wives of Raṭṭhapāla to adorn themselves. The next day he is received splendidly, and his father offers him all the jewels and treasures. But Raṭṭhapāla only says: "If you want to follow my advice, father, then load all the gold and ornaments on a cart and throw it into the Ganges where it is deepest. And why? Because nothing but pain and misery, wretchedness and sufferings will arise out of it." Neither will he have anything to do with the women, who throw themselves coaxingly at his feet. After he has finished his meal, he goes his way. Then he meets the king of the Kuru-land, who says that he can understand that a person who has become old or ill or poor or has lost his relatives becomes a monk, but he cannot understand why one who is young, happy and healthy should renounce the world. Raṭṭhapāla answers him in a speech on the vanity of existence and the insatiableness of desire, and convinces the Kuru-king in a Socratic dialogue, of the truth of the doctrine of Buddha.

Besides such magnificent compositions, we find sermons as dry as dust in which a series of technical expressions or a fundamental doctrine is explained in catechism style, *e. g.*, Nos. 43 and 44.[1] Some of these Suttas (*e. g.*, Nos. 127, 137, 140, 148, 151) have completely adopted the style of the enumerations of the Aṅguttaranikāya and of the definitions and classifications of the Abhidhammapiṭaka. The abovementioned Ākhyānas, in which the narrative proceeds vividly in a mixture of prose and verse, are very different from Suttas like No. 116, where a bare list of Paccekabuddhas (hermit-Buddhas who have attained

[1]) These two Suttas, which are called respectively the "great" and "small" Vedalla-Sutta, have nothing in common, beyond the question and answer form. It seems that the unexplained expression "vedalla" refers precisely to this form. Cf. above, p. 10, and C. A. *Foley* (Mrs. Rhys Davids), JRAS 1894, p. 321 ff.

enlightenment without proclaiming it to the world) is given first in prose and immediately afterwards in verse. This kind of mixture of prose and verse, which we came across occasionally in the Dīghanikāya also, belongs to a much later type, which we shall meet again in the Sanskrit Buddhist literature.

Apart from the fact that the Suttas of the Majjhimanikāya give us the best idea of the ancient Buddhist religion and the teaching methods of Buddha and his first disciples, we also value them because they afford us many an interesting glimpse of the every-day life of that ancient time, not only of the life of the monks themselves (as in Nos. 5, 21, 22, etc.) but of that of the other classes of the people too. Thus No. 51 gives us a good survey of the Brahmanical system of sacrifice, and valuable hints concerning the connection between bloody sacrifices, and government and priesthood. We repeatedly meet with enumerations of different kinds of ascetic practices which were popular in ancient India. In Nos. 12 and 14 we find a veritable pattern-card of ascetic abominations, and also in Suttas Nos. 40, 45, 51 and 60 we make the acquaintance of all sorts of queer saints of various sects. At that time there were, for instance, "dog-ascetics," and "ox-ascetics," whose asceticism consisted in feeding and living exactly after the manner of dogs and oxen. In reply to the question as to what will become of these ascetics in their future existence, Buddha replies that in the best case, the "dog-ascetic" might be re-born as a dog and the "ox-ascetic" as an ox, but that, just as likely they might both find themselves in hell. Several Suttas are of historical significance as throwing light on the relation of Buddha to the sect of the Jains, especially the Upāli-Sutta (No. 56),[1] but also Nos. 57, 101 and 104.

[1]) Treated in detail by Léon *Feer* in OC VI, Leyden, 1883, t. III, 67 ff., RHR t. 13, 1886, 74 ff. and JA 1887, s. 8. t. IX, 309 ff.; 1888, s. 8, t. XI, 113 ff, 123 ff. and t. XI, 209 ff. Cf. also R. *Chalmers* in JRAS 1895, p. 665 f.

No. 76 is of great interest, because it throws light on the relation of Buddha to the doctrines of other masters, especially free-thinkers and sophists, of his day. There are also occasional references to all kinds of superstitions, to social and legal conditions. Thus in No. 13, we find an enumeration of cruel punishments; Sutta 38 records all sorts of strange ideas upon birth and education of children, Nos. 28 and 37 throw light on the relationship between daughter-in-law and father-in-law, and so on.

In point of time the separate Suttas are often far removed from one another. While in some Suttas of the Majjhimanikāya, as in the ancient parts of the Mahā-Parinibbāna-Sutta, the Buddha appears purely as man and teacher, and only speaks of himself as of an ordinary mortal, who has gained certain knowledge, and who looks forward to entering into complete Nirvāṇa, and while, for instance in Suttas 26 and 36,[1] he relates in simple language a part of his autobiography, free from all miracles, in other Suttas (*e.g.*, No. 12) all kinds of magic powers and absolutely divine qualities are ascribed to Buddha. In the "Sutta of the astonishing events and miracles" (No. 123) the conception and birth of the Bodhisatta is described with all the miracles as they are known in the Buddha legend of the later non-canonical works (Nidānakathā, Lalitavistara, etc.), and as we have already found them in the Mahā-Apadāna-Sutta of the Dīghanikāya.[2] It is not rare in the Suttas for the Buddha, or even a saint like Moggallāna, to disappear, and "as a strong man stretches out his contracted arm or contracts his outstretched arm," to appear suddenly in the world of the

[1]) In the same way, Aṅguttaranikāya, III, 38.

[2]) See above, p. 42. According to *Windisch*, Buddhas Geburt, p. 104, Majjh. 123 is merely a shorter version of the Mahā-Apadāna-Sutta. There is, indeed, a most striking agreement between the two, except that Dīghanikāya 14 tells of the birth of Buddha Vipassi. On the importance of the Sutta Majjh. 123 in the development of the Buddha legend in the later texts, cf. *Windisch*, l. c., p. 107 ff.

gods or in Brahman's heaven (*e.g.*, Nos. 37, 49 and often elsewhere). One Sutta (No. 49) claims to prove absolutely that Buddha is mighty and exalted above all gods, even above the highest Brahman. Though in most of the speeches Buddha appears as the spokesman, yet in some of them disciples of Buddha are the principal speakers (*e.g.*, Nos. 15, 43 and 44). Not infrequently one of the disciples answers a question, but then lets Buddha confirm the corrrectness of the reply (*e.g.*, No. 126). However, the fiction that all the Suttas originated during the life-time of Buddha is not always maintained. Thus, in Nos. 84 and 94, in answer to the question where Buddha is now, a disciple receives the reply: "He has attained complete Nirvāṇa." Sutta No. 108 is immediately connected with the death of Buddha, Ānanda being asked whether, before his death, Buddha had not appointed a monk as the chief of the monastic community. Ānanda replies in the negative, but declares that the community is not, on that account, "without refuge," for the religion (dhamma) is its refuge,[1] and discipline shall be maintained in the community by the Pāṭimokkha ceremony[2] which was instituted by the Master. This, we may observe, is a Sutta concerned with the discipline of the order (vinaya) rather than with the religion (dhamma); this is also the case in other Suttas (*e.g.*, Nos. 103, 104 and 142).[3]

Whether, from the different methods by which certain points of the doctrine are treated in the Suttas, conclusions may be drawn as to their early or late composition—that

1) Obviously an allusion to the famous passage in the Mahā-Parinibbāna-Sutta, see above p. 39. Cf. also C. A. F. *Rhys Davids* in JRAS 1902, p. 476 f.

2) See above p. 22 ff.

3) K. E. *Neumann*, Reden Gotamo Buddhas III, Introduction, has based on this hypothesis that the Vinaya was originally included in the Suttapiṭaka and only took shape as an independent Vinayapiṭaka later. According to R. O. *Franke* (WZKM 29, 1915, p. 136) the Majjhimanikāya is "the very earliest work of the Vinaya literature," and he points out many passages (l. c., 139 ff.) in which the Majjh. speaks of the Vinaya.

must remain an open question.[1] For instance, the coarse presentation of the doctrine of Karman in Suttas Nos. 129 f., and 135 f., where the torments of hell are described with a minuteness which finds its counterpart in the descriptions of hell in the Purāṇas, may indicate a later date of composition. But it is also possible, that even in earlier times a more popular conception of the doctrine of Karman may have existed by the side of the purely philosophical one. The fact that the order already had a certain past history when the Majjhimanikāya was compiled, is indicated by a passage in No. 65, in which it is said that "formerly" there were fewer precepts and more monks, whereas "now" there are more precepts and fewer monks. The mention of the Yona-Kambojas in the Assalāyana-Sutta (No. 93) points to the existence of the Graeco-Bactrian Empire, that is, to the period shortly before Aśoka.

Suttas Nos. 41 and 42 may be taken as significant of the manner in which the collection originated. The latter, with the exception of a short introduction, is literally identical with No. 41. Elsewhere, too, the same sermons or dialogues recur, only in a different setting. Thus, for example, Nos. 132-134 are only different versions of one and the same sermon. These are probably sermons which were actually delivered by the monks;[2] if nothing better occurred to him, a monk would repeat an already existing sermon with slight alterations. The collectors then collected *everything*, from the lips of any preacher, on which they could possibly lay hands.[3]

[1]) Cf. C. A. F. *Rhys Davids* in JRAS 1902, 474 f.

[2]) We read in Sutta No. 115 that these sermons had certain titles (and the same sermons frequently had several titles). Aśoka also alludes to these titles of separate sermons, in his Bhabrū edict. See above, p. 16.

[3]) R. O. *Franke* has tried to trace a uniform fundamental idea and associations of thought underlying the various Suttas in the Majjhimanikāya too (WZKM 29, 1915, 134 ff.; ZDMG 68, 1914, 473 ff.) with a view to proving from it, that this book, too, is

III. The third great collection is the Saṃyuttanikāya,[1] "the Collection of Grouped Discourses." It consists of 56 groups (saṃyutta) of Suttas, each of which, in connection with a certain name or object, deals with various points of the doctrine. This, then, is not actually a division according to subjects, but only a feeble attempt at one. Thus the Devatā-Saṃyutta (I), contains sayings of deities (devatā), but the sayings refer to the most diverse subjects. The Māra-Saṃyutta (IV), consists of 25 Suttas, each of which relates a legend in which Māra the tempter appears in order to induce Buddha himself, or one of his disciples, to depart from the doctrine of salvation, in which he always fails. The Bhikkhunī-Saṃyutta (V), contains ten legends of nuns (bhikkhunī), whom Māra vainly tries to lure to apostasy. The Nidāna-Saṃyutta (XII), consists of 92 speeches and conversations, all of which, with endless repetitions, deal with the subject of the twelve Nidānas or the concatenation of causes and effects (paṭiccasamuppāda). The Anamatagga-Saṃyutta (XV), contains twenty speeches, of which all begin with the words: "The beginning of this Saṃsāra, O monks, is entirely unknown (anamataggo)," and explain this sentence by setting forth in ever varying comparisons and images the dreadful accumulation of sufferings in the cycle of migrations from existence to existence which has been going on from innumerable past

---

not a collection of sermons and dialogues, but the unified work of *one* author. The arguments in this case are, if anything, even less convincing than in the case of the Dīghanikāya. The very fact that we often find a "great" and a "small" Sutta on the same subject side by side in the Majjh. (*e. g.*, Cūḷa- and Mahā-Sīhanāda-Sutta), is evidence that the work is in the nature of a collection.

[1]) Edited by Léon *Feer*, London PTS 1884-1898, Indexes by Mrs. *Rhys Davids*, 1904. Translated by Mrs. *Rhys Davids* and F. L. *Woodward* (Book of the Kindred Sayings or Grouped Suttas), PTS, Parts I, 1917; II, 1922; III, 1925; into German by W. *Geiger* in ZB IV-VII, separately Vol. II, München 1925. The Bhikkhunī-Saṃyutta is also translated by Mrs. *Rhys Davids*, Psalms of the Sisters, pp. 180-191; Māra-Saṃyutta and Bhikkhunī-Saṃyutta into German by E. *Windisch*, Māra und Buddha, pp. 87 ff., 132 ff.

ages of the world's history. On the other hand, the 13 Suttas of the Kassapa-Saṃyutta (XVI), are united into a group only because the disciple Kassapa appears as speaker in all of them; in the same way the Sāriputta-Saṃyutta (XXVIII) contains ten speeches of Sāriputta. The 50 Suttas of the Nāga-Saṃyutta (XXIX) deal with the snake-demons (nāgas), enumerating the various kinds of snakes, and naming the deeds which cause one to be born again in one or other of the snake-forms. The 55 Suttas of the Jhāna- or Samādhi-Saṃyutta (XXXIV) deal with the modes of contemplation or meditations (jhāna, samādhi). The strong points and weaknesses, the virtues and vices of women (mātugāma) and the destinies which await them in the next life, are dealt with in the 34 Suttas of the Mātugāma-Saṃyutta (XXXVII). Legends of the great Moggallāna and a few of his speeches are contained in the 11 Suttas of the Moggallāna-Saṃyutta (XL). The hero of the Sakka-Saṃyutta (XI) is Sakka, the god Indra, who appears here, too,[1] as a devout Buddhist. There is surely an intentional piquancy in selecting Indra, the savage, infuriated Vṛtra-slayer of the Veda, as the exponent of the ethics of mildness and non-violence, and as a master in the art of self-command. To scare away the insolent demon who has sat upon his throne, he merely utters the polite words: "My dear friend, I am Indra, the prince of gods."[2] The last Saṃyutta is the Sacca-Saṃyutta (LVI), which deals in 131 Suttas with the four noble truths (sacca) of suffering, of the origin of suffering, of the cessation of suffering, and of the way to the cessation of suffering. Here we also find (LVI, 11) the famous Dhammacakkappavattana-Sutta, the "sermon of Benares," by means of which Buddha set the wheel of the religion (dhammacakka) in motion.[3]

---

1) As in the Sakkapañha-Sutta, s. above, p. 43.

2) XI, 3, 2, translated by *Warren*, Buddhism in Translations, 426 f.

3) It has often been translated, thus also by F. L. *Woodward*, Some Sayings of the Buddha, p. 7 ff.

It is evident that, in the grouping of these Suttas, at least three different principles are involved. The Suttas of a group treat either (1) of one of the chief points or principal branches of the Buddhist doctrine, or (2) they refer to some classes of gods, demons or men, or (3) some prominent personality appears in them as hero or speaker. These 56 Saṃyuttas or "groups" are also divided into 5 Vaggas or "divisions," and their contents embrace all branches of the religion of Buddha. In the first Vagga ethics and the Buddhist ideal of life are predominant, and in the next books epistemology and metaphysics are the main themes. We also find Suttas dealing with the life of the Master, others in which Buddha and Dhamma are already objects of veneration, and a few Suttas dealing with the discipline of the order (vinaya). The total number of Suttas, which are, as a rule, much shorter than those of the Majjhima- or of the Dīghanikāya, is 2889. The number of Suttas is so great, mainly because, according to some pattern or other, a subject is treated in all its different aspects—with continual repetition of the same phrases—until the subject, and the reader too, are completely exhausted. Thus, for example, the Saḷāyatana-Saṃyutta (XXXV) comprises no less than 207 Suttas, speeches and dialogues on the six senses. With untiring monotony it is here demonstrated that sight, hearing, smell, taste, touch and the organ of thought (manas) are perishable and full of suffering, and have nothing to do with the Ego, that the sense perceptions corresponding to the six sense organs are perishable and full of suffering, and have nothing to do with the Ego, and that the sense objects corresponding to the six sense organs are perishable and full of suffering, and have nothing to do with the Ego. Moreover, in the case of each single sense-organ, each single sense-perception, each single sense-object, the whole series of assertions is repeated literally, and every assertion forms a Sutta in itself. However tedious we may find this multiplication of Suttas, there are sure to have been sound, practical reasons for it in the use of the Suttas for religious exercises.[1] Even in this collection, however, we find many things which are to be appreciated also from the purely literary point of view, though it contains much more that is of importance only because it contributes to our knowledge of the doctrine of Buddha.

Valuable poetry is found especially in the first Vagga. It embraces Saṃyuttas I-XI, and is called Sagāthavagga, *i.e.*, " the Section with the song verses " (gāthā). Such Gāthās or verses appear occasionally, indeed, in all the sections, as in other Nikāyas, but they are so numerous in the first Vagga, that many of the Suttas consist entirely of verses. Thus, in the Devatā-Saṃyutta, we find many riddles and aphorisms in the form of questions and answers, *e.g.*, the following riddle:

Hast thou no little hut? Hast thou no nest?
Hast thou no line stretched out? Art free from ties?
"Nay, never hut is mine, nor any nest.
Nor line stretched out. Yea, I am free from ties."
What do I mean who speak to thee of 'hut,'
And 'nest,' and 'line stretched out,' and 'ties'?
"*Mother* thou meanest when thou sayest 'hut,'
And *wife* thou meanest when thou speak'st of 'nest,'
And *children*, when thou sayest 'line stretched out,'
And *men's desires*, when thou dost speak of 'ties'"!
O well is thee for whom no hut doth wait!
O well is thee who hast no nest at night!
Thou hast no line stretched out—O well is thee!
And happy thou who from all ties art free![2]

These riddles and aphorisms are not always in reference to Buddhist doctrines, as the following riddle will show:

[1] It is possible, as Mrs. *Rhys Davids* suggests to me, that the fact "that the varying Suttas were collected from different sources, from different vihāras or even laymen," may also have been a factor in the multiplication of Suttas.

[2] I, 2, 9, translated by Mrs. *Rhys Davids*, Kindred Sayings, I, p. 13 f.

What is the basis and support of men?
What here below is comradeship supreme?
What are the spirits who sustain the life
Of all such creatures as to earth are bound?
"Children are mankind's basis and support,
The wife is here below comrade supreme; [1]
The spirits of the rain sustain the life
Of all such creatures as to earth are bound." [2]

Just as, in an episode of the Mahābhārata,[3] Yudhiṣṭhira answers the questions of a Yakṣa, thereby gaining his favour, likewise, in Saṃyutta X, 12, Buddha satisfies a Yakṣa by the wise answers which he gives to his questions. It is especially the ballads (ākhyānas) in verse, or more often in the prose and verse form mixed, as we find them particularly in the Māra-Saṃyutta and the Bhikkhunī-Saṃyutta,[4] which are of great poetical value. Some of these short ballads about Māra and the nuns, which are remarkable also for the sake of their archaic language,[5] are among the most beautiful productions of ancient Indian poetic art. As an example, the Sutta (V. 3) of the nun Kisā-Gotamī ("Slender Gotamī") is translated here:

Thus have I heard. The Lord once sojourned at Sāvatthi in the Jeta grove in the garden of Anāthapiṇḍika. The nun Kisā-Gotamī, after she had dressed herself, went in the morning into the town of Sāvatthi, with her begging-bowl and robe, to beg for food. And after she had begged in Sāvatthi and had returned with the food which she had obtained through begging, she went, after her meal, into the dark forest, in order to spend

1) Cf. Aitareya-Brāhmaṇa: "A friend is the wife," s. above, Vol. I, p. 212 (English Edition).

2) I, 6, 4, translated by Mrs. *Rhys Davids*, l. c., p. 52.

3) III, 313, see above, Vol. I, pp. 352 f.

4) See *Windisch*, Māra und Buddha, pp. 87 ff., 132 ff., and *Feer* in JA 1883, s. 8, t. I, 410 ff.

5) By their language, too, the stanzas (gāthās) occurring in the Nikāyas, at least the majority of them, prove themselves as belonging to the oldest portions of the Tipiṭaka literature. Cf. *Rhys Davids* and *Carpenter*, Dīgha Nikāya edited, Vol. II,—Preface, p. VIII and above, p. 3, note 2.

the day there. Then, when she had retired far into the dark forest, she sat down at the foot of a tree, to stay there for the day.

Then Māra the evil one, desiring to cause the nun Kisā-Gotamī fear, terror and horror and to disturb her deep meditation, went to the place where the nun Kisā-Gotamī was. And after he had gone there, he addressed the nun Kisā-Gotamī in the verse:

" How now? Dost sit alone with tearful face,
As mother stricken by the loss of child?
Thou who hast plunged into the woods alone,
Is it a man that thou hast come to seek?"

Then the nun Kisā-Gotamī thought within herself, " Who is it, human or non-human, who has just uttered a verse?" And it occurred to the nun Kisā-Gotamī: " It is Māra the evil one, who, in order to cause me fear, terror and horror and to disturb me in my meditation, uttered the verse." But when the nun Kisā-Gotamī knew that it was Māra the evil one, she addressed Māra the evil one in the following verses:

" Past are the days when was she whose child
Was lost! Men to that past belong—for me!
I do not grieve, I am not shedding tears.
And as for thee, good sir, I fear thee not.
Lost on all sides is love of worldly joys.
The gloom of ignorance is rent in twain.
Defeating all the myrmidons of death,
Here do I bide (to rest), sane and immune." [1]

Then Māra the evil one knew that the nun Kisā-Gotamī had recognised him, and he vanished from the place, unhappy and despondent.

These poems can scarcely be anything but sacred ballads, counterparts of those Ākhyānas with which the epic poetry of the Indians originated.[2] If, with J. *Charpentier*,[3] we were to regard them as "little dramas," then they would be

---

[1]) The stanzas given in the translation of Mrs. *Rhys Davids*, l. c., p. 162 f.

[2]) Cf. above, Vol. I, pp. 311 ff., 471, 508 f. (Eng. Ed.). The technical term for these compositions consisting of a mixture of prose and verse seems, however, to have been g e y y a, not ā k h y ā n a. See above, p. 10.

[3]) WZKM 23, 1909, 33 ff. The fact that, as we shall see, a Buddhist drama

artistic creations of an exquisiteness with which we could hardly credit the Buddhist monks, so much the less as, in the entire Tipiṭaka, we do not find even the slightest trace of such sacred dramas having been performed. On the contrary, the monks are often forbidden, in the Buddhist texts, to take part in plays and similar performances. Had there been a sacred drama in existence, our texts would surely have made an exception in favour of religious performances of this nature. We shall frequently meet with these sacred ballads, always characterised by the same strong dramatic element. The secular and sacred ballads of this kind have surely contributed much towards the origin of the dramas, but these poems themselves should not, on that account, be called "dramas" any more than they can be called "epics," though both probably proceeded from them. The only doubtful point is whether the prose of these poems in the mixed form should always be regarded as being as ancient as the verses. To take an instance, the prose enwrapping the beautiful and impressive sayings on Karman (III, 2, 10; 3, 1) reads much like a commentatorial addition.

IV. The fourth great collection is the Aṅguttara-nikāya,[1] "the Collection of sermons arranged in ascending numerical order."[2] The Suttas, at least 2,308 in

---

existed later, proves just as little, as far as that early period is concerned, as do the dramatic performances in the Tibetan monasteries of to-day.

1) Edited by R. *Morris* and E. *Hardy*, London PTS 1855-1900, 5 vols., with Indexes by Mabel *Hunt*, forming Vol. VI. An analysis of the contents is given by E. *Hardy* in Vol. V, pp. 371 ff. Translated by E. R. J. *Gooneratne*, Part I (Eka-, Duka-, and Tika-Nipāta), Galle, Ceylon, 1913 ("Of that work perhaps the less said the better," Mrs. *Rhys Davids* in JRAS 1926, p. 348); Part II (Catukka-Nipāta) by A. D. *Jayasundara*, ed. by F. L. *Woodward*, Adyar, Madras, 1925; into German by the Bhikkhu *Ñāṇatiloka* (*i.e.*, Anton *Gueth*), 1911 ff. Cf. also E. *Leumann* in GGA 1899, pp. 586 ff.

2) Literally: "The yet-another-limb collection." In the Sanskrit canon an Ekottarāgama corresponds to the Aṅguttaranikāya (cf. Milindapañha VII, 3, 48: Ekuttaranikāya). Ekottara means "yet one more," and is therefore synonymous with aṅguttara. The title Dasuttara-Suttanta (Dīgha 34) means the "Up-to-ten Suttanta," *i.e.*, the discourse in which the Dhammas are enumerated from one to ten.

number,[1] are here arranged in eleven sections (Nipāta) in such a manner that Section I treats of things of which only one exists, Section II of things of which there are two, Section III of things of which there are three, and so on, to Section XI, treating of things of which there are eleven. Thus, for instance, in the "Section of two," there are Suttas on the two things one must avoid, on two dark and two bright things, two reasons for living in the forest, two kinds of Buddhas, and so on; in the "Section of three"—Suttas on the trinity of deeds, words and thoughts, three kinds of monks (those who have no desires, those who have some, and those who are free from all desire), the three messengers of the gods (old age, disease and death), the three reasons why death rules the world, three kinds of silence, three things which lead women to hell, and so on; in the "Section of four" Suttas on the four things which lead to liberation from existence (virtue, meditation, intuition and deliverance), four things by which man reaches hell, and four things by which he reaches heaven, the four causes (good and bad deeds in a former existence) of some women's being ugly and poor, others ugly and rich, others beautiful and poor, and yet others beautiful and rich and so on; in the "Section of seven" Suttas on seven requirements for meditation, seven miracles, seven kinds of wives, and so on; in the "Section of eight" Suttas on eight things by which the wife binds the husband and the husband the wife, eight kinds of alms, eight qualities which women must possess in order to be reborn as divine beings, eight causes of an earthquake, and so on; in the "Section of ten" Suttas on the ten powers of a Buddha, the ten fundamental questions (a summary of the whole doctrine of Buddha), ten reasons for the institution of the Pāṭimokkha, ten kinds of rich people, etc., etc.

---

[1]) In some cases it is not clear whether one or several Suttas should be assumed. Therefore 2363 is also a possible total.

Each of these eleven sections again falls into several divisions (vagga); and these frequently (though by no means always) comprise such Suttas as deal with one and the same subject. Thus the ten Suttas of the first division of the "Section of one" (Ekanipāta) deal with the relationship between husband and wife; I, Vagga 14 consists of 80 Suttas, in which are enumerated names of the most prominent male and female disciples, and their virtues; I, Vagga 20 contains 262 Suttas on the different kinds of meditation which lead to Nirvāṇa; V, Vagga 18 deals, in ten Suttas, with lay disciples (upāsaka), and so on. In this collection, as in the Saṃyuttanikāya, the Suttas are mostly short speeches and dialogues. Longer speeches are also found, and as in all Nikāyas, the prose is often interrupted by verses (gāthās). Very numerous are the Suttas and Gāthās which the Aṅguttaranikāya has in common with other texts of the canon, and these are sometimes actually quoted as extracts.[1)]

We give a few Suttas in translation, as specimens of this collection. We read in the "Section of two" (II, 4, 1-2):

"I shall explain to you, O monks, what constitutes a bad man, and what constitutes a good man. Hear, then, and pay heed, I shall speak."

"It is well, your reverence," said the monks, and listened to the Lord. And the Lord spoke thus:

"What, O monks, constitutes a bad man? A bad man, O monks, is ungrateful, he knows no gratitude. That is what is found in bad men: ingratitude, unthankfulness. The sumtotal of all that constitutes a bad man is this: ingratitude, unthankfulness. But a good man is grateful,

---

1) These parallel passages and quotations are recorded by E. *Hardy*, Vol. V, p. VIII f. But it is not always the Aṅgutt. which does the borrowing. Thus, for instance, the account of the admission of women into the order, *i. e.*, the founding of an order of nuns, is just as much in its right place in Aṅg. VIII, 51, as in Cullavagga X, 1 of the Vinayapiṭaka. On the other hand, the enumeration of the eight causes of an earthquake and the eight kinds of assemblies is absolutely in its right place in Aṅgutt. (VIII, 70), whilst the parallel passage in the Mahā-Parinibbāna-Sutta does not fit into the context at all (see above, p. 40).

he knows gratitude. That is what is found in good men: gratitude, thankfulness. The sumtotal of all that constitutes a good man is gratitude, thankfulness.

I shall name two beings to you, O monks, whose goodness one cannot repay. Which two? Mother and father. O monks, if a man were to take his mother on one shoulder and his father on the other, and if he lived to the age of a hundred years in this way, lived for a hundred years; and if he were to serve them, anointing them, massaging them, bathing them and rubbing them, and if they even eased themselves upon him—he would not have evinced sufficient gratitude towards his parents nor would he have repaid them for their benefits. And, O monks, if he were to set his parents in authority, in supremacy, to govern the whole of this great world filled with treasures of all kinds, he would not have evinced sufficient gratitude towards his parents nor would he have repaid them for their benefits. And why? O monks, parents bestow much good on their children, for they bring them into this world, nourish them, and explain this world to them.

But, O monks, if a man's parents are unbelievers, and if he lead them to perfect faith, stimulate and confirm them therein, or if they are wicked, he lead them to perfect virtue, stimulate and confirm them therein, or if they are miserly, he lead them to perfect self-sacrifice, stimulate and confirm them therein, or if they are without insight, he lead them to perfect insight, stimulate and confirm them therein—then, O monks, he has done well by his parents and has repaid his parents for their benefits, indeed more than repaid them."

Some of the Suttas of the Aṅguttaranikāya have the rare advantage of brevity. Thus we find, in the "Section of three" (III, 129) the speech of Buddha which may be warmly recommended to all those who believe in the humbug of a Buddhist "esoteric doctrine":

"Three things, O monks, act secretly and not openly. Which three? Womenfolk, O monks, act in secret and not openly. The incantations of the Brahmans act in secret and not openly. False doctrine acts in secret and not openly. These, O monks, are the three things which act secretly and not openly.

Three things, O monks, shine openly and not secretly. The disc of the moon, O monks, shines openly and not in secret. The disc of the sun shines openly and not in secret. The religion and discipline of the

Order proclaimed by Buddha shine openly and not in secret. These, O monks, are the three things which shine openly and not secretly."

A large number of Suttas deal with women, of whom the Buddhist monks, like the priests and saints of all other religions, have little good to say. Only Ānanda, the favourite disciple of Buddha, was always an enthusiastic champion of women. It was at his intercession that the Master, after long resistance and even then unwillingly, gave permission for the founding of an order of nuns—a partiality for which, according to the tradition,[1] he was still called to account at the council of Rājagaha. Once, so it is related in the "Section of four" (IV, 80), Ānanda, like a modern advocate of the emancipation of women, asked the Master :

"What is the reason, Lord, what is the cause for which women have no seat in the public assembly, pursue no business and do not earn their livelihood by some (independent) profession ?"

(Buddha replies thereto :) "Choleric, Ānanda, is womankind ; jealous Ānanda, is womankind ; envious, Ānanda, is womankind ; stupid, Ānanda, is womankind. That, Ananda, is the reason, that is the cause why women have no seat in the public assembly, pursue no business, and do not earn their livelihood by some (independent) profession."

One of the most beautiful speeches in the "Section of three" (III, 35) is that of the three messengers of the gods,[2] about whom King Yama asks the evil-doer in the nether world—old age, disease, death—whereupon he hands them over to the guardians of hell for punishment; ideas of hell are probably earlier than Buddhism. However, the

---

[1]) Vinayapiṭaka, Cullavagga XI, I, 10. Cf. *Oldenberg*, Buddha, p. 187.

[2]) Similarly in Majjhimanikāya No. 130, where, however, there are five messengers of the gods. Cf. *Oldenberg*, Buddha, p. 263 ; L. *Scherman*, Materialien zur Geschichte der indischen Visionsliteratur, Leipzig 1892, p. 60 f. Parallel passages from European literatures (*e.g.*, *Grimm's* Household Tales, Nr. 177 "The messengers of death," which was already known in the 13th century, and *La Fontaine's* fable VIII, 1 "La mort et le mourant") have been quoted by R. *Morris* in JPTS 1885, pp. 62-75. Cf. also *Grimm*, Kinder- und Hausmärchen, III 3, Göttingen 1856, p. 249.

number of passages of literary value in the Aṅguttaranikāya is not great. There are numerous monotonous and endlessly tedious sermons, which are by no means improved by the dry-as-dust tone of the enumeration. Thus, in the entire "Section of one" there is hardly anything to be found that is beautiful and edifying. It is remarkable that besides so many Suttas which refer to all departments of Buddhist ethics and psychology and sometimes also to the discipline of the Order (vinaya), there are also some Suttas which have nothing to do with the religion of Buddha, and are only inserted on account of the numerical principle. Yet such passages are sometimes not devoid of a certain humour, which is evoked by the enumeration of very heterogeneous things in one series. Thus, for example, it says in the "Section of eight" (VIII, 27):

> "There are here, O monks, eight powers! Which are they? Crying is the power of child, scolding is the power of women, weapons are the power of robbers, sovereignty is the power of kings, pride is the power of fools, humility the power of sages, reflection the power of scholars, meekness the power of ascetics and Brahmans."

Similar passages occur occasionally in Indian gnomic poetry. The idea of such enumerations probably belongs to ancient folk-lore, only that in the Aṅguttaranikāya, with real Indian pedantry, it became the principle of arrangement of an entire large work.[1)]

---

1) We find the same arrangement in the Thāṇaṅga and Samavāyaṅga Suttas of the Jains. A section in the Mahābhārata, V, 33, 56-106, on worldly wisdom (nīti), placed in the mouth of Vidura, is arranged on exactly the same numerical principle. Even more archaic is the Brahmanical riddle game (Mahābh. III, 134) in which Aṣṭāvakra vanquishes the sophist Vandin who, though well versed in the enumeration of the things of which there are one, two, three, and so forth, cannot get past thirteen, whilst Aṣṭāvakra enumerates all the things of which there are thirteen. Number riddles and number litanies of this kind are also to be found in the literatures of other peoples. The best known is the so-called "Catholic Vesper" in which Christian dogmas are enumerated according to numbers one to twelve: "Good friend, I ask thee, Good friend, what askest thou? Tell me, what is one? One and one is the Lord God, and so on (K. *Simrock*, Die deutschen

The fact that the Aṅguttaranikāya was compiled at a time when the Buddha had already become an omniscient demi-god, if not god, the sole fountain-head of all truth, is shown by the passage, in which the god Indra asks a few preaching monks where they have learnt such excellent things, whether from Buddha or through their own intuition, and they reply: If, near a great granary, one sees people carrying corn, some in a basket, others in their garment, yet others in their hands, then it really does not matter whence the corn is taken, for it all comes from the great granary. In exactly the same way, everything which is well said is said by the Lord Buddha. This is much more dogmatic than Aśoka's Bhābrū edict, which says: "All that Buddha has said, is well said," even more so than the word of a later Sanskrit work, the Divyāvadāna: "the heavens with the moon and the stars will fall, the earth with its mountains and forests will pass away, the ocean will dry up, but the Buddhas will never utter what is false.[1]

With this dogmatism the Aṅguttaranikāya is only a forerunner of the Abhidhammapiṭaka, for the texts of which it probably formed the foundation.[2]

The great number of Suttas in the Aṅguttaranikāya came about in the same way as in the Saṃyuttanikāya.[3]

With regard to the mutual relationship among these four Nikāyas or collections of Suttas—for the Khuddakanikāya has a totally different character—only so much is certain, that a whole series of Suttas occurs, not only in one, but in

---

Volkslieder, Frankfurt a. M. 1851, pp. 520 ff.). There is a similar number litany in the Passover Hagada of the Jews. Cf. K. *Kohler* in Zeitschrift für die Geschichte der Juden in Deutschland, 3, 1889, 234 ff. and G. *Léjeau* in Revue Celtique II, pp. 58 ff. There is a Greek fairy-tale (see J. G. v. *Hahn*, Griechische und Albanesische Märchen, Leipzig 1864, II, pp. 210 f.), which reminds us of Aṣṭāvakra.

1) Aṅgutt., Vol. IV, p. 163 f. Cf. *La Vallée Poussin*, Transactions of the Third Internat. Congress for the History of Religions, Vol. II, p. 36.

2) Cf. *Hardy* in Vol. V of the edition, Preface, p. ix f.

3) See above, p. 56.

several of these collections, and that, as regards the doctrines presented, there is no difference whatsoever among the four Nikāyas. In most cases it will be difficult to distinguish whether a Sutta originally occupied a place in the one or the other Nikāya. If, for example, the Sutta on the three qualities which lead women to hell, occurs in the Saṃyutta as well as in the Aṅguttaranikāya, it fits equally well into the first named collection in the "Section on women" as into the latter collection in the "Section of three." On the other hand, some sections of the Saṃyuttanikāya appear like extensions or illustrations of the Aṅguttaranikāya.[1] The Suttas of the Dīghanikāya often give us the impression of having originated through the extensions of shorter texts. Thus, for example, the tenth Sutta of the Majjhimanikāya (Satipaṭṭhāna-Sutta) recurs literally in Dīghanikāya No. 22 (as the Mahā-Satipaṭṭhāna-Sutta), only with a few additions after the style of a commentary. It has already been shown that the Mahā-Parinibbāna-Sutta probably attained to its great extent by means of additions. Some passages of the Dīghanikāya certainly fit better into the Aṅguttaranikāya.[2] The fact that the great number of Suttas in the last two Nikāyas is explained mainly by variations of one and the same theme with endless repetitions, has already been mentioned, and also that this is sometimes the case in the Majjhimanikāya too.[3] Moreover, the great length of many of the speeches in the Majjhima- and Dīghanikāya is explained by the continual repetitions. In all these collections we cannot avoid the impression that they owe their origin to practical needs, having been compiled for the use of the monks for religious practices—sermons, public

---

[1]) Cf. Saṃy. XXXVII, 4 with Aṅgutt. III, 127 and Saṃy. XXXVII, 5-9, and 14 24 with Aṅgutt. V, 230 and 115-120.

[2]) See above, p. 40.

[3]) See above, pp. 53 and 56.

recitations, hours of devotion and edification. The peculiarity of almost all these Suttas, which is so unpleasant to the Westerner, namely, the repetitions, so frequent as to become nauseous, proves that they were originally intended only for oral presentation.

These continual repetitions of the same words, sentences and whole paragraphs had the double purpose of impressing the speeches more deeply on the memory and of making them rhetorically more effective. As texts written down and intended for reading, they would probably have been quite as tedious to the Indians as they are to the Westerner. In the recitation the repetitions played a considerable part "as parts of a purely musical construction" and proved no more tiring to the ears of a Buddhist audience "than the repetitions of the motifs in the musical compositions of Bach or Wagner."[1] For this reason it is scarcely possible to translate these Suttas for Western readers exactly as they stand, with all the repetitions; but we must not forget that the Suttas were composed for Buddhist hearers, and not for Western readers.

Side by side with Suttas drawn out to inordinate lengths owing to the abundant repetitions, there are some brief and terse dialogues, in which an idea is presented with the utmost nicety and lucidity, and developed without a single superfluous word. Dialogues of this kind are to be found in all of the four Nikāyas, and we are pretty safe in assuming that they belong to the earlier parts of the canon. In style and language, too, there is no essential difference among the

[1]) P. *Tuxen* in Festgabe Jacobi, p. 98 ff., who adds that "even in individual cases the ancient authors showed a very well defined sense of musical effect, when they constructed their rhythm." This would also explain the extraordinary impression made by the recitation of the Pāli texts in the monasteries on hearers who follow the recital without being able to understand a single word of the contents. *Tuxen* testifies to this from his own experience.

four Nikāyas.[1] Though the Aṅguttaranikāya may be somewhat later than the other Nikāyas,[2] there cannot have been a very great interval of time between it and the others. There is even less foundation for assuming the Dīghanikāya to be "the earliest accessible source of Buddhist writing."[3] "The earliest accessible sources" of the doctrine of Buddha are only a few isolated Suttas appearing in different collections and are not afforded by any one collection; in fact they have to be culled from the whole of Buddhist literature, Pāli as well as Sanskrit. At all events all the four Nikāyas contain very ancient as well as more modern elements.

The literary merits also which are common to the Suttas of all the collections show that all the four collections are compiled from essentially the same elements. In all of them we find dialogues, in which the Buddha, when he carries on a discussion with an opponent, whether it be a Brahman or an adherent of another sect, does so in the same refined, skilful and ever polite and amiable manner. He first apparently puts himself entirely in the place of his opponent,

[1]) The description of the characteristics of early Buddhist prose given by *Oldenberg* (Zur Geschichte der altindischen Prosa, AGGW 1917, p. 39 ff.) may be applied with equal truth to all the four Nikāyas.

[2]) M. *Anesaki* (Transactions of the Asiatic Society of Japan, Vol. 35, 1908, Part 2, p. 83 f.) thinks that both the Pāli Aṅguttaranikāya and the Chinese Ekottarāgama bear traces indicating that this collection is later than the three others. Moreover, it contains the greatest number of quotations which are given *as* quotations. However, the Nikāyas or other collections are never cited as such, but only separate Suttas or portions of a collection. Thus, for instance, in Aṅg. X, 26, 2, a verse which occurs in Saṃy., IV, 3, 5 (I, p. 126) is not quoted as being taken from the Saṃy., but with the words: "Thus it was said by the Sublime One (bhagavatā) in the questions of the daughters (of Māra)." Aṅg. III, 32 quotes verses from the "Pārāyana" (not from the "Suttanipāta" in which we find the Pārāyana). In the same way, the quotation in Saṃy. 22, 4 from the "Sakkapañha" does not prove that it was taken from the Dīghanikāya. Cf. *Eliot*, I, p. 279 n. 1; *Rhys Davids* in Cambridge History, I, p. 194; Mrs. *Rhys Davids* in Prefatory Note to Indexes of Aṅgutt. Ed., Vol. VI.

[3]) R. O. *Franke*, ZDMG 69, 1915, 455. *Eliot*, I, p. 278, says of the Majjhimanikāya: "Taken as a whole it is perhaps the most profound and impassioned of all the Nikāyas and also the oldest."

sets out from the same points of view as he does, makes use of the same expressions, often also the same technical terms and, imperceptibly, leads his opponent over to the opposite standpoint. We may assume, with *Rhys Davids*,[1] that the writers of such dialogues must still have had a certain recollection of the kind of conversations which Buddha actually carried on. They give us at least as good an idea of the teaching method of Buddha as the Platonic dialogues of that of Socrates.

It was certainly also a part of the teaching method of Gotama Buddha to enthral and convince his audience by means of similes and parables. A simile or a parable is certainly not an argument; but often it has more effect on the mind, and even the intellect, of the hearer than a thousand arguments. Buddha was very well aware of this, so, he liked to embellish his speeches with similes, and his disciples followed him in this. Thus, we find in the Suttas of all the four collections a veritable flood of similes, and they are foremost in investing these speeches with a literary character and artistic value.

A beautiful example of a convincing simile is afforded by the dialogue of the Buddha with the son of Māluṅkyā,[2] in which the Buddha tells the enquiring disciple who asks for information concerning existence and non-existence and other metaphysical questions, that the answering of all these questions would leave no time for finding the way to salvation, to liberation from suffering, and he illustrates it by means of the following parable:

A man is hit by a poisoned arrow. His friends hasten to the doctor. The latter is about to draw the arrow out of the wound. The wounded man, however, cries: "Stop! I will not have the arrow drawn out until I

---

1) Dialogues of the Buddha, I, 206 f.

2) Majjh. No. 63; *Oldenberg*, Buddha, pp. 315 ff.; *Warren*, pp. 117 ff.

know who shot it, whether a warrior or a Brahman, a Vaiśya or a Śūdra, to which family he belonged, whether he was tall or short, of what species and description the arrow was," and so on. What would happen? The man would die before all these questions were answered. In the same way the disciple who wished for answers to all his questions about the beyond and so on, would die before he knew the truth about suffering, the origin of suffering, the cessation of suffering and the way to cessation of suffering.

No less apt are the parables of the Tevijja-Sutta (Dīghanikāya XIII, 15 ff.), in which Buddha wishes to show how foolish it is of the Brahmans to seek the way to salvation in union with Brahman, in spite of the fact that they are compelled to admit that neither they themselves, nor their teachers, nor the teachers of their teachers, nor the ancient ṛṣis of primeval times have ever seen this Brahman. It seems to him, says Buddha, just like a chain of blind people, of whom neither the first one nor the middle one, nor the last one can see. And this yearning for the unknown God appears to him as if a man were to say he loves a most beautiful maiden, but, in reply to the question as to who the fair one is, were unable to say to which caste, to which race she belongs, what her name is, whether she is tall or short, her complexion dark or fair, and where she lives; or as if a man wanted to erect a staircase to the balcony of a palace at a cross-road, without knowing whether this balcony is situated in the east or in the south, in the west or in the north, whether it is high or low or of medium height. In the Sāmaññaphala-Sutta (Dīghanikāya II, 69 ff., 78 ff.), in a series of beautiful similes Buddha compares the happiness of the monk who is freed from earthly fetters with the comfortable feeling of the debtor who has succeeded not only in discharging his debt, but also in earning a surplus for the maintenance of his family; of the invalid who, after severe suffering, recovers his health; of him who, having pined in captivity, at length regains his freedom; of the slave who is set free by his master; of the traveller who, on a dangerous road, wanders through a wilderness and at last reaches a village inhabited by human beings. And like a lake which receives its water from a spring, into which no water flows from any direction, on which the rain never falls, so that all its water is received only from the cool spring and it is filled throughout only with cool water, the monk is thoroughly impregnated and permeated with blissful calm.

Numerous, too, are the parables showing the vanity of enjoyments. In order to show how full of torment and suffering are the pleasures of the senses, seven forceful illustrations are set down in Sutta 54 of the Majjhima-nikāya:[1]

A butcher throws before a dog tormented by hunger, a bare and fleshless bone with which he cannot satisfy his hunger—like such a bare bone are the sensual pleasures, full of torment and sufferings, out of which only evils arise. As a bird of prey pounces upon a piece of meat and other birds attack him and ill-treat him—so only suffering and evil arise from sensual pleasures. The sage shrinks back before sensual pleasures as from a pit filled with glowing coals. Sensual pleasures are like a beautiful dream vision, which vanishes when one awakes, like a borrowed treasure, on account of which one is envied by those who do not know that it is only borrowed. A man comes into a forest, sees a tree laden with fruit, and climbs up in order to eat till he is satisfied; then a second man comes along, sees the same tree, and in order to gain possession of the fruit, sets about felling the tree: evil will befall the man up in the tree:—thus only suffering and torments and all kinds of evil arise from the gratification of sensual pleasures.

Occasionally the similes are connected in a very pleasing and homely manner with the given situation, *e.g.*, in Sutta 58 of the Majjhimanikāya. Prince Abhaya, urged on by Nigaṇṭha Nātaputta, the adversary of the Buddha, comes to the Master, in order to embarrass him with a very difficult question. He asks him whether the Buddha never utters an

---

[1] Sutta No. 22 of the Majjh. alludes to these seven similes, assuming that they are familiar.

unkind word. As the latter admits that he sometimes has to resort to unkind words, Abhaya retorts that there is then no difference between him and a common man, who also utters unkind speeches.

Now at that time (thus the Sutta continues) Prince Abhaya had a little boy, a tender infant, seated on his lap. Then the Master said to Prince Abhaya: "What thinkest thou, prince? If this boy, through thy carelessness or his nurse's, put a piece of wood or a little stone in his mouth, what wouldst thou do with him?"

"I should take it out, your reverence. And if I could not get it out at the first attempt, I should seize the boy by his head with my left hand, and with the right hand, bending my finger, I should take it out, even though it were bloody. And why? Because, your reverence, I should have compassion on the boy."

"In the same way, prince, the Tathāgata indeed utters no word which he knows to be untrue, incorrect, unprofitable, and at the same time disagreeable and unpleasant to others; neither does he utter any word which he knows to be true, correct, but unprofitable and at the same time disagreeable and unpleasant to others; but if the Tathāgata knows a word to be true, correct, salutary, and at the same time disagreeable and unpleasant to others, then the Tathāgata knows that it is opportune to utter such a word ..And why? Because the Tathāgata has compassion on the beings."

A very popular and frequently applied simile is that of the oil lamp, *e.g.*,

"O monks, just as an oil lamp, burning by means of the oil and the wick, if a person would pour fresh oil on it and renew the wick from time to time, would continue to burn for a long, long time thus fed and supplied with fuel,—even thus, O monks, grows the greed of the man who takes pleasure in the things of this world, which are but fetters." [1]

To the question of a village elder as to why the Buddha, though said to be benevolent and compassionate towards all beings, yet preaches his religion thoroughly to some, but less thoroughly to others, he answers with the parable: As the

---

[1]) Saṃyuttanikāya, XII, 53.

peasant first cultivates the good field, then the moderately good one, and finally the bad one, so the Buddha preaches his doctrine first to the monks and nuns, then to the lay-adherents and only last of all to the non-adherents.[1]

Humour, too, is not lacking in the parables, when, for instance, it is said in Majjh. 126: If one fills a trough with sand and water, however much one may twirl and stir it about, one will never obtain sesame-oil; however zealously one attempts to milk a cow by its horn, one will never obtain milk, and so on; in the same way, a monk will never reach the goal if he does not endeavour to do so in the right manner.

Some similes actually belong to the vocabulary of the Buddhist texts and probably of the Buddha and his disciples themselves. When they speak of desire, which is the origin of all suffering, they call this the "thirst," which leads from existence to existence. At this migration from existence to existence, the Saṃsāra, is the "ocean," on the "further shore" of which Nirvāṇa beckons. Desire and sin, the whole bustle of worldly life, is a "flood," and he who has attained Nirvāṇa is "rescued from the flood." The reward of good and bad deeds, the Karman, is the "fruit," and when treating of Karman, the simile of seed and fruit is always in the minds of the speakers. When the Buddha preaches, he "utters the roaring of a lion,"[2] and so on.

A popular simile,[3] which is also found outside the Nikāyas, is the following:

"Just as, O monks, if a man were to throw a one-holed yoke into the sea and the east wind were to cast it about to the west, the west wind

---

[1]) Saṃyuttanikāya, XLII, 7, 1-8. R. Otto *Franke* has compared this with Matth. 13, 12 ff., Mark 4, 12 and Luke 8, 10 (DLZ 1901, col. 2759).

[2]) In a cave near Turfan, A. *Grünwedel* (Bericht über archäolog. Arbeiten in Idikutschari, A. Bay A. Vol. 24, I, München, 1906, p. 125) found a picture representing a monk preaching; this is expressed by a little cloud, on which a little lion is standing, appearing before his face.

[3]) Majjhimanikāya, 129; Saṃyuttanikāya, 56, 47 f. The simile is very popular also in Buddhist Sanskrit literature (s. *Winternitz*, WZKM 27, 1913, 43 ff.) and it

to the east, the north wind to the south, and the south wind to the north; and there were a one-eyed turtle, which rose to the surface once in a hundred years; what do you think, O monks, would the one-eyed turtle place its neck into the one-holed yoke?" "Hardly, at the most perhaps once in a long time." "But it is easier for the one-eyed turtle to get its neck into the one-holed yoke, than for the fool, who has once sunk into the lower forms of existence, to be reborn as a human being. Why? because in the low forms of existence there is only mutual murder, and no good action."

These parables are of the utmost importance from the point of view of social history, for they often introduce us into the midst of the daily life of the ancient Indians, of the artisans, agriculturists and merchants, of whom Brahmanical literature, which moves almost entirely in the circles of priests and warriors, has so little to say.[1] We find similes of the coachman and charioteer, the dice-player, the preparation of sesame-oil, etc. In one simile (Majjh. 140) is described the whole of the work of the goldsmith, in another (Majjh. 125) the whole procedure of elephant-taming, and again in another (Majjh. 101) the whole process of curing a person wounded by a poisoned arrow.

However little they can be regarded as real proofs, the similes are, after all, the best kind of argumentation which we find in the Suttas. As for the rest, wherever a doctrine is to be proved, we do not find much more than accumulations of synonyms and dogmatic classifications and enumerations,[2]

occurs also in the Yoga-Vāsiṣṭha (s. G. A. *Jacob*, JRAS 1909, p. 1120 f.). The simile has nothing in common with the "camel going through the eye of a needle," which G. *de Lorenzo* and K. E. *Neumann* (Reden Gotamo Buddho's III, 334 note) have derived from it.

[1]) *Cf.* Mrs. *Rhys Davids*, "Buddhist Parables and Similes" (The Open Court, Chicago, Vol. XXII, 522 ff.), who rightly remarks that these similes furnish material sufficient for a large book, which ought to be written. The index of similes ("Similes in the Nikāyas, a Classified Index" in JPTS 1907 and 1908, by Mrs. *Rhys Davids*, is a highly useful preparation for such a book.

[2]) T. W. *Rhys Davids* has here the remark: "There are on the contrary many quite decent arguments and inferences." I have not found many.

which are most particularly characteristic of the Aṅguttara-nikāya, but occur in all the Nikāyas.

The method of proof in our Suttas cannot possibly be compared with that of Plato. Nor is the number of Suttas which, as dialogues, can bear comparison with the Platonic dialogues, very great. It is true that Karl *Fries*[1] has pointed out a number of remarkable parallels between Indian and Greek dialogues; but the parallels fail in just the most essential points. They are certainly not sufficiently striking to compel us to assume any mutual influence. The majority of the Suttas are indeed not "dialogues" in the real sense of the word, but rather the speeches of one principal speaker, usually Buddha, which are generally interrupted only by yes or no or by expressions of assent or approbation on the part of the other speakers. Even the best real dialogues in the Nikāyas will rarely remind us of the dialogues of Plato, but very often indeed of the dialogues of the Upaniṣads and the Itihāsa dialogues,[2] with which we became acquainted in the Mahābhārata.

2. *Narratives, Songs and Sayings.*

The Khuddakanikāya or "the Collection of the Smaller Pieces," usually reckoned as the fifth Nikāya of the Suttapiṭaka, but sometimes also classed with the Abhidhammapiṭaka, would more correctly be called "collection of miscellanies": for in this collection, besides several short works, we find also a few of the most extensive books of the Pāli-Canon. In contents and character, however, the texts incorporated into this collection differ very widely. In a very remarkable

[1]) Das philosophische Gespräch von Hiob bis Platon, Tübingen 1904, pp. 65, 76 ff. While K. E. *Neumann*, Reden Gotamo Buddho's III, p. 85, sees in Plato's Menon "a most astonishing reflection, distinctly recognisable down to the minutest details" of Majjh. 107, I absolutely fail to see anything of this "reflection."

[2]) See above, Vol. I, pp. 414 ff.

Sutta, which recurs several times,[1] we read a prophecy on the dangers which threaten the religion of Buddha in the future. One of these dangers is that the monks will no longer wish to hear and learn "the Suttantas proclaimed by the Tathāgata, deep, deep in meaning, reaching beyond this world, dealing with the Void,"[2] but will only lend their ear to the "profane Suttantas proclaimed by disciples, made by poets, poetical, adorned with beautiful words, beautiful syllables." From this we might conclude that the poetical pieces were not at first generally recognised, that their claim to be regarded as sacred texts was contested and that they were only later on combined into a Nikāya, namely the Khuddakanikāya. This assumption is based on the fact that the chief contents of this collection are works of poetic art—collections of aphorisms, songs, poems, fairy tales and fables. This collection was probably only concluded at a late period, and a few non-poetical texts, the authenticity of which is in a similar way, not universally recognised, might have been included afterwards.[3] There is no doubt that the works

[1]) Saṃyuttanik, XX, 7; Aṅgutt., IV, 160; V, 79, 5. Cf. *Rhys Davids*, Buddhist India 110 f.; *La Vallée Poussin*, Bouddhisme, p. 149. The passage is also very significant for the oral transmission of the Buddhist texts. When they were no longer heard and recited, they disappeared.

[2]) Suññata "void," *i.e.*, "devoid of independent reality." Here, as in a few other passages of the Pāli Canon, we already meet with the conception of the Void (śūnyatā), which in later times is the central idea of the philosophy of the Mahāyāna. *Cf.* C. A. F. *Rhys Davids*, A Buddhist Manual of Psychological Ethics, p. xlii f.

[3]) It is significant of the unstable character of the Khuddakanikāya as a canonical collection, that the Buddhists of Burma include in the Khuddakanikāya four texts which are not regarded as canonical in Ceylon, namely the Milindapañha, the Suttasaṃgaha (an anthology from the Suttapiṭaka), the Peṭakopadesa and the Netti. (Mabel H. *Bode*, Pali Literature of Burma, London, 1909, p. 4 f.) It is perhaps not a mere accident that in the Siamese edition of the Pāli-Canon (see above p. 21, note 1) eight texts of the Khuddakanikāya are missing: Vimānavatthu, Petavatthu, Theragāthā, Therīgāthā, Jātaka, Apadāna, Buddhavaṃsa and Cariyāpiṭaka. According to the Dīpavaṃsa, V, 37, the Mahāsaṃgītikas did not recognise the Paṭisambhidā, the Niddesa and a part of the Jātaka. The Khuddakanikāya as a whole does not appear in the Chinese Āgamas, but many of the texts are included in other collections. *Cf.* M. *Anesaki* in Transactions of the Asiatic Society of Japan, Vol. 35, part 3, 1908, p. 9.

combined in this collection originated at very different periods, and were not originally intended to form parts of one collection.[1] Even though the collection as such belongs to the latest compilations of the Canon, yet, in addition to comparatively modern fabrications, it also contains many of the oldest Buddhist poems. Indeed, it contains precisely all those works of Buddhist literature which are among the most important creations of Indian poetry. We propose to discuss the texts of the Khuddakanikāya not according to their probable age or their importance, but in the order in which they have come down to us in the manuscripts of the Buddhists of Ceylon.

1. At the head of this collection stands the Khuddakapāṭha,[2] "the Short Recitals." This is a compilation of nine short texts which the novice must know before all others, and which are used in the Buddhist cult as a kind of Mantras or "prayers." It must remain an open question whether the collection was intended as a little hand-book for novices or as a "prayer-book." The first four pieces are quite short. No. 1 is the Buddhist confession of faith, No. 2 an enumeration of the ten commandments for monks, No. 3 a list of the 32 parts of the body, for purposes of meditation on the loathsomeness and perishableness of the human body, and No. 4 contains the "questions of the novice." In ten questions (" What is one? What is two?" etc.) and answers, after the manner of the Aṅguttaranikāya, it explains the most important Buddhist terms. The five remaining pieces are

[1]) Otherwise it would be unaccountable, why the small Khuddakapāṭha should contain three Suttas (Maṅgala-Sutta, Ratana-Sutta and Metta-Sutta) which appear verbatim in the Suttanipāta too; or why the same stories should be told in the Cariyāpiṭaka from entirely different points of view from that of the Jātaka.

[2]) Edited and translated by R. C. *Childers*, in JRAS 1870, pp. 309-339; new edition by Helmer *Smith* and Mabel *Hunt*, London PTS 1915; translated by F. L. *Woodward*, Some Sayings of the Buddha, pp. 58 ff. He calls it "the Buddhist Layman's Prayer-Book." German translation by K. *Seidenstücker*, Breslau, 1910.

short Suttas, which, by their contents as well as the formula-like phrases and refrains, betray the liturgical purposes which they served. From the oldest times much importance has been attached in India to Maṅgalas, *i.e.*, all sorts of objects and ceremonies which are regarded as good omens or are supposed to bring good luck. Such Maṅgalas as good wishes, benedictions, feeding of Brahmans, garlands of flowers, music, singing, etc., were never missing at any sacrificial feast, marriage celebration, birth ceremony, and so on. In the Maṅgala-Sutta [1] (No. 5) Buddha teaches what he regards as the best Maṅgalas. We read, for instance:

"Honouring mother and father, cherishing of child and wife,
And a peaceful occupation: This is the best good omen.
Giving of alms and righteous life, to cherish kith and kin,
Doing deeds that bring no blame : This is the best good omen.
Ceasing and abstaining from sin, to shun intoxicating drinks,
Not neglecting religious duties: This is the best good omen."

The other Suttas, too, are permeated by the same spirit of a higher code of ethics. Thus the Ratana-Sutta (No. 6) by which, according to ancient custom, the Bhūtas, spirits of the earth and air, together with the three Ratanas or "jewels," [2] are worshipped. Of a similar nature is also Sutta 7, dedicated to the cult of the dead, a few verses of which are recited at cremations in Ceylon and Siam even at the present day. Sutta 8, of the "Hidden Treasure," in which it is demonstrated that a treasure of good works is the best treasure which the Buddhist can accumulate, and above all, the magnificent Metta-Sutta (No. 9), in which friendliness (mettā) towards

[1]) *Copleston*, Buddhism, p. 140, says of this Sutta: "It is constantly repeated now by the monks in Ceylon, and it is a great pity that nobody understands it." In Burma this Sutta is sung at times of epidemics by white-robed elderly men and women at cross-roads before images of Buddha. Ind. Ant. 8, 1879, pp. 82 and 329.

[2]) These are: Buddha, Dhamma (the religion) and Saṅgha (the monastic community).

all beings is praised as the true Buddhist cult, are on a still higher plane.

Seven of these nine texts are still used at the Buddhist Parittā-ceremony or "Pirit," as the Buddhists of Ceylon call it. The word Parittā means "protection, warding off," and already in the Tipiṭaka it is used in the sense of "Pirit" or "exorcism-formula, benediction." "At the present day in Ceylon, Parittā (Singhal. Pirit) has come to mean the recitation (or reading) by the Bhikkhus, of some thirty texts belonging to the Canon, for the purpose of banishing the influence of evil powers. The Parittā-ceremony is performed on all possible occasions, *e.g.*, at the building of a new house, in cases of death, diseases and so on."[1] I cannot help agreeing with K. *Seidenstücker* when he takes Suttas 5–9 to be old exorcism-songs, and, as the first four pieces also present a formula-like appearance, I do not regard it as unlikely that the Khuddakapāṭha was compiled for similar purposes as the Parittā-text-book still in use in Ceylon to-day.

2. The Dhammapada,[2] ("Religious Sentences"[3]) is the best known and the longest known work of Buddhist

[1]) *Seidenstücker*, l.c., p. 3. *Cf.*, M. *Grimblot* and Léon *Feer*, Extraits du Paritta in JA 1871, s. 6, t. XVIII, 225 ff. *Geiger*, Pali Literatur und Sprache, p. 16 f.; T. W. *Rhys Davids*, Dialogues III (SBB IV), p. 185 ff. The Milindapañha, p. 150 f., mentions Parittās as having been taught by Buddha. In Burma, too, there is a small collection of texts from the Suttapiṭaka, called Paritta or Mahā-Paritta, which is used for exorcisms, and is better known among the people than any other Pāli book (M. H. *Bode*, l.c., p. 3 f.).

[2]) Edited with a Latin Translation by V. *Fausböll*, Hauniae, 1855; 2nd ed., London, 1900; new edition by S. *Sumangala Thera*, London PTS 1914; translated into English by F. *Max Müller*, SBE, Vol. 10, part 1; by A. J. *Edmunds*, Hymns of the Faith, Chicago, 1902; by W. D. C. *Wagiswara* and K. J. *Saunders*, Way of Virtue, London, 1912 (Wisdom of the East Series); into German by L. V. *Schroeder* (1892), by K. E. *Neumann* (1893), by P. *Dahlke* (1919), by R. O. *Franke* (1928); into French by Fernando *Hû* (Paris 1878) and L. *Feer* (Bibl. or. elzév.); into Italian by P. E. *Pavolini* (Milano 1908, and Testi di morale buddhistica, Lanciano 1912, pp. 1-80). *Pavolini* (JSAI 25, 1912, p. 324) also mentions a Russian translation by N. *Gerasimov*.

[3]) According to the different meanings of *pada* and of *dhamma*, the title has been translated variously by "Footsteps of Religion," "Path of Religion," "Path of Virtue," "Sentences of Religion," "Worte der Wahrheit," etc. *Cf.* R. C. *Childers*

literature, which has been repeatedly translated into European languages, is much quoted in all works on Buddhism, and has always been held in high esteem owing to its profound moral value. In Ceylon the book has been used for centuries down to our own times by the novices as a text-book which they must have studied before they can receive the higher orders (upasampadā). For this reason there is not a monk in Ceylon who cannot recite his Dhammapada from beginning to end from memory. Buddhist preachers often take verses from the Dhammapada as the text of their sermons.[1)] It is an anthology of sayings which chiefly refer to the ethical doctrines of Buddhism. Of the 423 verses, every 10-20 are formed into a section (Vagga), as they deal with the same subject, or as a simile (*e.g.*, of the flower in Vagga 4, the "flower-section"), or sometimes a refrain runs through the verses of such a section. The formation and arrangement into Vaggas is probably the work of the compiler. In many cases, however, several verses together actually form a little poem, as, for instance the verses of the "Elephant-section," a few of which I quote from the translation by F. L. *Woodward.*[2)]

"As the elephant in battle bears the arrows at him hurled,
I must bear men's bitter tongues, for very evil is the world.

Tamed, they lead him into battle; tamed, the king his back ascends;
Tamed is he the best of beings, whom no bitter speech offends.

Dictionary, p. 117 f.; *Max Müller*, SBE, Vol. 10, part 1, p. xlv ff.; L. v. *Schroeder*, Transl., p. 131 ff.; R. O. *Franke*, ZDMG 46, 1892, 734 f.; WZKM 15, 1901, p. 396; PTS Dic., s.v. I have no doubt that "Dhammapada" is used in a collective sense, like "Udāna," "Itivuttaka," etc., and that it means "Collection of Words or Verses on Religion," "Dhamma Words," or "Religious sentences."

1) Cf. *Sumangala Thera* in the Foreword to his edition.

2) Some Sayings of the Buddha, p. 258 ff. (verses 320-322, 328-330).

Good are well-tamed mules, and good are Scindian steeds of lineage famed;
Good indeed the mighty tusker; best of all the man self-tamed."

"Hast thou found a fellow-traveller, upright, firm, intelligent?
Leaving all thy cares behind thee, gladly walk with him intent.

Hast thou found no fellow-traveller, upright, firm, intelligent?
As a king deserts his borders, by the enemy pursued,
Like the tusker in the forest, go thy way in solitude.

Better is the lonely life, for fools companions cannot be.
Live alone and do no evil, live alone with scanty needs,
Lonely, as the mighty tusker in the forest lonely feeds."

Couplets which together form a whole, are especially frequent, *e.g.*, verses 141 f.

"Not nakedness, nor matted hair, nor filth,
Nor fasting long, nor lying on the ground,
Not dust and dirt, nor squatting on the heels,
Can cleanse the mortal that is full of doubt.

But one that lives a calm and tranquil life,
Though gaily decked,—if tamed, restrained he live,
Walking the holy path in righteousness,
Laying aside all harm to living things,—
True mendicant, ascetic, Brāhmin he." [1]

Many of the most famous Buddhist sayings are in the Dhammapada. Thus the beautiful verses (153 f.), which Buddha is said to have uttered after he had gained enlightenment:

---

[1]) Translation by *Woodward*, l.c., p. 26.

"Thro' many a round of birth and death I ran,
Nor found the builder that I sought. Life's stream
Is birth and death and birth, with sorrow filled.
Now, house-builder, thou'rt seen! No more shalt build!
Broken are all thy rafters, split thy beam!
All that made up this mortal self is gone:
Mind hath slain craving. I have crossed the stream." [1]

A simple and yet splendid metaphor: lust, worldly desire, is the "builder of houses," who again and again constructs a new house, *i. e.*, a new body in a new rebirth. We repeatedly come across such simple but impressive metaphors and similes in the sayings. Thus the equanimity of the sage is compared with a deep lake, smooth as a mirror, or with an unshakable rock (81 f.). Or it says: As the spoon gets nothing of the flavour of the soup, so the fool derives no benefit from intercourse with the sage; it is only the sage who gains through intercourse with sages, as only the tongue enjoys the flavour of the soup (65 f.). Whoever speaks or acts with an impure mind, is pursued by suffering, as the wheel follows the foot of the draught-ox; whoever speaks or acts with a pure mind, is pursued by joy, as by his own shadow (1 f.). Or "Not quickly, as milk curdles, does the bad deed which one has committed, resolve itself into its consequences; burning, it follows the fool like fire which is covered with ashes" (71). We constantly meet with such images, and often they appear in pairs. We also find more elaborate verses with those plays on words (*e.g.*, 344) for which the Indians have always had a predilection.

More than half of all the verses of the Dhammapada have also been traced in other texts of the Pāli Canon, and there is scarcely any doubt that, generally speaking, the compiler of the anthology took them from the settings where we still

[1]) Translation by *Woodward*, l.c., p. xi.

find them to-day.[1] However, the collection has come to include some sayings which were originally not Buddhist at all, but were drawn from that inexhaustible source of Indian gnomic wisdom, from which they also found their way into Manu's law-book, into the Mahābhārata, the texts of the Jains, and into narrative works such as the Pañcatantra, etc. It is, in general, impossible to decide where such sayings first appeared.[2]

3. While the Dhammapada is merely a collection of verses, and it was only at a later period that narratives were added in the form of a commentary no longer belonging to the canon, relating on what occasion the single verses were uttered, the Udāna,[3] the collection of "pithy sayings," consists of verses and narratives. The work is divided into 8 Vaggas or "sections," each of which contains 10 Suttas. These Suttas are generally quite short narratives recounting some event of the time of Buddha, and ending with a pithy utterance which the Buddha, inspired by this event, is said to have "breathed out," *i.e.*, to which he gave vigorous expression. The standing phrase which introduced the actual Udāna, *i.e.*, "exhalation," generally a verse (Śloka, Triṣṭubh or Jagatī) and rarely a prose saying, reads: "Now when the Lord had gained knowledge of this matter, he uttered the following pithy saying on this occasion." Most of these utterances serve to glorify the Buddhist ideal of life, the deep blissful repose of mind of the saint (Arhat) torn away from all earthly things, the endless bliss of Nirvāṇa.

---

1) Cf. *Rhys Davids* in JRAS 1900, 559 f., and the concordance by R. O. *Franke*, in the appendix to his Translation, p. 93 ff.

2) Brahmanical sources may occasionally be assumed. Thus, verse 108 is probably a quotation from a Brahmanical text, which is given only to connect the following verses with it (109-115).

3) Edited by P. *Steinthal*, London, PTS 1885; translated (rather imperfectly) into English by D. M. *Strong*, London 1902; into German by K. *Seidenstücker* (1920). See also E. *Windisch* in JPTS 1890, p. 91 ff.; K. *Seidenstücker*, Das Udāna, I. Teil: Allgemeine Einleitung, Leipzig 1913; B. C. *Mazumdar*, JRAS 1911, p. 197 ff.

The book of the Udānas contains only a selection of the "pithy sayings" ascribed to Buddha. In other books of the Tipiṭaka also, there are utterances of this kind, called "Udāna," which are not always attributed to Buddha, but sometimes to a king, a deity or some other personage.[1] Quite a number of Suttas as well as of separate Udānas (without the Suttas belonging to them) are common to the Udāna and other collections.[2] In particular, it contains several Suttas relating to the life of Buddha, which are in agreement with the biographical texts of the Vinayapiṭaka and the Mahā-Parinibbāna-Sutta. However, they were probably not borrowed from these collections, but were based on earlier traditions on which the various collections have drawn.

It is an open question whether, as *Seidenstücker* thinks,[3] the majority of the Udānas in this collection are really "authentic words of the Master." We are safe, however, in granting that most of these short[4] and beautiful utterances certainly bear the stamp of antiquity, and that many of them are possibly the actual words of Buddha himself or of his most prominent disciples. On the other hand, there can be no doubt that the utterances themselves are, as a rule, older than the narratives into which they are inserted. Though a few of them may have come down from the very beginning in association with an introductory story, yet in the majority of cases it was the compiler who appended such a story to an old Udāna. This is why many of the Suttas only contain very simple, in fact sometimes silly stories, inappropriate to the

---

[1]) For instance, Vinayap. Mahāv. I, I, 5; Dīghanikāya XVI, 3, 10; Saṃyuttanik I, 3; III, 3; VII, 1; XXII, 55.

[2]) Cf. *Seidenstücker*, Allg. Einleitung, p. 62 f.

[3]) l.c., p. 36. *Seidenstücker* is probably right in saying that the metrical irregularities which Mr. *Mazumdar* (l.c.) has pointed out in some of the Udānas, must not be corrected, but are rather a sign of antiquity.

[4]) Only III, 10 and VI, 8 are not short sayings, but short homilies.

pathos of the utterances themselves. For instance, in one pithy saying (III, 7) we are told that even the gods envy the saint who is free from desire. To illustrate this, a story is told how Sakka and the other gods actually envy the Arhat Mahākassapa. Another pithy saying (VI, 9) compares people who are engrossed in worldly life and do not strive after that which is essential, with moths rushing into a flame. The corresponding story relates that Buddha once sojourned in Sāvatthi, and noticed a number of moths flying into the burning oil-lamps and being burnt. Or, again, Buddha sees the venerable Sāriputta teaching another monk by means of a sermon. This is sufficient pretext for his being made to utter the following pithy saying (VII, 2) :

> "The wheel is broken, since he has become desireless ;
> The river is dried up and flows no more,
> No longer does the broken wheel roll on : [1]
> The end of sorrow is attained."

In Section VIII we find a series of significant sayings, which are of great importance as bearing on the much discussed question of the true meaning of Nirvāṇa. Yet only one single, short, and insignificant story is given in illustration of the first four sayings. VIII, 10 repeats the legend of VIII, 9 : A monk who has attained complete Nirvāṇa, flies up into the air, where he is burnt so entirely that nothing is left of him, not even soot or ashes. What pathos to attach this childish legend to the beautiful and profound "pithy saying" :

> "As the fiery sparks from a forge, one by one are extinguished,
> And no one knows whither they have gone ;

[1]) The "wheel" is the wheel of recurring rebirths ; the "stream" means sensual desires. These similes are so familiar to the Buddhists that they have become inherent in the vocabulary of the language. Cf. above, p. 74.

So it is with those who have attained to complete emancipation,
Who have crossed the flood of desire,
Who have entered upon the tranquil joy (of Nirvāṇa)—
Of these no trace remains." [1]

In some cases there is not much more than a thread to connect the "pithy saying" with the corresponding story. On the other hand, there are a few Suttas, in which the narrative is more interesting and more significant than the "pithy saying." For instance, III, 2, tells the story of Nanda, the half-brother of Buddha, who, though a monk, still harbours thoughts of the wife he has left behind, and is taken by the Lord to Indra's heaven, where he sees the heavenly nymphs, and observes that, beside these, his wife only looks like a wretched she-ape. Then Nanda only practises his monastic vow so as to gain possession of the beautiful heavenly women, but finally Buddha puts him on the right path.[2] The story in II, 8, is of interest, because it shows that in comparatively olden times loving devotion (bhakti) to Buddha was regarded as productive of miracles. The parable of the blind men and the elephant, in VI, 4, is famous :

Some ascetics and Brahmans once met together, and began to quarrel. Some said : "The world is eternal," and the others : "The world is not eternal ;" some declared : "The world is finite," and the others : "The world is infinite ;" again some taught : "Body and soul are separate," and others : "Body and soul are but one." Some said : "The perfect man *is* after death," others maintained : "The perfect man *is* not after death" and so forth. Finally all this leads to a quarrel, and to harsh and insulting words. The monks tell Buddha of this quarrel, and then he tells them the following parable :

There was once a king, who had all those who had been born blind, brought together. When they were all assembled, the king commanded

[1]) Translation (rather free) by D. M. *Strong*, p. 129.

[2]) This theme later became the subject of an epic (Saundarānanda-kāvya) by Aśvaghoṣa.

an elephant to be shown to them. An elephant was brought, and they made some feel his head, others his ear, others his tusk, others his trunk, etc., and the last one the elephant's tail.[1] Then the king asked them: "How does an elephant look?" Then those who had touched the elephant's head, said: "An elephant is like a pot;" those who had touched the ear, said: "An elephant is like a winnowing basket;" those who had touched the tusk, declared: "An elephant is like a plough-share;" those who had touched the trunk, said: "An elephant is like the pole of a plough," etc.; and those who had felt the tail, maintained: "An elephant is like a broom." A great tumult now arose. Each one maintained: "An elephant is like this, and not otherwise; he is not like that, he is like this," until at last they came to blows, at which the king was mightily amused.

Even so, concluded Buddha, is the case of the ascetics and Brahmans, each of whom has only seen a portion of the truth, and who then maintain: "Thus is truth, and not otherwise; truth is not thus, but thus."[2]

4. Like most portions of the Udāna, the Itivuttaka,[3] ("Thus spake Buddha" sayings[4]) also consists of prose and verse. Yet here the relationship between the two is essentially different. The prose is not narrative prose, but the same idea, whether it is a doctrine or an admonition, is presented partly in prose, partly in verse. In many cases, in about 50 of the 112 short pieces of which the work consists, an idea is first briefly expressed in prose and then repeated in verse, only

---

1) The text reads: "He *showed* them the head," etc., but the meaning is, of course, that he told them to *feel* the elephant's head, etc.

2) The parable was also familiar to the Brahmanical philosophers, among whom "the rule of the blind men and the elephant" (andhagajanyāya) has become proverbial. Cf. G. A. *Jacob*, A Second Handful of Popular Maxims, Bombay 1902, p. 53, and JRAS 1902, p. 174; T. W. *Rhys Davids*, JRAS 1911, p. 200 f. It occurs also in the Jaina Syādvādamañjarī, see V. S. *Ghate*, Ind. Ant. 42, 1913, p. 251.

3) Edited by E. *Windisch*, London PTS 1889. Translated into English (Sayings of Buddha, with an Introduction and Notes) by J. H. *Moore*, New York 1908 (rather faulty); into German by K. *Seidenstücker*, Leipzig, 1922; into Italian by *Pavolini*, Testi di morale buddhistica, Lanciano 1912, pp. 97-111.

4) The title means "Sayings beginning with the words 'Thus was said (by the Lord).'" Every paragraph begins with the words: "This was said by the Lord."

deviating so far as the metrical form[1] demands. In a few cases only one verse has a counterpart in the prose, while several verses follow, to which nothing in the prose corresponds. In addition to these there are the numerous cases in which prose and verses supplement each other, whether the prose forms only a short introduction to the ideas expressed in the verses, or whether one aspect of an idea is treated in prose and the other in verse. In all these cases the spirit of the verses and of the prose is, on the whole, the same, and not infrequently an idea is expressed more clearly and more pointedly, and even more beautifully, in the prose than in the verses. Though here, too, there is no lack of formula-like phrases and repetitions so characteristic of the Buddhist Suttas, yet the style is, on the whole, free from excessive verbosity. Almost all the pieces are short. Both in the prose and the verses, the language is simple, natural and not excessively flowery. Elaborate similes are rare, but some beautiful metaphors occur. Thus the generous man, who gives liberally to pious beggars, is compared with the rain-cloud, which pours its water over hill and vale (No. 75). Bad company is avoided by the sage, as even the spotless quiver is defiled by the poisoned arrow (No. 76). The senses are the gates which must be well guarded (Nos. 28 and 29). Buddha calls himself the incomparable healer and surgeon, and the monks his children and heirs (No. 100). The language of the prose rises to the most lofty flights in the piece (No. 27) about friendliness towards all beings (mettā) :

"O Monks, all actions serving as the substratum of a new rebirth, by which one acquires merit, are not worth the sixteenth part of friendliness (mettā), which is the emancipation of mind; for friendliness radiates, shines and illumines, surpassing those actions as the emancipation of mind. O monks, just as all the lights of the stars are not worth the sixteenth

[1]) The metre of the Itivuttaka is dealt with by J. H. *Moore* in JAOS, Vol. 28, 317-330.

part of the moon-light, for the moonlight, surpassing them all, radiates, shines and illumines—so, O monks, all actions serving as the substratum of a new rebirth, by which one acquires merit, are not worth the sixteenth part of friendliness, which is the emancipation of mind; for friendliness radiates, shines and illumines, surpassing those actions as the emancipation of mind. Just as when, O monks, in the last month of the rainy season, in autumn the sky is clear and cloudless, the sun rises over the heavens, and, driving away the darkness which fills the atmosphere, radiates, shines and illumines, so, O monks, all etc.,......the emancipation of mind. And O monks, just as in the early morning, when the night is past, the morning star radiates, shines and illumines, so O monks, all etc., the emancipation of mind."[1]

Sometimes the prose adopts a personal note, which is missing in the verses. Thus, in No. 30f., Buddha says that two things cause him pain, namely, when a man has done no good, and when a man has done evil; and that two things give him pleasure, namely, when a man has done no evil, and when a man has done good. But the verses say only that he who has done evil in deeds, words and thoughts, shall descend to hell after death, while the virtuous one, who does good in deeds, words and thoughts, shall go to heaven after death. In the prose of No. 92 Buddha says very beautifully: Even if a monk takes hold of the hem of my garment and follows me step by step, but at the same time is greedy, passionate, malicious, etc., he is still far from me and I far from him. But if a monk dwells a hundred miles distant from me and is not greedy, not passionate, not malicious, etc., he is near me and I am near him. Then come the feeble, commonplace verses, in which it is said that the greedy man, the evil-doer, the malcontent, is far removed from the sage, who has attained calmness; while the good man, the calm man, the selfless man, is very near to the good one, the calm one, the selfless one. It seems almost as if a commentator had here welded together two texts, the one in prose, the other

---

[1] Cf. *Pischel*, Leben und Lehre des Buddha, p. 77 f.

in verse, though they have nothing in common but the words "near" and "far."

Indeed, cases are not rare in which the prose represents an independent Sutta, and the verses which follow it are only distantly connected with the prose, sometimes only by word consonances. Moreover, there are a few pieces in which the prose and the verse portions are entirely unconnected or even contradict each other. In all these cases we are probably dealing with later additions. Expressing an idea first in prose and then garbing it in verse, or commencing the presentation of a doctrine in prose and then continuing it in verse, seems to be an old form of Buddhist composition. Then when texts having this form were collected in the Itivuttaka, even prose texts and verses which were taken from elsewhere, were combined on the same pattern and inserted into the collection, possibly already by the first compiler, but perhaps not till later. It is a fact that in the Chinese translation of the Itivuttaka by Hsüan-Tsang many of the last pieces of our collection are missing,[1] and that a few of these last pieces are to be found in the Aṅguttaranikāya. It is very probable that they were taken thence. Furthermore, when we consider that a number of verses, combined with different prose pieces, appear twice, it may be regarded as indubitable that even in this very small collection earlier and later matters are combined. The additions include a few passages in which the prose only looks like a kind of commentary on the verse. In the old and authentic pieces,[2] however, the prose does not lag behind

---

[1]) Cf. *Watanabe*, Chinese Collection of Itivuttakas, in JPTS 1907, p. 44 ff.; A. J. *Edmunds*, Buddhist and Christian Gospels, I, 209 ff. On the other hand the Chinese Ityukta has 137 Suttas against 112 in the Pāli text. Cf. *Seidenstücker*, l.c., p. xvi ff.

[2]) *Moore*, wrongly regards the prose in general as a later ingredient. *Seidenstücker*, on the contrary, sees in the prose the nucleus of the work. It is probable that in the oldest passages of the Itivuttaka there is much which can be traced back to Buddha himself. However, A. J. *Edmunds* is far too optimistic in saying that: "If the Itivuttaka be not the words of Buddha, nothing is" (Buddhist and Christian Gospels, I, p. 83).

the verse either in value or in antiquity. In the later additions, too, it may happen that an old piece of prose has been combined with later verses.

5. If many pieces of the very oldest Buddhist poetry have been preserved in all the books of the Khuddakanikāya hitherto mentioned, this may be maintained with far greater certainty of the Suttanipāta [1] (the "Section of Discourses"); [2] for, though the whole collection as such cannot be proved as belonging to the very earliest of what ancient Buddhist poetry we have, yet certain of the essential parts of the collection can put forward this claim. The Suttanipāta is a collection of poetical Suttas in 5 sections. The first four sections (Uragavagga, Cūlavagga, Mahāvagga, Aṭṭhakavagga) contain 54 short poems, while section 5 (Pārāyana) is a long, independent poem, consisting of 16 shorter parts. Of these 5 sections, two, Aṭṭhakavagga and Pārāyana, are mentioned by their titles or quoted, both in other texts of the Pāli-Canon and in Sanskrit Buddhist texts.[3] There is an old commentary on these two sections, which has been included in the Canon (as Book 11 of the Khuddakanikāya) under the title of Niddesa. Moreover, single Suttas and numerous Gāthās, from all the five sections, can be traced in other texts of the Canon.[4] Among the texts especially

---

1) Edited by V. *Fausböll*, London PTS 1885 and 1893, and translated by the same scholar in SBE, Vol. 10, part 2, 1881. New edition of the text by Dines *Andersen* and Helmer *Smith*, London PTS 1913. Translated into German by K. E. *Neumann* (Reden Gotamo Buddho's IV, 1911). Cf. *Rhys Davids*, Buddhist India, p. 177 ff.; H. *Oldenberg*, Aus dem alten Indien, Berlin 1910, p. 25 ff.

2) Nipāta is a short section of a larger collection; thus the sections of the Aṅguttaranikāya are called Nipātas. *Neumann* translates it by "fragments," *Oldenberg* (l.c., p. 25) by "perhaps the isolated, occasional speeches."

3) The same two texts also occur in the Chinese Tipiṭaka, while the Suttanipāta as a whole has not been translated into Chinese. For this, see M. *Anesaki* in JPTS 1906-7, p. 50f.; Le Muséon, N. S., VII, 1906, p. 33 ff., and Transactions of the Asiatic Society of Japan, XXXV, 1908, part 3, p. 8 ff. Fragments of an Arthavargīya-Sūtra in Sanskrit have been discovered in Central Asia, s. A. F. R. *Hoernle*, JRAS 1916, 709 ff.

4) Cf. R. Otto *Franke*, in ZDMG 63, 1909, p. 1 ff., 23 ff., 255 ff., 551 ff.; 64, 1910,

recommended for study by King Aśoka in his Bhābrū edict, there are three which probably belong to the Suttanipāta.[1] Reasons, both of language and of subject-matter, also speak in favour of some of these Suttas reaching back to the time of the beginning of Buddhism and of many of them having originated at least in the circles of the first disciples of Buddha, not long after his death.

The significance of these compositions for the knowledge of the old doctrine of Buddha is just as generally acknowledged as their great antiquity, and next to the Dhammapada, the Suttanipāta is probably the most frequently quoted text in all works on Buddhism. Lastly, the high esteem in which the Suttas of this collection are held as works of poetic art is also general.

We find now shorter, now longer groups of verses, which are combined into a poem by the same idea and often also by the same refrain running through them. Side by side with prose sermons into which occasional verses are inserted, or sermons in verse but with a prose framework,[2] we also find the forms, popular from time immemorial, both of pure dialogue and of the ākhyāna or the ballad, in which dialogue-stanzas alternate with narrative-stanzas, and lastly of the ākhyāna composed of a mixture of prose and verse [3]—all

---

1 ff., 760 ff.; 66, 1912, 204, ff., 699 ff. *Franke* (WZKM 28, 1914, 261 ff.) endeavours to prove that the Suttanipāta has borrowed the Sela-Sutta (III, 7) and the Vāseṭṭha-Sutta (III, 9) from the Majjhimanikāya (No. 92 and No. 98). I do not believe that this proof is conclusive. But even if it were, it would only follow that the collection of the Suttanipāta is later than the collection of the Majjhimanikāya. As neither the Majjhimanikāya nor the Suttanipāta is a unified work, it does not follow that all the separate portions of the Suttanipāta are later than the Majjhimanikāya.

1) Cf. *Neumann*, Reden Gotamo Buddho's I, 567; IV, 71 f., 226, and Dharmananda *Kosambi*, Ind. Ant. 41, 1912, p. 37 ff.

2) E.g. Sundarikabhāradvāja-Sutta, Sela-Sutta, and others. Cf. *Oldenberg*, Zur Geschichte der altindischen Prosa, p. 77 ff.

3) I see no reason why we should use the expression "ākhyāna" only for the latter form of narrative poetry, and not for the ballad in general. According to Buddhaghosa the Suttanipāta consists of Gāthā, Geyya and Vyākaraṇa. (Paramatthajotikā, Introd.)

forms with which we are familiar from the ancient Brahmanical and epic poetry. In many cases there are still references or allusions to Brahmanical ideas. The Brāhmaṇa-Dhammika-Sutta (II, 7), the "Sutta of the Pious among the Brahmans," would be equally appropriate in an old Purāṇa. It describes how the Ṛṣis of olden days were the "true Brahmans," and lived abstemiously in every respect; how they were later allured by the wealth and the luxurious life of the kings, how they aspired after the same enjoyments, and were presented with beautiful women and wealth by King Ikṣvāku, and how all this led to the bloody animal sacrifices, at which even the innocent cow was killed. Intermingling of castes and deterioration of morals were the result of this. Here, then, Buddhism is represented as a return to the ancient true "Brahmanism." In the Sela-Sutta, too (III, 7), which relates the conversion of the Brahman Sela, there are passages which are quite in accord with verses of the Bhagavadgītā and Anugītā.[1] Thus the Buddhist monk who is faithful to his vow, is also held up as the "true Muni," [2] in several poems. The idea which we already met with in an old portion of the Mahābhārata,[3] that true Brahmanhood does not consist in birth, but in good conduct, is beautifully elaborated in the Vasettha-Sutta (III, 9), in 63 verses with the refrain "Him do I call a true Brahman." In other poems, again, in refined polemics, the Buddhist ideal of life is contrasted with the Brahmanic ideal, and presented as the higher one. Thus in the Āmagandha-Sutta (II, 2), where a Brahman who regards the observance of the dietary laws as the highest moral law and the tasting of forbidden meat as the most reprehensible

---

[1]) *Cf.* Suttanipāta 568 f. with Bhagavadg. IX, 18; X, 30 and Anug. 28, 2; 29, 1.

[2]) Muni, the ascetic, who has taken the vow of silence, is primarily a term applied to Brahmanical ascetics.

[3]) See above, Vol. I, p. 363. The theme of "the true Brahman" is also dealt with in the Dhammapada (Chapt. 26 = 383-423), in the Udāna I, and similarly in the Jinistic Uttarajjhayaṇa XXV. Cf. *Charpentier*, WZKM 24. 1910, 62 ff.

impurity, is told by Buddha that true impurity does not consist in the eating of meat, but:

"Torturing living creatures, murder, killing, tyrannizing,
Theft, lies and frauds, intercourse with a neighbour's wife,
This is impurity, and not the eating of meat."

"Being cruel and hard, slandering, betraying,
Being unmerciful, proud and covetous, giving nothing—
This is impurity, and not the eating of meat."

A poem like the Kasibharadvāja-Sutta (I, 4) seems to carry us back to the early days of Buddhism, when the monk was probably looked askance as an idler by the labouring people, by farmers and shepherds. Here the Brahman farmer Bharadvāja scornfully repels the begging Buddha, giving him to understand that he who will not work, neither shall he eat. Thereupon Buddha shows him that he too is working, and wherein his "ploughing" consists. In one of the most beautiful of these old poems, the Dhaniya-Sutta (I, 2), the comfort and happiness of the rich owner of herds, who rejoices in his prosperity and his domestic happiness, is contrasted with the quiet joy of the Buddha, without possessions, homeless, but free from all earthly bonds. In a magnificent dialogue the wealthy Dhaniya and the Buddha alternately utter a verse each with the same refrain, "Rain, O heaven, if thou wilt."

These poets find ever new methods of singing the same old song, that it is only the monk, removed from the world, who knows nothing and desires to know nothing of wife and child, of the joys and sorrows of this world, who is truly happy. What is said in the Dhaniya-Sutta in the form of a lively dialogue, we find again in the Khaggavisāna-Sutta (I, 3), the "rhinoceros-poem," in 41 vigorous stanzas with the refrain "He shall wander lonely as the rhinoceros," expressed with an earnestness and pathos, the impression of which cannot fail to affect even him who is far removed from this monkish conception of life.

The dialogue form is sometimes combined, as in the Ālavaka-Sutta (I, 10) and the Sūciloma-Sutta (II, 5), with the old riddle-poetry form which we have already met with in the Veda and the epic. Just as in the Mahābhārata,[1] here too, a Yakṣa appears as the questioner, and a sage replies to the questions by presenting the ethical doctrines of Buddhism.

The Suttanipāta contains not only didactic dialogues, but also a few narrative dialogues. Of these there are three, the Nālaka-Sutta (III, 11), the Pabbajjā-Sutta (III, 1), and the Padhāna-Sutta (III, 2), which are of special importance; for, they are precious remnants of that ancient sacred ballad-poetry from which the later epic version of the life of Buddha grew, in the same way as the heroic epic grew out of the secular ballads or Ākhyānas.[2] The chief peculiarity of these ballads is the conversational form. The dialogue was usually sufficient to bring the course of a narrative before the mind of the hearer. Where this was not the case, however, brief prose formulæ, a short introduction and a few short prose sentences were often inserted. The insertion of narrative-stanzas between the conversational stanzas was a further step in the development. We find this final step in the development of the ancient Indian Ākhyāna, which really formed the preliminary step to the epic, in the three Suttanipāta ballads abovementioned, dealing with scenes from the history of Buddha's youth. We find here the chief features of the later Buddha-legend already prepared. The Nālaka-Sutta deals with the events immediately after the birth of the Buddha-child:

The gods in heaven are in a state of pleasurable excitement. The divine seer Asita hears their outbursts of joy, and in answer to his question,

---

[1]) See above, Vol. I, p. 352 f.

[2]) See above, p. 40, note 1, p. 59, and Vol. I, p. 312 ff. Cf. also *Windisch*, Māra und Buddha, p. 3 ff., 222 f., 245 ff. and *Oldenberg*, Aus dem alten Indien, 45 ff.

receives the reply that in the Lumbinī-grove in the town of the Sakyas the Buddha has just been born for the salvation of the world. Then the sage descends from heaven to the palace of Suddhodana and desires to see the newly born boy. When he sees the boy, who is "radiant as fire, as the brightest of the stars, as the autumnal sun in the cloudless sky," being fanned by divine beings, he takes the child in his arms, and cries : "This is the incomparable one, the highest of men." At the same instant, however, he thinks of his own imminent end, and bursts into tears. In consternation the Sakyas ask whether any evil threatens the boy. The sage reassures them, and tells them that the boy will attain to the summit of complete enlightenment, but that he is sorrowful because he himself will not live to hear the preaching of the Lord. Before he departs, he exhorts his nephew Nālaka to follow the Buddha as soon as his call is heard.[1]

The second of these poems, the Pabbajjā-Sutta, describes the "departure" (pabbajjā) of the youthful Gotama from his home, and the meeting which, on his wanderings as a begging ascetic, he had with the king of Rājagaha. The third ballad, the Padhāna-Sutta,[2] describes a still later episode, how Māra, the evil one, after he has followed close on Gotama's heels for seven years, resumes the fight once again and endeavours to dissuade him from his struggle for knowledge, and to bring him back to the worldly life, and how Māra is ignominiously defeated. Though these ballads, as can be seen, are already rich in legendary features and mythical accessories, they may nevertheless be called simple and sober in comparison with the exaggeration of the later biographies of Buddha.

Nevertheless, even in the form in which they stand in the ballads of the Suttanipāta, these legends cannot belong

---

[1]) This legend has often been compared with that of Simeon, St. Luke 2, 25 ff., and it is indeed one of the most striking Buddhist parallels to the Gospels. *Cf.* especially *Pischel*, Leben und Lehre des Buddha, p. 23 ff. E. *Windisch* (in Festschrift Kuhn, p. 6 ff.) has discussed the variants of the legend, and traced Asita Devala back to Brahmanical literature. *Windisch* regards it as "not absolutely proved that the Simeon of St. Luke owes his existence to the Asita of the Buddhist legend."

[2]) This has often been compared with the Christian legend of the temptation of Christ.

to the oldest stratum of Buddhist tradition. They already pre-suppose a fairly long history of the Buddha legend. Among the latest parts of the Suttanipāta, however, are some of the prose narratives forming the framework for poems which in themselves bear the stamp of antiquity. *Fausböll* [1] indeed, has declared *all* the prose passages to be later additions. This can hardly be accepted. But K. E. *Neumann* is probably not far wrong when, in his translation, he simply omits some of the prose passages, regarding them, as he says using rather strong language, as "commentatorial priestly trash." When for instance, often in an entirely superfluous and clumsy manner, some Yakṣa or deity appears in order to introduce a dialogue, we are doubtless justified in calling such passages commentatorial additions.[2] At all events, the Suttanipāta, too, is a collection made up of earlier and later texts, and is certainly not a unified work,[3] even though a few of the poems included in the Suttanipāta, such as perhaps the 12 Suttas of the Uragavagga, may be the work of the same author.

6, 7. The two short works, Vimānavatthu and Petavatthu,[4] the "Stories of the Divine Palaces" and the "Ghost Stories," probably belong to the latest stratum of literature assembled in the Pāli-Canon. The truly great and profound doctrine of Karman, which has found expression in Brahmanical as well as Buddhist texts in so many beautiful sayings and legends,[5] is most clumsily explained by means of examples in these little stories, whose metrical form is their only

---

[1]) Preface, p. vii to his editio princeps of the text.

[2]) See, for example, I, 6; 10; II, 4; 5; III, 10.

[3]) *Cf.* R. O. *Franke* in Festschrift Windisch, p. 196 ff.

[4]) The Vimānavatthu, edited by E. R. *Gooneratne*, London PTS 1886. Petavatthu, ed. by J. *Minayeff*, London PTS 1888. *Cf.* L. *Scherman*, Visionslitteratur, p. 53 ff.; L. *Feer* in JA, s. 8, t. III, 1884, pp. 109 ff., 138 ff.; *Oldenberg*, Buddha, p. 345 note; W. *Stede*, Die Gespenstergeschichten des Peta Vatthu, Leipzig 1914, and Bimala Charan *Law*, The Buddhist Conception of Spirits, Calcutta 1923 (Calcutta Oriental Series).

[5]) *Cf.* above, Vol. I, pp. 258 f., 411 f., 441, 562 f.

poetical attribute. The stories, no doubt chiefly intended for laymen, are all made after one model. In the Vimānavatthu some divine being or other is asked by Moggallāna how he has gained possession of this or the other divine palace (vimāna) with all its splendours.[1] In reply the deity briefly recounts the good action which he had performed in one of his former existences, in consequence of which he gained this heavenly joy. In the Petavatthu a Peta (Sanskrit Preta, spirit of a dead person, which, restless and tormented, roams about in the neighbourhood of the earth as a ghost) appears, and is asked by Nārada, and sometimes by another person also, what action has brought about his unhappy lot, whereupon he relates it in a few brief words. One example (Petavatthu I, 2) will suffice:

(The wise Nārada says to a ghost:)

All golden is thy body, shining far through the wide world,
But thy mouth is that of a pig: what is the deed which thou hast done?

(Thereupon the ghost replies:)

Well curbed was I in deeds, unbridled only in words,
That is the reason why thou, Nārada, seest me in such disfigurement.
Therefore I tell thee, Nārada, as thou thyself hast seen it,
Do no evil with thy mouth, that thou may'st not acquire a pig's mouth.

The fact that in the Petavatthu (IV, 3) a king Piṅgalaka appears, who, according to the commentary of Dhammapāla, is supposed to have ruled in Surat 200 years after Buddha, proves that even the commentators of a later time place these texts at a considerable interval from the life-time

[1]) According to E. *Kuhn* and R. *Garbe* (Indien und das Christentum, p. 142) the Vimānavatthu is the source for the palace in the legend of Saint Thomas.

of Buddha. Even if we admit that the ideas of heaven and hell already existed in ancient Buddhism beside the ideal of Arhat and Nirvāṇa, and that the conceptions of the Petas may be traced back, in part, to very ancient popular superstition, we cannot ascribe great antiquity to these "poems."[1] Notwithstanding, even in these late books also, some ancient materials, Itihāsa-dialogues and ballads, have been incorporated.

8, 9. The miscellaneous character of the texts of the Khuddakanikāya is evidenced by the fact that the two above-mentioned texts, which are among the dullest productions of monk-poetry, are immediately followed by the Theragāthā and Therīgāthā,[2] the "Songs of the Elders," and "Songs of the Lady Elders,"[3] religious poems which, in force and beauty, are fit to rank with the best productions of Indian lyric poetry, from the hymns of the Ṛgveda to the lyrical poems of Kālidāsa and Amaru.

The Theragāthā and Therīgāthā are two collections, the

---

[1]) According to E. *Hardy*, ZDMG 53, 1899, 25 ff., the Petavatthu and the Vimānavatthu borrowed material which was useful for their purposes, from other works of the Khuddakanikāya, such as the Jātakas. See also E. *Hardy* in the preface to the edition of the commentary on the Vimānavatthu, London PTS 1901, p. xi. Nevertheless it is equally possible that the contrary was the case, and that the Jātaka-book borrowed from the Petavatthu and the Vimānavatthu; in fact the Jātaka commentary, No. 243, directly quotes from the Vimānavatthu.

[2]) Edited by H. *Oldenberg* and R. *Pischel*, London PTS 1883; translated by Mrs. *Rhys Davids*, Psalms of the Early Buddhists, I, Psalms of the Sisters, II, Psalms of the Brethren, London PTS 1909, 1913; into German by K. E. *Neumann*, Berlin 1899. Index to the Pādas of Thera- and Therī-Gāthā, by W. *Stede*, JPTS 1924-1927, p. 38 ff. *Cf.* E. *Müller*, JRAS 1910, 536 ff., Maria E. Lulius *van Good*, De Buddhistische Non, Leiden 1915, p. 142 ff.

[3]) The Theras and Therīs are the male and female "elders," primarily the first and most prominent male and female disciples of Buddha himself, and then those members of the order who were venerable by reason of their age and still more by their moral and spiritual qualities. Though Thera, fem. therī, Sanskrit sthavira, means "old," the title was determined rather by those qualities which inspire reverence, than by age or seniority. There was neither an honorary office nor privileges or duties of any kind in connection with this honorary title. *Cf.* T. W. *Rhys Davids*, ERE, Vol. 5, p. 252 f.

first of which contains 107 poems with 1,279 stanzas (gāthā) and the second 73 poems with 522 stanzas, which are ascribed by tradition to certain Theras and Therīs mentioned by name. This tradition is guaranteed to us both by the manuscripts and by the commentary of Dhammapāla, probably composed in the 5th century A.D., which also contains narratives in which a kind of life-history of each of these Theras and Therīs is told. These narratives, however, are either merely adapted from the verses, or they are pure inventions, or have been borrowed from various narrative works. They are entirely unauthentic; neither is the tradition of the names of the Theras and Therīs as the authors of the verses on the whole, trustworthy.[1] However, the tradition is right in assuming for these poems, not one author, but many authors, and certainly in ascribing the authorship of the songs partly to monks and partly to nuns. Some of the songs which are ascribed to various authors may, of course, in reality be the work of only one poet, and, conversely, some stanzas ascribed to one and the same poet, might have been composed by various authors; there may also be a few songs among the "Songs of the Lady Elders," composed by monks, and possibly a few songs among the "Songs of the Elders," composed by nuns[2] but in no case can these poems be the product of one brain. If the same

---

[1]) When, among the verses ascribed to Ānanda (Therag. 1018-1050) we also find verses referring to Ānanda, and among others, verses in praise of Ānanda, or when, in the verses ascribed to Moggallāna (1146-1208) the legends of Moggallāna related in Majjhimanikāya 50 are also interwoven, and so on, we see that the monks, who ascribed these verses to certain Theras and Therīs, knew just as little of the real composers of the songs as the compilers of the Anukramaṇīs knew of the composers of the Ṛgveda hymns (*cf.* above, Vol. I, p. 57 f.).

[2]) The redaction is by no means careful or skilful. We often find verses separated which clearly ought to come together in one poem, and *vice versa*, we find verses, which ought not to be together, combined to form a poem. We also frequently find the same verses again literally in different places. Some poems have been dismembered, and on purely external evidence some verses have been included in the Theragāthā and others in the Therīgāthā.

phrases frequently recur and the tone of the poems is, in many respects, uniform, it only proves that they all bear the stamp of the Buddhist mind, but not, as K. E. *Neumann* [1] considers, that "one man has left the impress of his mind on the whole."

There can be no doubt that the great majority of the "Songs of the Lady Elders" were composed by women. First of all, the monks never had so much sympathy with the female members of the community, as to warrant our crediting them with having composed these songs sung from the very hearts of women. We need only recall the difficulties which, according to tradition, Gotama placed in the way of his foster-mother when she desired to found the order of nuns, and the reproaches which are cast at Ānanda in several parts of the Canon on account of his friendly attitude towards women. For the same reason it would never have occurred to the monks to ascribe songs to the women, if an incontestible tradition had not pointed at this direction. Mrs. *Rhys Davids* [2] has pointed out the difference in idiom, sentiment and tone between the "Songs of the Elders" and the "Songs of the Lady Elders." One has only to read the two collections consecutively in order to arrive at the conviction that, in the songs of the nuns, a personal note is very frequently struck which is foreign to those of the monks, that in the latter we hear more of the inner experience, while in the former, we hear more frequently of external experiences, that in the monks' songs descriptions of nature predominate, while in those of the nuns, pictures of life prevail.[3]

---

[1]) In the Preface to his translation, p. vii. And the remarks of R. O. *Franke* in WZKM 24, 1910, p. 15 f., only prove that certain sets of verses are unified poems, but not that the whole is the work of one single author.

[2]) Psalms of the Sisters, p. xxiii ff.

[3]) *Oldenberg*, Literatur des alten Indien, p. 101 note, may be right when he explains the prevalence of the descriptions of nature in the "Songs of the Elders" by the fact that

Common to both collections are the religious ideals which are set up and the moral doctrines which are proclaimed. All these monks and nuns know of nothing higher than that profound calmness of mind for which even the gods envy the saint, which is won by the extinction of passion, hatred, and illusion and by the renunciation of all sensual inclinations and tendencies, and gives a foretaste of that highest bliss, Nirvāṇa, the end of all suffering in the consciousness of release from rebirth. Blessed is the monk who is equally insensible to joy and sorrow, who feels neither hunger nor cold: blessed the nun who can say of herself (Therīg. 76):

> " Now all the evil bonds that fetter gods
> And men are wholly rent and cut away.
> Purg'd are the Āsavas [1] that drugg'd my heart,
> Calm and content I know Nibbāna's Peace." [2]

These ideals, like the ethical doctrines, the noble fourfold path, gentleness and kindness towards all beings (mettā), non-violence (ahiṃsā), self-control, and so on, are common to these songs as well as to the sayings of the Dhammapada and the poems of the Suttanipāta. The distinctive feature of the songs of the monks and the nuns is, however, that they are personal confessions, or describe personal experiences. Proudly a monk relates how wife and child in vain endeavoured to disturb his peace—" Then my heart was set at liberty " (Therag. 299 ff.). Another one recalls to mind the courtesan whose blandishments he has resisted (Therag. 459 ff.). The

---

nature, as treated in these songs, is forest scenery, and the hermit life in the forest naturally played a greater part in the case of the monks than in that of the nuns. This is an additional argument in favour of the " Songs of the Lady Elders " having in reality been composed by the nuns themselves.

[1]) The Āsavas or " intoxicants " are: sensuality, longing for rebirth, false doctrine, and ignorance.

[2]) Translation by Mrs. *Rhys Davids*, Psalms of the Sisters, p. 53. Nibbāna = Nirvāṇa.

Songs of the Elders abound in attacks on the woman, the temptress—this snare, this bond—who never ceases to threaten to divert the monk from his holy living.[1] However numerous may be the women who come, boasts one monk, they shall not seduce me (Therag. 1211). Woman is the cause of all suffering, only he who steadfastly keeps away from her, can become a true hero (Therag. 738 ff.). A monk describes in a most gruesome manner, how he was led to the truth by the sight of the decaying corpse of a woman (Therag. 315 ff., 393 ff.). In contrast to these ugly pictures there are many more beautiful ones. We hear of a monk whose own mother led him to the truth, for which he thanks her in beautiful words.[2] In another song a monk consoles his mother by telling her that, after all, he has not died (Therag. 44). Another one relates how he eked out a miserable existence by picking up dead flowers, how he came to the Buddha and found liberation (Therag. 620 ff.). Yet another, according to tradition the son of a king's chaplain, tells how, proud of his noble birth, his wealth and his beauty, he lived a life of infatuation, until he saw the Buddha, and was converted (Therag. 423 ff.). A king, who has become a monk, compares his present life as a beggar with his erstwhile splendid court life (Therag. 842 ff.). Yet, in the Songs of the Elders, references to external experiences are comparatively rare. As a rule they only describe the inner life of the monks, mostly in short poems of a few verses each. However, in the verses ascribed to the Thera Talapuṭa,[3] we have also a long and splendid poem, the soliloquy of a monk striving after holiness. Some of the Songs of the Elders deal neither with

1) *Cf.* Therag. 267 ff., 279 ff., 453 ff., 459 ff., 1150 ff.

2) Therīg. 204-212, where the Thera Vaḍḍha is urged by his mother to become a monk, and Therag. 335-339, where Vaḍḍha thanks his mother, obviously belong to one poem. *Cf.* above, p. 101 note 2.

3) Therag. 1091-1145, s. *Oldenberg*, Literatur des alten Indien, p. 101 f., and Mrs. *Rhys Davids*, Psalms of the Brethren, p. 369 ff.

introspective self-expression nor external experience, but are merely verse sermons of general content.[1]

We have already remarked above, that pictures of real life are far more numerous in the Songs of the Lady Elders than in those of the Elders. Mad with grief at the loss of a child, a mother strays about, until, comforted and instructed by Buddha himself, she is admitted into the order. It happens more than once that women are brought into the order of nuns through the loss of children.[2] In one song we hear of a poor widow who (involuntarily) goes begging from house to house, and, by chance, comes to the nuns. Where she is sympathetically received and instructed, becomes a (voluntary) beggar, and through her kind teacher Paṭācārā, soon finds the way to Nirvāṇa. We hear repeatedly of former courtesans who became nuns, and the contrast between the life and conduct of the courtesan and the calm sanctity of the nun has a great artistic effect. In the midst of rejoicings and festivities, a beauty in festal array, comes to a convent and is instructed and converted by Buddha. Here, too, the contrast between the extravagant festive joy and the peace of Nirvāṇa is very effective.[3] We hear also of young girls of noble race, of matrons of advanced age, of a mother of ten children, who, instructed by Buddha himself or by some venerable nun, seek and find the way to Nirvāṇa. Moreover, we often hear how relatives vainly endeavour to dissuade a daughter from her decision to become a nun. The beautiful daughter of a rich man is courted by the sons of the wealthy people, even by princes, one of whom sends her father the message: "Eight times her weight in gold will I give for her, and stores of gems in addition." But she has heard the Buddha and prefers the life of a mendicant nun.

[1]) *Cf.* Mrs. *Rhys Davids*, Psalms of the Brethren, p. xxxi ff.

[2]) Therig. 133-138, 51-53, 127-132, 312-337.

[3]) Therig. 122-126, 25, 72-76, 145-150.

Neither is there any lack of tragedies. While Kisā-Gotamī [1] lies in the street, under labour pains, her husband dies in the jungle; she gives birth to a child, but wandering on she loses both her new-born babe and her elder child; at last she reaches her home, only to find her mother, father and brother dead, burning on one pyre: however, she now takes to the noble, eight-fold path, which leads her to "immortality," to the realisation of Nirvāṇa.[2] After the tragedy we have a comedy: The woman, who rejoices at being, by her conversion, released from the threshing of rice and from an unloved husband, expresses the incident humorously by saying that she is now rid of "three crooked things," mortar and pestle and her hunchbacked husband.[3]

The great importance of these pictures of life for our knowledge of the social conditions, especially of the social position of woman in ancient India, is self-evident. It need hardly be mentioned how largely, too, such pictures contribute to the animation of these poems, which always move in the same circles of ideas, namely the glorification of the Arhat ideal, though regarded from various points of view, thus giving the non-Buddhist reader the impression of a certain monotony.[4] Sure enough, in the "Songs of the Elders," the charming descriptions of nature are largely instrumental in making many of these religious poems real gems of Indian lyric poetry. The love of nature which we have already met with in the Rāmāyaṇa as a prominent feature of

[1]) Mrs. *Rhys Davids* (Psalms of the Sisters, p. 109) thinks that Kisā-Gotamī is here, not relating her own fate, but alluding to that of Paṭācārā, as told in the legend of the commentary to Therīg. 112 ff.

[2]) Therīg. 151-156, 16 f., 69, 102 ff., 338-365, 213-223.

[3]) Therīg. 11, perhaps a counterpart of Therag. 43, where a monk rejoices that he is freed from "three crooked things" (sickle, plough and spade).

[4]) Mrs. *Rhys Davids* (Psalms of the Brethren, p. 1) contests the very suggestion of monotony, because, as she has pointed out (Psalms of the Sisters, p. XXXVII f., Psalms of the Brethren, pp. XLII ff., 420 ff.) the one Arhat ideal is treated in various aspects.

Indian poetry, which we admire in the ornate epics and in the love lyrics, and even in the didactic gnomic poetry, was not foreign to these monks inspite of all their renunciation of the world. More poet than monk, they delight in lingering over the description of the forest and mountain scenery, in the midst of which the solitary sage pursues his meditations. When the thunder rolls and the torrential rain pours down out of the dark clouds, the liberated monk sits in bliss in his rock cave. Even the saint who is indifferent to pleasure and pain, does not refrain from describing the spring.[1]

The love of nature is also shown in many beautiful similes. The sage is compared to a rock, which stands firm, or to an elephant. The monk who is proud of his monk's robe is like the monkey in a lion's skin. The self-restrained monk sits like a lion in his den.[2] We find an elaborate accumulation of similes in one of the "Songs of the Lady Elders" (Therīg. 112ff.): As the peasant ploughs the field, sows the seed and reaps, so the nun desires to attain Nirvāṇa; while washing her feet she sees the water trickling down the rock, and, stimulated to reflection by this sight, she curbs her heart as one tames a noble steed; then she goes into the convent, takes the lamp, and with a needle, draws down the wick, and as the light of the lamp goes out, she attains Nirvāṇa. This artistic intertwining of similes already recalls the embellishments (alaṃkāras) of ornate poetry, and so do some very artificial word-plays which occasionally occur. A beautiful song, ascribed to Ambapālī, the former courtesan (Therīg. 252ff.) is also a very elaborate composition. Here the poetess, in the first two lines of each verse, describes the beauty of her body, and in the third line, the ravages which old age has made in the body which was so beautiful in youth,

---

1) Therag. 537 ff., 1062 ff., 1135 ff., 189 ff., 522 ff., 307 ff., 527 ff., *Cf.* C. A. F. *Rhys Davids*, The Love of Nature in Buddhist Poems: The Quest Review, April 1910.

2) Therag. 692 ff., 1000, 1080, 1081.

whereupon the refrain follows : " The word of the proclaimer of truth is not belied."

The refrain and the repetition of typical phrases are a characteristic feature of these poems.[1] The semi-dramatic dialogue form, too, is very popular. Thus one of the " Songs of the Lady Elders " (Therīg. 271 ff.) is a conversation between daughter and father, in which the daughter sets forth the advantages of the monastic life, and converts her father. Another of these songs (Therīg. 291 ff.) introduces a man—he was first a monk, then became a hunter, had a son, and now desires to become a monk again—in conversation with his wife, who is trying to dissuade him from his resolve ; she threatens to kill the child if he leaves her ; but he remains firm :

" And if thou throw the child to jackals or to dogs,
O wretch, thou wilt not turn me back,—not even for my son ! "

This is already a kind of ballad. And in the " Songs of the Elders " and the " Songs of the Lady Elders," especially in the latter, we find quite a number of real ballads with and without narrative stanzas. One of the longest of these ballads, which, at the same time, is extremely dramatic, is to be found among the "Songs of the Lady Elders" (Therīg. 312-337).

In amazement a Brahman asks his wife how is it that she does not weep, though she has lost her seven children, while she formerly used to weep day and night for the departed. She replies that she has learnt from Buddha how one can escape birth and death. Then the Brahman goes to Buddha and becomes a monk. He sends his charioteer back with a message to his wife that he has become a monk. The woman is about to give the charioteer a horse and carriage and a thousand pieces of gold for the glad tidings, but he says : " Keep the horse and carriage and

---

[1]) *Cf.* W. *Stede* in JPTS 1924-1927, p. 34 ff. *Stede's* " Synoptical Table of Repeated Pādas or ' Repertory ' Phrases," l.c., p. 197 ff., shows how numerous these repetitions are.

money, I too am going to become a monk." The daughter, too, whom the woman wishes to appoint as heir to the great treasures of the house, renounces, and declares her intention of becoming a nun.

Perhaps the most beautiful of these ballads is that of the nun Subhā, who is pursued in the forest by a rogue with declarations of love.

In glowing words he praises her beauty, depicts to her the terrors of the forest, and tries to tempt her to the delights of love. She rejects him :

"Lo ! thou art wanting to walk where no path is ; thou
seekest to capture
Moon from the skies for thy play ; thou would'st jump o'er
the ridges of Meru,
Thou who presumest to lie in wait for a child of the
Buddha ! "[1]

She declares that she has cast all worldly desires from her like glowing coals, like poison. She describes the perishableness and ugliness of the body ; even the eye is only a loathsome ball of flesh. With these words she tears out her eye [2] and hands it to the man. The latter is contrite and begs for forgiveness. The nun, however, goes to Buddha, and as soon as he looks at her, her eye shines forth as before (Therīg. 366-399).

One magnificent ballad relates how some robbers approach a monk, and, overwhelmed by his wonderful calmness and fearlessness, throw their weapons away, give up their trade, and become pious monks (Therag. 705ff.). The ballad of the robber Aṅgulimāla, which we came across in

---

[1]) Translated by Mrs. *Rhys Davids*, Psalms of the Sisters, p. 152.

[2]) When in the Christian legends St. Lucia and St. Bridget pluck out both their eyes because the young men fell in love with them on account of their beauty, it may quite well be mere chance coincidence. One need only think of St. Matth. 18, 9, to see that Buddhist influence can scarcely be assumed, as is the view of E. *Müller* (AR. III, 1900, p. 233). *Cf.* C. H. *Tawney*, Kathāsaritsāgara Transl., I, p. 248 note ; R. *Garbe*, Indien und das Christentum, p. 116 ; E. W. *Burlingame*, Buddhist Parables, New Haven 1922, p. 325 ff. ; and *H. Günter*, Buddha in der abendländischen Legende? Leipzig 1922, p. 220 f.

the Majjhimanikāya,[1] recurs verbatim in the Theragāthā (866ff.). Some of the ballads, dialogues between Māra and the nuns,[2] in the Therīgāthā, are in part counterparts to, and in part other versions of, those which we have found in the Bhikkhunī-Saṃyutta of the Saṃyuttanikāya. A number of other songs and verses of this collection can be traced in the four Nikāyas, in the Dhammapada and the Suttanipāta. In fact, in one passage (Therag. 145) similes of the Nikāyas are even assumed to be known, that is, they are directly quoted. But even if we were to see quotations or loans in all these cases, it would hardly prove the later origin of the two collections as such; for the passages in question might have been inserted later.

It is certain that, in the two collections, there is a considerable number of poems which must be of later origin. When, for instance, a monk relates that, only because he offered a single flower, he wandered through the heavens in eighty hundred million years and finally reached Nirvāṇa, it indicates a Buddha-cult such as we do not see fully developed prior to the later Mahāyāna-texts And when a seven-year-old saint performs miracles, when a monk multiplies himself a thousand times and flies through the air, when ten thousand gods in Brahma's heaven receive Sāriputta and do him honour,[3]—passages containing these and such other miracles, can scarcely belong to the oldest stratum of Buddhist poetry and thought. The two poems[4] which speak of the decay of the religion could only have originated centuries after the founding of the order and, as I believe, after the time of Aśoka. In the first poem the simple and pious life of the monks of former times is contrasted with the "present" life

---

1) No. 86, see above, p. 48.

2) Therīg. 182 ff., 189 ff., 196 ff.

3) Therag. 96, 429 ff., 563 ff., 1082 ff.

4) Therag. 920-948 and 949-980. *Neumann* compares these with Aṅguttaranikāya, V, 79 and 80.

of the monks. "They, who once forsook wealth, wife and child, now do evil for the sake of a spoonful of rice," eat what they like, carry on profane conversations, and, in return for vanities which they offer the people, expect rich gifts, collect herbs like physicians, adorn themselves like courtesans, are crafty, cunning, hypocritical and so on. In the second poem, in reply to the question as to what the monks of the future will be like, Phussa draws a picture which seems to indicate a period of the complete decay of Buddhism. The monks, it is said, will be filled with anger and hatred, envy and obstinacy, they will not want to know anything of the truth, will distort the word of the Lord, will accept gold and silver, will despise the virtuous and true monks, monks and nuns will live without discipline, and so on—a remarkable picture, which cannot possibly date from an ancient period. The song of Isidāsī in the "Songs of the Lady Elders" (Therīg. 400-447) seems to belong to the same period of decay. Here it is regarded quite as a matter of course that a girl only becomes a nun in consequence of some misfortune. That a man should become a monk, discard his monk's robe in order to marry and return to the monastic life after a fortnight, seems to be taken from real life, but probably from the life of a time at which Buddhism had already passed through many a crisis. The last of the "Songs of the Lady Elders" (Therīg. 448-521), too, is either a later addition, or else a poem much distorted by later additions and overburdened with quotations.[1]

For this reason the assertion of K. E. *Neumann* that these songs "were already collected and carefully preserved during Gotama's lifetime and soberly fixed soon after his death," is not only without proof, but it is quite impossible for one part of the songs, and improbable for

---

[1]) Mrs. *Rhys Davids*, too (Psalms of the Sisters, p. xviii f.) regards the last two "Songs of the Lady Elders" as products of later ornate poetry.

another. Nevertheless, it is possible that some of the songs were already composed by the very first disciples of Buddha. Thus the line which so frequently recurs in the "Songs of the Elders":

> "I find no delight in dying, I find no delight in life:
> The hour of death do I await, with mind alert and discerning." [1]

might very well have been uttered by one of the first disciples. It is possible that Mahāpajāpatī, Gotama's foster-mother, really sang the hymn in praise of Buddha (Therīg. 157-162) as is ascribed to her. Similarly, the verses (Therīg. 981-994) in which the ideal of a monk's life is so minutely described, might indeed have been composed by Sāriputta. The beautiful words:

> "Press on with earnestness and win the goal!
> This is the commandment that I give to you.
> Lo! now my going-out complete will be.
> From all am I released and utterly." [2]

could in reality have come down as the legacy of Sāriputta, his last exhortation to the disciples. And the celebrated lines, which recur in several parts of the Pāli Canon, and are ascribed to the great Moggallāna in this collection:

> "O transient are our life's experiences!
> Their nature 'tis to rise and pass away.
> They happen in our ken, they cease to be.
> O well for us when they are sunk to rest!" [3]

---

1) Therag. 196, 607, *cf.* 20, 1002.

2) Therag. 1017, translation by Mrs. *Rhys Davids*, Psalms of the Brethren, p. 349. The verse is ascribed to Revata, the brother of Sāriputta, in 658. Perhaps the verse is only an enlargement on the last words of the Buddha (Mahā-Parinibbāna-Sutta, Dīghanikāya XVI, 6, 7: appamādena sampādetha).

3) Therag. 1159, translation by Mrs. *Rhys Davids*, Psalms of the Brethren, p. 385. The verse is here said to have been spoken concerning the passing away of Sāriputta. In Mahā-Parinibbāna-Sutta, Dīgh. XVI, 6, 10, god Sakka recites the verse on the passing

are probably so old that Moggallāna or another of the first disciples of Buddha could have composed them. Here, as in all the collections of the Tipiṭaka, the old and the new are combined, and here too the scholar will have to determine the age of each portion separately on its individual merits.

10. This is especially true of the collection of Jātakas included in the Khuddaka-Nikāya, "stories of former births (of the Buddha)" [1] or "Bodhisatta stories," as they might be more briefly called. A "Bodhisatta," in Buddhist dogmatics, is a being (Pāli satta, Sanskrit sattva), who is destined to obtain enlightenment (bodhi), *i.e.* to become a Buddha.[2] Gotama the Buddha (*i.e.* the "enlightened one") is called "Bodhisatta" up to the time when he attained enlightenment, not only in his last earthly existence, but in all the countless existences which he experienced as man, animal or god, before he was re-born for the last time as the son of the Sakya prince. Now, a "Jātaka" is a story in which the Bodhisatta plays a part in one of his former existences, whether as the hero of the story or as a secondary character or as a spectator only. Hence every Jātaka begins with the words: "At such and such a time (*e.g.* at the time when Brahmadatta was reigning in Benares) the Bodhisatta was re-born in the womb of such and such a being (*e.g.* of the queen or of a female elephant)"; then follows the story. In this way it was

away of the Buddha; so also Saṃyuttanikāya I, p. 158: but Buddha himself speaks the verse in Saṃyuttanikāya II, p. 193. The verse occurs again in Saṃy. I, pp. 6 and 200, and Jātaka, Vol. I, p. 392. K. E. *Neumann* (Lieder der Mönche und Nonnen, p. 243) says: "This famous saying is so popular that it was recited to me in pure Pāli by a servant in Colombo, and, what is still more significant in this case, was excellently interpreted by him in a popular way."

[1]) This is the usual and probably correct explanation of the word "Jātaka," which is derived from jāta, "birth." H. *Kern*, Der Buddhismus, I, 328, translates Jātaka by "little story." *Speyer*, Jātakamālā, p. xxii, agrees with him. But see *Oldenberg*, DLZ, 1896, c. 261.

[2]) Others explain Bodhisatta by "One whose essence (sattva) is perfect knowledge," Cf. *La Vallée Poussin* in ERE, II, p. 739.

possible to change into a Jātaka any story which was told among the people or which was known from secular literature. One had only to make a Bodhisatta out of some human, animal or divine being which occurred in the story, and any story, however worldly and however far removed from the sphere of Buddhist thought, could become a "Buddhist" story. Now the Buddhist monks would not have been true Indians, if they had not taken into account the need, so deeply rooted in the soul of the Indian people, of hearing and relating stories, and if they had not utilised this need to gain followers for their religion. In fact, not only the Buddhist monks, but the preachers of all sects in India, have always done what the Christian monks of the West did centuries later. Gregory the Great had already recommended to these last-named the use of "example," of the narrative serving as argument, "quia nonnunquam mentes audientium plus exempla fidelium quam docentium verba convertunt."[1] The monks in India likewise maintained this principle. Just like the Christian preachers later, the Buddhist monks utilised for their purposes all kinds of stories, fairy-tales, fables, anecdotes, etc. Therefore a good idea of the Jātaka collection is given by books like the "Gesta Romanorum" or *Wesselski's* "Mönchslatein," in which the stories, culled from the sermons of the clergy of various centuries, are collected, with their varied contents, mixture of sacred legends and often very worldly stories. The more rigorous Buddhist Theras of the olden days do not seem to have been greatly in favour of this story-telling, for several passages of the canon[2] speak disapprovingly of the loud conversations of the monks, who tell one another stories of kings, robbers, ministers, arms, wars, women, gods and spirits, sea-faring adventures, etc. However, in one of the earlier Buddhist Sanskrit

---

1) Alb. *Wesselski*, Mönchslatein, Leipzig 1909, p. ix.

2) Vinayapiṭaka, Mahāvagga V, 6, 3; Dīghanikāya I, 17; IX, 3; XXV, 2; 21;

texts [1] we already read that the Buddha teaches by means of Sūtras, Gāthās, legends and Jātakas.

In ancient times it was not yet considered necessary to give the stories the form of "Jātakas." We still find isolated stories related, *e.g.* that of Dīghāvu ("Prince Longlived") in the Vinayapiṭaka,[2] without the hero being identified with the Bodhisatta. It was only at a later period that a Jātaka was made out of it. Yet there are also a few real Jātakas already to be found in the collections of the Suttas,[3] and they prove that the Buddhist monks, like their Christian colleagues in the Middle Ages, related these stories or used them as sermons.

Not all the Jātakas, however, were received into the canon when the work of combining them into a book was begun.[4] Indeed, it is difficult to determine how much of the Jātaka book, as we have it, belongs to the canon, for we do not possess the original canonical Jātaka, but merely a commentary on it. In this commentary, every single Jātaka consists of the following parts: (1) An introductory story, Paccuppannavatthu, *i.e.* "story of the present time," relating on what occasion the Buddha himself told the monks

---

[1] Saddharmapuṇḍarīka II, 44 (SBE., Vol. 21, p. 45).

[2] See above, p. 33, *cf.* Jātakas Nos. 371 and 428. In the same way the fable quoted above, on p. 32, is not a Jātaka whilst in Jātaka No. 37 the Bodhisatta is the partridge in the same story. Cf. *Rhys Davids*, Buddhist India, p. 195. E. W. *Burlingame*, JAOS, Vol. 38, Part 4, gives a list of ten Jātakas which are taken from the canon. *Rhys Davids*, JRAS 1919, p. 231, adds another three to the list. See also *Burlingame*, Buddhist Parables, p. 59 ff.

[3] Thus the Kūṭadanta-Sutta and the Mahāsudassana-Sutta in the Dīghanikāya and the Makhādeva-Sutta in the Majjhimanikāya are Jātakas.

[4] Majjhimanikāya, Sutta 81, is a Jātaka which does not occur in the Jātaka book. In the Milindapañha two or three Jātakas are mentioned, which cannot be traced in the collection; in the Dhammapada commentary, too, as well as in the Buddhist Sanskrit texts, there are some Jātakas which are absent in the collection. See also L. *Feer*, JA ser. 7, t. V, 1874, 417 ff.; VI, 1875, 244 ff. It is probable, though not yet proved, "that a Book of Jātakas, as contained in the Pāli Canon was not the exclusive possession of this particular school, but belonged to ancient Buddhism in general" (*Oldenberg*, NGGW 1912, p. 195).

the Jātaka in question; (2) a prose narrative, Atītavatthu, *i.e.* "story of the past," in which a story of one of the former births of the Buddha, in other words a Bodhisatta story, is told; (3) the Gāthās, *i.e.* stanzas, which, as a rule, form part of the "story of the past," but which are very often, too, a part of the "story of the present time";[1] (4) short commentary (Veyyākaraṇa) in which the Gāthās are explained word for word; and (5) the "connexion" (Samodhāna)[2] in which, finally (again by Buddha himself) the personages of the "story of the present" are identified with those of the "story of the past." This huge narrative work in the form of a commentary, the Jātakaṭṭhavaṇṇanā, or "elucidation of the meaning of the Jātakas,"[3] is the work of an unknown

---

1) The commentary generally calls these verses Abhisambuddha-Gāthās, *i.e.*, "verses spoken by the Buddha after his enlightenment." Cf. *Senart*, JA 1901, ser. 9, t. XVII, p. 385 ff.

2) As a rule the Samodhāna is in prose, but verses occur here and there.

3) Standard edition by V. *Fausböll*, Vols. I-VII (Vol. VII: Index by D. *Andersen*), London 1877-1897. A new edition, in Siamese characters, has been issued by their Majesties Queen Aunt and Queen Suddhasinninath of Siam in 1925 (10 vols.). Translations: Buddhist Birth Stories, or Jātaka Tales, translated by T. W. *Rhys Davids*, London, 1880 (contains Nos. 1-40). The Jātaka or stories of the Buddha's Former Births, translated from the Pāli by various Hands under the Editorship of E. B. *Cowell*, Vols. I-VI, Cambridge 1895-1907 (the translators are R. *Chalmers*, W. H. D. *Rouse*, H. T. *Francis*, R. A. *Neil* and *Cowell* himself): Vol. VII contains the Index. A considerable number of Jātakas have been translated by R. *Morris* in Folk-Lore Journal II-IV and Paul *Steinthal* Zeitschrift für vergleichende Litteraturgeschichte, N. F. VI, 1893, pp. 106 ff., VII, 1894, pp. 296 ff., X, 1896, pp. 75 ff., XI, 1897, pp. 313 ff. and Studien zur vergleichenden. Litteraturgeschichte I, 1901, pp. 475 ff., II, 1902, pp. 265 ff.; A. *Grünwedel*, Buddhistische Studien I, Berlin 1897 gives 55 Jatakas partly in extract, and partly in translation. Selections have been translated by Else *Lüders*, Buddhistische Märchen, mit einer Einleitung von H. *Lüders*, Jena 1921. A complete German translation by Julius *Dutoit* was published in Leipzig in 1908 ff. Literature on Jātakas: Léon *Feer*, JA 1875, s. 7, t. V, pp. 357 ff., t. VI, pp. 243 ff.; 1895, s. 9, t. V, pp. 31 ff., 189 ff.; 1897, s. 9, t. IX, pp. 288 ff.; S. *d'Oldenburg* JRAS 1893, pp. 301 ff.; R. O. *Franke*, Beitr. 22, 1897 pp. 289 ff., WZKM 20, 1906, pp. 317 ff.; T. W. *Rhys Davids*, Buddhist India, pp. 189 ff.; Album Kern, Leide 1903, pp. 18 ff.; *Oldenberg*, Literatur des alten Indien, pp. 103 ff; NGGW 1912, pp. 183 ff.; 214 ff.; 1918, pp. 429 ff.; 1919, pp. 61 ff., and Zur Geschichte der altindischen Prosa (AGGW 1917, pp. 79 ff.); S. *Lévi*, Les Jātakas (Conférences du Musée Guimet XIX, 1906); W. *Geiger*, Pāli Literatur und Sprache, pp. 20 f.; *Winternitz* in ERE, Vol. VII, pp. 491 ff.

Singhalese monk,[1] who took his materials from an earlier commentary on the Jātakas, the Jātakaṭṭhakathā. This last-named work, as indeed the Aṭṭhakathās in general, is said to have been written in Pāli immediately after the canon, brought to Ceylon with the canon itself, there translated into the Old Singhalese language, and then translated back again into Pāli by the compiler of the Jātakaṭṭhavaṇṇanā.[2] It is only the prose, however, which was translated into Singhalese and then translated back again; the Gāthās were preserved unchanged in Pāli. According to tradition, it is only these Gāthās, the stanzas, which were included in the canon.[3] This tradition is probably correct in so far as both prose and verse originally came down orally; but the prose naturally had a less stable form than the stanzas, so that when the canon was compiled, and later on, when it was written down, only the verses retained their original form, whilst, in the case of the prose, the rendering of it was at first entrusted to the reciters, and it was only at a later period committed to writing by commentators.

The majority of Jātakas, in fact, belong to that type of literary work which consists of a mixture of prose and verse,

---

[1]) According to the Gandhavaṃsa (JPTS 1886, p. 59), Buddhaghosa (5th century A. D.) is said to be the author of Jātakaṭṭhavaṇṇanā. T. W. *Rhys Davids*, in Buddhist Birth Stories, p. lxiii ff., had already, on good grounds, questioned the authorship of Buddhaghosa. E. W. *Burlingame* (Buddhist Legends, HOS, Vol. 28, pp. 49, 59f.) adds that both the language and the style of the Jātaka commentary differ from those of the authentic works of Buddhaghosa. See below.

[2]) *Burlingame* (JAOS 38, 1918, pp. 267 f.) declares this tradition to be unreliable, as it has been shown that Pāli sources were used for the commentary. But it is difficult to understand how and why so definite a statement could have been made without any historical background. It is quite feasible, in fact perfectly natural that, when translating into Pāli, the compilers should have accepted both canonical and noncanonical Pāli texts in their original Pāli form, without going to the trouble of translating the texts from the Singhalese.

[3]) Cf. *Rhys Davids*, Buddhist Birth Stories, p. lxxvii. It was hitherto thought that this Jātaka, which consists entirely of verses, had been preserved in manuscripts. Friedrich *Weller*, however (ZII 4, 1926, pp. 46 ff.), examined three manuscripts of Jātaka verses, and came to the conclusion that these manuscripts only contain extracts from the

a type which is such a favourite in Indian literature. It was ever a favourite method in ancient India to enliven narrative prose by verses, and to introduce or to garb narrative verses by explanatory prose passages. The teller of fairy-tales would insert into his story such fairy-tale verses as those familiar to us from our own fairy-tales. The writer of fables would give the moral or the point of the fable in one or two verses. The ballad poets and the singers, who recited their songs in alternating stanzas to correspond to the speeches of the dialogue, must often have prefaced them by a prose introduction, sometimes inserting explanations in prose, if occasion required it.[1]

We should, however, be mistaken in supposing that all the Gāthās which are included in the Jātaka commentary, belong to the canon. In accordance with a system of classification popular in India,[2] the Jātaka book is arranged according to the number of verses contained in them. The entire book consists of 2[illegible] sections (Nipātas), of which the first

Jātaka commentary, but not the ancient verse Jātaka which belongs to the canon. This serves to confirm the hypothesis put forward by J. *Hertel* (ZDMG 64, 1910, 58 ; WZKM 24, 1910, 23). *Weller* (l. c.; p. 54) raises the question as to whether a verse Jātaka ever existed at all. In the commentary itself, however, a distinction is often made between Pāli and Aṭṭhakathā, and in this case "Pāli" cannot refer to anything but the verse Jātaka. Moreover, the fact that the principle of division of the Jātaka book in 22 sections (Ekanipāta etc.) is based upon the verse Jātaka, and no longer agrees with the number of verses in the Jātaka commentary (see below), is further proof of the existence of the canonical verse Jātaka. *Senart* (JA 1901, s 9, t. XVII, pp. 385 ff., cf. *Oldenberg* NGGW 1911, p. 447f.) adduces still further arguments in favour of the verse Jātaka, arguments which have not been confuted by *Weller*.

1) *Cf.* above Vol. I, p. 101 and *Oldenberg*, The Prose-and-Verse Type of Narrative and the Jātakas (translated from NGGW 1911), in JPTS 1910-1912, pp. 19 ff. F. W. *Thomas* (JRAS 1903, pp. 402 f.) says: "The conjunction of a text in itself brief and obscure with an indispensable commentary is, one might say, the prevailing one in all periods of Indian literature down to the present......The figure of the poet who recites his verse in the middle of a prose narrative is still familiar in all parts of India, and may have been familiar to the earliest age."

2) For instance, the Theragāthās are also classified according to the number of verses.

contains 150 stories of one verse each, the second 100 stories of two verses each, the third 50 stories of three verses each, etc. In each subsequent section the number of verses increases, whilst that of the stories decreases.[1] Now, the number of Gāthās does not by any means always tallies with the title of the sections in question. Thus, for instance, in the "section of one," we find stories of 4, 5, 6, 10 and 11 stanzas, in the "section of two" there are some stories of from 3 to 10 stanzas, in the "section of twenty" there is one case of 44, in the "section of seventy" there are only two stories, one of 92 and the other of 93 Gāthās, in the "section of eighty" stories of 103 and 123 stanzas occur, and so forth. The only explanation of this is, that the classification is based on the verse-Jātaka, and not on the Jātaka commentary, and that the verse-Jātaka of the canon contained a far smaller number of Gāthās.

Nevertheless we may certainly say that, on the whole, the Gāthās have a stronger claim to be regarded as canonical than have the prose portions of the Jātakas. At all events the prose was more exposed to changes. In many cases it is nothing but the miserable performance of a very late period. It contains allusions to Ceylon, and not infrequently it is at absolute variance with the Gāthās.[2] Moreover, the language of the Gāthās is more archaic than that of the prose.

On the other hand, there is no chronological significance

---

[1]) In the original verse-Jātaka the number of verses must have tallied exactly with the title of the section (Eka-Nipāta, Duka-Nipāta etc.) otherwise the Pakiṇṇaka-Nipāta, "Section of mixed (number of verses)" would not have been inserted after Section XIII, neither would the Mahā-Nipāta, "Great Section," which contains only 10 stories, each consisting of a very large number of Gāthās, have been placed at the end, as Section XXII.

[2]) *Lüders* (NGGW 1897, pp. 40 ff.) has shown that the author of the prose of the Dasaratha-Jātaka (No. 461) did not understand the meaning of the Gāthās, and in ZDMG 58, 1904, 689 ff., that the Kṛṣṇa legend is presented "in a degenerate condition" in the prose of the Ghata-Jātaka (No. 355), "as so complicated a legend, separated from its home, was gradually bound to be in course of time." *Hertel*, too (ZDMG 60, 1906, 399 ff.), and *Charpentier* (ZDMG 62, 1908, 725 ff.), have pointed out contradictions

in the distinction between "stories of the present" and "stories of the past," for both are the work of one and the same commentator.[1] Very frequently, however, this commentator made use of good and old materials. It is for this reason that, especially in the prose of the shorter fables and fairy tales, we find very many stories excellently told, whilst in other Jātakas, especially in those which do not require prose, the prose narrative is extremely inferior and dull and frequently not at all in harmony with the Gāthās. It is not feasible to think that the same commentator on one occasion told his stories skilfully and humorously, and on another occasion in a dull and spiritless manner, but we must assume that, when he told them well, he used good old models or traditions. Therefore, in the prose, too, much that is old may have been preserved.

That this is actually the case, and that some of the Jātakas, even as regards the contents of the prose, belonged to Buddhist tradition in the second or third century B.C., is proved by the reliefs on the stone walls around the Stūpas of Bharhut and Sānchi;[2] these reliefs are extremely

between the prose and the verse. Such contradictions, however, assail us at every turn. In No. 128 the prose has a fable about a jackal, whilst both in the verse and the title, the animal is a cat. The fact that Jātaka No. 253 occurs in the Vinayapiṭaka with the same Gāthās, but different prose, is additional proof that, generally speaking, the prose of the Jātakas cannot claim to be authentic.

[1]) In his edition, *Fausböll* differentiates the Paccuppannavatthus from the Atīta-vatthus by printing the former in smaller type. But this distinction cannot by any means be maintained throughout. It is often clear that both were written or compiled at the same time. It is possible that the word-for-word explanation of the Gāthās was the work of a still later commentator. *Cf.* R. O. *Franke* in Bezz. Beitr. 22, 1897, 289 ff.; *Senart*, JA. 1901, s. 9, t. XVII, p. 406. It is perfectly natural that the "Stories of the present" tell chiefly of Kosala and sometimes of Magadha, *i.e.*, those districts where Buddha taught; on the other hand, when the scene of most of the Atītavatthus is laid in Benares, it is merely the result of a stereotyped convention. (It is only rarely that Taxila is the scene of the story; very occasionally the scene is laid in other cities of India, and once in Ceylon.) There is no justification for *Fausböll's* statement (Jātaka Ed., Vol. VII, p. viii) that the Atītavatthus are necessarily earlier on this account.

[2]) See above, p. 16, note 3, and see also S. d'*Oldenburg*, JAOS 18, 1897, pp. 183 ff.;

important from the point of view of the history of the Jātakas. These precious Buddhist monuments depict scenes from the Jātakas, including scenes which occur only in the prose, in fact in Bharhut the titles of the Jātakas are written above the reliefs.[1] These reliefs prove, then, that a number of narratives, which are also to be found in the Jātaka book, were in the 2nd (perhaps even in the 3rd) century B.C. technically called "Jātaka," and were regarded as Bodhisatta stories. They prove that even at that early time many worldly narratives, which were found already current by the Buddhist monks, were "Buddhistised," that accordingly they must have been known in India long before, and possibly belonged to the pre-Buddhist period.

If, therefore, a few prominent scholars[2] have assumed that the Jātakas offer us a picture of the narrative literature and the conditions of civilisation at the time of Buddha or a still earlier time, it is true only in a very limited sense. Some of the poems and a few of the prose narratives may perhaps reach back to such great antiquity. Some of the sayings and legends may indeed belong to the pre-Buddhist ascetic poetry. For the great mass of the verses, however, no greater

E. *Hultzsch*, JRAS 1912, pp. 399 ff.; B. M. *Barua*, Ind. Hist. Qu. II, 1926, 623 ff. and Calcutta Review, Dec. 1926, pp. 430 ff.

[1] In the Jātaka book, every Jātaka has a title, which is formed either after the hero of the narrative (usually the Bodhisatta) or another person, or from the first words of the first stanza. The same Jātakas, however, appear under various titles. *Cf.* Dines *Andersen* in Vol. VII, p. xv of the Jātaka edition. On the Bharhut stūpa, too, the titles are sometimes the same as those in the Jātaka book, but in other cases they differ. This makes it difficult to identify them. A list of the 27, or 29 Jātakas of the Bharhut stūpa which have been identified so far, is given by *Rhys Davids*, Buddhist India, p. 209, and *Hultzsch*, JRAS 1912, p. 406.

[2] Thus G. *Bühler*, on the Origin of the Indian Brāhma Alphabet, 2nd Ed., Strassburg 1898, pp. 16 ff.; R. *Fick*, Die soziale Gliederung im nordöstlichen Indien zu Buddhas Zeit, Kiel 1897 (English translation by S. *Maitra*: The Social Organisation in North-East India in Buddha's Time, Calcutta 1920); T. W. *Rhys Davids*, Buddhist India, 201 ff. and Mrs. *Rhys Davids*, Notes on Early Economic Conditions in Northern India, JRAS 1901, 859 ff.

antiquity than the 3rd century B.C. can conscientiously be urged, certainly not proved, and much of the prose assuredly belongs to the Christian era. We have already mentioned that not even all the Gāthās belonged to the canonical Jātaka. Now the last-named is not the work of a single, individual author, but is the product of the labours of compilers.[1] The compilers arranged the verses in such a manner as they thought proper, in order to form a narrative. Such procedure must have entailed many an error.[2]

From all this it can only be concluded that the position of the Jātaka book is probably no different from that of the Mahābhārata.[3] Not only every large section and every single narrative, but often also every single Gāthā, will have to be tested independently as regards its age. Some of the

[1]) It is quite impossible for the Jātaka Gāthās to be, as is the opinion of *Franke* (WZKM 20, 1906, p. 318, *cf.* ZDMG 63, 1909, p. 13) "when considered as a whole, the personal production of a single author," who "not only put them together, but very often composed them himself, adapted, altered and patched them up, and in fact endowed the complete work with the stamp of his own individuality." If we change the word "author" into "compiler" or "editor," there is some truth in these words of Franke; for the compilers of Indian literary collections have never scrupled to alter the verses of other poets and to add verses of their own composition to them.

[2]) Thus we may doubt whether the verses of Jāt. 61-65 were really intended as Gāthās for 5 different stories. The Gāthās of No. 377 and No. 487 probably belonged to one story, and in the same way those of Nos. 523 and 526. Cf. *Lüders* In Festschrift Windisch, pp. 228 ff. and NGGW 1897, 1. Jāt. No. 203 with 5 Gāthās, though it is included in the Section of two, is a snake incantation, in which, besides Buddha, Dhamma and Saṅgha, the "seven Buddhas" are also worshipped, though it is absurd to imagine that Gotama Buddha could have been worshipped as the seventh Buddha in the Atītavatthu, that is, at the period of one of his previous existences!

[3]) See above, Vol. I, p. 469. Even the manifold connections between the Jātakas and the Epics (*cf.* Vol. I, pp. 400 note 4, 401, 410 note 3, 415 note 1, 471 f., 473 note 1, and 508 f.) are of no use in determining the date, as the period of the epics is far too uncertain. Unfortunately, the fact that numerous Jātakas are mentioned and quoted in Book IV of the Milindapañha, and that in Book V of the same work, Jātaka reciters are mentioned side by side with the Dīgha and Majjhima reciters, does not help us. For these books belong to the later parts of the Milindapañha, which are missing in the Chinese translation, and are of uncertain date. The fact that in Milindapañha IV even fairy-tale verses which contain nothing Buddhistic, are quoted as "words of the Buddha," only proves that a few centuries after Christ, these verses were canonical, and every word of the canon was regarded as a word of Buddha. The fact that, even in these late books of the Milinda-

Gāthās may possibly date back to the Vedic period,[1] others should perhaps be regarded as a preliminary stage of epic poetry; [2] but the collection as we find it in the Jātakaṭṭhavaṇṇanā, cannot as such, be the "earliest" collection of Indian fables, fairy tales and narratives, as has often been affirmed.

Nevertheless, we are obliged to take our stand on this very Jātakaṭṭhavaṇṇanā, the only Jātaka-text known hitherto, for the following account of the contents of this collection of Buddhist tales, which is of the utmost importance not only for the history of Indian Literature, but also for the history of the literature of the world. The "stories of the present" it is true, can certainly be left aside. They are sometimes only duplicates of the "stories of the past," sometimes foolish and entirely worthless inventions, and at best narratives which have been borrowed from other parts of the canon, *e.g.* Vinayapiṭaka, Suttanipāta, Apadāna, or from other commentaries. So much the more valuable are the actual Jātakas or the "stories of the past."

Among the Jātakas of our collection, far more than 500,

pañha, deviations from the Jātaka book occur in the quoted Jātakas, shows the uncertainty of the transmission. The circumstance that a few Jātaka verses occur in *Patañjali's* Mahābhāṣya, and that the language of the latter shows points of contact with the language of the Jātakas (F. *Kielhorn* JRAS 1898, 17 ff. and R. G. *Bhandarkar* in OC IX, London 1892, I, 421 ff.), would indicate that some of the Jātakas originated in the 2nd century B.C.

[1]) For instance, if *Lüders* (Festschrift Windisch, pp. 228 ff.) has proved that some of the Gāthās of Jātakas Nos. 377 and 487, having reference to Śvetaketu, who is familiar to us from the Upaniṣads, date back to the Vedic period, then the statement is only true of these particular Gāthās, and we are *not* warranted to make the generalisation that the Gāthā poetry of the Jātakas forms "the connecting-link between the Vedic Ākhyāna and the epic poetry."

[2]) *Oldenberg*, in his researches as to the style of the Jātakas (NGGW 1918, 429 ff.; 1919, 61 ff.) comes to the conclusion that the Jātaka Gāthās represent a more ancient type of poetry than the epic. He is compelled to admit, however, that it is not possible to decide for certain whether that type which is more primitive as regards development is, at the same time, also the earlier as regards actual chronology.

in number,[1] all kinds and forms of narrative composition are represented. First, as regards the form, we find: 1. Narratives in prose with fable verses, fairy-tale stanzas, or aphorisms inserted here and there. Prose and verses easily join with one another, and together form such a beautiful whole that we cannot but assume that in these cases the Jātakaṭṭhavaṇṇanā used good old traditions for the prose also. 2. Ballads, (*a*) in dialogue form,[2] (*b*) in a mixture of conversational verses and narrative stanzas. The prose which we find in the Jātakaṭṭhavaṇṇanā, is, as a rule in these cases, the entirely superfluous and insipid fabrication of some commentator, and, as a matter of fact, is not infrequently in actual contradiction to the verses. 3. Longer narratives, beginning in prose and continued in verse, or in which prose narration alternates with narrative and conversational verses. Here prose is indispensable, but the prose of the Jātakaṭṭhavaṇṇanā is not a faithful copy of the original prose, but greatly enlarged on and disfigured by commentatorial additions.[3] 4. Collections of sayings on any subject, and 5. Regular

[1]) There are 547 numbers in the Jātaka book. But as, in some of these numbers, several narratives are included, while others only contain references to later Jātakas, and as sometimes the same narratives recur in different versions, the figure 547 does not agree exactly with the actual number of Jātakas. The Culla-Niddesa (p. 80) speaks of 500 Jātakas. Fa-hien, too (Record of the Buddhist Kingdoms, transl. by J. *Legge*, Oxford, 1886, p. 106), speaks of pictures illustrating "500 Jātakas" which he had seen in Ceylon. *Cf.* B. M. *Barua*, Ind. Hist. Qu. II, 1926, pp. 623 ff.

[2]) Dramatic as many of these ballads are—L. *Feer* (JA 1895, s. 9, t. V, pp. 47 ff.), for instance, calls the Chaddanta-Jātaka (No. 514) "un véritable drame," and the same could be said of many other Jātakas—we can scarcely look upon them as "dramas" in the true sense of the word. What has been said above, p. 59 ff, regarding the ballads of the Saṃyuttanikāya may be applied to these ballads also.

[3]) It is impossible to deny, as A. B. *Keith* does (JRAS 1911, 979 ff.; 1912, 435 ff.) that the Jātakas belong to the type of composition which consists of prose and verse; neither can we agree with *Oldenberg* (NGGW 1911, p. 444=JPTS 1910-1912, p. 22, but see note 3) in speaking of the prose-and-verse type as "*almost* the only prevailing one" in the Jātakas, even if we emphasize the "almost." Nor can we say with *Charpentier* (ZDMG 66, 1912, pp. 41 f.) that "in general" the Jātaka prose rests on ancient tradition, but only that this is sometimes the case. *Charpentier* (WZKM 27, 1913, pp. 92 f.) repeats his opinion, though without putting forward any new grounds.

epics, or epic fragments. In the latter two cases, the prose in the book is again a superfluous commentary, and mostly spiritless into the bargain.

As regards the contents, we find in the Jātakas: 1. Fables, most of which, like Indian fables in general, aim at teaching Nīti, *i.e.* worldly wisdom. Only a few of them have the moral tendency as evinced in the ascetic poetry, and only a very few are genuinely Buddhist. 2. Fairy tales, including many animal fairy tales, almost entirely in the style of the European popular fairy tales, and without the remotest reference to Buddhism. Only in a few cases have they been furnished with a Buddhist tendency, so to speak "Buddhistised," and some few may also be purely Buddhist inventions. 3. Short anecdotes, humorous tales and jokes, which have nothing Buddhist about them. 4. Novels and even long romances abounding in adventures, and sometimes with a greater or lesser number of narratives within the story. Here, too, there is nothing Buddhist, except that the hero is the Bodhisatta. 5. Moral narratives. 6. Sayings, and 7. Pious legends, all of which are only partly of Buddhist origin, while many of them belong to the common property of Indian ascetic poetry. Thus we can scarcely be much mistaken in saying that far more than one half of all the Jātakas, if we omit the commentary, is not of Buddhist origin. The explanation of this fact lies near at hand. The Buddhist monks were recruited from all classes; hence, there were many among them who were quite familiar with the popular tales and anecdotes of the workers, artisans and especially merchants; others, who knew well the old ballads and heroic songs of the warriors and yet others, who had often heard the sacred legends and myths of the Brahmans and forest hermits. When they became monks, they endeavoured as far as possible to connect these memories with the monkish and purely religious traditions. Now, it is precisely this which makes these Jātakas of so much greater importance in the history of Indian literature. The Buddhist preaching monks crammed into the Jātaka book everything that pleased them and their audience. As in contents and form, so in extent also, the Jātakas are very varied. By the side of short stories which hardly occupy half a printed page, there are extensive compositions of very many pages, some of which could equally well be called independent books.[1]

In the first sections, which contain the shorter Jātakas, we find most of the fables. Here again we meet with the hypocritical cat, which devours the mice, while pretending to be a pious ascetic.[2] Here we also find numerous fables, which recur in other Indian narrative works, Tantrākhyāyika, Pañcatantra, etc., and not a few of those fables of the world's literature whose home is difficult to determine, because they have become equally at home in the East and in the West. How the lion and the bull, the two friends, are separated by the jackal and kill each other, is told in Jātaka No. 349, in agreement with the frame narrative of Book 1 of the Tantrākhyāyika. The Jātaka book has several variants of the delightful story of the monkey which outwits the crocodile, which forms the frame story of Book IV of the Tantrākhyāyika.[3] As in Æsop's fable, the ass in Jātaka No. 189 has clothed himself in a lion's skin, while the Tantrākhyāyika

---

[1]) The numerous allusions in the Jātaka book, of one Jātaka to another, preceding as well as later ones, seems to me to confirm that the single Jātakas were in existence as independent texts long before they were combined to form a large collection. The long Jātakas of the last books, in particular, which in their turn are divided into sections, and to which reference is often made in earlier short Jātakas, were surely originally independent poems. *Cf. J. Dutoit*, Jātakazitate in den Jātakatexten, in Festschrift Kuhn, 345 ff.

[2]) Jāt. No. 128. The verse: "If one constantly raises aloft the banner of religion, like the raised sign of an inn, but sins in secret, it is called a cat's vow," agrees literally with Mahābh. V, 160, 13, and has also found its way into the law books (Manu IV, 195; Viṣṇu 93, 8). *Cf.* above, Vol. I, p. 406.

[3]) Nos. 57, 208. *Benfey*, Pantschatantra I, 420 ff. This fable has also been found among the Suahelis in Africa, s. R. *Köhler*, GGA., 1870, p. 1658; Kleinere Schriften, I, 515, and *Franke*, WZKM., 7, 1893, 215 f., 384 f. The frame-story of Book II of the Tantrākhyāyika, too, has a parallel in Jāt. No. 206, and there is a very beautiful relief of this on the Bharhut Stūpa (Cunningham, Pl. 27, Fig. 9).

gives him a panther's skin, and the Pañcatantra and Hitopadeśa a tiger's skin. Other well-known fables are those of the jackal which praises the crow's beautiful voice, and thereby gains some nice fruit ;[1] of the ox, which envies the pig on account of its good food, until he hears that the pig is being fattened only for the slaughter ;[2] of the cunning crane or ibis which pretends to lead the fishes into pleasant waters, but devours them all, until at last he receives his well merited punishment from the crab ;[3] of the parrot which is to watch over the chastity of a frivolous wife, and is killed by her for its indiscretion.[4] The fable of the dancing peacock which, by its impudent dance, forfeits its bride, the daughter of the bird-king,[5] is an ancient one. As the fable was already represented on a relief of the Stūpa of Bharhut in the 3rd century B.C., it must already at that time have been a Jātaka. Another relief on the same Stūpa is an

---

[1]) Jāt. No. 294. In No. 295 it is, conversely, the crow which flatters the jackal, thereby obtaining a morsel of ox carrion. In *La Fontaine*, Fables, I, 2, the fox praises the raven's beautiful voice, and thus obtains the cheese.

[2]) Jāt. No. 30, variant No. 286; *Benfey*, Pantschatantra I, 228 f. I. *Scheftelowitz* in ZB., VII, 1926, pp. 284 f.

[3]) Jāt. 38. *Benfey*, Pantschatantra I, 174 ff. ; Tantrākhyāyika I, 5; *La Fontaine*, Fables, X, 4. A gypsy version ZDMG. 42, 122 f.

[4]) Jāt. No. 198 (*cf.* No. 145); recurs in "Arabian Nights," "Gesta Romanorum," "Sindbad," and in *Chaucer* (Wife of Bath I, 231). *Cf.* JRAS., 1890, p. 504.

[5]) Jāt. No. 32. The fable seems to have migrated very early *viâ* Persia to Greece, where Herodotus (VI, 130) wove it into the history of Hippokleides. The hypothesis of C. H. *Tawney* (Journal of Philology XII, 1883, p. 121) that the story was brought to India by the Greeks when they ruled in Bactria, seems to me improbable, because it is more feasible for a fable to be transferred to human conditions, than for a fable to be made out of an anecdote. Moreover, the peacock, which, when it dances, bares its hind-quarters, is proverbially known in India as the type of shamelessness. Cf. *Böhtlingk*, Indische Sprüche No. 5233; *Benfey*, Pantschatantra, I, 280; J. G. V. *Hahn*, Sagwissenschaftliche Studien, Jena 1876, p. 69. S. J. *Warren*, in "Hermes," Vol. 29, 1894, pp. 476 f. says : "The details of the story as told by Herodotus are so exceptional, they are so reminiscent of an Indian svayamvara, where the maiden or the father selects a husband from among the assembled suitors, that one would assume Oriental origin, were it not for the fact that Herodotus narrated it all with such convincing certainty as if it had actually taken place."

illustration to Jātaka No. 383, which relates in four verses, how the cat, by flattering the cock and promising to be his submissive wife, endeavours to get him into her power. But the cock sees through her cunning, and drives her away. In three verses, the genuinely Buddhist doctrine is extracted from it: like the cat, so do crafty women act, when they want to seduce men, but the sage is equal to them, as the cock was equal to the cat. One of the few fables decidedly Buddhist in origin, is No. 278. Here the Bodhisatta is reborn as a buffalo, and as such exhibits unbounded patience: an impertinent monkey climbs on his back, befouls him, seizes him by the horns and does all kinds of mischief to him. Then the monkey does the same to another buffalo and is killed by him. In this way, as the prose commentary expressly says, the Bodhisatta preserves his virtue of patience, and yet the monkey is punished.[1]

Closely related to the fable is the animal fairy tale, a few beautiful examples of which are to be found in the Jātaka book. There is delightful humour in the story of the jackal All-tooth (Sabbadāṭha):

This jackal uses a magic spell, which he has heard accidentally, for making all four-footed creatures subject to him. In his arrogance he decides to go to war against the King of Benares. A lion had to stand on the backs of two elephants, and on the back of the former the jackal seated himself with the female jackal whom he had made his first queen, and thus, with great pomp, he marched towards the city of Benares. Impudently he challenges the king to yield his kingdom; all are in great terror, but through the cunning of the domestic priest (who is the Bodhisatta) the jackal with his animal host is annihilated. Then the people of Benares rush out of the city gate, in order to fetch meat, which, in a most un-Buddhistic manner, the Bodhisatta has told them to do, and what they cannot eat they dry. "At that time," thus concludes the

---

1) This Jātaka is represented in a fresco in a cave-temple of Ajantā, s. John *Griffiths*, The Paintings in the Buddhist Cave-Temples of Ajantā, London 1896, I, 12f., Fig. 27, p. 18.

Jātaka, in the true manner of the genuine animal fairy tales, "the drying of meat is supposed to have originated."[1]

More numerous than the purely animal fairy tales are the fairy tales of animals and human beings, in which the animals, as a rule, cut a better figure than the people, as, in the fairy tale of the wise partridge, which has learned the Vedas from a celebrated teacher. Many youths come to it in order to learn. The lion and the tiger are among its friends. It lives in a golden cage and is guarded by a lizard. One day there comes a wicked ascetic who has an interesting past career (he was formerly a porter, a hawker, a juggler, a hunter, a fencer, a bird-catcher, corn-measurer, dice-player and hangman's assistant), kills the young of the lizard and also the partridge, and, as a punishment, is torn to pieces by the tiger.[2] This class includes more especially those fairy tales, so widespread in universal literature, of grateful animals and ungrateful man, of which there are several in our collection. One of the prettiest is No. 73:[3]

There was once a king who had a wicked son, called Prince Rascal. He was like a poisonous snake, never spoke a pleasant word to anyone, and was "like grit in the eye." Once when he wishes to bathe during a great storm, the people bring him out into the river in order to let him drown. But he escapes on to a tree trunk in company with a snake, a rat and a parrot. All the four are pulled out of the water by an ascetic and taken home, where the pious man first attends to the animals as being the weaker, and only then attends to the prince. The latter is enraged at this. All the three animals promise the ascetic to prove their gratitude to him; so also does the prince, while, internally he vows vengeance on him. After some time the ascetic wishes to put the rescued ones to a

---

[1]) No. 241. Translated and discussed by A. *Grünwedel*, Buddhistische Kunst in Indien, 2nd Ed., Berlin, 1900, pp. 53 ff.

[2]) No. 438. Cf. E. *Windisch* in Gurupūjākaumudī, pp. 64 ff and *Fick*, Soziale Gliederung, etc., p. 198 (Social Organisation in North-East India, p. 301 f.).

[3]) See also Nos. 482 and 516. Cf. *Benfey*, Pantschatantra I, 193 ff. (where also the versions of Rasavāhinī, Chap. 3, and the Tibetan Karmaśataka are translated), 286, 608; II, 128 ff., Kathāsaritsāgara, 65, 45 ff.

test. The three animals immediately prove their gratitude, but the prince, who has meanwhile become king, causes the ascetic, as soon as he recognises him, to be whipped, and wants to have him executed. At every stroke of the whip the latter utters the verse:

> "True is the proverb which says: A log of wood,
> Washed up by the water, is better than many a man."

Questioned by the people regarding what he is saying, he relates the story. Thereupon all the people assemble and seize the tyrant, beat him to death, and crown the ascetic as king in his place.

The fairy tales of universal literature include also that of the ungrateful wife:

A man had once saved the life of his wife by giving her his own blood to drink. She, however, falls in love with a wretched cripple. In order to be able to belong entirely to the latter, she pushes her husband down from a hill. He is saved by a lizard, however, and in a strange way becomes king, in which capacity he has the opportunity of seeing his unfaithful wife again with her cripple lover, and of punishing her.[1]

World-wide circulation has also been attained by the humorously told fairy tale of the king who, by virtue of a spell, understands the language of beasts:

He should not betray the magic spell to any one; otherwise he must die. One day the king laughs at the comical conversation of ants and gnats. The queen enquires the cause of his laughter and importunes her husband to impart the spell to her, though he tells her that this would cause his death. The king is just about to give in to the insistence of his inquisitive wife. Then Sakka, the king of gods, appears in the form of a goat, and advises the king to give his wife a thrashing; then she will give up her request for the spell. The king follows the advice, and the desired effect is produced.[2]

---

1) Jāt. No. 193. Cf. *Benfey*, Pantschatantra I, 436 ff., II, 303 ff.; and Gaston *Paris* in ZVV, XIII, 1903, who traces the story in Oriental and Romance fairy-tale literature; *Chavannes*, Cinq Cents Contes, No. 12.

2) Jāt. No. 386. Similar in the Arabian Nights (cf. Orient und Okzident II, 133 ff.) and Gesta Romanorum (Grässe II, pp. 190 ff.). Regarding this story, so wide-spread in

We are reminded of the German fairy tales of "Table fill thyself," and similar magic things, by the fairy tale of the three brothers; the first of these has a magic axe which he needs to touch in order to obtain fire-wood, the second a drum by whose aid he can conquer all enemies, and the third a whey-pot, out of which, when it is turned, a great stream of whey issues.[1] A similar fairy tale is that of the youth who has wasted his whole fortune, and whose deceased father, reborn as the god Sakka, presents him with a pot which fulfils all wishes, but which he must take great care of, for only so long as the pot exists will he have a sufficiency of money. One day, in his intoxication, the youth repeatedly hurls the pot into the air in order to catch it again, but soon the pot lies smashed on the ground. From that moment his good fortune is at an end; he becomes so poor that finally, as a beggar clothed in rags, he remains lying against a wall and dies.[2]

Although so many fairy tales have found their way from India to the West, yet there can scarcely be any doubt that conversely, many a foreign fairy tale has wandered to India. That is possibly so, for instance, in the case of the mariners' fairy tales, which tell of shipwrecks and all kinds of strange sea-adventures. The female demons (Yakkhinīs), who lure the shipwrecked men and delight them with their love, in order to kill and devour them later, at once recall the Sirens and beings like Circe and Calypso.[3] A weird mixture of

---

the literature of the world, see also *Hertel*, Das Pañcatantra, pp. 284 f.; J. J. *Meyer*, Das Weib im altindischen Epos, 376. *Zachariae* also refers me to *Kuhn*, Barlaam und Josaaph, p. 81; R. *Köhler*, Kl. Schriften II, 610 f.; III, 539; Linguistic Survey of India VIII, 1, pp. 410 f. and others.

[1]) Jāt. No. 186. Cf. *Grimm*, Kinder-und Hausmärchen Nos. 36 and 54.

[2]) M. *Gaster*, JRAS., 1897, pp. 379 f. and Alfred *Forke*, Die indischen Märchen und ihre Bedeutung für die vergleichende Märchenforschung, Berlin 1911, pp. 8 f.; compare with it *Uhland's* well-known ballad "Das Glück von Edenhall."

[3]) Valāhassa-Jātaka, No. 196. The shipwrecked men are rescued by a winged horse (the Bodhisatta). Cf. Divyāvadāna, pp. 120, 524 ff.; Kāraṇḍavyūha, p. 52; Nāyā.

popular fairy tale and moral narrative is the Jātaka of Mittavindaka, who experiences wonderful adventures at sea, enjoys himself with ghostly women in magnificent palaces on islands in the middle of the ocean, and finally, because of his insatiable desire, or, according to a second version, because he ill-treated his mother, goes to a hell, where a wheel with sharp knives unceasingly revolves on his head.[1]

In the fairy tales of man-eating giants too, genuine popular fairy tale motifs mingle with moral tendencies. These cannibal fairy tales are associated with the name of King Kalmāṣapāda, familiar from Brahmanical literature, who became a cannibal through a curse. The real point of the Buddhist narrative however, is that the pious King Sutasoma is caught by the cannibal and again released by him, in order to redeem his promise to a Brahman, but again returns to the monster to be devoured, according to his promise, whereupon the cannibal, touched by such a love of truth, is converted.[2]

---

dhammakahão IX; *Charpentier*, JA., 1910, s. 10, t. XVI, pp. 606, 608; WZKM., 27, 1913, p. 93 Other Mariners' fairy-tales are No. 463 (of clever Suppāraka who, in spite of his blindness, is made first steersman, and bears himself splendidly) and No. 360 (of Garuḍa, who plays at dice with the king and elopes with his wife, with whom the royal singer after he has suffered shipwreck and has been cast on to the island of Garuḍa, later enjoys himself).

[1]) No. 439, with the variants and fragments belonging to it, Nos. 41, 82, 104 and 369. Cf. Kathāsaritsāgara 56, 141 ff. L. *Feer* (JA., 1878, s. 7, t. XI, pp. 360 ff.; 1892, s. 8, t. XX, pp. 185 ff.) has dealt with all the various Pāli and Sanskrit versions of this fairy-tale.

[2]) The numerous Buddhistic versions of this Jātaka No. 537 in Pāli, Sanskrit, Chinese and Tibetan literature, and its fore-runners in the epic-puranic tradition, have been treated in detail by K. *Watanabe*, in JPTS., 1909, pp. 236 ff. Cf. *Charpentier* in WZKM., 23, 1909, p. 161, note 3; 24, 1910, p. 396 note. *Pavolini* (GSAI., 25, 324) also refers to H. *Kern* in Versl. en Meded. der Kon. Akad. van Wetensch., Afd. Letterk. IV, 11, pp. 170 ff. J. S. *Speyer*, and after him R. *Garbe* (Contributions of Buddhism to Christianity, Chicago 1911, pp. 42 ff. and Indien und das Christentum, Tübingen 1914, pp. 101-111) seek to establish a connection between the Christian legend of Saint Christopher and this Jātaka; but the two legends have nothing in common but the conversion of a cannibal giant; the Christian legend bears no trace of the actual nucleus of the Buddhist fairy-tale. See also H. *Günter*, Buddha in der abendländischen Legende? Leipzig 1922, pp. 19 ff.

Superhuman beings of all kinds, snake and bird deities (Nāgas and Garuḍas), Yakkhas, Kinnaras [1] and so on, play a large part in the fairy tales. Some of these Jātakas have been elaborated into long fairy-tale compositions. Jātakas like No. 504, of the pair of Kinnaras who are in deep mourning, because they have been separated for one single night, or No. 485, of the Kinnara woman, who weeps so long for her beloved, who was shot by a king, until, through an elixir of life, he comes to life again, are really lyrico-dramatic fairy-tale compositions, in which the lyrical element prevails. A longer fairy-tale composition in prose and verse with inserted narratives is Jātaka No. 432, where the Bodhisatta is reborn as the son of a horse-headed man-eating Yakkha woman. Jātaka No. 543, which betrays itself as having been originally an independent work by its being divided into 8 sections (Khaṇḍas), is a long composition, of a mixture of prose and verse, dealing with the world of the Nāgas and Garuḍas, a strange mixture of popular fairy tale motifs and Buddhist dogmatics. The Vidhurapaṇḍita Jātaka,[2] the hero of which is the wise Vidhura, the minister of the Kuru king, is a real epic in 6 sections (Khaṇḍas) This Vidhura, who recurs several times in the Jātaka book, is none other than Vidura, known to us from the Mahābhārata, the half-brother and wise counsellor of Dhṛtarāṣṭra, who already in the epic appears as a knower of fables, parables and wise sayings.[3] Through this name, as well as the lifelike description of a game of dice, this Jātaka is in some way related to

[1]) Kinnaras are semi-human winged beings. Regarding the representation of them in Buddhist painting and sculpture, see *Grünwedel*, Buddhist. Kunst in Indien, pp. 44 ff.

[2]) Jātaka No. 545. English translation by Cowell and Rouse, Vol. VI, pp. 126-156. R. F. *St. Andrew St. John*, JRAS., 1896, 441-475, has translated the Jātaka according to a slightly diverging Burman version. It is also to be found in the Chinese Tripiṭaka, s. *Chavannes*, Cinq Cents Contes, III, p. 100.

[3]) Cf. above, Vol. I, pp. 323, 406, 408, 425, 472. We meet with Vidhura also in Theragāthā 1188 and Majjhimanikāya, 50.

the Mahābhārata, and is therefore of especial interest. Even taken on its own merits, however, it is an epic fairy tale composition of no slight poetic value.

The numerous short and often very witty anecdotes of the Jātaka book, have originally even less connection with Buddhism than the fables and fairy tales have. The ancient Indians were just as fond of laughing at all kinds of fooleries as we are of laughing at the silly tricks of the "wise men of Gotham," and the like. This is proved by narratives such as that of the son who, wishing to kill a mosquito on the head of his sleeping father, shatters the father's skull ;[1] or of the monkeys who are to water the trees, and do this by pulling up every tree by the roots, in order to see which requires more water and which less.[2] The fool is not infrequently a priest or a monk. Thus a Brahman mendicant monk comes to a place where two rams are fighting each other. As he sees the one ram jumping backwards before him, he imagines that the ram knows good manners, and wants to honour him. A merchant warns him that the ram is only taking a run prior to attack ; but already the animal comes running forward and knocks the monk over, who cries out lamentingly : "Help ! a saint is being murdered.[3] There is grim humour in the story of the wicked king Mahāpiṅgala (No. 240) :

This king was a great tyrant. When he died, the whole of Benares rejoiced—only the doorkeeper weeps. The Bodhisatta asks him the reason, and he replies : " I am not weeping because Mahāpiṅgala is dead, for every time he came down from the palace or went up, he gave me eight blows on the head, as with a sledge-hammer. Now I am afraid that, when he is in

[1]) Jāt. No. 44, with variant No. 45. Cf. *Benfey*, Pantschatantra I, 283, 292 f. ; II, 154 ff. ; *La Fontaine*, Fables VIII, 10.

[2]) Jāt. No. 46, illustrated on the stūpa of Bharhut.

[3]) Jāt. No. 324. A coarse joke, in which the avarice of the Brahmans is ridiculed, is to be found in Jātaka No. 113. The fact that it is not everyone who can profit by good advice, is discovered by an over-wise ascetic at his own cost, in Jāt. No. 376.

the other world, he will do the same to Yama, and Yama will send him back to earth, and then I will get my eight blows of the fist again, therefore I am weeping." The Bodhisatta consoles him: "The dead man will not return, he has been thoroughly burnt, the pyre has been extinguished with water, and the earth round about it has been well replaced."

Highly sarcastic is the anecdote of the monkey, who has stayed for some time in the palace of a king, who then sets him free. When he reaches his companions again, they surround him and wish to know how things go on in the world of human beings, of whose daily life he must have seen a great deal. The monkey describes the life of man in two verses:

"'The gold is mine, the precious gold!' so cry they, night and day:
These foolish folk cast never a look upon the holy way.
There are two masters in the house; one has no beard to wear,
But has long breasts, ears pierced with holes, and goes with plaited hair;
His price is told in countless gold; he plagues all people there."[1]

Then the monkeys do not want to hear any more, they cover their ears and run away. (Jāt. No. 219.) Remarkable on account of its relation to Greek literature, is the anecdote of the woman whose husband, son and brother are to be executed, and who is offered by the king the choice of the life of one of her three relatives. She decides for the brother, giving as a reason that she could easily obtain a husband and a son, but could never again obtain a brother. The same anecdote is told by Herodotus of the wife of Intaphernes, and Sophocles lets Antigone argue in the same way. The same idea recurs in India in the Rāmāyaṇa, in connection with an old Indian proverb which says that one can have everything in the world more easily than a real brother. The anecdote, therefore, is very old in India as well as in Greece; but it is just as little characteristically Indian as specifically Greek, so that it can hardly be determined where its actual home is to be found.

[1]) Translated by W. H. D. *Rouse*,

Only it seems certain to me that it could not have originated twice.[1]

This anecdote belongs to a class of narratives, which are just as popular in the narrative literature of all peoples, as those of foolish tricks, namely the narratives of ultra cleverness or skill, which finds expression in clever answers, especially answers to riddles, or in the skilful accomplishment of difficult tasks, or in wise judgments or in the accomplishment of wonderful works of art. We find numerous narratives of this kind in the Jātaka book, and many of them belong to universal literature. One of these, for instance, is the story of the wise judge, who gives all kinds of "Solomon-like" judgments, whereby he rescues a poor fellow—who unintentionally lames a horse, and causes a pregnant woman to have an abortion, and so on—and at the same time answers several riddles put by animals and men.[2] An artist, who can turn his hand to anything, is the hero of the charming Kusajātaka (No. 531):

Kusa, the son of King Okkāka, is as ugly as he is clever and wise. As he wishes to marry, he makes a most beautiful image of a woman in gold, and declares that he will only marry a girl who is as beautiful as the golden image. The image is taken from town to town, and at last Pabhāvatī, the daughter of the Madda king is discovered, who is as beautiful as the image. She is given in marriage to Kusa. Owing to the prince's ugliness, however, the queen-mother makes the condition that the married couple shall, till the conception, meet only at night. However, they cannot overcome the desire to see each other, and by various means they at

[1]) Jāt. No. 67. Cf. Herodotus, III, 119. Sophocles, Antigone, 909 to 912. *Pischel*, in Hermes, Vol. 28, 1893, 465 ff., believes that the anecdote is of Indian origin; Th. *Noeldeke*, in the same journal, Vol. 29, 1894, 155 f., is in favour of Persian origin; R. O. *Franke*, Theolog. Literaturzeitung, 1914, p. 166, is for Perso-Indian, Ind C. H. *Tawney*, Ind. Ant. X, 1881, 370 f., for Greek origin.

[2]) Jāt. No. 257, translated in German verse by *J. J. Meyer*, Kāvyasaṃgraha, pp. 46 ff. The same story is retold after the Tibetan Dsanglun by *Benfey*, Pantschatantra, I, 393 ff., and traced through universal literature down to Shakespeare's "Merchant of Venice." Cf. also *Tawney* in Journal of Philology, XII, 1883, 112 ff.

last succeed in seeing each other, which results in the princess's return to her parents, because she cannot bear such an ugly husband. But Kusa is filled with longing for his wife, and determines to win her back at all costs. He sets out on the journey to Sāgala, where the princess is staying. There he attracts the king's attention, first as a musician, by his beautiful lute-playing, then as a potter by marvellously formed figures, next as a basket-maker by valuable fans, again as a gardener by a magnificent garland, and finally as a cook by preparing a bone in such a way that a pleasant fragrance is diffused through the whole town ; he succeeds in coming into the presence of the princess, but is each time repulsed by her with scorn and contempt. Then Sakka sends seven kings who court Pabhāvatī, and King Madda is in great perplexity ; for if he were to give his daughter in marriage to one of the kings, the others would make war on him. Therefore he explains to the princess that he will have her cut into seven pieces, in order to give each of the seven kings a piece of her. In her terror she flees to Kusa, who is staying in the palace as a cook, and throws herself at his feet on the dirty floor of the kitchen. Kusa, the artist, now proves himself to be a great hero also. In the twinkling of an eye he conquers all the seven kings and captures them ; but as he is just as good as he is clever, he causes the king to give them his seven unmarried daughters in marriage. He himself returns home with his newly-recovered Pabhāvatī.[1]

In a shorter narrative the Bodhisatta is a master of the smith's craft, and obtains in marriage, the beautiful daughter of a smith, by fashioning a marvellous needle, enclosed in such a fine case, that the smiths of the village take the case to be the needle.[2] The Mahā-Ummagga Jātaka (No. 546) is, as it were, a reservoir of such stories of extraordinary cleverness and art. This is a lengthy romance in which numerous anecdotes, riddles and narratives are included, truly a popular book such as we still find in India to-day, which is of especial interest because it exhibits points of contact with

[1]) A Singhalese version of this tale has been translated into English by Th. *Steele*, An Eastern Love Story, London, 1871.

[2]) Jāt. No. 387. In a Chinese version of the story, the artistic smith makes such fine needles that they float on the water, similarly in the Sanskrit Divyāvadāna. *Cf.* A. *Schiefner*, Indische Künstleranekdoten, Mélanges asiatiques, VII (1875), pp. 519 ff.

the stories of the wise Ahiqār (Haikar or Heykar in the "Arabian Nights" and with the "Life of Æsop" of Planudes.[1]

The hero of this Jātaka is Mahosadha, who already as a boy, gives proof of great wisdom, and especially proves himself to be a clever judge. Thus, like King Solomon, he determines to which of two quarrelling women the child belongs, by allowing mother-love to decide. He draws a line on the ground and lays the child in the middle, ordering the one woman to pull the child by the hands and the other by the feet, so that it shall belong to the one who pulls it over the line to herself. They begin to pull and the child cries. Then the real mother lets go of the child, whereby the dispute is, of course, settled.[2] Whatever riddles and puzzling tasks the king may wish to have solved, Mahosadha is never at a loss. By laying a pole in the water and seeing which is the heavier end, he determines where the root and where the top of the tree was, out of which the pole has been made. Like a modern anthropologist, by observation of the sutures, he distinguishes between a male and female skull. He can also distinguish male from female snakes. When the king requires to have sent to him a white bullock with horns on its legs and a hump on its head, which raises its voice after three notes, nobody except Mahosadha knows that the king wants a white cock. The king commands that cooked rice shall be brought to him under the following conditions: it must be cooked without rice, without water, without a pot, without a stove, without fire and without fire-wood, and may not be carried across the street either by a man or a woman. Mahosadha accomplishes this also. The king asks for a string

1) Cf. *Benfey*, Kleine Schriften II, 192 ff. and B. *Meissner*, ZDMG 48, 174 ff.; V. *Jagic* and E. *Kuhn* in Byzantin. Zeitschr. I, 1892, 107 ff., 127 ff.; Th. *Zachariae*, ZVV 17, 1907, 174 ff. (cf. 16, 139; 145); WZKM 26, 1912, pp. 418 ff.; 30, 151 ff.; Kleine Schriften, Bonn und Leipzig 1920, pp. 55 ff.; M. *Bloomfield*, JAOS 36, 1916, pp. 65 ff.

2) This "Solomon's judgment" forms the nucleus of the Chinese play "Hoei-lan-ki or the chalk circle." It may be regarded as certain that this anecdote and the Judgment of Solomon in I. Kings 3, 16-28, could not have originated independently of each other. A. *Weber*, Indische Streifen III, p. 60, regards it as ont of the question that the Jews had borrowed it from the Indians, similarly *Garbe*, Contributions of Buddhism to Christianity, Chicago 1911, p. 12, note 16. On the other hand, Hugo *Cressmann* (Deutsche Rundschau, Vol. 33, 1907, pp. 212 ff.) has adduced very good reasons in favour of its Indian origin. Cf. also Th. *Benfey*, Kleine Schriften II, 170 f.; R. *Köhler*, Kleinere Schriften I, 531 ff.; H. *Gaidoz*, Mélusine, t. IV; R. *Engelmann* in Hermes, Vol. 39, 1904, 148 f.; T. W. *Rhys Davids*, Buddh. Birth Stories, p. xliv ff; *Zachariae*, Kleine Schriften, pp. 150 ff.

of sand for his swing. Mahosadha declares himself prepared to produce this, only he requests a sample of the old string of sand, in order to make it of the same thickness and length. He can also discover the thoughts of animals, *e.g.*, of a chameleon. The wise Mahosadha, who, through his displays of wisdom, has succeeded in becoming one of the king's counsellors, also chooses for his wife a supremely clever maiden,[1] who understands all his riddles. In an extremely clever manner, she manages the ministers who try to set traps for her and are jealous of Mahosadha. Mahosadha also shows himself to be a wise political counsellor in the fight against external enemies, and finally proves himself a splendid master-builder also, who builds a tunnel whose description reminds us of the most artistic Indian cave structures, such as those of Ajanta.[2]

The remarkable romance, which is, indeed, an independent book in itself,[3] concludes with a glorification of Mahosadha who, of course, is the Bodhisatta. Apart from the fact that it is as the Bodhisatta that Mahosadha possesses his great wisdom and skilfulness, there is nothing Buddhistic in the whole of the long romance.

Neither is there much that is Buddhistic to be found in the robber tales and other narratives of the Jātaka book, in which robbers, vagabonds, dice players and courtesans are the chief characters. All these narratives are very interesting from the point of view of the history of civilisation. The Bodhisatta himself is twice a highwayman.[4] One of these stories relates how, through a magic spell, a Brahman causes a

[1]) Cf. *Benfey*, Kleine Schriften II, 156-223; "Die kluge Dirne, die indischen Märchen von den klugen Rätsellösern und ihre verbreitung über Asien und Europa" and R. *Köhler*, Kleinere Schriften I, 445 ff.

[2]) In any case the description presupposes that really magnificent subterranean buildings were familiar to the narrator.

[3]) A Tibetan version, enlarged and deteriorated, of this Jātaka is given from the Kandjur by A. *Schiefner*, Indische Erzählungen (Mélanges Asiatiques, VII, 1876, 673 ff.). The Singhalese version: Ummagga Jātaka (The Story of the Tunnel) translated from the Singhalese by J. B *Yatawara*, London 1912, was not accessible to me.

[4]) Jāt. Nos. 279 and 318, cf. Nos. 419, 91, 193, 360. We hear of organised robber bands, and of entire robber villages. Cf. R. *Fick*, Social Organisation in North-East India, p. 274, and J. J. *Meyer* in the Introduction to his German translation of Daṇḍin's Daśakumāra-Carita, pp. 14 ff., 82 ff.

shower of precious stones to fall, how, for the sake of the treasure thus obtained, two gangs of robbers begin to fight and kill each other, so that only two remain, and how these two also, each wishing to have the sole possession of the treasure, kill each other—exactly like the rogues in *Chaucer's* "Pardoner's Tale."[1] Great is the number of stories that deal with the wickedness of women, a subject which is so inexhaustible to Indians. A whole cycle of such stories is to be found in Jātakas Nos. 61-66, while the Kuṇāla-Jātaka (No. 536) combines in one frame a whole collection of stories and sayings on the same subject. In endless variety, by ever new, sometimes extremely subtle stories, it is attempted to prove that every woman is inclined to conjugal infidelity provided a seducer is available. An especially subtle story is that of the Brahman who, in order to be quite sure, has a girl brought up in his house from the moment of her birth, and after she has grown up and has become his wife, has her strictly guarded in a tower surrounded by seven ramparts, but is, after all, deceived by her in the end; she, however, denies her infidelity, and even subjects herself to an ordeal, which she cleverly forges.[2] In the Kuṇāla-Jātaka, we find, among others, the story of Kaṇhā (*i.e.*, Kṛṣṇā or Draupadī), who, not content with her five husbands, commits adultery with a hunchbacked dwarf, which causes the Pāṇḍavas to renounce the world and retire to the Himālaya.[3] This Jātaka, the greater part of which is merely a sermon on the

[1]) Jāt. No. 48. Cf. R. *Morris* in Contemporary Review, May 1881; C. H. *Tawney* in Journal of Philology, XII, 1883, 203 ff.

[2]) Jāt. No. 62, translated and discussed by *Pischel* in "Philolog. Abhandlungen Martin Hertz zum 70. Geburtstag," Berlin 1888, pp. 74 ff. Cf. *Chavannes*, Cinq Cents Contes, Vol. I, No. 116, and J. J. *Meyer*, Isoldes Gottesurteil, Berlin 1914, pp. 112 ff.

[3]) Cf. above Vol. I, p. 472. The composition of the Kuṇāla-Jātaka is very confused, "Stories of the present" and "Stories of the past" being jumbled together, and the style, which is, in part, veritable ornate prose with very long compound words, is most peculiar, and reminds us of such works as the Divyāvadāna. Cf. *Oldenberg* in JPTS 1910-1912, p. 26, note 3.

wickedness of woman-kind, attributed to Buddha himself, also abounds in sayings against women, of which we may quote a few especially characteristic ones :

" Like poisoned draught or robber fell, crooked as horn of stag,
Like serpent evil-tongued are they, as merchant apt to brag.

" Murderous as covered pit, like Hell's insatiate maw are they,
As goblin greedy or like Death that carries all away."

" Women like flames devour their prey,
Women like floods sweep all away,
Women are pests, like thorns are they,
Women for gold oft go astray." [1]

Such stories, which were at all times immensely popular in India, could, of course, easily have a "Buddhistic" tendency tacked on to them, and be incorporated in Buddhist sermons. For it was only grist to the monks' mill, if, by such narratives, they could prove what a snare and danger every woman is to man, and how very carefully one must protect oneself against these temptresses.

Thus these often very immoral tales form the transition to the moral tales of the Jātaka book. Jātaka No. 527 [2] is a long moral story in the form of a ballad, which is so extremely dramatic that one could well imagine it as a short drama.

A prince catches sight of the wondrously beautiful wife of his commander-in-chief Ahipāraka, and falls passionately in love with her. But when he hears that she belongs to another, she is unattainable to him. In a melancholy, tender lamentation he gives expression to his feelings. Ahipāraka, though he loves his wife dearly, is prepared to yield her to the king, as he fears for the health of the latter. But the king refuses to commit a sin. In a most excellent, extremely dramatic dialogue, the king

[1]) Translated by H. T. *Francis.*

[2]) Ummadantī-Jātaka, cf. *Zachariae*, Bezz. Beitr. 4, 275 ff.

and his commander-in-chief vie with each other in nobility. Virtue finally triumphs, and the king renounces.

Some of the moral tales (as well as some of the fables) have an avowed pedagogical aim, and look as though they had been composed for children. Of this kind, for instance, is No. 484, of the Bodhisatta as a wise parrot, which not only eats rice from the field, but also carries some away in his beak, and in answer to the enquiry for his reason for doing this, replies : " I pay a debt, I give a loan, I lay down a treasure," meaning that he brings food to his old parents, nourishes his young ones, and gives food to other weak birds.

The " Consolatory stories," with a few of which we have already met in the Mahābhārata, are a kind of moral narratives.[1] The subject of but two such stories shall be given here :

No. 352. A man is inconsolable at the death of his father. Then the man's son is seen standing in front of a dead ox and giving it grass and water. The man naturally thinks his son has gone mad, but the latter says : " Here are at least still a head, feet and tail, so that the ox might be able to get up again ; but there is no longer either head, hand or foot of my grand-father's, it is you who seem to have lost your senses as you weep continually at his grave." Thereupon the father is comforted.[2]

No. 454. Kaṇha (the Kṛṣṇa of the legend) is inconsolable at the death of his son. Then his brother Ghata pretends to be mad, and runs through the town, crying : " Give me the hare ! " Kaṇha asks him what it is he wants. Ghata replies : " The hare in the moon." Kaṇha shows him that he is asking an impossibility, but Ghata declares that he too is asking an impossibility when he mourns for his son who is long dead, and wants to have him back. These words cure Kaṇha of his paternal grief.[3]

[1]) See above, Vol. I, pp 395 ff., 412 f.

[2]) This is a dialogue between the father and the son in eight verses, the meaning of which is quite clear even without the prose. On the stūpa of Bharhut there is a very beautiful relief (*Cunningham*, Stūpa of Bharhut, Pl. 47, Fig. 3), showing how the youth gives the cow grass to eat, and his father stands behind him. The same story in the Commentary to Petavatthu, s. Bimala Charan *Law*, The Buddhist Conception of Spirits, Calcutta 1923, pp. 21 f.

[3]) This, too, is a ballad in the form of a dialogue. The prose, which contains a deteriorated form of the Kṛṣṇa-legend is only a commentary. Cf. above p. 119 note, 2 and Vol. I, pp. 471 f. No. 372 also is a consolatory story.

The same purpose as these consolatory stories, namely to comfort those who sorrow for the departed, is pursued also by the consolatory verses of Rāma in the Dasaratha Jātaka (No. 461), which were probably taken from an old Rāma-ballad.[1] Apart from the prose commentary, this Jātaka does not really contain any narrative at all, but only moral sayings. In the same way, Jātaka No. 512, for instance, is nothing but a collection of sayings. Though the prose does relate a legend of the origin of the vice of drink, this legend is nothing but a silly commentators' invention. Only the verses are old which, for the edification of a king, describe, in forceful language, the frightful consequences of the drinking of spirituous liquor, verses which will delight the heart of every abstainer. The ironically used refrain "Therefore buy a full jug of this drink" seems, however, to have been taken from an old drinking song. The dialogue between the Kuru-king Yudhiṭṭhila (Yudhiṣṭhira) and his wise counsellor Vidhūra (Vidura) on the question of who is a "true Brahman," which could just as well be in the Suttanipāta,[2] also belongs to gnomic poetry. The commentator associates the Mahāmaṅgala-Jātaka (No. 453) with the Maṅgala-Sutta, but in reality it is a collection of sayings, which do not answer the question "What is the best Maṅgala?" but rather the question "What is happiness?"[3] The sayings are by no means entirely Buddhistic, but correspond more to the Brahmanical ideal of life. Thus also the sayings in Jātaka No. 473 in reply to the question as to how one can recognise a true friend, are not Buddhistic at

[1]) See above, Vol. I, pp. 508 ff. On Chinese-Buddhist versions of the Dasaratha-Jātaka and the Rāma story, see Vol. I, p. 513.

[2]) Jāt. No. 495, translated by *Fick*, Soziale Gliederung, etc., pp. 140 ff. (Social Organisation, etc., pp. 216 ff.), who has also already referred to the Vāseṭṭha-Sutta of the Suttanipāta.

[3]) In the commentary, the "Mahāmaṅgala-Sutta" is mentioned, but not the Khuddakapāṭha or the Suttanipāta, in both of which the Sutta appears. See above, p. 78, note 1, and p. 79.

all, but, on the contrary, resemble those which we find in Sanskrit gnomic poetry.[1]

The greatest bulk in the Jātaka book, especially in the last books, is occupied by legends. Some of these, exactly like some of the dialogues of the Upaniṣads and especially the Itihāsa dialogues of the Mahābhārata,[2] are merely frames for the speeches and sayings. Such is the extremely interesting dialogue in Jātaka No. 544, which is here given in extract :

King Aṅgati of Videha summons his three ministers and asks their advice as to what he should do. Alāta, the commander-in-chief, advises a gay and gallant war. Sunāma declares that a war is not necessary, it is better to enjoy music, dancing and pleasures. Vijaya, however, suggests hearing a pious ascetic or Brahman, and on the advice of Alāta, the king has the naked ascetic Guṇa Kassapa summoned. The latter appears, and proclaims coarsely materialistic doctrines like the following : There is no Karman, there are no ancestors, no parents, no teachers ; all beings are equal, and have their fate fore-ordained ; the giving of presents is of no use, punishment and reward in the Beyond are meaningless. Alāta declares himself in perfect agreement with these doctrines, and says : " I remember my former births : I was a cow-killer, a hunter, I took the life of many beings, and yet I have been born again in a respected family, and am now commander-in-chief." The slave Bījaka, who is present, assents with a sigh : " In a former birth I was good and generous, and yet I have been reborn the son of a courtesan, and am now a slave. I lose my game in the gamble of life, Alāta wins like a skilful player." King Aṅgata is convinced by these speeches, and commences a life of delight, no longer thinks of anything but enjoyments, and lets others rule his kingdom. Then his good and pious daughter Rujā appears, and proclaims the true doctrine : He who associates with bad companions, himself becomes bad. As the ship of a merchant sinks under a too heavy cargo, so the man who has gradually burdened himself with too great a load of sin, sinks into hell. Then she tells about her former births, in which, as a young man, she frivolously seduced women, and afterwards was reborn many times, in the

---

1) *Lüders*, ZDMG 61, 1907, pp. 641 ff., has shown that also many ancient Dharmaśāstra sayings are to be found in the Jātaka book.

2) See above vol. I, pp. 405, 414 ff.

worlds of human beings, animals, and hell, and endured terrible tortures. Then Nārada comes from heaven, and, like Rujā, teaches that there is a Karman, and a Beyond. But the king says : " If there is a Beyond, then lend me five hundred, I will give thee a thousand in the next world." Nārada replies : " I would indeed lend thee the five hundred but who will stand surety to me that thou wilt repay them when thou art in hell? Even in this world one lends money only to one worthy of confidence." Thereupon he gives a detailed description of hell and its torments. He concludes with a simile of the carriage, with which the human body is compared,[1] and finally converts the king.

Jātaka No. 530 is a similar Itihāsa dialogue, which, however, reads more like a passage from an old Purāṇa. Here it is announced to King Brahmadatta that the saint Saṃkicca, his former domestic priest, has come. The king goes to meet him, and asks him what the fate of sinners is in the Beyond. Saṃkicca replies with a sermon, which contains a detailed description of hell. The speeches are the essential part also in the legend of the two friends who were reborn consecutively as Cāṇḍālas, antelopes, sea-eagles, and finally as Citta, the son of a priest, and Sambhūta, the prince (No. 498). In these speeches Citta, recalling his death and former births, praises the ascetic life, and exhorts the king, his old friend, that, if he cannot renounce the world entirely, at least to rule justly, always bearing in mind that he, who is now king, was once poor and humble.[2]

Almost all these legends are in the form, already known to us, of sacred ballads. A large number of these poems tell of kings, who were stimulated to thought by some insignificant event or other, gave up the throne, renounced the world,

---

[1]) With this simile, cf. Ait. Ār. II, 3, 9 ; Śvet. Up. II, 9; Kaṭh. Up. I, 3 ff.; Sanatsujātīya VI ; Anugītā 36.

[2]) This beautiful specimen of the old ascetic poetry has been traced in other versions, including one among the Jains, by E. *Leumann* (in WZKM 5, 1891, 111 ff. and 6, 1892, 1 ff.). Jātaka No. 497, to which *Charpentier* has pointed out a Jain parallel (ZDMG 63, 1909, 171 ff.) also belongs to the ascetic poetry.

and led a quiet contemplative life as hermits[1] in the Himalayas. A king sees a mango tree bereft of its fruits, is thereby reminded of the transitoriness of all earthly things, and renounces the world. Another, by hearing the tinkle of two bangles on a girl's arm, is reminded of the fact that only the solitary man can find peace; a third, seeing vultures fighting for a piece of meat, and tearing one another, learns how contemptible greed is; a fourth, sees how a mad bullock rushes towards a cow and is pierced to death by a second passionate bullock, and learns to despise the desire of love. The result is always the same.[2] The legend of King Makhādeva (No. 9), whom the sight of his first grey hair impels to renounce the world, also belongs to this group. The most beautiful of these poems, however, is the Mahājanaka-Jātaka (No. 539), the hero of which is that wise King Janaka of Videha whom we have already met so frequently in the Upaniṣads and in the Mahābhārata. According to the Jātaka he is supposed to have pronounced his famous utterance: "Though the whole of Mithilā burn, nothing of mine burns,"[3] when the queen showed him the blazing town, in order to persuade him to return. How Janaka arrives at his decision of renouncing the world, how he first stays on the balcony of the palace in deep meditation, but is soon convinced that he must go away into solitude with the earthen begging-bowl instead of the golden coronation bowl, how his wives attempt to hold him back, how he is strengthened more and more in his resolve, how he remains unassailable and finally goes on his solitary way—all this is described with

---

1) In Buddhist dogmatics they are called Pacceka-buddhas, *i.e.* "Enlightened ones, who have attained enlightenment by themselves (without a teacher) and for themselves (not in order to become teachers)."

2) Nos. 408, 529, 539. Cf. P. E. *Pavolini*, sulla leggenda dei quattro Pratyekabuddha, OC XII, Rome 1899, I, 129 ff. and J. *Charpentier*, Studien zur indischen Erzählungslitteratur, I. Paccekabuddha-Geschichten (Uppsala Universitets Årsskrift 1908, Filosofi, Språkvetenskap och hist. vet., 4) Upsala 1908 and ZDMG 66, 1912, pp. 38 ff.

3) See above, Vol. I, pp. 414 f.

such thrilling force, as could only have been inspired by the very deepest conviction, combined with no mean poetical talent.

All these legends belong to that common stock of ancient Indian ascetic poetry from which, as we have seen,[1] many of the most beautiful legend poems in the Mahābhārata and the Purāṇas are culled. It has already been mentioned that the poem of Ṛṣyaśṛṅga (he is called Isisiṅga in Pāli), which belongs to the same literature, recurs in the Jātaka book, and that in the Naḷinikā-Jātaka (No. 526) the older form of the legend has still been preserved.[2] A duplicate of the same legend has been preserved in Jātaka No. 523, where the heavenly nymph Alambusā seduces the young saint Isisiṅga, who has never seen a woman, in the same way as Śāntā seduces Ṛṣyaśṛṅga in the older poem. In the prose introduction to this Jātaka it is related how Isisiṅga was born of an antelope. This introduction must be old, as a Bharhut relief already represents a scene in which a little boy born of an antelope is picked up by an ascetic (the father of Isisiṅga).[3] The Sāma-Jātaka (No. 540), the contents of which are given below, shows points of contact with the tragic story which King Daśaratha tells on his death-bed.[4]

Sāma is a pious hermit boy, who lives in the forest with his blind parents and devotes himself entirely to attending on them. One day, while he is fetching water for them, he is struck by a poisoned arrow which was aimed at him by King Piliyakkha of Benares, in the wantonness

---

[1]) See above, Vol. 1, pp. 320, 405 ff., and M. *Winternitz*, Some Problems of Indian Literature, Calcutta 1925, p. 21 ff.

[2]) See above, Vol. I, pp. 399 ff., 473 note, 520 f., 540.

[3]) *Cunningham*, Stūpa of Bharhut, Pl. 26, Fig. 7.

[4]) Rāmāyaṇa II, 63, 25 ff. Cf. above, Vol. I, p. 483, and *Charpentier*, WZKM 24, 1910, p. 397, note 2; 27, p. 94. *Oldenberg* (NGGW 1918, 456 ff.) has compared the epic tale with the Jātaka as regards style, and has shown that, in the Jātaka, the story is told with greater simplicity and less subtlety than in the Rāmāyaṇa.

of the chase. No curse, no angry word escapes the lips of the youth, but only a woeful lament at the fate of his poor parents, who are now bereft of their support. Remorsefully the king consoles him and promises to undertake the care of his parents. Sāma tells him in which direction his parents' hut lies, and, uttering expressions of thanks, falls unconscious. Filled with bitter remorse, the king bursts into lamentations and is comforted by a forest spirit, who tells him that he will be freed from his heavy guilt, if he goes to Sāma's parents and tends them like a son. Lamenting, the king takes the water pitcher, and goes to the parents' hut. By the footsteps of the approaching king, the old father recognises that it is not the expected son. Piliyakkha tells who he is, and the blind old man welcomes the king with friendly reverence, and offers him water and fruits as gifts of hospitality. The king asks whence he obtains fruits, as he cannot seek them himself, and the old man answers: We have a dear son, young and handsome, it is he who brings us water and fruits. Then the king announces the dreadful news: Your faithful son is dead, I have slain him. Mild, but full of piteous complaint are the words of the father. But the mother bursts into loud lamentations, and cannot understand the gentleness of her husband, who wishes the king no harm. The king comforts the parents, and begs of them to accept him in the place of a son; he will take care of them as Sāma did. But the parents only beseech him to lead them to their son's corpse, which the king does, though reluctantly. Before the corpse the blind parents burst into touching plaints, which however, end with conjurations.[1] The mother says: If it is true that Sāma always lived a virtuous life, then may the poison vanish, and may he stand before us in good health once more. The father repeats the conjuration with reference to his own virtues and those of his wife. The forest spirit also utters a similar conjuration. Then Sāma arises, stands fresh and well before his parents, and bids the astonished king welcome. He declares that he had only fainted; for those who honour their father and mother enjoy even in this world the support of the gods, and after death go to heaven. Then the king seeks Sāma's protection,

---

[1]) Such spells, or Saccakiriyās (literally "confirmations of truth") which consist of a person's referring to his virtue, and thereby performing a miracle, are not rare in the Buddhist legends; we also meet with them in the epic (thus in the Nalopākhyāna, Mahābhārata III, 68) and frequently in the later narrative literature. Cf. E. W. *Burlingame*, JRAS 1917, pp. 429 ff., and N. M. *Penzer*, New Edition of C. H. Tawney's Translation of Kathāsaritsāgara, I, 166 f.; II, 31 ff.; III, 179 ff.

and the latter preaches to him on the virtues which a king should practise.[1]

Exceeding kindness and gentleness, and self-sacrifice transcending by far the bounds of what is natural, characterise those legends whose purely Buddhistic origin is unmistakable. The legend of King Sivi (Sanskrit Śibi), who gives away his eyes, has already been mentioned.[2] Jātaka No. 440 tells of Prince Kaṇha, who gives away everything he possesses, in order to go to the Himālaya as a hermit. Sakka offers to grant the pious hermit his wishes; but he wishes only for calmness, freedom from hatred, desire and lust, and the most truly beautiful of all gifts:

> "If you would grant a boon to me,
> O Sakka, lord of every creature,—
> Let none, Sakka, on my account,
> Be harmed, whether in mind or body,
> At any time or place. This, Sakka,
> This would I choose as boon of boons."[3]

The moral of love for one's enemies is proclaimed in naive manner by the legend (No. 151) of the two kings who meet in a narrow pass. They are both equally just, equally old, equally famous, equally powerful—and the question is, who shall move aside to let the other pass. As the one not only returns good for good, but also good for evil, the precedence is granted to him. Another genuine product of Buddhism is the Khantivādi-Jātaka (No. 313), the Jātaka of the "patience

---

[1]) The legend is already to be found in the 3rd century B. C. on a relief on the Stūpa of Sānchi. A whole series of scenes is represented in the Gandhāra sculptures of Jamālgarhi. Cf. A. *Foucher*, L'art gréco-bouddhique du Gandhāra I, 279 ff.

[2]) See above, Vol. I, p. 409, and *Winternitz*, Some Problems of Indian Literature, p. 38.

[3]) Translated by T. W. *Rhys Davids* in SBE., Vol. 36, p. 310. The verse is quoted in Milindapañha, p. 384 (ed. Trenckner).

preacher," in which the Bodhisatta is whipped and mutilated by an enraged king, but he endures it all with patience, and forbears from any thoughts of revenge.[1] In many of these legends, which we might call "animal legends," the Bodhisatta is a good and noble animal. Here we find legends like that of the self-sacrificing male gazelle, which is prepared to sacrifice its life for the sake of a pregnant gazelle, and then is able to persuade the deeply moved king, not only to spare the herd of gazelles, but to give up hunting altogether;[2] of the hare which throws itself into the fire in order to serve itself as meat to the guest (No. 316);[3] of the monkey-chief, who makes himself into a bridge across the Ganges in order to save his retinue;[4] of the monkey who rescues a man who has fallen into an abyss, and whom this man,

---

1) The frequent occurrence of this legend in Buddhist literature and art bears witness to its great popularity among the Buddhists of all nations. Cf. A. *Attenhofer* in Festschrift Kuhn, pp. 353 ff.

2) Nigrodhamiga-Jātaka (No. 12). The Christian legend of Saint Placidus or Eustachius, who is said to have been converted through a stag, on whose forehead the sign of the cross was shining, is traced back to this Jātaka by some scholars. Cf. M. *Gaster*, JRAS., 1894, 335 ff.; J. S. *Speyer* in Theolog. Tijdskrift 40, 1906, 427ff.; E. *Kuhn* in Beil. Allg. Ztg. 9th Nov. 1906; R. *Garbe*, Contributions of Buddhism to Christianity, p. 30ff.; Indien und das Christentum, pp. 86 ff.; W. *Bousset* in NGGW 1916, 469 ff.; W. *Meyer*, ibidem, pp. 762ff.; *Clemen*, Theolog. Literaturzeitung 42, 1917, 257 ff.; H. *Günter*, Buddha in der abendländischen Legende? Leipzig 1922, pp. 7ff. I am not convinced that there is any connection between them.

3) Just as, in memory of this act of self-sacrifice, Sakka draws a hare in the moon, using a mountain as his pencil, so the Kalmuks have preserved the legend of "Sakimuni" as the "hare in the moon," s. T. W. *Rhys Davids*, Buddhism, London SPCK., 1890, p. 197. The "hare in the moon," however, is not familiar only in India, Tibet, Burma, China and Japan, but also in America. In India the idea is most likely earlier than Buddhism, at least as early as the Śatapatha-Brāhmaṇa XI, 1, 5, 3 and Śvetāśvatara-Upaniṣad II, 11. Cf. *Benfey*, Pantschatantra I, 348 f.; A. *Pfungst*, Aus der indischen Kulturwelt, Stuttgart 1904, pp. 122 ff.; I. *Scheftelowitz*, ZB., VII, 1926, pp. 270 f.; H. *Kunike*, Amerikanische und asiatische Mondbilder (Mythologische Bibliothek VIII, 4, 1916, pp. 24ff.); E. *Seler* in Zeitschrift für Ethnologie, 39, 1907, p. 10. Just as in Tantrākhyāyika III, 3, so in a Hottentot story, the hare appears as a messenger of the moon. Cf. W. H. I. *Bleek*, Reineke Fuchs in Afrika, Weimar 1870, pp. 54 ff.; A Brief Account of Bushman Folklore, London 1875, pp. 9 f.

4) Jāt. No. 407, illustrated on the Stūpa of Bharhut (*Cunningham*, Pl. 33, Fig. 4). H. *Kern* (Gurupūjākaumudī, pp. 98 f.) compares the old Cymric legend from the Mabinogi,

lusting after the flesh of monkeys, wants to kill, on account of which bad deed he is attacked with severe leprosy (No. 516); or the legend of the elephant which directs the lost wanderer to the path out of the forest and presents him with its teeth, whereupon the man, in his avarice, also cuts out the roots of the elephant's teeth, and causes it dreadful pain, but is soon swallowed up by the earth and descends into hell (No. 72).[1] Animal legends like the latter two, make it appear very probable that the above-mentioned tales of grateful animals and ungrateful human beings are all of Buddhist origin.

Probably the most famous, and, in the entire Buddhist world, the most popular of all these legends, is the last one in the Jātaka collection, the Vessantara-Jātaka (No. 547). This is in reality a regular epic, for the prose in it is nothing but a commentary, and it is easy to see how the commentator has done his best to spoil the story in the most spiritless and insipid manner. The hero of this epic, it is true, is not a warrior and conqueror, but a hero of generosity.

Prince Vessantara has taken a vow never to refuse to give anything which might be asked of him: "Should anyone ask me for my heart and eye, my flesh and blood, yea, my whole body, I shall give them up." As without consideration for the welfare of the land, he gives away a wonderful elephant, he is sent into banishment, whither he is followed by his faithful wife Maddī and his two little children. They have previously given everything away. In a four-horse carriage, their last possession, they drive away. Soon, however, they encounter a begging Brahman, to whom Vessantara gives the horses and carriage. On foot they wander on, carrying the children, and at last reach a hermitage in the forest, where they take up their abode. Then Sakka appears in the form of an ugly, wicked Brahman, who demands the children as slaves, and gets them.

---

in which King Bran makes himself into a bridge, over which his army reaches the bank of a river. In this case, however the agreement, though certainly striking, seems to me to be merely accidental.

[1]) The elephant is a general favourite in the animal legends. Cf. *Feer* in JA., 1895, s. 9, t. V, 31 ff., 189 ff. and *Foucher* on the Chaddanta Jātaka (No. 514) in Mélanges Lévi, pp. 231 ff.

Finally he asks for the wife also; Vessantara does not withhold even her from him; then only does Sakka make himself known, and all ends happily.

The legend is related in 786 stanzas with all the prolixity of an epic. The description of Vessantara's departure into banishment recalls vividly that of Rāma in the Rāmāyaṇa. The many and long descriptions of nature, such as the description of the forest and of the hermitage, also remind us of the Rāma epic. The poet lingers with especial pleasure over the story of the giving up of the children, who are treated so cruelly by the wicked Brahman, over the plaints of the little ones and the description of the mother's grief, how she seeks her children in vain. No wonder that, at the recitation or representation of these scenes—for in Tibet and Burma the Vessantara legend forms the subject of dramatic representations—the audience are dissolved in tears.[1)]

The hero of the Vessantara-Jātaka, as is general in the purely Buddhistic legends last discussed, is the Bodhisatta of the later dogma, to whom a certain number of "perfections"[2)] are ascribed; he already possesses certain

---

1) We meet with the legend of Vessantara in pictorial representations also. Cf. *Foucher*, L'art gréco-bouddhique, I, 283 ff. The Chinese traveller Song Yun relates that he saw a picture in Shâhbâz-Garhi reproducing the Vessantara legend, and that, whenever they saw this picture, the barbarians shed tears of pity for the pious man who had given away his children to the wicked Brahman. *Chavannes*, Cinq Cents Contes, t. I, p. x. P. *Dahlke* (ZB., I, 1914, p. 9) says: "This Vessantara legend is a favourite decoration in Buddhist temples. I have seen it represented from Ceylon to Cambodia. In the Wesak season it is...produced on the stage of the people's theatres, and never does it fail to produce its effect." R. *Fick* (Festgabe Jacobi, pp. 145 ff.) has compared the various versions of the Vessantara Jātaka, with a view to tracing its original form. He shows that the Jātakamālā probably used an earlier version than that of the Pāli Jātakā. A Soghdian version of the Jātaka has been published by R. *Gauthiot* (JA., 1912, s. 10, t. XIX, pp. 163 ff.).

2) Pārami or Pāramitā, "highest perfection," is the technical expression for the ten (or six) perfections which a Bodhisatta possesses, namely: Generosity, virtue (*i.e.* obedience to the commandments), renunciation of the world, wisdom, energy, patience, truthfulness, determination, friendliness towards all creatures, equanimity. Cf. R. Spence *Hardy*, Manual of Buddhism, 1860, pp. 98, 101 ff.; *Kern*, Manual, p. 66. The expressions pārami, pāramitā do not appear in the earliest texts, or in the Jātaka-Gāthās; but in the

super-human gifts, such as the recollection of former existences, extraordinary physical powers or mental faculties, and so on. This conception of the Bodhisatta as a higher being, generally plays only a secondary part in the texts of the Theravāda sect of the Hīnayāna, whose canon is the Pāli Tipiṭaka, while with the sects of the Mahāyāna, it has been developed all the more fully. It is no accident, therefore, that the Jātakas belong to the Mahāyāna just as much as to the Hīnayāna, and the question could be raised whether their actual native soil was not Mahāyāna Buddhism rather than Hīnayāna. Indeed we find Jātakas in the texts of all Buddhist sects. Most probably they did not originally belong to any sect; but as they were one of the chief media of propaganda, and carried Buddhism into extensive circles, especially the popular Buddhism, in which there could not have been much difference between the sects, they penetrated, along with this Buddhism, deep into the mind of the people. Even at the present day, there is no book so popular among the Buddhist peoples as the Jātaka. The Singhalese still listen the whole night through, to the recitation of the Jātakas without any trace of fatigue, and with unaffected delight. In Burma, too, the Jātakas are and have been for centuries the delight of both learned and unlearned, of monks and laymen alike;[1] and it is the same in every place to which Buddhism has penetrated. A. *Schiefner*[2] has given us an idea of the immense wealth of

---

Jātaka commentary (*e.g.* Nos. 515, 528, 529) it is expressly stated that the Lord told the story with reference to one of the "perfections." In other instances (*e.g.* Nos. 407, 547) the hero is clearly presented as the Bodhisatta endowed with the "perfections." Cf. *Rhys Davids*, JRAS., 1913, pp. 482 f.

[1]) Cf. R. Spence *Hardy*, Manual of Buddhism, London, 1860, p. 101; M. H. *Bode*, Pali Literature of Burma, London, 1909, p. 81.

[2]) Indische Erzählungen, Bulletin de l'Académie Impériale des Sc. de St. Pétersbourg 1876 and 1877 (Mélanges asiatiques, VII and VIII); Mahākātjājana und König Tschaṇḍa-Pradyota, ein Zyklus buddhistischer Erzählungen (Mémoires de l'Académie imp. des Sc. de St Pétersbourg, 1875). Cf. also W. R. S. *Ralston*, Tibetan Tales derived from Indian Sources, London, 1882, and W. W. *Rockhill*, Tibetan Buddhist Birth-Stories, Extracts and Translations from the Kandjur, JAOS. 18, 1897, pp. 1 ff.

Buddhist narratives in Tibetan literature, and Ed. *Chavannes*[1] has enlightened us as to the abundance of Chinese Buddhist narratives. Directly and indirectly the Jātakas have also enriched the literatures of many other peoples, and have therefore been of immense importance in universal literature, even though to-day we no longer believe, with Th. *Benfey*, that the entire fairy tale literature of the world is of Buddhist origin. Nevertheless, however largely the Brahmans, Jains and other sects might have contributed to Indian narrative literature, Buddhism alone pressed forward far beyond the limits of India as a world-religion, thus diffusing Indian civilisation and literature far and wide in all countries of the East and West.[2] On the other hand, it was Buddhism, too, which brought the Indians more than ever before into contact with other peoples; and it is not probable that it was only the Indians who brought their stories to those peoples every time; they, in their turn, must have received narratives from them too, especially from peoples who stood so high, intellectually, as the Greeks, Persians and Semites. In all probability, the Greek artists, who came to India in great crowds after Alexander's campaign and helped to build and ornament so many Buddhist monuments of art, also brought many Greek narratives and motifs to India. This is the more probable, as it is precisely the Jātakas which were in many cases pictorially represented on the Buddhist monuments. For, as the literature, so, Indian and non-Indian art too, was

---

[1]) Cinq Cents Contes et Apologues extraits du Tripiṭaka Chinois et traduit en français, t. I-III, Paris, 1910-1911. We see here that the books which were translated into Chinese in he 5th century A.D. contained numerous Jātakas which also occur in the Jātaka book; but it by no means follows that the Jātakas in question were necessarily translated from this Pāli work or from a Sanskrit collection corresponding to it.

[2]) *Chavannes*, Cinq Cents Contes I, p. xvi, still considers that Buddhism may be called "le plus vaste réceptacle de contes qu'il y ait eu au monde." *Charpentier* (Festschrift Kuhn, pp. 288 ff.) supposes that a collection of Jātakas may have been the source of the Greek Physiologus. H. *Günter*, Buddha in der abendländischen Legende?, pp. 65 ff., raises objections to this theory.

enriched by the Jātakas. They belong to the oldest subjects that were pictorially represented in India, and to-day they are still favourite themes for sculpture and painting in all Buddhist countries. We find them in the 3rd and 2nd centuries B.C. on the stone walls of Bharhut and Sānchi, in the 2nd century A.D. on those of Amarāvatī, and still later in the caves of Ajantā.[1] When the Chinese pilgrim Fa-hien travelled in Ceylon in the year 412 A.D. he saw how, at the festival of the sacred tooth, in Abhayagiri, the king of Ceylon had the five hundred Jātakas represented by figures ranged on either side of the street along which the procession passed, brightly coloured and grandly executed, looking as if they were alive. And Hsüan-Tsang relates of Stūpas seen by him, which had been erected in various parts of India in memory of the deeds of the Bodhisatta as recounted in Jātakas.[2] Many hundreds of reliefs which contain Jātaka illustrations, decorate the temples of Boro-Budur in Java (9th century),[3] of Pagan in Burma (13th century),[4] and of Sukhodaya in Siam (14th century).[5]

The Jātakas are of inestimable value, not only as regards

---

[1]) Besides the works of *Cunningham* and *Maisey*, which have been mentioned above, p. 16, note 3, cf. also A. *Grünwedel*, Buddhistische Kunst in Indien, 2nd. Ed., Berlin 1900, pp. 38 f., 59, and A. *Foucher*, L'art gréco-bouddhique du Gandhāra I, Paris, 1905, pp. 270 ff.

[2]) Cf. J. *Legge*, Record of Buddhistic Kingdoms being an account of the Chinese Monk Fâ-hien of his Travels in India and Ceylon, transl. Oxford, 1886, p. 106; and L. *Feer* in OC XI, Paris, 1897, I, pp. 151 ff.

[3]) A list of the Jātakas represented in Bharhut, Ajantā and Boro-Budur is given by S. d'*Oldenburg*, JRAS., 1896, 623 ff. and JAOS., 18, 1897, pp. 183 ff. The reliefs of Boro-Budur, according to d'*Oldenburg* (*loc. cit.*, p. 196 ff. in which he bases his theory on that of C. *Leemans*, Bôrô-Boudour dans l'île de Java, Leide, 1874) present 34 Jātakas arranged in the order of the Sanskrit work Jātakamālā. See also *Foucher* in BEFEO., IX, 1909, pp. 1 ff.

[4]) The Museum für Völkerkunde at Berlin possesses over a hundred reliefs of the Mangalacheti temple of Pagan. They have been discussed by A. *Grünwedel*, Buddhistische Studien I (Veröffentlichungen aus dem K. Museum für Völkerkunde, V, Berlin 1897).

[5]) L. *Fournereau*, Le Siam ancien, 2ième partie. AMG., Paris, 1908. The order of the pictures is that of the Pāli Jātaka collection.

literature and art, but also from the point of view of the history of civilisation. Though they cannot serve as documents for the social conditions at the time of Buddha, but at the most, for the period of the 3rd century B.C., and for the greater part, especially in their prose, only for the fifth or sixth century A.D., yet so much has remained unchanged in India throughout the centuries, that the picture of civilisation in the Jātakas may nevertheless be regarded as very "ancient." In any case the narratives of the Jātaka book afford us a glimpse into the life of classes of the Indian people, of which other books of Indian literature only rarely give us any information.[1]

The great importance of the Jātaka book in every respect, justifies our having lingered so long over this work, so that we can deal much more briefly with the other books of the Tipiṭaka which are yet to be mentioned.

11. Niddesa,[2] "Explanation," is the title of a commentary, which has already been mentioned, on sections of the Suttanipāta. It consists of the Mahā-Niddesa, the "Great Explanation," containing the commentary on the Aṭṭhakavagga, and the Culla-Niddesa, the "Short Explanation," which explains the Khaggavisāṇa-Sutta (Suttanipāta I, 3) as well as the Pārāyana. The inclusion of this commentary in the canon can certainly be due merely to its great antiquity in comparison to other Pāli commentaries. Indeed, we learn from the Niddesa how the sacred texts were explained at the lessons, in ancient times.[3] Grammatical

---

[1]) For this reason the data concerning the history of social conditions given by R. *Fick* and Mrs. *Rhys Davids* in the works mentioned above, p. 121, note 2, are very valuable even though, in judging them, we shall have to take a different point of view as regards chronology.

[2]) Mahā-Niddesa, ed. by L. de *la Vallée Poussin* and E. J. *Thomas*, PTS. 1916 and 1917; Culla-Niddesa, ed. by W. *Stede*, PTS. 1918. On the relation of this old commentary to Buddhaghosa's commentary, see M. H. B(ode) in JRAS. 1918, pp. 574 ff.

[3]) Cf. E. J. *Thomas*, Ind. Hist. Qu. II, 1926, pp. 495 ff.

and lexical explanations go hand in hand with instruction in the dogma. Important technical expressions are explained with reference to the doctrine, and passages from canonical texts are frequently quoted for this purpose. In order to explain a word, a long list of synonyms is given, and this is repeated every time the same word occurs. It is easy to understand how, in this way, these lists of words were impressed on the memory. Probably they formed the foundation for later dictionaries.

12. The Paṭisambhidāmagga,[1] "the Path to Analysis," consists of three large sections, each containing ten treatises on some important point of Buddhist doctrine. Thus, for instance, I, 1 deals with the 73 kinds of knowledge, among which, to give an example, there is the knowledge of the great pity of the Tathāgata; I, 3 deals with the regulating of the breath as an aid to mindfulness (sati), I, 7 with the Karman, II, 2 with the four noble truths, II, 4 on the love towards all creatures (mettā), III, 2 with the miraculous powers (iddhi) of the saints, and so on. All these subjects are treated in the form of questions and answers, after the fashion of the Abhidhamma texts. The work appears in the Suttapiṭaka, however, and not in the Abhidhammapiṭaka, because, at least in part, its form is that of the Suttas, as some sections begin with introductory stories ("Thus I have heard," etc.) and the address "O monks" (bhikkhave) is to be found here and there, as in the Suttas.[2]

13. Vast as the Jātaka book is, and abundant as are its contents, it does not by any means contain the entire wealth of Buddhist tales. Another narrative work which is just as copious as the Jātaka, though of lesser value from a literary

[1]) Ed. by Arnold C. *Taylor*, PTS. 1905 and 1907. Cf. C. A. F. *Rhys Davids*, JRAS. 1906, pp. 238 ff.

[2]) On archaisms in the text, see *Kosambi* in Ind. Ant. 41, 1912, p. 38 note.

point of view, is[1] the collection of "Apadānas" in the Khuddakanikāya, known as the Apadāna. The word apadāna (Sanskrit avadāna) means "heroic deed, glorious deed," the sense being extended also to glorious deeds of self-sacrifice and piety; and the Apadānas, like the Avadānas which are their counterpart in the Buddhist Sanskrit literature, are "tales of the heroic deeds," *i.e.*, the pious works of the saints (which often consist of very commonplace actions performed in adoration of a Buddha). The Apadānas, too, like the Jātakas, have a "Story of the present" and a "Story of the past." Whereas the Jātakas always describe a previous existence of the Buddha, the Apadānas, as a rule, deal with that of a saint, an Arhat. These stories are, therefore, legends of saints. The collection of Apadānas, written entirely in verse, begins with a Buddhāpadāna, containing a glorification of the Buddhas, of the "innumerable kings of the Dhamma, endowed with the 30 perfections,"[2] and Buddha himself is made to pronounce this glorification. Next comes the Paccekabuddhāpadāna, a glorification of the Paccekabuddhas, who go their solitary way, "like the rhinoceros." The entire "Sutta of the Rhinoceros" (Khaggavisāṇa-Sutta, from Suttanipāta I, 3) is inserted here. The main portion of the work, however, is the Thera-Apadāna, "the Glorious Deeds of the Elders," in 55 sections (vagga) consisting of 10 Apadānas each.[3] The last part is the Therī-Apadāna, "the Glorious Deeds of the Lady Elders," in 4 sections, consisting of 10 Apadānas each.[4] The "glorious deeds" are always related

---

[1]) Ed. by Mary E. *Lilley*, PTS. 1925 and 1927. Cf. L *Feer* in JA. 1883, s. 8, t. I, 406, 433 ff.; E. *Müller* in OC X, Genève 1894, I, 165 ff.; T. W. *Rhys Davids*, ERE., Vol. I, p. 603.

[2]) As each of the 10 Pāramitās or "perfections" is divided into three grades, *i.e.*, ordinary, superior and pre-eminent, there are 30 Pāramitās in all. (R. Spence *Hardy*, Manual of Buddhism, p. 101.)

[3]) Vagga 34 has only 7 Apadānas, hence the total of 547 instead of 550.

[4]) Extracts from the Therī-Apadāna have been published by E. *Müller* in his edition

by the saint in question himself. The first heroes of the Thera-Apadāna are the most famous disciples of Buddha: Sāriputta, the great Moggallāna, the great Kassapa and Anuruddha; side by side with these and other well-known names such as Upāli, Ānanda, Rāhula and Raṭṭhapāla [1] among the Theras, and Mahāpajāpatī Gotamī, Khemā, Paṭācārā. Kisā-Gotamī, and others, among the Therīs, we meet with a far larger number of names, which are only types and not real personages, *e.g.*, the Theras "Dispenser of fans," "Dispenser of clothes," "Dispenser of mangoes," "Worshipper of foot-prints," "Water-worshipper" (*i.e.*, the Thera who worshipped Buddha with a gift of water), Theras who are named after some flower offering, like Kimsukapupphiya, and the like. Most of these legends are made on one and the same plan. First of all the Thera (or Therī) tells of the adoration which he (or she) had offered to one of the previous Buddhas, the predecessors of Gotama Buddha, then he (or she) declares the prophecy uttered by that previous Buddha that he (or she) would hear the doctrine of the future Gotama Buddha, and finally relates how this prophecy has come true, and how he (or she) attained to the dignity of an Arhat. Only few of the Apadānas deviate from this stereotyped plan, for instance the very remarkable Buddhāpadāna (No. 387) with the secondary title Pubbakammapiloti, "the Interweaving of the Previous Deeds," in which the Buddha tells of his previous bad deeds in consequence of which he had to suffer countless reincarnations in hells, and the remains of which deeds caused him many an unpleasant experience even in his last existence.

The Apadāna is certainly one of the very latest works of

---

of the commentary on the Therīgāthā (PTS. 1892). The Apadāna of Mahāpajāpatī Gotamī has been translated into Dutch by Maria E. L. van *Goor*, de buddhistische non, pp. 204 ff.

[1]) The legend of Raṭṭhapāla in the Apadāna, who is familiar to us from the Majjhimanikāya, No. 82, has been compared with that in Buddhaghosa's commentary, by Mabel *Bode* in Mélanges Lévi, pp. 183 ff.

the Khuddakanikāya and of the canon generally, if we are really justified in including it in the canon. At all events, judged by its general character, it is much more closely allied to the Sanskrit Avadānas than to the remaining works of the Pāli Canon.[1] We must leave it to future research to find out, by means of a detailed comparison between the Apadānas and the Buddhist Sanskrit texts,[2] what place they occupy in the chronology of the history of Buddhist literature.

14. One of the shorter books of the Khuddakanikāya is the Buddhavaṃsa.[3] This contains poetical legends of the 24 Buddhas who are supposed to have preceded Gotama Buddha in the last twelve ages of the world (Kalpas). After an introductory chapter, one chapter is dedicated to each of the 24 former Buddhas.[4] In a somewhat dry manner, it is related in the case of each single Buddha, how he set the "wheel of religion" in motion and how—with but trifling differences—the principal events in the life of Gotama Buddha were enacted in the life of each one of the former Buddhas. It is Gotama Buddha himself who is telling the narrative, and

---

1) Not very many instances of actual agreement have been traced so far. Avadānaśataka VIII relates stories of ten holy women, but only three names coincide with those in the Therī-Apadāna. Cf. L. *Feer*, JA, 1884, ser. 8, t. III, p. 32.

2) E. *Müller* (Gurupūjākaumudī, pp. 55 ff.) after comparing the Dīpaṅkara legend in Apadāna No. 486 with the other versions of the same legend, has come to the conclusion that some of the Apadānas are later than the Sanskrit Avadānas. S. *Lévi* (JA, 1908, ser. 10, t. XII, pp. 167 ff.) concludes from the comparison of Therī-Apadāna No. 17, of Mahāpajāpatī Gotamī, with Kumāralāta's Kalpanāmaṇḍitikā ("Sūtrālaṃkāra") No. 68, that the author of the Apadāna must have been familiar with the Sanskrit poem. I am not convinced. As we have a plain story in the Apadāna, and an elaborate one in the Kalpanāmaṇḍitikā, it is just as likely that the last-named work used the raw material, either in the Apadāna or in a Sanskrit version corresponding to it, and created a work of art from it, as that the author of the Apadāna used the work of art, and made a dry extract of it.

3) Edited by R. *Morris*, London, PTS. 1882.

4) On the dogma of the multiplicity of Buddhas, see *Oldenberg*, Buddha, 370 ff. and *Kern*, Manual of Buddhism, 62 ff. Aśoka already mentions in one of his edicts that he had a stūpa of Buddha Konākamana (*i.e.*, Koṇāgamana, the 23rd Buddha of the Buddhavaṃsa) restored (*Bühler*, WZKM, 9, 1895, pp. 175 ff.).

speaking in the first person, he recounts who he himself was under each of the preceding Buddhas,[1] how he worshipped the Buddha, and how his own Buddhahood had been foretold by the Buddha of that time. The only part which is a little more imaginative and poetical, is the second chapter,[2] which deals with Dīpaṅkara, the first Buddha.

Gotama Buddha was at that time a rich Brahman named Sumedha, and he relates in verses (7-27) which are reminiscent of the Theragāthās, how he one day felt disgusted with the world, how he cast off the wretched body, as though it were dirt, and withdrew to a hermitage in the Himālaya. This was precisely the time when the Buddha Dīpaṅkara was carrying on his campaign of conquest throughout the world, and men and gods worshipped him. Sumedha, the hermit, comes too, and at a marshy spot loosens his plaited hair, spreads it out on the dirty ground, with his hempen garment and his cloak of skins, and lies face downwards,[3] inspired with the wish that the exalted Buddha Dīpaṅkara, with his host of disciples, may step over him without having their feet soiled by the mud. Prostrate on the ground, he resolves to become a Buddha one day, and bring salvation to the world. Dīpaṅkara approaches, and prophesies the future greatness of Sumedha. The inhabitants of the ten thousand worlds make a joyful noise, and signs and miracles happen, as is always the case when a future Buddha is foretold. But Sumedha determines to realise in himself all the ten perfections (Pāramitās), in order to fulfil the preliminary conditions of Buddhahood.

Thus this passage is actually a kind of preliminary history to the autobiography which Gotama Buddha later gives

---

[1]) Usually he was a Brahman or a warrior, but once also he was Sakka, the king of the gods, another time a lion, the king of beasts, twice a king of the Nāgas, once a Yakṣa, and several times an ascetic.

[2]) Translated by *Warren*, Buddhism in Translations, pp. 5-31. Translated from the Chinese (Abhiniṣkramaṇa-Sūtra) by S. *Beal* in JRAS 1873, pp. 277 ff. E. *Müller* (Gurupūjākaumudī, pp. 54 ff.) has compared the various versions of the Dīpaṅkara legend.

[3]) This scene has often been depicted on Buddhist monuments, probably it already appeared on the stūpa of Bharhut (S. J. *Fergusson*, Tree and Serpent Worship, Plate L; *Cunningham*, Stūpa of Bharhut, p. 134, No. 38; *Beal*, l.c., and *Ind. Ant.* 11, 1882, p. 146). Cf. *Foucher*, L'art gréco-bouddhique I, 273 ff..; A. *Grünwedel*, Bericht über archäologische Arbeiten in Idikutsari (ABayA 24, I, 1906), p. 90 f.

21

in Chapter 26, briefly summarising in 25 verses the chief events of his last earthly existence. A list of the Buddhas down to Metteyya, the future Buddha, and an account of the distribution of the Buddha relics form the conclusion of the book.

The commentator of the Buddhavaṃsa says that the work was proclaimed and recited by Gotama Buddha himself, and was handed down an uninterrupted line of Theras, to the time of the third Council, and again, since then, passed down an uninterrupted line of teachers and pupils. As the earlier texts are only familiar with 6 predecessors of Gotama, we shall not give credence to these statements of the commentator, but shall be compelled to class the Buddhavaṃsa among the latest productions of canonical Pāli literature. Moreover, it is replete with that Buddha-worship and Buddha-deification, which is foreign to the earliest texts of the Tipiṭaka, but is at its height in the Buddhist Sanskrit literature, especially that of the Mahāyāna.

15. The last book of the Khuddakanikāya is the Cariyāpiṭaka.[1] This is a collection of 35 Jātakas in verse, pursuing the express purpose of showing which Pāramitās or "perfections"[2] the Bodhisatta possessed in various of his previous existences. Each of the first two perfections, those of generosity and virtue, claims a whole chapter, consisting of ten stories each, while Chapter III contains 15 stories as examples of five further Pāramitās.[3] It is Buddha himself who is supposed to tell the stories. He records the event in brief, scanty words, sometimes only hinting so barely that a knowledge of the story is evidently already assumed, in fact,

---

1) Ed. by R. *Morris*, PTS. 1882; ed. in Devanāgarī characters with Introduction by Bimala Charan *Law*, Lahore, 1924.

2) See above, p. 152 and note 2.

3) The concluding verses prove that in reality all the ten Pāramitās were to be illustrated in the Cariyāpiṭaka. Perhaps the three missing ones (wisdom, energy and patience) are supposed to be included with the others, in Chapter III.

to a certain extent, the intention is merely to recall it. Most of the stories are such as appear also in the Jātaka book; but in this work only what is essential to illuminate some Pāramitā is told. Every trace of poetry is wiped away, every touch of humour is avoided, as though intentionally. The stories are often garbled, in order to make them into examples of some "perfection." Compare, for instance, the fable of the crocodile which is tricked by the monkey.[1] In Jātaka No. 208 (as in the Pañcatantra) it is humorously related how the crocodile, whose wife had a craving for a monkey's heart, lies in wait for the monkey, entices it in order to kill it, and is outwitted by the monkey, which says that it has not its heart with it, but has hung it up on a tree by the bank. The version of the same fable in Jātaka No. 57 is somewhat less humorous; but every vestige of humour is eradicated in Cariyāpiṭaka III, 7, where the Buddha relates:

> "When I was a monkey, which lived in a cave on the bank of a river, I was once prevented from going my usual way, because a crocodile threatened me. Just at the place where I was accustomed to take my stand in order to jump to the other bank, sat the murderous enemy, the crocodile, frightful to behold. It said to me: 'Come!' I said to it: 'I come,' and standing on its head, I reached the other bank. I told it no lie, but acted in accordance with my words. In the love of truth nobody is my equal. Such was my highest perfection of truth."

The fable has here shrunk to a meaningless skeleton, and the most important thing about it is the moral, which in this version (as n Jātaka No. 57, where it is also found) is entirely unfitting. In the same way, the Vessantara Jātaka, which, as we have seen, is an epic of 786 verses in the Jātaka book, is, in the Cariyāpiṭaka, I, 9, squeezed into 58 meagre verses, in which all the emphasis is laid on the miracles, such as the quaking of the earth, etc. Only five verses of the Vessantara epic are to be found word for word in the Cariyāpiṭaka also.

---

[1]) See above, p. 126.

As we do not know the Jātaka of the canon in its original form, it is difficult to say anything definite as to the relationship between the Cariyāpiṭaka and the Jātaka. One thing, however, which we do know, is that the doctrine of the Pāramitās does not appear in the earlier portions of the canon, but belongs to a later phase of the cult of Buddha. It is therefore likely that such works as the Cariyāpiṭaka and the Jātakamālā of Buddhist Sanskrit literature belong to the same later stage of development of Buddhism, and are really selections made for the purpose, from the abundant store of Jātaka literature, though perhaps not precisely from the Jātaka of the canon.[1] The Cariyāpiṭaka, however, has not come down to us in its original form, any more than the Jātaka itself. As a matter of fact, in the introduction to the Jātaka book, the Nidāna-Kathā,[2] we find the résumé of a Cariyāpiṭaka, which differs considerably from our text, and most likely represented an earlier recension of the work.[3] It is quite possible that various Jātakas were selected in the various monasteries as examples of the Pāramitās, and that the monks adhered only to a common stock of stories, and to the number 34.[4] At all events the Cariyāpiṭaka, as we have it to-day, is the work of an excellent monk who was anything but a poet, while, among the authors of the Jātakas as we have

---

[1]) There is no justification for the view that there was originally only a small collection of 34 Jātakas, which only later gradually grew into the large collection of 550 stories, in which case the Cariyāpiṭaka would be a résumé of this old Jātaka (Cf. *Pischel*, Leben und Lehre des Buddha, p. 61). Cf. *Oldenberg*, NGGW, 1912, 183 ff.

[2]) Jātaka, ed. *Fausböll*, I, pp. 45-47. *Rhys Davids*, Buddhist Birth Stories, pp. 54 ff.

[3]) *Charpentier* (WZKM 24, 1910, 351 ff.) has shown that the text of the Cariyāpiṭaka as we have it at present, was remodelled under the influence of the Jātaka commentary, and (we may add) deteriorated by it. I do not think it is possible to reconstruct an original Cariyāpiṭaka, as was attempted by *Charpentier* (*l.c.*, *Cf.* WZKM 27, 1913, p. 94).

[4]) The two recensions of the Cariyāpiṭaka have only 21 Jātakas in common with each other, and there are only 12 of these which they share with the Jātakamālā too. The fact that 34 was the original and traditional number, is proved not only by the Jātakamālā, but also by the name or epithet of Buddha Catustriṃśajjātakajña, "knower of the

them in the Jātaka book, there were, besides many a good monk and bad poet, a few distinguished poets also.

Thus we see again and again that the Khuddakanikāya combines books of very different periods, and most probably of different schools also, as well as all sorts of books whose canonical dignity was called into question.

The Abhidhammapiṭaka. Buddhist Scholasticism.

As the word Abhidhamma means "higher religion," or the "higher subtleties of religion," [1] it used sometimes to be translated by "metaphysics." In reality, however, Abhidhamma has nothing to do with metaphysics, and as to philosophy, it has no more and no less connection with it than the Dhamma as taught in the Suttapiṭaka. Indeed, the only difference between the books of the Abhidhammapiṭaka and those of the Suttapiṭaka is that the former are more circumstantial, drier, more learned, in a word, more scholastic. Both treat of the same subject. We shall look in vain for originality and profundity in the Abhidhamma books. Definitions and classifications are their strong point. The definitions, however, valuable as they are for the dictionary and the knowledge of Buddhist terminology, are disappointing in that they only turn on an endless series of synonyms. The classifications, too, however estimable for the attempt at creating a psychological basis of ethics which they contain, are rarely penetrating analyses of psychical processes; much

---

34 Jātakas," in Hemachandra's Abhidhānacintāmaṇi 233, in the commentary of which the old lexicographer Vyāḍi is quoted, who enumerates a list of Jātakas, the majority of which occur in the Jātakamālā. Cf. *Kern*, Manual, p. 66. The hypothesis suggested by some scholars (thus *Rhys Davids*, *l.c.*, p. liii f., but see *Charpentier*, *l.c.*, pp. 406 f.) that it was originally intended to elucidate each Pāramitā by 10 Jātakas, has no foundation whatsoever.

[1]) Buddhaghosa explains the abhi ("higher") in the word "Abhidhamma" as referring, not to the contents, but merely to the more detailed mode of treatment. *Cf. A. C. Taylor*, in JRAS, 1894, pp. 560 f. and *Rhys Davids* in SBE, Vol. 36, p. 237 note.

more frequently they are mere enumerations, unduly protracted, or arbitrarily created or banal categories. As a rule, all this yields nothing but dogmatism, hardly ever is there a trace of any research which could be called scientific. The form of these works is mostly that of questions and answers, after the style of a catechism.

The texts of the Abhidhamma, the beginnings of which are already to be found in the Suttapiṭaka (*e.g.* Majjhimanikāya 137 and 140, and in many of the Suttas of the Aṅguttaranikāya), are probably merely extensions of the Mātikās or "lists," (*viz.*, of the philosophical and ethical conceptions treated in the Suttapiṭaka) which are already mentioned in the Vinayapiṭaka.[1]

Book I of the Abhidhammapiṭaka, the Dhamma-Saṃgaṇi,[2] "Compendium of Dhammas," deals with the classification and definition of the Dhammas, *i.e.*, the psychical conditions and phenomena. Now, as in ancient Buddhism, ethics and psychology are just as inseparable as are philosophy and religion,[3] the English translator of this work, Mrs. Rhys Davids, is quite right in calling it "A Buddhist Manual of Psychological Ethics."[4] In the extremely valuable introduction to her translation,[5] this excellent authority on the philosophy of the Pāli texts, has been successful in her

---

1) The Dhamma-Saṃgaṇi begins with a Mātikā of this nature, and Mrs. *Rhys Davids* (Buddhist Manual of Psychological Ethics, 2nd Ed., pp. ix, cv-cxiii) believes that this one should be regarded as the sole source of the Abhidhammapiṭaka. The Puggalapaññatti and the Dhātukathā, however, also begin with Mātikās. The passages in which Mātikā is mentioned (*e.g.*, dhammadharo vinayadharo mātikādharo paṇḍito, Cullavagga I, 11, 1; XII, 1, 9), indicate that the word does not mean any one definite text, but, as in he case of dhamma and vinaya, a class of texts.

2) Edited by E. *Müller*, PTS. 1885.

3) Cf. Mrs. C. A. F. *Rhys Davids*, Buddhist Psychology, 2nd Ed., London, 1924, p. 138; Buddhist Manual, 2nd Ed., p. xxxviii ff.

4) Translation...of the...Dhamma-Sangaṇi (Compendium of States or Phenomena), on OTF 1900, second edition, 1923.

5) Also in her work "Buddhist Psychology," 2nd Ed., London, 1924. Cf. also A. B. *Keith*, Buddhist Philosophy, pp. 187 ff.

attempt to present the philosophy of ancient Buddhism in its main characteristics, as contained in the doctrine of the Nikāyas, and classified and summarised in this catechism, whose bare structure of enumerations is so difficult of comprehension, and to assign to that philosophy its rightful place in the general history of philosophical thought. It is not the intention of the Dhamma-Saṃgaṇi itself to give any systematic presentation of ethics or psychology; it presupposes a knowledge of the Dhamma, and only claims to be a manual for study for the use of advanced monks. In spite of the fact that it is a purely learned work, and anything but popular, it has been held in great regard in Ceylon. Evidence of this can be found in the report about a king of Ceylon in the 10th century, who had a copy of the work engraved on gold plates studded with jewels, and took it in grand procession to a vihāra he had built, where he worshipped it with offerings of flowers.[1]

By way of appendix to the Dhamma-Saṃgaṇi, an old commentary to Book III of the work has also been included in the canon, and tradition has even ascribed this commentary to Sāriputta.[2]

Book II of the Abhidhammapiṭaka, the Vibhaṅga,[3] "Classification," is merely a continuation of Book I. It presupposes the formulas and categories of the Dhamma-Saṃgaṇi, but new ones are added. Section I deals with the fundamental conceptions and fundamental truths of Buddhism, with which the Dhamma-Saṃgaṇi too begins, Section II deals with the knowledge of the sense impressions up to the highest knowledge of a Buddha and Section III with the things which

---

[1]) Mrs. *Rhys Davids*, Buddhist Manual, 2nd Ed., p. xxv.

[2]) Buddhaghosa calls this appendix (Text, pp. 234 ff.; cf. Mrs. *Rhys Davids l.c.*, pp. 334 ff.) a commentary (aṭṭhakathākaṇḍam or atthuddhāra). In the text itself, it has no especial title as though it were a part of the work.

[3]) Edited by Mrs. *Rhys Davids*, PTS, 1904.

hinder knowledge. The last section, which deals with the various conditions in human and non-human existences, contains a considerable mythological element.

Book III of the Abhidhammapiṭaka, called Dhātukathā,[1] "Discourse on the Elements," is a short text of 14 chapters, in questions and answers on the elements of psychical phenomena and their mutual relations.

In form and contents, Book IV, called Puggalapaññatti,[2] "Description of Human Individuals," is the book which is most closely allied to the texts of the Suttapiṭaka. In form it differs but little from the Saṅgīti-Sutta of the Dīghanikāya, and Sections 3-5 are for the most part to be found in the Aṅguttaranikāya too. Some chapters here read exactly like Suttas in one of the Nikāyas, and stand out favourably from their environment. We occasionally come across pretty similes. For instance (V, 3), five kinds of monks, in their relationship to woman, are compared with five kinds of warriors, and the simile, as is so often the case in the Majjhimanikāya, is carried on to the minutest detail. But it is only rarely that we come upon passages of undeniable literary value. Generally speaking, even the parables are as barren and tedious as the remaining parts of the book, the object of which is to classify individuals according to their ethical qualities. A few examples will suffice to give an idea of the spirit and style of the work, and of the type of definitions and classifications to be found in those portions which genuinely partake of the nature of the Abhidhamma.

"What sort of person is angry? What then is anger? That which is anger, being angry, and the state of being angry, hatred, hating, hatefulness, malice, the act of being malicious, maliciousness, hostility,

---

[1]) Edited by E. R. *Gooneratne*, PTS. 1892.

[2]) Edited by R. *Morris*, PTS. 1883; translated into English ("Designation of Human Types") Bimala Charan *Law*, PTS. 1923; into German by Bhikkhu *Nyānatiloka* ("Das Buch der Charaktere"), Breslau, 1910.

enmity, rudeness, abruptness, resentment of heart—this is called anger. He who has not got rid of this anger is said to be an angry person."

"What sort of person is crafty? What is meant by craftiness? Here a person becomes crafty and cunning. That which is craft, craftiness, state of being crafty, hardness, toughness, counterfeit, sham (—this is called craftiness).[1] The person in whom this craftiness remains unremoved is said to be a crafty person.

What sort of person is one having low inclination? Here is a person who, himself morally wicked and evil by nature, serves, follows, and worships another person who is also wicked and of evil disposition:—this is said to be a person having low inclination."

What sort of person is one having good inclination? Here is a certain person who, morally good and of virtuous habits, serves, follows and reveres another person of the same nature:—he is said to be a person having good inclination." [2]

Book V of the Abhidhammapiṭaka, the Kathāvatthu,[3] "Subjects of Discourse," is that book which more than all others in the Abhidhammapiṭaka, is of importance from the point of view of the history of Buddhism, and is the only work of the canon which is ascribed to a definite author.[4] As has already been mentioned above (p. 11 f.) it is said to have been compiled in connection with the Third Council, by Tissa Moggaliputta, the president of the Council. This tradition handed down by the chroniclers of Ceylon has been accepted as historical by prominent scholars, whilst others reject it as being entirely unauthentic.[5] Now

---

[1]) Missing in *Law*'s translation.

[2]) II, 1; 4; 25 f. Translation by B. Ch. *Law*.

[3]) Edited by A. C. *Taylor*, PTS 1894, 1897. Translated (Points of Controversy or Subjects of Discourse) by Shew Zan *Aung* and *Mrs. Rhys Davids*, PTS 1915. For an analysis of the work, see T. W. *Rhys Davids*, in JRAS 1892.

[4]) In the days of Buddhaghosa, it was indeed believed that Buddha himself had proclaimed the outlines of the work, and that Tissa had only elaborated the details. On the other hand, in the introduction to the Aṭṭhasālinī, *i.e.*, the commentary on the Dhammasaṃgaṇi, Buddhaghosa mentions that there were schools which did not acknowledge the Kathāvatthu as canonical.

[5]) For the tradition: *Oldenberg*, ZDMG 52, 1898, 633 f.; T. W. *Rhys Davids* in Cambridge History I, 194; *Mrs. Rhys Davids*, Points of Controversy, pp. xxx f.; Buddhist

as the Kathāvatthu in its present form is a patch-work,[1] I think it quite possible that Tissa Moggaliputta might have compiled a Kathāvatthu in the 3rd century B. C., but that the work was augmented by additional portions every time a new heresy cropped up.[2] The work, as we have it at present, and as Buddhaghosa commentated it in the 5th century A. D., consists of 23 sections, each of which contains 8-12 questions and answers, in which the most diverse false views are presented, confuted and rejected. (The commentary tells us which schools taught these false doctrines.) We find such questions as, for instance, the following:

Is there such a thing as a person (an individual soul) which can be regarded as a real or absolute substance? Does everything exist? Are there two kinds of cessation (of suffering)? Do the pupils of Buddha share in his superhuman powers? Can a householder be an Arhat? Can an Arhat lose his Arhat-hood as a result of Karman? Is virtuous behaviour unconscious? Can a person who has arrived at the right view (*i.e.*, the true faith) intentionally commit a murder? Is it correct to say that the Buddha lived in the world of human beings? Were the excrements and urine of the sublime Buddha more fragrant than all other fragrant things? Can animals be reborn among the gods? etc.

All these themes are discussed in questions and answers with an imaginary opponent; the final answer is in the negative, the opposite opinion being declared false. For the refutation of false doctrines, which, in the majority of

---

Manual of Psychological Ethics (1923), pp. xxiv f. ; *Geiger*, Pāli Literatur und Sprache, pp. 6 and 16. Against the tradition : I. P. *Minayeff*, Recherches sur le Bouddhisme, pp. 81 ff., 200 f.; *Barth* in RHR 42, 1900, pp. 72 f. = Œuvres II, 355 ; and *Keith*, Buddhist Philosophy, pp. 18 f. Max *Walleser*, who formerly (Die buddhistische Philosophie in ihrer geschichtlichen Entwicklung, I, Heidelberg 1904 (1925), pp. 20 ff., 95 f.) placed absolute reliance on the tradition, has now come to the conclusion (Die buddhist. Philosophie IV, Die Sekten des Buddhismus, 1927, p. 12) "that this text is very considerably later than the historical legend would have us believe."

[1]) Mrs. *Rhys Davids*, Points of Controversy, p. xxxi, speaks of "the 'patchwork-quilt' appearance" of the work.

[2]) *Cf.* *La Vallée Poussin*, ERE IV, p. 184.

cases, are differences of opinion among schools, and not so much the heresies of various sects, many passages are quoted from the Vinayapiṭaka and the Suttapiṭaka,[1] which shows that the Kathāvatthu is at any rate later than these Piṭakas. It also refers to passages in the first two books of the Abhidhamma, and to subjects which are treated in the Paṭṭhāna, but it quotes neither the Dhātukathā, nor the Puggalapaññatti, nor the Yamaka.

Even though the Kathāvatthu in its present form cannot be regarded as a work of the 3rd century B.C., it nevertheless throws interesting light on the development of Buddhist dogmatics during the later centuries. As far as the history of the Buddhist schools and sects is concerned, the information contained in the Kathāvatthu and the commentary on it, is only of value if taken in conjunction with the Chinese and Tibetan records of the schisms.[2]

We should be inclined to think that the Kathāvatthu formed the conclusion of the Abhidhammapiṭaka, but in the traditional enumeration of the texts, it comes fifth. The *sixth* is the Yamaka,[3] the "Book of double questions," so called because all the questions are presented and explained in two ways.[4] This work, which is very difficult to understand, is intended to dispel any doubts which might still arise after the first five books of the Abhidhamma.

The seventh and last book of the Abhidhammapiṭaka is the Paṭṭhāna-Pakaraṇa, the "Book of the Causal Relationships," or Mahā-Pakaraṇa, "the Great Book," the first

---

1) For a list of these passages, see *Taylor's* edition, pp. 633 ff.

2) *Cf. La Vallée Poussin*, JRAS 1910, pp. 413 ff.; *Walleser*, Die Sekten des alten Buddhismus, Heidelberg 1927.

3) Edited by Mrs. *Rhys Davids*, assisted by Cecilia *Dibben*, Mary C. *Foley*, Mabel *Hunt*, and May *Smith*, PTS 1911 and 1913.

4) Not even the title of the work is clear, s. Introductory Note, p. xv f. Mrs. *Rhys Davids* took great pains to obtain light on the meaning and method of the work, from learned monks in Burma. The answers to her questions are incorporated in a Pāli essay by the Thera *Ledi Sadaw* of Mandalay in the Appendix to the edition.

part of which is the Tika-Paṭṭhāna and the second part the Duka-Paṭṭhāna.[1] The entire work, deals with the investigation of the 24 kinds of relationships which are assumed between the (corporeal and psychical) phenomena : causal relationship, relationship of subject and object, relationship of the ruler and the ruled, contiguity, co-existence, etc. With the sole exception of Nirvāṇa, which is absolute, there is nothing which is not in some sense relative, *i.e.*, which is not related to something else in one of the 24 ways.[2] Mrs. Rhys Davids recommends the historian of Buddhistic ideas, and of logical and philosophical ideas in general, to study the first part of the Tika-Paṭṭhāna, in which these 24 kinds of relationships are enumerated, calling it "the one notable constructive contribution to knowledge in the Abhidhamma"; though, in general, she speaks rather sceptically about the value of this work of pure scholasticism.[3]

And Mrs. Rhys Davids, who has devoted years of patient and scholarly labour to the investigation of the texts of the Abhidhamma, yet concludes a general survey of the work accomplished, with these words of resignation: "As we leave this house of cloistered lives, of a closed tradition, of a past dominating present and future, we have a sense of rooms swept and garnished clean and tidy, of sealed windows, of drawn blinds, of no outlook towards the dawn." [4]

If we give credence to the tradition which dates the Kathāvatthu away back in the 3rd century B.C., we are compelled to date the earlier texts of the Abhidhamma still further back, and to assume that the scholastic activity of the

---

1) Tika-Paṭṭhāna, Parts I-III, ed. by Mrs. *Rhys Davids*, PTS 1921-1923; Duka-Paṭṭhāna I, ed. by Mrs. *Rhys Davids*, PTS 1906. The contents of the continuation of the Duka-Paṭṭhāna are given in the Tika-Paṭṭhāna, Part III, pp. 336 ff.

2) *Cf. Ledi Sadaw*, on the Philosophy of Relations, in JPTS 1915-1916, pp. 21 ff.

3) *Cf.* Foreword to Part I, p. v, and Editorial Note to Part II of the Tika-Paṭṭhāna.

4) JRAS 1923, p. 250.

monks began very early, immediately after the texts of the Suttapiṭaka. However, the authenticity of the Abhidhammapiṭaka is not universally recognised. It is disputed by the Sautrāntikas of the Hīnayāna, and the Sarvāstivādins have an Abhidharmapiṭaka in Sanskrit, the books of which differ entirely from those of the Pāli Abhidhammapiṭaka, though, as in the case of the latter, they are seven in number.[1] As even the report of the First Buddhist Council in the Vinayapiṭaka (Cullavagga XI) only mentions Vinaya and Dhamma, but not Abhidhamma, there are still doubts both as to the authenticity and the age of the Abhidhammapiṭaka.[2]

Among those sects, however, which recognise the Abhidhammapiṭaka as canonical, it is held in great esteem. In the Milindapañha it is related as a great marvel that young Nāgasena was so clever that he could at once be instructed in the seven books of the Abhidhamma, without having first learned the Suttas. In an inscription of about 262 A.D., engraved on a rock in the neighbourhood of the temple of Mihintale in Ceylon, we read among the rules for the monks of the monastery: 12 cells are to be allotted to expounders of the Abhidhammapiṭaka, 7 to preachers of the Suttapiṭaka, and 5 to readers of the Vinayapiṭaka.[3]

The study of the Abhidhamma is continued, especially in Burma, even at the present day, and numerous works have been written on it in the course of centuries.

---

1) *Cf. La Vallée Poussin*, Bouddhisme, Études et Matériaux, p. 55; Bouddhisme, p. 166; *Kern*, Manual of Buddhism, p. 126. *Walleser* (Buddhistische Philosophie, I, 17 ff.) tries to identify certain texts of the Pāli Abhidhammapiṭaka with similar ones in the Sanskrit, but can only take his stand on mere conjectures.

2) *Eliot*, Hinduism and Buddhism, I, 276 note 1, 291 f., thinks it possible, though not proved, that the Abhidhammapiṭaka was compiled in Ceylon, and not earlier.

3) R. Spence *Hardy*, Eastern Monachism, London 1860, p. 156.

NON-CANONICAL PĀLI LITERATU E.[1]

Apart from later additions, the greater part of the Pāli texts of the canon arose in India, and it was not until later that they were transmitted to Ceylon. The great bulk of the non-canonical Pāli literature, is, however, the work of the monks of Ceylon. The most notable exception is the Milindapañha,[2] "the Questions of Milinda." This work must have originated in north-west India, the only region where the memory of the great and wise ruler Milinda could have been sufficiently vivid as to warrant his being made the hero of a poem. This Milinda is none other than the Greek king Menandros, the most prominent of the rulers of the Græco-Indian empire, which, in the second century B.C., had separated itself from the Græco-Bactrian empire. The period of his reign was probably the first century B.C.,[3] and he

---

1) *Cf. Geiger*, Pāli Literatur und Sprache, p. 17 ff.

2) Ed. by V. *Trenckner*, London 1880; Vol. I of an edition in Siamese characters has been issued by Their Majesties Queen Aunt and Queen Suddhasinninath of Siam in 1925; translated into English by T. W. *Rhys Davids* in SBE, Vols. 35 and 36; into German (only the genuine parts) by F. O. *Schrader*, Berlin s.a. (1905), and (complete) by Bhikkhu *Nyāṇatiloka*, München 1919; Books I-III into French by L. *Finot*, Paris 1923 (Les Classiques de l'Orient VIII.). Extracts (similes and short parables) are translated by E. W. *Burlingame*, Buddhist Parables, p. 201 ff. Cf. *Barth* in RHR 28, 1893, 257ff. = Œuvres II, 170 ff.; R. *Garbe*, Beiträge zur indischen Kulturgeschichte, Berlin 1903, p. 95 ff.; T. W. *Rhys Davids* in ERE VIII, 1915, 631 ff. The title of the work is given in the MSS. as Milindapañhaṃ (neut.) or Milindapañhā (plur.), but the Buddhists of Ceylon generally say Milindapañho (masc.): *Trenckner* Ed., p. vi.

3) A. V. *Gutschmid*, Geschichte Irans und seiner Nachbarländer, Tübingen 1888, p. 104, gives the approximate dates of Menander's reign as 125-95 B.C. According to *Smith*, Early History, pp. 227 ff., 239, 258, Menander invaded India in about 155 B.C., "but *Gardner* places him about 110 B.C." H. *Raychaudhuri* (Political History of Ancient India, Calcutta 1923, pp 204 ff., 209), whose view is shared by L. D. *Barnett* (Calcutta Review, Feb. 1924, p. 250), places Menander in the first century B.C., and, (according to Benoytosh *Bhattacharya*, The Indian Buddhist Iconography, Oxford, 1924, p. xxi) R. C. *Mazumdar* is said to have proved "that a date prior to 90 B C. cannot be assigned to Menander." (Bhattacharya gives no reference, so I do not know Mazumdar's arguments.) See also *Rapson*, Cambridge History, I, 547 ff.

ruled over a great empire, which comprised not only the whole of the region of the Indus as well as Gujrat, but the Ganges province too. It may have been an historical event, the meeting and conversation of the Greek king with a celebrated Buddhist teacher, which led to the origin of the Milindapañha, or it may have been that the author of the dialogue merely took a pattern from so many dialogues in the Upaniṣads and Itihāsas, in introducing the great king in conversation with a sage: at all events, even if he was not himself a Buddhist,[1] Milinda-Menandros must have been closely connected with the Buddhist community. We can also assume as a certainty that the author of the Milindapañha, whose name, it is true, we do not know, lived at a time when the memory of the Greek king was still green. But as the Greek rule in India came to an end soon after the death of Menandros, it is scarcely feasible that his memory should have endured longer than a century at the most. Hence the work is more likely to have been written in the first century A.D., rather than in the second. The fact that the problems discussed in the Milindapañha are, in the main, identical with those forming the favourite themes in the canon, would also seem to indicate a comparatively early date.[2] Buddhaghosa,

---

[1]) An argument in favour of his having been a Buddhist, would be furnished by Plutarch's remarkable statement that, after the death of Menander, several Indian cities quarrelled about the possession of his ashes, which were eventually divided, whereupon each city erected a memorial over its own share. According to the legend, exactly the same thing happened at the death of Buddha (*Garbe*, l.c., pp. 102, 112 f., *Schrader*, l.c., p. xvi). Of course, it is possible that Menander was merely a sympathiser with the Buddhists, and presented the Order with great donations It is significant, though, that coins of Menander show the Buddhist wheel (S *Lévi* in RHR 23 ; 1891, p. 43 f.).

[2]) The themes discussed show remarkable similarity with those which play a prominent part in the Kathā-Vatthu. *Cf. Rhys Davids* in SBE, Vol. 36, pp. xx-xxvi. The allusion to the Thera Tissa (p. 71, SBE, Vol. 35, p. 110), "a master in the art of writing," who is said to have died many years before and "of whom people know only by his writings," would seem to point to a considerable, though not unduly protracted, interval of time between the author of the Milindapañha and Tissa Moggaliputta (if it is he who is meant) who lived in the 3rd century B. C.

too, the famous commentator of the fifth century, refers to the Milindapañha as an unimpeachable authority, on a level with the canonical texts.[1] In style, however, the Milindapañha shows an advance on the speeches of the Suttapiṭaka; and it is but few of the dialogues of the canon, as for instance that of the Pāyāsi-Sutta in the Dīghanikāya, which are as vivid and sprightly as those of the Milindapañha. These last-named are well able to bear comparison with the Dialogues of Plato.[2]

It is true that this praise, as well as the date I have assumed, cannot be applied to the entire work as we have it in the Pāli text, but only to the work in its original form; for there can scarcely be any doubt that, of the seven books which go to form the text, only a small part of the first introductory book and Books II and III are ancient and authentic. Even in Book III, later additions already appear to have crept in. By far the major portion of the work was not added until a later time, and probably not all at once. As it is the purpose of the work to dispel doubts of all kinds, which it does in somewhat incoherent fashion, it is, by its very nature, an eminently suitable receptacle for interpolation and additions. The most striking evidence of the spuriousness of Books IV-VII is the fact that they are absent in the Chinese translation, which is supposed to have originated between 317 and

---

[1]) *E.g.*, Atthasālini, pp. 112, 114, 119, 120, 122, 142; Visuddhi-Magga, p. 87; all these references are to passages in Books I-III of the Mil. f. *Rhys Davids* in SBE vol. 35, p. xiv ff.

[2]) A. *Weber*, Die Griechen in Indien (SBA 1890, p. 927) has raised the question whether the Milindapañha has not, perhaps, a closer connection with the Dialogues of Plato representing "so to speak, an intentional Indian counterpart to them." This is, however, unlikely, if only because the Milindapañha dialogue has so many models in the dialogues of the Upaniṣads, in the ascetic poetry of the Mahābhārata and in the Tipiṭaka, that there is no reason for supposing a Greek prototype. Neither does the Milindapañha show any trace whatsoever of a knowledge of the Greek language or of the Greek world of thought (*cf. Garbe*, l.c., p. 114). *Finot*, too, (Introduction to his French translation, p. 14) thinks that the style of the Milindapañha shows traces of Greek influence,

420 A.D.[1] In contents, too, Books IV-VII differ from Book I in character. Moreover, the last chapter of Book III forms a fitting conclusion to the work, and Book IV begins with a new introduction.[2]

The old poem probably began with the magnificent description of the city of Sāgala, the residence of King Milinda.[3] Then it was related how the well-informed and mighty Greek king one day, after he had reviewed his army, expressed a wish for a contest in speeches. But the king was so dreaded an opponent in speech contests with wise men, that it was not easy to find a Brahman or an ascetic who would venture to dispute with him. However, his courtiers took him to the monk Āyupāla, who lived in a hermitage in the vicinity of Sāgala. Even he is embarrassed by

---

[1]) *Cf.* Ed. *Specht* et S. *Lévi*, Deux traductions Chinoises du Milindapañho, OC IX London 1892, I, 518 ff. The "two translations" are in reality only two recensions of *one and the same* translation. Under the title of "the Sūtra of Nāgasena" this translation was already mentioned by Seng-yeou in the Catalogue compiled by him in 505 A.D., among the books which he saw with his own eyes; whereas under the title of "the Sūtra of the similes of Nāgasena," it was only familiar to him from the "old catalogue" of the 5th century. *Cf.* P. *Pelliot* in JA 1914, sér. II, t. IV, p. 379 ff. In a Chinese Buddhist Avadāna work of 472 A.D., the introductory book of the Milindapañha, embellished with anecdotes, appears as an independent story, which has the appearance of a late echo of the old dialogue (*cf.* J. *Takakusu* in JRAS 1896, pp. 1-21 and Ed. *Chavannes*, Cinq cents contes du Tripiṭaka Chinois III, 120 ff., No. 418). L. A. *Waddell* (in JRAS 1897, p. 227 ff.) on the strength of very doubtful Tibetan data, has attempted to show that this Chinese Avadāna is nearer to the original work, and that originally not Milinda, but a king Nanda of Magadha, was the hero of the book. "Nanda," however, is undoubtedly only a sanskritised form of the Greek Menandros. *Cf. Pelliot*, l.c., p. 380 f. *Rhys Davids* (ERE VIII, 632) thinks it possible that the Indian work, which was translated into Chinese, consisted of seven books, and that the concluding books were omitted by the Chinese translator. I regard this as most unlikely.

[2]) *Cf. Garbe*, l.c., p. 136 ff. E. *Schrader* (Introduction to his translation, p. xxiii f.) assumes that there were seven different recensions or revisions of this work. In my opinion, gradual interpolations and additions should be assumed, rather than revisions. I do not see sufficient reasons for declaring the whole of Book III to be spurious, as do *Garbe* and *Schrader*. *Senart* (JA 1892, sér. 8, t. xix, p. 343) and *Barth* (Œuvres II, p. 171) already declared the end of Book III (Trenckner's ed., p. 89) to be the final portion of the original work. Similarly *Pelliot*, JA, s. II, t. IV, 1914, p. 418.

[3]) The Pāli work begins with a few introductory *verses*, and towards the end of the introduction, too, we find a few verses. *Schrader* (pp. xxvi, xxxii) regards these verses as the remnants of a Pāli poem which originated in Ceylon. I think they are only Gāthās of the kind which occur so frequently in the Suttas of the Tipiṭaka, and which were at all times popular in India for the embellishment of prose narratives.

the king's very first question, and Milinda exclaims: "Empty, alas, is all India. All India is but vain gossip! There is no ascetic or Brahman who is capable of disputing with me and solving my doubts!" Just at that time the very learned and wise Buddhist monk Nāgasena was passing through villages and towns begging. He was famed far and wide for his wisdom, and in debate nobody could rival him. He had just come to Sāgala and had settled down in a hermitage. The courtiers take the king to him, and the personality of the sage at once makes a powerful impression on the king.[1]

Neatly arising from this situation, the first dialogue immediately introduces us to one of the main problems of Buddhism. King Milinda asks the sage his name. The sage says he is called Nāgasena, but that is merely a name, there is no ego, no person attached to it. This leads to a most excellent dialogue between the sage and the king, and finally the king has to confess that there is no permanent ego.[2]

The Buddhist doctrine that there is no permanent ego, no substance of soul,[3] but only a constant change of physical and psychical phenomena, can scarcely be reconciled to the belief in a cycle of rebirths, such as Buddha like the rest of his countrymen assumed, and still less does it harmonise with the doctrine of Karman, according to which all that an individual suffers or enjoys is the result of his own previous actions, a doctrine which plays so important a part in the ethics of

---

[1]) The passages which I regard as decidedly spurious in Book I, are the following: paragraph 3 (a table of contents, which refers to the entire Pāli work), paragraphs 4-8 (a Jātaka, which tells of the former births of Milinda and Nāgasena, and ends with a prophecy of Buddha), 11-14 (already recognised by *Rhys Davids* as a clumsy interpolation) and 16-36 (conception, birth, youth, conversion and attainment of Arhatship of Nāgasena).

[2]) *Cf. Oldenberg*, Buddha, p. 292 ff.; *Radhakrishnan*, Indian Philosophy, I, 391 f.

[3]) This is certainly the standpoint of the author of the Milindapañha. In the Canon we find sometimes a decided denial of the ego, at other times the doctrine that an ego does exist in a certain sense, and frequently the agnostic point of view that it is impossible to say either that there is a soul, or the contrary. *Cf.* M. *Walleser*, Die philosophische Grundlage des älteren Buddhismus I, 111 ff; Mrs. C. A. F. *Rhys Davids*, Buddhist Psychology (1924), pp. 156 ff., 278 ff.; *Radhakrishnan*, l.c., 382 ff., 390 ff.; *Keith*, Buddhist Philosophy, pp. 75 ff., 191 ff.

Buddhism. The first of these two questions forms the theme of the following conversation,[1] which I quote here because it shows the ability of the author of this work in elucidating even the most difficult problems in an ingenious manner, and by means of excellent parables:

The king said: "Lord Nāgasena, when a man is reborn, is he the same or is he another?" The Thera said: "He is neither the same nor is he another." "Give me a parable." "What do you think, great king, are you now as an adult the same as you were as a tender little boy, a little child lying flat on your back?" "No, lord, that tender little boy, that little child lying flat on its back was another, and I as an adult am now another." "If that is so, great king, then you have no mother, no father, no teacher, you have never been instructed, never learned the commandments, never gained wisdom. How then, great king, is the mother of the embryo in its four stages each time another, is the mother of the little child another, and the mother of the adult yet another? Is it another who takes instruction, and another who has learned something? Is it another who commits a crime, and another who is punished by having his hands and feet cut off?" "No, lord, but what would you reply?" The Thera said: "I myself, great king, was the tender little boy, the little child lying flat on its back, and I myself am now the adult. Through one and the same body all these are combined into one unity." "Give me a parable." "Great king, if a man lighted a lamp, would it burn all the night?" "Yes, lord, it would." "How now, great king, is the flame in the first watch of the night the same as the flame in the second watch of the night?" "No, lord." "And is the flame in the second watch of the night the same as the flame in the last watch of the night?" "No, lord." "How, great king, then was there one lamp in the first watch of the night, another lamp in the second watch of the night, and yet another lamp in the last watch of the night?" "No, lord, the lamp burned the whole night by means of one and the same (combustible)." "Exactly so, great king, the continuity of the phenomena[2] comes about, it is another who arises, and another who passes away, but

---

[1]) Ed. *Trenckner*, p. 40; SBE, Vol. 35, p. 63 ff. *Cf. Oldenberg*, Buddha, p. 301 *Keith*, Buddhist Philosophy, p. 169 f.

[2]) *i.e.*, of the beings, which, however, are in reality only ever changing phenomena.

at the same time there is something which unites them, and therefore a man enters into his last union with consciousness [1] neither as the same nor as another."

There is a whole series of parables to explain why, though there is no permanent ego, a man is yet responsible for his actions. The following parable is one of them: [2]

"Suppose a man has stolen another man's mangoes, the owner of the mango tree seizes him, takes him before the king, and says: 'Your Majesty, this man has stolen my mangoes;' now, if the thief says: 'Your Majesty, I did not steal this man's mangoes, the fruits which he planted, and those which I took away, were not the same fruits, I deserve no punishment, would this man be punished, great king?' 'Yes, lord, he would be punished.' 'And why so?' 'Because, whatever the man may say, he would be punished on account of the last mango which undeniably would not be there, had it not been for the former one."

In Book II there is a superabundance of excellent parables of this kind. In the authentic part of Book III, too, there is many an apt simile. When, for instance, Nāgasena, in reply to one of the king's questions, says that the end of suffering is brought about not only through renunciation in this life, but that, in addition, efforts in former existences are also needful, he illustrates it by asking the king whether he would delay the digging of wells until he was thirsty, or instruct his men to plough, sow and reap, when he was hungry, or have ramparts dug, walls erected and fortresses built, when the enemy was already before the gates.

These specimens will suffice to show the great value of the first and genuine part of the Milindapañha even as a literary production. It is indeed a masterpiece of ancient Indian prose. In Book II and the greater part of Book III,

---

1) *i.e.*, into his last rebirth, for it is the "consciousness" (viññāṇa), by means of which a new individual is formed in the womb. See *Oldenberg*, Buddha, pp. 255 ff., 301 *Keith*, Buddhist Philosophy, p. 78 f.

2) Ed. *Trenckner*, p. 46; SBE, Vol. 35, p. 72.

only such questions are raised, as relate to the most important points of Buddhistic ethics and psychology, fundamental questions which are of interest to any layman. Book IV, on the other hand, contains a system of apologetics which could not possibly be of interest to any but thorough-going scholars of the canonical texts. The dilemmas which are discussed in this work, frequently turn to very petty subjects of dogmatics, but especially to the person of Buddha, *e. g.*, what is the use of the veneration of relics, if the Buddha has passed away utterly ? How can the Buddha be omniscient, when we are told that he pondered ? Why did Buddha receive Devadatta into the Order, even though he knew that this monk would cause a schism ? Etc. The reason for these dilemmas is the juxtaposition of contradictory texts. At the same time, every word of the canon, even the most casual remark in the profanest stories in the Jātaka-Book, is regarded as a sacred word of Buddha, which must of necessity be true and good. If, in any of his former births, related in the Jātakas, the Bodhisatta had any faults or vices, the author of Book IV of the Milindapañha does his best to exonerate him. For, in his eyes, the Bodhisatta is entirely identical with the perfect Buddha. The authentic books do not bear the slightest trace of such a conception (neither does the Tipiṭaka). The question as to whether the Buddha ever existed at all,[1] which had already been broached in Book III, is again raised in Book V, and Nāgasena answers it by saying that his existence may be inferred from his teachings. This idea is worked out in a lengthy, very ornate and detailed parable making up the greater part of the book, in which Buddha, who has created his religion, is compared with a master-builder, who builds up a large city. Book VI presents a dilemma, which had already been

---

[1]) Ed. *Trenckner*, pp. 70, 73; SBE, Vol. 35, pp. 109, 113.

brought up for discussion in Book IV, but had not found any very satisfactory solution;[1] it is this: If, as the scriptures say, even laymen can attain to the state of an Arhat, why should a man take upon himself the strict monastic vows? The answer given here, is that laymen can attain to the state of an Arhat and Nirvāṇa only because they have already fulfilled the strict vows in former births. These strict vows, the thirteen Dhutaṅgas,[2] are then described in detail, and their exceptional value explained. This is apparently the real purpose of Book VI. In all the books of the Milindapañha the questions raised are generally answered in parables. Book VII is entirely a book of parables; there are no less than 67 parables[3] illustrative of the qualities essential for the monk who desires to attain to the state of an Arhat. Many of these parables already appear in the Tipiṭaka.

In Books IV-VII we find, on the one hand, a liberal sprinkling of quotations from the canon, and on the other, frequent allusions to traditions divergent from those embodied in the canon, and most likely belonging to a later period, and especially allusions to legends which appear only in the commentaries, in the commentary on the Jātaka and in those on the Vimānavatthu and Dhammapada.[4] These legends are permeated with a low conception of the doctrine

---

1) Ed. *Trenckner*, p. 242 ff.; SBE, Vol. 36, p. 56 ff.

2) They are very advantageous for a holy life, but are not compulsory for all monks. They are discussed in Section II of Buddhaghosa's Visuddhi-Magga. The term Dhutaṅga (or Dhūtaṅga) is not yet to be found in the Tipiṭaka, except in the Parivāra of later date (Vinayapiṭaka, ed. Oldenberg, Vol. V, p. 193, *cf.* p. 131). *Cf. Kern*, Manual of Indian Buddhism, p. 75 f.

3) The book begins with a table of contents (mātikā) which gives an additional 38 parables. The entire book was probably appended to the Milindapañha even later than the preceding books, and remained incomplete.

4) *Cf.* E. W. *Burlingame* in HOS, Vol. 28, p. 60 ff. Burlingame is wrong in concluding from these references that Books IV-VII of the Mil. "are as late as the beginning of the sixth century A.D." Not only is it not proved, but, in view of sundry deviations, it is unlikely, that the author of Books IV-VII of the Mil. derived his knowledge of the legends referred to, from these commentaries. *Cf.* also *Rhys Davids*, SBE, Vol. 35, pp. xl ff.,

of Karman, an exaggerated cult of the Buddha (Buddha-Bhakti) and a somewhat crude belief in miracles, which would seem to indicate a later period.

A work which is probably as early as the earliest portions of the Milindapañha, and which also possibly dates far enough back to have been written in India, is the Netti-Pakaraṇa, also called Netti-Gandha, or simply Netti, "The Book of Guidance" (*viz.*, to the True Religion).[1] This is the earliest work which offers a connected treatment of the whole of the teaching of Buddha; it is possibly earlier than the last two books of the Abhidhammapiṭaka,[2] and is ascribed to no less a person than Mahākaccāna, the disciple of Buddha, who, as far back as in the Majjhimanikāya, was proclaimed to be the best expounder of the word of Buddha.[3] The same Mahākaccāna is also said to have composed the Peṭakopadesa, "Instruction of the students of the Piṭakas,"[4] a continuation of the Netti, and most likely not much later than this last-named work. A commentary on the Netti was written by Dhammapāla (probably in the fifth century A.D.).

By far the major portion of non-canonical Pāli literature consists of commentaries. The monks in the monasteries of India and Ceylon, to whom we are indebted for the comparatively faithful transmission of the canonical texts, did not rest content with the study and teaching of these texts, but from the very outset endeavoured to explain them too. In the Suttas we find the earliest beginnings of exegetical activity, and

---

196, 284 ff., 297 f.; Vol. 36, pp 43 ff., 143 note, 304 note. The authentic parts of the Mil. contain only such quotations as could, for other reasons too, be regarded as belonging to the earliest part of the Canon. The enumeration of the seven books of the Abhidhamma (I, 26) appears in the spurious part of the introduction.

[1]) With Extracts from Dhammapâla's Commentary ed. by E. *Hardy*, PTS 1902.

[2]) *Cf.* Mrs. *Rhys Davids*, JRAS 1925, p. 111 f.

[3]) Majjh. 18 (I, 110 ff.), 133 (III, 194 ff.), 138 (III, 223 ff.).

[4]) Not yet published, but see Rudolf *Fuch's* Specimen des Peṭakopadesa, Berlin, Diss., 1908. *Cf.* Shwe Zan *Aung* in JPTS 1910-1912, p. 120.

there are a few commentaries in the canon itself.[1] Though we cannot believe the orthodox Buddhists of Ceylon, when they affirm that the Aṭṭhakathās, *i.e.*, the "explanations of the meaning" or "commentaries," have been handed down since the first Council with the texts of the Tipiṭaka, were translated into Singhalese by Mahinda, written down under Vaṭṭagāmani, and translated into Pāli by Buddhaghosa (5th century A.D.),[2] yet we can have no doubt that the exegetical and literary activity of the monks began in India immediately after the compilation of the texts, and, that Pāli, the language of the canon, was used also for the early commentaries. These ancient teachers are often cited in the commentaries of the 5th century, as Porāṇā, "the ancient ones." [3] But when the Theravāda school in India itself was more and more superseded by other Buddhist sects and schools, it was the monasteries of Ceylon,[4] which became permanent centres for the study of the Theravāda texts. Whatever Pāli commentaries were available were translated into Singhalese. Only the verses, partly memorial verses and partly verses of narrative passages, were left unchanged in Pāli. The monks of

---

[1]) B. Ch. *Law*, Life and Work of Buddhaghosa, p. 53 ff. The Sutta-Vibhaṅga in itself is a kind of commentary on the Pāṭimokkha. The Udāna and the Suttanipāta contain prose passages in the nature of commentaries. The Niddesa is an early commentary on parts of the Suttanipāta. A commentary ascribed to Sāriputta found its way into the Abhidhammapiṭaka as an appendix to the Dhamma-Saṅgaṇi.

[2]) *Cf.* L. Comrilla *Vijasinha* and R. C. *Childers* in JRAS 1871, p. 289 ff., *Kern*, Manual of Indian Buddhism, p. 8 f.; Th. *Foulkes* in Ind. Ant. 17, 1888, 123 f.; Dīpavaṃsa 20, 20f.; Mahāvaṃsa 33, 100 ff.; *Geiger*, Pāli Literatur und Sprache, p. 17 (para. 18).

[3]) Sometimes as Porāṇa-Kathā or Porāṇa-Aṭṭhakathā. Theras who compiled extracts from the Canon (therā dhammasaṃgāhakā) were also counted among the Porāṇas. One and the same verse is ascribed in the Milindapañha (p. 369) to these Theras, and in the Visuddhi-Magga (p. 270) to the "Porāṇā." *Cf.* Mrs. *Rhys Davids*, Visuddhi-Magga Ed., Vol. II, p. 764 f.; B. Ch. *Law*, Life and Work of Buddhaghosa, p. 64 ff.

[4]) Various monasteries had their own commentaries; besides the Mūla- or Mahā-Aṭṭhakathā of the "great monastery" (Mahāvihāra) of Anurādhapura, there was also one of the "northern monastery" (Uttaravihāra) in the same city of Ceylon, as well as an Andha-Aṭṭhakathā in Kāñcīpura in South India, and others. *Cf.* Mrs. *Rhys Davids*, Buddhist Manual of Psychological Ethics, 2nd Ed., p. xxviii.

Ceylon worked on independently in this direction, wrote Singhalese commentaries, tried their hand at Pāli also, especially Pāli verses, and attained to such a degree of perfection in this, that in the 5th century it was already possible for Buddhaghosa to write in an elegant Pāli style, and to set about translating or retranslating the Singhalese commentaries into the sacred Pāli language.

The exegetical and literary activity of the monks, however, extended to all the "three gems": Buddha, the religion (Dhamma) and the monastic community (Saṅgha). The Buddha legend was elaborated; they were not content with the ballads and occasional narratives of the Tipiṭaka, but wished to have a complete account of the Master's life. The religious texts were illustrated and explained in the same manner as was customary in India as far back as the time of the Brāhmaṇas, not only grammatically and lexically, but also by means of narratives and legends.[1] As the Brahmans in their Vedic schools, so also the monks in their monasteries, were true Indians, in that they felt a keen delight in the telling of stories. The numerous narratives contained in the canon were not sufficient for them. They lengthened and completed, they added what they gathered from oral transmission, they inserted what was familiar to them from other branches of literature, re-modelling it in the spirit of Buddhism, and they certainly also composed much that was new in imitation of old models. They also collected the legends on the origin, and made records concerning the history of the monastic order, with the discipline of which they dealt in the commentaries on the Vinayapiṭaka, so that the Aṭṭhakathās also contained the beginnings of a church history.

As regards the Buddha legend, we have seen that there was no actual Buddha biography contained in the canon, but

---

[1]) The Aṭṭhakathās contain Jātakas and other narratives, in the same way as the Arthavāda of the Brāhmaṇas (cf. above Vol. I, p. 208) contains Itihāsas and Ākhyānas.

only the beginnings of one. In the Vinayapiṭaka, in certain speeches of the Suttapiṭaka and in a few of the ancient ballads of the Suttanipāta, we found on the one hand records, more or less reliable, of the actual life of the Master, and on the other, the earliest beginnings of a Buddha legend and a Buddha epic. In the Buddhavaṃsa we found a kind of previous history, and in Chapter 26 of it, the epitome of a biography, of the Buddha. The Cariyāpiṭaka and the Jātaka, too, telling of the former existences of the Buddha, contain, at least in the view of the orthodox Buddhist, contributions to the history of the life of Buddha.[1] As far as Pāli literature is concerned, there is, however, no connected life story of the Buddha until we come to the Nidāna-Kathā,[2] the "Narrative of the Beginnings,"[3] which precedes the Jātakaṭṭhavaṇṇanā, the Jātaka commentary, and forms a part of this great commentary work.

This Nidāna-Kathā consists of three sections: 1. The story of the "beginnings in the remote past" (dūrenidāna), from the existence of the later Buddha as Sumedha at the time of the Buddha Dīpaṅkara down to his re-birth in the heaven of the Tusita gods; 2. The story of the "beginnings in the not very remote past" (avidūrenidāna), beginning with the descent of Buddha from the heaven of the Tusita gods, and ending with the attainment of Bodhi, *i.e.*, enlightenment; and 3. The story of the "beginnings in the present" (santikenidāna), relating the events from the enlightenment of

---

[1]) *Cf. Rhys Davids*, Cambridge History, I, 196 f.; J. *Dutoit*, Das Leben des Buddha, Leipzig 1906; E.H. *Brewster*, The Life of Gotama the Buddha. (Compiled exclusively from the Pali Canon.) With an Introductory Note by C. A. F. *Rhys Davids*, London 1926.

[2]) The text is to be found in Fausböll's edition of the Jātaka, Vol. I, pp. 1-94, translated by T. W. *Rhys Davids*, Buddhist Birth Stories, pp. 1-133; a free rendering of the contents of the Nidāna-Kathā in *Kern*, Der Buddhismus I., pp. 24-140, a translation of the dūrenidāna and avidūrenidāna in *Warren*, Buddhism in Translations, pp. 5-83. Two shorter passages, translated by J. *Dutoit*, Leben des Buddha, pp. 5 ff., 18 ff.

[3]) *i.e.*, of the beginnings of Buddha's career. *Nidāna* means "cause," "origin," hence also "beginning."

Buddha down to the story of the magnificent donation of the merchant Anāthapiṇḍika.

The first section is directly connected with the Buddhavaṃsa and the Cariyāpiṭaka, and is, in the main, a mere commentary on an extract from these two texts. Only the narrative of Sumedha, out of Chapter II of the Buddhavaṃsa, is completely included. We have seen how, countless æons before, the future Buddha, as Sumedha, pays homage to the Buddha of that time, namely Dīpaṅkara, and resolves to attain to the ten "perfections," in order to become worthy of Buddhahood.[1] After he had formed this resolve, he strove again and again in countless re-births for the fulfilment of these highest "perfections"—they are described in the Cariyāpiṭaka, which the author of the Nidāna-Kathā here quotes,[2] until finally, in his existence as Vessantara, by his boundless self-denying generosity, he has attained to the summit of perfection and is then re-born in the heaven of the Tusita gods.

While in Section I the prose is continually interrupted by verses from the Buddhavaṃsa and the Cariyāpiṭaka, the two next sections contain only a few occasional verse quotations. Section II commences with the "Buddha uproar" in heaven. The Tusita gods importune the Bodhisatta to be born again on earth for the salvation of the world, and, after due consideration, he decides to do so. Then follow the familiar legends of the conception of the Bodhisatta, who, as a white elephant, appears to penetrate into the womb of the dreaming Queen Māyā, of his miraculous birth in the Lumbinī-grove,[3] of the welcoming of the newly-born child and the prophecy of the seer Asita about his future greatness, the miracles of his childhood and boyhood, the four encounters of the prince,

---

[1]) See above, p. 161.

[2]) Though, as already observed above, on p. 164, in a version deviating from ours.

[3]) In all this, the Nidāna-Kathā has only slightly embellished the miracles told in Dīghanikāya, 14 and Majjhimanikāya, 123. The "white elephant," it is true, does not

through which he becomes acquainted with age, disease, death and renunciation of the world, the night scene in the seraglio which matures his resolve to renounce the world, his flight from the palace, achieved with numerous miracles and the aid of the gods, and his adopting the life of a mendicant monk, of his great feats of asceticism, of the milky rice of Sujātā, prepared with the aid of numerous miracles, from which the Bodhisatta, exhausted by his long fast, derives new strength, the meditation under the Bodhi tree, and the attacks of Māra, and finally the attainment of Bodhi, the highest knowledge, which is accompanied by numerous miraculous phenomena.

In Section III, too, which deals mainly with the first conversions and is less suited to the introduction of miracles, these latter are by no means absent. A week is spent by Buddha lost in meditation under the Bodhi tree, and the gods doubt whether he has really attained enlightenment. In order to dispel their doubts, he performs a few miracles, rises in the air, then stands beside his "throne" looking towards the East, and remains standing thus for a week, without blinking his eyes. Here the Nidāna-Kathā inserts the remark that on this spot the Animisacetiya, *i.e.*, the "shrine of the non-blinking," was later erected. Several other passages, too, mention fanes which are to recall events in the life of the Buddha, and which probably actually existed. The conversion of the two merchants Tapussa and Bhallika who became lay-disciples is already related in the Vinayapiṭaka (Mahāvagga I, 4). The Nidāna-Kathā adds, however, that

---

as yet appear in the Pāli Canon, though it is to be found on the rocks of Kalsi and Dhauli, which contain edicts of King Aśoka, the one on the Kalsi rock bearing the inscription: gajatame, "the best elephant." A relief on the East gate of the stūpa at Sānchi represents the conception of Buddha, showing how he penetrates into the womb of Māyā in the shape of an elephant. *Cf. E. Hultzsch*, The Inscriptions of Aśoka, pp. xiii, 26 f., 27 note 2, 50, 51; A. *Foucher*, The Beginnings of Buddhist Art, p. 92; *Windisch*, Buddhas Geburt, pp. 5 ff., 155 ff.

these first lay-disciples received a few hairs from the Buddha, over which relics they erected a shrine. The visit of the Buddha to his native town of Kapilavatthu is recounted in great detail, and there is no lack of miracles. Much space is also occupied by the narrative of the great merchant Anāthapiṇḍika, who presented the Jetavana-grove to the monastic order. With this narrative the Nidāna-Kathā breaks off, without its really being evident why the conclusion has been made at precisely this point.

The occasional references to the Nidāna-Kathā, in the "stories of the present" (Paccuppanavatthu) prove that the Nidāna-Kathā does not precede the Jātaka commentary by mere accident, but forms an essential part of it. However, as the author of the former work expressly says in one passage,[1] that he deviates from the Jātakaṭṭhakathā, and refers to the "other Aṭṭha-Kathās," it follows that he did not merely translate the Singhalese commentary, but revised it freely with the aid of other commentaries. Unfortunately we have no clue for a definite determination of the date of the Jātaka commentary, and consequently, not of the Nidāna-Kathā either. One thing, however, is certain. The many points of agreement between the Buddha legend as it is related in the Sanskrit sources, and the Nidāna-Kathā, prove that the last-mentioned work is based on the same *Indian* tradition as the former, and therefore probably also reaches back to commentaries which were brought from India to Ceylon, and that at a time before the Mahāyāna literature was developed in India. At all events the Nidāna-Kathā represents an earlier phase in the development of the Buddha legend than the Lalitavistara and similar Sanskrit works, even if the latter must be ascribed to an earlier time.

In the Gandhavaṃsa, a "History of the Books," probably

---

[1]) Jātaka, Ed. Fausböll, p. 62.

written in Burma in the 17th century, Buddhaghosa is said to be the author of the Jātaka commentary. If this were correct, he would belong to the 5th century A.D.; for, little as we know of this commentator, equally celebrated in Ceylon and Burma,[1] we may believe tradition as far as to assume that he lived in the reign of King Mahānāma of Ceylon. It is true that we find this report only in the continuation of the Mahāvaṃsa, which was not written until about the middle of the 13th century. It is, however, confirmed by the fact that a work by Buddhaghosa was already translated into Chinese in 489 A.D.[2] Out of all the legends that have been woven about this learned man, we might accept as an historical fact that, during the reign of King Mahānāma, he diligently studied the texts of the Tipiṭaka and the Singhalese Aṭṭha-Kathās or "commentaries" in the "great monastery" (Mahāvihāra) of Anurādhapura in Ceylon, where they were kept, and that later, as the first-fruits of his studies, he wrote a systematic work on the Buddha doctrine, the Visuddhi-Magga,[3] and afterwards revised, in the Pāli language, the commentaries on the chief texts of the Tipiṭaka.[4] It is

---

[1]) *Cf.* Bimala Charan *Law*, The Life and Work of Buddhaghosa, Calcutta and Simla, 1923 (Calcutta Or. Series, No. 9, E. 3); Max *Müller* in SBE 10 (I), pp. xii-xxiv; *Minayeff*, Recherches, 189 ff.; Thos. *Foulkes* in Ind. Ant. 19, 1890, pp. 105-122 and T. W. *Rhys Davids* in ERE II, 885 ff. The "biography" written by the monk Mahāmaṅgala in Burma, perhaps in the 14th century (*cf.* *Geiger*, Pāli Literatur und Sprache, p. 31, para. 40) and published by James *Gray*, Buddhaghosuppatti or the Historical Romance of the Rise and Career of Buddhaghosa, London, 1892, is purely legendary.

[2]) This Chinese translation of the Samantapāsādikā is the first work which has been proved to have been translated into Chinese from *Pāli*. Before this only Chinese translations from Sanskrit were known (J. *Takakusu* in JRAS 1896, 415 ff.)

[3]) There is a tradition that he wrote a work (which has not come down to us) Ñāṇodaya ("the dawning of knowledge") and the Atthasālinī in India, before departing for Ceylon. If there is any truth in this tradition, this atthasālinī could only have been the rough plan of his commentary on the Dhamma-Saṅgaṇi; for the Atthasālinī, which has come down to us, presupposes the Visuddhi-Magga, which was written in Ceylon. *Cf.* Mrs *Rhys Davids*, Buddhist Manual of Psychological Ethics, 2nd ed., p. xxvii.

[4]) He tells us himself (in the introduction to the Samantapāsādikā) that he not only translated the commentaries of the Mahāvihāra from the Singhalese, but compared

credible, too, that, as the legend has it, he was descended from a Brahman family in the neighbourhood of Bōdh-Gayā, became deeply learned in Brahmanical lore in early youth, but, in consequence of a disputation, was converted to Buddhism by the monk Revata, and was stimulated by his teacher to go to Ceylon to study the Singhalese commentaries.[1] He certainly wrote many of the works ascribed to him which made his name so great, that he was regarded as the commentator *par excellence*, and that commentaries were later ascribed to him which were the work of other authors, or whose authors were unknown. He himself, in introductory verses, mentions as his works the Visuddhi-Magga, the Samantapāsādikā (commentary on the Vinayapiṭaka), the Sumaṅgalavilāsinī (commentary on the Dīghanikāya), the Papañcasūdanī (commentary on the Majjhimanikāya), the Sāratthapakāsinī (commentary on the Samyuttanikāya) and the Manoratha-Pūraṇī (commentary on the Aṅguttaranikāya). In the Gandhavaṃsa there are also ascribed to him the commentaries Kaṅkhāvitaraṇī (on the Pāṭimokkhas), Paramattha-Kathā (on the seven books of the Abhidhammapiṭaka) and those on the Khuddaka-Pāṭha, Suttanipāta, Jātaka and Apadāna.[2]

There is scarcely any doubt that Buddhaghosa is also the author of the commentaries on the Abhidhammapiṭaka, or at least of the Atthasālinī (commentary on the Dhamma-Saṅgaṇi),

---

them with the commentaries of other monasteries, abbreviated and freely revised them. *Burlingame* (JAOS 38, 1918, 267 f.) pronounces the tradition according to which the Attha-Kathās were translated from Pāli into Singhalese, and translated back again from Singhalese into Pāli by Buddhaghosa and others, to be "unreliable and misleading," because Buddhaghosa and the compiler of the commentary on the Dhammapada availed themselves of common Pāli originals though independently of each other, and because both Dhammapāla and the compiler of the Jātaka commentary copied from Buddhaghosa's commentaries. Nevertheless, it is possible, indeed probable, that the 5th century translators, though translating from the Singhalese, used available Pāli texts as well (*e.g.*, of legends and tales).

[1]) On Buddhaghosa's date and life, see Appendix IV.

[2]) Gandhavaṃsa, JPTS 1886, p. 59.

the Sammoha-vinodanī (commentary on the Vibhaṅga) and the commentary on the Paṭṭhāna-Pakaraṇa, and most likely of the Kaṅkhāvitaraṇī and the Paramattha-Jotikā (commentaries on the Khuddaka-Pāṭha and the Suttanipāta).[1] On the other hand, the commentaries on the Jātaka and the Dhammapada are so very different in language and style from Buddhaghosa's commentaries, that he cannot possibly have written them.[2] As far as these two works are concerned, the designation "commentary" is, as a matter of fact, just as unsuitable as the expression "author." For, in both works, the actual commentary, *i.e.*, the grammatical and lexical explanation of the verses, occupies only a very small space, whilst narratives, or, to be more exact, sermons in the form of narratives,[3] constitute the major part. It will be more correct to speak

---

[1]) The Khuddaka-Pāṭha commentary has been proved to be the work of Buddhaghosa, by *Burlingame* in HOS, Vol. 28, p. 51f. An edition in Siamese characters of all the commentaries of Buddhaghosa (23 vols.) and of his Visuddhi-Magga (3 vols.) issued by H. H. the Supreme Patriarch of Siam, *Prince Vajiriyana*, in 1920-1922, has been generously presented to scholars by H. R. H. the Prince of Chandaburi. The following commentaries have up to now (1927) been published by the PTS: Samanta-Pāsādikā ed. by J. *Takakusu* assisted by M. *Nagai*, I, 1924, II, 1927; Sumaṅgala-Vilāsinī ed. by T. W. *Rhys Davids* and J. E. *Carpenter*, I, 1886; Papañcasūdanī ed. by J. H. *Woods* and D. *Kosambi*, I, Suttas 1-10, 1922; Manoratha-Pūraṇī, I, Eka-Nipāta, ed. by Max *Walleser*, 1924; Paramattha-Jotikā I, Khuddakapāṭha Commentary, ed. by Helmer *Smith* from a Collation by Mabel *Hunt*, 1915; Paramattha-Jotikā II, Suttanipāta Commentary, ed. by Helmer *Smith*, 1916-1918; Atthasālinī ed. by Ed. *Müller*, 1897; translated ("The Expositor") by Maung *Tin*, ed. and revised by Mrs. *Rhys Davids*, 1920-21; Sammohavinodanī, ed. by A. P. *Buddhadatta* Thera, 1923; Commentary to Paṭṭhānapakaraṇa in the edition of the Tikapaṭṭhāna by Mrs. *Rhys Davids*, 1921-1923; Puggalapaññatti-Atthakathā ed. by G. *Landsberg* and Mrs. *Rhys Davids* in JPTS 1913-1914, p. 170 ff.; Kathāvatthuppakaraṇa-Aṭṭhakathā ed. by J. P. *Minayeff*, in JPTS 1889; Yamakappakaraṇatthakathā ed. by Mrs. *Rhys Davids* in JPTS 1910-1912, p. 51 ff. Editions of Buddhaghosa's commentaries have also been published in Ceylon and in Burma. See *Geiger*, Pāli Literatur und Sprache, p. 19 f., para. 22. There is no mention in any Pāli source, of Buddhaghosa's having written a Sanskrit epic Padyacūḍāmaṇi also (see below in the chapter on Buddhist Sanskrit literature).

[2]) *Cf. Rhys Davids*, Buddhist Birth Stories, p. lxiii ff.; *Burlingame* in HOS, Vol 28, pp. 49, 59 f.; *Law*, Life and Work of Buddhaghosa, p. ix f.

[3]) Both in the Jātaka commentary and the Dhammapada commentary, the stories are made to issue from Buddha's own lips, as dhammadesanā, *i.e.*, "religious instructions" or "sermons."

of compilers or editors, who collected and edited these sermons or narratives.

In fact the commentary on the Dhammapada[1] forms a valuable supplement to the commentary on the Jātaka, and, like the latter, contains many an ancient, popular narrative theme, some of which are well known in universal literature, far beyond the borders of India. Thus we find here the story of a king of Benares who, like Harun al Rashid, wanders about the city at night, the tale of "Doctor Know-all," and so on. Here we also meet with the famous story of Kisā-Gotamī, the mother who strays about in despair with her dead child in her arms, and comes to the Buddha who tells her that he can restore her child to life if she will bring him a mustard seed; but this mustard seed must come from a house in which nobody has ever died. In vain the mother searches from house to house, until finally it dawns upon her that the Master was only endeavouring to teach her the great truth of the universality of death, and, comforted, she becomes a member of the community of Buddha. The legend proves itself genuinely Indian, owing to the fact that it belongs to the type of "consolatory stories" so familiar to us. For this reason, when we meet with a similar anecdote in the Alexander-legend, in a few versions of Pseudo-Kallisthenes as well as in Arabian, Jewish, Persian and Coptic narratives of

---

[1] Edited by H. C. *Norman*, 5 vols. (Vol. V, Indexes by Lakshmaṇa Shastrī *Tailang*), PTS 1906-1915. Translated (Buddhist Legends) by Eugene Watson *Burlingame*, with important introduction, in HOS, Vols. 28-30, Cambridge, Mass., 1921. Extracts have been edited by V. *Fausböll* in his edition of the Dhammapada (Hauniae 1855). Selections of tales have been translated by *Warren*, Buddhism in Translations, pp. 221 ff., 264 ff., 380 ff., 430 ff., 451 ff., into French by L. de *La Vallée Poussin* and G. de *Blonay* in RHR 26, 1892, 180 ff.; 29, 1894, 195 ff., 329 ff.; from a Burmese version by T. *Rogers*, Buddhaghosa's Parables, London 1870. *Cf. Burlingame*, Buddhaghosa's Dhammapada Commentary, and the Titles of its three hundred and ten Stories, together with an Index thereto and an Analysis of Vaggas I-IV, in Proceedings of the American Academy of Arts and Sciences, Vol. 45, 1910, pp. 467-550. On the subject-matter and motifs of the stories, s. *Burlingame* in HOS, Vol. 28, p. 29 ff.

Alexander, it is more probable that the Buddhist legend influenced the Greek legend; and Rohde's hypothesis of its having first originated on Greek soil, is less feasible.[1] On the other hand, when we read in the romance of Udena and Vāsuladattā,[2] how King Pajjota, in order to entice Udena into an ambuscade and to get him into his power, had a wooden elephant made, in which he concealed sixty warriors, we see in this an echo of the legend of the Trojan horse, which penetrated to Indian shores.

The plan of the work is as follows: To every verse or group of verses of the Dhammapada, it is recorded that the Master delivered "this sermon" (dhammadesanā), by which is meant the verse or the group of verses together with the narrative belonging to it, at such and such a place and with reference to this or that person or persons or event. Hereupon follows the story, which ends with the verse or verses, which are then explained word for word. All this, story, verses and explanation of words, is made to issue from Buddha's own lips. In the conclusion it is usually mentioned that after this sermon or these Gāthās a person appearing in the story or "many" or "a hundred thousand" persons (or monks) set their feet on the path of holiness, or attained to a higher stage of holiness. Not infrequently regular Jātakas, too, are inserted or added, telling of the deeds or experiences in a former existence of the hero of the story. The stories themselves are very varied. Side by side with very long stories or veritable novels, we find short, edifying legends, which are

[1]) The story is told in connection with Dhammapada 114, Ed. Norman II, 272 ff.; translation *Burlingame* in HOS, Vol. 29, 257 ff. *Cf.* E. *Rohde* in Verhandlungen der 30. Versammlung deutscher Philologen und Schulmänner zu Rostock 1875, p. 68 f, J. H. *Thiessen*, Die Legende von Kisāgotamī, Breslau 1880, and above, Vol. I, 395 f., 411 ff., Vol. II, p. 142.

[2]) Udenavatthu on Dhammapada 21-23, ed. Norman I, 161-231, transl. *Burlingame* in HOS, Vol. 28, 62 f., 247 ff. *Cf.* A. *Weber*, Indische Streifen I, 370 note, and III, 16, and *Rhys Davids*, Buddhist India, p. 4 ff.

invented in a dull and insipid manner merely for the elucidation of a verse; but on the other hand, there are also most interesting fairy tales and stories culled from popular literature. The chief doctrine which the stories seek to impress is that of Karman. The story of the death of Moggallāna is significant, and its interest is enhanced because, like many other narratives of the Dhammapada commentary, it indicates a very hostile attitude towards the "naked ascetics," *viz.*, the Jain monks.[1]

Opposition to the "naked ascetics" is also shown in the story of Visākhā,[2] which is interesting enough for several reasons; though its moral aims at nothing more than to show that the rich and pious lay-adherent is blessed with tremendous wealth, only because in a former existence she had done great honour to the Buddha of that time, and that, in her new existence also, she is working out a good Karman by spending her wealth in magnificent donations to the Buddhist monastic order. Some of the stories are merely versions of such as already occur in books of the Tipiṭaka. Thus, for example, the story of the Arhat Godhika,[3] who cuts his throat in order to enter Nirvāṇa, whereupon Māra vainly searches for a trace of him, is only a slightly different form of the legend related in the Saṃyuttanikāya.[4] As in the Jātaka book, in this collection, too, humour occasionally comes into its own; evidence of this is the fable of the obstinate donkey,[5] told in the

---

1) On Dhammapada 137. Translated by *Warren*, l.c. 221 ff., Ed. Norman, III, 65 ff.; transl. *Burlingame*, HOS 29, 304 ff.

2) On Dhammapada 53, *cf. Warren*, l.c., 451 ff., Ed. Norman, I, 385 ff.; transl. *Burlingame*, HOS 29, 59 ff.

3) On Dhammapada 57, *cf. Warren*, l.c., 380 ff., Ed. Norman, I, 431 ff.; transl. *Burlingame*, HOS 29, 90 ff.

4) IV, 3, 3, transl. by *Windisch*, Māra und Buddha, p. 113 ff.

5) On Dhammapada 13 f., Ed. Norman I, p. 123 ff., transl. *Burlingame*, HOS 28, 224 f.

form of a Jātaka, the substance of which is here briefly stated:

A merchant goes with a donkey from Benares to Taxila in order to sell pottery. While the man is selling his wares, the donkey grazes outside the city. He there converses with a she-ass who pities him greatly because he has to carry heavy loads so many miles, and because he has nobody to stroke his legs and back when he returns home. Through this talk the donkey becomes refractory and refuses to return to Benares. Even the threat of the whip avails nothing. At last the master perceives the she-ass, and guesses that she is the cause of the donkey's obstinacy, and he determines to make him tractable by means of the "eternal feminine." He promises him a beautiful she-ass as his wife. Highly delighted the donkey now willingly trots home. But after a few days he reminds his master of his promise. The latter says: "I will not break my promise, I will bring you a wife, but I can only give you food for yourself alone; you yourself must know whether or not that will be sufficient for you when there are two of you; through your both living together children will also be born; you yourself must know whether or not this will be sufficient for you when there are so many of you." No sooner had the master concluded his speech than the donkey lost all desire for a wife.

Quite a number of stories in this commentary on the Dhammapada have their parallels in the commentaries of Buddhaghosa, and over 50 stories are common to the commentaries on the Dhammapada and Jātaka respectively. In some cases there is word for word identity, in others we find varying versions of the Jātaka tales. The commentaries of Dhammapāla have borrowed about 25 stories from the commentary on the Dhammapada.[1] There is, of course, always the possibility that all these commentaries did not copy from one another, but made use of common sources. *Burlingame*, however, has succeeded in making it appear fairly likely that the Jātaka commentary is later than the commentaries of Buddhaghosa, the commentary on the Dhammapada is later

---

[1] *Burlingame*, HOS 28, 46 ff.

than that on the Jātaka, and that those of Dhammapāla are later still. Nevertheless it is probable that none of these commentaries was separated from the rest by any very considerable period of time.[1]

In the authentic commentaries of Buddhaghosa, too, similes and parables, and valuable traditions and tales, occur frequently, as for instance in the Atthasālinī,[2] the Papañcasūdanī,[3] Sumaṅgalvilāsinī,[4] and especially in the Manoratha-Pūraṇī. In the commentary on the Brahmajāla-Sutta, Buddhaghosa gives us a remarkable account of the daily life of the Buddha. Here, on the one hand, the Buddha already appears as a kind of demi-god, in the same way as in the Mahāyāna Sūtras; when he goes out begging for alms, soft winds clean the ground before him, clouds lay the dust with a light shower of rain, and then spread themselves above him like a canopy, rough places become even, and lotus flowers spring forth under his footsteps, rays of six different colours shine from his body, and so on; but on the other hand he leads the true life of a mendicant monk.[5] Stories of Jīvaka, the doctor, are interwoven with the commentary on the Sāmaññaphala-Sutta (I, pp. 132 ff.). And in the commentary on the Ambaṭṭha-Sutta (I, pp. 259 ff.) there is the legend of

[1]) *Burlingame*, l.c., p. 57 f., dates Buddhaghosa's commentaries as 410-432, the Jātaka commentary somewhat later, the Dhammapada commentary about 450 and Dhammapāla's commentaries towards the close of the 5th century. If Buddhaghosa had not lived until the second half of the 5th century (s. Appendix IV), the other commentaries would have to be placed in the 6th century.

[2]) Parables of the man who sleeps beneath a mango tree with his head covered up, of the blind and the lame man, and others in Atthasālinī, ed. Müller, pp. 271 f., 279 ff., translation ("The Expositor"), pp. 359, 367 ff., 555.

[3]) Tales, *e.g.*, I, pp. 201, 228, 230f. Three tales from the commentary on the Upāli-Sutta (Majjhimanikāya 56) translated into French by L. *Feer* in RHR 13, 1886, p. 77ff. and JA 1887, sér. 8, t. IX, p. 309 ff.

[4]) *Cf.* the parables in the commentary to Dīghanikāya 22; s. *Warren*, Buddhism in Translations, p. 353 ff.

[5]) Sumaṅgala-Vilāsinī I, p. 45 ff.; *Warren*, Buddhism in Translations, p. 91 ff.

the origin of the Sakyas and Koliyas, so interesting from the point of view of social history.

The princes of the race of Ikṣvāku (Pāli Okkāka), who had built up Kapilavatthu, are so proud that they cannot find any princes worthy of marrying their sisters. For fear of degrading their race, they therefore appointed their eldest sister as mother, and co-habited with the other sisters. Then the eldest sister is smitten with leprosy, is taken into the forest, and placed in a deep pit. At the same time, Rāma, a king of Benares, also becomes leprous, and goes into the forest after having left the kingdom to his eldest son. In the forest he cures himself by means of healing herbs, and then takes up his dwelling in a hollow tree. One day a tiger comes to the pit in which the princess lives. The latter screams in terror. King Rāma hears it and proceeds to the pit. He wants to pull her out, but in spite of her misery, the princess is so proud that she only allows him to rescue her after he has explained that he, too, is of princely blood. Thereupon he cures her and makes her his wife. However, he does not return to his country, .but builds a city for himself in the forest. He begets many sons by the Sakya princess. When these sons had grown to manhood, their mother sent them to Kapilavatthu, so that they could there marry the daughters of their maternal uncles. They go there and kidnap the princesses. When the Sakyas hear that the kidnappers of their daughters are relatives, they have no objection. This is how the race of the Koliyas originated.[1])

Buddhaghosa's commentary on the Aṅguttaranikāya, the Manoratha-Pūraṇī, contains about a hundred stories.[2]) Among these we find, for example, thirteen extremely interesting legends from the lives of the Therīs, the first female disciples of the Buddha, which are exceedingly valuable by way of supplements to the Therīgāthās.[3]) The garland of legends which the Buddhist narrators have woven around

[1]) The same story is also related in the Paramattha-jotikā, the commentary on the Suttanipāta, (and from this text, published by *Fausböll*, it has been translated into German by A. *Weber* (Ind. Stud. V, 412-437; Ind. Streifen I, 233-244).

[2]) Some of these have been translated by *Burlingame*, Buddhist Parables, Chap. IX.

[3]) *Cf.* Mabel *Bode*, Women Leaders of the Buddhist Reformation, in JRAS 1893, pp. 517-566.

their female saints, throws many side-lights on the actual life and feelings of those women who renounced the world in order to follow the Buddha. The section begins with the life-story, already told in the Vinayapiṭaka, of Mahāpajāpatī Gotamī, the aunt and foster-mother of Buddha, who became the first nun. This story, which has all the appearance of an historical event is followed by the wonderful legend of Khemā, the queen who is vain of her beauty, and, for a long time, turns a deaf ear to Buddha; but one day, in her presence, Buddha conjures up the apparition of a divine woman of the most entrancing beauty, who grows older and older before her eyes, until she stands there as a decrepit old woman, and finally sinks down dead; then she is reminded of the destiny which awaits her also, and she begs the king to allow her to enter the community of nuns. Another, Uppalavaṇṇā, is so beautiful that the princes of the whole of India woo her, and her father is in a terrible dilemma, out of which his brave daughter helps him by becoming a nun. The legend of Kisā-Gotamī and the mustard-seed also appears in this work. The most touching story is that of Paṭācārā, the gist of which is briefly given here:

Paṭācārā is the daughter of a wealthy merchant in Sāvatthi. She falls in love with a workman who is employed in the house, and allows him to seduce her. After she has become pregnant, she desires to return to her parents. The man consents, but postpones the departure from day to day until, finally, she goes alone. He follows her and overtakes her just at the moment when, seized by the pains of travail in the middle of the street, she gives birth to a child. Then they return again. The same thing happens at the birth of the second child. While the woman is again delivered on the way, a great storm arises. Her husband makes her a shelter out of sticks, but while he is cutting the grass for making a thatch he is bitten by a snake, and dies. Sadly the mother goes on her way with her two children. She comes to a stream, which she cannot cross with both children. So she leaves the elder boy behind on the bank and carries the younger one across, lays him down and returns to the elder one. While she is in the middle of the stream, a hawk flies towards the younger child.

She raises her hands to scare the bird away. The elder boy sees this, and, thinking that his mother is beckoning him to come to her, he goes into the water, and is carried away by the current. Meanwhile the hawk has made off with the younger child.[1] Full of grief the woman continues her journey to Sāvatthi. Arriving there she hears that her parents' house has been wrecked by a whirlwind and that her parents have perished. They are just being burnt on the pyre. Then the unhappy woman breaks into mourning and lamentation, tears her garments from her body, and strays about for days naked and mad. At last one day she comes across Buddha who is just preaching. And the Master lets his feeling of friendliness flow out over her, and says: "Sister, come again to your senses. Sister, let your understanding return to you!" As soon as she hears the words of the Master, shame overcomes her. A man throws her a garment, and she covers herself. A certain verse of Buddha's effects her complete conversion, and she later becomes one of the most respected nuns in the community.[2]

In some of these narratives we find fairy tale motifs which belong to the common stock of universal literature, whether they travelled forth from India or were received from foreign lands by the Indians themselves. Thus Uppalavaṇṇā, in a former existence (for Buddhist narratives never rest content with tracing the lives of their saints merely in their latest existence) was the maiden Padumavatī, born of a lotus blossom, under whose footsteps lotus blossoms spring forth. As the favoured wife of the king of Benares she excites the jealousy of the secondary wives; while the king is away on an expedition of war, the other wives steal her newly-born children, in whose place they put a block of wood, besmeared with blood, by her side. The king, on his return home, is told that Padumavatī is a witch and has given birth to a block of wood. She is rejected, but soon the children, who had been put out in

[1]) On a similar episode in an old French poem of Guillaume d'Angleterre see S. *Singer* in ZVV 4, 1894, p. 73. *Cf.* W. *Bousset* and W. *Meyer* in NGGW 1916, 501 ff., 768 ff.; 1917, 80 ff., 703 ff.

[2]) Text ed. *Walleser*, I, p. 356 ff.; translation by *Burlingame*, Buddhist Parables, p. 94 ff.

wooden boxes, are fished up and the truth comes to light. Similar stories are found in the fairy tale literature of East and West.[1] In another part of the Manoratha-Pūraṇī we meet with the story of the merchant Ghosaka, being a version of the story already familiar to us from the Jaimini-Bhārata, about the youth who was born under a lucky star, and the fatal letter which was exchanged by the maiden[2] Most of the stories are, however, merely edifying legends. One of them, for instance, tells of a merchant tempted by Māra, in the form of the Buddha, with a false doctrine; but the merchant recognises him as Māra, for Buddha could not have taught such a thing.[3]

In his commentaries Buddhaghosa makes frequent reference to his Visuddhi-Magga, and in the introductions to some of them,[4] he states expressly that he does not wish to repeat anything which has already been explained in that work. It would seem, therefore, that Buddhaghosa regarded the Visuddhi-Magga,[5] or "The Path to Complete Purification," as a preparation for his commentatorial labours. The

---

[1]) The same tale also in the Therī-Gāthā commentary. Cf. Ed. *Müller* in AR 3, 1900, 217 ff. and S. *Singer* in ZVV 4, 1894, 71 ff.

[2]) Translated by *Burlingame*, Buddhist Parables, p. 128 ff. The story is also to be found in the Dhammapada commentary (ed. Norman, 1, 168 ff., *Burlingame* in HOS 28, 262 ff.). Cf. E. *Hardy* in JRAS 1898, 741 ff.; J. *Schick*, Das Glückskind mit dem Todesbrief (Corpus Hamleticum I, 1), Berlin, 1912, pp. 15 ff., 45 ff., 66 ff. (Singhalese versions). See above, Vol. I, p. 585 (and *Grierson* in JRAS 1910, 292 ff.). In Kathā-Sarit-Sāgara, XX, 194 ff., we find only the last motif, namely the motif of the fate intended for the persecuted youth befalling the persecutor himself.

[3]) E. *Hardy* (in JRAS, 1902, 951 ff.) compares with it a Christian legend, in which Satan assumes the form of Christ, in order to teach a false doctrine to a monk, and *Garbe* (Indien und das Christentum, p. 111 f.) holds that the Christian legend is Buddhist in origin. However, the resemblance seems to me not very striking.

[4]) To Atthasālinī, Papañcasūdanī, and Manoratha-Pūraṇī.

[5]) Edited by C. A. F. *Rhys Davids*, 2 vols., PTS 1920-1921. A short table of contents by J. E. *Carpenter* in JPTS 1890, p. 14 ff., a detailed analysis and considerable extracts in English translation by H. C. *Warren* in JPTS 1891-1893, pp. 76-164, and "Buddhism in Translations," pp. 285 ff., 291 ff., 315 ff., 376 ff., 384 ff. Bhikkhu *Nyāṇatiloka* has translated "the Reflection on Death" from Chapter 8, into German in ZB VII, 1926,

author himself explains the title of the work, when he says: "Visuddhi here means the Nirvāṇa which is wholly and thoroughly purified, and freed from dirt of every description, and the path which leads to this purification is called Visuddhi-Magga." He says that it is his intention to expound this "Path to Complete Purification" in accordance with the teachings of the Mahāvihāra, *i.e.*, the traditions preserved in the "great monastery" of Anurādhapura. For the present, however, it is impossible for us to decide whether he had some definite work before him, which he merely revised,[1] or whether we should give him credit for being the first to offer a systematic presentation of the entire doctrine of Buddha, on the basis of the interpretations and explanations which had been handed down in the Mahāvihāra. Should the latter theory be correct, the clear and systematic arrangement and classification of the subject-matter according to the three points of view, morals (sīla), meditation (samādhi) and wisdom (paññā), would be his own work, whilst generally he was content to collect together with great diligence and industry, all that had accumulated during the course of the centuries, by way of explanation of the doctrine and legendary traditions. His style is clear and lucid, and, as in his commentaries, in the Visuddhi-Magga, too, he frequently enlivens the dry elucidations by

---

p. 75 ff. *Cf. Law*, Life and work of Buddhaghosa, p. 70 ff. "Buddhaghosa's monumental work, the Visuddhimagga ('The Path of Purity'), is an anthological Aṭṭhakathā and forms an indispensable text book in Burma" (Shwe Zan *Aung* in JPTS 1910-1912, p. 121).

[1]) If we are to believe the Japanese scholar M. *Nagai* (JPTS 1917-1919, p. 69 ff.) the Visuddhi-Magga is not the work of Buddhaghosa, but merely the revised version of a work written by a Thera Upatissa in the first century A.D., entitled Vimuttimagga, "The Path of Release," which was translated into Chinese between 505 and 520 A.D. by the Cambodian monk Saṅghapāla. Though very ingenious, the arguments of *Nagai* are not convincing. Until we are better acquainted with the Chinese translation of this work, I think it quite possible that it is merely a Chinese version of Buddhaghosa's work. According to *Nagai* himself, the contents of the Chinese Vimuttimagga bear a general resemblance to the Visuddhi-Magga, but are not free from Mahāyāna influence (l. c., p. 79). Like *visuddhi*, the word Vimutti also means "Nirvāṇa."

occasional parables and often by legends too. These last are not his own inventions, but he must have taken them from older sources. In style and contents, some of these legends are strongly reminiscent of the Tipiṭaka, and some do actually occur in canonical texts while most of the narratives, it is true, date from a later period, when Buddha worship was just as highly developed in the Hīnayāna as in the Mahāyāna. It is the spirit of the old Arhat ideal as it is illustrated, for instance, in the prose of the Udāna, by many legends; the same spirit is also found in narratives such as the legend of the Thera Mahā-Tissa, who is reminded of the impurity of the human body by the sight of the teeth of a beautiful woman while laughing, and by this thought, attains to the highest stage of holiness, that of an Arhat;[1] or that of the monk who lived for sixty years in his hermitage without noticing that the walls were covered with paintings; or of the monk who is so unworldly that for three months he goes daily begging for food and eating it in the house of his mother who is longing to see him but does not recognise him in his monk's robe, without once saying: " I am your son and you are my mother."[2] On the other hand, we find, especially in Part II, many legends which testify to a Buddha worship which recalls the Kṛṣṇa-Bhakti. For example, a frog hears the voice of Buddha who is preaching on the bank of the river, listens, and being trodden on by a shepherd, is literally translated to a better world; for he is immediately reborn as a god in a golden palace in the heaven of the thirty-three gods.[3] In this work we also find numerous miracle tales intended to show how saints attain to miraculous and magic powers by meditation. A monk rescues a snake which is

---

[1]) Edition Mrs. *Rhys Davids*, I, p. 20 f.; *Warren*, Buddhism in Translations, p. 297 f.

[2]) Ed. Mrs. *Rhys Davids*, I, 91 ff.; *Warren*, l. c., p. 434 ff.

[3]) Ed. Mrs. *Rhys Davids*, I, 208 f.; *Warren*, l. c., p. 301 f.

fleeing from a bird; he does this by quickly creating a hill, in which the snake disappears. The monk Bakkula is swallowed by a fish, but remains safe and sound, as he is destined to become an Arhat. Sañjīva was in the state of utter absorption, was taken for dead and laid on the pyre, but the flames could not burn him. The nun Uttarā, absorbed in meditation, was not even injured by boiling oil. The snake Nandopananda had wound herself around the mount Meru and stretched her heads up to the second heaven, then the holy Moggallāna came, transformed himself into a still larger snake, wound himself around Nandopananda and crushed her and the mount Meru into the bargain. Chapter 13 [1] gives a long and circumstantial account of the ages of the world and the destruction and restoration of the worlds, reminiscent of the Purāṇas, fancies which would scarcely have come from Buddhaghosa's brain, but are most likely faithful reproductions of earlier traditions.

As far as the dogmatical and philosophical contents of the Visuddhi-Magga and the commentaries are concerned, it is surely an exaggeration to set Buddhaghosa up as a philosopher who cut out new paths and made an original contribution to Buddhistic philosophy.[2] He was a man of astonishing erudition and of most extensive reading, who to this day enjoys a well-merited reputation among the Buddhists of Ceylon, Burma and Siam, but it is going too far to call him "a great teacher of mankind."[3] There is difference of opinion as to how far he is reliable in his commentaries as an expounder of the canonical texts. K. E. *Neumann* says on one occasion: "The moment the Buddhist patres ecclesiæ and doctores profundi try their hand at elucidating profound and obscure passages in the

---

1) Ed. Mrs. *Rhys Davids*, II, 411 ff.; *Warren*, l. c., p. 315 ff.

2) B. Ch. *Law*, l. c., 185 ff.

3) B. Ch. *Law*, l. c., 174.

canon, they simply talk moonshine."[1] Nevertheless, I believe that the same thing is true of Buddhaghosa as is true of other Indian commentators. We cannot follow them blindly, and yet, on the other hand, we must admit that they do sometimes help us over difficulties and if we neglected them, we should be depriving ourselves of one of the means of explanation.[2] I agree with Mrs. *Rhys Davids* when she says: " Buddhaghosa's philology is doubtless crude, and he is apt to leave cruces unexplained, concerning which an Occidental is most in the dark. Nevertheless, to me his work is not only highly suggestive, but also a mine of historic interest. To put it aside is to lose the historical perspective of the course of Buddhist philosophy."[3] Even if Buddhaghosa had no original contribution to make, we should yet be indebted to him for his faithful preservation of ancient traditions.

Not long after Buddhaghosa, Dhammapāla wrote his commentary Paramattha-Dīpanī, " Elucidation of the True Meaning," on those texts of the Khuddakanikāya which Buddhaghosa had not explained: the Itivuttaka, Udāna, Cariyāpiṭaka, Thera-Gāthā, Vimāna-Vatthu and Peta-Vatthu.[4] Padaratittha on the southern coast of India nearest to Ceylon, is mentioned as his native town, but in any case he must have studied at Anurādhapura too; for, like Buddhaghosa, he refers to the Attha-Kathās of the " great monastery " of Anurādhapura. Moreover, both commentators have similar conceptions

---

[1] Reden Gotamo Buddho's aus der mittleren Sammlung I, 1896, Preface.

[2] *Cf.* what has been said above, Vol. I, p. 71, on Sāyaṇa.

[3] A Buddhist Manual of Psychological Ethics, 2nd Ed., p. xxxi.

[4] This is the order in which they are enumerated in the Sāsanavaṃsa (ed. by M. *Bode*, PTS 1897), p. 33, where the commentary on the Netti is also ascribed to him. The following parts of the Paramattha-Dīpanī have up to now been published by the PTS: The Commentaries on the Peta-Vatthu, ed. by E. *Hardy*, 1894; on the Vimāna-Vatthu, ed. by E. *Hardy*, 1901; on the Therīgāthā, ed. by E. *Müller*, 1893; on the Udāna, by F. L. *Woodward*, 1926.

throughout, and follow the same method of explanation. For this reason it is impossible that any considerable period of time could have elapsed between these two.[1] In the commentary on the Therī-Gāthās we find a few legends about the Therīs, which are also to be found in the Manoratha-Pūraṇī; portions of the Therī-Apadāna are included in this commentary, and it contains some traditions which are undoubtedly of great antiquity. The legend of Bhaddā Kuṇḍalakesā, for instance, is reminiscent of conditions such as we imagine must have been prevalent at the time of the Buddha and his first disciples when the adherents of various sects travelled about from place to place, in order to challenge scholars and ascetics to philosophical contests:

Bhaddā is the daughter of the royal treasurer. One day she sees a robber who is being led to his death, and she falls in love with him. By means of bribery, the father succeeds in obtaining the robber's release, and marrying him to his daughter. But the robber cares only for the girl's jewels. He takes her to a lonely spot in order to rob her. However, she perceives his intention, and, pretending to embrace him, she pushes him over a cliff. After this adventure, she does not want to return to her father's house, but becomes a Jain ascetic. She is not satisfied with the doctrines of the Jains, and therefore goes to a place where some famous scholars are living, in order to dispute with them. As she does not find one who is her equal in a contest of speech, she wanders from place to place, and at the entrance to every village and town she sticks a branch of rose-apple in a sand-heap, saying to the village children: "If anyone would like to enter into a debate with me, let him trample the branch down." If anyone did so, the children were to report to her. If the branch was still standing upright after a week, she would pull it out, and go on her way.

---

1) On Dhammapāla, *cf.* T. W. *Rhys Davids* in ERE, Vol. 4, p. 701 f.; Gandhavaṃsa in JPTS 1886, pp. 57, 60; *Burlingame* in HOS, Vol. 28, p. 56 f.; *Law*, Life and Work of Buddhaghosa, p. 101 ff. The Dhammapāla who wrote commentaries on the Visuddhi-Magga and on the Dīgha-, Majjhima-, and Saṃyuttanikāyas (Sāsanavaṃsa, p. 33) is probably a different man. At all events the Dhammapāla with whom we are concerned, is not the same as the Dharmapāla, who lived in the monastery of Nālanda, and was the teacher of Hsüan-Tsang; s. *Hardy* in ZDMG 51, 1897, 105 ff.

In this way she came, among other cities, to Sāvatthi, where the great Sāriputta enters into debate with her and converts her to Buddhism. The Buddha himself consecrates her as a nun.[1]

Though *some* of these narratives are very beautiful, and though the commentary is most valuable by reason of its numerous quotations from the Apadānas, it cannot be denied that many of the stories are very stupid ; not infrequently they are only made up out of the verses, and sometimes they are so dull and insipid that, on one who has read the beautiful verses of the Therī-Gāthā, they often have the effect of a cold shower.

The commentaries on the Peta-Vatthu and the Vimāna-Vatthu[2] follow a similar arrangement to that of the Jātaka commentary and the commentary on the Dhammapada,[3] elucidating and enlarging on verses by circumstantial prose narratives. There are several valuable legends among them. We find a few interesting Consolatory Stories in the commentary on the Peta-Vatthu.[4] In some cases the stories in the commentary on the Vimāna-Vatthu are even of greater value than those in the Vimāna-Vatthu itself. As regards Dhammapāla as an exegetist, what has been said of Buddhaghosa might be applied to him also.[5]

The monks in the monasteries of Ceylon were not, however, merely occupied with the collection of legends and the explanation and elucidation of the canonical texts. From the earliest times onwards, they made it their business

---

[1]) Therī-Gāthā Commentary, p. 107 ff. The same story also in Manoratha-Pūraṇī, translated by *Burlingame*, Buddhist Parables, p. 151 ff. *Cf.* Mrs. *Rhys Davids*, Psalms of the Sisters, p. 63 ff., where many other stories from the Therī-Gāthā Commentary are also given, and Maria E. Lulius van *Goor*, De buddhistische Non, p. 142 ff.

[2]) Ed. by E. *Hardy*, London PTS 1894 and 1901.

[3]) The Dhammapada Commentary is quoted in the Vimāna-Vatthu Commentary, p. 165, and must therefore be of earlier date.

[4]) Legends from the Peta-Vatthu Commentary have been translated by B. Ch. *Law*, The Buddhist Conception of Spirits, 1923. For the Consolatory Stories (*Law*, l. c., 29 ff., 33, 64 ff.) *cf.* above, Vol. I, pp. 395 f., 412 ff.

[5]) *Cf.* Mrs. *Rhys Davids*, Psalms of the Sisters, p. xvi f.

also to record in the form of chronicles the chief events in the h[illegible] of the Buddhist monastic community. The account of the councils in the Culla-Vagga of the Vinayapiṭaka already betokens historical interest. The commentary on the Kathāvatthu[1] contains an account of the sects and schools, which is of paramount importance for the history of the schisms in the earliest Buddhist community. Moreover, the Singhalese Aṭṭhakathās, already mentioned several times, which were studied with much diligence by Buddhaghosa and were utilised by Dhammapāla too, contained sections on ecclesiastical history. These sections presumably formed the introductions to the Aṭṭhakathās, which deal with the Vinaya. Buddhaghosa followed them and drew upon them when he prefaced his Samanta-Pāsādikā, the commentary on the Vinaya-piṭaka, by an historical introduction.[2] The same Aṭṭhakathās are also the sources from which the historical and epic Pāli poems of Ceylon are derived; for the Pāli chronicles of Ceylon, the Dīpavaṃsa and the Mahāvaṃsa,[3] cannot be termed actual histories, but only "historical poems."

As it has never been the Indian way to make a clearly defined distinction between myth, legend and history historiography in India was never more than a branch of epic poetry. Thus the Buddhists regarded as history not only all the legends about the Buddhas of previous ages and the former

[1]) Buddhaghosa is not mentioned as the author, either at the beginning or in the colophons of the Commentary. At the beginning a long passage is cited word for word from the Dīpavaṃsa (ed. *Oldenberg*, p. 36).

[2]) Published by *Oldenberg* in his edition of the Vinayapiṭaka, Vol. III, 281 ff.

[3]) The Dīpavaṃsa, edited and translated by H. *Oldenberg*, London 1879. Mahāvaṃsa, edited and translated by G. *Turnour*, Ceylon 1837, Vol. I, containing the first 38 chapters; Turnour's translation is also prefixed to: The Mahāvaṃsa, Part II, containing Chapters XXXIX to C, translated by L.C. *Wijesiṃha*, Colombo 1889; critical edition by W. *Geiger*, PTS 1908, translated by the same scholar, PTS, Transl. Ser., 1912. *Cf.* H. *Jacobi* in GGA 1880, 851 ff; W. *Geiger*, Dīpavaṃsa und Mahāvaṃsa und die geschichtliche Überlieferung in Ceylon, Leipzig 1905, and ZDMG 63, 1909, 540 ff. (as against R.O. *Franke*, in LZB 1906, Sp. 1272 ff.; WZKM 21, 1907, 203 ff., 317 ff.). *Cf.* also *Oldenberg*, Aus dem alten Indien, Berlin 1910, 69 ff.

births of Gotama Buddha in the Buddhavaṃsa,[1] Cariyāpiṭaka and the Jātaka-book, but the whole of the Buddha legend as well. Taking a pattern from these legendary compositions and following on from them, the monks of Ceylon told the story of the introduction of Buddhism on the island, in the historical sections of the Aṭṭhakathās. They concocted legends[2] which were to connect the Buddhist community of Ceylon not only with that of India, but with Buddha himself, edifying legends telling how the Exalted One visited the island which was, at that time, inhabited only by demons and snake deities, how he flew over to it, accompanied by gods, in order to let the light of his doctrine shine forth, and to prepare for the subsequent greatness of the church of Ceylon. Pious legends of this nature led to mythical accounts of the first kings of Ceylon and also to semi-historical records of Asoka, Mahinda, the councils and the transmission of the sacred texts to the island. The nearer these records approach to the historical period, the more predominant do the real historical accounts become, though the legends are never altogether supplanted by history. Popular, secular narratives and anecdotes were also added to the ecclesiastical traditions.[3] Thus the historical sections of Aṭṭhakathās became, as it were, treasuries of ecclesiastical and secular traditions of all kinds, as well as of actual historical records.

[1]) The title signifies "history of the Buddhas;" for the Pāli word Vaṃsa (Sanskrit vaṃśa) means "line of a pedigree, or genealogy," hence also the "chronicle" or the "history" of a race, dynasty, line of teachers and so on; hence the meaning was extended to embrace any "history" going back to earliest beginnings, in such titles as Buddhavaṃsa, Dīpavaṃsa, Mahāvaṃsa, Thūpavaṃsa, Dāṭhāvaṃsa, etc., similarly in the Sanskrit titles Harivaṃśa, Raghuvaṃśa, etc.

[2]) But only *some* legends are inventions of the Singhalese monks. To a great extent, the historical as well as the legendary traditions of the Aṭṭhakathās go back to *Indian* sources (s. above, p. 184). Sten *Konow* (in Festgabe Garbe, p. 33 ff.) has shown this with regard to certain narratives (Dīpavaṃsa XV, Mahāvaṃsa XVII) which *a priori* would have been considered to be Singhalese in origin.

[3]) The reason for it is the same as that for the admission of so many secular stories in the Jātakas and in the commentaries in general. See above, p. 125.

Though these Aṭṭhakathās themselves have gone astray, their contents, as here described, may be deduced from the Pāli chronicles and Pāli commentaries which have come down to us.

The first, though very imperfect, attempt to mould into an epic the traditions stored up in the Singhalese Aṭṭhakathās is the Dīpavaṃsa, the "History of the Island." The author, whose name has not come down, but who probably wrote his work between the beginning of the 4th and the first third of the 5th century A.D.,[1] still betrays much awkwardness in the handling of language and metre. The offences against the laws of grammar and versification are numerous. It is evident that it is still an unaccustomed thing for a Singhalese to write in Pāli. He keeps slavishly to his models. He moulds his verses according to recollections of the Tipiṭaka, especially the Buddhavaṃsa, Cariyāpiṭaka and Jātaka.[2] His chief source of material was, however, the historical section of the Aṭṭhakathā[3] preserved in the "great monastery" of Anurādhapura, besides which he probably also used one or two other Aṭṭhakathās. This is most likely the reason why, not infrequently, the same subject is treated twice, or even thrice in different versions. Thus, for instance, immediately after a short, somewhat sketchy account of the three councils, follows a more complete, more finished account. These cannot possibly be cases of interpolation; the author found various versions available, and as he considered them

[1]) *Oldenberg*, Dīpavaṃsa, Introd., p. 8 f.

[2]) This has been proved convincingly by *Franke*, WZKM 21, 1907, 203 ff., though only as far as the form is concerned. The author could have taken only a very small portion of the subject-matter from the Tipiṭaka, as the latter gives no information about Ceylon. Cf. *Geiger*, ZDMG 63, 1909, 543.

[3]) This section of the Aṭṭhakathā, which was also a source of the Mahāvaṃsa, is quoted in the commentary on the latter, as Sīhalaṭṭhakathā-Mahāvaṃsa, *i.e.*, "the great History (of the Island of Ceylon) belonging to the Singhalese Commentary," and in the poem of the Mahāvaṃsa itself, as "the (Mahāvaṃsa) composed by the ancients." According to *Geiger*, Dīp. und Mah., p. 71, it was an independent chronicle; according to *Oldenberg* (Dīpavaṃsa, Introd., p. 4) with whom I agree, it was an historical introduction to a theological commentary.

of equal value, he passed them on. A poet, of course, would not have done so; but in other respects, too, the composition is as unsatisfactory as the language and metre. The narrator jumps straight from one subject to another without ado. Often gaps are left in the presentation. Some episodes are set out ballad-wise, whilst others are barely hinted at. In some cases, indeed, we find merely memorial verses in which a series of catch-words enumerates the chief points of a narrative or description. Obviously there were such verses in the Aṭṭhakathās, in which the setting forth of familiar scenes was left to the discretion of the reciters. Frequently also speeches follow upon speeches after the style of the primitive epic without any interceding narrative verses.[1] In some instances, as is so often the case in the ancient ballads, it can be seen from the context who the speaker is. But occasionally we have to assume that the reciter supplied the link between the speeches by means of prose narratives. In this, again, the author presumably only followed his models which were intended for recitation by monks at large assemblies.[2]

While the Dīpavaṃsa was thus closely connected even in form with its sources, and is only a feeble attempt at the composition of an epic, the Mahāvaṃsa, probably the work of a poet Mahānāma, who lived in the last quarter of the 5th century A. D.,[3] is a perfect epic. The poet wanted to create an ornate poem, a Kāvya, and he expressly states this in his poem. The historical work which the ancients composed,[4] says he, is in some places too verbose, and in

[1]) *Cf.* above, Vol. I, p. 324.

[2]) In two passages, IV. 47 and XII. 30-33, we also find the mixture of prose and verse as we must assume was to be found in the Aṭṭhakathā.

[3]) This seems very probable, from the Mahāvaṃsaṭīkā, see *Geiger*, Dīp. und Mah. 44 ff. *Cf.* V. A. *Smith* in Ind. Ant. 31, 1902, 192 ff.

[4]) It seems to me doubtful that this means the Dīpavaṃsa, as is assumed by *Geiger* (Mahāvaṃsa, Transl., p. xi). It certainly gives a false idea of the epic Mahāvaṃsa, if we designate it as a "commentary" on the Dīpavaṃsa, as is done by *Fleet* (JRAS 1909,

others too brief, and also contains many repetitions. He has, he says, avoided these faults and endeavoured to present the material in question in an easily comprehensible manner, so that the feelings of joy or of emotion may be aroused at the proper places. Indeed, in the Mahāvaṃsa the language and metre are handled with great dexterity. This is probably due not only to the talent of the poet, but also to the fact that the period between the origin of the Dīpavaṃsa and the Mahāvaṃsa coincides with the period of Buddhaghosa's literary activity, which made so lasting a mark on the Pāli literature of Ceylon. Neither is it possible to find fault with the presentation. There are no disturbing gaps, nor repetitions here. Where the Dīpavaṃsa is too brief, Mahānāma has extended and completed, again in other cases he has treated the theme more briefly. The Mahāvaṃsa is, as *Geiger* [1] says, "a work of art, created by a man who well deserves to be called a poet, and who mastered the frequently crude material, if not with genius, yet with taste and skill."

On the other hand, the Dīpavaṃsa and Mahāvaṃsa show great similarity with regard to the material and its arrangement, and even have a number of verses in common. Both epics commence with the story of Gotama Buddha, tell of his three visits to the island of Ceylon, which was at that time inhabited only by demons, namely Rākṣasas, Yakṣas, Piśācas and snakes, and relate how the Exalted One surveyed the whole world with his 'Buddha-eye" and caught sight of the beautiful island, how a terrible war broke out between the

p. 5) whose view is supported by *Geiger* (Mahāvaṃsa Transl. p. xi f.; Pāli Literatur und Sprache, p. 24). I consider Fleet's explanation of the passage in Mahāv. 38, 59 (ed. Turnour, p. 257 f., Cūlavaṃsa, ed. Geiger, I, p. 26) to which he refers, as erroneous. There is no question of the composition of a "Dīpikā" or a commentary, but it is merely related that King Dhātusena made a donation of 1,000 pieces of gold and commanded that, at the great Bodhi celebration in front of the memorial temple of the Mahāthera Mahinda, the monks assembled there should always expound the Dīpavaṃsa (in Singhalese) in return for which they should receive sweetmeats.

[1]) Dīp. und Mah., p. 19.

snake princes Great-belly and Small-belly, which threatened to destroy the island, how the Buddha in his boundless goodness felt pity, flew over to the island accompanied by gods, and let the light of his doctrine shine forth, whereupon hosts of snake demons and other demons were converted to the pure doctrine. Then the genealogical tree of Gotama's father Suddhodana is traced back to a mythical king of primeval times, and the history of Buddhism in India, especially the story of the councils, is related. The two epics dwell at some length on Aśoka, the great patron of Buddhism. With the account of the third council and the sending of Mahinda to Ceylon, the scene of the narrative changes, and is henceforth transferred entirely to Ceylon. From the union of an Indian princess with a lion, two children are produced, Sīhabāhu and Sīvalī. Vijaya, with whom the history of the kings of Ceylon begins, sprang from the marriage of this brother and sister. This wild prince is banished from his home, goes to sea with 700 companions, lands in Ceylon after manifold adventures on the seas, and becomes king of the island. The story of Vijaya and his immediate successors is told much more briefly in the Dīpavaṃsa than in the Mahāvaṃsa. Both works linger for some considerable time over King Devānampiyatissa, who ruled in Ceylon in the days of Aśoka, in whose reign Mahinda came to Ceylon (flying through the air, as we should expect), established there the religion of Buddha and erected the first Buddhist sanctuaries. Saṅghamittā, the sister of Mahinda, brings a branch of the Bodhi tree, the transplanting of which in Ceylon is described with especial attention to detail. Then the history of the kings of Ceylon, among them in somewhat greater detail Vaṭṭagāmani, who had the Tipiṭaka and its commentaries written down, is traced as far as Mahāsena, with whose death (352 A.D.?) [1] the narrative is cut short both in

[1]) This is the view of *Geiger*, The Mahāvaṃsa, Transl., p. xxxviii. 302 A.D. used to be assumed as the year of the death of Mahāsena. The chronology is by no means certain.

the Dīpavaṃsa and the Mahāvaṃsa; for the authentic work of Mahānāma ends with 37, 50. Everything which comes after that, is generally known in Ceylon as the Cūlavaṃsa,[1] "the little history," and consists of a series of addenda serving as a continuation of the Mahāvaṃsa and written by various authors. The first appendix is written by the Thera Dhammakitti, who lived during the reign of King Parākramabāhu (1240-1275).[2]

However, even though the subject-matter of the old Mahāvaṃsa moves within the same limits as that of the Dīpavaṃsa, Mahānāma has nevertheless inserted a considerable amount of new material within these limits. Above all, he has taken the story of King Gāmani the wicked (Duṭṭhagāmani), to whom only 13 verses are devoted in the Dīpavaṃsa, and developed it into an independent heroic poem (*Geiger* calls it the "Duṭṭhagāmani epic") in eleven cantos (22-32). In the first part he describes the warlike deeds of this mighty king, and not until the second part does he make him a hero of the faith, who atones for the streams of blood which he has caused to flow, by erecting sacred edifices, more especially the Mahāthūpa, "the great Stūpa," about the construction of which miracles are related. Mahānāma has also contrived to work into his composition a great number of fairy tale and romance motifs, some of which belong to universal literature. Whilst in the Dīpavaṃsa it is only mentioned that Vijaya and his companions were cast ashore in Ceylon, where they founded

[1]) Cūlavaṃsa, being the more recent part of the Mahāvaṃsa, ed. by W. *Geiger* I, PTS 1925. Cūlav. 37, 215 ff. deals with Buddhaghosa. Chapter 39 has been edited and translated by T. W. *Rhys Davids* (JRAS 1875, p. 191 ff., 201 ff. "The Reigns of Kaśyapa the Parricide and of Moggallāna the First"). In some MSS. the work consists of 90 chapters, and in others of 100 or 101. The title Cūlavaṃsa is nowhere to be found in the MSS. In 99, 76, the kings of Ceylon are divided into those of the "Great Dynasty" (mahāvaṃsa) and those of the "Lesser Dynasty" (cūlavaṃsa).

[2]) *Cf.* M. de Z. *Wickremasinghe* in JRAS 1896, 200 ff.; *Geiger*, Dīp. und Mah., p. 19. The coincidence of both the Dīpavaṃsa and the ancient part of the Mahāvaṃsa breaking off precisely at the death of Mahāsena, can only be explained by the fact that the

cities and established a kingdom, we are told in the Mahāvaṃsa (VII, 9 ff.) the most marvellous adventures of Vijaya and the ogress-sorceress Kuvaṇṇā, which vividly recall the experiences of Ulysses with Circe. A very interesting legend is that of King Eḷāra (21, 15 ff.):

This righteous prince had a bell fixed to his bed, and the rope of this bell hung in the open, so that everybody who had suffered some wrong could ring it.[1] First the rope is pulled by a cow, whose calf has been run over by the king's son. The king has his own son, his only son, crushed by the wheels of the same chariot. Then the king's aid is sought by a bird, whose young one has been killed by a snake, and the king has the snake killed. The bell rings for the third time; this time it is an old woman who is pulling the rope. She has laid some rice out to dry, and an unseasonable shower of rain has spoilt it. The king sees in this the punishment for a sin which he has recently committed. He does penance by fasting, whereupon Sakka orders the rain-god Pajjunna, only to send rain once a week at a certain hour of the night.[2]

It may probably be assumed that Mahānāma took all these materials which are missing in the Dīpavaṃsa, from the old Aṭṭhakathās, principally from the Sīhalaṭṭhakathā-Mahāvaṃsa, which was his chief source, even though he knew and used the Dīpavaṃsa as well. The fact that both epics are based on the historical sections of the old Aṭṭhakathās, is a

"Mahāvaṃsa" of the Aṭṭhakathā, the common source of both epics, was discontinued after the destruction of the "Great Monastery" of Anurādhapura which took place under Mahāsena, though Mahāsena had the monastery rebuilt. *Cf.* Mahāvaṃsa 37; Dīp. 22, 66 ff.; *Geiger*, Dīp. und Mah., p. 71.

[1]) "When the emperor Charlemagne......lived at Zürich, he had a pillar erected with a bell attached to it, so that anyone who desired administration of justice could pull it whenever the emperor was seated at his midday meal." *Grimm* Deutsche Sagen II, No. 453. Here, as in the similar legend of the sage Theodosius (Gesta Romanorum 105) it is a snake which demands and obtains justice against a toad. *Cf.* also the poem "Die Leidglocke" by F. *Rückert* in "Brahmanische Erzählungen;" E. *Hultzsch* in JRAS 1913, 529 ff., who, amongst other things, has traced a Tamil version of this story, and cites other parallels given by Th. *Zachariae.* See also *Benfey,* Pantschatantra I, 168 f.

[2]) Many other tales from the Mahāvaṃsa, which are of importance from the point of view of folk-lore, have been traced by *Geiger*. Dīp. und Mah., pp. 23-28. Some of these have interesting parallels.

strong argument in favour of our crediting them with a certain degree of reliability as historical sources. It is true, neither the Dīpavaṃsa nor the Mahāvaṃsa can be said to be a real work of history. Suffice it to point out[1] that neither of the two works even so much as mentions the name of Alexander the Great, that they have nothing but miracles to record of the great Aśoka, and that, in their narrative, this mighty conqueror is far more of a spiritual than a temporal hero. Even Gāmani the Wicked, whose popular cognomen shows clearly enough that he was essentially the very opposite of a pious model of virtue, is glorified in the Mahāvaṃsa above all as a religious hero! The purpose of both epics is primarily to serve for edification, and the Mahāvaṃsa is at the same time intended to be a Kāvya. Nevertheless, we should be doing these works an injustice if, as some critics have done, with expressions of indignation (which to me appear almost ridiculous), we label their authors as deliberate forgers and liars. Their authors certainly were nothing of that kind. They relate things which *they* looked upon as veracious history, though *we*, it is true, are compelled to regard much of it as myth, legend and fiction. Now, as they did not intentionally give false reports, we may believe much of what they tell us about historical times, and periods not too far removed from their own life-time. For instance, they were the first to give us information about Candragupta, the grandfather of Aśoka; and though this information does not tally exactly with the data of the Greeks, it is nevertheless in sufficient agreement with them to have made it possible by their aid to determine the year of Buddha's death, which means that we have been able to ascertain the most important date in the history of Indian literature. Sylvain *Lévi*,[2] too,

[1]) Cf. *Oldenberg*, Aus dem alten Indien, 77 ff.

[2]) JA sér. 9, t. XV, 1900, p. 429, and Journal des savants, 1905, p. 539. The theory of the reliability of the chronicles is also supported by Max *Müller*, SBE, Vol. 10 (I),

by comparing the Chinese annals with the Singhalese chronicles, has found that beginning at least from the 4th century A.D., the latter are, as historical sources, "solide, sinon impeccable."

There is also a greatly augmented recension of the Mahāvaṃsa, in 5,791 verses as against the ,915 verses of our text; and, though quite insignificant as a work of art, it is extremely instructive from the point of view of the history of literature, as showing how in India (for the Singhalese writers took their pattern from Indian models) epics were augmented by the insertion of more and more new themes.[1] A work of greater importance is the Mahāvaṃsa-Ṭīkā, written between 1000 and 1250 A.D., being the commentary on the Mahāvaṃsa. This is not merely an exegetic and dogmatic commentary, but it also contains numerous myths, fairy tales and legends by way of a supplement to the contents of the epic. These are culled partly from monkish and partly from popular traditions. For instance, the particularly interesting legends of Candragupta and Cāṇakya,[2] which the commentator, as he himself says, has taken in part from the Aṭṭhakathā of the "Northern Monastery," are of the popular variety. Otherwise he has drawn chiefly on the Aṭṭhakathā of the

pp. xiii-xxv; *Rhys Davids*, Buddhist India, p. 274 f.; H. O. *Norman*, JRAS 1908, 1 ff. In his researches on the history of the Canon, *Oldenberg* (see above, p. 1, note 1) has made many references to the data of Dip. and Mah. *Fleet* (JRAS 1909, pp. 987 and 1015) considers that the Dīpavaṃsa is based on local records of the time of Aśoka, and that the last words of Duṭṭhagāmaṇi are actually preserved in Mahāvaṃsa 32. A very low estimation of the historical reliability of the chronicles is held by V. A. *Smith* (Ind. Ant. 32, 1903, p. 365 f.) and R.O. *Franke*, JPTS 1908, p. 1. This scepticism has been refuted on excellent grounds by W. *Geiger*, (ZDMG 63, 1909, p. 550; The Mahāvaṃsa, Transl., pp. XII ff., XV ff., XX ff.). *Hultzsch* (JRAS 1913, p. 517 ff.) has succeeded in tracing synchronisms even between the later additions to the Mahāvaṃsa (for the period from the 10th to the 12th century) and the inscriptions.

[1]) The enlarged Mahāvaṃsa was discovered by E. *Hardy* (JPTS 1902-1903, p. 61 ff.) in a Cambodian manuscript, and has been discussed by *Geiger*, Dip. und Mah., p. 28 ff.

[2]) On this and other narratives see *Geiger*, Dip. und Mah., pp. 37-44, where analogies are indicated, especially the one presented by the legend of Cyrus.

"Great Monastery," at the same time using Buddhaghosa's commentaries Sumaṅgala-Vilāsinī and Samanta-Pāsādikā, and a great number of other works among which a Sahassavattha-ṭṭhakathā, "Commentary of the Thousand Stories" which is quoted several times, is especially worthy of notice.[1]

Also all the later works of ecclesiastical history of Ceylon are founded on the Aṭṭhakathās. Buddhaghosa drew on them for the historical introduction, already mentioned, to his Samanta-Pāsādikā.[2] This introduction, and the Nidāna-Kathā and the Mahāvaṃsa, are, in their turn, the foundation of the historical works, if we may call them so—for they contain more legendary lore than history—namely the Bodhi-vaṃsa, Dāṭhāvaṃsa and Thūpavaṃsa, which in later centuries were translated into Pāli or remodelled after Singhalese models. The Mahābodhivaṃsa or Bodhivaṃsa,[3] "the History of the Bodhi Tree," is a prose work (only at the ends of the chapters and towards the end of the whole work do we find Gāthās) which was written probably in the first half of the 11th century by a monk Upatissa. The Dāṭhāvaṃsa, "the History of (Buddha's) Tooth,"[4] is an epic in five cantos, in partly Sanskritised Pāli (with long compound words), written by the monk Dhammakitti at the beginning of the 13th century. The Thūpavaṃsa,[5] "the History of the Topes," is also a work of the 13th century. The work is available in both the

[1]) *Cf. Geiger*, Dīp. und Mah., p. 52 ff.

[2]) See above, p. 208.

[3]) Edited by S. A. *Strong*, PTS 1891. *Cf. Geiger*, Dīp. und Mah., p. 84 ff., Pāli Literatur und Sprache, p. 25.

[4]) Edited and translated by *Coomara Svāmy*; edited by *Rhys Davids* and R. *Morris*, JPTS 1884, p. 109 ff.; edited and translated by Bimalacharan *Law*, together with a Note on the Position of the Dāṭhāvaṃsa in the History of Pāli Literature by W. *Stede*, Lahore 1925 (PSS No. 7). *Cf.* J. Gerson da *Cunha*, Memoir on the History of the Tooth-relic of Ceylon, JBRAS XI, 1875, p. 115 ff. and *Geiger*, Dīp. und Mah., p. 88 ff. The Dāṭhādhātuvaṃsa mentioned in the continuation of the Mahāvaṃsa 37. 93, is probably (see Geiger, p. 19) the same work.

[5]) Two editions have appeared in Colombo, *cf. Geiger*, Dīp. und Mah., p. 92 ff.

Singhalese and Pāli languages. Vācissara calls himself the author. All these works are made after one pattern; they commence with the history of the former Buddha Dīpaṅkara, then of Gotama Buddha, the three councils, and so on, until finally they relate the history of the sanctuaries of which they treat. Similar works were also written in Burma, such as the Chakesadhātuvaṃsa,[1] "the History of the Six Hair Relic Shrines." Even so modern a work as the Sāsanavaṃsa, "the History of the Doctrine,"[2] which was written in Burma in 1861, by the monk Paññasāmi, follows the old pattern faithfully. Yet it is interesting to see from this work how Pāli literature continues even down to our own times. The Sāsanavaṃsa as well as the equally modern Gandhavaṃsa, "the History of the Books,"[3] written in Burma by a certain Nandapañña, are of great value from the point of view of the history of Pāli literature. The Gandhavaṃsa gives, in five chapters, a description of the canon according to the three Piṭakas and nine Aṅgas, the titles and sometimes the names of the authors of the later Pāli works, a description of the birthplaces of the writers, information about the causes which led to the writing of the books, and finally an account of the writing down of the canon.

We need not devote much space to the rest of the later Pāli literature of Ceylon and Burma. It is for the most part a learned, theological literature, closely connected with the canonical texts, though there is no lack of single poetical

[1]) Edited by *Minayeff* in JPTS 1885. The Sīmāvivādavinicchaya-Kathā, ed. by J. P. *Minayeff*, JPTS 1887, 17 ff., also contains ecclesiastical history.

[2]) Edited by Mabel H. *Bode*, PTS 1897. This work was the chief source for M. H. *Bode*, The Pali Literature of Burma, London 1909. *Cf.* by the same author, "A Burmese Historian of Buddhism," London 1898, and *Geiger*, Dīp. und Mah., p. 98 note.

[3]) Edited by *Minayeff*, Recherches, pp. 235 ff., and again in JPTS 1886, pp. 54-80. An index to this by Mabel *Bode*, JPTS 1896, p. 53 ff. According to M.H. *Bode* (Pali Literature of Burma, p. x) it is a work of the 17th century. The work is called Culla-Gandhavaṃsa, "Little History of the Books." There might, therefore, be a Mahā-Gandhavaṃsa also. *Cf.* E. *Hardy*, ZDMG 51, 1897, p. 111.

works. From the time of Buddhaghosa down to the revival of Pāli literature in the 12th century, we have in Ceylon scarcely more than a handful of names of authors and titles, while in Burma there is no Pāli literature at all before the 11th century.

Buddhadatta is said to have been a contemporary of Buddhaghosa. It is claimed that he, too, was born in India and lived at various times both in Ceylon and at Kāñcīpura and other places in South India. It is, however, questionable whether the legends about the meeting of Buddhadatta and Buddhaghosa were not merely invented with a view to enhancing the reputation of a much later writer. This later Buddhadatta is the author of a commentary on the Buddhavaṃsa and of comprehensive works on the Abhidhamma and Vinaya: the Abhidhammāvatāra, Rūpārūpavibhāga and the Vinaya-Vinicchaya.[1]

The poem Anāgatavaṃsa,[2] "the History of the Future One," *i.e.*, the future Buddha, is, as regards its contents, a sequel to the Buddhavaṃsa, the story of the past Buddhas, and perhaps belongs to an earlier period. The earliest description of the paradise of the future Buddha Metteyya, where human beings will attain to the mature age of 80,000 years, and where the maidens will be marriageable at the age of 500, when India will be teeming with human beings, like a poultry-yard swarming with fowls, etc., is already to be found in the Dīghanikāya (No. 26). The Anāgatavaṃsa gives a more detailed treatment of this Metteyya and his contemporary, the Cakravartin world-ruler Saṅkha, in the form of a

[1]) Buddhadatta's Manuals or Summaries of Abhidhamma, Abhidhammāvatāra and Rūpārūpavibhāga, ed. by A. P. *Buddhadatta*, PTS 1915. *Cf. Geiger*, Pāli Literatur und Sprache, p. 22, para. 25; B. Ch. *Law*, Life and Work of Buddhaghosa, p. 96 ff. There is, of course, the possibility that there was more than one Buddhadatta.

[2]) Ed. by J. *Minayeff* in JPTS 1886, p. 33 ff., and by E. *Leumann*, Maitreya-Samiti, das Zukunftsideal der Buddhisten, Strassburg 1919, p. 177 ff. (with explanatory notes).

prophecy which is made to issue from the lips of Gotama Buddha.[1]

A short summary of the rules of the Vinayapiṭaka is contained in the Sikkhās, the Khudda-Sikkhā by Dhammasiri, and the Mūla-Sikkhā by Mahāsāmi,[2] which, according to Burmese historical works, are said to have been written in 440 A. D., but are in all probability much more recent.[3] These compendia, together with the so-called Dvemātikā (consisting of Bhikkhu- and Bhikkhunī-Pāṭimokkha) and the Kaṅkhāvitaraṇī, are in Burma regarded as sufficient for those who have no time to learn the entire Vinayapiṭaka.[4] The Sārasaṃgaha by Siddhattha,[5] a pupil of Buddhappiya, and the Dhammasaṃgaha (or Saddhammasaṃgaha) by Dhammakitti,[6] which probably belong to the end of the 13th and the beginning of the 14th century,[7] are compendia which deal with the doctrine. The chief home of the study of the

[1]) According to the Gandhavaṃsa (JPTS 1886, pp. 61, 72), Kassapa is the author of the work, and Upatissa the author of an Aṭṭhakathā on it. Now both Kassapa and Upatissa are names of Theras and writers of various periods. *Cf. Geiger*, l.c., p. 25, para. 29. Visuddhi-Magga, p. 434, and Attha-Sālinī, p. 415, as well as Anāgatavaṃsa, v. 96, say of the future Metteyya, that the name of his mother is Brahmavatī and that of his father Subrahmā. It is not evident to me, however, that Buddhaghosa quotes from the Anāgatavaṃsa, as is assumed by Mr. *Rhys Davids* (Visuddhi-Magga Ed., pp. 761, 764). Hence we are not in a position to prove that the Anāgatavaṃsa is earlier than Buddhaghosa. As a matter of fact, there is also a recension of the Anāgatavaṃsa, which is written in the mixed prose and verse style, and yet another Anāgatavaṃsa which diverges from our work, and tells the story of the ten future Buddhas. (*Minayeff*, JPTS 1886, pp. 33 ff., 39 f.).

[2]) Ed. by Ed. *Müller* in JPTS 1883, p. 86 ff. At the end of the Khudda-Sikkhā itself, Dhammasiri from Ceylon is mentioned as the author. *Cf.* Gandhavaṃsa in JPTS 1886, p. 61.

[3]) *Rhys Davids* (JPTS 1883, p. xiii f.) considered them to be earlier than Buddhaghosa; Ed. *Müller* ascribes them to the 6th or 7th century; *Geiger* (Pali Literatur und Sprache, p. 24, para. 27) thinks that, judged by their language, they could scarcely have been written prior to the 11th century.

[4]) *Bode*, l.c., 5 f.

[5]) Des Sārasaṃgaha erstes Kapitel, Text und Übersetzung von K. E. *Neumann*, Leipzig 1891.

[6]) Ed. by N. *Saddhānanda* in JPTS 1890.

[7]) *Cf. Geiger*, l.c., p. 80.

Abhidhamma is Burma. There, too, the most important manual of Buddhist psychology and ethics, the Abhidhammattha-Saṃgaha, was written by the monk Anuruddha (probably in the 12th century).[1] Even at the present day this manual is still held in the highest possible esteem in Ceylon as well as in Burma, and has been more frequently commentated and translated in Burma than any other text of the Abhidhamma. Anuruddha is also the author of the Nāmarūpapariccheda, a philosophical poem of 1,855 verses.[2]

From among the learned works giving a poetical presentation of one or more points of the Buddhist doctrinal system, we call attention to the following. The Pañcagati-Dīpana, the "Illumination of the Five Paths,"[3] is a poem of 114 verses. It describes the great and small hells and the other worlds, and enumerates the actions by which human beings are reborn in one of the five conditions of life, namely as creatures of hell, as animals, spirits, human beings or gods. The same subject is treated in the Lokadīpasāra, which was written in the 14th century by Medhaṃkara in Burma.[4] In the 14th century one Dhammakitti wrote the Pāramī-Mahāśataka, a Pāli poem on the ten Pāramitās.[5] The Saddhammopāyana, "Ways and Means of the Good Religion,[6] deals, in 629 verses, with the fundamental doctrines of the Buddhist religion in general, and the ethical doctrines in

1) The text was published by T. W. *Rhys Davids* in JPTS 1884. A translation appeared under the title: Compendium of philosophy, being a Translation of the Abhidhammattha-Saṅgaha with Introductory Essay and Notes by Shwe Zan *Aung*, revised and edited by Mrs. *Rhys Davids*, PTS 1910. Transl. ser. *Cf. Bode*, l.c., p. 61 f. German translation by E. L. *Hoffmann* in ZB 7, 1926, 175 ff., 316 ff.

2) Ed. by A. P. *Buddhadatta* in JPTS 1913-1914, pp. 1-114.

3) Ed. by *Feer* in JPTS 1884, and translated by the same into French in AMG., t. V, 1883, 514 ff.

4) *Bode*, l.c., 35 f.

5) There were no less than 5 Theras by the name of Dhammakitti, who lived in the 13th and 14th centuries. *Cf.* M. de Z. *Wickremasinghe* in JRAS 1896, 200 ff.

6) Ed. by R. *Morris* in JPTS 1887, 35-98.

particular. The Pajja-Madhu, "the Verse Honey,"[1] is a short poem in praise of the Buddha, composed by Buddhappiya in the 13th century. In 104 elaborate stanzas in partly Sanskritised Pāli, the glory of the Buddha is described and his wisdom praised. Telakaṭāha-Gāthā, "the Verses of the Cauldron of Oil,"[2] is the title of another ornate poem on the good religion of the Buddha. The poet is supposed to have been a monk who, though innocent, was suspected by King Tissa of Kalyāṇi of carrying on an intrigue with his wife, and was condemned to be thrown into a cauldron of boiling oil. This was done, but the monk arose from the cauldron, and sang the 100 verses. Before he died, he recollected his former existence in which he was a cowherd and had thrown a fly into a pot of boiling milk. In the poem, the "hundred verses" are found only 98 stanzas in elegant Sanskritised Pāli, in which, however, no reference to the legend is contained. King Tissa of Kalyāṇi reigned in the 3rd century B.C., but, according to the evidence afforded by the language, the poem could hardly be earlier than the 12th century A.D.[3]

The Jinālaṃkāra by Buddharakkhita,[4] a poem of 250 stanzas, in which the Buddha legend is treated in the most bombastic Kāvya style, and which was written in the year 1156 A.D., is a regular specimen of ornate poetry. We find verses which can be read backwards as well as forwards, a stanza in

[1]) Ed. by E. R. *Gooneratne* in JPTS 1887, 1 ff. The poet is also the compiler of the Pāli grammar Rūpasiddhi.

[2]) Ed. by E. R. *Gooneratne* in JPTS 1884, 49 ff.

[3]) The legend is related briefly in the Mahāvaṃsa, 22, 13 ff., and in greater detail in the Rasavāhinī.

[4]) Edited with Introd., Notes and Translation by James *Gray*, London 1894. According to the Gandhavaṃsa (JPTS 1886, pp. 69, 72, *cf.* 65, 75) a Jinālaṃkāra was written by Buddhadatta and commented on by Buddharakkhita. A work like the Jinālaṃkāra with which we are concerned, could not have possibly been written by a contemporary of Buddhaghosa (see above p. 220 on Buddhadatta). The date "1,700 years after the death of Buddha" figures in the concluding verses of the poem, where Buddharakkhita refers to himself as the author. *Cf. Geiger*, l.c., p. 28.

which no consonant except "n" occurs, and other similar tricks. Mahāyānist doctrines are frequently found in the poem and it is full of Purāṇa-like exaggerations.

The Jinacarita[1] by the poet Vanaratana Medhaṃkara,[2] who lived in the reign of Bhuvanaka Bāhu I (1277-1288 A.D.), is a very mediocre poem on the life of the Buddha, in simple and natural, but not particularly beautiful, language. It looks almost like a somewhat clumsy versification of the Nidāna-Kathā. The Mālālaṃkāra-Vatthu, a Buddha biography written at an even later time (1773), has only become known through the English translation[3] of a Burmese translation from the Pāli.

Narrative works, too, have been written in Pāli down to the most recent times. The most important of these works is the Rasavāhinī,[4] a collection of 103 narratives, of which the first 40 are set in India and the remaining 63 in Ceylon. The work was originally written in the Singhalese language, was later translated into Pāli by a monk Raṭṭhapāla, and still later (in the 13th century) corrected by the Thera Vedeha.[5] In spite of this "correction," it is still written in bad Pāli, and in an extremely careless style. The Rasavāhinī is really a collection of sermons in the guise of edifying legends told in

[1]) Edited and translated by W. H. D. *Rouse* (JPTS 1904-5, p. 1 ff.), and by Ch. *Duroiselle*, Rangoon 1906.

[2]) According to Saddhamma-Saṃgaha IX, 22 (JPTS 1890, p. 63) and Gandhavaṃsa (JPTS 1886, pp. 62, 72).

[3]) By Bishop P. *Bigandet*, Life or Legend of Gaudama the Buddha of the Burmese, Rangoon 1858, 3rd ed., London 1880. *Cf. Rhys Davids*. SBE, Vol. 11, p. xxxii.

[4]) Selected stories have been edited and translated into German by F. *Spiegel*, Anecdota Palica, Leipzig 1845; Sten *Konow* in ZDMG 43, 1889, 297 ff.; the second decade by Magdalene and W. *Geiger* in SBayA 1918, into Danish by D. *Andersen*, openhagen 1891; into Italian by P. E. *Pavolini* in GSAI 8, 1894, p. 179 ff., 10, 1896, p. 175 ff.; into English (legends of Aśoka) by *Lakshmaṇa Śastrī* (with a "Prefatory Note" by H. C. *Norman*) in JASB 1910, p. 57 ff. *Cf. Gooneratne* in PTS 1884, p. 50 f.; *Pavolini* in GSAI 11, 1897, p. 35 ff.

[5]) He is also the author of the Samanta-Kūṭavaṇṇanā, a description of the Adam's Peak, published in Journal of the Buddhist Text Society, May 1893.

the favourite mixture of prose and verse. Each tale or sermon ends with an exhortation, *e.g.*, "O friends, never tire of doing good;" or, "Even a cruel tiger, feeding on the flesh of others, was wise, and he was admitted into heaven by reason of his compassion. Therefore be ever merciful towards men; for this will bring you blessings and happiness in the forms of existence." (II, 5). The Buddha-worship in some of the legends differs in no way from that of the Mahāyāna, nor from the Viṣṇu-Bhakti of the Bhāgavatas, *e.g.*, in the story of the snake that is tamed by the one word "Buddha." Side by side with many somewhat naïve legends, there are also in the collection a good number of stories of great merit, some of which are also interesting on account of their parallels in universal literature. Thus, here again, we find the universally known story of the grateful animals and the ungrateful human being, with which we already met in the Jātaka. Some of the stories are borrowed from earlier works, such as Buddhaghosa's commentaries, or the Mahāvaṃsa.

The Jātaka book was the inexhaustible source from which Buddhist poets, writers and compilers drew again and again. Thus the poet Sīlavaṃsa of Ava, in the 15th century, wrote a poem Buddhālaṃkāra, based on the Sumedha-Kathā in the Nidāna-Kathā. About the same time the poet Raṭṭhasāra of Ava produced a few poetical versions of Jātakas. Tipiṭakālaṃkāra, who was born in 1578 in Burma, wrote a poetical version of the Vessantara-Jātaka when he was a fifteen-year old novice.[1] Even the Rājādhirāja-Vilāsinī, a prose work written at the request of the Burmese king Bodōpayā, who ascended the throne in 1782, takes the Jātaka book as its chief source, though the author, in order to show his erudition, diligently used the entire literature from the Suttas down to the latest commentaries, as well as all sorts of learned Pāli

[1]) *Bode*, l.c., 48 f., 53.

and Sanskrit works on grammar, astronomy and other sciences.[1]

Buddhist Literature in Pure and Mixed Sanskrit

Now, though the Pāli literature of India, Ceylon and Burma, is an unusually rich and extensive literature, it must nevertheless be admitted that it does but represent the literature of one Buddhist sect, namely that of the Theravādins. Other schools and sects used other Middle Indian dialects,[2] and some of the most prominent schools produced works of literature written partly in Sanskrit and partly in a Middle Indian dialect assimilated to Sanskrit which, to use *Senart's* term, we may call "Mixed Sanskrit."[3] Many large works of this literature have come down to us, but in some cases only fragments remain. In the North and North-West of India there were great centres of learning, such as the universities of Nālanda and Takkasilā (Taxila) where for hundreds of years not only all branches of secular knowledge, especially medicine, but also the philosophical and theological literature of the Buddhists were cultivated with great zeal. Indian Pandits went thence to Tibet and China, learned Tibetan and Chinese, and translated Sanskrit works into these languages. Chinese pilgrims like Hsüan Tsang learned Sanskrit at Nālanda, and

¹) *Bode*, l.c., 78 ff.

²) According to Vinītadeva (8th century A.D.) the Sarvāstivādins used Sanskrit, the Mahāsaṅghikas Prākrit, the Sammitīyas Apabhraṃśa and the Sthaviravādins (*i.e.*, Theravādins) Paiśācī. *Cf.* Ryukan *Kimura*, A Historical Study of the Terms Hīnayāna and Mahāyāna and the origin of Mahāyāna Buddhism, Calcutta, 1927, p. 7; R. *Pischel* in SBA 1904, p. 808.

³) It was formerly generally called "Gāthā dialect" (see above, Vol. I. p 47 f.), which is the more inapt, as it is widely used in inscriptions too. *Cf.* S. *Lefmann* in ZDMG 29, 1875, 212 ff.; E. *Senart*, JA 1882, s. 7, t. XIX, 238 ff., 1886, s. 8, t. VIII, p. 318 ff.; *Kern*, SBE 21, p. XIV ff.; *Bühler*, Ep. Ind. I, 1892, 239, 377; II, 34; *Hoernle* and *Bhandarkar*, Ind. Ant. 12, 1883, pp. 89 f., 205f., 139 ff.; 17, 1888, p. 36 ff.; J. *Wackernagel*, Altindische Grammatik, I, Göttingen, 1896, p. XXXIX ff.

translated Buddhist texts into Chinese.[1] Some of the Sanskrit works which were produced there, and the originals of which are lost, would not be known to us but for the Tibetan and Chinese texts. The finds of manuscripts in Central Asia, include fragments not only of Sanskrit texts, but also of translations of Indian works in Central Asiatic languages.[2]

By far the greater part of this literature written in pure and "mixed" Sanskrit, and which, for the sake of brevity we term "Buddhist Sanskrit literature," either belongs to the Mahāyāna or has at least come under its influence to a greater or lesser degree.[3] For this reason, it is essential to premise a few remarks as to the schism of Buddhism into its two great sections, Mahāyāna and Hīnayāna, if we desire to attain to a true understanding of this literature.

[1]) *cf.* Phanindranath *Bose*, Indian Teachers of Buddhist Universities, Madras, 1923; The Indian Teachers in China, Madras, 1923; and Prabhatkumar *Mukherjee*, Indian Literature Abroad, in Ind. Hist. Qu, Vols. I-III, 1925-1927.

[2]) Thus fragments of Buddhist texts have been found in two languages hitherto unknown, which are now termed "Kuchean" and "Khotanese" after Kuchar and Khotan, the places in Eastern Turkestan where they were discovered, as the names "Tokharian," "North Aryan," "East Indian" and "Śakian," suggested by various scholars have not been generally accepted (*Cf.* Sten *Konow* in Festschrift Windisch, p. 96 f.; *Hoernle*, Manuscript Remains, I, p. IX ff.). Fragments in "Kuchean" have been published by S. *Lévi* in JA 1911, s. 10, t. XVII, 138 ff., 431 ff.; t. XIX, 1912, 101ff; JRAS 1913, 109 ff.; and in Hoernle, Manuscript Remains, I, pp. 357ff., 365 ff.; Fragments in "Khotanese" by *Konow* and *Hoernle* in Hoernle, Manuscript Remains, I, pp. 214 ff., 289 ff., 395 ff.; also by E. *Leumann*, Zur nordarischen Sprache und Literatur, Strassburg, 1912; Maitreyasamiti, Strassburg, 1919, and Buddhistische Literatur, Nordarisch und Deutsch, I, Leipzig, 1920 (AKM XV, 2). A Soghdian version of the Vessantara-Jātaka has been edited and translated by R. *Gauthiot* in JA 1912, s. 10, t. XIX, pp. 163 ff., 430 ff; see also Le Sūtra des causes et des effets du bien et du mal, éd. et trad. d'après les textes sogdiens, chinois et tibétains par R. *Gauthiot* et P. *Pelliot*, Paris (Mission Pelliot) I, 1920; II, 1926. Buddhist texts in the Uigurian language have been published by H. *Stönner* in SBA 1904, p. 1282 ff. and F. W. K. *Müller*, Uigurica I and II, in ABA 1908 and 1910. E. *Sieg* and W. *Siegling*, to which scholars is due the credit of having proved "Tokharian" ("Kuchean") to be an Indo-European language, (SBA 1908, p. 915 ff.) have published fragments of Buddhist Sanskrit texts from the finds at Turfan: Tocharische Sprachreste, I, Die Texte, Berlin and Leipzig, 1921.

[3]) For our earliest knowledge of this literature, which is preserved chiefly in Nepal, we are indebted to Brian Houghton *Hodgson*, who lived in Nepal from 1821 to 1843, and rendered equally signal services as a statesman, geographer, zoologist, ethnographer and

To the earlier Buddhist schools, whose main doctrines coincide with those of the Theravāda as it has come down in the Pāli Canon, individual liberation, Nirvāṇa, was the most complete salvation; and the state of the Arhat, who even during his mortal life is accorded a foretaste of Nirvāṇa, was the goal of all striving, a goal attainable only to the few, by the aid of certain spiritual experiences which can only be acquired in the monastic life. This doctrine is not rejected by the adherents of the Mahāyāna; but, though it is acknowledged to have originated with Buddha,[1] it is described as the

investigator of Indian languages and antiquities. He was instrumental in procuring numerous Buddhist manuscripts for Indian and European libraries, and especially for Paris, where they were turned to excellent use by Eugène *Burnouf* (Introduction à l'histoire du Buddhisme Indien, 2. ed., Paris, 1876). At about the same time (1824) as Hodgson made his discoveries which so essentially promoted the knowledge of Buddhist literature, the celebrated Hungarian Alexander Csoma de *Körös*, after wandering on foot from Hungary to Tibet, had just begun to open up the Buddhist literature of Tibet. Shortly afterwards, the Pāli literature of Ceylon, too, was opened by George *Turnour*. Information regarding the contents of numerous manuscripts of Buddhist Sanskrit literature is given by *Rājendralāla Mitra*, The Sanskrit Buddhist Literature of Nepal, Calcutta, 1882; C. *Bendall*, Catalogue of Buddhist Sanskrit Manuscripts in Cambridge, Cambridge, 1883; and *Haraprasāda Śāstrī*, A Descriptive Catalogue of Sanskrit Manuscripts in the Government Collection under the care of the Asiatic Society of Bengal, I, Buddhist Manuscripts, Calcutta, 1917. The Tibetan translations in the Kanjure are described by A. Csoma de *Körös*, Asiatic Researches, Vol. 20, Calcutta, 1836, and L. *Feer*, in AMG, t. 5, Paris, 1883. *Cf.* also H. *Beckh*, Verzeichnis der tibetischen Handschriften I, Handschriftenverzeichnis der Königl. Bibl. zu Berlin, Bd. 24, Berlin, 1914. A considerable amount of information about the later literature of Buddhism from Tibetan sources, is afforded us by Tāranātha in his work "History of Buddhism in India" completed in 1608, translated from the Tibetan into German by A. *Schiefner*, St. Petersburg, 1869; translated from the German in Ind. Hist. Qu. 3, 1927. On the Chinese translations see Bunyiu Nanjio's Catalogue of the Chinese Translations of the Buddhist Tripiṭaka, Oxford, 1883; E. Denison *Ross*, Alphabetical List of the Titles of Works in the Chinese Buddhist Tripiṭaka, being an Index to Bunyiu Nanjio's Catalogue and to the 1905 Kioto Reprint of the Buddhist Canon, Calcutta, 1910; and Probodhchandra *Bagchi*, Le canon bouddhique en Chine, les traductions, I, Paris, 1927. Sino-Indica Publications de l'Université de Calcutta, 1. Among the most famous translators are Dharmarakṣa, 265-313 A.D., Kumārajīva, 344-431 A.D., Hsüan-Tsang, 630-645 in India, his translations 645-661, and I-tsing, 671-695 in India, his translations 700-712. On Kumārajīva s. S. *Lévi* in JA 1913, s. 11, t. II, p. 334 ff. translated by Phanindranath *Bose*, Calcutta, 1922, and J. *Nobel* in SBA 1917, 206 ff.

[1]) Hsüan-Tsang gives a classification of the sacred writings of the Mahāyāna, in which the Śrāvaka-Piṭaka, *i.e.*, the Canon of the Hīnayāna, is also included. *Cf.* S. *Lévi* and Ed. *Chavannes* in JA, sér. 11, t. VIII, 1916, p. 5 ff.

Hīnayāna, *i.e.*, the lesser (hīna), the inadequate "vessel" (yāna), which does not suffice to steer all beings to the end of suffering. What they teach, is the Mahāyāna, the "great vessel," which is fit to conduct a larger number of beings, indeed the whole of the teeming mass of humanity, safely over the suffering of the world. This new doctrine which, according to the claims of its adherents, is based upon a profounder interpretation of the old texts, or upon the profounder teachings of Gotama Buddha, which he imparted only to the elect among his disciples, sets up the ideal of the Bodhisattva in the stead of that of the Arhat. Not only the monk, but every human being, can make it his aim to be reborn as a Bodhisattva, a "being destined for enlightenment," *i.e.*, a candidate for enlightenment, in order to bring salvation to all men. Now, if this aim is to be within the reach of the many, then there must be more convenient means of attaining it than are provided in the Hīnayāna. Thus, according to the teachings of the Mahāyāna, even in the householder in the midst of family life, the merchant, the artisan, the king, nay, even the labourer, the pariah, can attain salvation, on the one hand by practising pity and friendliness to all beings, by exceptional generosity and self-denial, and on the other hand by faithful and devoted worship of the Buddha, the Buddhas and the Bodhisattvas.[1] Though, as we have seen, Buddha is frequently described as a superhuman being, even in the Pāli Canon, it is nevertheless the enlightenment which

[1]) We see here the influence of the doctrine of Bhakti, known to us from the Bhagavad-Gītā, and it is most probable that it was the Bhagavad-Gītā itself which influenced the development of the Mahāyāna. *Cf.* above, Vol. I, p. 431 ff; *Kern*, Manual of Buddhism, p. 122. Some scholars assume that outside influences, too, contributed towards the moulding of the Mahāyāna; but a hypothesis of this nature is not necessary, and cannot be proved. *Cf.* S. *Lévi*, Mahāyāna-Sūtrālaṃkāra, II, p. 16 ff.: *Kennedy*, JRAS 1902, p. 377 ff.; *Eliot*, Hinduism and Buddhism, III, p. 445 ff.; A.B. *Keith*, Buddhist Philosophy, p. 217. On the Hīnayāna and Mahāyāna in general, see *La Vallée Poussin* in ERE VIII, 1915, 330 ff. and R. *Kimura*, A Historical Study of the Terms Hīnayāna and Mahāyāna *etc.*, Calcutta, 1927.

first makes him a superman, with power to perform many a miracle, and finally he enters into Nirvāṇa, leaving behind him only his doctrine, and at all events his relics, as objects of worship. The Lokottaravādins, who were still adherents of the Hīnayāna, went further than this. They regarded the Buddhas not as ordinary men, but as supernatural (lokottara) beings, who descend to earth for a certain period, in order to partake of all human experiences. In the Mahāyāna, on the other hand, the Buddhas are from the outset nothing but divine beings, and their sojourn on earth and their entry into Nirvāṇa are purely and simply sportive and a delusion. Furthermore, whilst the Hīnayāna already makes mention of a number of Buddhas, predecessors of Śākyamuni in earlier æons of the world's history, the Mahāyāna speaks of thousands, nay, milliards of Buddhas. In addition, the Mahāyāna Buddhists worship as divine beings countless myriads of Bodhisattvas, beings destined for enlightenment, endowed with the "perfections" (pāramitās), who in their pity towards human beings, refused to enter into Nirvāṇa. Add to these also Hindu deities, especially from the cycle of Śiva, which became associated with the Buddhas and Bodhisattvas, and with them filled the Buddhist pantheon. This newly originated mythology, the new Bodhisattva ideal, and the Buddha worship (Buddha-Bhakti) which now came more and more into prominence, all these combined form the popular side of the Mahāyāna. Even as this side was already prepared in the Hīnayāna, but found its further development under the influence of Hinduism, in the same way the philosophical side of the Mahāyāna is merely an elaboration of Hīnayāna doctrines under the influence of Brahmanical philosophy. Early Buddhism had explained the origin of suffering or the discords of existence by the Paṭiccasamuppāda,[1]

[1]) Sanskrit Pratītya-sam-utpāda, "the dependently-co-ordinated-origination" (Stcherbatsky). The usual translation "formula of causality" is not quite correct, for

i.e., the formula in which it is shown that all the elements of being originate only in mutual interdependence. The Hīnayāna derives from this formula the doctrine of Anattatā, of the "Non-Self," *i.e.*, the doctrine that there is no independent and permanent ego, but merely a succession of corporeal and psychical phenomena which change every moment. The Mahāyāna derives from the same formula the doctrine of Śūnyatā, *i.e.*, the doctrine that "all (is) void" (sarvaṃ śūnyam) meaning "devoid" of independent reality.[1]

Buddhist Sanskrit literature is, however, by no means exclusively Mahāyānist. There is also a number of important Hīnayāna texts, which are written in pure and mixed Sanskrit.

Remnants of the Sanskrit Canon.

In the first place the Sarvāstivāda school [2] of the Hīnāyana, which had its adherents more especially in Kashmir and Gandhāra, and spread thence to Central Asia, Tibet

the doctrine is not of a succession of cause and effect, but is that of a mutually interdependent conditionality. The established formula runs thus: "If there is this, then there appears that." *Cf.* Th. *Stcherbatsky*, The Conception of Buddhist Nirvāṇa, Leningrad, 1927, p. 39 ff.

[1]) *Stcherbatsky* (l. c., pp. 40 f., 42 f.) renders "Śūnyatā" by "relativity," because, according to this doctrine, nothing real can be stated of objects, but only relations. Max *Walleser* (Die buddhistische Philosophie, Vol. II. Heidelberg, 1911, p. III) calls this doctrine "negativity," because it simultaneously denies existence and non-existence.

[2]) The literal meaning of Sarvāstivāda is "the all-is doctrine," the doctrine that everything exists permanently. *I-tsing* (A Record of the Buddhist Religion, transl. by J. *Takakusu*, Oxford, 1896, pp. XXIV, 8 ff., 20) calls it Āryamūlasarvāstivāda, and he mentions the schools of the Mūla-Sarvastivādas, the Dharmaguptas, the Mahīśāsakas and the Kāśyapīyas, as its sub-divisions. The relationship between the Sarvāstivāda and the Mūla-Sarvāstivāda is, however, by no means clear. *Cf. Takakusu*, ERE XI, p. 198 ff.; *Lévi* in T'oung Pao, sér. 2, t. VIII, 1907, p. 114 f., N. *Dutt*, Early History of the Spread of Buddhism and the Buddhist Schools, p. 271 n. and table to p. 224. In the Buddhist dictionary Mahāvyutpatti, para. 275, a list of the schools begins with: Āryasarvāstivādāḥ,

and China, had a Sanskrit Canon of its own. Though no complete copy of this canon has come down to us, we know it firstly, from many fragments, large and small, which have been discovered among the manuscripts and block-prints brought from Eastern Turkestan by M.A. (Sir Aurel) Stein, A. Grünwedel, A. von Le Coq, P. Pelliot, and others;[1] secondly, from quotations in other Buddhist Sanskrit works, such as Mahāvastu, Divyāvadāna and Lalita-Vistara, and lastly, from Chinese and Tibetan translations.[2] The principal texts of the Mūla-Sarvāstivāda Canon were translated from Sanskrit into Chinese by the Chinese pilgrim *I-tsing* in the years 700-712.[3] There are, however, Chinese translation of single texts dating from the middle of the 2nd century onwards, and there were adherents of the Sarvāstivāda in India as early as the 2nd century B.C.[4] In wording and in the arrangement of the texts, the Sanskrit Canon evinces great similarity to the Pāli Canon, but on the other hand, there are many points of difference too. A feasible explanation of this is that both canons had a common source, probably

[1]) *Cf.* W. *Geiger*, Die archaeologischen und literarischen Funde in Chinesisch Turkestan und ihre Bedeutung für die orientalistische Wissenschaft, Erlangen (Rede beim Antritt des Prorektorats) 1912; H. *Oldenburg* in NGGW 1912, 171 ff.; H. *Lüders*, Über die literarischen Funde von Ostturkestan, in SBA 1914, p. 85 ff.; A. F. Rud. *Hoernle*, Manuscript Remains of Buddhist Literature found in Eastern Turkestan, I, Oxford, 1916.

[2]) *Cf. Oldenburg* in ZDMG 52, 1898, 654 ff., 662 ff.; M. *Anesaki* in OC XIII, Hamburg, 1902, p. 61; Le Muséon, N. S. VI, 1905, p. 23 ff.; VII, 1906, p. 33 ff.; JRAS 1901, p. 895 ff.

[3]) J. *Takakusu*, A Record of the Buddhist Religion by I-tsing translated, p. XXXVII. *Cf.* Ed. *Huber* in BEFEO VI, 1906, pp. 1 ff., 36; S. *Lévi* in T'oung Pao, sér. 2, t. V, 1904, p. 297 ff.; t. VIII, 1907, p. 110 ff. The Chinese "Tripiṭaka," though also divided into a Vinaya, Sūtra and Abhidharma, does not, however, mean the same as the Pāli Tipiṭaka, for it contains many non-canonical texts besides the canonical ones, in fact even Brahmanical philosophical treatises (s. *Takakusu* in JRAS 1896, p. 415). In the Tibetan Kanjur, too, which is also designated as a "Tripiṭaka" and consists of a Vinaya, Sūtra and Abhidharma, much is included which does not admit of comparison with the Tipiṭaka, and was certainly not a part of the Canon.

[4]) A Sarvāstivādin ācārya Buddhila is mentioned in inscriptions on the lion capitol in Mathurā dating from the 2nd century A.D., s. F.W. *Thomas*, Ep. Ind. 9, 1907-8, p. 135 ff.

the lost Māgadhī Canon, from which first the Pāli Canon branched off in one part of India, and then, later on, the Sanskrit Canon in another district.

Fragments of the Prātimokṣa-Sūtra of the Sarvāstivādins, as well as other texts of the Vinayapiṭaka of the Sanskrit Canon, have been found in Central Asia (Eastern Turkestan), and a few in Nepal too. It is also possible to reconstruct the Prātimokṣa-Sūtra from Chinese and Tibetan translations. Both the Sanskrit Canon of the Sarvāstivādins and the Vinayas of the Mahīśāsakas, Dharmaguptas and Mahā-Saṅghikas, show manifold divergences in separate details from the Pāli Canon and from one another, not only as regards the rules of the Prātimokṣa, but also as regards the rules of the Vinaya in general. Nevertheless, the original stock of rules is one and the same.[1] It is in the stories prefaced to the rules in order to relate on what occasion the Buddha proclaimed the rules in question, that the texts show greater divergences. The Mūla-Sarvāstivāda Vinaya contained many legends having reference to the conversion of Kashmir and North-western India to Buddhism.[2] Some of these legends are also to be

[1]) The Sanskrit text of the Prātimokṣa-Sūtra has been edited by L. *Finot* on the basis of the fragments of manuscripts found by *Pelliot* in Central Asia, and has been translated into French, with the Chinese version of Kumārajīva, by Ed. *Huber*, in JA ser. 11, t. II, 1913, pp. 465-558; a fragment from M. A. Stein's collection, by *La Vallée Poussin* in JRAS 1913, p. 843; a fragment in the Kuchean language, by S. *Lévi* in JA s. 10, t. XIX, 1912, 101 ff.; JRAS 1913, p. 109 ff.; Hoernle, Manuscript Remains, p. 357 ff. E. *Waldschmidt*, Bruchstücke des Bhikṣuṇī-Prātimokṣa der Sarvāstivādins, Leipzig 1926, has edited the fragments of manuscripts of the Prātimokṣa of the nuns, which were found at Turfan, and compared them with the corresponding texts of all the other schools. For the Tibetan version of the Prātimokṣa, see G. *Huth*, Die tibetische Version der Naiḥsargika-prāyaścittika-dharmāḥ, Strassburg 1891. See also *Oldenberg* in ZDMG 52, 1898, p. 644 ff.

[2]) Cf. J. *Przyluski* and S. *Lévi* in JA s. 11, t. IV, 1914, p. 493 ff. In addition, the reign of Kaniṣka is prophesied, the seven-day week is mentioned, among other things, from which *Lévi* (T'oung Pao, s. 2, Vol. VIII, 1907, p. 115 f.) concludes that the Mūla-Sarvāstivāda-Vinaya was not completed before the 3rd century A.D. However, as there were already Sarvāstivādins at a much earlier period (see above, p. 232), it is most likely that there was an earlier Sarvāstivāda-Vinaya too, and possibly the Mūla-Sarvāstivāda-Vinaya was merely a later version of that work.

found in the Divyāvadāna, which borrowed a large portion of its tales from the Vinayapiṭaka of the Mūla-Sarvāstivāda.[1] The Vinayapiṭaka also includes the Śikṣās and Saṅgha-karmans corresponding to the Pāli Sikkhās and Kammavācās, and fragments of these have been brought to light in Central Asia.[2]

The Nikāyas of the Pāli Canon find their parallel in the Āgamas of the Sanskrit Canon; the Dīrghāgama corresponding to the Dīghanikāya, the Madhyamāgama to the Majjhimanikāya, the Saṃyuktāgama to the Saṃyutta-nikāya, and the Ekottarāgama to the Aṅguttaranikāya. Fragments of various Sūtras of the Dīrghāgama (Saṃgīti-Sūtra, Āṭanātiya-Sūtra), of the Madhyamāgama (Upāli-Sūtra, Śuka-Sūtra), of the Saṃyuktāgama and the Ekottarāgama, have been found in Central Asia.[3] These fragments are not always in agreement with the corresponding Pāli texts. The comparison of the Chinese Āgamas with the corresponding Pāli Nikāyas, has also shown both agreement to a

[1]) Fragments corresponding to the Mahā-Vagga of the Vinayapiṭaka, found in the Stein collection, have been edited by *La Vallée Poussin* in JRAS 1913, p. 550 ff. A fragment of a Buddhist ritual of ordination, corresponding to the Culla-Vagga X, 17, in Sanskrit, was discovered by C. *Bendall* in Nepal and edited in Album Kern, p. 373 ff. Various fragments of the Vinaya, ed. by *Hoernle*, Manuscript Remains, pp. 4-16. A fragment of the Bhikṣuṇikā-dharma-vacana, ed. by Miss C. M. *Ridding* and *La Vallée Poussin* in BSOS I, 1920, p. 123 ff. See also S. *Lévi* in T'oung Pao, s. 2, Vol. VIII, 1907, p. 110 ff.; N. *Dutt*, Early History of the Spread of Buddhism and the Buddhist Schools, p. 280 ff.

[2]) Cf. *La Vallée Poussin* in JRAS 1913, 843 ff.; *Lüders* in SBA 1922, p. 243.

[3]) Fragments of the Āgamas of the Sanskrit Canon were discovered amongst the remains of MSS. found in Eastern Turkestan, and edited by R. *Pischel* in SBA 1904, pp. 808 f., 1138 ff.; S. *Lévi* in T'oung Pao, s. 2, Vol. V, 1904, p. 297 ff.; JA s. 10, t. XVI, 1910, pp. 433 ff., 450 ff.; JRAS 1911, p. 764 ff.; L. de *La Vallée Poussin* in JRAS 1911, p. 772; 1912, p. 1063 ff.; 1913, p. 569 ff.; *Hoernle*, Manuscript Remains, pp. 16-52. A fragment of the Sroṇa-Sūtras of the Saṃyukta-Āgama (cf. Saṃyuttanikāya 22, 49 f. = Vol. III, p. 48 ff.) has been edited by *La Vallée Poussin* from MSS. of Cecil *Bendall's* collection, in JRAS 1907, 375 ff. Quotations from the Saṃyukta and Ekottara Āgamas have been traced by S. *Lévi* in the commentary on Asaṅga's Mahāyāna-Sūtrālaṃkāra (ed. *Lévi*, on XVI, 21 f., 75). V. A. *Smith* and W. *Hoey* found Buddhist Sūtras in Sanskrit, written on bricks, in the ruins of Gopālpur, together with inscriptions which are dated between 250 and 400 A.D. (JASB, proceedings 1896, p. 99 ff.).

considerable extent, and notable divergences.[1] In the first place there is no agreement as regards the order of the Sūtras in the separate Āgamas. In the Saṃyuktāgama the division into Vargas and Saṃyuktas is totally different, and there are Saṃyuktas in the Pāli which are missing in the Chinese version; on the other hand, there are some in the Chinese which do not occur in the Pāli.[2] The greatest differences are those which we find between the Ekottarāgama and the Aṅguttaranikāya. On the whole it may be said that the points of agreement and the divergences prove that the Sanskrit Āgamas and the Pāli Nikāyas were compiled from the same materials, but were arranged in different ways in the different schools. Now in the Chinese Tripiṭaka there are also texts which, though bearing the same titles as the corresponding Pāli texts, are nevertheless essentially different. Thus there is a Brahmajāla-Sūtra, which was translated into Chinese by Kumārajīva, and is held in high esteem in China and Japan but which teaches Buddhist ethics in the spirit of the Mahāyāna. On the other hand, there are in the Abhidharma-Kośa-Vyākhyā, several quotations from a Brahmajāla-Sūtra, which must have corresponded to the Pāli text.[3] The Chinese Tripiṭaka contains ten different translations of the Mahā-Parinirvāṇa-Sūtra. Three of these translations belong to the Hīnayāna and seven to the Mahāyāna; and the only thing they have in common is the external form, inasmuch as they contain speeches which the

[1]) See especially M. *Anesaki*, The Four Buddhist Āgamas in Chinese, in Transactions of the Asiatic Society of Japan, Vol. 35, Part 3, 1908, and above, p. 232, note 3.

[2]) The Sagāthavarga in the three Chinese versions of the Saṃyuktāgama contains 318 Sūtras, out of which 244 coincide with those of the Pāli text. It is impossible to determine whether the quotations traced by *Anesaki* (Le Muséon, N. S. VII, 1906, 38 ff.) in the Chinese Mahā-Prajñā-Pāramitā-Śāstra, are derived from a Pāli or Prākrit text of the Saṃyutta and Suttanipāta. For the Saṃyukta Āgama, see also *Lévi* in T'oung Pao, s. 2, Vol. V, 1904, p. 297 ff.

[3]) Cf. *La Vallée Poussin* in JRAS 1908, 359 ff., *Anesaki* in ERE, Vol. V, p. 452.

Buddha is supposed to have uttered prior to his death (parinirvāṇa).[1]

The Sanskrit Canon also contained a "Kṣudraka" corresponding to the Khuddakanikāya.[2] We do not know whether this included all those texts which in the Pāli Canon are counted as belonging to the fifth Nikāya; but we do know that the Sanskrit Canon also contained the Sanskrit texts Udāna, Dharmapada, Sthavira-Gāthā, Vimānavastu and Buddha-Vaṃśa, corresponding to the Pāli texts Udāna, Dhammapada, Thera-Gāthā, Vimāna-Vatthu and Buddha-Vaṃsa. In the Chinese Tripiṭaka, it is true, there is no single text to correspond to the Suttanipāta; but more than half of the texts included in the Suttanipāta occur in the Āgamas, for instance the texts corresponding to the Aṭṭhaka-Vagga and the Pārāyana. Fragments of the Sanskrit version of the two last-named have been found in Eastern Turkestan too.[3] A collection corresponding to the Itivuttakas was translated into Chinese by Hsüan Tsang in about 650 A.D.[4] Considerable

[1]) Cf. F. Max *Müller* in SBE, Vol. 10 (I), p. xxxi note; J. *Edkins* in JRAS 1881, p. 66 ff.; R. *Kimura*, in JDL 4, 1921, 188 f. note, and Historical Study of the Terms Hīnayāna and Mahāyāna, p. 94 note. The Hīnayāna includes the translation of Po-fā-tsu (290-306 A.D.) and that of Fa-hien (between 317 and 420 A.D.); translated into Italian, after the last-named, by Carlo *Puini* in GSAI 21, 1908, p. 59 ff.; 22, 1909, p. 1 ff. The earliest Vaipulya-Parinirvāṇa-Sūtra was translated into Chinese by Dharmarakṣa (between 205 and 316 A.D.). Specimens of it are given by S. *Beal* in Ind. Ant. 5, 1876, p. 222 ff. and SBE Vol. 19, p. 365 ff.

[2]) A Kṣudraka is mentioned by Hsüan Tsang as the fifth Āgama of the Śrāvaka-piṭaka, s. *Lévi* in JA s. 11, t. VIII, 1916, p. 20. Nevertheless, the "four Āgamas" are especially emphasized as the real Āgamas, as for instance, when the Divyāvadāna makes frequent mention (pp. 17, 331, 333) of the *āgamacatuṣṭayam*, cf. *Oldenberg* in ZDMG 52, 654 f.

[3]) Cf. M. *Anesaki* in JPTS 1906-7, p. 50 f.; *Hoernle* in JRAS 1916, p. 709 ff.; 1917, p. 134. In the Sanskrit version of the Aṭṭhaka-Vagga (it is mentioned as the arthavargīyāṇi Sūtrāṇi in the Divyāvadāna, p. 20) prose narratives precede the verses, but there are none such in the Pāli. There are also other divergences from the Pāli text. The Sanskrit text is shorter.

[4]) K. *Watanabe* in JPTS 1906-7, p. 44 ff. In the Chinese Tripiṭaka there is a work Ṣaṭpāramitā-saṃnipāta-Sūtra (translated in 222 A.D.) which is a kind of Caryāpiṭaka; s. R. *Kimura*, A Historical Study of the Terms Hīnayāna and Mahāyāna, p. 129, note 1.

quotations, forming a parallel to passages from the Khuddaka-pāṭha, the Vimāna-Vatthu, Buddha-Vaṃsa and Dhammapada, are to be found in the Mahāvastu.[1]

We glean from one of the Mahāvastu quotations,[2] that there was a Dharmapada in the Sanskrit Canon, divided into Vargas, after the style of the Pāli Dharmapada. This Sanskrit version was not identical with that of the Pāli Canon, but both versions had an original stock of verses in common, and were arranged on one and the same principle. The collection of verses which belonged to the original Canon, also served as a prototype and as a foundation for more comprehensive anthologies, which were compiled in later times, and were widely propagated in Central Asia, Tibet and China. Thus, for instance, there is a Chinese anthology with the same 26 sections (Vargas) as the Pāli Dhammapada though it has 13 additional sections.[3] Fragments of a Sanskrit anthology have been found in Central Asia, which were at first regarded as passages from recensions of the Dharmapada, but which in reality belong to the Udāna-Varga, which is known to us from a Tibetan translation. This anthology was compiled by Dharmatrāta, who, according to Tāranātha, is supposed to have lived in King Kaniṣka's day. In the Tibetan version, it contains not only 375 verses, corresponding to verses of the Dhammapada, but also the greater part of the verses of the Udāna, and numerous verses which have parallels in the Suttanipāta and other portions of the Pāli Canon.[4] Another

[1]) Mahāvastu, ed. *Senart*, I, 290 ff.; II, 191 ff.; I, 250 ff.; Quotations from "the Dharmapada" (sing.) or "the Dharmapadas" (plur.): II, 212; III, 91, 156, 434 ff.

[2]) III. 434 ff. Here a Sahasravarga is quoted from "the Dharmapadas;" it contains 24 verses, whilst the Sahassa-Vagga in the Pāli consists of only 16 verses. On the Dharmapada in Nepal, Tibet and China, s. *Oldenberg* in ZDMG 52, 1898, p. 662 ff.

[3]) Cf. Max *Müller* in SBE, Vol. 10 (1), p. 2 ff.; S. *Beal*, Texts from the Buddhist Canon commonly known as Dhammapada, London 1902; and the important study on the Dharmapada recensions by S. *Lévi* in JA. s. 10, t. XX, 1912, pp. 203-204.

[4]) Fragments of the Udānavarga, from finds in Central Asia, have been published by R. *Pischel*, Die Turfan-Rezensionen des Dhammapada, SBA 1908, p. 968 ff.; S. *Lévi* and

anthology was written in a Prākrit dialect, which is a later form of the North-west Indian dialect familiar to us from the Shāhbāzgarhī rock edicts of Aśoka, and compiled after the pattern, and with the help of the Dhammapada or some similar verse collection of the Sanskrit Canon, or the original Canon. Fragments of this anthology have come down to us in a few leaves of a manuscript written in the Kharoṣṭhī script, which M. Petroffsky and J. L. Dutreuil de Rhins had found at Khotan, and brought to Europe.[1]

It is a certainty that there were Jātakas too, in the Sanskrit Canon; but it must remain an open question whether this Canon ever included a Jātaka Book or a large collection of Jātakas of its own. It is doubtful, too, whether the collection of "seven Abhidharmas," which is translated in the Chinese Tripiṭaka, is also derived from the old Canon,

La Vallée Poussin in JA s. 10, t. XVI, 1910, p. 444 ff.; t. XVII, 1911, 431 ff.; t. XIX, 1912, p. 311 ff.; JRAS 1911, p. 758 ff; 1912. p. 355 ff. The Tibetan version of the Udānavarga has been translated into English by W. W. *Rockhill*, London 1883, and the Tibetan text was published by H. *Beckh*, Berlin 1911. Cf. A. *Schiefner* Über Vasubandhus Gāthāsaṃgraha, in Mélanges Asiatiques VIII (Bulletin XXV, 1878), pp. 559 f., 590 ff.; *La Vallée Poussin* in GGA 1912, 191 f.; *Lüders* in SBA 1914, p. 102; and *Seidenstücker*, Das Udāna, I, 1913, pp. 37, 71 ff. A voluminous anthology, about five times as large as the Pāli Dhammapada, is the *Dharmasamuccaya* by *Avalokitasiṃha*, who has also drawn from Mahāyāna sources; on a MS. of this work, found in Nepal, see Dharma Aditya *Dharmacarya* in Ind. Hist. Qu. 1, 1925, 422 ff., 677 ff.

[1]) The old Kharoṣṭhī manuscript, important from the points of view both of language and palaeography, has been edited by *Senart* in JA s. 9, t. XII, 1898, pp. 193 ff., 515 ff. This edition was the foundation for the new edition by Benimadhab *Barua* and Sailendranath *Mitra*, Calcutta 1921. The fragments found by *Petroffsky* were identified by S. d'*Oldenburg*, St. Petersburg 1907. On the "MS. Dutreuil de Rhins," cf. Comptes rendus de l'académie des inscriptions, 14. mai 1895 et 15. avril 1898; *Senart*, OC XI Paris 1897, I, 1 ff.; G. *Bühler*, On the Origin of the Indian Brahma Alphabet, 2nd Ed., Strassburg 1898, p. 122 ff.; *Lüders* in NGGW 1899, p. 474 ff.; T. W. *Rhys Davids* in JRAS 1899, p. 426 ff.; R. O. *Franke* in ZDMG 60, 1906, p. 477 ff.; M. A. *Stein*, Ancient Khotan, Oxford 1907, I, 188; Jules *Bloch*, JA ser. 10, t. XIX, 1912, p. 331 ff.; *Konow* (Festschrift Windisch, p. 85 ff.) is of opinion that, though this anthology is composed in a dialect originating in the North-west of India, it was written in the neighbourhood of Khotan. Like *Bühler* (l.c.) he ascribes it to the 1st century A.D., whilst *Lüders* (SBA 1914, p. 101) thinks it was written in the 3rd century A.D. It is probably the earliest Indian manuscript which has been discovered so far.

for these Abhidharmas have nothing in common with the Abhidhammapiṭaka of the Pāli Canon save the number seven and a few titles.[1]

The Canon of the Mūla-Sarvāstivādins has thus only come down to us in an incomplete way, but as regards the other Buddhist sects, we do not know whether they had any set Canon at all. As far as we can see, each sect merely has one or several texts which pass as especially sacred, being regarded as a kind of "Bible," and which partly assimilated and partly displaced the old texts of a Tripiṭaka which they, too, acknowledged in principle.

The Mahāvastu.

One of the most important works which still belongs to the old school of the Hīnayāna is the Mahāvastu [2] or Mahāvastu-Avadāna.[3] The work calls itself a book " of the

[1]) J. *Takakusu*, JRAS 1905, p. 3 ff. and JPTS 1905, p. 67 ff. See above, p. 173.

[2]) The text has been edited by E'. *Senart* in 3 vols., Paris 1882-1897, with detailed surveys of the contents in the Introductions and a valuable commentary. A survey of the contents has also been given by Rājendralāla *Mitra*, Sanskrit Buddhist Lit. of Nepal, pp. 115-161. See also A. *Barth* in RHR 11, 1885, 160 ff.; 42 1900, 51 f. (=Oeuvres I, 376 ff,; II, 334) and Journal des savants 1899, 459 ff., 517 ff., 623 ff., E. *Windisch*, Die Komposition des Mahāvastu, in ASGW XXVII, 1909, 467-511; *Oldenberg* in NGGW 1912, 123 ff.; L. de *La Vallée Poussin* in ERE VIII, 328 ff.; Haraprasad *Śāstrī* in Ind. Hist. Qu. 1, 1925, 202 ff.

[3]) This is the title of the work in most of the colophons. In the text itself and also in some of the colophons, it is called Mahāvastu. Mahāvastu means "The great subjects," i.e., the main subjects of the Vinaya, that is to say the admission to the order, etc., and corresponds to the Mahā-Vagga of the Pāli Vinayapiṭaka and the Vinayavastu (beside Kṣudrakavastu, corresponding to the Culla-Vagga) of the Vinayapiṭaka of the Sarvāstivādins. *Cf. La Vallée Poussin*, l.c., Mahāvastu-Avadāna means "The legends pertaining to the main subjects of the Vinaya." H. *Zimmer* (in ZII 3, 1925, 201 ff.) seeks to prove that avadāna means the same as nidāna, "origin," "original cause," and he explains mahāvastu as "the great fact of salvation." I consider this erroneous. The fact that the Chinese translators occasionally confused *nidāna* and *avadāna* (*cf.* S. *Lévi* in JA 1912, s. 10, t. XX, p. 219) is no proof that these two expressions are identical. Moreover, in the Vinaya literature, vastu has the definite meaning of "subject of the Vinaya" and the "event" related in connection with this subject.

Vinayapiṭaka according to the text of the Lokottaravādins of the Mahāsāṅghikas." The Mahāsāṅghikas, *i.e.*, the adherents of the Mahāsāṅgha, "the great community," are according to unanimous tradition, the earliest schismatics. Among the sections into which they are subdivided, we find the Lokottaravādins, *i.e.*, those according to whose doctrine the Buddhas are "exalted above the world" (lokottara) and adapt themselves to worldly life only externally.[1] The biography of the Buddha, which is the chief content of the Mahāvastu, quite agrees with this doctrine, for it is profusely adorned with miracles. In this respect, to be sure, it differs little from those texts of the Pāli Canon which deal with the life of the Buddha. In both cases we hear of miracles accompanying the conception, birth and enlightenment, and the first conversions of the Buddha. The Mahāvastu agrees with the Nidāna-Kathā in that it treats the life of the Buddha in three sections.[2] The first of these begins with the life of the Bodhisattva at the time of Buddha Dīpaṅkara (I, 193 ff.) and tells of his existences at the times of the other former Buddhas. The second section (II, 1 ff.) introduces us to the heaven of the Tuṣita gods, where the Bodhisattva, there reborn, determines to attain rebirth in the womb of Queen Māyā, and tells of the miracles of the conception and birth of the prince, his departure from his home, his conflicts with Māra and the enlightenment which he finally attains under the Bodhi tree. Lastly, the third section (in Vol. III), agreeing in its main features with the Mahāvagga

[1]) "The perfectly enlightened ones have nothing in common with the world, but with the great Ṛṣis everything is exalted above the world," Mahāvastu I, 159, 2. "They wash their feet, though no dust clings to them, they sit in the shade, though the heat of the sun never oppresses them, they take nourishment, though hunger never troubles them, they use medicine, though they have no illness, etc;" *Windisch*, l.c., p. 470. According to Mahāv. I, 2, the Lokottaravādins belong to the "middle land" (madhyadeśa), *i.e.*, to the "sixteen countries" of Northern India. *Cf.* Mahāvastu I, 198.

[2]) See above, p. 186. However, the expressions *dūrenidāna*, *avidūrenidāna* and *santikenidāna* are not to be found in the Mahāvastu.

of the Vinayapiṭaka,[1] relates the history of the first conversions and the rise of the monastic community. This, too, is the reason why the Mahāvastu claims to belong to the Vinayapiṭaka, though apart from a few remarks on admission into the order, it contains next to nothing about the Vinaya, the rules of the Order. It corresponds to that part of the Vinayapiṭaka which tells the history of the rise of the Order.[2]

When we say that the main purpose of the Mahāvastu is to relate the life-story of the Buddha for the Lokottaravādins, this by no means exhausts the contents of the work, nor has any idea of its composition been given. Far from its being a specimen of artistic literature, the Mahāvastu should rather be described as a labyrinth, in which the thread of a connected narrative of the Buddha's life can only be discovered with some difficulty. This narrative is continually interrupted by other matters, especially numerous Jātakas and Avadānas, but also by dogmatic Sūtras. There is no apparent principle of systematic arrangement. Frequently there is not even an attempt made to establish any connection, however loose, between the various parts. Moreover, one and the same story, be it an episode of Buddha's life or a Jātaka, is very often told twice consecutively, first in prose and then again in verse, this latter form diverging sometimes more and sometimes less. Not only this, but in various places the same episodes recur

1) *Cf. Windisch,* l.c., 476 ff.

2) See above, p. 26 ff., and *Windisch,* l.c., pp. 473, 476 ff. Probably it is only this portion of the Vinayapiṭaka which has come down to us in the Mahāvastu. *Cf. Oldenberg* in NGGW 1912, 152. T. W. *Rhys Davids* (SBB III, 256 f.) advances the less likely theory that the Lokottaravādins revised only the introduction, because they took over the rules of the Vinaya themselves in their Pāli form, or in some form resembling the Pāli, just as they were, without any change. H. *Zimmer,* l.c., 209 ff., thinks that the presentation of Buddha's life with the preliminary conditions in previous existences, constitutes a "Vinaya" for those who wish to attain Buddha-hood (in the sense of the Mahāyāna, which, he says, is already foreshadowed in the Mahāvastu). There is no evidence anywhere for this use of the word vinaya.

several times with slight variations. Thus the legend of Buddha's birth is told no less than four times.[1] The language, too, is not unified. Though the entire work, the prose as well as the verse, is written in "mixed Sanskrit," this dialect is sometimes more and sometimes less akin to Sanskrit. In the verse it is more archaic.[2] As regards style, too, earlier and later portions of the work can be clearly distinguished.[3]

In spite of all this, and in spite of the fact that this work tells us scarcely anything new about the doctrine of the Buddha, nor even about special doctrines of the Lokottaravādins, this work is nevertheless of the utmost importance, because it has preserved many old traditions and old versions of texts which appear in the Pāli Canon too. Thus the departure of Prince Siddhārtha from his home (abhiniṣkramaṇa) is related in very archaic fashion, resembling the Majjhimanikāya (26 and 36).[4] Similarly we find there old versions of the "sermon of Benares," the Mahā-Govinda-Sutta (Dīghanikāya 19), the Dīgha-Nakha-Sutta (Majjhimanikāya 74), the Māra-Saṃyutta from the Saṃyuttanikāya, the Sahassa-Vagga from the Dhammapada, the Khuddaka-Pāṭha, the Pabbajjā, Padhāna and Khaggavisāṇa-Suttas from the Suttanipāta, and isolated portions of the Vimāna-Vatthu and of the Buddha-Vaṃsa.[5] The poems on the birth of the Buddha also main-

[1]) *Windisch*, Buddha's Geburt, pp. 106, 124 f.

[2]) *Oldenberg*, ZDMG 52, 663. Haraprasad *Śāstrī* (Ind. Hist. Qu. I, 1925, 204 f.) rejects the term "vernacularized Sanskrit" or "Sanskritized vernacular" as applied to the language of the Mahāvastu. He regards it as a dialect which was actually spoken in Northern India in the 2nd century B.C.

[3]) *Cf. Oldenberg* in NGGW 1912, 123 ff.

[4]) II, 117. Immediately after it there is a second, later setting of the same Abhiniṣkramaṇa-Sūtra.

[5]) *Cf. Oldenberg*, ZDMG 52, 659 ff., 665 ff. *Windisch*, Māra und Buddha, 316 ff., 322 ff.; J. *Dutoit*, Die duṣkaracaryā des Bodhisattva, Strassburg 1905; J. *Charpentier* in WZKM 23, 1909, 33 ff. (Māra-Saṃyutta und Mahāvastu); *Rhys Davids*, SBB III, p. 256 ff. (on the Mahā-Govinda-Sutta).

tain the old ballad style. They are remnants of that old Buddhist ballad poetry which we have already met with so often.

The Mahāvastu is more especially valuable as a treasure-trove of Jātakas[1] and other narratives. A good half of the work consists of Jātakas, which are related partly in pure prose, partly in mixed prose and verse, sometimes first in prose and then again in verse. Here again we meet with the Bodhisattva now as a world-ruling king, now as a merchant's son, a Brāhmaṇa, or a Nāga prince, as a lion, an elephant, and so on. Many of the Jātakas are versions of those which we find in the Pāli Jātaka book, sometimes almost literally identical, sometimes with greater or lesser deviations. Thus the Śyāmaka-Jātaka (II, 209 ff.), the touching story of the Brāhman's son whom King Peliyakṣa kills with an arrow, is only a version of the Sāma-Jātaka with which we are familiar. The Kinnarī-Jātaka (II, 94 ff.) corresponds in character, though not in contents, to the Kinnara fairy tales of the Jātaka book. The Kusa-Jātaka appears once (II, 420 ff.) in a recension deviating considerably from the Pāli, a second time (III, 1 ff.) in a metrical version, which shows points of agreement with the Pāli Gāthās.[2] The story of Nalinī, who seduces Ekaśṛṅga (*i.e.* "Unicorn") has, in the Mahāvastu (III, 143 ff.) been watered down to a very pious legend, though it has still preserved old features which have vanished in the prose of the

[1]) *Cf.* S. *d'Oldenburg* in JRAS 1893, 335 ff., A. *Barth* in Journal des savants 1899, 625 ff.; J. *Charpentier*; Paccekabuddhageschichten, pp. 2 ff., 12 ff., 25 ff. and in Le monde oriental, III, 1909, p. 34 ff. *Charpentier* shows how the text of the Mahāvastu can often be corrected with the help of the Pāli text.

[2]) See avove, pp. 147 f., 133, 136 f. The story of Amarā, the smith's daughter (II, 83 ff.) corresponds to the Pāli Jātaka No. 387. The Markaṭa Jātaka (II, 246 ff.) is the fable of the monkey and the crocodile (Jāt. No. 208), see above, pp. 126, 163. The Śyāmaka-Jātaka translated from the Chinese Tripiṭaka by Ed. *Chavannes*, Cinq cents contes, t. I, p. 156 ff. On the Kusa-Jātaka in the Mahāvastu see *Charpentier* in WZKM 27, 1913, 94 f.

Pāli Jātaka of Isisinga.[1] As in the Pāli Tesakuṇa-Jātaka (No. 521) there is in the Mahāvastu also (I, 271 ff.) the childless King Brahmadatta, who instead of a son, gets three eggs, from which three very wise birds come forth, which instruct him in the duties of a king (rājadharma).[2]

However, there are many Jātakas and Avadānas in the Mahāvastu, which have no parallels in the Pāli. A very favourite theme in these is the glorification of the exceeding self-denial and generosity of the Bodhisattva. As King Arka, for instance, he presents to the Buddha of that time, 80,000 grottos (cave-temples) constructed of the seven kinds of precious stones (I, 54). On another occasion he gives away his wife and child merely in order to learn a wise saying (I, 91 f.). As a potter he is more pious than King Kṛkin, as he kills no living being, and sets up his pots at cross-roads, in order to fill them with rice and beans for hungry people ; and when he hears that, during his absence, his parents have given to the Buddha the straw with which he had but lately re-thatched his hut, he rejoices for a whole month (I, 317 ff.). Some of the narratives remind us rather of the Brahmanical Purāṇas. Thus the description of hell at the beginning of the Mahāvastu shows various points of resemblance to that in the Mārkaṇḍeya-Purāṇa.[3] The Rāja-Vaṃśa, the "history of the kings" (to whose race Śākyamuni belongs), begins in the true manner of the Purāṇas with an account of

[1]) *Lüders*, NGGW 1901, p. 20 ff., and above, p. 147.

[2]) In Mahābhārata I, 229 ff., we meet with four wise birds, the sons of a ṛṣi, who know the Veda, and sing hymns to the god Agni. In the Mārkaṇḍeya-Purāṇa (see Vol. I, p. 560), four wise birds, sons of a ṛṣi, propound not only Yoga doctrines and all manner of other wisdom, but teachings of rājadharma too (Chapters 27-35).

[3]) See Vol. I, p. 562, and L. *Scherman*, Materialien zur Geschichte der indischen Visionslitteratur, p. 36. The visit of Maudgalyāyana (Pāli Moggallāna) to the eight hells, as well as his wanderings through the animal world, the world of the Pretas, the Asuras and the various classes of gods, may also be based on Pāli tradition, in which likewise Moggallāna is a saint who wanders through heaven and hell and all the worlds.

the creation (I, 338 ff.). The spirit of the Purāṇas is also breathed in the Jātaka (I, 283 ff.), in which a Ṛṣi Rakṣita, the Bodhisattva, attains to such miraculous powers, as a hermit, that he can touch the sun and the moon with his hands. The spirit of the Mahāyāna is very similar to that of the Purāṇas, and some narratives of the Mahāvastu exhibit that preference for phantasmagorias which is so characteristic of the Mahāyāna texts ; we find splendid magical pictures, which show the miraculous power of the saints, and are, at the same time, to serve for the glorification of the Buddhas. The " sunshade stories " (chattravastu I, 253 ff.) are of this kind. After the Buddha has delivered the city of Śrāvastī from a dreadful plague caused by Yakṣas, gods and spirits hold sunshades over the Exalted One in order to honour him. The Buddha, however, with his usual kindness, uses his magic power to cause a Buddha to appear under each sunshade, so that each god thinks that the Buddha is sitting under his sunshade.

Now, although the Mahāvastu belongs to the Hīnayāna and contains much which could just as well, or actually does, appear in the Pāli texts of the Theravādins, it also contains much which savours of the Mahāyāna. The reason for many such traits is probably that the conception of Buddha prevalent among the Mahāsāṅghikas and the Lokottaravādins does actually represent a transition to the Mahāyāna. In other cases, however, we are most likely right in assuming that interpolation took place.[1] Thus we find in the first volume

[1] Thus, for instance, the Avalokita-Sūtra (in two versions, II, 293 ff., 297 ff.), is cited as an independent Sūtra, in Śāntideva's Śikṣā-Samuccaya (ed. *Bendall*, pp. 89 f., 297 ff., with the title Avalokana-Sūtra), and in the Tibetan, too, it appears as an independent work. Hence it is probably interpolated in the Mahāvastu, the more so because, in the colophon at the end of the second version it is called parivāra (" accessory," see above, p. 33, the Parivāra of the Vinayapiṭaka). (See *Senart*, II, p. xxvi, note 3.) Though the text in the Śikṣā-Samuccaya agrees in the main with that of the Mahāvastu, there are nevertheless such striking divergences of particular passages, that it cannot possibly be an extract from the Mahāvastu.

(I, 63-193) a large section on the ten Bhūmis or steps, which a Bodhisattva must pass through, and a description of the virtues which he must possess in each of the ten steps.[1] Inserted into this section is a Buddhānusmṛti (I, 163 ff.), *i.e.*, a hymn to Buddha, which differs in no wise from the Stotras to Viṣṇu or Śiva in the Purāṇas. It is also in the spirit of the Mahāyāna when (II, 362 ff.) it is said that the purity of the Buddha is so great that the worship of the Exalted One is sufficient for the attainment of Nirvāṇa, and that one already acquires endless merit by merely walking round a stūpa and worshipping it by means of floral offerings, and so on. It reminds us of countless passages in Mahāyāna texts, when we read (III, 137 ff.) that, from the Buddha's smile, there radiate beams which illuminate the entire Buddha regions (Buddhakṣetra). The mention of a great number of Buddhas, and the saying that the Bodhisattvas are not begotten by father and mother, but originate immediately through their qualities,[2] also remind us of the Mahāyāna.

From the way in which the Mahāvastu is composed it follows that the date of the origin of the work is hard to determine. Many circumstances indicate great antiquity, notably the language itself, and the fact that the work belongs to the Lokottaravāda school. The fact that the work is written entirely in "mixed Sanskrit," whilst in the Mahāyāna texts this dialect alternates with pure Sanskrit, is a sign of higher antiquity: for, as Barth[3] says, Sanskrit is only an intruder as far as the Buddhist texts are concerned. Those numerous

[1]) The presentation of the Bhūmis in the Mahāvastu diverges from that in the texts of the Mahāyāna; hence this is probably a transition from the Hīnayāna to the Mahāyāna. A Tibetan Mahāyāna author, whose object is to prove that the doctrine of the Bhūmis was not a Mahāyānistic innovation, alludes to the fact that they already occur in the Mahāvastu. *Cf. La Vallée Poussin* in ERE II, 743 ff.; VIII, 330 note; J. *Rahder*, Daśabhūmika-Sūtra, Leuven 1926, p. iii ff.

[2]) *Cf. Windisch*, Buddha's Geburt, p. 97 note, 100 f. and p. 193 f.

[3]) Journal des savants, 1899, p. 459.

pieces which the Mahāvastu has in common with the Pāli Canon, and which hark back to a common earlier source, are undoubtedly old. Thus the Gāthās of the Khaḍgaviṣāṇa-Sūtra (I, 357 ff.) are probably earlier than those of the corresponding Khaggavisāṇa-Sutta in the Pāli Suttanipāta. But when in the Mahāvastu these verses are sung by 500 dying Pratyeka-Buddhas, the refrain "May he wander lonely like a rhinoceros" sounds strange enough coming from their lips, and it is not likely that the prose setting is as old as the Gāthās. The Mahāyānistic features mentioned above, as well as some passages which seem to be influenced by sculptures of the Gandhāra art, indicate the period belonging to the early centuries after Christ.[1] We are brought down to the fourth century A.D. by the references to the Huns, to the Chinese language and script, and the designation of the astrologer as "Horā-pāṭhaka" (III, 178).[2] The nucleus of the work is old, however, and probably originated as far back as the 2nd century B.C., even though it was enlarged in the 4th century A.D. and perhaps still later, by additions and interpolations. It is only the embellishment which is borrowed from the Mahāyāna, while only a weak admixture of actual Mahāyāna doctrines and none of the Mahāyāna mythology is to be found in the Mahāvastu.

---

1) For instance, in a flower miracle, the lotus blossoms fall in the shape of a circle around the halo of the Buddha. The halo was only introduced into India by Greek artists. *Cf. A. Foucher*, JA. 1903, s. 10, t. II, p. 208 f. and L'art grécobouddhique du Gandhāra, t. I, Paris 1905, p. 622. Also the numerous Buddhas under sunshades (see above, p. 245) are reminiscent of monuments of art.

2) According to *Senart* (1, p. 469 f.) we should regard Mahāvastu I, 120 as an allusion to the Mahāyāna school of the Yogācāras, which would indicate the 4th century. It is possible, however, that Yogācāra is used here merely with its general meaning of "practising Yoga." *Cf. La Vallée Poussin* in ERE VIII, 329 note 4; Haraprasad *Śāstrī* in Ind. Hist. Qa. I, 1925, 205.

The Lalita-Vistara.

While the Mahāvastu itself claims to be a work of the Hīnayāna, but has assimilated features of the Mahāyāna, the Lalita-Vistara[1] is regarded as one of the most sacred Mahāyāna texts, calls itself a Vaipulya-Sūtra ("discourse of great extent")—this being an ordinary term for Mahāyāna Sūtras—and exhibits all the peculiarities of a Mahāyāna Sūtra, although the work originally contained the life-story of the Buddha for the Sarvāstivādins of the Hīnayāna.[2] However, the mere title Lalita-Vistara, *i.e.*, "the detailed narration of the sport (of the Buddha)," corresponds to Mahāyānistic ideas. The life and work of the Buddha on earth is thus termed "the sport" (lalita) of a supernatural being.[3] Even in the introductory chapter, the Buddha appears as an exalted, divine being. It begins, indeed, after the manner of the Pāli Suttas, with the words: "Thus have I heard: once the Lord sojourned at Śrāvastī in the Jeta grove in the garden of Anāthapiṇḍada." However, whereas in the Pāli texts, the

[1]) First edition by Rajendralāla *Mitra* in Bibl. Ind. 1877 (very faulty); a better edition by S. *Lefmann*, Halle a. S. 1902 and 1908. Even this edition, however, needs correcting. *Cf.* Friedrich *Weller*, Zum Lalita-Vistara, Diss. Leipzig 1915, p. 8 ff. The English translation by Rajendralāla *Mitra* (Bibl. Ind. 1881-1886) only goes as far as Chapter XV; Chapters I-V translated into German by S. *Lefmann*, Berlin 1875; a complete French translation by Ph. Ed. *Foucaux* in AMG, t. 6 et 19 (Paris 1884, 1892).

[2]) Thus according to the Chinese tradition. *Cf.* S. *Beal*, The Romantic Legend of Sakya Buddha from the Chinese-Sanskrit, London 1875, Introd.; *Foucaux*, Lalita Vistara traduit, t. II, Introd. *Beal's* "Romantic Legend" is an abridged translation from the Chinese of the Abhiniṣkramaṇa-Sūtra, which has not come down in Sanskrit, but was translated into Chinese between 280 and 312 A.D. by Nie Tao-Tchen (s. *Bagchi*, l. c., I, p. 128) and in 587 A.D. by Jinagupta. It is said to be the biography of Buddha for the sect of the Dharmaguptas.

[3]) As regards the title, see *Lefmann*, Translation, p 70 ff., Edition, Vol. II, p. VI f., *Foucaux*, t. II, p. 3 and *Winternitz*, WZKM 26, 1912, p. 244. The work also calls itself a Mahā-Nidāna, *i.e.*, "a great (Sūtra treating) of the beginnings (of the Buddha's career,") and "Lalita-Vistara-Purāṇa," a term which is fitting in so far as the style of the work is not unlike that of the Purāṇas.

actual Sutta begins immediately after these or similar stereotyped introductory words, in which the Master is introduced to us surrounded by a few disciples, or at the most by a following of "five hundred monks," the Lalita-Vistara, like all Vaipulya-Sūtras of the Mahāyāna, first sketches a splendid picture of the Buddha, with divine brilliance shining around it. He is surrounded by 12,000 monks and no less than 32,000 Bodhisattvas, "all only bound to one more rebirth, all born with the perfections of a Bodhisattva, all rejoicing in the knowledge of a Bodhisattva, all in the possession of insight into magic sayings," and so on. While he sits absorbed in deep meditation in the middle watch of the night, a ray of light bursts forth from the parting of his hair, penetrates into the worlds of heaven and plunges all the gods into excitement. The gods immediately begin a song in praise of the exalted Buddha, and soon Īśvara and other gods appear before the Lord, throw themselves at his feet and implore him, for the salvation and blessing of the world, to reveal the excellent Vaipulya-Sūtra, called Lalita-Vistara, while, in extravagant terms, they praise the advantages of this text, which had also been revealed by former Buddhas. By maintaining silence, Buddha gives his consent. It is only after this circumstantial introduction, which occupies a whole, long chapter, that the actual narrative begins, the biography of Buddha, which forms the contents of the work. As a matter of fact, it begins where, in the Nidāna-Kathā, the second section (avidūrenidāna) begins :

The Bodhisattva sojourns in the heaven of the Contented (Tuṣita) gods in a magnificent heavenly palace. (The Bodhisattva receives over a hundred laudatory titles and the heavenly palace in which he lives, receives over a dozen.) Amid the sound of 84,000 drums he is invited to descend to earth in order to commence his work of salvation. After long consultations, in which the advantages and defects of a large number of royal families are weighed in the balance, the Bodhisattva decides to be reborn in the house of King Śuddhodana, and in the womb of Queen Māyā, as she possesses all the qualities of the mother of a Buddha. As perfect as her beauty (described down to the minutest detail) is her virtue and purity. She alone, of all the women of India, is able to bear the future Buddha, as the strength of ten thousand elephants is combined in her. With the aid of the gods the conception takes place, after the Bodhisattva has decided to penetrate into the womb in the shape of an elephant. The gods not only procure a heavenly dwelling as the confinement chamber for Māyā, but they also create a jewelled palace in her womb, so that the Bodhisattva shall not be defiled for ten months by the mother's womb. In this jewelled palace he has a beautifully soft seat. His body radiates in glorious beauty, and a light shines out for miles from the body of his mother. The sick come to Māyā Devī and are cured of their sufferings as soon as she lays her hand on their heads. "And whenever she looked to her right, she saw the Bodhisattva in her womb, as one sees one's own face in a clear mirror." While still in the womb the unborn Bodhisattva delights the gods with pious preaching, and the god Brahman obeys his every hint.[1]

In the same way as the conception, the birth of the Bodhisattva also takes place amid mighty miracles and signs. In the Lumbinī grove he is born of Māyā in the manner known to us from so many sculptures, not as an ordinary mortal, but as an omniscient, exalted being, as Mahāpuruṣa, "the Great Spirit." While lotus blossoms spring forth under each of his footsteps, the new-born one, proclaiming his greatness, takes seven steps in each of the six directions.[2]

Here the narrative is interrupted by a dialogue between Ānanda and the Buddha,[3] which declaims against those unbelievers who refuse to believe in the miraculous birth of the Buddha. The belief in the Buddha is taught as a necessary part of the religion; and we are reminded of the Kṛṣṇa of the Bhagavad-Gītā, when Buddha here says:

[1] Chapts. 2-6. The beginning of Chapt. 6 is translated by *Windisch*, Buddha's Geburt, p. 162 ff.

[2] In the Brāhmaṇas and Upaniṣads, the creator Prajāpati is called *Puruṣa* and Mahāpuruṣa, and later Brahman and Viṣṇu too. The seven steps of the new-born Buddha child are to be explained merely by the myth of the steps of Viṣṇu.

[3] Chapt. 7, ed. *Lefmann*, pp. 87-91.

"I do good to all who will believe in me. Those who seek refuge in me are as my friends. And the Tathāgata has many friends. But those friends of the Tathāgata speak only truth, not falsehood...To believe, O Ananda, may this be your aim. Thereto I admonish you."

It is surely no accident that this dialogue appears inserted just here. The reason is that, precisely with regard to legends of the conception and birth of the Buddha, the Lalita-Vistara differs very conspicuously from the accounts of the other schools by its exaggeration of the miraculous element. This is not so in the further account of the Buddha's life. In fact we find here very frequently an exceedingly close agreement with the oldest Pāli accounts, *e.g.*, those in the Mahāvagga of the Vinayapiṭaka,[1] and the Gāthās of the Lalita-Vistara sometimes appear to be more archaic than the corresponding Pāli texts. The two texts are in such cases not dependent on one another, but both reach back to a common older tradition. Here, too, however, the Lalita-Vistara has much that is entirely missing in the older accounts. Two episodes in particular are noteworthy. The one (Chapter VIII) relates how the Bodhisattva, as a boy, is taken to the temple by his foster-mother, and all the statues of the gods rise from their pedestals in order to fall at his feet. The other (Chapter X) tells of the Bodhisattva's first day at school:

With a following of ten thousand boys, with tremendous pomp and with all the gods participating, and with 8,000 divine maidens scattering flowers before him, the little Bodhisattva makes his entry into the writing school. The poor school-master cannot bear the glory of the Bodhisattva, and falls to the ground. A god raises him, and calms him by saying that the Bodhisattva, though omniscient and having no need to learn anything, yet, following the course of the world, has come to school. Then the

[1]) For the relationship of the Pāli tradition to the Lalita-Vistara, see *Burnouf*, Lotus de la bonne Loi, p. 864 ff.; *Oldenberg* in OC V, Berlin 1882, Vol. 2, pp. 107-122. *Cf.* also *Windisch*, "Māra und Buddha" and "Buddha's Geburt," and *Kern*, SBE Vol. 21, p. xi ff.

Bodhisattva surprised the school-master by asking him which of the 64, kinds of script he was going to teach him. And he enumerates them all including the scripts of the Cīnas (Chinese) and Hūṇas (Huns), scripts which the teacher does not even know by name. Finally the teacher begins to teach the ten thousand boys the alphabet. At every letter of the alphabet, however, the Bodhisattva gives utterance to a wise saying beginning with the letter in question.[1]

Chapters XII [2] and XIII also contain episodes, which are missing in the other biographies of the Buddha. On the other hand, the rest of the story (Chapters XIV-XXVI) differs but little from the legend as it is known from other sources:[3] namely, the four encounters by which the Bodhisattva becomes acquainted with age, disease, death and renunciation of the world, the flight from the palace, the meeting with King Bimbisāra, the apprenticeship of Gotama and his futile ascetic practices, the conflict with Māra, the final enlightenment and the proclaiming of the doctrine at the request of the god Brahman. The last chapter (XXVII), however, in the true manner of the Mahāyāna Sūtras, is devoted to the glorification of the Lalita-Vistara itself, and the enumeration of the merits and advantages which one gains by propagating and honouring it.

From all this it is very probable that the Lalita-Vistara is a recast of an older Hīnayāna text, the Buddha biography of the Sarvāstivāda school, enlarged and embellished in the spirit of the Mahāyāna. This supposition also explains the

[1]) E. *Kuhn* (Gurupûjâkaumudî, p. 116 ff.) has proved that these two legends of the little Buddha served as models for the apocryphal gospels, which relate similar stories of the little Jesus.

[2]) For this, *cf. Winternitz*, WZKM 26, 1912, p. 237 ff.

[3]) Here too, however, the Lalita-Vistara frequently distinguishes itself by its exaggerations. Whilst in our oldest record (Mahā-Vagga I, 1-4), for instance, Gotama spends the four weeks after his enlightenment, in meditation under various trees, in the Lalita-Vistara (ed. *Lefmann*, p. 377) he takes a "long walk" in the second week through thousands of worlds, and in the fourth week a "short walk," which extends only from the Eastern to the Western ocean.

character of the text, which is by no means the unified work of one author, but an anonymous compilation, in which very early and very recent passages stand side by side. In form, too, the work consists of unequal parts, a continuous narrative in Sanskrit prose, and numerous, often long, metrical passages in "mixed Sanskrit."[1] It is rarely that these verses form a part of the narrative; as a rule they are independent songs, which relate the subject-matter of the prose, in a shorter, simpler, and sometimes in a more or less deviating form. Some of these songs, such as the birth legend and the Asita episode in Chapter VII, the Bimbisāra story in Chapter XVI, the dialogue with Māra in Chapter XVIII, etc., are beautiful old ballads, which are derived from the same ancient sources as the above-mentioned (p. 96 f.) poems of the Suttanipāta. They belong to the old religious ballad poetry of the early centuries after the Buddha. Many prose passages, too, as for instance, the sermon of Benares (in Chapter XXVI) belong to the oldest stratum of Buddhist tradition. On the other hand, the later parts are found not only in the prose, but also in the Gāthās, many of which are composed in very artistic metres.[2]

When the Lalita-Vistara was finally edited, we do not know. It was formerly erroneously stated that the work had been translated into Chinese as early as in the first century A.D.[3] Actually, we do not even know whether the P'ou-yao-king, the biography of Buddha translated by

[1]) *F. Weller*, Zum Lalita Vistara, I, Über die Prosa des Lalita Vistara, Leipzig Diss. 1915, has made it seem probable that even the prose in the Lalita-Vistara was not originally written in Sanskrit, but in a dialect akin to the prose of the Mahāvastu, and that it was not sanskritized until later.

[2]) Thus the Vasantatilakā and the Śārdūlavikrīḍita are fairly frequent. See the list of metres in *Lefmann's* edition, Vol. II, p. 227 ff., and Introduction, p. xix ff.

[3]) By *B. Nanjio*, who regarded the Fo-pen-hing-king (68 A.D.) which has been lost long ago, as a translation of the Lalita-Vistara: but there is no proof whatsoever for such an assumption. *Cf. Bagchi*, l.c., I, p. 6.

Dharmarakṣa in the year 308 A. D., the supposed "second translation of the Lalita-Vistara," is really a translation of the text in question at all.[1] The Tibetan translation[2] is an accurate translation of the Sanskrit text, but it only originated in the 9th century. It may be assumed with certainty that a version, differing slightly from the Lalita-Vistara, was known to the artists who, from about 850 to 900 A.D., decorated the famous temple of Boro-Budur in Java: for these magnificent sculptures represent scenes from the Buddha legend in such a manner as though the artists had actually worked with a text of the Lalita-Vistara at their hand.[3]

The artists who adorned the Græco-Buddhist monuments of Northern India with scenes from the life of the Buddha, must already have been familiar with the Buddha legend, as it is related in the Lalita-Vistara. It is true that they did not work from texts, but from living, oral tradition. Not infrequently, however, the agreement between the pictures and the texts is so striking, that we must assume that the literary tradition, too, was sometimes influenced by art. Art and literature influenced each other.[4] Whilst the ancient Buddhist art of the time of Aśoka (reliefs of Bharhut, Sānchi,

[1]) It contains only 8 chapters. See *Winternitz*, WZKM 26, 1912, 241 f., and *Bagchi*, l.c., I, p. 87 f.

[2]) Edited and translated into French by Ph. E. *Foucaux* (Rgya-tcher-rol-pa, Version tibétaine du Lalitavistara), Paris 1847-48.

[3]) C. M. *Pleyte*, Die Buddhalegende in den Skulpturen des Tempels von Bōrō-Budur, Amsterdam 1901, and N. J. *Krom*, The Life of Buddha on the Stūpa of Barabuḍu according to the Lalitavistara-Text, The Hague 1926, have given extracts from the Lalita-Vistara in translation, by way of explanation of the sculptures. *Cf. Speyer*, Le Muséon, N. S. IV, 1903, p. 124 ff.; F. C. *Wilsen*, Die Buddha-Legende auf den Flachreliefs der ersten Galerie des Stūpa von Boro-Budur Java, verkleinerte Wiedergabe der Umrisszeichnungen, Leipzig 1923 (Veröffentl, des Forschungsinstituts für vergleichende Religionsgeschichte).

[4]) See A. *Foucher*, L'art gréco-bouddhique du Gandhāra, t. I, Paris 1905, p. 324 f., 616 ff.; *Grünwedel*, Buddhistische Kunst in Indien, p. 98, 104 f., 184; *Senart*, OC XIV, Alger 1905, I, 121 ff. and T. *Bloch*, ZDMG 62, p. 370 ff.

etc.) knows no representations of Buddha, but puts only symbols (*e.g.*, the wheel) in the place of the person of the founder of the religion, the representation of Buddha is one of the principal objects of the Gandhāra art. May this not be connected with the fact that the Buddha had, in the meantime, become an object of Bhakti, and that Buddha-worship had assumed the central position in the religion? Thus everything favours the supposition that the period of the development of the Gandhāra [1] art, that is, the first two centuries of the Christian era, is also the period of the earlier Mahāyāna texts which deal with the Buddha legend.

It is therefore only correct to say that the Lalita-Vistara offers us very old traditions concerning the Buddha legend, as well as some which are centuries later. It is an important source for ancient Buddhism only in those passages which agree with the Pāli texts and other Sanskrit texts such as the Mahāvastu. It is wrong, however, to regard the whole Lalita-Vistara as a good, ancient source for our knowledge of Buddhism, as has been done, notably by É. Senart in his "Essai sur la légende du Buddha." [2] Neither does the Lalita-Vistara give us information on the "popular Buddhism" of the early period, as Louis de La Vallée Poussin affirms.[3] It is, however, most informative as regards the

[1]) Scholars are practically unanimous in assuming that the Græco-Buddhist art of Gandhāra began shortly before the birth of Christ, and attained its perfection in the second century A.D., especially during the reign of Kaniṣka. See G. *Bühler* in Anzeiger der Kais. Akademie der Wissenschaften in Wien, Phil.—hist. Kl., 1896, p. 66 f.; A. *Grünwedel*, Buddhistische Kunst in Indien, Berlin 1900, p. 81; A. *Foucher*, L'art gréco-bouddhique du Gandhāra, I, Paris 1905, p. 40 ff.; II, 1918, pp. 401 ff., 486 ff.; V. A. *Smith*, Early History, pp. 255 ff., 252; History of Fine Art in India and Ceylon, Oxford 1911, p. 99 ("It is quite safe to affirm that the works of good quality belong to the first three centuries of the Christian era"); L. A. *Waddell* in JRAS, 1914, p. 140 f.; Sir J. H. *Marshall* in JRAS 1909, 1056 ff.; Cambridge History, I, 1922, p. 648.

[2]) 2nd Ed., Paris 1882, pp. XXXI *f.*, 456 *f.*

[3]) Bouddhisme, Études et Matériaux, pp. 37 and 42 f. According to *La Vallée Poussin*, the Pāli texts show us only an "aristocratic and philosophical Buddhism."

development of the Buddha legend from its earliest beginnings, when only the chief events in the life of the great founder of the religion are adorned with miracles, down to that boundless deification of the Master, in which, from the beginning to the end of his career, he appears mainly as a god above all gods. On this account the work is of immense value from the point of view of the history of religion. From the point of view of the history of literature, too, the Lalita-Vistara is one of the most important works of Buddhist scripture. Though it is not yet an actual Buddha epic, it contains all the germs of such an epic; and it is from the ballads and episodes as preserved in the earliest portions of the Lalita-Vistara, though probably not from the Lalita-Vistara itself, that Aśvaghoṣa, the greatest poet of the Buddhists, created his magnificent epic Buddha-Carita, "life of the Buddha." [1)]

The Poet Aśvaghoṣa[2)] *and his School.*

Until the year 1892, when the French scholar Sylvain Lévi published the first chapter of the Buddha-Carita, little more than the name of Aśvaghoṣa was known in Europe. To-day we know him as one of the most prominent poets of Sanskrit literature, as the most important predecessor of Kālidāsa, and as the creator of epic, dramatic and lyrical compositions; but of his life we know little. The traditions

[1)] I do not agree with S. *Lévi* when (JA 1892, s. 8, t. XIX, p. 202) he calls the Buddha-Carita "un abrégé substantiel du Lalita Vistara." At least the Lalita-Vistara in its present form cannot have been the model which Aśvaghoṣa used.

[2)] On Aśvaghoṣa in general, see S. *Lévi* in JA 1892, ser. 8. t.XIX, p. 201 ff.; 1908, s. 10, t. XII, p. 57 ff.; T. *Suzuki*, Açvaghosha's Discourse on the Awakening of Faith, Transl., Chicago 1900, Introduction; M. *Anesaki* in ERE II, 1909, p. 159 f.; and F. W. *Thomas*, Kavīndravacanasamuccaya, Bibl. Ind. 1912, p. 25 ff. A purely legendary biography of Aśvaghoṣa was translated into Chinese by Kumārajīva between 401 and 409 A.D.; it is published in extracts, by W. *Wassiljew*, Der Buddhismus, St. Petersburg 1860, p. 231 f.

embodied in the Chinese and Tibetan sources agree in asserting that Aśvaghoṣa was a contemporary of King Kaniṣka (2nd century A.D.).[1] Pārśva or his pupil Puṇyayaśas is mentioned as his teacher, and he is generally enumerated among the leaders or founders of the Mahāyāna.[2] In the Chinese lists of the Buddhist patriarchs in India, he always appears after Pārśva and Puṇyayaśas, and *before* Nāgārjuna and Āryadeva. It may be taken as certain that he was of Brahman family, and had enjoyed a thorough Brahmanical education before he went over to Buddhism. As a Buddhist he probably associated himself first with the Sarvāstivāda school,[3] but laid great stress on the Buddha-Bhakti and thus prepared the Mahāyāna. Sāketa (*i.e.*, Ayodhyā, the present-day Oudh) is generally given as his birthplace or home; but Benares and Patna are also mentioned. His mother was called Suvarṇākṣī. The Tibetan biographer of Aśvaghoṣa says of him: "There was no question which he would not have solved, no imputation which he would not have rejected; he overcame his opponents as frequently as a strong wind breaks rotten trees." According to the same account, he was also an excellent musician, who himself composed pieces of music and travelled about with a band of male and female singers in the bazaars. He played and sang with his choir melancholy songs about the vanity of existence, and, attracted by the beautiful melodies, the crowd stood still and listened. In this way he won many over to the religion.[4] The

[1]) According to Chinese sources, Aśvaghoṣa was the spiritual counsellor and Caraka was the medical adviser of King Kaniṣka. *Cf. Lévi* in JA 1896, s. 9, t. VIII, p. 447 f. On the period of Kaniṣka, s. Appendix V, and Vol. I, p. 513.

[2]) Perhaps this is only based on the fact that the authorship of the Mahāyāna-Śraddhotpāda was attributed to him.

[3]) See *Lévi*, JA 1908, s. 10, t. XII, pp. 90 ff., 184, and H. *Lüders*, Bruchstücke buddhistischer Dramen, Berlin 1911, p. 65. According to Vasubandhu he is supposed to have assisted Kātyāyanīputra with the commentary on the Abhidharma.

[4]) A. *Schiefner* in ABA 1859, p. 259 ff.

Chinese pilgrim I-tsing, who travelled through India in 671-695 A.D., speaks of the learned monks, who oppose the heretics with great success, promote the religion of the Buddha, and therefore receive respect above gods and men, and says that "of such persons in every generation only one or two appear," such men as "Nāgārjuna, Deva, Aśvaghoṣa of an early age."[1] I-tsing also relates that at his time in India, among other songs which were chanted at Buddhist sanctuaries, there was a collection of sacred texts compiled by Aśvaghoṣa. He mentions him also as a composer of songs, of the Sūtrālaṃkāra and of the Buddha-Carita.[2]

Of the Buddha-Carita[3] I-tsing says that "this extensive work......relates the Tathāgata's chief doctrines and works during his life, from the period when he was still in the royal palace till his last hour under the avenue of Sāla-trees." And he adds: "It is widely read or sung throughout the five divisions of India, and the countries of the Southern Sea.[4]

[1]) *Hsüan-Tsang* (Si-yu-ki, Buddhist Records of the Western World, transl. by S. *Beal*, II, p. 302 f.) calls Aśvaghoṣa, Deva, Nāgārjuna and Kumāralabdha "the four suns that illumined the world."

[2]) *I-tsing*, Record transl. by *Takakusu*, pp. 152 f., 165, 181.

[3]) The text has been edited by E. B. *Cowell*, Oxford (Anecdota Oxoniensia, Aryan Series, Vol. I, Part VII) 1893, and translated by the same scholar in SBE, Vol. 49. Translated into German by O. *Cappeller*, Jena 1922 (Religiöse Stimmen der Völker) and R. *Schmidt*, Hagen 1924; into Italian by C. *Formichi*, Açvaghoṣa, poeta del Buddhismo, Bari 1912. Contributions to the critical restoration of the text and explanation of the Buddha-Carita by O. *Böhtlingk* in BSGW 1894, 160 ff.; F. *Kielhorn* in NGGW 1894, p. 364 ff.; J. S. *Speyer* in Verslagen en Mededeelingen der Kon. Akademie van Wetenschappen, Afd. Lett., 3de Reeks, Deel XI, Amsterdam 1895, and JRAS 1914, p. 105 ff.; L. *Finot* in JA 1898, s. 9, t. XII, p. 542 ff.; *Formichi*, l.c., pp. 289-400, 409. E. *Leumann*, in WZKM 7, 1893, 193 ff.; NGGW 1896, 83 ff.; *Lüders* in NGGW 1896, 1 ff.; K. M. *Joglekar*, Ashvaghosha's Buddha-Charita, cantos I-V with a scholium by Dattatraya *Shastri Nigdukar*, and Introduction, Notes, and Translation, Bombay, 1912; A. *Gawroński*, Gleanings from Aśvaghoṣa's Buddhacarita, in Rocznik Oryentalistyczny I, Krakow 1914-15, 1 ff.; and Studies about the Sanskrit-Buddhist Literature, Krakow 1919, pp. 1 ff., 27 ff.; E. *Hultzsch* in ZDMG 72, 1918, 148 ff.; O. *Cappeller* in ZII 1, 1922, p. 1 ff.; E. H. *Johnston* in JRAS 1927, 209 ff.

[4]) This means the Malay Archipelago (Sumatra, Java, and the neighbouring islands). *Takakusu*, l.c., p. xxxix.

He clothes manifold meanings and ideas in a few words, which rejoice the heart of the reader so that he never feels tired from reading the poem. Besides, it should be counted as meritorious for one to read this book, inasmuch as it contains the noble doctrines given in a concise form." [1] We gather from the words of I-tsing that he knew the Buddha-Carita in the form in which it appeared in the Chinese translation,[2] where the epic consists of 28 cantos, and the narrative is continued down to the Nirvāṇa of the Buddha. As the Tibetan translation [3] also consists of 28 cantos, we must assume that the Sanskrit text, which consist of 17 cantos, and ends with the conversions in Benares, only represents a torso. In any case the work is a torso, for even of these seventeen cantos, only the first thirteen are old and authentic. The work was completed by a certain Amṛtānanda, who copied it at the beginning of the 19th century, and added the conclusion, because (as he himself admits) he could find no complete manuscripts.[4]

However, even with the mere torso which has come down to us, we can but fully endorse what the Chinese pilgrim has said in praise of the Buddha-Carita. Here we

---

[1]) *I-tsing*, l.c., p. 165 f.

[2]) This is the Fo-sho-hing-tsan-king, translated from Sanskrit into Chinese between 414 and 421 A.D. by Dharmarakṣa, and translated into English by Samuel *Beal* in SBE, Vol. 19. T. W. *Rhys Davids* (JRAS 1901, p. 405 f.) has asserted that this Chinese work is not a translation of Aśvaghoṣa's Buddha-Carita at all. Else *Wohlgemuth*, however (Über die chinesische Version von Aśvaghoṣas Buddhacarita, Diss. Leipzig 1916), has shown that the Chinese version is undoubtedly based on Aśvaghoṣa's poem, though some things have been added and others omitted, and that the recension on which it is based differed from the one which we know.

[3]) The Tibetan translation of the 7th or 8th century is far more accurate than the Chinese one, but on the other hand it does not (at least in the first canto) reproduce the original text of Aśvaghoṣa. *Cf.* E. *Leumann* in WZKM 7, 1893, p. 193 ff. and Friedrich *Weller*, Das Leben des Buddha von Aśvaghoṣa, Tibetisch und Deutsch, Leipzig 1926 (Gesang I-VIII übersetzt; in Veröffentlichungen des Forschungsinstituts für vergleichende Religionsgeschichte an der Universität Leipzig, II, 3); Part II, 1928.

[4]) Also a manuscript of the Buddha-Carita discovered by *Haraprasāda Śāstrī* only goes as far as the middle of Canto XIV (JASB, N. S., Vol. V, 1909, p. 47 ff.).

have indeed for the first time an actual epic of Buddha, created by a real poet, a poet who, filled with intense love and reverence for the exalted figure of the Buddha, and deeply imbued with the truth of the Buddha doctrine, is able to present the life and doctrine of the Master in noble and artistic, but not artificial language. His Sanskrit is faultless, even though it does not always comply strictly with the rules of Pāṇini.[1] The Buddha-Carita calls itself a Mahākāvya, or "great poem," *i.e.*, an ornate epic poem in the technical sense, and it is composed in the so-called Kāvya style, the beginnings of which we have already found in the Rāmāyaṇa.[2] Vālmīki and his immediate successors were the predecessors of Aśvaghoṣa, in the same way as the latter himself is a predecessor of Kālidāsa. All these three great poets have one thing in common: they are still very moderate in their use of the Alaṃkāras or "embellishments." Aśvaghoṣa is not only moderate in language and style, but he also uses restraint in the presentation of miracles in the Buddha legend. He always keeps himself far removed from such exaggerations as we find, for instance, in the Lalita-Vistara. In contrast to the chaotic disorder in texts like the Mahāvastu and the Lalita-Vistara, we find in the Buddha-Carita a well-planned, artistic arrangement of the material. Although the poet is quite familiar with the older sacred texts, he nevertheless assumes a certain amount of freedom in his attitude towards them. Not that he has made any alterations in the traditions; but he has the art of clothing the old familiar legends in a new poetical garment,[3] and of imparting original expression to the well-known doctrines of the Buddhist Sūtras. Aśvaghoṣa is always more of a poet than a monk, at least in the Buddha-Carita.

1) *Cf. Sukumar Sen* in Ind. Hist. Qu. II, 1916, p. 657 ff.

2) *Cf.* above, Vol. I, pp. 476, 489 f., 497, 506.

3) As *Windisch* (Māra und Buddha, p. 205) says, Aśvaghoṣa seems "almost intentionally to have avoided any resemblance to the wording of older texts."

How different from the Lalita-Vistara is, for instance, the highly poetical description of the excursions of the young prince in Cantos III and IV!

First of all there is a beautiful description of how, on hearing that the prince is going out, the women of the city, full of curiosity, hasten from their rooms to the house-tops and the windows. Hampered by their falling girdles, they scamper up in the greatest haste, pushing and jostling one another, and scaring away the birds on the roofs by the clattering of the girdles and rings. The lotus faces of the fair ones, leaning out of the windows, look as though the walls of the houses were decorated with real lotus blossoms.[1] Beautifully the poet then describes the encounter with the old man, whom the gods cause to appear. In consternation the prince asks:

"Who is the man who here approaches, O charioteer,
With white hair, and eyes sunk deep in their sockets,
Bent down on his staff, his limbs trembling?—
Is it a process of Nature, or the sport of destiny?"

Whereupon the charioteer replies:

"It is age which has broken him,—Age,
The thief of beauty and destroyer of strength,
The source of care and the end of joys,
The foe of the senses, the vanishing of memories.
He, too, has sucked at the mother's breast
As a little child, learned walking in the course of time,
Gradually he grew big and strong, a youth,
Gradually age has overtaken him."

After the prince, on his three excursions, has become acquainted with age, disease and death, he takes no more pleasure in anything. It is in vain that the family priest, at the King's request, invites the women and girls of the palace to apply all the arts of love in order to inveigle the prince and to drive away his sad thoughts. The prince remains unmoved

---

[1]) In the Raghuvaṃśa (VII, 5-12) Kālidāsa imitated this description of Aśvaghoṣa (Buddha-Carita III, 13-24), as has already been pointed out by *Cowell* (Buddha-Carita, Edition, Preface).

by all the sweet temptations. He only marvels at the gay doings of these women, and exclaims (IV, 60 f.) :

"How senseless seems to me the man who has seen
his neighbour ill and old and dead,
And yet remains happy and is not shaken by fear.
Thus, when a tree which, quite bereft of blossoms
and of fruits,
Is felled or falls,—the neighbour tree cares not."

The presentation of love scenes is one of the indispensable elements of an ornate court poem. The poet fulfils this requirement by describing the blandishments of the beautiful women, by which they seek to tempt the prince (IV, 24-53); and in the highly-coloured description of the night scene in the harem, which is the cause of the prince's flight from the palace,[1] the poet reveals his knowledge of the science of love. But a court poet must also be versed in the doctrines of Nītiśāstra, state-craft. Such doctrines are recited to the prince by the family priest (IV, 62-82), in order to distract him from his thoughts. Lastly, an ornate poem is not complete without a description of battle scenes. Our poet fulfils this requirement also, in Canto XIII, in which he gives an animated description of the battle of Buddha with Māra and his hosts.

The Saundarānanda-Kāvya,[2] a second poem by Aśva-

1 V, 48-62. This scene is related in its original version with regard to the youth Yasa in the Vinayapiṭaka (see above, p. 27). It has already been stated (see above, Vol. I, p. 490, note 3) that the similar scene in Rāmāyaṇa, V, 9, 11, was composed in imitation of Aśvaghoṣa.

2) The poem was discovered by *Haraprasāda Śāstrī*, and was also edited by him, Bibl. Ind., Calcutta 1910. A new critical edition, with notes, by E. H. *Johnston*, has just been published in the Punjab University Oriental Publications, Oxford University Press, London, 1928. *Cf.* *Haraprasāda Śāstrī* in JASB 5, 1909, p. 165 f.; F. W. *Thomas* in JRAS 1911, p. 1125 f.; A. *Baston* in JA 1912, s. 10, t. XIX, p. 79 ff.; *La Vallée Poussin* in BSOS 1918, p. 133 ff.; A. *Gawroński*, Studies about the Sanskrit Buddhist Literature, Krakow 1919, p. 56 ff.; Notes on the Saundarānanda, Critical and Explanatory, Second Series (Prace Komisji Orjental. Polskiej Akad. Um. Nr. 6.) W Krakowie 1922; E. *Hultzsch* in ZDMG 72, 1918, p. 111 ff.; 73, 229 ff.; 74, 293 ff.; C. W. *Gurner* in JRAS 1928, p. 131 f. From the concluding verses we may perhaps (with *Hultzsch*, ZDMG 73, 121 f.) assume that Aśvaghoṣa wrote the Saundarānanda first and the Buddha-Carita afterwards.

ghoṣa, also belongs to the same class of ornate court poetry. This work, too, is connected with the life story of the Buddha, but it amplifies those scenes and episodes in particular, which receive scanty attention or none at all, in the Buddha-Carita. Thus, in Canto I, the story of the founding of Kapilavastu is related in minute detail. The actual theme of this poem, however, is the story of the love-lorn Nanda, the half-brother of the Buddha, who is ordained as a monk against his will by the Buddha:

Just as Sundarī, the beautiful wife of Nanda, mourns and laments for her lost husband, so Nanda, too, longs to be back with his beloved. Vain are the attempts of the other monks to calm him. Even Buddha's words fail to change his mood. Then the Master takes him by the hand, and ascends with him to heaven. On the way they see in the Himālaya an ugly, one-eyed female ape, and Buddha asks him whether Sundarī is more beautiful than this, which Nanda of course enthusiastically affirms. Soon they see in heaven the Apsaras, the heavenly nymphs, and Nanda thinks that the difference between the last-named and his wife, is just as great as between her and the one-eyed ape. From that moment he has an ardent desire for the heavenly women, and, on his return to earth, devotes himself diligently to ascetic practices in order to reach heaven. Then Ānanda teaches him that even heavenly pleasures are empty and vain. At last Nanda is convinced, and goes to Buddha, in order to tell him that he no longer desires the heavenly women. Buddha rejoices greatly at this, and preaches to him (in several cantos) the principles of his doctrine. Now Nanda retires into the forest, practises the four great meditations, and becomes an Arhat. Thankfully he goes to Buddha and pays homage to him, but the Master exhorts him, now that he has attained his object, to preach the good doctrine to others, out of pity, and so as to lead them to liberation.[1]

---

[1]) In the Vinayapiṭaka (Mahāvagga 1, 54) and the Nidāna-Kathā (Jātaka ed. *Fausböll*, I, p. 91; *Rhys Davids*, Buddhist Birth Stories, p. 128) it is only related that Nanda was ordained as a monk by Buddha against his will. The legend of Nanda's ascent to heaven and his yearning for the Apsarases is told in Udāna III. 2, and in the Dhammapada Commentary I, 9 (Buddhist Legends, transl. by *Burlingame*, HOS, Vol. 28, p. 217 ff.). See also Spence *Hardy*, Manual of Buddhism, p. 204; and *Kern*, Der Buddhismus, I, 155 f. Some scenes from the Nanda legend are also to be found on reliefs, s. *Foucher*, L'art gréco-bouddhique, I, p. 464 ff.

In the concluding verses, the poet states emphatically that he has written his work, the aim of which is liberation, not for the sake of delectation, but with a view to perfect peace; he has given it the form of an ornate poem, only so as to be able to win over non-Buddhist hearers to Buddha's doctrine, and to make this doctrine palatable to them, just as one mixes a bitter medicine with honey to make it drinkable. Much space in the Saundarānanda is accordingly devoted to preaching, in which the poet makes use of much the same expressions which are familiar to us from the Tipiṭaka. The joys of solitude and meditation are extolled in this poem just as in other Hīnayāna works.[1] Nevertheless the Saundarānanda also alludes to doctrines which are peculiar to the Mahāyāna. Nanda is filled with the "great pity," which makes him search his heart, in deep commiseration, for means whereby he may release the beings from suffering (XIII, 8). Whilst the Tipiṭaka teaches often enough that everything is "transitory, without self, and full of suffering," Nanda attains to the realisation that everything is "transitory, empty (śūnya), without self, and full of suffering."[2] And at the end, it is not enough for Nanda himself to become a saint who attains to Nirvāṇa: he must also become an apostle.[3]

In the Buddha-Carita, too, Aśvaghoṣa's teaching is in the main that of the Hīnayāna, though traces of the Mahāyāna are not wanting. Book XVI contains the "Sermon of

---

[1]) The recommendation of *yogācāra* in XIV, 18, and XX, 68, does not refer to the yogācāra school of the Mahāyāna, but only to the advantages of the practice of Yoga (*Haraprasāda Śāstrī*, Preface, p. xii). Moreover, the tendency of the Hīnayāna, is seen clearly when Nanda pays homage to Buddha, and Buddha restrains him by saying that worship is due not to him, but to the Dharma (XVIII, 22).

[2]) XVII, 16-22. Cf. Vidhusekhara *Bhattacharya* in JRAS 1914, p. 747 f.

[3]) However, the Hīnayāna, too, valued highly the duty of instruction and conversion: this is shown, for instance, by the Sutta quoted above, on p. 62 f., from the Aṅguttara-nikāya.

Benares," which is only a poetical and expanded version of the text known from the Tipiṭaka, but it also speaks of the body as "empty, without a self" (śūnyam anātmakam, XVI, 28), calls the Buddha not only "the Self-born" (Svayambhū), "the Overlord of the Whole Dharma," but even the "Lord of the World" (XVI, 64; 69). And he even says that he has attained the Great Vehicle, the Mahāyāna, that has been set forth by all the Buddhas for establishing the welfare of all beings (XVI, 75; 85). Thus Aśvaghoṣa probably belongs to the period of the beginning of the Mahāyāna.

Both in the Buddhacarita and the Saundarānanda there are abundant allusions to Brahmanical legends and epic narratives, which serve to confirm the tradition that Aśvaghoṣa was of Brahman family.

The Vajrasūcī or "Diamond Needle,"[1] which is sometimes ascribed to Aśvaghoṣa, also reveals an intimate knowledge of Brahmanical literature. Unfortunately there are grave doubts as to whether he was actually the author of this little work, which is certainly interesting in any case. This work refutes the Brahmanical caste system very cuttingly. The author's method is extremely effective, for he takes up the Brahmanical standpoint, and seeks to prove from the Brahmanical texts themselves, by quotations from the Veda, the Mahābhārata and the law-book of Manu,[2] how frail the claims of the Brahman caste are. When B. H. Hodgson

---

[1]) Wujra Soochi or Refutation of the Arguments upon which the Brahmanical Institution of Caste is Founded, by the learned Boodhist Ashwa Ghoshu (published by Lancelot *Wilkinson* with the translation by B. H. *Hodgson*, which had already appeared in 1829 in the Transactions of the Royal Asiatic Society, Vol. III), also the Tunku by Soobajee Bapoo, being a Reply to the Wujra Soochi, 1839. A. *Weber*, "Über die Vajrasūcī" (ABA 1859, p. 205 ff., and Indische Streifen, I, 186 ff.). Cf. also B. H. *Hodgson*, Essays on the Languages, Literature and Religion of Napāl and Tibet, London 1874, p. 126 ff.; E. *Burnouf*, Introduction à l'histoire du Bouddhism Indien, 2ième éd., Paris 1876, p. 192 f., and S. *Lévi*, JA 1908, s. 10, t. XII, p. 70 f.

[2]) In the same way in Kumāralāta's Kalpanāmaṇḍitikā ("Sūtralaṃkāra" No. 77) the Brahmanical system is refuted by quotations from the law-book of Manu.

published a translation of this work, as far back as the year 1829, and L. Wilkinson edited the text in 1839, they were quite charmed with the democratic spirit with which the author defends the equality of all classes of men, "as they are equal as regards joy and sorrow, life, intellect, profession and trade, death and birth, fear and sexual love." For the sake of the quotations from Brahmanical texts, if on no other grounds, this work would be of great importance in the history of literature, if only we had any certain data about the author and the date of the work. There are some serious objections to ascribing the authorship to Aśvaghoṣa. The Vajrasūcī is not enumerated either by I-tsing or in the Tibetan Tanjur among the works of Aśvaghoṣa; and in the catalogues of the Chinese Tripiṭaka a Vajrasūcī, which is said to contain "a refutation of the four Vedas," and which was translated into Chinese between 973 and 981 A.D., is ascribed to a man named Dharmakīrti.[1]

Among the lyrical poems which are ascribed to Aśvaghoṣa, the only one we know is the Gaṇḍīstotra-Gāthā, which A. von Staël-Holstein[2] has attempted to reconstruct in the Sanskrit original on the basis of the Chinese transliteration. It is a beautiful poem, worthy of Aśvaghoṣa both in form and contents.

The scanty fragments, which are all that is left of his Śāriputra-Prakaraṇa show us that as a dramatist too, Aśvaghoṣa was a worthy predecessor of Kālidāsa.[3] This drama treats of

---

[1] Bunyiu *Nanjio*, Catalogue of the Chinese Translation of the Buddhist Tripiṭaka, No. 1303. Chinese *Fa-shang* is the translation of Sanskrit *Dharmakīrti*. For the philosophical work Mahāyāna-Śraddhotpāda, which has been erroneously ascribed to the great Aśvaghoṣa, see below in the chapter on "The Masters and Poets of the Mahāyāna."

[2] Bibliotheca Buddhica XV, St. Petersburg 1913. Cf. F. W. *Thomas* in JRAS 1914, p. 752 f.

[3] H. *Lüders* (Das Śāriputraprakaraṇa, ein Drama des Aśvaghoṣa, in SBA 1911, 388 ff.) discovered these fragments in palm leaf MSS. from Turfan. It is uncertain whether the fragments of two other Buddhist dramas discovered by *Lüders* (Königlich Preussische Turfan-Expeditionen, Kleinere Sanskrit-Texte I, Berlin 1911) were written by Aśvaghoṣa. For further information on this matter, see Vol. III in the chapter on the drama.

the conversion of Śāriputra and his friend Maudgalyāyana, which is already related in one of the most beautiful stories in the Mahāvagga of the Vinayapiṭaka.[1)]

Chinese authors also ascribe to Aśvaghoṣa a work entitled "Sūtrālaṃkāra" which was translated into Chinese by Kumārajīva in about 405 A.D., but which was really written by Aśvaghoṣa's junior contemporary Kumāralāta, and which, in Sanskrit, bore the title Kalpanāmaṇḍitikā or Kalpanālaṃkṛtikā. We glean this from the fragments of the work, which H. Lüders discovered in the finds of manuscripts in Turfan.[2)] Valuable though these fragments are, they are unfortunately so few in number, that even now we can only judge the work on the strength of the French translation of the Chinese version.[3)] The Kalpanāmaṇḍitikā is a collection of pious legends after the manner of the Jātakas and Avadānas, and they are told in prose and verse in the style of ornate poetry. Some of the legends are old acquaintances, for instance that of Dīrghāyus ("Prince Live-Long") and that of King Śibi. An old parable, which appears already in the Tipiṭaka, namely, that it is as difficult to be reborn as a human being, as for a one-eyed tortoise to put its neck into the hole

---

1) See above, p. 28. The disciples are called Sāriputta and Moggallāna in Pāli.

2) H. *Lüders*, Bruchstücke der Kalpanāmaṇḍitikā des Kumāralāta (Kön. Preuss. Turfan-Expeditionen, Kleinere Sanskrit-Texte II), Leipzig 1926. Both Kalpanāmaṇḍitikā and Kalpanālaṃkṛtikā appear as titles in the colophons. Both adjectives mean the same, and it is probable that Dṛṣṭānta-paṅktiḥ followed after them, so that the meaning of the title is: "A Series of Examples adorned by Poetic Invention." See *Lüders*, l.c., pp. 19, 26, and S. *Lévi* in JA, t. 201, 1927, p. 95 ff. The Chinese did not understand the somewhat extraordinary title, and (owing to the word alaṃkṛtikā) made a "Sūtrālaṃkāra" out of it. *Lüders* (l.c.) has advanced the hypothesis "that Aśvaghoṣa did actually write a work entitled Sūtrālaṃkāra, which was not translated into Chinese, but soon got lost, and was subsequently confused with the Kalpanāmaṇḍitikā which was known by the similar sounding title Chuang-yen-lun = Alaṃkāraśāstra." I am not convinced that this is the solution of the riddle. S. *Lévi* (l.c., p. 126 ff.) tries another solution and thinks it still possible that Aśvaghoṣa may be the author of the work.

3) Sūtrālaṃkāra traduit en français sur la version chinoise de Kumârajîva par Éd. *Huber*, Paris 1908. Cf. *La Vallée Poussin* in Le Muséon, N. S. X, 1909, 86 ff.

of a yoke cast into the ocean, is several times met with in this work, and one of the tales (No. 38) has been invented for the special purpose of elucidating this parable.[1] Other legends breathe rather the spirit of the Mahāyāna, or at least reveal a Buddha-worship which is more on the side of the Mahāyāna. An instance is No. 57, which is at the same time one of the most beautiful legends in the collection.

A man comes to the monastery, and desires to be admitted into the order. The disciple Śāriputra examines him, and finds that the man cannot claim to have done even the slightest good deed in any of his existences throughout æons, and he therefore declares him unworthy of being admitted into the order. Weeping, the man leaves the monastery. Then he meets Lord Buddha himself, whose heart is full of pity, and who desires to convert that man "like a mother, who loves her son." He lays his hands on the head of the rejected one, and asks: "Why do you weep?" The man tells him that Śāriputra has rejected him. Then the Buddha comforts him "with a voice that sounded like distant thunder," and declares that Śāriputra is not omniscient. The Lord himself brings the man back into the monastery, and before the assembled monks he tells of the Karman, the good deed which has entitled the man to liberation. Once in a former birth this person was a poor man, wandering about on the wooded hills to gather wood, when a tiger rushed upon him. Full of terror, he cried: "Honour to the Buddha!" For the sake of these words, the man shall participate in liberation. Buddha himself ordains him as a monk, and he soon becomes an Arhat.[2]

According to Hsüan-Tsang,[3] Kumāralāta was the founder of the Sautrāntika school, and came from Taxila. In

[1]) Cf. *Winternitz* in WZKM 27, 1913, 43 ff.

[2]) Another example of genuine Mahāyānistic Buddha-Bhakti is No. 68, where Gautamī attains Nirvāṇa through the grace of the Buddha, whereupon she actually worships him. Mortals and gods also hasten to worship the Buddha (and also Buddha's mother).

[3]) Si-yu-ki, transl. by S. *Beal*, II, p. 302 f. Cf. *Lüders*, l.c., p. 21. According to K'ouei-Ki, a pupil of Hsüan-Tsang, Kumāralāta was called "master of parables." Cf. *Lévi*, l.c., p. 95 f. "Kumāralabdha" is only a wrong retranslation of the Chinese name given for Kumāralāta. See *Lüders*, l.c., p. 20.

the work itself, the masters of the Sarvāstivādins are honoured, and many of the stories in the Kalpanāmaṇḍitikā are taken from the Canon of the Sarvāstivādins.[1] King Kaniṣka plays a part in two narratives, and he appears as a king of a past age.[2] Hence the work must have been written some considerable time after the death of Kaniṣka, and the poet could not have lived earlier than the end of the second century, when Aśvaghoṣa was already a very old man.[3] As far as we are able to glean from the few fragments extant, the language of the work is perfectly correct Sanskrit, and there are seldom deviations from grammar. It is a curious thing that, in one passage,[4] there are two Āryā verses in Prākrit in the midst of the Sanskrit verses. At all events it is very regrettable that we no longer possess the greater portion of the Kalpanāmaṇḍitikā in the original. It is not only in itself a work of literary distinction, the merits of which (as Lévi rightly remarks) are still recognisable even after two processes of translation ; but also from the point of view of the history of ancient Indian literature and culture, its importance should not be undervalued, for it mentions the epics Mahābhārata and Rāmāyaṇa, it confutes the philosophical doctrines of Sāṃkhya and Vaiśeṣika and the religious views of the Brahmans and Jains, and it contains all kinds of references to script, art and painting.

Just as the Chinese ascribed one of Kumāralāta's works to Aśvaghoṣa, some poems by Mātṛceta have likewise been ascribed

[1]) Cf. S. *Lévi* in JA 1908, s. 10, t. XII, 91 ff., 184. *Huber* (in BEFEO, 4, 1904, pp. 709 ff.) has traced three stories in the Divyāvadāna. The Sautrāntikas originated with the Sarvāstivādins, and it is therefore no contradiction for Kumāralāta, as a Sautrāntika, to honour the Sarvāstivāda teachers. (Cf. *Lüders*, l.c., p. 22.)

[2]) No. 14 and No. 31. Cf. *Lévi* in JA 1896, s. 9, t. VIII, 444 ff.

[3]) If Harivarman, a pupil of Kumāralāta, was really a contemporary of Vasubandhu, then Kumāralāta should be placed not earlier than the end of the 3rd century, and could not be a contemporary of Aśvaghoṣa. Cf. J. *Nobel* in SBA 1927, 229 ff.

[4]) In the 43rd story. Cf. *Lüders*, l.c., p. 45.

to Aśvaghoṣa in Tibet, and, according to the Tibetan historian Tāranātha, Mātṛceta is merely another name for Aśvaghoṣa.[1] It is probable that Mātṛceta was a somewhat senior contemporary of Aśvaghoṣa, and belonged to the same school of poets, and was therefore confused with him. King Kaniṣka at whose court it is generally assumed that Aśvaghoṣa lived, also invited the poet Mātṛceta to the court. Mātṛceta replied in a letter, called the Mahārāja Kanika-lekha,[2] which has come down in the Tibetan language; he asks the king to excuse him, as he is unable to come owing to his great age. The letter is a poem of 85 verses, containing chiefly admonitions to lead a moral life in the spirit of the Buddha. In verses running over with pity, the poet ends by imploring the king most earnestly to spare the creatures of the forest, and to give up the chase. When the Chinese pilgrim I-tsing (in the 7th century) was travelling in India, Mātṛceta was a very famous poet, and his hymns to Buddha were sung far and wide. The following legend, which I-tsing heard in India, testifies to his fame. Once when Buddha was walking through the forest, a nightingale began to sing sweet melodies, as though she were praising the glory of the Lord, whereupon the Buddha said to his disciples that this nightingale would once be reborn as Mātṛceta. His most famous hymns are the Catuḥ-Sataka Stotra, "the Hymn of Four Hundred

[1]) Ed. *Huber* (Sūtrālaṃkāra, pp. 63, 82) thought he had found a confirmation of the identity of Mātṛceta and Aśvaghoṣa, in the fact that Mātṛceta, too, cites the parable of the tortoise and the yoke in the ocean. However, even at the time, *Huber's* argument was not convincing (s. *Winternitz* in WZKM 27, 1913, 46 f.) and now that we know that Aśvaghoṣa is not the author of the "Sūtrālaṃkāra" at all, his argument falls to the ground entirely. See F. W. *Thomas* in OC XIII, Hamburg 1902, p. 40; ERE VIII, 1915, 495 ff.; *Hoernle*, Manuscript Remains, I, p. 59; *Lüders* in SBA 1914, p. 103.

[2]) Translated by F. W. *Thomas* in Ind. Ant. 32, 1903, 345 ff. I agree with *Thomas* in thinking that Maticitra, who is mentioned as the author of the letter, is identical with Mātṛceta, and that the King Kanika of the Kuṣa dynasty is identical with the Kuṣana King Kaniṣka, although both points are disputed by S. C. *Vidyābhūṣaṇa* (JASB 1910, p. 477 f.).

Verses," and the Śatapañcāśatika Stotra, "the Hymn of One Hundred and Fifty Verses." Fragments of both of these have come down to us in Central Asian manuscripts.[1] They are poems in ślokas, in simple and unadorned, but beautiful, language, and they evidently impressed the faithful more by their pious thoughts than by their form. It is delightful, ays I-tsing, to hear his "Hymn of 150 Verses" or "Hymn of 400 Verses" recited in the assembly of monks. "These charming compositions," he says further, "are equal in beauty to the heavenly flowers, and the high principles which they contain rival in dignity the lofty peaks of a mountain. Consequently in India all who compose hymns imitate his style, considering him the father of literature. Even men like the Bodhisattvas Asaṅga and Vasubandhu admired him greatly. Throughout India everyone who becomes a monk is taught Mātṛceta's two hymns as soon as he can recite the five and ten precepts (Śīla). This course is adopted by both the Mahāyāna and the Hīnayāna schools." I-tsing cannot find words sufficient to extol the merits of these poems, and he adds that there have been many commentators and imitators too. Thus the "Bodhisattva Jina" (an honourable title of the logician Dignāga) composed one verse to be placed before each of the one hundred and fifty verses of the Śatapañcāśatika Stotra, and in this way compiled a hymn of 300 verses, known as the "mixed Hymn of Praise."[2] I-tsing himself translated the "Hymn of 150 Verses" into Chinese, and there are Tibetan

[1]) W. *Siegling* has succeeded in reconstructing about two-thirds of the text of the Śatapañcāśatika-Stotra from the fragments of manuscripts from Turfan, and I am obliged to him for allowing me to peruse his manuscript which he was preparing for the press. Fragments from the collections made by *Pelliot* and Sir Aurel *Stein* have been published by S. *Lévi* (JA 1910, s. 10, t. XVI, 450 f.), *La Vallée Poussin* (JRAS 1911, 764 ff.) and *Hoernle*, Manuscript Remains, I, p. 58 ff. A few fragments of a "Tokharian" translation of the Buddha-Stotra are published by E. *Sieg* and W. *Siegling*, Tocharische Sprachreste I, pp. 216, 230 ff.

[2]) I-tsing, Record transl. by *Takakusu*, pp. 156, 157, 158, 166.

translations of both hymns.[1] A few specimens from the Śatapañcāśatika Stotra will serve to give the reader an idea of this pious poetry:

"How should I not, first of all, praise thee, and the great Compassion, by which thou, knowing its ills, hast been detained in mundane existence so long?"

"In laying the dust of passion thy speech acts as a raincloud; it acts like Vainateya (*i.e.* Garuḍa) in expelling the serpent of hatred.

Ever anew it acts as the midday in dispelling the darkness of ignorance; it acts as Śakra's (Indra's) thunderbolt in splitting in pieces the mountains of self-conceit."

"Towards an enemy intent on injury, thou art a friend intent on beneficence; towards one perpetually searching for faults, thou art bent upon searching for merits.

When there was an invitation to thee accompanied with poison and with fire: then there was visiting on thy part, with kindliness and with nectar.

Revilers are conquered by thee with forbearance, and injurers with blessing; and with veracity detractors, with friendliness the revengeful."[2]

The Maitreyavyākaraṇa, "the prophecy about Maitreya," or the Maitreyasamiti, "the Meeting with Maitreya," by the Vaibhāṣika Āryacandra, belongs to the same period, and perhaps also to the same school of poets, as the above-mentioned works. There is only one incomplete manuscript[3] of this

---

[1]) In the Tibetan version the Catuḥ-Śataka is called *Varṇanārhavarṇana*, "The Praise of Him Who Deserves Praise." The title is also found in Central Asian fragments in colophons (s. *Hoernle*, l.c., pp. 76, 81,83). F. W. *Thomas* has translated the first half of the poem from Tibetan (Ind. Ant., 24, 1905, 145 ff.). A list of the works which are ascribed to Mātṛceta in Tibetan, is given by *Thomas* in Kavīndravacana-Samuccaya, p. 27, and Ind. Ant., 32, 346 f.

[2]) Verses 59, 73 f., 122-124; for the text, see *Hoernle*, l.c., pp. 66 ff., 71; translation by *Hoernle* with slight alterations.

[3]) *Haraprasāda Śāstrī*, Descriptive Catalogue of Sanskrit MSS. in the Asiatic Society of Bengal, I, Calcutta 1917, p. 13 f. The name of the author is not mentioned here, but only in the colophons of Tokharian and Uigurian fragments, *cf.* F. W. K. *Müller* and E. *Sieg* in SBA 1916, 396, 414 f.; E. *Sieg* and W. *Siegling*, Tocharische Sprachreste, I, p. 125.

work, but it was translated repeatedly into Chinese, into the languages of Central Asia, and also into Tibetan, and it must have enjoyed great popularity for a long time, at least beyond the confines of India.[1] In the form of a dialogue between Gotama Buddha and Śāriputra (in other versions Ānanda) the work contains the prophecy about the coming of the future Buddha Maitreya, his birth, his appearance and the paradisaic life under him. In Central Asian versions it is sometimes called a "drama" (nāṭaka), and it seems to have been adapted for dramatic performances in Central Asia (perhaps at religious festivals).[2]

The Jātakamālā[3] by the poet Śūra or Āryaśūra,[4] resembles the Kalpanāmaṇḍitikā very closely as far as style is concerned. "Jātakamālā" or "Garland of Jātakas," is however, really a generic term. Various poets have written Jātakamālās, *i.e.*, they have produced free renderings of selected Jātakas in ornate poetical language, in a mixture of prose

---

[1]) E. *Leumann*, Maitreya-samiti, das Zukunftsideal der Buddhisten, Strassburg, 1919, gives the text and German translation of the version in the language which he terms "North-Aryan" (called by others "Tokharian"). The Chinese versions by Dharmarakṣa (between 255 and 316 A.D.), by Kumārajīva (about 402 A.D.) and by I-tsing (701 A.D.) have been translated into German by K. *Watanabe* (see *Leumann*, l.c., p. 227 ff.). The Kanjur contains three lives of Maitreya translated from the Sanskrit and one from the Pāli. See H. *Beckh*, Verzeichnis der tibetischen Handschriften, p. 188 f. and E. *Abegg*, Der Messiasglaube in Indien und Iran, Berlin und Leipzig, 1928, p. 132 ff. Fragments in "Tokharian" have been published by E. *Sieg* and W. *Siegling*, Tocharische Sprachreste, I, 107, 119, 125 ff., 155 ff., 164 ff., 254 f. (previously, too, in SBA 1908, 915 ff.), in Uigurian by F. W. K. *Müller* and E. *Sieg* in SBA 1905, p. 958; 1916, 395 ff.

[2]) See *Sieg* and *Siegling*, Tocharische Sprachreste, I, pp. 125, 255, and SBA 1916, 398. Expressions such as "interlude" and "all go out" in the Central Asian versions, do not, however, constitute a proof that the Sanskrit original was an actual drama. It is most desirable that *Haraprasāda Śāstrī* should give us further information about the contents of MS. No. 4806 in the Asiatic Society's collection.

[3]) Ed. by H. *Kern* in HOS, Vol. I, 1891; translated by J. S. *Speyer* in SBB, Vol. I, 1895. Cf. *Kern* in Festgruss an Böhtlingk, Stuttgart 1888, p. 50 f.; S. d' *Oldenburg* in JRAS 1893, 308 ff.; A. *Barth* in RHR 1893, t. 28, p. 260; K. *Watanabe* in JPTS 1909, p. 263 ff.; A. *Gawron'ski*, Studies about the Sanskrit Buddhist Literature, Krakov 1919, p. 40 ff.

[4]) According to *Tāranātha* this, too, is only another name of Aśvaghoṣa.

and verse. Āryaśūra, too, does not trouble to invent new stories, he re-tells the old legends in ornate, elegant language. The style, both in the prose and the verse, is the Kāvya style, but lofty and refined, more artistic than artificial. In the same way as the Jātakas were intended for the use of the monks in their sermons, so the Jātakamālā, too, is intended for the purposes of the preachers. Yet the poet, who was perhaps himself a court preacher, certainly had in view only monks who preached in court circles in which Sanskrit poetry was understood and appreciated. The work contains 34 Jātakas, which, like the 35 Jātakas of the Cariyāpiṭaka, are intended to illustrate the Pāramitās, or "perfections" of a Bodhisattva. Almost all the narratives occur also in the Jātaka book,[1] and 12 in the Cariyāpiṭaka. Among the few stories which are not found in the Pāli collection of Jātakas, is the first one, which tells how the Bodhisattva sees a hungry tigress who is about to devour her young ones, and kills himself so as to provide food for her. This very characteristic story is given here in brief extracts :

"Even in former births the Lord had shown his spontaneous and highest affectionateness towards all creatures, and had identified himself with all beings. Therefore one must cherish the greatest love for Buddha the Lord. Thus for instance, the following great feat of the Lord in a former birth is related, a deed which is praised by my revered teacher, a worshipper of the three jewels, who satisfied his teacher with his wisdom and virtue, and was a past master in the investigation of the virtues. At that time the Bodhisattva, who afterwards became the Lord, who in fulfilment of his extraordinary promises, had mercy on the world by gifts, words of love, acts of help, and other faultless streams of pity gushing forth from wisdom and love, was reborn in a very learned, powerful Brahman family, devoted to the fulfilment of their duties, and distin-

[1]) Some verses coincide with the Pāli Gāthās. See the table in *Speyer's* translation, p. 337 ff., S. d'*Oldenburg* in JRAS 1893, 328 ff.; J. *Charpentier* in ZDMG 64, 1910, 67 ff.; *Oldenberg* in NGGW 1918, 464 ff. R. O. *Franke* (Indogerm. Forschungen V, 1895, Anzeiger, p. 31 ff.) has also traced Pāliciam in the language of the Jātakamālā.

guished for the purity of their conduct." He grew up, and soon gained great mastery in all arts and sciences. Great wealth and honours fell to his lot. But he took no pleasure in the worldly life, and he soon retired into solitude. He lived in the forest as a pious hermit. One day, accompanied only by a pupil, he was wandering about on the hills. Then he saw in a rock cave a young tigress, exhausted by hunger, about to devour her young ones, which approached her confidingly for the milk in her udders.

" When the Bodhisattva saw her,
Then he trembled, brave though he was,
Full of pity for another's pain,
As the lord of the hills [1] in an earthquake.
Wonderful, how the pitiful
Remain brave, even when
Great sorrow comes upon themselves,
Yet at another's woe,
Though it be less, they are shaken."

Then he sends his pupil away to fetch meat, but this is only an excuse for remaining alone ; for he has already resolved to throw himself over the precipice, in order to save the lives of the tiger-cubs, and to serve as food for the tigress. His reason for this resolve is that this vain earthly body has no other value than that of being sacrificed for others. Moreover, by this means, he will afford an encouraging example to those who desire to do good in the world ; he will put to shame the selfish, point the way to heaven to well-doers, and himself attain perfect enlightenment immediately. He desires nothing else :—

" Not from ambition, nor desire for fame, not for
the joy of heaven, nor to win sovereignty,
Not for the sake of my own eternal bliss do I
do this,—no, only to benefit another.
As this is true, so may I always have the power of taking away
the sorrow of the world,
And bringing happiness to it, as the sun always brings
the light and drives away the darkness."

[1]) That is, Mount Meru.

With these words he casts himself down into the rock cave. The tigress is attracted by the sound, leaves her young ones, and throws herself upon the corpse of the Bodhisattva to devour it. When the pupil returns and sees this, he is deeply moved, and utters some verses full of worship for the Lord. Men, demi-gods and gods express their admiration for the Lord by throwing garlands of flowers, jewels, garments and sandalwood on the remaining bones.

The boundless pity of the Bodhisattva is also glorified in most of the other narratives.

I-tsing praises the Jātakamālā (or Jātakamālās) among the works which were particularly popular and much read in India at his time. Among the frescoes of the caves of Ajanta there are illustrations to the Jātakamālā with verses by Āryaśūra in inscriptions. Paleographically, these inscriptions belong to the 6th century A.D. As another work by Āryaśūra was already translated into Chinese in 434 A.D., the poet probably belongs to the 4th century A.D.[1]

A work of ornate poetry which deals once more with the life of Buddha, and which concludes with the same episode as Book XIII of the Buddha-Carita, is the Sanskrit epic Padyacūḍāmaṇi,[2] ascribed to a man named Buddhaghoṣa. The author of this Mahākāvya (in 10 Sargas) is certainly not the famous commentator, but some Buddhaghoṣa, who knew the epics of Aśvaghoṣa and Kālidāsa, and made liberal use of them,[3] or perhaps an anonymous writer, who simply assumed the name of Buddhaghoṣa.

[1] *I-tsing*, transl. by *Takakusu*, p. 162 f , H *Luders*, NGGW 1902, p. 758 ff.; B. *Nanjio*, Catalogue of the Chinese Tripiṭaka, No. 1349; Th. *Zachariae*, GGA 1888, p. 850; F. W. *Thomas* in Album Kern, p. 405 ff. Though the Chinese translation of the Jātakamālā mentions Āryaśūra as the author, it only contains 14 stories, see A. O. *Ivanovski* in RH d. 1903, t. 47, p. 298 ff. In the Tibetan Tanjur five other works besides the Jātakamālā, are ascribed to Āryaśūra; s. *Thomas*, Kavīndravacana-Samuccaya, p. 27 f.

[2] Ed. by M. *Ranga Acharya* and S. *Kuppuswami Sastri*, with a commentary by Pandits K. *Venkateśvara Sastri* and D. S. *Satakopa Acharya*, Madras, 1921.

[3] See *Kuppuswami Sastri's* "References to descriptions of same or similar things in Raghuvaṃśa, Buddhacarita, and Padyacūḍāmaṇi," prefixed to the Edition. The name of the author is mentioned only in the colophons. See B. Ch. *Law*, Life and Work of Buddhaghosa, p. 85 ff.

The Avadāna Literature.

The Jātakamālā is also called "Bodhisattvāvadānamālā," for "Bodhisattvāvadāna" is synonymous with Jātaka; and, indeed, the Jātakas are nothing but Avadānas the hero of which is the Bodhisattva. Thus, works like the Kalpanāmaṇḍitikā and Jātakamālā often coincide with the texts of the Avadāna literature, and numerous Jātakas are also contained in the Avadāna books.[1] Like the two above-mentioned works of Buddhist narrative literature, the Avadāna texts also stand, so to speak, with one foot in the Hīnayāna literature, and the other in that of the Mahāyāna.[2] The earlier works still belong entirely to the Hīnayāna; though they already exhibit that Buddha worship which is also met with in the later works of the Pāli Canon (Buddhavaṃsa, Apadānas) they as yet eschew the exaggerations and the mythology of the Mahāyāna, whilst the latest works of the Avadāna are already completely Mahāyānistic.

The word avadāna[3] means a "noteworthy deed," sometimes in a bad sense,[4] but generally in the good sense of "a heroic deed," "a feat," with the Buddhists a "religious

[1]) On the Avadāna literature in general, see E. *Burnouf*, Introduction à l'histoire du Bouddhisme, p. 207 ff.; L. *Feer* in the introduction to his translation, and J. S. *Speyer* in the foreword to his edition, of the Avadāna-Śataka, Vol. II.

[2]) We know through *I-tsing* (transl. *Takakusu*, pp. xxii f. and 14 f.) that the boundaries between Hīnayāna and Mahāyāna were often uncertain.

[3]) In Pāli apadāna, see above, p. 157 f. In Sanskrit, too, the secondary form apadāna is found. See *Burnouf*, Introduction à l'histoire du Bouddhisme Indien, p. 57; *Feer*, l. c., p. ix ff.; *Speyer*, l. c., p. 1 ff. The Chinese translators sometimes confuse *avadāna* with *nidāna*, but we must not, as H. *Zimmer* (ZII 3, 1925, 205 ff.) does, interpret *avadāna* as being synonymous with *nidāna* in the sense of "actions which causally determine as their consequences certain events which take place later in time." In the sense of "deed," "great deed," *avadāna* occurs not only in Jātakamālā I, beginning; III, 23; IV, 2, but also in the Rāmāyaṇa, in works of Kālidāsa and in other works written in classical Sanskrit.

[4]) For instance in Avadāna-Śataka V.

or moral feat" and then also the "story of a noteworthy deed, or feat." Such a "feat" may consist of the sacrifice of one's own life, but also merely of a gift of incense, flowers, ointments, gold and precious stones, or the erection of sanctuaries (Stūpas, Caityas, and so on). As these stories are, as a rule, intended to show that "black deeds bear black fruits, and white deeds white fruits," they are also Karman stories, which show how the actions of one existence are very closely connected with those of former or future existences. It is, of course, only from our standpoint that they are "legends": the Buddhists regard them as actual events, related by the Buddha himself, and are just as authentic as "words of the Buddha" (buddhavacana) as a Sūtra. Like the Jātakas the Avadānas, too, are a kind of sermons. It is therefore usually told, by way of introduction, where and on what occasion Buddha related the story from the past, and at the end, the lesson is deduced from the story by Buddha. A regular Avadāna, then, consists of a story of the present, a story of the past, and a moral. If the hero of the story of the past is the Bodhisattva, this kind of Avadāna can also be called a "Jātaka."[1] There is a special kind of Avadānas, namely those in which the Buddha, instead of telling a story of the past, gives a prophecy of the future. Like the usual story of the past, this story of the future serves to explain the present Karman.[2] There are also Avadānas in which both kinds of stories are combined, and finally also such in which a Karman already shows its good or bad fruits in the present existence.

All these kinds of Avadānas also occur sporadically in the Vinayapitaka and in the Sūtrapiṭaka, but are mostly to be found in large collections, which were compiled either purely

[1]) On Jātakas in the Avadāna literature, see S. d'*Oldenburg*, JRAS 1893, p. 304, and *Feer*, Les Avadānas Jātakas, JA 1884, s. 8, t. IV, p. 332 ff.

[2]) Hence the name Vyākaraṇa, "explanation," for the prophetic Stories of the Future.

for the purpose of edification or with literary ambitions as well.

The Avadāna-Śataka, or "the hundred Avadānas,"[1] is a work of the former category, presumably the oldest of these books. As it was already translated into Chinese in the first half of the 3rd century A.D., and on the other hand as the dīnāra is mentioned, we can, with a considerable degree of certainty, ascribe it to the 2nd century A.D.[2] The character of the narratives, and the fact that the Stories of the Present contain passages from a Parinirvāṇa-Sūtra and other Sūtras of the Sanskrit Canon of the Sarvāstivādins, are sufficient evidence that this work belongs to the Hīnayāna.[3] Though Buddha-worship plays a prominent part in the legends, there is no trace of the Bodhisattva cult and of Mahāyānistic mythology.

The Avadāna-Śataka consists of ten decades,[4] each of which deals with a certain subject. The first four decades contain narratives which are intended to show by which actions one can become a Buddha or a Pratyeka-Buddha.[5] All the narratives of the first decade and for the greater part also of the third decade, are of the nature of prophecies (Vyākaraṇas). The story is told of a pious deed by which a person, a Brahman, a princess, the son of an usurer, a rich merchant, a gardener, a king, a ferryman, a little girl, and so on, worships the Buddha ; a miracle usually takes place, and the Buddha pro-

[1]) Edited by J. S. *Speyer* (Bibliotheca Buddhica III), St. Petersburg 1902-1909. Translated into French by L. *Feer* (AMG., t. 18), Paris 1891. *Feer* had already previously translated and discussed separate sections of the work in a series of treatises (JA 1878-1884).

[2]) *Speyer*, Vol. II, Preface, p. xv. Works in which the Roman denarius is mentioned as dīnāra, could not have originated before the 1st century A.D., and were probably written later, see above, Vol. I, p. 464, note 2.

[3]) *Speyer*, l. c., p. xvi ff., and ZDMG 53, 1899, p. 120 ff. ; *Oldenberg* ZDMG 52, p. 672, NGGW 1912, p. 168 ff.

[4]) This division into Vargas (Pāli Vagga) of ten pieces each, is very popular in the Pāli texts, and therefore seems to be ancient Buddhist.

[5]) *i.e.*, Pāli Paccekabuddha, see above, p. 146, note 1.

claims smilingly that this person will, in a future age of the world, be a Buddha or (in Book III) a Pratyeka-Buddha. On the other hand, the stories in the second and fourth decades are Jātakas. The pious, virtuous and wonderful deeds are explained by the fact that the hero of these narratives is none other than the Buddha himself in one of his former births. Book V is a kind of Pretavastu, corresponding to the Pāli Petavatthu. A saint, usually Maudgalyāyana, looks around in the world of ghosts, and observes the sufferings of one of the (male or female) ghosts (Pretas). He asks the cause of his or her sufferings. The ghost refers him to the Buddha, who then relates the story of the "black deed," the refusal to give alms, the abuse of a saint, and so on, committed by that being in a former existence. Book VI relates stories of men and animals who, by means of some pious deed, are reborn as gods in heaven. The four last decades contain narratives which are to show which deeds qualify a person to become an Arhat. The Arhats of Book VII are all of the race of the Śākyas, those in Book VIII are women, those in Book IX men of blameless conduct, and those in Book X men who formerly did bad deeds and suffered for them, and only then attained the stage of an Arhat by means of a pious deed.

The tales in this collection are not only classified and compiled on a definite plan, but they are also narrated after one stereotyped pattern. This conventionality goes so far that certain phrases and descriptions of situations occur again and again in exactly the same words.[1] Thus every narrative begins with the following words:

"Buddha the Lord, honoured, highly esteemed, held in honour and praised by kings, ministers, rich people, citizens, masters of guilds, leaders of caravans, gods, Nāgas, Yakṣas, Asuras, Garuḍas, Kinnaras and great

[1]) Clichés of the same kind, also occur in Bengali poems, s. Dinesh Chandra Sen, History of Bengali Language and Literature, p. 585 f.

snakes, worshipped by Devas, Nāgas, Yakṣas, Asuras, Garuḍas, Kinnaras and great snakes, Buddha the Lord, the famous, highly meritorious one, accompanied by a community of disciples, and receiving as alms all necessary clothing, food, bed and shelter, refreshments and medicaments, went to.........and sojourned in........."

Every narrative, too, concludes with the words: "Thus spake the Lord, and with enraptured hearts the monks applauded the words of the Lord." When the moral of the story is summed up, it is always in the words :—

"So, O monks, the fruit of quite black deeds is quite black, that of quite white deeds quite white, that of mixed deeds is mixed. Therefore, O monks, give up the black and the mixed deeds, and take pleasure only in the quite white deeds......"

In the same way, a pious man, a rich man, a powerful king, a happy marriage, the education of a young man, the appearance of a former Buddha, and so on are always described in exactly the same words. That is, indeed, not only the case with a few short sentences, but even with long passages extending over several printed pages. One of the longest stereotyped pieces is, for instance, the description of the smile with which the Buddha utters the prophecy that somebody will become a Buddha ; for, before the Buddha prophesies the future, he invariably smiles. And when he smiles, blue, yellow, red and white rays burst forth from his mouth. Some of these rays descend to the hells, the others ascend into the worlds of heaven. And after they have travelled round the thousands and thousands of worlds, they return again to the Buddha from behind, and disappear in some part of the Buddha's body, which varies according to the subject of the prophecy. All this is very circumstantially described ; and this circumstantiality and prolixity is characteristic of the method of narration of the Avadāna-Śataka in general. Nevertheless, besides many commonplace and tedious, though always edifying, stories, it also contains many valuable narratives and noteworthy variants from the passages of Buddhist narrative literature familiar from other texts. Only a few examples can here be quoted in extracts, in order to give an idea of the character of the collection.

No. 28. A poor girl anoints the feet of the Buddha with ointment made of sandalwood oil. In consequence of this, the whole town is filled with the perfume of sandalwood. The girl is delighted with this miracle, falls at the Buddha's feet, and prays that she may become a Pratyeka-Buddha in a future birth. Buddha smiles, and prophesies that she will one day be a Pratyeka-Buddha named Gandhamādana ("Perfume-delighter").

No. 34 is a version of the legend of King Śibi, who gives away all his possessions. But it is not enough for him to satisfy human beings, he also wants to do good to the small creatures. Therefore he cuts his skin with a knife, and stands there to let the stinging flies satisfy themselves with his blood. Śakra sees this from his heaven, and, in order to put him to the test, appears before Śibi in the form of a vulture, as though he were about to attack him. The king only looks at him with friendliness, and says: "Take, my friend, whatever part of my body you require, I give it to you." Thereupon the god transforms himself into a Brahman and asks the king for both his eyes. Śibi says: "Take, great Brahman, what you will, I will not hinder you." Then Śakra assumes his true form, and prophesies that Śibi will attain perfect enlightenment.

No. 36 is the legend of Maitrakanyaka, a version of the Pāli Jātaka of Mittavindaka. But in this case the story takes quite a different turn from the Pāli version, owing to the fact that the Bodhisattva is the hero. Here, too, he goes to hell as a punishment for having offended his mother, and a glowing iron wheel revolves on his head. But while he suffers the dreadful torments, and it is foretold to him that he will have to bear the wheel for 66,000 years, until another shall come who has committed a similar sin, he feels pity for the creatures, and in order that nobody else shall have to suffer the same pains, he determines to bear the wheel on his own head for all eternity. In consequence of this merciful thought, the wheel vanishes from his head.[1]

No. 54. At the suggestion of his wives, King Bimbisāra has caused a Stūpa to be erected in his harem over some hairs and nail-parings which the Buddha had given him. The women worshipped this with incense, lamps, flowers, etc. But when Ajātaśatru murdered his father Bimbisāra,

1) See above, p. 182, and *Scherman*, Visionslitteratur, p. 69 ff.

and ascended the throne himself, he issued the strict command that no woman shall dare, on pain of death, to worship the Stūpa. Śrīmatī, however, one of the women of the harem, takes no notice of this command, and places a garland of lamps around the Stūpa. The enraged king kills her, she dies thinking of the Buddha, and is at once reborn in the heaven of the gods.

No. 100. Whilst the heroes of all the other Avadānas are contemporaries of the Buddha, the hero of this last story is a contemporary of King Aśoka. The link with the time of Buddha is established by the initial mention of a report of the passing away of the Buddha.[1] King Aśoka lived a hundred years after the passing of the Buddha. Aśoka had a son named Kuṇāla, who was so handsome that the king believed there could not be his equal in the whole world. One day, however, he hears from some merchants from Gandhāra, that a still handsomer young man exists. In their country, they say, there lives a youth named Sundara ("Beautiful") who is not only of faultless beauty, but wherever he goes, a lotus pond and a garden arise. The astonished King Aśoka sends messengers for Sundara, and convinces himself of this miracle. The king then asks what Karman has given the youth his advantages, and Upagupta,[2] one of the elders, replies as follows : At the time when the Buddha had just attained complete Nirvāṇa, the present Sundara had been a poor farmer, who prepared a refreshing bath and food for Mahā-Kāśyapa and his retinue of 500 monks when they went to the burial of the Lord and were bowed down with grief at the passing of the Master, and were quite exhausted by their long wanderings. He is now enjoying the fruit of that good deed.

Many of the narratives of the Avadāna-Śataka recur in other collections of Avadānas, and a few also in the Pāli Apadānas.[3]

[1]) This account is a passage from a Parinirvāṇa-Sūtra, and agrees fairly closely with the Pāli Mahā-Parinibbāna-Sutta. Another passage on the Parinirvāṇa is the introduction to No. 40.

[2]) Upagupta here takes over the rôle of the Buddha in the other Avadānas.

[3]) Thus, for example, the legend of Rāṣṭrapāla (No. 90) which corresponds partly to the Raṭṭhapāla-Sutta of the Majjhimanikāya, and partly to the Raṭṭhapāla-Apadāna. See Mabel *Bode* in Mélanges Lévi, p. 183 ff. Frequently it is only the titles which are identical, and the Apadāna shows great variations. See *Feer*, Avadāna Çataka, pp. 240 f., 313 f., 335, 340 ff., 354 f., 360 f., 372 f., 439 f.

The Karma-Śataka ("A hundred Karman stories"), is an old work which is very much like the Avadāna-Śataka, and has a number of narratives in common with it, but unfortunately it has only come down in a Tibetan translation.[1]

The Divyāvadāna ("The Heavenly Avadānas"),[2] is a later collection than the Avadāna-Śataka, but it also includes some very old texts. Though it begins with the Mahāyānistic benediction "Om, honour to all the exalted Buddhas and Bodhisattvas," and contains just a few obviously later additions in the spirit of the Mahāyāna,[3] as a whole it decidedly belongs to the Hīnayāna school. The Sanskrit Canon and single canonical texts such as Dīrghāgama, Udāna, Sthavira-Gāthā, and so on, are frequently quoted.[4] Some narratives begin and end exactly as in the Avadāna-Śataka, and a number of the stereotyped phrases and descriptions so characteristic of this book, also recur literally in the Divyāvadāna. They are probably derived from the Vinayapiṭaka of the Mūla-

[1]) *Feer*, l. c., pp. xxix f., 442 ff. ; *AMG.*, t. V, 382 ff., 404 ff., and JA 1901, s. 9, t. XVII, pp. 53 ff., 257 ff., 410 ff. ; *Speyer*, l. c., p. xix f. Another Tibetan Avadāna book translated from the Sanskrit, but the Sanskrit original of which is no longer extant, is the narrative work Dsanglun, well-known in universal literature, and translated into German with the title "Der Weise und der Tor" by I. J. *Schmidt* (St. Petersburg 1843). (On a Chinese version of this work, s. *Takakusu* in JRAS 1901, p. 447 ff.).

[2]) Edited by E. B. *Cowell* and R. A. *Neil*, Cambridge 1886. Long passages from it were translated by *Burnouf* in his "Introduction à l'histoire du Bouddhisme Indien." Four tales have been translated into German by H. *Zimmer*, Karman, ein buddhistischer Legendenkranz, München 1925. Critical notes on the text of the Divyāvadāna by J. S. *Speyer* in WZKM 16, 1902, 103 ff., 340 ff. "Studies in the Divyāvadāna" by James R. *Ware* in JAOS 48, 1928, 159 ff. The title of the work is not certain; it is only found in the colophons of some of the manuscripts. *Rājendralāla Mitra*, Nep. Buddh. Lit., pp. 304 to 316, describes a manuscript entitled "Divyāvadānamālā," which diverges greatly from our edition. Also a Paris manuscript described in the Edition, p. 663 ff, only partly agrees with our Divyāvadāna.

[3]) Thus Chapter 34 calls itself a "mahāyānasūtram" (Ed., p. 483) and the ṣaḍakṣarā vidyā, i.e., om maṇi padme hūṃ, is mentioned in Chapt. 33 (Ed., p. 613 f.). See *La Vallée Poussin*, Bouddhisme, p. 381.

[4]) See above, p. 233 f. and *Oldenberg*, ZDMG 52, 1898, pp. 653, 655 f., 658, 665. The four Āgamas are mentioned in Divyāvadāna, p. 333.

Sarvāstivāda school, from which, as S. Lévi [1] has shown, more than one-half of the stories is borrowed.

The composition of the work is, in fact, very confused and disconnected. There is no sign of any principle of arrangement. The language and style, too, are by no means unified. Most of the legends are written in good, simple Sanskrit prose, only interrupted here and there by Gāthās. In a few of the pieces, however, we also find the metres of ornate poetry and the genuine Kāvya style with its long compound words.[2] The compiler thus seems to have simply taken over the passages literally out of other texts. As a matter of fact, almost all the stories in the Divyāvadāna have been traced to other works. In addition to the Mūla-Sarvāstivāda-Vinaya, the compiler of the Divyāvadāna also made use of a "Book of King Aśoka,"[3] of the Saṃyuktāgama (which is known by the Chinese translation Tsa A-han King), and of Kumāralāta's Kalpanāmaṇḍitikā.[4] It stands to reason that, when the Divyāvadāna was compiled in this fashion, the various parts of the work belong to different periods. There are some passages which must certainly have been written prior to the 3rd century A.D. However, the collection as a whole, could not have been in existence earlier than the 4th century A.D.; for, not

[1]) "Les éléments de formation du Divyāvadāna" in T'oung Pao, s. II, Vol. VIII, 1907, 105 ff.

[2]) *Oldenberg* in NGGW 1912, 156 ff., has shown that, in the Divyāvadāna, just as in the Mahāvastu, there are two distinct styles, an earlier canonical one, and a later style.

[3]) It is not certain what the Sanskrit title of this work was. It was translated into Chinese as A-yu-wang-ch'uan (approximately Aśokarājāvadāna) by the Parthian Fa-k'in between 281 and 306, and in a shorter version as A-yu-wang-king (approximately Aśokarāja-Sūtra) in the year 512 by a certain Saṅghabhara or Saṅghabhaṭa.

[4]) See J. *Przyluski*, La légende de l'empereur Açoka (Açoka-Avadāna) dans les textes, Paris 1923 (AMG, Bibl. d'Études, t. 31); Éd. *Huber* in BEFEO 4, 1904, 709 ff.; 6, 1906, 1 ff. and *Speyer*, Avadānaśataka II, Preface, p. xvi f. A. *Gawron'ski*, Studies about the Sanskrit-Buddhist Literature, p. 49 ff., thinks that in the Aśoka cycle of the Divy. he is able to trace an acquaintance with Aśvaghoṣa's epics too.

only are Aśoka's successors, the kings of the Śuṅga dynasty down to Puṣyamitra (about 178 B.C.) mentioned in this work, but the dīnāra occurs several times, and this brings us at least to the first century A.D. and probably nearer to 400 A.D.[1] and lastly, some time must have elapsed after Kumāralāta, who lived a considerable time after Kaniṣka,[2] for a compiler to make such extensive use of his Kalpanāmaṇḍitikā.

However, it is valuable to know that precisely one of the most interesting legends in the Divyāvadāna, the Śārdūlakarṇāvadāna,[3] was translated into Chinese in 265 A.D. The substance of this Avadāna, remarkable in several ways, is as follows :—

When the Master was sojourning in Śrāvastī, Ānanda was in the habit of going daily to the town to beg for food. One day when he was returning from the town, he was thirsty, and saw a Caṇḍāla girl, named Prakṛti, fetching water from the well. "Sister," he said to her, "give me some water to drink." Thereupon Prakṛti replied : "I am a Caṇḍāla girl, honourable Ānanda." "Sister," said Ānanda, "I did not enquire about your family and your caste, but if you have water left, give me some, I want to drink."[4] Then the girl gave him a drink, and fell deeply in love with the saint. She declares to her mother that she will surely die if she cannot get Ānanda as her husband. Then her mother, who is a great sorceress, prepares a potent love-charm,[5] and bewitches Ānanda by means of mantras. The spell is successful, and Ānanda comes to the house of the Caṇḍālas, where the delighted Prakṛti has already prepared the couch. But at the moment of the greatest danger, Ānanda bursts into tears, and

[1]) See above, Vol. I, p. 464, note 2.

[2]) See above, p. 269.

[3]) Edition, p. 611 ff. See also *Rāj. Mitra*, Nep. Buddh. Lit., p. 223 ff.

[4]) The resemblance to St. John IV, 7 ff. (Jesus and the woman of Samaria) is certainly striking, but the whole of the rest of the story is so very different in the Gospel, that we can scarcely assume any connection between the two.

[5]) She does this in the same way as such magical rites were performed according to the Kauśika-Sūtra of the Atharvaveda (see above, Vol. I, p. 280) from time immemorial, and as they are familiar to witchcraft among all nations. See *Winternitz* in WZKM 26, 1912, 248 ff.

in his dire need prays to the Buddha. Buddha comes to his aid with *his* mantras; and Buddha's mantras render those of the sorceress powerless. Ānanda leaves the Caṇḍāla house, and returns to his monastery. The great sorceress explains to her unhappy daughter that the spells of Gautama are stronger than hers. But Prakṛti, the Caṇḍāla girl, was not cured of her love. She went into the town and now followed Ānanda daily when he went on his begging rounds. Again Ānanda, in his distress, appealed to the Master for help. Buddha sends for Prakṛti, and appears to agree to her desire of marrying Ānanda, but with great delicacy, he is able to induce her to take the vow of chastity, and become a nun. She not only has her hair cut off and assumes the garb of a nun, but she also enters into the complete understanding of the four noble truths, and entirely comprehends the religion of the Buddha.

Now when the Brahmans, warriors and citizens of Śrāvastī heard that Buddha had ordained a Caṇḍāla girl as a nun, they were very angry; they reported the matter to King Prasenajit, and the king immediately went to the Master in order to complain of this procedure. Many Brahmans, warriors and citizens of Śrāvastī were also assembled there. Then the Buddha told the story of Triśaṅku, the Caṇḍāla chief, who wished to marry his very learned son Śārdūlakarṇa to the daughter of the proud Brahman Puṣkarasārin. The Brahman rejects him with scorn. Now a most interesting dialogue is developed, in which Triśaṅku severely criticises the caste system and the Brahmanical ethical teachings. He points out to him that such differences as exist among the different kinds of animals and plants, cannot be shown among the castes. Moreover, according to the theory of the transmigration of souls and of Karman, there cannot be any castes, as everyone is reborn according to his actions, and so on. Finally Puṣkarasārin is convinced of the learning of Triśaṅku, whereupon he consents to the marriage. Now the Brahman's daughter was none other than Prakṛti, the Caṇḍāla girl, in a former birth. The Buddha himself was at that time Triśaṅku and Śārdūlakarṇa was Ānanda.[1])

[1]) Richard *Wagner* became acquainted with this legend by means of *Burnouf's* translation (Introduction, p. 205 ff.) and based the outline of his "Sieger" upon it. *Cf.* the sketch in Richard Wagner, Nachgelassene Schriften und Dichtungen, Leipzig, 1895, p. 161 f. How keen Wagner was to put Ānanda and Prakṛti on the stage, is shown by his letters to Matilde *Wesendonk* (21st edit., Berlin, 1904, p. 59 ff., 98, 197 and 242). As is well known, the "Sieger" finally became "Parsifal."

Chapters XXVI to XXIX should certainly be counted among the oldest portions of the Divyāvadāna : they contain a cycle of legends centring around the person of the great king Aśoka, and are based upon an ancient "Book of King Aśoka." This book probably originated in Mathurā between 150 and 50 B. C.,[1] but is no longer extant in its original form. We only know it from two different Chinese versions.[2] The Divyāvadāna did not only draw on the "Book of King Aśoka," which was already augmented at that time, but it also made use of the Kalpanāmaṇḍitikā.[3] These legends scarcely contain anything of much historical value ;[4] but they are all the more valuable from the purely literary standpoint. Above all, we find here the exceedingly dramatic legend of Upagupta and Māra. It is an extremely bold idea to allow Māra, the evil one, the tempter, to be converted by a Buddhist monk. The idea is still bolder when the saint Upagupta, who longs to see, face to face, the Buddha who had entered Nirvāṇa a hundred years before, beseeches Māra, whom he had converted, to appear in the guise of the Buddha, and when Māra does indeed, like a skilful actor, represent Buddha in so life-like a manner, that the saint sinks down before him in prayer. The whole of this story is so dramatic that we might believe it to be simply a Buddhist drama retold here. This passage is taken almost word for word from Kumāralāta's Kalpanāmaṇḍitikā, and in language, style and metre, it

---

1) *Przyluski*, l.c., pp. 13 ff., 92 f., 166.

2) See above, p. 285, note 3.

3) For a detailed treatment of the mutual relationship of the Kalpanāmaṇḍitikā, Divyāvadāna, A-yu-wang-ch'uan and A-yu-wang-king, s. H. *Lüders*, Bruchstücke der Kalpanāmaṇḍitikā des Kumāralāta, p. 71 ff.

4) Unless there is a historical nucleus underlying the persecutions of Jain monks, mentioned in Divy., p. 427, and the persecutions of Buddhist monks under Puṣyamitra, mentioned on p. 433 f. See *Rhys Davids*, JPTS 1896, p. 88 f.

is one of the best productions of ornate poetry.[1] One of the most beautiful legends in the Aśoka cycle is the touching story of Kuṇāla, the son of Aśoka, whose lovely eyes are poked out at the instigation of his wicked stepmother, without his feeling one moment's anger or hatred towards her who has done him so much injury.[2] The Divyāvadāna has many legends in common with the Pāli Canon. Thus Chapter XVII contains a passage from a Mahā-Parinirvāṇa-Sūtra.[3] Chapter III relates of the advent of the future Buddha Maitreya, combined with the legend of King Praṇāda.[4] In this it partly coincides with Dīghanikāya 26. The story of Pūrṇa, who goes as an apostle to the savage and violent Sroṇaparāntakas, determined to accept it with equanimity and gentleness if they despise him, strike him, or even want to kill him, corresponds to a familiar Pāli Sutta.[5] The story of the young son of a merchant, who gradually acquires enormous riches all on account of his having sold a dead mouse, corresponds to Jātaka No. 4.[6] The Avadāna of Rūpavatī is

---

1) Divyāvadāna Ed., pp. 356-364, transl. by *Windisch*, Māra und Buddha, p. 161 ff.

Cf. Éd. *Huber*, Açvaghoṣa, Sûtrâlaṃkâra traduit en Français, p. 263 ff. and BEFEO 4, 1904, p. 709 ff. *Lüders*, l.c., 77 ff. A Pāli form of this legend, quite inartistic and undramatic, has been published by C. *Duroiselle* (BEFEO 4, 1904, p. 414 ff.) from the Burmese work Lokapaññatti. It is curious that the monastery in which Upagupta, who later became Aśoka's teacher, lives, is endowed by the brothers Naṭa ("actor") and Bhaṭa ("soldier"), and is therefore called Naṭabhaṭika. *Lévi* (T'oung Pao 1907, p. 120) is not wrong in calling the Aśokâvadâna a kind of Mâhâtmya of the Naṭabhaṭika monastery of Mathurâ.

2) Divyâvadâna, p. 406 ff.; rendered in extracts by *Oldenberg*, Buddha, p. 348 ff., and E. *Hardy*, Aśoka, p. 65 ff.

3) Divy., pp. 200 ff., 706; s. *Windisch*, Māra und Buddha, pp. 35 ff., 43 ff.; *Oldenberg*, ZDMG 52, p. 658 f.

4) Divy., p. 55 ff.; s. E. *Leumann*, Maitreya-samiti, pp. 4, 173 ff. and E. *Abegg*, Der Messiasglaube in Indien und Iran, 1928, p. 153 ff.

5) Divy., p. 36 ff. L. de *La Vallée Poussin*, Bouddhisme, Paris, 1909, p. 275 ff., sees in Pūrṇa the type of the Mahâyânist Bodhisattva. However, both in the Divy. and the Pāli Saṃyuttanikāya 35, 88 (IV, p. 60 ff.) and the Majjhimanikâya 145 (III, 267 ff.) the stress is laid on the mildness and equanimity which characterise the perfect saint, the Arhat; and therefore it shows rather the Hīnayâna ideal of an Arhat.

6) Divy., p. 498 ff. A counterpart to the story of Dick Whittington and his cat. Also in Kathâ-Saritsâgara, I, 6.

reminiscent of the legends of the Jātakamālā: Rūpavatī cuts off her breasts in order to nourish with her flesh and blood, a woman who is near starvation and is about to devour her child. We see in her the Mahayāna ideal of a Bodhisattva when, in reply to an enquiry for the motive of her action, she answers:

"As true as it is that I sacrificed my breasts for the child's sake, not for sovereignty, not for enjoyments, not in order to attain heaven, not to become an Indra, not in order to rule a kingdom as a ruler, but for no other reason than to attain the highest perfect enlightenment, that I may tame the untamed, liberate the unliberated, comfort the uncomforted, and lead the unredeemed to the perfect Nirvāṇa,—as true as this is, may my female sex vanish, and may I become a man!" Scarcely had she uttered this, than she was transformed into a Prince Rūpavata, who later became king and reigned for sixty years. Reborn as a Brahmin, he sacrifices himself for a tigress.[1]

Chapter XXXVIII, which contains an ornate version of the Maitrakanyaka Avadāna after the Avadāna-Śataka (No. 36), is related in the same Kāvya style as the Jātakamālā.[2] It is in passages like this, that the Divyāvadāna resembles the Avadānamālās.

Poetical versions of Avadānas, partly selected systematically from the Avadāna-Śataka, partly taken from other sources, are the Kalpadrumāvadānamālā ("Wishing Tree Avadāna Garland," *i.e.*, a garland of Avadānas which grant all wishes), the Ratnāvadānamālā ("Jewel Avadāna Garland"), and the Aśokāvadānamālā ("Avadāna Garland of King Aśoka").[3] The Kalpadrumāvadānamālā begins with

---

[1]) *Cf.* Jātakamālā I, above p. 274 ff. In the Chinese Tripiṭaka, Rūpavatī is rendered by "Silver-white," see S. *Beal* in Ind. Ant. 9, 1880, 145 ff.

[2]) Divy., p. 586 ff. *Cf.* *Speyer*, Avadana-Śatāka, Ed. II, p. xii, and above, p. 282.

[3]) *Cf.* *Feer*, l. c., p. xxiii ff. *Speyer*, l. c., pp. xii ff., xxi ff.; Rāj. *Mitra*, Nep. Buddh. Lit., pp. 6 ff., 197 ff., 292 ff.; C. *Bendall*, Catalogue, p. 110 ff., and *Przyluski*, l. c., p. xiv f. A legend from the Ratnāvadānamālā is translated by Mahendra Lal *Dās* in the Journal of the Buddhist Text Society, 1894, Part 3.

a version of the last narrative of the Avadāna-Śataka. And as the Sthavira Upagupta[1] appears in conversation with King Aśoka, so all the legends in the Avadānamālās are inserted into the framework of a dialogue between Aśoka and Upagupta. The first part of the Aśokāvadānamālā contains legends of Aśoka himself; after these follow instructions in the form of stories which Upagupta relates to Aśoka. All the three collections differ from the Avadāna-Śataka, not only because they are written entirely in epic ślokas, but especially because they decidedly belong to the Mahāyāna, and recall the Purāṇas both in style and language. They possibly belong to the period in which the sectarian Purāṇas came into being.[2]

Another book, which has drawn liberally on the Avadāna-Śataka, is the Dvāviṃśatyavadāna ("The Avadānas in 22 sections"). Here too, Upagupta appears in conversation with Aśoka, but both of these soon give place to Śākyamuni and Maitreya. In this case, however, the legends are told in prose (with verses interspersed) and divided into sections according to the moral they teach ("meritorious actions," "hearing of the sermon," "generosity" and so on).[3]

The Bhadrakalpāvadāna ("Avadānas from the good age of the world") is a collection of 34 legends, which Upagupta relates to Aśoka. Like the Avadānamālās, it is entirely in

---

[1]) Upagupta is another name of Tissa Moggaliputta, the teacher of Aśoka (see above, p. 6, *cf.* A. *Waddell*, JASB proceedings 1899, p. 70 ff.).

[2]) About the 6th century A.D. and later. According to *Speyer*, l. c., p. xxxvi, who places them between 400 and 1000 A. D., they used the Jātakamālā. The *Mahājātakamālā* (or Bṛhajjātakamālā) excerpted by E. *Lang* (JA 1912, s. 10, t. XIX, p. 520 ff., *cf.* S. *Lévi* in Festschrift Vilhelm Thomsen, Leipzig, 1912, 162 ff.) also appears to belong to the Avadānamālās.

[3]) *Feer*, l. c., pp. xix f., xxvii; *Bendall*, Catalogue, p. 36. A specimen of it translated by *Feer* (AMG t. 5, 1883, p. 544 ff.). See also Rāj. *Mitra*, Nep. Buddh. Lit., p. 85 ff. The language of the Dvāviṃśatyavadāna is a popular Sanskrit, s. R. L. *Turner* in JRAS 1913, 289 ff.

verse. However, in plan and contents it is said to resemble the Mahāvagga of the Vinayapiṭaka to some extent.[1]

In the same way as, in the sectarian Purāṇas, there are large sections and entire works (Māhātmyas) consisting of legends which were invented to explain the origin of some feasts or rites (Vratas), so there are also similar Buddhist texts. A collection of such legends is the Vratāvadānamālā, "Garland of Avadānas on (the origin of) festivals or rites," which has only the framework of the dialogue between Upagupta and Aśoka in common with the previously mentioned Avadāna collections.[2]

The Vicitrakarṇikāvadāna is a collection with the most varied contents, containing 32 narratives, a few of which come from Avadāna-Śataka, and others belong to the type of the Vratāvadānas. The language, too, is as varied as the contents, now a barbaric Sanskrit, again good Sanskrit verses, and sometimes even Pāli.[3]

All these works are so far accessible only in a few manuscripts. Others are known only through the Tibetan and Chinese translations.[4] Not only books of Avadānas, but many single Avadānas of considerable length, however, have come down in manuscripts as well as in Chinese and Tibetan translations. An instance is the Sumāgadhāvadāna,

[1]) *Bendall*, Catalogue, p. 88 ff.; *Feer*, l. c., p. xxix; Rāj. *Mitra*, l. c., p. 42 ff.; *Speyer*, l. c., p. xxxvi. According to S. d'*Oldenburg*, who has translated the 34th tale, a version of Jātakamālā 31 (Jātaka No. 537) (JRAS 1893, p. 331 ff.), it is later than Kṣemendra (about 1040 A. D.).

[2]) Rāj. *Mitra*, l. c., pp. 102 ff, 221 ff., 231, 275 ff. Other texts of the same kind: *Ibid*, pp. 229 f., 232 f., 265 ff., 269 ff., 280 ff., L. *Feer*, Suvarṇavarṇa-Avadānam et Vratāvadānamālā, OC XII, Rome, 1899, I, p. 19 ff. These are obviously quite late Mahāyāna works.

[3]) *Speyer*, l. c., pp. xciii-c.

[4]) Based on Chinese Avadāna books (*cf.* *Feer*, l. c., p. xxx f.) are the "Contes et Apologues Indiens" by Stanislas *Julien*, Paris, 1860, (transl. into German by A. *Schnell*, Rostock, 1903.

the legends of Sumāgadhā, the daughter of the merchant Anāthapiṇḍada, who alienates her husband from the Jain monks, and, by a miracle, converts the whole town to the religion of the Buddha. In a former existence she had been the daughter of King Kṛkin, famous for his ten marvellous dreams.[1]

Lastly, mention must here be made of the extensive Avadāna book of the Kashmirian poet Kṣemendra, the Avadāna-Kalpalatā,[2] which was completed in 1052 A.D., and which is held in great esteem especially in Tibet.[3] Kṣemendra is a prolific writer and a verse-maker of astonishing fertility. We shall meet with him again in other places, for his activity was most versatile. Yet he is distinguished not so much by genius and taste, but by an iron determination. The huge collection of legends, too, in which Kṣemendra has recast the Buddhist Avadānas in the style of ornate court poetry, contains more edifying stories than skilfully and tastefully narrated ones. The Buddhist tendency to self-sacrifice is here brought to a climax with such subtlety, the doctrine of Karman is applied so clumsily, and the moral is pointed in such an exaggerated manner, that the story often achieves the reverse of the desired result. The collection consists of 107 legends, to which Somendra, Kṣemendra's son, has added not only an Introduction but also a 108th narrative (Jīmūtavāhana-Ava-

[1]) These dreams belong to universal literature. *Cf.* Jātaka No. 77, S. d'*Oldenburg* in JARS 1893, p. 509 ff., and Tsuru-Matsu *Tokiwai*, Studien zum Sumāgadhāvadāna, Diss. der Universität Strassburg 1898; Rāj. *Mitra*, l. c., p. 237. In Yaśomitra's Abhidharmakośavyākhyā the same Avadāna is quoted "from a Vinaya text."

[2]) The text, with the Tibetan transl., is published in Bibl. Ind., Calcutta, 1888 ff, by Sarat Chandra *Dās* and Hari Mohan *Vidyābhūṣaṇa*. A number of legends are translated in the Journal of the Buddhist Text Society, Vols. I-V, 1893-1897. *Cf.* also Rāj. *Mitra*, l. c., p. 49 ff.

[3]) Some Tibetan scholars, however, do not recommend this work, seeing that it was written by a layman; for Kṣemendra was not a monk.

dāna).[1] The legends are mostly known already from the older Avadāna books and also from other sources.[2]

The Mahāyāna-Sūtras.

The whole of the Buddhist Sanskrit literature discussed so far, belongs to the borderland which forms the transition between Hīnayāna and Mahāyāna Buddhism. We shall now turn to those works which belong entirely to the Mahāyāna.

The Mahāyāna does not possess a canon of its own, and cannot possess one, for the simple reason that the Mahāyāna does not represent one unified sect. There is, indeed, an account of a council which is supposed to have assembled under King Kaniṣka, but it is doubtful whether any canon was established at all at this council, and if so, in which language and by which sect.[3] It is true that a Chinese text translated by Hsüan-Tsang[4] makes mention of a "Bodhisattvapiṭaka" consisting of a long list of Mahāyāna texts, a Vinayapiṭaka and an Abhidharmapiṭaka, and the same text enumerates a lengthy list of Mahāyāna-Sūtras. How-

[1]) Somendra is an even worse poet than his father. In addition to the Bṛhatkathāmañjarī, IX. 18-1221, he also made use of Harṣa's drama Nāgānanda. See F. D. K. *Bosch*, de legende van Jimūtavāhana in de Sanskrit-Litteratuur, Leiden, 1915, p 115 ff.

[2]) Thus the Padmāvatī-Avadāna (No. 68) corresponds to the stories, familiar from the Pāli commentaries, of Padmāvatī, under whose feet lotus blossoms spring forth, and the Ekaśṛṅga-Avadāna (No. 65) corresponds to the Ṛṣyaśṛṅga legend which is so well known to us. Both are to be found also in the Mahāvastu, and *Lüders* (NGGW 1901, p. 26) shows that Kṣemendra recast the Ṛṣyaśṛṅga-legend on the model of the Mahāvastu. The Avadāna of Kṣemendra has been rendered in German verse by Hermann *Francke* (Ekasringa Prinz Einhorn, Leipzig, 1901).

[3]) The object of the alleged council of Kaniṣka was not to establish a Canon, but to collect explanations (commentaries). According to J. *Takakusu* (JRAS 1905, 414 f.) this council dealt with the Hīnayāna, and not the Mahāyāna.

[4]) See S. *Lévi* and Éd. *Chavannes* in JA 1916, s. 11, t. VIII, p. 5 ff. The Buddhist dictionary Mahā-Vyutpatti (Bibl. Buddh. XIII) 65, mentions 105 separate Mahāyāna texts, No. 12 of which is a "Bodhisattva-Piṭaka." This is also quoted in the Śikṣā-Samuccaya, pp. 190 and 311.

ever, as the text goes on to say that "there are hundreds of myriads of similar Mahāyāna-Sūtras," we are scarcely justified in regarding this as an attempt at a classification of "the Mahāyāna Canon." The so-called "nine Dharmas"[1] are not the canon of any sect, but a series of books which were compiled at different times and belonged to different sects, but which, at the present day, are all held in great honour in Nepal. The titles of these nine books are: Aṣṭasāhasrikā, Prajñā-Pāramitā, Saddharma-Puṇḍarīka, Lalita-Vistara, Laṅkāvatāra or Saddharma-Laṅkāvatāra, Suvarṇa-Prabhāsa, Gaṇḍavyūha, Tathāgataguhyaka or Tathāgataguṇajñāna, Samādhirāja and Daśabhūmīśvara.[2] All these works are also called "Vaipulya-Sūtras."

The most important Mahāyāna-Sūtra, and certainly the one which stands foremost as a work of literature, is the Saddharma-Puṇḍarīka, "the Lotus of the Good Religion."[3] He who wishes to become acquainted with Mahāyāna Buddhism, with all its characteristic peculiarities, with all its advantages and defects, should read this Sūtra. There is not much of the *man* Śākyamuni left in this work.[4] The Budhha now is actually nothing less than a god above all gods, an infinitely exalted being, who has lived since count-

---

[1] "Dharma" is here probably only an abbreviation of "Dharma-Paryāya" (religious texts). In Nepal a regular divine service is consecrated to these nine books (*Hodgson*, Essays, p. 13), a bibliolatry which is characteristic of the Buddhism of Nepal, and is also very conspicuous in the texts themselves.

[2] *Hodgson*, l.c.; *Burnouf*, Introduction, pp. 29 ff., 60 f.; *Kern*, Der Buddhismus, II, 508 ff.

[3] Edited by H. *Kern* and Bunyiu *Nanjio*, Bibliotheca Buddhica X, St. Pétersbourg, 1908 ff. Transl. into French ("Le Lotus de la bonne Loi") by E. *Burnouf*, Paris, 1852, into English by H. *Kern* in SBE, Vol. 21, 1884. The title is explained in the following manner by M. *Anesaki* (Buddhist Art in its Relations to Buddhist Ideals, 1914, p. 15 f.): "The lotus is a symbol of purity and perfection because it grows out of mud but is not defiled,—just as Buddha is born into the world but lives above the world; and because its fruits are said to be ripe when the flower blooms,—just as the truth preached by Buddha bears immediately the fruit of enlightenment."

[4] See *Anesaki* in ERE IV, p. 839; *La Vallée Poussin* in ERE VIII, 145 f.

less aeons in the past, and will live for ever. "I am the father of the world," he says of himself (XV, Gāthā 21), "the self-existent (Svayambhū), the physician and protector of all creatures, and it is only because I know how perverse and deluded the fools are, that I, who have never ceased to exist, pretend to have passed away." Thus it is only out of pity for the beings, out of consideration for the weakness of the human understanding, that he pretends to have entered Nirvāṇa. He is like that physician with many sons who were once attacked by a severe illness during their father's absence. The physician returns and prepares medicines for them. Only a few of his sons however, take them, the others reject them. In order to persuade these also to take the medicines, he goes to distant parts, and gives out that he is dead. The children, who now feel deserted, take the prescribed medicines, and recover their health. Buddha has recourse to a similar artifice when he apparently enters Nirvāṇa, but yet returns again and again in order to preach.[1] It is his preaching which forms the link between him and the human beings. The Buddha of the "Lotus" does not, however, preach like the Buddha of the Pāli Suttas, who wanders from place to place as a mendicant monk, in order to proclaim his doctrine ; on the contrary, he sits on the Gṛdhrakūṭa hill in a large assembly of monks and nuns, and in the midst of a still larger host of thousands of Buddhas and Bodhisattvas, gods and demi-gods ; and when he is about to "pour down the great rain of the religion, to sound the great drum of the religion, to raise the great banner of the religion, to light the great torch of the religion, to blow the great shell trumpet of the religion, to beat the great kettle-drum of the religion," a ray of light bursts forth from the

---

[1]) Chapt. XV, SBE 21, p. 304 ff.

hair between his eye-brows; this ray of light illuminates eighteen thousand "Buddha-lands" with all the Buddhas and all the beings in them, and permits the Bodhisattva Maitreya to see wonderful visions; for the Buddha of the "Lotus" is also a powerful magician, who loves to work upon the senses of his audience by means of splendid phantasmagorias.

The doctrine of this Buddha differs just as greatly from that of the Hīnayāna, as his personality differs from that of the Buddha of the old texts. Though it is true that he, too, desires to lead the beings to the "Buddha knowledge," to enlightenment, he gives them a single "vehicle," the "Buddha vehicle," which carries them to their goal. Everyone who has merely heard the Buddha's preaching, who has performed any kind of meritorious actions, who has led a moral life, can become a Buddha. Moreover, even those who worship relics, erect Stūpas, construct any kind of images of Buddha, whether jewelled, marble or wooden statues or frescoes, even children who in play make Stūpas of sand, or scribble figures of Buddha on the wall, those who offer flowers or perfumes at Stūpas or make music before them, even those who only by chance, have on some occasion thought of the Buddha with the thought "honour to the Buddha,"—all these will attain to the highest enlightenment.[1] It is only in appearance that there are three "vehicles," namely that of the disciples, that of the Pratyeka-Buddhas, and that of the Bodhisattvas, by means of which Nirvāṇa can be attained. In reality it is only by the mercy of the Buddha that all of them alike attain to enlightenment and become Buddhas. This is illustrated by one of those beautiful parables which are not rare in the Saddharma-Puṇḍarīka:

In a ruined old house lives a father with his children. Suddenly the house is on fire. The father is troubled about his children. It is true that

[1]) Chapt. II, Gathās 61 ff., 74 ff., SBE 21, p. 47 ff.

he is strong, and could take the little ones in his arms and escape from the house with them. But the house has only *one* door. The children, unconscious of the danger, run about in merry play, and do not pay heed to his cry of warning. It is to be feared that he and his children will all perish in the fire. Then a good plan occurs to him. Children love playthings. He calls out to them that he has all sorts of beautiful toys for them, little bullock-carts, little goat-carts, little antelope-carts, in front of the house. No sooner do the children hear these words, than they all rush out of the door and are saved. Now they ask their father for the promised little carts of three kinds. However, the father is a rich man, and gives them splendid, beautifully decorated bullock-carts instead. The children are merry and happy. Who will accuse the father of deception, because he promised the children three kinds of inferior carts, and only gave them the carts of the one, most splendid kind? Even so does the Buddha deal with men: by the promise of the three "vehicles" he lures them away from the burning, ruined house of this world, he rescues them, and gives them the one "vehicle," the most precious of all, the "Buddha vehicle."[1]

Again, in the parable of the "prodigal son," the Buddha is represented as the good, wealthy father, who means well towards his sons, the human beings:

A rich man has an only son, who roams about in foreign lands for fifty years. While the father grows richer and richer, and has become a great man, the son lives in foreign parts, poor and in reduced circumstances. As a beggar he at last returns to his home, where his father has been yearning for him all the time. The beggar comes to the house of his father, whom, however, he does not recognise in the great man, who, like a king, surrounded by a great retinue, sits before his mansion. When he sees the pomp and splendour, he flees for fear that he, the ragged beggar, might be ill-treated. His father, however, recognised him at once, and sends out servants to bring the beggar in. Trembling and shaking with fear, he is dragged in, and he falls unconscious. Then his father commands that he shall be released. Gladly the beggar gets up, and goes to the poor quarter of the town. Now the rich man thinks out a plan whereby he may win the confidence of his son. He sends workmen

[1]) Chapt. III, SBE 21, p. 72 ff.

to hire him for the humblest work in his house; he sometimes chats with him and gradually becomes intimate with him. In this way twenty years pass, without the father's making himself known. Not until the hour of his death does he cause all his relatives to assemble, and announce that the beggar, who has now become a trusted servant, is his own son; and he makes him the heir to all his wealth. The rich man is Buddha; the son who was lost and is found again, represents the human beings, whom Buddha, as the wise father, gradually draws to himself, and finally appoints as his fortunate heirs.[1]

The Buddha is also compared to a physician, as often as to a loving father. There is an especially detailed parable, in which the human beings are compared to persons born blind, whose eyes are opened by Buddha, the great physician.[2] The fact that the Buddha knows no partiality, but is an equally good father and physician to *all*, is shown by two beautiful similes: Even as a mighty rain-cloud gathers, and waters and refreshes by its moisture all the grasses, herbs and trees, even as the latter absorb the moisture of the earth and blossom forth in renewed vigour, so the Buddha appears in the world and refreshes all creatures, bringing them blessed repose. Again, even as the sun and the moon send down their rays equally over all the world, on the good and the bad, on the high and the lowly, so the preaching of the Buddha is for all the world alike.[3]

All these similes and parables would be still more beautiful, if they were not spun out to such length and with such verbosity, that the pointedness of the simile suffered from it. This verbosity is very characteristic of the whole work. It is a veritable whirl of words with which the reader is stunned;

[1] Chapt. IV, SBE 21, p. 98 ff. *Cf. La Vallée Poussin*, Bouddhisme, p. 317 ff. The parable of the "prodigal son" in the Gospel of St. Luke, 15 has such a very different tendency, that I do not believe that there is any connection between the two. *Cf. Garbe*, Indien und das Christentum, p. 46 and Carlo *Puini* in GSAI 27, 1915, 129 ff.

[2] Chapt. V, SBE 21, p. 129 ff.

[3] Chapt. V, SBE 21, pp. 119 ff., 122 ff., 128 ff.

and the idea is often drowned in the flood of words. The *numbers* are, however, still more immoderate and extravagant than the words. For instance, there was a Buddha who lived "forty hundred thousand myriads of tens of millions of ages of the world, as many as there are grains of sand in the river Ganges, and after he had attained to complete Nirvāṇa, his true religion still lasted hundreds of thousands of myriads of tens of millions of ages of the world, as many as there are tiny specks of dust in the whole of India, and a copy of the true religion after that, still lasted hundreds of thousands of myriads of tens of millions of ages of the world, as many as there are tiny specks of dust in the four continents," and there arose consecutively in the world "twenty hundred thousand myriads of tens of millions" of similar Buddhas.[1] The Buddha is glorified in the most extravagant manner, immoderate both in words and in numbers, especially in the splendid phantasmagoria of Chapter XIV, where, by the magic power of the Buddha, the earth opens and there suddenly appear from all sides many hundreds of thousands of myriads of tens of thousands of Bodhisattvas, each with a retinue as numerous as the sand of sixty Ganges rivers. While these countless Bodhisattvas pay homage to the Buddha, fifty ages of the world pass, during which great silence prevails, but which, by the magic power of the Lord, seem but a single afternoon. The Buddha tells the astonished Maitreya that all these countless Bodhisattvas were his pupils. The glorification of the text itself is equally immoderate and extravagant; for, strange as it is, the text refers at every turn to Buddha's preaching and expounding of the text, and to its propagation by the preachers. Thus (in Chapter XI) Śākyamuni causes a wonderful Stūpa to appear in mid-air, and from the interior of the Stūpa sounds the voice of a Buddha, who had died

[1]) Chapt. XIX, Text, p. 376 f., SBE 21, p. 356.

myriads of ages previously: "Excellent, excellent, Lord Sākyamuni, the religious discourse called 'Lotus of the Good Religion' has been well expounded by thee. Yes, so it is, so it is, Lord Buddha (Sugata)." The same chapter relates: The Bodhisattva Mañjuśrī proclaimed the "Lotus of the Good Religion" in the kingdom of the Nāgas at the bottom of the ocean, and the youthful daughter of the Nāga king heard the sermon, and understood all the doctrines. As a result she attains to enlightenment and changes her sex on the spot.[1] The merit of the preacher of the "Lotus" and of the faithful hearing of this sermon is praised again and again. Thus it is said in Chapter XXII:

"The religious discourse called 'Lotus of the Good Religion' is like a tank for the thirsty, like a fire for those who suffer from cold, like a garment for the naked, like the caravan leader for the merchants, like a mother for her children, like a boat for those who ferry over...like a torch for the dispelling of darkness."[2] Whoever writes down this book, or causes it to be written down, acquires endless merit. A female being who hears it, has lived as a female for the last time. He who, at the hearing of the sermon of the "Lotus" expresses his acclamation, will always exhale from his mouth sweet breath as from a lotus, and sandal-perfume will emanate from his limbs.

All these extravagances, and in particular all these glorifications of the texts in the texts themselves, are just as characteristic of all the Mahāyāna-Sūtras[3] as they are of the Purāṇas. In fact, it is the spirit of the Purāṇas of

[1]) SBE, Vol. 21, p. 250 ff.

[2]) SBE, Vol. 21, p. 388.

[3]) Amitāyurdhyāna-Sūtra 28 (SBE, Vol. 49, Part 2, p. 195) is significant: "If there be any one who commits many evil deeds, provided that he does not speak evil of the Mahāvaipulya Sūtras, he, though himself a very stupid man, and neither ashamed nor sorry for all the evil actions that he has done, yet, while dying, may meet a good and learned teacher who will recite and laud the headings and titles of the twelve divisions of the Mahāyāna scriptures. Having thus heard the names of all the Sūtras, he will be freed from the greatest sins which would involve him in births and deaths during a thousand Kalpas."

which we are reminded by every line of the Saddharma-Puṇḍarīka.[1] At times the Buddha of the Saddharma-Puṇḍarīka reminds us of the Kṛṣṇa of the Bhagavad-Gītā.[2] This does not, however, enable us to draw any conclusion as regards the chronology, as we cannot determine any sure date, either for the beginning of the Kṛṣṇa-cult, or for the Purāṇas.

It is altogether difficult to fix any definite period for the Saddharma-Puṇḍarīka, as it contains sections belonging to various epochs. The prose in pure Sanskrit, and the Gāthās in "mixed Sanskrit" could not possibly have originated at the same time,[3] because, in contents, they often diverge from one another. Both the prose and the Gāthās several times mention the work as a metrical composition. Probably it originally consisted only of verses, with *short* prose passages inserted by way of introduction and as a means of connecting the verses. The short prose passages were later enlarged, especially as the dialect of the verses had become obsolete. Without being actually a commentary, the prose served as an explanation.[4] It is significant that precisely those chapters which contain no Gāthās, have, on other grounds too, proved to be later additions. These are Chapters XXI-XXVI, which are devoted more to the adoration of Bodhisattvas, while the Saddharma-Puṇḍarīka on the whole serves for the glorification

[1]) The few points of agreement between the vocabulary of the Saddharma-Puṇḍarīka and that of the Śatapatha-Brāhmaṇa, which are pointed out by *Kern*, SBE 21, p. xvi f., are by no means sufficient to connect the work in any way with Vedic literature.

[2]) It seems to me, however, risky to assume that the "Lotus" was directly influenced by the, Kṛṣṇa-cult, the Vedânta and the Bhagavad-Gītā, as has been assumed by J. N. *Farquhar*, Outline of the Rel. Lit. of India, p. 114 f.

[3]) H. *Lüders* (Hoernle, Manuscript Remains, p. 161 f.) is of opinion that the original text was written in Prākrit, and was gradually Sanskritised.

[4]) We cannot, however, simply say that the prose is a résumé of the Gāthās, or that the Gāthās are an amplification of the prose. For instance, saposing that in Book I, we had only the prose, we should glean a meaning from it, whereas the Gāthās by themselves would remain inexplicable in some cases. In Book II, the main content is included in the Gāthās. In Book III (the parable of the father and the children), the prose diverges somewhat from the Gāthās, but the Gāthā narrative presents a better meaning.

of the Buddha Śākyamuni. One of these Bodhisattvas is Bhaiṣajyarāja, the ".Prince of the art of Healing" who in Chapter XXI utters protecting magic formulas (Dhāraṇīs) and in Chapter XXII, after he has, for twelve years, eaten sweet-scented substances and drunk oil, wraps himself in heavenly garments, bathes in oil, and burns himself. During twelve thousand years his body burns without ceasing; and the sole purpose of this magnificent sacrifice and splendid firework display, is to do honour to the Buddha and the Saddharma-Puṇḍarīka. Chapter XXIV is devoted to the Bodhisattva Avalokiteśvara, the great redeemer. He who invokes him, is delivered from every danger. The executioner's sword is shivered into fragments, if he who is sentenced to death, prays to him. All fetters are loosened if his name is but uttered. He rescues the shipwrecked and the caravan which is attacked by robbers. A woman who desires a son or a beautiful daughter, needs only to invoke Avalokiteśvara, and her wish is fulfilled. The chapter also contains a Gāthā passage of considerable length for the glorification of Avalokiteśvara. This, however, is also of more recent date; not *all* the Gāthās are earlier than the prose: some were added later.[1]

However, though the work contains later and earlier parts, it presents a much greater uniformity of character than, for instance, the Mahāvastu or the Lalita-Vistara. Whilst both the last-mentioned works contain many a passage which harks back to the very earliest period of Buddhist doctrine and poetry, the *whole* of the Saddharma-Puṇḍarīka only gives expression to a later phase of Buddhism.[2] Nevertheless

---

[1]) *Kern*, SBE 21, p. xviii f. Though the old Chinese translation contains Chapts. XXI-XXVI, they appear in a different order from that of the Sanskrit text. This proves that they are Pariśiṣṭas, Appendices, which did not originally belong to the work. *Kern*, l.c., p. xxi f.

[2]) It is significant that *Kern*, SBE 21, p. X ff., in order to prove that the

we shall most probably be right in placing the nucleus of the work as far back as the first century A.D., as it is quoted by Nāgārjuna, who probably lived towards the end of the 2nd century A. D.[1] The work was first translated into Chinese in 223 A.D. This translation has not come down to us, but we have those of Dharmarakṣa (286 A. D.) and Kumārajīva (about 400 A.D.) and that of Jñānagupta and Dharmagupta (601 A.D.).[2] In the preface to the last-named translation it is stated that Dharmarakṣa and Kumāragupta made their translations according to two different texts.[3] Moreover, the fragments of the Saddharma-Puṇḍarīka which have been found in Eastern Turkestan, and which present a text diverging from that of the Napalese manuscripts, afford a proof of the fact that there were two recensions of the work. On the whole it is a shorter text, and yet it contains some passages which are missing in our (Nepalese) text.[4] Whatever the exact date of the work in its original form may be, one thing is certain: the nature of the work as we know it, implies a mature development of Mahāyāna Buddhism, especially in the direction of Budha-Bhakti and the cult of relics and image-worship, and above all also an advanced stage of Buddhist art.

Saddharma-Puṇḍarika and the Lalita-Vistara contain materials which belong to the earliest period of Buddhism, can quote examples *only* from the Lalita-Vistara.

[1]) See *Eliot*, Hinduism and Buddhism, II, 52.

[2]) See B. *Nanjio*, Bibliotheca Buddhica X, 5, 1912, Preface, p. ii f.; *Bagchi*, I, pp. 87, 150, 186, 310, 322, 409; and N. D. *Mironov* in JRAS 1927, p. 252 ff.

[3]) *Kern* in SBE, Vol. 21, p. xxi note.

[4]) The Central Asiatic fragments have been published by *Hoernle* and *Lüders* in *Hoernle*, Manuscript Remains, pp. 132 ff., 138 ff., 162 ff. See also *La Vallée Poussin* in JRAS 1911, 1067 ff.; *Kern* in Preface to edition (Bibl. Buddh. X), p. v ff.; *Hoernle* in JRAS, 1916, p. 269 ff. According to N. D. *Mironov* (JRAS 1927, 252 ff.) there are two groups of fragments, one of which should, on palæographic grounds, be ascribed to the 5th and 6th centuries, and the other to the 7th century. Moreover, fragments of an Uiguric translation of the Saddharma-Puṇḍarika have been found in Central Asia, s. F. W. K. *Müller*, Uigurica II, in ABA 1911, p. 14 ff.; *Lüders* in SBA 1914, p. 99. *Bendall* ascribes a Nepalese MS. of the Saddh., which he discovered, to the 4th or 5th century (JRAS 1901, p. 124 note).

When there is such frequent talk of thousands or myriads of tens of millions of Stūpas, which are erected over the relics of a Buddha, or of hundreds of tens of milions of Vihāras, which are described as splendid buildings, furnished with the greatest comfort and luxury, there must have been at least many hundreds of Stūpas and Vihāras (topes and monasteries) in the land, and these must have been furnished with pictures of Buddha made of jewels, statues of Buddha made of wood and metal, and with reliefs and frescoes.[1] On the other hand, the Saddharma-Puṇḍarīka inspired Buddhist art.[2] It has always ranked foremost as a book of edification, among the Buddhists of China and Japan. The Chinese pilgrim I-tsing relates that the "Lotus of the Good Religion" was the favourite book of his teacher Hui-hsi; during a period of more than sixty years he read it through once daily, so that he read it twenty thousand times.[3] Even at the present day it may be found in every Buddhist temple in Japan: it is the most sacred book of the Hokke-shū or "Saddharma-Puṇḍarīka sect," founded by Nichiren in 1252 A.D., and one of the principal works upon which the Tien-tai school in China, and the Tendai sect in Japan also take their stand.[4]

The whole of a long Mahāyāna-Sūtra is also devoted to the Bodhisattva Avalokiteśvara, who is glorified in Chapter XXIV of the Saddharma-Puṇḍarīka. The complete title of this Mahāyāna-Sūtra is Avalokiteśvara-Guṇakāraṇḍa-Vyūha, "the detailed description of the basket of the qualities of

[1]) See particularly Chapt, II, Gāthās 77 ff., SBE Vol. 21, p. 50 f.

[2]) See M. *Anesaki*, Buddhist Art in its Relations to Buddhist Ideals, p. 16 f.

[3]) I-tsing, transl. by J. *Takakusu*, p. 205.

[4]) *Cf.* B. *Nanjio*, Short History of the Twelve Japanese Buddhist Sects, Tokyo, 1886, pp. 68 ff., 132 ff.; Yamakāmi *Sōgen*, Systems of Buddhist Thought, Calcutta, 1912, p. 4; K. J. *Saunders*, Epochs in Buddhist History, Chicago, 1924, p. 60 ff., 120 ff., 146 f.; Timothy *Richard*, The New Testament of Higher Buddhism, Edinburgh, 1910, p. 127; and W. M. *McGovern*, An Introduction to Mahāyāna Buddhism, London, 1922. pp. 208 f., 222. Extracts from the Chinese translation of the Saddh., which are said to contain the nucleus of the work, have been translated by T. *Richard*, l.c., pp. 147-261.

Avalokiteśvara," but it is usually briefly called Kāraṇḍa-Vyūha. There are two versions of this work, an earlier one in prose and a later one in Ślokas.[1] The latter is based on a theistic view of the world. It relates how, at the beginning of all things, Ādibuddha, the "first Buddha," also called Svayambhū, "the self-existent," and Ādinātha, "the First Lord," appeared and created the world through meditation. Out of his spirit arose Avalokiteśvara, who also takes part in the work of creation, creating the gods out of his own body. Not only does this introduction remind us forcibly of the Purāṇas, but the language and style of the metrical Kāraṇḍa-Vyūha are entirely those of the later Purāṇas. Now we know that in the fourth century A.D. there were already Buddhists who believed in Ādibuddha as God and Creator.[2] The cult of Avalokiteśvara, too, was already prevalent at that time, for the Chinese pilgrim Fa-hien, who came to India in the year 399 A.D., prayed to this Bodhisattva for deliverance, when he was overtaken by a storm on the voyage from Ceylon to China. The earliest pictures of Avalokiteśvara date from the 5th century.[3] For this reason it is possible that the metrical Kāraṇḍa-Vyūha was in existence even prior to the 4th century A.D., though this is not probable, since the Tibetan translation in the Kanjur, which originated in 616 A.D.,[4] is based upon the

---

1) The prose text is published by Satyavrata *Sāmaś'ramī*, Calcutta, 1873. (An edition which appeared in Serampore in 1872, is mentioned in the Catalogue of the Library of the India Office.) Cf. *Burnouf*, Introduction, pp. 196-206; Rāj. *Mitra*, Nep. Buddh. Lit., p. 95 ff.; 101 f.; *Bendall*, Catalogue, p. 9 ff.; Haraprasāda *Śāstrī*, Catalogue of... MSS. belonging to the Darbar Library, Nepal, Calcutta, 1895, p. 89; *La Vallée Poussin*, ERE II, p. 259 f.

2) This is proved by Maitreyanātha who says in the Mahāyāna-Sūtrālaṃkāra IX, 77: "There is no Adi-Buddha." Cf. *La Vallée Poussin* in *Garbe*, Indien und das Christentum, p. 182.

3) L. A. *Waddel*, JRAS, 1894, p. 57. *Cf.* A. *Foucher*, Étude sur l' iconographie Bouddhique de l'Inde (Bibl. de l'école des hautes études, t. 13), Paris, 1900, p. 97 ff.; and *La Vallée Poussin*, ERE II, p. 256 ff.

4) Thus according to *La Vallée Poussin*, ERE II, p. 259.

prose version which makes no mention of Ādibuddha. The prose version that contains a large section in the style of the Tantras, is probably not very old either.[1]

The fundamental idea, the glorification of the wonderful redeemer Avalokiteśvara, the "Lord who looks down," *i.e.*, who looks down with infinite pity on all beings,[2] is the same in both versions of the Kāraṇḍa-Vyūha. Avalokiteśvara here appears as the typical Bodhisattva, who refuses to assume Buddhahood until all beings are redeemed. Avalokiteśvara's one and only task is to bring the doctrine of salvation to *all* beings, to help all sufferers, to save them from every distress, and to exercise infinite pity that does not even shrink from sin,[3] and does not stop at the gates of hell. The early chapters of the Kāraṇḍa-Vyūha describe how he descends into the terrible hell Avīci, in order to release the tortured ones from their torment. No sooner has he entered, than the burning heat is transformed into

---

[1]) Unfortunately, I am unable to determine whether the Ratna-Kāraṇḍa-Vyūha-Sūtra, which was translated into Chinose by Dharmarakṣa in 270 A.D. and by Guṇabhadra between 435 and 468 A.D., (s. B. *Nanjio*, Catalogne No. 168 f. ; *Bagchi* 1, 96, 380 ; Alfred *Forke*, Katalog des Pekinger Tripiṭaka, Ostas. Sammlungen der k. Bibliothek zu Berlin, 1916, Nos. 623, 1069) is identical with the "Kāraṇḍa-Vyūha Sūtra", translated between 980 and 1001 A.D. (*Nanjio*, No. 782 ; *Forke* No. 548), and with one of the Sanskrit versions. A Ratna-Kāraṇḍa-Sūtra is quoted in the Sikṣā-Samuccaya (pp. 6, 356), and mentioned in Mahā-Vyutpatti, 65, 84. In the Kanjur, the Kāraṇḍa-Vyūha and the Ratna-Kāraṇḍa are, two different works, s. *Csoma de Körös* in AMG II, 243, 246.

[2]) The name is thus explained in the Kāraṇḍa-Vyūha itself, *Burnouf*, Introduction, p. 201 f. Other explanations of the name are also possible; see *La Vallée Poussin* ERE II, p. 256 f. H. *Zimmer*, ZII I, 1922, 73 ff., shows up the difficulties presented by all explanations of the name which have hitherto been suggested, but his own explanation : "The Master of Enlightenment, *i.e.*, he who has attained to perfect enlightenment, and yet does not become a Buddha, but remains a Bodhisattva until such time as all beings shall be released," is not at all convincing, for we ask ourselves in vain how Avalokita can possibly have the meaning of samyaksambodhi. On pictorial presentations of Avalokiteśvara, see A. *Foucher*, L'Iconographie Bouddhique de l'Inde, p. 97 ff. ; Alice *Getty*, The Gods of Northern Buddhism, Oxford, 1914, p. 64 ff.

[3]) Avalokiteśvara is made to say that it is better for a Bodhisattva to commit sin in the exercise of mercy, and to suffer in hell, than to disappoint any being in the which it has reposed in him. ERE II, p. 257 f.

a pleasant coolness; in place of the cauldron in which millions of the damned boil like pulse, a refreshing lotus-pond appears. The place of torture becomes an abode of joy.[1] From hell Avalokiteśvara goes to the abode of the Pretas and refreshes these ghosts, which are eternally tortured by hunger and thirst, with food and drink. One of his wanderings takes him to Ceylon, where he converts the cannibal witches (Rākṣasīs), thence he goes to Benares, where he preaches the doctrine to beings born as insects and worms, and then to Magadha, where he miraculously rescues the inhabitants from a dreadful famine. In Ceylon he appears as the winged horse Balāha, in order to bear away from the island the shipwrecked ones who had been allured by the witches, and to rescue them from destruction.[2]

Avalokiteśvara is not only a helper full of loving kindness, but he is also a cosmic being, out of whose body all the gods have come forth. "The sun and the moon came forth from his eyes, Maheśvara from his brow, Brahman and other gods from his shoulders, Nārāyaṇa from his heart, Sarasvatī from his two corner teeth, the winds from his mouth, the earth from his feet, Varuṇa from his stomach" (p. 14 f.). We see him as a genuine Bodhisattva, however, when his excellent qualities are praised: "Hear, O sons of a noble race! The Bodhisattva Avalokiteśvara, the Great Being, is a lamp for the blind, a sun-shade for those who are scorched by the great heat of the sun, a river for

---

[1]) *Cf.* E.B. *Cowell*, Journal of Philology VI, 1876, p. 222 ff. (reprinted also in Ind. Ant. VIII. 249 ff.); L. *Scherman*. Visionsliteratur, p. 62 ff. *Cowell* compares the apocryphal gospel of Nicodemus, and derives the Indian legend from the Christian one. My own opinion is that the points of agreement are not sufficiently great to warrant the likelihood of any historical connection. Similarly *Garbe*, Indien und das Christentum, p. 77 f. Avalokiteśvara's visit to hell is the prototype of the legend of King Vipaścit in the Mārkaṇḍeya-Purāṇa, see above Vol. I, 562 ff., and J. *Charpentier*, Paccekabuddhageschichten I, 118. The beautiful poem by the Austrian poetess Betty *Paoli*. "Der gute König in der Hölle" (Gedichte, Auswahl und Nachlass, Stuttgart 1895, 217 ff.) is based upon the Buddhist legend.

[2]) *Cf.* Jātaka No. 196, where the winged horse is identified with the Buddha of a former birth. In the Kāraṇḍa-Vyūha the merchant Siṁhala, cast adrift to Ceylon, is the Buddha Śākyamuni in a former birth.

those who are dying of thirst; he gives safety to those who are in fear of dangers, he is a physician to those who are tormented by sickness, he is a father and a mother to the unfortunate, he points the way to Nirvāṇa to those who have descended into hell. This is the nature of the qualities of this Exalted One. Fortunate are those beings in the world, who are mindful of his name. They escape from all suffering of Saṃsāra (from the first) to the last. Those people are very wise, who always honour Avalokiteśvara with gifts of flowers and incense" (p. 48 f.).

The major portion of Section II of the prose version of the Kāraṇḍa-Vyūha is after the style of the Tantras, and is devoted to the glorification of the "knowledge of the six syllables," *i.e.*, the protecting and benedictory prayer formula "Om maṇipadme hum." This famous prayer, which even at the present day is on every one's lips in Tibet, and which is written on all praying wheels and praying banners, is praised in the most extravagant manner in this work. We read:

"This great knowledge of the six syllables is the profound secret of Avalokiteśvara, and he who knows the profound secret, knows release (p. 67).

"Whoever will give me the great knowledge of the six syllables" says a Bodhisattva, "to that man I will willingly give the four continents, filled with the seven kinds of precious stones. O Lord, if there be no birch bark on which to write it down, no ink, and no quill, let him use my blood as ink, let him strip off my skin and use it instead of the birch bark, let him split my bones and make a quill of them. O Lord, this would not hurt my body. He will be a father and a mother to me, the teacher above all teachers (p. 69).

"O noble youth, I can count every single grain of sand in the four oceans, but it is not possible for me to count up the sum of merit which one acquires by a single recitation of the great knowledge of the six syllables" (p. 70).[1]

[1]) Cf. *La Vallée Poussin* in ERE II, 259; H. *Zimmer*, Kunst-form und Yoga im indischen Kultbild, Berlin, 1926, 167 ff. Om maṇipadme hum is probably a mode of addressing Maṇipadmā, the female counterpart of Avalokiteśvara; s. F. W, *Thomas* in JRAS 1906, 464, and *Eliot*, Hinduism and Buddhism, III, 396 f.

The Bodhisattva Avalokiteśvara is very closely related to the Buddha Amitābha, who is glorified in the Sukhāvatī-Vyūhas, "Detailed Descriptions of the Blessed Land," in much the same manner as Śākyamuni in the Saddharma-Puṇḍarīka and Avalokiteśvara in the Kāraṇḍa-Vyūha. Two works have come down to us in Sanskrit, one of considerable length and the other much shorter; both are entitled Sukhāvatī-Vyūha,[1] and diverge widely from each other, though both of them describe the "blessed land" of the Buddha Amitābha or Amitāyus.[2] Not only the introduction to the shorter text, but certain traits in the description of Sukhāvatī are different, and there is also an essential difference in their tendency. The longer Sukhāvatī-Vyūha teaches that those who have accumulated a large pile of good works, who direct their thoughts to enlightenment and think of Amitābha in the hour of death, go to the "blessed land," although those who merely direct their thoughts to Amitābha and his Buddha-land, may possibly also reach Sukhāvatī. On the other hand, the shorter text teaches that the "blessed land" is not the reward for good works, but that anyone who merely hears the name of Amitāyus and thinks of it in the hour of death, will be born in this Buddha-land. There seems to me to be no doubt that the longer text is the earlier one.

In the longer Sukhāvatī-Vyūha, Śākyamuni appears in Rājagṛha on the Gṛdhrakūṭa hill, surrounded by thousands of monks, disciples and Bodhisattvas. In conversation with Ānanda, he enumerates 81 Buddhas

[1] Both texts have been published by Max *Müller* and Bunyiu *Nanjio* (Anecdota Oxoniensia, Aryan Series, Vol. I, Part II, Oxford, 1883) and translated by Max *Müller* in SBE, Vol. 49, Part II. The shorter Sukhāvatī-Vyūha has been translated into French from Kumārajīva's Chinese version, by *Ymaizoumi* and *Yamata* in AMG II, 39 ff.

[2] On Amitābha, cf. *La Vallée Poussin* in ERE I. 98 f.; *Grünwedel*, Buddhistische Kunst in Indien, p. 169 f.; and Alice *Getty*, The Gods of Northern Buddhism, Oxford, 1914, p. 36 ff.

of the past. The last of these, named Lokeśvararāja, instructs the monk Dharmākara regarding the perfections of the Buddha-lands. It is this Dharmākara who, by prayers (praṇidhāna) in a former life, and by faithfully practising the virtues of a Bodhisattva through countless aeons, was re-born in the Sukhāvatī world in the West as Buddha Amitābha. There he radiates immeasurable light (hence his name Amitābha) and his span of life is immeasurable (hence his other name Amitāyus). In his "Buddha-land," the Sukhāvatī paradise, there is neither hell nor animal birth, nor Pretas, nor Asuras. This blessed land is filled with infinitely sweet scent. Jewel trees in many hundreds of thousands of colours grow there, also wonderful lotus blossoms. There are no hills there, the country is as flat as an open hand. Delightful rivers yield pleasant, sweet water, and the rippling of the water is the most glorious music. The beings who are born in Sukhāvatī are all endowed with the most beautiful qualities, physical and mental, and enjoy all imaginable pleasures. There is no difference between men and gods. There is no question of day and night. There is no darkness. Here Amitābha is continually praised. And whoever thinks of this Buddha with awe, whoever pays heed to the increase of his good deeds, whoever directs his thoughts to enlightenment, whoever prays reverently to be re-born in that world, to him Amitābha appears in the hour of his death, and he is born again in the blessed land. Indeed, even those who only think of Amitābha with one thought, are "born" there. The beings in Sukhāvatī are not, however, born of woman : they appear seated on lotus blossoms if they have firmly believed in Amitābha, or resting in the cups of lotus blossoms if their faith had not been quite firm. The beings in that blessed world live in happiness and calm, in perfect wisdom and sinlessness.

In the Sukhāvatī-Vyūha the splendour of Amitābha and his paradise are described with the same verbal extravagance and the same numerical immoderation as we find in all the Mahāyāna-Sūtras.

Of the twelve Chinese translations of the longer Sukhāvatī-Vyūha which are said to have existed, five have come down to us in the Chinese Tripiṭaka, the earliest of which was made between 147 and 186 A.D. The shorter Sukhāvatī-Vyūha was translated into Chinese three times, by Kumārajīva (402 A.D.), by Guṇabhadra (420-479) A.D. and by

Hsüan-Tsang (about 650 A.D.).[1] A third work, the Amitāyur-dhyāna-Sūtra,[2] which has come down only in the Chinese translation, deals less with the description of the blessed land, but devotes more space to the recommendation of meditations (dhyāna) on Amitāyus, by means of which one may reach that land. The loss of the Sanskrit original of this text is all the more regrettable, because it contains an interesting introduction, in which the story of Ajātaśatru and Bimbisāra is told, a story with which the Pāli accounts are also familiar.[3] For centuries, the three works on Amitāyus and Sukhāvatī have formed the basis of the faith of the majority of Buddhists in China and Japan, who found consolation and comfort in the belief in "Amida," as Amitāyus is called in Japan, and in the hope of the blessed land. This is especially true of the numerous adherents of the two Japanese sects Jodo-shu and Shin-shu.[4]

Just as the Sukhāvatī-Vyūha describes the blessed land of Amitābha, the Akṣobhya-Vyūha gives an account of the land of Buddha Akṣobhya,[5] and in the same way the Karuṇā-

[1]) Most of the Chinese translations bear titles, to which "Amitāyus-Sūtra" or "Amita-āyuṣa-vyūha" would correspond in the Sanskrit. *Cf.* Sukhāvatī-Vyūha ed. Anecdota Oxoniensia, p. iv ff. ; B. *Nanjio*, Catalogue, Nos. 23 (5), 25-27, 199, 200, 863 ; *Forke*, Kat. des Pekinger Tripiṭaka, Nos. 42, 429 f., 562, 635, 639 and p. 179 ; and *Bagchi* I, 24, 76 f., 192, 287. In the Tibetan Kanjur the title Amitābha-vyūha appears as well as Sukhāvatī-vyūha, s. *Csoma de Körös* in AMG II, 214, 243, 245.

[2]) Translated from Chinese by J. *Takakusu* in SBE, Vol. 49, part 2 p. 159 ff, Cf. *Saunders*, Epochs of Buddhist History, p. 85 ff.

[3]) Cf. *Kern*, Der Buddhismus, I, 243 ff. ; Spence *Hardy*, Manual of Buddhism, 1860, p. 317 f.

[4]) B. *Nanjio*, Twelve Japanese Buddhist Sects, pp. 104 ff., 122 ff. and Anecdota Oxoniensia, Vol. I, Part II, p. XVIII ff. See also H. *Haas*, "Amida Buddha unsere Zuflucht", Urkunden zum Verständnis des japanischen Sukhāvatī-Buddhismus, Leipzig, 1910, and *Saunders*, l.c., 176 ff.

[5]) This Sūtra has only come down in the Chinese translations by Lokakṣema (178-188) and Bodhiruci (693-713) and in the Tibetan Kanjur, and is counted as a part of the Ratnakūṭa ; s. *Nanjio* No. 28 ; *Bagchi* I, 43 ; Csoma de *Körös*, AMG II, 214. The same Ratnakūṭa also contains, a Mañjuśrī-Buddhakṣetra-guṇa-Vyūha, "Description of the qualities of the Mañjuśrī Buddha-land," which is lost in the Sanskrit ; s. *Forke*, Pekinger Tripiṭaka, p. 181 ; *Körös*, AMG II, 215. On Mañjuśrī s. *La Vallée Poussin* in ERE VIII, 405 f.

Puṇḍarīka, "the Lotus of Mercy,"[1] gives an account of the wonderland Padma of Buddha Padmottara, whose life lasted for thirty ages of the world. The Sūtra, which also contains legends after the style of the Avadānas, was translated into Chinese twice between 385 and 433 A.D. and once again in 558 A.D.[2]

Whilst the Mahāyāna-Sūtras which have so far been mentioned, are devoted mainly to the glorification of the Buddhas and Bodhisattvas, there is a series of other Sūtras which are rather in the nature of philosophical treatises. The earliest of these Sūtras, those which are regarded with the greatest reverence, and which are of the greatest importance from the point of view of the history of religion, are the Prajñā-Pāramitās, "the (Mahāyāna-Sūtras of the) Wisdom-Perfection."[3] They treat of the six "perfections" (Pāramitās)[4] of a Bodhisattva, but especially of Prajñā-Pāramitā, the highest perfection, called "wisdom." This wisdom consists of the knowledge of Śūnyatā, "emptiness,"[5] *i.e.*, the unsubstantiality of all phenomena, implying the conviction that all Dharmas or objects of thought, are only endowed with a conditional or relative existence.

---

[1]) Rāj. *Mitra*, Nep. Buddh. Lit., p. 285 ff.; *Bendall*, Catalogue, p. 73. The text published by the Buddhist Text Society, Calcutta, 1898, is unfortunately not accessible to me. A legend of the Karuṇā-Puṇḍarīka in the Tokharian (Kuchean) language, has been discovered and published by S. *Lévi* (Festschrift Vilhelm Thomsen, Leipzig, 1912, p. 155ff.).

[2]) *Nanjio* No. 142; *Bagchi*, I, 217 f., 239, 271. The introduction to the Tibetan version has been translated into French by L. *Feer* (AMG V, 1883, 153 ff.); see also *Körös* AMG II, 239 ff.

[3]) Prajñā-Pāramitā means both the perfection of "wisdom", and the writings treating of it.

[4]) Though in the Mahāyāna, as in the Hīnayāna, there are sometimes ten Pāramitās enumerated, yet more frequently there are only six, namely: charity, moral conduct, patience, energy, meditation and wisdom (Dharma-Saṃgraha 17; see above, p. 152 n. 2).

[5]) See above p. 231 and n. 1. In the Chinese life-story of Kumārajīva, the believer in Śūnya is compared to that foolish person who desires a thread so fine that it cannot be seen, and is not content until the artisan points into the air and says: "Here is the thread." *Cf.* J. *Nobel* in SBA, 1927, 216 f.

There is evidence of the fact that the Prajñā-Pāramitās belong to the earliest Mahāyāna-Sūtras. Firstly, the ancient dialogue form, which is familiar to us from the Pāli Suttas, is still more conspicuous in these than in other Mahāyāna-Sūtras, and secondly, Buddha (called Bhagavān, "the Lord") generally appears in conversation with one of his disciples, especially Subhūti.[1] In other Mahāyāna-Sūtras Buddha usually talks to a Bodhisattva. A Prajñā-Pāramitā was already translated into Chinese as early as 179 A.D. The Prajñā-Pāramitās appear to have originated in the South, and afterwards spread to the East and the North.[2]

According to a Nepalese tradition, there was first of all a Prajñā-Pāramitā-Mahāyāna-Sūtra of 125,000 "Ślokas,"[3] and this is supposed to have been abridged successively to similar Mahāyāna-Sūtras of 100,000, 25,000, 10,000 and 8,000 "Ślokas" respectively. According to another tradition, however, the Sūtra of 8,000 "Ślokas" is the original one, and was gradually enlarged more and more.[4] The latter tradition appears to be the likelier one. At any rate, a considerable number of Prajñā-Pāramitā texts of all lengths were already in existence in India, and their number increased even more in China and Tibet. Hsüan-Tsang translated 12 different Prajñā-Pāramitā-Sūtras in his Mahā-Prajñā-Pāramitā-Sūtra: the longest is that of 100,000 "Ślokas," and the shortest that of 150. In the Chinese Tripiṭaka, the first large

[1]) On Subhūti in the Mahāyāna and in Pāli literature, see M. *Walleser*, Die Streitlosigkeit des Subhūti, Heidelberg (Akad.) 1917.

[2]) We are justified in drawing this conclusion, from the prophecy which Buddha is made to utter (Aṣṭasāhasrikā p. 225 f.): "These Sūtrāntas, in which six Pāramitās are taught, will be current in the South after the passing away of the Tathāgata, from the South they will go to the East again, and from the East again to the North." *Cf. Anesaki* in ERE IV, 838 (where "west," instead of "east," is an error).

[3]) The Prajñā-Pāramitās are prose works, but it is customary in India to give the size of prose texts too, by "Ślokas," *i.e.*, units of 32 syllables.

[4]) *Cf.* Rajendralāla *Mitra*, Aṣṭasāhasrikā Ed., p. IV *f.*; *Burnouf*, Introduction, p. 414; Haraprasāda, Report I, 19 *f.* and Ind. Hist. Qu. 1, 1925, 211 *ff.*

section is made up of the Prajñā-Pāramitās.[1] In the Tibetan Kanjur, in which the Prajñā-Pāramitā texts constitute the Śer-phyin section in 21 books, there are translations of the Prajñā-Pāramitās of 100,000, 25,000, 18,000, 10,000, 8,000, 800, 700 and 500 "Ślokas," of the Vajracchedikā (with 300 "Ślokas") right down to an Alpākṣarā or Svalpākṣarā Prajñā-Pāramitā, "Prajñā-Pāramitā of (very) few syllables", and even a Bhagavatī-Prajñā-Pāramitā-sarva-Tathāgata-māta Ekākṣarī, "the sacred Prajñā-Pāramitā of One Syllable, of the mother of all Tathāgatas", in which the perfection of wisdom is concentrated in the one sound "a."[2] The following have come down to us in Sanskrit: Prajñā-Pāramitās of 100,000 "Ślokas" (Śatasāhasrikā),[3] of 25,000 (Pañcaviṃśatisāhasrikā),[4] of 8,000 (Aṣṭasāhasrikā),[5] of 2,500 (Sārdhadvisāhas-

[1]) The Daśasāhasrikā Pr. ("Pr. of 10,000") was translated into Chinese for the first time in 179 A.D., and then repeatedly till the 10th century; s. *Nanjio*, Nos. 5-8, 927; *Bagchi* I, pp. 40, 156, 186 f., 289. There are three translations of the Pañcaviṃśati-Sāhasrikā Pr. ("Pr. of 25,000"), (286, 291 and 404 A.D.), s. *Nanjio*, Nos. 2-4; *Bagchi* I, 86, 185 f. A Saptaśatikā Pr. ("Pr. of 700") was translated between 502 and 557 A.D., s. *Nanjio*, Nos. 21, 22; a Pañcaśatikā Pr. ("Pr. of 500") between 428 and 479; s. *Nanjio*, No. 16; *Bagchi*, I, 404; an Ardhaśatikā Pr. ("Pr. of 150") several times between the 7th and 10th centuries, s. *Nanjio*, Nos. 18, 879, 1033 f. The Vajracchedikā Pr. was translated first by Kumārajīva (405 A.D.) and then often, s. *Nanjio*, Nos. 10-15; *Bagchi* I, 192, 253, 255, 425. For other Prajñā-Pāramitās, s. *Nanjio*, No. 17; *Bagchi* I, 44 ff. Apart from the numerous Chinese translations of Indian texts, there is a still greater number of original Chinese works dealing with the Prajñā-Pāramitās; s. O *Franke* in OZ 4, 1915-16, 207 ff.

[2]) *Cf.* Csoma de *Körös* in Asiatick Researches, Vol. 20 (1836), p. 393 ff. and AMG II, 119 ff. For a bibliography of Chinese and Tibetan translations of Prajñā-Pārmitās, s. *Walleser*, Prajñāpāramitā, p. 15 ff.

[3]) Edited by Pratāpacandra *Ghoṣa* in Bibl. Ind. 1902-1914 (19 fasc.; more did not appear until 1926). *Cf.* Rāj. *Mitra*, Nep. Buddh. Lit. 177 ff.; *Bendall*, Catalogue, pp. 143-148. On Central Asiatic fragments of the Śatasāhasrkā Pr. in Chinese and Khotanese, s. *Hoernle*, *E. Chavannes* and S. *Lévi* in Hoernle, Ms. Remains I, 387 ff. Fragments of a Prajñā-P., which corresponds to the Śatasāhasrikā, but appears to be a shorter version, have been published by Pandit B. B. *Bidyabinod*, Fragment of a Prajñāpāramitā Ms. from Central Asia (Memoirs of the Archæological Survey of India, No. 32), 1927.

[4]) Rāj. *Mitra*, l.c. 193 f.; *Bendall*, l.c. 144 f.; Haraprasāda *Śāstrī*, Descriptive Catalogue of Sanskrit MSS. in the ...Asiatic Society of Bengal, I, p. 10 f.

[5]) Edited by Rājendralāla *Mitra* in Bibl. Ind. 1888; Chapt. XVIII translated by Haraprasāda *Śāstrī* in J.B.T.S. II, 1894; Extracts translated into German by Max *Walleser*

rikā),[1] of 700 (Saptaśatikā),[2] the Vajracchedikā Prajñā-Pāramitā, "the diamond cutter Prajñā-Pāramitā," *i.e.*, the Prajñā-Pāramitā,[3] cutting as sharp as a diamond and also the Alpākṣarā Prajñā-Pāramitā[4] and Prajñā-Pāramitāhṛdaya-Sūtras,[5] which are only used as protecting magic formulas (Dhāraṇīs).

In all probability the earliest of these writings is the Aṣṭasāhasrikā-Prajñā-Pāramitā, which was, on the one hand, expanded into the larger works, and the contents of which were, on the other hand, condensed in the shorter texts.[6]

Prajñāpāramitā, die Vollkommenheit der Erkenntnis, nach indischen, tibetischen, und chinesischen Quellen, Quellen der Religionsgeschichte, Göttingen 1914. In the Śikṣā-Samuccaya there are quotations from the Aṣṭasāhasrī Pr., as well as from a Mahatī Pr., an Ārya-Pr. and a Bhagavatī Pr.; s. *Bendall*, Śikṣāsamuccaya Ed., p. 369 and JRAS 1898 870 ff.

¹) *Bendall*, Catalogue, p. 123 f.

²) *Bendall*, l.c., p. 5 f.

³) Edited by F. Max *Müller* in Buddhist Texts from Japan, Anecdota Oxoniensia, Aryan Series, I, 1, 1881, and translated by the same scholar in SBE Vol. 49, part II, pp. 109-144; translated into French by C. de *Harlez* in JA 1891, s. 8, t. XVIII, 440 ff.; into German by *Walleser* l.c. pp. 140-158. Complete MSS. of the Sanskrit and of the Khotanese versions were discovered by Sir Aurel *Stein* in Eastern Turkestan, and the Sanskrit version has been edited and translated by J. E. *Pargiter*, the Khotanese version by Sten *Konow* (in Hoernle, MS. Remains I, pp. 176-195, and 214-288). The first fragments have been published, together with an Adhyardhaśatikā-Pr. (in a Sanskrit recension interspersed with Khotanese sections), by E, *Leumann* (Zur nordarischen Sprache und Litteratur, 56 ff., 84 ff.). The Tibetan version has been edited and translated into German by T. Y. *Schmidt* in Mémoires de l' Acad. de St. Pétersbourg t. IV, 1837. C. de *Harlez* has published and translated the Manchu version in WZKM 11, 1897, 209, ff., 331 ff.

⁴) Haraprasāda *Śāstrī*, Descriptive Catalogue of Sanskrit MSS...in the Asiatic Society of Bengal, I No. 16; Chinese translation, s. *Nanjio*, No. 797; Tibetan translation in the Kanjur, s. *Körös*, AMG II, 202.

⁵) Edited by F. Max *Müller* and B. *Nanjio* in Anecdota Oxoniensia, Aryan Series, Vol. I, Part III, 1884, and translated by Max *Müller* in SBE Vol. 49, Part II, p. 145 ff.; also by Shaku *Hannya* in EB II, 1922, 163 ff. Translated from the Tibetan by L. *Feer* in in AMG V, 176 ff. See below in the section on the Dhāraṇīs.

⁶) In the Abhisamayālaṃkāra-Kārikās it is said that the Aṣṭasāhasrikā was remodelled into the Pañcaviṃśati-sāhasrikā; s. Haraprasāda *Śāstrī*, Descriptive Cat. of Sansk. MSS. in the ...... As. Soc. of Bengal, I, p. 7 and Ind. Hist. Qu. I, 1925, 212. The Chinese translation of the Daśasāhasrikā is said to differ but little from the Aṣṭasāhasrikā, s. Haraprasāda *Śāstrī*, Descriptive Cat. p. 3; Ind. Hist. Qu. l.c.; *Walleser*, Prajñāpāramitā, p. 18.

The Aṣṭasāhasrikā contains in 32 chapters dialogues between Buddha and his disciples Subhūti, Śāriputra and Pūrṇa Maitrāyaṇīputra, and frequently Śakra, the prince of the gods, and sometimes a Bodhisattva joins them. The work begins with introductory verses, in which the Prajñā-Pāramitā, the perfection of wisdom, is personified and praised as "the sublime producer and the beloved mother of all heroes, she whose mind is fixed firmly on the highest goal", "as the kind grandmother of all beings" etc.[1] In the very first chapter we have an example of the dialectics which remind us of the Greek sophists, and which are characteristic of the Prajñā-Pāramitās. We read (pp. 4-6):

Then through the power of Buddha, the venerable Subhūti spoke thus to the Lord: "Now as to what you have said, O Lord: 'May it become clear to you, Subhūti, with regard to the wisdom-perfection of the Bodhisattvas, of the Great Beings,[2] how the Bodhisattvas, the Great Beings, are able to advance until they attain to wisdom-perfection'—when there is constantly mention of 'Bodhisattva, Bodhisattva', to what manner of object (dharma), Lord, does the term 'Bodhisattva' correspond? I do not see any object, Lord, which might be called 'Bodhisattva'. Neither do I see that object which is called 'wisdom-perfection.' Therefore, Lord, as I cannot find, perceive or see either a Bodhisattva or a Bodhisattva-object, and moreover, as I cannot find, perceive or see the wisdom-perfection,—what manner of Bodhisattva am I to teach, instruct, and in what manner of wisdom-perfection? Is it not, O Lord, perhaps precisely when his power of thought does not sink down, does not melt away, is not exhausted, does not become weak, when his mind does not lose all stability, does not entirely break down, when it does not take fright, does not tremble, does not grow fearful, on hearing such sermons and on receiving such doctrine and instruction, that he is a Bodhisattva who is fit to be instructed in wisdom-perfection? It is precisely this which is to be understood by the wisdom-perfection of a Bodhisattva, a Great Being. That is the instruction in wisdom-perfection, when he conducts himself thus, and his teaching, his instruction consists of this. Furthermore, O Lord, a Bodhisattva, a Great Being, who walks in the wisdom-perfection, who lives and has his being in the wisdom-perfection, must be trained in such a way that, as a result of

[1]) S. *Lévi*, L'Inde et le monde, Paris, 1928, p. 46, compares the Gnosis of the Gnostics, to this personified Perfection of Wisdom. We also think of the personification of Pistis Sophia. I am doubtful, however, whether these are more than coincidences.

[2]) Mahāsattva, "the Great Being," usual epithet of the Bodhisattva.

this training, he should not think anything by this thought which is fixed on enlightenment. And why is this so? Because it is so, that the thought is a non-thought, that the nature of the thought is shining in purity (*i.e.*, free from all contamination with non-real phenomena)."

Then the venerable Sāriputra said to the venerable Subhūti: "Venerable Subhūti, does such a thought which is a non-thought exist?"

To these words the venerable Subhūti replied to the venerable Sāriputra in the following words: "But, venerable Sāriputra, in the case of that which is non-thought, is there either a being or a non-being found or perceived?"

Sāriputra said: "No, venerable Subhūti."

Subhūti said: "If it is true, venerable Sāriputra, that neither a being nor a non-being is found or perceived in that which is non-thought, is there any sense in the question when the venerable Sāriputra says: "Does such a thought which is a non-thought exist?"

At these words the venerable Sāriputra addressed the venerable Subhūti in the following manner: "But, venerable Subhūti, what is this non-thinking?"

Subhūti said: "This non-thinking, venerable Sāriputra, is without change, without alternation."

Furthermore we read in the same chapter (p. 20 f.):

The Lord said: "Here, O Subhūti, a Bodhisattva, a Great Being, thinks thus: 'Immeasurable hosts of beings are to be led to complete Nirvāṇa by me, innumerable beings are to be led to complete Nirvāṇa by me.' Now neither those who are to be led to Nirvāṇa, nor those by whom they are to be led, do exist. He leads so many beings to complete Nirvāṇa, and there is no being which has attained to complete Nirvāṇa, and there is no one by whom such a being has been led to complete Nirvāṇa. And why so? That, Subhūti, is precisely the true nature of phenomena;[1] they are based upon deceptive appearances. Now, Subhūti, supposing a skilful magician or magician's apprentice were to conjure up a large crowd of people at a cross road, and after he had conjured up this large crowd of people, he were to cause it to vanish again,—what do you think, Subhūti, would anyone have been struck down, killed, destroyed, or caused to vanish, by anyone?"

[1]) Literally: "The Dharma-hood of the Dharmas."

In Chapter II Subhūti instructs the gods (p. 39 f.):

"O sons of gods, the beings are like an illusion (māyā), O sons of gods, the beings are like a dream. No, illusion and beings are not two different things, and do not form a duality; and dreams and beings are not two different things, and do not form a duality. Furthermore, O sons of gods, all objects of thought are like an illusion, like a dream. He, too, who has just entered the stream, (*i.e.*, the new convert) is like an illusion, like a dream... He, too, who is completely enlightened, is like an illusion, like a dream; the condition, too, of him who is completely enlightened, is like an illusion, like a dream....O sons of gods, even Nirvāṇa itself is like an illusion, like a dream, I say, how much more then every other object of thought."

Then the sons of gods said: "Noble Subhūti, you say that Nirvāṇa is like an illusion, like a dream?"

The venerable Subhūti said.: "Yes, O sons of gods, if there were another, more excellent object of thought than Nirvāṇa, I should still say that it is like an illusion, like a dream. No, O sons of gods, illusion and Nirvāṇa are not diverse, they do not form a duality, and also dreams and Nirvāṇa are not diverse, they do not form a duality."

The entire book continues in this strain. We are assured over and over again, that all phenomena are without being (śūnya), that even Buddhas, Bodhisattvas and the perfection of wisdom itself have no reality; but, at the same time, the Bodhisattva ideal is extolled time and again, as for instance in the beautiful words (p. 321 f.) which the Lord is made to say:

"O Subhūti, a Bodhisattva, a Great Being, who desires to advance to unsurpassable complete enlightenment, must behave alike towards all beings, must cultivate the same mind towards all beings; he must support the other beings with an impartial mind; he must support the others with thoughts of love, with kindly..., with friendly thought..., with thought which is free from pride..., he must support the others with thought which is not hostile, free from thoughts of harm..., he must support the others with thoughts free from injury. He must transfer to all beings the idea of the mother; he must support all beings, transferring to them the idea of the father, the idea of the son, the idea of the daughter (*i. e.*, he must look upon them, as if they were his mothers, his fathers, his sons, his daughters). In this way, therefore, Subhūti, a Bodhisattva, a Great Being, who desires to advance to unsurpassable complete enlightenment, must behave towards all beings : in this way he must train himself in being a protector of all beings. And he himself must be steadfast in suppressing all evil, he must give alms, observe the moral law, train himself in patience, he must show himself energetic, must devote himself to meditation and achieve the victory in wisdom, he must contemplate the formula of the causally conditioned origination both in regular and in inverted order, he must teach it to others, extol it in their presence, and enable them to take delight in it. "

While in reading the numerous long epistemological and metaphysical discussions on Śūnyatā, we often wonder what all this has to do with religion, such passages about the Bodhisattva as the above, remind us of the fact that the text before us is, after all, a religious book. This religious character of the book is emphasized also in several chapters, in which the great merit to be acquired by the hearing and understanding, the reading and writing, and the learning and teaching of the Prajñā-Pāramitā, is praised over and over again in extravagant fashion.[1]

As it was considered so great a religious merit to read and write these sacred books, it need not surprise us greatly that, as a result of endless repititions and phantastic embellishments of the scenes which introduced the speeches, more and more new works of this type, each one more voluminous than the last, came into existence.

[1]) In the Vajracchedikā, Chapt. 13, Buddha is made to say words to the effect that he who "selects merely one four-footed verse here from this sermon (the Vajr. contains 2 Gāthās in Chapt., 26 and one Gāthā in the last chapter), and explains it to others," acquires greater religious merit than a person who might sacrifice his life day by day for aeons, *cf. Walleser*, Prajñāpāramitā, p. 146 f., 149 ff. In the fragment of the Adhyardhaśatikā Pr. from Khotan (*Leumann*, Zur nordarischen Sprache und Litteratur, p. 89) it is even said that he who "even while still in the womb" hears this section of the Pr., is freed from all attacks and dangers, and never goes to hell or is reborn in any other evil form of existence.

Whilst the Aṣṭasāhasrikā relates in a few sentences that Buddha sojourned in Rājagṛha on the Gṛdhrakūṭa hill, surrounded by a host of monks, who were all arhats, the Satasāhasrikā-Prajñā-Pāramitā begins with a grandiose description of the scene on the Gṛdhrakūṭa hill :

The Lord is seated with his body erect and his legs crossed, ready for meditation, and becomes absorbed in that meditation which is called "King of all meditations," in which all absorptions are included. And after he had arisen, mindful and with a clear consciousness, from this absorption, he glanced over this Buddha-land with his heavenly eyes, and while so doing, he let a radiant light shine forth from the whole of his body and from every pore in his skin, and this radiant light illumined all the continents brilliantly. And all beings by whom this radiance was seen, became clear-sighted through it, and they were all confirmed in the unsurpassable complete enlightenment. Then the Lord thrust forth his tongue through the opening of his mouth, and produced a smile, and many hundreds of thousands of millions of milliards of rays of light emanated from his tongue. On each ray there arose lotuses of jewels, shimmering like gold, with a thousand petals, brightly hued, and beautiful to look upon, sweet, golden, with a pleasant scent, delicate and soft as Kācilindika.[1] And upon these lotuses sat the embodied Tathāgatas and preached the doctrine of the six perfections. But all beings by whom this doctrine was heard, were confirmed in the unsurpassable complete enlightenment. He again became absorbed in the Buddha-meditation which is called "lion's play." In this moment, hell, animal birth, and all evil forms of existence, were suspended in all the innumerable continents. All human beings and gods remembered their former births, approached the Lord and did homage to him. And at the same moment, those who had been born blind, in all the innumerable continents, recovered their sight, the deaf recovered their hearing, the insane had their sanity restored to them, etc.

All this is not stated in such short sentences, but is related with an endless mass of detail. We have already met with the peculiarity of the continual repetitions in the Pāli Suttas.

---

1) According to Mahā-Vyutpatti, 262, 39, a kind of garment.

This characteristic is exaggerated to such a degree in the longer Prajñā-Pāramitās, that it would be quite possible to write down more than one half of a gigantic work like the Śatasāhasrikā-Prajnā-Pāramitā from memory, as the same sentences and expressions constantly recur literally. For instance, in the introduction it is not only said that rays of light shine forth from the whole body of Buddha, and shed an infinite radiance of light over the whole world, but it is said of the toes, the ankles, and every limb and every little part of the body, that rays of light shine forth from them, and shed an infinite radiance of light over the eastern part of the world, the western part of the world, and so on— and the whole set of phrases is repeated for each part of the world, in the same words. In the same way, the writer is not content to say merely: "All is only name," but this "all" is amplified in minute detail, in never-ending series of sentences, until the whole of creation is completely exhausted. We can well comprehend people's holding the view that the world is not real and that everything is empty and vain, and that nothing can be expressed in words, and that "no" is the only possible reply to all questions:— but we would really regard it as an impossibility for book upon book, and for thousands of pages to be written from the standpoint of such a categorical negation of anything and everything: and yet, in the Prajñā-Pāramitās, the impossibility has become a reality. Our sole explanation of this verbosity for the sake of verbosity, is that these monks wrote so much, because it was regarded as a religious merit to write and read as much as possible of these sacred texts.[1] The substance of their writing did not matter. The actual doctrine is the same in the "Hundred-thousand Prajñā-Pāramitā"

---

[1] The same principle of repetition also appears in art, when entire rocks and caves are covered all over with pictures of Buddha. *Cf.* Grünwedel, Buddhist. Kunst in Indien, pp. 172, 182.

as in the Vajracchedikā-Prajñā-Pāramitā, a little work of but a few pages, in which the content of these texts appears in its most condensed form. In this work, too, we come across the same paradoxes as in the Aṣṭasāhasrikā-Prajñā-Pāramitā and the longer Prajñā-Pāramitās. Thus, for instance, we also read in the Vajracchedikā (Chapt. 13):

"The perfection of wisdom which has been proclaimed by Buddha, the same has been proclaimed by Buddha as a non-perfection also. What do you think, Subhūti, is there any doctrine (Dharma) which has been proclaimed by Buddha?" Subhūti said: "No, Lord, there is no doctrine which has been proclaimed by Buddha..." The Lord said: "What do you think, Subhūti, can Buddha, the saint, the completely enlightened one, be recognised by the thirty-two characteristics of a great man?" Subhūti said: "No, Lord, Buddha, the saint, the completely enlightened one, cannot be recognised by the thirty-two characteristics of a great man. And why not? Because the thirty-two characteristics of a great man, which have been proclaimed by Buddha, were proclaimed by Buddha as non-characteristics. Therefore they are called the thirty-two characteristics of a great man."

There are probably just as many (non-Buddhist) readers who will see a profound meaning in such utterances, as there are those who will regard them as pure nonsense.[1] In reality, they are probably neither the one nor the other, but views which frequently crop up in the history of philosophy, and which only become intelligible if we distinguish between

[1]) Among the latter is probably *Barth*, who says (RHR, t. 6, 1882, p. 117 Oeuvres I, 326) that in our text the Prajñāpāramitā is glorified, "transcendental wisdom, which knows that things are neither existent nor non-existent, that there is no reality which is not also a non-reality, wisdom which has been proclaimed and will be proclaimed by an infinity of myriads of Arhats and Bodhisattvas who have been and have not been, who will be and will not be; who, thanks to their knowledge of Buddha, and their view of Buddha, are perceived, apperceived, known of Buddha, who himself is neither existent nor non-existent." On the doctrines of the Prajñāpāramitās, *cf. Burnouf*, Introduction, pp. 111, 390, 404 ff., 412 ff., 430; W. *Wassiljew*, Der Buddhismus, p. 157 ff. and M. *Anesaki*, ERE IV, p. 837f.

a higher, transcendental, and a lower, empirical truth, as expressly taught by the Mahāyāna philosopher Nāgārjuna.

The great philosophers of the Mahāyāna, Nāgārjuna, Vasubandhu and Asaṅga, wrote bulky commentaries on the Prajñā-Pāramitās, which have, however, only come down to us in the Chinese Tripiṭaka and in the Tibetan Tanjur. Nevertheless it is very difficult for us to imagine that the immense sanctity which is attributed to these texts, can really be due to a valuation and an understanding of the metaphysical doctrines which they propound. It is more probable that it is precisely the dark and incomprehensible element in the doctrines taught by these texts, which has contributed to make them sacred. *Omne obscurum pro magnifico.*[1]

In the Buddhist dictionary Mahā-Vyutpatti (65, 4), a work called Buddhāvataṃsaka[2] is mentioned in a list of Mahāyāna-Sūtras, immediately after the Śatasāhasrikā, Pañcaviṃśatisāhasrikā and the Aṣṭasāhasrikā-Prajñā-Pāramitās. Both in the Chinese Tripiṭaka (Section IV, Hua-yen) and the Tibetan Kanjur,[3] there is a large body of writings entitled thus. It is the sacred scripture of the Avataṃsaka school which arose in China between 557 and 589 A.D., and of the Japanese Kegon sect.[4] According to Chinese sources, there

---

[1]) According to the Ādikarma-Pradīpa (s. *La Vallée Poussin*, Bouddhisme, E'tudes et Matériaux, Mémoires Ac. Belgique, 1897, p. 227), the reading and Sun-wise circumambulation of the Prajñāpāramitās and similar books are part of the Buddhist cult. Fa-hien, who visited India in the year 399 A.D., already mentions that the Prajñāpāramitās were an object of divine worship at his time; s. S. *Beal*, Si-yu-ki Buddhist Records of the Western World I, p. xxxix. In the Nepalese chronicle Vaṃśāvalī it is related, that during the reign of King Saṅkaradeva (12th century) on the occasion of a fire in a village, a widow fled to Patna, taking nothing with her except a small model of a Caitya, a manuscript of the Prajñāpāramitā, which is said to have been written in the year 188 A.D. in golden letters, and her little son; s. *Bendall* in OC Berlin, 1881, II, 190.

[2]) The title means: "Buddha Ornament; avataṃsaka is given as a synonym of alaṃkāra, in Mahā-Vyutpatti, 237, 48.

[3]) Section III, s. Csoma de *Kőrös*, AMG II, 208 ff.

[4]) *Cf.* B. *Nanjio*, Twelve Japanese Buddhist Sects, p. 57 ff.; *Eliot*, Hinduism and Buddhism, III, 282 f.; Y. *Sōgen*, Systems of Buddhist Thought, 287 ff.

are supposed to have been six different Avataṃsaka-Sūtras, the longest of which contained 100,000 Gāthās and the shortest 36,000. The latter was translated into Chinese in 418 A.D. by Buddhabhadra together with other monks. Śikṣānanda made a translation in 45,000 Gāthās, between 695 and 699 A.D.[1] Though no Avataṃsaka or Buddhāvataṃsaka Sūtra has come down in Sanskrit, there is a Gaṇḍavyūha-Mahāyāna-Sūtra,[2] which corresponds to one of the Chinese translations of the Avataṃsaka.[3] The main contents of the Gaṇḍavyūha are the wanderings of the youth Sudhana, who travels all over India on the advice of the Bodhisattva Mañjuśrī, in order to attain to the highest knowledge essential for enlightenment. He wanders from land to land, seeking instruction from various persons, monks and nuns, lay adherents both male and female, from a merchant, a king, a slave, a boy, also from the goddesses of the night, from Gopā, the wife of Śākyamuni and from Māyā, the mother of Śākyamuni,[4] until, finally, by the favour of Mañjuśrī, he attains to perfect knowledge,

---

[1]) *Cf. Nanjio*, l.c. and Catalogue, Nos. 87-89; *Bagchi* I, 343 f.; *Forke*, Pekinger Tripiṭaka, Nos. 1053, 1054. Isolated sections of the Avataṃsaka were translated into Chinese by Lokakṣema (178-188 A.D.), Dharmarakṣa (291-297 A.D.) and others, s. *Bagchi* I, 42, 89 f., 97, 220, 237, 286, 405; *Forke*, l.c., Nos. 1055-1057, 1059, 1065; for commentaries and explanatory writings on them, s. *Forke*, l.c., Nos. 1058, 1060-1064; Avataṃsaka Sūtra (according to Buddhabhadra's translation) epitomised by Japanese scholars and translated into English by D. T. *Suzuki* in EB I, I ff., 146 ff.

[2]) The text is not yet published. For table of contents, see Rāj. *Mitra*, Nep. Buddh. Lit., p. 90 ff.; *cf. Bendall*, Catalogue, pp. 23, 102; *Burnouf*, Introduction, p. 111; *Wassiljew*, Der Buddhismus, p, 171 ff.

[3]) At my request, my friend Dr. *Takakusu* compared the text of the Gaṇḍavyūha in the India Office with the text of the "Avataṃsaka-Sūtra in 40 chapters" (in Nanjio's Catalogue), and (in a letter of 4th Sept., 1912) he communicated to me the contents of the work, which coincides in the main with the table of contents given by Rāj. *Mitra*. According to D. T. *Suzuki* (EB I, 1 note), the third Chinese translation is "practically the same as the Nepalese Gaṇḍavyūha," whilst Śikṣānanda's translation "*also*" contains the Gaṇḍavyūha and the Daśabhūmaka. According to S. *Lévi* in JA, t. 203, 1923, p. 6 ff., the Gaṇḍavyūha is the last section of the Avataṃsaka. *Cf.* also *Watanabe* in JRAS 1907, 663; *Pelliot* in JA 1914, II, p. 118 ff.; *Eliot*, Hinduism and Buddhism, II, 54 f.; III, 283.

[4]) There is a remarkably large number of women among these teachers.

through the instrumentality of the Bodhisattva Samantabhadra.[1]

The Gaṇḍavyūha is quoted fairly frequently in the Śikṣāsamuccaya, whilst the "Avataṃsaka" is not quoted. For instance, there is a long quotation in Gāthās, in praise of the Bodhisattva who is resolved to become a Buddha, in order to show love and pity towards the beings and release them from suffering, to make hell empty, and to point the way to heaven. Another passage (in prose) treats of the cleansing of the city of the mind (citta-nagara) which a Bodhisattva must always bear in mind. In yet another passage we find Gāthās on the rare and blessed good fortune of seeing and hearing a Buddha.[2]

At the end of the Gaṇḍavyūha, both in manuscripts and in Chinese and Tibetan translations, we find the Bhadracarī-praṇidhāna-gāthāḥ, "the Prayer Verses concerning the Pious Life,"[3] a prayer in 62 melodious Dodhaka stanzas,[4] which ranks among the most beautiful expresssions of Buddhist piety, and has been used for purposes of worship in all countries of Mahāyāna Buddhism ever since the 4th century A.D.[5] It is also found as an independent text, and was

---

[1]) This is according to Rāj. *Mitra's* table of contents. However, in the communication of Dr. *Takakusu* from the India Office MSS. (mentioned above in note 3, p. 325) it is said : "At last he meets Samantabhadra who directs him to the one Buddha Amitābha of the West, from whom the earnest youth learns the highest truth and gets enlightened. In one text this last Amitābha section is omitted."

[2]) Śikṣās. 101 ff., 122 f., 310 f.

[3]) *Cf.* K. *Watanabe*, Die Bhadracarī, eine Probe buddhistisch-religiöser Lyrik untersucht und herausgegeben (mit deutscher Übersetzung von E. *Leumann*), Diss. Strassburg, 1912. According to *Watanabe*, Bhadra is an abbreviation of Samantabhadra, and the title should be translated : "The verses in which the pious wishes that distinguished the religious life of Samantabhadra, find expression." In the Śikṣā-Samuccaya it is quoted with the title Bhadracaryā (Gāthā).

[4]) On this metre (four Pādas of eleven syllables :— – ⏑⏑ – ⏑⏑ – ⏑⏑ – ⏓), so popular with the Mahāyāna Buddhists, s. *Watanabe*, l.c., p. 24 ff.

[5]) *Watanabe*, l.c., p. 10 ff. According to *La Vallée Poussin* in ERE II, 259 note, it belongs to the sacred books of the Sautrāntikas, but in ERE XII, 194, he counts it among the Tantras.

translated into Chinese several times in the 4th and 8th centuries, and into Tibetan in the 9th century. The language is a Prākrit with a strong leaning towards Sanskrit.

The prayer opens with verses in which homage is paid to all Jinas. Then come the pious wishes (praṇidhāna), in which the believer, after having renounced all evil, requests all the Buddhas to allow the wheel of the doctrine to revolve throughout all the aeons, in which he wishes good fortune and blessing for all beings, and prays on his own behalf, that he may ever lead a pious life, direct his thoughts to enlightenment, and that he may one day, as a Buddha, make an end to the sufferings of the world. In particular he implores the Bodhisattvas Samantabhadra and Mañjuśrī, whom he strives to imitate, and in conclusion he expresses the hope that he may at some future time behold Amitābha and attain to the Blessed Land (Sukhāvatī).

The Daśabhūmaka or Daśabhūmika-Sūtra or Daśabhūmīśvara,[1] is also regarded as a portion of the Avataṃsaka, but it is found just as frequently as an independent work. The subject-matter of this work is a discourse on the ten steps (daśabhūmi) by which Buddhahood may be attained. The speaker is the Bodhisattva Vajragarbha, who gives himself up to a deep meditation in a vast assembly of gods, Buddhas and Bodhisattvas, and is then invited by Śākyamuni to explain the "ten steps," while rays of light emanate in all directions from all the Buddhas present. Chapter I also contains Gāthās (in Sanskrit, not

---

[1]) The Sanskrit text has been edited, and the chapter on the seventh Bhūmi translated into English, by Johannes *Rahder*, Diss. Utrecht 1926 (J.-B. Istas, Leuven), Chapter VII also in Acta Or. IV, 214 ff. The text in Sanskrit and Tibetan with a French translation of Chapters I-VI (on the first six Bhūmis) had already previously been edited by *La Vallée Poussin* in Le Muséon 1907, 1910 and 1911, Chapt. VI also in Bouddhisme, Études et Matériaux, Théorie de douze causes (1913), p. 115 ff. *La Vallée Poussin* says (ERE II, 744) that Daśabhūmīśvara is the title of a recension augmented by Prākrit verses. *Rahder* does not make this distinction, but merely remarks that some MSS. have Gāthās in the last chapter. In the colophon in *Rahder's* edition, the title reads: Daśabhūmīśvara Mahāyānasūtraratnarāja. *Cf.* also Rāj. *Mitra*, Nep. Buddh. Lit., p. 81 ff.; *Bendall*, Catalogue, p. 4 f. It is frequently quoted in the Śikṣā-Samuccaya.

in the Gāthā dialect), though the actual treatise on the Bhūmis is entirely in prose. The doctrine of the "ten steps" is to be found in an earlier form in the Mahāvastu, but in the Mahāyāna it is a principal feature,[1] and the Daśabhūmaka is the most important work which treats of this doctrine. It was translated into Chinese in 297 A. D. by Dharmarakṣa.[2]

Like the Avataṃsaka, the R a t n a k ū ṭ a or "Heap of Jewels," also constitutes a large section both of the Chinese Tripiṭaka (II, Pao-chi)[3] and of the Tibetan Kanjur (IV, Kon-ts'egs).[4] In these works it is a collection of 49 Sūtras, including, among others, the long Sukhāvatī-Vyūha, the Akṣobhya-Vyūha, the Mañjuśrī-Buddhakṣetra-Guṇa-Vyūha, and also a Bodhisattva-Piṭaka, a Pitāputrasamāgama, "Meeting of the son (Śākyamuni) with his father (Śuddhodana),"[5] the Kāśyapa-Parivarta, and many Paripṛcchās, "Questions" (with the corresponding answers).

---

[1]) The doctrine of the Bhūmis is also to be found in the Lalita-Vistara, in the Aṣṭasāhasrikā-Prajñāpāramitā XVII ff., in Candrakīrti's Mādhyamakāvatāra and in Maitreyanātha's Mahāyāna-Sūtrālaṃkāra XX, XXI. For a detailed treatment s. T. *Suzuki*, Outlines of Mahāyāna Buddhism, Ch. 12, and especially *La Vallée Poussin* in ERE II, 743 ff.; VIII, 329 f.

[2]) Apart from this, it was translated into Chinese by Kumārajīva (406 A.D.), Bodhiruci (500-516) and Śīladharma (789). Kumārajīva also translated the Daśabhūmikavibhāṣāśāstra, a commentary on the first two Bhūmis, by Nāgārjuna. *Cf. Nanjio*, Nos. 88 f., 105, 110, 1180, 1194; *Bagchi* I, 87, 103, 186, 197 f., 258, 257; K. *Watanabe* in JRAS 1907, 663 f. A *Daśabhūmikleśacchedikā-Sūtra*, which is said to have been translated as early as in the year 70 A.D., has not come down, but the translation by Fo Nien (388-417) is extant, s. *Nanjio*, No. 375; *Bagchi* I, 171 f.; *Rahder*, l.c., pp. iii, viii, 217 f. The work treats of the same subject as the Daśabhūmaka, but is not identical with it.

[3]) Collected by Bodhiruci in 706-713 A.D.; s. *Nanjio*, No. 23, *Forke*, Pekinger Tripiṭaka, p. 179 ff. There is in Chinese also a short Ratnakūṭa-Sūtra, which treats of the Ratnakūṭa-samādhi; s. *Forke*, l.c., No. 846. Many shorter sections of the Ratnakūṭa were translated into Chinese from the 3rd to the 6th century A.D., s *Bagchi* I, pp. 24, 41-43, 96 f., 104 f., 210, 220, 252, 258, 350 f., 391. See also *Wassiljew*, Der Buddhismus, p. 167 ff.

[4]) *Cf.* Csoma de *Kőrös* in AMG II, 212 ff. and Marcelle *Lalou* in JA 1927, Oct.-Dec., p. 233 ff.

[5]) Extracts from it in the Śikṣā-Samuccaya.

We may take it that there was a Ratnakūṭa in Sanskrit too. According to Tāranātha the Ratnakūṭa-Dharma-Paryāya in 1,000 sections, had its origin during the reign of Kaniṣka's son.[1] On the other hand, the various single texts which are mentioned as portions of the Ratnakūṭa in the Chinese and Tibetan works, only occur as independent works in Sanskrit.[2] The Chinese and the Tibetan books agree in giving the K ā ś y a p a - P a r i v a r t a as section 43 of the Ratnakūṭa. Valuable fragments of the Sanskrit original of this work were found in the neighbourhood of Khotan, and have been published by *Baron* A. *von Staël-Holstein.*[3] It appears, moreover, that this Kāśyapa-Parivarta is identical with the original Ratnakūṭa.[4] The work was entitled Kāśyapa-Parivarta, because Kāśyapa the Great, Buddha's disciple, is the principal speaker.

In this work, which is said to have been translated into Chinese as early as between 178 and 184 A.D.,[5] the prose and the verses alternate in such a way that the verse portions

---

[1]) *Eliot*, Hinduism and Buddhism, II, 56 f.

[2]) Maitreyanātha quotes the Ratnakūṭa in his Mahāyāna-Sūtrālaṃkāra XIX, 29. The Ratnakūṭa is mentioned in Mahā-Vyutpatti 65, 39, but the single texts, too, are enumerated as independent works. Similarly, in the Śikṣā-Samuccaya, both the Ratnakūṭa and the works which it comprises, such as the Rāṣṭrapāla-Paripṛcchā, Ugra-Paripṛcchā, Akṣayamati-Paripṛcchā, and others, are cited. When the Śikṣ. quotes the Ugra-Paripṛcchā and the Ratnakūṭā side by side, on pp. 146, 196, or when in Śikṣ., p. 54 f. first the Ratnakūṭa, then the Rāṣṭrapāla-Sūtra, and then again the Ratnakūṭa are quoted, it follows that Śāntideva did not know the Ugra-Paripṛcchā and the Rāṣṭrapāla-Paripṛcchā as parts of the Ratnakūṭa.

[3]) The Kāçyapaparivarta a Mahāyānasūtra of the Ratnakūṭa class edited in the Original Sanskrit, in Tibetan, and in Chinese (The Commercial Press Ltd., Shanghai, 1926).

[4]) *Bendall*, Śikṣāsamuccaya Ed., p. 52 note 1, and *Staël-Holstein*. l.c., p. ff. xiv There is no colophon in the fragments, but the title Mahā-Ratnakūṭa-Dharmaparyāya occurs in a few fragments (pp. 82, 217, 227). However, the title "Kāśyapa-Section" remains unexplained, if the Ratnakūṭa and the Kāśyapa-Parivarta are one and the same work.

[5]) Three other translations were made between 265 and 420 A.D., 350 and 431 A. D., and at the close of the 10th century, s. A. *von Staël Holstein*, l.c., pp. ix f., xxi; *Nanjio*, Nos. 57, 1363; *Bagchi* I, 26 f., 41, 239.

(in Sanskrit with occasional Prākritisms) repeat what has already been said in prose. As far as we can glean from the fragments which have come down, the ideal of the Bodhisattva, and the doctrine of unreality (śūnyatā) are proclaimed again and again in the Kāśyapa-Parivarta in many a parable in the conversations between Buddha and Kāśyapa.

The first 22 fragments are reminiscent of the section of four in the Aṅguttara-Nikāya. Four good and four bad qualities, four good and four bad friends, etc., of a Bodhisattva are enumerated. The first of the four good qualities is a love of truth : "Not even in order to save their lives, do they utter a falsehood" (p. 8). Then come the comparisons (p. 56 ff.). As the vast earth is useful to all living creatures, unchanging and without seeking a reward, so also is the Bodhisattva. "As the element of water, O Kāśyapa, enables all the grasses, shrubs, herbs and trees to grow, even so the Bodhisattva, who is pure of heart, enables all beings to blossom forth, by the manifestation of his love (maitra), and continuing thus, enables all the luminous qualities of all beings to mature" (p. 58). In similar fashion the Bodhisattva is compared to fire, the wind, the moon, the sun, a lion, an elephant, a lotus, etc. There is a series of other similes in explanation of the Śūnyatā. Even as a physician heals the sick man, the Śūnyatā is a remedy for all who are entangled in heresies (p. 97). Then come fresh similes having reference to the Bodhisattva. "O Kāśyapa, just as the new moon is worshipped, and the full moon is not worshipped to the same degree, even so, Kāśyapa, a Bodhisattva should be honoured far more than a Tathāgata, by my followers. And why? Because the Tathāgatas arise from the Bodhisattvas" (p. 129).

Among the numerous Paripṛcchās which are included in the Chinese and the Tibetan Ratnakūṭa,[1] there is also the **Rāṣṭrapāla-Paripṛcchā**, or **Rāṣṭrapāla-Sūtra**.[2] The Sūtra consists of two parts, the first of

---

[1]) *Cf. Nanjio*, Catalogue, p. xiii ff.; *Kārōs* in AMG, II, 564 f.

[2]) Rāṣṭrapālaparipṛcchā, Sūtra du Mahāyāna, publié par L. *Finot.* (Bibliotheca Buddhica II.) St. Pétersbourg 1901. *Cf. La Vallée Poussin*, Le Muséon N. S. IV, 1903, p. 306 ff. This Sūtra has nothing in common with the Raṭṭhapāla-Sutta (see above, p. 48 f.) except the name Rāṣṭrapāla (= Pāli Raṭṭhapāla).

which is more dogmatic and contains Buddha's reply to "Rāṣṭrapāla's question" on the qualities (Dharmas) of a Bodhisattva, while Part II relates the Jātaka of Prince Puṇyaraśmi, whose story has a few features in common with the Buddha legend. Even in Part I, however, Buddha gives a brief account of his actions in former births, by way of elucidating the Bodhisattva-Dharmas, and fifty Jātakas are mentioned. Following abruptly after these Jātakas, is a prophecy of the future decay of the religion,[1] and this is the most interesting part of the Sūtra: for the picture here sketched in a very life-like and accurate manner, must necessarily reflect actual facts, and must contain a satirical description of the lax morals of the Buddhist monks. It says, for instance:

> "My monks will be without shame and without virtue, haughty, puffed up and wrathful...intoxicating themselves with alcoholic drinks. While they bear the banner of the Buddha, they will only be serving the householders...They themselves will have wives, sons and daughters like householders....'You are not to indulge in sensual pleasures, in order that you may not be born again as animals, ghosts or beings of hell,' thus they will preach to the householders, but they themselves will be uncontrolled, and so on."

This prophecy reminds us of similar ones in the Thera-Gāthās (see above, p. 111). The Chinese translation of the Rāṣṭrapāla-Paripṛcchā made between 585 and 592 A. D.,[2] proves that the conditions here described, already existed in the 6th century. The Sūtra is probably not much earlier than the Chinese translation, as is shown by the barbaric language, which particularly in the Gāthās is a mixture of Prākrit and bad Sanskrit, and by the elaborate metres and the careless style.

---

[1]) *Finot*, l.c., p. ix ff., 28 ff.

[2]) *Forke*, Pekinger Tripiṭaka, p. 181; *Nanjio*, No. 23 (18). A second translation was made between 980 and 1000 A.D., s. *Nanjio*, No. 873.

Many of the Paripṛcchās which are counted as belonging to the Ratnakūṭa, are also quoted in the Śikṣā-Samuccaya, thus for instance, the Ugra-Paripṛcchā or Ugradatta-Paripṛcchā, "Questions of (the householder) Ugradatta,"[1] from which, for example, a long passage on the advantages of a forest hermit's life is cited, the Udayana-Vatsarāja-Paripṛcchā, "Questions of the Vatsa king Udayana" (No. 29 in the Ratnakūṭa of the Kanjur), the Upāli-Paripṛcchā, "Upāli's Questions on Discipline,"[2] and others. It is interesting that women are made to ask quite a number of "questions," thus for instance, there is a Candrottarā-Dārikā-Paripṛcchā, "Questions of the Girl Candrottarā" (Śikṣ., p. 78 ff., on the evil consequences of lust), Dārikā-Vimalaśraddhā-Paripṛcchā (No. 40 in the Ratnakūṭa of the Kanjur), Sumati-Dārikā-Paripṛcchā (No. 30 in the Chinese Ratnakūṭa), etc.

Just as the Prajñā-Pāramitās proclaim first and foremost the Śūnyavāda, the doctrine of unreality, the Saddharma-Laṅkāvatāra-Sūtra, "the Revelation of the Good Religion in Laṅkā (Ceylon)," generally called briefly Laṅkāvatāra,[3] teaches principally a modification of the Śūnyavāda, the Vijñānavāda, the "Doctrine of Consciousness," *i.e.*, that doctrine which, though it also denies the reality of the external world, does at the same time recognise that the phenomena of consciousness have a subjective reality.

---

[1]) Translated into Chinese as early as in 181 A.D., and then again in 252 A.D., s. *Bagchi*, I. 47, 104 f.; *Forke*, Pekinger Tripiṭaka, Nos. 283, 1207. Śikṣās. pp. 196 ff., 367.

[2]) Vinaya-viniścaya-Upāli-paripṛcchā in the Kanjur (s. M. *Lalou* in JA 1927, Oct.-Dec., p. 252). Upāli is the expert of the Vinaya, at the council of Rājagṛha (Vinaya-Piṭaka, Culla-Vagga XI, 1, 7).

[3]) Edited by Bunyin *Nanjio*, Kyoto 1923 (Bibliotheca Otaniensis, Vol. I). An analysis of the doctrines contained in the Laṅkāvatāra Sūtra, especially in their relation to the Japanese Zen Buddhism, is given by D. T. *Suzuki* in EB IV, 199-298. *Cf.* G. *Tucci* in RSO X, 1923, 567 ff. and Memorie R. Acc. Lincei, ser. V, Vol. XVII, fasc. V, p. 170 ff.; J. W. *Hauer*, Das Laṅkāvatāra-Sūtra und das Sāṃkhya (Beiträge zur indischen Sprachwissenschaft und Religionsgeschichte 1927); and *Schayer* in ZB 8, 1928, 249 f. In the colophon of Chapt. II, the Sūtra is called Ṣaṭtriṃśatsāhasra, "consisting of 36,000 (Ślokas)."

In the form in which we have it, the work is either a very careless compilation, or else it has suffered very badly in coming down to us; moreover, it consists of portions which belong to various periods. It was translated into Chinese three times, by Guṇabhadra in 443 A.D., by Bodhiruci in 513 and by Śikṣānanda in 700-704.[1] In the first translation Chapters I, IX and X are missing, so that we may be justified in assuming that these three chapters were not written until between 443 and 513 A.D. The last chapter (Sagāthakam) consists entirely of verses, while the rest of the book is in prose with occasional Gāthās interspersed.[2]

Chapter I gives a very detailed description of the meeting of Buddha with Rāvaṇa, the king of the Rākṣasas in Laṅkā. Encouraged by the Bodhisattva Mahāmati, Rāvaṇa asks Buddha questions about the difference between true and false doctrine (Dharma and Adharma). With Chapter II, which has no connection whatsoever with Chapter I, Mahāmati, after he has praised Buddha and obtained permission to ask him questions, begins to ply Buddha with a long series of over one hundred questions: these questions bear on all the details of the doctrine, on release ("Whither does the released one go? Who is bound? By whom is he released?"), on Ālaya,[3] Manovijñāna and other main notions of the Vijñānavāda, on Śūnyatā, enlightenment, etc. But we also find such questions as: "How do food and drink of all kinds come into existence? How does copulation come about? What is the nature of a king, a ruler of the world (Cakravartin), a ruler of a district (Maṇḍalin)?...How is it that you are descended from the Śākya race, through whom and how are you a scion of Ikṣvāku?...Why are you alone seen in all lands?," etc. Buddha does not only deal with these questions and give his assent to them, but adds many

---

[1]) *Nanjio* Edition, Preface, p. viii f.; *Bagchi* I, pp. 254, 380.

[2]) Though Chapts. II-VIII appear in all the three Chinese translations, *Hauer*, l.c., p. 3, doubts whether Chapt. VIII, which is devoted entirely to the condemnation of meat-eating, belonged to the original work. As the question as to whether meat-eating is permissible is already discussed in II, 45, it is possible that Chapt. VIII too may have belonged to the nucleus of the work.

[3]) "The store-room of all ideas." *Cf.* O. *Rosenberg*, Die Probleme der buddhistischen Philosophie, Heidelberg, 1924, p. 235; Th. *Stcherbatsky*, Central Conception of Buddhism, pp. 65, 67, 100; *Strauss*, Indische Philosophie, p. 256.

more questions to the list, having reference to general knowledge (medicine, the arts, geography, etc.) which Mahāmati should have asked.[1] Then comes an enumeration of 108 subjects which have been explained by former Buddhas. The main portion of Chapters II-VII is entirely philosophic in content, and actually treats of the whole system of the Buddhist doctrine, mainly from the standpoint of the Vijñānavāda. The question: "What is Nirvāṇa?" and the various opinions on it, are discussed in two places.[2] In Chapter III, we find, among other things, a discussion on the paradoxical utterance of Buddha: "Between the night during which the Tathāgata attained to enlightenment, and the night during which he will be completely extinguished, in that time not one syllable was spoken by the Tathāgata, and he will not speak a single syllable: the Buddha word is a non-word" (p. 142 ff.). In the same chapter (p. 192 f.) we also come across a remarkable list of names of Buddha. We are told here that, just as in other cases there are several names for one and the same thing, *e.g.*, Indra and Śakra, hasta and pāṇi (both of which mean "hand"), etc., similarly, there are countless names for Buddha too; some call him Tathāgata, others Svayambhū, Nāyaka, Vināyaka, Pariṇāyaka, Buddha, Ṛṣi, Vṛṣabha, Brāhmaṇa, Viṣṇu, Īśvara, Pradhāna,[3] Kapila,[4] Bhūtānta (the end of the beings, death), Ariṣṭanemi,[5] Soma (moon), Bhāskara (sun), Rāma, Vyāsa, Śukra, Indra, Bali, Varuṇas and others again: Anirodhānutpāda (non-destruction and non-originating), Śūnyatā, Tathatā, Truth, Reality, Highest Being, Dharmadhātu, Nirvāṇa, That which is Eternal, the Four Noble Truths, etc. Chapter IV treats of the ten Bhūmis.

In Chapter VIII,[6] Mahāmati begs of the Lord to explain to him what is good or bad in the practice of eating meat, "so that we, I and the other Bodhisattvas, the Great Beings, may in the future and in the present so preach the doctrine that the beings who are still affected by the impres-

[1] Here there is a repetition of some questions which had already been asked previously. It is clear that the text is in disorder.

[2] Pp. 98 ff., and 182 ff. *Cf.* Th. *Stcherbatsky*, The Conception of Buddhist Nirvāṇa, p. 31 note; *Burnouf*, Introduction, p. 459 f.

[3] Original matter, a term of the Sāṃkhya philosophy.

[4] The founder of the Sāṃkhya philosophy.

[5] A Jain saint.

[6] It begins with the words: "Then the Bodhisattva, the Great Being, Mahāmati, questioned the Lord in the Gāthās." However, what follows is only prose; the verses seem to have been dropped.

sions surviving from a previous existence as a beast of prey, and who for that reason are greedy for meat, may renounce their greed for (the) taste (of meat), and in order that the meat-eaters may cast from them the greed for (the) taste (of meat), and that, as a result of a longing for the taste of the doctrine, they may treat all beings with a love as strong as that felt towards an only son, and thus gain the great Love (mahāmaitrī)." The eating of flesh is forbidden even by the adherents of false doctrines, and they themselves eat no meat, whilst under the Completely Enlightened One, who is all pity, people eat meat, and the eating of meat is not forbidden. Buddha's reply to this, is that the eating of meat should be avoided for innumerable reasons, first and foremost being the fact that every being is at some time or other connected with all other beings by rebirth as a father, brother, son, and so on. Legends are told, as evidence of the evil consequences of eating meat. In the Gāthās which follow the prose, not only meat, but also intoxicating drinks, onions and garlic are prohibited. Buddha admits that, in the future, there will be meat-eaters who will declare that the eating of meat is allowed by Buddha.[1] The Buddha however, forbids any kind of meat-eating, whether it be as a medicine or as a food, and he accounts it tantamount to eating the flesh of a son.

Chapter IX is a Dhāraṇī, a magic formula protecting people against snake-demons and ghosts of all kinds.[2]

The whole of Chapter X is a long philosophical treatise in 884 verses.[3] In this case, too, the doctrines put forth, are those of the Vijñānavāda. It is, however, expressly emphasized again and again, that all phenomena are unreal like a fata morgana, an illusion, a delusion. We are frequently reminded of the language of the Vedānta. As in the Gauḍapādīya-Kārikās, in which the Vedāntist doctrine of Māyā is first developed, this work (v. 443) also illustrates the non-reality of the

---

1) *Hauer*, Das Laṅkāvatāra-Sūtra, p. 3 f., regards these passages as allusions to Tantric cults. This is a possible, but not a necessary assumption. The practice of meat-eating may have arisen among Buddhists in the Northern districts even before there were Tantric cults.

2) Translated by J. W. *Hauer*, Die Dhāraṇī im nördlichen Buddhismus (Beiträge zur indischen Sprachwissenschaft und Religionsgeschichte, 2, 1927), p. 2 ff. Haraprasāda *Śāstrī* in JASB Proceedings, 1900, p. 100 ff., describes a "Laṅkāvatāra" Tantra, which, however, has nothing in common with the Mahāyāna-Sūtra.

3) The prose sentence at the beginning: "Then Mahāmati, the Bodhisattva, the Great Being, spoke to the Lord thus," is an absurd interpolation; for it is evident that a Buddha is made to say these verses.

world by the simile of the circle of fire, which originates when a burning stick is twirled round. Again and again we come across the instances of the "horn of a hare," the "ring-like apparitions before the shut eyes," and similar fictions and delusions of the senses, which are intended to show that everything is only illusion and that nothing is real, not even release (verse 623).[2] Sāṃkhyas, Vaiśeṣikas, naked sophists, and the theists, are mentioned as adherents of false doctrines (verse 723). The speaker in Chapter X is not Śākyamuni, but one of his predecessors, a Buddha of an earlier age, who says of himself: "I am descended from the family (gotra) of Kātyāyana, and have come from the Śuddhāvāsa heaven. I preach to the beings the doctrine which leads to the city of Nirvāṇa. I and those Tathāgatas have pointed to this very ancient path as leading to Nirvāṇa, in 3,000 Sūtras" (v. 772 f.). "And my mother is Vasumatī, my father is the Brahman Prajāpati, I am descended from the family of Kātyāyana, and my name is Jina the Pure (Viraja Jina). I was born in Campā, and so were my father and my grandfather also. The latter was called Somagupta, and was descended from the dynasty of the moon" (v. 798 f.).[1]

A few passages in Chapter X might possibly be of historical significance, if they were clearer; in particular the prophecy (X, 784 ff.): "Vyāsa, Kaṇāda, Ṛṣabha, Kapila, the Śākya leader, these and others will be there after my passing away. A hundred years after I have passed away, the Vyāsa who is well known from the (Mahā-)Bhārata, and also the Pāṇḍavas, the Kauravas, Rāma and then the Maurya (Chandragupta is meant) will live, and after that, the Mauryas, Nandas and Guptas, and then the barbarians, the meanest of the kings. At the end of the reign of the barbarians, there will be armed riots, and after they are ended, the Kali-Yuga will come, and at the end of the Kali-Yuga, the Good Religion will not be promoted by the people." In another passage (X, 813 ff.) the coming of Pāṇini, Akṣapāda, Bṛhaspati, of the teachers of Lokāyata, of Kātyāyana the writer of Sūtras, of Yājñavalkya, Vālmīki, Masurākṣa, Kauṭilya and Āśvalāyana, is foretold.

---

[1]) X, 558-628, translated into German by *Hauer*, Das Laṅkāvatāra-Sūtra, p. 7 ff.

[2]) S. Ch. *Vidyābhūṣaṇa* (JASB 1905, p. 161; JRAS 1905, p. 833 ff.) took these verses to be the words of the author of the book. His opinion is shared by *Hauer*, l.c., p. 4. Strange as this passage is, and it does really sound as though it were spoken by an author, this view is nevertheless impossible.

Whilst the last-named list is anything but chronological,[1] and can scarcely be of service in fixing any date, we are most likely justified in taking it that the passage about the Guptas, and the one about the succeeding reign of the barbarians, refer to the Hun invasions at the close of the 5th century.[2] From this we could infer that Chapter X was written not long before the time of the second Chinese translation (513 A.D.). The philosophy of the Vijñānavāda, which is taught in all parts of the Laṅkāvatāra, coincides with the doctrines of Maitreyanātha, Asaṅga, and the Mahāyāna-Śraddhotpāda, which may be ascribed to the 4th century A.D. at the earliest. It is, therefore, probable that the Laṅkāvatāra-Sūtra, even in its earlier form, was not in existence more than 50 or at the very most, 100 years before the Chinese translation of 443 A.D. At all events, from the point of view of the history of Indian philosophy from the 4th to the 6th century A.D., the importance of this work, which contains such numerous allusions to other systems of philosophy, should not be undervalued.[3]

Among the later Mahāyāna-Sūtras there is also the Samādhirāja, "(the Sūtra about the) King of Meditations," or the Candrapradīpa-Sūtra, as it is called after the principal speaker.[4] Here, in a dialogue between Candrapradīpa (or Candraprabha) and Buddha, it is shown how a Bodhisattva can attain to the highest knowledge by means of the various

---

[1]) *Cf.* E. H. *Johnston* in JRAS 1929, p. 86. ff.

[2]) *Cf.* above, Vol. I, 524 f.

[3]) Haraprasāda *Śāstrī* (Ind. Hist, Qu. I, 1925, 208 f.) speaks of the Laṅkāvatāra as a work belonging to the period before Kaniṣka. This is probably based upon the erroneous statement of Rāj. *Mitra*, Nep. Buddh. Lit., p, 113, that the work was already translated into Chinese in 168-190 A.D. H. *Śāstrī* (l.c.) calls attention to a paper published by Harinath *De*, "in which 20 different systems of thought were culled from the Laṅkāvatāra."

[4]) I do not know of any edition of the work. I only know it from quotations in the Śikṣā-Samuccaya and from the table of contents given by Rāj. *Mitra*, Nep. Buddh. Lit., pp. 207-221; s. *Bendall*, Catalogue, p. 22 f.; Śikṣā-Samuccaya, ed. Bendall, p. 368.

meditations, especially the highest of all, the "King of Meditations," and which preliminary conditions are necessary in order to prepare the spirit for this highest stage of meditation. Such preliminary conditions are worship of the Buddhas, complete renunciation of the world, gentleness and goodness towards all beings, entire indifference as to one's own life and one's own health if there is a question of sacrificing them for others, and lastly the knowledge of the non-reality of the world, the steadfast belief in the unreality (śūnyatā) of all phenomena. Passages of moral contents, mostly in Gāthās, are quoted by Śāntideva in the Sikṣā-Samuccaya, as for instance the beautiful verses about peace of mind (Śikṣ., p. 242 f.):

"*He* will never depart from the doctrine of the Blessed Ones (Sugatas *i.e.*, Buddhas), *that* hero will never fall into the power of women, *he* takes a delight in the commandment of the Blessed Ones—he who understands that real peace of mind is the true nature of Religion.

He will soon become a prince of men here, *he* will be a healing physician, a giver of good fortune, *he* will pull out completely the thorn (of pain) of the unfortunate,—he who understands that real peace of mind is the true nature of Religion.

He shines forth among the people, like the moon, by the power of his mildness, *he* is not angered, though he be ill-treated with clods of earth and with sticks, *he* remains unmoved, though he be pulled to pieces limb by limb,—he who understands that real peace of mind is the true nature of Religion."

In the Sikṣā-Samuccaya (p. 134) a verse is cited from the Jñānavatī section of the Samādhirāja, according to which the eating of meat, which is otherwise prohibited, is allowable by way of medicine. In a prose passage of some length, it is explained that it is more likely for a man who is burning from head to foot, and who is still alive, to think of sensual pleasures, than for a Bodhisattva to find rest, as long as there are still human beings in distress.[1] Legends are also told of saints

---

[1]) Śikṣ., p. 166. A long passage on morality is quoted on p. 100 f., and a passage on the advantages of a hermit's life, on p. 193 f.; a beautiful verse on maitrī, love, which is

who were successful owing to the "King of Meditations." This Sūtra corresponds to the Chinese Yüehtêng-san-mei-ching, which was translated in 450 and 557 A.D.[1]

The last work to be mentioned among the later Mahāyāna-Sūtras, is the Suvarṇa-Prabhāsa or "Splendour of Gold,"[2] the contents of which are partly philosophical and ethical, and which also contains many legends, but which, for a great part, already bears the stamp of a Tantra.

In Chapter I the Brahman Kauṇḍilya begs for a relic of Buddha, even though it might not be larger than a grain of mustard. The Licchavi prince Sarvalokapriyadarśana replies to him in the following verses: "When flowers will grow in the floods of the Ganges, when crows are red and Kokilas are the colour of conch-shells, when the Jambu tree bears palm nuts and the date tree mango blossoms,—then there will be a relic the size of a grain of mustard. When people will be well protected against the winter's cold with coats made out of the hairs of the tortoise,...When the feet of a mosquito will afford a firm support which will not waver,...When people will make a firm ladder out of a hare-horn, whereby to climb up to heaven,...When a mouse will climb up this ladder, and having eaten the moon up, will run around Rāhu,...When an umbrella made of Palāśa leaves will be large enough to protect people from the rain,...When ocean ships will career around upon the dry land with sail and mast,...When owls will carry away Gandhamādana hill with their beaks,[3] then there will be a

to be esteemed far above any cult, is quoted on p. 318. In the Śikṣ. the title is always Candrapradīpa-Sūtra.

[1]) Thus according to K. *Watanabe* in JRAS 1907, 663; *Nanjio*, No. 191. Both titles also occur in the Tibetan Kanjur, s. *Körös.* in AMG II, 249. The Śūraṅgamasamādhi, which is also quoted in the Śikṣā-Samuccaya, is a different work from the Samādhirāja.

[2]) Edited by Rai Sarat Chandra *Dās*, Bahadur, and Pandit Sarat Chandra *Śāstrī*, fasc. I, Calcutta 1898 (Buddhist Text Society of India). More does not seem to have been published. The complete title reads thus in the colophons: Suvarṇaprabhāsottamasūtrendrarāja. The fascicule contains Chapts. I-XV. Rāj. *Mitra*, Nep. Buddh. Lit., p. 241 ff., gives the contents of 21 chapters. *Cf. Burnouf*, Introduction, pp. 471 ff., 490; *Bendall*, Catalogue, p. 12 f.; M. *Anesaki* in ERE IV, p. 839. An edition of the Suvarṇa-Prabhāsa was prepared by the late Bunyiu *Nanjio*, and is being made ready for the press by his pupil Hotoku *Idzumi*, s. J. *Takakusu* in The Young East, May 1928, p. 404.

[3]) This list of impossible things is to be found, in part word for word, in Jātaka No. 425 (Aṭṭhāna-Jātaka, "the Jātaka of the Impossibilities"). *Cf.* Th. *Zachariae*, Kleine Schriften, Bonn 1920, p. 70 f.; She-Rab Dong bu or Prajnya Danda by Lu-Trub (Nāgārjuna

relic." The Brahman himself states the reason: It is impossible to find a relic of Buddha, even as small as a grain of mustard, as there is neither bone nor blood of Buddha's body, for the Completely Enlightened Tathāgata has only a Dharmakāya,[1] and consists only of the Dharma element, *i.e.*, he has only an immaterial "body" consisting of the absolute, and he is composed only of ideas, of spiritual (non-sensual) phenomena. A Buddha was never created and never passes away; only in order to bring the beings to maturity, he causes the vision of the complete Nirvāṇa to appear.

Chapter IV is on a lofty ethical plane, and contains many a beautiful passage such as the confession of sins,[2] and the praise of love (maitrī) towards all beings.[3] The doctrine of Śūnyatā is developed in Chapter VI. The major portion of the work consists, however, of a glorification of the Suvarṇa-Prabhāsa itself, and the merit of reading this book is extolled over and over again. In Chapter VIII the goddess Sarasvatī appears, and in Chapter IX Śrī Mahādevī, the great goddess Śrī, in order to magnify the Suvarṇa-Prabhāsa as a Dhāraṇī.[4] Chapter XIII is a kind of manual for kings (rājaśāstra), called Devendrasamaya, which Baladaketu recited to his son Ruciraketu when he was anointed as king.[5] Among the legends which are related in the Suvarṇa-Prabhāsa, there is also one about a prince who

---

ed. and transl. by W. L. *Campbell*, Calcutta 1919, p. 98 (vs. 194); and *Penzer-Tawney*, The Ocean of Story, IX, 152.

[1]) On the Mahāyāna doctrine of the three bodies (trikāya) of the Buddha, *viz.*, dharmakāya (the absolute), sambhogakāya (the superhuman body with which the Buddhas enjoy their glory, virtue and wisdom) and nirmāṇakāya (the assumed body, which the Buddhas assume, in order to carry out their work of releasing the beings, on earth), see *La Vallée Poussin* in ERE I, 97 f.; M. *Anesaki* in ERE IV, 839 f.; P. *Masson-Oürsel* in JA 1913, sér. 11, t. 1, p. 581 ff.; *Rosenberg*, Die Probleme der buddhistischen Philosophie, p. 236 ff.; W. Montgomery *McGovern*, An Introduction to Mahāyāna Buddhism, London 1922, p. 75 ff. I-tsing's Chinese translation of the Suvarṇa-Prabhāsa has a chapter on the doctrine of Trikāya, which does not appear in the Sanskrit text, and which, in the opinion of *Anesaki* (l.c.) was probably interpolated by an adherent of Vasubandhu. On Dharmadhātu see Th. *Stcherbatsky*, Central Conception of Buddhism, pp. 59, 97.

[2]) P. 12 ff., quoted in Śikṣā-Samuccaya, pp. 160-164. This passage has been published by H. *Stönner* (SBA 1904, 1310 ff.) from a block print found in Idikutschari (Eastern Turkestan).

[3]) P. 19 ff., quoted in Śikṣā-Samuccaya, p. 217 f.

[4]) It is justified to a certain extent, when *La Vallée Poussin*, Bouddhisme, E'tudes et Matériaux, Mémoires etc., 1897, p. 127, describes the Suvarṇa-Prabhāsa as a Māhātmya of Dhāraṇīs.

[5]) It is not easy to see how this section crept into this pious work. It reminds us of similar sections in the Purāṇas.

kills himself in order to serve as food for a hungry tigress,[1] whereupon the prince's father has his son's remains preserved in a golden casket, and has a Stūpa erected over them. In other places, however, Tantric ritual is also taught, and female deities, Hārītī, Caṇḍikā, etc., are mentioned.

The Suvarṇa-Prabhāsa enjoys a great reputation and is popular in all countries where Mahāyāna Buddhism prevails. In Central Asia, too, fragments of this work have been discovered.[2] It is said to have been explained in China by Kāśyapa Mātaṅga as early as during the reign of Ming-ti (58-75 A.D.).[3] If this statement is not a mere fiction with a view to extolling the work, there must have been a Suvarṇa-Prabhāsa in those days which diverged widely from the present text. The Chinese translation by Dharmakṣema (414-433), Paramārtha and his pupils (552-557) and I-tsing (703) have come down to us.[4]

The Masters and Poets of the Mahāyāna.

Tāranātha[5] says that the adherents of the Hīnayāna declare the Śatasāhasrikā-Prajñā-Pāramitā to be the latest of the Mahāyāna-Sūtras, and the work of Nāgārjuna,[6] and

---

1) See above, p. 274 f. According to a Mongolian version translated by I. J. *Schmidt*, Grammatik der mongolischen Sprache, St. Petersburg 1831, p. 142 ff.

2) A passage from it in the language of Khotan, s. in E. *Leumann*, Buddhist. Lit. Nordarisch und Deutsch, 1920, p. 58 ff. A few Central Asiatic fragments of the Sanskrit text have been published and translated by F. W. *Thomas* in Hoernle, MS. Remains, p. 108 ff. An Uiguric translation appeared in Bibl. Buddhica in 1914. For fragments of Uiguric texts, s. F. W. K. *Müller*, Uigurica, in ABA 1908, p. 10 ff.; *Lüders*, SBA 1914, p. 99; in the colophon it is expressly stated that the work was translated from the Indian language into Chinese, and from the Chinese into Turkish.

3) *Bagchi* I, p. 4.

4) *Bagchi* I, 220, 422; *Forke*, Pekinger Tripiṭaka, Nos. 121, 127. In the Tibetan Kanjur, s. AMG II, 315 f. The West Mongolian recension (Altan Gerel) has been published by Erich *Haenisch*, Leipzig 1929.

5) Geschichte des Buddhismus in Indien, aus dem Tibetischen übersetzt von A *Schiefner*, St. Petersburg 1869, p. 71.

6) On Nāgārjuna, see A. *Grünwedel*, Mythologie des Buddhismus in Tibet und der Mongolei, Leipzig 1900, p. 29 ff.; *Eliot*, II, 84 ff.; Satis Chandra *Vidyābhūṣaṇa* in Proc.

it is not impossible that this Prajñā-Pāramitā is indeed an apocryphal Sūtra which was produced by Nāgārjuna's school. It is more likely, however, that this statement is due to a confusion between the text of the great Prajñā-Pāramitā and the Prajñā-Pāramitā-Sūtra-Śāstra which was ascribed to Nāgārjuna, *i.e.*, the commentary on the Pañcaviṃśati-Sāhasrikā-Prajñā-Pāramitā. At all events Nāgārjuna cannot possibly have been the founder of the Mahāyāna, as was so often supposed in former days; for there is no doubt that Mahāyāna-Sūtras were in existence long before his time.[1] According to Hsüan-Tsang,[2] Aśvaghoṣa, Nāgārjuna, Āryadeva and Kumāralabdha (=Kumāralāta) were contemporaries, and he calls them "the four suns which illumined the world." According to Kalhaṇa's Rājataraṅgiṇī (I, 173), the Bodhisattva Nāgārjuna was "the only lord of the land" in Kashmir at the period of the kings Huṣka, Juṣka and Kaniṣka. Tāranātha says that he was born in the days of Kaniṣka. It is a good working hypothesis, though nothing more, that he lived in the latter half of the 2nd century A.D.[3] On the other hand, so many legends have been woven about his life, that doubts have even been expressed as to whether he was a historical personage at all.

According to the biography of Nāgārjuna translated into Chinese by Kumārajīva (in about 405 A.D.), Nāgārjuna was born as a Brahman in Southern India, studied the four Vedas and learned all sciences. He was also, however, said

---

IOC, Vol. II, p. 125 ff.; Max *Walleser*, The Life of Nāgārjuna from Tibetan and Chinese Sources (Hirth Anniversary Volume, Asia Major I, 421 ff.); P. L. *Vaidya*, E'tudes sur Āryadeva et son Catuḥśataka, Paris 1923, p. 46 ff.; *Keith*, Buddhist Philosophy, p. 229 f.

1) In the Prajñā-Pāramitā-Sūtra-Śāstra and Daśabhūmi-Vibhāṣā-Śāstra (both translated into Chinese by Kumārajīva in about 405 A.D.), Nāgārjuna quotes numerous Mahāyāna-Sūtras; s. R. *Kimura* in Ind. Hist. Qu. III, 1927, p. 412 ff.

2) Si-yu-ki, Buddhist Records of the Western World transl. by S. *Beal*, II, 97 ff., 302 f.; Hwui Li, The Life of Hiuen-Tsiang, transl. by S. *Beal*, 1911, p. 199.

3) Cf. *Kern*, Manual of Indian Buddhism, p. 122 f.; *Keith*, Buddhist Philosophy, p. 229; *Walleser* in *ZB* VI, 1924-25, pp. 95 ff., 237 ff.

to be a great sorcerer. By his magic art he was able to make himself invisible, and, accompanied by three friends, he secretly entered into the royal palace, where they began to violate the women. They were discovered, Nāgārjuna's three companions were sentenced to death, but he himself escaped after he had first vowed to become a monk. He fulfilled his vow, studied the whole of the three Piṭakas in 90 days, and grasped their meaning; yet he was not satisfied with this, but began to seek other Sūtras, until at last he received the Mahāyāna-Sūtra from a very aged monk in the Himalaya. With the aid of a Nāgarāja, a serpent-king, he also found a commentary on it. He zealously propagated Buddhism in Southern India. He directed the religion, says the biographer, for over 300 years.[1] The Tibetans even go as far as to let him attain the age of 600 years.

Kumārajīva describes Nāgārjuna not only as a great magician, but also as well versed in astronomy, medicine, the production of precious stones, and other worldly things. The poet Bāṇa (7th century A.D.) relates in the Harṣacarita, that Nāgārjuna received a necklace of pearls from a snake-king, which served as a remedy for snake-bite and in fact all pains. In the Tibetan chronicles Nāgārjuna appears almost exclusively as a mighty magician.[2] In spite of all this, we

---

[1]) *Wassiljew*, Der Buddhismus, p. 232 ff. According to *Walleser* (Hirth Anniversary Volume, p. 443 ff.) it is not certain whether we possess the authentic text of Kumārajīva's biography.

[2]) Thus especially in No. 16 of the "Stories of the 84 Magicians," translated by *A. Grünwedel* (Baessler-Archiv, V, 1916, 161ff.). A medical writer Nāgārjuna is named as the author of the Uttara-Tantra on the Suśruta; s. J. *Jolly*, Medizin (Grundriss), pp. 16, 125, and in ZDMG 53, 1899, 378. About Nāgārjuna, the author of Tantras, who lived in the 7th century, see below. Alberūnī says of the alchemist Nāgārjuna, the author of the Rasaratnākara, that he lived a hundred years before his time. P. C. *Ray* places him in the 7th or 8th century A.D. In the Rasaratnākara we find dialogues between Nāgārjuna and King Śālivāhana (for Śālivāhana or Sātavāhana as a friend of Nāgārjuna, see below), and at the beginning of Chapter III, which deals with quicksilver, we read that the goddess Prajñā-Pāramitā appeared to Nāgārjuna in a dream, and revealed to him the ingredients for a recipe. *Cf.* P. C. *Ray*, A History of Indian Chemistry, I, Calcutta 1903,

may safely assume that he came from Vidarbha (Berār) and was born as a Brahman, for his writings give evidence of an intimate acquaintance with Brahmanical learning. So great was the reputation which he enjoyed, that even after the lapse of centuries, numerous works for which people desired to assure special authority, were ascribed to him.[1] The fact of his being the founder of one of the most important schools of the Mahāyāna, namely the Mādhyamaka school, accounts for this high degree of veneration: for there is not a shadow of a doubt that he is the author of the Mādhyamika-Kārikās or Mādhyamika-Sūtras [2] which present in a *systematic* manner the Śūnyavāda which is taught in the Mahāyāna-Sūtras.

The work consists of 400 memorial verses (Kārikās) in 27 chapters, on which the author himself has written a commentary, the Akutobhayā "The Safe One." Nāgārjuna was perhaps the first, or at all events one of the first, to make use of this style of presentation which is so greatly favoured in the scientific literature of the Indians, to wit—memorial verses

pp. xxiv, xcii ff.; II, 1909, pp. xx, xxiii ff., xxxviii ff., 6 ff. Most likely the Buddhist philosopher, the Tantric writer, the medical writer and the alchemist were four different men, who were confused owing to the identity of the names.

1) For the works ascribed to Nāgārjuna, s. *Nanjio*, col. 369 ff.

2) Mūlamadhyamaka-Kārikās (Mādhyamika-Sūtras) de Nāgārjuna avec la Prasannapadā, commentaire de Candrakīrti, publié par L. *de La Vallée Poussin*, St. Pétersbourg (Bibliotheca Buddhica IV), 1903 ff. *La Vallée Poussin* has translated Chapt. 24 of the Commentary, in Mélanges Charles de Harlez, Leiden 1896, p. 313 ff. Chapt. I (on Causality) and Chapt. XXV (on Nirvāṇa) with the Commentary of Candrakīrti, transl. by Th. *Stcherbatsky*, The Conception of Buddhist Nirvāṇa, Leningrad 1927, pp. 63-212. A summary of the contents of Candrakīrti's Commentary, the text of Chapt. I, and a translation of Chapts. II, V and VII, are given by Satis Chandra *Vidyābhūṣaṇa* in JBTS V, 1897, part 4, p. 7 ff.; II, 1894 and 1896, part I, p. 13 ff : 1897, part I, 23 ff. ; part III, p. 21 ff. The Kārikās with the Akutobhayā have been transl. from Tibetan by Max *Walleser*, Die mittlere Lehre (Mādhyamikaśāstra) des Nāgārjuna, Heidelberg 1911. The same scholar has also translated the Chinese version of the Mādhyamika-Śāstra, the Cuṅ-lun, by Kumārajīva, Heidelberg 1912, and edited the Tibetan version of the Akutobhayā in photographic reproduction according to the Peking edition of the Tanjur, in "Materialien zur Kunde des Buddhismus," Heft 2, Heidelberg 1923.

with a commentary by the author himself. The Akutobhayā has not come down in Sanskrit, and our knowledge of it rests upon the Tibetan translation. The commentaries by Buddhapālita and Bhāvaviveka have also come down in Tibetan translations only. The commentary entitled Prasannapadā, "The Clear-Worded,"[1] by Candrakīrti, who on several occasions argues against his two predecessors, is the only one which we possess in Sanskrit. The Mādhyamika system, which is taught by Nāgārjuna and his pupil Āryadeva, and which found one of its chief exponents in Candrakīrti derives its name "the middle doctrine"[2] from the fact that it declares nothing either positive or negative, but merely relativity. The work begins with the famous eight negations, but it is here expressly stated that they mean the same as the doctrine of causally dependent origination:[3]

> "No passing away and no origination, no destruction and no everlasting continuance, no unity and no multiplicity, no coming and no going: I revere the Completely Enlightened One, the best of teachers, him who has thus taught the causally dependent origination, the salutary cessation of the world of phenomena."

There was an obvious objection to this, and Nāgārjuna himself makes his opponent voice it in Chapter XXIV: If everything is "empty," and there is neither origination nor

---

1) In the opinion of *Stcherbatsky* (Nirvāṇa, p. 67, note 1), it is so entitled "not without some dose of irony, since...its extreme dialectical subtlety...is equalled by no other work in the whole domain of Northern Buddhist literature." Buddhapālita's commentary is edited in Tibetan by M. *Walleser* in Bibl. Buddhica XVI.

2) Whilst in the "Sermon of Benares" the "middle way" is understood in the ethical sense (avoidance of the extremes of worldly life and exaggerated asceticism), the expression has a metaphysical meaning in this case: the avoidance of extreme statements regarding existence and non-existence.

3) The reproach that the Mādhyamikas are nothing but Nāstikas or "Nihilists," is firmly rejected by Candrakīrti (Madhyamaka-Vṛtti, p. 368). On the system of the Mādhyamikas, cf. *La Vallée Poussin*, Bouddhisme, pp. 189 ff., 290 ff., and ERE VIII, 235 ff., *Anesaki* in ERE IV, 838; Y. *Sōgen*, Systems of Buddhistic Thought, p. 194 ff.; P. L. *Vaidya*, Études sur Āryadeva, p. 31 ff.

passing away, then there can also be no "four noble truths" and no rule of life based on the knowledge of these truths, no fruit of good and evil deeds, no Buddha doctrine (Dharma), no monastic community, and finally also no Buddha. Thus the entire religion of the Buddha collapses into nothingness. Thereupon Nāgārjuna replies: The doctrine of the Buddha rests on two truths, one conventional truth, in which the deeper meaning remains hidden, and one truth in the highest sense. He who does not know the distinction between these two truths, does not understand the profound substance of the Buddha doctrine. The highest truth can be taught only when based on the truth of every-day life, and without the assistance of this highest truth, it is not possible to understand Nirvāṇa.

The same doctrines are expounded by Nāgārjuna in more concise form in two shorter works, Yuktiṣaṣṭikā, "Sixty Arguments,"[1] and Śūnyatā-Saptati, "Seventy Verses on Unreality."[2] The Pratītya-Samutpādahṛdaya treats of the "Secret of the causally dependent origination" in 7 Āryā stanzas.[3] The Mahāyāna-Viṃśaka[4] is a short philosophical treatise, in which it is taught that, from the standpoint of absolute truth, there is neither Saṃsāra nor Nirvāṇa, and that everything is mere illusion and dream. The Vigraha-vyāvartanī, which is frequently quoted by Candrakīrti, is a work on logic. In the case of other works which are attributed to Nāgārjuna, it is more or less doubtful whether

---

[1]) Yukti-ṣaṣṭikā, die sechzig Sätze des Negativismus nach der chinesischen Version übersetzt von Phil. *Schaeffer*, Heidelberg 1923 (Materialien zur Buddhismus, 3. Heft). It is extant in Tibetan also.

[2]) Extant in Tibetan in the Tanjur. The work seems to have been the prototype for Vasubandhu's Paramārtha-Saptati and Īśvarakṛṣṇa's Sāṃkhya-Saptati.

[3]) Tibetan text with French translation by *La Vallée Poussin* in Bouddhisme, E'tudes et Matériaux, Théorie des douze causes, Gand 1913, p. 122 ff.

[4]) Tibetan and Chinese with English translation, edited by Susumu *Yamaguchi* in EB IV, 56 ff., 169 ff.

they are really his. This applies, for instance, to the Dharma-Saṃgraha, which is ascribed to him, and which has come down in Sanskrit.[1] This is a short and very useful glossary of Buddhist technical terms, but it is one which any monk might have compiled.[2]

The Suhṛl-Lekha or "Letter to a Friend,"[3] has a more rightful claim to be regarded as a work of the great master, though it contains no Mādhyamaka doctrines whatsoever. As a matter of fact, there is nothing in the epistle which could not just as well be in the Pāli Canon, and certain verses coincide word for word with the Dhammapada and similar texts, other verses agreeing with Brahmanical sayings. The Chinese pilgrim I-tsing praises this work of Nāgārjuna very highly, and reports that in his day it was widely read and memorised in India.[4] The Chinese mention Sātavāhana as the friend, to whom the letter is addressed.[5] Now Sātavāhana is not the name of a king, but

---

[1] Edited by Kenjiu *Kasawara*, *Max Müller* and H. *Wenzel* (Anecdota Oxoniensia Aryan Series, Vol. I, Part 5), Oxford 1885. Half the termini of the Dharma-Saṃgraha are also to be found in the *Dharma-Śarīra-Sūtra*, a block-print of which was brought from Idikucchari by *Grünwedel* and published by H. *Stönner* (SBA 1904, p. 1282 ff.). The Dharma-Saṃgraha has much in common with the Buddhist lexicon Mahā-Vyutpatti (edited by J. P. *Minayeff* in Bibl. Buddhica XIII, 1911), the period and author of which are entirely unknown. As Kaniṣka and Aśvaghoṣa are mentioned, and as allusions to Greek astrology occur in the Mahā-Vyutpatti, the work cannot be earlier than the 3rd or 4th century A.D.; s. F. W. *Thomas* in Ind. Hist. Qu. II, 1926, 501 ff.

[2] In the Chinese version the name of the author is not mentioned. *Cf. Kasawara* Dharma-Saṃgraha Edition, p. 68.

[3] The complete title is Ārya-Nāgārjuna-bodhisattva-suhṛllekha. Translated into English, after the Chinese translation of Guṇavarman (424-431 A.D.), by S. *Beal* in Ind. Ant. 16, 1887, 169 ff. Other Chinese translations by Saṅghavarman (about 433 A.D.) and by I-tsing (about 700 A.D.); s. *Nanjio*, Nos. 1440, 1441; *Bagchi* I, 375, 377. Translated into English, after the Tibetan version, by H. *Wenzel* in JPTS 1886, p. 1 ff., and into German, Leipzig 1886. The Sanskrit original has not come down.

[4] *Cf.* I-tsing, transl. *Takakusu*, p. 158 ff.

[5] *Cf.* Hwui Li, The Life of Hiuen-Tsiang, tr. by S. *Beal*, p. 135; Th. *Watters*, on Yuan Chwang's Travels in India, II, 200 f., 206. A legend related by Bāṇa (Harṣacarita transl., by E. B. *Cowell* and F. W. *Thomas*, London 1897, p. 252) also mentions Sātavāhana as the friend of Nāgārjuna.

the title adopted by the rulers of the Āndhra dynasty, which held sway in Southern India from the middle of the 3rd century B.C. until the beginning of the 3rd century A.D. The first prominent Āndhra sovereign, who called himself Sātavāhana, and who favoured both Brahmans and Buddhists, was Gautamīputra (119-128 A.D.). His successor was Rājā Vāsiṣṭhīputra Śrī Pulumāyi, who reigned over 30 years. In the period which we have assumed for Nāgārjuna, Gautamīputra Yajñaśrī, who reigned in 166-196 A.D., would come into question.[1]

There are no ground for denying Nāgārjuna the authorship of the commentaries Prajñā-Pāramitā-Sūtra-Śāstra and Daśa-Bhūmi-Vībhāṣā-Śāstra.[2] The short treatise Eka-Śloka Śāstra,[3] which has come down only in Chinese, and which sets out to prove that true existence (svabhāva) is non-existence (abhāva), is perhaps rightly ascribed to Nāgārjuna. On the other hand, it is not very likely that the Prajñā-daṇḍa,[4] which has come down in Tibetan, a book of 260 sayings, only very few of which are Buddhist at all, and the majority of which merely teach general morality and wisdom, with many an allusion to the fables in the Pañcatantra, was the work of Nāgārjuna.

---

1) *Cf. Smith*, Early History, p. 221 ff. Max *Walleser* (ZB VI, 96 ff.) makes it seem probable that the statement, according to which in the Tibetan version, Udayana is the king to whom the letter is addressed, is based upon an error. He assumes (l. c., p. 103) that Vijaya Śrī Sātakarṇi, who ascended the throne in 213 A.D., was Nāgārjuna's friend.

2) Both commentaries, as well as the Madhyamika-Śāstra, were translated into Chinese by Kumārajīva ; s. *Bagchi* I, 197 f., 428.

3) Translated from the Chinese by H. R. Rangaswamy *Iyengar* in the Mysore University Journal for Arts and Science 1, 1927, No. 2. A short treatise consisting of 9 Kārikās, entitled Yogāvatāra, is ascribed to Nāgārjuna only in one Sanskrit manuscript, and in the Tibetan version is ascribed to Dignāga ; s. Vidhushekhara *Bhattacharya* in Ind. Hist. Qu. IV, 1928, 775 ff.

4) She-rab Dong-bu or Prajnya Danda by Lu-Trub (Nāgārjuna) edited and translated by Major W. L. *Campbell*, Calcutta 1919.

One of Nāgārjuna's pupils was Deva or Āryadeva, also known as Kāṇadeva, "the one-eyed Deva" and Nīlanetra, "the blue-eyed."[1] Hsüan-Tsang relates the following of him: The Bodhisattva Deva came from the land of Siṃhala (Ceylon), in order to discuss the difficulties of the doctrine with Nāgārjuna. He asked a pupil to announce him to the Master. Nāgārjuna sends his begging-bowl out, filled with pure water. Deva throws a needle into it. The pupil takes the bowl back, and Nāgārjuna is much delighted at this "eloquent silence." In reply to the question of his astonished pupil, the master says, that the bowl with the water signified his own pure knowledge; by throwing the needle in, Deva wanted to say that he has reached the very bottom of this knowledge. Deva is shown in, and approaches the Master very modestly. Nāgārjuna was very well satisfied with the discussion he had with Deva, and as he himself was already old and feeble, he appointed him as his successor.[2] Deva's biography was translated into Chinese by Kumārajīva (in about 405 A.D.) together with those of Aśvaghoṣa and Nāgārjuna, and is just as legendary as these last named. Legend has it that he died at the hands of a murderer. The pupil of one of the heretical teachers whom Deva had defeated in disputation, waylaid him and pierced him through with a sword, as he sat in the forest absorbed in meditation. Before his death he instructed the murderer, and restrained his pupils who were about to pursue the murderer, with these words: "Everything is unreal. Reflect upon the true meaning of all things in the world of phenomena. Where is the oppression or

---

[1]) He is said to have been named thus, owing to two blue spots, resembling eyes, on his cheeks. According to the legend, he became one-eyed in the following manner: In order to demonstrate that a golden statue of Maheśvara is not the god himself, he tore out the left eye of the statue; but, in order to show that he had not done this out of pride, he tore out one of his own eyes, when Maheśvara paid him a visit the next day.

[2]) *Cf.* Hwui Li, The Life of Hiuen-Tsiang, tr. by S. *Beal*, p. 135; Th. *Watters*, On Yuan Chwang's Travels in India, II, 200 ff.

cruelty? Who is pierced or murdered? If you recognise the true nature of all things, then there is neither murdered nor murderer. Who is a friend and who is a foe? Who is the murderer and who is the murdered?"[1] Both Hsüan-Tsang and I-tsing mention Āryadeva along with Aśvaghoṣa and Nāgārjuna, as one of the great men who lived "in ancient times." Most probably he lived at about the turning-point of the second and third centuries A.D.[2]

Many works are ascribed to Āryadeva.[3] His most famous work is Catuḥ-Śataka,[4] which, like the Mādhyamika-Sūtra, consists of 400 Kārikās. With Candrakīrti's commentary, it belongs to the fundamental works of the Mādhyamika school. Deva defends Nāgārjuna's doctrines not only as against other Buddhist schools, but also against Brahmanical systems, especially the Vaiśeṣikas. The importance of distinguishing between the two kinds of knowledge, is very emphatically brought out by Āryadeva in these verses:

"Love for the religion is prescribed by the Tathāgatas for such as long for heaven; on the other hand, the highest truth is prescribed for such as seek deliverance.

---

[1]) *Cf. Wassiljew*, Der Buddhismus, p. 234 f.; Y. *Sogen*, Systems of Buddhist Thought, p. 187 ff.

[2]) See above, p. 258. According to Kumārajīva's statements, H. *Ui*, The Vaiśeṣika Philosophy, London, 1917, p. 43, calculates the time of Nāgārjuna between 113 and 213, and that of Deva between 163 and 263, whilst Harivarman, the pupil of Kumāralāta and author of the Satyasiddhi-Śāstra (which has come down only in Chinese) is said to have lived in about 260 or 270 A.D.

[3]) See *Nanjio*, Col. 869 ff.

[4]) It is often quoted by Candrakīrti, under the title Śataka or Śataka-Śāstra, in the Madhyamaka-Vṛtti. *Cf. La Vallée Poussin* in Le Muséon, N.S.I., 1900, 236 ff. The Catuḥśataka has come down in its entirety in the Tibetan version. Fragments of the Sanskrit original of the text and commentary have been discovered and edited by Haraprasada *Śāstrī* in Memoirs of the Asiatic Society of Bengal, Vol. III, No. 8, pp. 449-514, Calcutta 1914. Chapter VII with Extracts from the Commentary of Candrakīrti, reconstructed from the Tibetan Version, with an English Translation, by Vidhushekhara *Bhattacharya*, in Proc. IV OC, Vol. II, pp. 831-871. P. L. *Vaidya*, Études sur Āryadeva et son Catuḥśataka, Paris 1923, p. 69 ff., has reconstructed the Sanskrit text of the last 9 chapters (VIII-XVI), on the basis of the Tibetan version, in as far as the Sanskrit text

He who desires to acquire religious merit, cannot always talk of unreality (śūnyatā). Does not a medicine, wrongly used, become a poison ?

Just as one can make a thing clear to a barbarian (mleccha) only if one uses his language, even so one cannot explain anything to the common people unless one uses the common language." [1]

Down to the present day, Nāgārjuna's Mādhyamika-Śāstra together with Āryadeva's Catuḥ-Śataka or Śata-Śāstra and the Dvādaśa-Nikāya-Śāstra, form the ground-work of the faith of the Sanron sect in Japan.[2]

Only fragments have come down to us of the Cittaviśuddhi-Prakaraṇa,[3] "Section of the Purification of the Mind," a didactic poem containing among other things controversial arguments against the Brahmanical ceremonial system. The following is declared against the belief that bathing in the Ganges washes away sins : If salvation could be attained by means of Ganges water, then fishermen would all attain salvation, and more particularly the fishes, which are in the Ganges day and night. It is doubtful, however, whether this work in its present form, in which Tantric ideas, and expressions for the days of the week (vāra) and the zodiac (rāśi) which were borrowed from Greek astronomy, occur, can be ascribed to the ancient Āryadeva.[4]

---

was not extant, and has added a French translation (p. 129 ff.). Hsüan-Tsang translated the work into Chinese. A complete Italian translation of the text and commentary, from the Chinese, has been published by G. *Tucci* in Studi e materiali di storia delle religioni, 1925. For a comparison of the Chinese text with the Sanskrit original and the Tibetan version, s. *Tucci* in RSO X, 1928, 521 ff.

[1] Verses 192-194 in P. L. *Vaidya's* Text.

[2] *Cf. Nanjio*, Twelve Japanese Buddhist Sects, p. 44 ff.; W. M. *McGovern*, Introduction to Mahāyāna Buddhism, p. 205 ff.

[3] Haraprasāda *Śāstrī* has also discovered these fragments, s. JASB 67, 1898, 175 ff.

[4] *Cf. LaVallée Poussin*, Bouddhisme, p. 383, note 1 and Haraprasāda *Śāstrī* in Ind. Hist. Qu. I, 1925, p. 464 : "The book has been revised by another Āryadeva in later times, for at the end are mentioned images not known in the great Āryadeva's time, and there was one Āryadeva in Bengal who wrote also in Bengali." For this reason it is im-

There are in the Chinese Tripiṭaka two short treatises translated by Bodhiruci (508-535), which are ascribed to Āryadeva, and which constitute a kind of commentary on those sections of the Laṅkāvatāra which deal with heretical doctrines of Nirvāṇa.[1] There is another short treatise by Āryadeva the Hastavāla-Prakaraṇa or Muṣṭi-Prakaraṇa, the Sanskrit text of which F. W. Thomas has endeavoured to reconstruct on the basis of the Chinese and Tibetan translations.[2] In this work it is taught, in 5 memorial verses, that all phenomena are mere illusion, and a sixth verse explains the distinction between the two truths.

Hitherto it has usually been thought that the founder of the Yogācāra school of Mahāyāna Buddhism was Asaṅga or Āryāsaṅga. It is now, however, probable that the tradition according to which several of his works are supposed to have been revealed to Asaṅga by the future Buddha Maitreya in the Tuṣita heaven, rests upon the fact that Maitreyanātha, briefly called Maitreya, was a historical personage, the teacher of Asaṅga, and the real founder of the Yogācāra school.[3] This

---

possible to deduce from this work the chronological data, which were deduced by H. *Jacobi*, JAOS 31, 1910, p. 2.

[1]) Nanjio, Nos. 1259, 1260. *Cf.* G. *Tucci* in T'oung Pao, 2 série, Vol. XXIV, 1926, p. 16 ff.

[2]) JRAS, 1918, 267 ff. The Chinese translations, which were used by *Thomas*, of Paramārtha and I-tsing (*Nanjio*, Nos. 1255, 1256) are here published by H. *Ui*. Digṇāga seems to be the author of the commentary on the Kārikās, for which reason the whole work appears among the works of Dignāga.

[3]) The Tibetan Bu-ston, in his "History of Religion," ascribes 5 Śāstras to Maitreya: (1) Sūtrālaṃkāra in 7 chapters, (2) Madhyānta-Vibhaṅga, (3) Dharma-Dharmatā-Vibhaṅga, (4) Mahāyāna-Uttaratantra-Śāstra, and (5) Abhisamayālaṃkāra-Kārikā. He ascribes to Asaṅga the three works Pañcabhūmi, Abhidharma-Samuccaya and Mahāyāna-Saṃgraha; s. *Stcherbatsky* in Le Muséon, N.S., VI, 1905, 144 f. In the Chinese Tripiṭaka a whole series of works is ascribed to Maitreya, s. *Nanjio*, col. 368. It is true that the tradition that Asaṅga received the revelation from Maitreya in the Tuṣita heaven, was already taken to China by Paramārtha (499-569), and was believed by Dharmapāla (528-560), Prabhākaramitra (630-632), who translated the Mahāyāna-Sūtrālaṃkāra-Śāstra into Chinese, as well as by Hsüan-Tsang and I-tsing. However, see below, p. 354, note 1.

school teaches the Vijñānavāda, *i.e.* that nothing exists outside consciousness. Thus, like the Sūnyavāda, it denies the reality of the world of phenomena, but yet, in a certain sense, recognises an existence contained in thought and consciousness. The sole Absolute, however, which embraces this conciousness which in its turn includes in itself all psychic processes (ālayavijñāna), is Bodhi, the one and only truth, which is *one*, though revealed in the endless multiplicity of the Buddhas. But this Bodhi is only attainable to the Yogācāra, *i.e.* to him who practises Yoga, and even to him only in stages, after he has gone through all the ten stages (daśabhūmi) of the career of a Bodhisattva. The practice of Yoga, which, in Hīnayāna Buddhism also, plays no unimportant part,[1] is here associated systematically with Mahāyāna Buddhism.[2]

At all events, the Abhisamyālaṃkāra-Kārikās, also known as the Prajñā-Pāramitopadeśa-Sāstra, are certainly the work of Maitreyanātha. The text is usually to be found at the beginning of the manuscripts of the Pañcaviṃśatisāhasrikā-Prajñā-Pāramitā, which was translated into Chinese between 261 and 316 A.D.[3] In all probability, the text of the Mahāyāna-Sūtrālaṃkāra, which is composed of memorial verses

---

[1] For instance, the Manual of a Mystic being a Translation from the Pāli and Sinhalese work entitled the Yogavachara's Manual, by F. L. *Woodward*, ed. by Mrs. *Rhys Davids*, London, PTS 1916, is a Hīnayāna manual of Yoga.

[2] On the teachings of the Yogācāra school or the school of the Yogācāryas, *cf.* *La Vallée Poussin*, Bouddhisme, p. 200 ff.; D. T. *Suzuki*, Outlines of Mahāyāna Buddhism, London 1907, pp. 60 ff., 125 ff.; S. *Lévi* in the introduction to his translation of the Mahāyāna-Sūtrālaṃkāra; Y. *Sōgen*, Systems of Buddhistic Thought, p. 210 ff.; Otto *Rosenberg*, Die Probleme der buddhistischen Philosophie, Heidelberg 1924 (Materialien zur Kunde des Buddhismus 8), p. 235 f.; J. *Masuda*, Der individualistische Idealismus der Yogācāra-Schule (Materialien zur Kunde des Buddhismus 10), Heidelberg 1926. Th. *Stcherbatsky*, The Conception of Buddhist Nirvāṇa, p. 31 ff.

[3] *Cf.* Haraprasāda *Śāstrī* in JASB 1910, p. 425 ff., and Descriptive Catalogue of Sanskrit MSS... Asiatic Society of Bengal 1, 1917, p. 7 ff. The section on Trikāya in Chapt. VI of the Abhisamayālaṃkāra with commentary, translated into French by P. *Masson Oursel* in JA, 11 sér., I, 1913, p. 598 ff. S. *Lévi* (Rapport sur la mission dans l'Inde et au Japon in Comptes Rendus de l'Académie des inscr. et belles lettres, Paris 1899, p. 83) mentions a

(Kārikās), which was discovered by S. Lévi and attributed to Asaṅga by the same scholar, is also the work of Maitreyanātha.[1] Without being a great poet, the author of these memorial verses certainly has the art of writing Buddhist Sanskrit skilfully, and also of utilising elaborate metres side by side with Ślokas and Āryā stanzas. However, he is decidedly more of a philosopher than a poet. Even when, in the last two chapters he glorifies the perfections of the Buddhas, and concludes with a hymn (verses 43-61), there is more erudition than enthusiastic worship in the enumeration of all the perfections of the Buddhas. Only in Chapter IX, in which Maitreyanātha expends all his mental energy in elucidating the conception of Bodhi and Buddhahood, is the dry-as-dust tone occasionally enlivened and elevated by more imaginative and picturesque language. Thus, for instance, Bodhi, by which the Buddhas enlighten the world, is compared with the sun, in a series of metaphors (IX, 20 ff.).

The Yogācāra-Bhūmi-Śāstra or Saptadaśa-Bhūmi-Śāstra, too, of which only a portion, the Bodhisattva-Bhūmi,[2] has

---

commentary by Haribhadra (10th century) on the Abhisamayālaṃkāra. However, according to Haraprasāda *Śāstrī* (JBORS 5, 1919, 176 f.), the monk Haribhadra, who lived under Dharmapāla, the second king of the Pāla dynasty, is the author of the commentary Abhisamayālaṃkārāvaloka on the Aṣṭasāhasrikā-Prajñā-Pāramitā.

[1]) Asaṅga, Mahāyāna-Sūtrālaṃkāra, Exposé de la doctrine du grand vehicule selon le système Yogācāra, Édité et traduit par Sylvain *Lévi*, t. II (Bibliothèque de l'École des hautes études, t. 159, 190), Paris 1907, 1911. On the style and contents of the work, *cf.* St. *Schayer* in ZII 2, 1923, 99 ff. H. *Ui* (ZII 6, 1928, 215 ff.) has made it seem very probable that Maitreyanātha, and not Asaṅga, was the author of the Mahāyāna-Sūtrālaṃkāra; even previously, Haraprasāda *Śāstrī* (Ind. Hist. Qu. I, 1925, 465 f.) had declared Maitreyanātha to be the founder of the Yogācāra school, and placed him between 150 and 265 A.D. In the work itself Asaṅga is not mentioned as the author, but it is described as being "proclaimed by the Bodhisattva Vyavadātasamaya ('Purifier of the doctrine'). This might be an epithet of Asaṅga just as well as of Maitreyanātha. According to S. *Lévi*, both the Kārikās and the commentary are the work of Asaṅga. H. *Ui* (l.c., 220 ff.) shows that Vasubandhu is the author of the commentary.

[2]) Bodhisattvabhūmi, a Text-Book of the Yogācāra School; an English Summary with Notes etc., by C. *Bendall* and L. *de La Vallée Poussin*, Le Muséon, N. S. VI, 1905, p. 38 ff.; VII, 1906, p. 213 ff.; XII, 1911, p. 155 ff.; Unrai *Wogihara*, Asaṅga's

come down in Sanskrit, is among the works which are supposed to have been revealed to Asaṅga by the mythical Maitreya: probably, however, it is one of Maitreyanātha's works. It is a prose work after the style of the Abhidharma texts. The Bodhisattva-Bhūmi, "The Bodhisattva step," is the fifteenth of the seventeen steps taught in this large work: the last step is that in which no trace of the Karman remains.[1]

The Tibetans attribute the Yogācāra-Bhūmi-Śāstra to Asaṅga. Hsüan-Tsang, too, who took Asaṅga's work to China, appears to have regarded it as a work of this master. At all events the name of Asaṅga[2] as the teacher of the Yogācāra-Vijñānavāda has become more famous than that of his teacher Maitreyanātha. It is true that his works have only come down in Chinese translations: Mahāyāna-Samparigraha, translated by Paramārtha (563 A.D.),[3] Prakaraṇa-Āryavācā, Mahāyānābhidharma-Saṃgīti-Śāstra, translated by Hsüan-Tsang (625 A.D.),[4] and a commentary on the Vajracchedikā, translated by Dharmagupta (590-616 A.D.).[5]

Asaṅga, more properly Vasubandhu Asaṅga, is the eldest of three brothers, who were born as the sons of a Brahman of the Kauśika family in Puruṣapura (the present-day Peshāwar) in the extreme North-West of India. They probably lived in the 4th century[6] and were all three originally adherents of

---

Bodhisattvabhūmi, Strassburger Diss., Leipzig 1908. The text of the Bodhisattvabhūmi is also edited by J. *Rahder* in the Appendix to the edition of the Daśabhūmi-Sūtra (1926). *Cf.* also U. *Wogihara* in ZDMG 58, 1904, 451 ff. On Yogācārya- and Yogācāra-Bhūmi, s. *Ui*, l.c., p. 224 f.

[1]) *Cf.* E. *Leumann* in ZDMG 62, 1908, p. 89 ff.

[2]) About him, *cf.* M. *Anesaki* in ERE II, 62; *Wogihara*, l.c.; *Lévi* in the introduction to the Mahāyāna-Sūtrālaṃkāra; N. *Péri*, A propos de la date de Vasubandhu, p. 31 ff.; *Winternitz* in WZKM 27, 1913, 33 ff.

[3]) It is the principal work of the Shōron sect in Japan; s. *McGovern*, Introduction to Mahāyāna Buddhism, p. 209.

[4]) *Nanjio*, No. 1199.

[5]) *Nanjio*, No. 1168; *Bagchi* I, 258.

[6]) N. *Péri*, A propos de la date de Vasubandhu (BEFEO XI, 1911, Nos. 3-4) has adduced sound arguments in favour of Vasubandhu's having lived in the 4th century A.D.

the Sarvāstivāda school. The youngest, Vasubandhu Viriñcivatsa, was not prominent in literature. So much the more important was the middle one of the three brothers, Vasubandhu, one of the most prominent figures in the history of Buddhist literature.[1] He combined great independence of thought with astonishing erudition. His chief work, the Abhidharmakośa, has unfortunately not come down in the Sanskrit original. We only know the Abhidharmakośa-

J. *Takakusu* (JRAS 1905, 33 ff.) had placed Vasubandhu between 420 and 500 A.D., but stated later (JRAS 1914, p. 1013 ff.), without definitely going over to *Péri's* side, that he was inclined to assume that Vasubandhu lived earlier. *Wogihara* (Asaṅga's Bodhisattvabhūmi, p. 16) places Vasubandhu between 390 and 470, and Asaṅga between 375 and 450, but in ERE XII, 1921, 595 f., he states 420-500 as the period of Vasubandhu's life. *Lévi* places Asaṅga's activity in the first half of the 5th century. It appears, however, that there were two Vasubandhus, both of whom dealt with Abhidharma and the elder of whom was the teacher and the younger the pupil of Manoratha. This view was put before me, and was supported by sound arguments in great detail, as early as the year 1922, by the Japanese scholar T. *Kimura* when he visited Prague, and also in a long letter. However, I cannot say that I am fully in agreement with his grounds for assigning the dates 420-500 A.D., to the later Vasubandhu, the author of the Abhidharmakośa. Cf. *Watters*, On Yuan Chwang's Travels in India, I, 211 ff.; *La Vallée Poussin*, Bouddhisme, Études et Matériaux, Cosmologie, p. viii ff. and Abhidharmakośa, traduit et annoté, I, p. 26 (note to I, 13), II, p. 70 (note to III, 27), III, p. 7 (note to IV, 3); *Stcherbatsky*, The Central Conception of Buddhism, p. 2, note 2. According to K. B. *Pathak* (Ind. Ant. 41, 1912, 244) Vasubandhu lived under Kumāragupta and Skandagupta; the monk Buddhamitra, who is mentioned in an inscription, is identified by him with Vasubandhu's teacher, who, according to Paramārtha, was called Buddhamitra. *Smith*, Early History, pp. 320, note 2, 325, 346 f., agrees with N. *Péri*, and places the life-time of Vasubandhu, the author of the Kośa, in the period of the reign of Chandragupta I and Samudragupta (about 280-360 A.D.). Hsüan-Tsang says that the Abhidharmakośa was written during the reign of Vikramāditya or his son Bālāditya, s. *Watters* I, 210.

[1]) *I-tsing* (transl. *Takakusu*, p. 181) classes Asaṅga and Vasubandhu among the celebrated men of the "middle ages," *i.e.* the period between the time of Aśvaghoṣa, Nāgārjuna and Āryadeva on the one hand, and his own time on the other. The Indian monk *Paramārtha* (499-569 A.D.) compiled a biography of Vasubandhu, in which that of his brother Asaṅga is also included. It has been translated from the Chinese by J. *Takakusu* in T'oung Pao V, 1904, pp. 1 ff.; given in extracts by W. *Wassiljew*, Der Buddhismus, p. 235 ff. Still more fabulous than the Chinese is the Tibetan biography in *Tāranātha's* History of Buddhism, p. 107 ff. Paramārtha took the works of Asaṅga and Vasubandhu from Magadha to China in the year 539. Hsüan-Tsang, too (s. *Watters* I, 354 ff.), relates legends of Asaṅga and Vasubandhu.

Vyākhyā, Yaśomitra's commentary on the work,[1] and on the other hand the Chinese and Tibetan versions. the earliest Chinese translation is that of Paramārtha, written between 563 and 567 A.D. A second translation (651-654 A.D.) is by the celebrated Hsüan-Tsang. The Abhidharmakośa treats, in 600 memorial verses (Kārikās) together with the author's own commentary (Bhāṣya), of the entire field of ontology, psychology, cosmology,[2] ethics and the doctrine of salvation. The last chapter, which is given either as Chapter IX or as an appendix to Chapter VIII, and which is not composed of memorial verses, treats of the Buddhist doctrine of the soul (denial of a permanent soul), and is directed against the Pudgalavādins, those who believe in a permanent soul.[3] Though the Abhidharmakośa is written from the standpoint of the Sarvāstivāda school of the Hīnayāna, it is nevertheless an authority for *all* schools of Buddhism. We can learn far more from the Kośa with its commentary, about the dogmatics of the ancient Buddhist schools, than from any other work, and it affords us a sidelight upon the debates between the Vaibhāṣikas and the

[1]) Sphuṭārthā Abhidharmakoçavyākhyā, the Work of Yaçomitra First Koçasthāna, ed. by S. *Lévi* and Th. *Stcherbatsky*, Bibl. Buddhica XXI, 1918. L. *de La Vallée Poussin* has translated the Sanskrit text of Yaśomitra's Vyākhyā, making use of the Tibetan version of Vasubandhu's own commentary and the Chinese versions by Paramārtha and Hsüan-Tsang, into French : L'Abhidharmakośa de Vasubandhu traduit et annoté, hitherto 5 vols., Paris 1923-1926. *Cf.* also *Burnouf*, Introduction, pp. 397 ff., 502 ff.; Rāj. *Mitra*, Nep. Buddh. Lit., p. 3 ff.; *Bendall*, Catalogue, p. 25 ff., S. *Lévi* in ERE I, p. 20; *La Vallée Poussin* in ERE IV, p. 129 ff.

[2]) Chapter III, which deals with cosmology, has already been reconstructed in Sanskrit, and translated into French, by *La Vallée Poussin* in Bouddhisme, Études et Matériaux, Cosmologie : Le Monde des Êtres et le Monde-Réceptacle (Mémoires de l'Académie Roy. de Belgique, classe de lettres, etc., II. série, t. VI, 1914-1919) according to the Tibetan version. In the appendix to this work, *La Vallée Poussin* gives an analysis and the extant fragments of the Prajñapti-Śāstra (Lokaprajñapti and Kāraṇaprajñapti) by Maudgalyāyana, belonging to the Abhidharma of the Sarvāstivādins. *Cf.* also *La Vallée Poussin* in ERE IV. 129 ff.

[3]) It has been translated from the Tibetan by Th. *Stcherbatsky*, The Soul Theory of the Buddhists, in Bulletin de l'Académie des Sciences de Russie, Petrograd 1919, pp 824 ff., 937 ff. The Pudgalavādins are here called Vātsīputrīyas.

Sautrāntikas. Moreover, the work is rich in quotations from the earlier literature.[1] In the 7th century the Abhidharmakośa was so widely read in India that, in a description of a hermitage of Buddhist monks, Bāṇa says that the parrots explained the Kośa to one another.[2] This work gave rise to an extensive literature of commentaries, and in China and Japan it is largely used as a text-book. It is also the final authority, when controversies regarding points of dogma arise.[3]

There is a book of sayings, thoroughly Hīnayānist in character, extant only in Tibetan and ascribed to Vasubandhu, called the Gāthā-Saṃgraha, with a brilliant commentary, from which A. Schiefner[4] has given a few specimens. The 24 Gāthās are sayings in the true manner of the Dhammapada. Provided that the work is correctly ascribed to him, the commentary shows us the philosopher Vasubandhu also as a humorous preacher. Merely a short specimen of this :

"A jackal followed a lion, because he desired the remains of the meat which the lion had devoured. As the lion had once, when he was hungry, slain a great boar, he told the jackal to carry this load. Now as the jackal was too feeble, and could not carry this load, but was afraid that the lion might in wrath, kill him, he had no pleasure in complying with the lion's

---

[1]) Some passages from the Abhidharmakośa-Vyākhyā have been compared with corresponding passages in the Pāli Canon, by *La Vallée Poussin* (JRAS 1906, p. 443 ff.). *La Vallée Poussin's* book, La morale bouddhique, Paris 1927, is based largely upon the Abhidharmakośa. *Cf.* also Y. *Sōgen*, Systems of Buddhistic Thought, pp. 109 ff.

[2]) Harṣacarita VIII; s. Harṣacarita transl. by E. B. *Cowell* and F. W. *Thomas*, p. 236.

[3]) *Cf.* O. *Rosenberg*, Die Probleme der buddhistischen Philosophie, pp. xv, 87 ff., 41, 93. Hwui Li (The Life of Hiuen-Tsiang, transl. by S. *Beal*, p. 80) says of Vasubandhu : " His deep reasoning and ornate style were the admiration of all Western students. The very spirits and demons also studied and followed his teaching." Hwui Li (*loc. cit.*, p. 79 f.) also reports : The Kashmiri Saṅghabhadra wrote a Kośa-Kārikā-Śāstra in 25,000 Ślokas and 80 myriads of words. He died before he could have the meeting with Vasubandhu which he had desired. However, when later on, Vasubandhu became acquainted with Saṅghabhadra's work, he praised it highly, and said it should be called the Nyāyānusāra-Śāstra, because it was in such close agreement with his own teachings.

[4]) Über Vasubandhu's Gāthā-Saṃgraha, Mélanges asiatiques VIII (Bulletin, t. XXV, St. Petersburg 1878), p. 559 ff.

request. But as he knew the lion was proud, he said : 'It is needful to do two things in carrying this load, to groan and to bear the burden ; I cannot do both at the same time, you will have to undertake one of them.' As the lion was proud and did not want to groan, he asked the jackal to groan, while he could carry the load himself. So the lion carried the load, but the jackal followed the lion, groaning. In the same way I also bear the burden of presenting the doctrine, but you are not able to say, in agreement with me, 'It is so.' "[1])

In the Abhidharmakośa already, Vasubandhu adduces many arguments against the teachings of Brahmanical philosophy, and he attacks the Vaiśeṣikas in particular. He wrote an especial work in order to refute the Sāṃkhya philosophy, the Paramārtha-Saptati, " Seventy (verses) on the Highest Truth." This work, the Sanskrit original of which is lost also, seems to be a confutation of Īśvarakṛṣṇa's Sāṃkhya-Saptati, though Paramārtha speaks of a heretic Vindhyavāsa as the author of the Sāṃkhya work attacked by Vasubandhu. Strange to say, the Chinese also ascribe a commentary on Īśvarakṛṣṇa's work to Vasubandhu.[2)]

It was not until the latter part of his life that Vasubandhu was converted to the Mahāyāna by his brother Asaṅga. Now, as his biographer relates, he regretted his former calumniation of the Mahāyāna so deeply that he wanted to cut off his tongue. But his brother demonstrated to him that it would be a much better penance if he would now employ his tongue, which he had formerly employed in attacking the Mahāyāna doctrine, with equal skill in expounding the Mahāyāna. Vasubandhu did this, and after the death of Asaṅga, wrote a large number of commentaries on Mahāyāna-

[1]) *Schiefner, loc. cit.*, p. 582.

[2]) See *Takakusu* in T'oung Pao 1904, pp. 15 ff., 461 ff. ; BEFEO, t. IV, 1904, p. 1 ff. ; JRAS 1905, p. 16 ff. *Takakusu's* assumption that Vindhyavāsa is another name for Īśvarakṛṣṇa is not tenable, see S. N. *Dasgupta*, History of Indian Philosophy, I, Cambridge 1922, p. 218, note 3.

Sūtras, on the Saddharma-Puṇḍarīka,[1] the Mahā-Parinirvāṇa-Sūtra[2] and the Vajracchedikā-Prajñā-Pāramitā.[3] It was at this time that he also wrote the two classical treatises on idealism, the Viṃśatikā and Triṃśikā,[4] in which in a subtle manner, he refutes the belief in the reality of the objective world, but defends the doctrine of the reality of pure consciousness (Vijñānamātra). The Tibetan Bu-ston also mentions the following works of Vasubandhu : Pañcaskandha-Prakaraṇa, Vyākhyāyukti, Karma-Siddhi-Prakaraṇa and commentaries on Maitreya's Mahāyāna-Sūtralaṃkāra, on the Pratītya-Samutpāda-Sūtra and the Madhyānta-Vibhāga.[5] Towards the end of his life, he is said to have become a devotee of Amitābha and to have written a work entitled Aparimitāyus-Sūtropadeśa, in which he gave expression to the longing for Sukhāvatī.[6] Paramārtha concludes his biography of Vasubandhu with these words :

"The sense conveyed in his compositions is fine and excellent ; there is no one who, on hearing or seeing it, does not believe and pursue it. Therefore all those who study the

[1]) Translated into Chinese between 508 and 535, s. *Nanjio*, Nos. 1232, 1233; *Bagchi* I, 250, 258.

[2]) Translated between 386 and 550, s. *Nanjio*, Nos. 1206, 1207.

[3]) Translated between 386 and 534, s. *Nanjio*, No. 1231.

[4]) The Sanskrit originals of these two treatises the Viṃśatikā with the author's commentary, and the Triṃśikā with Sthiramati's commentary, were discovered by S. *Lévi* and edited by him for the first time : Vijñaptimātratāsiddhi, deux traités de Vasubandhu, Viṃśatikā et Triṃśikā, Paris 1925 (Bibliothèque de l'École des hautes études, sc. hist. et phil. 245). The Viṃśatikā with the author's commentary has been translated into French from the Tibetan, by *La Vallée Poussin* (Le Muséon 1912, pp. 53-90). A good idea of the subject-matter of these two important philosophical treatises, is given by Surendra Nath *Dasgupta* in Ind. Hist. Qu. IV, 1928, p. 36 ff. There were as many as ten different commentaries on the Vijñapti-mātratā-triṃśat-kārikā in India : these were translated by Hsüan-Tsang, who afterwards melted them down to *one* work with Dharmapālas commentary Vijñapti-mātratā-siddhi-Śāstra. Dharmapāla was the teacher of Hsüan-Tsang's teacher. *Cf.* H. *Ui*, The Vaiśeṣika Philosophy, London, OTF, 1917, p. 2, and L. *de La Vallée Poussin*, Vijñapti-Mātratāsiddhi, La Siddhi de Hiuan Tsang, Paris, 1928.

[5]) See *Stcherbatsky* in Le Muséon, N.S. VI, 1905, 144 ff. According to G. *Tucci* (Ind. Hist. Qu. IV, 1928, 630 ff.) the Vādavidhi, which others ascribe to Dignāga, is also a work of Vasubandhu.

[6]) *Cf.* *U. Wogihara* in ERE, XII, 596.

Mahāyāna and Hīnayāna in India and in all the frontier countries use the works of Vasubandhu as their text-books. There are no teachers of any other schools (of Buddhism) or of the heretical sects who, on hearing his name, will not become quite nervous and timid. He died in A-yu-ja (Ayodhyā) at the age of eighty. Though he lived an earthly life, his real nature is indeed difficult to be understood."[1]

A work which attempted a synthesis of the teachings of the Mādhyamika and Vijñānavāda schools, is the Mahāyāna-Śraddhotpāda, "The Origin of the Mahāyāna Faith." It is attributed to Aśvaghoṣa, but cannot possibly have been written by the poet of the Buddhacarita. It must remain an open question whether it was attributed to the great poet with a view to securing a greater reputation for the book, or whether there was an Aśvaghoṣa II in about the 5th century A.D., who wrote this philosophical work, which gives evidence of an advanced stage of development of Mahāyāna philosophy.[2] The work has come down only in two Chinese versions, one by Paramārtha (about 553 A.D.) and one by Śikṣānanda (about 700 A.D.).[3] It is entirely unknown in

[1]) J. *Takakusu*, The Life of Vasubandhu by Paramārtha (A.D. 499-569). Extrait du "T'oung-pao," 1904, p. 27.

[2]) In the year 1912 I repeatedly had the opportunity to converse with my friend Prof. *Takakusu* verbally as well as by letter, regarding the question of the authorship of the Mahāyāna-Śraddhotpāda. In a letter of the 18th July, 1912, he wrote to me : "Either the poet Aśvaghoṣa is different from the philosopher Aśvaghoṣa (for Buddhists generally believe there were more than one Aśvaghoṣa) or that Śāstra of a different origin has been attributed to him simply because of his great renown. I think the latter is the case, *for an earlier Catalogue of Chinese texts omits the name Aśvaghoṣa.* In any case the Mahāyāna-Śraddhotpāda does not belong to him. Nor do the contents show any probability of his authorship. It is later than Laṅkāvatāra in which Nāgārjuna's appearance is prophesied by Buddha, and only a step earlier than Vijñānamātravāda." R. *Kimura*, Hīnayāna and Mahāyāna, Calcutta, 1927, pp. 41, 180 ff., is inclined to attribute the work to the beginning of the 5th century A.D. On the doctrines of the Mahāyāna-Śraddhotpāda, *cf.* Y. *Sōgen*, Systems of Buddhistic Thought, p. 252 ff.; S. N. *Dasgupta*, History of Indian Philosophy, I, 129 ff.; K. J. *Saunders*, Epochs in Buddhist History, p. 97 ff. ; *Stcherbatsky*, Nirvāṇa, p. 32 ; *McGovern*, Introduction to Mahāyāna Buddhism, p. 60 ff.

[3]) It has been translated into English, after the second Chinese version, by *Teitaro Suzuki*, Açvagosha's Discourse on the Awakening of Faith in the Mahāyāna, Chicago, 1900.

Sanskrit, and is not quoted either by the great masters of the Mahāyāna or their commentators. In a biography of Hsüan-Tsang, the Mahāyāna-Śraddhotpāda is ascribed to the celebrated Aśvaghoṣa, but it is said that Hsüan-Tsang translated it *from Chinese into Sanskrit,* and thus propagated it throughout the five empires of India.[1] Even at the present day the work is much studied in the schools and monasteries of Japan and it is a favourite work of reference.

Buddhapālita and Bhāvaviveka (or Bhavya),[2] who belong to the school of Nāgārjuna and Āryadeva and wrote commentaries on their works, lived and worked at the beginning of the 5th century A.D. Buddhapālita is the founder of the Prāsaṅgika school, which followed the method of leading an opponent *ad absurdum,* whilst Bhāvaviveka founded the Svātantra school, which seeks to prove the correctness of the Mādhyamika doctrines by means of independent (svatantra) arguments. Their works have come down only in Tibetan translations.

In the 5th century A.D. there lived Sthiramati,[3] Dignāga (or Diṅnāga), and somewhat younger Dharmapāla, teachers who arose from Vasubandhu's school. Sthiramati wrote a commentary on the Kāśyapa-Parivarta, or Ratnakūṭa,[4]

Suzuki regards the poet Aśvaghoṣa as the author. It has been translated into English, after Paramārtha's Chinese version, by Timothy *Richard,* The New Testament of Higher Buddhism, pp. 37-125. On the Chinese translations, s. *Suzuki,* l.c., p. 38 ff., and *Bagchi,* I, 423.

1) *Cf.* J. *Nobel,* Kumārajīva, in SBA, 1927, p. 231, note. This account would speak in favour of the view, held by a few Japanese scholars, especially *Senshoi Murakami,* that the Mahāyāna-Śraddhotpāda is a Chinese, and not a Sanskrit work. There was a heated controversy on this question in Japan, s. EB I, 1921, pp. 88, 103 ff.

2) *Cf.* P. L. *Vaidya,* Études sur Āryadeva, p. 26 ff.; *Stcherbatsky,* Nirvāṇa, p. 66 f.

3) The question of the date of Sthiramati is very complicated, and it is probable that there was more than one author of this name. One Sthiramati was a pupil of Guṇamati, and lived before 425 A.D. *Cf.* N. *Péri,* La date de Vasubandhu, Extrait du BEFEO 1911, p. 46 ff.; H. *Ui* in ZII 6, 1928, p. 218 f.; and A. V. *Staël-Holstein,* The Kāçyapaparivarta, p. xvi f.

4) Extant in Chinese and Tibetan translations, s. A. V. *Staël-Holstein,* l.c., p. xiv f.

and on Vasubandhu's Triṃśikā. Dharmapāla wrote a commentary on the Vijñaptimātratā-Siddhi. The greatest and most independent thinker among the successors of Vasubandhu is Dignāga, the founder of Buddhist logic, and one of the foremost figures in the history of Indian Philosophy.[1] Only *a single one* of Dignāga's works, the Nyāyapraveśa, has come down in Sanskrit; we know the others only from the Tibetan translations.[2] The principal work of his successor Dharmakīrti,[3] the Nyāyabindu, has come down to us in Sanskrit.

One of Dharmapāla's pupils is Chandrakīrti, who must accordingly have lived in the 6th century, and not, as is usually taken for granted,[4] in the 7th. According to Tāranātha, he was born in Southern India at Samanta, even in childhood showed great intellectual gifts, entered the monastic order, studied all the Piṭakas, and began to study the works of Nāgārjuna under Kamalabuddhi, the pupil of Buddhapālita and Bhavya. After completing his studies, he lived as a Pandit in Nālandā, and wrote numerous works on

[1]) According to Tāranātha, Dignāga was a pupil of Vasubandhu. Works by him were translated into Chinese in 557 and 569 A.D. *Randle*, Fragments from Diṅnāga, p. 3, says: "All that can be said with certainty is that he lived somewhere between 350 A.D. and 500 A.D." *Cf.* Th. *Watters*, On Yuan Chwang's Travels in India, II, 209 ff.; *Keith*, Buddhist Philosophy, p. 305 ff.; and *Stcherbatsky*, Nirvāṇa, p. 35. Translations of Dignāga's works on logic are to appear shortly, by Prof. *Stcherbatsky*, who wrote to me about it on 26th April, 1929: "You will be astonished to find among the Indians, especially Dignāga, a comprehensive system of critical philosophy. It has long been my conviction that we here have before us a most excellent achievement of the Indian mind, this conviction has now grown stronger than ever before, and I hope to be in a position to present it clearly."

[2]) The Tibetan text of the Nyāyapraveśa is edited by Vidhushekhara *Bhattacharya* in GOS No. XXXIX, Baroda, 1927. The Sanskrit text is to be edited by A. B. *Dhruva* in GOS. The Sanskrit fragments which are available in quotations have been collected and translated by H. N. *Randle*, Fragments from Diṅnāga, London, 1926.

[3]) *Cf. Keith*, Buddhist Philosophy, p. 308 ff. The trio Nāgārjuna, Āryadeva and Asaṅga, together with the trio Vasubandhu, Dignāga and Dharmakīrti, are called by the Tibetans "the six ornaments of Jambudvīpa," s. *Grünwedel*, Mythologie des Buddhismus in Tibet, p. 36. Dignāga and Dharmakīrti more properly belong to the history of secular philosophy; for further information on them, see Vol. III.

[4]) *Cf.* P. L. *Vaidya*, Études sur Āryadeva, p. 52 ff.

Mādhyamika philosophy. He is the principal representative of the Prāsaṅgika school, and carried on the work of Nāgārjuna and Āryadeva.[1] His chief work is the Madhyamakāvatāra, "Introduction to the Middle Doctrine," which has come down to us in the Tibetan Tanjur.[2] Chandrakīrti frequently refers to this work of his own, in the abovementioned commentary Prasannapadā on the Mūla-Madhyamaka-Kārikās. In this commentary he gives evidence of exceptional erudition, in the numerous quotations, which are very important for us, because many of the texts which he cites, have not come down to us in Sanskrit. Chandrakīrti is not only a learned scholastic, but a good writer as well. The numerous verse quotations, which occur especially frequently at the end of a chapter, put life into the narration. His commentary on Āryadeva's Catuḥśatikā is a work of even greater literary merit. In this treatise, the presentation of the dogmas and philosophical doctrines is continually flavoured by means of examples, comparisons and parables.[3]

For instance, the fact that there are more causes for grief than for joy, is explained in the following way: "It is just like the wooing of a princess who holds a self-choice of a husband (svayamvara). The many who come to woo her, suffer grief; for she is the cause of joy to *one* only, not for all. Though many desire her, they do not win her, hence they are unhappy."

In order to explain that there is nothing which is impure in itself, the following is related: An astrologer declared to a certain king, that rain would fall, and that everyone who used this rain-water, would become mad. Then the king had his own well closed. The rain fell, all the people used the water, and became mad. As they were all mad, they all

1) *Stcherbatsky*, Nirvāṇa, p. 66, describes him "as a mighty champion of the purely negative method of establishing Monism."

2) The Tibetan text edited in Bibl. Buddhica, IX, 1912, by L. *de La Vallée Poussin*, and translated by the same scholar in Le Muséon, N.S. VIII, 1907; XI, 1910; XII, 1911. *Cf.* also Le Muséon, I, 1900, 226 ff.

3) Similarly Book IV of the Sāṃkhya-Sūtra contains a whole collection of "little stories" (Ākhyāyikās).

thought that they were all sane, and only the king was considered to be mad. When the king saw how things were, he too used that water, so that the people should not think him mad, laugh at him, or even kill him.

Another example: If only *one* person in the world were to pass urine, he would be avoided as one avoids a leper. But as all people pass urine, it does not occur to anyone to see anything unclean in it.[1]

A contemporary and opponent of Chandrakīrti, whose teachings he refuted, was Candragomin, who enjoys an immense reputation in the Buddhist world as a grammarian, philosopher and poet. According to Tāranātha,[2] who has much that is legendary to relate of him, he composed an enormous number of hymns and learned works. Of his poetical works we have only a religious poem in the form of a letter to his pupil, the *Siṣyalekha-Dharma-Kāvya*.[3] Buddhist doctrines are here presented in elegant Kāvya style. His drama Lokānanda has come down to us only in the Tibetan version in the Tanjur.[4]

As the most prominent among the later teachers of Mahāyāna Buddhism, who also shone as poets, we have to mention Śāntideva, who probably lived in the 7th century A.D. According to Tāranātha, he was born in Saurāṣṭra (in

---

[1]) Catuḥśatikā by Ārya Deva edited by Haraprasāda *Śāstrī*, pp. 458, 459.

[2]) Geschichte des Buddhismus, p. 156 ff.

[3]) Edited by I. P. *Minayeff* in Zapiski IV; *cf.* H. *Wenzel*, JRAS, 1889, p. 1133 ff; *Bendall*, Catalogue, p. 31 f.; *Kern*, Manual, p. 11.

[4]) I-tsing (Record, transl. by J. *Takakusu*, pp. 164, 183) speaks of a Candra or Candradāsa, who was a holy man, a kind of Bodhisattva, who composed a musical play about Prince Viśvāntara (=Pāli Vessantara), to which all people " in the five realms of India " sing and dance, and who was still alive when he came to India (in 673] A.D.). S. *Lévi* (BEFEO 3, 1903, p. 41 f.) has identified this Candra with Candragomin. This identification has, however, been refuted on good grounds, by B. *Liebich* (Das Datum Candragomin's und Kalidasa's, Breslau 1903). *Liebich* (WZKM 13, 1899, 308 ff.) dates Candragomin between 465 and 544 A.D., which would approximately fit in with our dating of his contemporary Candrakīrti. Candragomin was a pupil of Sthiramati. *Péri*, l. c., (Extrait, p. 50, note 2) places Candragomin in the beginning or the first half of the 7th century. However, in the first half of the 7th century Candragomin's Grammar is already used by the writers of the Kāśikā. On Candragomin as a grammarian, s. Vol. III.

the present-day Gujarat) as a king's son, but was instigated by the goddess Tārā herself to renounce the throne, whilst the Bodhisattva Mañjuśrī, in the form of a Yogin, initiated him into the sciences. He acquired great magic powers, and was for a time the minister of King Pañcasiṃha, but finally he became a monk. He was a pupil of Jayadeva, the successor of Dharmapāla in Nālandā. Tāranātha ascribes to him the works Śikṣā-Samuccaya, Sūtra-Samuccaya and Bodhicaryāvatāra.[1]

The Śikṣā-Samuccaya, "the Sum Total of the Doctrine,"[2] is a manual of Mahāyāna Buddhism, which consists of 27 Kārikās (memorial verses) and an extensive commentary compiled, together with the Kārikās, by the author himself. I say intentionally that the commentary was "compiled" by Śāntideva, for it consists almost entirely of quotations and extracts from the sacred texts, which he has grouped around his Kārikās and arranged in chapters.

---

1) Tāranātha, Geschichte des Budhdismus, übers. von *Schiefner*, p. 162 ff. The biography of Śāntideva, which Haraprasāda *Śāstrī* (Ind. Ant. 42, 1913, pp. 49-52) found in a Nepalese manuscript of the 14th century, agrees in the main with Tāranātha. In this MS. Rājā Mañjuvarmā is mentioned as his father. It is said here that he had the additional name "Bhusuka," because he was well versed in the meditation called "Bhusuka." He is also said to have been the author of a Tantra, and Haraprasāda found works of the Vajrayāna school and songs in the Old Bengali language, which are attributed to a certain Bhusuka. This biography, too, speaks of *three* works of Śāntideva. The assumption of P. L. *Vaidya* (Études sur Āryadeva, p. 54) that by Śikṣā-Samuccaya, the text of the Kārikās is meant, and by Sūtra-Samuccaya the commentary containing the quotations from Sūtras, is indeed very tempting: nevertheless, I regard it as far more likely that the statement about the *three* works of Śāntideva is merely based upon an erroneous interpretation of the verses Bodhicaryāvatāra V. 105 f., where Śāntideva recommends the study of his Śikṣā-Samuccaya or the Sūtra-Samuccaya of Nāgārjuna; s. *Winternitz* in WZKM 26, 1912, 246 ff. *Cf.* also P. L. *Vaidya*, l. c., p. 54 ff. and *Keith*, HSL, pp. 72 f., 236.

2) Edited by C. *Bendall* (Bibl. Buddhica I), St. Petersburg 1902. Translated by C. *Bendall* and W. H. D. *Rouse*, London 1922 (Indian Texts Series). The work was translated into Tibetan between 816 and 838, but was probably written as early as the middle of the 7th century. (*Bendall*, Introduction, p. v f.). *Bendall*, Introd., p. xxxi ff. gives a short summary of contents. The edition rests on a single manuscript.

The work betrays an extraordinary degree of erudition and reading, but little originality. Śāntideva himself confesses this modestly in the introductory words to his book: "I have nothing new to say here, nither have I any skill in the writing of literary works. Therefore my efforts are not for the benefit of others, but my only desire is to perfect my own mind. Nevertheless, the longing for clearness is fostered by this my work, so as to make the good real; and if another who is of the same mind as myself, should see this longing, then this my work will not have been in vain."[1] The book is, nevertheless, extremely suitable as an introduction, especially to the ethical doctrine of the Mahāyāna, and is also of great value on account of the numerous, often long, extracts from texts which are no longer extant, the more so as Śāntideva, in those cases in which we can judge of his work, proves to be very accurate and very reliable in his quotations.

The fundamental idea of the work and the nucleus of Mahāyāna morality, is expressed in the first two Kārikās:

"If to my neighbour as to myself
Fear and pain are hateful,
In what does my ego differ,
That I should guard it more than another's?
Do you wish to attain the end of suffering,
And the goal of happiness ?
Then let your faith be as a firmly planted root,
And direct your mind towards enlightenment."

By means of numerous extracts from the Mahāyāna-Sūtras, it is shown how salutary *Bodhicittam* is, *i.e.*, thought directed towards enlightenment, the Will to Enlightenment, the resolve to embark on the career of a Bodhisattva, in order to become a Buddha in the future. Whoever has formed this resolution,

[1] The same verses are to be found also in the introduction to the Bodhicaryāvatāra.

however, must carry self-denial, self-sacrifice for the sake of others, to the extreme. He must be prepared not only to give up his temporal possessions but even his salvation in the Beyond, for his neighbour. He must not shrink from taking the sins and sufferings of the beings in hell upon himself. The Bodhisattva must say:

> "I take the sufferings of all beings upon myself, I am firmly resolved to do this, I bear them, I do not turn back, I do not fly, I do not shudder, I do not quake, I do not fear, I do not shrink back and do not despair. And why? It is necessary that I take the burden of all beings upon myself. It is not my choice. For I have vowed to deliver all beings...I must liberate all beings from the jungle of birth, from the jungle of old age, from the jungle of disease ..from the dense jungle of heresy, from the jungle of the loss of good deeds, from the jungle which has grown up through ignorance...I am not concerned with my own liberation only. For, with the boat of resolve of omniscience, I must rescue all beings from the flood of Saṃsāra...I am resolved to spend endless myriads of ages in every single place of torture...And why? Because it is bettter that I alone suffer, than that all these beings should sink into the places of torture. I give myself as ransom," etc.[1]

But next to active pity, the pure way of life of the Bodhisattva must also include all the other perfections (Pāramitās), above all, meditation, which leads to the highest wisdom, *i.e.*, to insight into the "unreality" (Sūnyatā) of all phenomena, and faith, which finds expression in Buddha-worship, in the erection of Stūpas, etc. Yet here, too, his mind should ever strain at the liberation of the beings. "May I lead all beings into the city of Nirvāṇa!" Let this be his constant thought.[2]

Of the many texts quoted in the Sikṣā-Samuccaya,[3] we here call attention only to a few, which are represented by

---

1) Text, p. 280 ff., quotation from a Vajradhvaja-Sūtra. Cf *La Vallée Poussin*, Bouddhisme, pp. 322 f., 337 f.

2) According to the Ratnamegha-Sūtra quoted on page 348.

3) They are recorded in the edition by *Bendall*, p. 367 ff.

a considerable number of quotations or by fairly long extracts. A long passage is quoted from the Ākāsa-Garbha-Sūtra, on the sins (the five principal iniquities of a king, the eight iniquities of an Ādikarmika-Bodhisattva, and so on, p. 59 ff.). One short passage and one longer one on sin and confession, are quoted from the Upāli-Paripṛcchā (pp. 164 f., 168 ff.). Quotations from the Ugra- or Ugradatta-Paripṛcchā [1] are fairly numerous, *e. g.*, on the duties of married life (p. 78) and on the life of a hermit in the forest (p. 198 ff.). We find a long passage on the virtues of a Bodhisattva from the Vimala-Kīrtinirdeśa,[2] which is quoted several times (p. 324 ff.). The Avalokana-Sūtra, which occurs in the Mahā-Vastu, is quoted by Śāntideva as an independent text (*e. g.* p. 297 ff.). A long passage from the Ratnolkā-Dhāraṇī [3] on the virtues of a Bodhisattva, shows us a "Dhāraṇī" which is not a mere magic formula, but scarcely differs from a Sūtra. The quotation is also interesting owing to the enumeration of vocations and ascetic orders (p. 331 ff.). Other works quoted, are: Tathāgatayuhya-Sūtra, Daśabhumika-Sūtra, Dharma-Saṃgīti-Sūtra, several recensions of the Prajñā-Pāramitā, Karuṇā-Puṇḍarīka, Gaṇḍavyūha, Candra-Pradīpa-Sūtra, Ratnakūṭa-Sūtra,[4] Ratnamegha, Laṅkāvatāra, Lalita-Vistara, Śālistamba-Sūtra,[5] Saddharma-Puṇḍarīka, Suvarṇa-Prabhāsa, etc.

---

[1]) See above, p. 332.

[2]) The Sūtra has been translated from Chinese, by Karichi *Ôhara* in the Japanese monthly publication Hansei Zasschi XIII, 1898, XIV, 1899, and again by *Hokei Isumi* in EB II-IV (1922-1928). It was translated into Chinese by Kumārajīva in 406 A.D., s. *Bagchi* I, 188.

[3]) P. 327 ff. Cf. *Bendall*, JRAS 1901, p. 122 ff.

[4]) On these Sūtras, see above, p. 327 ff.

[5]) This is a principal source for the doctrine of the Pratītya-Samutpāda; it is edited by *La Valée Poussin*, Théorie des douze causes, Gand 1913, p. 68 ff. Cf. also *La Vallée Poussin* in JRAS 1901, p. 307 f. and E. *Hardy* in JRAS 1901, p. 573.

Although the Śikṣā-Samuccaya is the work of a not very original scholar, and the Bodhicaryāvatāra [1] that of a prominent poet, yet there can scarcely be a doubt that they are both by the same author. Apart from external reasons,[2] these two works, which are so fundamentally different from each other in character,[3] are nevertheless both on exactly the same doctrinal standpoint. In both, the ethical ideal is the Bodhisattva, who has formed the resolve one day to attain enlightenment, who strives to reach this, the highest goal, firstly by infinite pity for the beings, and secondly by worshipping the Buddhas, and who sees the highest wisdom in the conviction of the unreality of the world of phenomena (Śūnyatā).

But while in the Śikṣā-Samuccaya there is often only a loquacious learnedness which shows itself in a flood of quotations, the Bodhicaryāvatāra ("the Entrance into the Bodhi-Life," *i.e.*, "into the way of life leading to enlightenment") not infrequently rises to the loftiest flights of religious poetry.

---

1) Edited by I. P. *Minayeff* in Zapiski IV, 1889, reprinted in JBTS 1894. Prajñākaramati's commentary (including text) edited by *La Vallée Poussin*, Bibl. Ind 1901-1914, Chapt. IX also in Bouddhisme, Études et Matériaux, Mémoires de l'Acad Belgique, t. 55, 1898, pp 253-388. Translations · Into French by *La Vallée Poussin*, Paris 1907 (Extrait de la RHR X-XII, 1905-1907; and by L *Finot*, Paris 1920 (Les classiques de l'Orient II); into English (abridged) by L. D *Barnett*, London, 1909 (Wisdom of the East); into German by Rich. *Schmidt*, Paderborn 1923 (Dokumente der Religion V), into Italian by G *Tucci*, Torino 1925. In the Chinese Tripiṭaka the Bodhicaryāvatāra is erroneously attributed to Nāgārjuna, s. *Lévi* in BEFEO II, 253 ff.

2) *Cf Bendall*, Introduction to the edition of the Śikṣā-Samuccaya, p. iii ff Śāntideva included in the Bodhicaryāvatāra a few passages occurring in the Śikṣā-Samuccaya as quotations, *e. g.*, Śikṣās, p. 155 ff. in Bodhic. VI, 120 ff. In the Bodhic. V, 105, Śāntideva recommends the study of the Śikṣā-Samuccaya.

3) *Barth* (RHR 42, 1900, p. 55 = Oeuvres II, 338) terms the Śikṣā-Samuccaya "la scholastique verbeuse et délayée usque ad nauseam," whilst he values the Bodhicaryāvatāra very highly as a counterpart to the "Imitatio Christi" of Thomas à Kempis (RHR 1896, p. 259 f. = Oeuvres II, 172). The Bodhicaryāvatāra does not, it is true, teach how to imitate Buddha, but teaches how to become a Buddha. Cf. *La Vallée Poussin*, Bouddhisme, p. 297 ff.; C. H. *Tawney* in JRAS 1903, 593 f; Foucher in RHR 1908, t. 57, p. 241 ff.

It is certain that, here too, Śāntideva refrains from pursuing any literary aims in his work; but he gives such fervent and inspired expression to his religious feelings, that he becomes a poet almost in spite of himself.

The work begins with a glorification of bodhicittam, the Will to Enlightenment, the determination to become a Buddha for the sake of the salvation of the beings. Thus it reads, I, 8:

"If you would overcome the many hundreds of sufferings of existence,
If you would deliver all beings from their sufferings,
If you would enjoy many hundreds of delights,
Then never, never cease to direct your minds to Bodhi."

In inspired words, the poet describes his feelings after he has thus directed his mind towards enlightenment. He expresses his fervent joy at the good deeds of all beings and at their liberation, he prays to the Buddhas of all parts of the world, that they may light the lamp of religion for all those who are in ignorance, he beseeches all Bodhisattvas to defer their Nirvāṇa, he prays for the salvation of all beings, and finally offers himself for all beings:

"By the merit which I have ever acquired,
By good deeds, may I bring to all beings
Relief from all their sufferings!
I desire to serve as medicine, doctor and nurse
To all the sick as long as their sickness lasts."

"I desire to be a protector to those who need protection,
A guide to those who wander in the desert,
And a ship, a landing-stage and a bridge
To those who seek the shore.
A lamp to those who need a lamp,
A couch to those who need a couch,
A slave to all beings who need a slave." [1]

---

[1]) III, 6; 7; 17; 18.

Chapters IV-VIII deal with the duties which the Bodhisattva takes upon himself. Whoever has vowed to strive for Bodhi, on him are the hopes of all beings, and he is responsible for the welfare of all beings. He must be diligent in all the perfections (Pāramitās). Above all, he must be prepared to sacrifice himself entirely. He must, however, also obey all the commandments of the religion, and fulfil all the rules of good conduct, as they are laid down in the sacred texts, which he must therefore study diligently.[1]

Our worst enemies are wrath and hatred and passion. These must be overcome. They harm us, not our enemies. We must love our enemies like all other creatures. For if we love the creatures, we delight the Buddhas, but if we injure them, we injure the Buddhas. If others wrong me, it is only the fruit of some action (Karman)—then why should I be angry with them? One must not hate even those who destroy or despise Buddha-pictures, Stūpas, or even the good religion itself. He who does good to the beings, does good to the Buddhas and Bodhisattvas, who have so often annihilated their bodies and have gone to hell for the sake of the beings. Therefore one should do good only, even to those who have done much evil to us.[2] From the outset the Bodhisattva aims at making no difference between his ego and his neighbour: to identify his ego absolutely and entirely with that of others, is a kind of spiritual exercise in which the Bodhisattva is particularly active.

> "I must destroy others' suffering, for it hurts like one's own pain;
> I must do good to others, as they are beings like myself."

In the same way as a man loves his hands and feet, because they are limbs of his body, so all other living beings have a right to his love, as they are all members of the same

[1]) Here (V. 103 ff.) some texts are specially recommended for study.

[2]) See particularly VI, 19; 38; 68; 120; 124; 126.

world of the living. It is only a habit to regard our body, which does not really exist at all, as our ego; in exactly the same way we can form the habit of regarding our neighbour as our ego.[1]

With admirable eloquence, which can only spring from the most sincere conviction, Sāntideva succeeds in representing it as a matter of course, that for the pious disciple of Bodhi, there is complete "equality between one's neighbour and one's ego" (Parātmasamatā), and that he finally reaches the "transformation of one's neighbour into one's ego" (Parātmaparivartana).[2]

Chapter IX is less attractive, and is purely erudite in its content: here the philosophical doctrine of the unreality of the world of phenomena (Śūnyatā) is developed according to the Mādhyamika system, incompatible though the negativism of this system appears to us with the devotion and self-sacrifice for other beings, as taught in the first chapters of the work, yet Sāntideva, too, utilises the doctrine, already familiar to us, of the differentiation between the two truths as a means of bridging the contradiction. Everything in the world is indeed vain and transitory, but only the delusion concerning the ego (ātmamoha) is harmful, whilst the delusion concerning the duties (Kāryamoha) is beneficent.[3] Nevertheless, it is strange enough that, after all the doctrines of active pity, the only conclusion at which the poet can arrive, is (IX, 152 f.):

> As all existence is so empty and transitory,
> What can be gained, what can be taken away?
> Who can be honoured, who blamed?
> How can there be joy and sorrow, beloved objects

[1]) See VIII, 90 ff.

[2]) *Cf. La Vallée Poussin*, ERE II, 749, 752 f.

[3]) *Cf. La Vallée Poussin*, Bouddhisme, Études et Matériaux, Mém. Ac. Belg. 1898, p. 109 ff.

Or objects of hatred? And greed, and non-greed,
Seek where you will, you will never find them.

After this excursion into the metaphysics of silence,— for that is really the true essence of the doctrine of unreality— namely that the answer to any question can only be a silence —the poet comes back to the earth in the concluding chapter (X), and the work ends with an earnest prayer for the welfare of all beings, even for the beings in the hells, and with entreaties to the Bodhisattva Mañjuśrī.[1]

The fact that there are no less than eleven commentaries on the Bodhicaryāvatāra, speaks eloquently for the popularity of the work, though these commentaries have come down only in Tibetan translations.[2]

In the 8th century Śāntarakṣita wrote a large philosophical work Tattva-Saṃgraha,[3] in which, from the standpoint of the Svātantrika Yogācāra school, he criticises numerous other philosophical systems of his day, both Buddhist and non-Buddhist. He himself does not mention the names of the teachers whom he attacks, but we learn them from the commentary which his pupil Kamalaśīla wrote on the work. Among Buddhist teachers we find there Vasumitra, Dharmatrāta, Ghoṣaka, Buddhadeva, Saṅghabhadra, Vasubandhu, Dignāga and Dharmakīrti. Besides these, teachers of the Lokāyata, the Jain philosophy, and of Sāṃkhya, Nyāya and

---

1) In the days of Tāranātha there were doubts as to the authenticity of this chapter, and the commentator Prajñākaramati did not explain the chapter, though it was known to him. However, all the MSS. and the other commentaries have it, and it certainly seems to me to be a far better conclusion to the work, than if it ended with Chapter IX. *Cf. La Vallée Poussin*, Bodhicaryāvatāra traduit p. 143 f.

2) The titles of the commentaries are given by P. L. *Vaidya*, Études sur Āryadeva, p. 56 f.

3) Tattvasaṅgraha of Śāntarakṣita with the Commentary of Kamalaśīla. Edited by *Embar Krishnamacharya* in GOS Nos. XXX, XXXI, Baroda 1926. The General Editor Dr. Benoytosh *Bhattacharyya* deals in detail, in the Foreword, with the life and works of Śāntarakṣita and Kamalaśīla, and the authors cited in the commentary; *cf. Winternitz* in Indologica Pragensia I, 1929, p. 78 ff.

Mīmāṃsā are also named. The Madhyamakālaṃkāra-Kārikās, with the author's own commentary, are a shorter work of Śāntarakṣita. The work has come down only in the Tibetan translation.[1] Tibetan sources also allow us to glean something as to the life of Śāntarakṣita. He came from Nālandā to Tibet, where he founded the monastery of Sam-ye in the year 749 A.D., the first proper Buddhist monastery in Tibet. He lived there for thirteen years, and died in 762 A.D. Padmasambhava, who is usually mentioned as the founder of Lamaism, is said to have been the brother-in-law and collaborator of Śāntarakṣita.[2]

Lastly, among the later Buddhist writers, we may mention Advayavajra, who lived in the 11th or at the beginning of the 12th century, and wrote a large number of short didactic poems on the Mahāyāna and Vajrayāna.[3]

Māhātmya, Stotras, Dhāraṇīs and Tantras.

Repeated reference has already been made to the great similarity between the Mahāyāna-Sūtras and the Purāṇas. We have seen that in the ancient Purāṇas, many texts which were connected with the cult of the Hindu gods, were included or appended, such as Māhātmyas, Stotras and Kalpas.[4] In the same way there is also a Buddhistic "Purāṇa," the Svayambhū-Purāṇa, which is not really a Purāṇa, but a Māhātmya. It is a glorification of the holy places in Nepal, especially the Svayambhū-Caitya near Kaṭhmandu. The work is a manual for pilgrims, and therefore also contains descriptions of ceremonies (*e.g.*, for the worship of Nāgas so as to obtain rain) and many a legend attaching to the various

---

1) See P. L. *Vaidya*, l. c., p. 57 f.

2) See B. *Bhattacharyya*, GOS No. XXX, pp. x ff., xvi ff.

3) Advayavajrasaṃgraha, edited with an Introduction by Haraprasāda *Śāstrī* in GOS No. XL, Baroda, 1927.

4) See above, Vol. I, p. 533.

holy places. Thus for instance in Chapter IV the Maṇicūḍāvadāna [1] is told by way of glorifying the river Maṇirohiṇī. In the Svayambhū-Purāṇa, Svayambhū, "the Self-Existent," which is in Hinduism one of the names of the god Brahman, appears as the king and teacher of the world, seated on a wondrous lotus, the root of which had been planted in bygone ages by an earlier Buddha. There are five different recensions of the work, which differ from one another more in their external form than in contents.[2] None of the recensions can, however, lay claim to very great antiquity. Perhaps the work was not written earlier than the 16th century.

Just as this Māhātmya is composed in the true manner of the Viṣṇuite and Śivaite Māhātmyas, similarly the sole difference between the Buddhistic Stotras or hymns, and those which are dedicated to the worship of Viṣṇu or Śiva, lies in the names of the divine beings which are the objects of adoration. Some of these Stotras are the works of well known poets in the ornate style of poetry and in elaborate metres, others are litanies after the manner of those which we find in the Purāṇas. A few of such Stotras also gained admittance to earlier texts, such as the Mahāvastu, Lalita-Vistara and others. The hymns of Mātṛceta have already been mentioned. We have a collection of four hymns (Catuḥstava) of Nāgārjuna

---

1) Translated by L. *de La Vallée Poussin* in JRAS 1894, p. 297 ff. This self-sacrifice legend is also to be found in one manuscript as an independent Avadāna, as well as in one manuscript of the Divyāvadānamālā (s. Rajendralala *Mitra*, Nep. Buddh. Lit., pp. 162 ff., 314) and in Kṣemendra's Avadāna-Kalpalatā (s. JBTS, Vol. I, part 3, 1893).

2) According to S. *Lévi*, the "Svāyambhuva-Mahā-Purāṇa" which has come down in a Paris MS., contains the best recension. It is written in prose and verse in various metres. S. *Lévi* gives a detailed analysis of the work in Vol. I, p. 208 ff., of his book Le Népal (AMG, Bibliothèque d'études, t. 17-19, Paris 1905). The "Bṛhat-Svayambhū-Purāṇa" edited by Haraprasāda *Śāstri* in Bibl. Ind. (1894-1900) is written entirely in Ślokas and in execrable Sanskrit. Book X has been edited by *La Vallée Poussin* (Université de Gand, Recueil de Travaux publiés par la faculté de phil. et lett. 9e fasc., Gand & Louvain 1893). Cf. also Raj. *Mitra*, Nep. Buddh. Lit., p. 249 ff.; Haraprasāda *Śāstrī* in JBTS II, 1894, part 2, p. 33 ff.; and *Hodgson*, Essays, p. 115 ff.

in the Tibetan translation.[1] King Harṣavardhana (600-647 A.D.), who, under the influence of the Chinese pilgrim Hsüan-Tsang, leaned more and more strongly towards Buddhism during the last years of his life, composed a Suprabhāta-Stotra,[2] a morning hymn in praise of Buddha, in 24 verses, and an Aṣṭa-Mahā-Śrīcaitya-Stotra,[3] a "hymn in praise of the eight great shrines," in 5 stanzas. The poet Vajradatta, who lived under King Devapāla in the 9th century, is the author of the Lokeśvara-Śataka, the "Hundred (stanzas) in praise of Lokeśvara."[4] Legend has it, that the poet became a leper owing to a curse. He implored Lokeśvara, *i.e.*, Avalokiteśvara, to help him, and each day he composed an elaborate Sragdharā stanza in praise of him. When three months had gone by, and he had completed the hundredth stanza, the Bodhisattva appeared to him, and he was healed.[5] In this very elaborate poem Avalokiteśvara is described in the greatest detail from his fingers to his toes, his fifty names are enumerated, and his qualities, his love and his mercy glorified.

The Paramārthanāma-Saṃgīti[6] is a hymn of the type which occurs as early as in the Yajurveda, the Mahābhārata and very frequently in the Purāṇas,[7] that is to say, a litany consisting of an enumeration of names and laudatory epithets of the deity. Another work which is composed mainly for

[1]) The French translation by *La Vallée Poussin* was printed in Le Muséon in 1914, but all the copies were destroyed at the time of the burning of Louvain; s. P. L. *Vaidya*, Études sur Āryadeva, p. 49.

[2]) Edited by *Minayeff* in Sapiski de la Société Archéologique, t. II, fasc. III, 236 f.

[3]) Translated into Sanskrit by S. *Lévi* (OC, Genève, 1894, II, 189 ff.) on the basis of a Chinese transcription.

[4]) Edited and translated into French by Suzanne *Karpelès* in JA, 1919, s. 11, t. XIV, pp. 357-465.

[5]) A similar legend is told about Mayūra, the poet of the Sūryaśataka.

[6]) Raj. *Mitra*, Nep. Buddh. Lit., p. 175.

[7]) *Cf.* above, Vol. I, pp. 185, 397, note 1.

devotional purposes, is a poem in 9 stanzas, the Sapta-Buddha-Stotra, "Praise of the Seven Buddhas," in which the six Buddhas of previous ages, from Vipaśyin down to Kāśyapa, and then Śākyamuni and the future Buddha Maitreya are worshipped and invoked one after the other; likewise the Naipālīya-Devatā-Kalyāṇa-Pañcaviṃśatikā, by an otherwise unknown "poet" Amṛtānanda, a litany of 25 stanzas, in which the "Nepalese deities," *i.e.*, a motley list of Buddhas, beginning with Svayambhū, Bodhisattvas, Hindu gods and goddesses, Buddhist personifications, Tīrthas and Caityas, are invoked, amid praises, to send down blessings (kalyāṇa).[1]

A large number of Stotras are dedicated to the Buddhist goddess Tārā, "the Rescuer," the female counterpart of Avalokiteśvara. A poem in praise of Tārā, composed in polished Kāvya style by the Kashmiri poet Sarvajñamitra is the Sragdharā-Stotra or Ārya-Tārā-Sragdharā-Stotra in 37 verses. Sragdharā, "(female) wearer of the wreath," is an epithet of Tārā as well as the name of the metre in which the poem is written. The poet lived in the first half of the 8th century. According to the legend, he was a man widely famed for his generosity (according to Tāranātha,[2] a son-in-law of the King of Kashmir), who finally, after he had given away all his treasures, went forth into the world as a mendicant monk. Once he met an old Brahman on the way, who complained to him that he was poor and needed money for his daughter's marriage. In order to procure the money for this man, Sarvajñamitra sold himself to a king who was just

---

1) The two Stotras have been translated by H. H. *Wilson*, Works, II, pp. 5 ff., 11 ff. *Cf. Winternitz* and *Keith*, Catalogue of Sanskrit Manuscripts in the Bodleian Library, Vol. II, p. 257; Raj. *Mitra*, Nep. Buddh. Lit., p. 99.

2) Geschichte des Buddhismus, p. 168 ff. In Rājataraṅgiṇī IV, 210, there is mention of the monk Sarvajñamitra, who appeared as a second Jina, and lived in the Kayya-Vihāra built by Kayya. Kayya was a king of Lāṭa, and was subject to King Lalitāditya, who reigned in Kashmir in the 8th century. *Cf.* S. Ch. *Vidyābhūṣaṇa* in JASB 1, 1905, p. 156 ff.

preparing a great human sacrifice for which he needed a hundred persons. When the poet heard the lamentations of his fellow-sufferers with whom he was to be sacrificed, he sang the hymn to Tārā, and the goddess came and rescued the hundred victims. Whilst the Sragdharā-Stotra has some poetical value, the Ārya-Tārā-Nāmāṣṭottaraśataka-Stotra, "the Song of praise consisting of 108 names of the noble Tārā," is a mere litany of names and titles of the goddess; and the Ekaviṃśati-Stotra, "the song of praise in 21 verses," is only a loose stringing together of invocations to the goddess Tārā.[1)]

The Bhakti-Śataka, "the Hundred (stanzas) on Bhakti," [2)] by Rāmacandra Kavibhāratī, a Brahman of Bengal, who came to Ceylon under King Parākramabāhu (about 1245 A.D.) and was converted to Buddhism, affords an example of how the Brahmanical-Indian idea of Bhakti or the love for God, was transferred to Buddha. In this work the Buddha is worshipped and praised, in the ornate style of poetry and in elaborate metres, as the only teacher, redeemer and dispenser of mercies, in precisely the same fashion as Rāma, Kṛṣṇa or Śiva in Brahmanical Bhakti poems. The work might just as

---

1) These three Stotras have been edited and translated by G. *de Blonay*, Matériaux pour servir à l'histoire de la déesse Buddhique Tārā (Bibl. de l'école des hautes tudes, fasc. 107), Paris, 1895. The Sragdharā-Stotra (with commentary and two Tibetan ersions) is also edited in Bauddha-Stotra-Saṃgraha, Vol. I, edited by Satis Chandra *Vidyābhūṣaṇa*, Bibl. Ind., 1908. In the introduction, the editor enumerates no fewer than 6 texts relating to Tārā. 62 of these have come down only in Tibetan translations. A great devotee of this goddess was Candragomin who has been mentioned above (p. 365), and to whom a Tārā-Sādhana-Śataka is ascribed (*Blonay*, l.c., p. 17 f.). The cult of Tārā was introduced in about the 6th century A.D. Hsüan-Tsang mentions statues of "Tārā-Bodhisattva," which he had seen in India. In the year 778 A.D. Ārya-Tārā was already worshipped in Java, where she has a gorgeous shrine. *Cf. Waddell* in JRAS, 1894, p. 63 ff. and OZ I, 178 ff.; *Blonay*, l.c., pp. 3, 5, 17; H. *Kern* in OZ II, 1914, p. 481, note 1.

2) Edited by *Śīlaskandha* in Ceylon in 1885, and published by the Buddhist Text Society of India, Darjeeling 1896, and by Haraprasāda *Śāstrī* with an English translation in JBTS I, 1893, part 2, pp. 21-48; translated into German by Rudolf *Otto*, Texte zur indischen Gottesmystik II, Jena 1917, pp. 141-160. *Cf.* Haraprasāda *Śāstrī* in JASB Proceedings, 1890, p. 125 ff. and JBTS I, 1893, part III, p. iv ff.

well belong to the Mahāyāna as to the Hīnayāna, for it is essentially a Hindu poem as far as ideas are concerned. By way of example, I give a few verses (31-34) in translation:

"Be gracious, O Lord, ruler of the gods, ruler of the world, conqueror, O Buddha, who deservest to be worshipped by the world, to be worshipped by me, to be worshipped by the good, O enemy of sin, enemy of mundane existence, enemy of lust, enemy of darkness! To thee verily am I devoted (bhakta) with body, speech, and thought.

He is a son of thy family, he is devoted to thee, he bears the burden of thy teaching, he is a disciple, he takes refuge with thee, he is thy slave,—he who never on any account swerves from thy command.

Doing good to the world, O Buddha, is worship to thee, doing evil to it, O Lord of the world, is pain to thee. O Jina, how should I, when doing evil to the world, not be ashamed of saying that I am devoted to thy lotus-feet!

Where is my mercy, where my sympathy, where my love, as I am doing evil, and not good, to that very world for whose benefit thou hast, in a hundred ways, given away wealth, men, power, life, body and kingdom?"

The Dhāraṇīs [1] or "Protective Spells" [2] constitute a large and important part of Mahāyānist literature. The need for incantations, benedictions, and magic spells, which was supplied in the very earliest times by the Vedic mantras, especially those of the Atharvaveda,[3] played far too great a part in the mind of the Indian people, for Buddhism to have been able to dispense with them. We have already seen how

---

1) *Cf. Burnouf*, Introduction, pp 466, 482 ff.; *Wassiljew*, Der Buddhismus, pp. 153 ff., 193 ff., 217; *La Vallée Poussin*, Bouddhisme, Études et Matériaux, Mémoires Acad. Belg. 1898, p. 119 ff.; L. A. *Waddell* in OZ I, 1912, 155 ff.; Ind. Ant. 43, 1914, 37 ff., 49 ff., 92 ff.; J. *Hauer*, Die Dhāraṇī im nördlichen Buddhismus, Tübingen 1927, and G. *Tucci* in Ind. Hist. Q. IV, 1928, 553 ff.

2) Dhāraṇī is a synonym of rakṣā and the Pāli parittā, "protecting magic formula," "talisman." *Cf. Kern* in OZ II, p. 481, note 2. According to the Saddharma-Puṇḍarīka, p. 399, the Dhāraṇīs are taught "for the protection, safety and shelter of the preachers." Dhāraṇīs are also used as amulets.

3) Above, Vol I, pp. 109 ff., 119 ff. The tale in the Śārdūlakarṇāvadāna (Divyāvadāna, p. 613) is characteristic of the need for magic formulas, s. above, p. 286 f.

the Buddhists of Ceylon used some of their most beautiful Suttas as Parittās or Pirits.[1] In a similar manner the Mahāyāna Buddhists in India also transformed some of the Sūtras themselves into magic formulas. In addition to these, there were also endless invocations to the divine beings of Buddhist and Hindu origin, so numerous in the Mahāyāna, and—last, but not least—the mysterious words and syllables already so popular in the sacrificial mysticism of the Yajurveda.[2] The protective and salutary magical power of a Dhāraṇī is primarily due to its containing some piece of wisdom *in nuce*, and not to any occult mystical significance of the words and syllables, though it is true that the Dhāraṇīs do also include "magic words" (mantrapadāni) of this kind.

For instance, the Prajñā-Pāramitā-Sūtras in their shortest form were used as Dhāraṇīs: thus the Alpākṣarā Prajñā-Pāramitā, etc.[3] Special mention should here be made of the Prajñā-Pāramitā-hṛdaya-Sūtras, the shorter text of which we have in the ancient palm leaves, which have been kept since the year 609 A. D. in the monastery of Hôriuzi in Japan. These Sūtras teach the "heart" (hṛdaya) of the Prajñā-Pāramitā, *i.e.*, the "Mantra which alleviates all pain," which contains the perfection of wisdom, and says: "O Enlightenment, which hast gone, gone, gone to the other shore, completely gone to the other shore,[4] hail!" Even though this saying is, to a certain extent, supposed to present the essence of the negativist doctrine of the Prajñā-Pāramitā-Sūtras, its spiritual level is no higher than that of the Uṣṇīṣa-Vijaya-Dhāraṇī, which has also come down on the palm leaves of Hôriuzi, and only consists of a series of senseless

[1]) See above, p. 80.

[2]) See above, Vol. I, p. 185 ff.

[3]) See above, p. 316.

[4]) This is nothing but a false etymology of *pāramitā*.

invocations.[1] Many Prajñā-Pāramitā texts appear amongst the Dhāraṇīs in the Tibetan Kanjur.[2] There are also Dhāraṇīs in the Kanjur, whose function is to help people to understand the Śatasāhasrī Prajñā-Pāramitā and other long Prajñā-Pāramitās.[3]

There is not always a clear line of demarcation between Dhāraṇīs and Sūtras. There are Mahāyāna-Sūtras which are nothing but recommendations of Dhāraṇīs. Thus the Aparimitāyuḥ-Sūtra,[4] which we have not only in Sanskrit and Old Khotanese, but also in Chinese and Tibetan translations, is nothing more than the glorification of a Dhāraṇī. The Ratnolkā-Dhāraṇī, which is quoted in the Śikṣā-Samuccaya, might just as well be classed as a Mahāyāna-Sūtra. It is a long work; in which Mahāyāna doctrines are expounded, among other things the doctrine that a Bodhisattva should not aspire to salvation immediately, but is to be reborn again and again in various professions and sects, for the sake of the

---

[1]) *Cf.* The Ancient Palm Leaves containing the Prajñāpāramitā-hṛdaya-sūtra and the Uṣṇīṣa-vijayadhāraṇī edited by F. *Max Müller* and Bunyiu *Nanjio* (Anecdota Oxoniensia, Aryan Series, Vol. I, Part III), Oxford 1884 and SBE, Vol. 49, part II, p. 145 ff. Prajñā-Pāramitā-Hṛdaya-Sūtra translated from the Tibetan into French by L. *Feer* in AMG V, 176 ff. *Cf.* Haraprasāda *Śāstrī* in Ind. Hist. Q. I, 1925, p. 469.

[2]) *Cf. Körös* in AMG II, 305, 307, 312, 314.

[3]) In a MS. of Dhāraṇīs (Rāj. *Mitra*, Nep. Buddh. Lit., p. 292) there is also a Pañcaviṃśatikā-Prajñā-Pāramitā-hṛdaya. Another Dhāraṇī of this kind, is the Prajñā-Pāramitā-naya-Śata-Pañcāśatikā (or Adhyardha-Śatikā-Prajñā-Pāramitā) fragments of which have been found in the neighbourhood of Khotan, in Sanskrit, interspersed with sections in Khotanese. These fragments have been edited by E. *Leumann*, Zur nordarischen Sprache und Litteratur, Strassburg 1912, p. 84 ff.; reprinted and compared with the Tibetan and Chinese texts, by *Shōun Toganoo*, Kyoto 1917. There is also a Pratītya-Samutpāda-Dhāraṇī (*Körös*, AMG II, p. 321) which is intended to help one to understand the doctrine of causally dependent origination.

[4]) The Old Khotanese Version together with the Sanskrit Text and the Tibetan Translation ed. by *Sten Konow* in Hoernle, Manuscript Remains, 1, pp. 289-329 (with English translation); Aparimitāyur-Jñāna-Nāma-Mahāyāna-Sūtram nach einer nepalesischen Sanskrit HS. mit der tibetischen und chinesischen Version herausgegeben und übersetzt von *Max Walleser* Heidelberg (Sitzungsber. der Akademie) 1916. According to the Chinese Version, the title reads: Ārya-Aparimitāyuḥsuviniścita-tejo-rāja-dhāraṇī-sūtra. Cf. *Hoernle* in JRAS 1910, 834 ff., 1293; 1911, 468 ff., and E. *Leumann*, Zur nordarischen Sprache und Litteratur, pp. 75, 82 f.

welfare of the beings: a long list of these professions and sects is enumerated.[1]

The Megha-Sūtra[2] is a good example of a Sūtra with Dhāraṇīs, written for the purposes of magic. It begins, like other Mahāyāna-Sūtras, with the words: "Thus have I heard; once the Lord sojourned in the palace of the serpent princes Nanda and Upananda," etc. It then relates how the snake deities offer adoration to the Buddha and the Bodhisattvas, whereupon one of the snake princes asks the Exalted One the following question:—

"How, Lord, can all the pains of all snakes be alleviated, and how can the snakes be so pleased and delighted, that they may send down torrents of rain over India in due season and may thereby cause all grasses, shrubs, herbs and trees to grow, all seeds to sprout and all juices to flow forth, so that the people of India be blessed with happiness?" Pleased with the question, the Buddha replies: "By *one* religious exercise (Dharma), O snake-prince, all the pains of all snakes can be alleviated altogether, and they be blessed with happiness." "Which is this one religious exercise?" "It is friendliness (maitrī). The gods and men, O snake-prince, who thus live in friendliness, are not burnt by fire, not injured by the sword, not carried away by water, not killed by poison, not overcome by the enemy's host. They sleep calmly and calmly they waken, they are protected by their own virtue......Therefore, O snake-prince, you must act in friendliness with your body, in friendliness in your speech, in friendliness with your mind. And further, O snake-prince, you must use the Dhāraṇī called Sarvasukhandadā ('the all-hail-bringing'). This alleviates all the pains of all the snakes, brings all salvation, then brings the torrents of rain down over India here in due season, and causes all grasses, shrubs, herbs and

---

1) See C. *Bendall* in JRAS 1901, p. 122 ff. The Nārāyaṇa-Paripṛcchā, too, which is several times quoted in the Śikṣā-Samuccaya, is described as a Dhāraṇī in the colophon of a MS. (Haraprasāda *Śāstrī*, Descriptive Catalogue of Sansk. MSS. in Asiat. Soc. of Bengal, 1, p. 16 f.). On an Āryācala-Mahākrodharāja-Guhya-Dhāraṇī-Sūtra in Sanskrit, Tibetan, Chinese and Japanese, s. C. *Puini* in GSAI 3, 1889, p. 38 ff.

2) *Cf.* C. *Bendall*, JRAS 1880, p. 286 ff. A Mahā-Megha-Sūtra was translated into Chinese as early as between 397 and 439 A.D., other translations were made between 589 and 618, and 746-771. *Cf.* B. *Nanjio*, Catalogue, Nos. 186-188, 244, 970. In the Tibetan Kanjur it is translated among the Sūtras (Mdo), s. *Kőrös*, AMG II, 264 ff.

trees to grow, all seeds to sprout and all juices to flow forth. And how goes this Dhāraṇī ?"

Then follow the actual Dhāraṇīs, which consist of numerous invocations to female deities (as "holder," "supporter," etc.), to Buddhas and Bodhisattvas, between which sentences (such as "Shake off the evil," "Cleanse the paths") and exorcisms against snakes (such as "Come, O great snakes...rain in India") are inserted, and lastly, of syllables scattered here and there (such as "sara sire sire suru suru nāgānāṃ java java jivi jivi juvu juvu," etc.). A description of the magic rites which are performed with these Dhāraṇīs is added, and it ends with the assurance that, in times of drought, there are no better means of inducing rain to fall, than the use of this Sūtra.[1]

Similarly, the Dhāraṇīs often appear as parts of Sūtras which relate the circumstances under which they were proclaimed. There are, however, also numerous Dhāraṇīs which have come down singly in manuscripts, and on the other hand, large collections of Dhāraṇīs.[2] We find there exorcism formulas against the influence of ill-omened constellations, against poison, snakes and demons, spells for the healing of diseases and the lengthening of life, magic spells for bringing luck in war, others which cause a person to be reborn in

---

[1]) A much simpler form of a snake charm which, however, is to serve as a means of warding off snake-bite, is already to be found in the Vinaya-Piṭaka, Culla-Vagga V, 6, where the snakes are appeased by the Buddhist friendliness (metta, maitrī). *Cf.* also Jātaka 203, Dīgha-Nikāya 32, and Aṅguttara-Nikāya IV, 67 (Vol. II, p. 72). A Sūtra, similar to the Megha-Sūtra, is the Diśa-Svāstika-Sūtra, which has come down to us in the Uiguric language in a fragment from Turfan (Ṭiśastvustik by W. *Radloff* and Baron A. von *Staël-Holstein*, Bibl. Buddhica XII, St. Petersburg, 1910).

[2]) *E.g.* Dhāraṇī-(mantra)-saṃgraha, Raj. *Mitra*, Nep. Buddh. Lit., p. 80 f. Other single Dhāraṇīs and collections of Dhāraṇīs, l.c., pp. 93 f., 174, 176, 267 f., 288, 291 f. Numerous MSS. of Dhāraṇīs are also included in *Bendall's* Catalogue. *La Vallée Poussin*, JRAS 1896, p. 433 f., assumes that a "Vidyādhara-Piṭaka" quoted in the Ādikarma-Pradīpa and in the Śikṣā-Samuccaya, p. 142, is the same as a Dhāraṇī-Piṭaka. According to Hsüan-Tsang, a Dhāraṇī-Piṭaka of this kind was contained in the Canon of the Mahā-Sāṅghikas (*Kern*, Manual, p. 4).

the Sukhāvatī paradise, to ensure against a bad rebirth, and to secure release from sin; there are also such by which a person can conjure up a Bodhisattva or protect himself from unbelief. It is not only the elements which can be influenced by Dhāraṇīs, but they bring about the birth of a son or a daughter according to the wish of the expectant mother. The collection of five Dhāraṇīs entitled "*Pañcarakṣā*" is extremely popular in Nepal. These "Five Protecting Spells" are as follows: (1) Mahā-Pratisarā, for protection against sin, disease and other evils, (2) Mahā-Sahasrapramardinī, against evil spirits, (3) Mahā-Māyūrī, against snake-poison, (4) Mahā-Śītavatī, against hostile planets, wild animals and poisonous insects, and (5) Mahā(rakṣā)mantrānusāriṇī against diseases.[1] The Mahā-Māyūrī, frequently entitled Vidyārājñī, "Queen of Secret Sciences,"[2] takes its name from the notorious hostility of the peacocks (mayūra) towards the snakes, but it was also used as a general remedy for diseases. In Chapter V of the Harṣacarita, Bāṇa tells us how Harṣavardhana entered the palace of his father who was lying sick unto death, and that all kinds of sacrifices and ceremonies were performed, and that among other things, the Mahā-Māyūrī was recited.[3] Most probably this Dhāraṇī can be traced back to the same sources as the verses in the Mora-Jātaka (No. 159) and the

---

1) *Cf.* Rāj. *Mitra*, Nep. Buddh. Lit., pp. 164 ff., 173 f. *Winternitz* and *Keith*, Catalogue of Sanskrit MSS. in the Bodleian Library, Vol. II, p 257 ff. In the Nepalese courts of justice, the Buddhists are sworn on the Pañcarakṣā (*Hodgson*, Essays, p. 18).

2) *Cf.* J. *Przyluski* in BEFEO 23, 1923, p. 308 f.

3) Harṣacarita, transl. by E. B. *Cowell* and F. W. *Thomas*, p. 137. Furthermore, a verse by Rājaśekhara in Jalhaṇa's Sūktimuktāvalī contains an allusion to the Māyūrī vidyā:

darpaṃ kavibhujaṅgānāṃ gatā śravaṇagocaram |
viṣavidyeva māyūrī Māyūrī vāg nikṛntati ||

"The speech of (the poet) Mayūra destroys the pride of the poets, when it comes within reach of their ears, just as the peacock science against poison (destroys the pride) of the snakes (when it comes within reach of their ears)"; Cf. G. P. *Quackenbos*, The Sanskrit Poems of Mayūra, CUIS 1917, Intron., p. 5.

similar incantations in the snake-charms which we have in the Bower manuscript.[1]

Moreover, the Dhāraṇīs penetrated to a great extent into the ancient Mahāyāna-Sūtras. We have found them in Chapters XXI and XXVI, *i.e.* those chapters which were added at a later time, of the Saddharma-Puṇḍarīka, and also in the last two chapters of the Laṅkāvatāra, chapters which are missing in the earliest Chinese translation of 443 A.D. Thus we see that they are a later element in the Mahāyāna-Sūtras. Nevertheless we should not regard them as a very modern product of Buddhist literature, for we already find them in Chinese translations made as early as in the 4th century A.D.[2] And if the passage in the longer Sukhāvatī-Vyūha (VIII, 33) where it says that the beings in Sukhāvatī receive Dhāraṇīs, was already included in the text which was translated into Chinese in the 2nd century A.D., we should be compelled to assume that there were Dhāraṇīs as early as that period. It is not possible, however, to trace the Dhāraṇīs back to the early days of Buddhism, much less to Buddha himself.[3] It is true that Buddha lived in an environment of people who believed in the power of magic spells: but if

---

[1]) *Cf. Waddell* in OZ I, 166 ff. The Mahā-Māyūrī (in a longer and a shorter form) has been translated into Chinese repeatedly, by Śrīmitra (307-342 A.D.), by Saṅghapāla (516 A.D.), I-tsing (705 A.D.) and Amoghavajra (746-771 A.D.). *Cf.* K. *Watanabe* in JRAS 1907, p. 261 ff., *Lévi* in JA 1915, s. 11, t. V, pp. 19 ff., 26; and *Bagchi*, I, pp. 320, 417.

[2]) Śrīmitra (307-342 A.D.) translated more Dhāraṇīs than anything else, s. *Bagchi*, I, 319 f.

[3]) Thus *Waddell* in OZ I, 155 ff. The expression Dhāraṇī first occurs in the Lalita-Vistara and Saddarma-Puṇḍarīka. *Waddell* (Asiatic Quart. Review, N.S., 1,1913, p. 293 ff.) compares the Dhāraṇīs with the magic formulas of the Nestorian Christians, and is of opinion that these formulas are derived from Chaldean ones, and that even the Buddhist magic formulas came to India from Chaldea and Iran. This is very unlikely, when we take the universality of protecting magic formulas into consideration; we need only compare, for instance, ERE III, 392-472, and VIII, 245-321. J. W. *Hauer* (Die Dhāraṇī, etc. 1927) has pointed out the similarity between the Dhāraṇīs and the Mithras liturgy, but he is right in not assuming anything beyond a parallel development.

there is one thing which we *do* know of Buddha, it is that he desired to bear a new message to his compatriots, a message which was at variance with the old Brahmanical cult of sacrifices and magic. The Dhāraṇīs belong to a period at which Buddhism in India began to be more and more assimilated to Hinduism,[1] while outside India it tended to make compromises and to become contaminated by the popular religions of the countries in question. In the course of time the difference between the Dhāraṇīs, and the Mantras belonging to the Tantras, became more and more obliterated, and finally the Dhāraṇīs were completely supplanted by the Mantras. In the Tibetan Kanjur the Dhāraṇīs are to be found both among the Sūtras (Mdo) and the Tantras (Rgyut).[2] The numerous fragments of Dhāraṇīs in various languages of Central Asia, which have been found in Eastern Turkestan,[3] and also the large amount of space which the Dhāraṇīs occupy in the Tibetan Kanjur and the Chinese Tripiṭaka, are evidence of the great popularity and wide propagation of this literature in all Buddhist countries.

Mantrayāna and Vajrayāna are branches of the Mahāyāna, from which they are not separated by any hard and fast line of demarcation. Mantrayāna is the "vehicle" in which

---

[1]) It is significant that there is a Gaṇapati-Dhāraṇī, addressed to the Śivaite god Gaṇapati, in spite of the fact that it is "proclaimed by Buddha"; s. Rāj. *Mitra*, Nep Buddh. Lit., pp. 89 f., 292.

[2]) *Körös* in AMG II, 249, 318 ff., 561 ff.

[3]) A fragment of a Nīlakāṇṭha-Dhāraṇī, brought from Central Asia by M. A. *Stein*, Sanskrit text in Brāhmī script and in Sogdienne transcription, has been edited by *La Vallée Poussin* and R. *Gauthiot* in JRAS 1912, 629 ff This Dhāraṇī was already very popular in China between 650 and 750 A.D., s. *Lévi* in JRAS 1912, 1063 ff. Dhāraṇīs in Uiguric language (Uṣṇīṣa-Vijayā, Sitātapatrā) have been edited from Central Asian block prints, by F. W. K. *Müller*, Uigurica II, in ABA 1911, pp. 27 ff., 50 ff. A Jñānolkā-Dhāraṇī in the Khotanese language, has been edited by E. *Leumann*, Buddhistische Literatur Nordarisch und Deutsch, Leipzig 1920 (AKM XV, 2), p. 151 ff. A Central Asian fragment of a Mahā-Pratyaṅgirā-Dhāraṇī in Sanskrit, containing invocations to Tārā, has been edited by *Hoernle*, in Hoernle Manuscript Remains, I, p. 52 ff.

the Mantras, words and syllables of mysterious power, are the chief means of attaining salvation. Vajrayāna is the "vehicle" which leads men to salvation not only by using Mantras, but by means of all things which are denoted by the word vajra. Now vajra is a word with many meanings. It means "diamond," and denotes everything which is hard and impermeable, which cannot be cleft, nor burnt, nor destroyed. Vajra also means the "thunderbolt," the weapon of the god Indra, who appears in Buddhist mythology as Vajrapāṇi, "he who holds the Vajra in his hand." It is also the name for the weapon of the ascetics and monks when fighting against hostile powers. Then again, the Śūnya, the indescribable absolute, which is taught by the Mādhyamikas to be the sole reality, and also the Vijñāna or consciousness, which according to the Yogācāryas is the sole reality,—both of these are described as being indestructible as a Vajra. Lastly, in the mystic language of some of the adherents of the Vajrayāna, and that of the Śāktas, Vajra also means the male organ, just as Padma, "the lotus," serves as a term to describe the female sexual organ. Furthermore the Vajrayāna teaches a monistic (Advaita) philosophy. All beings are Vajra beings (vajrasattva), and the one and only Vajrasattva is immanent in all beings. In addition to the "three bodies" (Trikāya) of a Buddha, the Śāktas have a fourth body, the "body of happiness" (sukhakāya), with which the eternal Buddha embraces his Śakti, Tārā or Bhagavatī. This "highest bliss" (mahāsukha) is attained by the adepts of the Buddhist Śākta religion, in like manner as the non-Buddhist Śāktas,[1] by a ritual connected with the enjoyment of meat, intoxicating liquors and sexual intercourse. Thus the Vajrayāna is a queer mixture of monistic philosophy, magic and erotics, with a small admixture of Buddhist ideas.

---

[1] See above, Vol. I, 594.

We have seen that there is no rigid boundary-line between the Mahāyāna and the Mantrayāna-Vajrayāna: and the same may be said of the Mahāyāna-Sūtras and the Tantras,[1] the literature of the Mantrayāna and Vajrayāna. As we have already seen, there are some Mahāyāna-Sūtras which contain Tantric sections,[2] and the Tantras treat not only of the rites of the Vajrayāna, but also of the ritual of the Mahāyānist cult (the erection of Stūpas, construction and setting up of images, Stotras and daily sacrifices), as well as sections on the philosophical doctrines of the Mahāyāna. The only thing which distinguishes the Buddhist Tantras from the Tantras of the Śāktas,[3] is the sparse element of Buddhism which is still to be found in them. There are four classes of Buddhist Tantras: Kriyā-Tantras, which treat of ceremonies at the building of temples, erection of images of gods, etc.; Caryā-Tantras, which teach the practical cult; Yoga-Tantras, which deal with the practice of Yoga, and Anuttarayoga-Tantras, which deal with higher mysticism.[4]

Among the first class of Tantras we have the Ādikarma-Pradīpa.[5] This is a work which, in the style of the

---

1) Cf. *Burnouf*, Introduction, pp. 465 ff., 486 ff., 578 f.; *Wassiljew*, Der Buddhismus, p. 201 ff.; *La Vallée Poussin*, Bouddhisme, Études et Matériaux, Mém. Acad. Belg., t. 55, 1898, pp. 72 ff., 130 ff., 162 ff.; Bouddhisme, pp. 343 ff., 378 ff.; OC Paris 1899, I, 241 ff.; ERE XII, 193 ff.; J. *Woodroffe*, Shakti and Shâkta, 2nd Ed., Madras, 1920, pp. 30, 116 ff.; J. N. *Farquhar*, Outline of the Religious Literature of India, pp. 209 ff., 272 f.; Benoytosh *Bhattacharyya* in Ind. Hist. Qu. III, 1927, p. 733 ff., and Sādhanamālā, II, Introduction. Extracts from texts of Tantras are contained in the anthology Subhāṣita-Saṃgraha, edited by C. *Bendall* in Le Muséon, N. S. IV, 1903, and V, 1904.

2) See above, pp. 309, 339.

3) See above, Vol. I, 591 ff.

4) *Cf. La Vallée Poussin* in JRAS, 1901, p. 900 f.

5) Edited with Introduction and analysis of contents, by *La Vallée Poussin*, Bouddhisme, Études et Matériaux, Mém. Acad. Belg. 1898, pp. 177-232. The Kriyā-Saṃgraha-Pañjikā by Kuladatta, in which detailed prescriptions are given for the erection of monasteries (Vihāras) is most probably also a ritual work of similar nature. (Rāj. *Mitra*, Nep. Buddh. Lit., p. 105 ff.), and Haraprasāda *Śāstrī*, Descriptive Catalogue of Sanskrit MSS. in As. Soc. of Bengal, I, 119 ff.

Brahmanical manuals of ritual (Gṛhya-Sūtras, Karma-Pradīpas) describes the ceremonies and religious acts which the "Ādikarmika-Bodhisattva," *i.e.* the adherent of the Mahāyāna and candidate for enlightenment, has to perform. The work consists of a Sūtra text (Mūla-Sūtra) with a running commentary, and contains precepts on the initiation ceremonies for the disciple (who can be a layman or a monk), sprinklings, washings and prayers, rules for rinsing the mouth, cleaning the teeth, morning and evening devotions, offerings of water for the departed (Pretas), almsgiving, meals, worshipping of the Buddhas and other sacred beings, reading of the Prajñā-Pāramitā, meditations, and so on, as they are to be performed at the various times of the day by the candidate (the beginner as opposed to the accomplished Yogin).

The Aṣṭamīvrata-Vidhāna, too, which contains the rules for the ceremonies to be performed on every eighth day of every half month, belongs to the Kriyā-Tantra texts. Mystical diagrams and intertwinings of the fingers are employed, and sacrificial gifts and prayers (with mysterious syllables such as "hrum hrum hrum phaṭ phaṭ phaṭ svāhā") are addressed not only to Buddhas and Bodhisattvas, but to Śivaite deities also.[1]

In the Tantric ritual literature we have also the Sādhanas or works on magic ritual. These teach the methods by which a person can attain to Siddhi, *i.e.* "perfection" or mysterious powers, and become a Siddha, "an accomplished one." The virtue of these Siddhis is that the Siddha has the power of making himself small, large or light, at his own will, can penetrate into other bodies, can rise and move about in the air can converse with heavenly beings, can obtain everything he desires, can have gods and goddesses, men and women in his

---

1) *Cf.* H. H. *Wilson*, Works, II, p. 81 ff.

power, has the power of healing diseases by merely looking at the sufferer, and also of attaining omniscience and Nirvāṇa at will. The methods taught in the Sādhanas consist of using the Mantras according to very detailed instructions, the use of certain positions of the fingers (Mudrās) ; and most specially is it emphasized that the Sādhaka is to become absorbed in meditation (Dhyāna) on some deity, and is to bring that deity before his mind in so intensive a fashion that he becomes entirely identified with it.[1] For the purposes of this identification it is essential that the deity be accurately described in every detail. These descriptions were utilised by the sculptors and painters in the construction of images of the gods. It is for this reason that the Sādhanas, which are collected in such works as the Sādhanamālā or Sādhana-Samuccaya,[2] are of the very greatest importance from the point of view of Buddhist iconography. The deities which are worshipped in these Sādhanas, are the Dhyāni-Buddhas and their "families," and also numerous forms of Tārā and other female deities. There is also a Buddhist god of love, Vajrānaṅga, an incarnation of Mañjuśrī, who is invoked in Sādhanas (Nos. 59 and 60) where it is taught how a man can get a woman into his power. The essential content of the Sādhanas is magic. It is true that the preparations for the magic ritual also include Yoga exercises, meditations, devotion (pūjā), confession of sins, love (maitrī) and mercy (karuṇā). For this reason we find, for instance, in the very long

---

[1] *Cf. La Vallée Poussin* in EBE VIII, 406.

[2] Sādhanamālā, ed. by Benoytosh *Bhattacharyya* in GOS, Nos. XXVI, XLI, Baroda 1925, 1928. *Cf.* F. W. *Thomas*, Deux collections Sanscrites et Tibétaines de Sādhanas, Muséon IV, 1903, No. 1; Vidhushekhara *Bhattacharyya* and K. S. Ramaswami *Sastri* in Ind. Hist. Qu. II, 1926, 626 ff. and III, 161 ff.; A. *Foucher*, Étude sur l'iconographie bouddhique (Bibl. de l'école des hautes études 13, II, 1905); Benoytosh *Bhattacharyya*, The Indian Buddhist Iconography mainly based on the Sādhanamālā and other cognate Tantric Texts and Rituals, Oxford, 1924.

Tārā-Sādhana,[1] not only meditations and Mantras, but also a confession of sins, the confession of faith in the "three jewels," the vow to walk in the path of the Buddhas, the Brahmavihāra absorptions, *i.e.* the yielding to the feelings of love, pity, sympathy in joy, and equanimity, together with detailed definitions of these qualities. The language of the Sādhanas is a very frequently defective Sanskrit, and the metre of the verses is very irregular. Of the 312 Sādhanas contained in the Sādhanamālā, some are in prose and are quite short, others are longer, with verse Mantras, and a few are entirely in verse. Every single Sādhana is an independent work. Most of them are anonymous, whilst in a number of cases, the name of the author of the Sādhana is mentioned. The authors mentioned in them belong to the 7th-11th centuries A.D., as far as their period can be determined. As a manuscript of the Sādhanamālā was written in the year 1165, the collection must have been compiled in the 11th century.

The authors mentioned in the Sādhanamālā also appear in other places as authors of Tantras. One Sādhana (No. 159 which is dedicated to the worship of the Prajñā-Pāramitā, is attributed to Asaṅga. It is scarcely feasible, however, that Asaṅga himself should already have written Tantric works, though there seems to be a historical connection between the Yogācāra school and the rise of the Vajrayāna.[2] The Nāgārjuna who is mentioned as the author of Sādhanas and

---

[1]) No. 98. Text and English translation by B. *Bhattacharyya*, The Indian Buddhist Iconography, p. 169 ff.

[2]) Tāranātha (Geschichte des Buddhismus, p. 201) says that Tantrism was handed down by secret means from the time of Asaṅga until the time of Dharmakīrti, and Benoytosh *Bhattacharyya* (Ind. Hist. Q. III, 736 f. and Sādhanamālā, III, pp. xxiii ff., xxvii f.) believes that Asaṅga actually had something to do with the rise of the Vajrayāna. It seems to me that Tāranātha's statement is accounted for by the mere fact that the adherents of the Vajrayāna had an interest in ascribing a greater antiquity to their doctrines. S. *Lévi* thought he could detect an allusion to Tantric rites in Mahāyāna-Sūtrālaṃkāra IX, 46 (which he attributed to Asaṅga). I am unable to see this allusion.

numerous Tantric works, is not the founder of the Mādhyamika system, but a teacher, who probably lived about the middle of the 7th century. It is said of him that he brought a Sādhana from the land of Bhoṭa (Tibet ?). Many of his Tantric works are to be found in the Tanjur.[1] A great Tantra teacher, to whom a Sādhana is also attributed, is Indrabhūti (about 687-717 A.D.), the author of Jñānasiddhi and numerous other Tantric works.[2] He was a king of Uḍḍiyāna (Orissa ?) and father of Padmasambhava, the founder of Lamaism. Padmavajra,[3] whose Guhyasiddhi has come down to us in Sanskrit, was a contemporary of Indrabhūti. In this work, which is written in the "Sandhā-language,"[4] all the secret rites of the Vajrayāna are described and recommended. Lakṣmīṃkarā, who, in her Advayasiddhi, proclaimed novel, monistic doctrines, which were called Sahajayāna, and which are even at the present day prevalent among the Bāuls in Bengal, was a sister of Indrabhūti. She refutes asceticism, ceremonies and the worship of images, and recommends only meditation on the body in which all the gods dwell.[5] Another prominent Tantra authoress is Sahajayoginī Cintā (about 761 A.D.), and indeed it is no rare thing to find women among the writers of Tantric works.[6]

---

1) *Cf.* B. *Bhattacharyya*, Sādhanamālā II, pp. xlvi, cvi ff.

2) B. *Bhattacharyya*, l.c., pp. xli ff., li ff., xcviii f. [23 of his works are translated in the Tanjur. In Sanskrit only the Kurukullā-Sādhana (Sādhanamālā No. 174) and the Jñānasiddhi have come down. On the latter (an edition is to appear in GOS) s. *Bhattacharyya*, l.c., p. lii f.

3) B. *Bhattacharyya*, l.c., pp. xxvii, xlvii ff.

4) Haraprasāda *Śāstrī* called this language Sandhyā-bhāṣā or "twilight-language," Panchcowrie *Banerjee* (Visva Bharati Quarterly, 1924, p. 265) called it the language of the borderland between the ancient Āryāvarta and the actual Bengal. Vidhushekhara *Bhattacharya* (Ind. Hist. Q. IV, 1928, p. 287 ff.) has, however, shown that the correct name is Sandhā-bhāṣā, and means "intentional speech," *i.e.*, enigmatical speech in which a secret meaning is intended.

5) B. *Bhattacharyya*, l.c., p. liv f.

6) B. *Bhattacharyya*, l.c., pp. liv ff., lviii f.

The earliest Tantras are difficult to distinguish from the Mahāyāna-Sūtras. It may be that Mahāyāna doctrines mingled with Tantric rites, or perhaps works which were originally Sūtras, were remodelled into Tantras. Among the earlier Tantras we have the Tathāgata-Guhyaka or Guhyasamāja, which was a very authoritative work as early as in the 7th century. It was an authority for Indrabhūti,[1] and even in the Sikṣā-Samuccaya a Tathāgata-Guhya-Sūtra is quoted several times.[2] The passages quoted, however, teach a pure Mahāyāna morality, and appear to have been culled from a Mahāyāna-Sūtra rather than from a Tantra, for instance:

"In whom does the Will to Enlightenment arise, O Lord?" He said: "In that one, O great king, who has formed the immutable resolve to obtain it." He said: "O Lord, and who has this immutable resolve?" He said: "He, O great king, in whom the great pity has arisen." He said: "In whom, O Lord, has the great pity arisen?" He said: "In him, O great king, who does not desert any living being." He said: "In what way, Lord, is no living being deserted?" He said: "O great king, it is by renouncing one's own welfare."

In another passage it is explained: All beings are released from everything evil and from all ills by the contact of a Bodhisattva who is permeated with the Dharmakāya. This is illustrated by the parable of the "medicine girl:"[3]). Jīvaka the king of physicians, had taken all the medicaments and formed them into a girl. All the sick people who came to him, were then united with this girl, after which they were immediately healed.

---

[1]) According to one tradition, Asaṅga is even supposed to have written an introduction to the work. *Cf.* B. *Bhattacharyya*, l.c., pp. xxvii f., xxxv.

[2]) According to *Watters* (s. Sikṣāsamuccaya, ed. C. *Bendall*, p. 274, note), the work cited by Sāntideva corresponds to the Chinese translation made in about the year 1000 A.D. [*Nanjio*, Nos. 23 (3), 1043], in which the title corresponds to a Tathāgatacintya-guhya-nirdeśa, and which is a Mahāyāna-Sūtra entirely different from the Tantra described by Rāj. *Mitra*. K. *Watanabe* (JRAS 1907, p. 664) says that Nanjio No. 1027 corresponds to the Śrīguhyasamāja-Tantrarāja, and adds: "Some parts of the original text which are not fit for publication as Dr. Rājendralāla Mitra indicates...are omitted in the Chinese."

[3]) A counterpart to the "poison girl" well known in narrative literature.

Then, in another quotation, the ten things are enumerated, by means of which a Bodhisattva acquires power : " Here, O great king, a Bodhisattva gives up his body and his life, but he does not give up the good religion. He bows his head before all beings, and does not allow his pride to rise. He has patience with the feeble beings and does not put any difficulties in their way. He gives the best, excellent food to those beings who are suffering from hunger. He gives security to those beings who fear. He is full of zeal for the complete healing of the sick. He satisfies the poor with riches. He repairs the shrines of the Tathāgata by lumps of plaster. He brings glad tidings to the beings. He shares his possessions with the poor and the unfortunate. He bears the burden of those who are weary and exhausted."[1])

It is true that the Tantra described by Rājendralāla Mitra[2]) also begins with instructions as to various kinds of meditation, but, for the most part, it merely teaches Mantras and Yantras, and as a means to the highest perfection the enjoyment of meat, as well as daily sexual intercourse with young and beautiful Caṇḍāla girls. Whether this Tantra is a later variant of an earlier Mahāyāna-Sūtra, or whether it is entirely different from the work cited in the Śikṣā-Samuccaya, can only be decided by a comparison of the Chinese translation with the Sanskrit manuscripts.[3])

The Pañcakrama[4]) is said to be an extract from the Guhyasamāja. It is an Anuttarayoga-Tantra, and deals more

---

[1]) Śikṣā-Samuccya, pp. 7 f., 158 f., 274.

[2]) Nep. Buddh. Lit., p. 261 ff.

[3]) Haraprasāda *Śāstrī* (Descriptive Catalogue of Sanskrit MSS. in the...As. Soc. of Bengal, I, 1917, pp. 17-21 and 72) describes 3 MSS. of the work, in which the Vajrapāṇi-Guhyakādhipati and the Bodhisattva Śāntimati appear in conversation. Śāntimati is also addressed in a quotation in Śikṣā-Samuccaya, p. 242. H. *Śāstrī* assumes that the earliest of the three parts of the work is a Mahāyāna-Vaipulya-Sūtra, whilst the later parts belong to the Vajrayāna. *Cf.* also B. *Bhattacharyya* in Ind. Hist. Q. III, pp. 737, 742 f. and Sādhanamālā II, pp. xxvii f., xxxv.

[4]) Edited, with an Introduction, by *La Vallée Poussin*, Études et Textes Tantriques (Recueil de Travaux publiés par la faculté de philosophie et lettres, Université de Gand, fasc, 16), Gand et Louvain 1896. *Cf. Burnouf*, Introduction, p. 497 ff. *La Vallée Poussin* in OC Genève 1894, I, pp. 137-146. and Bouddhisme, Études et Matériaux, Mém.

with Yoga than with the actual Tantric usages. As the name implies, the Pañcakrama is a presentation of the "five stages," the last of which is the final possession of the highest Yoga. The preliminary stages consist of the purification of body, speech and mind, so that these receive the "diamond nature"[1] of the body, the speech and the mind of the Buddhas. However, the means for attaining the five stages are magic circles, magic formulas, mysterious syllables and the worshipping of Mahāyānist and Tantric deities. In this manner, the Yogin reaches the highest stage of all, where all differences cease and where no duality of any kind exists. Of this Yogin it is said (VI, 30 ff.):

> "He feels towards his enemy as towards himself; his mother is to him as his wife; a harlot is to him as his mother; a Brahman woman is to him as a Ḍombī (a female musician of the lowest caste); the skin of an animal is to him as a garment; a blade of straw is like a precious stone, wine is like urine, food is like mud, an insult like a hymn of praise, Indra like Rudra, day like night, what he has seen is like a dream, things which exist are like things which have been destroyed, pain is like pleasure, his son is like a rascal, heaven is like hell—and thus even good and evil are one and the same to him."

Śākyamitra is mentioned as the author of Section III of the work, which consists of five sections: the other four sections are attributed to Nāgārjuna, which probably means the Tantra writer of this name (see above, pp. 392 f.). Śākyamitra is mentioned by Tāranātha as a contemporary of Devapāla of Bengal (about 850 A.D.).[2]

A work which describes itself as a Mahā-Vaipulya-Mahāyāna-Sūtra and as belonging to the Avataṃsaka, is the

---

Ac. Belg. 1898, p. 146: "manuel qui se présente comme un extrait ou résumé du Guhyasamāja-Tantra."

[1]) For the nature of Vajra, see above p. 388.

[2]) A Pañcakramopadeśa Śrīghaṇṭa is mentioned in the Catalogue of Buddhist Sanskrit MSS. in the Royal Asiatic Society, by E. B. *Cowell* and J. *Eggeling* (JRAS, 1876, reprint p. 28).

Mañjuśrī-Mūla-Kalpa.[1] Nevertheless, as far as its contents are concerned, the work is entirely in the spirit of the Mantrayāna. In the major portion of the work, Śākyamuni speaks in a large assembly, but addresses himself only to Mañjuśrī. In the first three chapters Mañjuśrī himself speaks, and in the last two chapters the goddess Vijayā. Śākyamuni gives Mañjuśrī instructions as to magic rites with Mantras, Mudrās, Maṇḍalas, etc. In Chap. IX, for instance, the "great king of sciences," the Mantra of Mañjuśrī, is taught, which includes all sciences within itself, by means of which one can attain all things, which destroys all the Mantras of evil-doers, blots out all sins, etc.—this is the "kllhuṃ" Mantra. In Chapter XIV the same powers are claimed for the "bhrūṃ" Mantra. There is very little trace of Buddhism in this manual of magic, though the worship of the "three jewels" is mentioned in Chap. 47. The work was translated into Chinese as a Mahā-Vaipulya-Sūtra between 980 and 1000 A.D. and into Tibetan as a Tantra in the 11th century.[2]

The (Ekallavīra-) Caṇḍa-Mahāroṣaṇa-Tantra[3] explains on the one hand (in Chapt. XVI) the Pratītya-Samutpāda according to the philosophical doctrines of the Mahāyāna,[4] whilst on the other hand, the cult of Yoginīs, such as

---

[1]) Edited by T. Gaṇapati *Śāstrī* in TSS, Nos. LXX and LXXVI, 1920, 1922. *Cf.* J. *Przyluski* in BEFEO, t. XXIII, 1923, p. 301 ff. and B. *Bhattacharyya*, Sādhanamālā II, p. xxxivf.

[2]) *Körös* in AMG II, 313 f. It is frequently cited by Tibetan scholars. The Bodhisattva Mañjuśrī also occurs in the titles of other Tantra works. The Mañjuśrīnāma-saṃgīti (edited by *Minayeff* in his Russian work on Buddhism, Petrograd 1887) admits of a double interpretation, one purely philosophical and the other Tantric with allusions to Śākta rites. Thus according to *La Vallée Poussin* in ERE XII, 194.

[3]) Considerable extracts from MSS. of the work, are given by Haraprasāda *Śāstrī*, Descriptive Cat. of Sanskrit MSS. in...the As. Soc. of Bengal, I, pp. 131-141. Caṇḍaroṣaṇa is an emanation of Akṣobhya. On his secret cult see B. *Bhattacharyya*, Indian Buddhist Iconography, p. 60 ff.

[4]) See *La Vallée Poussin*, Théorie des douze causes, 1913, p. 125 ff.; JRAS, 1897, 466 ff.; OC XI, Paris, I, 244; ERE XII, 196.

Mohavajrī, Piśunavajrī, Rājavajrī, etc., and that of female deities with sexual actions, are recommended.

It is shown how the six perfections can be attained by means of sexual union. In one passage Bhagavatī asks: [1]) "O Lord, can the dwelling of Caṇḍamahāroṣaṇa be attained without a woman, or is that not possible?" The Lord said: "That is not possible, O goddess."..."Enlightenment is attained by means of bliss, and there is no bliss without a woman"......"I am the son of Māyā, and I have assumed the form of Caṇḍamahāroṣaṇa; you are the exalted Gopā, [2]) who are one with the Prajñā-Pāramitā. And all women in the universe, are regarded as incarnations of her, and all men as incarnations of myself."

The ritual of the "great bliss" (mahāsukha) is described in the Śrīcakrasambhāra-Tantra,[3]) which we have only in Tibetan. The book teaches the Mantras, the meditations, the pictures of the divine couples which one has to present to one's mind, the sacrificial ritual and the symbolical significance of the Mantras connected with the Mahāsukha.

As regards the immoral character of this literature and these cults, we should neither exaggerate it, nor should we seek to deny it. There is no doubt that the ritual of the Vajrayāna has led to gross abuses; on the other hand, we must admit that it has a mystic, philosophical background. The Vajrayāna teaches a monistic philosophy. Just as Śiva and Pārvatī are one, Buddha and his Śakti, Tārā or Bhagavatī or Prajñā-Pāramitā, are one. This unity is symbolised figuratively by the intimate embrace (yuganaddha, Tibetan

---

[1]) "The Exalted One (feminine)" is the personified Prajñā-Pāramitā, wisdom conceived as a goddess. On strīpūjā, *cf.* Haraprasāda *Śāstrī* in JASB, Vol. 67, 1898, p. 175.

[2]) Gopā is the consort of Gotama. Because the accomplished Buddha, before he withdrew from the world in order to attain to Bodhi, was happy in the harem united to Gopā, sexual union is also recommended to his adherents as a means of attaining to Bodhi.

[3]) Ed. by *Kazi Dawa-Samdup* in Tantrik Texts, Vols. VII (Introduction and English translation) and XI (Tibetan text). *Cf.* H. *Zimmer*, Kunstform und Yoga im indischen Kultbild, Berlin 1926, 67 f., 74 ff.

yabyum) of the gods and goddesses, who, for the most part, are merely male and female personifications of abstract ideas. The sexual union, in which the man is regarded as the incarnation of Buddha, and the woman as that of Bhagavatī, in reality serves the same symbolical purpose as those pictures in the cult.[1]

In his "History of Buddhism in India," Tāranātha[2] gives us a good idea of the spirit of the Tantra Buddhism. Though he also speaks of Mahāyāna and Tripiṭaka, of Buddhist science and Buddhist self-sacrifice, it is nevertheless Siddhi, the magic art acquired by means of Mantras and Tantra rites, which plays by far the more prominent part. Just as the contents of the Tantras present a medley of Buddhism and Hinduism, of religion, philosophy, occultism and magic, popular belief and hair-splitting, erudite argumentation, truly Indian cults and cults savouring of foreign influence, thus, the history of Buddhist Tantra literature too, is a very complex one. When Tāranātha says that at the time of the Pāla dynasty of Bengal, that is to say, from the 9th to the 11th century, Yoga and magic were paramount in Buddhism, his statement is probably not far from the truth. Most likely the Buddhist Tantras did not come into being until the 7th or 8th century under the influence of the Śivaite Tantras, and belong to the period at which Buddhism was almost entirely assimilated to Hinduism. The very names of the deities in the Buddhist Tantras betray their dependence upon the Śivaite Tantras. The Mahākāla-Tantra is in the form of a dialogue between Śākyamuni and a goddess, and it is said that it was "proclaimed by Buddha." However, it contains

---

[1]) *Cf. La Vallée Poussin*, Bouddhisme, Études et Matériaux, Mém. 1898, p. 141 ff.

[2]) Tāranātha was born in 1573, and completed his work, which was written on the basis of Indian and Tibetan sources, in the year 1608. Translated into German by A. *Schiefner*. He describes regular competitions in magic (*e.g.*, on p. 189 ff.).

explanations as to the mystical significance of the letters of which the name Mahākāla, *i.e.*, Śiva, is composed, and on the means of finding hidden treasures, gaining a kingdom, obtaining the desired wife, and even Mantras and magic rites, by which one can make people insane, enslave them, and kill them.[1] The Saṃvarodaya-Tantra, again, in spite of the form of a dialogue between Buddha and the Bodhisattva Vajrapāṇi, is more of a Śivaite than a Buddhist work. The Liṅga cult and the worshipping of Śivaite gods are expressly recommended in it.[2]

The lands where Tantrism was the most widespread, and perhaps where it originated, are Assam and Bengal.[3] From the 8th century onwārds it proceeded from this territory in a veritable triumph to Tibet and China, where it mingled with native cults. Vajrabodhi and Amoghavajra went to China in about 720 A.D., and contributed largely towards the propagation of the Tantras.[4] In Japan, where only the Mantrayāna, and not the Vajrayāna, obtained a footing, the Shin-go sect takes its stand upon the Tantras.[5] In the later Tantras we again find traces of Tibetan and Chinese influences, and in the case of some cults, it is expressly stated that they were brought from Cīna (China) or Mahācīna (Tibet). In the Tārā-Tantra Buddha and Vasiṣṭha are described as great Bhairavas. Buddha was a form of Viṣṇu, and obtained the position of a creator, after his initiation into the Mantras of Ugra-Tārā. Tārā is Buddha's Śakti, and a

---

[1] *Burnouf*, Introduction, p. 480; Rāj. *Mitra*, Nep. Buddh. Lit., p. 172 f.; E. B. *Cowell* and J. *Eggeling*, Catalogue of Buddhist Sanskrit MSS., p. 37 f.

[2]) *Burnouf*, Introduction, p. 479 ff.

[3]) *Cf.* B. *Bhattacharyya* in Ind. Hist. Q. III, 744; Buddhist Iconography, p. xxvii; Proceedings of Madras Or. Conf. p. 138; Sādhanamālā II, p. xxxvi ff.

[4]) *Cf.* L. *Wieger*, Histoire des croyances religieuses et des opinions philosophiques en Chine, 1922, p. 535 ff. The most important text of Mantra-Buddhism in China, namely the Mahā-Vairocana-Abhi-Sambodhi, was brought to China by Śubhakarasiṃha (died in 735 A.D.); s. *Anesaki* in ERE IV, 840.

[5]) B. *Nanjio*, Twelve Japanese Buddhist Sects, p. 78 ff.

form a wisdom (Prajñā). Vasiṣṭha, however, is said to have learned the knowledge of Tārā in Cīna from the lips of Buddha. The Tantric manual Tārā-rahasya by Brahmānanda also teaches the cult of Tārā in agreement with the usages of Mahācīna.[1] At this late period it also occasionally happened that the Hindu Tantras were influenced by the Buddhist ones.[2] It is related in the Hindu Tantras Rudrayāmala and Brahmayāmala that Vasiṣṭha, in spite of all his ascetic endeavours, did not succeed in causing the goddess Pārvatī to appear to him. In the end his Guru tells him that he should go to Mahācīna, the land of the Buddhas. He follows this advice, and seeks the help of Mahādeva Buddharūpa, who teaches him the Pañcatattva ritual.[3] Tantras still continued to be written even in very late times. Thus for instance there is a Kālacakra,[4] which already mentions Mecca and Islam.

The Sanskrit in which the Tantras are written, is, as a rule, just as barbarous as their contents. Inferior as they may be from the literary point of view, they are nevertheless extremely important owing to their great popularity over a wide area, and the great influence which they exerted over the spiritual life of Western India and of considerable portions of Asia.

---

[1]) On Tārā-Tantra and Tārā-Rahasya, s. Haraprasāda *Śāstrī*, Notes of Sanskrit MSS., 2nd Series, I, 1900, pp. xxix f., xxxii f. Thus the cult of Mañjuśrī was taken from India to China, but became so oppular there, that people in India said Mañjuśrī lived in China, and his cult was then again taken from China to Nepal. I-tsing (Record, transl. by J. *Takakusu*, p. 169) calls attention to an Indian book, probably a Tantra, in which China is praised because it is the home of Mañjuśrī. Cf. *La Vallée Poussin* in ERE VIII, 405 f.

[2]) It is, however, quite contrary to the facts, when B. *Bhattacharyya* (Sādhanamālā II, pp. lxvi ff., lxxviii) assumes that the Tantras first came into existence in Buddhism, and went over into Hinduism afterwards.

[3]) Cf. *Woodroffe*, Shakti and Shākta, p. 104 ff.

[4]) Only extant in Tibetan, s. *Burnouf*, Introduction, p. 480 f.

Buddhist Literature and Universal Literature.

Just as Buddhism became one of the great religions of the world, a great part of Buddhist literature belongs to universal literature. We have already seen, on various occasions, that Buddhist fables, anecdotes, fairy tales and legends not only migrated to the Far East with Buddhism, but also frequently have their parallels in European literatures, though it is not always certain that the Buddhist narratives migrated to Europe, for the reverse may sometimes have been the case.[1] We have also seen that the Buddha legend has some features in common with the legend of Christ,[2] and that certain speeches and parables in the Suttas of the Tipiṭaka and the Mahāyāna Sūtras are, more or less strikingly, reminiscent of passages in the Christian gospels.[3]

The question as to how far these points of agreement between Buddhist and Christian literature actually exist, and what significance is due to them, is sufficiently important to warrant our treating of them once more as a whole. Are they more or less accidental similarities, resemblances which may be explained by the fact that the respective legends, similes and utterances have arisen out of the same situations and religious moods, or is it a question of the actual dependence of the one literature upon the other? Were the Christian gospels influenced by the Buddhist sacred texts, which date from pre-Christian times? Or were later Buddhist texts, like the Lalita-Vistara and the Saddharma-Puṇḍarīka, influenced by the Christian gospels? These questions have repeatedly been the subject of research and have been answered in most varying ways.

---

[1]) See above, pp. 64 note 2, 109 note 2, 126 f., 130 f., 132 note 2, 134 ff., 150, notes 2, 3, 4, 193 f., 200 f., 214 f.

[2]) See above, pp. 97 notes 1 and 2, 252 note 1, 286 note 4.

[3]) See above, pp. 29 note 1, 74 note 1, 299 note 1.

Rudolf Seydel,[1] in particular, thought he could prove such numerous coincidences between the Buddha legend and the life of Jesus according to the gospels, that he framed the hypothesis that the Evangelists, besides using an "original text" of St. Matthew and an "original text" of St. Mark, had also made use of a poetical gospel, Christian though influenced by Buddhism, and had taken from this all those legends, parables and utterances which have parallels in the Buddhist texts. He considered this hypothesis to be necessary, because the points of agreement (in his opinion) do not appear singly but massed together, and actually form groups, indeed, a connected whole. A single stick, he says, can easily be broken, but it is more difficult to break a bundle, or indeed a bundle of bundles. This is well said! But if the stick is no stick, but only the phantom of a stick, then even a bundle, or a bundle of bundles of such "sticks" is of no use to us. In reality it is not difficult to show, and has repeatedly been shown, that the majority of the "parallels" indicated by Seydel will not bear closer examination.

The Dutch scholar *G. A. van den Bergh van Eysinga*[2] has approached the problem of the Indian influences on the Christian gospels far more cautiously than Seydel. He begins by eliminating everything which could easily be explained by the similarity of circumstances under which the texts originated, similarity of religious development, and finally on general human grounds. Nevertheless, even according to this scholar there still remain actual parallels which can only be explained as loans. He is, however, of opinion that we are

---

[1]) Das Evangelium von Jesu in seinen Verhältnissen zu Buddha-Sage und Buddha-Lehre, Leipzig 1882; Die Buddha-Legende und das Leben Jesu nach den Evangelien, erneute Prüfung ihres gegenseitigen Verhältnisses, 2. Aufl. mit ergänzenden Anmerkungen von Martin Seydel, Weimar 18.7.

[2]) Indische Einflüsse auf evangelische Erzählungen, Göttingen 1904, 2. Aufl. 1909. (I quote from this edition.)

not justified in assuming that there was any dependence upon written texts, but by mere oral transmission at the time of the Roman Empire, Indian subjects, themes and ideas reached the West, and certain of these features were borrowed in the formation of the legends of the earliest Christianity. Of the 51 parallels which Seydel believed to have found, Bergh van Eysinga regards only nine as worthy of discussion, and only six as more or less important.

What Seydel undertook to produce with inadequate material, for Buddhist literature was but very incompletely known in his day, namely, a "Buddhist-Christian Gospel Concordance," was once again attempted later, on the basis of a far more accurate knowledge of the Pāli and Sanskrit texts, by the American scholar *Albert J. Edmunds.*[1] He expressly states that he is not out to prove the dependence of the Christian sacred scriptures upon the Buddhist texts, but only to compare the two religions, "as such a comparison will finally have the effect of making them respect each other." Nevertheless he inclines to the view that Christianity, as the more eclectic religion, borrowed from Buddhism, and that St. Luke, in particular, was acquainted with a Buddha-epic. On the other hand, it is precisely Edmunds' comprehensive collection of all the passages in both literatures which can possibly be dragged in, as it were, for comparison, which shows most clearly, firstly, that there is no instance in which a loan on the part of the four gospels must necessarily be assumed, secondly, that in most instances there is only a similarity of ideas, which does not presuppose a literary connection, and thirdly, that in the best cases, only a possibility of mutual influence can be admitted, and that this *possibility* amounts

[1]) Buddhist and Christian Gospels now first compared from the Originals by A. J. *Edmunds*, edited by M. *Anesaki*, 4th Ed., Philadelphia 1908-9; A. J. *Edmunds*, Buddhist Texts quoted as Scripture by the Gospel of John, 2nd Ed., Philadelphia-London 1911; and Buddhist Loans to Christianity in The Monist, January 1912, p. 129 ff.

to *probability* only in very few cases. Very frequently, indeed, Edmunds' comparison of the texts shows how very much greater the differences are than the points of contact.

We need only to read the texts, compared by Edmunds,[1] on the miraculous conception and birth of Christ and of Buddha, and the differences become obvious. It is true that there are miracles in both cases ; but as the history of religion, mythology and folk-lore teach us, the birth of great men is attended by miracles everywhere. Greek mythology affords far closer parallels to the virgin birth than does the Buddhist legend.[2] As a matter of fact, Buddha is conceived and born of a married queen, and not of a virgin at all. Again, the texts about the temptation of Buddha by Māra and of Christ by Satan [3] show more differences than points of agreement, and the temptation of Zoroaster by Ahriman proves that it cannot be a question of the mere borrowing of texts, but at most a matter of connections in religious history, harking back to far earlier times. Likewise in the legend of the transfiguration of Jesus, as compared with the account in the Mahā-Parinibbāna-Sutta of the radiance of the Buddha's body, I can see only a striking parallel, of great interest from the point of view of the history of religion, but not a loan from Buddhist literature.[4]

---

[1]) I, 107 f., 167 ff.; St. Luke I, 35; Majjhimanikāya 38 and 123.

[2]) *Cf.* H. *Gunkel*, Zum religionsgeschichtlichen Verständnis des Neuen Testaments, Göttingen 1903, p. 65 ff.; *Garbe*, Indien und das Christentum, p. 31 f.; *Günter*, Buddha in der abendländischen Legende ? 194 ff.; *Haas*, Buddha in der abendländischen Legende ? 17 ff.; W. *Printz* in ZDMG 78, 1925, 119 ff.

[3]) *Edmunds*, I, 198 ff.; also *Pischel*, Leben und Lehre des Buddha, p. 26 f., denies the connection in this instance. Similarly *Götz*, "Der Katholik" 1912 (IV, 9), 485 ff.; *Beth*, Theolog. Studien und Kritiken 1916, 202 ff.; *Carpenter*, Buddhism and Christianity, p. 180; and E. *Leumann*, Buddha und Mahāvīra, reprinted from ZB 1921, p. 60 ff. On the other hand, *Garbe*, loc. cit., 50 ff., regards the points of agreement as so striking, that he deems it necessary to trace the Gospel narrative back to the Buddhist temptation stories, "for a devil in the flesh does not appear anywhere else in the Bible, but occurs constantly in the Buddhist Canon." *Cf.* J. *Charpentier* in ZDMG 69, 1915, 441 f.

[4]) *Edmunds*, II, 123 ff.; Mark IX, 2 ff.; Luke IX, 30 f.; *Rhys Davids*, Dialogues

In his comprehensive work[1] on Indian influences on Christianity and Christian influences on the Indian religions, *Richard Garbe* assumes a loan from Buddhist tradition on the part of Gospel narratives, in four cases only: the story of Simeon in the temple, the legend of the temptation, St. Peter walking on the sea, and the miracle of the loaves. With regard to the parallel to the "widow's mite," Garbe assumes that the Christian legend is the original one, and that it was taken over by the Buddhists.

It will never be possible to give a conclusive answer to these questions. Any decision in this matter is more or less subjective, for parallels are never equations. In each instance there are both resemblances and divergences. In the vast mass of literature which has accumulated on this problem and which is well-nigh overwhelming,[2] some scholars

---

of the Buddha, II, p. 146; *Dutoit*, Leben des Buddha, p. 283 f. *Bergh van Eysinga*, p. 73, alludes to the transfiguration of Moses (Exodus XXXIV, 29 ff.).

[1]) Indien und das Christentum, Tübingen 1914. In his earlier studies (Deutsche Rundschau, Vol. 144, 1910, 73 ff., Vol. 149, 1911, 122 ff., and Contributions of Buddhism to Christianity, Chicago 1911), *Garbe* had taken up a more sceptical attitude. Joh. B. *Aufhauser*, Buddha und Jesus in ihren Paralleltexten, Bonn 1926, has confronted the parallel texts, giving the Gospel legends in the Greek text and the Indian legends in German translations, for the cases treated by *Garbe*.

[2]) *Cf.* Hans *Haas*, Bibliographie zur Frage nach den Wechselbeziehungen zwischen Buddhismus und Christentum (Veröffentlichungen des Forschungsinst. f. vergl. Religionsgeschichte an der Universität Leipzig No. 6) and *Aufhauser*, Buddha und Jesus, Introduction. Besides *Seydel*, *Bergh van Eysinga*, *Edmunds* and *Garbe*, other supporters of the theory of the dependence of the canonical Gospels upon the Buddhist texts or traditions, are H. *Kern* (DLZ 1882, col. 1276) and R.O. *Franke* (DLZ 1901, col. 2757 ff.), who have a prehistoric ("Aryan") connection in mind; also: O. *Pfleiderer*, Die Entstehung des Christentums, 2 Aufl., München 1907, p. 198 f., Ernst *Kuhn* in the Appendix to Bergh van Eysinga's work (p. 102 ff.) and R. *Pischel* (DLZ 1904, col. 2938 ff.) who confidently asserts: "The question as to whether Indian influences are at all to be found in the narrative literature of the Gospels can no longer be denied at the present day"; also K. E. *Neumann*, Reden Gotamo Buddho's III, 112, 256 note, 258 note, 259 note, 260 note, 331 note and elsewhere (cf. the criticism of *Günter*, Buddha, 259 ff.); K. *Seidenstücker* in his German translation of Udāna II, 8; VII, 9; VIII 5; 9; 10 and introduction p. xxii; in a few cases also H. *Haas*, "Das Scherflein der Witwe" and seine Entsprechung in Tripiṭaka, Leipzig 1922 (Veröffentlichungen etc. No. 5) and Buddha in der abendländischen Legende? Leipzig 1923 (Veröffentlichungen etc. No. 9). A. *Weber* (Griechen in Indien, SBA 1890,

emphasize above all, the divergences, whilst others lay stress upon the resemblances. The question of chronology, moreover, can rarely be decided in such a way as to exclude all doubt. All that can be said with certainty[1] is that, centuries before the birth of Christ, numerous trade connections and manifold intellectual relations were already in existence between India and the West, and that there is a possibility of Christianity's having been influenced by Buddhism. We also know that, from the 2nd and 3rd centuries A.D., representatives of various religions, Syrian Christians, Zoroastrians and Buddhists, met one another, especially in Eastern Turkestan. At this period it was just as much possible for Christian themes to find their way into Buddhist tales, as for Buddhist ideas to

---

p. 928 f.) and H. *Oldenberg* (Theolog. Litztg. 1905, col. 65 ff., Aus dem alten Indien, p. 47 f.) regard it as an open question. An entirely or almost entirely negative attitude is taken up by T. W. *Rhys Davids*, SBE XI, 165 f.; J. Estlin *Carpenter*, The first three Gospels, their Origin and Relations, 2nd Ed., London 1890, pp. 136 ff., 161 ff., 174 ff., 203 ff., 237 f.; "Buddhist and Christian Parallels" in "Studies in the History of Religions" presented to Crawford Howell Toy, New York, 1912 (not accessible to me) and Buddhism and Christianity (London 1923), p. 179 f.; E. *Hardy*, Der Buddhismus, new ed. by Rich. *Schmidt*, Münster i. W. 1919, p. 175 ff.; E. W. *Hopkins*, India Old and New, New York and London 1902, p. 120 ff.; E. *Windisch*, Māra und Buddha, pp. 6 ff., 214 ff., 312 and Buddha's Geburt, p. 195 ff.; *La Vallée Poussin*, Revue biblique 1906, p. 353 ff., Bouddhisme, p. 5 ff.; L'histoire des religions de l'Inde et l'Apologétique, London 1912 (not accessible to me); S. *Lévi* in Revue critique 1908, N. S. 65, p. 382; A.B. *Keith* in JRAS 1910, 218 f.; History of Sanskrit Lit., 501 ff.; Edv. *Lehmann*, Der Buddhismus als indische Sekte als Weltreligion, Tübingen 1911, p. 78 ff.; G. *Faber*, Buddhistische und Neutestamentliche Erzählungen, Leipzig 1913; A. *Götz* in "Der Katholik" 1912 (IV, 9), 74 ff., 254 ff.; (IV 10), 16 ff.; 1915, 363 ff.; Karl *Beth* in DLZ 1915, 893 ff., 957 ff. and Theologische Studien und Kritiken 1916, 169 ff.; Carl *Clemen* in Zeitschrift für die Neutestamentliche Wiss. 1916, 128 ff.; DLZ 1917, 668 ff.; OZ IX, 185 ff. and RGG I, 1332 ff.; Joh. B. *Aufhauser*, Christentum und Buddhismus im Ringen um Fernasien, Bonn and Leipzig 1922, p. 349 ff.; Edward J. *Thomas*, The Life of Buddha, 1927, p. 237 ff. J. *Kennedy* (JRAS 1917, 209 ff., 469 ff.) seeks the origin of all legends in the West. H. *Günter* (Buddha in der abendländischen Legende? Leipzig 1922) is inclined to explain all the Buddhist-Christian parallels on the grounds of the "relationship of life," *i.e.* the similarity of religious moods and experiences in the two religions; R. *Fick* in GGA 1924, p. 172 ff. agrees with him, but is more in favour of a "non liquet."

[1]) *Cf. Bergh van Eysinga*, loc. cit., 83 ff.; *Edmunds*, Buddhist and Christian Gospels, I, pp. 111-164, and R. *Stübe* "Indien und der Westen," in M. Kern's "Das Licht des Ostens," p. 242 ff.

be incorporated in Christian legends. On the other hand, it is very improbable that Christian ideas penetrated to India as early as in the 1st century A.D. It is true that J. *Dahlmann*[1] was at pains to prove that there is an historical basis for the Acts of St. Thomas, that a Christian mission was at work in Northern India as early as the 1st century A.D., and that Mahāyāna Buddhism developed under Christian influence—but his arguments are by no means convincing. The mention of historical names, such as Gundaphorus and Gad only proves that the background of the legend is historical, but not that the nucleus of the legend itself is necessarily so. There is not the least proof of Christian missions in India in the 1st century, and it is highly improbable that Christianity influenced the origin of the Mahāyāna.[2] It is not likely that anything much about Christians was known in India prior to the 3rd century.[3] It must be admitted, however, that the Buddhist texts can scarcely ever be dated with any degree of certainty. Moreover we have always to reckon with the possibility that a legend might have originated at an early period, even though it was not written down until later. We see, then, that these are very complex questions, and each case must be decided on its own merits. It is only such elaborate monographs as those of *Hans Haas*[4] on the "widow's mite" and *William Norman Brown*[5] on the miracle of walking on the sea, which can pave the way for a tolerably satisfactory result.

---

1) Indische Fahrten, Freiburg i.B. 1908, II, 100, 129 ff., 152 ff.; Die Thomas-Legende, Freiburg i.B. 1912; cf. Alfons *Väth*, Der hl. Thomas der Apostel Indiens, Aachen 1925, and J. *Charpentier*, The Apostle of India, in Kyrko-historisk Årsskrift 1927, 21 ff.

2) *Cf. Winternitz* in DLZ 1913, 1750 ff. and *Garbe*, Indien und das Christentum, 128 ff., 159 ff.

3) *Cf.* A. *Harnack*, Die Mission und Ausbreitung des Christentums in den ersten drei Jahrhunderten, 4. Aufl. Leipzig 1924, p. 698.

4) "Das Scherflein der Witwe" (s. above p. 406 note 2).

5) The Indian and Christian Miracles of Walking on the Water, The Open Court Company, Chicago, London 1928.

The Buddhist parallel to the story of the "widow's mite" is the legend of the poor girl who gives the monks the whole of her possessions, two copper coins which she has found in the dust-heap, and is praised for it by Buddha, her gift being valued as highly as that of the rich man who gives all his estates and treasures as alms. She does not go without a reward for her good deed, for soon afterwards she is discovered by a passing king, who immediately falls in love with her and makes her his queen. There is no doubt that the Buddhist narrative, in the form in which we know it from the Chinese translation of the Kalpanāmaṇḍitikā,[1] is far inferior to the Gospel story, so beautiful in its simplicity, of the widow's two mites. As the Buddhist tale is first attested by the Chinese translation of 402 A.D., and can scarcely be earlier than 200 A.D., it is not impossible that the Buddhists learned it from Christians, and made it end like a fairy tale. It is also possible, however, that an earlier and better form of the Buddhist legend has been lost. The agreement with regard to so small a detail as the "*two* mites" makes it highly probable, nevertheless, that the Buddhist and Christian stories did not originate independently of each other.

Similarly, the parallel to St. Peter's walking on the sea, is not found until the time of the later Buddhist literature: we have it in the Jātaka commentary. Just as in Matth. XIV, 28 ff. St. Peter walks on the sea, and begins to sink as soon as his faith wavers, similarly, in the "Story of the present" of Jātaka No. 190, a believing layman walks across the river as long as he thinks joyfully of Buddha, and begins to sink as soon as this joyful mindfulness of Buddha diminishes at the sight of the waves. In this instance the details

[1]) Sūtrālaṃkāra, trad. Huber, p. 119 ff.; Mark XII, 41 ff.; Luke XXI, 1 ff.; *Bergh van Eysinga*, p. 50 ff.; *Lehmann*, loc. cit., p. 88 ff.; *Götz* in "Der Katholik" 1912 (IV, 10), 18 f.; *Clemen* in OZ IX, 186 f., 199 f.; *Garbe*, Indien und das Christentum 88 f.; *Haas*, l. c.

coincide so strikingly, that it is highly improbable that the two legends originated independently of each other. As the Indian legend is not an isolated one, whilst as far as the New Testament is concerned, it occurs only in St. Matthew, it is very likely that the Christian legend was derived from an Indian source. We must assume, it is true, that the narrative which has come down to us in the Jātaka commentary, is based upon a much earlier tradition.[1]

Again, the parallel to the miracle of the feeding of the multitude, does not occur earlier than in the Jātaka commentary. Just as Jesus feeds 5,000 people with five loaves and two fishes, the Buddhist narrative tells us that 500 monks were fed with a cake which increased of itself. There is, however, a considerable difference between the two. In the Gospel we have a miracle which Jesus performs in order to feed a multitude of poor people, and in which he raises his eyes to heaven, and blesses, whilst in the Jātaka commentary we have a comical, not to say silly, fairy-tale, in which the miracle is performed by a saint in order to convert a miser. Indeed, the miracle of Jesus has more in common with the miraculous feeding of the children of Israel with quails and manna (Exodus XVI, cf. Numbers XI, 31 f.) than with the Buddhist fairy-tale.[2] There is also an account of a miracle of feeding in

---

[1]) *Cf.* W. N. *Brown*, loc. cit.; *Edmunds* II, 257 f.; *Bergh van Eysinga*, p. 52 ff.; *Carpenter*, First Three Gospels, p. 203 ff.; Buddhism and Christianity, p. 180; *Garbe*, Contributions, p. 12 f.; Indien und das Christentum, 56 ff.; *Götz*, l. c., 19 ff.; *Beth* in DLZ 1915, col. 1900; Theolog. Studien 1916, 214 ff.; *Clemen* in Zeitschr. für die neutestamentliche Forschung 1916, 137; *Charpentier* in ZDMG 69, 441; *Günter*, Buddha in der abendländischen Legende? 218 f.; *Haas*, Buddha in der abendländ. Legende? 25 f.

[2]) Matth. XIV, 16 ff.; XV, 32 ff.; Jātaka, No. 78. *Cf. Edmunds* II, 258 ff.; *Garbe*, Indien und das Christentum, 59 f.; *Charpentier* in ZDMG 69, 441; *Carpenter*, Buddhism and Christianity, p. 180; *Clemen* in OZ IX, 185 f.; Zeitschr. f. d. neutest. Wiss. 1916, 137 f.; *Beth* in DLZ 1915, 900 f.; Theolog. Studien 1916, 219 ff.; *Günter*, l.c., p. 214; *Haas*, "Scherflein der Witwe," 37 f. The Rasavāhinī, in which similar legends occur (*Lehmann*, l.c., p. 90 ff.) is quite a late work (see above, p. 224 f.). In his book "Unter Brahmanen und Parias," Leipzig 1923, p. 68 f., J. A. *Sauter* tells of a miracle

the Mahāyāna-Sūtra Vimala-Kīrti-Nirdeśa.[1] Many Bodhisattvas have assembled for a pious conversation. It is time for the meal, and by his miraculous power, Vimalakīrti causes a being from the world of sweet perfumes to produce a tiny fragment of food, which satisfies the whole assembly, and yet does not grow smaller. This miraculous feeding differs as widely from that of the Jātaka as it does from that of the Gospel. Finally, if we remind ourselves of the fairy-tale motif of "Table, fill thyself!", which has its counterpart even in the Mahābhārata[2] in the self-filling pot which was the gift of the sun-god, we shall come to the conclusion that all these miracles of feeding are but variations of a motif which could quite well crop up afresh as a new invention at different times and in different places.

There is a far more striking similarity between the legend of Asita and that of Simeon in St. Luke. In spite of some differences, which, here too, are undeniable, I regard it as fairly probable that the author of the Christian narrative was acquainted with the Buddhist legend.[3] It is possible, too, that there is a connection between the legend of Buddha who, as a boy, goes apart from his companions, and after being missed by his family, is found absorbed in deep meditation, and the story of the twelve-year old Jesus who, instead of returning to Nazareth with his parents, remains behind in the temple in Jerusalem and converses with the teachers.[4] I

---

of feeding which he says he witnessed himself, on the part of Dayanandi Svami, who fed and satisfied twenty guests with two handfuls of rice.

[1]) Communicated by *Haas*, "Das Scherflein der Witwe," p. 89 ff.

[2]) See above, Vol. I, p. 346 f.

[3]) See above, p. 96 f. *Cf. Bergh van Eysinga*, 28 ff.; *Edmunds* I, 181 ff.; *Pischel* in DLZ 1904, 2938 ff.; *Garbe*, l.c., 48 ff.; *Charpentier* in ZDMG 69, 441. The divergences between the two legends are emphasized by *Götz* in "Der Katholik" 1912 (IV, 9), 429 ff.; *Beth* in DLZ 1915, 898 f.; Theolog. Studien 1916, 192 ff.; *Clemen* in Zeitschr. f. d. neutest. Wiss. 1916, 134 f.; *Carpenter*, Buddhism and Christianity, 179 f.; and by *Günter*, l. c., p. 203 f. (on the other hand, cf. *Haas*, Buddha in der abendländischen Legende? 24).

[4]) St. Luke II, 41 ff.; Lalita-Vistara XI; Nidāna-Kathā, Jātaka Ed., p. 58; *Rhys*

also consider it within the realm of possibility that the beatification of the mother of the Lord by a woman in St. Luke XI, 27f. is connected with that in the Nidāna-Kathā.[1]

It is less probable that the parable of the "prodigal son" in the Saddharma-Puṇḍarīka is connected with that in St. Luke. Even Seydel[2] says: "The parable of the 'Lotus' has in reality nothing in common with the Christian parable, except that a wandering son returns in poverty, and above all, the tendency of the comparison is entirely different in the two parallels." Also the similarity between the legend of Jesus and the woman of Samaria in the Gospel of St. John, and that of Ānanda and the pariah girl in the Divyāvadāna is none too great.[3] Besides, in both cases they are Buddhist texts of post-Christian times.

Even the death of Christ has been compared with Buddha's entrance into Nirvāṇa. Seydel has pointed out that both events are accompanied by an earthquake, while Edmunds goes so far as to emphasize the fact that Jesus and Buddha both die in the open-air![4] And yet the difference between the two religious texts is nowhere shown so clearly

---

Davids, Buddhist Birth Stories, p. 75; *Kern*, Der Buddhismus I, 39 f. *Cf. Bergh van Eysinga*, p. 33 f.

1) Jātaka I, p. 60; *Rhys Davids*, Buddhist Birth Stories, p. 79 f.; *Seydel*, Die Buddhalegende, p. 26 f.; *Bergh van Eysinga*, p. 48 ff. It is true enough that such beatitudes also occur elsewhere in poetry (*Neumann*, Lieder der Mönche und Nonnen, p. 309 note; *Lehmann*, Der Buddhismus, p. 85); nevertheless, it is a remarkable coincidence that both Buddha and Jesus append to the benedictions a remark concerning that whereof true blessedness consists. The connection is denied by *Götz* in "Der Katholik" 1912 (IV, 10), 16 f., and doubted by *Garbe*, l. c., p. 32 f.

2) Das Evangelium von Jesu, p. 230; cf. above, p. 298 f.; J. M. *Carter*, JRAS 1893, p. 393 f.; *Bergh van Eysinga*, p. 67 ff.; *Edmunds* II, 260 f. *Seydel*, l. c., p. 232 f., has, however, compared the allegory of the man who was born blind (John IX) with Saddharma-P. V. (see above, p. 299), though the Indian *parable* has nothing in common with the Christian *legend*, except that a man who was born blind occurs in both.

3) See above, p. 286 f.; *Bergh van Eysinga*, p. 57 ff.

4) *Seydel*, l. c., p. 280 ff.; *Edmunds* II, 169 f.; cf. *Windisch*, Māra und Buddha, p. 60 ff.

as here. What a vast difference between the Mahā-Parinibbāna-Sutta and the 27th chapter of St. Matthew! Here the heart-rending tragedy of a martyr and a victim of fanaticism, there the calm passing of a sage—a glorious Euthanasia. In the Gospel of St. Matthew, the earth opens and quakes, and the graves yawn in horror at the crime which was being committed; in the Mahā-Parinibbāna-Sutta the earth quakes in token of her jubilation that the complete Nirvāṇa of the Lord, a beautiful event, has taken place.

When we come to the single utterances and parables of Jesus and Buddha, it is still more difficult to prove a probable connection than it is in the instance of the legends. It is mostly only a question of resemblances,[1] or of such general ideas that they could easily occur and actually do occur, in the sacred books of all religions; when, for instance, Majjhimanikāya 110, where there is talk of the sowing and reaping of good works, is compared with the parable of the sower (St. Matth. XIII, 18 ff.), or when, in the Sutta of the "real treasure,"[2] a similar idea is expressed as in Matth. VI, 19 f.: "Lay not up for yourselves treasures upon earth, where moth and rust doth corrupt," etc.

When we sum up all that has been brought to light by the comparison of the four gospels with the Buddhist texts, it is seen that the differences greatly outweigh the points of agreement. There is a great difference to be seen in the whole character of even those legends which bear comparison. Whilst in Buddhism all the miracles are explained by

[1]) For instance, above, pp. 29 note 1, 74 note 1, 109 note 2; *cf. Neumann*, Lieder der Mönche und Nonnen, p. 359 note. There is greater similarity between St. Matth. XVII, 19, where there is talk of removing the mountain by faith, and Aṅguttaranikāya VI, 24, where it is said that the monk could cleave the Himalaya by meditation (*Edmunds* II, 40). Nevertheless, even this agreement is most probably only an accidental one. Cf. also *Garbe*, Indien und das Christentum, p. 30 ff.

[2]) Khuddakapāṭha VIII, translated by *Winternitz*, Der ältere Buddhismus (Religionsgesch. Lesebuch, 2, Aufl.) 1929, p. 105 f. *Cf.* Edmunds I, 222.

the Karman, the act working through the rebirths, the Christian miracles are only the outcome of God's mercy and omnipotence. Edv. Lehmann [1] says very aptly: "For the taste of Indians the events in the Christian narratives will always seem to be insufficiently justified by reason and for us Christians the Indian narratives, even from the purely aesthetic point of view, will appear to have an almost unbearably efficient sequence of cause and effect."

Whilst we have thus seen that doubts as to an historical connection on the strength of any of the parallels cited from the canonical gospels are more than justifiable, and whilst we can at the very most speak of the possibility of such a connection, we find in the apocryphal gospels which originated in the 2nd and 3rd centuries A. D., a whole series of legends, the loan of which from Buddhist literature may be asserted with as great a degree of probability as is at all possible in questions of this kind. The tales of the Bodhisattva, who is taken to the temple in his boyhood, and before whom the statues of the gods arise, so as to fall down at his feet, and that of the Bodhisattva's first day at school, coincide so exatly with the stories of the childhood of Jesus as related in the pseudo-St. Matthew's gospel, Chapter XXIII and in St. Thomas's gospel, Chapts. VI-VIII and XIV, that the dependence of the Christian legend upon the Buddhist one, could only be doubted by persons who refute any such dependence on principle. Or take such legends as the following: in Pseudo-Matth., Chapt. XIII, it is said of the child Jesus that, while still in his mother's womb, a light shone forth from him, so that the dark cavern into which Mary entered, was illuminated and became bright as day, and that the Saviour's mother was in no wise stained with blood through the

[1]) Der Buddhismus, p. 98.

birth of the child, and felt no pain: in the proto-gospel of St. James, Chapt. VI, it is told of the six-months old Mary, that she walked towards her mother with seven steps; in the same gospel, Chapt. XVIII, it is related that the forces of nature and the activities of mankind came to a sudden standstill at the birth of Jesus; in Pseudo-Matth., Chapt. XX, a palm-tree inclines its branches down to the ground at the command of the infant Jesus, in order to offer its fruits to Mary, who is thirsty and exhausted. It is so very obvious to anyone acquainted with the legend of Buddha, that these wonder-tales must be assumed to be of Indian origin, that even among Christian theologians, there are only few who doubt an historical connection.[1]

It has also been attempted to trace some of the mediæval legends of the Christian saints back to Indian sources. Māra appears in the form of Buddha in two different Buddhist legends, on one occasion it is in order to seduce a pious man, in which he does not succeed; and the other time, Upagupta causes Māra, whom he has converted, to appear in the form of Buddha.[2] Christian legends tell of several monks to whom the devil appeared in the guise of the Saviour. The Christian legend of the

---

[1]) See above, p. 251; *Bergh van Eysinga*, p. 75 ff.; *Garbe*, Contributions, p. 19 ff.; Indien und das Christentum, p. 70 ff.; *Charpentier* in ZDMG 69, 442; E. *Hennecke*, Neutestamentliche Apokryphen, 2. Aufl., Tübingen 1924, p. 95 f. Even *Götz* in "Der Katholik," 1912 (IV, 9), 271, says: "An influence on the part of Indian and presumably also Buddhist traditions on the apocryphal writings of semi-Christian elements of the West is, then, an historical fact." J. *Kennedy* in JRAS 1917, 508 ff., explains the undeniable resemblances between the apocryphal stories of the childhood of Jesus and the Buddhist legends, by the hypothesis of Christian-Gnostic influences on Buddhism. Among those who make it their principle to deny any connection whatsoever, even in this case, we may mention *Clemen* in Zeitschr. f, neutestament. Wiss. 1916, 131 ff. and *Günter*, l.c., 74 ff., 78 f., 91 f.; see, however, *Haas*, Buddha etc., pp. 12 f., 22 f. As early as in 1762 the Augustine hermit Georgius pointed out that a similar story to that told of the five-year old Jesus and Zakchaios in the Gospel of St. Thomas, was told in Tibet about Buddha, see L. *Conrady*, Das Thomasevangelium (Thelog. Studien und Kritiken, Gotha 1903), p. 403 ff.

[2]) See above, pp. 201 and 288.

presumptuous monk Valens, to whom the devil appeared in the shape of Christ, whereupon the monk worshipped the devil and related that Christ had appeared to him, is traced by Garbe [1] to the Buddhist narratives, especially as "the monstrous idea of the apparition of the devil in the shape of the Saviour is not to be found anywhere in Christian literature except in this one isolated instance." Günter [2] has shown, however, that "the monstrous idea" occurs frequently enough in Christian legendary literature. For this reason it is just as much possible for the legends to have originated independently of each other in Christianity and in Buddhism, as for the theme to have migrated to the West from India, where a legend of this nature was translated into Chinese as early as in the year 401 A. D.[3]

Garbe and others before him have also traced the legends of St. Eustace and St. Christopher back to Buddhist Jātakas. Nevertheless, in spite of Garbe's arguments, I cannot bring myself to believe that this is a case of an actual connection.[4]

On the other hand, it is a fully established fact that one of the favourite books of the whole of Christendom in the Middle Ages, the story of Barlaam and Josaphat, was composed by a devout Christian on the basis of the Buddha legend, with which he might have become acquainted from the Lalita-Vistara.[5] This story, which is otherwise

---

1) Indien und das Christentum, p. 111 ff.

2) Loc. cit., p. 234 ff.; cf. *Haas*, Buddha in der abendländischen Legende? p. 32.

3) *Chavannes*, Cinq cents contes et apologues, t. II, p. 86 (No. 206).

4) *Cf.* above, pp. 132 ntoe 2,150 note 2, and *Garbe*, Indien und das Christentum, p. 86 ff.; 101 ff.; *Haas*, l.c., p. 9.; *Günter*, l.c., p. 7 ff.; *Charpentier* in ZDMG 69, 442 f.; *Beth*, Theolog. Studien 1916, 197 f.

5) *Max Müller*, Essays III, p. 538 f. (cf. *Foucaux*, Lalita Vistara trad. II, 43 ff.) quotes a few passages from which it seems evident that the author "heard the story not only, as he says, from the lips of people who had brought it to him from India, but that he even had the text of the Lalita-Vistara before him."

entirely imbued with the spirit of Christianity, has a Buddhist setting: the main features of the Buddha legend, the three excursions, at which the Bodhisattva becomes acquainted with age, disease and death, recur in it, a few of the interpolated parables (e.g. that of the "man in the well") are familiar from Indian literature, and references to India occur in the story itself.[1] In Eastern Iran or in Central Asia, where, as we know through the finds of Sir Aurel Stein, Grünwedel and v. Le Coq in Khotan and Turfan, Zoroastrians, Buddhists, Christians and Manicheans lived together in closest proximity, a Christian monk[2] could easily become acquainted with the Buddha legend, and be stimulated by it to compose a work which was to impart Christian doctrines. This work was presumably written in the 6th or 7th century, first in the Pahlavi language and afterwards translated into Arabic and Syriac. The Georgian and Greek translation might be traced back to the Syriac text. The Greek text gave rise to Arabian, Hebrew, Aethiopian, Armenian, Ecclesiastical-Russian and Rumanian versions, which came into being in

[1] As early as in the year 1612 the Portuguese Diogodo Conto compared the Barlaam-Josaphat legend with that of Buddha (Ind. Ant. XII, p. 288 f.). It was, however, Laboulaye who first asserted the Buddhist origin of the legend, in Journal des Débats of the 26th July 1859. The proof was then furnished by Felix Liebrecht (in Jahrbuch für romanische und englishe Literatur II, 1860, p. 314 ff. and in his book "Zur Volkskunde", Heilbronn 1879, p. 441 ff.). The whole history of the story has been traced throughout universal literature, by E. *Kuhn* ("Barlaam und Joasaph, eine bibliographisch-litterargeschichtliche Studie," ABayA XX, München 1897). Kuhn (p. 39) believes, however, that the author "made very free use of the entire Buddhist tradition, and not of one particular text like the Lalita Vistara." Cf. also the literature cited in V. *Chauvin*, Bibliographie des ouvrages Arabes III, 1898, p. 83 ff., and H. G. *Rawlinson* in JBRAS 24, 1915, p. 96 ff. Even *Günter*, l.c., p. 92 ff., cannot but admit that Josaphat is the Bodhisattva, though he is very anxious to minimize the influence of the Buddhist legend over the Christian one, and prefers to assume nothing more than a "distant indirect influence" (p. 41).

[2] It has been supposed by A. v. *Le Coq* (SBA 1909, p. 1205) that the Buddha legend was first brought to Europe, not by Christians, but by Manicheans. The actual author of the story, however, can only have been a Christian, as the doctrines contained in the book are specially Christian. It was just as possible for Christians to become acquainted with the subject as it was for Manicheans.

later times. The numerous European translations and recensions (Lope de Vega has even dramatised the story) can be traced back to the Latin text translated from the Greek. German recensions have been in existence since 1220 A.D. In course of centuries the characters in this work had grown so familiar to the Christian peoples, that they were regarded as pious Christian men who had really lived and taught, so that the Catholic Church finally made the two heroes of the story, Barlaam and Josaphat, into saints. Josaphat, however, is none other than the Bodhisattva.[1)]

It is not only pious narratives such as that of Kisā-Gotamī[2)] which wandered from India to the West, but also many secular fables, and narrative motifs as are to be found in the Jātaka, the Dhammapada commentary and Buddhaghosa's commentaries.[3)] Even down to our own day, the Indian legend of Buddha has so well preserved its ever youthful freshness and vitality, that again and again it has inspired poets, including Western poets, to compose epic and dramatic renderings of this immortal theme.[4)] Thus *Edwin Arnold's* epic "The Light of Asia" was in the 19th century, still capable of inspiring such enthusiasm that it saw over sixty editions in England and over a hundred in America, and really

1) In Greek the prince is called Jōasaph, the Arabic Jūdāsaf, which is derived from Būdāsaf, *i.e.*, Bodhisattva. In Arabic, Syriac and Pahlavi, " f " and " b " are easily confused in the script. The sage Barlaam is called Balaubar in Arabic, which might be derived from Bhagavān. (Kuhn, loc. cit., pp. 17, 19, 34 f.) Barlaam and Josaphat already appear as saints in the " Catalogus Sanctorum " of Petrus de Natalibus, who died in about 1370. Even in more recent times, the legend of Barlaam and Josaphat has been made the subject of a romance for children and also of a drama in Germany ; s. *Slepčević,* Buddhismus in der deutschen Litteratur, p. 33 ff.

2) See above, p. 58 f.

3) See above, p. 200 f. ; also *Günter*, l. c., 107 ff., admits that a steady stream of Indian motifs, including such as we find in the Jātaka-Book, poured into the European literatures from the 12th century onwards.

4) On the influence of Buddhism on German literature, see Pero *Slepcevic* Buddhismus in der deutschen Litteratur (Diss. der Universität Freiburg in der Schweiz), Wien 1920.

laid the foundation for this poet's fame.[1] Whilst Edwin Arnold kept closely to the Indian legend, the German poet *Joseph Viktor Widmann*, in his "Buddha,"[2] has left little of the ancient Indian legend. On the other hand, much of the spirit and mentality of Buddhism is embodied in the beautiful epic poem "The Saint and the Animals" by the same poet. The Buddha legend was made the theme of a drama in Germany by *Ferdinand Hornstein*, whose "Buddha"[3] was produced at the Hoftheater in Munich in 1900.

Under the influence of the philosophy of Schopenhauer, Richard Wagner felt strongly attracted towards the Buddhist doctrine of salvation and morality of pity. "You know that I have become a Buddhist in spite of myself," he wrote to Mathilde Wesendonk on the 22nd February, 1859; and on the 9th July of the same year, he wrote to the same friend, full of enthusiasm about Buddhism: "Yes, child, this is a philosophy compared with which all other dogmas must appear petty, narrow and inadequate!"[4] Three years prior to that, he had already sketched out a Buddhist musical drama "The Victors," in which he intended to dramatise the legend of Ānanda and the Caṇḍāla girl Prakṛti. A year later he embodied the ideas of this sketch, which was never completed, in "Parsifal." Not only here, but in others of Wagner's works, too, we have sufficiently frequent instances of a perfectly clear expression of the Buddhist view of life.

[1]) *Cf.* E. F. *Oaten*, Sketch of Anglo-Indian Literature, London, 1908, p. 84 ff.; Leon *Kellner*, Die englische Literatur im Zeitalter der Königin Viktoria, Leipzig 1909, p. 404 ff., and Beil. Allg. Zeitung 1889, Nos. 30 ff.; Artur *Pfungst* translated "The Light of Asia" into German (Leipzig 1887).

[2]) Epische Dichtung in 20 Gesängen, Bern 1869. As the poet himself wrote to me (in a letter of the 27th August 1905), this poem of Buddha was "really only modern free-thinking views disguised in that Oriental garb." *Cf.* also *Slepćević*, l.c., p. 55 ff.

[3]) Legende in 3 Akten, Musik von Robert v. Hornstein, München 1899. See *Slepćević*, l.c., p. 69 ff. Angelo de *Gabernatis* and A. *Obolonsky* (Le Prince Siddhartha, drama en 5 actes et 22 tableaux, Tours 1899) have also dramatised on life of Buddha.

[4]) See Richard Wagner uhd Mathilde Wesendonk, 21. Aufl., Berlin 1904, p. 59 f., 77 f., 105, 161 f.

In the "Götterdämmerung" ("The Twilight of the Gods,") Brunhilde says:

"Wisst ihr, wohin ich fahre?
Aus Wunschheim zieh'ich fort,
Wahnheim flieh'ich auf immer;
Des ew'gn Werdens offne Thore
Schliess' ich hinter mir zu...
Von Wiedergeburt erlöst,
Zieht nun die Wissende hin." [1])

These thoughts are Buddhist through and through.

During the last years of his life, Wagner's mind was occupied with the personality of the Buddha, though there is no sufficient evidence to justify the rumour, spread abroad after his death, that he had worked at a musical drama "Buddha." [2])

Like Richard Wagner, the Danish poet Karl Gjellerup found Buddha by way of the philosophy of Schopenhauer. He drew upon K. E. Neumann's translations, but also made himself acquainted with Buddhism through his own independent study. Though his beautiful prose poem "The Pilgrim Kamanita" [3]) is entirely an invention of the poet's own, the figure of Buddha himself has been sketched lovingly according to the sources, and, what is more important, the whole poem

[1]) "Do you know whither I go?
I bid farewell to the land of desires.
I flee for ever from the land of illusions;
I close behind me the open portals
Of never-ending existence...
Released from re-birth,
She who has gained knowledge now departs."

[2]) See above, p. 287, note 1; H. *Lichtenberger*, Richard Wagner, Dresden und Leipzig 1899, pp. 357 f., 499 f.; Max *Koch* in Studien zur vergleichenden Literatur geschichte 3, 1903, 412 ff.; *Slepčević*, l.c., p. 40 ff.

[3]) "Pilgrimen Kamanita," Kopenhagen 1906; Der Pilger Kamanita, ein Legendenroman, 7-10. Tausend, Frankfurt a. M. 1917. Also translated into English.

is instinct with the true spirit of Buddhism. The delicate poetical description of the Buddhist paradise Sukhāvatī is full of charm, and there is no harm in the poet's having woven this picture, which is a part of the Mahāyāna, into his poem, which is mainly based upon the Pāli sources. In the drama "The Wife of the Perfect One,"[1] Gjellerrup has endowed Buddha, who first appears in the play as Prince Siddhārtha, but later on as the Enlightened One, with more worldly traits, and above all, more attachment to his family, than the Buddha of the legend really possessed. It would scarcely be possible to find in Buddhist texts a counterpart to the scene in which Buddha yields the sovereignty to his half-brother Nanda. The Buddha of the texts never troubled about such matters. Neither could we find in any Buddhist text such words as Buddha is made to speak, in the last scene in the drama, when he hands his weapons to Nanda, and passes him the swords, with the words:

> "Draw it in a just cause only! But then
> Wield it well, and win, so that wrong may not triumph!"

The true Buddha had no dealings with the sword. For him there is no "just cause," for the sake of which we are justified in doing violence, for he knew, what we have learned but yesterday, that the "just cause" is always merely another name for our own cause, however unjust that cause may be.

Fritz Mauthner, too, in his prose work "The Last Death of Gautama Buddha,"[2] has made Buddha utter many a very un-Buddhistic speech.

Among the works which serve Buddhist propaganda, "The Gospel of Buddha" by *Paul Carus* may be mentioned.

[1] "Den fuldendtes Husfru," Kopenhagen 1907; 'Das Weib des Vollendeten, ein Legendendrama, Quelle & Meyer, Leipzig. This drama was also staged in Germany.

[2] "Der letzte Tod des Gautama Buddha," München und Leipzig 1913. The poem is based upon the Mahā-Parinibbāna-Sutta in K. E. *Neumann*'s translation.

In this work, edifying passages from the most varied sources, from earlier and later Pāli texts, from the various biographies of Buddha and European works on Buddhism have been combined to form a mosaic which, from a scholarly point of view, is not always faultless, but is eminently suited to affect people's minds in the religious sense. Since its publication in the English language in America in 1894, this work has seen numerous editions, and it has been translated into many languages. In Ceylon and Japan the work is read in Buddhist schools and temples for purposes of edification.[1]

Whilst Paul Carus lays no claim to erudition, the Italian indologist *Luigi Suali* has recently (1924) retold the Buddha legend in beautiful, poetical language, in his book "Il Illuminato,"[2] on the basis of an accurate knowledge of the original sources. Without the slightest thought of propaganda, he has allowed himself to become absorbed in the very spirit of the legend, and with a loving hand, has portrayed the Buddha with all his human, super-human and super-divine qualities, such as he has lived for over two thousand years, and still lives to-day, in the faith of devout Buddhists.

We may also mention *Lafcadio Hearn*,[3] who has brought us into closer contact with Japanese Buddhism, in many of his sketches and tales. Free from any propagandist intentions, he has with love and sympathy, and with consummate art, given us an insight into Buddhist thought and sentiment as they still exist, even to-day, in the hearts of the devout Buddhists of Japan.

[1]) See Das Evangelium des Buddha nach alten Quellen erzählt von Paul *Carus*, illustriert von O. *Kopetzky*, 2. deutsche Auflage von Karl *Seideastücker*, Chicago und London, The Open Court Publishing Company, 1919. The translation was made according to the 18th English edition. Paul *Carus* died on 2nd Febr. 1919.

[2]) I only know the German translation : "Der Erleuchtete, das Leben des Buddha" (aus dem Italienischen übersetzt von Dora *Mitzky*), Frankfurt a. M. 1928.

[3]) "Gleanings in Buddha Fields," "Out of the East," and others, which are well known in German translations also.

There is not much of importance to be found in the propaganda literature which serves the Neo-Buddhist movement. Translations of Pāli texts are the best thing which we owe to it. *Paul Dahlke*'s "Buddhist Stories"[1] may be mentioned, and also the lyric poems of *Hans Much.*[2] But though the latter are Buddhist in sentiment, this European monastic poetry is very feeble when compared to the Thera-Gāthās and Therī-Gāthās, the songs of the ancient Buddhist monks and nuns.

Nevertheless, whatever our views of the new Buddhist movement may be, we cannot but admire the vitality of Buddhism and of the works of Buddhist literature, which have ever and again inspired the minds of thinkers and poets of all nations, and still continue to do so. I hope, too, that I have succeeded in showing in the above chapters, that there is still much in Buddhist literature which well merits being introduced into European literatures and made the common property of universal literature.

1) "Buddhistische Erzählungen," Dresden 1904.

2) "Ich nahm meine Zuflucht...Flugsamen aus einem abendländischen Buddhagarten," Leipzig 1920; "An Buddhas Hand, Leider der Erweckung im Felde," 1917, in "Buddhistische Weisheit" von Georg *Grimm* und Hans *Much*, 1920.

SECTION IV.

JAIṄA LITERATURE.

Jinism and its Literature.

Buddhist texts frequently mention Nigaṇṭha Nātaputta as a rival and opponent of Gotama Buddha. This is none other than the saint known and venerated by the name of Mahāvīra, *i.e.*, "the great hero," the founder or reformer of the sect of the Jainas, which had developed out of the far older sect of the Nigaṇṭhas (*i.e.*, the Fetter-less), under the leadership of Vardhāmāna Mahāvīra, probably not long before the appearance of Gotama.[1] The religion of the Jainas, Jinism,[2] has so much in common with Buddhism that, for a long time, it was

[1]) On the strength of the unanimous tradition of both Buddhists and Jainas, we may take it as certain that Mahāvīra was a senior contemporary of Buddha, and that both were contemporaries of Kings Bimbisāra and Ajātaśatru of Magadha. The year of Mahāvīra's death is, however, at least as uncertain as that of Buddha's. Appendix VI. H. *Jacobi* (Ind. Ant. 9, 1880, 158 ff.; SBE 45, p. xx ff.) has made it seem very probable that Mahāvīra was not the founder but only the reformer of an earlier sect of the Nigaṇṭhas founded by Pārśva. Nevertheless, when the tradition says that Pārśva lived exactly 250 years before Mahāvīra, we are not by any means justified in taking this as a certain historical fact.

[2]) The epithets "Enlightened One" (Buddha) and "Victor" (Jina) were applied to Gotama as well as to Mahāvīra (and other founders of religions). However, whilst "Buddha" came to be the name of Gotama, "Jina" came to be the usual name of Mahāvīra, and his adherents called themselves "Jainas", *i.e.*, disciples of the Jina." It has grown customary to use the expressions "Jainism" and "Jainistic." However, as we never say "Bauddhism" and "Bauddhistic," we ought by rights to say "Jinism" and "Jinistic" just as we say "Buddhism" and "Buddhistic." Scholars like A. *Weber* and Th. *Benfey* still considered the Jainas as a Buddhist sect. It has been proved by *Jacobi* (SBE 22, Introd., and in the introduction to his edition of the Kalpa-Sūtra) that this view is erroneous.

considered merely as a Buddhist sect. Nevertheless, it presents a marked divergence from the Buddhist religion in such essential points, that it must be regarded as an independent creed. Jinism [1] lays far more stress than Buddhism on asceticism and all manner of cult exercises, and in contrast to the Buddha, Mahāvīra taught a very elaborate belief in the soul. All that the two religions have in common, is the ancient Indian "ascetic morality" which we have already characterised more than once; the points of contact, too, between Buddhist and Jaina literature, are precisely those which they both share with the whole of Indian ascetic poetry. It is the Jainas, however, who far more than any other Indian religion, emphasize the commandment of Ahiṃsā, non-violence.

An essential difference between the two religions is, however, that Jinism has always remained a national Indian religion, whilst Buddhism developed into a world religion. It is true that, according to the belief of the Jainas, their religion is a "world religion" in the sense that it is a religion not only for human beings of all races and classes, but even for animals, gods and denizens of hell. Notwithstanding, the Jainas have retained the Indian system of castes and classes in its entirety,[2] and Jinism has a much stronger tendency than Buddhism to adapt itself to Brahmanism and

[1]) *Cf.* G *Bühler*, Ueber die indische Sekte der Jainas (Almanach der k. Akademie der Wissenschaften, Wien 1887); translated into English by J. *Burgess*, On the Indian Sect of the Jainas, with an Outline of Jaina Mythology, London 1903; H. *Jacobi* in ERE VII. 1914, 465 ff.; Mrs. Sinclair *Stevenson*, The Heart of Jainism, Oxford and London 1915; Puran Chand *Nahar* and Krishnachandra *Ghosh*, An Epitome of Jainism, Calcutta 1917; Helmuth v. *Glasenapp*, Der Jainismus, Berlin 1925. A. *Guérinot*, La religion Djaina, histoire, doctrine, culte, coutumes, institutions, Paris 1926. A presentation of the Jaina religion from the view-point of an enthusiastic European is given by Herbert *Warren*, Jainism in Western Garb as a Solution to Life's Great Problems, Arrah 1912, second ed. 1916. On the history of the Jainas, see also A. *Guérinot*, Répertoire d'Epigraphie Jaina précédé d'une esquisse de l'histoire du Jainisme d'après les inscriptions, Paris (Publ. de l'Ecole française d'Extrême-Orient) 1908, and J. *Charpentier* in Cambridge History I, 150 ff.

[2]) H. v. *Glasenapp*, Der Jainismus, pp. 314 ff., 316 ff.

Hinduism, and also it is confined within the frontiers of India. The Jainas themselves explain the close relations of their religion with Brahmanism by asserting that their religion is the oldest of all religions, and the religion of the Brahmins is merely a degenerate form of it. Although, as has already been mentioned, Jinism is older than Buddhism, the canonical literature of the Jainas has not come down to us in its earliest form. Unfortunately only parts of it have been preserved, and in its present form it only dates back to a comparatively recent period. It is solely for this reason that we deal with it here *after* Buddhist literature.

With rare exceptions, the sacred books of the Jainas are written in a dry-as-dust, matter of fact, didactic tone, and as far as we know them hitherto, are seldom instinct with that general human interest which so many Buddhist texts possess. Hence, important as they are for the specialist, they cannot claim the interest of the general reader to anything approaching so great an extent. If, for these reasons, the following treatment of Jinist literature [1] occupies a comparatively small space, we shall be giving only a faint idea of the exceedingly wide range of literary activity of the Jaina monks, to which the catalogues of Jaina manuscripts [2] and the very numerous

[1]) The first to open up the rich treasures of the Jaina libraries was G. *Bühler*, who in the years 1873-1878 acquired a large collection of Jaina manuscripts for the royal library at Berlin. This collection formed the basis of the first comprehensive and epoch-making accounts of the literature of the Jainas, by Albrecht *Weber*, Ind. Stud. 16, 1883, pp. 211-479; 17, 1885, pp. 1-90 (translated into English by H. W. *Smyth* in Ind. Ant., vols. 17-21, 1888-1892) and HSS. Verz. II, 1888-1891. *Cf.* E. *Windisch*, Geschichte der Sanskrit-Philologie (Grundriss I, 1 B), p. 346 ff.; A. *Guérinot*, Essai de bibliographie Jaina, Paris 1906 (AMG, bibl. d'études, t. 22); Addenda to it JA 1909, s. 10, t. XIV, 47-148; 1912, s. 10, t. XIX, 373 ff., and B. *Geiger* in GGA 1908, 124 ff.; *Guérinot*, La religion Djaina, pp. 69-90; H. v. *Glasenapp*, Der Jainismus, pp. 81-134 and Die Literaturen Indiens (in "Handbuch der Literaturwissenschaft"), p. 118 ff. For important data on Jain authors, see J. *Klatt* in Ind. Ant. 11, 1882, pp. 245-256 and Specimen of a Literary-Bibliographical Jaina-Onomasticon, Leipzig 1892. The little book by U. D. *Barodia*, History and Literature of Jainism, Bombay 1909, has no scientific value.

[2]) The following accounts of Jaina MSS. are of great importance :— those by R. G.

editions of texts that have appeared during the last decades in various collections, bear testimony.[1]

The literature of the Jainas is also very important from the point of view of the history of the Indian languages: for the Jainas always took care that their writings were accessible to considerable masses of the people. Hence the canonical writings and the earliest commentaries are written in Prākrit dialects (Māgadhī and Māhārāṣṭrī).[2] It was not until a later period that the Jainas—the Śvetāmbaras from the 8th century, and the Digambaras somewhat earlier—used Sanskrit for commentaries and learned works as well as for poetry. Some of these authors write a simple, lucid Sanskrit, others compete with the classical Sanskrit poets in their use of an elaborate Sanskrit in the Kāvya style, whilst yet others affect a Sanskrit shot with Prākritisms, approaching the vernacular.[3]

Bhandarkar, Report 1883-4; P. *Peterson*, 3 Reports, Report IV and Rep. V; by *Jacobi*. *Klatt* and *Leumann*. ZDMG 33, 693 ff., 478 ff.; 45, 454 ff.; 47, 308 ff.; WZKM 11, 1897, 297 ff.; F. L. *Pullé*, Catalogo dei manoscritti giainici della Bibliotheca n.c.di Firence 1894 and OC X, 1894, II, p. 15 ff.; A. B. *Keith*, Catalogue of Prākrit Manuscripts in the Bodleian Library, Oxford 1911, col. 1-45; *Rai Bahadur Hiralal*, Catalogue of Sanskrit and Prakrit MSS. published under the Orders of the Government of the Central Provinces and Berar, Nagpur 1926; H. D. *Velankar*, A Descriptive Catalogue of Saṁskṛta and Prākṛta Manuscripts in the Library of the Bombay Branch of the Royal Asiatic Society, Vols. III-IV, Jain and Varnacular Literatures, Bombay 1930.

[1]) A collection of the canonical writings, "Āgama-Saṃgraha," was printed between 1875 and 1885 in Calcutta, Bombay, Benares and Ahmedabad in 45 volumes. Numerous texts have appeared in the Śrī-Jaina-Jaso-Vijaya-Granthamālā published by the great Jaināċarya Vijaya Dharma Sūri; learned societies, such as the Jaina Dharma Prasāraka Sabhā in Bhavnagar, the Jaina Vidyā Prasāraka Varga in Palitana, the Jaina Jñāna Prasāraka Varga in Bombay, the Jaina Vidyā Śālā in Ahmedabad, the Āgamodaya Samiti in Mehsana, and others, and wealthy patrons such as Sheṭh Devchand Lalbhai Jhaveri in Bombay, Sheṭh Bhagabāi Mansukkhāi in Ahmedabad, and others, have assisted towards the publication of Jain texts. See E. *Hultzsch* in Ind. Ant., Vol. 39, 1910. p. 228; *Jacobi* in AR 13, 1910, 615 ff., and 18, 1915, 275 f. We are indebted to the Digambara Jainas also, for such valuable publications as the "Sacred Books of the Jainas" and "The Library of Jaina Literature," both of which are appearing in Arrah.

[2]) See above I, p. 48, and W. *Denecke*, in Festgabe Jacobi, p. 160 ff.

[3]) See M. *Bloomfield*, Some Aspects of Jaina Sanskrit, in Festschrift Wackernagel, 1923, p. 220 ff.

At a later time, from the 10th to the 12th century, there is a return of poetry to the Apabhraṃśa dialects adapted to the vernacular.[1] Lastly, in quite recent times, the Jainas also use various modern Indian languages, and they have enriched more especially Gujarati and Hindi literatures, as well as Tamil and Kanarese literatures in the south.

The Canons (Siddhānta) of the Jainas.[2]

The most important schism within the Jaina religion, namely, into the two great sects of the Śvetāmbaras, *i.e.*, " those clad in white ", and the Digambaras, *i.e.*, " those clad in air " or " naked ", occurred as early as in the first century A.D. The collective term given by the Jainas to their sacred books, is Siddhānta or Āgama. Both sects are unanimous in calling the twelve Aṅgas, *i.e.*, " limbs " (of the body of the religion) the first and most important part of their Canon. Hitherto, however, we have a detailed knowledge only of the Siddhānta of the Śvetāmbaras. It consists of the following texts :—

I. The twelve Aṅgas: 1. Āyāraṃga-Sutta[3] (Ācārāṅga-Sūtra) ; 2. Sūyagaḍaṃga (Sūtrakṛtāṅga) ; 3. Ṭhāṇaṃga

---

[1]) See above I, p. 49, and *Jacobi*, Zur Frage nach dem Ursprung des Apabhraṃśa, in Festschrift Wackernagel, p. 124 ff.

[2]) On the Canon and its history see *Jacobi* in the introductions to his edition of the Kalpa-Sûtra, p. 14 ff. and to SBE, Vols. 22 and 45, and ZDMG 28, 1 ff.; *Hoernle* in the introduction to his translation of the Uvāsagadasāo, p. vii ff. and Proceedings ASB 1898, p. 39 ff. (French Le Muséon, N.S., VII, 1906, 109 ff.); G. *Bühler*, WZKM 1, 1887, 165 ff.; 2, 1888, 141 ff.; 3, 1889, 233 ff.; 4, 1890, 313 ff; A. *Barth*, RHR 3, 1881, 89 ff.; 11, 1885, 185; 19, 1889, 280 ff.; 20, 332; 29, 1894, 25 ff.; 45, 1902, 178; Oeuvres I, 306 ff., 344 ff., 397; II, 59 ff., 192 ff., 378 ff.; P. C. *Nahar* and K. C. *Ghosh*, An Epitome of Jainism, Calcutta 1917, Appendix C; J. *Charpentier* in the introduction to his edition of the Uttarâdhyayana-Sûtra (Upsala 1921) and W. *Schubring*, Worte Mahâvīras, Göttingen 1927, p. VIII f. and 1 ff. Selected passages from canonical texts translated into German by W. *Schubring*, Die Jainas (in Religionsgeschichtliches Lesebuch von A. Bertholet, 2. Aufl., Nr. 7) Tübingen 1927.

[3]) The titles are given in their Prâkrit form, with the traditional Sanskrit translation beside them in brackets.

(Sthānāṅga) ; 4. Samavāyaṃga ; 5. Bhagavatī Viyāhapannatti (Vyākhyā-Prajñapti) ; 6. Nāyādhammakahāo (Jñātādharma-kathāḥ) ; 7. Uvāsagadasāo (Upāsakadaśāḥ) ; 8. Aṃtagaḍadasāo (Antakṛddaśāḥ) ; 9. Aṇuttarovavāiyadasāo (Anuttaraupapātikadaśāḥ) ; 10. Paṇhāvāgaraṇāiṃ (Praśna-Vyākaraṇāni); 11. Vivāgasuyaṃ (Vipāka-Srutam) ; 12. Diṭṭhivāya (Dṛṣṭivāda).

II. The twelve Uvaṃgas (Upāṅgas) or "secondary limbs" : 1. Uvavāiya (Aupapātika) ; 2. Rāyapaseṇaijja or Rāyapasenaiya (Rājapraśnīya) ; 3. Jīvābhigama ; 4. Pannavaṇā (Prajñāpanā) ; 5. Sūrapannatti or Sūriyapannatti ; 6. Jaṃbuddīvapannatti (Jambūdvīpa-Prajñapti) ; 7. Caṃdapannatti (Candraprajñapti) ; 8. Nirayāvalī ; 9. Kappāvadaṃsiāo (Kalpāvataṃsikāḥ) ; 10. Pupphiāo (Puṣpikāḥ) ; 11. Pupphacūliāo (Puṣpacūlikāḥ) ; 12. Vaṇhidasāo (Vṛṣṇidaśāḥ).

III. The ten Païṇṇas (Prakīrṇas, *i. e.*, "scattered pieces"): 1. Caüsaraṇa (Catuḥśaraṇa) by Vīrabhadra ; 2. Āurapaccakkhāṇa (Āturapratyākhyāna) ; 3. Bhattaparinnā (Bhakta-Parijñā) ; 4. Saṃthāra (Saṃstāra) ; 5. Taṃdulaveyāliya (Tandulavaitālika) ; 6. Caṃdāvijjhaya ; 7. Deviṃdatthaa (Devendrastava) ; 8. Gaṇivijjā (Gaṇi-Vidyā) ; 9. Mahāpaccakkhāṇa (Mahā-Pratyākhāyāna) ; 10. Vīratthaa (Vīrastava).

IV. The six Cheya-Suttas (Cheda-Sūtras); 1. Nisīha (Niśītha) ; 2. Mahānisīha (Mahā-Niśītha) ; 3. Vavahāra (Vyavahāra) ; 4. Āyāradasāo (Ācāradaśāḥ) or Dasāsuyakkhandha (Daśāśrutaskandha), also called briefly Dasāo (Daśāḥ) ; 5. Kappa (Bṛhat-Kalpa) ; and 6. Paṃcakappa (Pañca-Kalpa). Instead of the last-named the Jīyakappa (Jita-Kalpa) by Jinabhadra is also mentioned.

V. Individual texts : 1. Nandī or Nandi-Sutta (Nāndī-Sūtra) ; 2. Aṇuogadāra (Anuyogadvāra).

VI. The four Mūla-Suttas (Mūla-Sūtras) : 1. Uttarajjhāyā (Uttarādhyāyāḥ) or Uttarajjhayaṇa (Uttarādhyayana) ; 2. Āvassaya (Āvaśyaka) ; 3. Dasaveyāliya (Daśavaikālika); 4. Piṃḍanijjutti (Piṇḍa-Niryukti). The third and fourth

Mūla-Suttas are also sometimes given as Ohanijjutti (Ogha-Niryukti) and Pakkhi (Pākṣika-Sūtra), and sometimes the Piṃḍanijjutti and Ohanijjuti appear in the list of the Cheya-Suttas. [1]

Indeed, with the exception of the Aṅgas, the lists and titles of the canonical texts are not always mentioned in the same way. The list of the Païṇṇas, in particular, is very indefinite. Sometimes Nandī, Aṇuogadārā and Paṃcakappa are placed at the head of the Païṇṇas. The traditional number of books in the Siddhānta is 45, but the number of texts mentioned in various places varies between 45 and 50. In the Canon itself, *viz.*, in the Thāṇaṃga, in the Nandī and in the Pakkhi-Sutta, we find lists of canonical works, in which the only distinction made is either between Aṅgas and Aṅgabāhiriyas ("texts standing outside the Aṅgas") or between Aṅgapaviṭṭha ("belonging to the Aṅgas") and Aṇaṅgapaviṭṭha ("not belonging to the Aṅgas"). The last-mentioned include the names of works which occur in the Siddhānta either as independent texts or as sections of well-known texts, but also works which no longer exist in the Siddhānta.[2]

The language of this Canon is a Prākrit which is known as Ārṣa (*i.e.*, "the language of the Ṛṣis") or Ardha-Māgadhī (*i. e.*, "half-Māgadhī"). Mahāvīra himself is said to have preached in this language. There is, however, a difference between the language of prose and that of verses. As was the case with the Pāli verses in the

[1]) See *Weber*, Ind. Stud. 17, 85.

[2]) See *Weber*, Ind. Stud. 16, 222 ff., 369 f., 372 f.; 17, 10 ff. Some texts which *Weber* still thought were lost, have come to light since. In a few cases, too, gaps have been filled by other texts. *Cf. Schubring*, Worte Mahâvîras, p. 13. A list which is strikingly different from the traditional one, is that by Rajendralala *Mitra*, Notices of Sanskrit Manuscripts III, Calcutta 1874, p. 67. *Nahar* and *Ghosh*, Epitome of Jainism, Appendix C, p. xxxvii, describe the Nandi and the Anuogadāra as "Cūlikā Sūtras," and enumerate in addition to the 45 "Āgamas" another 86 works, otherwise unknown, as "Jain Nigamas or Upaniṣads,"

Buddhist Canon, here too, the verses present more archaic forms. The most archaic language is to be found in the Āyāraṃga-Sutta, and next to this, in the Sūyagaḍaṃga-Sutta and the Uttarajjhayaṇa. Ardha-Māgadhī is quite different from Jaina-Mahārāṣṭrī, the dialect of the non-canonical Jaina texts.[1]

Regarding the antiquity and the authority of the Canon, the Śvetāmbara Jainas themselves have the following tradition :

The original doctrine was contained in the 14 Puvvas (Sansk. Pūrvas, *i. e.*, "old texts"), which Mahāvīra himself had taught to his disciples, the Gaṇadharas or "heads of schools." The knowledge of the "old texts" was, however, soon lost. Only one of Mahāvīra's disciples handed them down, and they were only preserved during six generations more. Now in the second century after Mahāvīra's death, there was a terrible famine in the land of Magadha, which lasted for twelve years. At that time the Maurya Candragupta was king of Magadha, and the Thera Bhadrabāhu was the head of the Jaina community. Owing to the famine Bhadrabāhu emigrated with a host of his adherents to Karṇāṭa in South India, and Sthūlabhadra—the last one who had a knowledge of all the 14 Puvvas—became head of the community which remained behind in Magadha. During the absence of Bhadrabāhu it was evident that the knowledge of the sacred texts was threatening to lapse into oblivion. A Council was therefore convened at Pāṭaliputra,[2] at

[1] R. *Pischel*, Grammatik der Prākrit-Sprachen (Grundriss I, 8) paragraphs 16-21. *Cf. Jacobi.* Kalpasūtra, p. 17 ff.; *Weber*, Ind. Stud. 16, 232 ff. According to the belief of pious Jainas, Mahāvīra was understood by all creatures, whatever their language was.

[2] If *Sten Konow* (Acta Or. 1, 1922, p. 20 ff.) is right in his explanation of the Hāthīgumphā inscription of Khāravela, then this inscription would furnish a confirmation of the Jaina tradition regarding the Council of Pāṭaliputra and the Diṭṭhivāya, and King Khāravela (170 B.C.?) would in that case have compiled a recension of the Aṅgas in 64 sections. Konow's explanation is ingenious, but very much open to doubt.

which the 11 Aṅgas were compiled, and the remnants of the 14 Puvvas were united to form a twelfth Aṅga, the Diṭṭhivāya. When the adherents of Bhadrabāhu returned to Magadha, there was a great gulf fixed between those who had emigrated and those who had stayed at home. The latter had grown accustomed to wearing white garments, whereas the former, in pursuance of the strict requirement of Mahāvīra, still persisted in going naked. And this is how the great schism between the Digambaras and the Śvetāmbaras came about.[1] Consequently the Digambaras also refused to acknowledge the Canon, as they declared that, in their eyes, the Puvvas and the Aṅgas were lost. In the course of time the Canon of the Śvetāmbaras was reduced to a state of disorder, and was even in danger of being lost altogether. Hence, in the year 980 (or 993) after the death of Mahāvīra (*i.e.*, about the middle of the 5th or the beginning of the 6th century A.D.) a Council was held at Vallabhi in Gujarat, presided over by Devarddhi Kṣamāśramaṇa, the head of a school, for the purpose of collecting the sacred texts and writing them down. The twelfth Aṅga, containing the remnants of the Puvuas, had already gone astray at that time. This is why we find only eleven Aṅgas in the recension which has come down to us, and which is supposed to be identical with that of Devarddhi.

Thus we see that, according to the tradition of the Śvetāmbara Jainas themselves, the authority of their sacred texts does not go beyond the 5th century A.D. It is true that they assume that the texts which were written down at the Council of Vallabhi, are based on those old texts that had been compiled at the Council of Pāṭaliputra, and which can be traced back to Māhavīra and his disciples. The Gaṇadharas or heads of schools, who were still pupils of Mahāvīra, especially

¹ The Digambaras relate a legend about the origin of the schism, which differs from the legend told by the Śvetāmbaras. *Cf.* H. v. *Glasenapp*, Der Jainismus, p. 347 ff.

Ajja Suhamma (Ārya Sudharman), are said to have compiled the Master's words in the Aṅgas and Upāṅgas. Certain individual texts are, however, ascribed to later authors even by tradition, for instance the fourth Upāṅga is ascribed to Ajja Sāma (Ārya Syāma), who is said to have lived 376 or 386 years after Mahāvīra's death,[1] the fourth Cheda-Sūtra, the Piṃḍanijjutti and the Ohanijjutti to Bhadrabāhu (2nd century after Mahāvīra's death), the third Mūla-Sūtra to Sejjaṃbhava (Śayyambhava), who counts as the fourth head of the school after Mahāvīra,[2] and the Nandī, which is actually attributed to so late a writer as Devarddhi, the president of the Council of Vallabhi, in the 10th century after the death of Mahāvīra.[3] Even the Digambaras admit that the first disciples of Mahāvīra knew 14 Puvvas and 11 Aṅgas. They relate, however, that not only was the knowledge of the 14 Puvvas lost at an early period, but that, as early as 436 years after Mahāvīra's Nirvāṇa, the last who knew all the 11 Aṅgas died, and the teachers who succeeded him knew less and less Aṅgas as time went on, until the knowledge of these works was completely lost 683 years after Mahāvira's Nirvāṇa.

Even though the tradition of the Jainas themselves would not appear to be in favour of investing their sacred texts with a very great antiquity, there are nevertheless good reasons for attributing their first origin, at least in part, to an earlier age, and for assuming that Devarddhi's labours consisted merely of compiling a Canon of sacred writings partly with

---

[1]) He is reckoned as the 23rd head of a school after Mahâvîra, and is said to be identical with the teacher Kâlaka famous in legend, who lived at the time of Gardabhila (74-61 B.C.). *Cf. Weber*, Ind. Stud. 16, 392 f. and J. *Charpentier*, Uttarādhyayanasūtra, Introd., p. 27, and Cambridge History, I, 167 f. In the Commentary on the Kalpa-Sūtra, however, a distinction is made between 3 Kâlakâcāryas; s. *Jacobi* in ZDMG 34, 1880, 250 ff.

[2]) The year 98 after the death of Mahāvīra is mentioned as the date when the Dasaveyâliya was written. *Cf. Weber*, Ind. Stud. 17, 77.

[3]) *Cf.* also *Glasenapp*, Der Jainismus, p. 99 f.

the help of old manuscripts, and partly on the basis of oral tradition. As a matter of fact, there are inscriptions of the 1st and 2nd centuries A.D. which prove that, even at that early period, the Jainas were split into Śvetāmbaras and Digambaras, and that there were schools (gaṇa) where the successive teachers were enumerated just as in our texts. As the same inscriptions also mention monks with the title of Vācaka, *i.e.*, "reader," there must have been sacred texts at any rate in those days. Inscriptions and bas-reliefs prove that the legend of Mahāvīra as known in the first century A.D. was very similar to that found in our texts. The fact that the Śvetāmbaras did not alter in their Siddhānta those rules which require that Jaina monks shall go naked, shows that they did not venture to make any arbitrary alterations in the texts, but handed them down as faithfully as they could.[1] Lastly, it is also an eloquent argument in favour of the trustworthiness of the Jaina tradition, that it should coincide exactly with the Buddhist tradition in many remarkable details.[2]

So much is certain: the works of the Siddhānta cannot have originated at one period. The Canon which Devarddhi compiled, and which has come down to us, is the final result of a literary activity that must have begun as soon as the organisation of the Order and the monastic life were firmly established. This was in all probability the case not long after the death of Mahāvīra. The earliest portions of the Canon may therefore quite possibly belong to the period of the first disciples of Mahāvīra himself, or at the latest to the 2nd century after Mahāvīra's death—the period of the Maurya Candragupta, in which tradition places the Council of

---

1) *Jacobi*, ZDMG 40, 97; SBE 22, xxxvii ff.; *Charpentier*, Uttarādhyayanasūtra, Introd., 25 ff.

2) *Jacobi*, SBE 45, XV ff.; *Oldenberg*, Buddha, 5. Aufl., p. 95 f. *Bhandarkar* (Report 1883-4, 124 ff.), relying on the tradition of the Digambaras, believes that the Jainas did not receive any written sacred books until 683 years after the death of Mahāvīra (that

Pāṭaliputra—whilst the latest portions should probably be dated nearer the time of Devarddhi.[1] Scholars have only just begun to distinguish between the earlier and the later strata of the Canon.[2]

As is usual in India in the compilation of collections of texts, here also, the principle followed in the compilation and arrangement of the Canon is often, not the contents, but something purely external. It is numbers which play a particularly prominent part. Thus, to correspond to the 12 Aṅgas there had to be 12 Upāṅgas,[3] or texts were grouped according to the number of sections they contained. Groups of ten (Dasāo, "decades") are special favourites, and the compilers of the Canon tried all possible methods of achieving the number 10.

We now proceed to examine the individual works in the Canon, and shall deal more fully with those which are of greater importance from a *literary* point of view.

The first A ṅ g a is the Ā y ā r a ṃ g a-S u t t a.[4] In two lengthy sections (śruta-skandha) it treats of the way of life (āyāra, Sansk. ācāra) of a monk. The first section, which makes a very archaic impression, is most decidedly earlier than

would be 216 A.D., but according to Bhandarkar 139 A.D.), when the last of the teachers who knew any portion of the sacred writings from memory, was dead. On the other hand, *Jacobi* (SBE 22, xxxvii ff.) thinks that we might place the writing of the works of the Jaina Canon towards the end of the 4th or beginning of the 3rd century B.C.

[1]) As the commentaries mention variants and books which have got lost, not even the redaction of Devarddhigaṇi has come down to us unchanged, and some additions were surely made later. *Cf. Weber*, Ind. Stud. 16, 229 ff.

[2]) In this connection the investigations of W. *Schubring* (Ācārāṅga-Sūtra Erster Śrutaskandha 1910, and Worte Mahāvīras, 1926, p. 2 ff.) are valuable.

[3]) *Schubring*, Worte Mahāvīras, p. 8, assumes that there were originally only 5 Upāṅgas.

[4]) Edited by H. *Jacobi*, London PTS 1882 and translated by the same scholar in SBE, Vol. 22. The first Śrutaskandha, the Bambhacerāiṃ (brahmacaryāṇi, "Rules for the holy life") has been newly edited by W. *Schubring* in AKM XII, 4, Leipzig 1910, and translated into German by him in "Worte Mahāvīras," pp. 66-121. Edition with commentary in the AUS series.

the second, and yet even the first is a mosaic pieced together from heterogeneous elements. Here again we meet with the mixture of prose and verse which we so frequently encountered in Buddhist literature. Now we have long series of stanzas, now long prose passages without verse, then again a rapid change between prose and verse, and often it is only fragments of verses, some long, some short, which are inserted into the prose passages.[1]

These sermons consist mainly of exhortations and warnings, *e.g.*, the warning against any kind of killing or injury of living creatures, for instance :

"I speak thus. All Saints (Arhats) and Lords (Bhagavats) in the past, in the present and in the future, they all say thus, speak thus, announce thus and declare thus : One may not kill, nor ill-use, nor insult, nor torment, nor persecute any kind of living being, any kind of creature, any kind of thing having a soul, any kind of beings. That is the pure, eternal, enduring commandment of religion, which has been proclaimed by the sages who comprehend the world."

"You yourself are the (being) which you intend to kill ; you yourself are the (being) which you intend to ill-use ; you yourself are the (being) which you intend to insult ; you yourself are the (being) which you intend to torment ; you yourself are the (being) which you intend to persecute.[2] Therefore the righteous one, who has awakened to this knowledge, and lives according to it, will neither kill nor cause to kill." [3]

The essential difference between the monastic rules of the Jainas and the Buddhists is, that those of the Jainas lay much

---

[1]) *Schubring* in his edition and his translation of the Bambhacerāiṃ, has made an attempt to separate out the mosaic-like portions of the work, metrical and prose passages, and to throw light on the very entangled assortment of texts. Though he has brought much ingeniousness to bear on his task, he has only succeeded in part. *Cf. Jacobi* in AR 18, 1915, 283 ff.

[2]) The intended meaning is : The consequences of the action return to yourself.

[3]) I, 4, 11 ; 5, 5, 4. This kind of repetition and accumulation of synonymous or almost synonymous expressions is just as popular in the Jinistic sermons as in the Buddhist ones.

more stress on severe asceticism, and even go as far as to recommend religious suicide. If a monk suffers from cold, he should rather freeze to death than break his vow. However ill and weak he may be, he should rather die than break his vow of fasting. He is to go naked, so as to expose himself to the pricking of the blades of grass, to the inclemency of the weather and the bites of the flies and mosquitoes. A long verse passage (I, 7, 8) includes, it is true, the famous ascetic rule, which is known to the Brahmins and Buddhists also, *viz.*, "He should not desire life, he should not long for death": this is, however, immediately followed by the characteristic rules on the various methods by which the accomplished sage is to starve himself to death by slow degrees. This passage is followed by a long narrative poem—really a mosaic of verses, in which it is often doubtful whether they *are* verses—the Ohāṇasuyaṃ (I, 8),[1] describing in a very graphic manner the ascetic life of the "Great Hero:"

He wandered naked and homeless. People struck him and mocked at him—unconcerned, he continued in his meditations. In Lāḍha the inhabitants persecuted him and set the dogs on him. They beat him with sticks and with their fists, and threw fruits, clods of earth and potsherds at him. They disturbed him in his meditations by all sorts of torments. But "like a hero in the forefront of the battle," Mahāvīra withstood it all. Whether he was wounded or not, he never sought medical aid. He took no kind of medicaments, he never washed, did not bathe and never cleaned his teeth. In winter he meditated in the shade, in the heat of summer he seated himself in the scorching sun. Often he drank no water for months. Sometimes he took only every sixth, eighth, tenth or twelfth meal, and pursued his meditations without craving.

Section II of the Āyāraṃga is a much later work, as can be seen by the mere fact of the sub-divisions being described as Cūlās, *i.e.*, "appendices." The subject-matter of the first

---

1) Translated in its entirety by *Jacobi* in SBE, Vol. 22, p. 79 ff., and *Schubring*, Worte Mahāvīras, p. 115 ff.

two Cūḷās is dry rules for begging and wandering, and the daily life of the monks and nuns. In the rules as regards begging, and in the dietary regulations, the main point is that only such food is to be taken as does not in any way entail the destruction of life. In the rules for speaking (II, 4) the essential point is that the monk shall utter no falsehood, nor anything which may hurt. The third Cūḷā contains the materials for a biography of Mahāvīra, which have been utilised in Bhadrabāhu's Kalpa-Sūtra, and which recur there in part. The book ends with twelve verses, the contents of which are somewhat reminiscent of the Buddhist Theragāthās.

The second Aṅga, the S ū y a g a ḍ a ṃ g a,[1] treats of the pious life of the monks, and is mainly devoted to the confutation of heretical opinions. This Aṅga, too, consists of two books, the second of which is probably only an appendix, added later, to the old Aṅga which we have in the first book. This is composed in verses, Ślokas and also more artificial metres;[2] the similes, too, show that the author was desirous of proving himself to be a poet. Some of these similes are turned quite prettily, as for instance, when it says: As birds of prey swoop down upon young, unfledged birds and carry them off, thus unscrupulous people seek to entice young monks (I, 14, 2 ff.) The explicit purpose of the book is to keep young

[1]) Published with various commentaries in the Āgama-Saṃgraha, Vol. 2, Bombay 1880; with Śīlāṅkācārya's commentary, Bombay 1917 for AUS. Translated into English by *Jacobi* in SBE, Vol. 45, and selected sections into German by *Schubring*, Worte Mahāvīras. Sūtrakṛtāṅga is a false Sanskritisation; for, as *Schubring* (Worte Mahāvīras, p. 12) has rightly observed, *sūtra*, "text," is *sutta* in Prākrit, and not *sūya*. He therefore explains sūyagaḍaṅga as the Aṅga of the Sūcākṛt or "philosophers," and is thinking of the meaning *dṛṣṭi* which is given by lexicographers both for *sūcā* and *sūci*. It is true that neither *sūcikṛt* nor *dṛṣṭikṛt* occurs anywhere else in the sense of "philosopher." The Nijjutti says that there are three names of the Aṅga: sūtagaḍaṃ, suttakaḍam and sūyagaḍam. The last is explained thus by Śīlāṅka: *sūcākṛtam iti svaparasamayārthasūcanaṃ sūcā sāsmin kṛteti*. This is right. The title means: "The Aṅga in which the distinction (between the true and the false doctrines) is made."

[2]) Vaitālīya stanzas and Yamakas occur, cf. *Jacobi*, ZDMG 38, 593; 40 101,

monks away from the heretical doctrines of other teachers, to warn them of all dangers and temptations, to confirm them in their faith and thus lead them to the highest goal. The work begins with a condemnation of the doctrines of the Buddhists and other heretics, and the principal teachings of Mahāvīra are set forth in opposition to these. It is true, nevertheless, that what is here said about Karman and Saṃsāra does not differ greatly from the "heretical" doctrines. For instance, such sentences as the following (I, 2, 1, 13) might be found equally well in a Buddhist text:

"It is not myself alone who suffers, all creatures in the world suffer; this a wise man should consider, and he should patiently bear (such calamities) as befall him, without giving way to his passions." [1]

There is a graphic description of the cares and dangers with which the monastic life is fraught, but by which the novice should not allow himself to be repelled. His friends and relatives seek to hold him back, and paint the joys of family life to him in attractive colours. Kings and ministers, Brahmins and warriors endeavour to entice him to return to the world, but he is to withstand all these temptations. Critics and heretics attack him, and he should stand up to them courageously. Most especially, however, the young monk should beware of the blandishments of women, who use their utmost endeavours to fascinate him in every manner imaginable. By way of warning, there is a description, not devoid of humour, of the plight of men who have been caught in the web of women.

"And then they make him do what they like, even as a wheelwright gradually turns the felly of a wheel. As an antelope caught in a snare, so he does not get out of it, however he struggles.

"Afterwards he will feel remorse like one who has drunk milk mixed

---

[1]) I, 2, 1, 13, translated by *Jacobi* in SBE, Vol. 45, p. 251.

with poison; considering the consequences a worthy monk should have no intercourse with women."...

..." Now hear the pleasures of Śramaṇas which some monks enjoy.

" When a monk breaks the law, dotes (on a woman), and is absorbed by that passion, she afterwards scolds him, lifts her foot, and tramples on his head."...

" But when they have captured him, they send him on all sorts of errands: 'Look (for the bodkin to) carve the bottle-gourd, fetch some nice fruit.

' (Bring) wood to cook the vegetables, or that we may light a fire at night; paint my feet, come and meanwhile rub my back !...

' Reach me the lip-salve, fetch the umbrella and slippers, the knife to cut the string, have my robe dyed bluish !...

' Fetch me the pincers, the comb, the ribbon to bind up the hair, reach me the looking-glass, put the tooth-brush near me "...

..." Pregnant women order their husbands about like slaves to fulfil their craving.

" When a son, the reward (of their wedded life), is born, (the mother bids the father) to hold the baby, or to give it to her. Thus some supporters of their sons have to carry burdens like camels.

" Getting up in the night they lull the baby asleep like nurses; and though they are ashamed of themselves, they wash the clothes like washermen." [1]

Like the authors of so many of the texts of the Purāṇas and Buddhist Suttas, a section of this Jaina Aṅga, too, dwells with truly Sadistic complacency on the fantastic description of the hells and the most gruesome torments of hell (I, 5, 1 f.). However, the author invariably reverts to polemics. Thus, for instance, he assails Brahmanical ritual, in the following terms (I, 7): If it were true that perfection can be attained by ablutions with cold water, then fishes, tortoises and snakes would attain the highest perfection; and if water really washed away the evil deed, then it must needs wash away the good deed also. Brahmins assert that perfection is to be

---

[1] I, 4, 1, 9 f.; 2, 1 ff., translated by *Jacobi* in SBE, Vol. 45, pp. 272 f., 275 ff.

attained by the daily lighting of the fire; if this were true, smiths and artisans of a similar nature would attain the highest sanctity.

It is possible that this book is the work of a single author. It is more probable, however, that a compiler united various poems and sermons on the same theme, to form one book. On the other hand, Book II, written in prose, is merely a somewhat clumsy conglomeration of appendices. These, too, are for the most part polemical in content and have only been appended because they deal with the same kind of themes as the old Aṅga. Nevertheless, even this book is of importance as contributing to our knowledge of the life of religious sects in India.[1]

In the third Aṅga, the Ṭhāṇaṃga,[2] as in the Aṅguttara-Nikāya of the Buddhists, various themes of the religion are dealt with in numerical order from 1 to 10. These enumerations sometimes contain parables in a nutshell, as for instance: There are four kinds of baskets, and also of teachers; there are four kinds of fishes, and also of mendicants; there are four kinds of balls, and also of men, etc. Occasionally, too, enumerations occur which are not directly connected with religion, *e.g.*, the ten themes of mathematics (in Sūtra 747). This Aṅga also contains important literary data regarding the Siddhānta, especially a table of contents of the Diṭṭhivāya which has gone astray.[3]

The fourth Aṅga, the Samavāyaṃga,[4] is in a way a

---

[1]) On the heretical doctrines dealt with in the Sūyagaḍaṃga, s. *Jacobi*, SBE 45, p. xxiii ff. Sūyagaḍa II, 1, as has been shown by *Schubring* (Worte Mahāvīras, p. 17 f.) is closely related to Āyāra I (Bambhacerāiṃ) both in wording and mode of expression.

[2]) Edited in the Āgama-Saṃgraha, Vol. 3, Benares 1880, with a Sanskrit and a Prākrit commentary; with Abhayadeva Sūri's commentary, Bombay 1918-1920. The title means "The Aṅga of the items," *i.e.*, of the subjects enumerated under numbers 1-10. *Cf.* E. *Leumann*, GGA 1899, 588, 592.

[3]) *Cf. Weber*, Ind. Stud. 16, 267 ff.

[4]) Edited with commentary in the Āgama-Saṃgraha, Vol. 4, Benares 1880; with Abhayadeva Sūri's commentary, by the AUS, Bombay 1918.

continuation of the third, the subject-matter of the first two-thirds of the work being arranged in numerical groups, [1] just like the Ṭhāṇaṃga, except that in this case the numbers do not stop at 10, but go a long way beyond 100, as far as a million.

The work begins with an enumeration of the twelve Aṅgas and a table of contents of the fourteen Puvvas. At the conclusion, however, we find very exact data regarding not only the contents but also the extent of all the twelve Aṅgas, including the Samavāya itself. There is evidence of the fact that the Aṅga in its present form is either a late work or that it contains portions of later date, in such things as the enumeration, under the number 18, of the eighteen kinds of Brāhmī script, the enumeration, under number 36, of the thirty-six sections of the Uttarajjhayaṇa, and the mention of so recent a work as the Nandī. The data in regard to the extent of the Aṅgas do not tally with their present extent, and some of the figures given are very fantastic. [2]

The fifth Aṅga, the Bhagavatī Viyāha-Pannati, "the holy teaching of explanations," usually entitled briefly "Bhagavatī," [3] contains a bulky, circumstantial presentation of the dogmatics of Jinism, partly in the form of questions and answers, Mahāvīra replying to the questions of his principal disciple Goyama Indabhūti, and partly in the form of dialogue-legends (itihāsa-saṃvāda). The contents are a motley mixture of ancient doctrines and traditions, with numerous later additions containing frequent allusions to other works, more especially to the Pannavaṇā, the Jīvābhigama,

---

[1]) Hence the title samavāya, *i.e.*, "group," "aggregate."

[2]) *Cf. Weber*, Ind. Stud. 16, 285 ff.

[3]) Vivāha-Pannatti is only a corrupt form of Viyāha-P. Edition with Abhayadeva's commentary by the AUS, Bombay 1918-1921, 3 Vols. *Cf.* A. *Weber*, Ein Fragment der Bhagavatī, in ABA 1865, 367-444; 1866, 155-352; and W. *Schubring*, Worte Mahāvīras, p. 10, 18 ff. Portions of the Viyāha-Pannatti have been translated into German by *Schubring*, Die Jainas (Religionsgesch. Lesebuch).

the Uvavāiya, the Rāya-Paseṇaijja, the Nandī and the Āyāradasāo. This work gives a more vivid picture than any other work, of the life and work of Mahāvīra, his relationship to his disciples and contemporaries, and his whole personality. Side by side with reports concerning apparitions of deities and the miraculous powers of Mahāvīra, we also find purely human traits, such as in the following account of the meeting of Mahāvīra with his mother :

(The Brahman Usabhadatta and his wife Devāṇandā went on pilgrimage to Mahāvīra.) "Then milk began to flow from the breast of the Brahman woman Devāṇandā, her eyes filled with tears, her arms swelled beside her bangles, her jacket stretched, the hairs of her body stood erect, as when a Kadamba unfolds itself in response to a shower of rain ; thus she gazed at the holy monk Mahāvīra without averting her eyes. "Why, Master," said the venerable Goyama to the holy monk Mahāvīra, "does the Brahman woman Devāṇandā gaze...(thus)...without averting her eyes ?" "Hear, Goyama," said Mahāvīra, "the Brahman woman Devāṇandā is my mother, I am the son of the Brahman woman Devāṇandā. That is why the Brahman woman Devāṇandā gazes at me with tender love, the cause of which is that I first originated in her." (It is then related how Devāṇandā was received into the Order by Mahāvīra himself.)

We are probably also justified in regarding many of the doctrines, and particularly the similes and parables contained in this book as traces of the founder's own peculiar manner of expression.

'Numerous parables,' which have been handed down faithfully as such, show Mahāvīra endeavouring to make his meaning comprehensible to his hearers. He must condescend very low to the level of their intelligence, and draw on incidents familiar to them from their daily lives. Thus, for instance, the old man, to whom a blow from an axe causes the same pain as grief causes to an elemental being (19, 3); the immense number of glances fixed upon a dancing girl,

---

[1] 9, 33, after the translation by *Schubring*, Die Jainas (Rel. Leseb.), p. 4.

the crowdedness and yet isolation of which corresponds to the kindred qualities of the single points of space (11, 10); the goat-shed, which is as full of the excrements of the goats, as origination and decay are taking place at every point of space (12, 7). Souls and substances permeate one another, as water permeates a sunken ship (1, 6)" etc.[1]

It is quite likely that Mahāvīra delivered the speeches about Saṃsāra and Kamma as they are written down here, *e.g.*:

"As each mesh in a piece of netting, which is set in a row of meshes, without a gap, occupying a regular and co-ordinated position in contact with the other meshes, reacts on the next mesh in regard to heaviness, drag, full-weight and closeness, even so in every single soul in many thousands of reincarnations, each one of many thousands of forms of life reacts in regard to heaviness, drag, full-weight and closeness on the life next to it" (5, 3).

"This soul of yours, Goyama, has already been incarnated as a mother, father, brother, sister, wife, son, daughter and daughter-in-law, as a foe, adversary, murderer, injurer and opponent, as a prince, royal heir, governor, mayor, magistrate, millionaire, master of guild, commander and merchant,—as a slave, messenger, servant, serf, pupil and domestic, in relation to all souls, and all souls have already been incarnated...(as the same)...in relation to your soul, and that more than once or an endless number of times" (12, 7).

"Just as if a man should eat food which tastes delicious, well cooked in a saucepan, and containing the desired quantity of each of the eighteen principal ingredients, but nevertheless mixed with poison, and after having consumed it, though he is in good health, yet changes...(to a condition which is bad in every respect)..., even thus, Kālodāi, souls change...(to a condition which is bad in every respect)...if they take unto themselves the hurting of beings, untrue speech, misappropriation, sexual stimulation, possession, anger, pride, deceit and greed, love and hate, strife, slander, gossip and back-biting, dislike and liking, lying and deception, and that thorn of false belief. Thus it comes about, Kālodāi, that souls perform evil deeds, from which evil fruits ripen. But if a man eats delicious

[1] *Schubring*, Worte Mahāvīras, p. 21 f.

food...mixed with wholesome substance, and though he is not in good health when he consumes it, but yet changes afterwards...(to a condition which is good in every respect), even so, Kālodāī, souls change, when they incorporate abstinence from hurting...from false belief, that thorn... (to a condition which is good in every respect)...Thus it comes about Kālodāī, that souls perform good deeds, from which good fruits ripen" (7, 10).[1]

The legendary portion of the work also gives an account of the predecessors of Mahāvīra, and of pious ascetics who attained great divine dignity through their severe castigations. Considerable space is also devoted to the descriptions of the heavenly worlds of the gods, which are granted as a reward to the pious, and the hells with their torments, to which the wicked are doomed. Among the legends, those dealing with the predecessors and contemporaries of Mahāvīra are specially important, namely those of the disciples of Pārśva and of Jāmāli and Gosāla Makkhaliputta, the founders of sects, to which Book XV of the Bhagavatī is devoted. This section is a good example of the way in which one sect presents the life of the founder of a hostile sect. The nucleus of history in the background of this presentation, appears to be the fact that the two hostile sects, the Nigaṇṭhas, *i.e.*, the adherents of Pārśva and Mahāvīra, and the Ājīvikas, *i.e.*, the adherents of Gosāla, were originally very closely connected, before they came to a parting of the ways.[2] It would seem that this Book XV of the Bhagavatī was originally an independent text, and indeed the whole of the fifth Aṅga has the appearance of a mosaic, into which various texts were inserted little by little.

The sixth Aṅga is entitled Nāyā-Dhammakahāo,[3] which

---

[1]) After the translation by *Schubring*, Die Jainas (Rel. Leseb.), p. 15 f., 19 f.

[2]) In the Appendix to his translation of the Uvāsagadasāo *Hoernle* has translated the story of Gosāla Makkhaliputta from Bhagavatī XV. *Cf.* also *Hoernle*, ERE 1, 261, and B.M. *Barua* in Calcutta Review, June 1927, p. 355 ff.

[3]) Edited with Abhayadeva Sūri's Commentary, Bombay 1916 by the AUS. *Cf.* P.

probably means "Examples and religious narratives."[1] Book I of this Aṅga consists of 21 chapters, each one of which as a rule presents a complete, independent narrative. Most of these tales are of the type which lays more stress on some parable incorporated in them than on the tale itself; some are, indeed, nothing but parables spun out and enlarged to form narratives. As an instance of this type, there is Chapter 7, in which the following is related:

A merchant had four daughters-in-law. In order to put them to the test, he gives each of them five grains of rice with orders to preserve them carefully until he shall ask for them back again. The first daughter-in-law throws the grains away, and thinks to herself: "There are plenty of grains of rice in the larder, I shall give him others instead." The second thinks in the same way, and eats the grains. The third daughter-in-law preserves them carefully in her jewel-casket. But the fourth one plants the grains, and reaps; she again sows the harvest and reaps again, until at the end of five years she has accumulated a large store of rice. Then the merchant returns and punishes the first two daughters-in-law, assigning them the meanest tasks in the household; he entrusts the third one with the guarding of the entire property; but he gives the entire management of the large household into the hands of the fourth daughter-in-law.—These four women represent the monks some of whom do not keep the five great vows at all, others neglect them, the better ones observe them conscientiously, but the best of whom are not content with observing them, but propagate them also.[2])

Steinthal, Specimen der Nāyādhammakahā, Diss. Leipzig 1881; W. *Hüttemann*, Die Jñāta-Erzählungen im sechsten Aṅga des Kanons der Jinisten, Strassburg 1907.

[1]) This is how the Jainas themselves explain the title. The nāyas (Sansk. jñāta) are a certain kind of stories, "they are to lay such emphasis upon either a certain definite *subject of their action* or a definite *passage in the narrative*, that the hearer will recognise that *everything* depends on *this* point of the narrative" (Hüttemann, loc. cit., p. 47 f.). There is already a classification of the nāyas to be found in the Thāṇaṃga 4, 3 (s. *Leumann* in ZDMG 46, 1892, 602 f.). *Weber* explains the title otherwise: "Stories for the Dharma of Nāya," *i.e.*, of Jñātṛ; according to his descent, Mahāvīra is also called Jñātṛputra or Nāyaputta (in the Buddhist Pāli texts Nātaputta).

[2]) E. *Leumann* (WZKM 3, 1889, 331 f.; GGA 1899, 588) has compared the parable of the talents in St. Matth. 25 and St. Luke 19, 12 ff. It is, however, scarcely feasible to

Side by side with legends and parables of this nature, we also encounter regular novels, tales of travellers' adventures, mariners' fairy-tales, robber tales and the like, in which the parable only appears in the form of a moral clumsily tacked on to the end.[1] In Chapter 8 the legend of Mallī, the only female Tīrthakara[2] is told, with that morality which, though sickly to our taste, is so characteristic of the monastic conception of life :

Mallī, the daughter of the king of Mithilā, is of wondrous, incomparable beauty. Six princes learn of her beauty, each in a different way, and woo her. One of them, the king of the Kuru land, gets to know of Mallī through a portrait which an artist has painted of her, after he had seen only the princess' great toe.[3] Mallī's father refuses all the six princes. They are infuriated, and combine to wage war against the king. Mithilā is besieged, and the king is helpless. Then Mallī advises the king to invite each one of the princes into the city, promising each one her hand. Owing to her power of clairvoyance, she had already foreseen everything long before, and had a "puzzling house"[4] constructed; then she made a figure which bore an exact resemblance to herself, and put it into this house. This figure had an opening on the head, into which she put remnants of

assume any historical connection between the Jinistic and the Christian parable. Thus also *Garbe*, Indien und das Christentum, p. 43 f. Note ; and now also *Leumann*, Buddha und Mahāvīra, ZB 1921, p. 55 ff.

[1]) In the mariner's fairy tale in the ninth Jñāta story, the winged horse also occurs, as in the Valāhassa-Jātaka (No. 196). See above, p. 131 f., and *Charpentier*, WZKM 27, 1913, 93.

[2]) According to the hagiology of the Jainas, there are 24 Tīrthakaras, "preparers of the path," also called Jinas, "victors" of whom Ṛṣabha was the first and Mahāvīra the last. All of them possessed perfect knowledge (kevalajñāna), and ever again proclaimed anew the religion which had sunk into corruption. With the Digambaras, the 19th Tīrthakara is a man, Malli, like all the others, but according to the Śvetāmbaras, a woman, Mallī. *Cf.* Mrs. *Stevenson*, Heart of Jainism, p. 50 ff., 56 f. ; H. v. *Glasenapp*, Der Jainismus, p. 247 ff., 284 and in Festgabe Jacobi, p. 337.

[3]) This episode reminds us of the Buddhist stories of famous artists, above, p. 136 f., and the entire narrative betrays a highly cultivated art.

[4]) Mohanaghara, "a house intended for confusion," namely a house in which a second house, and in the latter a third house stands, with net-work walls, so that the princes could be led into the house, without knowing of one another, and yet could all see the same figure.

her meals every day. She took care to conceal the opening carfeully with lotus blossoms. The princes were conducted into this "puzzling house." While they are admiring the figure of the princess through a wall of netting, Mallī herself appears. She opens the figure, and a terrible stench is spread about, so that the princes hastily cover their faces and turn away, whereupon the beautiful princess moralises on the fact that the inside of her lovely body is even much more loathsome than the inside of this figure. They should therefore not set any store on the enjoyment of love. She then tells the story of her former births, in which the six princes also played a part, and announces that she has decided to become a nun, whereupon the six princes also renounce the world.

If is a favourite theme in Jinist legends in general, as in this particular instance, to follow up the fate of persons through various rebirths. In Chapter 13, a pious layman who had lapsed into heresy for lack of a suitable teacher, was reborn as a frog, in spite of his many good works. In this existence he is crushed by a horse's hoof, but is just able to summon his remaining strength sufficiently to repeat the formula of worship to Mahāvīra, and is consequently reborn immediately as a god in heaven.[1] Chapter 16 contains the legend of Dovaī, *i.e.*, Draupadī, in the form of a story of rebirth. This is a monkish corruption of the legend from the Mahābhārata of Draupadī's marriage to the five brothers.[2]

Book II of this Aṅga is a complete contrast to Book I both in form and contents, and is more closely associated with the seventh and the ninth Aṅgas. Curiously enough, the

[1]) The same legend is also told in the Paīnna Bhattaparinnā (cf. K. v. *Kamptz*, Über die vom Sterbefasten handelnden älteren Paīnna des Jaina-Kanons, p. 31); similarly in the Visuddhi-Magga, above, p. 203.

[2]) E. *Leumann*, OC VI Leiden 1883, 3, 539 ff., believes that an archaic tradition is embodied in the Jinistic form of the legend. That is certainly not the case. See also *Weber*, HSS. Verz. II, 2, 473 f. Leumann (loc. cit. 551 f.) discusses Chapter 14 of the Aṅga, which he compares, as the Indian "Herod legend," with that part of the Kṛṣṇa legend which is told in the Bhāgavata-Purāṇa 10, 2-4. There is, however, only a very slight connection between the legend of the massacre of the innocents and the pious Jinistic legend.

story of the goddess Kālī is here told as a Dhammakahā, "sermon,"[1] though it is eminently unsuitable for this purpose.

The seventh Aṅga, Uvāsagadasāo,[2] *i.e.*, "the ten (chapters on the duties) of the lay adherent" also contains narratives for the most part. Legends are told of ten pious householders, most of whom are wealthy merchants, who impose on themselves certain forms of self-denial, take the vows enumerated by Mahāvīra, and become pious lay adherents. By dint of their asceticism they actually attain to miraculous powers while they are still lay adherents: finally they die a voluntary death by starvation as genuine Jaina saints, and are reborn as gods in the heaven of the pious. Just as in the Purāṇas and the Buddhist Mahāyāna-Sūtras, ten stories of this kind are included in one and the same frame, being told by the venerable, Suhamma to Jambū. The legends are all told after a stereotyped pattern in the most monotonous manner imaginable, so much so that in the later stories there is often only a catchword given by way of allusion to the earlier stories. The part that has the greatest claim upon our interest, is Chapter VII, in which the story is told of the wealthy potter Saddālaputta, who had been an adherent of Gosāla Makkhaliputta, but seceded from him and went over to Mahāvira. The description of how Mahāvīra convinces the potter of the truth of his doctrine, is in places reminiscent of the best Buddhist dialogues. It is obvious, however, that the whole work was only compiled for devotional purposes.[3]

[1]) See *Schubring*, Worte Mahāvīras, p. 6, 13.

[2]) Ed. in the original Prākṛt with the Sanskrit Commentary of Abhayadeva and an English Translation with notes by A. F. R. *Hoernle*, Calcutta, Bibl. Ind. 1885-1888. Edited with Commentary of Abhayadeva Sūri by the AUS, Bombay 1920. *Cf. Leumann*, WZKM 3, 1889, 328 ff.; *Barth*, RHR 19, 1889, 284 = Oeuvres II, 61 f. There is a metrical, elaborated version of the contents of this Aṅga, namely the Vardhamānadeśanā in Prākrit-Gāthās (with interlinear version in Sanskrit); s. *Weber*, HSS. Verz. II, 2, 492.

[3]) This is also expressly stated at the conclusion of the book: "The seventh Aṅga,

The next two Aṅgas, composed on the same plan, can lay just as little claim to literary merit. The eighth Aṅga, Aṃtagaḍadasāo,[1] *i.e.*, "the ten (chapters) on the (pious ascetics) who have made an end," originally consisted of ten chapters, but is now divided into eight sections. The ninth Aṅga, too, Aṇuttarovavāiyadasāo, *i.e.*, "the ten (chapters) on the (pious ascetics) who have attained to the very highest (regions of heaven)," is now divided into three sections with thirty-three lessons, instead of the original ten lessons. As we learn from Ṭhāṇaṃga 10, the original contents of these two Aṅgas were totally different from the present contents.[2] On the ground of their form, if for no other reason, these works must be denied any claim to literary excellence. Not only are the legends related after a stereotyped pattern, but they often present merely a skeleton, which the reciter is left to fill in with set words and phrases like clichés. For instance, one passage reads: "There was once a city named Campā, a shrine Puṇṇabhadda, a forest. Description."[3] What is meant is, that a complete description of the city, the shrine and the forest is to be inserted here, as it stands in the first Upāṅga. Another instance is the part about the Thera Suhamma, one of Mahāvīra's disciples, where there is a mere indication that a detailed description of this holy man is to be given, which can be found in the sixth Aṅga. In those cases where they

Uvāsagadasāo, forms a book of the sacred scripture. Its ten chapters ... are recited in exactly ten days. Thus the whole book is read completely. It is however, permitted to do this with the Aṅga in two days."

1) The 8th, 9th and 11th Aṅgas with Abhayadeva Sūri's Commentary are edited in one volume by the AUS, Bombay 1920. The Antagaḍa-dasāo and Aṇuttarovavāiyadasāo translated from the Prākrit by L. D. *Barnett*, London OTF 1907.

2) See *Schubring*, Worte Mahāvīras, p. 6 ff.

3) We find something similar in the Canon of the Sarvāstivādins; s. above II, 280 f., 284 and *Speyer*, Avadānaśataka II, p. xvi f. The "Varṇakas" occur in all the texts of the Canon.

are given in full, these "descriptions" (vannaa, varṇaka) are composed in an ornate style characterised by the conglomeration of long compound words. In all probability they belong to the earlier poetical portions of the Canon. Even the earliest commentaries read these descriptions as ornate prose. Prof. Jacobi[1] attempted to find in them traces of a long metre not arranged to form stanzas, but himself remarks that, though they are metrical, they are more closely akin to prose than to actual poems. However, even where the descriptions are given in the text itself, *e.g*, that of the marriage of Prince Goyama, they are very tedious, and mostly consist of nothing but endless enumerations. The only time when the narrative becomes more poetical is, when the prince announces his resolve to become a monk, and his parents endeavour to dissuade him from this course. The words in which Goyama begs for admittance into the monastic order, in the eighth Aṅga—"The world is in flames, the world is being burnt by old-age and death"—put us in mind of the famous "Fire Sermon" of Buddha. This Aṅga is of importance from the point of view of Indian mythology and history of religion, because it embodies the Kṛṣṇa-legend in a corrupted Jaina version, related so as to suit Jaina requirements. The story of the downfall of the city of Dvāravatī and the death of Kṛṣṇa is told as in the Mahābhārata, only Kṛṣṇa is made into a pious Jaina.

[1]) Ind. Stud. 17, 389 ff.; *cf. Schubring*, ZII 2, 178 ff and Worte Mahâvîras, p. 3 ff., who regards this metre (veḍha, veṣṭaka) as a forerunner of the āryā. He too, observes: "The absence of a division into stanzas which is caused by the varying lengths of the Veḍhas, gives a Veḍha text the character of rhythmic prose" It is true that in the Anuogadāra (p. 233 f. of the 1924 Bombay edition) veḍha is mentioned after gāhā (gāthā) and siloga (śloka), but it is not certain whether it here means a metre, because, after veḍhasaṃkhā we find nijjuttisaṃkhā, etc. *Cf. Leumann*, Jītakalpa in SBA 1892, p. 1196. We must bear in mind that, from the Indian point of view, the metre is no criterion of poetry, as prose can just as well be poetry as can verses, so that it really does not make much difference whether we read these passages as verses or rhythmic prose

The ninth Aṅga gives a hopelessly monotonous account of how the saints again and again attain to the highest perfection by starving themselves to death. To our minds at least, it is not very edifying to have the "beauty of asceticism" illustrated by a minute description of every single part of the body, accompanied by a series of drastic comparisons, in order to show how lean and emaciated it had grown. It is a remarkable contradiction: this exaggerated love of death on the part of the Jaina saint, and on the other hand, the equally exaggerated fear of killing any living thing, even though it might be only a worm or a green herb.

The tenth Aṅga, the Paṇhā-Vāgaraṇāiṃ, "Questions and Explanations,[1] treats in ten "Gates" (dāra) firstly of the five "great vows" (not to hurt any living being, not to lie, not to steal, not to be unchaste, not to be attached to possessions), and then of the five virtues corresponding to these. It is a purely dogmatic presentation, which does not correspond either to the title of the work or to the table of contents in the Ṭhāṇaṃga 10 and in the Nandī. Thus a later work took the place of the old Aṅga which had got lost.[2]

The eleventh Aṅga, Vivāgasuyam, *i.e.*, "the text of the ripening (of actions),"[3] contains legends on the retribution of good and evil deeds after the manner of the Buddhist Karman stories in the Avadāna-Śataka and Karma-Śataka. Goyama Indabhūti, the oldest pupil of Mahāvīra, sees various unhappy people, and at his request Mahāvīra explains by what actions in a former birth the person has deserved such mis-

[1] Edited with Abhayadeva Sūri's Commentary, by the AUS, Bombay, 1919.

[2] *Cf. Weber*, Ind. Stud. 16, 326 ff.; *Schubring*, Worte Mahāvīras, p. 13.

[3] For edition (together with Aṅgas 8 and 9) s. above, p. 450, note 1. According to Ṭhāṇaṃga 10, where this Aṅga is called Kamma-Vivāga-Dasāo, it originally contained only 10 chapters, whilst it contains 20 to-day. "This extension is made for the purpose of setting the reward for previous merits beside the evil consequences of previous guilt" (*Schubring*, Worte Mahāvīras, p. 6).

fortune, through what bad rebirths the person has already passed, what is still in store for him, and by what means he may finally attain to a good rebirth again. There is, for instance, a certain Umbaradatta, who is afflicted with all manner of horrible diseases. Why? Because when he was a doctor, in a previous existence, he had prescribed meat diet to a patient, thus causing the killing of numerous living creatures. He will still be born again in worse incarnations, as a dog, etc., but finally he will nevertheless be born again as a merchant.

In regard to the contents of the twelfth Aṅga, the Diṭṭhivāya ("Doctrine of the various views"), which went astray, there is nothing beyond all kinds of information given in other texts.[1] Five divisions of the Diṭṭhivāya are distinguished: (1) Parikammaṃ (Parikarmāṇi); these are said to be 16 "Preparations" for the right understanding of the Sūtras, after the analogy of the 16 arithmetical operations; (2) Suttāi (Sūtrāṇi), 88 (4 × 22) Sūtras, in which the heretical doctrines are confuted; (3) Puvvagae (Pūrvagatam), the 14 Puvvas; (4) Anuyoga, legends of the Tīrthakaras and other great men; and (5) Cūliyā (Cūlikāḥ) or "Addenda."[2] The existence of twelve Upāṅgas is additional evidence of the fact that twelve Aṅgas once existed.

There is an Upāṅga to every Aṅga. Nevertheless the connection is merely external. The subject-matter of the

---

[1]) Thus in the fourth Aṅga, in the Nandī and the Cheda-Sūtras. A short text, after the manner of a Tantra, seems to have stood at the beginning of this Aṅga; s. *Leumann* OC VI, Leiden 1883. III, 2, 558 ff. A Karma-Grantha by Candrarṣi and a work by Śivaśarmasūri called Karma-Prakṛti, old texts in Prākrit Gāthās on the doctrine of Karman, are said to have been taken from the Diṭṭhivāya; s. H. v. *Glasenapp*, Die Lehre vom Karman in der Philosophie der Jains nach den Karmagranthas dargestellt, Leipzig 1915, p. 9 f. The Siddhapañcāśikā by Devendra Sūri, is an extract from the Diṭṭhivāya in 50 Gāthās; see *Weber*, HSS. Verz. II, 2, 534 ff.

[2]) *Cf. Weber*, Ind. Stud. 16, 349 ff.; *Guérinot*, La Religion Djaina, p. 71, and H. v. *Glasenapp*, Der Jainismus, p. 93 ff.

twelve Upāṅgas is purely dogmatic and mythological, and they are not very interesting from a literary point of view.

The first Upāṅga is the Uvavāiya.[1] The first part describes the departure of Mahāvīra for the Puṇṇabhadda shrine, and the pilgrimage of King Kuṇiya Bhiṃbhasāraputta to the same place, in order to hear Mahāvīra's sermon.[2] The sermon deals with the retribution of good and evil deeds in the four forms of existence (as denizens of hell, animals, human beings and gods), and also with the duties of monks and laymen. In the second part, which has no connection whatsoever with the first, Goyama Indabhūti journeys to the Master, in order to question him regarding the various re-births. It is then taught in the form of questions and answers, how every being which has done evil, has to bear the consequences, and the beings which have not sinned so grievously, reappear in a world of the gods under certain circumstances. The various circumstances which lead to the "attainment of an existence" (uvavāya) in one of the twelve worlds of the gods, are enumerated in 16 categories. The last site lies beyond the borders of the universe, and is destined for those who have attained to complete knowledge. These mansions of the blessed are described in great detail:

"The same form which the enlightened one had at the last moment, when leaving this earthly existence, that same form he has yonder, only that it is intensified in its soul-atoms. From the form which was large or small in the last existence, one-third will be lacking in the size and bulk of the enlightened one....They are without a body, densely compact of

---

[1]) Das Aupapātika-Sūtra, erstes Upāṅga der Jaina, 1. Teil. Einleitung, Text und Glossar von E. *Leumann*, AKM VIII, 2, Leipzig 1883. Complete edition in the AUS series. The Sanskritised form "Aupapātika" given by the commentaries is erroneous. Uvavāiya stands for upapādika, "dealing with the upapāda (uvavāya)"; uvavāya means "the attainment of an existence." *Cf.* S. *Lévi* in JA, 1912, sér. 10, t. XX, 502 f. The Digambaras call the 9th Aṅga Anuttaraupapādikāṅga, s. *Bhandarkar*, Report 1883-4, p. 107.

[2]) The descriptions (varṇaka) are given completely in the first two Upāṅgas.

soul-atoms, they cherish a right belief and a right knowledge as regards objects in particular as well as in general. By reason of their being able to exercise omniscience, they recognise the nature of all things and their temporal qualities; with a never-ending, penetrating, keen glance of their intellect, they look in every place. Neither among human beings nor among all the gods is there such illimitable bliss as has begun for the enlightened one. The bliss of the gods, multiplied in duration to eternity, even though it were endlessly augmented in its fulness, is not so great as the blissfulness of liberation....As a savage, who becomes acquainted with the manifold beauties of a city, cannot describe them, because he lacks something with which to compare them, so, too, the blissfulness of the enlightened ones is incomparable, there is no comparison, and yet I shall mention something which can be compared with it in a certain sense. As a man, when he has eaten food containing all desirable ingredients, no longer experiences thirst and hunger, as though he had sated himself with the celestial beverage, so the enlightened ones who have come to the unique extinguishing, dwell sated for all time, rapturous in the possession of illimitable blissfulness without end."[1)]

As a work of literature, the second Upāṅga, the Rāyapaseṇaijja,[2)] is of greater importance. It is true that it begins with a long and tedious story, in the style of the Purāṇas, of the pilgrimage of the god Sūriyābha to Mahāvīra, but the nucleus of the work is really the dialogue, included in this tale, between King Paësi and the monk Kesi, concluding with the conversion of the free-thinking king. This is a splendid, lively dialogue, in which Kesi endeavours to prove to Paësi that there is a soul independent of the body, whilst

---

[1)] 170 f., 178 ff. After the translation of W. *Schubring*, Die Jainas (Rel. Leseb.), p. 29 f.

[2)] Rājapraśnīyasūtram, edited with Malayagiri's Commentary by the AUS, Bombay 1925. On the contents s. *Leumann* OC VI, Leiden 1883, III, 2, 490 ff. The Sanskrit translation of the title, Rājapraśnīya, is probably erroneous. Presumably the work originally treated of a king Prasenajit, in whose place Paësa was inserted; see *Weber*, Ind. Stud. 16, 382 ff. On a Buddhist version of the Paësi dialogue in the Dīgha-Nikāya see above II, 44.

Paësi thinks that he has established the contrary by means of experiments. He says, for instance, that he has had a thief sentenced to death, cut up, and hacked to pieces, and found no trace of any soul; whereupon Kesi retorts that he is even simpler than certain people who wanted to make a fire and chopped up the fire-sticks.

The next two Upāṅgas again take the form of questions (by Goyama) and answers (by Mahāvīra). The third Upāṅga, Jīvājīvābhigama, "the doctrine of the living and the lifeless things,"[1] gives in 20 sections a comprehensive classification of living creatures and a description of the universe in all its details (oceans, islands, palaces of gods, etc.). The section dealing with the continents (dīva) and the oceans (sāgara) is connected with the Jambuddīva-Pannatti, and is an interpolation.[2]

The fourth Upāṅga, Pannavaṇā,[3] which describes itself as a work of Ayya Sāma,[4] also gives in 36 chapters a classification of the living beings, containing under "human being" a geographical-ethnographic outline, in which the Aryans (ariya, ārya) and the barbarians (milikkha, mleccha) are enumerated with their habitations.

The fifth, sixth and seventh Upāṅgas are "scientific" works, dealing with astronomy, geography, cosmology and the division of time. Curiously enough, the Canda-Pannatti, which is counted as the seventh Upāṅga, according to its title an astronomical theory of the heavens based upon the

---

[1]) Jīvājīvābhigamōpāṅga with Malayagiri's Commentary edited in JPU 50, Bombay 1919. See *Weber*, Ind. Stud. 16, 388 ff. The title is usually given as Jīvābhigama, but Jīvājīvābhigama seems to be more in keeping with the contents of the work.

[2]) *Cf.* W. *Kirfel* in ZII 3, 1925, p. 50 ff. According to the data in the Ṭhāṇaṃga and in the Nandī, there was an independent text Dīvasāgara-Pannatti in the Canon.

[3]) Pannavaṇā Bhagavatī with Malayagiri's Commentary and Sanskrit translation by Nārakacandra, publ. Benares 1884; Śyāmācārya-dṛbdhaṃ śrīman-Malayagiryācārya-vibi-[illegible]vivaraṇa-yutaṃ śrī-Prajñāpanopāṅgam, Bombay 1918, AUS,

[4]) See above, p. 433, note 1,

moon, is completely identical in all available manuscripts with the Sūra-Pannatti,[1] the description of the heavens based upon the sun. Originally it was most probably a text preceding the Sūra-Pannatti and a work separate from this text. The Sūra-Pannatti contains a systematic presentation of the astronomical views of the Jainas. It deals with the orbits which the sun describes during the year, with the rising and setting of the sun, with the speed of the course of the sun through each of its 184 circuits, the light of the sun and moon, the measure of the shadow at various seasons of the year, the connection of the moon with the lunar mansions (Nakṣatras), the waxing and waning of the moon, the velocity of the five kinds of heavenly bodies (the sun, the moon, planets, Nakṣatras and Tārās), the qualities of the moonlight, the number of suns in Jambudvīpa, etc. As the work deals with the sun as well as with the moon, it almost looks as though the original Canda-Pannatti had been worked into the Sūra-Pannatti.

The sixth Upāṅga, the Jaṃbuddīva-Pannatti, "the description of Jambudvīpa,"[2] the central continent, contains the mythical geography of the Jainas. In the description of Bharatavarṣa (India), however, the legends of King Bharata occupy much space.[3]

Upāṅgas 8-12 are sometimes also comprised as five sections of one text entitled Nirayāvalī-Suttam. Probably they originally formed one text, the five sections of which were

[1] Sūryaprajñapti-Upāṅgam with Malayagiri's Commentary, edited by the AUS, Bombay 1919. *Cf. Weber*, Ind. Stud. 10, 254 ff.; 16, 401 ff.; HSS. Verz. II, 2, 573 ff.; G. *Thibaut* in JASB 1880, 49, 107 ff., 181 ff.; *Leumann* in OC VI, Leiden 1883, III, 2, 490 ff. and *Schubring*, Worte Mahāvīras, p. 13. In Ṭhāṇaṃga 4, 1 Canda-Pannattī, Sūra-Pannattī, Jaṃbuddīva-Pannattī and Dīvasāgara-Pannattī are enumerated as Aṅgabahiriyas.

[2] Jambūdvīpa-Prajñapti with Sānticandra's Commentary in JPU, Nos. 52 and 54. *Cf.* on the mythical geography of the Jainas, W. *Kirfel*, Kosmographie der Inder, Bonn und Leipzig 1920, p. 208 ff. and H. v. *Glasenapp*, Der Jainismus, p. 225 ff.

[3] According to *Leumann* (ZDMG 48, 82) these legends "can be called an exactly parallel text to Viṣṇu-Purāṇa II and Bhāgavata-Purāṇa V."

then counted as five different texts, in order to bring the number of Upāṅgas up to twelve. They are all of legendary contents, and deal with life in the beyond. The eighth Upāṅga, Nirayāvaliyāo,[1] "the series of hells," relates how the ten half-brothers of the king of Campā, Kuṇiya or Ajātaśatru, were killed by their grandfather Ceḍaga of Vesāli in the battle against him, and after their death were re-born in the various hells (niraya). The Buddhists relate that Ajātaśatru killed his father Bimbisāra, the contemporary of Buddha, and that he was altogether a bad, cruel ruler. The Jainas endeavour to show him in a better light, obviously because he favoured their order. The ninth Upāṅga, Kappāvaḍaṃsiāu, gives an account of the ten sons of the same princes whose story was told in the eighth Aṅga: like their grandmothers they were converted to the ascetic life, and each one reached a different heaven. The tenth Upāṅga, Pupphiāo, gives an account of ten gods and goddesses, who drove earthwards in their heavenly chariots (puṣpakāḥ) from their heavenly world, in order to pay homage to Mahāvīra, whereupon the latter tells Goyama Indabhūti their previous history. In the eleventh Upāṅga, Pupphacūliāo, ten similar stories are told, or rather they are indicated merely by catchwords. The twelfth Upāṅga, Vaṇhidasāo, deals with the conversion of the twelve princes of the Vṛṣṇi dynasty by the saint Ariṭṭhanemi The first of the legends deals with Nisaḍha, son of Baladeva and nephew of Kaṇha (Kṛṣṇa) Vāsudeva, and is thus connected with the Kṛṣṇa legend.

The ten Paiṇṇas or "scattered pieces" correspond to the Vedic Pariśiṣṭas, and are, like the latter, mostly metrical, and deal with all kinds of subjects pertaining to the Jaina religion.

[1]) Nirayāvaliyāsuttam, een Upāṅga der Jaina's. Met inleiding......van S. *Warren*, Amsterdam 1879. Nirayāvalikasūtram with Candrasūri's Commentary, publ. by the AUS, Ahmedabad 1922.

The Caüsaraṇa deals in 63 verses with the prayers by means of which one may take the "fourfold refuge," namely, that of the saints (Arhat), the perfected (Siddha), the living pious (Sādhu) and of religion (Dharma). The first verses, however, prescribe the six daily duties (ṣaḍāvaśyakam) essential for the purification of one's mode of life.[1] Virabhadda (Vīrabhadra) is mentioned as the author of the Caüsaraṇa. There is a whole series of Païṇṇas which deal with the voluntary death of the sage:[2] Bhattaparinnā, "the dispensing with food," in 172 verses; Saṃthāra, "the pallet of straw," upon which the sage, sick unto death, stretches himself in order to meditate, in 122 verses; Āura-Paccakkhāna, "the sick one's refusal" (of the pleasures of life), and Mahā-Paccakkhāna, "the great refusal," a formula of confession and renunciation in 143 verses. "The death of the fool" (bālamaraṇa) is the involuntary death from various causes of ordinary people who are strangers to the Jaina doctrine, and also the suicide of such people. The "death of the semi-sage" is that of the lay adherent who, though he does not die by voluntary fasting, dies after making a confession, on a bed known to be his death-bed. In contrast to these the "death of the sage" is the solemn passing of the man who is sick unto death, by means of voluntary fasting, after he has completed his confession and all vows and penances. Though the texts mentioned really contain nothing but the

---

[1]) These are : (1) sāmāiaṃ (sāmāyikam), "equanimity," obtained by desisting from all evil, (2) caüvīsaīthaa (caturviṃśatistava), "the glorification of the twenty-four" (Tīrthakaras), (3) vaṃdana, "the veneration" (of the Guru), (4) paḍikkamaṇaṃ (pratikramaṇa), "confession," (5) kāussagga (kāyotsarga), penance through certain postures of the body, and (6) paccakkhāṇaṃ (pratyākhyāna), "the refusal" (of certain pleasures), *i. e.*, the vow to renounce certain pleasures.

[2]) *Cf.* Kurt von *Kamptz*, Über die vom Sterbefasten handelnden älteren Paīnna des Jaina-Kanons, Diss. Hamburg 1929. The "death of the fool" and the "death of the sage" are also dealt with in Bhagavatī II, 1, 48 in detail; s. *Weber*, Bhagavatī, in ABA 1866, p. 266 f.

rules for attaining death by fasting, they are nevertheless in the form of didactic poems, and mostly in verse, and make use of plays on numbers and all kinds of figures of ornate poetry. They also contain sermons, which are adorned with poetical comparisons, as for instance the following:

> "Even as a needle through which a thread has been drawn, cannot get lost in the rubbish heap, so also a soul does not disappear in Saṃsāra. Souls which do not renounce the world, and which are lacking in character and good qualities, plunge into Saṃsāra, just as birds with a broken wing and without tail-feathers fall into the ocean. A dog which licks a bone, does not reach the marrow, and persuades himself that he is happy, whilst in reality he is only keeping his throat dry. Similarly a man takes for bliss intercourse with women, which in reality, serves to exhaust him. A sinner who makes a sincere confession, is like the bearer of a burden, whose burden is taken from him."[1]

In the Bhattaparinnā and the Saṃthāra there are also numerous legends of grievous sinners who did penance and became saints, of martyrs, of strange destinies in the cycle of re-births, etc.[2]

The other Païṇṇas deal with very varied themes: the Taṃdula-Veyāliya,[3] in mixed verse and prose, is a dialogue between Mahāvīra and Goyama on physiology and anatomy, the life of the embryo, the ten ages of man, the measure of length and that of time, the number of bones and sinews,

[1]) Bhattaparinnā 86, 141 ff., Mahāpaccākkhāṇa 80, according to the translation of *Kamptz*, loc. cit., p. 23 f.

[2]) K. v. *Kamptz*, loc. cit., p. 24 ff.

[3]) Usually witten Taṃdula°, Tandula°, sometimes also Taṇḍula°. The explanation of the title (in Sanskrit it is both Tandulavaikālika and Tandulavaicārika) is doubtful. Vijaya Vimala explains it as follows: tandulānāṃ varṣaśatāyuṣkapuruṣapratidinabhogyānāṃ saṃkhyāvicāreṇopalakṣitaṃ tandula vaicārikaṃ nāmeti, "an examination of rice grains (tandula = taṇḍula), characterised by the number of rice grains, to be eaten day by day, by a man who lives for a hundred years." Does the title refer to the great number of details, dealt with in the work? Editions in the AUS, and Pratnapūrvadharanirmitaṃ śrī-Tandulavaicārikaṃ śrīmad-Vijaya-Vimalagaṇi-dṛbdha-vṛtti-yutaṃ sāvacūrikaṃ ca Catuḥśaraṇam, Bombay 1922, JPU 59.

etc. The Caṃḍā-Vijjhaya (or Caṃḍā-Vejjhagā)[1] deals in 174 verses with teachers and pupils, and with discipline in general. The Devindatthaa in 300 verses contains a classification of the kings of gods according to their groups, residences, etc. The contents of the Gaṇi-vijjā, in 86 verses, are astrological. The Vīrathaa contains an enumeration in 43 verses of the names of Mahāvīra.

In reality, however, as has already been observed above, the list of the Païṇṇas is quite indefinite. A Gacchāyāra (Gacchācāra), "School rules,"[2] is also enumerated as a seventh or eighth Païṇṇa, and a Maraṇa-Samāhī (Maraṇa-Samādhi), "Death-Meditation," as a tenth Païṇṇa. The Gacchāyāra contains rules of life for teachers, monks and nuns, and is an extract from the Cheya-Suttas Mahā-Nisīha and Vavahāra. The Maraṇa-Samāhī, of course, also belongs to the texts which deal with the "death of the sage." Sometimes, however, also 20 or more texts are counted among the Païṇṇas.[3]

The six Cheda-Sūtras[4] did not, perhaps, form a group in the Canon until a late period, as it is not always the same

[1]) After *Schubring*, Worte Mahāvīras, p. 2, note 2: candrakavedhyaka, "the apple of the eye which is to be bored through" = "hitting the mark." (?)

[2]) Gacchācāraprakīrṇakam with Vānararṣi's Commentary, publ. by the AUS, Bombay 1923. *Cf. Weber*, Ind. Stud. 16, 445 f.; *Schubring*, Das Mahānisīha-Sutta, p. 50 f.

[3]) According to tradition (*cf.* Nandisūtra 44 and Vijaya Vimala Gaṇi in the Commentary on the Tandulavaicārika) there were no less than 84,000 Prakīrṇakas of each one of the pupils of Ṛṣabha and 14,000 of each one of the 14,000 Sādhus who had still been taught by Mahāvīra himself. One of them is said to have been Vīrabhadra, the author of the Caüsaraṇa. The edition, Catuḥśaraṇādi-Maraṇasamādhy-antaṃ Prakīrṇakadaśakaṃ chāyāyutam, Bombay, saṃvat 1983, AUS 46, contains: Caüsaraṇa, Āurapaccakkhāṇa, Mahāpaccakkhāṇa, Bhattaparinnā, Tandulaveyāliya, Saṃthāra, Gacchāyāra, Gaṇivijjā, Devindatthya and Maraṇasamāhī. An older edition Bhavnagar, saṃvat 1966, contains: Caüsaraṇa, Āurapaccakkhāṇa, Bhattaparinnā and Saṃthāraga. *Cf. Weber*, Ind. Stud. 16, 426 ff.; *Schubring*, Worte Mahāvīras, p. 2 f.; K. v. *Kamptz*, loc. cit., pp. 5-8.

[4]) The meaning of the word is not clear. Cheda means "cut." As *cheda* and *mūla* in Jaina discipline mean two kinds of penances, *Schubring* (Kalpasūtra, p. 8, and OLZ

texts which are placed in this group. The nucleus of this group, however, Cheda-Sūtras 3-5, belongs to the earliest portion of the Canon. These three texts are treated by tradition as one book (śrutaskandha) and called Dasā-Kappa-Vavahār Side by side with an assortment of legendary material, the contents of the Cheda-Sūtras are what we have met with under the name of Vinaya in Buddhist literature, namely, the rules of life for the monks and nuns and the prescriptions as regards atonements and penances, and in fact the entire discipline of the Order. The fourth Cheda-Sutra, entitled Āyāradasāo ("the ten sections on behaviour"), also known as Dasāo or Daśāśrutaskandha, is ascribed by tradition to Bhadrabāhu, and the eighth section of this Dasão has long been known by the title "Kalpa-Sūtra of Bhadrabāhu."[1]

Bhadrabāhu is reckoned as one of the earliest teachers and most prominent authors among the Jainas. He is said to have been the sixth Thera after Mahāvīra, and to have died 170 years after Mahāvīra's Nirvāṇa. Tradition has it that he was the last who knew the Puvvas that had gone astray, and he is said to have extracted the third and fourth Cheda-Sūtras from the ninth Puvva. Besides the Dasāo, the Nijjuttis (Niryuktis), concise metrical explanations of certain parts of the Canon, are also attributed to him.

Three different texts are united to form a whole in the Kalpa-Sūtra, and it does not seem feasible that Bhadrabāhu was the author of all three. Section I contains the Jina-

1924, 484) assumes that the expressions Cheda-Sūtra and Mūla-Sūtra are derived from these. Nevertheless, the Mūla-Sūtras, at least in their present form, have nothing to do with penances.

[1]) A very faulty translation by J. *Stevenson* appeared as early as 1848, a critical edition by H. *Jacobi*, AKM VII, 1, Leipzig 1879, an English translation by the same scholar in SBE, Vol. 22. Edition with the Commentary Subodhikā of Vinayavijaya Gaṇi, pupil of Kīrtivijaya Gaṇi, Bombay 1911, JPU 7.

caritra, "the biographies of the Jinas."[1] The main portion of this section is the biography of Mahāvīra, which is told in great detail, with great diffuseness, with descriptions in the Kāvya style and with exaggerations beyond all measure, reminding us of the Lalita-Vistara. The conception, transference of the embryo,[2] and birth of Mahāvīra are presented in the same way as in the Āyāraṃga-Sutta. Then come the 14 dreams of Devānandā, the mother of Mahāvīra, and the interpretation of them, Mahāvīra's life at home, his twelve years' ascetic life, and the activity which he displayed during nearly thirty years as an accomplished sage (Kevalin). The biographies of Mahāvīra's predecessors, the remaining Jinas down to Pārśva, which follow after the biography of Mahāvīra, are composed absolutely after the pattern of the last-mentioned, and were intended for liturgical purposes.[3]

Section II of the Kalpa-Sūtra consists of the Therāvalī, a list of schools (gaṇa), their branches (śākhā) and heads of schools (gaṇadhara). This list goes far beyond Bhadrabāhu, hence could not possibly have been written by him. Inscriptions from the 1st century A.D. prove, however, that the names in this list are historical, and not mere inventions.

Section III is probably the oldest nucleus of the Kalpa-Sūtra. It contains the Sāmācārī or "Rules for the ascetics,"

[1]) A manuscript of this Jinacaritra preserved in the Museum für Völkerkunde at Berlin, contains very interesting miniatures representing the principal events in the life of Mahāvīra. They have been described by W. *Hüttemann* in Baessler-Archiv, Vol. 4, 1914, p. 47 ff. For the life of Mahāvīra, *cf.* Mrs. *Stevenson*, Heart of Jainism, p. 21 ff.; H. v. *Glasenapp*, Der Jainismus, p. 296 ff.; Harisatya *Bhattacharyya*, Lord Mahavira, a short sketch of the Life of Bhagwan Mahavira, and Kamta Prasad *Jain*, Lord Mahavira and Some Other Teachers of His Time: Jain Mittra Mandal Tracts, Nos. 43 and 47, Delhi 1926 and 1927.

[2]) This transference of the embryo is borrowed from the Kṛṣṇa legend, but is already presented on sculptures of the Jainas in Mathurā as early as in the 1st century B.C.

[3]) When the images of the Jinas or Tīrthakaras are worshipped in the Jaina temples, hymns are sung to them, one of which summarises the happy moments of their lives, and it is precisely of these that the biographies of the Jinas treat.

namely, the rules for the rainy season (Pajjusan). Another point in favour of the assumption that this is the oldest portion of the work, is the fact that the complete title of the "Kalpa-Sūtra" is Pajjosavaṇākappa (Sanskrit Paryuṣaṇā-Kalpa), though in reality it only fits this third part. Even at the present day the Kalpa-Sūtra is read aloud to the laymen every year during the Pajjusan days. The tradition which maintains that the Jinacaritra, Therāvalī and Sāmācārī were not contained in the original Canon under the title "Kalpa-Sūtra," but were added to the Siddhānta later by Devarddhi, is most probably right.[1]

The old, genuine Kalpa-Sūtra is the fifth Cheda-Sūtra, which is also called Bṛhat-Kalpa-Sūtra or Bṛhat-Sādhu-Kalpa-Sūtra.[2] It is the principal work on the rules and regulations for the monks and nuns. A necessary supplement to it is the Vavahāra, the third Cheda-Sūtra. The Kalpa-Sūtra teaches the liability for punishment, and the Vavahāra the meting out of the punishment. The Nisīha, the first Cheda-Sūtra, containing regulations for punishment for various transgressions against the rules of daily life, is a later work.[3] It has embodied the major portion of the Vavahāra in its last sections, and has numerous similar Sūtras in common with Cūlas I and II of the Āyāraṃga. Probably both

[1]) According to one tradition, all three Cheda-Sūtras 3-5 are the work of Bhadrabāhu. *Weber* (Ind. Stud. 16, 472 ff.) adduces sound reasons for the theory that the whole of this "Kalpa-Sūtra" is erroneously ascribed to Bhadrabāhu. *Cf.* also *Oldenberg*, ZDMG 34, 1880, 755. At any rate it is worth noticing that biographical passages are inserted in the Chedas just as is the case in the Buddhist Vinaya-Piṭaka. It is possible that there was an earlier Mahāvīra biography which was supplanted by this "Kalpa-Sūtra." B. M. *Barua*, Calcutta Review, Oct. 1924, p. 52, is of opinion that "the original purpose of the Jinakalpa was rather biographical or historical than liturgical."

[2]) Das Kalpasūtra, die alte Sammlung jinistischer Mönchsvorschriften, Einleitung, Text, Anmerkungen, Übersetzung, Glossar von W. *Schubring* (Indica; herausg. von E. *Leumann*, Heft 2), Leipzig 1905.

[3]) Vavahāra- und Nisīha-Sutta, edited by W. *Schubring*, Leipzig 1918, AKM XV, 1. The title Niśītha is a false Sanskritisation of Nisīha, which probably corresponds to Sanskrit niṣedha, "prohibition."

these works originated in one and the same earlier source. The P a ṃ c a k a p p a does not appear to be in existence any longer. Sometimes, however, the J ī y a k a p p a by J i n a b h a d r a,[1] a detailed, metrical compilation of the cases in which the individual transgressions are valid, is called the sixth Cheda-Sūtra, though it is a later work on monastic discipline. The P i ṇ ḍ a-N i j j u t t i and O h a-N i j j u t t i, which also deal with discipline, are also occasionally classed among the Cheda-Sūtras. A still later work than these two N i j j u t t i s is the M a h ā-N i s ī h a-S u t t a, which appears as the second, and sometimes as the sixth Cheda-Sutta, but which in reality can scarcely be attributed to the Canon with correctness. The principal contents of the text which we have before us and which perhaps took the place of an earlier canonical Mahā-Nisīha that went astray, are rules regarding confession and penance, which are emphasized as the most important steps towards liberation. Ethical sections deal with the suffering of the beings, in connection with the doctrine of Karman, with the sin of breaking the vows, especially the vow of chastity, with good and bad monks, etc. Legends, some of which are original inventions and others taken from earlier sources, are also inserted. Both language and subject-matter, *e.g.*, the occurrence of Tantric sayings, the mention of non-canonical writings, etc., seem to indicate a late origin of this work.[2]

Four canonical texts, the first three of which are not unimportant even from the literary point of view, are described

[1]) Jinabhadra's Jītakalpa, edited with extracts from Siddhasena's Cūrṇi, by E. *Leumann*, SBA 1892, 1195 ff. It is often called Yati-Jītakalpa, to distinguish it from the Srāddha-Jītakalpa, dealing with the penances for laymen.

[2]) W. *Schubring*, Das Mahānisīha-sutta, Berlin 1918 (ABA 1918 Nr. 5). According to one tradition, Haribhadra is supposed to have taken part in the compilation of the Mahā-Nisīha, which is not likely, although he occupied himself with the text; s. *Schubring*, loc. cit., p. 5 f. Chapter 8 of the Mahā-Nisīha has been worked up by Devendra Sūri in 519 Āryā stanzas with the title Susaḍhakahā; s. *Schubring*, loc. cit., p. 48 ff.

as Mūla-Sūtras.[1] Above all, the first Mūla-Sūtra, the Uttarajjhayaṇa or Uttarādhyana-Sūtra,[2] as a religious poem, is one of the most valuable portions of the Canon. The work, consisting of 36 sections, is a compilation of various texts, which belong to various periods. The oldest nucleus[3] consists of valuable poems—series of gnomic aphorisms, parables and similes, dialogues and ballads—which belong to the ascetic poetry of ancient India, and also have their parallels in Buddhist literature in part. These poems remind us most forcibly of the Sutta-Nipāta. Several sections are sermons in series of aphorisms, admonitions to the pupils, elaborations on the cares which the monk must endure with patience, on the four most precious things (birth as a human being, instruction in the religion, faith in the religion, strength in self-control),

[1]) Why these texts are called "root-Sūtras" is not quite clear. Generally the word mūla is used in the sense of "fundamental text" in contradistinction to the commentary. Now as there are old and important commentaries in existence precisely in the case of these texts, they were probably termed "Mūla-texts." The explanation given by *Charpentier* (Uttarādhyayana-Sūtra, Introduction, p. 32): "Mahāvīra's own words," does not seem to me to be justified in any way. *Schubring* (Worte Mahāvīras, p. 1, cf. also OLZ 1924, 484 and above, II, p. 461, note 4) is of opinion that "the Mūla-Sūtras are," as their name indicates, "intended for those who are still at the beginning (mūla) of their spiritual career." *Guérinot* (La Religion Djaina, p. 79) translates Mūla-Sūtra by "traités originaux."

[2]) Edited with an Introduction, Critical Notes and a Commentary by Jarl *Charpentier*, in Archives d' Études Orientales, Vol. 18, Uppsala 1922. Indian editions appeared with Śānti Ācārya's Commentary in JPU Nos. 33, 36 and 41, in the AUS series, and recently again by Munī Śrī Jayanta Vijaya, a pupil of Vijaya Dharma Sūri, with a Commentary by Upādhyāya Kamalasaṃyama from the Kharatara Gaccha, Agra, 1923-1927, 3 vols. English translation by *Jacobi* in SBE, Vol. 45. *Leumann* (WZKM 5, 1891, p. 112, n. 1) assumes that the title "The later (uttara) readings" should be explained with reference to the sixth Aṅga, to which the work is closely related in contents. However, uttara can also mean "answer," and perhaps the title means "answer readings" having reference to a tradition according to which, during the last rainy season before his death, Mahāvīra recited, "the 36 explanations of questions not asked," which, according to the commentary, is supposed to be an allusion to the Uttarajjhayaṇa. *Cf.* also *Charpentier*, l.c., Introduction, p. 33 f.

[3]) The earlier sections contain "an abundance of archaic and curious forms" of Prākrit, s. R. *Pischel*, Grammatik der Prākrit-Sprachen, in "Grundriss" 1, 8, para. 19.

on Karman and sin, on the voluntary death of the sage and the involuntary death of the fool, on true and false ascetics, etc. We find here many sayings which excel in aptitude of comparison or pithiness of language. As in the Sutta-Nipāta and the Dhammapada, some of these series of sayings are bound together by a common refrain. A few instances are given here:

"As the burglar caught in the breach of the wall, perishes by the work the sinner himself had executed, thus people in this life and the next cannot escape the effect of their own actions."

"As a charioteer, who against his better judgment leaves the smooth highway and gets on a rugged road, repents when the axle breaks; so the fool, who transgresses the Law and embraces unrighteousness, repents in the hour of death, like (the charioteer) over the broken axle."[1]

Section VII consists mainly of parables. Here we meet with the parable of the three merchants, which reminds us of the Biblical parable of the talents:

"Three merchants set out on their travels, each with his capital; one of them gained there much, the second returned with his capital, and the third merchant came home after having lost his capital. This parable is taken from common life; learn (to apply it) to the Law.

"The capital is human life, the gain is heaven; through the loss of that capital man must be born as a denizen of hell or a brute animal.[2]

Whilst all the other sections are reckoned as a matter of course to be the words of Mahāvīra, Adhyāya VIII is expressly ascribed to Kapila, and forms an independent poetical discourse entitled "Kāvilīyaṃ."[3] It contains admonitions to the monks to cast off all things which fetter the soul, to give

[1]) IV, 3; V, 14 f. Translated by *Jacobi* in SBE, Vol. 45, pp. 18, 22.

[2]) VII, 14-16. Translated by *Jacobi* in SBE, Vol. 45, p. 29. *Cf.* Matth. 25, 14; Luke 19, 11; *Jacobi*, l.c., p. xlii, who calls attention to the fact that the agreement with the Hebrew gospel (s. Neutestamentliche Apokryphen, published by E. *Hennecke*, p. 20) is still more striking; *Edmunds*, Buddhist and Christian Gospels, II, 268 ff.; *Garbe*, Indien und das Christentum, p. 42 ff.; and *Hertel* in "Geist des Ostens" 1, 1913, 247 f.

[3]) An interesting legend of Kapila Muni, the son of the Brahmin Kāśyapa and of

up all hate, to renounce all the joys of life, and not to kill any living thing. There are sayings to be found there, such as are familiar to us in other branches of ascetic literature, *e.g.*:

"And if somebody should give the whole earth to one man, he would not have enough; so difficult is it to satisfy anybody.

"The more you get, the more you want; your desires increase with your means. Though two māṣas[1] would do to supply your want, still you would scarcely think ten millions sufficient.

"Do not desire (women), those female demons, on whose breasts grow two lumps of flesh, who continually change their mind, who entice men, and then make a sport of them as of slaves.

"A houseless (monk) should not desire women, he should turn away from females; learning thoroughly the Law, a monk should strictly keep its rules."[2]

The whole of Chapter XVI, too, is devoted to the commandment of chastity.

Just as in the Sutta-Nipāta, so, too, in the Uttarajjhayaṇa we meet with a number of beautiful old Itihāsa dialogues and ballads of ascetic poetry. Here again we come across one of the Buddhist Pratyeka-Buddha legends in the beautiful ballad of King Nami, in which the ideal of asceticism is put forward as against that of the warrior and ruler.[3] Likewise in the ballad of Harikeśa, in a vivacious dialogue between a proud Brahmin and a despised ascetic of low-caste origin, the contrast is set forth between the formalism and ceremonialism of the priestly religion on the one hand, and the self-control and the virtuous life of the pious monks on the other.[4] In

Yaśā, is told by Śānti Sūri in the Commentary (reproduced by *Jacobi* in SBE, Vol. 45, p. 31, note 1). This Kapila does not appear to have any connection with the Kapila of the Sāṃkhya system.

1) Small coins. *Cf.* Yayāti's saying, above, I, 380.

2) Uttar. VIII, 16-19, translated by *Jacobi* in SBE, Vol. 45, p. 34 f.

3) Adhyāya IX. The legend of Citta and Sambhūta, well-known from the Jātaka, is to be found in Adhyāya XIII. See above, II, 145.

4) Adhyāya XII, compared by *Charpentier* (ZDMG 63, 1909, 171 ff.) with its Buddhist counterpart (Jātaka No. 497).

the splendid dialogue, too, between the Purohita and his sons, the ascetic ideal is set forth against the Brahmanic ideal as the better and higher one. The fact that we find this conversation also in the Mahābhārata, the Purāṇas and in the Jātaka,[1] in part even literally, proves that it belongs to general Indian ascetic poetry. The dialogue in Adhyāya XXIII, in which a pupil of Pārśva and a pupil of Mahāvīra converse regarding the advantages and differences of their respective creeds which are so closely related, is of interest from the point of view of the history of Jinism. In this instance the dialogue is carried on in part in the form of riddles, which remind us of the Brahmodyas. In the majority of these ballads, the dialogues are the principal part. Only in Adhyāya XXII the narrative portion of the ballad is the more interesting, firstly because the tale is connected with the Kṛṣṇa legend by the names that occur in the legend, and secondly on the strength of the content itself, which is as follows:

In the city of Sauryapura there lived two mighty princes. The first, Vasudeva by name, had two wives, Rohiṇī and Devakī, each of whom bore him a son, Rāma and Keśava. The second, Samudravijaya by name, had a son Ariṣṭanemi by his wife Śivā. Keśava sought Rājīmatī, the daughter of a mighty king, as a wife for Ariṣṭanemi, and she is granted him. Ariṣṭanemi sets forth with great pomp to fetch his bride; but on the way he sees many animals confined in cages and enclosures, and learns, in answer to his question, that these animals are all to be slaughtered for his marriage-feast. He is so deeply shocked by this, that he resolves to take the vow of an ascetic. When Princess Rājīmatī hears of it, she breaks forth into lamentations, but then resolves, in her turn, to become a nun. In her wanderings as a nun, she one day takes refuge in a cave during a torrent of rain. She believes herself to be alone, and undresses herself, in order to dry her garment. Now the ascetic Rathanemi, Ariṣṭanemi's elder brother, had previously taken refuge in the same cave. Now

[1]) Adhyāya XIV; see above, I, 417 ff., 561; Jātaka 509 and *Charpentier*, ZDMG 62, 1908, 725 ff.

when he sees Rājīmati in her nude beauty, he is seized by passion and makes advances to her. However, she reproves him, and admonishes him not to wish to "drink that which another has spat out." Reminded of his vow by her forcible words, "he returned to religion, like an elephant spurred on by the goad." [1]

As a contrast to these poetical passages, the last Adhyāyas (XXIV and XXVI-XXXVI) contain only dry sermons, partly catechistical enumerations, partly erudite elucidations of various points of Jaina dogmatics, and partly regulations for the life of the monks.

The second Mūla-Sūtra is the Āvassaya or Āvassaga (Saḍāvāśyaka-Sūtra) which has come down only in conjunction with the Nijjutti.[2] The Sūtra consists of six sections (Adhyāyas), which correspond to the six Āvassayas, *i.e.*, the six "essential" (āvaśyaka) daily duties of a Jaina (desisting from all evil, glorification of the Tīrthakaras, veneration of the teacher, confession, asceticism and renunciation of sensual pleasures).[3] Attached to the formulas with which these duties are performed, there are stories which have come down in the old commentaries.[4]

The third Mūla-Sūtra, Dasaveyāliya,[5] is said to have been written by a certain Sejjaṃbhava. Legend tells that this man was enlightened by the apparition of a picture of the

1) The extended form of this legend in the Commentary of Devendra, has been edited and translated by *Charpentier* (ZDMG 64, 1910, 397 ff.).

2) Śrī Āvaśyaka Sūtra, Part I, with Niryukti (gloss) by Śrutakevalin Śrī Bhadrabāhu Svāmin, along with the Commentary by Śrī Malayagiri Sūri, Bombay 1928, AUS No. 56.

3) See above, p. 459, note 1, *Cf.* B. L. *Garr*, Sāmāyika or A Way to Equanimity, Arrah, 1918.

4) *Cf.* E. *Leumann* in OC X, Genève 1894, I, 125 and "Die Āvaśyaka-Erzählungen" (herausgegeben), erste Hälfte, Leipzig 1897 (AKM X, 1). There are, belonging to the text of the Āvaśyakas, besides the Nijjutti, two old commentaries, the Cūrṇi and Haribhadra's Ṭīkā. Haribhadra's Commentary (Hāribhadrīyāvaśyaka-Vṛtti) has been published with elucidations, by Hemacandra Sūri, a pupil of Abhayadeva Sūri, Bombay 1920, JPU 53. *Cf.* also *Weber*, Ind. Stud. 17, 50 ff.

5) E. *Leumann* (ZDMG 46, 1892, 581-663) has not only translated the Sūtra, but has also edited the Niryukti and examined the contents of its narrative portions.

Jina, and left his house when his wife became pregnant. She bore a son, whom she named Mānaka. When the boy was eight years old, he asked after his father, and when he heard that the latter had become an ascetic, he went forth to seek him and become his pupil. As the father knew that his son had only six months more to live, he taught him the Dasaveyāliya within that period, whereupon he gave up the ghost by means of deep meditation.[1] The Sūtra consists of sayings pertaining to the monastic life, some of which remind us of the sayings in the Dhammapada, whilst others contain only rules for monastic discipline. Section II is connected with the ballad of Rājīmatī in the Uttarajjhayaṇa; they are verses in which she admonishes Rathanemi who wishes to seduce her. This Sūtra, too, is connected with an abundant narrative literature which is contained in the commentaries.

As the fourth Mūla-Sūtra the Piṃḍa-Nijjutti[2] is usually mentioned, sometimes also the Oha-Nijjutti,[3] and occasionally the Pakkhi.[4] The Piṃḍa-Nijjutti and the Oha-Nijjutti are ascribed to Bhadrabāhu, and are sometimes counted among the Cheda-Sūtras. They treat of the pious life, and of subjects of discipline. The Pakkhi or the Pākṣika-Sūtra is a liturgy in verse for the Pakkhi-Paḍīkamaṇaṃ (Pakṣi-Pratikramaṇa), *i.e.*, the fourteen days' confession.[5] The confession of the "five great vows" (mahāvrata), with which the work

[1]) He is said to have died 98 years after the Nirvāṇa of Mahāvīra. The legend is told at the end of the edition of the Daśavaikālika-Sūtram (Bombay 1919). *Cf.* also *Peterson*, Report IV, p. cxviii.

[2]) Bhadrabāhusvāmi-praṇītā Piṇḍaniryuktiḥ, Malayagiryācārya-vivṛtā, publ. in JPU, Bombay 1918.

[3]) Oghaniryuktiḥ, Bhadrabāhusvāmi-viracita-niryukti-śrīmat-pūrvācāryaviracita-bhāṣya-yutā......śrīmad-Droṇācāryasūtrita-vṛtti-bhūṣitā, publ. by the AUS, Bombay 1919. *Cf. Weber*, Ind. Stud. 17, 61, 82 ff.

[4]) Pākṣikasūtram with Yaśodeva Sūri's Commentary, publ. in JPU No. 4, Bombay 1911. *Cf. Weber* in HSS. Verz. II, 819 ff.; Ind. Stud. 17, 85.

[5]) *Cf.* Mrs. *Stevenson*, Heart of Jainism, p. 166; H. v. *Glasenapp*, Der Jainismus, p. 374 f.

begins, also includes the worship of the "patient ascetics" (khamāsamaṇa), who are accounted the authors of the "sacred scriptures which stand outside the Aṅgas" (aṅga-bāhiram), and of the twelve Aṅgas, which gives rise to a solemn enumeration of all the sacred writings (sutta-kittanam).[1]

The Nandī and the Aṇuogadāra[2] are sometimes counted among the Païṇṇas, but they are usually mentioned either before or after the Mūla-Sūtras as independent texts standing outside the groups. They are in prose with occasional verses. The Aṇuogadāra is in the form of questions and answers. The Nandī (probably "auspicious introduction") which, according to tradition, was written by Devarddhi, the redactor of the Siddhānta, in person,[3] begins with a hymn of praise to Mahāvīra, and is followed by an enumeration of the twenty-four Tīrthakaras and the eleven Gaṇadharas (heads of schools) and a Therāvalī (list of teachers) which ends with Dūsagaṇi, the teacher of Devarddhi. Both works are huge encyclopædias, dealing with everything which should be known by a Jaina monk. The survey of the Canon which they give, is of great importance. They do not, however, deal exclusively with themes pertaining to religion, but treat also of profane

[1]) Ritual books such as Śrāddha-Pratikramaṇa-Sūtra (publ. with Devendra Sūri's Commentary, Bombay 1912, JPU 8), and Śramaṇa-Pratikramaṇa-Sūtra (publ. with Commentary, Bombay 1911, JPU 2), and Sāmācārī-Prakaraṇam (pūrvācāryavihitam...... Yogaviśeṣavākyayutam, ed. Bombay 1911, JPU) may also be described as semi-canonical. *Cf. Weber*, Ind. Stud. 16, 369 ff.; 17, 71 ff.

[2]) Nandīsūtram, śrīman-Malayagiryācārya-praṇīta-vṛtti-yutam, śrīmad-Deva-vācaka-kṣamāśramaṇa-nirmitam, ed. AUS, Bombay 1924. Anuyogadvārāṇi......Hemacandrasūri-nirmita-vṛtti-yutāni, ed. AUS, Bombay 1924. *Cf. Weber* HSS.-Verz. II, 672 ff., 692 ff.; Ind. Stud. 17, 1 ff. A specimen of Malayagiri's Commentary to the Nandī (the refutation of Theism) is given by F. O. *Schrader*, Über den Stand der indischen Philosophie zur Zeit Mahāvīras und Buddhas, p. 62 ff.

[3]) Against the authorship of Devarddhi, the argument is brought forward that the Nandī contains data on the Canon which do not agree with its present form. But, then, do we possess the Canon in exactly the form in which Devarddhi edited it? *Cf. Weber*, Ind. Stud. 17, 2, 17 ff.; *Charpentier*, The Uttarādhyayanasūtra, Introd., p. 18.

branches of knowledge. Both texts contain an interesting enumeration of the "false tradition" (micchāsuaṃ, mithyā-śrutam) or "worldly" (loïe, laukika) sciences, which begins with Bhārahaṃ (Mahābhārata) and Rāmāyaṇaṃ, but mentions, besides some hitherto unexplained titles, among others Koḍillayaṃ (Kauṭilīya Arthaśāstra), Ghoḍayamuhaṃ (the Kāma-Sūtra of Ghoṭakamukha, a predecessor of Vātsyāyana), Vaïsesiyam (the Vaiśeṣika system of philosophy), Buddha-Sāsaṇaṃ (the doctrine of Buddha), Kāvilaṃ (the system of Kapila), Logāyataṃ (Lokāyata, system of materialism), Purāṇa, grammar (vāgaraṇaṃ), Bhāgavayaṃ (Bhāgavata-Purāṇa), Pāaṃjali (Pātañjali), mathematics (gaṇiaṃ) and drama (nāḍayāī, nāṭakāni) and lastly "the four Vedas together with the Aṅgas and Upāṅgas."[1] There are entire sections dealing with moods in poetry (kāvyarasa), including love lyrics in illustration of the subject, with grammar (compound words, word-formation), the division of time, etc.

So much for the Canon of the Svetāmbara Jainas. Hitherto little is known about the Siddhānta of the Digambaras.[2] They, too, recognise the twelve Aṅgas. The title of the sixth Aṅga reads Jñātṛ-Dharma-Kathāṅga. They, too, include in the twelfth Aṅga the fourteen Pūrvas, which form one of the five sections of this Aṅga. Section I of the Dṛṣṭivāda, the Parikarmāṇi, includes among others Candra-prajñapti, Sūryaprajñapti and Jambūdvīpaprajñapti. Those texts which do not belong to the Aṅgas are called the fourteen Aṅgabāhyas ("standing outside the Aṅgas") or Prakīrṇakas ("Miscellanea"), and are said to have been written "for the

[1]) Nandī, p. 194, sūtra 41, Aṇuogadāra, p. 86, sūtra 41. *Cf.* with this list *Weber*, Ind. Stud. 17, 9 and Bhagavatī, ABA 1866, 248; *Charpentier*, l.c., p. 29 f.

[2]) A complete survey of the Canon of the Digambaras is given by *Bhandarkar*, Report, 1883-4, p. 106 ff., according to Sakalakirti's Tattvārthasāradīpaka. *Cf.* also *Weber*, HSS.-Verz. II, 3, 823 f. and *Guérinot*, p. xxx f.; J. L. *Jaini* in SBJ, Vol. V, Preface, p. 12 ff.

benefit of the simple-minded." The first four Aṅgabāhyas, according to their titles: Sāmāyika, Caturviṃśatistava, Vandana and Pratikramaṇa, correspond to sections of the second Mūla-Sūtra. Besides these, the only texts to be found among the Aṅgabāhyas which also occur in the Canon of the Śvetāmbaras, are the Daśavaikālika, Uttarādhyayana and Kalpa-Vyavahāra (probably corresponding to the Dasākappa-Vavahārā of the Śvetāmbaras). It is feasible to assume that those texts which are common to both sects, present the earliest portions of the sacred writings of the Jainas. Nevertheless, the question of how far the subject-matter of texts bearing the same titles is correspondingly similar, remains to be investigated.

The Digambaras of the present day have, in addition, a "secondary Canon," which might perhaps be more correctly termed a "substitute Cannon," and which they also describe as "the four Vedas." This "Canon" consists of a number of important texts of later times, which are classified into four groups: (1) Prathamānuyoga, legendary works, to which belong the "Purāṇas" (Padma-, Harivaṃśa-, Triṣaṣṭilakṣaṇa-, Mahā- and Uttara-Purāṇa) which will be mentioned below; (2) Karaṇānuyoga, cosmological works: Sūrya-Prajñapti, Candra-Prajñapti and Jayadhavalā; (3) Dravyānuyoga, philosophical works of Kunda-kunda, Umāsvāti's Tattvārthādhigama-Sūtra with the commentaries and Samantabhadra's Āptamīmāṃsā with the commentaries; (4) Caraṇānuyoga, ritual works: Vaṭṭakera's Mūlācāra and Trivarṇācāra and Samantabhadra's Ratnakaraṇḍa-Śrāvakācāra.[1]

[1]) *Cf. G. Bühler*, in Ind. Ant. 7, 1878, p. 28 f.; *Farquhar*, Outline, 218 f.; *Guérinot*, La religion Djaina, p. 81 ff., 85 f. A somewhat divergent division of the Anuyogas is given by S. C. *Ghoshal* in SBJ, I, p. xi.

The Non-canonical Jaina Literature.

As the Jaina Canon was written down at so late a period, it is not possible to fix a definite line of demarcation between the canonical and the non-canonical literature. At all events the non-canonical literature already begins before the completion of the Canon, and it has continued through all the centuries down to the present day.

The language of the post-canonical Jaina works is partly Prākrit—the so-called Jaina-Māhārāṣṭrī—and partly Sanskrit. In general it may be said that the earlier works were in Prākrit, and that later, certainly not until the centuries of the Christian era, Sanskrit was also used. Side by side with Sanskrit, however, in which language some Jaina authors reached a great perfection, though others wrote it rather clumsily, Prākrit and the Apabhraṃśa dialects were still used, even in the later centuries, and lastly the modern Indian languages too: for the Jains, more than any other sect, have in their writings, and especially in their exceptionally comprehensive narrative literature, never addressed themselves exclusively to the learned classes, but made an appeal to other strata of the people also. As is still the case at the present day, it was among the merchant classes in particular that they found their most loyal lay adherents.

It is extremely difficult to establish a chronology of the earlier non-canonical Jaina literature from the 1st to the 8th century A.D. It is true that we possess a large number of so-called Paṭṭāvalīs, Therāvalīs, genealogical lists of the teachers and heads of schools, which frequently contain very exact chronological data. On the other hand, these lists often contradict one another: sometimes there are external reasons why credence should not be given to them, and yet it is scarcely feasible to regard them as pure invention. A further difficulty is that frequently the same names occur several times, so that it would be necessary to devote a separate investigation to each single author and each individual work.

It may be assumed as certain that, long before the final compilation of the Canon under Devarddhi, the Jaina monks began to write explanations of the sacred texts. The earliest commentaries, the Nijjuttis or Niryuktis, are in some instances very closely interwoven with the Sūtras, or they even supplanted the latter. The Piṇḍa-Nijjutti and the Ogha-Nijjutti appear in the Canon itself, and the Ogha-Nijjutti is even supposed to have been taken from one of the Pūrvas.[1]

Bhadrabāhu, who is said to have died 170 years after the death of Mahāvīra, has already been introduced to us above, as the author of a Kalpa-Sūtra, and tradition is unanimous in naming him as the author of Nijjuttis on 10 works of the Canon.[2] The Digambaras tell us, however, that there were two Bhadrabāhus, the first of whom died 162 years after the Nirvāṇa of Mahāvīra (*i.e.*, 365 B.C.) and the second 515 years after the Nirvāṇa (*i.e.*, 12 B.C.).[3]

Kundakunda,[4] who, according to the Paṭṭāvalīs of the Digambaras, lived in the 1st century A.D., calls himself

1) See above, pp. 462, 465, and *Charpentier* in ZDMG 70, 1916, 219 f.

2) On Āyāraṃga, Sūyagaḍaṃga, Sūriyapannatti, Uttarajjhayaṇa, Āvassaya, Dasaveyāliya, Dasāsuyakkandha, Kalpa-Sūtra, Vavahāra and Ṛṣibhāṣita-Sūtra. Cf. *Bhandarkar*, Report, 1883-4, p. 131 f.; *Peterson*, Report IV, p. lxxxiv.

3) *Cf.* H. *Jacobi* in the Introduction to the Bhadrakalpa-Sūtra, p. 10 ff.; J. *Klatt* in Ind. Ant. 11, 1882, p. 245; Satis Chandra *Vidyābhūṣaṇa*, History of Indian Logic, Calcutta 1921, p. 164 f. If a recent Śvetāmbara tradition makes him a brother of Varāhamihira, it refers to the author of a Bhādrabāhavī Saṃhitā, a work on astronomy, which is later than Varāhamihira. *Cf. Jacobi*, loc. cit., p. 13 f. It is yet an entirely different Bhadrabāhu who wrote the Bhadrabāhu-Saṃhitā, a work on the right of succession: text and Engl. translation by J. L. *Jaina*, Jaina Law, in the Library of Jaina Literature, Vol. IV, Arrah, 1916.

4) He belongs to the Draviḍa-Saṃgha, *i.e.*, the Jaina community of the South. He has also the epithets Vakragrīva, Elācārya, Gṛdhrapiccha, and his original name is said to have been Padmanandin. According to a Digambara-Paṭṭāvalī, he is the fifth in the genealogical tree of teachers beginning with Bhadrabāhu. The school which he founded s first mentioned in an inscription of 797 A.D. *Cf.* A. *Guérinot*, Répertoire d'Épigraphie

a pupil of Bhadrabāhu, perhaps referring thereby to Bhadrabahu II.[1] He wrote his learned works only in Prākrit. Umāsvāmin, who is called Umāsvāti by the Śvetāmbaras, and who is recognised by both sects as a great authority in matters pertaining to the faith, is according to the Digambaras, a pupil of Kundakunda. Vaṭṭakera and Kārttikeya Svāmin, too, probably belong to the first centuries of the Christian era. Siddhasena Divākara, who is by some also ascribed to the earlier centuries of the Christian era, and by others to a period as late as the 7th century A.D., is celebrated both as a logician and a lyrical poet.[2] Vimala Sūri, who, according to his own statements, composed his Rāma-epic Paümacariya in Prākrit 530 years after the Nirvāṇa,[3] is certainly a very early Prākrit

Jaina, Paris 1908, p. 42 ff. ; *Peterson*, Report II, 80 ff., 158 ff.; Report, IV, p. xix f.; *Hiralal*, Catalogue, p. vi f. It is not so likely that he is also the author of the famous Tamil book of sayings Kurral, as is believed by *Chakravartinayanar* (SBJ, III, p. ix f.). He wrote three of his works for his royal pupil Śivakumāra Mahārāja. This prince is identified by K. B. *Pathak* (Ind. Ant. 14, 1885, p. 15) with the Kadamba king Śiva Mṛgeśa Mahārāja (5th century A.D.), by *Chakravartinayanar* (SBJ, III, p. xii ff.) with Śivaskandavarman of the Pallava dynasty.

1) *Cf.* W. *Denecke* in Festgabe Jacobi, p. 163 f.

2) According to a Śvetāmbara tradition he is said to have converted King Vikramāditya in the year 470 after Mahāvīra (57 B.C.) (*Klatt* in Ind. Ant. 11, 1882, p. 247), whereas the Digambaras state 714 to 798 after Mahāvīra (187-271 A.D.) as his time. Vṛddhavādi Sūri is named as his teacher. He is supposed to be a contemporary of Siṃhagiri (who is 15th in the Kharatara-Gaccha-Paṭṭāvali, in which Samantabhadra is the 19th) and of Pālitta. For the legends about Siddhasena and King Vikramāditya, s. *Weber*, Ind. Stud. 15, 278 ff. He is said to have received the name Kumudacandra at his consecration. See *Peterson*, Report IV, p. cxxxi f. *Jacobi* (Ind. Stud. 14, 376) thinks that this may be merely an invention on the part of the commentator, who was anxious to interpret the concluding verse of the Kalyāṇamandira-Stotra as alluding to the name of the author. *Jacobi* (Samarāicca Kahā, Ed., Introduction, p. iii) considers 670 A.D. as his probable date. The arguments adduced by S. Ch. *Vidyābhūṣaṇa*, History of Indian Logic, p. 173 f., for placing him in about 480-550 A.D. are not convincing. L. *Suali*, Introducione allo studio della Filosofia Indiana, Pavia 1913, p. 38 f., agrees with Vidyābhūṣaṇa, who already previously (Mediaeval School of Indian Logic, p. 14 f., and Nyāyāvatāra, Introduction, p. iv) gave the date as 533 or as 550 A.D. See also *Hiralal*, Catalogue, p. xii ff.

3) That is, according to the usual calculation, in the year 4 A.D. As in the work itself the terms dīnāra and lagna occur, and there is mention of Yavanas and Śakas,

poet. During the first centuries, at all events prior to the 5th century A.D., Pālitta (Pādalipta)[1] wrote a religious novel in Prākrit. It is possible that the poet Mānatuṅga,[2] who, according to some of the lists of teachers, lived as early as at the beginning of the 3rd century A.D., also belongs to the early period of classical Sanskrit poetry. Devanandin or Jinendrabuddhi, who is usually called by his honorific name Pūjyapāda, and who is famous as a grammarian, poet and erudite writer, lived between the 5th and 7th centuries.[3]

The second half of the 7th and the first half of the 8th century A.D. was a period of lively philosophical disputes. Kumārila, the great Mīmāṃsā philosopher and representative of Brahmanical orthodoxy, attacked the Buddhist and Jinistic logicians, including among the last-named the prominent teachers Samantabhadra and Akalaṅka, whilst Prabhācandra and Vidyānanda defended their co-religionists against Kumārila.[4]

Jacobi (Bhavisatta Kahā, p. 59,* Upamitibhavaprapañcā-Kathā Ed., Preface, p. x) thinks that the work can have originated "in the 2nd or 3rd century A.D. at the earliest." In this case we should have to assume that, in Vimala's days, a later date was assumed as the date of Mahāvīra's death, than that now usually assumed, *i.e.*, 527 B.C. *Leumann* regards the date 4 A.D. to be incontestable, as he tells me in a letter. See above I, 513 f.

1) According to the Paṭṭāvalis, Vṛddhavādin, Pādalipta (Pālitta) and Siddhasena Divākara were contemporaries. (*Klatt*, Ind. Ant. 11, 251.)

2) In the chronology of the heads of schools in the Kharataragaccha-Paṭṭāvalī, he appears as the 23rd, immediately before Devarddhi, as whose date 980 after Vīra (453 A.D.) is given, whilst Samantabhadra appears as the 19th (*Klatt*, Ind. Ant. 11, 247). In the Tapāgaccha-Paṭṭāvalī Samantabhadra is the 16th and Mānatuṅga the 20th in the list (loc. cit. 252).

3) *Bhandarkar*, Early History of the Dekkan, second Ed., p. 59, places him about 678 A.D., B. Lewis *Rice* in JRAS 1890, 245 ff., about the middle of the 5th century A.D. A Digambara Paṭṭāvalī gives 251 A.D. as his date. See *Hoernle* in Ind. Ant. 20, 1891, 351; *Klatt*, Specimen of Jaina Onomasticon, p. 45 f., and *Jacobi* in ZDMG 60, 290. That he lived before Samantabhadra is shown by K. B. *Pathak* in Ann. Bh. Inst. 11, 1930, pp. 53 f., 153.

4) Akalaṅka lived during the reign of the Rāṣṭrakūṭa-King Sāhasatuṅga Dantidurga, and Prabhācandra until the reign of Amoghavarṣa I. According to S. Ch. *Vidyābhuṣaṇa*, History of Indian Logic, p. 193 f., he lived in the 9th century A.D. See K. B. *Pathak*

In the 8th century, probably between 705 and 775 A.D., there also lived one of the most distinguished and prolific writers of the Jainas, Haribhadra,[1] a pupil of Jinabhadra (or Jinabhaṭa) and Jinadatta,[2] from the Vidyādharakula. He was born at Citrakūṭa, the present-day Chitore,

---

in JBRAS 18, 219 ff.; OC IX, London 1891, I, 186 ff., and Ann. Bh. Inst. 11, 1930, p. 149 ff.; 12, 1931, p. 123 ff. There is an inscription, first edited by Lewis *Rice* in 1889, in Śravaṇa Belgola (Mysore) in which it is reported that an Ācārya by the name of Prabhācandra died the voluntary death of an ascetic on the mountain Kaṭavapra. The inscription is not dated, but on palaeographical grounds is said to be not later than 750 A.D., probably earlier. E. *Leumann* in WZKM 7, 1893, p. 382 ff., was the first to express the conjecture that this Prabhācandra and the Digambara author and logician are identical, and J. F. *Fleet* (Ep. Ind. 4, 1896-97, p. 22 ff.) agrees with him. A. *Venkatasubbiah* (JBRAS 3, 1928, 144 ff.), however, is right in saying that there is no proof of this identity. In Digambara Paṭṭāvalīs one Prabhācandra is mentioned with the date 396 A.D. and another with the date 1250 A.D.; see *Hoernle* in Ind. Ant. 20, 1891, pp. 351, 354. There are 4 or 5 different writers named Prabhācandra, s. *Hiralal*, Cat., p. xxviii.

1) Thus according to the researches of Muni *Jinavijayaji* (The Date of Haribhadrasūri, in Proc. I. OC, Poona, Vol. I. 1920, p. cxxiv ff.), with whom *Jacobi* (Samarāicca Kahā Ed., pp. i-iv) agrees. *Peterson* (3 Reports, p. 3 f. and Appendix I, 284) quotes a Prākrit verse, out of the Gāthāsahasrī written in 1630, according to which the famous Haribhadra is said to have died in 535 of the Vikrama era, *i.e.*, in 478 A.D. Another tradition, which can be traced till the 13th century, gives 529 A.D. as Haribhadra's date (*Klatt*, Ind. Ant. 11, pp. 247, 253). However, as writers of the 6th and 7th centuries are mentioned in works attributed to Haribhadra, these dates cannot be correct. Perhaps Mahāvīra's Nirvāṇa was reckoned differently in those days. (See above p. 424, note 1, and *Jacobi*, Upamitibhavaprapañcā-Kathā Ed., Preface, p. viii ff.) S. Ch. *Vidyābhūṣaṇa* (History of Indian Logic, p. 208 ff.) has certainly assumed that the younger Haribhadra, who wrote in about 1120 A.D., is the author of the works Ṣaḍdarśanasamuccaya, Daśavaikālika-niryukti-ṭīkā, Nyāyapraveśaka-Sūtra and Nyāyāvatāra-vṛtti, but this is in contradiction to the entire tradition. Muni *Jinavijayaji* has established, however, that Uddyotana in his Prākrit poem Kuvalayamālā, completed in 779 A.D., calls Haribhadra his teacher. As he quotes authors who lived in the second half of the 7th century, he must have lived in the 8th century. Śāntarakṣita (8th century A.D.) quotes in Tattvasaṃgraha an Ācārya Sūri, whom Benoytosh *Bhattacharyya* (GOS, Vol. 30, p. lxxv) identifies with Haribhadra Sūri.

2) Haribhadra says of himself in the colophons at the end of some of his works, that he obeys the command of Jinabhaṭa, a teacher of the Śvetāmbaras, and that he is the pupil of Ācārya Jinadatta, the ornament of the Vidyādharakula (gaccha). See *Jacobi*, Samarāicca Kahā Ed., p. iv. Besides the famous Haribhadra there are at least 8 other Jaina writers of the same name, s. *Klatt*, Specimen of a Literary Bibliographical Jaina Onomasticon, pp. 5, 8 f.; Muni *Kalyāṇavijaya* in the Introduction to his edition of Haribhadra's Dharmasaṃgrahaṇi, Bombay, 1918 (JPU 23) and *Jacobi*, Sanatkumāracaritam, p. VII, Note 3.

as the son of a Brahmin, and was instructed in all branches of Brahmanical learning. Proud of his enormous erudition, he declared that he would become the pupil of any man who could tell him a sentence the meaning of which he did not understand. This challenge was inscribed on a plate which he wore on his stomach, whilst another legend has it that he laid gold bands around his body to prevent his bursting owing to so much learning. One day he heard the Jaina nun Yākinī reciting a verse, the meaning of which he did not understand. He asked her to explain the meaning to him. She referred to a teacher Jinabhaṭa, who promised to instruct him, if he would enter the Jaina Order. So Haribhadra became a monk, and thenceforth called himself the "spiritual son" (dharmaputra) of the nun Yākinī. He soon became so well-versed in the sacred writings of the Jainas, that he received the title Sūri (honorific epithet of learned Jain monks), and his teacher appointed him as his successor. According to an unauthenticated tradition, he wrote no less than 1,444 works. Hitherto 88 of his works have indeed been found in manuscripts, and 20 of these are also printed. In all probability he soon wandered away from his birthplace Citrakūṭa, for his life as a monk was spent for the most part in Rājputāna and Gujarat. A Brahmin by birth, Haribhadra was thoroughly well versed in Brahmanism, but he also had a considerable knowledge of the Buddhist doctrines, which may have given rise to the various legends, according to which he secretly procured a knowledge of Buddhism through his pupils and his nephews Haṃsa and Paramahaṃsa, in order to be able to refute its doctrines thoroughly.[1] Haribhadra wrote both in Sanskrit and Prākrit. He was an eminent composer in

---

1) On the numerous legends and anecdotes which are told regarding the life of Haribhadra, see *Klatt* in Ind. Ant. 11, p. 247; *Hertel*, Jinakirtis "Geschichte von Pāla und Gopālā," p. 141 ff.; *Glasenapp*, Der Jainismus, p. 107 f.; *Jacobi*, Samarāicca Kahā Ed., pp. iv-xviii.

verse and in prose, and also wrote systematic scientific treatises (Prakaraṇas) and comprehensive philosophical works. Probably, he was also the first to write commentaries to the Canon in Sanskrit. Among his commentaries, those to the two Mūla-Sūtras Āvassaya and Dasaveyāliya have come down to us. While utilising the ancient Prākrit commentaries, he retained the narratives (Kathānakas) in their original Prākrit form.

Sīlāṅka or Sīlācārya, who lived about a century later, and wrote commentaries on the first two Aṅgas in about 862 or 872 A.D., already translated all the Prākrit sources which he used, including the narratives, into Sanskrit. He also wrote a Mahāpuruṣa-Carita in the year 869 A.D.[1]

In the 9th century Jinasena, the friend of King Amoghavarṣa I (815-877 A.D.) wrote the Ādi-Purāṇa. At the beginning of the 10th century (906 A.D.) the poet Siddha, usually called Siddharṣi, wrote his famous allegorical romance in which the existence of the beings is set forth in symbolical terms. At the end of the 10th and the beginning of the 11th century, the Digambara Amitagati wrote two famous didactic poems and a number of other works. Round about the same time, the Digambara Nemicandra, the teacher of the minister Cāmuṇḍarāya, in Southern India, wrote the Gommaṭasāra and other erudite works on the Jaina religion. In the 11th century Śānti Sūri and Devendragaṇin wrote their exhaustive commentaries on the Uttarajjhayaṇa,[2] and the famous Abhayadeva, pupil of Jineśvara, his commentaries on nine Aṅgas. His commentary on the 6th Aṅga was written in 1064 A.D.[3] Maladhāri-Hemacandra Sūri, who wrote

1) H. *Jacobi*, Sanatkumāracaritam, p. xiii.

2) On this commentary, see *Charpentier*, Uttarādhyayana, Introduction, p. 53 ff.

3) He is said to have died in 1075 or 1082 A.D. See *Klatt* in Ind. Ant. 11, 258. There are, however, no less than 6 Jaina authors by the name of Abhayadeva, s. *Peterson*, Report IV, p. iii ff.

commentaries and didactic poems at the beginning of the 12th century, was a pupil of Abhayadeva.

Somewhat later than the last-named, and far more celebrated, is the great H e m a c a n d r a,[1] also called Hemācārya, the pupil of Devacandra. He was one of the most versatile and prolific of writers, and worked in the most varied domains, both as a poet and a scholar. It is due to him that Gujarat became a main stronghold of the Śvetāmbara Jainas and has remained so for centuries, and that Jaina literature flourished so exceedingly there in the 12th and 13th centuries. He was not, however, only the author of Jinistic works, but, in addition, he provided his co-religionists with important text-books on temporal branches of learning (grammar, lexicography, poetics and metrics), so that he was called "the Omniscient of the Kali Age" (Kalikālasarvajña). He was born at Dhundhūka, a town in the neighbourhood of Ahmedabad (Gujarat) in 1089 A.D. as the son of a merchant. His parents were pious Jainas, and in his early childhood he was already destined for the life of a monk. As a Jaina teacher he spent the greater part of his life in the capital of Gujarat. His patron was at first the Caulukya king Jayasiṃha Siddharāja (1094-1143). This king favoured literature and science, and was a devout worshipper of Śiva, but he was so much devoted to philosophy that he called teachers of various sects to his court. Among these teachers was Hemacandra, who, owing to his great erudition, not only attracted the attention of the king, but attempted to win the king's sympathy for the Jaina religion; with a view to achieving this end, he made it his business to emphasize more specially the points of agreement between the Jaina religion and authoritative Brahmanical works. Jayasiṃha's successor was Kumārapāla, who was originally also a devotee of Śiva, but

1) See G. *Bühler*, Ueber das Leben des Jaina-Mönches Hemchandra, des Schülers des Devachandra aus der Vajraśākhā : Denkschriften der Kais. Akademie der Wissenschaften in Wien 1889; also *Jacobi*, ERE VI, 591.

was converted to Jinism by Hemacandra. After his conversion, which is said to have taken place in 1159 A.D., he endeavoured to make Gujarat a model Jaina state. He personally renounced the sport of hunting, and prohibited in his entire realm the slaughter of animals, the eating of meat and the drinking of intoxicants, dice-playing, animal fights and betting. In addition he erected Jaina temples, and favoured the literary and scientific efforts of the Jainas. During the reign of these two kings Jayasiṃha and Kumārapāla, Hemcandra enjoyed a period of intense literary productivity. He died in the year 1172 A.D. at the age of 83 years.

There is scarcely any province of Indian literature in which the Jainas have not been able to hold their own. Above all, they have developed a voluminous narrative literature, they have written epics and novels, they have composed dramas and hymns; sometimes they have written in the simple language of the people, at other times they have competed, in highly elaborate poems, with the best masters of ornate court poetry, and they have also produced important works of scholarship.

The Nijjuttis, which have already received mention, consist of very concise explanations in Āryā-verses and Jaina-Māhārāṣṭrī. They are probably memorial verses which served as an aid to the memory of the teachers in their oral interpretation of the sacred texts. At a later date, these Nijjuttis were extended to form exhaustive commentaries in Prākrit (Bhāṣyas and Curṇis). These in their turn formed the foundation for the Sanskrit commentaries (Ṭīkās, Vṛttis, Avacūrṇis), which were compiled between the 11th and 12th centuries A.D. These various strata of commentaries are often so much intermingled that it is difficult to distinguish them from one another.[1]

---

1) See *Leumann* in ZDMG 46, 1892, 556 ff.

The value of all these commentaries lies in their serving as a depositary of very many ancient, historical or semi-historical traditions on the one hand, and of a great mass of popular narrative themes on the other. Like the Buddhist monks, the Jaina monks, too, delighted at all times in adorning their sermons with the telling of stories, in converting worldly stories into legends of saints, in elucidating Jinistic doctrines by means of "examples," thus exploiting the inborn Indian love for fables in order to win over and retain as many adherents as possible for their religion. As we have seen, a part of these stories had already found a place in some texts of the Canon in the form of legends and ballads. The majority of them is to be found dispersed in great masses throughout the commentary literature which extends down the centuries. The narratives contained even in the later Sanskrit commentaries hark back to earlier sources: evidence for this is provided by the fact that the writers frequently do not tell them in the Sanskrit which would be their natural medium of narration, but in Prākrit, *i.e.*, the language in which the stories had come down to them from their predecessors.[1]

As is the case with the Buddhist Jātakas, this narrative literature imbedded in the Commentaries, contains many popular themes, including some which occur also in other Indian and non-Indian literatures, and form part of the common treasury of universal literature. Much of this kind is already to be found in the narratives of the Nijjuttis.

Thus in the Nijjutti to the Dasaveyāliya we find the story of the fatal purse:

Two poor brothers are returning from a business journey with a purse full of money. On the way, each of them plans to kill the other, so as to

1) An older form of Jaina-Māhārāṣṭrī appears in the Cūrṇis, Kathānakas and Āvaśyaka narratives. Moreover, the language of the verses differs from that of the prose. See H. *Jacobi*, Über das Prakrit in der Erzählungs-Litteratur der Jainas (RSO, Vol. II, Roma 1909, p. 231 ff.).

be the sole possessor of the money. They are, however, ashamed of their intentions, and confess to each other, whereupon they throw the purse into the pond. It is swallowed by a fish, the fish is bought by the sister of the two brothers and the purse found by the maid-servant in the fish's stomach. A quarrel arises between the maid-servant and the woman, in the course of which the woman loses her life.[1]

It is in the same Nijjutti that we find the following humorous dialogue, which also points to the fact that at the period of these old commentaries there must already have been monks of very dubious character.

"O Monk, your cloak has so many folds."
"Yes, it serves me as a net when I catch fish." "You eat fish?"
"I eat them along with my brandy." "You drink sweet brandy?"
"Oh yes, with the harlot." "What, you go to harlots?"
"After I have crushed my enemies." "You have enemies, then?"
"Only those whose houses I rob." "You are a thief, then?"
"Only because of the game of dice." "How, are you a gambler?"
"Am I not, after all, the son of a slave mother?"[2]

The accounts of the schisms, in **Haribhadra**'s commentary on the Āvassaya and **Śānti Sūri**'s commentary on the Uttarajjhayaṇa,[3] are of great interest from the point of view of the history and development of the Indian sects. For instance, when we meet, in one of these accounts, with a wandering monk who has bound a copper wire around his garment, and runs about with the branch of a Jambu-tree,

---

1) *Leumann* in ZDGM 46, p. 602.

2) *Leumann*, loc. cit., p. 607. The story also occurs in the second narrative of Hemavijaya's Kathā-Ratnākara (German translation by Joh. *Hertel*, I, p. 10). A similar Sinhalese-Buddhist dialogue, in J. E. *Seneviratne*, The Life of Kalidas, Colombo 1901, p. 20 f.; in Vallabhadeva's Subhāṣitāvalī 2402; Kṣemendra's Lokaprakāśa (*Weber*, Ind. Stud. 18, 366 f.); *Böhtlingk*, Indische Sprüche, 2. Auflage, Nr. 4588. *Cf.* the story "Ein Wort gibt das andere" in J. P. *Hebel*, Schatzkästlein, Stuttgart, 1888, p. 168 f., and Th. *Zachariae*, Kleine Schriften, Bonn, Leipzig 1920, p. 195 ff.

3) E. *Leumann*, Ind. Stud. 17, 91 ff.; *Charpentier*, Uttarādhyayana-Sūtra, Ed., Introduction, p. 48 ff. *Leumann* edited one part of the Āvaśyaka narratives (mainly after Haribhadra's commentary on the Āvassaya) in AKM X, 2, Leipzig 1897.

offering as a reason for his behaviour, that his garment might burst owing to the fulness of his erudition, and that he has no equal in the whole of the Jambu-continent (*i.e.*, in the whole of India), we are reminded of similar pictures from the lives of Indian sophists in the Upaniṣads and the Buddhist texts.

The commentaries on the Uttarajjhayaṇa are especially remarkable for their wealth of narrative themes.[1] The Nijjutti ascribed to Bhadrabāhu, consisting of nearly 600 verses, is the earliest commentary. The Cūrṇi by an unknown author, is later. The most important commentaries, however, are those by Śānti Sūri and Devendragaṇin. The earlier of the two is Śānti Sūri, who died in about 1040 A.D. In his commentary, entitled Śiṣyahitā, the narratives are only retold in quite a short form: but this work forms the foundation for the Sukhabodhā, completed in the year 1073 A.D. by Devendragaṇin, who tells the stories in leisurely and ambling fashion. There is a Sanskrit recension of the tales from this commentary included in the commentary by Lakṣmīvallabha, the date of whom is not known.

More than the Buddhists, the Jainas were at pains to appropriate to themselves all the favourite popular themes from Brahmanical and general Indian literature, so as to be in a position thus to offer their adherents within the fold of their own religious community, all that they could find elsewhere too. At times they established but a very slight connection between these ancient themes and the Jaina religion: in other cases, however, they completely changed

1) The most interesting tales from these commentaries have been published by H. *Jacobi*, Ausgewählte Erzählungen in Māhārāṣṭrī, Leipzig 1886, and translated into English by J. J. *Meyer*, Hindu Tales, London. 1909. See also *Jacobi*, ZDMG 42, 493 ff., and Appendix to Hemacandra's Pariśiṣṭaparvan, pp. 1-28; J. *Charpentier*, ZDMG 64, 397 ff.; 66, 88 ff.; 67, 668 ff. The legend of the saint Pārśva, the 23rd Tīrthakara, has been edited and translated by *Charpentier*, from Devendragaṇin's Commentary, in ZDMG 69, 1915, 321-359.

and spoilt them, in order to give them a Jinistic appearance. At all events, many a gem of the narrative art of ancient India has come down to us by way of the Jaina commentary and narrative literature, which would otherwise have been consigned to oblivion, and in other cases the Jainas have preserved interesting versions of numerous legends and tales which are known from other sources also.

For instance the Jainas incorporated the Kṛṣṇa-cult into their religion at a very early period, and consequently also interwove the Kṛṣṇa-legend with their own treasury of legends. As early as in the eighth Aṅga we met with a Jinistic form of the legend of the destruction of the city of Dvāravatī and the death of Kṛṣṇa. This is told in greater detail in Devendra's commentary on the Uttarajjhayaṇa.[1]. It is in the same commentary that we find the ancient legend of the descent of Gaṅgā and the destruction of the sixty thousand sons of Sagara,[2] which is familiar to us from the epics. The great attractiveness of this epic legend for the Jaina narrator lay in the fact that the death of the sons was such a convenient peg on which to hang consolatory speeches, with pious thoughts as to the transitoriness of all earthly things. Moreover, their death is justified by Karman in the Jinistic sense. This is also used as an opportunity to introduce a Consolatory Story, which is but a variant of the Buddhist legend of Kisā-Gotamī and the mustard-seed.[3] The Paccekа-Buddha stories, which Devendra tells as a connected whole in his commentary, show points of contact

---

[1]) See above, p. 470, note 1; *Jacobi* in OC VII, Wien, 1886, Berichte, p. 75 ff.; ZDMG 42, 1888, 493 ff. and E. *Hardy*, ZDMG 53, 1899, 41 ff.

[2]) R. *Fick*, Eine jainistische Bearbeitung der Sagara-Sage. Diss. Kiel 1888. A. *Holtzmann*, Indische Sagen (Nr. VI : "Dass Meer") has treated the legend according to the Mahābhārata (III, 100-109). On the same legend in the Rāmāyaṇa, see above I, p. 480.

[3]) See above, p. 198 f.

with Buddhist literature. In the story of the fourth of these royal saints, namely King Naggaï, the story of Kaṇayamañjarī is inserted, who has been regarded as the prototype of Sheherezade.[1] One of the most charming romances which Devendra has preserved for posterity, is that of Mūladeva, the Jack of all trades, and the courtesan Devadattā.[2] Connected with Mūladeva, who, by the way, seems really to have lived and to have been the author of a Kāma-Śāstra,[3] there is also the interesting robber tale of Maṇḍiya, who excites the pity of the people as a beggar by day, whilst he reduces the city to a state of terror as a murderous robber and burglar by night. Another robber tale is the prose narrative of Agaladatta, of which, however, a far more beautiful, and undoubtedly earlier poetic setting has come down to us in Devendra's commentary.[4]

Many interesting tales are also to be found in Haribhadra's commentaries. In the Āvaśyaka narratives, for instance, we meet with the pretty legend of Vāsudeva, who sees only the good in all things:

A deity transforms himself into the carcass of a dog, with beautiful teeth, lying by the roadside. All the passers-by draw back, disgusted at the stench of the carcass. Then Vāsudeva comes along, gazes calmly at the carcass, and exclaims: "How gloriously this dog's teeth gleam!"[5]

---

1) See P. E. *Pavolini* in GSAI 12, 159 ff. *Charpentier*, Paccekabuddha-Geschichten, p. 146 ff., and J. J. *Meyer*, Two Twice-Told Tales, Chicago (Decennial Publications), 1903. The text according to Bhāvavijaya's Commentary on the Uttarajjhayaṇa is given by *Charpentier* (JA 1911, s. 10, t. XVIII, 201-255). The story of Kaṇayamañjarī is also translated into German by Hertel, Indische Märchen, Jena 1919, p. 271 ff.

2) Translated by *Charpentier*, Paccekabuddhageschichten, p. 62 ff.

3) See *Charpentier*, loc. cit., p. 57 ff.; P. E. *Pavolini*, GSAI 9, 175 ff. and M. *Bloomfield*, The Character and Adventures of Mūladeva: Proceedings of the American Philosophical Society, Vol. 52, 1913, 616-650.

4) Transl. into German verse by J. J. *Meyer*, Kāvyasaṃgraha, p. 72 ff. Italian transl. by A. Ballini, Agaḍadatta, Firenze 1903.

5) J. J. *Meyer*, Hindu Tales, p. 88, note 1. According to K. *Seidenstücker* ("Der Buddhist," 2, 1910, 456 f., quoted by *Günter*, Buddha, p. 86 f.) the legend of the dog's carcass is Buddhist, as it is told in the Commentary on the Udāna-Varga. The same

The Jainas did not rest content with adopting popular epic themes such as the Kṛṣṇa-legend, the legend of Draupadī, and others, into their sacred writings and the commentaries on them, but they also created poems of their own, which were to serve their adherents as a complete substitute for the great epics Rāmāyaṇa and Mahābhārata. The earliest poem of this kind is the Prākrit epic P a ü m a c a r i y a (Padma-Carita)[1] by the poet V i m a l a S ū r i, which was written, according to the data given by the poet himself (CXVIII, 103), 530 years after the demise of Mahāvīra. It is written in pure Jaina-Māhārāṣṭrī and in the Āryā metre, which is the real metre of Prākrit poetry. The "Life of Padma"—Padma is the name of Rāma in the poem, though the name Rāma also occurs frequently enough—is told in 118 cantos,[2] which are only in partial agreement with the Rāmāyaṇa. It is no part of the author's intention to follow Vālmīki, whom indeed he puts down as a liar, but he wants to tell the story of Rāma in such a way as to fit in with the "history of the world" according to Jinistic tradition, and as it was communicated by Goyama (Gautama), the principal pupil of Mahāvīra, to King Seṇiya (Bimbisāra) in accordance with Mahāvīra's own instructions. As the author says (CXVIII, 118), there is much that he already found in the Pūrvas.

---

legend, in which Jesus plays the part of Vāsudeva, has been retold by *Goethe* (in the "Noten und Abhandlungen zum besseren Verständnis des westöstlichen Diwans") after the Persian poet *Nisami*. The story of Śatānīka and Pradyota from Haribhadra's Commentary on the Āvaśyakas, is given by *Hertel*, Jinakīrtis "Geschichte von Pāla und Gopāla," p. 98 ff. The text of the stories of the former existences of Jina Ṛṣabha after Haribhadra's Commentary on the Āvaśyaka-Niryukti (AUS, Bombay 1916) reprinted in Jaina Jātakas, ed. by Banarsi das *Jain*, Lahore 1925, p. xix ff.

1) Edited by H. *Jacobi*, Bavnagar 1914. The fact that I am in a position to give more detailed information regarding this work is due to the courtesy of my friend Prof. *Leumann*, who kindly placed the manuscript of his abridged translation of Cantos I-XXXI at my disposal, and also gave me valuable information by letter.

2) In the colophons of I-XXXV they are called uddesa (uddeśa), and after that, pevvam (parvan).

Canto I contains a table of contents. In the Introduction (Canto II) the following is related :

It was in the days when King Seṇiya, *i.e.*, Śreṇika Bimbisāra, reigned in the Magadha city of Rājapura. Now in the city of Kuṇḍagrāma the Jina Mahāvīra was born as the son of Prince Siddhārtha and his consort Triśalā; at the age of 30 years he left his home, and attained to perfect knowledge. Once Mahāvīra preached a sermon upon souls and transmigration, on the Vipula hill in the presence of gods, men and animals. Among those present was king Seṇiya. When the latter had returned home, he dreamed about the Jina, and the next morning he made the following reflection :

" How is it possible that the demon heroes in all their mighty strength were defeated by the monkeys? And the demons with Rāvaṇa at their head, who, according to the Jaina faith, were certainly of noble descent, are said to have eaten meat! Then again it is said that, in spite of all the disturbances, Rāvaṇa's brother Kumbhakarṇa slept for half a year, and then after his awakening, devoured elephants, etc., whereupon he again slumbered for half a year. Then again Indra, though he rules over gods and men, is said to have been taken captive to Laṅkā by Rāvaṇa! At that rate we might as well affirm that the lion is overcome by the gazelle, the elephant by the dog. These Rāmāyaṇa stories are most certainly lies." [1]

In order to obtain enlightenment on these matters, the king with his retinue repairs to Goyama, and requests him to instruct him correctly regarding the life of Padma, as it seemed to him that the absurdities which are related regarding Rāma, Rāvaṇa and others, were not worthy of belief. Goyama declares his willingness to impart to the king that which Mahāvīra himself proclaimed, for " that which bad poets relate about Rāvaṇa, is indeed lies, I shall instruct you first as to place and time, and then as to the lives of the great men " (III, 14-17).

The narrative begins (III, 18) as in a Purāṇa,[2] with a description of the universe and the history of Ṛṣabha, the first Jina, who lived in the

---

1) After *Leumann's* rendering of II, 99-119. In the following extracts, too, for the portions given in quotation marks Professor *Leumann's* German translation has been freely used.

2) The work calls itself a " Purāṇa " in the Introduction (I, 32) and at the end (CXVIII, 111).

Kṛta age, when there were only three castes, Kṣatriyas, Vaiśyas and Śūdras. The origin of the Vidyādharas, "holders of spells," a kind of demigods, is related (III, 144 ff.; *cf.* V, 13 ff.), also the origin of the Brahmins (IV, 64 ff.), of the Ikṣvāku dynasty and the dynasty of the moon (V, 1 ff.). Then comes the history of the second Jina with all manner of preliminary stories (V, 48 ff.).

The story of the "race of monkeys" is told in Canto VI. On the monkey island there is the city of Kiṣkindhāpura. The "monkeys" are in reality a race of Vidyādharas, which is so-called, because it has monkeys by way of a badge on the arches of gates, banners, and the like. Canto VII treats of Indra, of the guardians of the universe Soma, Varuṇa, Kubera and Yama, the Asuras, Yakṣas etc., Vaiśramaṇa (who is distinct from Kubera) and the birth of Rāvaṇa, his sister Candramukhā and his brothers Bhānukarṇa and Vibhīṣaṇa. Rāvaṇa and his brothers acquire enormous magic powers by virtue of asceticism. The Rākṣasas, whose prince Rāvaṇa is, are not man-eating demons, however, but adherents of the race of the Vidyādharas. Rāvaṇa's mother hangs around his neck a wondrous string of pearls, in which his face is reflected nine times, hence his epithet of Daśamukha, "the man with ten faces" (VII, 95 f.).[1] The succeeding cantos tell of all manner of heroic deeds of Rāvaṇa. This Rāvaṇa is a great devotee of the Jinas; he restores ruined Jina shrines, and establishes the Jina faith (XI, 1 ff.).

In Canto XI Goyama replies to the king's question as to how the sacrifice of animals originated. A Brahmin had a son Parvata and a pupil Nārada. Owing to blameworthy ascetic practices, Parvata was born again as a Rākṣasa, and in the guise of a Brahmin he introduced animal sacrifices. Nārada, however, who is a pious Jaina, declares that these sacrificial acts should be interpreted in the spiritual sense: "The sacrificial animals which are to be killed, are the passions, the sacrificial fee which is to be paid, is truth, forbearance and non-violence, the blessing (to be expected) is (not heaven, but) Nirvāṇa; those, however, who really slaughter sacrificial animals, go to hell like hunters." (XI, 75-81).

---

1) This is obviously a realistic explanation of the epithet of Rāvaṇa, who in Rāmāyaṇa, III, 9 f., is a ten-headed monster, and is therefore called Daśagrīva or Daśānana. See Chintāharan *Chakravarti* in Ind. Hist. Qu. 1, 1925, 779 ff. G. *Ramadas* (Ind. Hist. Qu. 5, 1929, 281 ff.) has shown that in many passages in the Rāmāyaṇa Rāvaṇa has only *one* head and *one* face. The interpretation of the "monkeys" as Vidyādharas with monkeys on their banner, is also realistic.

Cantos XII and XIII tell of a fight between Rāvaṇa and the god Indra. Indra is defeated and is brought in triumph to Laṅkā, but is then released. The reason for his humiliation is that in a previous incarnation he had molested a monk. Indra places his son on the throne, becomes a monk, and attains to bliss. Rāvaṇa visits shrines on the Meru hill, where the gods are just paying homage to Anantavīrya, who has attained to perfect knowledge, and he hears the sermon of the latter upon Karman, generosity, the duties of monks and the duties of laymen (XIV). This sermon is also responsible for the conversion of Hanumant, whose descent and whose fights as the ally of Rāvaṇa, are related in Cantos XV and XIX. Through Rāvaṇa Hanumant receives a thousand wives. Canto XX treats of the Jinas, the rulers of the world, the Baladevas and the Vasudevas. It is not until Canto XXI that King Janaka is mentioned, and the story of Daśaratha and the actual Rāma epic begins: it is only in its main features that this story agrees with Vālmīki's Rāmāyaṇa: as regards the details there are many divergences.

Daśaratha is presented by each of his wives Aparājitā and Sumitrā with a son, whose birth has been announced by three lucky dreams. The first is named Padma,[1] and the second Lakṣmaṇa: his sons Bharata and Śatrughna are born to him by Kaikeyī (XXV, 1-13).

Whereas the heroes of the Rāmāyaṇa move in an entirely Brahmanical atmosphere, in the Paüma-Cariya the religion of the Jina is everywhere very much to the fore. The kings are generally pious laymen, who retire from the world in their old age, and become Jaina monks. As in all narrative poems of the Jainas, the preliminary stories, *i. e.*, the stories of the previous existences of the heroes, are told with a great wealth of detail. Daśaratha takes up the reins of government, because his elder brother Anantaratha has become a monk (XXII, 100-105). A festival in the Jaina temple is described (XXIX, 1-18) at which King Daśaratha with his sons performs the ablution of the Jina images, and after an eight days' fast worships the Jinas. After the ablution he sends the water to his wives, and the young women, the daughters-in-law, pour it over the heads of their mothers-in-law. Now the principal wife did not receive the water which was intended for her, and feels herself slighted, so that she wishes to hang herself. The king, however, surprises

---

[1]) It is noteworthy that it is only Rāma who has received another name, whilst the other names remain unchanged.

her. While she is explaining things to him, the chamberlain comes with the water, and pours it over her head, whereupon she calms down. But the king reproaches the chamberlain with his thoughtlessness, whereupon the latter excuses himself on the ground of old age :

" The body goes slowly like an old cart,
The eyes are short-sighted like bad friends,
The ears are deaf like bad sons,
The teeth have fallen out like spokes out of the wheel,
The hands find it difficult to grasp, like elephants taking a bite,
The legs are unreliable like bad women ;
Only the crutch is like the beloved of the heart."

These words are a warning for the king, intimating that he, too, is ripe to say farewell to worldly things.

There are, however, also many divergences in the epic, which have no connection with the Jaina faith. Sītā does not come forth out of the earth, as in the Rāmāyaṇa, but is born in a natural way by Videhā, the wife of King Janaka. Sītā is betrothed by Janaka to Padma (Rāma) because the latter has aided him in the fight against the Mlecchas of Ardhabarbara (the land of the semi-barbarians) and has distinguished himself. The story of the bending of the bow is told differently. The bow is brought by the Vidyādharas, who insist upon Sītā's being given in marriage to the Vidyādhara prince Candragati ; but at the self-choice of a husband arranged by Janaka, Rāma is the only man who succeeds in bending the bow.

Daśaratha wishes to become a monk and to entrust Padma-Rāma with the responsibility of governing. Bharata, too, desires to withdraw from the world, but is persuaded by Kaikeyī and Padma to take over the reins of government. He makes a vow, however, in the presence of the Jaina monk Dyuti, to renounce the world as soon as Padma returns home, and he governs as a pious Jaina layman, without giving himself up to pleasure. The main story—the stealing of Sītā, the sending of Hanumant, the fights with Rāvaṇa and his defeat, the bringing home of Sītā, the discontent of the people, the banishment of Sītā, and the lamentations of Padma, the birth of Kuśa and Lava—is ever and again interrupted by incidental stories (upākhyāna). Finally Padma attains to perfect knowledge, and enters Nirvāṇa.

Vimala's work probably served as a model for all the later adaptations of the Rāma legend among the Jainas. In the year 678 A.D. Raviṣeṇa wrote his Padma-Purāṇa,[1] which is merely a slightly extended recension of the Paüma-Cariya in Sanskrit, agreeing with it in all essential points. The Sanskrit epic, too, begins with a description of the world, especially the world of the Vidyādharas, and a glorification of the first Tīrthakara Ṛṣabha. Here, too, the "monkeys" are Vidyādharas, who have the picture of a monkey emblazoned on their banner.[2] As in the Paüma-Cariya, Parvan XX treats of the Tīrthakaras, and the actual story does not begin until Parvan XXI, with Daśaratha. Here, too, Padma is the name given to Rāma, and Kuśa and Lava are called Lavaṇa and Aṅkuśa etc.[3] It goes without saying that, in a Jaina poem sermons are also inserted, *e. g.*, XXVI, 54 ff., on the dreadful consequences of killing and of the eating of flesh, with a description of hells appended.

Later adaptations of the Rāma legend are to be found in Parvan 68 of the Uttara-Purāṇa and in Hemacandra's Triṣaṣṭiśalākā-Puruṣa-Caritra, Parvan 7 of which is also called "Jaina-Rāmāyaṇa."[4] Hemacandra, too, begins with the stories of the Rākṣasas and monkeys, and depicts Rāvaṇa as a great and mighty ascetic. It is not until Sarga IV that the

1) Edited by Pandit Darbārī Lāla *Nyāyatīrtha Sāhityaratna* in MDJG Nos. 29-31, 1928. See *Bhandarkar*, Report 1883-84, pp. 117 f., 417 ff., and Hiralal, Catalogue, p. xxi. Chintaharan *Chakravarti* has given a synopsis of the contents in the Bengali language: on this see Batakrishna *Ghosh* in Ind. Hist. Qu. 5, 1929, 157 ff.

2) VI, 1. 215.

3) 123 Parvans in the edition of the Padma-Purāṇa correspond to the 118 sections of the Paüma-Cariya. How exactly Raviṣeṇa follows Vimala is shown, for instance, in Padma-Purāṇa I, 43 f., where the 7 objects of the "Purāṇa" are enumerated in almost literal agreement with Paüma-Cariya I, 32 f. It is very desirable, however, that a careful comparison of all the Jinistic adaptations of the Rāma legend be made.

4) It has been printed in India as "Hemacandra's Rāmacaritra" or "Jaina-Rāmāyaṇa," thus in Poona 1890. On this, see D. Ch. *Sen*, The Bengali Ramayanas, Calcutta 1920, p. 26 ff., and above, I, p. 514, Note 1. For the various versions of the Rāma legend in which Sītā is the daughter of Rāvaṇa, see also W. *Stutterheim*, Rāma-Legenden und Rāma-Reliefs in Indonesien, München 1925, p. 92 f.

story of Rāma, Lakṣmaṇa and Sītā begins, and this ends in the last Sarga (X) with Rāma's entrance into Nirvāṇa. In the year 1596 A.D. Devavijayagaṇin, a pupil of Rājavijaya Sūri, wrote a Rāma-Caritra in prose. The author himself says that he is following Hemacandra's "Rāmāyaṇa." [1]

The Mahābhārata also has repeatedly been adapted by the Jainas. The earliest work of this nature which has come down to us, is the Harivaṃśa-Purāṇa [2] in 66 Sargas by Jinasena, who himself mentions in the concluding verses, that he completed his work in the year 705 of the Saka era, *i.e.*, 783 A.D. In this Purāṇa not only are the legends of Kṛṣṇa and Balarāma told in a Jinistic setting, but Gautama, the pupil of Mahāvīra, is made the narrator of the story, and in many places sermons on the Jaina doctrine are inserted. The legend of Ṛṣabha, the first Jina, is told by way of introduction, and, connected with the story of Kṛṣṇa, we have the legend of Ariṣṭanemi or Nemi, Kṛṣṇa's cousin. Nemi is the 22nd Jina, and wanders around the world preaching. The story of the Kauravas and Pāṇḍavas and the descendants of Kṛṣṇa and Balarāma is also told. The Kauravas and Karṇa are converted to the Jaina religion. Finally the Pāṇḍavas also become ascetics, and like Nemi, attain to Nirvāṇa.

1) See *Bhandarkar*, Report 1882-83, pp. 94, 229. Rajendralala *Mitra*, Notices of Sanskrit MSS., VI, 1882, p. 70 ff. tells of a Puṇyacandrodaya-Purāṇa by Kṛṣṇadāsa, which similarly treats the subject-matter of the Rāmāyaṇa. A Jaina-Rāmāyaṇa in the Kanarese language is said to have been written in the 12th century, see *Guérinot*, p. 270.

2) Edited by Paṇḍit Darbārī Lāla *Nyāyatīrtha Sāhityaratna* in MDJG, 32 and 33. The complete title is Bṛhad-Harivaṃśa-Purāṇa or Ariṣṭanemipurāṇasaṃgraha-Harivaṃśa. An analysis of the work is given by Rajendralala *Mitra*, Notices of Sanskrit MSS., Vol. VI, 1882, pp. 74-97. See *Peterson*, Report IV, 167 ff.; *Leumann* in WZKM 11, 1897, p. 307; *Hiralal*, Catalogue, pp. xxii, 688, 715. On the dates given in the Praśasti, see *Peterson*, Report IV, p. 176; *Bhandarkar*, Early History of the Dekkan, 2nd ed., p 65; *Hoernle* in JRAS 1904, p. 644; K. B. *Pathak* in Ind. Ant. 15, 141 ff.; *Fleet* in Ep. Ind., VI, 195 ff.

Another Harivaṃśa in 39 Sargas was written by Sakalakīrti and his pupil Jinadāsa in the 15th century.[1] Among his predecessors Jinadāsa mentions Raviṣeṇa and Jinasena Ācārya, and he honours Bhadrabāhu, Kundakunda along with other Munis and his teacher Sakalakīrti, who is praised in the concluding verses as the "ornament of the Kundakunda race."

In about 1200 A.D. the Maladhārin Devaprabha Sūri wrote a Pāṇḍava-Carita[2] in 18 Sargas, in which the contents of the 18 Parvans of the Mahābhārata are given in a concise form, though remodelled in many of its details. The lengthy Sarga 6 contains the story of the game of dice, and the Nala episode—it is here called "story of Nala and Kūbara," the latter being the name of Nala's brother—is related by Vidura as a warning example. Sarga 16 tells the legend of the Jina Ariṣṭanemi in connection with the Pāṇḍava legend, and Sarga 18 relates how Baladeva reaches heaven and Ariṣṭanemi and the Pāṇḍavas enter Nirvāṇa. A Pāṇḍava-Purāṇa,[3] which is also known as "Jaina-Mahābhārata," was written by Śubhacandra in 1551 A.D. In the opening verses the author

1) The first 14 Sargas were written by Sakalakīrti, the rest by Jinadāsa. See *Bhandarkar*, Report 1883-84, pp. 123 and 433 f.; *Leumann* in WZKM 11, 1897, 312; *Hiralal*, Catalogue, p. 715 f. In Bhandarkar's MS. only Jinadāsa is mentioned as the author. Sakalakīrti lived in about 1464 A.D., and Jinadāsa therefore in the second half of the 15th century. *Hiralal*, Catalogue, pp. 715 f., 760 ff., 768, also mentions Harivaṃśa-Purāṇas by Raviṣeṇa, Śrībhūṣaṇa, Dharmakīrti and Rāmacandra. Besides these Sanskrit epics there is a Harivaṃśa-Purāṇa in the Apabhraṃśa language, which was written by the poet Dhavala in the 10th or 11th century. See *Hiralal*, Catalogue, pp. xlviii f., 716, 762 ff.

2) Published in Km. 93, Bombay 1911. Earlier editions appeared in the Jaina-Śāstra-Kathāsaṃgraha and the Caritra-Saṃgraha in Ahmedabad in 1884. See *Peterson*, 3 Reports, Appendix 1, 131-134. Devaprabha is a pupil of Municandra Sūri, whose teacher was Candra Sūri, who wrote a commentary on the Āvaśyaka-Sūtra in the year 1165 A.D.; s. *Peterson*, Report IV, pp. xxvii f., lii.

3) See *Peterson*, Report IV, 156 ff.; *Leumann* in WZKM 11, 1897, p. 306. There is also a Pāṇḍava-Purāṇa in 18 Sargas by Vādicandra, s. *Leumann*, l. c. It would certainly be worth while to compare the various Jaina versions of the Mahābhārata carefully with one another and with the old epic.

does honour to the teachers Kundakunda, Samantabhadra, Pūjyapāda, Akalaṅka, Jinasena and Guṇabhadra. Devaprabha's epic was done into prose with inserted verses in 1603 A.D. by Devavijaya Gaṇin, pupil of Rājavijaya Sūri.[1] Among the verses many have been taken literally from Devaprabha's work, whilst many others belong to the gnomic poetry and are known from other sources.[2]

It is, however, the biographies of the 63 "Great Men," [3] that is to say the 24 Tīrthakaras, and their contemporaries, the 12 Cakravartins or rulers of the world, and the 27 heroes (9 Baladevas, 9 Vāsudevas and 9 Prativāsudevas) of antiquity, which constitute the favourite substitute, most popular among the Jainas, both for the heroic epics and for the Brahmanical Purāṇas. These works are usually called "Purāṇas" by the Digambaras, whilst among the Śvetāmbaras they go by the name of "Caritras." Among the earliest of these works is the Triṣaṣṭilakṣaṇa-Mahā-Purāṇa,[4] "the Great Purāṇa of 63 Excellent Men," also named briefly Mahā-Purāṇa,[5] by Jinasena and Guṇabhadra, containing the biographies of all of the 63 men. It consists of the Ādi-Purāṇa in 47 chapters, of which 42 are written by Jinasena and the last 5 by his pupil Guṇabhadra, and the Uttara-Purāṇa, which is exclusively from the pen of Guṇabhadra. The Ādi-Purāṇa,

1) Edited by Haragovind *Das* and Bechar *Das* in YJG Benares V. E. 2438 (1911).

2) Thus for instance, there is on p. 133 the well-known verse from the Pañcatantra: "One should not act rashly, one should act after mature reflection, otherwise repentance will follow, as in the case of the wife of the Brahman because of the ichneumon."

3) See *Glasenapp*, Der Jainismus, p. 247 ff. The earlier tradition in the Samavāyaṃga 54 and in Śīlācārya knows only 54 "excellent men" (uttamapurisa), as it does not count the Prativāsudevas especially. *Cf.* Banarsi Das *Jain*, Jaina Jātakas, p. II.

4) A survey of the contents and the position of the work in Jaina literature is given by *Glasenapp* in Festgabe Jacobi, p. 331 ff., based on the edition of the text by Pandit Lālārām *Jain* in the Syādvādagranthamālā with a Hindī translation Indore, Vik. S. 1973 and 1975. See *Bhandarkar*, Report 1883-84, pp. 118 ff., 422 ff.; *Hiralal*, Catalogue, p. xxii ff.

5) There is, however, also a "Mahā-Purāṇa" by Malliṣeṇa, written in 1047 A.D.; s. K. B. *Pathak*. Ind. Ant. 40, 1911, 46 ff.

or the "first Purāṇa," contains the story of Ṛṣabha, the first Tīrthakara, and of the first Cakravartin, whilst the Uttara-Purāṇa contains the life-stories of all the remaining "Great Men." The work does not, however, consist only of these life-stories of saints and heroes, and the episodes interwoven with them (stories from former incarnations of the principal personages, stories about their contemporaries, etc.), but in the true manner of the Brahmanical Purāṇas, this "Great Purāṇa," too, is at the same time an epic poem, which claims to give a "history of the world," and presents at the same time an encyclopædia of all that is edifying to the pious Jaina and that is worthy of his knowledge. Thus, for instance, in the Ādi-Purāṇa (38-40) the Saṃskāras, the "consecrations," which accompany the life of the individual from his conception until his death, are described in fair agreement with the corresponding Brahmanical rites. Chapter 41 treats of the interpretation of dreams. A short treatise on town planning is to be found in Chapter 16, a treatise on the duties of the warrior and the art of governing (Nīti) in Chapter 42. On the other hand, there are, in various places, hymns of considerable poetical value.

Like the Paüma-Cariya, the Maha-Purāṇa, too, traces its origin back to Mahāvīra himself, who communicated its contents to Gautama, who in his turn imparted them to King Sreṇika. The knowledge of the sacred legends is said to have been transmitted by Gautama to those versed in the Aṅgas and Pūrvas, and in several passages the Aṅgas are cited as an authority. The real source of the work is, however, the Prathamānuyoga, that is, the third part of the Dṛṣṭivāda, which has gone astray, though we do not know how far the legends of the Mahā-Purāṇa agree with those of the original Dṛṣṭivāda.[1]

---

[1] *Glasenapp*, Festgabe Jacobi, p. 336 ff., points out numerous divergences of the Mahā-Purāṇa both from the tradition of the Śvetāmbaras and from other Digambara traditions.

The authors of the Mahā-Purāṇa took pains to obliterate the difference between Jinism and the older religion as far as possible by retaining the names of the saints and heroes, by the use of Brahmanical terms and even by the adoption of Brahmanical rites. The underlying tendency in all this was to cause Brahmanism and Hinduism to appear as merely a decayed form of the true faith, namely the Jaina religion, which had existed from time immemorial.[1]

We have fairly accurate information regarding the time when the Mahā-Purāṇa was written.[2] It is stated at the end of the work that it was consecrated on the 23rd June, 897 A.D. during the reign of the Rāṣṭrakūṭa-king Kṛṣṇa II Akālavarṣa by Guṇabhadra's pupil Lokasena. Jinasena, the author of the Ādi-Purāṇa, was a pupil of Vīrasena, and was highly honoured by King Amoghavarṣa I, who reigned from 815 to 877 A.D. According to this, then, the work was undoubtedly composed in the 9th century. Jinasena, the author of the Ādi-Purāṇa, is not, however, identical with Jinasena, the author of the Harivaṃśa-Purāṇa.[3] An allusion to Guṇāḍhya's Bṛhatkathā in the Ādi-Purāṇa, is worthy of notice.[4]

One of the favourite stories in the Uttara-Purāṇa is that of Jīvandhara, which has also been treated several times by later poets both in Sanskrit and in Tamil. By way of a

---

1) See *Glasenapp, loc. cit.*, p. 339 ff.

2) Through the Praśasti at the end of the Uttara-Purāṇa. See *Bhandarkar, loc. cit.*, and Early History of the Dekkan, p. 69 f.

3) In the Maṅgala of the Harivaṃśa (quoted by *Hiralal*, Catalogue, p. xxii) Raviṣeṇa, Kumārasena, Vīrasena and Jinasena are mentioned with praise. The teacher of this Jinasena is Kīrtisena of Punnāṭa Gaṇa. According to this, Jinasena, the pupil of Vīrasena, and author of the Ādi-Purāṇa, would have lived before the Jinasena of the Harivaṃśa, that means before 783 A.D., which is scarcely possible. Unless there is some mistake, we must assume that there were teachers named Vīrasena and Jinasena both before and after the author of the Harivaṃśa. The name Jinasena frequently occurs as the name of an author; s. *Hiralal*, Catalogue, pp. xxiii, 644, 651, 707.

4) I, 115. See A. *Venkatasubbiah* in Ind. Hist. Qu. 5, 1929, 31 ff., and Kamta Prasad *Jain*, *ibid*, p. 547 ff.

specimen, we here give the contents of this legend, which is told in Chapter 75.[1]

Queen Vijayā, the consort of King Satyandhara of Rājapura, is warned in dreams that she is about to be visited by both joy and sorrow. Soon afterwards a being from the heavenly world of the gods descends into the womb of the queen, "just as a beautiful flamingo would descend upon a pleasant lake covered with autumnal lotus-flowers." Soon after this, the king is bereft of his throne, and killed by his treacherous minister Kāṣṭhāṅgāraka.[2] The queen, protected by a friendly female elf (Yakṣī) gives birth to a son on a cremation-ground, "as the sky brings forth the moon." The Yakṣī, who places jewel-lamps (*i.e.*, shining jewels used as lamps) around the newly-born child (to protect it from evil demons) consoles the queen in her grief with a speech on the transitoriness of all things and the destinies brought about by deeds in former births. The merchant Gandhotkaṭa, to whom it had been prophesied by an ascetic that he will have a long-lived son if he exposed his newly-born child, who would die just after birth, comes along, and hears the voice of the boy born by Vijayā. He exclaims "Jīva, jīva" ("live, live") for which reason the boy receives the name Jīvandhara. When the queen recognised Gandhotkaṭa, she entrusted her child to him, begging him to take care of the boy. The merchant takes the child to his wife Nandā, who considers it as her own. Vijayā was taken by the Yakṣī to a hermitage of ascetics, and lived there in secret, consoled by the Yakṣī with stories and pious instructions concerning the religion of the Jina. Two younger wives of King Satyandhara, and the wives of the four most faithful followers of the king, also bear sons, who are all brought up together by Gandhotkaṭa, and Nandā also bears another son Nandāḍhya, who grows up with the seven boys. As he advances in years, Jīvandhara evinces exceptional wisdom. For instance he weeps, as children do, because his food was too hot. When the ascetic who is present, admonishes him, telling him that a sensible child should not weep, the boy replies, asking him whether he is not aware that weeping has the following advantages: The mucus collected in the body flows out, the eyes become clear, and the food becomes thoroughly cooled. The ascetic, who

---

1) After E. *Hultzsch*, The Story of Jīvandhara, in Quarterly Journal of the Mythic Society 12, 1922, 317-318. The text of this Jīvandhara-Caritra is edited by T. S. *Kuppusvami Sāstrī*, Tanjore 1907 (Sarasvativilasa Series 11).

2) *I.e.* "charcoal-burner," probably an allusion to the man's former occupation.

had formerly been a king, becomes the teacher of Jīvandhara and the other boys.

In consequence of his good deeds in previous incarnations, Jīvandhara, after he has attained to manhood, wins eight beautiful women as his wives one after another. The Vidyādhara prince Garuḍavega wishes to marry his charming daughter Gandharvadattā, a pious devotee of the Jinas. He arranges a self-choice. The princess appears in the hall which has been erected for this purpose, with a lute, on which she plays beautifully, accompanying the music by song. Jīvandhara steps into the hall to take part in a musical contest. However, he returns as being unsuitable the lutes which are handed to him, and asks whether he may have the princess's lute. She hands it to him, and he now plays and sings far more beautifully, whereupon she hands him the wreath and selects him as her husband.

Jīvandhara gives further proof of exceptional wisdom and bravery. He decides the quarrel between two maidens, Suramañjarī and Guṇamālā, as to the goodness of their perfumes, by scattering the powders, whereupon it is seen that the bees swarm to the more sweetly scented powder, that of Suramañjarī. He also tames a furious elephant. On this occasion Suramañjarī falls in love with the prince, and he accepts her as his second wife. He rescues a dog, which is being persecuted by bad boys, from its tormentors. The dog remembers its former incarnation, and transforms itself into a Yakṣa, who thenceforth becomes a faithful friend to the prince; he also gives him a ring, by the aid of which he can assume any kind of form he desires. Padmottamā, the daughter of King Dharmapati, is bitten by a poisonous snake. The king promises his daughter to the man who will cure her of the snake's poison. Jīvandhara alone is able to do this with the help of his Yakṣa friend, and he wins this princess, too, as his wife. A few days later he comes to a lovely grove, where he worships in a Jaina temple. All of a sudden a Campaka tree begins to burst forth in red blossoms, the cuckoos begin to sing charmingly, the pond by the temple fills itself with limpid water, the water-lilies open, bees approach in swarms, and the doors of the Jaina temple fly open of their own accord. Now it had been prophesied that the merchant Subhadra should give his daughter Kṣemasundarī in marriage to the man at whose coming all these miracles should take place. So Kṣemasundarī, too, became the wife of Jīvandhara. He wins a fifth wife, Hemābhā, owing to his skill in archery. Princess Śrīcandrā observes a pair of doves enjoying themselves and falls into a swoon, for she remembers that she had been a dove ina previous existence and had lost her husband. After a long search, and with the assistance of Jīvandhara, the former husband of the princess is found in the person of Nandāḍhya, Jīvandhara's half-brother, who is again married to her. Jīvandhara stays away from his family for 16 years, because in a former birth he had separated the young one of a flamingo from its parents for 16 months. At last comes the reunion with his mother, which is described very touchingly. She enlightens him regarding the fact that he is the son of King Satyandhara who was killed, and asks him to seize the reins of government. He promises to do this when the right moment shall have come.

By the aid of his magic ring he comes to Rājapura as a merchant. There the merchant Sagaradatta gives him his daughter in marriage, as he was her destined husband according to prophesy on the part of the astrologers. Disguised as an old and wandering Brahman ascetic, he comes one day into the audience hall of Kāṣṭhāṅgāraka and is entertained by him. After leaving the hall, he offers the princes a powder which has the power to make people docile to one's wishes. The princes laugh, and say he should make the maiden Guṇamālā, who has become a man-hater since Jīvandhara declared her perfume to be inferior, docile. He boasts that he will win Guṇamālā. He goes to her and announces his arrival. She asks: "Whence have you come, and whither are you going"? He replies: "I have come afterwards, I shall go again before." As the waiting-maids laugh at this reply, he says: "Do not laugh, old age brings perversity in its train; will this not be your lot also?" Guṇamālā asks again: "Whither are you going?" He answers: "I shall go so long, until I reach a worthy maiden." When she heard this, she said jokingly: "He is old in body and in years, but not in his heart," gave him a place of honour, ate with him and said: "Now go quickly where you want to go." He praised her, and said: "You have said well, my dear one," rose with an effort, supported by his stick, and sat down upon her couch, as if she had said that he was to do this. When the waiting-maids saw this, they exclaimed: "Just see this impertinence!" and were about to drive him away. But Guṇamālā has a feeling that this is no ordinary Brahman, and restrains the maids, saying: "What harm is there? The Brahman is my guest, let him stay here." At the end of the night he sang sweet melodies, which reminded Guṇamālā of Jīvandhara's singing at Gandharvadattā's self-choice. Finally he discloses his identity, and receives Guṇamālā as a wife from her parents. The merchant Gandhotkaṭa arranges a feast.

Soon after this Jīvandhara wins Ratnavatī, the daughter of King Videha, as his eighth wife, this time again through his skill in drawing the bow. Kāṣṭhāṅgāraka and other persons of evil intent, try to carry away his wife in a fight. Jīvandhara notices this, reveals his identity to the former vassals of Satyandhara as the son of the old king, fights with them against Kāṣṭhāṅgāraka, defeats his army and cuts off his head. After he has duly worshipped the Jinas, he is anointed king, celebrates his marriage with Ratnavatī, crowns Gandharvadattā as first queen, and lives happily as a good sovereign with his mother, his wives and friends, enjoying the reward of his former good deeds. One day he meets a Jaina monk, and takes the monastic vow upon himself. His brothers do likewise. While he is living with them in the forest, he notices a herd of monkeys fighting furiously among themselves, and he is filled with disgust at the world. After a meeting with Mahāvīra, he renounces his kingdom in favour of Prince Vasundhara, son of Gandharvadattā, and becomes a monk. His companions do the same, whereupon his mother and his eight wives become nuns.

The Śatruñjaya-Māhātmya[1] by Dhaneśvara, who, according to his own statement, wrote his work in Valabhī at the desire of Śīlāditya, King of Surāṣṭra,[2] is a work after the style of the Māhātmyas of the Purāṇas. This is an epic, mostly in Slokas, in 14 Sargas, the theme of which is the glorification of the sacred mountain Satruñjaya. It begins with a cosmology, then tells of the adventures of a King Mahīpāla, whereupon the story of the first Jina Ṛṣabha follows. It tells of the fights of the two brothers Bharata

1) A. *Weber*, Ueber das Çatrunjaya Mâhâtmyam AKM I, Nr. 4, Leipzig 1858; transl., with appendices, by J. *Burgess*, Ind. Ant. 30, 1901, 239 ff.; 288 ff.

2) The text has Śilāditya. Between 605 and 766 A.D. there were six different rulers of the Valabhī dynasty named Śīlāditya (s. *Duff*, p. 380). Though there are a few quite definite chronological data in the work itself (I, 13 f.; XIV, 101 ff.; 165 ff.; 281 ff.) these contradict one another to such an extent that it is not possible to assign an exact date to the work, See *Weber*, l.c., p. 8 ff., 15, 39 ff. According to XIV, 283, Dhaneśvara was "the moon in the ocean of the Moon-Gaccha" (śaśigacchâmbudhiśaśī). A Dhaneśvara of the Candragaccha is mentioned in the list of teachers by Abhayadeva, the teacher of Āsaḍa. The last-named lived in about 1191 A.D.; hence Dhaneśvara, the teacher of Devendra Sūri, the teacher of Bhadreśvara, the teacher of Abhayadeva, would have lived in about 1100 A.D.

and Bāhubali and the pilgrimages and pious foundations of Bharata, especially the shrines erected on the Śatruñjaya mountain. In Book IX we come across the Rāma legend, whilst in Book X to XII the story of the Pāṇḍavas, connected with the Kṛṣṇa legend and the legend of the Jina Ariṣṭanemi, is told. The stories told in Book X about Bhīmasena refer, however, to a Bhīma totally different from that of the Mahābhārata. He is a thief and a good-for-nothing, though a keen adventurer, about whom, for instance, the following is told:

A merchantman vessel, on which he is sailing overseas, runs aground in mid-ocean on a coral-reef. A parrot indicates a way of rescue. One of them must be prepared to die, swim to a mountain and there startle up the Bhāraṇḍa birds.[1] Bhīma undertakes this, and saves the ship, but remains alone on the mountain. The helpful parrot gives him a means of escape. He is to cast himself into the ocean, allow himself to be swallowed by a fish and thrown ashore. This takes place, and he lands in Ceylon. After manifold adventures he acquires a kingdom, but renounces it after some time, in order to withdraw as a hermit on Raivata, one of the peaks of the sacred Śatruñjaya. Book XIV contains the legend of the Jina Pārśvanātha and at the end a long prophecy of Mahāvīra, which contains all manner of historical allusions, the significance of which is, however, not yet explained.

Corresponding to the Purāṇas of the Digambaras, the Śvetāmbaras have the Caritras, some of which describe the lives of individual Jinas, whilst others treat of the lives of all 63 Śalākāpuruṣas[2] or "excellent men." The work of the last-named type which enjoys the greatest reputation

[1]) According to Mahābhārata VI, 7, 13, there live in the northern Kuru-land the Bhāruṇḍa birds, which have sharp teeth and are very strong, and throw the corpses of men who live to the age of thousands of years, into mountain caves. According to XII, 169, 10, they have human faces. The Pañcatantra (s. *Benfey*, Das Pantschatantra I, 111 f., 538; II, 360 f., 526) tells of Bhāraṇḍa birds with two beaks.

[2]) Śalākā (Pali salākā) means "arrow" or "little stake," also the small bamboo sticks which are used by the Buddhist monks as an identity badge. Śalākāpuruṣa would probably mean "legitimised, characterised men," so that Śalākāpuruṣa and Lakṣaṇapuruṣa

among the Śvetāmbara Jainas, is the Triṣaṣṭi-Śalākā-puruṣa-Carita,[1] "The Lives of the 63 Excellent Men" by the famous Jaina monk Hemacandra. This work, which was written at the desire of King Kumārapāla between 1160 and 1172 A.D., the latter being the year of Hemacandra's death, contains in 10 Parvans the legends about the 24 Jinas, the 12 Cakravartins, the 9 Vāsudevas, the 9 Baladevas and the 9 Viṣṇudviṣas (enemies of the 9 incarnations of Viṣṇu). The language of the work, which the author himself describes as a Mahākāvya, "a great ornate epic," and which in bulk if in nothing else, seems to vie with the Mahābhārata,[2] is simple and unaffected. The description "Mahākāvya" is justified by many beautiful comparisons, such as when, for instance, the poet (I, 70) compares the buffaloes carrying water, with clouds which have fallen to earth, and many a pretty description of seasons, love-scenes, and so on, in the style of ornate poetry. The main purpose of the work is, however, instruction and edification; for, as the author himself says (I, 29): "To sing in praise of the pious, leads to liberation." The narrative is often interrupted by long instructive discourses on subjects of religion and morality. There is often mention of the doctrine of Karman, and all the stories of the rebirths of the great men and their destinies, are instances of the effects of good and bad deeds. In the case of each one of the "excellent men," his destinies in his former existences are related. In the main, they are the same legends as are to be found in the earlier Jinistic epics and Purāṇas.[3] It is

are synonymous. The Commentary on Abhidhānacintāmaṇi III, 364, however, explains: puruṣeṣu jātarekhā ity arthaḥ, "which form as it were lines of demarcation among the monks."

[1]) The text has been published by the Jaina-Dharma-Prasāraka-Sabhā (in a new edition), Bhavnagar 1906-1913.

[2]) Even the division into Parvans seems to indicate the proud comparison with the Mahābhārata.

[3]) See *Glasenapp*, Der Jainismus, p. 259 ff.

still a matter for more detailed investigation as to what earlier sources Hemacandra drew upon for his poem.[1]

Parvan I begins, after the usual benedictions, with the life of Ṛṣabha, the first Tīrthakara, in his previous existences.[2] Parvan X, which also occurs as an independent text in manuscripts, entitled Mahāvīra-Caritra, "Life of Mahāvīra," is of greater significance. It contains the life-story of Mahāvīra, which agrees on the whole with the accounts in the Kalpa-Sūtra and the Āyāraṃga, but gives far greater detail. We find here also detailed data, which are probably based on earlier traditions, and which are for that reason important from the historical point of view, regarding King Śreṇika Bimbisāra, the contemporary of Mahāvīra and Buddha.[3] In the form of a prophecy of Mahāvīra, Hemacandra also describes in a lengthy passage the ideal reign of his pious pupil, King Kumārapāla, who ascended the throne 1669 years after the Nirvāṇa of Mahāvīra.[4] Interwoven with the more or less historical accounts of King Śreṇika and his son, Prince Abhaya, there are also many interesting tales, such as the story of the master-thief Rauhiṇeya, who by

1) We are tempted to think of the Triṣaṣṭilakṣaṇamahāpurāṇa, but the Caüpannamahāpurisacariya, a work written in Prākrit prose by Śīlācārya in the year 868 A.D. must also be taken into consideration. On this little-known work which has not yet been published, s. *Peterson*, 3 Reports, p. 38, App. p. 91; Banarsi Das *Jain*, Jaina Jātakas, p. iii ff. and *Jacobi*, Sanatkumāracaritam, p. xiii. According to *Jacobi* in E RE VII, 466b, the legend-collection Vasudevahiṇḍi would be one of the sources of Hemacandra's work. Vasudevahiṇḍi is the work of Saṅghadāsa Gaṇin (the first part, which also contains the Dhammillahiṇḍi, is published as No. 80 of the Ātmānanda-Jaina-Grantharatnamālā, Bhavnagar 1930). See also *Peterson*, Report 1882-83, p. 58; 3 Reports, p. 184 f.; *Guérinot*, p. 75 and *Farquhar*, Outline, pp. 278, 280, erroneously state Hemacandra to be the author of the Vasudevahiṇḍa (= Vasudevahiṇḍi).

2) On Parvan I, see L. *Suali* in SIFI VII, 3 ff. An English translation of Canto I of Parvan I has appeared in the Punjab Sanskrit Series No. 8. Jaina Jātakas or Lord Ṛshabha's Pūrvabhavas...translated by Amūlyacharan *Vidyābhūshaṇa*, revised and edited with Notes and Introductions by Banarsi Das *Jain*, Lahore, 1925.

3) See Helen M. *Johnson* in JAOS 45, 1925, 301 ff.

4) See *Bühler*, Ueber das Leben des Jainamönches Hemachandra, pp. 37 ff., 78 ff.

reason of his boldness and artfulness, succeeds in eluding all pursuit, but who in the end would almost have been outwitted by Prince Abhaya himself, had he not by a mere chance heard a few words of Mahāvīra, which save his life. This causes him to hear the sermon of the Jina and to become a monk, and he enters into heaven as a sage.[1]

The **Pariśiṣṭa-Parvan** or **Sthavirāvali-Carita**,[2] *i.e.*, "Appendix-Section" or "Lives of the Series of the Elders," the appendix to the Triṣaṣṭi-Śalākā-puruṣa-Carita, has a still greater wealth of fairy-tales and stories of all kinds. This book treats of the history of the Daśapūrvins, *i.e.*, the earliest teachers of the Jaina religion, who were still knowers of the ten Pūrvas. Whilst with the exception of the last two Tīrthakaras, Pārśvanātha and Mahāvīra, the personages of the Triṣaṣṭi-Śalākāpuruṣa-Carita belong throughout to mythology or epic poetry, the Sthavirāvali-Carita contains the life-stories of the Elders (Sthaviras, Theras), *i.e.*, the disciples of Mahāvīra, whose names and sequence in accordance with the unanimous tradition of the Śvetāmbaras may be regarded as historical. It is true that the stories by themselves alone seldom contain any historical nucleus. Hemacandra took them from earlier works of legendary lore and commentaries, especially those of Haribhadra. Frequently enlivened by proverbs and colloquialisms of the common people, the stories reveal clearly their popular origin. Hemacandra translated them from the Prākrit without making many alterations.

---

1) See Helen M. *Johnson*, in JAOS 44, 1924, p. 1 ff. The great popularity of this story is shown by the fact that it has again been remodelled in extended form as an independent work by a more recent poet Devamūrti (15th century) in the Rauhiṇeya-caritra (Jamnagar 1908, 2nd Ed. by the Ātmānanda-Sabhā, Bhavnagar 1916) ; translated into English by Helen M. *Johnson* in Studies in Honor of M. Bloomfield, New Haven, 1930, p. 159 ff. ; *cf.* JAOS 45, 1924, 73 ff.

2) Edited by H. *Jacobi*, Calcutta, Bibl. Ind., 1891. Extracts translated into German by J. *Hertel*, Erzählungen aus Hēmacandras Pariśiṣṭaparvan, Leipzig, 1908.

There are many interesting parallels to be found among the stories of the Pariśiṣṭa-Parvan, not only to such stories as are familiar to us from other Indian works, but also to such as form part of universal literature. The story of the twins Kuberadatta and Kuberadattā, the children of the courtesan Kuberasenā, is a kind of Oedipus tragedy. The time-honoured theme of incest committed unconsciously, is here diluted, even more than in the Christian legend of Saint Gregory, into a pious monastic legend. What appeals to the Indian narrator is, not so much the tragic situation, as the subtlety of the complicated relationship. When a monk writes stories, it is conceivable that the wickedness of womankind will furnish him with inexhaustible material for the most subtle stories of adultery. There is an abundance of such stories in the Pariśiṣṭa-Parvan, including some, the individual motifs of which often recur in universal literature.[1] The tale of Sthūlabhadra and the nun Kośā (VIII, 110-193) is one of the characteristic monastic stories :

Three monks each made a vow in the presence of the master. The first said that he would sit in front of a lion's den throughout the four months of the rainy season; the second said that he would sojourn for the same length of time in front of the hole of a snake, the mere sight of which is fatal; the third declared that he would sit on a well-wheel throughout the rainy season. Then the monk Sthūlabhadra comes along, and says he will spend the four months in the house of the courtesan Kośā (whose lover he had been before he became a monk), without violating his vow of chastity. He not only succeeds in this, but Kośā is also converted to the Jaina faith. At the end of the rainy season the four monks return to the master, who declares that Sthūlabhadra has accomplished the greatest feat. The other monks are jealous at this, and the one who had sat in front of the lion's den, declares that, before the beginning of the next

---

1) Thus the motif of the ordeal of the adulteress, among others, in the narrative II, 446-640, translated into German by J. J. *Meyer*, Isoldes Gottesurteil, Berlin 1914, p. 130 ff. The Ṛṣyaśṛṅga legend is imitated in the story of Valkalacīrin, I, 90-258.

rainy season, he will perform the same feat as Sthūlabhadra. He repairs to Kośā, who sees through him: he falls an easy victim to her, but is at length brought back to repentance and to the monastic life by Kośā herself, who finally becomes a nun.

Side by side with such stories there are also purely Jinistic legends, some of which read like historical or biographical accounts. Thus it is related in Book V, how Sayyambhava wrote the Daśavaikālika-Sūtra, in order to give his son, who, he knows, must die in six months, the chance of grasping the essence of the Jaina doctrine in the shortest possible time, without studying the other sacred texts. The legends told in Books IX and XIII also have reference to the compilation of the Canon. The stories in Book VIII relating to the royal dynasty of the Nandas are of some historical interest, though the legends themselves probably contain but little actual history. At any rate the fact that the last Nanda prince was overthrown by Candragupta, the founder of the Maurya dynasty (*ca.* 317 B. C.) is historical. According to the legend, Candragupta, who was of low descent on the maternal side, only succeeded in pushing his way to power and consolidating his throne, because he had the astute Brahman Cāṇakya as his minister. There were many popular tales current about this man, and Hemacandra did not fail to make use of them, though Cāṇakya was of all men thoroughly unsuitable as an example for a pious Jaina to imitate. From time immemorial, however, the Jainas have always taken pains to make every hero of the popular stories into one of their own also. Nevertheless, it is so remarkable that they should have done this even in the case of Cāṇakya, that crafty, unscrupulous intriguer and despotic politician, who shrank back from no trick however bad, that we are inclined to believe, with the tradition, that Candragupta really favoured the Jaina faith, and that, for this reason, he and his famous minister were extolled by the Jainas. It is true that Hemacandra succeeded in making a pious Jaina of even this man. Indeed, this out and out worldly man, who shortly before his death, takes his revenge on his enemy, nevertheless retires at the end of his days to the vicinity of a dung-heap, in order to starve himself to death, in the true manner of a Jaina saint. Owing to the rascality of a rival, who sets fire to the dung-heap, he is, however, burnt against his will. After his death, he curiously enough becomes a goddess.

The Caritras which describe the life of individual Jinas, are numerous. Among these, Ṛṣabha, the first, Śāntinātha, the sixteenth, Ariṣṭanemi or Neminātha, the twenty-second, Pārśva, the twenty-third, and of course the last Jina, Mahāvīra himself, are most especially honoured by the Jainas, and their biographies are among the most popular themes of narrative poetry.

Even in the Canon there are already Mahāvīra-Caritas, descriptions of the life of the last Jina. Hemacandra's Mahāvīra-Carita forms Parvan X of his Triṣaṣṭi-Śalākāpuruṣa-Carita. A Mahāvīra-Cariyam in Prākrit was written in the year 1082 A.D. by Guṇacandra Gaṇin,[1] and another in 1085 A.D. by Devendra Gaṇin,[2] also known as Nemicandra.

The life of Ṛṣabha is, as we have seen, told in the introductory sections of the Rāma epics. Kṛṣṇa and the heroes of the Mahābhārata are supposed to be contemporaries of the Jina Neminātha, about whom legends are told in all adaptations of the Mahābhārata. Furthermore it is the legend of Neminātha which has been made the theme of innumerable poetic versions, beginning with the early one in the Uttarajjhayaṇa.[3] In later times there are at least a dozen life-stories of Neminātha.

1) Edited in AUS Granthoddhāra 1929. Cf. *Peterson*, Report V, p. xiii f.

2) Edited in Jaina-Ātmānanda Granthamālā, No. 50. The work also contains Apabhraṃśa stanzas, s. *Jacobi*, Sanatkumāracaritam, p. xxii. The author is probably the same as that of the commentary on the Uttarādhyayana-Sūtra.

3) See above, p. 469 f.

Thus in the 11th century we have a Neminātha-Carita in Sanskrit by Sūrācārya and one by Maladhāri-Hemacandra. In the year 1159 A.D. Haribhadra, a pupil of Śrīcandra, who himself was a pupil of Jinacandra, completed his Nemināhacariu in Apabhraṃśa.[1] The author was a contemporary of Hemacandra, and completed his work, which he had written at the request of the minister Pṛthivīpāla, on the day of the conversion of King Kumārapāla. The legend of Neminātha is the same in all the presentations. Haribhadra, however, is at pains to depict romantic scenes after the manner of the ornate poetry, to interweave descriptions of nature, etc. He takes such a delight in doing this, that the entire first half of the poem treats only of the previous births of Nemi and Rājīmatī, and insufficient attention is devoted to the actual legend of the Tīrthakara. Interwoven with the story of the second reincarnation, there is a Sanatkumāra-Carita, which relates the legend of the fourth Cakravartin Sanatkumāra,[2] the contemporary of the fifteenth Tīrthakara. The narrative is full of romance, the scene of which is laid partly on earth, and partly in the world of the Vidyādharas and gods. After many amorous adventures and numerous victorious fights, after he had become a ruler of the world (Cakravartin) famed for his incomparable beauty, and after he had lived happily for 300,000 years, old age approached him suddenly. Then he renounced the world, devoted himself to rigorous asceticism, died the voluntary death through fasting and entered into the Sanatkumāra-heaven. The poet evidently wanted to show that he could apply all the subtleties of the Kāvya style in Apabhraṃśa just as well

[1] *Cf.* H. *Jacobi*, "Sanatkumāracaritam," ein Abschnitt aus Haribhadras Nemināthacaritam eine Jainalegende in Apabhraṃśa, in ABayA XXXI, 2, München 1921. This Haribhadra is also the author of Mallināthacarita in Prākrit.

[2] *Cf. Glasenapp*, Der Jainismus, p. 279.

as in Prākrit, for the legend itself had been treated often enough before him.[1]

The life-story of Neminātha is also treated by the poet Vāgbhaṭa in his Nemi-Nirvāṇa,[2] a Mahākāvya in 15 cantos. The poem Nemidūta[3] by Vikrama, the son of Sāṅgaṇa, is a most artificial work. The theme of this poem is the lament of Rājīmatī, after her husband had become a monk. The work is an example of the "Completing of verses":[4] The last line of each verse is taken from Kālidāsa's "Meghadūta," whilst the first three lines are composed by the poet himself. This appears to be a very modern work.

An earlier work of the same kind is the Pārśvābhyudaya,[5] a poetical life-story of Pārśvanātha by Jinasena, who wrote the Ādi-Purāṇa in the 9th century. In this poem the entire "Meghadūta" has been incorporated by inserting one or two lines from Kālidāsa's in each verse, whilst Jinasena composed the rest.

The number of poetical life-stories of Pārśvanātha, the predecessor of Mahāvīra, is very great. The Pārśvanātha-Caritra[6] by Bhāvadeva Sūri, who probably wrote

1) Thus already by Devendra in his commentary on the Uttarajjhayaṇa in the year 1073 A. D., and only one year earlier than Haribhadra, Śrīcandra wrote a Sanatkumāracarita in Prākrit. As there are several writers named Śrīcandra, it is not certain whether this is the same one who wrote a Kathākośa. Cf. *Hiralal*, Catalogue, p. xlix ff. and *Jacobi*, l.c., p. xiii.

2) Edited in Km., 56, 1896. The poet lived under Jayasiṃha of Gujarat (1093-1154) and is also the author of a work on poetics (Vāgbhaṭālaṃkāra).

3) Edited in Km., Part II, pp. 85-104. *Cf.* P. *Pavolini* in GSAI 18, 329 ff.; E. *Hultzsch*, Kālidāsa's Meghadūta, Ed. London 1911, p. vi f.

4) Samasyāpūraṇa, a poetical exercise consisting of one or two lines of a stanza being given to which the poet must compose the remaining lines.

5) The Meghadūta as embodied in the Pārśvābhyudaya with the Commentary of Mallinātha, with a literal English Translation Ed. by K. B. *Pathak*, Poona 1894 and edited with a commentary by *Yogirāṭ Paṇḍitācārya*, Bombay NSP 1909. Cf. *Guérinot* in JA 1909, s. 10, t. XIV, pp. 72, 75; E. *Hultzsch*, l.c., p. vii, and T. S. Kuppuswami *Śāstri* in Ind. Ant. 36, 1907, 285 ff.; *Hiralal*, Catalogue, p. xxiii.

6) Edited by *Haragovindadāsa* and *Becaradāsa*, Benares 1912, YJG 32. An analysis

it in 1255 A.D.,[1] tells with an exceptional wealth of detail, not only the life-story of this saint in his last incarnation, but also his previous nine existences.

Marubhūti and Kamaṭha are sons of a court priest. Marubhūti hears a pious sermon, and renounces the world and the pleasures of the senses. Kamaṭha commits adultery with the neglected wife of his brother. Marubhūti denounces him to the king, and causes the adulterer to be punished. Kamaṭha kills his brother in revenge. Marubhūti dies with gloomy thoughts, and is therefore reborn as an elephant. As such he is converted by the king, who had withdrawn into solitude, and from that time onwards he lives a pious life. As an elephant he is killed by Kamaṭha who had in the meantime been reborn as a snake.[2] As the elephant is just meditating upon religion, he is reborn in heaven, whilst Kamaṭha descends to hell. In the succeeding incarnations the former Marubhūti is reborn now as a god in some heaven, now as a prince who after ruling justly and piously, retires from the world. Reborn as a snake, as a wild Bhīl and as a lion, Kamaṭha ever and again kills the former Marubhūti, and ever and again descends to hell. At length in the tenth reincarnation the former Marubhūti is reborn as a prince in Benares, amidst all manner of miracles and signs proclaiming the future Jina. While his mother was pregnant with him, she saw a snake at her side one night (pārśvataḥ), hence the prince received the name Pārśva. The former Kamaṭha is reborn as Kaṭha, the son of a Brahman, is very poor and becomes an ascetic. One day Pārśva sees Kaṭha seated between five fires performing ascetic practices, and throwing a large snake into the fire. Pārśva rescues the snake, which then reappears as the Nāga king Dharaṇa, whilst Kaṭha is reborn as an Asura. The sight of a picture of the former Jina Nemi causes Pārśva to give up wealth and

---

of the work is given by M. *Bloomfield*, The Life and Stories of the Jaina Savior Pārçvanātha, Baltimore, 1919. Bloomfield also gives numerous parallels from Indian and world-literature.

1) At the end of the work the author says that he completed the work in the year 1312. The era is not stated. If it is the Saṃvat era, 1255 A. D. would be the corresponding date. If this date is correct, Yaśas, whom he names as his teacher, cannot be identical with Yaśodeva Sūri, who wrote a commentary on the Pākṣika-Sūtra in 1124 A.D.

2) It is one of the favourite themes in Jinistic legend literature to trace the destinies of two sworn enemies through many rebirths. *Bloomfield, loc. cit.*, p. 13 ff.

power, tear out his hair, and wander forth as an itinerant monk. At the age of 30 years he attains perfection. Like Māra in the Buddha legend, the Asura Meghamālin (the former Kaṭha) attacks Pārśva, in order to disturb him in his meditation, but he is protected by the snake king Dharaṇa. At length the Asura repents, and becomes a pious layman. Pārśva becomes a Kevalin (possessor of the perfect knowledge), visits his parents, and finally attains Nirvāṇa. After his passing, he enters the highest heaven, and is much honoured by Sakra. His corpse is cremated by the gods, and Sakra erects a jewelled Stūpa over his ashes.

The legend of Pārśvanātha, however, forms merely the frame, into which numerous stories, fables and fairy-tales are inserted in the manner so familiar in Indian narrative literature. Not a few of these stories are also known from other Jinistic and secular narrative works (such as Pañcatantra, Vetālapañcaviṃśati, and others), *e.g.*, the story of the Gold-man, who is killed, and transforms himself into a gold treasure (II, 959 ff.), of the Brahman who builds castles in the air (II, 1015 ff.), of the patient Hariścandra (III, 556 ff.), the parable of the four daughters-in-law [1] (VI, 389 ff.) and others. The story of the emperor Suvarṇabāhu not only contains themes of the Śakuntalā legend, but actually reveals (IV, 41) an acquaintance with the drama of Kālidāsa. One of the most interesting stories is that of King Vikrama as a parrot (III, 105 ff.)[2]

The mighty King Vikrama who is endowed with all the virtues, learns from a sage the magic art of penetrating into another body. At the same time with him a Brahman learns the same art. The latter, a scoundrel, seizes the opportunity when Vikrama leaves his own body and enters that of an elephant, to penetrate into the body of the king, and to give himself out as the king. When the real King Vikrama is aware of this, he enters into the body of a parrot, allows himself to be caught by a

1) Already in Nāyādhammakahāo, Chapt. VII; see above, p. 446.

2) Cf. *Bloomfield, loc. cit.*, p. 74 ff., and the treatise "On the Art of Entering Another's Body" in Proceedings of the American Philosophical Society, Vol. LVI, 1, 1917.

hunter, and causes this man to sell him to the queen. As a parrot he becomes the queen's favourite and converses with her ; they ask each other riddles, and he recites to her all kinds of wise sayings and instructions on the religion of the Jina. The riddles are erudite rather than popular. One of the simpler riddles is that of the queen : " It makes snakes poisonless, the gods powerless, lions motionless, and yet children hold it in their hands, what is it ?" The parrot guesses it at once : "A painter's brush." After so many proofs of sagacity the queen no longer doubts that the wise parrot is none other than the real King Vikrama, her husband. One day Vikrama's soul leaves the parrot's body, and enters into the body of a lizard. When the queen sees the dead body of the bird, she begins to lament, and wishes to burn herself with it. In order to prevent the self-immolation of the queen, the false king enters into the parrot's body, which enables the real king to assume his own body and to appear before the queen in all his splendour.

Like other Indian narrative works, the Pārśvanātha-Caritra also contains many gnomic sayings both on morality and on worldly wisdom. There are more than a thousand of them, many of which are well-known from other sources too. A few examples are given here :

" It is better for a man to be cast into a dungeon, better to wander in strange lands, better to live in hell,—than to have two wives." (II, 833.)

" Better is death, better to beg, better to serve one's enemies, if one meets with a misfortune through the visitation of fate,—than to seek help from relatives." (III, 785.)

" The wise ones know how much sand there is in the Ganges and how much water in the ocean, they know the dimensions of a great mountain,—but the thoughts of a woman they cannot fathom." (VII, 82.)

Other Pārśvanātha-Caritras (or Caritas) are written by Vādirāja (1025 A.D.), the teacher of the Western Calukya King Jayasiṃha II Jagadekamalla,[1] by Māṇikyacandra (1217

---

[1]) Cf. *Hultzsch*, in ZDMG 68, 1914, p. 698 and Quarterly Journal of the Mythic Society, 12, 1922, p. 319; A. *Venkatasubbiah* in ZII 7, 1929, 179 ff.

A.D.),[1] by Sakalakīrti (15th century),[2] by Padmasundara (1565 A.D.)[3] and by Udayavīra Gaṇin.[4]

Māṇikyacandra and Sakalakīrti also wrote Śāntinātha-Caritas, life-stories of the 16th Tīrthakara.[5] A Śāntinātha-Caritra in Sanskrit verses was written by Devasūri in 1282 A.D.[6] Devasūri was the teacher of Tilakaprabha, the teacher of Vīraprabha, whose pupil Ajitaprabha wrote a great epic Śāntinātha-Caritra.[7] The date of a Śānti-Purāṇa by *Aśaga*[8] is not known.

The Sumatinātha-Caritra by Somaprabha (second half of the 12th century) in Prākrit treats of the life of the 5th Tīrthakara.[9]

A voluminous Prākrit poem Supāsanāha-Cariyaṃ[10] by Lakṣmaṇa Gaṇin, deals with the story of the 7th Tīrthakara. This work, composed in the year 1143 A.D., also contains 68

---

1) *Peterson*, 3 Reports, p. 157 ff.; Report IV, p. xci. He also wrote a commentary on Kāvyaprakāśa.

2) See above, p. 496 and Note 1; and *Bhandarkar*, Report 1883-84, pp. 122 f.; 433.

3) Pārśvanāthakāvya, s. *Aufrecht*, Bodl. Cat., p. 392.; *Peterson*, 3 Reports, p. 255 ff.; Report IV, p. lxxv.

4) Date not known; s. *Bloomfield*, *loc. cit.*, p. i f. The contents of a Pārśvanātha-Caritra written in the year 1597 A.D. is given by Major James *Delamaine* (Transactions of the Royal Asiatic Society I, 1827, p. 428 ff.). The name "Bṛddha Tapā Gaccha" given by him as the name of the author is probably based on some error.

5) Cf. *Kielhorn* in Ind. Ant. 10, 1881, p. 101. *Bhandarkar*, Report 1883-84, pp. 121 f., 430 ff.

6) This was corrected by Pradyumna Sūri. It is an abridged translation into Sanskrit, of Śrīśānti-vṛtta, which was written in Prākrit, by an earlier Devasūri, who is said to have written a Stuti on his teacher Municandra in Apabhraṃśa, a Syādvādaratnākara and a Pramāṇagrantha and lived from 1068 to 1169 A.D. Cf. *Klatt* in Ind. Ant. 11, 254; *Peterson*, Report 1882-83, p. 59 f., Report IV, p. lv f.; *Jacobi*, Sanatkumāracaritam, p. xxii.

7) Edited by *Muni Indravijaya* in Bibl. Ind. 1909 f. On Ajitaprabha and his genealogical tree of teachers, s. *Peterson*, Report V, p. i f.

8) *Aufrecht*, Bodl. Cat., p. 372 f.

9) *Cf. Muniraja Jinavijaya*, Kumārapāla-Pratibodha Ed. GOS No. XIV, p. v.

10) Edited by Pandit Haragovind Das *Seth*, Benares 1918. *Cf.* P. D. *Gune* in Proc. IOC Poona 1922, p. 161 f., and *Jacobi*, Sanatkumāracaritam, p. xxii.

Apabhraṃśa verses. A Vimala-Purāṇa by Kṛṣṇadāsa,[1] deals with the life of the 13th Tīrthakara. The story of Dharmanātha, the 15th Tīrthakara, is treated by the poet Haricandra in the great epic Dharmaśarmābhyudaya.[2] The epic is an imitation of Māgha's Śiśupālavadha. The legend of the 12th Tīrthakara is treated by Vardhamāna Sūri in the Vāsupūjya-Caritra.[3] In this case the biography is quite stereotyped, but it forms the frame for a series of instructive and edifying stories. The life-stories of the five "Great Men" Ṛṣabha, Neminātha, Śāntinātha, Pārśvanātha and Vardhamāna Mahāvīra are contained in the epic Mahāpuruṣa-Caritra[4] in five Sargas by Merutuṅga, the author of the Prabandhacintāmaṇi (1306 A.D.). The work has come down, in manuscripts, with a commentary which was probably written by the poet himself, and in this commentary the work is also called Upadeśaśata and Dharmopadeśaśataka.

Not only the Tīrthakaras themselves, but other holy men too, have been glorified in Caritras. A famous legendary hero is Śālibhadra, a contemporary of Mahāvīra and King Śreṇika, whose story is told briefly and simply in Hemacandra's Mahāvīra-Caritra (Triṣaṣṭiśalākāpuruṣa-Caritra X, 57 ff.). Dharmakumāra treated this legend in 1277 A.D. in the epic Śālibhadra-Carita,[5] which was revised by Pradyumna Sūri[6]

1) See *Aufrecht*, Bodl. Cat., p. 372 f.

2) Edited in Km. 8, 1888. Cf. *Peterson*, Report II, 77 f., 141 ff. It is impossible to determine the period of the poet, as there were several poets named Haricandra. As, however, he utilised not only Māgha but also Vākpati's Gaüḍavaha (s. *Jacobi*, WZKM 3, 1889, 136 ff.) and as the Jīvandhara-Campū is based upon the Uttara-Purāṇa, he must have written later than 900 A.D. (s. E. *Hultzsch*, Ind. Ant. 35, 1906, 268).

3) *Cf.* A. *Ballini* in RSO I, 1906-07, 41 ff., 169 ff., 439 ff. and II, 1908-09, 39 ff., 289 f.

4) *Cf. Weber*, HSS Verz. II, 3, 1024 ff.; *Peterson*, 3 Reports, p. 266 f.; Report IV, p. xcviii and Report VI, 43 ff.

5) Edited in YJG No. 15, Benares 1910. Detailed treatment of it by M. *Bloomfield* in JAOS 43, 1923, p. 257 ff.

6) He was an excellent Sanskrit scholar and obviously a specialist in Kāvya. Among other things he worked up the Prabhāvaka-Caritra (1278 A.D.), the Śāntinātha-Carita by

and supplied with all the subtleties of ornate poetry. The story terms itself a Dānadharma-Kathā, "a narrative about the religious duty of giving alms," and also a Dānāvadāna,[1] "story of notable deeds of alms-giving." The subject-matter of the legend is as follows:

In his former incarnation Śālibhadra was the son of a poor widow, a shepherd boy named Saṃgama, who delighted in giving himself up to religious meditations while minding the flocks. On a feast-day he sees that delicious food is being prepared in all the houses, and he asks his mother to prepare a festive meal for him too. With great difficulty the poor woman succeeds in preparing a meal of this kind. However, before Saṃgama eats it, there comes an ascetic who is just about to break his fast, and the boy gives him the meal which has been prepared for himself. (According to the Jaina faith, it is the most meritorious form of alms-giving to offer food to an ascetic after his fast.) In consequence of this good deed, Saṃgama is reborn in Rājagṛha as Śālibhadra, the son of Bhadrā and Gobhadra, endowed with incomparable beauty and all virtues. When he had reached manhood, his father selects 32 beautiful virgins as his wives, and he leads a happy life. His father Gobhadra became an ascetic, died the voluntary death by starvation, and reached heaven. As a god, he procures immense wealth for his son Śālibhadra. "As rich as Śālibhadra" became proverbial, just as we say "as rich as Crœsus." One day, however, owing to the sight of King Śreṇika who, in spite of all his power, is nevertheless only an ordinary mortal, he becomes enlightened, and becomes a Pratyekabuddha. He repairs to the teacher Dharmaghoṣa, who instructs him in the religion, and finally, after he has renounced the world, he is reborn as a god in heaven.

This simple legend is told in 7 cantos in the ornate style of Sanskrit poetry. Numerous sayings, maxims on morality and practical wisdom, are inserted into the narrative.

Devasūri (see above, p. 516, Note 6) and the Samarāicca-Kahā in a similar fashion, s. *Bloomfield loc. cit.*, p. 258. Pradyumna Sūri is also the author of the Vicārasāra-Prakaraṇa in Prākrit (edited with a chāyā by Māṇikyasāgara, Mehsana 1923). Cf. *Peterson*, 3 Reports, 270 ff.; Shankar P. *Pandit*, Gauḍavaho Ed. BSS, p. cliv.

1) Avadāna is used here in the sense in which it is generally known to the Buddhists only. See above, p. 277 f.

All these "life-stories" are purely legendary. Notwithstanding, in the life of Mahāvīra and perhaps also in that of Pārśva we meet with many a historical trait. At any rate the stories of historical royal dynasties and personages in the history of the Order, as we found them in Hemacandra's Pariśiṣṭa-Parvan, reveal a certain historical interest, which is also evinced already in the canonical texts in the beginnings of a biography of Mahāvīra and his first disciples, as well as in the list of the Sthaviras and their schools with their branches, in Bhadrabāhu's Kalpa-Sūtra. There are many such lists of teachers (P a ṭ ṭ ā v a l ī s) in later centuries.[1] Semi-historical legends regarding the schisms are told in Haribhadra's and Śantisūri's commentaries.[2] Works such as the G u r v ā v a l ī - S ū t r a,[3] a list of the teachers of the Tapāgaccha, by D h a r m a s ā g a r a G a ṇ i n, and the T h e r ā v a l ī[4] by M e r u t u ṅ g a, deal exclusively with ecclesiastical history.

The so-called P r a b a n d h a s are also of semi-historical character, for they deal with historical personages, though they are collections of anecdotes rather than real biographies or history. Nevertheless they should not be entirely rejected as historical sources, even though they can be used only with extreme circumspection.[5] The P r a b h ā v a k a - C a r i t r a, "Life of the Prominent"[6] written by P r a b h ā c a n d r a

1) Paṭṭāvalīs have been edited, or extracted, by J. *Klatt*, Ind. Ant. 11, 245 ff.; 293 f.; 23, 169 ff.; *Hoernle*, Ind. Ant. 19, 233 ff.; 20, 341 ff.; 21, 57 ff.

2) See above. p. 485 and *Leumann*, Ind. Stud. 17, 91 ff.; *Jacobi*, ZDMG 38, 1ff. Jacobi also attributes historical value to the Bhadrabāhu-Carita by Ratnanandin (15th or 16th century).

3) Text in *Weber*, HSS. Verz. II, 2, 651 f. and 3, 997 ff. and *Guérinot* in JA 1912, s. 10, t. XIX, 605 ff.

4) *Bháu Dáji* in JBRAS 9, 1867, p. 147 ff.

5) Cf. *Bühler*, Hemachandra, p. 4 ff.

6) Edited by Hīrānanda M. *Sharmā*, Bombay NSP 1909. *Cf.* J. *Klatt* in WZKM 4, 1890, p. 63 ff., 67 f.; *Bühler*, Hemachandra, pp. 4, 52 ff.; Sankar P. *Pandit*, Gauḍavaho Ed., Introduction, p. cxlviii ff.; *Jacobi*, The Upamitibhavaprapañcā

or Candraprabha, and revised in the year 1277 A. D. by the well-known Kāvya specialist Pradyumna Sūri, is a continuation of Hemacandra's Pariśiṣṭa-Parvan. It contains the life stories of 22 Jaina teachers, poets and authors, including Haribhadra, Siddharṣi, Bappabhaṭṭi, Mānatuṅga, Śāntisūri and Hemacandra.

The Prabandhacintāmaṇi or "Wishing-Jewel of Stories" by Merutuṅga,[1] completed in 1306 A. D. and the Prabandhakośa or "Treasury of Stories" by Rājaśekhara,[2] completed in 1349, can only be termed quasi-historical-biographical works. Under the semblance of "history," Merutuṅga's work contains a motley collection of stories, legends and anecdotes associated with historical and literary personages. Kings Bhoja, Vikramāditya and Śīlāditya are extolled as the patrons of the most excellent poets and scholars, and in doing this the author sticks at no anachronism. Thus for instance Varāhamihira, the great astronomer of the 6th century A. D. is made without further ado a contemporary of King Nanda in the 4th century B. C. Side by side with many naïve little tales, there are, however, also many clever and witty anecdotes. Life at the courts of the Indian princes, and especially the literary contests which were organised at these courts, are very vividly described. The stories about Hemacandra and King Kumārapāla, personages not far removed from the period of the author, are also not devoid of a certain amount of historical value. Rājaśekhara's Prabandhakośa

Kathā, Edition, pp. xii, xcix ff. and S. Krishnaswami *Aiyangar* in JBRAS, N.S., 3, 1928, p. 101 ff.

1) Edited by Rāmacandra *Dīnanātha*, Bombay 1888; translated from Sanskrit by C. H. *Tawney*, Bibl. Ind. 1901. How unreliable Merutuṅga is, even in passages where he is apparently stating exact dates (day, month and hour) is shown by R. *Sewell* in JRAS 1920, 333 ff Cf. *Bühler*, Hemachandra, p. 4 ff.

2) I do not know of any edition of this work. Cf. *Bühler*, Hemachandra p. 4 ff. Shankar P. *Pandit*, Gaüḍavaho Ed., Introduction, p. cliii ff, ; E. *Hultzsch*, Report of Sanskrit MSS. in Southern India, III, Madras 1905, p. vi f.

contains the life-stories of 24 persons, namely ten Jaina teachers (including Hemacandra), four poets (Śrīharṣa, Harihara, Amaracandra and the Digambara Madana Kīrti), seven kings and three other personages.

Another semi-historical work is the Tīrtha-Kalpa,[1] also called Kalpa-Pradīpa and Rājaprasāda, by Jinaprabha Sūri, written between 1326 and 1331 A. D. This work gives a description of the Jinistic places of pilgrimage, together with the names of their founders, the kings by whom they were restored, and also the dates of the years. In spite of all the legendary matter which the work contains, we should nevertheless not be justified in denying that it has some slight historical significance, for in any case it is based upon earlier sources and in part tells of events belonging to the author's own period. It is written partly in bad Sanskrit and partly in Jaina-Māhārāṣṭrī.

The Jaina monks and authors have always been tellers of tales far rather than historians. We have already seen that the commentaries to the sacred texts contain not only a mass of traditions and legends, but also numerous fairy-tales and stories, and moreover that the legendary poems, the Purāṇas and Caritras were often only a frame in which all manner of fairy-tales and stories were inserted. Now, in addition to all this, the Jainas have produced a vast fairy-tale literature, in prose and in verse, in Sanskrit, Prākrit and Apabhraṃśa. All these works, be they stories in plain prose or in simple verse, or elaborate poems, novels or epics, are all essentially sermons. They are never intended for mere entertainment, but always serve the purpose of religious instruction and edification.

1) Edited by D. R. *Bhandarkar* and Kedarnath *Sāhityabhūṣaṇa* in Bibl. Ind., fasc. 1, 1923. *Cf. Peterson*, Report IV, pp. xxxvii, 91 ff. and G. *Bühler*, A Legend of the Jaina Stūpa at Mathurā in SWA 1897 and Ind. Ant. 26, 1897, 194 f.

The earliest religious novel (dharmakathā) was Taraṅgavatī by Pādalipta (Pālitta) Sūri. "The author of the Taraṅgavatī" (Taraṅgavaīkāro) is already mentioned in the Aṇuogadāra, and for this reason the work must have been written before the 5th century A. D. However, the original has not come down to us but only a shorter version, written 1,000 years later, in 1643 Prākrit stanzas, entitled Taraṅgalolā.[1] The subject-matter of this romantic love-story, which ends in a pious sermon, is briefly as follows :

A nun who is conspicuous for her beauty, tells the story of her life. She was the charming daughter of a rich merchant. One day she sees a couple of ducks in a lotus pond, and falls into a swoon : for she remembers that in a previous life she had been a duck like this, and that, out of love for a drake killed by the hunter, she had burned herself with him. She longs for the husband of her previous life, and after many love-sorrows, she finds him, by the aid of a picture which she paints of the couple of ducks. The man carries her off, on their flight they are captured by robbers, and they are to be sacrificed to the goddess Kālī. They are rescued, and the parents agree to the marriage. The wedding takes place. Soon afterwards they meet a monk who delivers a lecture to them on the religion of the Jina. Through the encounter with the monk, who in his previous life had been the hunter who killed the drake, they are so much affected that they renounce the world, and become monk and nun.

The ancient Taraṅgavatī was one of the prototypes of the Prākrit poem Samarāicca Kahā[2] by Haribhadra, described by the poet himself as a Dharmakathā, "religious

1) The Taraṅgalolā was translated into German by E. *Leumann*, "Die Nonne," in ZB III, 1921, 193 ff., 272 ff. (an off-print was also published). According to *Leumann*, Pādalipta lived as early as in the 2nd or 3rd century A. D.

2) Edited by H. *Jacobi* in Bibl. Ind. (1908) 1926, Vol. I, Text and Introduction. The introduction contains a detailed table of contents of the work. See also *Jacobi* in RSO II, 1909, pp. 233, 236, and *Peterson*, 3 Reports, 118 ff. An abstract of Haribhadra's work was made by Pradyumna, in 1214 A.D., in his Samarādityasaṃkṣepa (ed. by H. *Jacobi*, Part 1, Ahmedabad 1905). *Cf.* A. *Guérinot*, JA 1909, s. 10, t. XIV, nr. 1078.

novel." It is on this work that Haribhadra's fame as a poet primarily rests. The Samarāicca Kahā is a religious novel not only because the heroes and heroines after all sorts of adventures renounce the world at last, and enter the Order, and because copious instructions on religion are inserted in all convenient places, but also because, underlying the main narrative and most of the inserted narratives, there is the doctrine of Karman, according to which even the slightest peccadillo must have its effects in future rebirths. There is often a very great disparity, at least to our minds, between the sin and the atonement. The poet traces the fate of a hero and his opponent through nine rebirths (Bhava). In the introduction he quotes eight stanzas, in which the subject-matter of the main narrative is summarised very briefly. These stanzas are ascribed to "the ancient teachers," whence it follows that Haribhadra took the main theme from earlier sources. In the numerous stories, parables and fairy-tales inserted, we come across many themes which we find often in Indian narrative literature, and some of which belong to universal literature.

Thus in the course of a sermon the parable of the "man in the well" [1] is told. It is a very common occurrence in Indian ascetic poetry for a king to be forcibly reminded, by some chance sight, of the vanity of existence, and to renounce the world. For instance, a king sees a snake devouring a frog, but itself devoured by a sea-eagle, which in its turn is devoured by a boa constrictor. This sight causes him to renounce the world and become an ascetic. King Yaśodhara sees his first white hair,[2] and resolves to become a monk. In the night he sees how his wife leaves the bedroom, approaches a hunchbacked watchman, who insults and misuses her, and how she gives herself up to this man.[3] In order to prepare his

[1]) See above, Vol. I, p. 408.

[2]) Thus also in Jātaka No. 9, see above, p. 146.

[3]) *Cf. Hertel*, Jinakīrtis "Geschichte von Pāla und Gopāla," pp. 84 f., 92, where there is also reference to parallels from Indian and universal literature.

mother gently for his plan to become a monk, he departs somewhat from the truth, and tells her of a dream in which he had become a monk. Now, with a view to averting the evil consequences of the dream, his mother advises him to disguise himself as a monk and sacrifice a number of animals to the "family goddess" (obviously Kālī). The king naturally refuses to slaughter, but is prepared to make a compromise. He has a cock made of dough, and this fowl is beheaded in front of the image of the goddess, whereupon he eats the "meat" of the cock. Owing to this he brings upon himself a bad Karman,[1] in consequence of which he has to go through various animal births (peacock, antelope, fish, sheep) with his mother, until at length, reborn as a pair of fowls; they have the good fortune to hear the sermon of a famous monk, remember their previous births, and in their next existence, born as the twins of a queen, to become monk and nun. At the end of their lives they enter heaven as gods.

On the whole it is rather tiresome always to follow the wanderings of the same persons from one rebirth to another, the one always killing the other, the one going to heaven and the other to hell or being reborn as an animal, in one instance even as a coconut-palm. However, we also meet with some interesting tales, romantic love-stories, such as that of Sanatkumāra and Vilāsavatī, who are reunited after a long separation and after inexpressibly sorrowful adventures (shipwrecks etc.). The story, too, of Dharaṇa and Lakṣmī is a pretty fairy-romance, full of adventures on land and sea, with many familiar fairy-tale motifs. Thus we find here the motif of the ungrateful wife : Dharaṇa and Lakṣmī are wandering in the forest. The woman is nearly dying of thirst. Dharaṇa draws blood from his arm, and cuts off some flesh from his thigh, so as to nourish his wife. Soon afterwards, nevertheless, she tries to get rid of her husband, in order to follow a robber, to whom she has taken a fancy.[2]

The destinies in the course of the reincarnations are often passing strange. A merchant is reborn as a pig in his own house and is slaughtered for the festive meal. Reborn in the same house as a snake, he remembers his previous existence, but is not angry with the cook who slaughtered him as a pig. Thereupon in his next rebirth he again becomes a man, in fact he is reborn as the son of his own son. When he is one year old, he remembers his previous existence. He sees that his daughter-in-law has now

1) For, in the belief of the Jainas, even sins of thought have their consequences.

2) See above, p. 130.

become his mother, and that his son is now his father, and is at a loss to know how to address them. Hence he does not speak at all, and is called "the dumb one." When he has reached the age of twelve years, an all-knowing monk invites him to come and be instructed by him. Then he breaks his vow of silence, and follows the monk into the religious life. The fate of the nun Susaṃgatā is tragic. In one of her former births she had given a female friend a love-potion for a lover. For this slight sin she was reborn, in succession, as an elephant, a monkey, a bitch, a cat, a Caṇḍāla girl and lastly as a Śabara girl. The savage Śabaras drove her away from their village. Whilst she is wandering in the forest, she meets some monks, to whom she does honour. For this she becomes a queen in her next existence, the consort of the king of Kosala. A remaining portion of the Karman was, however, still left. Thus it happened that a female demon (Yakṣī) who was in love with the king, assumed the form of the queen, and succeeded in persuading the king that the real queen was a demon. She is driven away, and is about to commit suicide. Then she meets a monk, who tells her about her previous existences. After some time the king, who had in the meantime discovered the truth, finds her again, but both of them now renounce the world, and enter the Jaina Order.

The Samarāicca Kahā is written in prose with inserted verse passages of varying length (usually in the Āryā metre). The language is Jaina-Māhārāṣṭrī. In the verses it does not differ from the dialect used generally in Jaina-Prākrit, in the prose it is mingled here and there with peculiarities of Śaurasenī. On the whole the style is simple and lucid, not so elaborate as in the novels of Bāṇa and Subandhu; nevertheless long compound words in the descriptions, and the use of ornate poetical figures of speech show that the author was well-versed in the rules of poetic art.

This literary form, namely the Dharmakathā or religious novel, reaches its culmination in the allegorical Sanskrit novel Upamitibhavaprapañcā Kathā, [1] "the narrative in

1) Edited by P. *Peterson* and H. *Jacobi* in Bibl. Ind. 1899 to 1914; new edition Bombay 1918 and 1920 in JPU 46 and 49. German translation (Books I-III) by W. *Kirfel*, Leipzig 1924 (Indische Erzähler Nr. 10). Italian transl., by A. *Ballini* in GSAI, Vols. 17-19 and 21-24. See also *Jacobi*, Upamitibhavaprapañcae Kathae specimen, Bonnae

which the manifoldness of existence is presented in parable," by the poet Siddharṣi. The following anecdote about the poet is told in the Prabhāvaka-Caritra XIV:

Siddha was a cousin of the poet Māgha. He was married to Dhanyā, a woman of good family, but in the course of time he got into bad company, took to gambling and spent the nights with evil companions. One day his mother saw her young daughter-in-law weeping, and asked her what was the cause of her grief. The young woman said that her husband never came home before midnight. The mother-in-law comforted her, and promised to exhort her son. The next time that Siddha returned home late, she did not open the door to him, but told him to go to a place where doors were open at that time of night. Then Siddha went to the Jaina monks whose doors are always open. They recognised the future Prabhāvaka in him, and received him with due ceremony. He became a Jaina monk, and it was in vain that his father tried to dissuade him from his resolve. After he had learned with the Buddhists for some time and had become their adherent, he was brought back to the Jaina faith again by his old teacher.

As Siddharṣi completed his work, according to his own statement, in 906 A.D., whereas the poet Māgha lived in the second half of the 7th century, this pretty anecdote is devoid of any historical foundation. In the Praśasti, the appendix to his poem, Siddharṣi mentions in his genealogy of teachers the names of Sūryācārya of the Nirvṛtti Kula, Dellamahattara and Durgasvāmin, a wealthy Brahman who had become a Jaina monk, and who died at Bhillamāla (the present-day Bhīnmāl in Southern Mārwāḍ),[1] but he then speaks with enthusiasm and great respect of the Ācārya Haribhadra as the teacher to whom he is indebted for the enlightenment in

1891 (Festschrift der Universität) and A. *Ballini*, Contributo allo studio della Upamitibhavaprapañcā Kathā di Siddharṣi (Rendiconti della Reale Accademia dei Lincei, Scienze morali, storichee filol. s. V, Vol. 15), Roma 1906. In the MSS. both Upamiti and Upamita occur as the title.

1) In the Jaina temple of the same town Siddharṣi first recited his poem and the nun Gaṇā, a pupil of Durgasvāmin, wrote it down.

the true religion and of whom he has spoken in Book I of his poem as the "Awakener of the knowledge of the religion" (Dharmabodhakara).[1] These words would lead one to believe that Haribhadra must have been the immediate teacher of the poet. Nevertheless this is impossible, if the date for Haribhadra assumed above is correct. Neither has the later tradition, e.g., in the Prabhāvaka-Caritra, any knowledge of Haribhadra and Siddharṣi having been contemporaries. There is, therefore, nothing for it but to assume that Siddharṣi pays Haribhadra so great a toll of veneration only because he has derived the greatest inspiration from his writings. Haribhadra's Samarāicca Kahā did indeed serve as a model for Siddharṣi.

The work is a novel in prose with numerous verse passages, some long and others short, mostly Ślokas, only at the end of the individual books more elaborate metres also make their appearance.[2] Like all Indian novels it consists of a frame story with inserted tales. As in all narrative poems of the Jainas, here too, the destinies of a being are traced through numerous reincarnations. The original trait of this poem is, however, that it does so in the form of an allegory, or rather of allegories : for it is not only the main narrative, but the separate stories also, which are in part allegories. On the other hand the form of an allegory is not strictly adhered to.[3] The poet himself distinguishes between two kinds of personages : "outward" companions of the hero, and "inward" companions. It is only the latter which are personifications; and they are indeed the main characters in the "drama of

1) He adds : "He who, foreseeing what is to come, wrote for my sake the Lalitavistarā, his commentary on the Caityavandana." On a MS. of this commentary, s. *Kielhorn* in Ind. Ant. 10, 1881, p. 101.

2) *Cf. Jacobi*, Ed., Preface, p. xxiii ff.

3) This constitutes the difference of this work from Bunyan's "Pilgrim's Progress," with which it has sometimes been compared.

mundane existence" (saṃsāranāṭaka), which the poet intends to unroll before the pious hearer.

The poet commences with an allegory in which he describes his own career. In the city of "Without-beginning-and-without-end" there lives an ugly, wretched beggar, who is suffering from all diseases, and whose name is Virtueless (Niṣpuṇyaka). The wretched food which he was able to procure by begging, scarcely served to satisfy his hunger, and only increased his illness. In this city the famous king "Stand-firm" ruled. The beggar came to his palace, and was admitted by the door-keeper "Resolver-of-one's-own-Karman" out of pity. The beggar feels very happy indeed at the sight of the splendour of the palace. The cook "Awakener-of-the-knowledge-of-religion" and his beautiful daughter "His pity" bring the beggar the tasty and curative food "The great good" and treat him with the eye-salve "Pure sight" and the mouth-lotion "Creating-joy-in the-Truth." Little by little he is cured, but for a long time he is unwilling to give up his old bad diet. Then the cook "Awakener-of-the-knowledge-of-religion" engages "True Insight" as his nurse, and at length he realises the impurity of his former food, he cleans his begging bowl, and "Virtueless" is transformed into "Rich-in-Virtues." He is now desirous of making this wondrous remedy available to others too, but as the people who had previously known him, do not want to listen to him, "True Insight" advises him to place the three remedies in a wooden bowl and place it in the courtyard of the royal palace, so that everyone may help himself. In the concluding verses of Book I the explanation of the allegory is then given: The city "Without-beginning-and-without-end" is Saṃsāra. The beggar "Virtueless" is the poet himself. The King "Stand-firm" is the Jina, his palace is the Jaina religion. The cook "Awakener-of-the-knowledge-of-religion" is "the Master who awakened me, and his daughter is the great pity which he extended towards me."[1] Knowledge is the eye-salve, the true faith is the salutary lotion, and the good life is the best diet. It is "True Insight" which allows one to find the path to virtue, and the wooden bowl with the food, the lotion and the eye-salve is the following story.

There is a city "Way-of-man," which has been in existence since all eternity, and in which, as in the narrative of Samarāditya,[2] many events

1) As the poet himself says in the Praśasti, this refers to the master Haribhadra.

2) An allusion to Haribhadra's Samarāicca Kahā. I cannot help confessing that, after all this, I find it very difficult to believe that Haribhadra should not have been really Siddharṣi's teacher.

take place. In this city there reigns the mighty king " Maturing-of-deeds " (Karmapariṇāma), [1] a rulerof unlimited powers, who mercilessly inflicts severe punishments. For his own entertainment he has the beings who act the drama of the world-wandering, wearing the most diverse masks. He makes them scream as denizens of hell, dance before him in agonies of pain, act the parts of crows, cats, mice, lions, elephants, buffaloes, lice, ants, and other large and small animals of all kinds ; whilst others again are compelled to act human rôles, such as hunchbacks and dwarfs, dumb and blind men, old men and invalids, the unfortunate, persons separated from their dear ones, poverty-stricken persons and tormented ones, as faithless women, ignoble men, etc. And this drama amuses the mighty king immensely. The principal wife of this king is " Effect-of-Time " (Kālapariṇati), and he has to ask her advice on all occasions. She too takes delight with her husband in the drama of the world-wandering. She wishes for a son, and a son is born, who receives from his father the name " Man-as-he-should be " (Bhavyapuruṣa) and from his mother the name " Well-disposed " (Sumati). Now in the city of Way-of-man " there lives a great sage named Sadāgama, *i.e.*, " The true doctrine." The king is very much afraid of this man, because he spoils the king's drama, as he has already liberated many of the actors and taken them to a city called " Blissful-rest " (Nirvṛti, meaning Nirvāṇa) situated outside the realm, where they live in the greatest happiness. Nevertheless the female attendant " Rich-in-Insight " succeeds in effecting a meeting of the prince with Sadāgama. The parents give their consent to Sadāgama's undertaking the boy's education. Once when Sadāgama is reciting his doctrines on the market-place, a great tumult arises. It is seen that the thief " Wandering-Soul " (Saṃsārijīva) is being led to the judgment-seat. (It is the Emperor Anusundara who appears in the form of this thief, in order to relate his experiences in countless rebirths for the instruction of his relatives.) " Rich-in-Insight " takes pity on the thief, and advises him to seek the protection of Sadāgama. The executioners have to release him, and he now relates his experiences for the instruction of " Rich-in-Insight " and Prince " Well-disposed." Now there comes the story of Saṃsārijīva, *i.e.*, the soul wandering in the cycle of rebirths.

He relates how he was first of all born as a plant in the world "Motionless," how he then came to the city " Home-of-beings-with-one-sense organ"

1) The law that every deed must have its consequences.

and ever and again wandered to and fro among the lowest organisms, the earth-bodies (stones, minerals, etc.), the water-bodies (hoar-frost, snow, fog, etc.), fire-bodies and wind-bodies,[1] and suffered many sorrows and torments. He was then reborn among the various animals from the very lowest insects, worms, etc., up to the elephants. At length he was reborn in the world of human beings as Nandivardhana, a king's son. Though he had an invisible friend "Dawn-of-virtue," to whom he was indebted for many successes in life, yet his most intimate "inner" friend was Vaiśvānara, *i.e.*, "Fire-of-anger." This friend always supplied him with the pill "Cruel Thoughts." For this reason the efforts of excellent teachers and counsellors, such as the sage Vidura, who sought to improve him by means of moral narratives (allegory of Sparśana, the sense of touch) and speeches, proved fruitless. The influence of Vaiśvānara grew even stronger, when he succeeded in marrying him to "Violence" (Hiṃsā), the daughter of King "Bad-Will" and Queen "Merciless."

Fortified by the pills of "Cruel Thoughts" and encouraged by the glances of his wife "Violence," he kills innumerable wild animals in the chase, but also wins great fame in fights with robbers and foes. After many adventures (the scene of some of them is laid, not in the world of allegory, but in the real world, love-stories, etc.) he becomes king. Under the influence of his evil "inner" friends he perpetrates many cruelties, he kills an ambassador, his father, his mother, his wives, and finally also his rescuer and benefactor. He flees and meets a young man: a quarrel ensues between them, the result of which is that they pierce each other with their swords. Thereupon both of them are reborn in the "Abode of the worst sinners," and after that, as lions, falcons, ichneumons, always as foes. At length Saṃsārijīva comes into the world as a prince again, Prince Ripudāraṇa. Now it is "Pride" and "Falsehood" that become his friends, and they exert paramount influence over him, so that "Dawn-of-virtue" does not stand much chance against them. After his father has become a monk, he becomes king, refuses to pay due respect to a ruler of the world, is humiliated by a sorcerer and slain by his servants. In the subsequent rebirths he pays the penalty of his misdeeds in hell and as animals, until he is once again reborn among human beings, this time as the son of the merchant Vāmadeva. "Falsehood," "Deceit" and "Theft" are now his friends. He robs a merchant, is hanged, and is then again reborn in hell and in the

1) In the belief of the Jaina, all these are beings having souls.

animal world. After a long time he again makes his appearance in the world as the son of a merchant, his "inner" companions now being "Dawn of Virtue" and "Avarice" (Sāgara). Through the latter he acquires enormous wealth. He makes friends with a prince, and goes on a sea-voyage with him. In order to secure the riches of this prince, he wants to kill him. The sea-god, however, rescues the prince, and throws the merchant into the sea. He is cast up on shore, wanders about in a wretched condition, and finally, when he wants to bury a treasure, he is devoured by a Vetāla. More rebirths in hell and in the animal world follow. Reborn as Prince Ghanavāhana, he grows up with his cousin Akalaṅka. The latter becomes a pious Jaina, and through him Ghanavāhana, too, comes into contact with Sadāgama. But Mahāmoha, *i.e.*, "The Great Infatuation," and Parigraha, *i.e.*, "Longing-for-possession" also seek his friendship, and finally obtain complete mastery over him. Hence he becomes a violent ruler, is deposed, and perishes miserably. After many rebirths in hell and in the animal world, he is at length reborn in Sāketa as Amṛtodara, and now begins Saṃsārijīva's ascent to higher forms of existence. He is converted to the Jaina faith, and attains to the world of gods and of men, by turns. Reborn as King Guṇadhāraṇa, he is reunited with Sadāgama and Samyagdarśana ("Right Faith"); he becomes a pious layman and a good ruler, especially after he has brought home the ten virgins "Patience," "Pity," "Gentleness," "Love of Truth," "Straightness," "Honesty," "Chastity," "Liberation," "Science" and "Desirelessness" as brides. At the end of his life he becomes a monk, and is then reborn alternately as god or man. Finally, in his last incarnation Saṃsārijīvin is the world-ruler Anusundara. Now at length the retinue of the "Great Infatuation" is powerless, and only the good qualities are his "inner" companions; he attains to the highest knowledge, and remembers his former existences. Now, in the form of the thief condemned to death, he relates his fortunes in the cycle of rebirths. Then he becomes absorbed in meditation, and rises, as a god, to the highest heaven.

All this is told with great verbosity, and numerous stories and sermons are interwoven with the narrative wherever convenient. Siddharṣi says that he chose the allegory, in order to attract the readers, and for the same reason he wrote in Sanskrit, and not in Prākrit, because Prākrit is for the uneducated, whilst even the educated are to be won over to the doctrine from their heretical views. He adds, however, that he wishes to write an easy Sanskrit which will be universally understood. The language is, indeed, smooth and clear, never bombastic and rarely obscure. As is usually the case with the Jainas who write in Sanskrit, he uses Prākritisms and popular expressions.[1] The great popularity which this poem enjoyed among the Jainas is shown by the fact that, only 100 years after its appearance, extracts and abridgments were made from it,[2] and that even Hemacandra uses names in one of the stories in the Pariśiṣṭa-Parvan [3] which presuppose that Siddharṣi's work was universally known.

There were also religious novels written entirely in verse. A romantic epic of this kind is the Bhavisatta Kahā [4] in Apabhraṃśa by a poet Dhaṇavāla (Sanskrit Dhanapāla), a Digambara Jaina layman, who belonged to the merchant caste of Dharkaṭa. The period of the author is unknown, but it is probable that he used Haribhadra's Samarāicca Kahā as a model. The explicit aim of the narrative is the glorification of the Pañcamīvrata, a vow which is fulfilled on the fifth day of one of the three months Kārttika, Phālguna or Āṣāḍha, and extends, accompanied by various religious exercises, over 5 years. In order to show the fruits of the fulfilment of these religious exercises, the story of Bhavisatta (Bhaviṣyadatta) is told.

1) *Jacobi*, Ed., Preface, pp. xxii, xxvii-xxxv gives many examples of this.

2) Such as those by Vardhamāna (who suffered the voluntary death by starvation in about 1032 A.D.), Devendra Sūri and Haṃsaratna. *Cf. Jacobi* in JRAS 1909, 421 ; on Vardhamāna, s. *Peterson*, Report IV, p. cx.

3) II, 315 ff. It is said here of a wealthy merchant, that his father was "Ocean" (Samudra) and his mother "Deceitful" (Bahulā). In the Upamitibhavaprapañcā Kathā, Sāgara, "Ocean" is the personification of avarice, and Bahulikā that of deceit. *Cf. Jacobi, loc. cit.*, 421 ff.

4) Bhavisatta Kahā von Dhanavāla, eine Jainalegende in Apabhraṃśa herausgegeben von H. *Jacobi* in ABayA XXIX, 4, München 1918 ; partly edited by the late C. D. *Dalal* and completed with Introduction, Notes, Glossary etc., by the ate Pandurang Damodar *Gune* in GOS Nr. 20, Baroda 1923 ; *cf. Gune* in Proc. I. OO Poona 1922, p. 158f. The work is especially important for our knowledge of the Apabhraṃśa language. The author is distinct from Dhanapāla, the author of the Pāīyalacchī.

The main theme of the poem is a fairy-tale, the hero of which, Bhavisatta, experiences strange adventures. Deserted upon a lonely island by his treacherous step-brother, he comes to a deserted city, discovers a princess with the help of a god, marries her, and they live joyfully for 12 years. Bhavisatta is home-sick, and one day the ship of the wicked step-brother lands again on the island. Bhavisatta wishes to return to his home with his wife, but is again outwitted by the step-brother, who carries off his wife, but leaves Bhavisatta himself on the island. With the help of a Yakṣa he is, however, brought home on the chariot of a god in the nick of time, and is reunited with his wife who has remained faithful to him throughout. In Part II fights after the manner of the Mahābhārata and the Rāmāyaṇa are described, whilst in Part III the preliminary stories of the principal characters in their former births are told.

The Malayasundarī Kathā,[1] in which an unknown poet has worked up popular fairy-tale themes into a Jaina legend, appears to be a romantic epic in Prākrit of a similar nature. A veritable deluge of the most phantastic miracles and magic feats, almost takes away the reader's breath in this work. Countless motifs well-known in the fairy-tale literature are interwoven with the novel, which relates how Prince Mahābala and Princess Malayasundarī find each other miraculously, how they are ever and again separated from each other, and ever and again reunited. Since all the wonderful destinies are explained as the consequences of some deeds in previous existences, and as Prince Mahābala finally attains to omniscience as a pious monk, and Malayasundarī becomes a famous nun, the magic fairy-tale has come to be a pious Jaina legend. This fairy-tale romance must have been very popular, for, as late as in the 15th century Māṇikyasundara wrote a Mahābala-Malayasundarī-Kathā,

[1]) I know the contents of the work only from *Hertel*'s German translation of the Malayasundarīkathoddhāra written by Dharmacakra in the 14th century, an extract in Sanskrit prose with interspersed verse passages in Sanskrit and Prākrit, based upon the Prākrit epic, s. *Hertel*, Indische Märchen, Jena 1919, pp. 185-268.

which, in its turn, served as a prototype for a M a l a y a-s u n d a r ī-C a r i t r a in Sanskrit stanzas by J a y a-t i l a k a. The last-named work again formed the basis of a Gujarātī poem in the 18th century.[1]

Distinct from these novels there are the C a m p ū s or ornate novels in prose and verse, written after the model of Bāṇa's "Kādambarī." Foremost among these is the Y a ś a s-t i l a k a[2] by the Digambara Jaina S o m a d e v a S ū r i, written in about 959 A.D. The contents of this religious poem in prose and verse, based upon Guṇabhadra's Uttara-Purāṇa, are briefly as follows :

King Māridatta has ascended the throne at an early age and is entirely given up to sensual pleasures. At the advice of his family priest he prepares to offer a great sacrifice to his family goddess Caṇḍamāridevatā, consisting of a pair of every living creature, including human beings. Māridatta himself is to perform the sacrifice. Then the servants drag in a youth and a maiden, a pair of ascetics whom they have selected for the human sacrifice. At the sight of them a change comes over the king. It occurs to him that these might be the twin children of his own sister, who were said to have renounced the world and joined the Jaina community. He asks these two to tell him their history, and it is revealed that they are indeed his relatives. The major part of the story deals with their experiences in various rebirths, but many explanations regarding the doctrines of the Jaina religion are interwoven. Many famous poets, such as Bhāravi, Bhavabhūti, Bhartṛhari, Guṇāḍhya, Vyāsa, Bhāsa, Kālidāsa, Bāṇa, and others, are mentioned, all of whom are supposed to have done honour to the Jaina religion. The last three sections also form an independent book, entitled U p ā s a k ā d h y a y a n a ("Readings for Laymen"), which serves as a work of edification for Jaina laymen. The work ends with the conversion of Māridatta and his family goddess to the Jaina religion.

Poems of the same category are T i l a k a m a ñ j a r ī[3] by the Śvetāmbara Jaina D h a n a p ā l a, who wrote about

1) *Cf. Hertel, loc. cit.*, p. 377 ff.

2) Edited with a commentary in Km. 70, 1901. *Cf. Peterson*, Report II, 33 ff., 147 ff., and *Haltzsch* in Quarterly Journal of the Mythic Society, 1922, p. 318 f.

3) Edited in Km. 85, Bombay 1903. *Cf. Jacobi* in GGA 1905, 379 Merutuṅga

970 A.D., and Gadyacintāmaṇi,[1] "Wishing-jewel of prose" by the Digambara Jaina Oḍeyadeva Vādībhasiṃha (beginning of the 11th century A.D.).[2] The subject-matter of this novel, as well as that of Kṣatracūḍāmaṇi[3] by the same author, is the legend of Jīvandhara with which we are familiar from the Uttara-Purāṇa. The same legend has also been treated in the form of a Campū by the Digambara Jaina poet Haricandra in his Jīvandhara-Campū.[4]

Just as the legends of the Jinas, thus other legends and fairy-tale themes, too, have been worked up into ornate epics. Thus, for instance, the legend of King Yaśodhara, which we know already from Haribhadra's Samarāicca Kahā, has been treated by Vādirāja Sūri[5] in the Yaśodhara-Carita,[6] an epic in 4 cantos. Vādirāja's source was, however, again Guṇabhadra's Uttara-Purāṇa. On the other hand, according to his own statements, Māṇikya Sūri

(Prabandhacintāmaṇi, Transl. by Tawney, p. 60 f.) tells a pretty story about the origin of the work.

1) Edited by T. S. *Kuppuswāmi Sāstri*, Madras 1902.

2) His teacher was Puṣpasena, a fellow-pupil of Vādirāja, the author of the Yaśodhara-Carita. Both were pupils of Somadeva Sūri, author of the Yaśastilaka. Vādībhasiṃha is an epithet of several teachers. *Cf. Hultzsch* in ZDMG 68, 1914, 697 f. and A. *Venkatasubbiah* in JBRAS, N.S., 3, 1928, 156 ff. According to him Śrīvijaya Oḍeyadeva is identical with Vādībhasiṃha.

3) Edited by T. S. *Kuppuswāmi Sāstrī*, Tanjore 1903 (Sarasvatī-vilāsa Series No. 3); *cf.* Ind. Ant. 36, 1907, 285 ff. and *Hultzsch* in Quarterly Journal of the Mythic Society, 1922, p. 318.

4) Edited by T. S. *Kuppuswāmi Sāstrī*, Tanjore 1905 (Sarasvatī-vilāsa Series No. 4); s. *Hulzsch* in Ind. Ant. 35, 1906, 268 and Quarterly Journal of the Mythic Society, 1922, p. 318. The author is probably identical with Haricandra, the author of the Dharmaśarmābhyudaya. A famous Tamil adaptation of the same legend is Jīvakacintāmaṇi by the poet Tiruttakadevar, who probably lived before Oḍeyadeva. *Cf.* also *Glasenapp*, Der Jainismus, p. 119 f.

5) The same who wrote the Pārśvanātha-Carita in the year 1025; s. above p. 515.

6) Edited by T. A. *Gopinatha Rao*, Tanjore 1912 (Sarasvatī-vilāsa Series No. 5). *Cf. Hertel*, Jinakīrtis "Geschichte von Pāla und Gopāla," pp. 91 ff., 146 ff.

used Haribhadra's narrative as a source, in his Yaśodhara-Caritra.[1)] Surasundarī-Cariaṃ[2)] by Dhaneśvara, the pupil of Jineśvara Sūri and Buddhisāgara Sūri,[3)] written towards the end of the 11th century, is a voluminous romantic epic in Prākrit. Mṛgavatī-Caritra[4)] by Maladhāri-Devaprabha, containing one of the many versions of the legend of Udayana and his wives Vāsavadattā and Padmāvatī, is another fairy-tale epic. The author, who probably lived in the 13th century, himself says that he drew upon the Siddhānta and its commentaries. He has indeed made use of Haribhadra's Āvaśyaka commentary and Hemacandra's Pariśiṣṭa-Parvan.

Mahīpāla, the hero of the Mahīpāla-Caritra[5)] by Cāritrasundara, who probably wrote in the middle of the 15th century, is a genuine fairy-tale king. All manner of narratives, fairy-tales and legends are here combined to form an ornate epic in 14 cantos.

Mahīpāla is skilled in all arts, and gives numerous proofs of exceptional cleverness. For instance, when a Yakṣa, posing as the "double" of the real husband, tries to appropriate a woman, he decides who is the real husband, by saying that the real husband is the one who can crawl into a water-jug and out again. This can, of course, only be done by the Yakṣa, the demon, who is thus proved to be the false husband.[6)] When he is

1) Edited by Hīrālāl *Haṃsarāj*, Jamnagar 1910. There were several authors named Māṇikya Sūri, one in the 13th and one in the 16th century, and it is not possible to ascertain which of them is the author of the Yaśodhara-Caritra. *Cf. Weber*, HSS. Verz., II, 3, 1067 ff.; *Hertel*, l.c., p. 81 ff., 138 ff.

2) Edited with Notes by *Muniraj Shree Raje Vijayjee*, Benares 1916 (Jaina Vividha Sahitya Shastramala No. 1).

3) These two were pupils of Vardhamāna Sūri, who died in 1031 A.D., so that Dhaneśvara must have lived not later than towards the close of the 11th century. However, there are 5 other teachers named Dhaneśvara.

4) Edited by Hīrālāl *Haṃsarāj*, Jamnagar 1909; *cf. Hertel*, l.c., p. 105 ff., 150 ff.

5) Edited by Hīrālāl *Haṃsarāj*, Jamnagar 1909; *cf. Hertel*, l.c., p. 72 ff., 188 f.

6) Parallels from Indian and universal literature are cited by *Hertel*, l.c., p. 74, Note 2.

cast into the ocean by a treacherous minister, he saves himself by swimming on the back of a large fish which carries him ashore. There he wins a beautiful wife, a magic bed which transports him to any place he desires, a magic staff which makes him invincible, and an incantation by means of which he can assume any form he desires. He changes himself into a hunchback, gives himself out as an astrologer, and shows the king a book which he says can be read by any person who has been legitimately begotten, but not by one who has been begotten in adultery. The king, the court priest and the prime minister in turn have a look at the book, none of them can read anything in it, but each one pretends that he can read it, and praises the clearness of the script.[1] Moreover, Mahīpāla is the only man who can weigh an elephant and also can tie up a post from the shore. Finally, of course, Mahīpālā becomes a monk and a saint, and attains to release, after having lived to the age of 500 years.

The Kathānakas or little stories, so many of which were included in the commentaries, were frequently also written down as independent works, and sometimes they were elaborated into ornate poems.

The Kālakācārya-Kathānaka,[2] which is generally recited by the monks at the end of the recital of the Kalpa-Sūtra, is a Prākrit poem in prose and verse. The narrative is probably based on an old tradition, and it is quite possible that it contains an historical nucleus.[3] It is the story of the king's son Kālaka, who is converted to the Jaina religion, and attains to the high degree of Superior of the Order.[4] His younger sister, the nun Sarasvatī, is abducted by Gardabhilla, ruler of Ujjayinī, and dragged into his harem. Kālaka feigns madness, incites the people to rebel against the ruler, and

[1]) Parallels from universal literature are given by *Hertel*, l.c., p. 77, Note 2.

[2]) Edited and translated by H. *Jacobi*, ZDMG 34, 1880, 247-318 ; supplements to it, ZDMG 35, 675 ff., and *Leumann*, ZDMG 37, 493 ff. There is also a Kālakācāryakathānaka by Bhāvadeva Sūri in 102 Prākrit verses. On the same legend in Sanskrit *cf.* *Bhâu Dâji* in JBRAS 9, 1867, 139 ff.

[3]) *Cf.* Sten *Konow* in SBA 1916, p. 812 f.

[4]) He is identical with Ayya Sāma (Ārya Syāma), who is said to have written the fourth Upāṅga. See above, pp. 433 and Note 1 ; 456.

wanders to Śakakūla, whose rulers, the Sāhis, he causes to go to war against Gardabhilla and to conquer Ujjayinī. In the narrative portions the language is simple enough, but in the descriptions an ornate style prevails, which reminds us of Subandhu and Bāṇa and the ornate Campūs. Unfortunately the date of the work is unknown, and not even the name of the author has come down.

Another work of unknown date is the Uttama (-Kumāra)-Caritra-Kathānaka, "The Story of the Life of (Prince) Most Excellent,"[1] a fairy-tale full of the most wonderful adventures, inserted into the frame-work of a Jinistic sermon. It is to be found in one prose-version and several metrical ones. The language is Sanskrit, but the occurrence of dialectal words proves that the work originated in Gujarat.

A pious fairy and wonder tale of the same nature is the Pāpabuddhi-Dharmabuddhi-Kathānaka, "The Story of Evil-mind and Pious-mind."[2] King Evil-mind believes only in power and wealth and not in the consequences of religious merit. The minister Pious-mind, who, owing to his pious works in the previous life, attains to fabulous good fortune and wealth, with the help of all kinds of magic things (a wishing-pot which always supplies food, a cudgel which itself invisible drives all foes away, an umbrella which cures all diseases, etc.) proves the contrary to him. Finally a monk enlightens both of them as to their destinies in their former incarnations, and both the king and his minister become Jaina

1) The prose version edited and translated into German by A. *Weber* in SBA 1884, 1, 269 to 310, the metrical recension, Uttamakumāra-Caritra, in 686 Ślokas by Cārucandra the pupil of Bhaktilābha, is edited by Hīralāl *Haṃsarāj*, Jamnagar 1908 (2nd Ed., 1911); *cf. Weber*, HSS. Verz. II, 3, 1080 f., and *Hertel* in Festgabe Jacobi, p. 135 ff.

2) Edited and translated into Italian by E. *Lovarini* in GSAI 3, pp. 94-127; s. *Hertel*, *loc. cit.*, pp. 66 ff., 136, who quotes two recensions of the story in Sanskrit prose (one of these entitled Kāmaghaṭakathā, "Story of the Wishing-Pot," edited by Hīralāl *Haṃsarāj*, Jamnagar 1909) and two in Gujarātī verses,

monks. In the case of this story also, the time and the author are unknown.

In the Campakaśreṣṭhi-Kathānaka, "Story of the merchant Campaka,"[1] by Jinakīrti, who wrote in about the middle of the 15th century,[2] we have the fairy-tale of the lucky child who is saved from destruction by the fatal letter exchanged at the last moment. This is the tale, widely known both in the East and in the West, with which we are familiar from the Brahmanical and Buddhist literature, and with which we thus meet among the Jainas also. In this case it forms the frame-story for three inserted stories. The first of these is the fairy-tale of King Rāvaṇa, who vainly tries to defy a decree of fate. The third story of the merchant who has hitherto deceived everyone, but is himself at last deceived by a courtesan, is not lacking in humour.[3] Another work of the same author is the Pāla-Gopāla-Kathānaka, the "Story of Pāla and Gopāla," a pious Jaina legend, with which all kinds of well-known themes of novels and fairy-tales (of the two brothers who go on their wanderings, and after many adventures attain to honour and fame; of the grateful and helpful animals; of the woman who tries to seduce the chaste youth, and when she cannot succeed, accuses him of having made an attempt on her honour, etc.) are interwoven.[4] The same Jinakīrti is also the author of a didactic poem

1) First analysed by A. *Weber* in SBA 1883, pp. 567 ff., 885 ff.; edited and translated into English by *Hertel* in ZDMG 65, 1911, pp. 1-51, 425-470; a German translation in "Indische Märchenromane" I (Indische Erzähler, Bd. 7, Leipzig 1922). The story is to be found among the Jainas also in Kathākośa (translated by C. H. *Tawney*, p. 169 ff.) and in Merutuṅga's Prabandhacintāmaṇi; *cf.* J. *Schick*, Das Glückskind mit dem Todesbrief (Corpus Hamleticum I, 1), pp. 75 ff.; 96 ff.; 160 ff., and see above, I, 585; II, 201.

2) *Cf. Klatt*, Specimen of a lit.-bibl. Jaina Onomasticon, p. 15; *Duff*, p. 254; *Peterson*, Report IV, p. xxxiii, and *Hertel*, Jinakīrtis "Geschichte von Pāla und Gopāla," p. 1.

3) Similarly Gesta Romanorum, Cap. 118. *Cf. Köhler* and *Gildemeister* in Weber, l.c., p. 591 f. and 890 f.

4) Joh. *Hertel*, Jinakīrtis "Geschichte von Pāla und Gopāla," Leipzig 1917 (BSGW 69. Bd. 1917, 4 Heft).

Dāna-Kalpa-Druma,[1] in which the importance of almsgiving is presented, and lavishly illustrated by means of stories.

The Aghaṭa-Kumāra-Kathā, the "Story of Prince Aghaṭa" is also based upon the fairy-tale of the lucky child and the fatal letter which is exchanged. There are three different recensions of this pretty fairy-tale, a longer and a shorter one in verse, and a prose version.[2]

The Ambaḍa-Charitra, "The Adventures of Ambaḍa,"[3] by Amara Sūri, is a very phantastic magical fairy-tale. The world of ideas in which this fairy-tale moves, is Śivaite rather than Jinistic. Ambaḍa is a great magician, who can fly through the air, change men into animals and change them back again, and himself assume any form he likes. By means of his magic arts he succeeds in carrying out seven difficult tasks of the witch Gorakhā, and in winning 32 beautiful wives, untold wealth and a kingdom. It is not until the last chapter that the hero Ambaḍa is converted from the Śivaite faith to the Jaina faith ; he becomes at first a pious layman and finally a monk, who, after his voluntary death by starvation, reaches heaven. It is true that a great magician Ambaḍa (or Ammada) is already mentioned in the Ovavāiya, the first Upāṅga, but the story itself is undoubtedly modern, and is associated with the "Thirty-two Throne-stories" (Siṃhāsanadvātriṃśikā), which belong to the cycle of legends of King Vikramāditya.[4]

Another novel, consisting of a frame-story and a few inserted stories, is the Ratnacūḍa-Kathā, "Story of

1) Edited in JPU No. 9, Bombay 1919.

2) The last-named is translated into German by Charlotte *Krause*, Indische Novellen I (Indische Erzähler Bd. 4), Leipzig 1922. The shorter metrical version appeared in Bombay NSP 1917 entitled Aghaṭa-Kumāra-Caritra. The two other versions were accessible to the translator in MSS.

3) Edited by Hīralāl *Haṃsarāj*, Jamnagar 1910; translated into German by Charlotte *Krause*, l.c.

4) *Krause*, l.c., 155 f. ; 162 ff.

Ratnacūḍa,"[1] by Jñānasāgara Sūri, who lived in the middle and the second half of the 15th century. The frame-story contains the witty and entertaining story of the city of rogues, Anītipura, in which King "Unjust" rules, whose prime minister is "Unwise" and whose court priest is "Restless," and in which only thieves, rogues and deceivers reside. Amongst the inserted stories we have that of the clever boy Rohaka, who, like Mahosadha in the Mahā-Ummagga-Jātaka,[2] is able to perform many seemingly impossible feats, owing to his intelligence. Here, too, we meet once more with the story of Somaśarman who builds castles in the air, which is familiar from the Pañcatantra. Some of the didactic passages inserted occasionally in these narratives, are also of interest: a long discussion on dreams and their interpretation; the instructions given by the father to his son Ratnacūḍa when the latter sets forth on his travels, and which present a curious mixture of worldly wisdom and superstition; an enumeration of the auspicious omens when going on a journey, and an enumeration of the thirty-two characteristic marks of the body of a great man.

In later times the Jainas also compiled Books of stories, in which the stories either appear in the form of stories inserted into a frame-story, in the manner familiar in Indian narrative literature, or else they are just told one after another. A work belonging to the former category is Samyaktvakaumudī, "The Moonshine of Perfection," by an unknown author.[3] The only connection of this book

---

1) Edited in YJG, Bhavnagar 1917; translated into German by *Hertel*, Indische Märchenromane, I. (Indische Erzähler, Bd. 7), Leipzig 1922, p. 97 ff.

2) See above, p. 137 ff.

3) A. *Weber*, Ueber die Samyaktvakaumudī, eine eventualiter mit Tausendundeinenacht auf gleiche Quelle zurückgehende indische Erzählung, SBA 1889, 731 ff. According to *Weber*, l.c., p. 733, the time of the work would be limited by the date of the poet Bilhaṇa (end of the 11th century) who is mentioned in it, and by the date of one of the three MSS (1433 A.D.). If, however, the Bilhaṇa referred to is not the Kashmiri poet,

of fairy-tales and stories with the Jaina religion is the frame, in which the merchant Arhaddāsa tells his eight wives, and they in turn tell him, how they attained to perfection (samyaktva) in the religion. At the same time these stories are overheard by a king, who roams about at night with his minister, after the fashion of Harun al Rashid, and by a thief. The story of King Suyodhana who, in order to set a trap for his faithful deputy, breaks into his own treasury, is recognised by the deputy as a thief, and is warned by seven stories told on successive days, but is finally unmasked as a thief and deposed by the people, reminds us of the "Arabian Nights" and still more of the Sindbad book.[1]

A rich mine of tales, part of which also belong to universal literature, is to be found in the Kathā-Kośa, the "Treasury of Stories," collected by an unknown compiler.[2] The language of the tales is bad Sanskrit with verses in Prākrit. Everywhere there is a strong Jinistic tendency. For instance, a sea-faring story replete with wonderful adventures is transformed into a pious legend. The last story in the book, that of Nala and Davadantī is a curious Jinistic adaptation and extension of the Nala episode of the Mahābhārata. Some of the stories are quite naïve and even insipid through their tendency. However, along with them we find many a most charming fairy-tale, such as that of the maiden Garden-beautiful:

This maiden has a wicked step-mother, who makes her do all kinds of heavy work. Once when she has led the cows out to pasture, and has

but the poet and minister whom Āśādhara mentions as his contemporary, then the work should be placed between the 13th and 14th centuries. As there are, however, two recensions of the text, the dating becomes even more uncertain.

1) The similarity with "The Arabian Nights" is very remote, but Jātaka No. 432 is very similar. *Cf.* also *Pullé*, GSAI 4, 161 ff.

2) Translated from Sanskrit MSS. by C. H. *Tawney*, London OTF, 1895. Unfortunately there are no clues whereby to determine the date of this compilation. It is certainly not old, though it probably made use of old sources.

fallen asleep, she is awakened by a black snake, which begs her to protect it from the snake-charmer. The girl protects the snake, which then asks her to wish for something. She says, "Make a shade above my head, so that I can mind the cows in comfort." Then the snake conjures up a beautiful garden which accompanies Garden-beautiful wherever she goes. In this garden the king finds her one day, falls in love with her, and makes her his queen. The step-mother lies in wait for her, so as to make her own daughter the queen, but the snake rescues Garden-beautiful from all dangers.[1]

As in other Indian narrative works, there are gnomic sayings to be found in the Kathā-Kośa too. One of these is worthy of mention :

> "The father should cherish his little son until he is five,
> And punish him until his fifteenth year he reaches;
> But when the son has reached the sixteenth year of his life,
> The father should ever treat him as a friend."

There is also a Kathā-Kośa in Apabhraṃśa, containing 53 tales in an equal number of chapters, by Śrīcandra, who wrote either in the 10th or 12th century,[2] also a Kathānaka-Kośa written in 1092 A.D. by Jineśvara,[3] the pupil of Vardhamāna. In the 14th century Rājaśekhara wrote his Antara-Kathā-Saṃgraha, "Collection of various narratives,"[4] a book of stories which he took mostly from earlier works, especially from the commentaries

---

1) *Tawney*, l.c., p. 85 ff., where many parallels from fairy-tale literature are pointed out, among others No. 11 ("Brüderchen und Schwesterchen") in *Grimm*, Kinder-und Hausmärchen.

2) According to the Praśasti, he wrote at about the period of King Mūlarāja of Anhilawāḍ: but there are two kings of this name in the Cālukya dynasty, the first of whom reigned from 941 to 996 A.D., and the second from 1176 to 1178 A.D. He traces his genealogy of teachers back to Kundakunda in the fifth degree; s. *Hiralal*, Catalogue, p. xlix ff.

3) The same author also wrote a Līlāvatī-Kathā in the year 1035 A.D. *Cf. Bhandarkar*, Report 1882-83, p. 46, and *Peterson*, Report IV, p. xliv.

4) Tales 7-14 have been given, and translated into Italian, by F. L. *Pullé*, Uno progenitore Indiano del Bartoldo, Venezia 1888. The text of the first 22 tales has been edited by *Pullé* in SIFI I, 1 ff.; II, 1 ff., Firenze 1897-98. *Cf.* also *Weber*, HSS. Verz., II, 3, 1077 ff.

on the canonical texts. Here, among others, stories of the clever solver of riddles, of a "Judgment of Solomon"[1] etc., are to be found. The book Kathā-Mahodadhi, "The great ocean of stories,"[2] compiled in the year 1448 by Somacandra, contains 157 stories partly in Prākrit, partly in Sanskrit with Prākrit verses. In the year 1464 Subhaśīla Gaṇin, pupil of Lakṣmīsāgara Sūri, wrote his Pañcaśatī-Prabodha-Sambandha, "Book of 500 stories serving to awaken the Faith."[3] Inspite of the title, the book contains nearly 600 stories, anecdotes, legends, fables, fairy-tales, etc., some of which allude to historical personages, kings and authors of both ancient and modern times, such as Nanda, Sātavāhana, Bhartṛhari, Bhoja, Kumārapāla, Hemasūri and others. The same Subhaśīla Gaṇin also wrote the Bharatādi-Kathā[4] or Kathā-Kośa in the year 1452 and several other narrative works. In about 1530 Nemidatta wrote a book of narratives entitled Ārādhanā-Kathā-Kośa.[5] In 1600 Hemavijaya wrote his Kathā-Ratnākara, "Ocean of Stories,"[6] a book of

---

1) *Cf. Zachariae*, Kleine Schriften, pp. 65 ff., 190 f.; *Garbe*, Indien und das Christentum, p. 25 f.; *Glasenapp*, Der Jainismus, pp. 272, 472. The story of the "Judgment of Solomon" has been translated according to the Antarakathāsaṃgraha by L. P. *Tessitori* in Ind. Ant. 42, 1913, 148 ff., together with another Jinistic recension (from Malayagiri's commentary on the Nandī-Sutta). *Hertel* (Geist des Ostens 1, 1913, 189 ff.) compares the Jinistic recensions with the Hebrew one, and endeavours to prove what, in my opinion, is impossible to prove, namely that the Jaina recension "is in contents the primary one, from which the other variants can then be derived."

2) *Cf. Weber*, HSS. Verz. II, 3, 1101 ff.; *Peterson*, 3 Reports, 18 f.; 316 ff. *Alsdorf*, Kumārapālapratibodha, p. 201 f., gives the story of Sthūlabhadra.

3) *Cf. Weber*, Ind. Stud. 16, 159 f., and HSS. Verz. II, 3, 1112 ff.; *Pavolini* in GSAI 13, 89 ff., who deals with the stories of Draupadī, Kuntī, Devakī and Rukmiṇī which are told in this work, and A. *Ballini* in SIFI, Vol. VI, Firenze 1904 (Text and translation of the first 50 tales). A cycle of 16 tales deals with Suratrāṇa Pīroja, *i.e.*, Sultan Fīrūz II (1220-1296) and his friend Jinaprabha Sūri; s. *Ballini* in OC XIII, Hamburg 1902, p. 41 ff.

4) See *Weber*, l. c..

5) *Peterson*, Report IV, p. 139 ff.; *Alsdorf*, Kumārapālapratibodha, p. 189 f. Nemidatta or Brahmanemidatta wrote a Śrīpālacarita in the year 1528 A. D.; s. *Bhandarkar*, Report 1883-84, pp. 123, 435.

6) Translated into German by Joh. *Hertel*, München 1920 (Meisterwerke orientalischer

258 stories. With the exception of a very few metrical narratives, the work is written in elaborate Sanskrit prose, in which stanzas in Sanskrit, Māhārāṣṭrī, Apabhraṃśa, old Hindī and old Gujarātī are interspersed. It is only the opening stanzas and the moralising introductions to the individual tales, and a very few edifying stories, which betray the fact that the compiler is a Jaina monk. Most of the narratives are similar to those in the Pañcatantra and other books of stories of this kind, tales of the artfulness of women, tales of rogues, tales of fools, fables and fairy-tales, anecdotes of all descriptions, including some which hold up Brahmans and other holy men to scorn. As in the Pañcatantra there are numerous wise sayings interspersed with the tales. The tales are, however, loosely strung together, and not inserted into a frame. There are also many interesting stories in the Dharma-Kalpa-Druma, "The wishing-tree of religion,"[1] a bulky narrative work in Sanskrit verses, written by a certain Udayadharma in about 1450 A.D. or later.

The mass of narratives and books of narratives among the Jainas is indeed vast.[2] They are of great importance not only to the student of comparative fairy-tale lore, but also because, to a greater degree than other branches of literature, they allow us to catch a glimpse of the real life of the common people. Just as in the language of these narrative works there are frequent points of agreement with the

---

Literature 4 & 5). *Cf. Hertel,* Das Pañcatantra, p. 140 f.; Ein altindisches Narrenbuch in BSGW 64, 1912, pp. 41, 43; Jinakīrtis "Geschichte von Pāla und Gopāla," p. 58 ff. Geist des Ostens, 1, 1913, p. 249 ff., and Indische Märchen, pp. 90 f., 169 ff., 374 f., 377.

1) *Cf. Hertel* in ZDMG 65, 1911, 429 ff.; 441 ff.; Ein altindisches Narrenbuch, p. 58 ff., and Indische Märchen, p. 111 ff. (*cf.* 375 f.). There was an Udayadharma, who wrote the Vākyaprakāśa (edited in the Stotra-Ratnākara, Mehsana 1913, Part I) in 1450 A.D., but also another who lived 99 years later; s. *Hertel* in ZDMG 65, 429 Note.

2) *Cf. Weber,* HSS. Verz. II, 3, 1090-1136. On the achievements of the Jainas in Indian narrative literature, s. *Hertel,* on the Literature of the Śvetāmbaras of Gujarat, Leipzig 1922.

vernaculars of the people, their subject-matter, too, gives a picture of the real life of the most varied classes of the people, not only the kings and priests, in a way which no other Indian literary works, especially the Brahman ones, do.

As poets, the Jainas have also contributed their share to the literature of the Drama.[1] Only a few of the dramas written by Jainas can, however, be described as actually Jinistic. Rāmacandra, the pupil of Hemacandra, was an exceptionally prolific writer of dramas. He is supposed to have composed no less than 100 Prakaraṇas (dramas). One of his pieces, the Nirbhaya-Bhīma-Vyāyoga, "The spectacular play of the fearless Bhīma,"[2] treats the story of the giant Baka, who is killed by Bhīma, taken from the Mahābhārata. A theme from the Mahābhārata is also treated by Vijayapāla, the son of Siddhapāla, a contemporary of Kumārapāla, in the drama Draupadī-Svayamvara.[3] Hastimalla, a pupil of Govindabhaṭṭa, wrote in about 1290 A.D. in the South of India several dramas, thus a Mahābhārata-drama, Vikrānta-Kaurava, in 6 acts, and a Rāma-Sītā-drama, Maithilī-Kalyāṇa in 5 acts.[4]

The Mudrita-Kumudacandra-Prakaraṇa,[5] "The Drama of Kumudacandra who has been Silenced," by Yaśaścandra, is a genuine Jinistic drama. This five-act drama describes how the Digambara teacher Kumudacandra was defeated by the Śvetāmbara teacher Devasūri in a disputation which took place in the presence of King Jayasiṃha. This disputation is said to have taken place in the year

---

[1] *Cf. Hultzsch* in NGGW 1921, 36 ff., and ZDMG 75, 1921, 61 ff.

[2] Edited in YJG No. 19, s. *Hultzsch*, l. c., p. 62 f.

[3] Edited by *Muni Jinavijaya*, Jaina-Ātmānanda-Sabhā, Bhavnagar 1918; s. *Hultzsch*, l.c., p. 67 f.

[4] These two plays have been edited in MDJG, Nos. 1 and 5.

[5] Edited in YJG No. 8, Benares 1905.

1124 A.D.[1] Thus the poet was probably a contemporary of King Jayasiṃha, who reigned in Gujarat from 1094 to 1142 A.D. The Jaina poet J a y s i ṃ h a wrote in the year 1229 A.D. the H a m m ī r a - M a d a m a r d a n a, [2] "The Breaking of the Pride of Hammīra," a drama in 5 acts describing how the pride of Hammīra, that is, Amir Shikār or Sultan Samsu-d-dunyā, was broken, and the attack of the Mahomedans on Gujarat was repulsed. The piece is not Jinistic in itself, but the brothers Vastupāla and Tejaḥpāla, the famous ministers of the Caulukya-king Vīradhavala, who play a part in the drama itself, were pious Jainas. As such they are glorified by Jaysiṃha in a panegyric in verse, the V a s t u p ā l a - T e j a ḥ p ā l a-P r a ś a s t i, engraven on a stone slab in a temple founded by Tejaḥpāla, and by U d a y a p r a b h a S ū r i in the panegyric S u k ṛ t a-K ī r t i k a l l o l i n ī.[3]

Between 1229 and 1232 A.D. Y a ś a ḥ p ā l a wrote an allegorical drama M o h a-R ā j a-P a r ā j a y a, "The Defeat of King Delusion,"[4] in 5 acts, in which the conversion of King Kumārapāla to Jinism and his wedding with Princess Kṛpā-Sundarī, "Mercy the Beautiful," daughter of King "Understanding" are presented, Hemacandra being named as the priest who consecrates the marriage before the Arhat. This play in which many characters, mostly allegorical, play a part, is of interest not merely from the literary point of view,

---

[1]) Thus according to the Prabhāvaka-Caritra, xxi, 86 ff., Deva Sūri, famous as the author of works on logic, died in 1169 A.D. *Cf. Hultzsch* in ZDMG 75, 1921, p. 61 f., and *Jacobi*, Sanatkumāracaritam, p. viii.

[2]) Edited by Ch. D. *Dalal* in GOS No. 10, Baroda 1920; cf. *Hultzsch* in NGGW 1921, p. 48 ff., and S. R. *Bhandarkar*, Report II, pp. 16 ff., 72 ff.

[3]) Both Praśastis are edited in GOS No. 10 as appendices.

[4]) Edited by *Muni Chaturavijayi* with Introduction and Appendices by C. D. *Dalal* in GOS, No. 9, with English translation, Baroda 1918. *Cf. Bühler*, Hemachandra, pp. 4, 32, 55, 81; *Kielhorn*, Report on the Search of Sanskrit MSS. in the Bombay Presidency 1880-81, Bombay 1881, No. 50; *Hultzsch* in NGGW 1921, p. 39 ff.; *Munirāja Jinavijaya* in GOS, No. 14, p. xiv f., and *Dalal* in the introduction to the edition.

but also as throwing light on the history and the social conditions of Gujarat in the 13th century.

The story of the robber Rauhiṇeya, well-known from the narrative literature, is treated in the drama Prabuddha-Rauhiṇeya[1] by Rāmabhadra Muni. This drama in 6 acts was performed at a festival in a temple of Ṛṣabha which had been erected by two contemporaries of the Cāhamāna prince Samarasiṃha in about 1185 A.D. Most probably the poet may be ascribed to about the same period. The Jaina teacher Bālacandra, who is also known as a writer of commentaries, is the author of a drama Karuṇā-Vajrāyudha,[2] in which the legend of the compassionate King Śibi, who protected the dove from the falcon, is treated. The name of the compassionate king is, however, Vajrāyudha here, as in an ancient Jaina legend.[3] It is also a Jinistic legend which constitutes the plot of the drama Dharmābhyudaya[4] by Meghaprabhācārya. This piece, which was acted at a festival in a temple of the Jina Pārśvanātha, calls itself at the end, a "Shadow-play" (chāyānāṭyaprabandha). The time of the author is unknown.

Since ancient times the Jainas have vied with the poets of other sects in another literary form also, namely the sphere of religious lyric poetry. There is a large number of hymns (Stutis, Stotras) in praise of Mahāvīra, the other Jinas, and some to the ancient Jaina teachers also, both in Sanskrit and in Prākrit; some of them were written solely for purposes of the cult, others, on the other hand, are worthy of being appreciated as lyrical poems too.

---

1) Edited in the Jaina-Ātmānanda-Granthamālā, No. 60, Bhavnagar 1917; s. *Hultzsch* in ZDMG 75, 1921, p. 66 f.

2) Edited by *Muni Chaturavijaya* in Jaina-Ātmānanda-Grantharatnamālā, No. 56, Bhavnagar 1916; s. *Hultzsch*, l. c., p. 68 f.

3) Prākrit text by J. J. *Meyer*, Hindu Tales, p. 301 f.

4) Edited in the Jaina-Ātmānanda-Grantharatnamālā, No. 61, Bhavnagar 1918; s. *Hultzsch*, l. c., p. 69 f.

Many of them are quite short, others are poems of considerable length.[1] The earliest known hymn is the Uvasaggahara-Stotra,[2] a hymn to Pārśva in 5 stanzas ascribed to Bhadrabāhu.

One of the most famous Stotras, used both in the cult and for purposes of magic, is the Bhaktāmara-Stotra[3] by Mānatuṅga. This poem enjoys a great reputation among both the Śvetāmbaras and the Digambaras, as both sects class the poet among their own writers. This in itself seems to indicate that Mānatuṅga belongs to a comparatively early period. According to some lists of teachers, he might have lived as early as the beginning of the 3rd century A.D. Other traditions, on the other hand, point to the 5th, 7th, 8th or 9th century as his period.[4] The Bhaktāmara-Stotra is an ornate poem, but not so elaborate, by a long way, as the hymns of Bāṇa and Mayūra. In this hymn the Jina Ṛṣabha is extolled as the incomparable saint, set on a level with the highest deities, and his name is invoked as a protection in all perils. Thus we read of him:

"Hundreds of women bear hundreds of sons,
But no mother bore a son to equal thee:
Stars there are in every region of the sky, but
Only the East brings forth the sun with its
Flaming network of rays, the thousand-rayed divinity." (22)

---

1) Collections of Jaina Stotras have been edited in Km., Part VII, 1890; Jaina-Stotra-Saṃgraha in YJG Nos. 7 and 9, 1905; Stuti-saṃgraha with Avacūri, Bombay NSP 1912; Stotra-Ratnākara I, II, edited by Yaśovijaya-Jaina-Saṃskṛta-Pāṭhaśālā, Mehsana, Bombay NSP 1913 and 1914; Pañcapratikramaṇādi-Sūtrāṇi in Sanskrit, Prākrit and Gujarātī, Ahmedabad 1915; some also in MDJG No. 21. *Cf. Weber*, HSS. Verz. II, 3, 931-944; *Guérinot*, p. 208 ff.

2) *Jacobi*, Kalpasūtra of Bhadrabāhu, Introd., p. 12 f.

3) Edited and transl. into German by *Jacobi* in Ind. Stud. 14, p. 359 ff. Text also in Km., Part VII. The title is formed from the opening words of the first verse.

4) The anecdote mentioned below, and related by Merutuṅga in Prabandhacintāmaṇi (transl. by *Tawney*, p. 66) makes Mānatuṅga a contemporary of Bāṇa, the friend of King Harṣadeva (606-647 A.D.), though also the friend of King Bhoja in the 11th century. In

"Thou art Buddha, because the gods praise the awakening of thy mind.

Thou art Śaṃkara, because thou workest out the salvation of the three worlds;

Creator art thou,

Because through thy doctrine thou hast created a pathway to salvation;

Thou, O Lord, art Puruṣottama, the highest of all the beings." (25)

"He who bears thy name in his heart as a charm against snakes, can trample on the most furious poisonous snake with his bare feet; he who goes on pilgrimage to the lotus-grove of thy feet, conquers the hosts of the enemy; with his thoughts fixed on thee, the traveller sails fearlessly over the ocean" (38-40).

"Men whose bodies are fettered from head to foot in mighty fetters, and whose legs are sorely ground by thousands of heavy chains, are at once released of themselves from the pains of the prison, if they are ever mindful of thy name as an incantation." (42)

It is probably this verse 42 which gave rise to the legend that is related by the commentators. In order to purify himself of leprosy, so the story goes, Mayūra composed his 100 stanzas to the Sun-god (the Sūrya-Śataka). Bāṇa, who was jealous of him, hereupon had his hands and feet cut off, and composed 100 stanzas to the goddess Caṇḍikā (the Caṇḍikā-Śataka) by means of which his limbs were restored to him and grew on again. Then Mānatuṅga, in order to prove that the Jaina religion is also quite capable of performing great miracles, had himself fettered with 42 iron fetters and locked up in a house; then he composed the 44 verses of the Bhaktāmara-Stotra, and became free and quit of all his fetters.

another Paṭṭāvalī, Mānatuṅga is called "Mālaveśvara-Caulukya-Vayarasiṃha-devāmātyaḥ." If by Vayarasiṃha the Mālava Vairisiṃha I, the successor of Kṛṣṇa Upendra, who founded the Paramāra dynasty in the year 825, is meant, this brings us to the 9th century, whilst yet another tradition gives 743 A.D. as his date. Cf. Note 1, p. 551 and above, p. 478 and Note 2.

On the strength of this miracle he converted King Bhoja to the Jaina religion.[1]

Mānatuṅga is also the author of the Bhayahara-Stotra,[2] a hymn to the Jina Pārśvanātha, in Prākrit.

The celebrated Siddhasena Divākara, too, is among those Jaina writers who are claimed by both Digambaras and Śvetāmbaras. Just as the Bhaktāmara-Stotra, his Kalyāṇa-Mandira-Stotra[3] consists of 44 stanzas; it is also a hymn to Pārśvanātha, and is written in the same metre. It is, however, far more artificial in style than the poem of Mānatuṅga, who never uses such ambiguities (Śleṣas) as Siddhasena, who has probably imitated his predecessor,[4] and is really more of a scholar than a poet. A less artificially elaborated poem is the Dvātriṃśikā-Stotra or Vardhamāna-Dvātriṃśikā,[5] a hymn to Vardhamāna Mahāvīra in thirty-two Sanskrit stanzas with the refrain : "He the only highest spirit, the prince of Jinas, is my refuge." In these verses all the qualities of the Jina are enumerated according to the Jaina theory, and the names and epithets of the great deities of Hinduism are attributed to him, though they are used in a

1) *Cf. Bühler*, Ind. Ant. 1, 1872, 114 f.; *Klatt*, Ind. Ant. 11, 252; *Weber*, HSS. Verz. II, 3, 932 Note; *Peterson*, Report IV, p. xcii f.; *Jacobi*, Ind. Stud., 14, p. 360 f.; G. P. *Quackenbos*, The Sanskrit Poems of Mayūra, New York 1917, pp. 16 ff., 265 f. In the 14th century verses by Mānatuṅga were already used as incantations.

2) In 1309 A.D. Jinaprabha Sūri wrote a commentary on it. *Cf. Peterson*, Report 1882-83, p. 52; *Weber*, HSS. Verz. II, 3, p. 933 f. The text does not seem to be printed.

3) Edited and transl. into German by *Jacobi* in Ind. Stud. 14, 376 ff. Text also in Km., Part VII. The Paramajoti-Stotra, an old metrical translation in the old Braj dialect, of the Kalyāṇamandira has been published by L. P. *Tessitori* in Ind. Ant. 42, 1913, 42 ff.

4) Thus according to *Jacobi*, l.c., p. 377 f. But the Jainācārya *Vijaya Dharma Sūri* wrote to me on 25th April 1922 : "Siddhasena, Divākara, the author of Kalyāṇamandir, lived before Mānatuṅga...I cannot say how far the argument of my old friend Dr. Jacobi that Kalyāṇamandir appeared after Mānatuṅga, will hold good."

5) Edited with a commentary (Avacūri) by Udaya-Sāgara-Sūri and explanations in Gujarātī, by the Jaina Dharma Prasāraka Sabhā, Bhavnagar 1903. The edition printed in 1922 is not known to me. I am not in a position to decide whether this Dvātriṃśikā is also a part of the Dvātriṃśad-Dvātriṃśikā, "Treatise consisting of 32 with 32 verses each," as there is no text of the last-named accessible to me.

different sense. He is "the Lord of the three worlds," "the Knower of the three times," he is Śiva ("the Bringer of Salvation"), he is Buddha ("He who has awakened to Knowledge"), he is the "Ancient One" and "Manifold, though he is but One,"[1] he is Hṛṣīkeśa, Viṣṇu, Jagannātha, Jiṣṇu;[2] but he has no trident, no bow, no disc, no bird, no lion, no bull, there is no Gaṅgā on his head, he has no Lakṣmī, etc.[3] In both poems Siddhasena Divākara shows himself to be a past master in the use of Sanskrit. A legend has it that by means of the Kalyāṇa-Mandira-Stotra the poet split the Liṅga (Phallus) of the god Rudra in the Mahākāla temple at Ujjayinī, whereupon the image of Pārśvanātha stepped forth out of the middle of it.[4]

Like Siddhasena Divākara, Samantabhadra and Vidyānanda (or Vidyānandin Pātrakesarin) also were at the same time authors of learned works on logic, and of Stotras. Samantabhadra wrote a hymn in praise of all the 24 Jinas, entitled Bṛhat-Svayambhū-Stotra or Caturviṃśati-Jina-Stavana,[5] beginning with the praise of the first Jina who is here called Svayambhū, the Self-existent. Vidyānandin is the author of the Pātrakesari-Stotra,[6] an elaborate hymn in praise of Jina Mahāvīra in 50 stanzas.

There are quite a number of Stotras in which all the 24 Jinas are extolled. Thus the poet Bappabhaṭṭi,[7] who

1) God (Brahman, Ātman) is thus described in the Brahmanical philosophy.

2) Names of the god Viṣṇu; but, according to the commentary, Viṣṇu also means "he who penetrates all things by his knowledge," Hṛṣīkeśa, "Commander of all the organs of the senses," Jiṣṇu "Conqueror of the passions," Jagannātha "Lord of the world" is, of course, also the Jina.

3) Attributes of the god Viṣṇu.

4) Told in the Prabhāvaka-Carita, VIII, 144 ff. *Cf. Peterson*, Report IV, p. cxxxi f.

5) Published in DJGK I. See also *Hiralal*, Catalogue, p. 639 f.

6) Published in DJGK I, and with (the author's own?) commentary in MDJG No. 13 p. 100 ff. It is also called Bṛhatpañcanamaskāra-Stotra.

7) There are several "Life-stories of Bappabhaṭṭi," one in Prabandhakoṣa, one in the Prabhāvaka-Carita (XI) and an independent Bappabhaṭṭi-Sūri-Carita. *Cf. Shankar*

lived from 743 to 838 A.D. and is said to have converted King Āmarāja, the son and successor of Yaśovarman of Kanauj, wrote not only a Sarasvatī-Stotra,[1] but also a Caturviṃśati-Jina-Stuti[2] in 96 Sanskrit verses.

The most celebrated is the hymn in praise of the 24 Jinas by the poet Śobhana,[3] who lived in the second half of the 10th century. The poem is usually called, with intentional ambiguity, "Śobhana-Stuti," which can mean "Hymn of Śobhana" as well as "Beautiful hymn." It is in very artificially ornate language with variegated metres and most perilous tricks in the matter of figures of speech. One such trick, for instance, consists of the second and fourth line of each verse being identical syllable by syllable, and yet having a different meaning.

Dhanapāla,[4] Śobhana's brother, wrote a commentary on the poem, and himself composed a hymn to Ṛṣabha, Ṛṣabha-Pañcāśikā.[5] This is a Prākrit poem in 50 stanzas. In the first 20 verses there are allusions to events in the life of Ṛṣabha, whilst the following verses are exclusively devoted to the praise of Ṛṣabha. Though the style is very artificial, the poem is not lacking in warmth of imagination, and here and there we meet with beautiful metaphors. Thus the poet calls life an ocean, upon which Ṛṣabha is the boat, or a forest full of robbers, namely the passions, against which one

Pandurang Pandit, Gauḍavaha, Ed., Introd., pp. cxxxv-clxi; *Bhandarkar*, Report 1883-84. p. 14 f.; *Peterson*, Report IV, p. lxxxii; S. Krishnaswami *Aiyangar* in JBRAS N. S., 3, 1928, p. 101 ff. According to the Bappabhaṭṭi-Carita, Siddhasena Sūri was his teacher, and the poet Vākpati his contemporary.

1) *Peterson*, 3 Reports, p. 212.

2) Edited in Stutisaṃgraha with Avacūri, Bombay NSP 1912.

3) Edited and transl. into German by *Jacobi* in ZDMG 32, 1878, 509 ff. Text also in Km., Part VII.

4) Probably he is the same author who wrote the Prākrit dictionary Pāïyalacchī in 972 A.D., and also the Tilakamañjarī.

5) Edited and transl. into German by *Klatt* in ZDMG 33, 1879, 445 ff. Text with Sanskrit translation in Km., Part VII.

can find protection only with Ṛṣabha, or a night of false belief, in which Ṛṣabha rises like the sun. The world is to him a chess-board [1] with human chess-men or a stage from which all the actors make their exit at the end. Dhanapāla was a Brahman and it was not until after he had been converted to Jinism by his brother Śobhana that he wrote the hymn.

Ajiyasantithaya (Ajita-Śānti-Stava) by Nandiṣeṇa, [2] who lived perhaps even earlier than the 9th century, is a Prākrit poem in rare, artificial metres. In this hymn, which is recited by special singers at the confession festivals, Ajita, the second, and Śānti, the 16th Tīrthakara, are glorified together, because, according to the legend, both of them spent the rainy season in the caverns of the Śatruñjaya mountain, and, as the commentator tells us, the poet, while on a pilgrimage, was inspired to compose the hymn, by the sight of the shrines dedicated to them. The same two Tīrthakaras are also glorified by the very erudite Jinavallabha, [3] who died in 1110 A.D., in the Ullāsikkamathaya, [4] by Vīra Gaṇin in the Ajiyasantithaya in Prākrit, and by Jayaśekhara in the Ajita-Śānti-Stava in Sanskrit. As late as in the 16th century Śānticandra Gaṇin imitated Nandiṣeṇa in his Ṛṣabha-Stava, perhaps also in his Ajita-Śānti-Stava. [5]

1) This is perhaps the earliest mention of the game of chess; s. *Klatt*, l. c., p. 465 f.

2) *Cf.* W. *Schubring* in ZII 2, 1923, p. 178 ff.

3) According to Sumati Gaṇin, who was a pupil of Jinapati Sūri who died in 1221 A.D., and wrote life-stories of the heads of his school, Jinavallabha was versed in Pāṇini's grammar, in the Mahākāvyas and Alaṃkāra-Śāstras, in dramatic literature, in astronomy, logic and the works of Jayadeva and Abhayadeva. He was the successor of the last-named as head of the school, enjoyed a great reputation in Citrakūṭa (Chitore) and had various temples built in honour of the Jinas. *Cf. Klatt*, Jaina-Onomasticon, p. 34 f.; *Bhandarkar*, Report 1882-83, p. 47 f., and L. G. *Gandhi* in the Introduction to GOS, No. 37, Baroda 1927.

4) It is also called Ajita-Śānti-Laghustavana. *Cf. Weber*, HSS. Verz. II, 3, 931 ff. and *Schubring*, l.c. Jinavallabha also wrote a Mahāvīra-Stotra (edited in Km., Part VII), a Praśnaśata, "A hundred questions," which are answered in the commentary (edited in Stotra-Ratnākara, Part II), and a number of erudite works; s. *Bhandarkar*, l. c.

5) *Schubring*, l.c.

In the 11th century the celebrated commentator A b h a y a- d e v a wrote a J a y a t i h u y a n a - S t o t r a.[1] The legend has it that the poet, who was seriously ill, recovered his health through this hymn, and that he restored to the light of day a statue of Pārśvanātha which had been hidden for centuries.[2]

It is probably the same V ā d i r ā j a,[3] who wrote the Pārśvanātha-Carita in 1025 A.D. and later the Yaśodhara-Carita, who is also the author of some Stotras of philosophical contents, a J ñ ā n a l o c a n a - S t o t r a,[4] an E k ī- b h ā v a-S t o t r a,[5] and an A d h y ā t m ā ṣ ṭ a k a.[6]

The great H e m a c a n d r a also indited a few Stotras. At the request of King Kumārapāla he wrote a V ī t a r ā g a- S t o t r a,[7] "A poem in praise of the Passionless One," *i.e.*, Mahāvīra, which is at the same time a poetical manual of the Jaina religion and was perhaps Hemacandra's first attempt to make the king acquainted with the fundamental doctrines of Jinism.[8] The work consists of 20 short sections (Prakāśas or Stavas)[9] generally of 8 or 9 Ślokas each, or sometimes

1) Edited with a Sanskrit commentary, Ahmedabad 1890.

2) *Cf. Klatt* in Ind. Ant. 11, p. 248; *Peterson*, 3 Reports, pp. 25 f., 245 ff.

3) This is Vādirāja II whose teacher was probably Kanakasena Vādirāja I who lived about 1000 A.D.; Vādirāja II wrote also a commentary on Akalaṅka's Nyāyaviniścaya; s. A. Venkatasubbiah in ZII 7, 1929, 179ff. and above, pp. 515, 535.

4) Published in MDJG No. 21, p. 124 ff. In the last verse the author calls himself "the son of Pomarāja."

5) Published in Km., Part VII.

6) Published in MDJG No. 13, p. 131.

7) Edited with two commentaries, the Vivaraṇa by Prabhānanda, Abhayadeva's pupil, and an Avacūri by a pupil (name not mentioned) of Viśālarāja, in JPU No. 1, Bombay NSP 1911; in the title of the edition Viśālarāja is mentioned as the author of the Avacūri, but at the end of it, the author, who himself says that he wrote in 1455 A.D., does honour to Viśālarāja as his teacher.

8) *Cf. Bühler*, Hemachandra, pp. 36 and 85.

9) N. G. *Javeri* says in the Foreword to the Edition, that Hemacandra wrote 32 cantos at the request of Kumārapāla, of which 20 are contained in the Vītarāga-Stotra and 12 in the Yoga-Śāstra.

more. The language of the work is exceptionally lucid and simple. It begins as follows:

"He who is the highest spirit, the highest light, the Highest of the Most High, whom they call the Sun-hued beyond the darkness;

from whom all trees of sin have been uprooted with their roots, before whom gods, demons and men bow their heads;

from whom proceeds all knowledge which furthers the welfare of men, whose wisdom illuminates the present, future and past forms of existence;

in whom knowledge, joy and Brahman are united,—in him one should believe, about him one should meditate, in him do I take refuge."

The concluding verses, (20, 6-9) read:

"These are eyes which take delight in thy countenance, these are hands which offer thee worship, these are ears which hear thy praises: May these ever be with me!

If this my speech, feeble though it be, but seek with ardent desire to comprehend thy excellence, then all hail to it! Why should I desire any other?

Thy servant am I, thy slave, thy footman, thy bondman. Say 'Yes' and give thy consent, O Lord! I say no more.

By this hymn to the Passionless One from the pen of the celebrated Hemacandra, may the King Kumārapāla attain the desired reward!"

In imitation of Siddhasena Divākara's Dvātriṃśikā, Hemacandra wrote two Mahāvīra-Stotras, hymns to Mahāvīra, consiting of 32 verses (Dvātriṃśikas) each: the one is entitled Ayogavyavacchedā, and the other Anyayogavyavacchedā.[1] These two poems also contain instructions regarding the religion.

At the beginning of the 14th century Jinaprabha Sūri wrote a Caturviṃśati-Jina-Stuti and several other hymns.[2] Muni Sundara

[1]) Both texts are edited in Km., Part VII, pp. 102 ff., 104 ff.

[2]) They are printed in Km., Part VII, Caturviṃśatijina-Stuti also in "Stutisaṃgraha with Avacūri." In 1309 A.D. he wrote a commentary on Mānatuṅga's Bhayahara-Stotra. There is also a Caturviṃśatijinabhavastava by Guṇavijaya Gaṇin, printed in Jaina-Stotra-Saṃgraha II, YJG 9, and a Jinacaturviṃśatikā by Bhūpāla Kavi in Km., Part VII.

Sūri (died 1379 A.D.) wrote a large collection of hymns, entitled Jina-Stotra-Ratna-Kośa.[1] The first Prastāva contains 23 Stotras in praise of various Jinas in connection with their monuments at various sacred places. Mānatuṅga's Bhaktāmara-Stotra had many imitators. Bhāvaprabha Sūri wrote a Nemibhaktāmaram[2] with allusions to the legend of Neminātha and Rājīmatī. Dharmaghoṣa, a pupil of Devendra (died 1270 A.D.), is the author of a Yamaka-Stuti,[3] and probably also of a Caturviṃśat-Jina-Stuti.[4] Whether it is the same or a much earlier Dharmaghoṣa[5] who is the author of the Isimaṇḍala or Ṛṣimaṇḍala-Stotra,[6] must remain an open question. This work is a hymn in Prākrit stanzas in praise of the ancient Jaina teachers Jambusvāmin, Śayyambhava, Bhadrabāhu, etc. A Vītarāga-Stotra in 25 verses, also entitled Ratnākara-Pañcaviṃśatikā, after the author Ratnākara, is of unknown date.[7]

1) Edited in Jaina-Stotra-Saṃgraha II, YJG No. 9. The third Stotra is dated Saṃvat 1476 (1419 A.D.); but the editor of the Adhyātmakalpadruma states Saṃvat 1436-1503 (1379-1446 A.D.) as the period of the author's life.

2) This and other Bhaktāmara Stotras, imitations of Mānatuṅga's celebrated Stotra, are printed in Stotra-Ratnākara, Part I, Bombay 1913, and in Bhaktāmara-Stotra, Part I, Bombay 1926 (AUS 45). Other Stotras by Bhāvaprabha Sūri are to be found in Jaina-Stotra-Saṃgraha I, YJG 7.

3) *Cf. Klatt* in Ind. Ant. 11, 255; *Peterson*, 3 Reports, pp. 17, 310 ff. The same author also wrote a Śrāddhajīta-Kalpa, a work on atonements; s. *Weber*, HSS. Verz. II, 3, 881 f.

4) Edited in Stotra-Ratnākara, Part I.

5) *Peterson*, Report IV, p. lxiii ff., names no less than 7 different Jaina writers by the name of Dharmaghoṣa.

6) A commentary written on this work in 1496 A.D. by Padmamandira, contains numerous legends on the Jaina teachers honoured in Isimaṇḍala. Some of these legends are also known from Hemacandra's Pariśiṣṭa-Parvan. *Cf. Peterson*, Report 1882-83, App. p. 93 f.; *Bhandarkar*, Report 1883-84, pp. 130 ff., 443 ff.; *Weber*, HSS. Verz. II, 3, 944 Note 2. Gāthās 155-218 and a portion of the commentary have been reprinted by *Jacobi* in the Edition of the Pariśiṣṭa-Parvan, Appendix, pp. 29 ff. and 37 ff.

7) Edited in "Stuti-Saṃgraha with Avacūri" and prefixed to the Edition of Muni Sundara's Adhyātmakalpadruma, Bombay NSP 1906.

As from the nature of the case, the glorification of the Jinas admitted of no variation as regards the subject-matter, the poets were at pains to introduce a change in the form. Hence it is precisely in this hymn poetry that the style of the ornate court poetry was most developed. Some of the hymns are very highly elaborated. A specimen of a very artificially constructed hymn is the Siddhipriya-Stotra[1] by Devanandin. Throughout this hymn the verses are rhymed in such a way that the same syllables in each of two consecutive lines, have a different meaning.[2] There is also a Mahāvīra-Stava in Prākrit, where the same words occur three times over with a different meaning each time, or a Nemi-Jina-Stava, in which no consonants occur except "l" and "m." In Jayatilaka Sūri's Caturhārāvalī-Citrastava there are verses in which the syllables are to be read in the shape of certain figures (of a cross, a lotus-petal, a Svastika, etc.).[3] Attempts were also made to introduce a greater variety of metres, and poets went to the length of selecting a new metre for nearly every stanza in one and the same poem. What is still more curious is that these poems would be written in several languages, each stanza in a different language. Ṣaḍbhāṣānirmita-Pārśvajinastavana by Dharmavardhana (about 1200 A.D.) and Ṣaḍbhāṣāvibhūṣita-Śāntināthastavana by Jinapadma (1325-1344 A.D.) are poems written in six languages, and belong to this category. The languages are Sanskrit, Māhārāṣṭrī, Māgadhī, Śaurasenī, Paiśācī and Apabhraṃśa. The first-named poem has even two stanzas written half in Sanskrit and half in Prākrit.[4]

---

1) Edited in Km., Part VII, p. 30 ff.

2) In Verse 20 the relative pronoun *ya* is even extended by the suffix *ka*, only to make the rhyme muninā‿yakena, munināyakena possible. These tricks make it improbable that this Devanandin is identical with the old Pūjyapāda.

3) These hymns are contained in Part II of the Stotra-Ratnākara, Bombay 1913.

4) *Cf.* W. *Schubring* in Festgabe Jacobi, p. 89 ff.

Many of the Stotras mentioned above could equally well be termed didactic poems: on the other hand, it is not easy to separate the genus didactic poetry from the narrative literature, as this too is mostly instructive. The didactic poetry also forms the bridge to the purely learned works. For it is often difficult to decide whether to include certain manuals of religion and morals, as a rule written in verse, in the purely erudite literature or in the didactic poetry. In the Canon we already find aphorisms along with stories, and in many of the narrative works of the Jainas, as in Indian narrative literature in general, aphorism and narrative are closely interwoven.

One of the earliest non-canonical didactic poems is Praśnottara-Ratnamālā,[1] "The Jewel-Garland of Questions and Answers," consisting of brief questions and answers, and written in Ślokas, in the simplest possible style. The morality taught in these questions and answers, is general human morality and not specifically Jinistic, and it is as simple as the language in which it is couched. We find verses like the following:

8. "What does one fear? Death. Who is in even worse plight than the blind man? The passionate man. Who is a hero? He who is not disconcerted by the arrows of the glances of beautiful women.

10. "What is unfathomable? The conduct of women. Who is intelligent? He who is not deceived by this. What is poverty? Discontent. What is lack of dignity? Entreating.

"What is hell? Dependence upon another. What is good fortune? The renunciation of all desires. What is truth? The welfare of the beings. What do the beings like best? Life.

---

1) The title is also Vimala-Pr., *i.e.*, "Praśnottaramālā of Vimala," sometimes also "Ratnamālikā," edited in Km., Part VII, 121 ff.; a Prākrit recension by P. E. *Pavolini* in GSAI 11, 153-163. In 1373 A.D. Devendra and Maṇibhadra wrote a commentary on "Vimalacandrasūri's Praśnottararatnamālā," in which a story is told in connection with each question. *Cf. Weber*, HSS. Verz. II, 3, 1118 ff.

26, 27. "What shall I tell you, that is as difficult to find on earth as a wishing-jewel? Certainly it is the fourfold good. And what is the special name given to it by those who have driven away the darkness of ignorance? Gifts, accompanied by friendly speech; knowledge without arrogance; heroism coupled with forbearance, and wealth hand in hand with self-sacrifice. This fourfold good is indeed difficult to find."

It is no wonder that this didactic poem is also claimed by Buddhists and Brahmans as belonging to their own writings.[1] The Jainas ascribe it to a Śvetāmbara Vimala[2] or Vimalacandra, but sometimes also to King Amoghavarṣa,[3] who reigned in the 9th century and was a friend of the Digambara Jinasena.

Another early work is Uvaēsamālā, "Garland of Instructions,"[4] a didactic poem in 540 Prākrit stanzas, containing moral instructions for laymen and monks, by Dharmadāsa, who according to tradition is said to be a younger contemporary of Mahāvīra. This is scarcely possible, as the language of the Uvaēsamālā corresponds to the later Jaina Māhārāṣṭrī. At all events, there were commentaries on this work as early as the 9th century, and, as is

---

1) There is a Tibetan recension in the Tanjur with the title Praśnottararatnamālā, edited in Tibetan and German by *Schiefner*, Petropoli 1858; a Sanskrit and a Tibetan recension with French translation have been published by Ph. Ed. *Foucaux*, Paris 1867. *Cf.* A. *Weber*, Indische Streifen I, 210 ff., where two versions are translated into German, and Vidhushekara *Bhattacharya* in Ind. Hist. Qu. 5, 1929, 143 f. It is significant that the text in the Tanjur begins with an invocation to Mañjuśrī, a Bombay edition, in which Śaṅkara is mentioned as the author, with an invocation to Gaṇeśa, and the Jinistic version with that to Mahāvīra.

2) Haridas *Śāstrī* (Ind. Ant. 19, 1890, 378 f.) is of opinion that this Vimala is identical with the author of the Paümacariya. This admits of neither refutation nor proof. In the last verse the author is called simply Sitapaṭaguru, *i. e.*, "the teacher clad in white." A Calcutta edition erroneously gives Asitapaṭa as the name of the author, s. *Weber*, l. c., p. 212, 220 Note 3.

3) *Cf. Bhandarkar*, Early History of the Dekkan, 2nd edition, p. 68f. J. F. *Fleet* in Ind. Ant. 33, 1904, 198 ff.

4) Edited by L. P. *Tessitori* in GSAI 25, 1912, 167-297. *Cf. Jacobi*, AR 18, 1915, p. 285 f. A number of stanzas are taken from the Mahānisīha-Sutta; s. *Schubring*, Das Mahānisīha-sutta, p. 51 ff.

proved by the numerous commentaries, it must have enjoyed considerable popularity.[1]

There is also S ī l o v a ē s a m ā l ā by J a y a k ī r t i, the pupil of Jayasiṃha, in 116 Prākrit Gāthās, the date of which is not known. All we know is that in the year 1337 A.D. Somatilaka Sūri wrote a commentary on it, Śīlataraṅgiṇī, consisting of narratives.[2]

There are two didactic poems by the famous P ū j y a p ā d a; I ṣ ṭ o p a d e ś a, "The desired Instruction,"[3] and S a m ā d h i ś a t a k a, "A Hundred Verses on the Absorption (in meditation)."[4]

Haribhadra wrote 32 Aṣṭakāni,[5] poems of 8 verses each, on the "Great God" (mahādeva), *i.e.*, the Jina free from all passions, on the cult, knowledge, renunciation, etc. He is also the author of an U p a d e ś a p a d a in Prākrit.[6]

G u ṇ a b h a d r a, the author of the Uttara-Purāṇa, also wrote an ethical poem Ā t m ā n u ś ā s a n a[7] in 270 stanzas.

The didactic poems of the Digambara A m i t a g a t i are greatly appreciated by the Jainas. An earlier work of his is S u b h ā ṣ i t a r a t n a s a ṃ d o h a, "The Collection of

---

1) The poet Siddharṣi, too, wrote a commentary on Uvaēsamālā. This commentary is available in two recensions, one of which contains stories also; s. *Jacobi*, Upamitibhava-prapañcā Kathā, Ed., Preface, p. xi; *Weber*, HSS. Verz. II, 3, 1082 ff. There is also an U v a ē s a m ā l ā in 505 Prākrit stanzas by M a l a d h ā r i - H e m a c a n d r a, the senior contemporary of the famous Hemacandra; s. *Weber*, l. c., 1081 f.

2) *Cf. Weber*, HSS. Verz. II, 3, 1085 ff. The Sthūlabhadra legend from this commentary is given by *Alsberg*, Kumārapālapratibodha, p. 90 ff.

3) Edited in DJGK I, in MDJG No. 13 (with Āśādharā's commentary), and in Granthatrayī, SJG No. 20, Calcutta V. S. 2449 (1922); translated into English by Champat Rai Jain, Hardoi 1925.

4) Edited in SJG. Vol. I, Bombay 1905. The same volume also contains P u r u ṣ ā r t h a s i d d h y u p ā y a by A m ṛ t a c a n d r a who, according to a Digambara Paṭṭāvalī, wrote in 904 A.D. The two works are also printed in DJGK I.

5) Edited together with Yaśovijaya's Aṣṭakaprakaraṇa, Haribhadra's Saḍdarśanasamuccaya and Rājaśekhara's Saḍdarśanasamuccaya Surat 1918

6) *Cf. Peterson*, 3 Reports, pp. 34 f., Extract 46.

7) Edited in DJGK I, p. 55 ff.

Gems of Beautiful Aphorisms,"[1] in 32 chapters, each of which treats of a special subject, and is, as a rule, written in a unified metre. The language, style and metres are those of the ornate poetry. In elaborate verses the poet deals with the entire ethics of the Digambara Jainas, gives rules of conduct for both monks and laymen, and subjects the tenets of the Brahmanical religion to a severe and caustic criticism. It is but rarely, however, that we come across an original expression for those thoughts with which we are so familiar from the ascetic poetry, on the world of the senses and its dangers, on error and truth, the right mode of life, death and transitoriness, the wickedness of women, the sin of eating flesh, drinking intoxicants, honey, etc. A very few specimens will suffice to give an idea of this work which at any rate is important from the point of view of Jinistic ethics:

Chapter IV contains warnings against a v a r i c e, beginning with the verse:

> " The sun grows cold, and hot the cool moon grows,
> The cloud grows firm, the ocean is satiated with the water of the streams,
> The wind stands still, the heat of the fire gives up its glow,—
> But never does the ardour of avarice cease to glow."

Among the sins which are enumerated as following in the wake of avarice, are man's tilling the soil with a plough, sewing garments, producing paintings, and doing other things which we should call useful professions. Chapter VI deals with the favourite theme of ascetic poetry, the "investigation of the virtues and faults of women." The female body is described by this poet-monk as the sum of all impurity, in his eyes woman is "the treasury of all sufferings," "the bolt barring the city of heaven, the path to the dwelling of hell," "the axe for the pleasant grove of piety, the hoar-frost for the lotus of virtues, the root of the tree of sins, the soil

---

1) Edited in Km. 82; edited and transl. by R. *Schmidt* and J. *Hertel* in ZDMG 59, 1905 and 61, 1907. *Cf. Hertel*, WZKM 17, 1903, 105 ff. and *Leumann*, ZDMG 59, 578 ff. According to Hertel (WZKM 17, 110 ff.) Amitagati was influenced by Bhartṛhari.

for the creeper of deceit" etc. The warning against the blandishments of courtesans takes up an entire chapter (XXIV). We read here, for instance (XXIV, 21):

> "As a thief of the wealth which bestows all delights, called penance,
> As a man-murdering pest, skilled in bringing all sufferings,
> As a snare to catch the mad elephant called man,
> The whore, the saleable woman, was sent to earth by fate."

The Āptas, *i.e.*, the sinless beings who have cast off passion, hate and delusion, are dealt with in Chapter XXVI. These "released ones" are the true gods; and here the poet indulges in the most damning expressions against the Brahmanical gods, who lust after women, drink intoxicating drinks and are entirely given up to sensual pleasures, and can therefore not be counted as Āptas. At the end of this chapter Amitagati protests that he has not laid such stress on the faults of the gods "from motives of eloquence, hate or passion," but he has merely endeavoured "to know the all-knowing, faultless Āpta." "And yet the saviour of the three worlds, as he dwells in the Beyond, cannot be known in this world. As long as the sun does not rise, so long all darkness has not been banished." The essence of the true religion is shown in Chapter XXVIII, where, for instance, we read (V. 6):

> "The king of hills may waver,
> And cold the fire may grow,
> The rock may swim in the water,
> And the moon send forth rays of heat,
> The sun may rise in the West—
> But in the killing of beings
> Religion can never consist."

Twenty years after the Subhāṣitaratnasaṃdoha, in 1014 A.D., the second great work of Amitagati, Dharmaparīkṣā,[1] "Examination of the Religion" was completed. This is a dogmatic-polemical work, which is, however, so closely interwoven with narratives, that it may be included among the narrative literature as well. The obvious aim of

---

1) N. *Mironow*, Die Dharmaparīkṣā des Amitagati. Diss. Leipzig 1903. See also *Bhandarkar*, Report 1884-87, pp. 13 ff., 134 ff.

the author in this book is, not only to instruct and convert, but also to entertain at the expense of adherents of other religions, the plan of the work being as follows: A Jaina converts his Brahman friend by doing all kinds of absurd things or telling incredible stories, in order to bring home to his astonished friend that the Brahmanical legends tell even more incredible and more absurd things. This is a peg on which Amitagati succeeds in hanging a large number of popular anecdotes. They are gleaned either from oral tradition or from a book of tales in Prākrit. In the language, too, there are traces of their having been translated from Prākrit. Other tales are taken from the epic-Purāṇic tradition, but are sorely corrupted. Among the popular narratives, two interesting types are especially represented: stories of fools and marvellous tales of lies.

Among the first-named category the most interesting is the story of the four fools who meet with a saint, who greets them. The fools begin to quarrel as to who it was whom the saint had greeted. They ask the saint, and he says: "The most foolish among you." Now they cannot agree as to who is the most foolish among them. So they go to the town, in order to ask the citizens to decide, and each of them relates some piece of stupidity which he has committed. The first one allowed his eyes to be burned out by a lamp, only in order not to disturb his two wives in their sleep. The second let his two bad wives break his legs. The fourth had his cheek pricked through, from fear of his mother-in-law. The third, however, behaved in a fashion similar to the man in Goethe's poem "Gutmann und Gutweib." Once he was lying in bed with his wife. "Then they decided to act on his suggestion, that the one who spoke first must give the other ten sweet cakes. As they were thus lying quietly, a thief entered the house, and stole everything there was to steal. When the thief had already laid hands on the wife's under-garments, the wife said to the husband: "What? Are you going to look on quietly even now?" Then the husband demanded the promised ten cakes, because she had been the first to break the silence." [1]

---

1) *Mironow*, l.c., p. 21. *Cf.* R. *Pischel*, ZDMG 58, 1904, 363 ff.; *Hertel*, Ein altindisches

As to the marvellous tales à la Munchausen (Münch-hausen), we mention only the following: A man sees a beautiful tree and wishes to taste its fruits. But the tree is too tall. So he cuts off his head, throws it on to the tree, where it eats as much fruit as it wants. Then he fastens his head on to his neck again.

Remarkable are the sagas and legends which Amitagati cites from the Mahābhārata and the Rāmāyaṇa. Only few of these are told in the form in which we know them from the two epics. Most of them are pieced together from fragments of the most various traditions in such a way that they appear as absurd as possible. Yet most likely he did not invent these corruptions of the Brahmanical legends himself, but probably they had already been changed by the Jainas in this fashion at an earlier time.[1] Amitagati tells the following satirical story regarding the origin of the Mahābhārata :

Vyāsa certainly knew that his poem was full of lies, but he ventured to dish up the inconsistent and senseless stuff to mankind, after he had convinced himself, by an experiment, of the stupidity of men. He placed a pot on the bank of the Gaṅgā and began to heap sand over it. Immediately the people came along and followed his example, so that after a short time the place where the first pot stood, could no longer be determined.

Indeed Amitagati is none too scrupulous in his criticism of Brahmanism. The Brahmanical pantheon is condemned just as ruthlessly here as in the Subhāṣitaratnasaṃdoha.[2]

Narrenbuch, p. 37 ff. The story frequently recurs in India (*e.g.* Vetālapañcaviṃśati, ed. *Uhle*, 23, 63, and often in modern Indian versions). The earliest known version in the Chinese Tripiṭaka (E. *Huber*, BEFEO 4, 1091; cf. *Zachariae*, ZVV 1906, 136 Note), takes us back as far as the year 492 A.D. The propagation of the anecdote, which is also known in Arabic variants and in Baluchi, has been traced, as far as Europe is concerned, by R. *Köhler* (Jahrbuch für romanische und englische Litteratur 12, 348 ff.). *Goethe* took the theme from a Scottish ballad.

[1]) According to *Mironow*, l.c., p. 49 ff., he used Raviṣeṇa's Padma-Purāṇa and Śubhacandra's Pāṇḍava-Purāṇa (or " Jaina-Mahābhārata ").

[2]) And this is additional proof of the fact that the two works are by one and the same author. According to *Mironow*, l.c, p., 41, the Subhāṣitaratnasaṃdoha appears to have been used in the last two sections of the Dharmaparīkṣā.

Here, too, the narrator revels in dwelling on the infamous deeds of the gods, especially their amorous adventures. He is, moreover, very hard on Brahmanical ethics, and attacks the caste system in particular. He devotes far less space to the refutation of the Buddhist doctrines, and it is Mahāyāna Buddhism that he attacks. In his presentation of Jinistic ethics he tells, among other things, a version of the parable of the "Man in the Well." Most especially characteristic of Amitagati's standpoint are, however, the legends that he tells of the origin of Jinism and the heretical doctrines. This "historical" retrospect concludes with the statement that, though some good is certainly contained even in the heretical doctrines, this is always borrowed from Jinism.

A third book by Amitagati is Y o g a s ā r a.[1] This is a didactic poem in simple Ślokas, treating of various aspects of the religion, in 9 chapters, but consisting mainly of moral instructions. A few specimens are given here:

"An action performed by anger and the other passions counts as an action performed by the soul, just as a battle won by the foot-soldiers counts as a battle won by the king." (II, 34.)

"We see the soul-less body of our neighbour, but not his soul; whence then should affection come at a good deed, whence aversion at a harmful one?" (V, 11.)

"Enemies, fathers, wives, relatives, brothers and children oppress and delight my body, not my soul." (V, 12.)

"The possessor of knowledge is not spotted by sins, any more than the sun by eclipses. Knowledge is not touched by the objects of the senses, any more than the mail-clad warrior is pierced by the enemy." (IX, 30.)

"Just as in spite of the difference among cows, there is no difference to be found in the milk, thus in spite of the difference among men, there is no difference in the true knowledge." (IX, 77.)

1) Edited with a Hindī explanation in SJG, No. 16, 1918.

Among the works of Amitagati there is also a D v ā t r i ṃ-ś a t i k ā,[1] a poem in 32 stanzas of highly ethical value, which partly has the form of a prayer in which the Āpta, the perfect saint or Jina, is invoked as "god" (deva) or "god of gods" (devadeva), and partly contains only religious-moral contemplations. It begins with the beautiful verses:

"May my self always have love (maitrī) for all beings, pleasure in the company of the virtuous, deepest compassion for the creatures in pain, and indifference towards him who is perversely inclined, O God!

"May I, by thy grace, O Lord of Jinas (Jinendra), possess the power to separate, like the sword from its sheath, my soul which is faultless and possessed of infinite power, from the body!

"May my mind, O Lord, be always equal in sorrow and in joy, towards enemy and friend, in union and in separation, in the house and in the forest, and may all selfishness be banished from my heart!"

One of the most important didactic poems of the Jainas is the Y o g a ś ā s t r a[2] by H e m a c a n d r a. The work consists of a text in simple Ślokas and a commentary short (vṛtti) in ornate Kāvya style, which also contains stories.[3] The first four chapters, which constitute more than

1) Edited in MDJG No. 13, p. 132 ff.; and in DJGK I; also under the title S ā m a-y i k a P ā ṭ h a, with an English translation by *Ajit Prasada* in the Jaina Scripture Gift Series No. 2. Yet another work of Amitagati, the P a ñ c a s a ṃ g r a h a, is printed in MDJG No. 25.

2) It is also called Adhyātmopaniṣad. The first four chapters belong to the daily reading of the Jaina monks, and are therefore frequently to be found copied out separately, whilst manuscripts of all 12 chapters are rare (*Peterson*, 3 Reports, p. 31; *Weber*, HSS. Verz., II, 3, 913 ff.); they are edited and transl. into German by E. *Windisch* in ZDMG 28, 1874, 185-262. An edition with Italian translation has been begun by F. *Belloni-Filippi* in GSAI 21, 1908, 123 ff. The edition by Vijaya Dharma *Sūri* in Bibl. Ind. (fasc. 1, 1907 to fasc. 6, 1921) is also not complete. A complete edition with the author's own commentary was published by the Jaina Dharma Prasāraka Sabhā, Bhavnagar 1926.

3) These narratives look like brief summaries of the legends told in the Triṣaṣṭiśalākāpuruṣa-Carita, from which *Belloni-Filippi* concludes that this work was written earlier, whilst *Bühler* (Hemachandra, pp. 36, 43) agrees with the tradition (s. *Peterson*, Report IV, p. 7) in regarding the Yogaśāstra as the earlier work. On the Brahmadatta-Kathānaka in Hemacandra's commentary, s. *Pavolini* in GSAI 7, 339 ff.; on the Abhayarājarṣi-Kathānaka in the same, which is connected with the Udayana legend, s. *Hertel*, Jinakīrtis "Geschichte von Pāla und Gopāla," p. 127 ff.

three-quarters of the entire work, give a brief summary of the Jaina doctrine as far as it concerns laymen, "and the very copious commentary extends this summary into the clearest and most comprehensible presentation of the system which has ever been written."[1] The duties of a king of the Jaina faith are also often discussed here, for Hemacandra wrote this work at the request of King Kumārapāla, and it contributed largely towards winning the king over to the Jaina religion. In this "Yogaśāstra," Yoga does not, however, mean merely "meditation" or "absorption," but "religious exercise" in general, the whole "effort" which the pious must make. The work contains a complete doctrine of duties. The actual Yoga, the ascetic exercises and absorptions which lead to release, are relegated to the last eight chapters, the explanation of which takes up only about one-tenth of the whole commentary. "It is remarkable that the Jain-Yoga is preceded by a very lengthy exposition of those very exercises which, according to the explicit statement of the author, are useless to attain Mukti, though they enable one to catch a glimpse of the future and are supposed to endow one with supernatural powers. It appears that even Hemacandra believed in their efficacy, and perhaps gave himself up to them. If he devotes a long chapter to describing them, he probably did so with regard to the fondness of the king for Yoga exercises, of which he speaks in the commentary on XII, 55."[2] The subject-matter of the first four chapters coincides in the main with that of Amitagati's Subhāṣitaratnasaṃdoha. Though, however, Hemacandra moves in the same spheres of thought, he is certainly more ingenious and more original.[3] More often than in Amitagati's

---

1) *Bühler*, l. c., p. 36.

2) *Bühler*, l. c., p. 36.

3) Hence it is not so likely that he was influenced by Amitagati as is assumed by *Hertel* (WZKM 17, 106).

work we meet with ideas, images and metaphors which are not quite so stereotyped. For instance, the following invocation of Mahāvīra (1, 3) is very pretty :

> " Hail to the Jina hero's eyes
> Whose pupils are rigid with pity
> And wet with tears, from pity
> Even for him who has committed sin."

He is very severe in his attack on Brahmanical morality as taught more especially in the Law-book of Manu. He is well versed in Brahmanical literature, and he quotes verses from Manu to show convincingly that they proclaim a morality which is incompatible with the command of Ahiṃsā (the sparing of all living creatures) and is therefore not worthy of the name of morality. This Ahiṃsā is inculcated again and again, for instance in II, 50 f. :

> " Ahiṃsā is like a loving mother of all beings,
> Ahiṃsā is like a stream of nectar in the desert of Saṃsāra,
> Ahiṃsā is a course of rain-clouds to the forest-fire of suffering,
> The best healing-herb for the beings tormented by the disease
> Called the perpetual return of existence, is Ahiṃsā." [1)]

Of course, in the eyes of Hemacandra too, women are "the torches on the way to the gate of Hell, the root of all troubles and the primal cause of dissension " etc., wherein he agrees not only with Amitagati, but with all monastic poets. In Hemacandra's work too we come across vivid and excellent metaphors of the kind so frequent in Indian gnomic poetry, thus when he says that " the tree of arrogance must be uprooted by the floods of the stream of gentleness " (IV, 14). Some of the verses on the transitoriness and vanity of human

---

1) It is, however, very characteristic of Hemacandra that, at the request of the same King Kumārapāla, whom he sought to win over to ascetic morality by the Yogaśāstra, he also wrote a Laghvarhannīti-Śāstra, " Short Manual of the Art of Governing for Jainas," which cannot be said to be entirely in conformity with the principle of Ahiṃsā. More will be said of this Nīti-Śāstra in Vol. III.

existence also remind us of the best sayings of Bhartṛhari, such as for instance IV, 58 :

> "Fortune wavers like the wave,
> The meeting of friends is like a dream ;
> Youth is like the panicle of a blade of grass,
> Whirled on high by each gust of wind."

A contemporary of Hemacandra is Jinadatta Sūri (1075-1154 A.D.), a pupil of Jinavallabha Sūri. He wrote Upadeśarasāyana Rāsa,[1] a didactic poem in the form of a dancing-song in 80 verses, Kālasvarūpakulakam, a didactic poem in 32 rhymed verses in Apabhraṃśa, and a Caccarī (Carcarī),[2] also a kind of dancing-song in praise of his teacher Jinavallabha Sūri, who had had moral sayings engraven on various shrines.

A younger contemporary of Hemacandra and King Kumārapāla is Somaprabha, the author of the Kumārapāla-Pratibodha,[3] a didactic poem and collection of tales,

---

1) Among the devotees of Kṛṣṇa, Rāsas are dancing-songs, in which the love of Kṛṣṇa and Rādhā is sung. Among the Jainas, they are ballads, often with a bearing on historical personages, frequently in Old Gujarātī.

2) All three poems are edited with a Sanskrit introduction by Lalchandra Bhagwandas *Gandhi*, Three Apabhraṃśa Works of Jinadatta Sūri with Commentaries, in GOS No. 37, Baroda 1927. In the same volume are published as appendices : a Saṅghapaṭṭaka by Jinavallabha Sūri, a Gaṇadharasārdhaśataka (*cf.* also *Weber*, HSS. Verz. II, 3, 981 ff.) and a Sugurupāratantrya by Jinadatta, and a hymn written in 1113 A D. by Jinarakṣita, the pupil of Jinadatta, in praise of his teacher. A Gaṇadharasaptati, written for the purpose of exorcising a man possessed by a spirit, is mentioned by *Bhandarkar*, Report 1882 83, p. 48 f. Another Jinadatta, who lived in the first half of the 13th century, wrote an encyclopædia Vivekavilāsa, s. *Bhandarkar*, Report 1883-84, pp. 156, 458 ff.

3) Edited by *Munirāja Jinavijaya*, Baroda 1920 (GOS No. 14). *Cf. Peterson*, Report IV, p. 12 f.; P. D. *Gune* in Proc. I. OC, Poona 1922, p 159 ff., and Ludwig *Alsdorf*, Der Kumārapālapratibodha, ein Beitrag zur Kenntnis des Apabhraṃśa und der Erzählungslitteratur der Jainas (Alt- und Neu-Indische Studien) Hamburg 1928. In the last verse the title is given as Jinadharmapratibodha, in the colophon Kumārapālapratibodha, which is probably to be explained as an abbreviation for Kumārapāla-Jinadharma-pratibodha, "Awakening of the religion of the Jina in Kumārapāla." Hemakumāracaritra also appears to be a title of the same work, s. *Alsdorf*, l. c., p. 1, Note 1.

in verse and prose, for the most part in Prākrit, but also partly in Sanskrit and Apabhraṃśa. According to the statement of the author himself, the work was written in the year 1184 A.D., and consists of five Prastāvas (" Recitals, sermons ") by which Hemacandra who is made the speaker, is supposed to have converted King Kumārapāla. Prastāva I deals with the 5 commandments as to conduct: avoidance of killing, of gambling, adultery, fornication, drinking and theft; Pr. II with the worship of gods and teachers, Pr. III with the four duties: generosity, virtue, asceticism and meditation, Pr. IV on the 12 vows of the Jaina layman,[1] and Prastāva V on the four passions (anger, pride, deceit and greed) and various other points of the doctrine. The separate teachings are illustrated by stories, of which there are 54 in all. Most of the stories told here occur in other Jaina works too.[2]

As an example of the vice of gambling the story of Nala is told.[3] The story of King Pradyota of Ujjayinī serves to elucidate the sin of adultery. The story belongs to the cycle of the Udayana legends. It is also told here how Prince Abhaya of Rājagṛha becomes the prisoner of King Pradyota owing to trickery. As a captive he does the king an important service on three occasions, and each time the king grants him a wish with the exception of his liberty. When he rescues the king from his distress the fourth time, and the king again offers to grant him a wish Abhaya says: " Whilst you sit upon the elephant Nalagiri as a driver and I sit on the lap of (your consort) Śivadevī, burn me with the (fire-proof) wood of the chariot Agnibhīru." By demanding such impossibilities, he indicates to the king that he has only the one wish for liberty. The king recognises this and sets him free, whereupon Abhaya takes leave of him with this oath: " If I do not take you prisoner, O King, in broad daylight in the middle of the town amidst loud cries, may I go into the fire." By means of a ruse he does actually take the king prisoner.[4]

---

1) *Cf.* Mrs. S. *Stevenson*, The Heart of Jainism, p. 205 ff.; *Glasenapp*, Der Jainismus, p. 202 ff.

2) See *Alsdorf*, l. c., p. 7 ff.

3) Pp. 47-76 of the edition.

4) Pp. 76-83 of the edition, *cf. Alsdorf*, l. c., p. 140 f. and P. D. *Gune* in Ann. Bh. Inst. II, 1920, p. 1 ff.

As an instance of the vow of virtue, the story is told of Sīlavatī, the virtuous wife of the rich merchant Ajitasena. She understands the language of the birds and performs all kinds of seemingly absurd actions and gives seemingly absurd answers : it turns out, however, that the apparent absurdities are in reality proofs of great intelligence.[1]

Prastāva V contains two long narratives in Apabhraṃśa. The one is the J ī v a-m a n a ḥ-k a r a ṇ a-s a ṃ l ā p a-K a t h ā, "The Story of the Conversation between Soul, Mind and Senses."[2] This is an elaborately worked out allegory (105 stanzas), in which King Ātman (Soul), his consort Buddhi (Insight), his minister Manas (Mind) and his five court officials, the Five Senses, appear : Manas and the five Senses carry on a heated debate as to the origin of suffering, whereupon Ātman takes the lead, and in a long speech describes the terrible sufferings of Saṃsāra and extols the happiness of those whose mind is directed towards the Jina, the Munis and pity on all beings, "who avoid the striving after possession, as one avoids robbery, which brings suffering in its wake, kingly power, as a snare or poison, sensual pleasure and a loving woman, as a piece of wood, wealth as a fetter, inclination to adornment as a burden ; who, making no difference between themselves and others, have taken upon themselves the burden of the discipline of the Order."[3]

The second long story in Apabhraṃśa is the story of Sthūlabhadra[4] in 106 verses. Sthūlabhadra is the last successor of Mahāvīra, who still knew the 14 Pūrvas. Stories about him and his enemy, the learned Brahman Vararuci, are already told in the Pariśiṣṭa-Parvan.[5] We also find here the story of the monks, each of whom fulfils another, more difficult vow, whilst Sthūlabhadra takes upon himself and fulfils the vow that he will spend four months in the house of the courtesan Kośā, without violating his vow of chastity. The vain attempts of Kośā to entangle the monk in the bonds of love, are described in accordance with all the rules of the Kāma-Śāstra. In the end the king gives Kośā to his charioteer as a wife. In order to amuse her, this man performs a remarkable trick : he cuts a mango from the tree with two arrows shot into one another, whereupon Kośā does a still more wonderful trick : she

1) Pp. 220-229 of the edition ; *cf. Alsdorf*, l. c., p. 141 f.

2) Pp. 422-437 of the edition ; *cf. Alsdorf*, l. c., pp. 6, 10 ff., 80 ff., 92 ff.

3) *Alsdorf*, l. c., p. 100.

4) Pp. 443-461 of the edition ; *cf. Alsdorf*, l. c., pp. 6, 19 ff., 100 ff., 118 ff.

5) Pariśiṣṭa-Parvan VIII, 110-193, see above, p. 507 ff.

dances upon the point of a needle which is sticking at the top of a heap of mustard-seeds. Then the charioteer is astonished, but she says that Sthūlabhadra performed a far more marvellous trick, when he lived with her and yet did not violate his vow of chastity.

Somaprabha is a poet well versed in all the arts of the Alaṃkāra-Śāstra : this is evidenced by the extremely artificial hymn to Pārśva in Apabhraṃśa.[1] Another work by Somaprabha which is very artificial and at the same time reveals great Sanskrit erudition, is the Śatārthakāvya written between 1177 and 1179 A.D. This is a single verse in the Vasantatilakā metre, which is explained by the poet himself in 100 different ways.[2]

The same Somaprabha is also the author of the didactic poem S i n d ū r a p r a k a r a or S ū k t i m u k t ā v a l ī,[3] written in 1199 A.D., a book of moral sayings very popular among the Jainas.

It is, on the other hand, a later S o m a p r a b h a, who wrote the Ś ṛ ṅ g ā r a v a i r ā g y a-T a r a ṅ g i ṇ ī[4] in about 1276 A.D. This is a didactic poem in 46 elaborate stanzas written in the most perfect Kāvya style. In this erotic-ascetic poem, the charms of women and the blandishments of love are described with all the arts of the Kāma-Śāstra, as a warning against them as being an obstacle to peace of mind and release.

1) P. 471 f. of the edition ; *cf. Alsdorf*, l. c., pp. 45 f., 126 ff.

2) *Munirāja Jinavijaya*, Kumārapāla-Pratibodha, Ed., Introduction, p. vii f.

3) Edited in Km., Part VII, pp. 35-51 ; translated into Italian by *Pavolini* in SIFI II, 33-72, Firenze 1898 with Introduction by F. L. *Pullée* ; *cf. Weber*, HSS. Verz. II, 3, p. 1132 ff.; *Bhandarkar*, Report 1882-83, pp. 42, 225 f. *Munirāja Jinavijaya*, l. c., p. vi, who says : " This work is well-known among the Jainas and is repeated by heart by many a man and woman of the Jain community."

4) Edited in Km., Part V, 1888, 124 ff. Trans. into German as " A true Capuchin's Sermon against Women " by R. *Schmidt*, Liebe und Ehe im alten und modernen Indien, Berlin 1904, p. 36 ff. According to verse 33 (" he whose thoughts are bent on Śiva, should not even stay in the vicinity of women") and verse 39 (" the city of Śiva " in the sense of " release ") it appears to be an originally Śivaite poem, which has been

Śīladūta, "Virtue as a Messenger," [1] by Cāritrasundara, is a very elaborate didactic poem composed on the principle of the completion of verses (samasyāpūraṇa) in imitation of Kālidāsa's Meghadūta. In the last verse the poet mentions the date when his poem was completed, which corresponds to the year 1420 A.D.

Anthologies of moral sayings have also been compiled by Jainas. Thus the Gāthā-Kośa by Municandra Sūri [2] (died 1122), a book of Prākrit verses, from which Peterson has culled a few remarkable sayings, *e.g.*:

> " Heaven and hell, the atmosphere and the whole earth
> Do the wise ones know, —the doings of women they know not."
> " The path of the fish in the water, the bird's flight through the air
> The wise ones know, —the heart of a woman they know not."

Gāthāsahasrī by Samayasundara,[3] is a more comprehensive anthology of more recent date (1630). All of these "thousand stanzas," partly in Sanskrit, partly in Prākrit, are compiled from earlier works by Haribhadra, Devendra and others. There are also memorial verses among them, the contents of which deal with ecclesiastical history. A saying taken from a work by Devendra is deserving of mention :

> " You cannot tread two paths at once,
> You cannot sew with a needle with two points;
> You cannot enjoy both at the same time :
> The pleasure of the senses and release in the Beyond."

appropriated by the Jainas. The commentator explains Śiva as a synonym for mukti, " release."

1) Edited in YJG. No. 18, Benares 1909. *Cf.* F. *Belloni-Filippi* in GSAI, 28, 1916, 153 ff.

2) *Peterson*, 3 Reports, 12 ff., 297 ff.

3) *Peterson*, 3 Reports, 3 ff., 281 ff. Samayasundara is also the author of Visaṃvādaśataka, a compilation of a hundred verses which contain discrepancies to be found in the sacred texts (l. c., p. 10).

Bhavavairāgyaśataka,[1] a collection of a hundred verses on the vanity of existence, the inconstancy of all earthly goods, the wretchedness of Saṃsāra, etc., as the sole remedy for which the Jaina religion is recommended, is an anthology of Prākrit verses.[2]

Great is the number of the purely erudite works, some of which are works on the dogmas of the Jaina religion, others on philosophy, and more especially logic. The Jainas play a by no means unimportant part in the history of Indian philosophy. The Upaniṣads taught the eternal existence of the soul, which is the only existing being. Earlier Buddhism taught that there is no independent self, but only a constant becoming and passing away of psychical and physical phenomena, from which Mahāyāna Buddhism developed the doctrine of Śūnyavāda or Nāstivāda, "the doctrine of It-is-not." Midway between these two stand the Jainas, who proclaim the Syādvāda, "the doctrine of It-can-be," saying: "There is something which exists eternally, objects are eternal as matter, but this matter can assume all possible forms and qualities." At an early period the Jainas rendered very great services in the development of logic and atomism, the Nyāya and the Vaiśeṣika philosophy. Bhadrabāhu taught a syllogism consisting of ten parts already in the Āvasyaka-Niryukti, and Syādvāda in the Sūtrakṛtāṅga-Niryukti.[3] According to the Āvaśyaka-Sūtra, the Jaina teacher Rohagutta is supposed

---

[1]) Edited and translated by L. P. *Tessitori* in GSAI 22, 179-211 ; 24, 405 ff.

[2]) Other anthologies such as the earlier Vajjālagga by Jayavallabha (with Sanskrit Version ed. by J. *Laber* in Bibl. Ind., Fasc. I, 1914, Fasc. II, 1923) and the more modern collection Prākrita-Sūktaratnamālā (Collection of Ancient Prakrit Popular Poems with Sanskrit Equivalents and English Translation) compiled by Puran Chand *Nahar*, Calcutta 1919 (Jaina Vividha Sāhitya Shāstra Mālā No. 11) are of the quite general character, and not specifically Jinistic, though they are compiled by Jainas.

[3]) *Cf. Jacobi* in Transactions of the Third Congress for the History of Religion, Oxford 1908, II, p. 59 ff. ; S. Ch. *Vidyābhūṣaṇa*, History of Indian Logic, p. 164 ff. ; H. *Ui*, Vaiśeṣika Philosophy (OTF), London 1917, p. 83. S. *Dasgupta*, History of Indian Philosophy I, Cambridge 1922, p. 173 ff.

to have occasioned a schism in the year 18 A. D. and founded the Vaiśeṣika.[1]

The earliest Digambara author who is also cited with esteem by the Śvetāmbaras, is K u n d a k u n d a, who wrote only in Prākrit. Of the 83 treatises (pāhuda, prābhṛta) which he is said to have written, only seven are known. P a ñ c a t t h i y a s ā r a (Pañcāstikāyasāra)[2] or P a v a y a ṇ a s ā r a P a ñ c a t t h i y a s a ṃ g a h a (Pravacanasāra Pañcāstikāyasaṃgraha)[3] consists of two parts, which are really independent works.[4] The first and longer section contains the doctrine of the 5 Astikāyas or groups of existence: souls (Jīva), non-souls (pudgala), principles of rest and motion (dharma and adharma) and space (ākāśa). The second section treats of the path to release. This work, together with Pavayanasāra, and Samayasāra, forms a "trilogy" (Prābhṛtatraya or Nāṭakatraya). P a v a y a ṇ a s ā r a (Pravacanasāra)[5] in Prākrit Gāthās, is a much prized book on Jinistic dogmatics, psychology and ethics. On S a m a y a s ā r a (Kernel or Essence of the Doctrine")[6] in 414 Prākrit stanzas, there are Sanskrit commentaries by Prabhācandra, the pupil of Akalaṅka, and Amṛtacandra, who commented on the principal works of Akalaṅka in about 904 A.D. N i y a m a s ā r a[7] is a

---

1) *Cf. Weber*, Ind. Stud. 17, 121 ff.; *Jacobi* in SBE, Vol. 14, p. xxxvii; *Ui*, l. c., p. 35 ff.

2) The Building of the Cosmos or Pañchâstikâya Sâra (The five Cosmic Constituents) by Svami Sri Kundakundacharya ed. with Philosophical and Historical Introduction, Translation, Notes and an Original Commentary in English by A. *Chakravartinayanar*, Arrah 1920 (SBJ, Vol. III). Text also edited by *Pavolini* in GSAI 14, 1901, pp. 1-40 and in Rāyacandra-Jaina-Śāstramālā, Bombay 1904.

3) The title of the work is given thus in the colophons.

4) Each of the two parts has an introductory formula and a conclusion of its own.

5) More recent editions have appeared in India. *Cf. Bhandarkar*, Report 1883-84, pp. 91 ff., 379 ff.

6) Edited with a Sanskrit commentary in SJG No. 3, Benares 1914. *Cf. Peterson*, Report II, p. 161 ff., and *Hiralal*, Catalogue, p. 702; on Amṛtacandra Sūri s. *Peterson*, Report IV, p. ix.

7) *Cf. Bhandarkar*, Report 1883-84, p. 102 f.

work on the discipline to which the seeker after salvation must submit himself. To Kundakunda is also ascribed Chappāhuḍa (Ṣaṭprābhṛta),[1] six chapters on the Jaina doctrine, but this work contains views which differ from the views of the teacher known from his other works. The author calls himself "pupil of Bhadrabāhu," which may mean Bhadrabāhu II, who lived in the 1st century A.D., so that the author may nevertheless have been a contemporary of Kundakunda.

It was probably in one of the early centuries of the Christian era that Vaṭṭakera wrote his Prākrit works Mūlācāra and Trivarṇācāra on the moral conduct of a pious Jaina. There is a commentary Ācāravṛtti on the Mūlācāra, written by Vasunandin, who observes by way of introduction that Vaṭṭakera intended to give in his work a brief summary of the Āyāraṅga for his pupils.[2]

Kārttikeya Svāmin, whose Kattigeyāṇupekkhā (Kārttikeyānuprekṣā)[3] enjoys a great reputation among the Jainas, probably also belongs to this earlier period. This work treats in 12 chapters of the 12 Anuprekṣās or meditations, to which both monk and layman must devote themselves, in order to emancipate themselves little by little from Karman.[4] These are reflections on the transitoriness of all

---

1) Edited with a Hindī commentary by *Bābū* Sūrajbhān *Vakīl*, Benares 1910. Commentary on it by Amṛtacandra Sūri and by Śrutasāgara. *Cf. Peterson*, Report II, pp. 80 ff., 158 ff., and W. *Denecke* in Festgabe Jacobi, p. 163 f.

2) Mūlācāra with Vasunandin's commentary edited in MDJG Nos. 19 and 23. In one manuscript Mūlācāra is ascribed to Kundakunda. *Cf. Peterson*, Report II, pp. 74 ff., 134 ff.; *Hiralal*, Catalogue, p. xiv f. and *Denecke*, l. c., p. 162. Vasunandin quotes Amitagati and is quoted by Āśādhara, and must therefore have lived between the 10th and 13th centuries.

3) Printed with a Hindī commentary in Bombay 1904. *Cf. Peterson*, Report IV, p. 142 ff.; *Bhandarkar*, Report 1883-84, pp. 113 ff., 398 ff. (where the text of Chapter XII is given); *Hiralal*, Catalogue, p. xiv.

4) *Cf.* Mrs. S. *Stevenson*, The Heart of Jainism, p. 156 ff.; *Glasenapp*, Der Jainismus, p. 206 f.

things, the helplessness of all beings, the sufferings of the beings in the cycle of rebirths, the soul which goes on this journey alone and can only be released alone, the difference of everything else (body, friends, relatives and possessions) from the soul, the impurity of the body, the influx (āsrava) of Karman and the means whereby one can stem this influx, the annihilation of Karman and the purification of the soul by mortifications, the countless uncreated worlds, the precious treasure of illumination, which is difficult of attainment, and lastly the duties of laymen and monks, which are set forth in Chapter 12.

The Digambara U m ā s v ā m i n, who is called U m ā s-v ā t i by the Śvetāmbaras[1] and described as a pupil of Ghoṣanandi Kṣamāśramaṇa, was, according to tradition, a pupil of Kundakunda. The Digambaras also give him the epithet Gṛdhrapiccha, "Vulture's feather," which Kundakunda had too, and the title "Reciter" (Vācakaśramaṇa or Vācakā-cārya). According to the Digambara-Paṭṭāvalīs he lived from about 135 to 219 A.D., whilst the statements of the Śvetām-baras not only contradict those of the Digambaras, but even contradict one another.[2] In any case he is earlier than Siddhasena Divākara, who wrote a commentary on the principal work of Umāsvāti. He is said to have written no less than 500 books, but his most famous work, which he wrote in Pāṭaliputra, is the T a t t v ā r t h ā d h i g a m a-S ū t r a,[3] "the Manual for the Understanding of the True Nature of

1) He is said to be called so because his mother was called Umā Vātsī and his father Svāti.

2) *Cf. Klatt*, Jaina-Onomasticon, p. 4 f.; *Peterson*, 3 Reports, p. 328 f.; Report IV, p. xvi f.; *Jacobi* in ZDMG 60, 1906, 288 f.; *Vidyābhūṣaṇa*, History of Indian Logic, p. 168 ff.; L. *Suali*, Introductione alla Studio della Filosofia Indiana, Pavia 1913, p. 36 ff.; J. L. *Jaini* in SBJ II, p. vii; *Farquhar*, Outline, p. 164 f. Neither are the statements of the Digambaras free from ambiguity. J. H. *Woods*, The Yoga-System of Patanjali (HOS Vol. 17), p. xix, makes it appear probable that Umāsvāti quotes from the Yoga-Sūtra.

3) Edited with the Commentary, by *Vakil* Keshavlal Premchand *Mody* in Bibl. Ind. 1903-1905, together with a few minor works of Umāsvāti in the appendices; with a

Things," a Sanskrit manual, which is recognised as an authority by both Śvetāmbaras and Digambaras, and even at the present day is read by all Jainas in private houses and temples. By reading this book once through one is said to acquire just as much religious merit as by fasting for one day. The logic, psychology, cosmography, ontology [1] and ethics of the Jainas, are treated in these Sūtras and in the Commentary appended by the author himself, in the closest possible agreement with the Canon, more especially with Aṅga VI and Pūrva II. Even to-day it may still serve as an excellent summary of Jaina dogmatics. It is true that the Commentary, which expresses views that are not in harmony with those of the Digambaras, is not recognised by this sect as the work of Umāsvāmin. It is doubtful, therefore, whether the Digambaras are justified in claiming him as one of their own. He probably belongs to a period at which there was not yet so wide a gulf between the two sects as was the case later. The large number of commentaries which have been written on this work by both Śvetāmbaras and Digambaras, bear witness to its significance and great popularity; these include commentaries by such notable teachers as Siddhasena Divākara, Samantabhadra and Haribhadra. The last-named also wrote a commentary on Śrāvakaprajñapti,[2] a systematic treatise of the Jaina religion for lay adherents, in Prākrit. Praśamarati-Prakaraṇa,[3] "Treatise on the Joys of Peace of

---

commentary in Hindī, also in Rāyacandra-Jaina-Śāstramālā, Bombay 1906; with Introduction, Translation, Notes and Commentary in English by J. L. *Jaini*, Arrah 1920, SBJ, Vol. 2; Text of the Sūtras also in *Bhandarkar*, Report 1883-84, p. 405 ff.; and in DJGK I; translated into German and explained by H. *Jacobi* in ZDMG 60, 1906, 287 ff., 512 ff.; *cf. Peterson*, Report II, 78 ff., 156 ff.

[1]) On the classification of the animals according to Tattvārthādhigama, *cf.* B. N *Seal* in the Appendix to B. K. *Sarkar*, The Primitive Background of Hindu Sociology, Allahabad 1914, p. 323 ff.

[2]) Ed. by B. K. Premchand (*Mody*), Bombay 1905.

[3]) Edited in the Appendix to the Edition of Tattvārthādhigama, Bibl. Ind.; also in Amadavada, Saṃvat 1960; with Tīkā and Avacūrī, Bhavnagar, Saṃvat 1966; edited

the Soul," is a religious-philosophical work, also possessing literary merit.

Like Umāsvāti, Siddhasena Divākara, too, is regarded by both Śvetāmbaras and Digambaras as one of their own. He wrote a commentary on the Tattvārthādhigama-Sūtra,[1] and is said to have written 32 different works on logic, 21 of which are known.[2] His Nyāyāvatāra,[3] which treats of the means of acquiring knowledge (pramāṇa) and of methods (naya) in 32 Sanskrit verses, is a fundamental Jaina work on logic. It forms a part of the Dvātriṃśad-Dvātriṃśikā.[4] The Sammatitarka-Sūtra[5] is a general work on philosophy, which also deals with logic.

A commentary on Umāsvāti's work, entitled Sarvārthasiddhi,[6] was also written by Pūjyapāda Devanandin.

In the first half of the 8th century A.D. lived the Digambara Samantabhadra,[7] who again wrote a commentary

---

with Commentary and translated into Italian by A. *Ballini* in GSAI, 25, 1912, 117 ff.; 29, 1918-20, 61 ff.

1) Tattvānusāriṇī Tattvārthaṭīkā was printed in Ahmedabad. Siddhasena Gaṇin, who also wrote a Tattvārthaṭīkā, quotes Siddhasena Divākara. *Cf. Peterson*, 3 Reports, Extracts p. 83 ff.; *Hiralal*, Catalogue, p. xii ff. Distinct from these two is Siddhasena Sūri, who in 1185 A.D. wrote a commentary on Nemicandra's Pravacanasāroddhāra; *cf. Weber* HSS. Verz. II, 3, 850; *Peterson*, Report IV, p. cxxx ff.

2) Ekaviṃśatidvātriṃśikā, Nyāyāvatāra and Sammatisūtra were published in Siddhasena-Divākara-Kṛta-Granthamālā, Bhavnagar 1909: Sammatitarka-Prakaraṇa with commentary by Abhayadeva is published in YJG No. 13, Benares 1919. Abhayadeva's exhaustive commentary has also been published in Gujarātapurātattvamandira-Granthāvalī 10, 16, 18, 19, Ahmedabad, 1923-1928.

3) Edited with Commentary and an English translation by Satis Chandra *Vidyābhūṣaṇa*, Calcutta, 1909.

4) *Cf.* S. Ch. *Vidyābhūṣaṇa*, History of Indian Logic, p. 174 ff.

5) Edited with Abhayadeva's commentary Tattvabodhinī in YJG, No. 13; with Tattvārthavidhāyinī in the Ārhatamata-Prabhākara Series, Poona 1926.

6) Edited in Kolhapur 1904, s. *Jacobi* in ZDMG 60, 290.

7) Thus according to K. B. *Pathak* in Ann. Bh. Inst. XI, 1930, 149 ff., who proves that Samantabhadra lived after Dharmakīrti and before Kumārila. S. Ch. *Vidyābhūṣaṇa*, History of Indian Logic, p. 182 f., states his period as 600 A.D. According to a Vaṃśāvalī he is supposed to have lived in 419 A.D.; s. *Hiralal*, Catalogue, p. x ff. On Samantabhadra's

on Umāsvāti's Tattvārthādhigama-Sūtra. The introduction to this commentary is entitled Devāgama-Stotra or Āptamīmaṃsā,[1] in which the Jinistic philosophy of Syādvāda is explained. The work was known to the philosophers Kumārila and Vācaspatimiśra. Another philosophical work by Samantabhadra is Yuktyanuśāsana.[2] Ratnakāraṇḍaśrāvakācāra,[3] also called Upāsakādhyayana, is a manual of morals for the lay adherent, in 150 Sanskrit verses.

Not far removed from Samantabhadra in point of time is Akalaṅka,[4] or Akalaṅkadeva, who wrote Tattvārtharājavārttika,[5] a commentary on the Tattvārthādhigama-Sūtra, and Aṣṭaśatī, a commentary on Samantabhadra's Āptamīmāṃsā. He is also the author of works on logic, Nysyāviniścaya, Laghīyastraya and Svarūpasambhodhana.[6] A treatise on expiatory rites, Prāyaścittagrantha (or Prāyaścittavidhi) is also ascribed to him.[7] His views are opposed by Kumārila, the great philosopher of Brahmanical orthodoxy, whilst Vidyānanda Pātrakesarin[8] and Prabhācandra defend Akalaṅka against Kumārila. Vidyānanda wrote Aṣṭasahasrī,[9] a commentary

---

life, character, and time, see Pandit Jugala Kiśora *Mukhtara* in MDJG No 24, 1925. Samantabhadra is also called, "Kavi" and is the author of a Svayambhū-Stotra, s. above, p. 552.

[1]) Edition in Jaina Grantha Ratnākara and in SJG Vol. 1, Bombay 1905; in SJG 10, Benares 1914, and in DJGK I. On the contents of the work, cf. *Vidyābhūṣaṇa*, l.c., p. 184 f.

[2]) Edited in SJG Vol. 1; MDJG No. 15; and in DJGK I.

[3]) Text with English translation (after the Hindī translation) by Champat Rai *Jain*, The Householder's Dharma, Arrah 1917; text only in DJGK I; text with commentary by Prabhācandra in MDJG No. 24.

[4]) *Cf. Hiralal*, Catalogue, p. xxvi ff.

[5]) Edited in SJG 4, Benares 1915.

[6]) Laghīyastraya and Svarūpasambodhana are edited in MDJG No. 1.

[7]) Edited together with three other treatises on Prāyaścittas in MDJG No. 18 (Prāyaścitta-Saṃgraha). But it is doubtful whether Akalaṅka is really the author of this treatise; s. *Hiralal*, Catalogue, p. xxvi.

[8]) *Cf. Hiralal*, Catalogue, p. xxviii f.

[9]) Edited in Gāndhīnāthāraṅga-Jaina-Granthamālā, Bombay 1915.

on Aṣṭaśatī, also Tattvārthaślokavārttika,[1] a commentary on Umāsvāmin's work, Āptaparīkṣā and Patraparīkṣā,[2] Pramāṇanirṇaya and Pramāṇaparīkṣā.[3] Based upon Akalaṅka's Nyāyaviniścaya there is a work on logic, the Parīkṣāmukha-Sūtra,[4] by Māṇikyanandin;[5] and Prabhācandra, who calls himself a pupil of Padmanandin (*i.e.*, Kundakunda), wrote a commentary on the last-named work: this commentary is entitled Prameyakamalamārtaṇḍa, and is a well-known work on logic. The same author also wrote another work on logic, Nyāyakumudacandrodaya. It has been believed hitherto that this is the same Prabhācandra who was a pupil of Akalaṅka in the 8th century. According to the epilogue (praśasti) of the first work, however, this work was written in Dhārā in the reign of King Bhoja (1019-1060 A.D.).[6] One Prabhācandra wrote commentaries on the Tattvārthādhigama-Sūtra by Umāsvāmin, the Samayasāra by Kundakunda, Pūjyapāda's Samādhiśataka and on Samantabhadra's Ratnakaraṇḍa and Svayambhū-Stotra.[7]

---

1) Edited in Gāndhīnāthāraṅga-Jaina-Granthamālā, Bombay 1918.

2) Edited in SJG 1,2, Benares 1913; Āptaparīkṣā also in DJGK I.

3) Edited in SJG 10, 1914.

4) Edited in SJG I, Bombay 1905; also in DJGK I. *Cf.* S. Ch. *Vidyābhūṣaṇa*, History of Indian Logic, p. 188 ff.

5) According to a Digambara Paṭṭāvalī (*Hoernle* in Ind. Ant. 20, 1891, p. 352) Māṇikyanandin lived in 528 A.D. *Cf.* also *Hiralal*, Catalogue, p. xxviii. A later Māṇikyanandin was the teacher of Meghacandra, who died in 1163 A.D., s. Lewis *Rice*, Epigraphia Carnatica, Vol. XII, p. 134.

6) Thus according to A. *Venkatasubbiah* in JBRAS, N.S., 3, 1927, p. 144 ff. But according to K. B. *Pathak* in OC IX, London 1892, I, 213 (s. above, p. 478 and note 4) Jinasena mentions Akalaṅka in the Ādi-Purāṇa (838 A.D.) and speaks of Prabhācandra as the author of Candrodaya. In the introduction to Nyāyakumuda-Candrodaya, Prabhācandra says that he is the pupil of Akalaṅka and that he also wrote Prameyakamalamārtaṇḍa. According to this, Prabhācandra would have to have lived at the end of the 8th or beginning of the 9th century. As the works themselves are not accessible to me, I am not in a position to settle the question.

7) Neither can I decide to which Prabhācandra these commentaries should be

At the close of the 8th or the beginning of the 9th century the Digambara Śubhacandra wrote a philosophical treatise in Sanskrit verses, entitled Jñānārṇava, "The Ocean of Knowledge" or Yogapradīpādhikāra.[1]

Among the Śvetāmbaras we must mention the famous Haribhadra, who wrote a large number of works both on general philosophy and the Jaina doctrine. In the former category there is Ṣaḍdarśanasamuccaya, "A summary of the Six Philosophical Systems."[2] Haribhadra here deals with the systems of Buddhism, Nyāya, Sāṃkhya, Vaiśeṣika and Jaimini, in a short appendix also with the materialism of Cārvāka, and only one short section, the fourth, is devoted to Jinistic metaphysics. Lokatattvanirṇaya ("Investigation of the True Nature of the World)," [3] a philosophical text in Sanskrit verses, is also not an exclusively Jinistic text. In fact Haribhadra goes to the length of saying that Lord Mahāvīra is not his friend and the others are not his foes; that he is not biassed in favour of Mahāvīra and feels no hatred for Kapila and the other philosophers, but that he is desirous of accepting whosesoever doctrine is the true one.[4] He also proved his unbiassedness by writing a commentary on the Nyāyapraveśa of the Buddhist Dignāga.[5] On the other hand, other works such as

---

ascribed, or the short treatise Arhatpravacana, printed in MDJG Nr. 21, p. 114. ff. Jaina authors named Prabhācandra lived in the 12th, 13th and 16th centuries too. *Cf. Hiralal*, Catalogue, pp. xxviii, 625 f., 629, 648, 671, 702, 704, 714. See above, p. 478 note 4.

1) Edited in Rāyacandra-Jaina-Śāstramālā, Bombay 1907. *Cf. Weber*, HSS. Verz., II, 3, 907 ff.; *Guérinot* in JA 1912, s. 10, t. XIX, 373 ff.

2) Edited by F. L. *Pullée* in GSAI 1, 47 ff.; 8, 159 ff.; 9, 1 ff.; edited with Guṇaratna's (or Guṇākara Sūri's) Commentary, by *L. Suali* in Bibl. Ind. 1905 ff.; edited together with Aṣṭaka-Prakaraṇa and with works of Yaśovijaya and Rājaśekhara, Surat 1918; also edited with Guṇaratna's Commentary in Jaina-Ātmānanda-Granthamālā 49, Bhavnagar, V. S. 2444 (1917).

3) Edited and translated into Italian by L. *Suali* in GSAI Vol. 18, 263 ff. Text also edited, Bhavnagar 1902.

4) *Cf. La Vallée Poussin*, JA 1911, s. 10, t. XVII, 923 ff.

5) See N. D. *Mironov* in Festgabe Garbe, p. 37 ff.

Yogabindu,[1] Yogadṛṣṭisamuccaya,[2] Dharmabindu, etc., contain presentations of the Jaina doctrine. Dharmabindu[3] is a manual of practical morals and asceticism in three sections, the first of which treats of the duties of the layman, the second of the rules for the monks, and the third of the bliss of the saint in Nirvāṇa. The author here uses the Sūtra style in the manner of the Brahmanical Dharma-Sūtras. He availed himself of Umāsvāti's works.[4]

In about 904 A. D. Amṛtacandra[5] wrote the works Puruṣārthasiddhyupāya or Jinapravacanarahasyakośa[6] in 226 Sanskrit verses, Tattvārthasāra,[7] Tattvadīpikā and commentaries on Kundakunda's works. In the year 933 A. D. Devasena, who was born in 894 A. D., wrote a manual of the Digambara faith entitled Darśanasāra,[8] and in the same year a Śrāvakācāra, a manual of rules of life for the layman.[9] He is also the author of an

---

1) Ed. with Comm. by L. *Suali*, Bhavnagar 1911.

2) Edited by L. *Suali* in JPU 12, Bombay 1912.

3) Edited and translated into Italian by L. *Suali* in GSAI, Vol. 21, 223 ff.; edited together with Municandra's Commentary by the same scholar in Bibl. Ind. 1912 (fasc. 1, Adhy. 1, 2); edited with Municandra's Commentary and detailed Indices, in AUS, Ahmedabad 1924. The title "Drop of the Religion" is an expression of modesty: As the drop of water is to the ocean, so is this work to the religion of the Jina. An abridgment of Haribhadra's Muṇivaicariya is Munipaticaritrasāroddhāra: s. F. *Belloni-Filippi* in GSAI, Vol. 25, 137 ff., 26, 163 ff.

4) *Jacobi* in AR 18, 1915, 277 f. mentions also the following works of Haribhadra; Anekāntajayapatākā with the author's commentary printed in YJG, Ahmedabad; Śāstravārttāsamuccaya (together with Saḍdarśanasamuccaya and Aṣṭakāni in one vol.), Bhavnagar 1908; Aṣṭaka-Prakaraṇa with Abhayadeva's Aṣṭakavṛtti published in Ahmedabad; Upadeśapada, Part I, Palitana 1909; Ṣoḍaśa-Prakaraṇa with Commentary, Bombay 1911.

5) *Cf. Peterson*, Report IV, p. ix.

6) Edited in Rāyacandra-Jaina-Śāstramālā, Bombay 1905, and in SJG, Vol. 1, Bombay 1905.

7) Edited in SJG Vol. 1; also in DJGK I, where we find also a philosophical poem Nāṭakasamayasārakalaśāḥ by Amṛtacandra.

8) Edited by Nathuram *Premi*, Bombay 1920, *cf. Peterson*, 3 Reports, pp. 22 ff., 374 ff.

9) *Cf. Hiralal*, Catalogue, p. xlvii f.

Ārādhanasāra, "Essence of Worship,"[1] and of a Tattvasāra.[2] All these books are written in Prākrit verses, Srāvakācāra being in the Dohā metre which is otherwise not used in scientific works. The Ālāpapaddhati is a short manual of Jaina dogmatics in Sanskrit verses with commentary.[3]

Cāmuṇḍarāya, who won great fame by his warlike deeds as the minister and general of the Gaṅga princes Mārasiṃha II (died 974 A. D.) and Rācamalla or Rājamalla II (974-984 A. D.), but devoted himself to pious works in his later years, erected the famous colossal statue of Gommaṭa[4] in Śravaṇa Belgola (Mysore) in about 980 A. D., and wrote the Cāmuṇḍarāya-Purāṇa in the Kanarese language[5] in the year 978 A. D., mentions Ajitasena and Nemicandra as his teachers. The last named, who must thus have lived at the close of the 10th and the beginning of the 11th century, has the epithet of Siddhānta-Cakravartin, *i.e.*, "He who like a ruler of the world, has a mastery over the totality of the sacred writings," and is a very erudite Digambara writer, who deals with the whole system of the Jaina religion in his works. He mentions Abhayanandin, Indranandin, Vīranandin[6] and Kanakanandin as his teachers. Davvasaṃgaha (Dravyasaṃgraha), "Compendium of Substances,"[7] in 58 Prākrit

[1]) Edited with Commentary in MDJG, No. 6, Bombay, Vik. S. 1973 (1916).

[2]) Edited in MDJG No. 13, p. 145 ff.

[3]) Printed in DJGK I.

[4]) Gommaṭa or Bāhubali, the son of the first Jina Ṛṣabha, is highly honoured especially by the Digambaras.

[5]) *Cf.* S. Ch. *Ghoshal* in SBJ, Vol. I, Introduction, and A. *Venkatasubbiah* in Ind Hist. Qu. VI, 1930, 290 f.

[6]) Vādirāja, author of the Pārśvanātha-Kāvya, mentions Vīranandin as a celebrated author; s. A. *Venkatasubbiah* in Ind. Hist. Qu. VI, p. 294.

[7]) With a Commentary by Brahmadeva, edited with Introduction, Translation, Notes and an original Commentary in English, by Sarat Chandra *Ghoshal*, Arrah 1917, SBJ, Vol. I. Bṛhat-Dravyasaṃgraha, edited in Rāyacandra-Jaina-Śāstramālā, Bombay 1906-07; Laghu-Dravyasaṃgraha is an abridgment made by the author himself; s. *Guérinot* in JA 1912, s. 10, t. XIX, p. 377 f.

verses, deals not only with the substances, the living (jīva) and the lifeless (ajīva), but also with release, its causes and conditions, morals and the importance of meditation. Gommaṭasāra[1] is a bulky work, in which the author explains the essence (sāra) of the Jaina doctrine for Gommaṭarāya,[2] *i.e.*, Cāmuṇḍarāya. The work, which has the title Pañcasaṃgraha[3] also, consists of two parts, the Jīva-Kāṇḍa in 734 and the Karma-Kāṇḍa in 972 Prākrit verses. The Jīva-kāṇḍa deals with the Jīvas, the "souls," their classification, their origin and nature. It is a kind of natural history of the living beings and this word is to be taken in the comprehensive Jinistic sense.[4] On the whole it is nothing but dry-as-dust, purely scientific enumerations, descriptions and calculations. Only rarely do we light upon a simile, such as in Verse 202 : " As a bearer of burdens bears a burden in a shoulder-pannier, thus the soul bears the burden of Karman, for which the body serves as the shoulder-pannier." There is scarcely any detail in the religion and philosophy of Jinism which does not find a place in the Jīva-Kāṇḍa. Chapter IX deals with the activity of the soul in connection with thought, speech and action, and the origin of Karman, various kinds of speech and the ten kinds of truth (Verse 222). Chapter XI deals with the denizens of hell, which have their origin in sin, with the passions, etc. Chapter XII deals with knowledge, and the various types of knowledge. Space is also here devoted to the knowledge which is acquired by the reading of the sacred scriptures, and a survey of the

---

1) Edited in 4 vols. in Gāndhī-Harībhaī-Devakaraṇa-Jaina-Granthamālā No. 4 with the Sanskrit Commentaries by Abhayacandra (on Jiva Kāṇḍa) and Keśavavarṇin (on Karma-Kāṇḍa) and a Commentary in Hindī, Calcutta ; also with Introduction, translation in Sanskrit and English and with a Commentary in English by J. L. *Jaini* in SBJ, Vols. V and VI, Lucknow 1927. Karma-Kāṇḍa edited in Rāyacandra-Jaina-Śāstramālā, Bombay 1928 ; *cf. Hiralal*, Catalogue, p. xxxiv ff.

2) So called because he erected the Gommaṭa statue.

3) " Compendium of the 5 Things," namely binding (bandha) of the soul to the Karman, that which is bound, that which binds, the cause of the binding, and the kinds of binding.

4) *Cf.* Mrs. *Stevenson*, Heart of Jainism, p. 94 ff. ; *Glasenapp*, Jainismus, p. 252 f.

sacred texts (Aṅgas, Pūrvas, etc.) is given. The Karma-Kāṇḍa treats of the nature of Karma and its relationship to the soul. Cāmuṇḍarāya himself wrote a commentary on the work in the Kanarese language.

The works Labdhisāra, "The Essence of Attainment" (of the things which lead to perfection) and Kṣapaṇāsāra, "The Essence of Annihilation" (of the Kaṣāyas or sinful passions : anger, pride, falseness and greed.),[1] which are connected with each other, form a sequel to Gommaṭasāra. Trilokasāra,[2] "The Essence of the Three Worlds," is a complete cosmology. Nemicandra is also said to have written a work Pratiṣṭhāpāṭha on the erection and consecration of statues.[3]

It is not Cāmuṇḍarāya, the pupil of Ajitasena and Nemicandra, but a certain Cāmuṇḍa-Mahārāja,[4] the pupil of Jinasena, who wrote Cāritrasāra,[5] a manual of morals and the path of salvation according to the faith of the Digambaras.

Vardhamāna Sūri[6] is the author of Ācāradinakara,[7] a work on the daily life of the Jaina with all details.

---

1) The two works are edited together, with Sanskrit and Hindī Commentaries, in Gāndhī-Haribhaī-Devakaraṇa-Jaina-Granthamālā, No. 5, Calcutta.

2) *Cf.* Rajendralala *Mitra*, Notices of Sanskrit MSS., Vol. 6, 1882, p. 97 ff.; S. Ch. *Ghoshal* in SBJ, Vol. I, p. xlii, f. The edition by Pandit Manohara Lala *Śāstrī* mentioned by A. *Venkatasubbiah* (Ind. Hist. Qu. VI, 1930, p. 298) is not accessible to me.

3) *Ghoshal*, l. c., p. xliii f.

4) It is true that both have the epithet Raṇaraṅgasiṃha, "Lion on the stage of battle." Hence both of them must have been generals. However, there were three political personages named Cāmuṇḍarāya in the 11th century, who are distinct from the founder of the Gommaṭa statue; s. A. *Venkatasubbiah* in Ind. Hist. Qu. VI, 1930, pp. 296 ff., 299 note 1.

) Edited with explanation in Hindī, by *Lālā Rāmajī* in SJG 20 (Gāndhī-Haribhaī-Devakaraṇa-Jaina-Granthamālā 6), Calcutta.

6) The same who, according to the Kharatara-Gaccha-Paṭṭāvalī, died the voluntary death by starvation in Saṃvat 1088 (1031 A. D.)? (*Klatt* in Ind. Ant. 11, 248.)

7) According to this work (edited several times in India) *Glasenapp* (Der Jainismus, p. 408 ff.) describes the rites of the daily life of the Jainas.

In the year 1015 A. D., Jinacandra Gaṇin, who later called himself Devagupta, wrote a Navapaya (Navapada-Prakaraṇa) in Prākrit with a Sanskrit commentary. He is also the author of a Navatattva-Prakaraṇa,[1] a treatise on the nine Tattvas or fundamental truths: souls (jīva), the lifeless (ajīva), merit (puṇya), sin (pāpa), influx (āsrava) of the Karman into the soul, warding off (saṃvara) this influx, binding (bandha) of the Karman, the gradual vanishing away (nirjarā) of the Karman and release (mokṣa).[2] The work consists of only 14 Prākrit Gāthās, on which Abhayadeva wrote a commentary in about 1063 A. D. and Yaśodeva between 1108 and 1117 A. D. It is perhaps only one of the recensions of the semi-canonical work Nava Tatta[3] on the nine fundamental truths.

Another semi-canonical work is Jīvaviyāra (Jīvavicāra),[4] "Investigation as to the Living Beings," in 51 Āryā verses by Śānti Sūri (died, 1039 A. D.). In this work the beings are classified into such as are in the state of release, and such as are still in the cycle of rebirths: the latter are again classified into lifeless and living, these being

---

1) Edited with the two Commentaries in Ātmānanda-Grantha-Ratnamālā, No. 10, Bhavnagar 1912. *Cf. Peterson*, 3 Reports, p. 16, App. 280 ff.; Report IV, p. xxxiv.

2) *Cf.* Mrs. *Stevenson*, Heart of Jainism, p. 94 ff., 299 ff. Sometimes only 7 Tattvas are enumerated, *i.e.* puṇya and pāpa, being contained in āsrava and bandha, are not counted separately; *Cf. Jacobi* in ZDMG 60, 1906, p. 293.

3) The author and the date of this work, of which there are recensions of 30, 50 and 60 Prākrit stanzas, are not known. An extended recension names Maṇiratna as the author. *Cf. Weber*, HSS. Verz., II, 3, 841 f.; *Guérinot*, La religion Djaina, p. 85 f. The Kalpa Sūtra and Nava Tatva, two works illustrative of the Jaina Religion and Philosophy, translated from the Māgadhī by J. *Stevenson*, London 1848. Neither this book nor the texts printed in Ahmedabad in 1871 and in Bombay in 1905 were accessible to me. The relationship of these texts to one another and to Devagupta's work should be investigated.

4) Edited and translated into French by A. *Guérinot* in JA, 1902, s. 9, t. XIX, pp. 231 ff. Edited with Pāṭhaka Ratnākara's Commentary by the Yaśovijaya-Jaina-Saṃskṛita-Pāṭhaśālā, Ahmedabad 1915. A commentary by Kṣamākalyāṇa is mentioned by *Aufrecht*, Bodl. Cat., p. 377.

in their turn subdivided into denizens of hell, animals, human beings and gods. The work is therefore at one and the same time a treatise on Theology, Zoology, Botany, Anthropology and Mythology.

Maladhāri Hemacandra Sūri, the pupil of Abhayadeva, wrote a Jīvasamāsa[1] in the year 1107 A.D. and a Bhavabhāvanā[2] in 531 Prākrit Gāthās in the year 1113 A. D. He is also the author of commentaries on the Anuyogadvārā-Sūtra,[3] Haribhadra's Āvaśyakavṛtti,[4] and on Jinabhadra's commentry on the Āvaśyaka-Sūtra.[5]

The great Hemacandra is the author of a philosophical work Pramāṇa-Mīmāṃsā, "Examination of the Means of Proof."[6] Mahesara Sūri, who calls himself a pupil of Hemahaṃsa Sūri, and who wrote Sañjamamañjarī,[7] a work on ethics, in Apabhraṃśa, is possibly a contemporary of Hemacandra, at all events earlier than 1309 A. D. The work consists of only 35 Dohā verses, but is furnished with an exhaustive commentary containing a great mass of quotations from Sanskrit, Prākrit and Apabhraṃśa works which make it valuable. The work teaches self-control (sañjama, Skr. saṃyama) as the only "gate to release." Another Apabhraṃśa poem in 77 Dohā verses is Vairāgyasāra[8] by Suprabhācārya.

---

1) *Cf. Peterson*, Report 1882-83, App., p. 63.

2) With an (anonymous) commentary in Sanskrit, s. *Peterson*, 3 Reports, p. 155 f.; *Weber*, HSS. Verz. II, 3, 855 ff.

3) Edited with the text, Bombay 1924.

4) Edited in JPU 53, Bombay 1920.

5) *Cf. Bühler*, Leben des Hemachandra, p. 74 f.; *Peterson*, Report IV, cxl f.

6) Edited with the author's own commentary, in Ārhata-Mata-Prabhākara, No. 1, Poona 1925.

7) Text with translation into Sanskrit by P. D. *Gune* in Ann. Bh. Inst. I. 1919-21, p. 157 ff. Mahesara Sūri is also the author of a Kālakācārya-Kathānaka, of which there is a manuscript written in the year 1309.

8) Discovered and edited by H. D. *Velankar* in Ann. Bh. Inst. 9, 1928, p. 272 ff.

Syādvādamañjarī,[1] which was written in the year 1292 A.D. by **Malliṣeṇa**, is a commentary on the 32 verses of Hemacandra's Anyayogavyavacchedikā, but is at the same time an independent philosophical work which frequently levels criticism at other systems, for instance the Śūnyavāda of the Buddhists. When Malliṣeṇa completed the work, he had, as he himself tells us, the collaboration of Jinaprabha Sūri.

In the first half of the 13th century, **Āśādhara**, who is highly esteemed both as a poet and a scholar, wrote a number of Stotras, one narrative work and several learned works. According to the very detailed panegyric (praśasti) at the end of his Dharmāmṛta, he was friend of King Arjunadeva of Mālava. The sage Udayasena said of him: "Great is Āśādhara, the swan on the lotus of the Vyāghreravāla family, the son of Sallakṣaṇa, and the Kālidāsa of the Kali age of the world," and the poet-prince Vilhaṇa,[2] the war and peace minister of Vijayavarman, King of the Vindhyas, said of him: "Noble Āśādhara! Know that, as a son of Sarasvatī you are naturally my brother and friend." The principal work of Āśādhara is **Dharmāmṛta**, "Nectar of the religion,"[3]

Another author who wrote learned works in Apabhraṃśa (Yogasāra, Paramātmaprakāśa, Śrāvakācāra Dohaka and Dohāpāhuḍa) is Joīndu (Yogīndra), who wrote before Hemacandra; s. A. N. *Upadhye* in Ann. Bh. Inst. 12, 1931, 132 ff. Yogasāra is published in MDJG No. 21, p. 55 ff. (with Sanskrit translation).

1) Edited in Chowkhambā Sanskrit Series, No. 9, fasc. 32, 33, Benares 1900 and in YJG No. 30, Benares, Vīra S. 2438 (1911) and in Ārhata-Mata-Prabhākara No. 3, Vīra S. 2452 (1925). The chapter which contains a criticism of the proofs of the existence of God, translated into German by H. *Jacobi*, Die Entwicklung der Gottesidee bei den Indern, Bonn 1923, p. 102 ff. *Cf.* *Weber*, HSS. Vers. II, 3, 940 ff.; *Peterson*, Report IV, p. lxxxix; *Barth*, RHR 45, 1902, p. 173 = Oeuvres II, 376.

2) This Vilhaṇa, who is also mentioned in inscriptions of the kings of Mālava, has, of course, no connection with the Kashmiri poet Bilhaṇa, who lived from about 1070 till 1090. *Cf.* *Kielhorn* in Ep. Ind. 9, 1908, 107 f.

3) There appears to be no edition of the work, but manuscripts are existent. See for this and other works of Āśādhara, *Bhandarkar*, Report 1883-84, pp. 103 ff., 390 ff.; *Hiralal*, Catalogue, pp. XXXVI, 644, 669, 682, 706 (Sarasvatī-Stotra), 709 (Siddhacakra-Stotra). A Triṣaṣṭi-Smṛiti contains stories of 63 great men according to the Jaina-Purāṇas.

which, in two parts, Sāgāra and Anāgāra-Dharmāmṛta, treats of the duties of the layman living in the house and of the homeless ascetic. He himself wrote a commentary on his work in the year 1243 A.D.[1]

D e v e n d r a S ū r i,[2] a pupil of Jagaccandra, wrote probably at the period of Vastupāla, minister of king Vīra Dhavala of Gujarat (died 1241 A.D.) and of his brother Tejaḥpāla (died 1251 A.D.) a V a n d ā r u-V ṛ t t i, a commentary on the Srāddhapratikramaṇa-Sūtra.[3] He is also the author of a S i d d h a p a ñ c ā ś i k ā,[4] an extract from the Diṭṭhivāya in 50 stanzas, and in the year 1241 A.D. he wrote U p a m i t i b h a v a p r a p a ñ c ā - K a t h ā-S ā r o d - d h ā r a,[5] an extract from Siddharṣi's famous poem. First and foremost, however, he is the author of the first 5 K a r m a g r a n t h a s.[6] The Karmagranthas are six books in Prākrit verses, in which the entire doctrine of Karman which is very intricate in the religion of the Jainas, is treated in all its details. The books are as follows: Karmavipāka, Karmastava, Bandhasvāmitva, Ṣaḍaśītikā, Sataka and Saptatikā. Book VI consists of 70 verses by C a n d r a m a h a t t a r a, to which his teacher (?) Devendra Sūri added a further 19 verses. Candramahattara is also the author of the P a ñ c a- s a ṃ g r a h a,[7] a compendium of the whole doctrine of

---

1) His Jinayajña-Kalpa is dated 1228 A. D., the Sāgāra-Dharmāmṛta 1239 A. D. Āśādhara was a contemporary of no less than five successive kings of Mālava, from Vindhyavarman to Devapāla's son Jaitugideva; s. *Kielhorn* in Ep. Ind. 9, 1908, 107 f.

2) *Cf. Peterson*, Report IV, p. lvii f. He is said to have died in the year 1270 A. D. in Mālava; s. *Klatt* in Ind. Ant. 11, p. 255.

3) Edited in JPU No. 8, Bombay 1912.

4) *Cf. Weber*, HSS. Verz. II, 2, 534 ff.

5) *Cf. Peterson*, Report VI, pp. x f., 40 ff. On the basis of Chapter VIII of the Mahā-Nisīha he wrote a Susaḍha Kahā in 519 Āryā stanzas; s. W. *Schubring*, Das Mahānisīha, p. 48 ff.

6) Edited in Vol. 4 of Prakaraṇa-Ratnākara, Bombay 1880; with the author's commentaries on Books 1-5 and commentary by Malayagiri on Book 6, by the Srī-Jaina-Dharma-Prasāraka Sabhā, Bhavnagar 1909-1911. *Cf. Weber*, HSS. Verz. II, 3, 837 ff.

7) Edited with Malayagiri's Commentary, by *Hīralāla Haṃsarāja*, Jamnagar 1909, 4 vols.

Karman. Śivaśarma Sūri's Karmaprakṛti[1] in 475 Gāthās, is a more exhaustive work. If the tradition is to be believed, all these works can be traced back to the Diṭṭhivāya. They have all been commented on by Malayagiri, who also wrote commentaries on several canonical works.[2]

In the 15th century Sakalakīrti, who probably died in about 1464 A.D., wrote Tattvārthasāradīpaka,[3] a large work in 12 chapters on the entire system of the Jaina religion. The first chapter teaches how the soul attains to the 5 kinds of knowledge by annihilating the Karman. One of these is attained through sacred books, which on this occasion are completely enumerated, with exact information as to the number of words, and in the case of the Aṅgas and Pūrvas even the number of syllables. A second work by Sakalakīrti is Praśnottaropāsakācāra,[4] in which the duties of lay adherents are taught in the form of questions and answers.

Round about 1494 A.D. Śrutasāgara, the pupil of Vidyānandin, wrote a Jainendrayajñavidhi, a ritual work after the style of the Brahmanical Prayogas, a Tattvārthadīpikā, and a commentary on Kundakunda's Ṣaṭprābhṛta.[5] Kupakṣakauśikasahasrakiraṇa, "The Sun for the Owls of the heretical

---

1) Edited with Malayagiri's Commentary, JPU, No. 17, Bhavnagar 1912.

2) On Malayagiri *cf. Peterson*, Report IV, p. lxxxviii. A manuscript of Malayagiri's Commentary on Karmaprakṛti is dated 1395 A. D., a manuscript of the commentary on the Nandī-Sūtra is dated 1235 A.D., a MS. of the commentary on the Vyavahāra-Sūtra is dated 1253 A. D.; s. *Petreson*, 3 Reports, Appendix, pp. 35 f., 49 f., 70 f., 157. On all the works on the doctrine of Karma mentioned here, s. H. v. *Glasenapp*, Die Lehre von Karman in der Philosophie der Jainas nach den Karmagranthas zusammengestellt, Leipzig 1915; also *Glasenapp*, Der Jainismus, pp. 167, 184.

3) *Cf. Bhandarkar*, Report 1883-84, pp. 106 ff., 393 ff.

4) *Bhandarkar*, l. c., p. 116 f.

5) *Cf. Bhandarkar*, l. c. p. 117 and *Peterson*, Report II, pp. 8 ff., 158 ff. and Report IV, p. cxxiii f.

Doctrine," [1] by the Śvetāmbara **Dharmasāgara**, is a polemic treatise against the Digambara Jainas. This treatise, written in 1573 A.D. in Prākrit, with a commentary in Sanskrit by the same author, violently refutes the doctrines of the Digambaras, especially their views on going naked and the exclusion of women from release.

We would also mention **Vinayavijaya**, the son of Tejaḥpāla, who in the year 1649 compiled **Lokaprakāśa**,[2] a comprehensive encyclopædia of everything a Jaina needs to know.

Yaśovijaya (1624-1688) of the Tapāgaccha, is a prominent Jaina teacher, reformer and author of the 17th century.[3] He endeavoured to unite the two sects of the Digambaras and Śvetāmbaras, by seeking to prove that the Kevalin, the completely Enlightened, so long as he leads a physical life, must take nourishment, that women can attain to release, and that the ordinary objects of usage of the monks, garments etc., are not to be counted as "possessions," and that the saintly life does not exclude life in the world. Even at the present day he is still cited as a model and a saint. His name is borne by two educational institutions (Pāṭhaśālās) in Benares and Mehsana, and by the collections of texts (Granthamālās) published by them.[4] Among his works we mention **Adhyātmaparīkṣā** in Prākrit with a Sanskrit commentary by the author himself, **Jñānabinduprakaraṇa**[5]

---

1) The title of the treatise is also Pravacana-Parīkṣā. It is dealt with by A. *Weber* in SBA 1882, p. 793 ff.

2) Edited by *Hiralāla Haṃsarāja* in 3 vols., Jamnagar 1910. The same author also wrote a commentary on the Kalpa-Sūtra in the year 1639. *Cf.* H. D. *Velankar*, Descriptive Catalogue of Sanskṛita and Prākṛta MSS. in the Library of the Bombay Royal Asiatic Society, Vols. III-IV, 1930, pp. 386 f., 446.

3) On him *cf. Jacobi* in AR, 18, 1915, 271, 278 f. and *Glasenapp*, Der Jainismus, pp. 72, 109, 342.

4) Edited in JPU No. 5, Bombay 1911.

5) A manuscript written in the year 1675, described by *Peterson*, 3 Reports, p. 192 f.

and Jñānasāra or Aṣṭakaprakaraṇa.[1] He also revised the Dharmasaṃgraha[2] which was written by Mānavijaya in the year 1681. This is a bulky work on the duties of the householder and the ascetic.

In our own times, too, the Jainas not only turn their attention to the editing of texts, which are being published in numerous series, and are most generously made accessible to European scholars also, but they are still productive in literature proper, and are writing original works in Sanskrit and the vernaculars on Jaina philosophy and dogmatics. The publication of a series of valuable editions in the Yaśovijaya-Jaina-Granthamālā is the immortal legacy of the great Jaina saint and teacher Vijaya Dharma Sūri,[3] who also wrote a number of works in Gujarātī, Hindī and Sanskrit (Pramāṇa-Paribhāṣā, Jaina-Tattva-Jñāna). A pupil of this saint is Muni Nyāyavijaya, from whose pen two works in Sanskrit have appeared: Adhyātma-Tattvāloka[4] and Nyāya-Kusumāñjali.[5]

The Jainas have extended their activities beyond the sphere of their own religious literature to a far greater extent than the Buddhists have done, and they have memorable achievements in the secular sciences to their credit, in

---

1) Published together with Haribhadra's Aṣṭaka and other works, Surat 1918.

2) Edited in JPU, Nos. 26 and 45, Bombay 1915 and 1918. The work is very rich in quotations. According to the index 103 works and 26 authors are quoted.

3) On the life and works of *Vijaya Dharma Sūri*; s. L. P. *Tessitori*, A Jain Achārya of the present day, Calcutta 1917, A. J. *Sunavala*, Vijaya Dharma Suri His Life and Work, Cambridge 1922; *Vijaya Indra Sūri*, Reminiscences of Vijaya Dharma Sūri, Allahabad, 1924; Sayings of Vijaya Dharma Suri translated by Charlotte *Krause*, Bhavnagar 1930.

4) The spiritual Light, with Gujarātī Translation and Explanatory Notes, translated into English by Motichand Jhaverchand *Mehta*, Bhavnagar 1930.

5) With Introduction in English and Translation and Notes in English and Gujarātī by Hiralal Rasikadās *Kāpadiā*, Baroda 1922.

philosophy, grammar, lexicography, poetics, mathematics,[1] astronomy and astrology, and even in the science of politics. In one way or other there is always some connection even of these "profane" works with religion. In Southern India the Jainas have also rendered services in developing the Dravidian languages, Tamil and Telugu, and especially the Kanarese literary language. They have, besides, written a considerable amount in Gujarātī, Hindī and Marvārī. Thus we see that they occupy no mean position in the history of Indian literature and Indian thought.

---

1) On the great interest taken in Mathematics by Jainas of ancient and modern times, s. D. M. *Roy* in Ann. Bh. Inst. 8, 1926-27, p. 145 ff.; Bibhutibhusan *Datta*, The Jaina School of Mathematics, in Bulletin of the Calcutta Mathematical Society, Vol. XXI, 2, 1929, p. 115 ff.

APPENDIX I (on page 1).

THE YEAR OF BUDDHA'S DEATH. DID A GOTAMA BUDDHA LIVE ?

Much as has already been written about the year of Buddha's death, it is by no means firmly established as yet. According to the Singhalese tradition, 544 B.C. would be the death-year, but this is rejected by most European scholars as incompatible with the chronology of the kings of Magadha. According to M. de Z. *Wickremasinghe*, there used to be in Ceylon too, an era beginning with 483 B.C. as the year of Buddha's death, whilst 544 B.C. as the death-year cannot be traced back further than about the middle of the 11th century.[1] However, all the seemingly convincing evidence which we thought we had acquired in favour of various dates between 477 and 487 B.C., has in every case proved to be uncertain and doubtful. *Cf.* J. F. *Fleet*, JRAS 1909, 1 ff., 323 ff., 981 ff.; 1910, 1308 ; 1912, 239 ff.; *Oldenberg*, AR 13, 1910, 611 ff., V. Gopala *Aiyer*, Ind. Ant. 37, 1908, 341 ff.; W. *Geiger*, The Mahavamsa, Transl., p. xxii ff.; J. *Charpentier*, Ind. Ant. 43, 1914, 130 ff.; T. W. *Rhys Davids* in Cambridge History I, 171 ff.; E. *Hultzsch*, Inscriptions of Aśoka (1925), p. xxxii f., xxxv; H. *Jacobi*, Buddhas und Mahāvīras Nirvāṇa und die politische Entwicklung Magadhas zu jener Zeit, in SBA 1930, p. 557 ff. K. P. *Jayaswal* (JBORS I, 1915, 67 ff., 97 ff.; *cf.* III, 1917, 425 ff.; IV, 1918, 264 ff.) again endeavoured to prove, on the basis of a new reading of the Hāthīgumphā inscription of Khāravela, that the year 544 B.C. is the year of Buddha's death, and V. A. *Smith* (JRAS 1918,

---

[1]) *Cf.* W. *Geiger*, The Mahāvaṃsa, Transl., p. xxviii.

543 ff.; Early History, 4th ed., 49 f.) agreed with him, though he is also compelled to say: "I do not believe that the date can be fixed with anything like certainty." *Jayaswal*'s readings and calculations have, however, been shown to be untenable, by R. C. *Majumdar* (Ind. Ant. 47, 1918, 223 f.; 48, 1919, 187 ff.; *cf.* R. P. *Chanda*, Ind. Ant. 48, 214 ff.; K. G. Śankara *Aiyar*, Ind. Ant. 49, 1920, 43 ff.). A. B. *Keith*, too (Buddhist Philosophy, p. 32) refutes *Jayaswal*'s argumentation, but even he declares the usual dating 487-477 to be uncertain, and says that "the case against the traditional date is insufficient to justify its rejection out and out."[1] When we take into consideration that there is sufficient evidence to show that Buddha was a contemporary of kings Bimbisāra and Ajātaśatru, whom we can place with a fair amount of certainty in the 6th and 5th centuries B. C., then we are at least justified in saying that the best working hypothesis is to place the life of Buddha into this period too.[2]

It is true that we are taking it for granted that Gotama Buddha did really live. R. Otto *Franke* (ZDMG 69, 1915, 455 f.)—like E. *Senart* and A. *Barth* before him—doubts even this, and is of opinion that "the so-called doctrine of Buddha is perhaps only the collection of a bundle of didactic elements from the vast treasury of philosophical thoughts" which came into being in India in the centuries preceding the Christian era. In another passage (OZ 4, 1915-16, p. 10) the same scholar says: "For me Gotama Buddha is not a bit less mythical than his six 'mythical predecessors'"; "Buddha" according to him is but a dogmatical conception, and all the seven Buddhas are but "paradigmata of the dogmatical Buddha," who to him is apparently nothing more than "a form, grown

1) *Cf.* also E. J. *Thomas*, The Life of Buddha, p. 27; G. P. *Malalasekara*, The Pali Literature of Ceylon, London 1928, p. 15; Mrs. *Rhys Davids*, Sakya or Buddhist Origins, London 1931, p. 434.

2) *Cf.* also Appendix VI.

nebulous, of an ancient conception of the deity," "perhaps of the philosophical conception of the pantheistic divinity," perhaps a form of this divinity, which was especially associated with trees. How improbable and how baseless is this hypothesis compared to the assumption that Gotama Buddha is an historical personage, who enjoyed such great veneration that myths and legends were woven around him! True, we know very, very little about the real life of Gotama. On the other hand, tradition and even monuments afford us a few facts which there are no grounds to doubt. *Oldenberg* (Reden des Buddha, p. xx f.) is right when he says that there is no reason to doubt the accounts that Buddha belonged to the Sakya race and was born at Kapilavatthu, in all other respects so insignificant a place. At any rate this tradition was already so firmly established in about 250 B.C., that king Aśoka went on a pilgrimage to Buddha's birthplace, and recorded the memory of this pilgrimage in an inscription on the column found in 1896 near the Nepalese village of Paderia. The inscription reads: "When King Piyadasi had been anointed 20 years, he came here in person and paid his devotion here, because the Buddha, the sage born of the Sakya race, was born here."

It was also in the vicinity of Kapilavatthu, near Piprāvā, on the Nepalese frontier, that Mr. W. C. *Peppé* found in 1898 a reliquary chest containing a crystal urn with remains of bones which were formerly regarded as actual relics of the Buddha.[1] The readings and explanation of the inscription which is written round the rim of the lid of the urn, certainly admits of various interpretations. Even if the explanation: "This is the reliquary treasure of the Lord Buddha of the Sakyas," is, as I believe, the correct one, this does not constitute a proof of the "authenticity" of the relics; it only

[1]) *Cf.* e.g., R. *Pischel.* Leben und Lehre des Buddha, 4th Ed., by J. *Nobel*, 1926, p. 48f.

shows that at Aśoka's time (the script is that of the Aśoka inscriptions) people *believed* that these were relics of the Buddha.[1] Yet, this belief would scarcely have arisen, unless a man venerated as a saint, as a "Buddha," had actually lived in the days before Aśoka.

Even when we eliminate all legendary and mythical elements from the tradition, the Buddhist texts still afford us a life-like and very plausible picture of the personality of Gotama and his career as the founder of a religion and as a preacher.[2] If the personality of the Buddha, with its strong reaction on the contemporaries, had never existed, it would indeed be passing strange that in Buddhist literature it is precisely the picture of the Master which is so living. "It is no exaggeration to say," says Sir Charles *Eliot* (I, 297), "that the Buddha is the most living figure in Hindu literature. He stands before us more distinctly not only than Yājñavalkya and Śaṅkara, but than modern teachers like Nānak and Rāmānuja, and the reason of this distinction can, I think, be nothing but the personal impression which he made on his age."

In addition to this, the accounts of the Buddhists regarding Gotama Buddha and his contemporaries are in striking agreement with those of the Jainas regarding Mahāvīra, and the two currents of tradition supplement each other.[3] Lastly, when we call to mind that it has repeatedly happened in India, down to quite modern times, that founders of a religion or of a religious sect are deified even during their own lifetime, then we can only call it exaggerated, barren scepticism to doubt that Gotama Buddha lived just as certainly as did Keshub Chunder Sen,

---

1) *Cf.* R. O. *Franke* in OZ 4, 1915-16, 1ff.; E. J. *Thomas*, The Life of Buddha, 160ff.

2) See also E. J. *Thomas*, The Life of Buddha, p. 225f.

3) *Cf. Oldenberg*, Buddha, 5th Ed., Berlin 1906, p. 95f. As to whether Buddha is historical, *ibid*, p. 98ff.

the founder of the "Brahmo Samaj of India," who died in 1884, and who was worshipped as a deity by some of his adherents as early as in the year 1868.[1]

If we wish to regard Buddhism, with *Franke*, as "only a collected bundle of general Indian doctrines," we should still have to explain why this "bundle," in spite of all the changes of Buddhism, shows such individual traits, if there was not an individual, a creative personality, who bound this "bundle" into something entirely new and special, and stamped the impress of his personality upon it. Even if we were unable to give credence to the Buddhist chroniclers, and could not determine the exact date of the Buddha, but were compelled to limit ourselves to affirming that his doctrine came into being before Aśoka's time, we cannot doubt the personality of the founder[2] any more than that of Kālidāsa, whose date we can also determine only approximately.

APPENDIX II (on page 13).

What is Pāli?

Wilhelm Geiger, Pāli Literatur und Sprache, p. 5, does not explain the words *anujānāmi bhikkhave sakāya niruttiyā buddhavacanaṃ pariyāpuṇitum* (Culla-Vagga V, 33) like the translators in SBE, Vol. 20, p. 150f., "I allow you, O brethren, to learn the word of the Buddhas each in his own dialect,"

1) J. C. *Oman*, Brahmans, Theists and Muslims of India, London 1907, p. 122f.

2) *Franke* admits in a later essay (ZDMG 69, 1915, p. 456) that such a personage existed, when he says: "Let us content ourselves with the conviction that it was no ordinary mind which evolved what we call the earliest Buddhism, and with the fact that he was an Indian Aryan of (be it said provisionally) one of the pre-Christian centuries but not the latest of those centuries." Why this "Indian Aryan" should not have been called Gotama and received the epithet "Buddha," it is really difficult to see.

but according to the commentary of Buddhaghosa: "I order you to learn the word of the Buddha in *his* own language" (*i.e.* in Māgadhī, the language spoken by the Buddha). Consequently, *Geiger* regards Pāli as an attempt to reconstruct the word of the Buddha in Buddha's own language. According to this the Pāli Canon would be identical with the Canon of Pāṭaliputra not only in content, but also in language. I do not think, however, that *Geiger's* explanation of Culla-Vagga V, 33 is tenable. *Geiger* is of opinion that, in the translation "I allow you" etc., we would expect a *vo* after *anujānāmi*, to which *sakāya* would refer However, this *vo* can, I think, be supplied easily enough from the vocative *bhikkhave*, especially when we remember that the expression *anujānāmi bhikkhave* occurs on almost every page of the Vinaya-Piṭaka, and has become stereotyped. If *Geiger's* explanation were correct, we should also expect that not only the translation into Sanskrit, but also the learning of the word of Buddha in the dialects of the monks of various districts, would have been forbidden. Then again, the stern words attributed to Buddha, in which he rejects the suggestion that the word of Buddha should be translated into the language of the Veda or set in verse after the manner of the Veda, because that would not contribute to the conversion of the unconverted nor increase the number of the converted, are additional evidence that the chief concern was to propagate the word of Buddha as widely as possible, which is only possible if the monks in various districts preach the word of Buddha in the languages of those districts.[1]

E. J. *Thomas* (The Life of Buddha, p. 253 f.) explains this passage differently. He translates *nirutti* by "grammar"

---

[1]) *Geiger's*, *i.e.*, Buddhaghosa's explanation of the passage is also rejected by Friedrich *Weller* in ZB, N. F. 1, 1922, p. 211ff. (to which *Geiger* replies in the same publication, p 218f.) and by A. B. *Keith* in Ind. Hist. Qu. 1, 1925, p. 501.

and *chando* by "metre," and makes Buddha say: "I order you, monks, to master the word of Buddha (Buddhavacanam) in its own grammar." He does not think it possible that *sakāya niruttiyā* can mean "each in his own dialect," and believes that the passage in question only contains a prohibition to versify the Canon. Even if this explanation be accepted, it is difficult to see why a versification of the word of Buddha should be detrimental to the propagation of the doctrine. Moreover, *nirutti* does not mean "grammar," but "linguistic expression."[1] *Chandas* may mean "metre" just as well as "Veda." *Chandas* has the latter meaning in *Sāvitthī chandaso mukhaṃ* too (Vinaya-Piṭaka, Mahā-Vagga VI, 35, 8 and Sutta-Nipāta 568). *Oldenberg* and *Rhys Davids* have taken it in the sense of "Veda dialect," and refer to the use of "*chandasi*" by Pāṇini. Buddhaghosa, too says: *chandaso āropemā ti vedaṃ viya sakkaṭa-bhāsāya vācanāmaggam āropema.*[2] The translation: "I allow you, O monks, to learn the word of the Buddha each in his own language" also accords well with Majjhima-Nikāya 139 (III, pp. 234f., 237) wherein it is said that the "middle way" which leads to rest, is for a man not to insist unduly on his own provincial dialect (janapadanirutti) and at the same time not to diverge from general linguistic usage.[3]

The commentaries frequently use the word "Pāli" in the sense of "canonical text" in contrast to the Attha-Kathā, sometimes also in the sense of "language of the canonical texts;" in the Jātaka commentary "Pāli" often means the Jātaka-Gāthās. Curiously enough the term "Pāli" is

---

1) *Cf.* Dīgha I, 202; Saṃyutta III, 71; *Childers*, Dictionary of the Pali Language s.v. nirutti: "use or expression of a language." PTS. Dic. s.v.: "way of speaking, expression."

2) The form chandaso from the neuter chando is difficult to explain.

3) It is said here that, for instance, a different word is used for "bowl": pātī patta, vittha, sarāva, dhāropa, poṇa, pisila, and that each one considers his word as the only correct one, but that in the interests of peace it is best for each one to use the word which is current in his land.

used at the present day by the country people of Eastern Bengal to denote the verse portions in their prose narratives (Rūpa-Kathās and Gīta-Kathās).[1]

Phonetic peculiarities of the Māgadhī dialect in Pāli have already been indicated by E. *Kuhn*, Beiträge zur Pāli-Grammatik, Berlin, 1875, p. 9, E. *Müller*, Grammar of the Pali Language, London, 1884, and R. *Pischel*, SBA 1904, p. 807. E. *Windisch* (OC XIV, 1906, p. 252ff.) endeavoured to prove that Māgadhī forms the foundation of Pāli. S. *Lévi* (JA 1912, s. 10, t. XX, p. 495ff.) attempted to trace remnants of an earlier Māgadhī Canon. According to *Lüders* (Bruchstücke buddhistischer Dramen, p. 41) it would be more correct to speak of "Old Ardha-Māgadhī" as the foundatian of Pāli. "This dialect agrees in essentials with the Māgadhī of the Aśoka Inscriptions, but in part it already represents a more advanced stage of development" (*Lüders* in SBA 1927, p. 123). The demonstration by P. V. *Bapat* (Ind. Hist. Qu. 4, 1928, 23ff.) that Pāli cannot be derived from Ardha-Māgadhī, as the last-named shows a later stage of development of Prākrit than Pāli, refers only to Jaina Ardha-Māgadhī. Paiśācī elements in Pāli have been pointed out by *Konow* (ZDMG 64, 1910, 114ff.), *Grierson* (Bhandarkar Comm. Vol., p. 117ff.) and Nalinaksha *Dutt* (Early History of the Spread of Buddhism, p. 249ff.). *Konow* localises Pāli and Paiśācī in the district of the Vindhya hills. This leads us to the district of Ujjein, where Pāli had already been localised by *Westergaard*, E. *Kuhn* and R. O. *Franke* (Pali und Sanskrit, Strassburg 1902, 127ff.). *Grierson* regards Paiśācī as the local dialect of Kekaya and Eastern Gandhāra. Kekaya, especially Takṣaśilā was at the time of the Buddha famous for learning. *Grierson* concludes from this that Pāli is the literary form of the

---

[1]) *Cf.* Ind. Hist. Qu. 4, 1928, 6ff., and Dineshchandra *Sen*, Eastern Bengal Ballads, Vol. III, part 1, Calcutta, 1928, p. lxv ff.

Māgadhī language, which was in those days used in India as *Koiné*, and was in particular utilised in Takṣaśilā as the language of instruction. *Cf.* also *Eliot* I, 282ff.

According to S. K. *Chatterji* (Origin and Development of the Bengali Language, 1926, I, 55ff.) the phonetics and morphology of Pāli show most resemblance to Śaurasenī, but have adopted archaic forms from north-western and other Aryan dialects.

Oldenberg (Vinaya Piṭaka I, Intrōduction, p. 1 ff.) held the view that Buddhism was not introduced to Ceylon by Mahinda, as related in the Singhalese chronicles, but spread gradually over the Island from the neighbouring Kaliṅga land, and that Pāli is the language of the Kaliṅga land. There are, however, no proofs for this.

T. W. *Rhys Davids* (PTS Dic., Foreword) is of opinion that Pāli is based upon the dialect of Kosala, as it was spoken in the 6th and 7th centuries B. C. But what do we know of the dialects of these centuries ?

Max *Walleser* (Sprache und Heimat des Palikanons, Heidelberg 1924, and ZB VII, 1926, 56ff.) made an unfortunate attempt to explain Pāli as the " language of Pāṭaliputra" even by way of etymology.[1]

There is nothing to support the assumption that Pāli originated in Ceylon. Though Singhalese has much in common with Pāli, we should rather assume that it is the Pāli which influenced Singhalese. *Cf.* W. *Geiger*, Literatur und Sprache der Singhalesen (Grundriss I, 10), p. 91.

Cf. Geiger, Pali Literatur und Sprache, pp. 1-5 ; H. *Reichelt* in Festschrift für Wilhelm Streitberg, 1924, p. 244 ff. ; A. B. *Keith* in Ind. Hist. Qu. I, 1925, 501ff. ; W. *Wüst*, Indisch (Grundriss der indogermanischen Sprach-und Altertumskunde II, 4, 1), p. 44 f. and Mrs. *Rhys Davids*, Sakya or Buddhist Origins, p. 429ff.

---

[1]) E. J. *Thomas* (Ind. Hist. Qu. 4, 1928, 773 ff.) also rejects this hypothesis.

APPENDIX III (on page 16).

Bhābrū-Bairat-Edict of Aśoka.

The small boulder which contains the inscription of Bairat, is now preserved in Calcutta in the Asiatic Society of Bengal, and for this reason the inscription is described by E. *Hultzsch* (Corpus Inscriptionum Indicarum, Vol. I, Inscriptions of Asoka, New Edition, p. xxv) as "Calcutta-Bairat Rock-Inscription," as there is also another rock inscription of Bairat. The boulder was discovered in 1840 on an eminence in the neighbourhood of Bairat. As the discoverer stated that Bairat was not far from "Bhabra," the inscription was also called the "Bhabra edict." Bhabra is, however, only an erroneous name for Bhābrū, which is, as a matter of fact, 12 miles from Bairat. Many scholars have devoted themselves to identifying the texts mentioned in the inscription, in the Canon, and appreciating their historical significance. *Cf.* E. *Hultzsch*, l. c., pp. xliii f., 172ff. ; *Senart* in JA 1884, s. 8, t. III, p. 478ff. ; 1885, t. V, p. 391ff. ; and 1887, t. IX, p. 498ff. with an excellent facsimile of the inscription ; H. *Oldenberg*, Vinaya Piṭakam Ed., Vol. I, p. xl note ; K. E. *Neumann*, Reden Gotamo Buddhos I, pp. 135, 324, 567 and WZKM 11, 1897, p. 159f. ; T. W. *Rhys Davids* in JPTS 1896, p. 93ff.; JRAS 1898, p. 639f. ; Buddhist India, p. 169f. ; Dialogues of the Buddha, SBB II, 1899, Preface, p. xiii f. ; S. *Lévi* in JA 1896, s. 9, t. VII, p. 475ff. ; E. *Hardy* in JRAS 1901, p. 311ff. and Aśoka, p. 58ff. and V. A. *Smith* in JRAS 1901, p. 574 ; Asoka, 3rd Ed., p. 157 ; *Kern*, Manual, pp. 2 and 113 ; *Pischel* in SBA 1904, p. 807f., A. J. *Edmunds* in JRAS 1913, 385ff. ; *Kosambi* in Ind. Ant. 41, 40 ; *Barua* in JRAS 1915, p. 805 ; Ind. Ant. 48, 8ff.; *Eliot* I, 290f. ; F. *Weller* in Asia Major 5, 1930, p. 166.

The texts recommended by Aśoka are :—

(1) *Vinaya-samukase*, probably " the principal sermon of the Vinaya-Piṭaka," *i.e.*, the sermon of Benares, which in numerous passages (Vinaya-P., Mahā-Vagga I, 7, 6 ; 8, 2 etc., Udāna V, 3) is called sāmukkaṃsikā dhammadesanā, " the most excellent sermon." Thus according to A. J. *Edmunds* in JRAS 1913, p. 385. *Oldenberg* and *Rhys Davids* (SBE 13, p. xxvi f.) explained it as "Abstract of the Vinaya" and assumed that this referred to the Pātimokkha. B. M. *Barua* translates : " Excellent treatise on Vinaya moral discipline."

(2) *Aliya-vasāṇi*, the dasa ariya-vāsā, "the ten rules of life of the noble one " which are taught in the Saṃgīti-Suttanta and in the Dasuttara-Suttanta of the Dīgha-Nikāya (III, pp. 269 and 291) and in the Aṅguttara-Nikāya X, 19 (Vol. V, p. 29).

(3) *Anāgata-bhayāni*, " the five future dangers," which are taught in the Aṅguttara-Nikāya V, 77-80 (Vol. III, p. 100 ff.).

(4) *Munigāthā*, probably the Muni-Sutta in the Sutta-Nipāta 206 to 220.

(5) *Moneyasute*, doubtless the moneyyāni in the Itivuttaka 67, also in Aṅgutt. III, 120 (Vol. I, p. 273).

(6) *Upatisapasine*, "Questions of Upatissa." As Upatissa is a name of Sāriputta, and as the Sāriputta-Sutta in Sutta-Nipāta 955-975 contains questions of Sāriputta, which are answered by Buddha, I have no doubt that this is what is meant. Thus already *Neumann* and now also *Walleser*.

(7) *Lāghulovāde musāvādam adhigichya bhagavatā Budhena bhāsite*, " the exhortations to Rāhula, which were uttered by the Lord Buddha in regard to lying," in Majjhima-Nikāya 61. As there is also a second Rāhulovāda-Sutta (Majjhima 62), Aśoka also states the subject-matter of the text recommended by him. Thus Aśoka must have known both texts.

The significance of the Bairat Edict should neither be overrated nor yet under-estimated. It is overrating it to conceive of it, as *Barua*, l. c. has done, "as a rare historical document, which conclusively proves the existence of the Buddhist Canon in the third century B.C., in the same form, and with almost the same titles to its different passages, as we have now." On the other hand, it is under-estimating it, when *Barth* (RHR 5, 1882, 239 f.=Oeuvres, I, p. 342) declares that the titles do not prove that there was a Canon in existence in those days, but that on the contrary they show that though Buddhism had a literature, it had not yet a Canon. Similarly *La Vallée Poussin*, Bouddhisme, Études et Matériaux (Mémoires Acad. Belgique, 55, 1898), p. 32 f., says that the titles prove nothing for the antiquity of the Pāli Canon; according to him they prove merely the antiquity of Sūtras and Vinayas which are related to the Pāli texts, and that Aśoka does not allude to a definite Canon. The very words of the edict: "Whatever has been uttered by the Lord Buddha, all that is well said,"[1] make it appear probable that there was something in the nature of a Canon in existence, wherein that which was regarded as having been uttered by Buddha, was collected, and which, therefore, to the minds of believers, bore the stamp of genuineness. When Aśoka says that, though everything which the Lord uttered is good, he especially recommends a few selected texts not only to the monks and nuns, but also to the lay adherents of both sexes, it seems as though he must have been acquainted with a considerable number of such texts. We shall therefore not be unduly bold in arguing from the Edict that, at the time when it was written, there was a canonical collection of Sutta and Vinaya texts in the Māgadhī language. As the texts enumerated by Aśoka appear in various books of the Pāli Canon,

[1]) The dictum of Aṅguttara IV, 164: "All that is well said, that is the word of Buddha" (similarly Śikṣāsamuccaya, p. 15) represents a later stage of development.

it is, to say the least of it, very probable indeed, that the Pāli Canon, as far as the Sutta and Vinaya-Piṭaka are concerned, was very closely related to the Māgadhī Canon. The exaggerated scepticism of *Minayeff*, Recherches, p. 84 ff., has already been confuted by *Oldenberg*, ZDMG 52, 1898, 634 ff.

According to T. *Bloch*, ZDMG 63, 1909, 325 ff., the purpose of the inscription of Bairat was to institute public recitals of the texts named and to make a foundation for this. Unfortunately, however, there is nothing to this effect in the inscription.

As to the correctness of the readings and interpretations of the Edict given by Max *Walleser* (Das Edikt von Bhabra, Materialien zur Kunde des Buddhismus, Heft 1, Leipzig, 1923; Nochmals das Edikt von Bhabra, ibidem Heft 9, Heidelberg 1925 and ZII 3, 1924, 113 ff.), I am just as little convinced as Joh. *Nobel* in OLZ 1924, 361 ff., and E. *Leumann* in ZII, 2, 1923, 316 f.

APPENDIX IV (on page 190f).

Time and Life of Buddhaghosa.

Th. *Foulkes* (Ind. Ant. 19, 1890, p. 122) already gave expression to the conjecture that Buddhaghosa never lived at all, but that the existing commentaries were ascribed to the "Voice of Buddha." V. A. *Smith*, too (Ind. Ant. 34, 1905, p. 185) says, "Personally I do not believe in the existence of Buddhaghosa, 'The Voice of Buddha,' as an historical personage." L. *Finot* (La légende de Buddhaghosa, in Cinquantenaire de l'école pratique des hautes études, Paris 1921, p. 101 ff.) goes further, and attempts to prove that there is no historical foundation for Buddhaghosa's journey from Magadha to Ceylon, and that the commentaries are the work of several

Singhalese translators, who have been grouped by tradition around the more or less authentic name of Buddhaghosa. We admit that the accounts of Buddhaghosa which have come down to us are 800 years later than he himself, that they are full of legends, that the accounts of Buddhaghosa's journeys to Burma and Pegu have no sort of historical background, and likewise that some commentaries have been ascribed to him erroneously. However, in the case of Śaṅkara, too, there are only quite legendary so-called "biographies," and many works are ascribed to him, which he could not have written, and yet no one doubts that a philosopher Śaṅkara really existed. At all events the name Buddhaghosa is quite trustworthy, as this name already occurs in inscriptions of Mathurā in the first centuries of the Christian era (*Foulkes*, l. c., p. 105ff.). *Cf.* P. *Pelliot* in T'oung Pao 21, 1922, p. 243 f., and *Pe Maung Tin* in JRAS 1923 265 ff. *Pelliot* (l. c. and BEFEO 4, 149, 412) has pointed out that, at the beginning of the fifth century Fa-hien and Tche-mong made the acquaintance of a Brahman Raivata in Pāṭaliputra, who is possibly identical with Buddhaghosa's teacher. The fact that Buddhaghosa knew the Vedas and was versed in Sāṃkhya and Yoga, lends probability to the tradition that he was originally a Brahman; s. *Maung Tin*, l. c.

The period of the reign of King Mahānāma of Ceylon was formerly assumed to be 410-432 or 413-435, and the life-time of Buddhaghosa was accordingly set in the first half of the 5th century. This view was still held by *Burlingame* (HOS Vol. 25, p. 58). According to the chronology of W. *Geiger* (The Mahāvaṃsa transl., p. xxxvi ff.), which is based upon the foundation of the date 483 B. C. as the year of Buddha's death, 458-480 A. D. would be the dates of Mahānāma's reign, and thus also Buddhaghosa's time. This chronology, however, given only "provisionally" by *Geiger* himself, seems rather doubtful to me. The account of Chinese annals of an embassy which King Mahānāma of Ceylon sent to the emperor of China in the year 428 A. D. (S. *Lévi*, JA 1900, s. 9, t. XV, p. 412f.)

speaks rather in favour of the date 410-432. *Geiger* refers to the fact that, according to his chronology King Meghavaṇṇa of Ceylon reigned from 352 to 379 A. D., and according to a Chinese account (*Lévi*, l. c., p. 316 f.) this king sent an embassy to Samudragupta, who reigned from 326 to 375 A. D. (*Smith*, Early History, in the 4th edit. gives 330-380). However, even the old dating of Meghavaṇṇa, *viz.*, 304-332 A.D. would not contradict the Chinese account, if the embassy had taken place between 330 and 332 A. D. *Smith*, Early History, p. 345, does, it is true (obviously on the basis of *Geiger's* chronology), give the date of about 360 A. D. for King Meghavaṇṇa's embassy.

APPENDIX V (on page 257).

The Date of Kaniṣka's Reign.

The date of the reign of King Kaniṣka is of the utmost importance for the study of the History of Buddhism and Buddhist literature. Now though there are numerous dated coins of Kaniṣka, and inscriptions in which Kaniṣka is mentioned, there is no sure means of determining according to which era these dates should be reckoned. There are also traditions about Kaniṣka in Tibet, China and Mongolia. Deriving their material from Indian sources, the Chinese give much edifying information concerning Kaniṣka, but they do not give us any synchronisms with Chinese History. Hence even now we have nothing beyond hypotheses as to Kaniṣka's time. Epigraphical, numismatical, archaeological and literary evidence points more and more to the 2nd century A. D. as the time when Kaniṣka reigned, and to round about 125 A. D. as the probable date of his accession. The view, still maintained by a few scholars, that Kaniṣka is the founder of the Saka era, which began in 78 A. D., is less likely to be correct.

In view of the importance and the difficulty of this question, I give below a summary of the almost overwhelming literature on the problem, which is still further complicated by the fact that there were probably two rulers named Kaniṣka.

(1) The view that Kaniṣka is *the founder of the Vikrama era in 58 B. C.* will find but few supporters now-a-days. It was represented by Alexander *Cunningham* (Archaeological Survey of India, Reports, Vol. II, 1871, p. 68 note, 159 ff.; III, p. 31), [1] J. F. *Fleet* in his Introduction to the English translation of G. Bühler's 'Indian Palaeography' in Ind. Ant. 33, 1904, and in JRAS 1906, 979 ff.; 1903, 334; 1913, 95ff., 965 ff.; 1914, 992 ff.; O. *Franke* in ABA 1904, 61 ff., J. *Kennedy* in JRAS 1912, 665ff., 981ff.; 1913, 369ff., 661 ff., 1054 ff.; S. *Lévi* JA 1896, s. 9, t. VIII, 444 ff., 1897, s. 9, t. IX, 1 ff.,[2] assumes the *1st century B.C. and the beginning of our era* as Kaniṣka's time. The same view is also held by L. D. *Barnett* in JRAS, 1913, 193, and in Calcutta Review, Feb. 1924, p. 252.

(2) The view that Kaniṣka is *the founder of the Śaka era in 78 A.D.* was first put forward by *J. Fergusson* in JRAS, 1880, 259 ff. and by H. *Oldenberg* in Zeitschrift für Numismatik 8, 1881, 289 ff. (English translation in Ind. Ant. 10, 1881, 213 ff.), and is still defended at the present day by E. J. *Rapson* (Cambridge History I, pp. 581, 583 ff.), Daya Ram *Sahni* in JRAS, 1924, 399 ff., L. *Bachhofer* in OZ, 1927, 21 ff., 1930, 10 ff., Hari Charan *Ghosh* in Ind. Hist. Qu. 4, 1928, 760 ff.; 5, 1929, 49 ff. *The first century A.D.* is assumed as Kaniṣka's time by L. A. *Waddell* in JRAS, 1913, 947 ff., on archaeological grounds, and by J. Ph. *Vogel* in Ep. Ind., VIII, 173 ff. on palæographical grounds.

1) *Cunningham* changed his opinion later, and placed Kaniṣka about 80 A.D.

2) The same Chinese sources on which *Lévi* takes his stand, are utilised by Ed. *Specht* in JA 1897, s. 9, t. X, p. 152 ff., for fixing the date as the end of 1st or the beginning of the 2nd century A.D.

(3) *The end of the 1st and the beginning of the 2nd century A.D.* is assumed by many scholars, s. H. *Oldenberg* in NGGW, 1911, 427 ff. (English translation in JPTS, 1910-11, p. 1 ff.), AR, 17, 1914, 646 ff., Ed. *Specht* in JA 1897, s. 9, t. X, p. 152 ff., A. M. *Boyer* in JA 1900, s. 9, t. XV, 526 ff., H. *Lüders*, Die Inschrift von Āra in SBA, 1912, 824 ff. (English translation in Ind. Ant., 42, 1913, 132 ff.); F. W. *Thomas* in JRAS, 1913, 627 ff., 1011 ff.; 1914, 748 ff., GGA, 1931, 1 ff., and M. A. *Stein* in Ind. Ant., 34, 1905, 77 ff.: "Palæographical and other considerations make it appear probable that the date of Kaniṣka's accession may be somewhat later than the beginning of the Śaka era." According to R. D. *Banerji*, who has formulated all the theories advanced up to that time (Ind. Ant., 37, 1908, 27 ff.) Kaniṣka crossed the Indus in the year 91 A.D. and died in 123 A.D.

(4) *The 2nd century A.D.* is supported on archaeological grounds by A. *Foucher*, L'art gréco-bouddhique du Gandhāra I, 1905, p. 623, II, 1918, p. 505 ff., Sir John *Marshall* in JRAS, 1914, 973 ff., 1915, 191 ff., Guide to Taxila, 2nd Ed., Calcutta, 1921, p. 17, V. A. *Smith*, History of Fine Art in India and Ceylon, Oxford, 1911, p. 99.[1] The most decided supporter of the view that Kaniṣka did not come into power until after the year 125 A.D. and that the Kaniṣka era begins with the year 128-29 A.D., is Sten *Konow* (ZDMG, 68, 1914, 97; SBA, 1916, 787 ff.; Ep. Ind., XIV, 1918, 130 ff.; Acta Or., II, 1923, 130 ff.; III, 1924, 52 ff.; JBRAS, N. S. 1, 1, 1925, p. 1, ff.; Ind. Hist. Qu., 3, 1927, 851 ff. and lastly in Kharosthi Inscriptions, Corpus Inscriptionum Indicarum, Vol. II, part I, Calcutta, 1929, pp. lxxv ff., lxxx ff., xciii f.). V. A. *Smith*, Early History, 271 ff., gives approximately 120-160 A.D., and R. *Kimura* (Ind. Hist. Qu., 1, 1925, 415 ff.)

[1] Earlier views are discussed and criticised by *Smith* in JRAS 1903, p. 3 ff.

140-180 A.D. as the time of Kaniṣka's reign. *Cf.* also A. V. *Staël-Holstein* in SBA, 1914, 643 ff.; E. *Windisch* Philologie und Altertumskunde in Indien, Leipzig, 1921 (AKM, XV, 3), p. 26 ff., who again gives a survey of the various theories, and *Keith*, Hist. Sansk. Lit., p. xxvii.

(5) *The 3rd century A.D.* is supported only by D. R. *Bhandarkar* (JBRAS, 20, 1899, 269 ff.), R. G. *Bhandarkar* (JBRAS 20, 1900, 385 ff.), R. C. *Majumdar* (Ind. Ant., 46, 1917, 261 ff. and JDL, 1, 1920, 65 ff.).

For a second Kaniṣka, who was probably the grandson of the great Kaniṣka and lived in the 3rd century, s. *Lüders* l.c.; Satis Chandra *Vidyabhushana* in JASB 6, 1910, 477 ff.; *Kimura* l.c.; Daya Ram *Sahni* l. c.; Hari Charan *Ghosh*, Ind. Hist. Qu., 5, 1929, p. 70, and Sten *Konow*, Kharoshthi Inscriptions, p. lxxx f.

APPENDIX VI (on page 424).

The Year of the Death of Mahāvīra.

According to the usual chronology of the Śvetāmbara Jainas, Mahāvīra died 470 years before the beginning of the Vikrama era, *i.e.*, in 527 B.C., but according to the Digambaras, in 605 B.C. These dates are probably based upon erroneous calculations, for they are as difficult to reconcile with the one and only firmly established fact, namely that Buddha and Mahāvīra were contemporaries and lived in the reigns of Kings Bimbisāra and Ajātaśatru, as they are with other traditions of the Jainas themselves. There is a tradition of the Jainas, which can be traced as far back as the 11th century A.D., according to which Candragupta was anointed king 155 years after the death of Mahāvīra. Now it is true that even the date of Candragupta's coronation is by no means certain. Otto *Stein* (Archiv Orientální 1, 1929, 354 ff., 368 ff.) has shown that Candragupta cannot have been crowned king before 318-17 B.C. If we assume 317 B.C., hypothetically, as the coronation year, then the Nirvāṇa of Mahāvīra would have taken place in 473-72 B.C., and that of Buddha in 480-79 or 483-82 B.C., according to whether we assume 28 or 25 years as the length of Bindusāra's reign. J. *Charpentier* (Ind. Ant., 43, 1914, 118 ff., 125 ff., 167 ff. and Cambridge History, I, 150 ff.) has attempted to prove that Buddha died in 477 B.C. and Mahāvīra in 467 B.C. H. *Jacobi*, who formerly (The Kalpasūtra of Bhadrabāhu Ed., Introduction, p. 6 ff.) had likewise assumed the date 467 B.C., now accepts (Buddhas und Mahāvīras Nirvāṇa und die politische Entwicklung Magadhas zu jener Zeit in SBA, 1930, p. 557 ff.) 484 B.C. as the year of Buddha's death and 477 B.C. as that of Mahāvīra, as a " sure foundation " for the history of Magadha, and he sets out from the year 322 B.C. as the year of Candragupta's coronation. S. V. *Venkateswara*, JRAS, 1917, 122 ff., has tried to prove that Māhavīra could not have died earlier than 437 B.C.

None of these datings can be reconciled with the tradition, preserved in three different passages in the Pāli Canon (Dīgha III, 117, 210; Majjhima II, 243f.) and also in the Chinese Dīrghāgama (s. S. *Behrsing* in Asia Major VII, 1931, p. 1ff), that the Nighaṇṭa Nātaputta died a short time before Gotama. *Jacobi* SBA 1930, 558 ff., assumes that this report was only invented in order to connect with it the story of the quarrels in the community of the Nighaṇṭas after the death of the Master. Of course, this is possible, but I have grave doubts that such a report which, as the Chinese translation shows, belongs to an earlier Canon, should be mere invention. I should prefer to say that the real date of Mahāvīra's Nirvāṇa is still unknown.

Cf. also K. B. *Pathak* in Ind. Ant. 12, 1883, p. 21f.; *Hoernle* in ERE I, 261; *Smith*, Early History (4th ed.), pp. 34, 48f., and *Guérinot*, La religion Djaina, p. 41.

ADDITIONS AND CORRECTIONS

P. 3, L. 16, read *pāṭimokkha.*

P. 8 note 2, add : That the canon was written down under Vaṭṭagāmani is not only related in the Dīpavaṃsa and Mahāvaṃsa, but also, with more details in the Nikāyasaṃgraha, composed at the end of the 14th or the beginning of the 15th century A.D. See G. P. *Malalasekera,* Pali Literature of Ceylon, London 1928, p. 43f. It is likely enough that some commentaries may have been written down even before Vaṭṭagāmani, but canonical texts were learnt by heart by the monks and transmitted orally, even in much later times; see *Malalasekera,* l.c., p. 44ff.

P. 9 note 2, L. 2, read *abhidhamma* for *abhdhamma.*

To p. 12ff. : On the value of the Pāli Canon for our knowledge of early Buddhism, see also Friedrich *Weller* in Asia Major 5, 1930, p. 149ff.; *Winternitz* in Studia Indo-Iranica, Ehrengabe für Wilhelm Geiger, Leipzig 1931, p. 63ff.; Bimala Churn *Law* in Ann. Bh. Inst. 12, 1931, p. 171ff.

P. 12, L. 1, read *not* for *oot.*

P. 16 note 3, L. 4, after *Barua* add : *and* K. G. *Singha.*

„ „ „ L. 5, after "Calcutta, 1926" add : *Cf.* J. Ph. *Vogel* in JRAS 1927, 592ff.

P. 21, L. 16, read *Bhikkhunīvibhaṅga.*

P. 21 note 1, L. 10f., instead of "*new edition in preparation*" read *second edition, 1929.*

P. 25 note 1, L. 6, read *Frankfurter* for *Frankfurier.*

P. 35 note 2, L. 2, read *translated by* T. W. *and* C. A. F. *Rhys Davids.*

P. 36, L. 21, read *entertainments* for *conversations.*

P. 39, L. 13, read *Nirvāṇa.*

P. 41 notes, L. 6, read *Mahā-Parinirvāṇa-Sūtra, see Carlo.*

To p. 42, L. 10: *Cf.* Friedrich *Weller*, Der chinesische Dharmasaṃgraha. Mit einem Anhang über das Lakkhaṇa-suttanta des Dīghanikāya, Leipzig 1923.

P. 48, L. 22, read *reins* for *reigns.*

To p. 53, L. 3 : An enlarged version of Majjhimanikāya No. 135 (Cūḷa-Kammavibhaṅga) which also exists in the Chinese Madhyama-Āgama and in two other Chinese recensions, is the Mahā-Karmavibhaṅga, discovered by S. *Lévi* in a Nepalese MS. See Annual Bibliography of Indian Archaeology for the Year 1929 (Leyden, Kern Institute, 1931), p. 1 ff.

P. 53 note 2, L. 3, read *Bhābrū.*

P. 54 note 1, L. 4, after 1925 add : *and Vol. I, 1930.*

P. 59, L. 17, read *when I was she.*

P. 78 note 2, add : On the relative date of the text cf. B. Ch. *Law* in Ann. Bh. Inst. 12, 1931, p. 176 f.

P. 80 note 2, L. 5, read *L. von Schroeder.*

" " , L. 8, read *GSAI* for *JSAI.*

P. 94, L. 7 from below, read *Vāseṭṭha-Sutta.*

P. 98 note 3, add : See also Bimala Churn *Law* in Ann. Bh. Inst. 12, 1931, 173 ff.

P. 116 note 3, L. 6 from below, read *Franke in Bezz. Beitr.*— At the end of the note add : See also Gokuldās *De* in Calcutta Review, June 1929, 265 ff.; August 1929, 246 ff. ; Jan. 1930, 78 ff. ; July 1930, 65 ff. ; Feb. 1931, 278 ff.

P. 118 notes, L. 11, add : See *Winternitz* in Ind. Hist. Qu. 4, 1928, 1 ff.

P. 119, L. 6, read *tally* for *tallies.*

P. 120 note 2, add : and Oct. 1927, p. 56 ff. ; cf. J. Ph. *Vogel* in JRAS 1927, p. 592 ff. ; Gokuldās *De*, "Bharhut Jātakas" in a New Light, in Calc. Rev., August 1929, p. 246 ff.

P. 121 note 1, add : See also A. *Coomaraswamy* in JRAS, 1928, 390 ff.

,, note 2, L. 2, read *nordöstlichen* for *nordostlichen* and add : B. C. *Sen*, Studies in the Buddhist Jātakas, Calcutta 1930, still takes the whole of the Jātaka book as evidence for the "history" of the time of Buddha. Gokuldas *De*, Jātaka-Gleanings bearing on Ancient Indian Culture and Civilisation (Calcutta Review, Sept. 1931, p. 361 ff.; Oct. 1931, p. 106ff.), is more cautious, in taking his "gleanings" from the Gāthās only.

P. 131f. note 3, add : In the Saṃkha-Jātaka (No. 442) and the Mahājanaka-Jātaka (No. 539) we meet with a goddess of the sea, Maṇimekhalā, who saves shipwrecked seafarers. This goddess has a temple in Kānchī (near Madras). See S. *Lévi* in Ind. Hist. Qu. 6, 1930, 597 ff.

P. 133 note 3, add : On the relation between the Jātaka and the Mahābhārata, see above Vol. I, p. 472 note 4; H. *Lüders* in SBA, 1929, 269 ; N. B. *Utgikar* in JBRAS, N.S., Vol. IV, nos. 1, 2.

P. 156 note 2, add : See also B. Ch. *Law* in Ann. Bh. Inst. 12, 1931, p. 173f.

P. 170 note, L. 2, after "pp. 6 and 16" add : Dwijendra Lal *Barua* in Ind. Hist. Qu. 7, 1931, 367ff.

P. 170 note 2, add : See also B. Ch. *Law* in Ann. Bh. Inst. 12, 1931, p. 177f.

P. 174 note 1, add : G. P. *Malalasekera*, Pali Literature of Ceylon, London 1928, and B. Ch. *Law* in Ann. Bh. Inst. 13, 1931-32, pp. 97-143.

P. 174 note 2, add : A new theory on the composition of the Milindapañha has been suggested by Mrs. *Rhys Davids*, The Milinda Questions—An Inquiry into its Place in the History of Buddhism with a Theory as to its Author, London 1930. She thinks that there is *one* author of the book who first edited the conversation between Milinda and Nāgasena, which she considers to have actually taken place, then—about ten years later—wrote the dialogues on the Dilemmas, and still later, as "a grey-haired man," the book of the Similes. I am not convinced, and see no reason to change my views expressed on pp. 174-83. For an analysis of the work see also B. Ch. *Law* in Ann. Bh. Inst. 13, 1931-32, pp., 105-22.

P. 177 note 1, L. 1, read *Milindapañho* for *Milindapaũho*.

P. 177 note 2, L. 1, read *F. O. Schrader* for *E. Schrader*.

P. 183 note 1, add : For an analysis of the contents of the Netti, see B. Ch. *Law* in Ann. Bh. Inst. 13, 1931-32, p. 97ff.

,, note 4, read *Fuchs* for *Fuch's*, and add at the end of the note : B. C. *Law* in Ann. Bh. Inst. 13, 1931-32, p. 105.

P. 190 note 1, add : *Cf. Maung Tin* in JRAS, 1923, 265ff.

P. 214 note 2, add : It is now probable that an older Thera Dhammakitti (I), who lived in the reign of Parakkamabāhu I, was the author of the first part of the Cūḷavaṃsa ending with the death of Parakkamabāhu I in 1186 A.D., while chapters 80ff. were written by another Dhammakitti (II), who may be the same who wrote the Dāṭhāvaṃsa in 1211 A.D. The second part of the Cūḷavaṃsa deals with the period 1186-1333 A.D. and the third part, probably composed by the Thera Sumaṅgala in the second half of the 18th century, with the period from 1333 to 1781 A.D. See W. *Geiger* in Ind. Hist. Qu. 6, 1930, 206ff.

P. 215 note 2, add : On the sources of the Mahāvaṃsa see also W. *Geiger* in ZII 7, 1929, 259ff., who shows that Mahānāma probably also used a chronicle of Rohaṇa, and puññapotthakāni (books containing lists of pious foundations), besides popular (oral) traditions.

P. 216f. note 2, add: On Mahāvaṃsa and Cūḷavaṃsa as sources of history, see also W. *Geiger* in Ind. Hist. Qu. VI, 1930, 208ff.

P. 220 note 1, L. 3, after "p. 96ff." add: and Ann. Bh. Inst. 13, 1931-32, p. 122f.

„ note 1, add at the end: A paper on Buddhadatta, by S. *Jambunathan* in Journal of Or. Res., Madras, April 1928, pp. 111-17, is quoted in BB. I, No. 130.

P. 221 note 1, L. 7, read Mrs. *Rhys Davids*.

P. 222 note 1, add: See also B. C. *Law* in Ann. Bh. Inst. 13, 1931-32, p. 123ff.

P. 222 note 3, add: *Cf.* B. C. *Law* in Ann. Bh. Inst. 13 1931-32, p. 141ff.

P. 224 note 1, add: *Cf.* B. C. *Law* in Ann. Bh. Inst. 13, 1931-32, p. 134ff.

P. 227 note 1, add: Buddhist texts are known to have been translated into Chinese already in the second century A.D., if not earlier. The earliest Tibetan translations date from the second half of the eighth century A. D.; see A. H. *Francke*, Antiquities of Indian Tibet, Vol. II, The Chronicles of Ladakh and Minor Chronicles (Archaeological Survey of India, New Imp. Series, Vol. 50), Calcutta 1926, p. 86.

P. 227 note 2, L. 2, read *Kucha* for *Kuchar*.

P. 229, L. 18, read *even the* for *even in the*.

P. 229 note 1, add: Nalinaksha *Dutt*, Aspects of Mahāyāna Buddhism and its Relation to Hīnayāna, London 1930 (Calcutta Oriental Series No. 23).

P. 230 note 1, L. 2, read *causality* for *cusality*.

P. 232 note 1, L. 3 and note 2, L. 1, read *Oldenberg* for *Oldenburg*.

P. 233 note 2, add: On the legendary matter, Jātakas and Avadānas, in the Mūla-Sarvāstivāda Vinaya, see also J. *Przyluski* in Ind. Hist. Qu. 5, 1929, p. 1ff.

P. 235 note 1, add: The Chung-Tsi-King (Chinese version of the Saṃgītisutta) of the Dīrghāgama has been translated into German and discussed by Siegfried *Behrsing* in Asia Major 7, 1931, pp. 1-149. *Cf.* above, p. 45 note 2.

P. 235 note 3, add: The Chinese Fan wang king or "Brahmajāla-Sūtra," a Vinaya work of the Mahāyāna, translated by Kumārajīva from an unknown Sanskrit text, has been edited and translated into French by J. J. M. *De Groot*, Le code du Mahâyâna en Chine son influence sur la vie monacale et sur le monde laique (Verhandelingen der Kon. Akademie van Wetenshappen te Amsterdam, Afd. Lett. Deel I, No. 2) 1893. Another Brahmajāla-Sūtra in the Chinese Dīrghāgama, as well as the Brahmajāla-Sūtra in the Tibetan Kanjur, corresponds to the Pāli text in the Dīghanikāya.

P. 237, L. 6, read *Dhammapada* for *Dharmapada.*

P. 237 note 4, add: Fragments of Udānavarga translations in Kucean language are discussed by E. *Sieg* and W. *Siegling* in BSOS VI, 2, p. 483ff.

P. 238 notes, L. 4, read *Schiefner* for *Schiefnen.*

P. 239 note 2, add: See now also Bimala Churn *Law*, A Study of the Mahāvastu, Calcutta and Simla 1930, and Supplement.

P. 240, L. 1, Mm. Haraprasāda *Śāstrī* (Calcutta Review, Sept. 1930, p. 441f.) would translate: "Vinayapiṭaka according to the text of the Mahāsaṅghikas who declare the Buddha to be lokottara." For, he says, all the Mahāsaṅghikas believe the Buddha to be lokottara, and in the list of the eighteen sects "Lokottaravādins" are not mentioned. But Vasumitra and Bhavya mention the Lokottaravâdins as a sect of the Mahāsaṅghikas. See Mrs. *Rhys Davids,* Points of Controversy, p. xxxvi f. and Max

Walleser, Die Sekten des alten Buddhismus, Heidelberg 1927, pp. 28, 78.

P. 240, L. 3, read *Mahāsaṅgha* for *Mahāsāṅgha*.

P. 243 note 2, L. 1 : read *above* for *avove*.

P. 247 note 2, add: See also B. C. *Law*, A Study of the Mahāvastu, Supplement, p. 17f., and A. B. *Keith*, A Note on the Mahāvastu, in *Law's* book, p. vii.

P. 260 note 2, add : On the style and language of Aśvaghoṣa's poems *cf. Keith*, HSL, p. 56 ff.

P. 262 note 1, add: On the relation between Vālmīki and Aśvaghoṣa, s. Vol. I, p. 512 f., and C. W. *Gurner* in JASB, Vol. XXIII, 1927, p. 347ff. (BB I, no. 102).

P. 262 note 2, L. 4, after "1928" add: An English translation of the Saundarananda by E. H. *Johnston* has been published in the same series, London 1932.

P. 266 note 1, add: It seems to me quite impossible that such texts as the Nairātmya-paripṛcchā, the Gurupañcāśikā, and similar Mahāyāna and Tantra texts which are ascribed to Aśvaghoṣa (s. S. *Lévi* in JA 213, 1928, 204 ff.; 215, 1929, 255 ff.) could be works of the poet. Either they are apocryphal, or their author is another Aśvaghoṣa. *Cf.* J. *Przyluski* in Acad. roy. de Belgique Bulletins de la classe des lettres, 1930, 425ff.

P. 267 note 1, add: It is possible that Aśvaghoṣa is also the author of a lyrical drama treating the legend of Rāṣṭrapāla, s. S. *Lévi* in JA 213, 1928, 200ff.

P. 267 note 2, add : Pages 267ff. were already printed when I saw Joh. *Nobel's* paper "Kumāralāta und sein Werk" (NGGW, 1928, 295ff.; see also S. *Lévi* in JA 213, 1928, 193ff.; 215, 1929, 271ff., and L. de *La Vallée Poussin*, Vijñaptimātratāsiddhi (Buddhica I, 1) Paris 1928, p. 223f.) which makes it most probable that Kumāralāta's Kalpanāmaṇḍitikā Dṛṣṭāntapaṅkti is not identical with the Sūtrālaṃkāra, but an imitation of it prepared for the use of the Sautrāntikas, and that Aśvaghoṣa is the author of the "Sūtrālaṃkāra" translated by Kumārajīva. On the other hand the colophons of the Turfan fragments leave no doubt that Kumāralāta is the author of the Kalpanāmaṇḍitikā, s. J. *Przyluski* in Acad. roy. de Belgique Bulletins de la classe des lettres, 1930, 425ff. H. *Lüders* (Kātantra und Kumāralāta, SBA 1930, 531f.) has also discovered fragments of a grammar by Kumāralāta.

P. 270, last line, read *Catuḥśataka Stotra.*

P. 277 note 3, add: *Cf. Winternitz* in Comm. Wogihara, p. 7ff.

P. 285 note 4, add: J. *Przyluski* (Ind. Hist. Qu. 5, 1929, p. 5) does not think it probable that the Vinaya is the source of the Divyāvadāna. He holds that "the compilers of the Vinaya of the Mūlasarvāstivādins are likely to have borrowed......from the ancient collection of fables of which our Divyāvadāna is only a late recension."

P. 286 note 3, add: J. *Przyluski* in JA 210, 1927, p. 115ff.

P. 293 note 1, L. 2, read *JRAS* for *JARS*.

P. 294 note 4, add: On the Bodhisattvapiṭaka see also Haraprasād *Śāstrī* in B. C. *Law*, Buddhistic Studies, 1931, p. 846ff.

P. 295, L. 4, add: As there is no Mahāyāna Canon, there is also no special Vinayapiṭaka of the Mahāyāna, though there are Sūtras which treat of Vinaya subjects. Such Sūtras are the Chinese *Brahmajāla-Sūtra* (translated into French by M. *de Groot*, Le code du Mahâyâna en Chine (see p. 622 above addition to p. 235 note 3) and the *Bodhisattva-Prātimokṣa-Sūtra* (edited by Nalinaksha *Dutt* in Ind. Hist. Qu. 7, 1931, 259ff.). See also N. *Dutt*, Aspects of Mahāyāna Buddhism and its relation to Hīnayāna, p. 290ff.

P. 305 note 4, add: On the great importance of the Saddharmapuṇḍarīka in Japan, see M. W. de *Visser*, Ancient Buddhism in Japan Sūtras and Ceremonies in use in the Seventh and Eighth Centuries A.D., Paris 1928 (Buddhica, sér. I, t. III), pp. 1ff., 43.

P. 306 note 3, L. 1, read *Waddell*.

P. 307 note 1, L. 7, read *Śikṣā-Samuccaya*.

P. 307 note 3, L. 2, read *being in the hope*.

P. 315 note 1, add: See now also the valuable "Note on the Prajñāpāramitā" by Nalinaksha *Dutt*, Aspects of Mahāyāna Buddhism, London 1930 (Calcutta Oriental Series No. 23), p. 323ff., and the survey of the Prajñāpāramitā literature by Tokumyo *Matsumoto*, Die Prajñāpāramitā-Literatur nebst einem Specimen der Suvikrāntavikrāmi-Prajñāpāramitā (Bonner Orientalistische Studien Heft 1), Stuttgart 1932. N. *Dutt*, l. c., pp. 39f., 328 dates the Aṣṭasāhasrikā "as early as the first century B. C." According to *Matsumoto* (l. c., p. 22) the earliest Chinese translation of the Aṣṭasāhasrikā Pr. dates 172 A. D. He thinks (l. c., p. 31) that the Prajñāpāramitās originated in Kashmir between the birth of Christ and the time of Kaniṣka.

P. 315 note 2, add: On a list of Prajñāpāramitās in the Tibetan Kanjur, see also Marcelle *Lalou* in JA 215, 1929, pp. 87-102.

P. 316 note 2, add: The Sanskrit text of the Saptaśatikā Prajñāpāramitā has been edited by G. *Tucci* (Memorie della R. Accademia Nazionale dei Lincei, Vol. XVII), Roma 1923, and, together with Hsüan Tsang's Chinese version, by Jiryo *Masuda* in Comm. Wogihara, p. 185ff.

P. 316 note 6, add: N. *Dutt*, l. c., 328ff., by a comparison of the Prajñāpāramitā versions, comes to the conclusion that "the relation between the Aṣṭa. and the Sata.

can be hardly called that of abridgment or expansion, as it can be said between the Śata. and the Pañcaviṃśati." Verbal agreements show "that the Aṣṭa. and the Śata. deal with identical topics, but the arrangement and the emphasis laid on a particular topic are quite different. Besides this, the Śata. introduced new topics like bhūmis and expositions of the various śūnyatās, samādhis, etc., which were only enumerated or referred to in the Aṣṭa. So it may be said that the Śata. utilised the Aṣṭa. and not *vice versa.*" On the other hand, "the Pañcaviṃśati is clearly an abridgment of the Śata. effected by an omission of set enumerations and repetitions." Dr. Dutt is certainly right in saying "that the generalisations regarding abridgment and expansion of the Prajñāpāramitās are not possible and that each book must be judged by its contents." About the Daśasāhasrikā and Aṣṭasāhasrikā in Chinese, s. *Dutt,* l. c., p. 323f. *Matsumoto,* in his list of Prajñāpāramitā texts (l. c., p. 2ff.). does not mention a Daśasāhasrikā at all.

P. 321, L. 4, read *Śatasāhasrikā.*

P. 322 note 1, add : N. *Dutt,* l.c., p. 332ff., would explain the tiresome repetitions in the Prajñāpāramitās as due to the desire of philosophical writers of first wiping out from the minds of the readers old ideas, in order to implant new ideas in their place, but who "sadly lacked the knowledge of *artful* repetitions," and therefore became tiresome. I think that the writers of the Pr. wrote for religious purposes rather than for philosophical teaching.

P. 326 note 5, L. 2, read *Sautrāntikas* for *Santrāntikas.*

P. 327 note 1, add: See also J. *Rahder,* Glossary of the Sanskrit, Tibetan, Mongolian and Chinese Versions of the Daśabhūmika-Sūtra, Paris 1928 (Buddhica, sér. 2, tome I) and The Daśabhūmika-Sūtra (Gāthā portion) Edited by Johannes *Rahder* and Shinryu *Susa* in EB 5, No. 4, July 1931.

P. 328 note 1, add: On the Bhūmis and the literature on them see now N. *Dutt*, Aspects of Mahāyāna Buddhism, p. 238ff.

P. 332 note 1, add: The Ugradatta Paripṛcchā seems to have been a book of conduct for use by the lay Bodhisattvas, s. N. *Dutt*, Aspects of Mahāyāna Buddhism, p. 299.

P. 332 note 2, add: The Sanskrit text of a Nairātmyaparipṛcchā, formerly only known in a Tibetan and in a Chinese version, has been discovered by S. *Lévi* (see JA t. 213, 1928, p. 207ff.). A reconstruction of the Sanskrit text from the Tibetan version has been edited by Sujitkumar *Mukhopadhyaya* in Visva-Bharati Studies, No. 4, Calcutta 1931.

P. 332 note 3, add: See now also Daisetz Teitaro *Suzuki*, Studies in the Lankavatara Sutra, London 1930 (*cf.* EB V, 1929, pp. 1-79), also Haraprasād *Śāstrī* and S. N. *Dasgupta* in B. C. *Law*, Buddhistic Studies, 1931, pp. 840ff., 859ff.

P. 333, L. 9: The last chapter should not be called "Sagāthakam," but (if it had any title at all) it should be "Gāthāḥ." This is also the meaning of the colophon: ity āryasaddharma-Laṅkāvatāro nāma mahāyānasūtraṃ sagāthakaṃ samāptam. *Cf. Suzuki*, Studies in the Lankavatara Sutra, p. 22.

P. 335 note 3, add: Of the 884 Gāthās of Chap. X, 200 occur also in the main part of the work. *Suzuki*, Studies in the Lankavatara Sutra, p. 21ff., describes this Gāthā chapter as "nothing but a heap of rubbish and gems."

P. 336, L. 6, read [1)] for [2)].

P. 336, L. 18, read [2)] for [1)].

P. 339 note 2, add: The new edition of the Suvarṇaprabhāsa Sūtra, prepared by the late Professor Bunyiu *Nanjio* and after his death revised and edited by H. *Idzumi*, The Eastern Buddhist Society, Kyoto 1931, has since been published.

P. 341 note 2, L. 4, read: An Uiguric version of the Suvarṇaprabhāsa has been edited by W. W. *Radloff* and S. E. *Malov* in Bibl. Buddh. XVII, 1913ff., and translated into German by the same in Bibl. Buddh. XXVII, 1930.

P. 343 note 2, add: A Sanskrit biography of the Siddhas, found by G. *Tucci* (JASB, N.S., XXVI, 1930, 138ff.), contains also some information on Nāgārjuna, or rather on the different authors and teachers of this name. On the confusion of the Mādhyamika Nāgārjuna and the Tāntrika Nāgārjuna s. also Nalinaksha *Dutt* in Ind. Hist. Qu. 7, 1931, 635ff.

P. 346, L. 3 from below, add: The Vigraha-Vyāvartanī is a polemical treatise; it has been translated from the Tibetan by Susuma *Yamaguchi* (JA 215, 1929, pp. 1-86), who also notes the differences of the Chinese translation. The Tibetan text and an English translation from the Chinese and Tibetan has been published by G. *Tucci* in Pre-Dinnāga Buddhist Texts on Logic from Chinese Sources, GOS No. XLIX, 1929.

P. 346 note 1, L. 2, read *Materialien zur Kunde des Buddhismus.*

P. 346 note 4, add: A reconstruction of the Sanskrit text from the Tibetan and Chinese versions, and an English translation, with Introduction and Notes, has been published by Vidhushekhara *Bhattacharyya* in Visva-Bharati Studies No. 1, Calcutta 1931. The Pandit leaves it an open question whether the author of the work is the old Nāgārjuna of about 200 A.D., or the second Nāgārjuna who "is believed to have flourished in about the first half of the seventh century A.D."

P. 347 note 1, L. 2, after "Oxford 1885" add: Different from the Sanskrit Dharmasaṃgraha, but closely related to it is the Chinese Dharmasaṃgraha, see F. *Weller*, Der chinesische Dharmasaṃgraha, Leipzig 1923.

P. 348, L. 11, read *grounds* for *ground*.

,, L. 12, read *Sūtra* for *Śūtra*.

P. 350 note 4, add: See now also the Catuḥśataka of Āryadeva Sanskrit and Tibetan texts with Copious Extracts from the Commentary of Candrakīrti. Reconstructed and edited by Vidhushekhara *Bhattacharya*, Part II, Visva-Bharati Series, No. 2, Calcutta 1931. An English translation from the Chinese of Āryadeva's *Śataśāstra*, a work which is similar to the Catuḥśataka, though the subjects are differently arranged, has been published by G. *Tucci* in Pre-Diṅnāga Buddhist Texts on Logic from Chinese Sources, GOS No. XLIX, 1929. Another Madhyamaka text of Āryadeva, the *Akṣara-Śatakam*, has been translated after Chinese and Tibetan materials by Vasudev *Gokhale*, Heidelberg 1930 (Materialien zur Kunde des Buddhismus 14).

P. 351 note 4, add: See also *La Vallée Poussin* in BSOS VI, 2 (1931), p. 411ff.

P. 353 note 3, add: The Sanskrit text and Tibetan translation of the Abhisamayālaṃkāra-Prajñāpāramitā-Upadeśa-Śāstra have been edited by Th. *Stcherbatsky* and E. *Obermiller* in Bibl. Buddh. XXIII, 1929. It is, according to *Stcherbatsky*, "the fundamental work for the study of the Buddhist doctrine of the Path towards moral perfection and the attainment of the condition of a Buddhist Mahāyānistic Saint, and of a Mahāyānistic Buddha in the blessed

Nirvāṇa." *Stcherbatsky* explains *abhisamaya* as a synonym of *mārga*, and says: "*Alaṃkāra* is the name for a literary form popular with the Buddhists. It means that the work in question contains no full and detailed exposition of the doctrine, it is not a mahāśāstra, like the Abhidharmakośa, but it is only a short summary of the salient points of the system contained in the prajñāpāramitā sūtras." The Alaṃkāras are always composed in memorial verses (kārikās) which, like the Brahmanical Sūtras, again require a commentary. See also *Tucci*, On some Aspects of the Doctrines of Maitreya(nātha) and Asaṅga, Calcutta 1930, p. 10ff., and in JASB N.S. XXVI, 1930, p. 127.

P. 354 note 1, add: See also Hakuju *Ui*, Maitreya as an Historical Personage, in Lanman Studies, p. 95ff. Here he says (p. 99) that it " is still a question" whether the authorship of the commentary on the Mahāyāna-Sūtrālaṃkāra belongs to Asaṅga or to Vasubandhu. He ascribes to Maitreya the works: Yogācārabhūmi, Yoga-vibhaṅga-śāstra (now lost), Mahāyāna-Sūtrālaṃkāra, Madhyāntavibhaṅga, Vajracchedikā-Pāramitā-śāstra, and Abhisamayālaṃkāra. G. *Tucci*, On some Aspects of the Doctrines of Maitreya(nātha) and Asaṅga, Calcutta 1930, and in JASB, N.S., XXVI, 1930, p. 125ff., supports, by new evidence, the view that Maitreya or Maitreyanātha is an historical personage and the author of six works, including the Mahāyāna-Sūtrālaṃkāra, and the Yogacaryā-bhūmi-śāstra (this is the correct title). He is of opinion that Maitreya is the author of the Kārikās of all the six works, while Asaṅga, his chief pupil, wrote the commentaries on them. E. *Obermiller*, in the introduction to his translation of the Uttaratantra of Maitreya (The Sublime Science of the Great Vehicle of Salvation, being A Manual of Buddhist Monism, The Work of Ārya Maitreya with a Commentary by Āryāsaṅga. Translated from the Tibetan, in Acta Orientalia, Vol. IX, 1931, pp. 81-306), states that the following five works are ascribed to Maitreya by Tibetan tradition, *viz.*, Sūtrālaṃkāra, Madhyānta-vibhaṅga, Dharma-dharmatā-vibhaṅga, Abhisamayālaṃkāra, and Uttaratantra. *Obermiller* gives a summary analysis of all these works. As the commentary on the Abhisamayālaṃkāra is ascribed to Asaṅga, and as both text and commentary must have been composed by the same author, *O.* inclines to the opinion that all the 5 treatises which show a great resemblance with each other as regards style, though they are written from different points of view (1-3 from Yogācāra-Vijñānavāda, 4 and 5 from Mādhyamika point of view), were written by Asaṅga, and that the tradition of Asaṅga having heard them from Maitreya in the Tuṣita heaven is only meant to give a divine sanction to the works.

P. 354 note 2, add: An edition of the Bodhisattvabhūmi, being the 15th section of the Yogācārabhūmi, has been published by Unrai *Wogihara*, Tokyo 1930.

P. 355f. note 1, add: The question of Vasubandhu's date has recently been discussed by J. *Takakusu*, Taiken *Kimura*, and Genmyo *Ono* (in Lanman Studies, pp. 79ff., 89ff., 93f.) who agree in assigning the author of the Abhidharmakośa to the 5th century (420-500 A. D.). T. *Kimura* speaks here also of two Vasubandhus. *Takakusu's* chief arguments are *argumenta ex silentio*: Kumārajīva (383-414 in China) and Fa-hien (399-414 in India) know nothing of Vasubandhu and his Abhidharmakośa. The sources on which N. *Péri* relies, are declared by *Takakusu* to be "spurious." On the other hand, H. *Ui* (Lanman Studies, p. 101f.) gives the following dates: Maitreya 270-350, Asaṅga 310-390, Vasubandhu 320-400, which Takakusu considers too early by 100 years.

P. 357 note 1, Line 2, after "1918" add: Second Koçasthāna ed. by U. *Wogihara*, Th. *Stcherbatsky*, and E. *Obermiller*, Bibl. Buddh., 1931. The Tibetan version of the Abhidharmakośakārikāḥ and Abhidharmakośabhāṣyam has been edited by Th. *Stcherbatsky* in Bibl. Buddh. XX, 1917 and 1930.

P. 358 note 4, add: A similar work is the Śīlaparikathā, a moral treatise of 11 verses, which is ascribed to Vasubandhu, and preserved in the Tibetan Tanjur only; s. Anathanath *B asu* in Ind. Hist. Qu. 7, 1931, 28ff.

P. 360 note 5, add: A fragment of the Sanskrit text of the Commentary on the Pratītya-Samutpāda-Sūtra has been published by G. *Tucci* in JRAS, 1930, p. 611ff. Instead of "According to G. Tucci," etc. read: H. R. Rangaswamy *Iyengar* (JBORS 12, 1926, p. 587 ff.; Ind. Hist. Qu. 5, 1929, p. 81ff.) and G. *Tucci* (Ind. Hist. Qu. 4, 1928, p. 630ff.) have proved that the Vādavidhi also is a work of Vasubandhu, and not as A. B. *Keith*, in agreement with Satis Chandra *Vidyabhushana*, tried to prove (Ind. Hist. Qu. 4, 1928, p. 221ff.) the work of Dharmakīrti.

P. 362 note 1, add: The whole extremely complicated problem of the authenticity of the Ta Tch'eng K'i Sin Louen (this is the Chinese title of the Mahāyānaśraddhotpādaśāstra) has been fully discussed by Paul *Demiéville*, Sur l'authenticité du Ta Tch'eng K'i Sin Louen (Extrait du Bulletin de la Maison Franco-Japonaise, tome II, No. 2, Tôkyô 1929).

Mr. *Demiéville* sees no reason to deny the Indian origin of the work which (he thinks) must be later than the Laṅkāvatāra, but earlier than Asaṅga and Vasubandhu. Else it would be difficult to explain why they are never quoted in the work. On the other hand it is strange that the work, so famous in China and Japan, is never alluded to in any Sanskrit text, nor in any Chinese or Tibetan translations of Buddhist Sanskrit works.

P. 363, L. 10, read *Candrakīrti*.

P. 363 note 2, add : The Nyāyapraveśa has also been edited by N. D. *Mironov* in T'oung Pao, 1931, pp. 1-24.

P. 364, L. 5 and L. 11, read *Candrakīrti*.

P. 364, L. 7, add note to Prasannapadā : Chapters I and XXV of the Prasannapadā have been translated by Th. *Stcherbatsky* in his work The Conception of Buddhist Nirvāṇa (Leningrad 1927), pp. 79-212 ; Chap. X by St. *Schayer* in Rocznik Orjentalistyczny, Lwów 1930, VII, 26-52, and Chapters V, XII, XIII-XVI by St. *Schayer*, Ausgewählte Kapitel aus der Prasannapadā in Polska Akademja Umiejetności, Mémoires de la Commission Orientaliste Nr. 14, w. Krakowie 1931. An analysis of Chap. XXIV was given by *La Vallée Poussin* in Mélanges Charles de Harlez, Leiden 1896.

P. 364 note 2 : An edition of the Sanskrit text of the Madhyamakāvatara is now being published in the Journal of Oriental Research, Madras, Vol. VI, 1932 (Supplement).

P. 365, L. 7, read *Candrakīrti*.

P. 366 note 1, L. 15, read *Keith*.

P. 367, L. 4, read *neither* for *nither*.

P. 369, L. 2, read *Ākāśa-*

P. 369, L. 11, read *Vimalakīrtinirdeśa*.

To p. 369, L. 12: The Avalokita-Sūtra in the Mahāvastu II, 363 ff., agrees with the Avalokana-Sūtra quoted by Śāntideva in general, but differs from it in so many details that Śāntideva's text cannot possibly be a quotation from the Mahāvastu.

P. 369, L. 19, read *Daśabhū-*

P. 369, L. 19, read *Tathāgataguhya-Sūtra.*

P. 370 note 1, add: A Mongolic translation of the Bodhicaryāvatāra ed. by B. J. *Vladimircov* in Bibl. Buddh. XXVIII, 1929.

P. 375 note 3, add: *Cf.* Vidhushekhara *Bhattacharya* in Ind. Hist. Qu. 6, 1930, 757ff.

P. 377 note 1, L. 1, read *The Tibetan text with a French translation*; and add at the end of the note: The first and the last of the four hymns, Sanskrit and Tibetan Texts, have been edited, with an English translation, by G. *Tucci* in JRAS, 1932, p. 309ff.

P. 385 note 2, add: The Mahā-Māyūrī has been translated into Chinese by Kumārajīva, and three times more. See also G. *Tucci* in JASB, N.S. XXVI, 1930, p. 129.

P. 391 note 2, add: See also P. C. *Bagchi* in Ind. Hist. Qu. 6, 1930, 576ff.

P. 392 note 2, L. 3, read *Sādhanamālā, II.*

P. 392 note 2, add: G. *Tucci* also (JASB XXVI, 1930, p. 129 ff.) is of opinion that the Tantras go back to the times of Harivarman and Asaṅga (4th century A.D.) because they allude to a " Somasiddhānta " which he identifies with the " Tantric sect " of the Kāpālikās. I am afraid, the use of the terms " Tantric " and " Tantras " is too vague to allow any safe dating of Tantra literature. In line 3 of the note read Sādhanamālā II (instead of III).

To p. 393, L. 9, Uḍḍiyāna is probably not Orissa, but the Swat country; s. P. C. *Bagchi* in Ind. Hist. Qu. 6, 1930, p. 580f.

P. 393 note 4, add: See also P. C. *Bagchi* in Ind. Hist. Qu. 6, 1930, 389ff. The Sandhā-bhāṣā is also used in the *Dohākośa*. Sahajayāna poems written in Apabhraṃśa, s. Les chants mystiques de Kāṇha et de Saraha. Les Dohā-Koṣa (en apabhraṃśa, avec les versions tibétaines) et Les Caryā (en vieuxbengali)...édités et traduits par M. *Shahidulla*, Paris 1928. Kāṇha lived about 700, Saraha about 1000 A.D.

P. 394 note 2, L. 1, read *C. Bendall*.

P. 395 note 3, add: None of the passages quoted from a Tathāgataguhya-Sūtra in the Sikṣāsamuccaya occur in the Guhyasamāja Tantra or Tathāgataguhyaka edited by Benoytosh *Bhattacharyya*, Baroda 1931 (GOS No. 53). The latter is a genuine Tantra. In the colophons it is called "Guhyasamāja Mahāguhyatantrarāja." It is a work belonging to the Yogatantra class. Dr. Bhattacharyya would ascribe this Tantra to Asaṅga, but his arguments are very weak indeed.

P. 397 note 1, add: See also Marcelle *Lalou*, Iconographie des étoffes peintes (paṭa) dans le Mañjuśrīmūlakalpa, Paris 1930 (Buddhica, sér. 1, t. VI). B. *Bhattacharyya* (GOS, Vol. LIII, p. xxxiii ff.) would ascribe the Mañjuśrīmūlakalpa in its original form to the second century A.D. But his arguments are by no means convincing.

To p. 399, L. 22: Some scholars (see *e.g.*, G. *Tucci* in JASB N.S. XXVI, 1930, p. 128ff.) claim a higher antiquity for the Tantras. But no real Tantra can be proved to have existed before the 7th century A.D. Neither the Suvarṇaprabhāsa nor the Mahāmāyūrī can be called "Tantras." Nor are the Kāpālikas a "Tantric sect." All we can say is that some of the elements of Tantrism are already found in earlier works.

P. 400 note 4, add: On foreign elements in the Tantra, see also P. C. *Bagchi* in Ind. Hist. Qu. 7, 1931, 1ff.

P. 401 note 1, L. 3, read *popular* for *oppular*.

P. 401 note 1, add: A goddess Lāmā often appears in Buddhist Tantras connected with the cult of Ḍākinīs and Yoginīs. Lāmā is the same as Tibetan Lhamo, "she-devil." On this Lāmā and on Tibetan influence on the Tantras s. also G. *Tucci* in JASB N.S. XXVI, 1930, p. 155ff.

P. 406 f. note 2, add: See also W. *Wüst*, Buddhismus und Christentum auf vorderasiatisch-antikem Boden, in Zeitschrift für Missionskunde und Religionswissenschaft, 1932, 33ff.

P. 411, L. 1, read: *Vimalakīrti-Nirdeśa.*

P. 419 note 3, L. 2, read *Angelo de Gubernatis.*

P. 422 note 2, add: The Italian original was published in Milano in 1925.

P. 427 note 2, add: Also Franklin *Edgerton*, Notes on Jaina Māhārāṣṭrī, in Lanman Studies, p. 27ff.

P. 427 note 3, add: Also *Bloomfield*, On Diminutive Pronouns in Jaina Sanskrit, in Lanman Studies, p. 7ff.

P. 428, L. 7, read *Canon* for *Canons.*

P. 429, L. 21, read *Mahā-Pratyākhyāna.*

P. 430, L. 3, read *Ohanijjutti.*

P. 432, L. 20, read *Puvvas* for *Puvuas.*

P. 432, L. 2 from below, read Mahāvīra.

P. 443, L. 21, add:[1]

P. 443, L. 26, read "*Numerous parables, which* for "*Numerous parables,*" *which.*

P. 449, note 2, add: A new edition of the Uvāsagadasāo by P. L. *Vaidya* has been published at Poona 1930.

P. 470, L. 12, read *Ṣaḍāvaśyaka-* for *Saḍāvāśyaka-.*

P. 474, L. 16, read *Canon* for *Cannon.*

P. 489 note 2, read *pavvam* for *pevvam.*

P. 494 note 4, L. 4, read *Stutterheim.*

P. 498 note 1, L. 1, read *Glasenapp*.

After p. 503, L. 17, add: Another "Mahāpurāṇa" is the *Tisaṭṭhimahāpurisagaṇālaṃkāra* in Apabhraṃśa by the poet *Pupphayanta* or *Puṣpadanta*. This Mahāpurāṇa also consists of two parts, an Ādipurāṇa in 37, and an Uttarapurāṇa in 65 Chapters. It was completed in 965 A. D. Puṣpadanta is also the author of two other Apabhraṃśa works, a *Nāgakumāracariu*, and a *Jasaharacariu* (Yaśodharacarita).[1] The subject of the latter is the life of Yaśodhara, which has also been treated in Somadeva Sūri's Yaśastilaka and Vādirāja Sūri's Yaśodharacarita.

1) Jasaharacariu of Puṣpadanta. Critically edited with an Introduction, Glossary and Notes by P. L. *Vaidya* (The Ambādās Chaware Digambara Jain Granthamālā or Karanjā Jain Series edited by Hiralal Jain, Vol. I), Karanja, Berar 1931. On the Tisaṭṭhimahāpurisaguṇālaṃkāra, see Introduction, p. 19 ff. and also *Hiralal*, Catalogue, p. xliii ff.

P. 506 note 2: The Ādīśvaracaritra, the first book of the Triṣaṣṭiśalākāpuruṣacaritra, has been translated into English by Helen M. *Johnson*, Baroda 1931 (GOS No. 51).

P. 540, L. 8, read *Caritra* for *Charitra*.

P. 543 note 1, add: But No. 13 in *Grimm*, Kinder-und Hausmärchen, has more in common with the Kathākośa story, as A. *Wesselski*, Versuch einer Theorie des Märchens, Reichenberg i. B. 1931, p. 75 ff., has shown.

P. 548 note 4, add: Translated into German by H. *Jensen* in Das indische Schattentheater bearbeitet von G. *Jacob*, H. *Jensen*, H. *Losch*, Stuttgart 1931, p. 48 ff.

P. 558 note 2, add: As to the relative pronoun *yaka*, see M. *Bloomfield* in Lanman Studies, p. 9 ff.

P. 561, L. 3, read *There is also a S.*
P. 561 note 3, L. 1, read *Āśādhara's.*
P. 561 note 5, Ll. 1 and 2, read *Ṣaḍdarśanasamuccaya.*
P. 581, L. 15, read *Nyāyaviniścaya.*
P. 581, L. 16, read *pasambodhana.*
P. 583, L. 3, read *Jñānārṇava.*
P. 586, L. 6, read *Cāmuṇḍarāya.*
P. 594, L. 14, read *Dharma* for *Dhārma.*
Addition to Appendix II: The latest discussions on the problem of Pāli and its home are those by R. *Siddhārtha*, Origin and Development of Pāli Language with special reference to Sanskrit Grammar, and by A. B. *Keith*, The Home of Pāli, in B. C. *Law*, Buddhistic Studies, p. 641 ff., and p. 728 ff.

ADDITIONAL CORRECTIONS

P. 304, L. 13, read *Nepalese.*
P. 304, L. 20, read *Buddha-Bhakti.*
P. 314, L. 17, read *Sūtra.*
P. 343 note 2, L. 2, read *Nāgārjuna.*
P. 353, L. 15, read *Abhisamayālaṃkāra-Kārikās.*

INDEX

COMPILED BY W. GAMPART, PH.D.

Some Important Publications

History of Indian Literature, Vol. I, by Prof. M. Winternitz. Demy 8vo, pp. 653. Rs. 10-8.

Contents:—Introduction—Veda—National Epics—Puranas—Tantras.

Some Problems of Indian Literature, by the same author. Royal 8vo, pp. 130. Rs. 2-8.

Contents:—The Age of the Veda—Ascetic Literature in Ancient India—Ancient Indian Ballad Poetry—Indian Literature and World Literature—Kautiliya Arthasastra—Bhasa.

Selections from Avesta and old Persian, First Series, Part I, by I. J. S. Taraporewala, B.A., Ph.D., Sometime Professor of Comparative Philology, Calcutta University. Demy 8vo, pp. 255. Rs. 6.

History of Bengali Language and Literature (in English), by Rai Bahadur Dineschandra Sen, B.A., D. Litt. Demy 8vo, pp. 1067. Rs. 16-12.

A comprehensive view of the development of the Bengali Language and Literature from the earliest times down to 1850.

History of Bengali Language, by Bijaychandra Mazumdar, B.L., Lecturer in Anthropology, Comparative Philology and Indian Vernaculars in the University of Calcutta. *Second Edition.* Demy 8vo, pp. 323. Rs. 7.

The Vaishnava Literature of Mediaeval Bengal, by Rai Bahadur Dineschandra Sen, B.A., D.Litt. Demy 12mo, pp. 312. Re. 1-6.

The book contains a connected history of the influence of Vaishnava Literature of the Mediaeval Age on the development of Bengali Language with concluding chapters on the relation between the Buddhistic and Vaishnava creeds and similarity between Vaishnavism and Christianity.

Bengali Literature in the Nineteenth Century (*Premchand Roychand Studentship Thesis, 1917*), by S. K. De, M.A., D.Lit. Demy 8vo, pp. 530. Rs. 8-6.

The Origin of Bengali Script ((*Jubilee Research Prize, 1913*), by Rakhaldas Banerjee, M.A. Demy 8vo, pp. 122. Rs. 3.

Elements of the Science of Language, by I. J. S. Taraporewala, B.A., Ph.D. Demy 8vo, pp. 520. Rs. 10.

Indian Writers of English Verse, by Mrs. Latika Basu, B.Lit. Demy 8vo, pp. 165. Rs 2.

The Linguistic Speculations of the Hindus, by Prabhatchandra Chakravarti, M.A., Ph.D. Demy 8vo, pp. 511. 1933. Rs. 6.

Contents:—Introductory—Philosophy of Language—Origin of Speech—Evolution of Sound—Sentence—Parts of Speech—Division and Denotation of Words—Roots—The Sanskrit Language—Prakrit and Apabhramsa—Sound and Sense—History of Word and Meaning—Logic and Language.

Sino Indica, by Prabodhchandra Bagchi, M.A., D.Lit.:—

Vol. I (*Le Canon Bouddhique en Chine*), Part I. Royal 8vo, pp. 436+lii. Rs. 15.

Vol. II (*Deux Lexiques Sanskrit-Chinois*), Part I. Double Crown 8vo, pp. 336. Rs. 15.

Asoka (*Carmichael Lectures*, 1923), by Prof D. R. Bhandarkar, M.A., Ph.D. Second edition, *revised and enlarged*. Demy 8vo, pp. 406+xxviii. Rs. 5.

Political History of Ancient India (From the accession of Parikshit to the extinction of the Gupta Dynasty), by Hemchandra Raychaudhuri, M.A., Ph.D. Third Edition, *revised and enlarged*. Royal 8vo, pp. 496. Rs. 7-8.

Indian Ideals in Education, Philosophy and Religion and Art (*First Series of Kamala Lectures*), by Annie Besant, D.L., with a Foreword by the Hon'ble Sir Ewart Greaves, Kt. Demy 8vo, pp. 135. Re. 1-8.

Philosophical Discipline (*Third Series of Kamala Lectures*), by Mahamahopadhyaya Ganganath Jha, M.A., D.Litt. Demy 8vo, pp. 179. Re. 1-8.